THE ROUTLEDGE COMPANION
TO PHILOSOPHY AND FILM

The Routledge Companion to Philosophy and Film is the first comprehensive volume to explore the main themes, topics, thinkers, and issues in philosophy and film. The *Companion* features sixty specially commissioned chapters from international scholars which are organized into four clear parts:

- Issues and concepts
- Authors and trends
- Genres and other types
- Film as philosophy

Part I is a comprehensive section examining key concepts, including chapters on acting, censorship, empathy, depiction, ethics, genre, interpretation, narrative, spectatorship, and style. The second part covers authors and scholars of film and significant theories. Part III examines genres such as documentary, experimental cinema, horror, comedy and tragedy. The final part includes chapters on key directors such as Tarkovsky, Bergman and Terrence Malick, and on particular films including *Gattaca* and *Memento*.

The Routledge Companion to Philosophy and Film is essential reading for anyone interested in philosophy of film, aesthetics and film, and cinema studies.

Paisley Livingston is Professor of Philosophy at Lingnan University, Hong Kong. He is the author of *Art and Intention: A Philosophical Study*, and coeditor (with Berys Gaut) of *The Creation of Art: New Essays in Philosophical Aesthetics*.

Carl Plantinga is Professor of Film Studies in the Communication Arts and Sciences Department at Calvin College, USA. He is the author of *Rhetoric and Representation in Nonfiction Film*, and coeditor (with Greg M. Smith) of *Passionate Views: Film, Cognition and Emotion*.

Routledge Philosophy Companions

Routledge Philosophy Companions offer thorough, high quality surveys and assessments of the major topics and periods in philosophy. Covering key problems, themes, and thinkers, all entries are specially commissioned for each volume and written by leading scholars in the field. Clear, accessible and carefully edited and organised, *Routledge Philosophy Companions* are indispensable for anyone coming to a major topic or period in philosophy, as well as for the more advanced reader.

The Routledge Companion to Aesthetics, Second Edition
Edited by Berys Gaut and Dominic Lopes

The Routledge Companion to Philosophy of Religion
Edited by Chad Meister and Paul Copan

The Routledge Companion to the Philosophy of Science
Edited by Stathis Psillos and Martin Curd

The Routledge Companion to Twentieth Century Philosophy
Edited by Dermot Moran

The Routledge Companion to Philosophy and Film
Edited by Paisley Livingston and Carl Plantinga

Forthcoming:

The Routledge Companion to Nineteenth Century Philosophy
Edited by Dean Moyar

The Routledge Companion to Philosophy of Psychology
Edited by John Symons and Paco Calvo

The Routledge Companion to Ethics
Edited by John Skorupski

The Routledge Companion to Metaphysics
Edited by Robin Le Poidevin, Peter Simons, Andrew McGonigal, and Ross Cameron

The Routledge Companion to Epistemology
Edited by Sven Bernecker and Duncan Pritchard

The Routledge Companion to Seventeenth Century Philosophy
Edited by Dan Kaufman

The Routledge Companion to Eighteenth Century Philosophy
Edited by Aaron Garrett

The Routledge Companion to Philosophy and Music
Edited by Andrew Kania and Theodore Gracyk

THE
ROUTLEDGE COMPANION
TO PHILOSOPHY AND FILM

Edited by
Paisley Livingston and Carl Plantinga

Taylor & Francis Group

LONDON AND NEW YORK

First published 2009
by Routledge
2 Park Square, Milton Park, Abingdon, Oxon OX14 4RN

Simultaneously published in the USA and Canada
by Routledge
270 Madison Ave, New York, NY 10016

Routledge is an imprint of the Taylor & Francis Group, an informa business

Typeset in Goudy Oldstyle Std 10.5/13pt by Fakenham Photosetting Ltd,
Fakenham, Norfolk
Printed and bound in Great Britain by MPG Books Ltd, Bodmin

British Library Cataloguing in Publication Data
A catalogue record for this book is available from the British Library

Library of Congress Cataloging in Publication Data
The Routledge companion to philosophy and film / edited by Paisley Livingston
and Carl Plantinga.
p. cm. -- (Routledge philosophy companions)
Includes bibliographical references and index.
1. Motion pictures. 2. Motion pictures--Philosophy. I. Livingston, Paisley, 1951- II.
Plantinga, Carl R.

PN1994.R574 2008

791.43--dc22

2008017372

ISBN10: 0-415-77166-8 (hbk)
ISBN13: 978-0-415-77166-5 (hbk)

CONTENTS

CONTENTS

CONTENTS

CONTRIBUTORS

Richard Allen is Professor and Chair of Cinema Studies at New York University. He is author of *Projecting Illusion* (1995) and *Hitchcock's Romantic Irony* (2007) and coeditor of *Film Theory and Philosophy* (1997) and *Wittgenstein, Theory and the Arts* (2002) among other books.

Dudley Andrew is Professor of Film and Comparative Literature at Yale University, where he directs the graduate film program. Specializing in French film and culture and issues of world cinema, he has written books on the history of film theory and is currently at work on the specificity of the cinematic image and reflections around the writing of André Bazin.

Giorgio Biancorosso was a Mellon Fellow at the Society of Fellows in the Humanities at Columbia University in 2001–3 and is now an Assistant Professor in Music and Film Theory, Music Department, the University of Hong Kong. Biancorosso is completing a book, under contract with Oxford University Press, called *Musical Aesthetics through Cinema*. He has written for the journals *Music and Letters*, *ECHO*, and *Future Anterior* and the collections *Bad Music* (2004), *Wagner and Cinema* (forthcoming), and *Popular Music and the Postmodern Auteur* (forthcoming).

Ronald Bogue is Distinguished Research Professor of Comparative Literature at the University of Georgia. His books include *Deleuze and Guattari* (1989), *Deleuze on Cinema* (2003), and *Deleuze's Way: Essays in Transverse Ethics and Aesthetics* (2007).

David Bordwell is Jacques Ledoux Professor Emeritus of Film Studies at the University of Wisconsin, Madison. He has written many books on film aesthetics, including *The Way Hollywood Tells It* (2006) and *Poetics of Cinema* (2007).

Noël Carroll is a Distinguished Professor of Philosophy at the Graduate Center of the City University of New York. His most recent books are *The Philosophy of Motion Pictures* and *On Criticism*. He is presently working on *A Short Introduction to Humor*.

Francesco Casetti, born in Trento, on 2 April 1947, is Full Professor at Università Cattolica of Milano, where he also serves as Chair of the Department of Media and Performing Arts. He is the author of *Inside the Gaze: The Fiction Film and Its Spectator* (1999), *Theories of Cinema, 1945–1995* (1999), and *Eye of the Century: Film, Experience, Modernity* (2008). Coeditor (with Roger Odin) of the special issue of *Communications*, 51 (1990) ("Télévisions/Mutations"), he has been a visiting professor at many universities, including, most recently, Yale, and is President of the Association of Film and Television Teachers in the Italian Universities.

Jinhee Choi is Lecturer in Film Studies at the University of Kent, UK. She is the coeditor of *Philosophy of Film and Motion Pictures* (2005) with Noël Carroll and is completing a monograph on contemporary South Korean cinema.

Amy Coplan is Associate Professor of Philosophy at California State University, Fullerton. Her research interests include philosophy of emotion, philosophy of film, feminism, and ancient Greek philosophy. She has published articles on various types of character engagement, including empathy, sympathy, and emotional contagion, as well as on Terrence Malick's *The Thin Red Line*, the popular television show *House*, and horror films. She is currently editing a collection on the film *Blade Runner* for the Routledge series, Philosophers on Film, and co-editing an interdisciplinary collection titled *Empathy: Philosophical and Psychological Perspectives* (forthcoming).

Angela Curran is Assistant Professor of Philosophy at Carleton College, Minnesota. Her work in aesthetics has investigated topics in Aristotle's aesthetics and the philosophy of film, and her current project is on Aristotle's account of our emotional engagement with art. She is the coeditor of *Philosophy of Film: Introductory Text and Readings* (2005).

David Davies is Associate Professor in the Department of Philosophy at McGill University, Montréal. He is the author of *Art as Performance* (2004) and *Aesthetics and Literature* (2007) and editor of *The Thin Red Line* (2008) in the series Philosophers on Film. He has published articles on philosophical issues in the philosophies of film, photography, literature, and the visual arts and on topics in metaphysics, philosophy of mind, philosophy of language, and philosophy of science. He is currently working on a book on the philosophical foundations of the performing arts.

Carol Donelan is an Associate Professor in the Department of Cinema and Media Studies at Carleton College, Minnesota, where she teaches courses in film history and theory, film modes and genres, directors, national cinemas, and television studies. She has published articles on the politics of gender in cinema and on teaching film theory in a post-film, post-theory era. Her research interests include melodrama and the history of moviegoing and film exhibition in small towns and rural areas.

Susan Dwyer is Chair and Associate Professor of Philosophy at the University of Maryland, Baltimore County. Previously she taught at McGill University, Montréal. She specializes in ethics and public policy, moral psychology, and feminist theory.

Chris Falzon teaches philosophy at the University of Newcastle, Australia. He is the author of *Foucault and Social Dialogue* (1998) and *Philosophy Goes to the Movies* (2002, 2nd ed. 2006).

Dan Flory is Associate Professor of Philosophy at Montana State University, Bozeman. His publications include several essays on philosophy, film, and critical race theory. He has also guest-edited two volumes of the journal *Film and Philosophy*. Currently President of the Society for the Philosophic Study of the Contemporary Visual Arts, his most recent publication is *Philosophy, Black Film, Film Noir* (2008).

Don Fredericksen is Professor of Film and Director of Undergraduate Studies in Film at Cornell University and author of a recent book on Bergman's *Persona* (2005), coauthor of a book on Wajda's *Kanal* (2007). He also practices as a psychotherapist who is convinced, contra Münsterberg, that the unconscious exists.

Jonathan Frome is an Assistant Professor of Film and Media Studies at the University of Texas at Dallas. His research focuses on how media generate emotion and why various media tend to generate different emotions. He is also interested in documentary film and animation. His website is www.jonathanfrome.net

Richard Fumerton received his PhD from Brown in 1974 and is currently the F. Wendell Miller Professor of Philosophy at the University of Iowa. His research has focused mainly on epistemology, but he has also published in metaphysics, philosophy of mind, philosophy of science, value theory, and philosophy of law. He is the author of *Metaphysical and Epistemological Problems of Perception* (1985), *Reason and Morality: A Defense of the Egocentric Perspective* (1990), *Metaepistemology and Skepticism* (1996), *Realism and the Correspondence Theory of Truth* (2002), and *Epistemology* (2006) and the coeditor (with Diane Jeske) of *Philosophy through Film* (forthcoming).

Berys Gaut is Reader in Philosophy at the University of St Andrews. He holds a PhD from Princeton University and is author of *Art, Emotion and Ethics* (2007) and *A Philosophy of Cinematic Art* (forthcoming). He is coeditor of *Ethics and Practical Reason* (1997), *The Routledge Companion to Aesthetics* (2001, 2nd ed. 2005), and *The Creation of Art* (2003). He has also published numerous articles on aesthetics, the philosophy of film, ethics, political philosophy, and Kant's moral philosophy.

Mette Hjort is Professor and Program Director of Visual Studies at Lingnan University, Hong Kong. She has published *Stanley Kwan's "Center Stage"* (2006), *Small Nation, Global Cinema* (2005), and *The Strategy of Letters* (1993). She has also edited and coedited numerous volumes on film.

Patrick Colm Hogan is Professor in the Department of English, the Program in Comparative Literature and Cultural Studies, and the Program in Cognitive

Science at the University of Connecticut. He is the author of ten books, including *Cognitive Science, Literature, and the Arts: A Guide for Humanists* (2003), *The Mind and Its Stories: Narrative Universals and Human Emotion* (2003), and *Understanding Indian Movies: Culture, Cognition, and Cinematic Imagination* (2008). He is also the editor of *The Cambridge Encyclopedia of the Language Sciences* (forthcoming).

Robert Hopkins is a member of the Department of Philosophy in the University of Sheffield. His research interests lie in various topics in aesthetics, epistemology, and the philosophy of mind. As well as work on film, he has published on pictorial representation, the senses, sensory imagining, the epistemology and objectivity of aesthetic judgment, and the aesthetics of painting and sculpture.

Andrew Kania's principal research is in the philosophy of music, film, and literature. He is the editor of *Philosophers on* Memento, and, with Theodore Gracyk, *The Routledge Companion to Philosophy and Music* (both forthcoming). He recently won the inaugural Essay Prize of the British Society of Aesthetics.

Joseph G. Kickasola is Associate Professor and Director of the Baylor Communication in New York program, Baylor University. He is the author of *The Films of Krzysztof Kieslowski: The Liminal Image* (2004). His publications include articles in *Quarterly Review of Film and Video, Journal of Moving Image Studies*, and various film studies anthologies. He lives in New York City.

Deborah Knight is Associate Professor of Philosophy at Queen's University at Kingston, Canada. Her research focuses on philosophy of art, philosophy of film, and philosophy of mind. She has recently published on *The Matrix, The Age of Innocence, Dark City*, and *Blade Runner*.

András Bálint Kovács is Head of the Film Department at Eötvös Loránd University, Budapest, Director of the National Audiovisual Archive, and Artistic Advisor for Béla Tarr's production company, T&T Filmműhely. He has taught at several universities, including the University of Paris (la Nouvelle Sorbonne) and the University of Stockholm. He translated Deleuze's *Cinéma I–II* into Hungarian. His books include *Screening Modernism: The European Art Cinema 1950–1980* (2007), *Les mondes d'Andrei Tarkovsky* (1987), *Metropolis, Paris (On German Expressionism and the French New Wave)* (1992), *Tarkovszkij* (1997), *Film and Narration* (1997), *Collection of Essays* (2002), and *Trends in Modern Cinema* (2005).

Joseph Kupfer is Professor of Philosophy at Iowa State University, teaching and publishing in ethics, social-political philosophy, and aesthetics. Recent work includes aesthetics of nature, virtue theory, articles and book on philosophy in film, *Visions of Virtue in Popular Film* (1999), as well as a book on virtue and vice in personal life, *Prostitutes, Musicians, and Self-Respect* (2007).

Brian Laetz is a doctoral student at the University of British Columbia. He works in aesthetics and epistemology, and he is writing a dissertation on art and evolution. He also has an interest in genres and has written on horror and fantasy.

Brian Lewis is Dean of the Faculty of Applied Sciences, Professor of Communication, and founder of the Leonardo Institute at Simon Fraser University. He teaches film production, documentary media, and film theory and history. His current research looks at emerging communication technologies, together with their public and policy implications.

Paisley Livingston is Chair Professor of Philosophy and Dean of Arts at Lingnan University, Hong Kong. He previously taught at McGill University and at Aarhus University and the University of Copenhagen. His books include *Ingmar Bergman and the Rituals of Art* (1982), *Literary Knowledge* (1988), *Literature and Rationality* (1991), *Models of Desire* (1992), and *Art and Intention* (2005). He coedited *The Creation of Art* (2003) with Berys Gaut. Professor Livingston's *Cinema, Philosophy, Bergman: On Film as Philosophy* is forthcoming.

Dominic McIver Lopes is Distinguished Professor of Philosophy at the University of British Columbia. He is author of *Understanding Pictures* (1996) and *Sight and Sensibility: Evaluating Pictures* (2005) and is now completing a book on computer art.

Aaron Meskin is Senior Lecturer in Philosophy at University of Leeds. Before moving to Leeds in 2005, he taught at Texas Tech University. He has published articles on aesthetics and the philosophy of art in *The Journal of Aesthetics and Art Criticism*, *The British Journal of Aesthetics*, and *Philosophy and Phenomenological Research*, as well as in a number of collections. He is the editor of the aesthetics/philosophy of art section for the online journal *Philosophy Compass*, and he recently coedited *Aesthetics: A Comprehensive Anthology* (2007). He also serves on the Executive Committee of the British Society of Aesthetics and is on the Board of Trustees of the American Society for Aesthetics.

Carl Plantinga is Professor of Film Studies at Calvin College, USA. His research interests extend from the history and theory of documentary film, to the nature of film spectatorship, to film theory and the philosophy of film generally. He is the author of *Moving Viewers: American Film and the Spectator's Experience* (2009) and *Rhetoric and Representation in Nonfiction Film* (1997) and coeditor of *Passionate Views: Film, Cognition, and Emotion* (1999). He serves on the Board of Directors of the Society for Cognitive Studies of the Moving Image and is Associate Editor for *Projections: The Journal for Movies and Mind*.

Trevor Ponech is Associate Professor of English at McGill University, Montréal, and author of *What Is Non-Fiction Cinema?* (1999). His recent work on the ontology of cinema appears in *The Journal of Aesthetics and Art Criticism* and *The British Journal of Aesthetics*.

Stephen Prince is Professor of Communication at Virginia Tech. He is the author of numerous books on film, which include *Classical Film Violence* (2003) and *Savage Cinema* (1998). His new book project looks at American film in the age of terrorism.

Johannes Riis is Associate Professor of Film Studies at University of Copenhagen, Denmark. His publications have centered on film acting and psychologically based film theories. He is currently working on an historical study of acting styles that rely on realist techniques.

William Rothman received his PhD in philosophy from Harvard University, where he taught film studies for many years. He is currently Professor of Motion Pictures and Director of the Graduate Program in Film Studies at the University of Miami. His books include *Hitchcock: The Murderous Gaze* (1982), *The "I" of the Camera* (1988; expanded edition 2004), *Documentary Film Classics* (1997) and *Reading Cavell's* The World Viewed: A Philosophical Perspective on Film (2000). He is the editor of *Cavell on Film* (2005).

Neven Sesardic is Professor of Philosophy at Lingnan University in Hong Kong. His main interests are philosophy of science and philosophy of biology. His book *Making Sense of Heritability* was published in 2005, and his articles have appeared in leading philosophical journals, such as *The British Journal for the Philosophy of Science*, *Ethics*, and *Philosophy of Science*.

Jeff Smith is a Professor in the Department of Communication Arts at the University of Wisconsin, Madison, and the author of *The Sounds of Commerce: Marketing Popular Film Music* (1998). His scholarship on film music has appeared in several edited anthologies, including *Post-Theory: Reconstructing Film Studies* (1996), edited by David Bordwell and Noël Carroll; *Passionate Views: Film, Cognition, and Emotion* (1999), edited by Carl Plantinga and Greg M. Smith; *Music and Cinema* (2000), edited by James Buhler, Caryl Flinn, and David Neumeyer; and *Soundtrack Available: Essays on Film and Popular Music* (2002), edited by Arthur Knight and Pamela Robertson Wojcik.

Murray Smith is Professor of Film Studies at the University of Kent, UK. He is the author of *Engaging Characters: Fiction, Emotion, and the Cinema* (1995) and *Trainspotting* (2002) and the coeditor of three anthologies: *Thinking through Cinema: Film as Philosophy* (2006), *Film Theory and Philosophy* (1997), and *Contemporary Hollywood Cinema* (1998). He has published widely on the relationship between ethics, emotion, and films, including essays in *The Journal of Aesthetics and Art Criticism* and *Cinema Journal*.

Aaron Smuts earned his PhD in philosophy at the University of Wisconsin, Madison, where he also studied film. He works in a variety of areas in the philosophy of art and ethics, widely construed. Aaron is particularly interested in horror, humor, philosophy of film, analytic existentialism, and well-being. Recently he has written for *American Philosophical Quarterly, Asian Cinema Journal, Contemporary Aesthetics, Kinoeye, Film and Philosophy, Film-Philosophy, The Journal of Aesthetic Education, The Journal of Aesthetics and Art Criticism, Philosophy Compass, Philosophy and Literature,* and *Stanford Encyclopedia of Philosophy*. He is currently a Visiting Assistant Professor in the Department of Philosophy at Temple University.

Vivian Sobchack is Professor in the UCLA School of Theater, Film and Television. She has published widely in film studies and is author of *Screening Space: The American Science Fiction Film* (1997), *The Address of the Eye: A Phenomenology of Film Experience* (1992), and *Carnal Thoughts: Embodiment and Moving Image Culture* (2004).

Robert Stecker is Professor of Philosophy at Central Michigan University. He is the author of *Artworks: Definition, Meaning, Value* (1997), *Interpretation and Construction: Art, Speech and the Law* (2003), and *Aesthetics and the Philosophy of Art: An Introduction* (2005). He has written numerous papers in the areas of aesthetics, the philosophy of mind and language, and the history of modern philosophy.

Kevin W. Sweeney is an Associate Professor of Philosophy at the University of Tampa. He is an associate editor of *Film and Philosophy*. He has published articles on film theory, silent comedy, and horror. Recently he edited an anthology of interviews with Buster Keaton, *Buster Keaton: Interviews* (2007).

Stéphane Symons studied philosophy, liberal studies, and international politics at the University of Leuven, Belgium and the New School for Social Research, New York. He recently finished his doctoral thesis on the philosophy of Walter Benjamin. He is currently employed by the Institute of Philosophy at the University of Leuven and the Research Fund Flanders. His main academic interests are twentieth-century German and French philosophy and aesthetics.

Folke Tersman is Chair Professor of Practical Philosophy at Uppsala University, Sweden and has previously taught at the University of Stockholm and University of Auckland, New Zealand. His main interest lies in moral philosophy, and in particular metaethics. His recent publications include *Moral Disagreement* (2006).

Katherine Thomson-Jones is Assistant Professor in the Department of Philosophy at Oberlin College. As well as having published several articles in aesthetics, she is the author of *Aesthetics and Film* (forthcoming) and the coeditor of *New Waves in Aesthetics* (2008).

Maureen Turim is author of *Abstraction in Avant-garde Films* (1985), *Flashbacks in Film: Memory and History* (1989), and *The Films of Oshima Nagisa: Images of a Japanese Iconoclast* (1998). She has published more than eighty essays in anthologies and journals on a wide range of theoretical, historical, and aesthetic issues in cinema and video, art, cultural studies, feminist and psychoanalytic theory, and comparative literature. Her current book project, entitled *Desire and Its Ends: The Driving Forces of Recent Cinema, Literature, and Art*, will look at the different ways desire structures narratives and images in various cultural traditions, and the way our very notion of desire may be shaped by these representations.

Malcolm Turvey is an Associate Professor of Film Studies at Sarah Lawrence College and an editor of *October*. He has published widely on film theory and avant-garde film. A book on film theory, *Doubting Vision: Film and the Revelationist Tradition*, is forthcoming. He is currently at work on a book about European avant-garde film of the 1920s, titled *The Filming of Modern Life*.

Thomas E. Wartenberg is a Professor of Philosophy at Mount Holyoke College, where he also teaches in the Film Studies program. He is the author of, among other works, *Unlikely Couples: Movie Romance as Social Criticism* (1999) and *Thinking on Screen: Film as Philosophy* (2007) and the editor of a number of anthologies on the philosophy of film, most recently, *Thinking through Cinema: Film as Philosophy* (2006), with Murray Smith. His most recent book is *Existentialism: A Beginner's Guide* (2008).

George Wilson is Professor of Philosophy and Cinematic Arts at the University of Southern California. He has written a book on point of view in film (*Narration in Light*, 1986) and a book on the philosophy of action (*The Intentionality of Human Action*, 1989). He has published articles in the philosophy of language, Wittgenstein on rule-following, and film theory and interpretation.

PREFACE

The recent surge of interest in film in academia has seen the emergence of film studies as a legitimate academic discipline, and a concomitant rise in film scholarship and courses in film offered at colleges and universities. Yet film has also become a medium of interest in other disciplines, especially in philosophy, which is currently witnessing a "boom" in the general area of philosophy and film.

One reason for this trend pertains to the expansion of the topics typically covered within the field of philosophical aesthetics: whereas film was largely ignored in the philosophy of art even twenty years ago, today leading aestheticians have made extensive philosophical investigations of film a central part of their work. Courses are now offered in the philosophy of film; film is regularly discussed in courses in aesthetics; and books examining film from the standpoint of philosophical aesthetics have begun to multiply.

Another reason why philosophers are contributing to the burgeoning literature in the area of philosophy of cinema is that many publications in the area of "film theory" emerging from film studies have constituted an implicit or explicit challenge to central philosophical assumptions and methods. To mention two central examples, film semioticians' statements about the conditions of possibility of cinematic meaning have prodded some philosophers to assess these broad claims in light of arguments and findings from philosophy of language, cognitive science, and linguistics, just as the tenets of psychoanalytic film theory have generated responses from philosophers informed about the philosophy of mind and psychology. Philosophy of cinema has in part emerged, then, as a critical engagement and dialogue with work in film theory, and vice versa.

Another significant recent trend has been the emergence of a sizeable literature, authored by professional philosophers, exploring the philosophical significance of individual films and genres. Although the precise sense in which a film can "be" philosophical or contribute to philosophical knowledge is a matter of lively ongoing debate, it is uncontroversial to observe that a range of films, including popular ones, resonate in fruitful ways with traditional and contemporary philosophical issues. Reference to films in the context of the undergraduate philosophy curriculum has the dual payoff of vividly illustrating philosophical issues and generating excitement and discussion about them, both for philosophy majors and nonmajors.

The Routledge Companion to Philosophy and Film has been designed to function as a textbook and a reference work for undergraduates, graduate students, and faculty who wish to study cinema and philosophy. The conjunction of film *and* philosophy in this companion's title should be understood as embracing both the philosophical study of cinema and the investigations of films' philosophical dimensions, implications, and pedagogical value.

Given the open-ended and interdisciplinary nature of this emerging field of inquiry, our target readership is not comprised exclusively or even primarily of philosophers.

Our ambition has been instead to build a bridge between philosophers working in this area and film students and scholars with theoretical or philosophical inclinations. The fact that philosophical scholarship on film often goes ignored in film and media studies is an unfortunate consequence of the artificial boundaries often drawn between the disciplines. This volume has been designed to bridge this gap by aiming the entries at students and faculty in both disciplines, and at those from other disciplines who are simply interested in the topics presented. For that reason the volume's entries cover topics and thinkers familiar to philosophers and to film and media scholars, with the hope that further mutual interests will develop.

These general ambitions orient the volume's division into four parts. The first part, "Issues and concepts," provides detailed coverage of the most central questions and concepts in the area. Philosophers and film theorists writing these entries offer a systematic, argumentative perspective on these key topics, well-grounded in knowledge of the history of the literature, yet not organized or presented in the form of historical narratives or exegetical discussion. The second part, "Authors and trends," provides crucial information in the form of intellectual histories and author studies. This part was designed to provide incisive and crisp surveys of the central contentions of the most influential philosophers and theorists who have contributed significant generalizations about the cinema. Part III, "Genres and other types," deals with some of the categories of films that have been salient to filmmakers, audiences, and critics, as well as to philosophical commentators. While there could be no attempt to be comprehensive here, the entries cover some of the most salient of the genres and types that have elicited philosophical interest.

The fourth part of the *Companion*, "Film as philosophy," provides a number of selected "case studies" focusing on individual films, filmmakers, and philosophical themes in films. While this section is obviously not designed to offer detailed coverage of all of the philosophically significant moments in the complex history of world cinema, it does provide examples of the ways in which films have philosophical significance, and these entries also provide the reader with examples of philosophically oriented interpretations of films. With eleven entries, the aim is not comprehensiveness, but rather the provision of significant case studies demonstrating the usefulness of film as a source of and stimulus to philosophical analysis. It is our hope that this part may be of special pedagogical use in the undergraduate curriculum.

The editors of this *Companion* have no illusions about having covered all of the relevant topics falling beneath the broad rubric of philosophy and film. The topics actually covered were usually the result of choices rooted in principle but also depended on the availability of suitable authors willing (and able) to work within our timeframe, and on other practical considerations. It is our hope that our contributors have provided a great deal of insight into the subjects covered, as well as a point of entry to many other topics in this wide and rapidly expanding field.

ACKNOWLEDGMENTS

Paisley Livingston is very thankful to Carl Plantinga for inviting him to join him in this project. Work on the book was supported by two different grants from the Research Grants Council of the Hong Kong Special Administrative Region, China: Paisley's research on Ingmar Bergman and philosophy was supported by a CERG (Competitive Earmarked Research Grant) (Project No. LU3401/06H), and work on the collection more generally was funded by an Academic Programme Research Grant (DA07B7). Paisley is very grateful for this support.

Carl Plantinga is thankful to Calvin College for supporting this book in the form of a Calvin Research Fellowship and for a leave of absence for the fall of 2007. He also thanks Lingnan University, and especially Mette Hjort, for the opportunity to become a visiting scholar at Lingnan during that time.

We are both grateful to Solly Leung for his dutiful assistance. Thanks as well to James Thomas for careful copy-editing work.

Part I

ISSUES AND CONCEPTS

1
ACTING

Johannes Riis

The centrality of acting to film narratives raises several issues, some related to the ontology of actors and characters, others to realism and the role of acting styles, and others pertaining to the performance's contribution to a film's artistic merit. This entry surveys some of the most influential and pertinent ideas and issues related to these topics.

Acting in images

In film, the value of acting depends on the abilities of others, such as cinematographers and editors; to probe deeper into the nature of acting's contribution we need to see performances relative to images and the sound track.

First, our experience of a performance as a part of the film implies that acting causally affects the image and sound track. Computer-generated images, which are based on *motion* or *performance capturing*, illustrate even more pointedly the relation of acting to images. Andy Serkis' performance as Gollum in the trilogy of *The Lord of the Rings* is a case in point. Even though we look at a fantasy creature with an outward appearance created from scratch at a computer, not unlike the object of a painting, Gollum's quirky movements and gestures and his uncanny postures all rely on Serkis' acting technique.

The idea that photographic pictures are fundamentally different from other pictures has been highly contested, and it is clear that moving pictures share with other pictures many aesthetic properties. A painter and a film director who wish to depict a certain posture will face similar decisions concerning, for example, how to frame, compose, and light the figure, and the painter may instruct a model to hold a certain pose, not unlike the director who asks the actor to behave in a certain manner. We are looking at images in both cases, and they both rely on the techniques of a painter and a director; yet one of them also relies on acting technique as the actor moves within the picture frame.

Kendall L. Walton's concept of transparency may shed light on the kind of causal relation that is possibly at work in images of a performance (Walton 1984). Elaborating upon an idea first expressed by André Bazin, Walton points out that photographic pictures will show what happened in front of the camera and thereby manifest a counterfactual dependency between the content of the picture and the objects in front of the camera, whereas a painting depends on what the painter believes he or she has observed and what he or she intends to be the pictorial content.

Second, acting implies that someone plays a role as part of a fictional narrative. It may be defined, as James Naremore has put it, as "a special type of theatrical performance in which the persons held up for show have become agents in a narrative" (Naremore 1988: 23). Other kinds of performances, such as singing on stage, might also entail a narrative function, but acting entails that the person "held up for show" tries to enact the role of agent in a narrative. What acting shares with other kinds of performances is the evaluation by the audience: the question is whether the claim to center stage, as it were, is justified by the performer's abilities.

Third, the performance is carried out for the purpose of a film audience. Public service television is in some countries used to broadcast successful stage performances at large theaters, but this is an example of performance as an object of distribution in an audio-visual medium. In film performances, we have distinct expectations concerning the relation of acting to film technology. Comparative studies of scenes which are based on the same play and use cinematography in similar ways show that a performance can be more or less "calibrated" to framing and camera movements (Jacobs 1998), and small nuances of performance can alter a remake (of an earlier film) in thematically important ways (McDonald 2004: 27–32). Acting is an integral and distinct part of the work in question.

Historically, a prevalent use of film technology has allowed for counterfactual dependency on acting, but only empirical study can reveal the extent to which acting accounts for valuable properties such as character expressiveness. Nevertheless, the pictorially inclined may point out that our experience of a performance is affected, for example, by the use of editing, and that acting therefore is a kind of raw material for the editor, subject analogously to the so-called Kuleshov effect. Although the premise is true, it does not follow that editing constructs the expressive content of acting, and the Kuleshov effect should not be trusted as proof in this regard. Lev Kuleshov, an editor and director in post-Revolutionary Russia, did an experiment in which a close-up of the actor Ivan Mozhukin was intercut with various objects. The reactions of the spectators who viewed the intercut shots ostensibly showed that it was the editing, rather than Mozhukin's acting, that created meaning. The footage used in the Mozhukin experiment has been lost, but two similar experiments of Kuleshov indicate that he used this preexisting footage for pedagogical purposes, to illustrate cutting on eye-lines, rather than to prove a theoretical point (Tsivian *et al.* 1996: 359). We should be skeptical of any references to the Kuleshov experiment with regard to acting and expressiveness. First, it is often assumed that Mozhukin took part in what could have been a semi-scientific experiment, when in fact, by the time the "experiment" was conducted, he had fled the country, due to the Revolution (see Albéra 1995: 76). Second, it is often assumed that Mozhukin was inexpressive and that it therefore was the editing that created the illusion that he was emoting. Yet it is rather implausible that Kuleshov would have picked an inexpressive performance by Mozhukin, even if he could find one. An inexpressive glance in a close-up does not cut easily with shots of other objects, since the spectator has no reason to ask for an offscreen cause of an expression.

We are better off with a more recent model of how acting and editing may work together, supplied by Noël Carroll in his theory of point-of-view editing. Carroll implies that facial expressions are somewhat ambiguous. To communicate emotions in a precise manner in cinema, the film structure known as point-of-view editing has been developed (Carroll 1993).

Dualism of actor and character

Acting offers spectators the pleasure of letting us see and hear the artistic agent as part of the film, but it remains unclear whether we can claim to watch an actor and a character at the same time.

According to most accounts, our awareness of the performer need not interfere with the spectator's comprehension of or immersion in the narrative. Naremore provides a striking example from *The King of Comedy* (1983), in which the extras on location (or, alternatively, the fictional bystanders) stop to watch celebrity Robert De Niro and Sandra Bernhard (or their fictional characters). Thus, filmmakers may play upon our ability to notice nuances of role-playing to dramatize the theme of celebrity in yet another form, leaving the spectator to linger over the ambiguities of identity and role-playing (Naremore 1988: 285). This kind of experience presupposes a distinction between what George M. Wilson calls photographic and what he calls dramatic representation. According to Wilson, "there is a complex, dynamic interaction between these types of representation which makes it impossible, in analyzing a film, to unfuse the interaction, to treat them as discernibly separate and distinct" (Wilson 1986: 140).

Established practices in the film industry, such as casting according to type and the promotion of certain actors to stardom, exemplify how the interaction often works. For instance, we may analyze the role of star image in a performance by looking for a selective use, a problematic or a perfect fit (Dyer 1979: 143–9). One model for understanding type casting and star images is to assume that we form a composite or extract that finds its basis in particularly powerful roles. Thus, in a discussion of Humphrey Bogart, Stanley Cavell suggests that Bogart's screen personality, as established across a range of roles, became so powerful as to render character names subordinate; "'Bogart' *means* 'the figure created in a given set of films'" (Cavell 1979: 28). There may be other reasons than good acting for attaining stardom; numerous star studies have examined individual stars and their historical and industrial context (see, for example, Studlar 1996; Basinger 2007).

Underlying the actor and character dualism is a necessary distinction between two sets of actions and attitudes. Acting, as noted initially, means that a performance is carried out for the benefit of an audience, and that the performer becomes an agent in a narrative. This means that we cannot make the mistake of attributing a fictional murder to an actual actor; character beliefs and desires are kept distinct and separate. Conversely, it means that we may admire an actor's performance, even though we do not approve of morally repulsive actions his or her character performs.

Similarly, actor and character do not share an emotional experience, even when the actor uses realist techniques. For instance, the American actor Lindsay Crouse contends that good acting occurs when "what is going on in the scene dovetails exactly with something that you [the actor] have to do … it is your life in that moment" (quoted in Zucker 1995: 20). Thus, a fictional event in a scene comes to stand for an actual event that she wishes to perform. However, that does not mean that actor and character share an emotional experience. An emotion which has the concern for role and audience as part of its content – the actor's emotion – is most plausibly viewed as different from one that does not. An actor's emotional experience is bound to reflect that he or she is playing a role, since what the role requires (or offers, demands, etc.) is the origin of the need for applying a realist technique in the first place.

The question is how we may acknowledge two distinctive sets of actions, beliefs, and desires, as well as a constant interaction between photographic and dramatic representation. I suggest we distinguish between two ways of understanding the actor and character dualism and, for lack of better terms, I will call them the duck/rabbit and the realist model.

According to the duck/rabbit model, actor and character are distinct and separate because they result from mutually exclusive perspectives, and we can only see one at a time, not unlike the famous trick-drawing of a duck and a rabbit. That is, we see in parts of the picture either an actor or a character, two distinct agents: pictorial information is anchored to one agent from the very outset. The distinction between two different pictorial contents leaves unexplained how an actor's previous roles can make themselves felt, but one might hypothesize that properties drift from one agent to the other because actor and character are identical in outward appearance in the images. For instance, Stephen Heath argues that "expression" or "figure of acting" is the result of circulation between several levels: agency of action; the actor, who supplies the body; the actor's image; the character as a specific individual (Heath 1981: 179–82). The question, however, is whether Heath makes too much of the fact that we look at a picture, since Heath's levels could be applied to any agent. For instance, I may describe myself as an agent; I have a body, I can pretend to be someone else, and other people form an image of me. In this case, we would not necessarily claim that meaning circulates as Heath describes it.

According to a realist model the spectator stores information watched in the film with the photographed actor. Instead of being seen as belonging to a fictional entity, an actor's character beliefs and desires can be viewed as the actor's pretense. In other words, acting (or dramatic representation) might be viewed as a certain mode in which actions can be carried out. Not unlike everyday life's playful actions or use of irony, it is a benign and nondeceptive way of carrying out actions. We are unlikely to attribute what we might call pretense-actions to a nonexisting agent, for the same reason that we keep track of the agent who uses irony or does an imitation of us in everyday life.

Whereas the duck/rabbit dualism implies a kind of perceptual mistake when we are affected by previous roles or star promotional material, the realist model can view previous roles as ways of setting up expectations of the actor, given a new role and new set of circumstances. However, the realist model may face difficulties when encountering roles played by multiple actors. In, for instance, *Palindromes* (2004), we assume continuity of character beliefs and desires while recognizing eight distinct actresses; arguably, we assume that each actor has an intention to play the protagonist from where the previous one left off.

Technique

When trying to assess the value of actors' contributions, we are probably better off looking for performance technique rather than, for instance, asking questions about authorship. The script and the director's choices set up a framework within which the actor works, not unlike the constraints facing, for example, musicians and ballet dancers.

Acting technique could be viewed, simply, as that which allows the actor to perform a given role, or parts of it. Admittedly, such an inclusive definition does not distinguish between roles that are demanding and those that appear easily performed. Technique, however, can be taken to mean many things. A role can showcase skills that we would not normally take to be part of a contemporary acting school's core curriculum but are valued by spectators; this is clear, for instance, in musicals and martial arts films. A role can also entail the kind of actions that we are used to performing in our everyday life, for instance, driving a car or opening a door, and such actions can appear anything but artful. To account for the way in which mundane actions can sometimes be considered aesthetically valuable properties of a performance, we are probably best served with an inclusive and nonnormative view of acting technique.

Film performances need not be technically demanding to serve the role and the film; nonprofessional acting is a case in point. The French director Robert Bresson aimed for the portrayal of character actions as automatic and habitual – an acting style that often contrasted strikingly with what was at stake in his narratives. Bresson therefore preferred amateurs, whom he would ask to repeat an action over and over, until their relation to objects and characters "were right because they will not be thought" (Bresson 1977: 12). When a director works with child actors, Vsevolod Pudovkin recommends (drawing on his experience in cinema in the 1920s and early 1930s) that they be given a counterinstruction in the middle of a take in order to deliver a genuine surprise or confusion, thereby creating what he calls real-life conditions (Pudovkin 1954: 119). Although these kinds of performances feed the idea that technique is altogether unnecessary in film acting, they can be taken to demonstrate that a limited technical repertory is sometimes sufficient to perform the role in a style appropriate to a particular scene or film.

Technically demanding roles may require that the actor combine deliberate control of gestures and speech patterns with an emotional experience. To communicate the role's state of mind in a clear and characteristic way, the actor may develop a certain manner of speaking or gesturing; an emotional experience can then serve to remove signs of volition and suggest that emotions underlie the gesture or line. The highly influential Konstantin Stanislavsky has written extensively on actors' means for fostering emotions and conveying character, based on his groundbreaking work as a stage director in the early twentieth century (Stanislavsky 1987, 1989). In his chapter on scenic speech in *Creating a Role*, he advises the actor to distinguish between *logical* and *psychological* pauses. In a logical pause, the verbal meaning of a line is rendered lucid by demarcating a thought, whereas in a psychological pause the actor brings a subtext to the following line or word by using emotion-provoking imagery. In the same chapter, Stanislavsky also gives advice on how to deliver a soliloquy in a manner that will give the impression of increasing force without sacrificing clarity, by means of upward steps in tone of voice. This technique, along with psychological and logical pauses, is recognizable in, for example, Laurence Olivier's delivery of soliloquies in *Hamlet* (1948).

Other acting theorists and pedagogues have downplayed the need for deliberate control and careful execution of a plan, thus giving the actor more room to let emotions affect their performance. One of the most prominent is Lee Strasberg, who claimed that in a performance the actor should be "really thinking something that is real to him at that particular moment" (Strasberg 1991: 46). Whereas Stanislavsky felt that getting too personally involved would jeopardize the buildup toward a climax, as well as the capacity for repetition (Stanislavsky 1989), Strasberg's approach is possibly more suited for cinema (Carnicke 1999, see also Carnicke 1998). One of Strasberg's coteachers and an important twentieth-century director, Elia Kazan, developed strategies for maintaining control of structure and climaxes, while getting performances that have captivated audiences in large part because the actors, most notably Marlon Brando and James Dean, did not concentrate on the execution of a deliberate plan. Through improvisations and by relating "the events in the material to their own life," Kazan ensured that actors had an intense emotional experience (Kazan 1999: 81, 137). Stretching the emotional moment by cutting back and forth between close-ups, the climax of the scene is controlled at the editing table rather than in the performance alone (Kazan 1999: 70–1).

By attending to what actors, directors, and acting instructors prefer in terms of methods, exercises, and training, we gain a heuristic for analyzing a given performance. Unless one reads what Sergei Eisenstein has to say about expressive movement, one is unlikely to describe the performance by Nicolai Cherkasov, in the final scene of *Ivan the Terrible I* (1944), as a series of bodily conflicts, in which the actor works against gravity and the inertia of a prior movement (Eisenstein 1988: 52–6). Once we recognize the technique, however, Eisenstein's description goes a long way toward explaining what lends the performance a sense of both artificiality and forcefulness. The conflict of movement taxes Cherkasov's physique to an extent that it would be impossible to simultaneously employ imagery with psychological pauses, and the scene is a fine example of a technique first developed by Vsevolod Meyerhold in a "nonempathetic" approach to acting that was later pursued also by Bertolt Brecht (see also Leach 1993).

An actor can use different techniques for different roles, even different scenes, and two actors can come up with similar techniques, even though only one of them has been trained for it. In other words, we also have to rely on traditional film analysis and a critical eye. A case in point is André Bazin's comparison of the acting style that Humphrey Bogart developed in the early 1940s, with what Bazin calls the Kazan school of acting. If we suppose that actors face common constraints, some of them due to the psychological mechanisms at work in emotions, we should also expect different performances to draw on similar techniques. In this perspective, the technique possibly at work in the performances of Bogart and the Kazan school serves to convey what Bazin saw as a shared sense of interiority (Bazin 1985: 100).

By attending to acting techniques, we may also become better at understanding styles. Techniques are applicable to different roles by different performers, and when this occurs, there will be interesting differences and similarities that will lead us to speak of, say, a group style or period style. More importantly, we need to discern when different performances reflect differences of style rather than, for instance, differences of role or narrative. Stylistic terms, as pointed out by Rudolf Arnheim, can be arrived at in two ways: either by means of a bottom-up approach in which we identify characteristic and recurrent patterns in a predefined empirical body, or by means of a hypothesis-driven approach in which we assume the existence of certain constraints which artistic choices help overcome (Arnheim 1986: 264). For example, we may look for uses of logical and psychological pauses in trying to identify an actor's characteristic style; to explain a certain use of camera and editing, we may hypothesize that realist acting techniques are difficult to use because especially intense emotions easily distort the structure of the whole.

By looking for techniques, we need not assume that all acting styles are historically contingent codes for representing characters in a world similar to ours. Not all acting styles aim at realism in this sense, and some that do not may still successfully engage the audience relative to an agent in a narrative. Prior to and well into the nineteenth century, a stage actor was expected to play a role as though he or she were a *speaker*, someone able to move the audience by use of eloquent, oratory techniques, for instance, illustrating words in gesture (Christiansen 1975: 196). Good acting in such styles relied on "how the actor negotiates the intermediate stages of the gesture to reach its limits, or how the actor makes effective transitions from one gesture to another," as well as the ability of the actor to adjust to musical accompaniment (Mayer 1999: 18). Early film acting bore traces of performance techniques that first served to engage a theater audience. In the 1910s and 1920s, actors would use broad gestures and extended postures in order to stretch a narrative climax, as though the spectator were momentarily looking at a still picture, in what has been coined a *pictorialist* style (Brewster and Jacobs 1997). In the early 1930s, predefined, rather mask-like expressions – which were originally used to empower a stage actor's eloquent speech by making its emotional content unequivocal – could be applied to film roles that exemplified high moral standards (Riis 2004).

In studying acting, it is important that we do not take for granted what we might call a behaviorist thesis, according to which the actor just behaves as called for in the script and as suggested by the director. This assumption will soon have us focusing too much on the techniques of casting actors, framing, and editing, at the expense of acting. Perhaps adequate to technically undemanding roles, a behaviorist assumption does not serve the appreciation of most acting in film. It is through the actor's balancing of deliberate control and emotional experience, a balancing which can take a variety of forms, that the ability to convey the emotional life of characters is achieved. This ability is at the heart of good acting.

See also Rudolph Arnheim (Chapter 27), Bertolt Brecht (Chapter 30), Noël Carroll (Chapter 31), Digital cinema (Chapter 7), Emotion and affect (Chapter 8), Sergei Eisenstein (Chapter 35), Realism (Chapter 22), and Style (Chapter 25).

References

Albéra, F. (1995) *Albatros: des Russes à Paris, 1919–1929*, Milano: Mazzotta; and Paris: Cinémathèque française.

Arnheim, R. (1986) "Style as a Gestalt Problem," in *New Essays on the Psychology of Art*, Berkeley: University of California Press.

Basinger, J. (2007) *The Star Machine*, New York: A. A. Knopf.

Bazin, A. (1985) "The Death of Humphrey Bogart," in J. Hillier (ed.) *Cahiers du cinéma: The 1950s*, London and New York: Routledge and Kegan Paul.

Bresson, R. (1977) *Notes on Cinematography*, trans. J. Griffin, New York: Urizen Books.

Brewster, B., and Jacobs, L. (1997) *Theatre to Cinema: Stage Pictorialism and Early Film*, Oxford and New York: Oxford University Press.

Carnicke, S. M. (1998) *Stanislavsky in Focus*, Amsterdam: Harwood Academic Publishers.

—— (1999) "Lee Strasberg's Paradox of the Actor," in A. Lovell and P. Krämer (eds.) *Screen Acting*, London and New York: Routledge.

Carroll, N. (1993) "Toward a Theory of Point-of-View Editing: Communication, Emotion, and the Movies," *Poetics* 14: 123–41.

Cavell, S. (1979) *The World Viewed: Reflections on the Ontology of Film*, Cambridge, MA: Harvard University Press.

Christiansen, S. (1975) *Klassisk skuespilkunst. Stabile konventioner i skuespilkunsten 1700–1900*, Copenhagen: Akademisk Forlag.

Dyer, R. (1979) *Stars*, London: British Film Institute.

Eisenstein, S. M. (1988) "The Montage of Film Attractions," in R. Taylor (ed.) *S.M. Eisenstein: Selected Works*, vol. 1: *Writings, 1922–34*, Bloomington: Indiana University Press.

Heath, S. (1981) *Questions of Cinema*, Bloomington: Indiana University Press.

Jacobs, L. (1998) "Keeping Up with Hawks," *Style* 32: 402–26.

Kazan, E. (1999) *Kazan on Kazan*, ed. J. Young, London: Faber and Faber.

Leach, R. (1993) "Eisenstein's Theatre Work," in I. Christie and R. Taylor (eds.) *Eisenstein Rediscovered*, London and New York: Routledge.

Mayer, D. (1999) "Acting in the Silent Film: Which Legacy of the Theatre?," in A. Lovell and P. Krämer (eds.) *Screen Acting*, London and New York: Routledge.

McDonald, P. (2004) "Why Study Film Acting: Some opening Reflections," in C. Baron, D. Carson, and F. P. Tomasulo (eds.) *More Than a Method: Trends and Traditions in Contemporary Film Performance*, Detroit: Wayne State University Press.

Naremore, J. (1988) *Acting in the Cinema*, Berkeley: University of California Press.

Pudovkin, V. I. (1954) *Film Technique and Film Acting*, trans. I. Montagu, London: Vision Press.

Riis, J. (2004) "Naturalist and Classical Styles in Early Sound Film Acting," *Cinema Journal* 43: 3–17.

Stanislavsky, K. (1987) *Creating a Role*, trans. E. R. Hapgood; ed. H. I. Popper, New York: Theatre Arts Books.

—— (1989) *An Actor Prepares*, trans. E. R. Hapgood, New York: Routledge.

Strasberg, L. (1991) "A Dream of Passion: The Development of the Method," in J. Butler (ed.) *Star Texts: Image and Performance in Film and Television*, Detroit: Wayne State University Press.

Studlar, G. (1996) *This Mad Masquerade: Stardom and Masculinity in the Jazz Age*, New York: Columbia University Press.

Tsivian, Y., Thompson, K., and Tsivian, E. (1996) "The Rediscovery of a Kuleshov Experiment: A Dossier," *Film History* 8: 357–64.

Walton, K. L. (1984) "Transparent Pictures," *Critical Inquiry* 11: 246–77.

Wilson, G. M. (1986) *Narration in Light: Studies in Cinematic Point of View*, Baltimore, MD: Johns Hopkins University Press.

Zucker, C. (1995) *Figures of Light: Actors and Directors Illuminate the Art of Film Acting*, New York: Plenum Press.

2
AUTHORSHIP
Aaron Meskin

Directors play a significant role in ordinary thought and talk about film. We often choose to watch films on the basis of who directed them ("I'll see anything Tim Burton directs"), and we commonly evaluate and interpret them in light of other works in the director's oeuvre ("It's the best he's directed since *Edward Scissorhands* [1990], and it shows that his films have not, in fact, become more sentimental"). We also compare one director's oeuvre with another's (e.g., Hawks' films with Ford's and Lucas' movies with those of Spielberg). Perhaps even more basically, we regularly identify films by reference to their director ("Have you seen the new Scorsese film?").

It is also a commonplace that the director is typically the most important figure involved in the making of a film. As Bordwell and Thompson put it, "Within most film industries, the director is considered the single person most responsible for the look and sound of the finished film" (Bordwell and Thompson 1993: 13). And it is natural to think that it is precisely *because* the director is typically so central to the making of films that it makes sense to talk and think about them in the ways sketched above.

These considerations might tempt one to think that film directors are enough like literary authors that we may gain significant insight into the workings of film by (1) borrowing our best theories of authorship from the literary domain and applying them to cinema; and (2) identifying film directors as typically standing in the authorship role. Perhaps, as Ernest Hemingway stands to the novel *To Have and Have Not* (1937) so Howard Hawks stands to the 1944 film of the same name. Moreover, there is a well-established film-critical tradition that does just this. From the defense of *la politique des auteurs* by figures such as François Truffaut to Andrew Sarris' articulation of the auteur theory, a wide range of critics and theorists have explicitly treated many of the major directors of mainstream and "art" cinema as authors (Truffaut 2000; Sarris 2000, 2003). But although this might eventually prove to be a fruitful strategy, a number of considerations should give us pause before pursuing it.

First, although it is certainly true that directors figure heavily in ordinary discourse about film, they are not the only ones who play a significant role in our talk and thought about cinema. The category of the "Julia Roberts movie" seems just as robust and important to our thought as that of the "Altman film." And Rudolf Arnheim suggested that in certain cases, such as *Anna Christie* (1930), "we have indirect experimental proof that the leading actress was the main author of the film," because without Garbo there would have been "a totally different film" (Arnheim 1997: 68). (See Dyer [1979] for an influential work that highlights the importance of film stars.) In certain other cases, screenwriters seem to be especially important. *Being John Malkovich* (1999) and *Eternal Sunshine of the Spotless Mind* (2004) are as well known as Charlie Kaufman films as they are as by their directors Spike Jonze and Michel Gondry, respectively. Moreover, screenwriters literally produce written texts, so their claims to be the authors of films seem – at least in one way – on firmer ground than those of directors. (For an early defense of the view that the screenwriter "is the primary creative source," see Koch [2000].) In still other cases – especially but not only during the heyday of the Hollywood studio system – producers such as David O. Selznick, as well as film companies such as Hammer Film Productions, were especially significant. (See Schatz [1988] for an key work emphasizing the importance of studios and producers.) The Academy Award for Best Motion Picture is, after all, given to the producer or producers of the film! So it is not at all clear that directors really are the only – or even best – candidates for being cinematic authors.

Second, film is simply a very different sort of thing than literature. Even though texts go into the making of most films, films themselves are not linguistic texts. There is no language of cinema in any literal sense of "language" (Currie 1993, 1995a). And films are typically (though not essentially) made collaboratively – in most cases by very large groups. Literature – on the other hand – is at least primarily a matter of texts (oral literature may be the exception) and is typically (though not essentially) produced by individuals. (See Stillinger [1991] and Inge [2001] for dissenting views about literature.) *Pace* certain semiotic approaches then, literature seems a poor model for understanding the cinema, and adapting theories of the literary author to the cinematic case may seem especially misguided. In addition it is true that the term "author" is not usually applied to the makers of films in colloquial English. Perhaps, then, films have no authors at all or, at least, no authors in any literal sense of the word.

Skepticism about the very idea of film authorship might also be engendered by a few more considerations. There is the broadly genealogical worry that the very idea of cinematic authorship and the director-as-author thesis largely appear to be fairly recent products of the aforementioned film-critical movements. A reminder that directors didn't always seem to be as important as they do now, and that early advocates of auteurism sought to elevate the status of certain directors in order to advance the causes of film and film criticism, may undercut the apparent naturalness of the director-as-author position. There may also be worries that the very notion of authorship or, at least, the traditional notion of authorship is only really applicable in the sphere of the high or fine arts and, hence, is somehow inappropriately applied to film, which is often characterized as a popular or mass art. For example, in a discussion of television authorship, Rosalind Coward suggests that "the study of the author seems a peculiarly limiting way of approaching the mass media" (Coward 1987: 79).

Pauline Kael famously excoriated auteur theorists for following a rigid and misguided approach to film criticism, criticizing them for "their truly astonishing inability to exercise taste and judgment within their area of preference" (Kael 2005: 109). Any approach to film that leads to such misguided critical evaluation looks questionable. More importantly, there is a significant current of thought that is decidedly skeptical about authorship in any domain. Roland Barthes famously proclaimed "the death of the author" (Barthes 2002), and another famous French theorist, Michel Foucault, optimistically predicted a time when even "the author function will disappear" (Foucault 2002: 22). Although these two authors (!) were primarily concerned with the case of literature, the relevance of their arguments to the question of cinematic authorship is obvious and their influence has been huge.

So it appears there is a deep tension in our thinking about film and authorship. On the one hand, treating some if not all directors as authors is tempting, and there is a long and distinguished history of making just such an identification. Furthermore, it must be said that despite Kael's skepticism, the director-as-author thesis has paid off critically. The directors and films championed by Truffaut (e.g., Renoir, Bresson, Cocteau, Ophuls and their movies) and Sarris (e.g., Flaherty, Ford, Hawks, Hitchcock, Keaton and theirs) have to a very large extent survived the test of time. The recognition of the very significant artistic successes of American moviemaking during the height of the Hollywood studio system seems due in large part to the writings of the auteur theorists. And this must weigh in favor of the director-as-author view. But, on the other hand, there is something deeply unintuitive about treating directors as authors. The analogy between authors of novels and directors of full-length films seems to obscure difference rather than illuminate similarity. And the very notion of authorship seems as if it may be an outdated and perhaps limiting romantic concept. How then to proceed?

One traditional philosophical approach would be to start by arguing for a definition of the author concept. Armed with such a definition, one would then seek to apply it to the case of film. Does any person or group of persons involved in the making of films meet the criteria for authorship laid out in the definition? If so, films have authors, and the person or persons who fit the criteria are such. If not, they don't. Although I am suspicious of such a strategy – philosophy doesn't have the greatest record when it comes to definition, and the history of failure may have a psychological basis (Ramsey 1998) – I admit that such an approach may ultimately be useful. (Livingston [1997, 2005] offers the most compelling advertisements for such an approach that I know. See below for brief discussion.) Nevertheless, I believe that we will gain more insight into the debate about cinematic authorship (and get a firmer grasp on what cinematic authorship is) by first considering why the issue of authorship matters. But before we get on with that, let me address some of the aforementioned skeptical views about cinematic authorship. For if there are good arguments against the existence of film authors, we might save ourselves a lot of trouble.

Skepticism about (cinematic) authorship

As should be clear from the discussion above, much of the skepticism that auteurism and related views faced focused on specific theses about actual authors (i.e., the director-as-author view and the related claim that solo authorship is common in film). Such forms of skepticism do not seek to do away with the notion of authorship altogether – far from it. Defenders of multiple-authorship views, for example, do not doubt that films have authors – they are simply critical of common views of how many persons typically fill that role (Gaut 1997; Sellors 2007). Other critics of the director-as-author view may simply be in favor of identifying a *different* figure as the standard author of a film or, perhaps, holding that various figures may fill that role in different circumstances. Even someone sympathetic to auteurism, such as Ian Cameron, is sympathetic to the latter view: "Given a weak director the effective author of a film can be its photographer … composer … producer … or star" (Cameron 2000: 54–5; see also Arnheim 1997: 68).

Some more robustly skeptical views about cinematic authorship can be dismissed rather quickly. Is there any inconsistency in applying the idea of authorship to works of mass or popular culture? In short the answer is no. Stephen King and Danielle Steel work in the sphere of mass culture, and they are clearly authors in at least some important sense. If commercial films were produced by some process akin to that involved in making cars or computers, then it might be reasonable to deny authorship to them. But even at the height of the studio system, this is not how films were made (Bordwell and Thompson 1993: 10). And, of course, not all film falls into the categories of mass or popular culture.

The genealogical worry may be swiftly dismissed too. Cinema is a relatively young art form. It should not be surprising that the appropriate theoretical apparatus for understanding it took some time to discover. And the purposes for which the idea of cinematic authorship was initially used are simply irrelevant to the validity of the concept. In response to the suggestion that colloquial English doesn't typically involve the application of the term "author" to films, it is worth noting that it is not the case that the only relevant literal usages of the term apply to the makers of texts. A quick perusal of the OED unearths a wide range of literal uses. Moreover, the issues that underlie the debate about cinematic authorship are live ones even if films do not literally have authors: the question may be about the film artist (as Gaut argues), or about the value of treating films *as if* they had authors, or about whether there is anything significantly analogous to literary authorship in the case of filmmaking.

Stephen Heath's influential criticism of the idea of the cinematic authorship focuses on the putative way in which "the notion of the author … avoids … the thinking of the film text in relation to ideology" (Heath 1986: 217), and he suggests that the notion of the film author is inconsistent with the much needed development of "a theory of the subject" (217), by which he seems to mean a theory that would address both viewers and filmmakers in relation to ideology. Heath gestures at a significant problem with auteur theory – it could, in certain modes, be rather one-dimensional in its approach. A narrow critical focus on directors and their oeuvres might involve a concomitant failure to attend to the role of the film industry and the social conditions in which films are produced, as well as the ways in which viewers receive films. But this is not reason to reject the idea that films have authors. It merely provides a good reason to reject the idea that authorship is the *only* thing worth studying when it comes to film. For example, in the article about which Heath's essay comments,

Edward Buscombe suggests augmenting auteur theory with an attention to "the effects of the cinema on society … the effect of society on the cinema … the effects of films on other films" (Buscombe 1986: 32). Heath's suggestion that simply adding these approaches to the auteur theory is impossible rests on the assumption that "the notion of the author itself is a major ideological construction" (Heath 1986: 217), but this is tendentious, since it is not at all clear that the author concept is inherently epistemically defective, nor that it has an essential link to social domination. (See Carroll [1998] for the characterization of ideology that underwrites my skepticism about Heath's claim.) Nor is there an inconsistency between a belief in cinematic authors and the practice of ideological criticism. Careful attention to the ways in which films reflect, express, and instill ideology may go hand in hand with the view that they are authored. What is true is that many of the most plausible accounts of ideology in cinema are not *explicitly* concerned with authorship (e.g., Carroll 1996). But this does not imply inconsistency – at most it suggests that we may not have a unified "Grand Theory" of cinema. So Heath's concerns are misplaced. It should be noted, too, that Heath himself suggests that "the author … may return as a fiction" (Heath 1986: 220), so his skepticism is itself ambivalent.

But what about the aforementioned "death of the author"? If the author is dead then the cinematic author is dead as well and debates about the nature and number of film authors are moot. As mentioned above, Barthes and Foucault have certainly been influential, but it is not even clear whether they were arguing that authors do not exist, will not exist, or should not exist. (See Lamarque [1990] for relevant discussion.) Barthes, for example, claimed that "the sway of the Author remains powerful" (2002: 4). But if the author and/or author function currently exists, then theorists interested in developing accounts of cinematic authorship still have a legitimate area of inquiry.

Perhaps more importantly, their arguments for the death-of-the-author conclusion – insofar as those can be made out – are unpersuasive. I shall ignore the purely predictive reading of the death thesis, since it is hard to know what possible arguments could support such crystal ball pronouncements. With respect to arguments for the extant nonexistence of the author the case does not seem much better. For example, Foucault's discussion of authorship and the author function emphasizes the social, legal, and moral status associated with it: "the author function is linked to the juridical and institutional system that encompasses, determines, and articulates the universe of discourses" (Foucault 2002: 17). Authorship, on his account, is then a constructed and therefore contingent social role: "Texts, books, and discourses really began to have authors … to the extent that authors became subject to punishment, that is, to the extent that discourses could be transgressive" (14). But if we focus on the social role of authorship and, in particular, the moral and legal status of those people who produce works of literature and film, then it is obvious that the social role of the author still exists (Lamarque 1990). In many contexts filmmakers are still subject to moral, legal, and religious censure for what they produce. Films may still transgress. The juridical and institutional systems that allegedly underwrite the author function are still in place.

This leaves us with the most interesting of the claims suggested by Barthes and Foucault – the normative view that we would be better off in some sense if authorship disappeared or came to an end. There *might*, in fact, be some advantages to such a development (although pretty clearly there would be some serious drawbacks to doing away with copyright law), but Barthes and Foucault do not make the case for this. Rather they argue that the elimination of the author would be hermeneutically liberatory and "truly revolutionary" (Barthes 2002: 6). The author, Foucault states, "is a certain functional principle by which, in our culture, one limits, excludes, and chooses" (Foucault 2002: 21), and here he is talking about meaning or signification which – on his view – would be better left to "proliferate" to some significant extent (21). But, in the first place, the degree to which authorship limits and excludes is often overstated. Even a cursory glance at the contemporary philosophical work on interpretation should make evident the degree to which a commitment to the importance of authorship is consistent with interpretive pluralism (Stecker 2006). And, in the second place, it is not at all obvious how valuable the proliferation of meaning would really be. In many practical contexts (e.g., with traffic signs and shouts of warning or distress) it is crucial that meaning doesn't proliferate. Similarly in scientific contexts – a little too much proliferation of meaning and the cooperative pursuit of knowledge is jeopardized. Limitation and exclusion of meaning are often good things. And as Foucault recognizes, "it would be pure romanticism … to imagine a culture in which the fictive would operate in an absolutely free state" (Foucault 2002: 22). The upshot is that there are significant reasons for being skeptical of the claim that we would be better without the social role of the author and that, hence, all versions of the death of the author thesis are suspect. Friends of auteurism have nothing to worry about from Foucault and Barthes. Skepticism about the very idea of film authorship can be put safely aside.

Why does (cinematic) authorship matter?

So what is at stake in the debate about film authorship? Once we know how different sorts of films are made, what difference does it make whether we identify an individual or group as author or deny that films have authors altogether?

We may gain some insight into why the issue matters by considering the place of authorship in literature. For authorship – though an almost irredeemably contested notion – seems to play a central role in ordinary and critical appreciation of literature. In particular, some notion of authorship seems to play an important role in our engagement with literature *as literature* – authorship matters (or, at least, seems to matter) in the contexts of literary evaluation, interpretation, and stylistic attribution. (It also matters legally and morally – more on this below.) And it is natural to think this relevance carries over to the cinematic realm and that film authorship is just as central to ordinary and critical engagement with cinema; that is, that it plays an important role in film evaluation, interpretation, and stylistic attribution. Examination of the debate on film authorship in light of these activities helps clarify what is at stake in the debate about cinematic authorship.

17

Evaluation

Although this is tendentious, many philosophers would agree that to evaluate a work of art as art is, at least in part, to evaluate the achievement of the artist who made it (Dutton 1979; Currie 1989). The artists who make literary works are their authors, so if the general principle is true then authorship matters in the context of literary evaluation. This is not the whole story about literary evaluation of course, but it does point to an important connection between authorship and evaluation – a connection that is manifest in much of the discussion of cinematic authorship. Evaluative concerns were central to the early development of the auteur theory. Truffaut's influential distinction between mere *metteurs en scène* and *auteurs* was primarily a matter of defending and explaining certain critical evaluations; namely, his negative assessment of the dominant mode of postwar French cinema and his valorization of the films of the directors mentioned above. Andrew Sarris' "premises" of the auteur theory – "the technical competence of a director as a criterion of value," "the distinguishable personality of the director as a criterion of value," and "interior meaning, the ultimate glory of the cinema as an art" (Sarris 2000: 69) – are clear expressions of the evaluative concerns underlying his commitment to the director-as-author thesis, as is his suggestion that although directors "do not always run true to form," it is "almost always" the case that bad directors make bad films (68). And Kael's critical remarks, mentioned above, are an expression of her negative assessment of the evaluative dimension of the auteur theory. Moreover, authorship isn't just relevant to the evaluation of *individual* cinematic works or specific bodies of work like Hollywood films of the studio era. It is plausible that the very idea of applying the concept of authorship to cinema was centrally tied up with the establishment of film – especially commercial film – as on an artistic par with the other arts. So the debate about authorship centrally has evaluative significance.

Interpretation

The dominant view among philosophers who have addressed themselves to interpretation in the literary context is that authorship of some sort or other (i.e., actual, implied, postulated) plays a role in interpretation. Only the most extreme forms of conventionalism or anti-intentionalism about interpretation reject any appeal to authors whatsoever, and it is noticeable that the most vigorous recent philosophical defender of an anti-intentionalist approach to literary and artwork interpretation argues that "an author's intentions seem to be essential to her work's identity and thereby central to the identification of the appropriate object of interpretation" (Davies 2006: 233). This should also reinforce the point that thinking authorship has *something* to do with interpretation is not thereby to think that the actual author's semantic intentions fully determine acceptable interpretation.

These reflections on the literary case suggest that the question of cinematic authorship may matter for interpretive or hermeneutic reasons. And, in fact, the interpretive significance of authorship seems central to much of the writings of auteur theorists, as well as their critics. A concern for the interpretive significance of authorship is clearly manifest in the work of Peter Wollen, whose auteur structuralism is centered around discerning structures implicit in the bodies of films produced by particular directors – structures whose varying manifestations are key to "decoding" or deciphering their films. So, for example, Wollen states that, "the auteur theory enables us to reveal a complex of meanings in films such as *Donovan's Reef*" (Wollen 1986: 142). Robin Wood's version of auteurism, as expressed in his writings on Ford and Hawks, shows a significant concern for the role that directors' intentions and values may play in the interpretation and understanding of their films (Wood 1986, 2000). The philosopher Gregory Currie appeals to the "implied author" of certain films (i.e., the author as he/she/they seem from the evidence of the work) to explain our ability to grasp certain sorts of cinematic unreliability (Currie 1995b). Even some critics of traditional author theory have argued that "the 'fiction' of the author enables us to locate an author of the fiction ... who in 'his' notional coherence provides the means for us to grasp the text in the moments of its production before us" (Nowell-Smith 1986: 223).

Style

Style and stylistic attribution are central to our engagement with literature and the other arts. So, for example, we interpret, evaluate, and identify literary works in virtue of our recognition of the various styles that they manifest. The same is true of cinema, and one key role that authorship plays in film criticism and theory is to underwrite certain sorts of judgments about film style. Now it is not the case that all forms of film style (e.g., universal film styles such as the realist style) have much to do with authorship. But our concern for the individual styles that are manifested in works of the cinema (i.e., the styles of film artists such as Godard and Hitchcock) seems to mirror our concern for the individual styles of authors found in great works of literature. Moreover, one very important – arguably dominant – view about individual literary style connects it to the personality or character of the author or implied author of the work of literature (Robinson 1985).

What is more, a concern for style and the connection between individual style and personality is a key aspect of the auteurist view. Sarris writes that "Over a group of films, a director must exhibit certain recurring characteristics of style which serve as his signature" (Sarris 2000: 69). Bazin distinguishes between the auteur (e.g., Hitchcock) and the *metteur en scène* (Huston) who lacks a "truly personal style" (Bazin, quoted in Buscombe 1986: 23). And Perkins claims that the "most telling argument for a critical belief in the 'director's cinema' is that it has provided the richest base for useful analyses of the styles and meanings of particular films" (Perkins 1993: 185).

Legal and moral aspects of authorship

I have to this point focused on the broadly artistic aspects of cinematic authorship. This is reflective of the literature on the topic. But authorship is not purely an aesthetic category – it also has legal and moral significance. (See Salokannel [2003] for a useful discussion of some of the legal aspects of cinematic authorship.) So, for example, authors are typically – at least in the first instance – treated as the legal owners of the works they produce. And in virtue of ownership and the possession of copyright, authors are treated as having certain legal rights. Copying and adaptation of copyrighted works typically require the consent of the author. Moreover, authors often have the right to be identified as authors, and they have certain rights to object to the way in which their works are treated. These rights, of course, can be transferred; for example, it is common in the academic world for all or some of these rights to be assigned to a publisher. But it is the author who initially holds copyright and the rights that go with it.

Even more significantly for the case of film, in some legal jurisdictions works produced as part of employment may be treated as owned and authored by the employer. US copyright law counts the typical commercially made film as a "work made for hire" and states that in "the case of a work made for hire, the employer or other person for whom the work was prepared is considered the author for purposes of this title" (17 USC §201 [b]). Laws vary of course, as do their application to film. In the European Union the principal director is typically treated as the (or a) film's author – there is some variation within the European Union about whether or not other makers count as authors (Salokannel 2003: 167). The key points to take from this are that authorship is not purely an artistic or aesthetic category – it is of legal significance too.

And of moral significance. Plagiarism and film piracy are not simply legal affronts: they seem to be moral affronts to the author as well. More centrally, it is widely (although not uncontroversially) held that the intimate relationship in which authors stand to their works underwrites certain sorts of author-focused moral evaluations. It is natural to treat the author of a racist work of literature or film as to some extent morally responsible for that racism. And the author of a work that is designed to foment hatred and violence or to honor something that is despicable is commonly morally censured. The fascist sympathies of *Triumph of the Will* (1935) have seemed to many to provide reason to morally criticize Leni Riefenstahl. There are, of course, substantive debates about the ethical evaluation of art and literature (and, in particular, whether it is real authors or manifest and/or implied authors who are appropriately ethically evaluated on the basis of works); my only point is that the idea of authorship plays a role in these debates.

One potential upshot of considering the legal and moral aspects of authorship is the recognition that authorship may be fragmented (i.e., distinct notions of authorship or distinct aspects of the authorship role may pull apart in certain circumstances). In fact, I think there is a significant potential for this sort of fragmentation in the case of film, and I shall return to this below.

Two issues in film authorship

Now that we have a sense of what is at stake in the debate about cinematic authorship, let us briefly turn to a consideration of two issues about film authors: (1) How many authors do films typically have? And (2) are film authors real or constructed?

Individual or collaborative authorship?

Let us assume that it makes sense to say that films have authors. It would be a mistake to ask whether films in general are singly or multiply authored, for it is plausible that such a question would be ill-formed. There are many kinds of films and many kinds of filmmaking practices. Surely the only reasonable position is that some films have individual authors and some are authored by groups. In addition, it is plausible that there are (or could be) entirely unauthored films. Cases to consider here are accidentally produced films (see Gaut 1997: 169n14) or "traffic jam" films that, as Livingston puts it, are "the unintended result of disparate and unintentional activities" (Livingston 1997: 138). (Perhaps such films could not be [good] works of art.)

That some films have individual authors seems hard to deny. Some homemade digital films are entirely made by one person. The same is true of certain experimental and avant-garde films (e.g., Brakhage's 1963 *Mothlight*). Other films are almost entirely made solo (i.e., at the most only certain technical processes are carried out by others), and it does not seem that, for example, sending Super 8 stock out to be developed undercuts one's status as the sole author of a film. Louis Lumière is often treated as a solitary filmmaker, and other early pioneers such as Le Prince also seem to have worked largely alone. On the other hand, there are cases where it seems difficult to deny multiple authorship. The close working relationships between the Coen brothers and the Brothers Quay suggests that their films are multiply and, in fact, collaboratively authored. Other cases of multiple, although perhaps noncollaborative, authorship can be found in certain omnibus films such as *New York Stories* (1989), which is composed of three shorts made by three distinct filmmaking teams. And some films have been produced by collectives such as Newsreel.

But although it should be fairly uncontroversial that there are both singly and multiply authored films, the question of what is typical or standard is tendentious. The view that most popular films are individually authored (if authored at all) is dominant, but there is a significant minority who argue that multiple authorship is typical for commercial "mainstream" film (e.g., Gaut 1997; Sellors 2007). The sheer number of people involved in the making of a standard studio film seems to weigh in this direction. How could one person (even the director) possibly count as *the* author of a standard Hollywood film? One might worry that the popularity of the single-author hypothesis (the view that a great many popular films are authored by a single individual) rests on confusion or a failure to take seriously the ways in which mainstream films are made.

But this would be a mistake. The defenders of the single-author hypothesis are not blind to the essentially collaborative nature of mainstream filmmaking (see, for example, Perkins 1993: 158ff.). And some sorts of collaborative or at least cooperative production do seem consistent with solo authorship or artistry. The editors of academic journals in the humanities often make (or, at least, suggest) changes to articles before they are published. But the idea that such a journal article is, therefore, authored by a group rather than an individual seems perverse. The situation is the same in the literary context. Although some editors may make such significant contributions that they may deserve coauthorship status (Gordon Lish's contributions to Raymond Carver's stories and Maxwell Perkin's editing of Thomas Wolfe are notable cases), it does not seem plausible that every novel that has been edited is thereby coauthored. Individual authorship does not require that a text or artwork be produced solely by a single person. As Livingston writes: "some items can be collectively produced … without having been collaboratively or jointly authored" (Livingston 2005: 75).

So how can the collective or collaborative production that is standard in film be made consistent with solo authorship? A variety of suggestions are made in the literature (notably, these are typically in service of a director-as-author thesis as well). V. F. Perkins claims that directors are "in charge of relationships, of synthesis" and are, therefore, "in charge of what makes a film a *film*" (Perkins 1993: 184), moreover, that the "director's authority is a matter not of total creation but of sufficient control" (184). Bordwell and Thompson suggest that "usually it is through the director's control of the shooting and assembly phases that the film's form and style crystallize" (Bordwell and Thompson 1993: 16). Peter Wollen argues that we may focus on the structures found in groups of films produced by a single director and treat everything else as irrelevant, i.e., mere "noise" contributed by producers, camera operators, and actors (Wollen 1986: 143–4). Livingston, who has argued that *some* studio films are singly authored, points to the "high degree of control" and "huge measure of authority" that some directors have (Livingston 1997: 144) and the fact that some films express a director's "sensibility and attitudes so vividly" (Livingston 2005: 85).

Although one may tease apart at least two different broad strategies here (Gaut distinguishes the "sufficient control" strategy from the "restriction" strategy [Gaut 1997: 155–8]), perhaps the most plausible argument for solo authorship combines the two, appealing to the director's significant (and, hence, sufficient) control over the factors that determine the artistically or cinematically relevant aspects of the film.

Can such a strategy be successful in shoring up a solo authorship view of film? There are two broad ways one might challenge this sort of argument for solo authorship – one could dispute the empirical claim about the typical degree and extent of directors' control or one could dispute the broadly conceptual claim about what suffices for authorship. Gaut offers both sorts of challenges. Although he admits that some architects might be properly seen to be solo authors/artists in virtue of their sufficient control over the artistically relevant features of the buildings they design, the case of film is simply different: "the director's degree of control over the work is not that of the architect's" (Gaut 1997: 158) and, hence, is not properly seen as a solo author/artist. (Presumably no other person involved in the making of a film has the requisite degree of control either.) Gaut also suggests that sufficient control may not be enough to establish solo authorship – the fact that the director is the person with the greatest degree of responsibility for the look and sound of the finished film does not imply that he or she is the only author for "if there are others who make a significant artistic difference to the work, then it is only fair to acknowledge them as artistic collaborators" (157). It remains to be seen whether defenders of the single-author view can successfully meet these challenges.

Defenders of certain versions of the multiple-authorship view face their own challenges. Gaut goes so far as to argue that the "actors of films are among its co-creators" (158); hence, they count as coauthors. He bases his claim on the fact that film performances are "internal to the film" (163) and that screen actors partially determine the nature of the characters they play. But at least two considerations weigh against the actor-as-author view. In the first place, Gaut's reasoning would seem to be extendable to cases of photographic portraiture, and it is counterintuitive that subjects of photographic portraits typically count as coauthors. More significantly, actors' performances are "internal" to films in virtue of their being represented cinemato-graphically. But it is simply hard to see how *this* could provide a basis for a legitimate authorship claim – the grounds of performance internality simply don't seem the right ones to underwrite a claim of authorship. The topic is a rich one for future research.

Cinematic authors and/or author constructs?

I have already mentioned Foucault's invocation of the "author function" rather than the author itself. Foucault's usage reflects an important trend in recent thinking about both literary and cinematic authorship – a shift from thinking of authorship as a role filled by actual individuals or collectives to thinking of them as constructs or fictions or something of the sort. Peter Wollen distinguishes between the real individuals Fuller, Hawks, and Hitchcock, on the one hand, and "'Fuller' or 'Hawks' or 'Hitchcock', the structures named after them" (Wollen 1986: 147), and this distinction is taken up by Geoffrey Nowell-Smith, among others, who states that "What the play with inverted commas aims to do is to distinguish the author as empirical origin (John Ford, the man with the eye-patch who isn't Raoul Walsh) from the author as effect of the text ('John Ford')" (Nowell-Smith 1986: 222). Seymour Chatman explicitly borrows the idea of the "implied author" from literary theory to make sense of the way in which a collabo-ratively produced film may seem as if it is the unified product of a single controlling intelligence (Chatman 2005: 191–2).

The issue of the ontological status of authors is a huge one (see Livingston [1997] and Gaut [1997] for discussion in the context of film), but we need not see it as one of forced choice. That is, we can and should allow that there are both real empirical authors and authors as they are seen in their works (i.e., author constructs or implied authors). In some but not all works of fiction, there are additionally full-fledged fictional authors; that is, it is true-in-the-fiction that they are authored by some agent or agents. The character David Holzman (played by L. M. Kit Carson) is portrayed as the sole maker and author of *David Holzman's Diary* (1967), even though it was directed by Jim McBride.

But this limited pluralism about authorship does not settle the disputes about evalu-ation, interpretation, and stylistic attribution that underlie the authorship debates. So, for example, does film interpretation properly concern itself with the intentions of the actual cinematic author(s) or, rather, the intentions of the author construct (i.e., the author as manifest in the work)? Is the attribution of individual cinematic style (e.g., Kurosawa's style) concerned with the actual director's personality or character or, rather, the personality of the implied author (Kurosawa as he appears from the evidence of the film or body of films)? It is, of course, also possible that both concerns are legitimate. How are we to decide?

I have already mentioned one argument in favor of the significance of the implied cinematic author – the suggestion that recognition of and appeal to the author construct provides the best explanation of the apparent unity and coherence that many films present us with. This, I believe is not persuasive. The assumption seems to be that unity is only attributable as an effect of an individual maker, but this assumption is flawed. There are a range of ways that groups may organize themselves to produce unified and coherent outputs – the use of a project manager (or lead author!) is a common strategy in the academic context. Moreover, it is not obvious that the implied author of a film is best thought of as an individual. Gaut argues that "were we to construct just one author for each film, it would be so different from people as we know them that its use ... would systematically distort our responses to cinema" (Gaut 1997: 160). So it does not seem that appeal to an implied author can comfortably explain the apparent unity of many films. And, as Gaut points out, appeal to collective authorship may help us explain why some films give the appearance of disunity and internal contradiction (165–6).

Let me offer two other reasons to be skeptical of the appeal to implied authors or author constructs. The first is that one of key motivations for the shift away from actual author to author construct looks to be questionable. Fans of author constructs often point to the frequent apparent mismatch between the character or personality of the real person(s) who made a work and the character or personality expressed in the work. For example, D. W. Griffith made films that appear to express viciously racist ideas, but some have suggested that he is not properly seen as a racist (Curtis 2003). The possibility of mismatch suggests to some that we are not and should not be concerned with the attitudes of the actual person(s) who made the film, when it comes to interpretation and stylistic attribution. Perhaps the right thing to say is that Griffith's films express the attitudes of Griffith-as-he-is-seen-from-his-films (i.e., the views of the Griffith construct or "Griffith"), rather than those of Griffith himself. (See Robinson [1985] for a classic statement of the general form of argument in the case of literature.) But this mismatch argument seems to rely on the idea that character traits are broad or "global," that is, that they are consistently manifested across a wide range of relevant domains. Recent work on character has called this assumption into question (Doris 2002). And if character traits are narrow or "local," then a mismatch between a trait exhibited in fiction-writing or filmmaking and a trait exhibited in other contexts should not trouble us. If character traits are more like *courage in a particular context* than *courage simpliciter* (62), then there should be nothing surprising about the fact that the style of a director's cinematic oeuvre may express different character traits than are expressed by him or her in other contexts and activities. After all, we all know people who are nice in one sort of situation and nasty in another.

The second reason for being skeptical of the appeal to implied authors or author constructs rests on the claim that the concept of authorship seems to be a broadly explanatory notion. Authors make works of literature. The psychological states of authors play a role in explaining the individual styles that the works they produce exhibit (cf. Wollheim 1987: 26–36). It is because authorship is, at least in part, a causal-explanatory notion that authors seem appropriately blamed and praised for certain moral aspects of the works they produce. But author constructs, fictive authors, and implied authors cannot play an appropriate explanatory role. It is Hawks who has causal relations with real-world entities, not "the fiction of Hawks," nor Hawks-as-he-seems-to-be-on-the-basis-of-his-films (Gaut 1997; see also Stecker 1987). Films may have implied authors, but these will do little work in explaining what needs explaining.

Trends and new directions

In an important paper on the topic, Livingston offered a definition (or "partial analysis") of cinematic authorship:

> Cinematic author = the agent or agent(s) who intentionally make(s) … an action the intended function of which is to make manifest or communicate some attitude(s) by means of the production of apparently moving images projected on a screen or other surface. (Livingston 1997: 141)

I do not have the space to address this account in detail (for objections, see Sellors 2007; and Gaut 1999: 171). But it is worth noting that Livingston's account is part of a very recent trend that seeks to apply the tools of the theories of action, agency, and communication to the question of cinematic authorship. Additional work by Livingston on authorship more generally, as well as recent work by C. Paul Sellors and Trevor Ponech, is part of this promising turn (Livingston 2005; Sellors 2007; Ponech 1999). Further clarification about the nature and possibility of authorship under the massively collaborative conditions of ordinary filmmaking requires careful development and deployment of theories of collective and complex action and intention.

Let me suggest two other directions for further exploration. First, theorists interested in cinematic authorship may find it useful to examine the nature of authorship in certain nonliterary contexts where collaboration is standard, such as scientific publishing. Recent articles testify to significant growth in the mean number of authors in scientific papers, as well as the stunningly large numbers of authors that certain papers may have (King 2007; Greene 2007). I do not claim that attention to scientific publishing will straightforwardly answer questions about cinematic authorship. It is certainly possible that conceptual confusion about authorship is as – or more – endemic in that domain than in the domain of film theory. Nonetheless, there is an important model here of how authorship is theorized and attributed in a collaborative setting. One particular payoff from attending to this domain might be a richer account of the notions of lead and primary authorship (and, along with it, secondary or additional authorship). For it is very tempting to think that appeal to such notions would enrich the discussion of cinematic authorship.

Second, I mentioned above the possibility that authorship seems to have the potential to exhibit a sort of fragmentation in the sphere of filmmaking. What do I mean? Compare the paradigmatic case of literary authorship. In the literary context, the author role is a complex and unifying functional role that is typically filled by a single individual. That is, the interpretive, evaluative, moral, legal, and even individuating functions of literary authorship are typically all located in a single individual. But we have already seen that in the film case legal authorship may pull apart from other authorship roles. I suggest that in very ordinary cases of filmmaking other sorts of fragmentation of the authorship role may occur. An agent (e.g., composer) who is partly artistically responsible for a film (i.e., who deserves some credit for its artistic merit) may be in no way morally responsible for it (perhaps because the relevant ethical content was generated in the editing process after the score's composition was completed). It is easy to think of many other such cases. In this way authorship in film can exhibit a kind of disunity that is not typical in literature. It is not simply that no one person involved in the making of a film stands in the authorship role, it is that no single group of people might be properly seen as standing in the authorship role (although different subgroups might be seen as performing one or more aspects of the authorship role). There may, of course, be much less extravagant ways of putting this point. But my suggestion is that this dimension of filmmaking (the way in which various aspects of the authorship role that are unified in the literary case may come apart in the film case) is one to which theorists of cinematic authorship should attend.

Acknowledgments

Thanks are due to the editors, Stephen Meskin, and Andrew Kania for their comments on previous versions of this chapter.

See also Ethics (Chapter 10), Interpretation (Chapter 15), Narrative closure (Chapter 19), Style (Chapter 25), and Ingmar Bergman (Chapter 51).

References

Arnheim, R. (1997) *Film Essays and Criticism*, trans. B. Benthien, Madison: University of Wisconsin Press.

Barthes, R. (2002) "The Death of the Author," trans. S. Heath, in W. Irwin (ed.) *The Death and Resurrection of the Author?*, Westport, CT: Greenwood Press.

Bordwell, D., and Thompson, K. (1993) *Film Art: An Introduction*, 4th ed., New York: McGraw-Hill.

Buscombe, E. (1981) "Ideas of Authorship," in J. Caughie (ed.) *Theories of Authorship*, London and New York: Routledge.

Cameron, I. (2000) "Films, Directors and Critics," in J. Hollows, P. Hutchings, and M. Jancovich (eds.) *The Film Studies Reader*, London: Arnold.

Carroll, N. (1996) "Film, Rhetoric and Ideology," in *Theorizing the Moving Image*, New York: Cambridge University Press.

—— (1998) *A Philosophy of Mass Art*, Oxford: Oxford University Press.

Chatman, S. (2005) "The Cinematic Narrator," in T. Wartenberg and A. Curran (eds.) *The Philosophy of Film: Introductory Text and Readings*, Malden, MA: Blackwell.

Coward, R. (1987) "Dennis Potter and the Question of the Television Audience," *Critical Quarterly* 29: 79–87.

Currie, G. (1989) *An Ontology of Art*, London: Macmillan.

—— (1993) "The Long Goodbye: The Imaginary Language of Film," *British Journal of Aesthetics* 33: 207–19.

—— (1995a) *Image and Mind: Film, Philosophy and Cognitive Science*, New York: Cambridge University Press.

—— (1995b) "Unreliability Refigured: Narrative in Literature and Film," *Journal of Aesthetics and Art Criticism* 53: 19–29.

Curtis, B. (2003) "D.W. Griffith in Black and White," *Slate Magazine*. Available at http://www.slate.com/id/2076307 (accessed 7 March 2008).

Davies, S. (2006) "Author's Intentions, Literary Interpretation, and Literary Value," *British Journal of Aesthetics* 46: 223–47.

Doris, J. (2002) *Lack of Character: Personality and Moral Behavior*, Cambridge: Cambridge University Press.

Dutton, D. (1979) "Artistic Crimes: The Problem of Forgery in the Arts," *British Journal of Aesthetics* 19: 304–14.

Dyer, R. (1979) *Stars*, London: British Film Institute.

Foucault, M. (2002) "What is an Author?," in W. Irwin (ed.) *The Death and Resurrection of the Author?*, Westport, CT: Greenwood Press.

Gaut, B. (1997) "Film Authorship and Collaboration," in R. Allen and M. Smith (eds.) *Film Theory and Philosophy*, Oxford: Clarendon Press.

Greene, M. (2007) "The Demise of the Lone Author," *Nature* 450, 1165 (20 December 2007).

Heath, S. (1981) "Comment on 'The Idea of Authorship'," in J. Caughie (ed.) *Theories of Authorship*, London and New York: Routledge.

Inge, M. T. (2001) "Collaboration and Concepts of Authorship," *PMLA* 116: 623–30.

Kael, P. (2005) "The Idea of Film Criticism," in T. Wartenberg and A. Curran (eds.) *The Philosophy of Film: Introductory Text and Readings*, Malden, MA: Blackwell.

King, C. (2007) "Multiauthor Papers Redux: A New Peek at New Peeks," *Science Watch* 18. Available at http://archive.sciencewatch.com/nov-dec2007/sw_nov-dec2007_page1.htm (accessed on 6 March 2008).

Koch, H. (2000) "A Playwright Looks at the 'Filmwright'," in J. Hollows, P. Hutchings, and M. Jancovich (eds.) *The Film Studies Reader*, London: Arnold.

Lamarque, P. (1990) "The Death of the Author: An Analytic Autopsy," *British Journal of Aesthetics* 30: 319–31.

Livingston, P. (1997) "Cinematic Authorship," in R. Allen and M. Smith (eds.) *Film Theory and Philosophy*, Oxford: Clarendon Press.

—— (2005) *Art and Intention: A Philosophical Study*, Oxford: Oxford University Press.

Nowell-Smith, G. (1981) "Six Authors in Pursuit of *The Searchers*," in J. Caughie (ed.) *Theories of Authorship*, London and New York: Routledge.

Perkins, V. F. (1993) *Film as Film: Understanding and Judging Movies*, London: De Capo Press.

Ponech, T. (1999) "Authorship and Authorial Autonomy: The Personal Factor in the Cinematic Work of Art," *Canadian Aesthetics Journal* 4. Available at http://www.uqtr.ca/AE/vol_4/trevor.htm (accessed 6 March 2008).

Ramsey, W. (1998) "Prototypes and Conceptual Analysis," in M. R. DePaul and W. Ramsey (eds.) *Rethinking Intuition*, Lanham, MD: Rowman and Littlefield.

Robinson, J. (1985) "Style and Personality in the Literary Work," *Philosophical Review* 94: 227–47.

Salokannel, M. (2003) "Cinema in Search of Its Authors: On the Notion of Film Authorship in Legal Discourse," in V. W. Wexman (ed.) *Film and Authorship*, Piscataway, NJ: Rutgers University Press.

Sarris, Andrew (2000) "Notes on the Auteur Theory in 1962," in J. Hollows, P. Hutchings, and M. Jancovich (eds.) *The Film Studies Reader*, London: Arnold.

—— (2003) "The Auteur Theory Revisited," in V. Wexman (ed.) *Film and Authorship*, New Brunswick, NJ: Rutgers University Press.

Schatz, T. (1988) *The Genuis of the System: Hollywood Filmmaking in the Studio Era*, New York: Pantheon.

Sellors, C. P. (2007) "Collective Authorship in Film," *Journal of Aesthetics and Art Criticism* 65: 263–71.

Stecker, R. (1987) "Apparent, Implied, and Postulated Authors," *Philosophy and Literature* 11: 258–71.

—— (2006) "Interpretation and the Problem of the Relevant Intention," in M. Kieran (ed.) *Contemporary Debates in Aesthetics and the Philosophy of Art*, Malden, MA: Blackwell.

Stillinger, J. (1991) *Multiple Authorship and the Myth of Solitary Genius*, New York: Oxford University Press.

Truffaut, F. (2000) "A Certain Tendency of the French Cinema," in J. Hollows, P. Hutchings, and M. Jancovich (eds.) *The Film Studies Reader*, London: Arnold.

Wollheim, R. (1987) *Painting as an Art*, Princeton, NJ: Princeton University Press.

Wollen, P. (1981) "The Auteur Theory," in J. Caughie (ed.) *Theories of Authorship*, London and New York: Routledge.

Wood, R. (1981) "Shall We Gather at the River? The Late Films of John Ford," in J. Caughie (ed.) *Theories of Authorship*, London and New York: Routledge.

—— (2000) "Hawks de-Wollenized," in J. Hollows, P. Hutchings, and M. Jancovich (eds.) *The Film Studies Reader*, London: Arnold.

Further reading

See John Caughie (ed.) *Theories of Authorship* (London and New York: Routledge, 1981); and V. W. Wexman (ed.) *Film and Authorship* (Piscataway, NJ: Rutgers University Press, 2003). A recent and useful collection on the topic is B. K. Grant (ed.) *Auteurs and Authorship: A Film Reader* (Malden, MA: Wiley-Blackwell, 2008).

3
CENSORSHIP
Susan Dwyer

For individuals at all points on the political spectrum, and especially for those engaged in any form of expressive enterprise – from comic book illustrators, to film directors, to performance artists – censorship typically carries very negative connotations. Indeed, for many, censorship is the very antithesis of freedom and creativity. However, we can and should conceive of censorship more neutrally – simply as the imposition of constraints. On such a construal, censorship is not obviously always a Bad Thing. This point is crucial for any effective argument *against* particular instances of censorship. For, if we simply define censorship as something always to be rejected, then we have merely asserted what potential censors deny, and we have provided no *reasons* to reject censorship. Moreover, a neutral construal of censorship better allows us to grasp that there are different agents of censorship, that censorship can and does have a range of targets and motivations, and that (apparently paradoxically) constraints of some kind may well be part of the very creative enterprise itself.

Here I shall be concerned only with censorship as it has affected and continues to affect film. Obviously, there is much else to be said about the censorship of the press, art, and literature (see "Further reading" in this chapter and "Pornography").

Agents of censorship

The agent of censorship is not always, and perhaps not typically, the state. To be sure, across the globe and through time, governmental bodies are and have been engaged in the imposition of constraints on film, ranging from outright prohibition to what, in United States jurisprudence, are called time, place, and manner restrictions. But nonstate actors, such as film industry associations, advertisers, and advocacy groups, can be just as and sometimes even more powerful controllers of what films get made, distributed, and exhibited.

State censorship

When the state undertakes to prohibit or restrict public access to expressive materials, it can run afoul of a variety of constitutional protections. Most democratic constitutions embody protections for speech, for the press, and for expression more generally.

In the United States, the government must demonstrate that a proposed instance of censorship is motivated by a "compelling state interest" (increasingly cast in terms of fighting the "war on terror") and that this particular act of censorship represents the least intrusive means to protect that interest. In addition, the government may not practice "prior restraint" – that is, prohibit some form of expression before it is published. Material is legally actionable only when it is in the public domain.

The history of film is interesting in this regard. For it was not until 1952 that the United States Supreme Court conceded that motion pictures fell under the protection of the First Amendment. The controlling case prior to this was *Mutual Film Corporation v. Industrial Commission of Ohio*, 236 US 230 (1915), which concerned Ohio's attempts to suppress D. W. Griffith's *The Birth of a Nation* (1915). In this case, the Supreme Court contended that motion pictures are "a business pure and simple, originated and conducted for profit ... [and] not to be regarded ... as part of the press of the country or as organs of public opinion" (245). And so the Court upheld Ohio's law that stated, in part, that "only such films as are in the judgment and discretion of the board of censors of a moral, educational or amusing and harmless character shall be passed and approved." It was several decades later, in *Joseph Burstyn, Inc. v. Wilson*, 343 US 495 (1951) that the Supreme Court reversed itself, opining that motion pictures – in this instance, Rossellini's *The Miracle* (1948) – could not be constitutionally denied an exhibition license, on the grounds that they were sacrilegious. Most importantly, in *Burstyn*, the Court recognized that cinema is "a significant medium for the communication of ideas ... [and that] the importance of motion pictures as an organ of public opinion is not lessened by the fact that they are designed to entertain as well as inform" (502). (However, prior restraint on movies, manifested by the power of local and state censorship boards to prohibit screenings without first going to court, was not invalidated until 1965 [*Freedman v. Maryland*, 380 US 51].)

In the wake of the Second World War, the United States government targeted Hollywood, in particular screenwriters and directors, during the infamous operations of the House on Un-American Activities Committee (HUAC). First in 1947, and then again in 1951, HUAC investigated individuals and examined films for the presence of what it deemed subversive (that is, pro-communist) messages. The HUAC hearings were extremely controversial; some members of the movie industry refused to cooperate, resulting in their imprisonment, while others testified against their peers. Careers and lives were literally ruined during these years (Gladchuk 2007). Studio heads were called before the Committee. Here, in a passage worth contrasting with the contemporary context, is Jack L. Warner, then the head of Warner Bros:

> Our company is keenly aware of its responsibility to keep its product free from subversive poisons. With all the vision at my command, I scrutinize the planning and production of our motion pictures. It is my firm belief that there is not a Warner Bros. picture that can fairly be judged to be hostile to our country, or communistic in tone or purpose. (Congress, HUAC, 1947: 11)

While state censorship of the movies has been typically quite direct, the *Family Movie Act* of 2005 (part of the *Family Entertainment and Copyright Act* of 2005) is a very recent example of indirect state action. The *Family Movie Act* indemnifies the manufacturers of DVDs for home consumption against copyright violation charges if they make "imperceptible" (read, *delete*) certain scenes from films without the copyright holder's permission, as long as the alteration is clearly noted.

The ethical issues here are quite interesting. Arguably, the defensible motivation behind the Act is to support parents and caretakers in protecting children from images and language that is unsuitable for them. However, the Act would also seem to undermine the moral rights of filmmakers. In contrast to several European nations, the United States (as a common law nation) does not recognize the moral rights of artists as legal rights (Holland 2006). Copyright law, and thus the protection of a creator's product, is largely justified in economic terms – no one may profit from my labor, pretending it is theirs. Copyright protections are not legally understood in terms of the artists' moral interest in maintaining the integrity of their work and in not having their name associated with mutilated or distorted versions of that work.

Industry associations

Ironically, the most influential nonstate agent of censorship in the domain of film is the Motion Picture Association of America (MPAA). Initially called the Motion Picture Producers and Distributors of America (MPPDA), this industry body supported the establishment, in 1930, of the so-called Hays Code. Code "seals" were denied to any film that contained action or dialogue in violation of the thirty-some rules articulated in the Code, with the effect that such films could not be distributed or shown by any member company of the MPPDA. The Hays Code articulated the following general principles, here paraphrased:

1 No picture shall be produced that will lower the moral standards of those who see it. Hence the sympathy of the audience should never be thrown to the side of crime, wrongdoing, evil, or sin.
2 Correct standards of life, subject only to the requirements of drama and entertainment, shall be presented.
3 Law, natural or human, shall not be ridiculed, nor shall sympathy be created for its violation, which are supplemented by quite specific rules governing the presentation of crime, including murder, sex, nudity, dress, vulgarity, and national feelings. (MPPDA 1982 [1930]: 324)

In 1968, the MPAA replaced the, by then, dated Hays Code with a ratings system. Again, this move by the industry itself was intended to preempt any state control or censorship of movies.

Ratings systems

Ratings systems are operative in the United States, the United Kingdom, and India, among other moviemaking nations. In the United Kingdom, the 1912 British Board of Censors was renamed the British Board of Film Classification in 1985. It currently uses eight classifications for film, primarily designed to provide parents with guidelines about what material might be suitable for their children to see, and to clearly isolate sexually explicit material as available only to persons over eighteen years of age.

India – which has the largest movie business in the world, producing almost eight hundred films a year – also has a Central Board of Film Classification (CBFC), which imposes ratings. But prior restraint is alive and well in India. For example, the CBFC requires that no mouth-to-mouth kissing scenes, and certain words survive editing cuts. Proposals made in 2004 to liberalize *The Cinematograph Act* of 1952 have not yet been enacted.

In the United States, movies can receive any of the following ratings: G (Suggested for General Audiences); PG13 (Parental guidance suggested); R (Restricted, persons seventeen years of age or younger not admitted unless with parent or guardian); NC-17 (persons seventeen years of age or younger not admitted). The last rating in this list was not introduced until 1990 – *Henry and June* (1990) was the first film to receive it – when the MPAA decided to cease using X as a rating for movies with significant sexual content. The reason for this change was that the X rating was not trademarked by the MPAA, meaning that any filmmaker could use it. During the 1970s and 1980s, producers of pornography adopted the X rating for their films and so in the public's view the rating became synonymous with pornography. Hence, while the MPAA had applied the X rating to films such as *A Clockwork Orange* (1971) and *Taxi Driver* (1976), it chose to adopt the trademarked NC-17 rating to dissociate any of its sanctioned films from pornography.

As evidence of the power that the MPAA wields, the public is largely unaware of how the ratings system works in the United States. *This Film Is Not Yet Rated* (2006) exposes what its director, Kirby Dick, takes to be the secrecy and arbitrariness surrounding the MPAA ratings procedure. The names of the ten to thirteen members of the Ratings Board remain confidential, as do Board deliberations. Critics say this shields the Board and the MPAA from being accountable to filmmakers and the public for its ratings decisions. The MPAA, however, claims that anonymity is required to prevent Board members from being pressured by filmmakers and others to give movies particular ratings.

Critics like Kirby Dick also complain that Board members are not especially qualified to judge movies. Indeed, on its website, which in response to Kirby Dick's film now contains information about the ratings scheme, the MPAA says, "There are no special qualifications for Board membership, except that the members must have shared parenthood experience, must be possessed of an intelligent maturity, and most of all, have the capacity to put themselves in the role of most American parents" (MPAA 2008a: online). By itself, this might seem unproblematic. However, it is worth noting two things.

First, the rating a movie receives determines whether and how it will be distributed and exhibited. Exhibition and distribution companies have substantial influence. Just fifteen companies control all the movie theaters in the United States, and the top five companies (Regal Entertainment Group, AMC Entertainment, Carmike Cinema, Cinemark USA, Loews Cineplex Entertainment) own 45 percent of the screens and 25 percent of exhibition sites (Eliasburg 2005). And these companies are loath to pick up movies that are rated NC-17. As a result, filmmakers have cut material from their movies in order for the Board to grant a more economically viable rating. In the face of criticism of the power of the ratings system, the MPAA emphatically points out that moviemakers are not *obliged* to submit their films for rating and that films may be released unrated. However, such films are likely to have difficulty finding a distributor.

Second, it would appear that the Board employs a double standard in assessing the respective suitability of representations of violence and representations of sexuality. It is prepared to give an R rating to films that contain extreme violence – like *The Departed* (2006), *Hostel* (2005), and *Saw* (2004) – but it gives the NC-17 rating to films that depict pubic hair or male frontal nudity. For example, both *The Cooler* (2003) and *Eyes Wide Shut* (1999) were cut or digitally altered in order to receive a more congenial rating. Many critics claim that the MPAA rating system is at base a form of protectionism, ensuring a market for United States products from the major production companies while significantly restricting the market for independent, art-house, and foreign films (Lewis 2000: 189).

It is important not to forget the pragmatic and economic motivations for censorship. The average Hollywood movie now costs approximately $100 million to produce, promote, and advertise (MPAA 2008b). Hence production companies take very big financial risks. It would be naïve not to grant that script revisions, cuts and so on may be, for the most part, economic and not artistic or ideological decisions at all. Lewis (2000) argues that "film censorship only incidentally and superficially regards specific film content ... The MPAA supervises the regulation of film content solely to protect studio products in the marketplace" (2–3).

Advocacy groups

Though hardly financial behemoths akin to the corporations that control the production, distribution, and exhibition of motion pictures across the world, particular interest or pressure groups are also effective agents of censorship. Organized, grassroots opposition to certain films can be quite powerful, since it typically arises suddenly and relatively unpredictably. Notable examples have been Queer Nation's protests of *Basic Instinct* (1992) (for its portrayal of gays and lesbians), Women Against Violence Against Women's protests of *Dressed to Kill* (1980) (as encouraging violence against women), and Greek Orthodox opposition to *The Da Vinci Code* (2006) (as an insult to Christianity), and Johnson (2005) reports an anonymous source who claims that Paramount gave into pressure from the Council on American Islamic Relations, which objected to the fact that a terrorist in *The Sum of All Fears* (2002) was depicted as a Palestinian. (The Palestinian character was replaced by a neo-Nazi.)

Public controversy can, of course, be good publicity. Viewers will see movies precisely because they want to know what the all the fuss is about. Still, it is worth noting that local pressure has kept a variety of films (and other expressive works) out of libraries and schools (Sova 2001). Targets here have been *The Tin Drum* (1979), *1900* (1976), and *Schindler's List* (1993).

Targets of censorship

As the discussion above reveals, representations of sex and sexuality, race, ethnicity, violence, and religion have been the primary targets of state and nonstate efforts at censorship. However, it is important to note that the discussion has primarily focused on film in developed Western nations. In these regions, censorship is typically explicitly motivated by the desire to protect children from images that may be harmful to them and tacitly motivated by financial and moralistic concerns. Moreover, in these locations censorship is more likely to be the work of the film industry itself, rather than the state, since most forms of expression enjoy strong protection from governmental interference.

The same cannot be said for other nations, China in particular, where political views and certain historical perspectives are more often than not the targets of state censorship. Films banned recently in China include *Seven Years in Tibet* (1997), for treatment of a free Tibet; *Memoirs of a Geisha* (2005), for fear of provoking anti-Japanese sentiment; *Brokeback Mountain* (2005), for depictions of homosexuality; and *The Departed* (2006), for the suggestion that China may use nuclear weapons against Taiwan. Chinese director Ye Lou's *Summer Palace* (*Yihe yuan*) (2006) has also been banned by the Chinese government, since it deals in part with the 1989 student uprising at Tiananmen Square, and Ye has been banned from making films in China for five years.

Somewhat ironically, China's censorship committee, unlike the MPAA's ratings board, includes "filmmakers, such as playwrights and directors, and … scholars on film study, film critics, and experts on film technology" (Liu 2007: online). Still, until 2006, filmmakers were obliged to submit full screenplays to the committee prior to beginning shooting. Allegedly motivated by the desire not to hold up production and to support the growing Chinese film industry, the government now requires only a short plot summary to be submitted for approval, unless the "film story is related to significant revolutionary or historical subjects, religion, diplomacy, minors, or judicial system, a complete script still must be submitted to the state bureau" (ibid.).

Arguments against censorship

We have been working with a neutral construal of censorship, according to which censorship is just the imposition of some constraints or other – on content, on exhibition venues and so on. Still, it is true that censorship is typically thought to be a bad thing. To understand why censorship is problematic, when it is, we need to understand what it is that censorship threatens or damages, or alternatively, what values protections of expression protect.

Why is freedom of expression valuable?

Freedom of expression has been variously defended in terms of the necessity of maintaining a "marketplace of ideas" for the discovery and/or testing of the truth (Mill 1859), the bad consequences thought likely to ensue upon the suppression of expression, the role of free expression in democratic self-governance (Meiklejohn 1948), and the connection, thought to exist, between a person's ability to express herself freely (and to hear others do so) and her dignity and moral autonomy (Dwyer 2001; Dworkin 1992).

It is not obvious that these justifications are or need be mutually exclusive. But one point of difference among them deserves mention. The last idea – namely, that freedom of expression is connected with human dignity – has it that freedom of expression is a good, in and of itself. However, all the other justifications just mentioned are consequentialist – that is, they appeal to the likely outcomes of allowing or not allowing free expression. According to these views, then, the value of free expression is a function of the value of the end to which it is thought to be a (necessary) means; for example, the discovery of truth, the avoidance of tyranny, or the possibility of democracy. No matter how freedom of expression is defended, it is rarely defended as an absolute value, as one that may never be permissibly infringed.

What counts as a sufficiently compelling reason to limit expression in any particular instance will depend on how freedom of expression is defended in the first place. Suppose, for example, that freedom of expression is defended on the grounds that it is essential to the pursuit of truth. Then, one might argue for the restriction of some form of expression by showing that it plays no role in furthering that goal.

When it comes to defending the freedom of artistic expression, especially that at work in popular movies, we need to be particularly careful. For it is not at all clear that the typical products of Hollywood, or Bollywood, for that matter, contribute to the search for truth, are essential for a marketplace of ideas, or directly support democracy. It would seem that the firmest ground on which to defend the liberty of filmmakers is that which connects human artistic expression to human dignity and autonomy itself.

This may appear to invest Hollywood movies with more gravitas than they deserve. However, it is important to think about the influence that movies have on individuals and the popular imagination more generally.

What responsibilities does the movie industry have?

In the face of complaints about violence, say, in contemporary movies, many people reply, "But it is just a movie! It is just entertainment!" Our question now is whether this is a plausible position for the film industry to adopt, such that filmmakers need not be concerned with the content of their creations (over and above their potential to entertain) or with the ways in which their creations may be interpreted. Is it reasonable for filmmakers to disregard the effects that the portrayals of women and ethnic and racial minorities may have on viewers' attitudes toward members of these groups?

As Valenti (2000) notes, it is paradoxical of filmmakers and industry executives to say both (1) that their product is just for fun *and* (2) that their product is a serious instance of meaningful expression that falls under First Amendment protection. Films are one thing or the other. It is in the interests of filmmakers to cleave to the second claim. However, if they do, then (arguably) they must assume some responsibility for the likely effects and influences of their creations.

Ironically, this was recognized in the Preamble to the previously mentioned Hays Code. It is worth quoting at length.

> Motion picture producers recognize the high trust and confidence which have been placed in them by the people of the world and which have made motion pictures a universal form of entertainment.
>
> They recognize their responsibility to the public because of this trust and because entertainment and art are important influences in the life of a nation.
>
> Hence, though regarding motion pictures primarily as entertainment without any explicit purpose of teaching or propaganda, they know that the motion picture within its own field of entertainment may be directly responsible for spiritual or moral progress, for higher types of social life, and for much correct thinking.

Further:

> Hence the MORAL IMPORTANCE of entertainment is something which has been universally recognized. It enters immediately into the lives of men and women and affects them closely; it occupies their minds and affections during leisure hours; and ultimately touches the whole of their lives.
>
> The motion pictures, which are the most popular of modern arts for the masses, have their moral quality from the intention of the minds which produce them and from their effects on the moral lives and reactions of their audiences. This gives them a most important moral quality.
>
> Hence, the larger moral responsibilities of the motion pictures.

Naturally, the film industry and individual filmmakers cannot be held individually responsible for the ways a particular person may interpret or react to a movie. Still, it would appear to be somewhat cavalier of filmmakers to claim that their creations have no influence whatsoever and that therefore they need not be concerned with these matters. Human social attitudes are formed under all manner of environmental influences, and it would seem to behoove the motion picture industry occasionally to examine what contribution it is making to this pool of influence.

Self-censorship and creativity

The last point brings us finally to the role that constraints in the form of self-censorship might play in the creative enterprise itself. Presumably, expressive artists want their creation to succeed in some sense or other. There may be a message to convey, a set of emotions to evoke, a motivation to get into gear. Consider films such as *Philadelphia* (1993) (raising awareness of the stigma attached to AIDS), *Norma Rae* (1979) (concerning labor rights), and documentaries like *An Inconvenient Truth* (2006). Additionally or alternatively, a filmmaker's primary purpose might be to amuse, horrify, or titillate. And, finally, the intentions of the creative artist might simply be to concretely express him- or herself.

Succeeding in realizing any of these intentions and desires requires doing or saying one set of things rather than another. Quite trivially, this means that the artist is always working with a set of self-imposed constraints. If anything goes, then there can be no meaning. In addition to this perfectly straightforward point, it might be argued that constraints play a special role both in the manifestation of creativity and in the aesthetic value of a completed artwork.

Elster (2000) importantly distinguishes between different types of self-imposed constraints; they may be invented by the artist him- or herself (as when novelist Georges Perec produced *La Disparition*, which contained not one instance of the letter *e*), or they may be chosen by the artist from the prevailing parameters of various genres (as when a director decides to make a romantic comedy or horror movie). Elster also emphasizes that a chosen set of constraints does not fully determine the final creative product, for an artist may continue to make choices within those constraints. Elster contends that artists make such choices in order to improve the aesthetic value of their creations. This is no doubt true in some cases, however, we may question, as Levinson (2003) does, whether Elster's picture of artistic creativity entails an overly rational and self-conscious view of the artist at work.

A slightly different example of how working with constraints is related to creativity is provided by Hjort's discussion of Lars von Trier's film *The Five Obstructions* (2003) (see "Further reading" in this chapter, "Dogme 95," and "*The Five Obstructions*"). This film shows how Danish director, Jorgen Leth, remakes his short film *The Perfect Human* (*Det perfekte menneske*) (1967) in accordance with a number of technical and conceptual obstructions provided by von Trier. The obstructions pose significant challenges to Leth, and yet, in every instance, he produces a new version of *The Perfect Human*, each one a manifestation of profound creativity that would not have been possible without those very constraints.

See also Authorship (Chapter 2), Pornography (Chapter 47), and Violence (Chapter 26).

References

Congress, HUAC (1947) *Hearings Regarding the Communist Infiltration of the Motion Picture Industry*, 8th Congress, 1st session, 20 October.

Dworkin, R. (1992) "The Coming Battles over Free Speech," *The New York Review of Books* 11 (June): 55–8, 61–4.

Dwyer, S. (2001) "Free Speech," *Sats: The Nordic Journal of Philosophy* 2: 1–18.

Eliasburg, J. (2005) "The Film Exhibition Business: Critical Issues, Practice, and Research," in C. C. Moul (ed.) *Concise Handbook of Movie Industry Economics*, Cambridge: Cambridge University Press.

Elster, J. (2000) *Ulysses Unbound: Studies in Rationality, Precommitment, and Constraints*, Cambridge and New York: Cambridge University Press.

Gladchuk, J. J. (2007) *Hollywood and Anti-Communism: HUAC and the Evolution of the Red Menace*, New York: Routledge.

Holland, B. L. (2006) "Note: Moral Right Protection in the United States and the Effect of the *Family Entertainment and Copyright Act* of 2005 on U.S. International Obligations," *Vanderbilt Journal of Transnational Law* 39: 217n.

Johnson, B. (2005) "In the Fray: Hollywood's Last Taboo," *The Wall Street Journal* (Eastern edition) (13 July): D10.

Levinson, J. (2003) "Elster on Creativity," in B. Gaut and P. Livingston (eds.) *The Creation of Art: New Essays in Philosophical Aesthetics*, New York: Cambridge University Press.

Lewis, J. (2000) *Hollywood v. Hard Core: How the Struggle Over Censorship Saved the Modern Film Industry*, New York: New York University.

Liu, W. (2007) "Censoring Movies Done according to Script," *ChinaDaily.com.cn*. Available at www.chinadaily.com.cn/cndy/2007-08/31/content_6070081.htm.

Meiklejohn, A. (1948) *Free Speech and Its Relation to Self-Government*, New York: Harper.

Mill, J. (1859) *On Liberty*, London: J. W. Parker and Son.

MPAA (Motion Picture Association of America) (2008a) *Film Ratings*. MPAA website. Available at www.mpaa.org/FilmRatings.asp.

—— (2008b) *Research and Statistics*. MPAA website. Available at www.mpaa.org/researchStatistics.asp.

MPPDA (Motion Picture Producers and Distributors of America) (1982 [1930]) "The Motion Picture Production Code of 1930," in G. Mast (ed.) *The Movies in Our Midst*, Chicago and London: University of Chicago Press.

Sova, D. B. (2001) *Forbidden Films: Censorship Histories of 125 Motion Pictures*, New York: Checkmark Books.

Valenti, F. M. (2000) *More Than a Movie: Ethics in Entertainment*, ed. L. Brown and L. Trotta, Boulder, CO: Westview Press.

Further reading

J. Green and N. J. Karolides (eds.) *Encyclopedia of Censorship*, rev. ed. (New York: Facts on File, 2005) contains exhaustive account of censorship of all kinds across the world. Lee Grieveson, *Policing Cinema: Movies and Censorship in Early-Twentieth-Century America* (Berkeley: University of California Press, 2004) gives a subtle theoretical analysis of early censorship in the United States. See also R. J. Haberski, *Freedom to Offend: How New York Remade Movie Culture* (Lexington: University Press of Kentucky, 2007); and Mette Hjort (ed.) *Dekalog 1: On The Five Obstructions* (London: Wallflower Press, 2008). *Index on Censorship* is a magazine devoted to the basic human right of the freedom of expression. See also C. Lyons, *The New Censors: Movies and the Culture Wars* (Philadelphia: Temple University Press, 1997).

4

CONSCIOUSNESS

Murray Smith

[T]here is some deceiver both very powerful and very cunning, who constantly uses all his wiles to deceive me. There is therefore no doubt that I exist, if he deceives me; and let him deceive me as much as he likes, he can never cause me to be nothing, so long as I think I am something ... this knowledge ... I maintain to be more certain and evident than all I have had hitherto.

(Descartes 1968: 103)

Notwithstanding Descartes' confidence in his own consciousness, and James' influential characterization of conscious experience as a flowing "stream" (James 1950: 239), for much of the twentieth century, consciousness was put on the back burner of scholarly debate (though debate was hardly extinguished – consider Broad [1925], Ryle [1949], as well as the tradition of phenomenology – discussed elsewhere in this volume). Numerous forces conspired to put it there, but three factors might be singled out as particularly important. First, Freud. Notions of an "unconscious" dimension to the mind and behavior certainly existed before psychoanalysis, but there is little doubt that Freud and his followers put the notion at center stage, making it the fulcrum of the psychoanalytic theory of mind. Within the tradition of psychological behaviorism, consciousness perhaps fared even worse. While psychoanalytic theorists may routinely doubt the reliability of conscious avowals and states of minds, behaviorism denies, or at least remains agnostic about, their very existence, restricting itself to observable behavior, the billiard balls of stimulus and response. Even the advent of cognitive psychology – the paradigm-shifting force which overturned behaviorism and in certain ways began to rehabilitate the study of consciousness – continued (and continues) in its own way to keep consciousness at arm's length. The dominant framework within cognitive psychology conceives of mental activity as *computation*, and the mind as an *information processor*; and to the extent that our chief model of an information-processing device – a computer – lacks consciousness, so the analogy does not make *conscious* computation very salient. A great deal of cognitive theory has concerned itself with information processing which is always or normally nonconscious – like the brain computations allowing you to see this page and to make sense of the words you are reading. Of these traditions, the first and the third – psychoanalysis and cognitivism – have exerted considerable influence on the study of film. Perhaps it is not surprising, then, that the relationship between consciousness and film remains largely uncharted territory. The goal of this essay is to provide a preliminary map of the terrain, with some suggestions concerning lines of future inquiry.

Despite the situation I describe above, the study of consciousness has been all the rage for a decade or more, to the extent that "consciousness studies" has now established itself, with all the paraphernalia of an academic discipline – journals, symposia, conferences, dedicated departmental centers and graduate-level courses, a steady flow of book publications, along with internal debates and controversies, which sometimes spill into the public domain (for overviews, see Flanagan 1992 and Carter 2002). What explains this resurgence? The emergence of cognitive theory made reference to internal states – thoughts, intentions, beliefs, feelings – respectable once more, while also engendering a new confidence that the nature of mind, so conceived, could become the subject of scientific investigation. Moreover, the initial emphasis on nonconscious states – or computations for which consciousness did not appear to be an important feature – eventually led back to consciousness, in the form of the question: if our minds can crunch so much information nonconsciously, why would we have evolved consciousness at all? In short, what are the functions of consciousness?

One way of approaching this question is to consider the types of cognition that involve consciousness (Baars 1997). Our thinking becomes highly conscious when we face challenging or novel tasks. Learning to type, or drive a car, initially requires great conscious deliberation over the sequence of movements and steps involved. Mastery of such tasks is characterized in part by greater speed and fluidity in their execution, which goes hand in hand with an attenuation of conscious attention. As I type this sentence, I don't consciously think about the location of individual letter keys – that aspect of the task has become automatic for me, freeing up processing capacity for the more demanding job of coming up with an overview of consciousness and its relationship with film. And once a skill like typing or driving has been mastered, finding ourselves becoming conscious of it usually impedes performance. But some tasks always seem to require conscious attention, as V. S. Ramachandran notes:

> Imagine you are driving your car and having an animated conversation with your friend sitting next to you. Your attention is entirely on the conversation, it's what you're conscious of. But in parallel you are negotiating traffic, avoiding the pavement, avoiding pedestrians, obeying red lights and performing all these very complex elaborate computations without being really conscious of any of it unless something strange happens, such as a leopard crossing the road ... Intriguingly it is impossible to imagine the converse scenario: paying conscious attention to driving and negotiating traffic while unconsciously having a creative conversation with your friend. (Ramachandran 2003: 35–6)

Ramachandran characterizes the conversation which requires conscious attention as "creative" in character, but any use of language – beyond the smallest of small talk and the most vacant of affirmatives – depends upon such attentiveness.

Consciousness also appears to be closely associated with detailed, fine-grained perception and cognition. Thus parts of the visual field that we fixate foveally, in the course of consciously exploring it, will either be immediately available in consciousness, or poised for access in working memory, while those parts of the field which hover unscanned in peripheral vision are registered much more roughly. So it is that we can be blind to very significant elements in a visual array before us if we have devoted little or no conscious attention to them, a phenomenon captured in the related concepts of "inattentional blindness" and "change blindness" (Mack and Rock 1998; Levin and Simons 1997; Rensink *et al.* 1997). (Inattentional blindness and change blindness refer to the failure to perceive, respectively, stable features of a visual array, and apparently striking changes to a visual array.) These forms of perceptual "blindness" play an important role in relation to principles of image composition in film, as well as principles of continuity editing. The conventions of continuity editing keep our attention fixed on elements carefully controlled for continuity; other details across a sequence may be less consistent, but perceptual blindness makes it unlikely that we will pick them up. (The phenomenon of "blindsight" – registration of the information by the visual system with absolutely no conscious awareness of vision – might appear to undermine this relationship between consciousness and perceptual detail, but in fact it supports it. Blindsight demonstrates that perception can occur without consciousness, but the "resolution" of such unconscious perception is coarse, compared with that delivered by conscious perception.) Broadly, then, it seems that consciousness attends certain types of cognition in novel situations, where detail and vividness of perception and flexibility of mind and action are at stake, providing an adaptive advantage over creatures lacking such attributes. Given the centrality of novelty and vividness to artistic practice and experience, we should not be surprised to find consciousness playing a crucial role in relation to art – a point I return to in the final section.

The question of the function(s) of the conscious mind has come to be known as one of the "easy problems" in debates around consciousness. The hard problem arises from the very fact that consciousness exists (Chalmers 1996; Clark 2001). A brain is a complicated thing, but it is made of nothing more than flesh and blood. How does it give rise to a conscious mind? How can meaning emerge from meat, subjectivity from synaptic firing? There are a variety of responses to the hard problem, each generating new problems. Substance dualism, which owes its modern philosophical origin to Descartes, holds that consciousness doesn't arise from physical matter; it somehow coincides with it in human beings, residing as the "Ghost in the Machine" (Ryle 1949). Physicalists generally hold that consciousness supervenes on material brain states, prompting the search for the "neural correlates of consciousness," that is, the specific brain states which correlate with – and thus are plausible candidates for the causation of – conscious states of mind. But as many skeptics would maintain – physicalists among them – we still don't have a clue as to *how* it could be that a physical event, no matter how complex, could give rise to glimmers of consciousness. As David Chalmers puts it, "How could a physical system such as a brain also be an *experiencer*? ... We do not just lack a detailed theory; we are entirely in the dark about how consciousness fits into the natural order' (Chalmers 1996: xi). Chalmers himself adopts *property dualism*: there may be no separate nonmaterial substance constituting consciousness, but it is irreducible to any currently conceivable physical explanation. A more extreme skepticism – the "new mysterian" – holds that an understanding of the relationship between matter and mind is permanently out of our reach, in the same way that calculus is beyond the ken of guinea pigs. Smart as we are relative to other species, there are going to be some problems which are beyond our comprehension, just because we don't have the right neural equipment (McGinn 2006). Still another response to the hard problem goes by the name of "panpsychism," arguing that the solution to the hard problem lies in not restricting consciousness to ourselves, or even to animal life in general; if we meat machines possess consciousness, perhaps consciousness is much more widely distributed in the physical universe than your average physicalist is wont to admit (Chalmers 1996; Strawson 2006). One other colorful member of the troupe warrants mention here: the eliminativist thesis that consciousness – at least as traditionally understood, as intrinsically private and ineffable subjective experience, the unique "what it is like" to be a certain individual in a state and situation – does not exist (Dennett 1991). None of these arguments is easy to swallow: the interest in the hard problem of consciousness seems inversely proportional to the plausibility of available solutions to it.

Consciousness analyzed

Although reference to "consciousness" in general is standard in the contemporary debate on consciousness, implicit in that description are numerous types and levels of conscious experience. Breaking the overarching concept of consciousness down into various subtypes marks an important step toward its understanding. The first distinction we might draw lies between perceptual or "primary" consciousness (Edelman 1992), on the one hand, and self-consciousness, on the other. For an entity to have perceptual consciousness, it must have conscious awareness of some object or phenomenon – the increasing intensity of light, let us say, as the sun rises. Such consciousness might be momentary and episodic, or more continuous. One step on from this, an entity which possesses a conscious perceptual sensitivity to the state of its body we might say possesses "sentience." Another elaboration involves the integration of perception with memory, setting the stage for personal identity, conceived in the Lockean tradition as an at least partly continuous, temporally extended conscious experience. But fully fledged self-consciousness involves a level of awareness well beyond, even if continuous with, these basic levels of consciousness. To have self-consciousness is to have knowledge of, and to attend to, the nature of one's being in the world. Classically, the emphasis has lain on our awareness of ourselves as thinking, free-willing agents, transcending our status as physical, animal beings. A more contemporary picture would lay emphasis on the embodied nature of human existence, acknowledging our place in the physical and biological realms, while emphasizing the character and limitations of such embodiment. Such self-consciousness does not eradicate or transcend more basic forms of consciousness in human experience, however. Much of the time we consciously attend to the task at hand, whether that be a relatively humdrum exercise (fixing a nail to a wall), or a more demanding and notionally "exalted" activity, such as focusing intently on an aesthetic object (a film or a piece of music, say). At the very least, for much of the time self-consciousness drops into the background as we extend ourselves into the world; indeed, constantly sustained and intense self-consciousness is probably pathological and maladaptive.

Consciousness varies around other axes too. Consciousness comes in different grades; we can be conscious of things to different degrees. Watching a film, I am most conscious of those elements that grab my attention from moment to moment, like the flow of conversation and play of facial expressions between two characters. But at the same time I have some awareness of a large array of secondary and peripheral factors, such as the score and sound design of the film, the quality of the light in the depicted space, and objects in the space behind the characters. Theorists of film music often mark just this distinction in contrasting "hearing" with "listening," where the latter describes focused attention on the soundtrack, the former a still conscious but more peripheral, and "lower grade," form of attention (Kalinak 1992: 3). The dynamic and flexible nature of the stream of perceptual consciousness ensures that at any given moment, however, the items occupying the spotlight of conscious attention may change – a change in ambient sound breaks through into conscious awareness, and I ask myself, why do things sound different? Has a door been opened off screen?

Psychologists of emotion have also marked a distinction between "declarative" and "representational" memory which hinges on the degree to which the memory can be brought to consciousness. A declarative memory is one which we can describe and discuss in language, a memory, of which – whatever its veracity – we feel we have a more or less complete understanding. I can recall vividly the occasion of my learning about the sudden and untimely death of a colleague. I know how it made me feel and I know why, and I can describe both the qualia of the state and its causes. Representational memories, by comparison, are elusive but potent states. Visiting a house I was familiar with in an earlier phase of life, I experience a definite unease, but I can neither recall nor articulate the cause of the unease. The sights and sounds of the house trigger certain memory associations; I consciously experience a certain kind of emotion, but cannot bring to consciousness the earlier experiences causing the emotion. Greg Smith (2003) and Karen Renner (2006) have both argued that films may exploit this form of memory through "emotional markers" – filmic motifs, like musical cues or lighting schemes, which redundantly mark a character or an action with a particular emotional tone without drawing great attention to themselves. The upshot of this strategy is that spectators have an intense experience of the emotion in question, with a very incomplete conscious knowledge of the devices in the film which have given rise to this experience. Although the model of mind here is not psychoanalytic, and in particular does not posit a mechanism of repression whereby certain experiences are actively "buried" beneath conscious attention, the concept of representational memory does acknowledge the existence of *unconscious* sources of conscious states of mind – mental states which are not merely currently non- or only peripherally conscious, like the objects of secondary awareness as I watch a scene in a film, but largely or wholly unavailable to consciousness.

To complete our sketch of the varieties of conscious experience, we need to acknowledge the place of dreaming as a form of consciousness. Dreaming as a form of consciousness?! Well, yes – insofar as we experience things in dreaming, it is a form of consciousness. The claim will only seem odd because of the legacy of psychoanalysis, which explains the functions of dreaming by recourse to its particular conception of the unconscious. Contemporary psychological research into dreaming, however, paints a very different picture, identifying the functions of dreaming in terms of memory and learning – dimensions of mind which often enter into fully conscious, waking experience. So there are *two* conceptual revisions at stake here: first, simply appreciating that while there is obviously an important difference between dreaming and being awake, when we dream we do not lack consciousness – as we do during other phases of sleep. And second, emerging evidence suggests that dreaming has evolved to enhance aspects of the conscious mind, not to provide a playground for experiences repressed by the conscious mind. The idea that film viewing is akin to dreaming goes back pretty well to the origin of cinema, and psychoanalytic film theory has erected elaborate theories on the basis of what was originally an evocative metaphor. This revised "cognitive" conception of the dreaming mind, brought within the orbit of conscious cognition, raises an intriguing question. We certainly don't literally fall into a dream state when we watch films; but is it possible that we do enter a neural-cum-mental state distinct in certain ways from the mental state we possess when we engage with the world? A state so systematically in contrast with our waking navigation of the world that it warrants identification in the way that we identify dreaming as a distinct type of mental experience? Or to pose a parallel question, is there a distinctive mental state which constitutes the "aesthetic attitude" (Beardsley 1981) – a form of consciousness systematically distinct from ordinary, "interested" consciousness, characteristically prompted by films and other aesthetic works?

Consciousness in the history of film

A phenomenon as central to human existence and identity as consciousness is bound to be manifest in the history of an art form in innumerable ways. We can, nevertheless, pick out a number of ways in which the idea or the fact of consciousness has not merely been present in film but is an explicit object of fascination or inquiry. The conscious mind – or at least the particular types of conscious state that comprise it – is integral to the earliest extended work of film theory in English, Hugo Münsterberg's *The Photoplay* (2002 [1916]). Münsterberg focused on the way in which the development of technique and form over the first two decades of cinema sought (on his view) to mimic the mental mechanisms of attention, memory, and emotion. Few subsequent theorists put such an emphasis on the role of these basic conscious mental processes in shaping cinematic form; and, as we have seen, psychoanalytic theory played down their relevance, stressing instead the idea that a film, like a human subject understood in psychoanalytic terms, should be understood in terms of the dynamics of the unconscious. Some recent theory has shown a renewed appetite for conscious mental processes, in terms of their significance for both the design of films and the experience of film viewing, but little work shows much interest in the fact that these mental processes *are* conscious. Such research has focused on the functional roles of various types of perception, memory, and emotion, rather than their qualitative character *as* conscious experiences. The real successors to Münsterberg's early ruminations are not to be found in any body of film theory, but in particular traditions of filmmaking.

The most obvious stamping ground for the representation and exploration of the conscious mind has been the tradition of art cinema (Kawin 1978; Bordwell 1985). One of the defining features of such cinema, and one that can be traced back to its roots in the 1920s movements of German expressionism and French impressionism (Abel 1984), is an emphasis on the rendering of subjective experience. Filmmaking in this mode confirmed the thrust of Münsterberg's thesis, but expanded the range of mental states given expression to include fantasy and dream states (which, to reiterate a point above, we may regard as an important form of conscious experience). Broadly speaking, art cinema also expands the techniques through which subjectivity can be rendered, and often makes them highly salient. It is not that such techniques are wholly absent in the classical tradition of filmmaking; indeed, in certain periods and genres, they have been highly visible. But by and large, it is within art cinema that subjectivity itself has been dramatized.

One director who confronted a particular conception of human consciousness in the classic, postwar era of European art cinema was Michelangelo Antonioni. Antonioni's *L'Eclisse* (1962), the third of his famous trilogy, bears the marks of the widespread influence of Sartrean existentialism during this period. The film is restrained in its overt rendering of the subjectivities of its central characters, instead directing our attention to their outward behavior and the surface of the physical world. But the diffuse discontent and unfocused anxiety of the characters make themselves felt, hanging like a cloud over the entire film. András Kovács has argued that the characters suffer from the angst characteristic of those living in the disenchanted state described by Sartre – the absence of any traditional metaphysical guarantee leaves them facing "Nothingness," all too conscious of the contingency of the world, their fragile and insignificant place within it, and the weight of their own decisions in shaping their destinies (Kovács 2006).

Consciousness has also been explored in the still more rarefied atmosphere of avant-garde filmmaking. The movement known as structural filmmaking – essentially the manifestation of sixties art world minimalism in the context of avant-garde film – was given an early and influential interpretation as a "metaphor for consciousness." The stripped down form of a film like *Wavelength* (1967) was held to represent, and invite the spectator to contemplate, nothing less than human "apperception" (self-consciousness) itself. The gradual, "stammering" zoom across the loft space that forms the backbone of *Wavelength* represents, on this argument, not merely certain objects and the occasional event but, at a deeper level, the conscious subjectivity itself which might apprehend particular objects and events. Only by drastically minimizing what we normally perceive and cognize *through* consciousness can consciousness itself become the focus of consciousness (precisely, self-consciousness), via the agency of the film-as-metaphor. Only by eliminating or attenuating the action available to be viewed through a window are we likely to attend to the window itself. In proposing this interpretation of Snow's work, Annette Michelson (1971; see also Peterson 1994) was in part inspired by the repeated use of cinema as an analogy for conscious experience in philosophical and psychological writings – an image found in the writings of William James, Henri Bergson, and Edmund Husserl and still active today in the work of Oliver Sacks (2004). Citing Gérard Granel, Michelson likens the method of phenomenology to "an attempt to film, in slow motion, that which has been, owing to the manner in which it is seen in natural speed, not absolutely unseen, but missed, subject to oversight" (Granel 1968: 108, quoted and translated by Michelson 1971: 30; Michelson, p. 37, also describes Münsterberg's *The Photoplay* as "an early and remarkable attempt at a phenomenological analysis of the cinematic experience"). Reciprocally, structural filmmaking offers back to philosophy this metaphor, now incarnate in film itself. (See also the comparable analysis of Derek Jarman's *Blue* presented by Vivian Sobchack in her overview of phenomenology and film, this volume, p. 437.)

Such filmic reflections on consciousness are not, however, the unique possession of such ostentatiously serious traditions of cinema as art and avant-garde cinema. Consciousness has been fertile material for Hollywood as well. Many contemporary science-fiction films thematize aspects of consciousness: in different ways, *2001: A Space Odyssey* (1968) and *I Robot* (2004) both dramatize the possibility that a computer might develop consciousness and assert independent agency on the basis of it. On one reading, *Blade Runner* (1982) takes as its subject the centrality of memory, and awareness of death, in human consciousness (a theme central to the philosophy of Heidegger, in the form of "being-toward-death" – Heidegger 1962; Mulhall 2002). Scott's film about the hunting down of a group of advanced, renegade androids explores the impact of doubt about the reliability of memory, uncertainty as to the duration of a human life, and the ever-present threat of death (and the demise of consciousness). We also find within contemporary Hollywood the "comedy of consciousness," in films which exploit some of the absurdities implicit in our confused and often paradoxical assumptions about consciousness. Films like *All of Me* (1984), *The Man with Two Brains* (1983), and *Being John Malkovich* (1999) create humor from the dualist idea that the conscious mind can be decoupled from its physical seat and relocated in other bodies, and even objects (a joke that resonates with the doctrine of panpsychism – that consciousness, in different grades, is pervasive in the universe). In *Being John Malkovich*, Malkovich's personality makes its way through several individual bodies, finally arriving, in rather sinister fashion, in the body of a child; while in *All of Me*, the soul of the character played by Lili Tomlin cohabits with Steve Martin in "his" body, before taking up residence in the body of Victoria Tennant (with a brief stay in a bucket along the way) (M. Smith 2006).

Qualia and (film) art

In 1982 Frank Jackson introduced the world to Mary the color scientist (Jackson 1982; Ludlow *et al.* 2004). Mary has been raised in an artificially contrived black-and-white world, but as an expert color scientist she has nevertheless acquired a complete understanding of all there is to be known about the physics of color. One day Mary is exposed to colored objects: does she now learn anything new – that is, does she obtain new *knowledge*? Jackson (and many others) held that she does, and that no amount of propositional knowledge concerning the physical underpinning of color experience will deliver knowledge of (for example) what it is like to see red, the distinctive subjective "raw feels" that constitute conscious experience. The character of conscious experience as given by qualia is as such *sui generis* and, according to Jackson, exposes the falsity of physicalism as a metaphysical doctrine (the thesis that reality is constituted wholly by physical elements, their properties, and their relations).

How does Jackson's thought experiment, and the "knowledge argument" that it supports – that knowledge of the qualia that constitute conscious experience is a distinctive, irreducible form of knowledge – bear upon the making and appreciation of films? Like all art forms, film trades in the domain of phenomenal experience. The visual arts furnish us with novel visual experiences; the sonic arts provide us with new aural experiences; and the literary arts, while not directly rendering novel perceptual experiences, instead evoke phenomenal experiences through the imaginative positing of actual and fictional agents, spaces, and situations. Films characteristically work on all of these fronts. This emphasis on the conscious, quali-tative character of our experience of art may strike many contemporary literary and art theorists as peculiar, or worse, naïve and even pernicious. But remove conscious qualia in the domain of art and you truly have, to adapt Kant's well-known phrase, a system without purpose. The knowledge argument matters for a theory of art because it impinges on what we understand art to provide us with, and how we value it. If art can provide us with knowledge, and if it is uniquely or especially well-placed to furnish us with particular kinds of knowledge, then phenomenal knowledge – knowing what it is like to perceive and experience from a particular point of view – must be a frontrunner. If the knowledge argument fails, then its failure critically undercuts one of the grounds for attributing to art a special and unique epistemic role in human existence.

What, then, can we say about the kinds of qualia created by different sorts of art? And how do the arts go about creating such qualia? Yasujiro Ozu's *The Flavour of Green Tea Over Rice (Ochazuke no aji)* (1952), provides a good starting point. The title of the film refers to the traditional and simple meal of rice with green tea. The meal – which is shared in harmony by a married couple, who have been rowing over the course of the film – is symbolically laden, representing the virtues of a quiet, unpretentious, and relaxed attitude to life. But what is key here is the way that whatever symbolic value the meal has is embodied in the *taste* of the meal, or rather, for viewers of the film, in the way that the taste of the meal is evoked by the film. What this brings to mind is another, rather more famous instance of the evocation of a specific taste in a work of narrative: Proust's description of the madeleine in the opening pages of *A la recherche du temps perdu* (*Remembrance of Things Past*) (Proust 1981 [1913–27]). What both examples remind us of is the extent and depth of connectedness between the subjective experience of something as apparently simple as a taste, and the network of memory, cultural association and symbolism it can become integrated with: the way a whole life can be conjured up by a taste or a smell, and the way "thick" percepts and sensations like this – qualia laden with, or better, constituted by, memory, association, beliefs, desires, values – can be created and evoked by works of art. Other films which similarly evoke a dense network of associations through sensory imagery include Ozu's *An Autumn Afternoon*, the Japanese title of which is *Samma no aji* – literally, "The Taste of Samma," evoking "the brief season in late summer when *samma*, a variety of mackerel, is at its most savory" (Bordwell 1988: 370–1); Sergei Parajanov's *The Colour of Pomegranates* (*Sayat Nova*) (1968); and Trần Anh Hùng's *The Scent of Green Papaya* (*Mùi đu đủ xanh*) (1993).

The work of Stan Brakhage takes us into the matter of art and qualia from a different angle. Brakhage was an experimental filmmaker whose films can most straightforwardly be likened with abstract expressionism. Some of Brakhage's films are purely abstract; many contain representational elements, but even where they do so, the films retain a strongly abstract quality, in the sense that they put before us fields of textured light whose primary role is not to depict objects, characters, or events. In a famous passage from his essay "Metaphors on Vision," Brakhage asks us to:

> Imagine an eye unruled by man-made laws of perspective, an eye unprejudiced by compositional logic, an eye which does not respond to the name of everything but which must know each object encountered in life through an adventure of perception. How many colors are there in a field of grass to the crawling baby unaware of "Green"? How many rainbows can light create for the untutored eye? (Brakhage 1963: 25)

Brakhage's films work against our natural inclination to find objects in the visual arrays we are presented with, instead presenting us with colors, forms, and textures which refuse to "attach" themselves to stable depicted objects. It is in this sense that the films create an "adventure of perception," in which we are confronted with strikingly novel visual experiences. Comparing Brakhage's art with the example of *The Flavour of Green Tea Over Rice*, we can mark a distinction between Brakhage's ambition to create radically new qualia – ones which cannot be adequately described through familiar concepts or predicates like "green" – and Ozu's ambition to evoke for us a familiar quale, even as he renews our awareness of it and bestows special significance upon it.

One way in which this conception of the distinctive knowledge furnished by art has been articulated is through the notion of *defamiliarization*, first propounded by Viktor Shklovsky in 1919. Ordinary cognition, Shklovksy argues, works to "automatize" the perception of objects and execution of tasks with which we have become familiar.

48

And so ... life fades into nothingness. Automatization eats away at things, at clothes, at furniture, at our wives, and at our fear of war.

If the conscious life of many people takes place entirely on the level of the unconscious, then it's as if this life had never been.

And so, in order to return sensation to our limbs, in order to make us feel objects, to make a stone feel stony, man has been given the tool of art. The purpose of art, then, is to lead us to a knowledge of a thing. (Shklovsky 1991: 5–6)

Shklovsky's account of ordinary cognition, then, prefigures in outline one of the central ideas in cognitive neuroscience – that we become most conscious of an activity when it is novel. The vocation of art to defamiliarize or "make strange" ranges across all aspects of experience, from simple object perception to emotionally charged personal relationships and social events. The contrast between Brakhage and Ozu can be illuminated in these terms as well: where Brakhage works at (or even before) the level of object perception, Ozu focuses upon the experiences of family and community life. The contrast should not be oversimplified, however: many of Brakhage's films represent existential themes like birth and death, and as we have seen, Ozu shows the interpenetration of perception, emotion, memory, and personal life. Each filmmaker is concerned with "life" in the broadest sense but tackles the task of representation through a different point of entry.

The role of art in creating new qualia, and renewing our awareness of familiar qualia, does not end with the art object itself and the perceiver's engagement with it. On this view of the function of art, one of the major roles of criticism is to *evoke* the qualia characteristic of particular works of art. Criticism in this mode sustains the focus on and renewal of the qualia of experience achieved by art, by describing and evoking *what it feels like* to engage with particular works of (film) art. The aim of such criticism is to describe, and thereby enable us to imagine, the set of "phenomenal information properties" (Dennett 1991) that, taken together, uniquely characterize a given work of art. And here the target of such description will be both the qualia represented by the work (the taste of green tea over rice), as well as the unique qualia furnished by the work itself (*The Flavour of Green Tea Over Rice*). The role of criticism in this respect is perhaps most obvious in the form of impressionistic passages, where critics attempt to capture the experience of viewing a film through metaphor and adjectival description. But, in this respect at least, such impressionistic criticism is continuous with more technical analysis. For those with the relevant knowledge, describing a cue within a film score as a "major seventh with a sharp attack and equally rapid decay," or a film sequence as an example of "metrical montage at a tempo of 10 frames a second," will serve to bring to mind the characteristic feel of the sequences in question. Again, it is important not to misunderstand the contrast here between impressionistic and more technical analysis: technical analysis enables precise description where it is possible, but there may be aspects of perceptual experience beyond the reach of such analysis (Raffman 1993), and this is where more indirect, especially metaphorical, description may play an essential role. Not all impressionistic analysis is mere *belle lettrisme*. The vocation of art is the creation of novel and highly nuanced adventures in perception and cognition. The work of artists like Brakhage and Ozu is the call to which evocative criticism is the response, and the savoring of the qualia of conscious experience is central to both enterprises.

See also Hugo Münsterberg (Chapter 39), Avant-garde film (Chapter 48), Phenomenology (Chapter 40), and Edgar Morin (Chapter 38).

References

Abel, R. (1984) *French Cinema: The First Wave, 1915–29*, Princeton, NJ: Princeton University Press.

Baars, B. J. (1997) *In the Theater of Consciousness: The Workspace of the Mind*, Oxford: Oxford University Press.

Beardsley, M. C. (1981) *Aesthetics: Problems in the Philosophy of Criticism*, second edition, Inianapolis: Hackett Publishing Company.

Bordwell, D. (1985) *Narration in the Fiction Film*, Madison: University of Wisconsin Press.

—— (1988) *Ozu and the Poetics of Cinema*, Princeton, NJ: Princeton University Press.

Brakhage, S. "Metaphors on Vision," *Film Culture* 30 (special issue).

Broad, C. D. (1925) *The Mind and Its Place in Nature*, London: Routledge and Kegan Paul.

Carter, R. (2002) *Exploring Consciousness*, Berkeley: University of California Press.

Chalmers, D. J. (1996) *The Conscious Mind: In Search of a Fundamental Theory*, New York: Oxford University Press.

Clark, A. (2001) *Mindware: An Introduction to the Philosophy of Cognitive Science*, Oxford: Oxford University Press.

Dennett, D. (1991) *Consciousness Explained*, Boston: Little, Brown, and Company.

Descartes, R. (1968) *Discourse on Method* and *The Meditations*, trans. F. E. Sutcliffe, Harmondsworth: Penguin.

Edelman, G. (1992) *Bright Air, Brilliant Fire: On the Matter of the Mind*, Harmondsworth: Penguin.

Flanagan, O. (1992) *Consciousness Reconsidered*, Cambridge, MA: MIT Press.

Granel, G. (1968) *Le Sens du temps et de la perception chez Husserl*, Paris: Gallimard.

Kalinak, K. (1992) *Settling the Score: Music and the Classical Hollywood Film*, Madison: University of Wisconsin Press.

Heidegger, M. (1962) *Being and Time*, trans. J. Macquarrie and E. Robinson, Oxford: Blackwell.

Jackson, F. (1982) "Epiphenomenal Qualia," *Philosophical Quarterly* 32: 127–36.

James, W. (1950) *The Principles of Psychology*, vol. 1, New York: Dover.

Kawin, B. F. (1978) *Mindscreen: Bergman, Godard and First-Person Film*, Princeton, NJ: Princeton University Press.

Kovács, A. B. (2006) "Sartre, the Philosophy of Nothingness, and the Modern Melodrama," in M. Smith and T. E. Wartenberg (eds.) *Thinking through Cinema: Film as Philosophy*, Malden, MA: Blackwell.

Levin, D. T., and Simons, D. J. (1997) "Failure to Detect Changes to Attended Objects in Motion Pictures," *Psychonomic Bulletin and Review* 4: 501–6.

Ludlow, P., Nagasawa, Y., and Stoljar, D. (eds.) (2004) *There's Something about Mary: Essays on Phenomenal Consciousness and Frank Jackson's Knowledge Argument*, Cambridge, MA: MIT Press.

Mack, A., and Rock, I. (1998) *Inattentional Blindness*, Cambridge, MA: MIT Press.

McGinn, C. (2006) *Consciousness and Its Objects*, Oxford: Clarendon.

Michelson, A. (1971) "Toward Snow," *Artforum* 9: 30–7.

Mulhall, S. (2002) *On Film*, London: Routledge.

Münsterberg, H. (2002 [1916]) *The Photoplay: A Psychological Study*, in A. Langdale (ed.) *Hugo Münsterberg on Film: The Photoplay: A Psychological Study and Other Writings*, New York: Routledge.

Peterson, J. (1994) *Dreams of Chaos, Visions of Order: Understanding the American Avant-garde Cinema*, Detroit: Wayne State University Press.

Proust, M. (1981 [1913–27]) *Remembrance of Things Past*, trans. C. K. Scott, M. Kilmartin, and T. Kilmartin, London: Chatto and Windus.

Raffman, D. (1993) *Language, Music, and Mind*, Cambridge, MA: MIT Press.

Ramachandran, V. (2003) *The Emerging Mind: The Reith Lectures 2003*, London: Profile Books.

Renner, K. (2006) "Repeat Viewings Revisited: Emotion, Memory, and *Memento*," *Film Studies: An International Review* 8: 106–15. (Special issue, "Film, Cognition, and Emotion," edited by Daniel Barratt and Jonathan Frome.)

Rensink, R. A., O'Regan, K. J., and Clark, J. J. (1997) "To See or Not to See: The Need for Attention to Perceive Changes in Scenes," *Psychological Science* 8: 368–73.

Ryle, G. (1949) *The Concept of Mind*, London: Hutchinson's University Library.

Sacks, O. (2004) "In the River of Consciousness," *New York Review of Books* 51 (January 15).

Shklovsky, V. (1991) *Theory of Prose*, trans. B. Sher, Elmwood Park: Dalkey Archive Press.

Smith, G. M. (2003) *Film Structure and the Emotion System*, New York: Cambridge University Press.

Smith, M. (2006) "Film Art, Argument, and Ambiguity," in M. Smith and T. E. Wartenberg (eds.) *Thinking through Cinema: Film as Philosophy*, Malden, MA: Blackwell.

Strawson, G. (2006) *Consciousness and Its Place in Nature: Does Physicalism Entail Panpsychism?*, Exeter, UK: Imprint Academic Press.

5

DEFINITION OF "CINEMA"

Trevor Ponech

Definitions and essences

Philosophical and scientific requests for definitions often arise as "what is" questions. Here, *noûs* consists in proposing noteworthy features in virtue of which a thing or kind of thing, K, is to be identified. Proposals of that sort are apposite when users' ideas about what it is a K-designating term picks out are sketchy, muddled, conflicting, or contraindicated by available evidence. The primary goal is to enhance theoretical understanding of K; if possible, to discover what is so special about it. The method is to learn what makes it true that something is K or an instance of K. Such a definition might further support legislating what a term ought to mean to competent users. Consider the International Astronomical Union's 2006 redefinition of "planet," informed by recent scientific research. Heretoforth, "planet" refers to a celestial body which, among other characteristics, has cleared the neighborhood around its orbit of other bodies (IAU 2007: 13–14). Certain items people believed or desired to be planets – notably, Pluto – now belong to a new category, "dwarf planet," the members of which haven't cleared their neighborhoods. The IAU has fixed the extension of a pair of terms on the basis of what a planet evidently is, after all.

An ambitious answer to a "what is" question might take aim at a target's essence. Essentialism is multiform. One important type of essentialist definition tries to list individually necessary and jointly sufficient conditions or properties. To be a K, an item must satisfy or have each of these; together, they are enough to identify that item as a K. A bachelor is an adult, male, unmarried person. Knowledge is justified true belief. Formulating a statement of necessity and joint sufficiency is a powerful tool for achieving conceptual precision and logical rigor; it clarifies and renders coherent the very idea of K. But strongly realist, explicitly naturalistic definitions suppose that certain concepts and their associated words have a less abstract, nonmental anchor in empirical reality. Of examples of nature's kinds we might ask, what is it about this physical thing or sample of stuff that makes it a K (brain, tree, sample of gold, planet)? The realist's response is that empirical investigation is conducive to knowledge of essences, that is, packages of precisely similar inner features possessed uniformly across particular objects or individual samples. All samples of gold have the atomic number 79, melt at 1,073°C, and resist corrosion by chemical agents other than aqua regia. This property cluster is a candidate for gold's real essence. A real essence is a mind-independent package of properties whereby an item is what it is. Disappearance of just one of these properties would end that item's existence (Elder 2005). Granted, we always risk misidentifying things' inner natures or encountering tough to classify cases. However, with Locke, one might be skeptical about our ability to discover essences without being antirealist about essences themselves (1979: III.vi.9).

What is cinema?

Aesthetic philosophers and cinema scholars disagree over the conceptual content of the term "cinema." Not that experts' minds utterly fail to meet. They routinely make correct, intelligible use of this word, relative to prevailing beliefs, habits, practices, and conventions. Imagine I tell a colleague during projection of an immaculate 35-mm VistaVision print of *The Searchers* (John Ford, 1956), "Now that's cinema!" She will likely grasp that I am expressing how impressive I find the motion picture image's visible magnitudes – its size, luminosity, vivacity, and depth on the big screen. We make sense of one another's cinema-talk by drawing upon our shared resources. These include generally recognized paradigm cases, mutual tacit assumptions about what it is like to have various sorts of viewing experiences, plus common knowledge of the intermeshing technological, economic, and artistic developments commonly associated with cinema history.

So what's the problem? The definition of "cinema" is controversial because people dispute both the nature of cinema and how, if at all, a definition beyond lexicology or social-history, in which ontology does the heavy lifting, could illuminate and unambiguously determine once and forever the reference of "cinema." Whether cinema has an essence is the debate's crux.

CINEMA is distinct from the word "cinema." Speakers of different languages can share my CINEMA concept, yet associate it with other lexical units (*cinéma, Kino, cinematografo, eiga, diàn ying*). It is a public concept insofar as different people can share it, in whole or in part. My CINEMA concept is similar, for instance, to Noël Carroll's concept. Another philosopher might have a CINEMA concept so similar to Carroll's that it makes sense to say they possess the same concept. We tell one CINEMA concept from the next not principally by whose brains they are lodged in but by their content. Roughly, content comprises whatever a concept is about or refers to beyond itself, along with the constraints on its applicability. CINEMA, as I understand it, refers to the aforementioned screening of *The Searchers*, among other things; it does not refer to moving imagery produced by flipbooks, because flipbook displays are not made of light.

CINEMA is a mental item which sorts external objects, states of affairs, or events. Someone equipped therewith has a tool for differentiating between cinematic and noncinematic things and has ideas, however rudimentary, about what properties or conditions make it true that something is a candidate for cinemahood. Opinions differ

53

regarding how to establish CINEMA's content. Let's turn to some of these differences, deferring awhile discussion of whether it is plausible that cinema could have a real essence to which CINEMA might refer.

Some essentialist conceptions

Classic attempts to pinpoint cinema's unique, distinguishing features often start from a quintet of precepts, adoption of which is understandable, given cinema's most salient and familiar forms during the late nineteenth through mid-twentieth century. Theorists throughout much of the twentieth century tended to construct CINEMA concepts atop empirical assumptions to the effect that cinematic items paradigmatically if not necessarily are [a] pictorial images [b] made photographically with a camera, said images being [c] recorded, stored, and exhibited using flexible film strips, [d] their public exhibition normally employing a projector casting light through film strips and onto a screen so as [e] to produce the impression of movement. These presuppositions – plus the culturally overwhelming popularity of pictorial imagery and the longevity of early twentieth-century cinema's dominant technologies – help explain why "film," "movie," "motion picture," and "cinema" are still used synonymously.

One grand old definition nominates as cinema's essence *photogénie* (Delluc 1920; Epstein 2004; Morin 2005). When its proponents talk about "cinema," they have in mind things matching [a] through [e]. They do not, however, conceptualize the empirical quintet itself as marking the cinematic. Their idea is that something which is [a], [b], [c], [d], and [e] is apt to have a certain other, definitive property. *Photogénie* eludes precise analysis but seems generally thought a capacity to trigger archaic affective responses. First published in 1956, Edgar Morin's anthropologically inspired reflection on the nature of cinema treats *photogénie* as a sort of partnership between rationality and superstition. People of modern, industrialized societies harbor a residual propensity toward magical, supernatural thinking; imaginatively and emotionally, they remain in the thrall of phantoms, doubles, divinities, and occult forces. Thanks to the thaumaturgical technologies they employ, movies, in their most popular form, possess an "inner power" (Morin 2005: 7) to arouse the *homo demens* in us. This power derives from their being at once realistic and ethereal. Moving, photopictorial imagery of persons and things makes viewers feel that the image's objects are both absent and present, as if these objects' mystical doubles or lifelike shadows had broken free of the bodies that cast them. Projected across the screen, the image is, moreover, "dematerialized, impalpable, fleeting," its ghostly charm magnified (34–5).

In declaring *photogénie* cinema's essence (7), Morin primarily means "essence" teleologically, as that anthropocentric purpose explaining cinema's existence. His essentialism is thus only as defensible as his sweeping, a priori teleological speculation that cinema's invention is the expression and fulfillment of "the imaginary man," that part of us which lives in and through myths, fantasies, and dreams. Were this social function a necessary, nonaccidental condition for the emergence and persistence of cinematic phenomena, it still wouldn't suffice to divide cinema from noncinema. Morin himself believes numerous cultural artifacts, including photography, share cinema's *raison d'être* and power to elicit archaic, magical thinking. The implied solution to this problem relies on the empirical quintet. Movies' "inner power" to trigger archaic thinking depends on – is perhaps reducible to – their being moving pictorial images and so on. Let these jointly distinguish cinema from noncinema. But now, instead of *the* essence, *photogénie* is at most part of a package of reputed defining features, albeit a specially valued one which might explain cinema's development and nearly universal appeal.

Elucidating human nature is Morin's ulterior motive for pondering cinema's nature. Other theorists are driven principally by normative aspirations. As movie cameras, film stocks, optical systems, and engineering strategies for integrating them evolved, so did arguments, not yet concluded (Scruton 2002; Gaut 2002), about whether these burgeoning technologies' confluence could produce art versus mechanical records and reproductions. During the late 1920s and the 1930s – the silent era's tipping point and denouement – Rudolf Arnheim (1957) published several defenses of cinematic art. These generally rely upon various premises regarding cinema's *Material*, its medium. Arnheim believes cinema's medium is necessarily the moving or animated image projected from a film strip. Significantly, he does not consider [b] photographic imagery a necessary feature of the medium. Furthermore it is possible that he would permit modifying [a] to include nonpictorial imagery, as suggested by his express approval of abstract movies (5). However, [b] troubles Arnheim. Though recognizing it as a key artistic resource, he'd rather cinema abandon photographic representation to become "a pure work of man" by taking the form of "animated cartoon or painting" (213).

Why? As Carroll (1988a: 27) explains, Arnheim shares his opponents' premise that mechanically recording reality indeed is antithetical to creativity and expressivity, hence to art. His mission is to show that cinema is not art's mechanical antithesis. He proceeds by citing the medium's alleged failures and limitations: the absence of sound and color, the fragmentation of the spatial-temporal continuum, the lack of three-dimensionality, lessening of depth perception, and the loss of constancy of size (Arnheim 1957: 127–30). Arnheim thinks these deficiencies differentiate cinema from other media and, crucially, that they prove that film neither perfectly reproduces reality nor replicates human perception. Instead, the medium, imperfectly, idiosyncratically molds, transforms the world according to its own principles. If one skillfully seizes upon these as working principles, one can decisively turn cinema to expressive ends and thereby leverage it into art. But Arnheim's CINEMA concept does not postulate [a]–[e] as cinema's real essence. His argument is not that the quintet describes necessary and sufficient conditions for membership in a certain category of physical object or substance. Cinema's "true meaning" as *art form* is what he claims to have ascertained (210–11). That there exists a medium actually, not essentially, comprising the quintet is an empirical given. And given its inherent properties and constraints, we can figure out how to exploit that medium so to realize a unique, authentic art form. Following Arnheim, this medium dictates that film art must reject extraneous properties like sound, recorded dialogue, and color photography, should embrace montage, and ought to avail itself to photographic and nonphotographic techniques that promise to bring cinema closer to being animated painting.

Arnheim's normative interest in establishing the content of CINEMATIC ART qualifies him as a "medium-essentialist." Medium-essentialism posits an art form's essence – in the sense of its telos, i.e., its specific aims, effects, and style – on the basis of empirical observations regarding whatever is taken to be the art form's distinctive physical medium (Carroll 1996: 50). André Bazin, whose writings of the 1940s and '50s influenced Morin, similarly proposes a medium-essentialist CINEMATIC ART concept. Unlike Arnheim, Bazin makes a strong claim regarding the nature of cinema's medium. Journalist, rather than academic, Bazin does not argue about necessary-sufficient conditions and properties. Nonetheless, he apparently believes he has isolated three necessary features accounting for a fundamental difference between cinema and the material bases of other art forms. To wit, cinema is [a] pictorial imagery, [b] produced by photographic means and displayed so as [e] to produce the impression of movement. The linchpin of Bazin's CINEMA concept is [b]. Photography endows imagery with "objectivity," by which he intends an automatic, natural, mind-independent ontological connection between the image and its object. Photography by the same token endows film with a unique relation to motion and change: "[C]inema is objectivity in time … the image of things is likewise the image of their duration" (Bazin 1967: 14–15). Bazin goes so far as to invite the thought that, owing to its objectivity, a photograph does not just resemble its model, it *is* the model, having snatched something of the model's existence or identity from time's corrupting effects (14). Unequivocally, though, he concludes that cinema's telos is realism. This realism is partly a psychological phenomenon, because it has the power to satisfy the desire to preserve existence against time. It is also aesthetic, cinema's objectivity having the power to fulfill the perennial figurative artistic ambition to make ever more lifelike representations of reality, untrammeled by convention and artifice. Authentically cinematic art is that which embraces technologies, styles, and content – long takes, deep focus, camera movement, panchromatic film, and sound recording; characters, settings, or problems drawn from ordinary life – consistent with fulfilling this realist telos versus, say, Arnheim's expressivist medium-essentialism.

Not every essentialist definition advocates a teleology. Gregory Currie offers one he considers no more prescriptive "than the claim that water is essentially H_2O" (1995: 1). That analogy is telling, because Currie holds cinema to be "something like a 'natural kind'" (Currie 1998: 357). He concedes that, relative to our contemporary, pluralistic attitudes to cinematic technology and art, his CINEMA concept is stipulative: He would reserve "cinema" for a naturally identified category comprising just some of the many sorts of items intelligibly collected under this term. His stereotypical examples of cinema are projected from film prints. But to fall under Currie's CINEMA concept, it is necessary and sufficient that something be a photographically produced pictorial representation delivered onto a surface so as to produce, or have the power to produce, an apparently moving image (1995: 2, 4).

Identifying [a]-[b]-[e] of the quintet as cinema's essence, Currie's CINEMA concept reprises the core tenets of Bazin's definition – although extravagant metaphysical ideas about the image's identity with its object play no role here. Currie is also adamant that his definition embodies no aesthetic recommendations for maintaining cinema's artistic purity. He means only to restrict the extension of "cinema" to a familiar quasi-natural kind. Though artifacts, instances of cinema are like instances of gold because "cinema," like "gold," can be used to pick out something possessing a certain cluster of mind-independent properties. Owing to natural regularities governing reflected light and its interactions with photosensitive receptors, photographically generated imagery is automatically, all things being equal, pictorial imagery of some real object. The image's existence and visible condition naturally depend on, and naturally afford information about, its object's condition. The specifically cinematic image can likewise preserve transtemporal information (1995: 69). If its object moves, the image changes correspondingly, such that viewers have perceptual experiences as of the object's movement taking just so long to occur and as of one stage of its trajectory following another.

Some nonessentialist conceptions

Nonessentialists generally charge that, considered as art form, material basis, and sociohistorical phenomenon, cinema is richer and more complex than essentialists fathom.

It has become commonplace since the late 1960s to observe that cinema, from an historical perspective, derives from so many technological, cultural, and artistic sources, and is so open to technological and stylistic change that it is implausible to ascribe to it a single, immutable essence. Alluding to its multifarious origins – including prephotographic optical devices like the magic lantern and phenakistoscope, painting, cartoon strips, theatrical melodrama, pulp novels, and magic shows – Peter Wollen (1969: 153) denies any one dimension of cinema can be nonarbitrarily validated as grounding or mandating a specifically cinematic aesthetics. His own CINEMA concept holds cinema a "strikingly mixed and impure" (153) semiotic system. Its impurity, consistent with its mixed origins, is reflected in a movie's being a "text" constructed of iconic, indexical, and symbolic signs. Medium-essentialisms err by unilaterally anchoring CINEMATIC ART in one kind of sign at the others' expense. Bazin's realism skews toward indexical signs, the significance of which depends on their causal or existential bonds to what they signify; Arnheim's expressivism skews toward symbolic signs, the significance of which depends on human agency and conventions. In fact, says Wollen, only by considering the interactions of a triad of signs can we begin to understand cinema's aesthetics (141).

Wollen's CINEMA concept is not about medium-specifying material parts and properties. It pertains to a type of signification, a form of production and exchange of meaningful signs. Conceived as cinematic text, a movie is a locus of signifying properties, functions, and processes. Cine-semioticians' paradigmatic texts frequently match the empirical quintet. Wollen himself confines discussion to movies fitting the stereotypical empirical profile insofar as his focus is projected film texts of a predominantly indexical-iconic character, those largely comprising signs standing in an existential relationship to their objects as well as resembling them (165). But officially, semiotics doesn't identify CINEMA with any cluster of necessary empirical properties.

Indeed semiotics is generally presumed "absolutely non-essentialist" for regarding cinema as sociohistorically instituted (Nowell-Smith 1976: 40). Cinema is described as a specific discursive form delimited by the conjunction of two sorts of determinants. On one hand are socially constructed "codes" – like those allegedly governing meaning production and comprehension through continuity editing – prevailing at particular historical moments. These arbitrary signifying practices, conventions, and rules operate within yet transcend individual movies. On the other hand are the technical and material determinants serving to "inscribe" movie texts and the codes guaranteeing their meanings. These, too, change historically. For example, safety film and digital editing supersede nitrate stock and cutting-and-splicing.

Though widely embraced by theorists, premises to the effect that movies are language-like texts, and cinema, a signifying system, attract intense philosophical criticism (Carroll 1988b; Currie 1993; Harman 1999). Furthermore, cine-semiotics is hardly free of essentialist tendencies. Its vanguard theorist proposes that cinema's unique, identifying feature is the "imaginary signifier" (Metz 1982). Sarah Bernhardt, live on stage, could be, but need not be, a signifier. She might represent Phèdre, or simply greet the audience as herself. Regardless, she and her public are co-present at a proximal spatiotemporal location. Bernhardt photopictorially recorded in a movie is necessarily a signifier, namely, the-image-of-Bernhardt. It is unclear how Bernhardt, the image's referent, is a real part or property of the signifier itself. That the-image-of-Bernhardt is an imaginary signifier evokes the putative fact that it is both absent, since Bernhardt is not there in the room; and present to audiences, as a manifestly real screen image consisting of her "phantom," "double," or "replica" (45). This indexical-mimetic phantom moves about, even makes sounds. Thanks to this vivacity, only cinematic representation contains signifiers that are absent, yet present to much the same degree that on-stage Bernhardt is present. Explicitly psychoanalytic, with intimations of *photogénie* and Bazinian realism, the further claim is that cinematic imagery, fascinating spectators with absent presence, is an especially powerful trigger of pleasurable psychic responses.

Noël Carroll offers an alternative nonessentialist CINEMA concept as a class of artifacts conceived and constructed by human agents with sociohistorically varying practical, communicative, and artistic aims in mind. Membership involves satisfying five necessary but not jointly sufficient conditions. The venerable empirical quintet is virtually banished from this definition. No particular medium – no specific material basis, physical process, implement, technology, or congeries thereof – figures in the definition. No particular entrenched social function – representation, art-making, gratification of primordial human desires – is associated with that which identifies cinemahood. Carroll also disavows interest in grounding a CINEMATIC ART concept, noting that his five conditions have no implications regarding which if any formal and stylistic features befit uniquely, authentically cinematic artworks (1996: 72).

Let "cinema" designate any image that is [1] two-dimensional, [2] presented in a detached display, [3] mechanically generated from a [4] template, and [5] produced by such means that the impression of movement is technically possible. Condition [1] differentiates cinematic artifacts from sculptures, music boxes, and the like. Display detachment concerns the way in which cinematic like other imagery involves spatial dislocation. Unlike windows, mirrors, and magnifying lenses, movie pictures do not connect us spatially with their depicta. Merely by looking at movie imagery of it, one can't orient one's body to Mt Aconcagua's direction. A template, [4], is any mass-producible storage, recording, exhibition, or transmission format, including but not limited to DVDs, videocassettes, MPEG files, broadcast signals, and film prints. Coupling templates with appropriate optical systems generates two-dimensional images in detached displays. Though a sort of "performance," this coupling process differs from live theatrical performance: its achievement consists of the technology operating, or being operated by somebody, according to its mechanical specifications. Finally, [5] accommodates commonsense empirical as well as philosophical (Sparshott 1979: 321) intuitions that movement is a defining feature of cinema. Trouble is, some movies contain no movement. Hollis Frampton's *Poetic Justice* (1971–2) is a film of a shooting script sitting on a tabletop; Michael Snow's *One Second in Montréal* (1969) consists exclusively of still photos. Yet these movies share with orthodox ones the property of having been produced using technologies making a certain result, moving imagery presented in a detached display, a possibility. Their makers could have employed their chosen technology to generate moving images, had they preferred. While categorically impossible for drawings, paintings, or photographic stills to be moving imagery, "movement in a film image is an artistic choice which is always technically available" (Carroll 1996: 64).

This definition is strikingly inclusive and not at all parochial. No style of imagery is deemed more cinematic or more artistically valuable than another. No restrictions are imposed on the means by which conditions [1] through [5] are satisfied. Cinema might be instantiated photographically or digitally, by cell animation, or by relatively heteroclite methods like joining strips of clear and opaque leader. Apropos, Carroll's definition dissociates cinema from depiction. Indeed he prefers the less freighted term "moving image" to "cinema" for its distance from connotations of an art form, but also for its applicability to pictorial items (photographically or otherwise made), as well as purely abstract, nonpictorial ones. He would regroup under CINEMA both *The Searchers* and Ernie Gehr's *History* (1970), made without a camera by exposing raw stock to dim light and consisting of scintillating beads of illumination distributed within a depthless black space. Moreover, Carroll's definition regards cinema as protean: novel technologies of moving-image production, dissemination, and spectatorship constantly emerge, accompanied by new formal possibilities; imagemaking practices, and imagemakers' communicative and artistic aims and strategies undergo continuous historical mutation.

Conditions [1]–[5] individuate a concept capable of distinguishing instances of cinema from painting, sculpture, photography, and live theater in all its manifestations. Carroll believes [1]–[5] necessary if CINEMA is to be a distinct, coherent concept, reliably enabling us to identify instances of cinema, but denies they are sufficient to differentiate cinema from noncinema. The five jointly grant cinemahood to arguably precinematic items like mass-produced flipbooks and series of still photographs animated by zoetrope devices. And they leave open whether certain esoteric items satisfying the five conditions – e.g., a radically minimalist pitch-black "movie" made with underexposed film – are cinematic. These classification problems are endemic. Cinema, being a protean class of artifacts, cannot be identified with reference to closed, preexisting boundaries awaiting discovery and conceptualization. Hence an essential definition is unavailable, meaning decisions about how to classify hard cases must be outsourced. Invoking a tactic he advocates while discussing definitions of "art" (2001), Carroll recommends considering history and context. Hence, were it "part of an intelligible, ongoing filmworld conversation" (1998: 329), we would be warranted in taking aboard the radically minimalist candidate, its berth secured by its relevance and contribution to practices, concerns, and interests generative of more clear-cut cases of cinema.

The nature of cinema?

Nonessentialism conceives cinema's identity as mutable insofar as its constitutive technologies, practices, and conventions are variable. Relative to gold, it is hard to believe cinema has a real essence. Essentialist definitions seem naïve and illiberal for treating some selection of historically contingent properties, like the empirical quintet or part thereof, or adventitious functions, practices, and values, like one or another strain of realism, as real essences. Perhaps cinema is ultimately a projection of our CINEMA concepts. "[C]inema has not yet been invented," muses Bazin (1967: 21), alluding to a Platonic CINEMA *eidos*, a "myth of total cinema," awaiting full instantiation. More mundanely, CINEMA's content is up to us. What counts as cinema is up to us, too. Objects so counted are of our conception and making.

Someone might concede cinema's inexpugnable conceptual and historical dimensions yet still use "cinema" to pick out items having a possible real essence. Principally, these are artifacts. Some philosophers hold artifacts in low ontological esteem, reasoning that, even if they do genuinely exist, they cannot have essences because an artifact's being the kind of thing it is perforce derives from our attitudes and doings, not from nature. Critics find this argument tendentious, given that we are part of nature (Baker 2004; Elder 1995) – as is every physical part, particle, and process composing the artifact. Moreover, there are methods of categorizing artifacts other than with reference to their anthropocentric functions, histories, and meanings.

One way to categorize artifacts is with reference to their intrinsic physical properties. Thus an artifactual kind, like a natural kind, can be identified with a collection of objects each of which possesses a precisely similar package of inner properties. Because essentially intention-involving, the causes of an artifact's nature, the clustering of its identifying properties, and the multiplication of similar artifacts differ from those underlying instances of gold and tigers. We needn't posit or know these intentions in order to collect members of an artifactual kind. Hypothesizing the aforementioned property clusters does the job, too.

Cinema's identifying property cluster might be that of a stroboscopic-luminescent field or visual display (Ponech 2006, 2007). Described synchronically, the stroboluminescent display (SLD) is a delimited, spatially contiguous field of resolving elements comprising points of light – "pixels" – plus any nonilluminated areas and intervals separating them. These pixels have intensity, brightness, and color. Diachronically, an SLD manifests for the duration of its existence a kind of dynamic or movement: it has the property of "stroboscopy," consisting of the continuous, high-frequency redistribution of illumination across a reflective or light-emitting surface. During this cycle of phase changes, usually sixty or more per second, pixels refresh, that is, they independently vary their brightness, intensity, and color. "Cinema" might be defined as any such stroboluminescent field or display, whatever its provenance, engineering specifications, or function. Ordinarily, SLDs are vehicles for achieving or presenting expressive and communicative acts, including artworks. In the preponderance of ordinary instances, the active play of light comprising the display is informed by some template, to borrow Carroll's term, which itself has been given a certain structure or content in an effort to adapt it to serve expressive purposes in conjunction with an SLD. But from a naturalistic perspective, being an SLD, rather than being an SLD with a certain psychohistory or one coupled with a template, is what counts decisively toward cinemahood.

Perhaps cinema is only contingently an artifact. It is not inconceivable that an SLD could spring into existence in a mind-independent, arational way, the result of a mindless cosmic accident. Absent sentient beings to make, exploit, and view it, the SLD would still have the parts, properties, dispositions, and causal powers by virtue of which it is an SLD, versus a tree, tiger, gold sample, or airplane. In contrast, concepts like ART, LITERATURE, MUSIC, and MOVIE presumably cannot be grounded in strictly internal property packages uniformly observable across individual physical things. A material artifact's, α's, also fitting the MOVIE (ART, etc.) concept, depends upon a network of complex psychohistorical events and relations obtaining between α and the relevant thoughts and actions of some cultural agent(s). Psychohistorical facts – facts about why and by whom they were made – are (partially) constitutive of α's being a movie (art, literature, etc.). The concept CINEMA need make no essential reference to agency. To be sure, we employ what amounts to an anthropic principle when identifying candidate SLDs. That there could exist cosmologically large or microphysically tiny SLDs seems a given. But the ones of interest to us are those we can pick out on the basis of their effects on us. That anthropic principle does not turn the SLD into something subjective or lacking properties that do not depend on us, on our consciousness of and responses to it. It is a mind-independent object, possessing just the complex qualities that it has. One such property is its power or disposition to appear to percipients such as ourselves as (part of) a spatiotemporally contiguous, delimited stroboscopic field.

Essentialism – the belief that certain traits are indispensable to an object's or sort of object's existence – is philosophically contentious. It is difficult to establish that things have the essences attributed to them and to demonstrate that our apparent knowledge of real natures is not ultimately a projection of our capacities and conventions of individuation, identification, and categorization. These framework debates are not the only ones troubling stroboluminescence's candidacy for cinema's real essence. Whether the foregoing description of this property cluster is true awaits empirical verification. Which if any of the items we label "cinema" are SLDs is also a live empirical question. Another question is why we should accept stroboluminescence as a constraint on what we mean by "cinema." Cinema-talk is mostly about works, canons, institutions, practices, traditions, revolutions, representations, experiences. A reductive, naturalistic CINEMA concept ignores cinema as a human phenomenon.

A nuclear definition of "cinema" does not reduce cinema as we know it to some putative essence. Stroboluminescence is another in a line of proposed restrictions on identifying and individuating *one* basic unit of analysis in the humanistic study of that totality of works, canons, institutions, etc. This restriction is nonetheless latitudinarian. It eschews medium-essentialism and dissociates cinemahood from any particular technology, causal chain, or cognoscenti "conversation." Yet a naturalistic definition contains the resources for adjudicating hard cases, thereby excluding flipbooks, zoetropes, and, *pace* Carroll, lightless cinematic displays. It also clarifies that which is so special about cinematic artifacts. They are dynamic. Movement – change, if you prefer – is deep within their nature. Cinematic motion is most apparent in the redistribition of patterns of illumination such that reidentifiable items seemingly undergo displacement within the display space. Stroboluminescence, rather than unspecified means, underlies this identifying technical possibility.

See also Medium (Chapter 16), Ontology (Chapter 20), Film as art (Chapter 11), Realism (Chapter 22), Semiotics and semiology (Chapter 42), Rudolph Arnheim (Chapter 27), and Edgar Morin (Chapter 38).

References

Arnheim, R. (1957) *Film as Art*, Berkeley: University of California Press.
Baker, L. R. (2004) "The Ontology of Artifacts," *Philosophical Explorations* 7: 99–112.
Bazin, A. (1967) *What Is Cinema?*, trans. H. Gray, Berkeley: University of California Press.
Carroll, N. (1988a) *Philosophical Problems of Classical Film Theory*, Princeton, NJ: Princeton University Press.
—— (1988b) *Mystifying Movies: Fads and Fallacies in Contemporary Film Theory*, New York: Columbia University Press.
—— (1996) "Defining the Moving Image," in N. Carroll (ed.) *Theorizing the Moving Image*, Cambridge and New York: Cambridge University Press, 49–74.
—— (1998) "The Essence of Cinema?," *Philosophical Studies* 89: 323–30.
—— (2001) "Identifying Art," in N. Carroll, *Beyond Aesthetics: Philosophical Essays*, Cambridge and New York: Cambridge University Press, 75–100.
Currie, G. (1993) "The Long Goodbye: The Imaginary Language of Film," *British Journal of Aesthetics* 33: 207–19.
—— (1995) *Image and Mind: Film, Philosophy, and Cognitive Science*, Cambridge: Cambridge University Press.
—— (1998) "Reply to My Critics," *Philosophical Studies* 89: 355–66.
Delluc, L. (1920) *Photogénie*, Paris: De Brunhoff.
Elder, C. L. (1995) "A Different Kind of Natural Kind," *Australasian Journal of Philosophy* 73: 516–31.
—— (2005) *Real Natures and Familiar Objects*, Cambridge, MA: MIT Press.
Epstein, J. (2004) "On Certain Characteristics of *Photogénie*," in P. Simpson, A. Utterson, and K. J.

Shepherdson (eds.) *Film Theory: Critical Concepts in Media and Cultural Studies*, vol. 1, London and New York: Routledge, 52–6.

Gaut, B. (2002) "Cinematic Art," *Journal of Aesthetics and Art Criticism* 60: 299–312.

Harman, G. (1999) "Semiotics and the Cinema: Metz and Wollen," in L. Braudy and M. Cohen (eds.) *Film Theory and Criticism: Introductory Readings*, 5th ed., New York: Oxford University Press, 90–8.

IAU (International Astronomical Union) (2007) *Information Bulletin* 99. Available at http://www.iau.org/fileadmin/content/lbs/ib99.pdf (accessed 11 May 2007).

Locke, J. (1979) *An Essay Concerning Human Understanding*, ed. P. H. Nidditch, Oxford: Clarendon; and New York: Oxford University Press.

Metz, C. (1982) *The Imaginary Signifier: Psychoanalysis and the Cinema*, trans. C. Britton, A. Williams, B. Brewster, and A. Guzzetti, Bloomington: Indiana University Press.

Morin, E. (2005) *The Cinema, or the Imaginary Man*, trans. L. Mortimer, Minneapolis: University of Minnesota Press.

Nowell-Smith, G. (1976) "Moving on from Metz," *Jump Cut: A Review of Contemporary Media* 12–13: 39–41.

Ponech, T. (2006) "The Substance of Cinema," *Journal of Aesthetics and Art Criticism* 64: 187–98.

—— (2007) "Cinema Again: A Reply to Walley," *Journal of Aesthetics and Art Criticism* 65(4): 412–16.

Scruton, R. (2002) "Photography and Representation," in A. Neill and A. Ridley (eds.) *Arguing about Art: Contemporary Philosophical Debates*, 2nd ed., London and New York: Routledge, 195–214.

Sparshott, F. E. (1979) "Basic Film Aesthetics," in G. Mast and M. Cohen (eds.) *Film Theory and Criticism: Introductory Readings*, 2nd ed., New York: Oxford University Press, 321–44.

Wollen, P. (1969) *Signs and Meaning in the Cinema*, London: Martin Secker and Warburg.

6
DEPICTION
Robert Hopkins

Depiction is the kind of representation that pictures – ordinary, "still" pictures – display. A picture depicts whatever it is a picture of. There are many kinds of representation: along with listing pictures, we might include words, theatrical performances, hand gestures, or road signs. Not all of these represent in the same way. Depiction is the way of representing that distinguishes pictures from other representations. That's not to say that every picture depicts. Some purely abstract pictures don't represent anything at all. Nor is it to say that a picture depicts everything it represents. A painting might depict a woman who in turn symbolizes the sufferings of Russia. The picture in some way represents Russia's suffering, but it does not depict it. Nonetheless, every representational picture depicts at least some of what it represents. That's what it is to be a picture of something.

We describe cinema films as "moving pictures," and rightly so. Films represent, and films involve pictures. It's likely, then, that they represent depictively, that they depict at least some of what they are about. But what is depiction? Can we give an account that leaves room for the idea that cinema depicts? Can we say what is special about depiction in film, as opposed to still pictures? Can a single account apply equally to all film – traditional fiction film, documentary, old-style animation, and computer-generated imagery (CGI) – or do the diverse ways in which movies are made prevent that? Finally, how much of what a film represents is depicted?

Moving and still depictions

Freeze a film at any moment, and the result is a picture of whatever that sequence in the film represents. True, if the sequence involves considerable movement, the picture might be blurred. True too, not everything the sequence represents might appear in the picture – what the flung fist is aimed at, or why, might be lost. But that we can generate pictures by freezing cinema images, and that the resulting pictures represent much of what the unfrozen sequences do, strongly suggests that films are themselves pictures, that they depict at least some of what they represent. However, before we can be certain of this, we need to say something about the obvious difference between ordinary pictures and film – the former are "still," the latter "move." Can we give an account of this difference that allows both to depict?

We might think that what distinguishes moving from still pictures is their content: only the former represent time. That would be a mistake. A painting of an execution might show the moment before the guillotine drops, and an illustration on a safety card might show the process by which the plane is to be evacuated. Since moments are points in time, and processes occupy periods of it, both pictures represent time. Yet neither counts as moving. A second suggestion would be that, while moving pictures are themselves spread across time, still pictures are not. Only in the latter are all the parts of the picture present at once. Only for the former does it make sense to talk of the picture having a beginning, middle, and end. However, this proposal is also flawed. Most pictures don't change interestingly over time. But consider a picture that does: a neon sign that lights up bit by bit, to reveal a cowboy on a horse. There's a perfectly good sense in which this picture is *not* all present at the beginning of the process, and we can sensibly talk of the beginning, middle, and end of its appearing. Nonetheless, all we have here is a still picture, revealed bit by bit. True, that the process of revealing the picture has a beginning, middle, and end does not show that the picture itself does, but then we could raise that quibble for the case of film. True too, the natural way to take the example *does* involve the whole picture being present at once at the end of the process, if not before. However, we can imagine the example tweaked so that this is not so. Perhaps earlier bits switch off as later ones light up.

Rather than turning on whether they have temporal content, or whether they extend over time, the distinction between still and moving pictures is instead a matter of the *relation between* properties of the representation and its content. Any representation will have properties that determine what it represents. In the case of pictures, those properties include the distribution of paint on a canvas or that of light projected onto a screen. These properties can change over time, or remain stable. The paint can fade, but may well not do so. The pattern projected might alter, but it might not (think of a long shot of an unchanging scene). The difference between still and moving pictures is that only in the latter does development (stability or change) in properties of the representation determine development (stability or change) in properties represented. How the picture develops over time dictates how its objects are represented as developing.

Thus the neon sign does not count as a moving picture because, although it changes over time, that does not dictate that the cowboy does. In contrast, even an exceptionally stable movie, such as Warhol's film of John Giorno asleep, does count as moving because, if nothing on the screen changes for ten minutes, nothing in the scene represented changes for ten minutes either. This is not to say that a neon sign couldn't count as a moving picture. We can easily alter the example so it does. If two differently positioned neon tubes represent the cowboy's rope, one lighting up as the other fades, the result might be a moving picture of the rope rising and falling. Nor is it to say that moving pictures always involve the straightforward relations between representation and content that we find in the Warhol. Flashbacks, flashforwards and the like show that the time of the image and that of the world in the film can be much more obliquely related than that. In these cases, how the images evolve still determines how the world represented does, just not in the most straightforward way.

If this is the difference between moving and still pictures, we can indeed allow that both depict. The difference turns on something purely structural: the way certain properties of the representation relate to certain properties represented. Why should depiction not provide the way to fill out that structure?

So film usually depicts. But must it? Can there be cinematic representations that fail to represent in the way still pictures do? There are two possible sources of nondepictive cinema. One source is film that doesn't represent at all. In a famous sequence toward the end of *2001: A Space Odyssey* (1968) the screen is filled for long minutes with dazzling but indecipherable patterns of colored light, accompanied by a soundtrack of pure noise. Perhaps these patterns depict the strange scenes the remaining astronaut witnesses in his last journey. Even if so, they might have been used otherwise, to create a sort of symphony in light. Some filmmakers have explored such extreme abstraction. The other source is film that represents without pictures, such as Derek Jarman's *Blue* (1993), for the entire duration of which the screen is a radiant blue. Although Jarman perhaps intended the undifferentiated image to reflect his own experience as he lost his sight, it is not clear that it *depicts* the world as experienced by someone going blind.

Despite these examples, it is clear that almost all film depicts. Cases such as *Blue* raise the question where cinema stops and other forms of representation, such as Radio Theater, begin. Purely abstract cinema, if there is such a thing, lies outside the realm of representation altogether. Where film does represent, and does so in ways that are clearly cinematic, it seems always to do so at least in part by depicting things. And, while we might wonder whether a work without pictures could count as film, we'd have no doubts over a work composed entirely of images. The earliest movies were just that.

What is depiction?

Although confined almost exclusively to the discussion of still pictures, there has been considerable debate over the nature of depiction. Here there is space to describe only some of the available positions (for more, see Hopkins 1998: chapters 1 and 2).

Some (Goodman 1969; see also Kulvicki 2006) say that depiction is symbolic. It is just as much a matter of convention what a picture depicts as what a word means. In consequence, there can be different systems of picturing, just as there can be different languages. The obvious difference between systems that count as pictorial and those that count as linguistic reduces to formal properties of the systems involved. Our task as theorists of depiction is then to identify these formal differences. This view is likely to have appeal for those who take seriously the idea of a language of cinema. Such thinkers need not locate that language in cinema's capacity to depict. Perhaps cinema represents in various ways, and perhaps it is the nondepictive ways that are language-like (Metz 1985). But since depiction has some claim to be fundamental to cinema, if it were conventional, all cinema would bear important similarities to language (Eco 1985).

The central challenge for the symbolic view is to explain the sense in which cinema and the other kinds of picturing count as *visual*. This cannot reduce to the fact that we take in pictures by looking at them: the same is true of written language. Nor can it lie in whatever formal features are supposed to distinguish depictive symbols from those of other kinds. There seem to be important parallels between the way things are presented in pictures and the way they are presented in vision. Not only can the same sorts of property be represented in each, but space is given in pictures in ways strikingly similar to the way it is given by sight (Hopkins 1998, 2004). Yet there is nothing conventional (or language-like) about the way vision represents the world. Some will deny this, claiming that the culture one is raised in determines the nature of one's visual experience. But even if this is true, it is not enough to render vision conventional. For a practice to be conventional is (i) for it to be one of two or more equally good solutions to a problem, all of which are available to a given community; and (ii) which is adopted by each member of that community in part because it is adopted by the others, it being common knowledge that this is so (Lewis 1969). Even if (i) is true of a particular way of seeing the world, (ii) is not. Thus picturing bears striking parallels to seeing, and seeing is not conventional. This strongly suggests that depiction is not conventional, at least not all the way to the core.

What, then, is the relation between picturing and seeing that supports these parallels? One answer (Schier 1986; Lopes 1996) appeals to the perceptual processing that pictures trigger. The same neuropsychological mechanisms that are involved in visually recognizing, say, a dog, are involved in understanding a picture of one. Since the parallel claim is not plausible for the (written) word "dog," or for a dog description, pictures are visual in a sense in which words are not. Understanding them requires that we deploy the same mechanisms responsible for face-to-face recognition of the things they represent.

This could not be the whole story. We don't, except in very unusual circumstances, mistake pictures of dogs for dogs. So there must be more going on when we see dog pictures and grasp what they depict than simply the engagement of the mechanisms by which, in general, we recognize dogs. The recognition theorist will say that pictures not only engage our capacity to recognize objects such as dogs, they also engage our capacity to recognize flat surfaces. Thus our perceptual system delivers conflicting results about what is before us – that it's a dog, and that it's a flat surface. The conflict is overcome by judging that what we're seeing is not a dog, but a picture of one.

How, though, does this reconciliation figure in conscious experience? It's not as if we're presented with something contradictory, something that both looks to be a dog and looks to be a flat surface, and then just form the belief that it's a picture. Dog pictures don't look contradictory any more than do other representations, such as dog descriptions. True, in the former case there are, in a sense, two aspects to what we see before us. True, too, that is not so in the same way when we read the description of a dog. In the picture case, a dog is somehow *seen*; it is present to us in experience, as it is not in the case of words. But though our experience of pictures involves these two aspects, it integrates them in a harmonious way. How does it do so? What is our experience of pictures like? If we can answer, we might hope to define depiction as representation that gives rise to that experience. We would then not need the claims about perceptual processing that constitute the recognition theory.

Although various thinkers agree that experience holds the key to depiction, they disagree about how that experience should be described. Following Richard Wollheim (1987) let's call that experience "seeing-in." We see things in variegated surfaces, and it is in virtue of this that those surfaces *depict* those things. Disagreements aside, there are two claims all those who back an experiential theory should accept.

First, seeing-in cannot alone define depiction. We see things in surfaces that don't depict at all, such as clouds and flames. And we sometimes see in pictures things they do not depict, as when we see the face of a friend in a portrait painted long before she was born. At most, then, depiction is seeing-in plus something else. The extra is generally agreed to lie in the surface's history. Perhaps someone marked the surface intending that person or thing to be visible in it. Perhaps the surface was the product of a mechanism, such as a camera, designed to produce surfaces in which whatever provides the initial input can be seen. Either way, a "standard of correctness" has been set – something making it *right* to see one thing, rather than another, in the surface. Depiction is seeing-in governed by some such standard of correctness (Wollheim 1987: chapter 2).

Second, seeing-in is a special form of seeing. If we don't, in a perfectly ordinary sense, *see* the marks before us, then we're not seeing things in them, but hallucinating. Equally, however, seeing-in can't simply reduce to seeing the marks. For we see the marks even when seeing them only as blotches on a surface, and that is precisely to *fail* to see something in them. So, while seeing-in involves seeing the marks, it must also involve something else. The questions are what this extra is, and how it combines with seeing the marks to form a coherent experience.

Answers to these questions amount to a characterization of seeing-in. Wollheim's own characterization hardly adds to the sketch I used to introduce the idea. According to him, just as there are two aspects to the pictures we see, so there are two aspects to our experience of them. One aspect somehow presents us with a marked surface, the other with something else, such as a dog. To see a dog in the marks just is to have an experience with these two aspects. Nothing more informative about it can be said. Dissatisfied with Wollheim's caution, others have tried to say more. Some have claimed that seeing-in involves the interpenetration of ordinary seeing by a special kind of imagining (Walton 1990). Others say it is an experience of resemblance. When we see a dog in the marks, we see the marks as resembling a dog in some respect. There is then disagreement about what that respect might be (Peacocke 1987; Budd 1993; Hopkins 1998).

Any of the various accounts of depiction in still pictures will transfer, without further strain, to film. Anyone wanting to define depiction in cinema will therefore have to engage with the debate about depiction in general. Let us not pursue further which view is to be preferred. I am simply going to assume that some form of experiential account is correct. Doing so offers the easiest, and in some cases the only, way to pursue some further issues concerning depiction in film.

Seeing film as pictures

One striking kind of picture is *trompe l'œil*, pictures so lifelike that we mistake them for the objects they depict. We fail to see these images as pictures. Usually this occurs only under special viewing conditions. A flat ceiling might be painted so as to appear made of ornately formed plasterwork. The fact that it is impossible to get closer to the detail helps sustain the illusion. Many realistic pictures are seen in conditions that make it impossible for them to fool the eye in this way. We see the craquelure, the ink strokes, or the light glinting off the photographic paper. Many other pictures could hardly sustain illusion under any conditions – think of stick figures, cubist painting, and caricature. Nonetheless, while among still pictures it is rare for the eye to be fooled, it does sometimes occur. Some pictures, then, are illusionistic: the experience we have before them (under the right conditions) matches that we would have before what they depict.

What of cinema pictures? Some (Allen [1995] is a recent, sophisticated example) claim that they too sustain illusion. Of course, almost any film viewer knows not to take what is before her as real. She doesn't *believe* she's seeing the events shown. But, according to this view, she nonetheless has illusory experience of the film. Her visual experience when watching matches that she would have before those events. There is illusion in experience here, if not in belief.

No doubt cinematic pictures could be shown in conditions which would enable them to fool the eye. But in the conditions under which they are usually viewed, we do not have illusory experience of them. As we sit in the cinema, we are fully aware, visually as well as in belief, that what is before us is an illuminated screen. In part, this is a matter of context: we see the dark room that contains the screen. But in part it is simply a matter of the appearance of the projected image itself. For all that cinema pictures lack the obvious textures of canvas, paper, crayon, or paint, they are composed of lights that vary in intensity far less than does the light reflecting off most objects viewed in the flesh. Often the scale of the images does not match that of things seen in real life. And changes in apparent size, as the camera moves, are not usually accompanied, as they would be in reality, by any sense of our own movement. In these and other ways, cinematic images make plain that we are looking at pictures, not things. If moving pictures differ from still ones in this respect, it is only by degree. With still pictures, we are often aware both of the features, such as what colored paint lies where, that fix what they represent and of those that don't, such as the grain of the canvas (Lopes 2005: chapter 1). Perhaps cinema images differ in that we find it hard to see the content-fixing features. We are frequently aware of them only by seeing in them the content they fix, and see what is before us as a picture only by seeing other features, such as the shape and size of the screen. Or perhaps we can after all see what content-fixing features there are, but a far narrower range of features play that role, little more than what color is projected where. However that may be, that we do see film images as pictures seems beyond doubt.

What do we see in film?

So we experience films as pictures. But what, exactly, do we see in those pictures? In particular, does what we see in a film depend on how it was made?

There are various means by which films are made. We might, as in documentary, make a photographic record of real events and use the film to inform the audience about them. We might, as in traditional animation, photograph hand-drawn pictures. We might avoid photography altogether, using CGI techniques to create pictures directly. (Even where CGI does begin with photography, many aspects of what the finished picture shows were not present in the original scene.) But historically the vast majority of films have been made another way. Actors, with the aid of sets, props, and perhaps live special effects, act out the events the film seeks to narrate. (Call those events *the story told*.) The complex events involving the actors, sets, props and the like are themselves recorded photographically. (Call those *the events filmed*.) Since photographic recording and acting (etc.) are both forms of representation, the film, or each of the sequences of which it is made, thus begins life as the representation of a representation. The second kind of representation here clearly bears strong points of contact with that found in theater. So call it *theatrical representation*. (That is not to assume that there aren't important differences between the two.) Call movies made in this way *two-tier* films.

What do we see in two-tier film? Often our experience reflects the film's making. We see in the images before us the events filmed, representing the story told. For instance, in *The Searchers* we see John Wayne on a horse, representing a cavalryman, Ethan Edwards, searching for his niece. That we sometimes see films in this tiered way is shown by our ability to focus on the quality of the acting. Unless we see the actor in the picture before us, we can have no sense of his contribution. But unless we see him as representing such and such a person, undergoing certain travails, we can have no idea of what his contribution is intended to achieve.

We often see films in this tiered way, but do we always do so? The alternative is that our experience does not acknowledge the different tiers of representation involved in the making of the film. The level of events filmed drops out, and all we see in the film is the story told. Do we, in fact, ever undergo this "collapsed" form of seeing-in? Perhaps whether we do in part depends on who "we" are. The film critic may spend her time pondering how the camera has been used, and the quality of the acting. She is, perhaps, professionally obliged to see films in the tiered way. The question, however, is whether any of us ever do anything else. (And note that the question concerns our actual experience of film. It is obvious that some subject *could* see in two-tier film nothing more than the story told. Just consider showing a two-tier film to someone brought up in a culture where all film is very realistic CGI.)

Now, not only is much film two tier, but the lower tier, the theatrical represen-tation, is often illusionistic. The story told is represented by the events filmed in an illusionistic way: someone watching the events filmed from the camera's viewpoint would have visual experiences matching those she would have before the events in the story themselves. Perhaps illusion, so defined, is more aspiration than reality for many films. Certainly it is not always even aspiration: some films refuse to attempt illusion at this level. But that it is often at least aspired to is the only way to make sense of the tremendous care usually taken to get the sets and costumes right, to act convincingly, and to ensure that items of studio equipment, such as sound booms, are not visible in the filmed scene.

Illusionistic representations, be they pictorial or theatrical, are hard to see for what they are. Looking at them, we seem to see what they represent. We don't, therefore, seem to see a representation of that thing. Moreover, this fact about illusionistic representations carries over to *pictures of* them. Consider again our *trompe l'œil* painting of ornate plasterwork. Suppose we create an accurate picture of this illusionistic picture, e.g., by photographing it. What will we see? There's no reason to think the photograph is illusionistic, so presumably we will see it as a picture in which we see something else. But will we see in the photograph another picture, in which in turn we see plasterwork? If we approach the photograph knowing what it shows, perhaps we will. However, our seeing-in might just as easily collapse: we might simply see ornate plasterwork in the photograph. So, where picture 1 accurately depicts picture 2, and picture 2 is an illusionistic depiction of object O, not only do we seem to see O (rather than a picture of one) when looking at picture 2, but we seem to see a picture of O (and not a picture of a picture of O) on looking at picture 1. Nothing here turns on the fact that the illusion is pictorial. We would expect just the same in the case of an accurate depiction of an illusionistic *theatrical* representation. But two-tier film is (often) just that. It is made by creating a photographic record of the events filmed. Photographic pictures have a strong tendency to accuracy (the camera does not lie). But what is recorded in two-tier film is (often) a theatrical representation that is illusionistic. So we should expect to see in two-tier film only the story it tells. Our experience of two-tier film does indeed collapse.

Note two things. First, the claim is not that we *cannot* see two-tier films any other way. Of course we can, and often do. All we need do is bring to bear our knowledge of how such films are made. We attend to what is before us *as* the photographic representation of a series of events that themselves represent. For instance, where a moment before we saw only Ethan's remorse, now we see how Wayne uses his eyes to convey that emotion. We can slip between tiered and collapsed seeing-in, depending on where we direct our attention.

Second, I have not claimed that the images composing two-tier film are illusionistic. The illusionism is at the level of the theatrical telling of the story, not that of the depiction of that telling. So nothing here contradicts the claim of the last section, that we do not have illusionistic experience of film. Indeed, there is a sense in which illusion in two-tier film is not a feature of our experience of it at all. When seeing-in collapses, we are blind to a feature of the film's making, i.e., that it was made by photographing a theatrical representation of the story told. But our experience does not misrepresent the facts. We don't see the picture as made in some way other than it was. Collapsed seeing-in need not suggest anything about how the movie was made. Thus, while illusion in the film's making leads seeing-in to collapse, collapsed seeing-in is not itself illusory.

The unity of cinematic representation

Why does it matter whether seeing-in collapses? It matters because it bears on one final issue: how far we can hope to tell a unified story about representation in film. (In fact, I think it matters in other ways too. See Hopkins 2008.)

The unity of cinematic representation might fail in two ways. It could be that single films represent in more than one way. Or it could be that different films, whether they represent in one way or many, represent in different ways from each other. The fact that some, but only some, films are two tier makes both threats real. The natural thing to say about two-tier films is that they display two kinds of representation. They depict, since they are a photographic record of the events filmed. But the events filmed represent the story told in another way, one we dubbed "theatrical." As a result, the film itself can only, it seems, represent the story told in dog-legged fashion, by depicting events that themselves theatrically represent that story. But if this is true of some film, it is hardly true of all. Traditional cartoons are made by photographing pictures, not theatrical representations; documentaries are made by photographing the very events the film narrates; and CGI offers a way to make pictures without photographing anything at all. If the making of a film dictates how it represents, films made differently must represent differently.

If seeing-in collapses, however, both threats can be avoided. The idea is that even in two-tier film all we see, at least often, is the story told. If so, we experience these films in the same way we experience others. In traditional cartoons all we see is the story they tell: the sufferings of various comic characters. The same is true of CGI. We see, say, massed armies, and do not even attempt to get our experience to reflect the process by which the image was generated. Finally, consider documentary. Here, at least sometimes, we take what we see in the image really to have occurred. But, despite that difference from the other cases, we still see in the film only the events it narrates. We see, for instance in the famous sequence at the start of *Triumph of the Will* (1935), Hitler's plane landing in Nuremberg. Riefenstahl filmed Hitler's plane, not a representation of it, and that is what we see in her movie.

Where experience is unified across different types of film, we can hope that representation will be. Just as depiction by still pictures is a matter of generating a certain experience, seeing-in, so is depiction by film. Just as still pictures depict what we see in them, so do films. And what is seen in all films, regardless of how they are made, is simply the story they tell – be it pure fiction, fact told by means of actors, or fact told by recording the events themselves. Cinematic representation is thus unified, and, for all we've said so far, is nothing but depiction.

I close with four comments on this proposal. First, cinematic representation may just be depiction, but that is not to say that there are no differences between it and depiction by still pictures. We've already seen one, in our discussion of the distinction between moving and still images. We are now close to another. The proposal is that cinematic representation is something like telling a story in pictures. It is a way of narrating a story by showing the viewer pictures in which she sees (nothing but) the events that compose the tale. Individual still pictures sometimes tell a story, but it's a different challenge to do so in moving images. Depiction in cinema might be distinctive in the narrative structures it uses to accomplish this. Examples would be linear and other forms of storytelling, flashbacks, jump cuts, and reverse angles.

Second, I don't deny that we *can* construe two-tier film as involving two kinds of representation, and therefore as involving different forms of representation from other film. The facts about how two-tier film is made, and indeed our ability to see it in the light of those facts (i.e., to undergo "tiered" seeing-in), make that only too plausible. What I've done is to articulate a theoretical perspective on cinema which makes sense of it as displaying just one kind of representation. From another perspective, it displays several. We should not think that only one of these perspectives offers us the truth. Both are right.

Third, in developing that perspective, I relied on the idea that much two-tier film is illusionistic (at the theatrical tier). But I conceded that not all is. Some film refuses to aspire to illusion. Think of films where the acting is deliberately mannered, or where there are constant references to the fact that this is merely acting, and the whole is merely a film (e.g., the *Austin Powers* series). Some film falls short of illusion through incompetence – through bad acting, poor sets, or accidentally leaving sound booms in view. And some falls short of it, however illusionistic it otherwise is, by using actors so familiar that we struggle not to see them as the celebrities they are, rather than the characters they convey (see Cavell [1979] on the "persona"). In all these cases, lack of illusion in theatrical representation of the story told makes it hard to see that story in the picture, rather than an acting-out of it. If the theoretical perspective I've offered is to apply to all cinema, something needs to be said about these cases.

Fourth, and finally, I am not saying categorically that all representation by cinema can be brought under one heading. There are other sources of cinematic content that I have not considered. Language is the most obvious, whether it be spoken by the protagonists, added by a narrator, or simply used in the titles that sometimes introduce scenes and convey background. But the narrative structures mentioned above might also complicate matters. Even the use of music in film might sometimes bear on what it represents. Considering these sources of cinematic meaning might lead us to conclude that cinema does indeed involve various kinds of representation. My point here is limited to that part of cinematic meaning that derives from pictures. That those pictures are made in various ways does not, in itself, show that cinematic representation has several forms, rather than one.

See also Digital cinema (Chapter 7), Music (Chapter 17), Narrative closure (Chapter 19), and Documentary (Chapter 45).

References

Allen, R. (1995) *Projecting Illusion: Film Spectatorship and the Impression of Reality*, Cambridge and New York: Cambridge University Press.
Budd, M. (1993) "How Pictures Look," in D. Knowles and J. Skorupski (eds.) *Virtue and Taste: Essays on Politics, Ethics and Aesthetics*, Oxford, UK; and Cambridge, MA: Blackwell.

Cavell, S. (1979) *The World Viewed: Reflections on the Ontology of Film*, exp. ed., Cambridge, MA: Harvard University Press.

Eco, U. (1985) "Articulations of the Cinematic Code," in B. Nichols (ed.) *Movies and Methods: An Anthology*, vol. 1, Berkeley and Los Angeles: University of California Press.

Goodman, N. (1969) *Languages of Art*, 2nd ed., Oxford: Oxford University Press.

Hopkins, R. (1998) *Picture, Image and Experience: A Philosophical Inquiry*, Cambridge and New York: Cambridge University Press.

—— (2004) "Painting, Sculpture, Sight and Touch," *British Journal of Aesthetics* 44(2): 149–66.

—— (2008) "What Do We See in Film?," *Journal of Aesthetics and Art Criticism* 66(2): 159–69.

Kulvicki, J. (2006) *On Images: Their Structure and Content*, Oxford and New York: Clarendon.

Lewis, D. (1969) *Convention: A Philosophical Study*, Oxford: Basil Blackwell.

Lopes, D. (1996) *Understanding Pictures*, Oxford: Clarendon; New York: Oxford University Press.

—— (2005) *Sight and Sensibility: Evaluating Pictures*, Oxford and New York: Oxford University Press.

Metz, C. (1985) "On the Notion of a Cinematographic Language," in B. Nichols (ed.) *Movies and Methods: An Anthology*, vol. 1, Berkeley and Los Angeles: University of California Press.

Peacocke, C. (1987) "Depiction," *Philosophical Review* 96: 383–410.

Schier, F. (1986) *Deeper into Pictures*, Cambridge and New York: Cambridge University Press.

Walton, K. (1990) *Mimesis as Make-Believe: On the Foundations of the Representational Arts*, Cambridge, MA: Harvard University Press.

Wollheim, R. (1987) *Painting as an Art*, London: Thames & Hudson.

7

DIGITAL CINEMA

Berys Gaut

A brief history

We should distinguish between full and partial digital cinema. The cinematic process, from planning to screening, can be divided into five phases: pre-production, production, post-production, distribution, and exhibition. Partial digital cinema is digital at one or more of these phases, but not at all of them; full digital cinema is digital at all of these phases.

Digital cinema began in the post-production arena, where films were digitally processed and manipulated, usually as a way of creating special effects or animation. One of the earliest partially digital films was *TRON* (1982), which employed digital sequences to simulate a kind of computer game. *Jurassic Park* (1993) and *Forrest Gump* (1994) brought digital special effects to popular awareness, and George Lucas' Industrial Light and Magic studio created the effects in these and many other pictures. Digital color grading (allowing manipulation of film color by digital means) was widely employed from the late 1990s, in preference to chemical grading, and digital editing gradually became standard. *Toy Story* (1995) was the first digital-animated feature film, created by Pixar Studios (originally Lucasfilm Computer Development Division). In the production process, some of the first widely distributed films to be shot with digital cameras were the two earliest Dogme 95 films, *The Idiots* (1995) and *The Celebration* (1995), and many independent filmmakers adopted digital shooting thereafter. In distribution and exhibition, 1999 saw both four widely publicized digital screenings of Lucas' *The Phantom Menace* (though the film was shot on conventional film, and later digitized), and the Sundance Film Festival's acquisition of a digital projector. (Before this point, digitally produced films were transferred by laser recording back onto conventional celluloid for commercial screenings.) And in pre-production, animatics (animated storyboards) were increasingly employed in the 1990s. By the late 1990s there were experimental fully digital films, and the first commercial fully digital films appeared in the new century: Mike Figgis' *Timecode* (2000) was one of the earliest, and George Lucas' *Attack of the Clones* (2002), shot on digital video, brought fully digital cinema to popular attention.

So fully digital cinema, involving all parts of the filmmaking and distribution processes, is less than ten years old. But it is likely to become the dominant form of cinema within the next two decades, given its exclusive adoption by influential filmmakers such as George Lucas and Robert Rodriguez, and given the fact that it is cheaper to produce and distribute than conventional film. It is also likely to accelerate the dispersion of filmmaking practice away from Hollywood, and to lead to an increasing democratization of the filmmaking and film distribution process, particularly through the Internet.

What is digital cinema?

So what precisely is this new type of cinema? Cinema is the medium of moving images. Moving images have been constructed by several methods over the course of history. The oldest method employs objects to cast shadows onto a backdrop, as in traditional Javanese shadow plays. Handmade images have also been used, as in Émile Reynaud's films, regularly screened from 1892 in Paris; these were composed of hand-painted images, projected onto a screen. Most familiar are moving photochemical images, traditional photographs, pioneered by several figures in the late 1880s and 1890s. More recently, video images have been used, constituting electronic cinema. Video can employ analogue or digital images. An analogue image is one that is completely specifiable only by continuously varying values. Object-generated, handmade, photochemical images and predigital video images are all analogue.

In contrast, a digital image is one that is composed of discrete values, typically integers (whole numbers). The digital image, when it is a mechanical recording of some object, is produced by *digitizing* a continuously varying value, such as light waves emanating from objects: the waves are sampled thousands of times a second, and the amplitude of the wave at each sample point is recorded as an integer. These integers are stored as a *bitmap*. A bitmap is composed of a grid of picture elements (pixels), and each point of the grid has an integer assigned to it that is generated by sampling the light emanating from the part of the object that the pixel represents. These integers are stored as binary digits (bits), i.e., as integers to base 2. At each point of the pixel grid, one out of millions of integers, representing colors, is stored: a common digital standard is 24-bit color; i.e., any one of 2^{24} (more than 16.7 million) colors can be represented at any point in the pixel grid. Digital cinema is the medium of moving images generated by bitmaps.

It follows from this account that digital images can be directly subject to computational manipulation: computers are designed to process binary digits and hence can process bitmaps. Analogue images, in contrast, can be subject to computational manipulation only after they have been digitized. It follows from their computability that digital images can be easily and infinitely manipulated without degradation: for any numerical array, there is an algorithm which can transform it into any other numerical array, and information stored as numbers suffers no degradation in being reproduced. In contrast, analogue images, such as traditional photographs, are relatively difficult and cumbersome to manipulate, and their reproduction, involving an analogue copy of an analogue original, leads to *generational loss*: a photograph of a photograph has less information than does the original photograph. And whereas there is a fixed amount of information in a digital image (given by its bitmap), this is not true for the analogue image, since there is a potentially infinite amount of information in a continuously varying value. Finally, given the possibility of direct computer processing in real time, digital cinema can be interactive, whereas traditional photochemical film cannot. (For useful accounts of some of the technical aspects of digital cinema and imagery, see McKernan [2005] and Monaco [2000: chapter 7]; and for digital animation, see Kerlow [2004].)

So, digital cinema is radically distinct from traditional analogue, photographic cinema. A number of philosophical and theoretical questions can be raised about these differences. I will consider four: whether digital cinema constitutes a new medium; the nature and implications of interactivity; the kind of realism available in digital cinema; and the possibility of single authorship in digital cinema.

A new medium?

Is digital cinema a new medium, distinct from traditional cinema? Is it even a medium? Timothy Binkley argues that it is not a medium at all, since the digital image is an abstract object, a bitmap, and media are physical – the medium of painting is paint, for instance. In contrast, "The computer is not a medium" (Binkley 1997: 114). However, Binkley's assumption about media always being physical (what we might call their *material*) is mistaken: literature is a medium, but it is composed of semantic structures, not physical ones. Rather, a medium is a set of practices for using material, whether symbolic or physical, so digital imagery can constitute a medium (Lopes 2004: 110).

One might suppose that digital cinema cannot be a new medium, since cinema is the medium, and digital cinema is only one kind of cinema; and media cannot contain other media. But that assumption is false: we can properly talk of the medium of printing, but also of the media of woodcuts, engraving, etching, lithography, and so on, which are all types of printing. So, one medium can contain other media: media can, as I will say, *nest*. And given the distinctiveness of digital imagery, which we noted in the previous section, there is good reason to believe that it constitutes a new medium, but one which nests in the wider medium of cinema, along with other media such as shadow plays, handmade cinema (e.g., Reynaud's cinema), traditional photochemical films, and analogue electronic cinema.

How distinct is this medium? According to W. J. T. Mitchell, the digital image is a radically distinct type of image. He holds that talk of digital photographs is only metaphorical: "Although a digital image may look just like a photograph when it is published in a newspaper, it actually differs as profoundly from a traditional photograph as does a photograph from a painting" (Mitchell 1992: 4). To support this claim, he appeals to various features of the digital image that we noted earlier, such as the existence of a fixed amount of information and the ease and speed with which it can be manipulated. He also notes that "A digital image may be part scanned photograph, part computer-synthesized shaded perspective, and part electronic 'painting' – all smoothly melded into an apparently coherent whole" (Mitchell 1992: 7).

Mitchell's supporting reasons are true and important. One can generate digital images by three main methods. First, one may employ mechanical capture techniques: these include not just (what we ordinarily call) photography, but also two and three-dimensional scanning techniques, and techniques such as motion capture, which record a performer's body and/or facial motions. Second, one can handcraft the image, using a graphics editing tool, for instance; one can digitally "paint" an image, using Adobe Photoshop or Corel Painter. Third, one can have a computer synthesize an image by running a set of algorithms: for instance, rendering is the process of a computer generating an image by running algorithms specifying perspectival and shading relations on a 3D computational model of an object (and that model can in turn be produced by capture, hand construction, or synthesizing techniques). And all three techniques can, as Mitchell maintains, be combined seamlessly. For instance, the character of Gollum in *The Lord of the Rings* trilogy (2001, 2002, 2003) was generated by motion-capturing the body movements of Andy Serkis and editing them; animators then used traditional key-frame animation techniques to "paint" an image on top of these recorded movements, and a computer rendered the three-dimensional virtual model into a series of two-dimensional views, which were themselves then further manually adjusted (Jackson 2004). These techniques were pushed further in *King Kong* (2005), where motion capture was used on Serkis' face as well as his body (Jackson 2006). The resulting images do, indeed, come across largely as seamless, in the sense that the viewer can see no trace of the various techniques that were used in their making. So the digital image can be produced by three kinds of techniques (capture, computer-synthesis, and painting) in any proportion, and with a seamlessness to the image that does not betray its origins. Given this mixture of techniques, we can refer to the digital image as a mélange (or blended) image – that is, it can be produced by any of three distinct techniques, and each technique may vary in its importance in the making of a particular image.

The fact that the digital image is a mélange image is an important one: it shows that digital images are very different from traditional photographs and supports the claim that digital cinema is a radically new medium. However, Mitchell is incorrect in saying that it follows from these facts that digital photographs do not, strictly speaking, exist. For one option with a mélange image is to use only one of these generation techniques, rather than using all three, and this one might be the capture technique, that is, in one of its varieties, very similar to that used by a traditional photograph. The crucial difference between a digital camera and a traditional camera is the replacement of a photochemical film with an electronic sensor (a charge-coupled device); the lenses, optical systems, shutter mechanisms, and so on, can be identical. So we can still allow that digital photographs exist, while holding that the digital image is very different from the analogue image, in part because it can be generated by nonphotographic means.

Finally, one might suppose that, though digital cinema is a new medium, it does not follow that it is a new *artistic* medium. The telephone was a new medium of communication, but it was not an artistic medium. What more is required for a medium to be an artistic one, that is, to form the basis for an art form? Plausibly this – that one can create artistic effects in the medium that are either impossible or prohibitively difficult in other media. On this criterion, digital cinema counts as a new artistic medium. For consider the ideal of photoreal animation. Photoreal animation is animation where the animation image of something is visually indiscernible from how a photograph of that thing would look, if it existed with the properties that the animation image ascribes to it. For instance, the animation image of King Kong looks visually indiscernible from how a photograph of King Kong would look, if he existed with the properties that the animation image ascribes to him. In contrast, a traditionally drawn cartoon of King Kong can easily be visually discriminated from a photograph of what he would look like, if he existed. Much digital animation is now driven by the photoreal ideal, and it has been successfully realized several times. Photoreal animation is an artistic achievement, affecting how one responds to the image in artistically relevant ways (for instance, the greater realism of the animation helps promote empathy with Kong and engagement with his plight). And photoreal animation is all but impossible in traditional animation: imagine the superhuman difficulty of drawing frames of Kong so that they look like photographs of him. So there is at least one aesthetically relevant effect that is distinctive of the medium of digital cinema. There are many more, most strikingly those arising from interactivity; but they occur also in the realm of special effects, where these do not depend on animation. It follows, then, that digital cinema is not only a new medium, but also a new artistic medium.

Interactivity

Since computers can process information in real time, digital cinema can be interactive – and much of it is. The latter claim may seem surprising, but recall that cinema is the medium of moving images; so videogames, which are composed of digital images, are a part of digital cinema on this definition, as are massively multiplayer online role-playing games, such as *World of Warcraft*. There are also virtual worlds that support moving images, such as *Second Life*; live-action interactive movies, such as *I'm Your Man* (1992); and digital interactive dramas, such as *Façade* (2005). The history of digital cinema recounted in the first section concerned only noninteractive digital cinema; interestingly, the history of interactive cinema is older: the first videogame was produced in 1962 or arguably 1958 (Poole 2004: 15), though the quality of early videogame graphics was far inferior to that of noninteractive digital cinema.

Little work of philosophical distinction has been produced on interactivity; but of that which has been undertaken, one central topic concerns the issue of what is meant by "interactivity," and another concerns the implications of interactivity for our engagement with works. One mooted distinction is between weakly interactive and strongly interactive works. In the case of a DVD with a chapter selection function, the viewer can choose which parts of the film to access and in which order. This gives her more control over the order in which she views the film than the viewer in a movie theater has. However, the structure of the work still exists independently of the viewer's activities: such works are weakly interactive. But this kind of interactivity is the same as that provided by a table of contents and the index of a book, so it does not represent a radical departure from traditional works (though Rafferty [2003] sees even this form of interactivity as a threat to the integrity of film, since it shifts control away from the director to the viewer). In contrast, in strongly interactive works, the structural properties of the work are partly determined by the viewer's own choices: in the case of interactive cinema, the images and sounds shown are partly determined by the viewer's decisions, and there need be no fixed canonical order to their showing. This kind of interactivity is a radically new departure, unlike the weaker sort. It depends on the fact that interactive works can be specified by a set of rules with a certain provenance: these rules, in the case of computer programs, are algorithms, which determine, given a certain input and the interactor's choices, what the output will be (Lopes 2001; see Saltz 1997, for a different account of interactivity).

Audiences interact with strongly interactive works in a very different way than they do with traditional works. In a literal sense, constructivism is true for interactive works: the images on the screen partly depend on viewer's choices, so the viewer is part author of the particular images she sees (though the work itself, determined by a set of algorithms, is still independent of her choices). And, whereas the traditional audience of a work is forced to a more contemplative attitude toward what is being enacted before it, interactors typically have a pragmatic attitude, since they must determine how they are (make-believedly) to act. In particular, this means that they can feel a wider range of emotions than is appropriate in noninteractive works: it makes sense to feel guilty, for instance, about what one may make-believedly have done in a videogame (Tavinor 2005). And, though Lopes argues against the point, interactors are plausibly like performers of musical works and plays: just as, within the permissible boundaries specified by the work, performers have to make certain choices that partly determine the properties of the performance they give, so interactors make certain choices, within the rules specified by the work, that partly determine the properties of their interactions with the works (what they see and hear).

Realism

Is digital cinema different in respect of realism from traditional film? The question cannot be answered simply, since the notion of realism is one that has many aspects.

One sense of "realism" is that of *transparency*: some philosophers, most prominently Kendall L. Walton, have argued that photographs are transparent in the sense that, when we look at a photograph, we literally see the object photographed. Look at a photograph of your ancestors and you literally see them. The claim is general: it would apply to all photographs, both traditional and digital. However, crucial to Walton's defense of photographic transparency is that features of the photograph are counterfactually dependent on features of the subject in a way that is not mediated by the photographer's beliefs. Nonphotographic pictures, in contrast, are mediated by the artist's beliefs about her subject: for this reason, Walton holds that (with the exception of a few mechanically executed paintings and drawings), handmade pictures are not transparent (Walton 1984). So, on this view, nonphotographic digital images are opaque, i.e., not transparent. Given the prevalence of mélange images in digital cinema, Walton's view has the consequence that digital cinema is sometimes transparent, sometimes opaque, and that certain aspects of a single image may be transparent and other aspects opaque. And digital images may seem transparent, even though they are opaque. Lopes, in contrast, has argued that not just photographs, but also handmade pictures of actual objects, can be transparent (Lopes 1996: chapter 9). This has the advantage of preserving a unitary account of transparency for all digital images, whether photographic or not, of actual objects, but it inherits the problems of Walton's account and then adds several counterintuitive consequences of its own. An alternative account is also unitary, but holds that all pictures, whether photographic or nonphotographic, are opaque; this has the advantages of preserving a unitary account of pictures in respect of transparency, while avoiding the counterintuitive consequences of Lopes' account (Gaut forthcoming: chapter 2).

Another sense of realism is *ontological realism*: from the existence of a photograph, it follows that its subject existed. Photographs have a causal relation to their subjects; handmade pictures have an intentional relation to them. From the obtaining of a causal relation, it follows that the subject of the photograph existed at the time the photograph was made: one cannot photograph something that does not exist, such as King Kong. From the obtaining of an intentional relation, it does not follow that the subject existed at the time that the picture was made: I can make a painting of Kong. So photographs, whether traditional or digital, can only be of what is actual. (A traditional animated film is a photograph of an actual animation drawing or painting; live-action photographic fiction films are photographs of people, such as actors, who are make-believedly someone else; and in both cases audiences can also make-believe that the photographs are images of fictional things.) Nonphotographic digital images or aspects of digital images that are not photographic, in contrast, can be of what is not actual. So traditional film is ontologically realistic, but digital film is not in all cases. (And note that these features show only that the subject existed, not that the subject possessed the properties it seems to possess: there is plenty of scope for manipulation in both traditional and digital film.) The traditional film image is, in Peirce's terms, an index (has a causal relation to its referent), whereas many digital images are merely icons (resembling their subjects but lacking a causal relation to them) (Prince 1996).

A third sense of realism, *perceptual realism*, is that in which a realistic depiction looks like the object it depicts. How to make that claim precise is notoriously difficult, but a plausible view is that the picture and its object resemble each other in respect of their possession of those visual properties that trigger the capacity to recognize the object depicted. A horse picture resembles a horse in that both trigger the visual horse-recognition capacity. Pictures have greater realism, the greater is the number of properties that they depict in this fashion (Currie 1996: chapter 3). This view grounds the claim that certain filmmaking styles are more realistic than others. Renoir's deep-focus, long-take style is more realistic than Eisenstein's montage style, since looking at a deep-focus-style film is more like looking at the subjects depicted than looking at a montage-style film is like looking at the subjects it depicts. On this construal of realism, digital cinema has a greater capacity for realism than does traditional film, since it can, for instance, make takes of much greater length than can traditional film, which is limited to a film length of about fifteen minutes, due to the bulkiness of the film roll in the camera. Digital films have been composed of one take that is the length of the entire film, over one and a half hours: for instance, Figgis' *Timecode* and Alexander Sokurov's *Russian Ark* (2002).

A fourth sense of realism is that of *illusionism*. It is sometimes claimed that the cinema spectator is under an illusion, understood as a false belief, of one sort or another, such as that she is really in the presence of the events depicted. Most of these claims are straightforwardly false: if, for instance, the spectator believed that she were really in the presence of the ravenous monster in a horror film, she would be fleeing the movie theater, not contentedly munching on her popcorn. However, the viewer of digital cinema may well be under illusions in respects that the viewer of traditional film is standardly not. For instance, the viewer may assume that she is seeing an image of an actor moving in a real location, but the set has in fact been created purely digitally. Or she may assume that she is seeing an image of actors moving, whereas she is seeing purely digitally created characters: in *The Lord of the Rings* and *King Kong*, for instance, "digital doubles" are used at several points, where placing actors in the scene would have been too dangerous. Even close inspection may fail to reveal whether a digital double is used, especially in long shots. Digital creation and manipulation of characters and sets, then, give a much greater scope for illusionism in digital cinema than in traditional film.

A fifth sense of "realism," already adverted to, is *photorealism*, and it can be achieved comparatively easily in digital cinema, unlike traditional film. An animation image is photoreal when it looks like a photograph of a real object. Digital animation employs features such as motion blur and lens flare so that its images look like photographs of real objects: here the standard of realism is not that the image looks like the object would in real life, since motion blur and lens flare are artifacts of the camera and are not something that we see when observing a scene through our own eyes. Rather, the notion of photorealism is a derivative one: it takes the *photograph* as the standard of reality and tries to make the animated image look like a photograph. Traditional handmade animation can pursue the photoreal ideal too, but as noted earlier, it is one that is all but impossible for it to achieve. Photoreal animation is a central means for achieving the realism of fantasy and special effects digital movies.

Finally, there is what we can call *epistemic realism*: an image is epistemically real just in case it provides strong (though defeasible) evidence that what it apparently depicts really happened. Traditionally, photographs have been accorded great evidential authority: we accept a photograph as providing much stronger evidence for something's having occurred than we would a drawing or painting, however meticulous, of that scene. A traditional film can be viewed as constituting good evidence that certain actors were at certain locations in the past. But a digital photograph can be subject to so much manipulation that it can be systematically misleading about what it is a photograph of, as in the case of digital manipulation of models to make them look more glamorous. As Barbara Savedoff has noted, the rise of the digital photograph threatens the general "destruction of photographic credibility" (Savedoff

1997: 212). And obviously the wider category of the digital image may provide no evidence whatsoever for something's having occurred (such as King Kong's fall from the Empire State Building). The problem is made worse by the achievability of the photoreal ideal: we may think we are looking at a photograph of something, though it is in fact a mere animation frame.

So, digital cinema has greater powers to achieve realistic-looking images than traditional film. The irony, though, is that when viewers come to know of these powers, they have every reason to be suspicious about whether what they seem to have evidence for happening really did happen. In this sense, digital cinema's pursuit of realism is a self-defeating project: the informed viewer increasingly has reason for a suspension of judgment about the evidential authority of the digital image.

Authorship and control

Is it possible to have a single author of a digital film? More weakly, does digital cinema extend the degree of directorial control over films? Some directors have thought so: Robert Rodriguez, for instance, has said of digital cinema that "It's the speed and power of almost having a paintbrush in your hand" (Waters 2005: 16). Technological achievements appear to support this view. The mélange image, as we have seen, increases the power of filmmakers to manipulate the image. With Gollum and King Kong, a combination of motion capture, motion editing, and key-frame animation allowed increased control, relative to the actor, over a character's actions, since only aspects of the actor's performance were incorporated into the character's actions.

However, though the filmmakers collectively have more control over the image, it is not true that the director's control is increased relative to that of all other collaborators. On the contrary, even a brief glance at the credits of most digital films shows a large increase in the number of people credited with working on a film. This is hardly surprising, given the technically and artistically demanding nature of many of the tasks associated with digital filmmaking. Digital films are currently more, not less, collaborative than traditional films. And, as I have argued elsewhere, traditional films are, if they involve at least one actor distinct from the director, essentially collaborative, and the single authorship view is false of them. One reason is that the actor is an expressive agent, and hence the director is not in the same position as, say, the author of a novel, who creates characters without having to rely on the recording of others' expressive actions (Gaut 1997; for the best defense of the single authorship view, see Livingston 1997).

One might suppose that increased collaboration in digital cinema is merely a feature of the current state of technology and that technical progress will one day result in all of these digital tasks being performable by the director. This may be so, since it is impossible to forecast the path of technical development. So suppose that such developments result in a director being able to modify on his own all features of the digital image, and that he did choose to modify every single feature. Then, if the actor's contribution is still visible in the finished product, it would still not be a single authored film, since there would be at least two expressive agents involved in the final film. Or, alternatively, the modification might be so extensive that nothing was left of the actor's contribution. In that case the film would be the equivalent of an animated film, and there is no doubt that animated films can be the products of a single individual. So such digital films would have a single author, but only for the same reason that animated films can have a single author, due to the absence of actors' expressive contribution.

Digital cinema creates new possibilities for collaboration in performance. One can now unbundle an actor's role: Serkis' voice and bodily and facial movements were incorporated into the Kong character, but other aspects, such as his particular physical look, were discarded. And the role of Kong was in effect collectively acted. The motion-capture footage was edited to alter aspects of Serkis' performance – a motion editor talks of "performance change" and of "keeping the tension in the eyes" of Kong (Jackson 2006). Key-frame animators added further nuances to the performance, particularly around the face, where the motion-capture technology was insufficiently precise to record emotional subtleties and in scenes where it was impossible for the real actor to do what Kong was doing. So, here again, digital cinema has saliently different features from traditional film, but it is not in virtue of its enhancing single authorship, but in expanding the role of collaboration in film.

See also Realism (Chapter 22), Authorship (Chapter 2), Definition of "cinema" (Chapter 5), Film as art (Chapter 11), Interpretation (Chapter 15), and Medium (Chapter 16).

References

Binkley, T. (1997) "The Vitality of Digital Creation," *Journal of Aesthetics and Art Criticism* 55: 107–16.

Gaut, B. (1997) "Film Authorship and Collaboration," in R. Allen and M. Smith (eds.) *Film Theory and Philosophy*, Oxford: Oxford University Press.

—— (forthcoming) *A Philosophy of Cinematic Art*, Cambridge: Cambridge University Press.

Jackson, P. (dir.) (2004) *The Lord of the Rings* (extended DVD version). (See esp., "The Taming of Smeagol," appendix 3; "Visual Effects" on MASSIVE, appendix 6.)

—— (dir.) (2006) *King Kong*, Disc 2, 2006: *Post-Production Diaries*, esp., "Bringing Kong to Life: I & II."

Kerlow, I. (2004) *The Art of 3D Computer Animation and Effects*, 3rd ed., Hoboken, NJ: John Wiley.

Livingston, P. (1997) "Cinematic Authorship," in R. Allen and M. Smith (eds.) *Film Theory and Philosophy*, Oxford: Oxford University Press.

Lopes, D. (1996) *Understanding Pictures*, Oxford: Oxford University Press.

—— (2001) "The Ontology of Interactive Art," *Journal of Aesthetic Education* 35: 65–81.

—— (2004) "Digital Art," in L. Floridi (ed.) *The Blackwell Guide to the Philosophy of Computing and Information*, Oxford: Blackwell.

McKernan, B. (2005) *Digital Cinema: The Revolution in Cinematography, Postproduction and Distribution*, New York: McGraw-Hill.

Mitchell, W. (1992) *The Reconfigured Eye: Visual Truth in the Post-Photographic Era*, Cambridge, MA: MIT Press.

Monaco, J. (2000) *How to Read a Film*, 3rd ed., New York: Oxford University Press.

Poole, S. (2004) *Trigger Happy: Videogames and the Entertainment Revolution*, New York: Arcade Publishing.

Prince, S. (1996) "True Lies: Perceptual Realism, Digital Images, and Film Theory," *Film Quarterly* 49:

27–38. Reprinted in L. Braudy and M. Cohen (eds.) *Film Theory and Criticism*, 6th ed. (New York: Oxford University Press, 2004).

Rafferty, T. (2003) "Everybody Gets a Cut: DVDs Give Viewers Dozens of Choices – And That's the Problem," *New York Times Magazine* (4 May): 58, 60–1. Reprinted in N. Carroll and J. Choi (eds.) *Philosophy of Film and Motion Pictures* (Oxford: Blackwell, 2006).

Saltz, David. (1997) "The Art of Interaction: Interactivity, Performativity, and Computers," *Journal of Aesthetics and Art Criticism* 55: 117–27.

Savedoff, B. (1997) "Escaping Reality: Digital Imagery and the Resources of Photography," *Journal of Aesthetics and Art Criticism* 55: 201–14.

Tavinor, G. (2005) "Videogames and Interactive Fiction," *Philosophy and Literature* 29: 24–40.

Walton, K. (1984) "Transparent Pictures," *Critical Inquiry* 11: 246–77.

Waters, R. (2005) "Hollywood Sees Power Shift from Film-set to Desk-top," *Financial Times* (20 June): 16.

8

EMOTION AND AFFECT

Carl Plantinga

Why should anyone be concerned about the affective experiences of film viewers? We could list at least the following reasons: (1) a pleasurable affective experience is one of the primary motivations for film viewing; (2) emotions provide narrative and character information and are necessary to fully understand a narrative film; (3) emotions and affects, whether pleasurable or not, are a central element of the phenomenological experience of the cinema; (4) emotions are intimately tied to cognitions, and for this reason affective experience, meaning, and interpretation are firmly intertwined; and (5) emotions as experienced in films have powerful rhetorical functions and contribute to a film's ideological effects.

In the 1970s and 1980s film theorists approached questions of cinema and affect nearly exclusively from the standpoint of psychoanalysis. Psychoanalytic film theory certainly dealt with human affect but focused on desires and pleasures, rather than emotions (Plantinga and Smith 1999; Plantinga forthcoming). Of typical emotions – such as fear, pity, admiration, disgust, and compassion – psychoanalytic theory has little to say. Neither could psychoanalytic film theory shed light on affective phenomena such as mimicry and emotional contagion. This essay focuses on cinematic affect from what might be termed a cognitive or naturalistic perspective, derived from contemporary developments in psychology, aesthetics, and film and media theory.

Emotions and affects

A human emotion is a complex phenomenon, but is probably best thought of as a mental state accompanied by physiological and autonomic nervous system changes, subjective feelings, action tendencies (that is, tendencies toward certain behaviors in response to emotions), and outward bodily behaviors (facial expressions, body postures, gestures, vocalizations, etc.). Emotions are intentional in the sense that they are directed toward some "object" (which may or may not be real or correctly understood by the person having the emotion). In some cases, such as phobias or delusions, the emotion is powerful and real, but its object is not. Robert C. Roberts calls an emotion a "concern based construal," that is, it is a person's perception or judgment of a state of affairs rooted in that person's concerns (Roberts 2003: 65–83). To take a simple example, Ann becomes fearful when she construes that her cabbie is driving dangerously fast; her concern is for her safety. Jane experiences guilt when she mulls on the fact that she has stolen a cookie from the cookie jar; her construal is that she is blameworthy and her concern is that she not be a "bad" person. This may seem to make an emotion a simple phenomenon, but such is not the case; emotions are complex, episodic, dynamic, and structured (Goldie 2000: 12–16).

There is also considerable debate about whether emotions, as mental states, should be considered to be judgments or beliefs, rather than something broader like generalized "perceptions" or "impressions." Roberts, for example, writes that the construals that in part make up emotions may be unconscious, and often have an immediacy reminiscent of sense perception: "They are impressions, way things appear to the subject; they are experiences and not just judgments or thoughts or beliefs" (Roberts 2003: 75, 84–7, 89–92). Derek Matravers identifies the view that an emotion must necessarily be a belief "narrow cognitivism" (Matravers 1998: 14); Jenefer Robinson takes a similar position (Robinson 2005). Both favor a broader view in which the mental state characteristic of an emotion need not imply belief.

"Affect" is a broader category than "emotion." Affects are any felt bodily state, including a wide range of phenomena, including emotions, moods, reflex actions, autonomic responses, mirror reflexes, desires, pleasures, etc. Emotions are a special case of affect because they are intentional, that is, they "take" an "object" and represent a relationship between a person and her or his environment. For example, the object of my fear might be a charging rhinoceros. The object of my jealously is that man or that woman chatting up my spouse. My fear and jealously are intentional because they are about something and are directed at something (Goldie 2000: 16–28). Affects, on the other hand, lack this intentionality or *aboutness*. My indigestion and feelings of nausea are *caused* by eating too many tacos, perhaps, but my indigestion is not *about* those tacos in the way that my jealously is about that threatening lothario. The indigestion is merely a matter of a stimulus and response and is not an intentional relationship. Noël Carroll holds that affects are more structurally primitive than emotions and reserves the term "emotion" for affects that have a complex structure that integrates computation (or what Roberts would call a construal) with feelings (Carroll 2008).

Moods, another type of affect, are thought to be longer lasting and more diffuse than emotions proper. Thus a mood may last for hours or days, and it may take no object whatsoever, when, for example, one is in a good or a bad mood for no apparent reason. The claim that moods take no object is not without problems, as Peter Goldie points out (Goldie 2000). Sometimes bad moods follow negative emotions, and good moods follow positive emotions. There is a sense, then, in which the object of the emotion is *also* the object of the mood. It is also worth noting that moods and emotions, however conceived, impact each other. A person in a giddy mood is primed to experience certain emotions because moods influence construals. A giddy person is more likely to construe events or situations in ways that giddiness makes salient – as amusing or exciting or benign. Likewise, emotional experience can also alter subsequent moods.

Emotions at the cinema

What kinds of emotions do spectators have at the movies? One question we might ask is whether "filmic emotions" are different in kind from emotions had outside the movie theater. Many film and communication scholars hold that filmic emotions are similar in many ways to garden-variety emotions. Some maintain that spectator responses to fictional events closely approximate responses to actual events, as though the spectator entertained the illusion that the events were actually happening to her (Tan 1996: 82) or as though the spectator were a "side participant" in actual events (Gerrig and Prentice 1996). Tan claims that the emotions spectators have at movies are "witness emotions," comparable to those we might have in witnessing actual events, and that the spectator imagines that she or he is "in the scene." Richard Gerrig and Deborah Prentice, similarly, write that spectator emotions approximate those that an actual "side participant" might have.

These claims, however, neglect important differences between spectator emotions and "extrafilmic" witness emotions. Emotional responses, I have argued, are concern-based construals, in which the emoting party responds to elements of her environment in relation to her concerns. This construal is often automatic and immediate, in part the result of commonplace "assumptions" that are largely unconscious. We can call these background assumptions the emoter's "mental set." In the case of the movie spectator, what elements of the spectator's mental set inflect emotional response away from "real-world" emotional responses?

There are at least two elements of the spectator's mental set that significantly alter response: (1) the realization that the spectator cannot affect the events in any way; and/or (2) (in the case of narrative fiction) the understanding that what she sees is in fact fictional and not actual. To discuss the first element, one should understand that emotions are often accompanied by "action tendencies" that are suppressed or disabled in a film viewing environment. Emotions evolved in part as adaptive mechanisms that enable us to quickly detect threats and/or affordances, or in other words, opportunities in the environment, and to mobilize action. Thus the threat of a tiger leads to actions designed to enhance the possibility of survival, such as flight. Disgust initiates avoidance tendencies; and pity, the desire to assuage the hurt in the other. The spectator of any traditional film understands that no action will influence the events depicted on the screen. This gives the emotions a different phenomeno-logical feel and makes the negative emotions, at least, less laden with anxiety, since emotional response is freed from any immediate need or responsibility to act. Second, the spectator's mental set (for fictions) also includes the knowledge that what she sees is fictional and not actual. Film viewing, whether in the movie theater, at home, in a commercial airliner, or on an iPod or cell phone, rarely ever involves the illusion that what is seen is actually occurring at the time of the viewing, and this fact vitiates the analogy to being an actual witness to an event. Again, this is precisely what allows films to be emotionally powerful without threatening the spectator's safety and comfort. The assumption of fictionality allows spectators the enjoyment of scenes involving rampaging dinosaurs, raging battles, and scenes in which characters undergo extreme emotional distress. Such scenes would be unpleasant and unbearable for most in actual life, but with the potential to provide pleasure in the realm of fiction film spectatorship. The institutions of fiction, of which the film and media industries are important components, prompt the spectator to approach a film in the context of social convention and of play (M. Smith 1995b).

If it is true, in fact, that narrative fiction films and the institutions that provide them invite the audience to relate to the film as a work of fiction, then this raises an interesting question: Why do spectators have any emotional responses at all? If we know that serial killer Anton Chigurh in *No Country for Old Men* (2007) does not actually exist, why is he such a frightening figure? Why have compassion for Dorothy in *The Wizard of Oz* (1939) if we understand that she is a mere fiction? This so-called "paradox of fiction" has intrigued philosophers since Colin Radford argued that if emotions do depend fundamentally on belief, then perhaps our emotional responses to fiction are irrational and undesirable, since we do not believe the fictional events or characters to be real (Radford 1975). Two prominent "solutions" to the paradox are the pretense theory and the thought theory. Pretense theory contends that spectators and readers of fiction have emotions, or perhaps "quasi-emotions," within the context of a game of make-believe (Walton 1990). Thought theory contends that spectators or readers can have genuine emotional responses to propositions or imaginations they do not necessarily believe to be true (Scruton 1974; Lamarque 1981; Carroll 1990: 59–88).

But one might also point out that the paradox is most difficult to resolve for "narrow cognitivists," and less difficult for those with a broader perspective on the emotions. If emotions sometimes result from impressions or perceptions that do not rise to the level of belief, then the paradox begins to dissolve because it depends on the faulty premise that emotions are necessarily dependent on belief. We respond to fictions with actual emotions because the human mind/brain is modular, with various systems operating more or less independently. Fictions engage parts of the brain that generate automatic affective and emotional responses, while eliciting high-order cognitive processing that precludes viewers from responding as though the fictions were actual events. If human responses were solely the result of rationalistic deliberations and separate from automatic and unconscious "built in" psychic and bodily mechanisms, perhaps the paradox of fiction would seem more troublesome.

To return to the question of how cinematic emotions differ from extracinematic emotions, we might say that cinematic emotions differ in at least the two ways described above. It should also be remembered that the emotions had at the cinema do not all take as their object a fictional character or narrative events. Spectators may also have artifact emotions that take as their object the film itself, and metaemotions that take as their object the spectator's own prior response, or that of an audience. A fascination with the construction of a film narrative or production design, admiration for the skill with which a scene is constructed, or outrage at racist or homophobic stereotypes, all are artifact emotions. Metaemotions are important as well, as a spectator can have pride or satisfaction for having responded compassionately to a character's plight (Feagin 1983), for example, or can become disgusted with herself for responding to the same scene if it is later deemed to be sentimental.

Fiction emotions can be either direct or sympathetic/antipathetic. The direct emotions take as their object the unfolding narrative itself. Examples are anticipation, curiosity, surprise, suspense, and fascination. Tan proposes that "interest" is not only the primary direct emotion at the cinema, but is a global and long-lasting emotion that functions to rivet the spectator's attention to the screen (Tan 1996: 85–120). Sympathetic and antipathetic emotions take as their object the character, behavior, or situation of a film character, ranging from "pro-emotions" like pity, compassion, and admiration to "con-emotions" such as anger, disgust, and contempt.

There are good reasons to believe that fiction, artifact, and metaemotions in response to films have strong similarities to extrafilmic emotions, but can be altered or inflected by various filmic strategies. Thus, for example, audience contempt for and disgust at Dr Chilton in *The Silence of the Lambs* (1992) is elicited by his behavior, which arguably constitutes sexual harassment of a sympathetic protagonist Clarice (Jodie Foster) and demonstrates both sexist patronization and an untempered drive to retain power. Such patterns for the elicitation of disgust and contempt exist for the spectator both inside and outside the movie theater. Yet in many ways the filmmakers amp up the disgust and contempt by the way Dr Chilton is framed in relation to Clarice, in tight two-shots that emphasize an unwelcome intimacy that is forced on Clarice, and in directing the audience's attention to unpleasant features of Chilton's appearance, facial expressions, and vocal intonations. Movies are typically more "hyperrealist" – exaggerated, clear, focused, and simplified – than realist (Carroll 1996b: 86–7). (It should also be noted that films have the capacity not only to clarify and intensify emotional response, but may also complicate responses in intriguing ways by employing techniques that elicit contradictory or discordant affective charges.)

The study of how particular film genres elicit emotion also promises to shed light on the types of emotions spectators have at the movies. The most sustained study in this regard, from a cognitive/analytic perspective, has been Carroll's *The Philosophy of Horror*. There Carroll posits that "art horror" combines disgust with fear, both directed at an "impure being," or monster, that threatens the safety of sympathetic characters. Carroll also proposes a solution to the "paradox of horror," which is related to the "paradox of tragedy" (Hume 1965; Feagin 1983) and like the latter, a subspecies of what might be termed the "paradox of negative emotion." Why do audiences, in their consumptions of fictions, willingly subject themselves to negative emotions such as fear and disgust, given that these emotions are typically among those that bring displeasure, discomfort, and distress? Do film audiences actually enjoy fear and disgust as "art emotions," or, as Carroll suggests, are audiences willing to abide these unpleasant emotions because their curiosity about this monster – this categorically impure being, together with a narrative of gradual disclosure, brings a pleasure that is strong enough to outweigh the displeasures of fear and disgust? Carroll's view has generated intense debate (e.g., Feagin 1992; Gaut 1995; Yanal 1999), and the paradox of negative emotion remains a formidable issue.

Narrative and character

Film and television are typically experienced through audio-visual displays that appeal to the senses in ways that differ from literature. This has implications for affective response, a topic further discussed in the following section. But it makes sense first to examine the ways in which narrative films employ narrative and character, common to both film and literature, in the elicitation of spectator emotion. Most theorists of filmic emotions see narrative and character engagement as central to the spectator's emotional response to a film. Emotions occur in time and, like narratives themselves, constantly evolve as situations change and as various bodily affects run their course. Thus the spectator's concern for a character in relation to evolving narrative situations is typically seen as the backbone of spectator emotion. Emotional response is typically rooted in the spectator's appraisal of the narrative in conjunction with character goals and desires. We name emotions in accordance with particular kinds of "concern-based construals," and those construals, in turn, accord with conventional paradigm scenarios. Thus certain narrative paradigms, often corresponding with particular genres, tend to elicit pity, fear, elation, compassion, etc.

Sympathy or antipathy for various characters provides a compass for the spectator in light of which she construes the narrative situation. Thus at the end of *The Silence of the Lambs*, when Hannibal tells Clarice that he plans to dine on Dr Chilton's liver, the spectator may experience a rather grim satisfaction, rather than abject horror, because the spectator has been led to detest Dr Chilton. Had Hannibal informed Clarice that he planned to dine on *her*, spectator response would have been far different (and manifestly unpleasant), because the spectator has been led to sympathize with her.

One issue of contention has been the degree to which spectator emotions are identical with the presumed emotions of a sympathetic protagonist. Spectator identification or engagement, sympathy, and empathy all are essential in any discussion of film affect. Since they are discussed at length in another essay in this volume (see "Empathy and character engagement" in this volume), only brief mention will be made here. The film theorist who most strongly promotes the "identification hypothesis," that is, the view that spectator and protagonist emotions are largely identical, is Torben Grodal, whose "PECMA flow model" of emotion elicitation in film (the acronym "PECMA" standing for perception, emotion, cognition, and motor action) combines cognitive theory with neuroscience. For Grodal, spectator emotional response depends fundamentally on the viewer's identification with characters. In viewing a film, the spectator adopts the character's goals, mentally simulates the character's situation, and responds to the film based on that simulation. Grodal's model is a "flow" model in that it compares the temporal experience of the viewer to that of one flowing down a narrative river that leads to the film's end. The protagonist becomes the viewer's mental raft, so to speak. The viewer assesses the protagonist's goals, progress, blockages, and obstacles, just as the passenger might assess the progress of a raft on which she rides. The viewer responds accordingly as the viewer and protagonist float down the narrative river together. The viewer projects him- or herself into the protagonist, responding much as the protagonist would (Grodal 1997, 2006).

One objection to this view is based on counterexamples to the thesis that the viewer's mental responses match the fictional feelings of the film's protagonist. There are many instances in which the spectator's goals and desires conflict with those of even the most sympathetic protagonist. One thinks of Ethan Edwards' (John Wayne) obsessive and racist desire to kill his own niece, Debbie (Natalie Wood) in *The Searchers* (1956) because she has become the mate of the hated Indian chief Scar. Or one thinks of the spectator's desire that Rick (Humphrey Bogart) in *Casablanca* (1942) overcome his cynical narcissism, forgive Ilsa (Ingrid Bergman), and help the war hero Laslow escape Casablanca. In both cases, the spectator's goals and desires do not match those of the protagonist, at least until the film's ending. Or consider films with flawed protagonists such as *Five Easy Pieces* (1970), *Unforgiven* (1992), or *Erin Brockovich* (2000), warped protagonists in films such as *The Godfather: Part II* (1974), conflicted, confused, and morally ambiguous protagonists such as Deckard in *Blade Runner* (1982) or Johnny Cash in *Walk the Line* (2005). The spectator can understand these protagonists as flawed, warped, confused, conflicted, and morally ambiguous only because the spectator responds to them from an egocentric perspective and does not wholly take on the protagonists' goals and desires, as if from the inside.

The view that spectators invariably respond to characters, whether sympathetic or not, from an exterior perspective we might call "ineliminable egocentrism," or what Carroll calls "assimilation" (Carroll 1990: 88–96) or, in relation to sympathetic characters, "solidarity" (Carroll 2008). It is plausible that the film's narration constructs a preferred or intended trajectory of emotional responses that is congruent with the responses of a sympathetic protagonist, but never identical (Plantinga forthcoming). Spectator responses, as elicited by the film, often have a similar valence to those of a sympathetic protagonist, but also differ, and sometimes markedly. For example, while many spectators will have a great deal of sympathy for Erin (Julia Roberts) as she battles corporate polluters in *Erin Brockovich* her tendency for impulsive anger and foul language are shown to detract from her effectiveness. While Erin is neither amused by nor disdainful of herself during her angry outbursts, the spectator is led to judge these outbursts as mild yet amusing faults that need correction. In these cases, Erin is merely angry, while the spectator may be slightly disdainful, disappointed, and/ or bemused.

The viewer's "relationship" with a favored character is one of sympathy, together with an assimilation of the character's situation. The spectator's psychic "relationship" with a sympathetic protagonist is both internal and external. The internal part consists of the viewer's simulation of the character's thoughts, together with automatic processes such as mimicry and emotional contagion (M. Smith 1995a; Plantinga 1999; Carroll 2008). The external part involves an assessment of the character's broader situation, incorporating information sometimes unavailable to the character, and incorporating the character's assessment of, and response to his situation. Given this simultaneously internal and external engagement with a character, then, neither the thoughts nor the feelings of the spectator can possibly be identical with those of the character, since the response necessarily involves that external portion of character engagement (M. Smith 1995a).

The film theorist Greg M. Smith takes an alternative approach to a focus on narrative and character as primary elicitors of emotion. Smith has built his theory of affect elicitation at the cinema on the importance of moods in film. Smith argues that the "primary emotive effect of film is to create mood" (G. Smith 2003: 42). Where emotions are intense, brief, and intermittent, moods have longer duration. Emotions depend on moods as "orienting states" that prepare the viewer for the specific emotional responses that are cued through various stylistic techniques. Smith rejects the centrality of narrative and character in emotion elicitation, claiming that the advantage of the mood-cue approach is in its focus on the cues offered by film style, rather than primarily by narrative and character. Stylistic elements cue emotions by way of associations, rather than by way of the appraisals associated with narrative and character, and it is affective experience via association and other less prototypical means that most interests Smith. Thus Smith turns, first, to the stylistic cues designed to elicit emotion, and thus differs from the majority of theorists/philosophers, who would put narrative and character at the center of emotion elicitation, and who would argue that moods and stylistic cues in films gain their salience in relation to overarching character goals and narrative situation.

Affect and style

A cinematic work is viewed in the form of some kind of audio-visual display, and as such, film viewing is sensual in a way that reading literature is not. Any account of affect elicitation in the movies must take in account the sensual nature of the audio-visual display, or the means by which films appeal to the senses of sight and hearing. Research into this aspect of filmic experience is in a preliminary stage. The perceptual realism (Prince 1996) that the medium often employs allows a film to take advantage of various perceptual processes with strong affective impacts. Films draw their power in part from the automatic bodily processes that they invoke in the spectator. Linda Williams' essay, "Film Bodies: Gender, Genre, and Excess," explores the excesses of violence, sexual desire, and weeping elicited by horror, pornography, and melodrama, respectively (Williams 1999). Williams calls these "body genres," but this would seem to imply that some genres appeal simply to the mind. *All* films appeal to the corporeality of the viewer. This has been acknowledged recently in film studies with books such as Vivian Sobchack's *Carnal Thoughts: Embodiment and Moving Image Culture* (2004) and Carl Plantinga's *Moving Viewers: American Film and the Spectator's Experience* (forthcoming) and in philosophy, for example, in Carroll's *The Philosophy of Motion Pictures* (2008) and work by Amy Coplan (2006).

Coplan ably describes the affective importance of perceptually realistic images of human bodies – and especially of the human face – in her entry in this volume ("Empathy and character engagement"). But there are other ways in which films, through their visual and aural appeals, have a strong affective charge. Spectator responses to movements, sounds, colors, textures, and spatial configurations – not to mention certain kinds of pictorial content – are in large part automatic and prereflective. The human brain did not evolve to interact with the visual media, or indeed, with representations of any sort, but adapted itself to the more immediate environmental data to which humans must daily respond for their survival and flourishing. Thus the spectator's responses to the audio-visual media are rooted, in part, in those natural perceptual responses that have developed over long periods of human history, and that in some cases have been conventionalized through decades of filmmaking.

The filmmaker can affect the spectator through all of the various parameters of film style, from shot composition, to movement, to editing, to color, to sound and music. A few examples will suffice to demonstrate the various effects and devices through which films provide affect. Music resonates with or otherwise impacts our very physiologies through rhythm, dynamics, tempo, and pitch. It affects spectators in physical ways that researchers are only beginning to understand. *Auditory entrainment*, or what is also sometimes called the "Frequency Following Effect," for example, is an auditory "mirror" effect. Physiological functions of the body, such as the heartbeat or brainwaves, tend to synchronize with the rhythmic patterns of audio, whether it is a complex musical score or a lone heartbeat (Vickers 2004). A mere heartbeat on the soundtrack, slowly increasing in volume and/or tempo, can elevate suspense and anxiety in response to a film scene, in part by elevating the spectator's heartbeat (Stern *et al*. 1972). Auditory entrainment is one of the ways in which sound, and especially music, can have direct bodily effects on the spectator.

Other examples would include the startle response and other forms of perceptual surprise and disorientation (Baird 2000; Choi 2003); erotic attraction and other visceral responses to various sorts of content; affective mimicry or mirror responses in relation to the human face, voice, posture, and gesture (Plantinga 1999; Carroll 2008); perceptual and physiological effects of color and shading; kinesthetic or movement effects; and proxemic patterns (closeness and distance responses). Although many of these responses are automatic and immediate, they relate to more complex emotions in a variety of ways. Affects may enable or intensify emotions, and may color experience in subtle ways by complicating, nuancing, or deepening the affective experience of a scene (Plantinga forthcoming).

Rhetoric and ideology

The cognitive or naturalistic approach to affect in film studies is in its infancy, and it has not yet approached questions of the rhetoric and ideology of emotion in film sufficiently. How does affect play into the ability of movies to confirm or alter values, beliefs, and/or ideologies? Psychoanalytic film theory, conjoined with Marxist thought, sought out the spectator's deepest motivations for viewing films and related spectator pleasure and desire to broad ideological concerns. If such theories are judged by some to be unsatisfactory in their determinism and conceptual flaws, they nonetheless made these issues a central feature of inquiry. Cognitive and analytic theorists and philosophers, on the other hand, have so far been preoccupied with developing basic theories of emotional response to films, a preoccupation that is justified if one considers such fundamental theories to be prolegomena to considerations that run further afield.

Cognitive theorists have made preliminary forays into this territory, however, suggesting avenues from which questions of rhetoric and ideology in relation to affect might be examined from a broadly cognitive perspective. Carroll, for example, has defended the "images of women" approach to feminist film criticism, suggesting that the repetition of sexist stereotypes and paradigm scenarios (such as the "fatal woman" scenario of *Fatal Attraction* [1987] or the "spider woman" scenario of many films noir) may "warp the emotions" of viewers by negatively influencing the conventional emotional responses of men to women (Carroll 1996b: 270).

Murray Smith (1996) and Plantinga (1997) have both criticized what they see as the misplaced suspicion of emotion in Brechtian criticism (see "Bertolt Brecht," in this volume). Carroll is no doubt correct that stereotypes and paradigm scenarios have the capacity to alter conventional emotional responses on a broad scale; Plantinga offers a theory of the means by which fiction films make those stereotypes both salient and emotionally powerful (forthcoming). He focuses on the "gatekeeper" emotion of socio-moral disgust, and then generalizes to a consideration of the means by which various emotions can be used to elicit judgments of persons rooted in stereotypes and to make salient and pleasurable conventional ways of responding to narrative scenarios.

See also Consciousness (Chapter 4), Empathy and character engagement (Chapter 9), Spectatorship (Chapter 23), Bertolt Brecht (Chapter 30), Noël Carroll (Chapter 31), Cognitive theory (Chapter 33), Phenomenology (Chapter 40), Psychoanalysis (Chapter 41), and Horror (Chapter 46).

References

Baird, R. (2000) "The Startle Effect: Implications for Spectator Cognition and Media Theory," *Film Quarterly* 53: 12–24.

Carroll, N. (1990) *The Philosophy of Horror*, New York and London: Routledge.

—— (1996a) "The Power of Movies," in *Theorizing the Moving Image*, Cambridge: Cambridge University Press.

—— (1996b) "The Image of Women in Film: A Defense of a Paradigm," in *Theorizing the Moving Image*, Cambridge: Cambridge University Press.

—— (2008) *The Philosophy of Motion Pictures*, Maldon, MA, and Oxford: Blackwell.

Choi, J. (2003) "Fits and Startles: Cognitivism Revisited," *Journal of Aesthetics and Art Criticism* 61: 149–57.

Coplan, A. (2006) "Catching Character's Emotions: Emotional Contagion Responses to Narrative Fiction Film," *Film Studies: An International Review* 8: 26–38.

Feagin, S. L. (1983) "The Pleasures of Tragedy," *American Philosophical Quarterly* 20: 95–104.

—— (1992) "Monsters, Disgust and Fascination," *Philosophical Studies* 65: 75–84.

Gaut, B. (1995) "The Enjoyment of Horror: A Response to Carroll," *British Journal of Aesthetics* 35: 284–9.

Gerrig, R. J., and Prentice, D. A. (1996) "Notes on Audience Response," in D. Bordwell and N. Carroll (eds.) *Post-Theory: Reconstructing Film Studies*, Madison: University of Wisconsin Press.

Goldie, P. (2000) *The Emotions: A Philosophical Exploration*, Oxford: Clarendon Press.

Grodal, T. (1997) *Moving Pictures: A New Theory of Genres, Feelings, and Cognition*, Oxford: Oxford University Press.

—— (2006) "The PECMA Flow: A General Model of Visual Aesthetics," *Film Studies: An International Review* 8: 1–11.

Hume, D. (1965) "Of Tragedy," in J. V. Lenz (ed.) *Of the Standard of Taste and Other Essays*, Indianapolis and New York: Bobbs-Merrill.

Lamarque, P. (1981) "How Can We Fear and Pity Fictions?," *British Journal of Aesthetics* 21: 291–304.

Matravers, D. (1998) *Art and Emotion*, Oxford: Clarendon Press.

Plantinga, C. (1997) "Notes on Spectator Emotion and Ideological Film Criticism," in R. Allen and M. Smith (eds.) *Film Theory and Philosophy*, Oxford: Oxford University Press.

—— (1999) "The Scene of Empathy and the Human Face on Film," in C. Plantinga and G. M. Smith (eds.) *Passionate Views: Film, Cognition, and Emotion*, Baltimore, MD: Johns Hopkins University Press.

—— (2006) "Disgusted at the Movies," *Film Studies: An International Review* 8: 81–92.

—— (forthcoming) *Moving Viewers: American Film and the Spectator's Experience*, Berkeley: University of California Press.

Plantinga, C., and Smith, G. M. (1999) "Introduction," in C. Plantinga and G. M. Smith (eds.) *Passionate Views: Film, Cognition, and Emotion*, Baltimore, MD: Johns Hopkins University Press.

Prince, S. (1996) "True Lies: Perceptual Realism, Digital Images, and Film Theory," *Film Quarterly* 49: 27–37.

Radford, C. (1975) "How Can We Be Moved by the Fate of Anna Karenina?," *Proceedings of the Aristotelian Society* (suppl. vol.) 49: 67–80.

Roberts, R. C. (2003) *Emotions: An Essay in Aid of Moral Psychology*, Cambridge: Cambridge University Press.

Robinson, J. (2005) *Deeper Than Reason: Emotion and Its Role in Literature, Music, and Art*, Oxford: Oxford University Press.

Scruton, R. (1974) *Art and Imagination*, London: Routledge and Kegan Paul.

Smith, G. M. (2003) *Film Structure and the Emotion System*, Cambridge: Cambridge University Press.

Smith, M. (1995a) *Engaging Characters: Fiction, Emotion, and the Cinema*, Oxford: Oxford University Press.

—— (1995b) "Film Spectatorship and the Institution of Fiction," *Journal of Aesthetics and Art Criticism* 53: 113–27.

—— (1996) "The Logic and Legacy of Brechtianism," in D. Bordwell and N. Carroll (eds.) *Post-Theory: Reconstructing Film Studies*, Madison: University of Wisconsin Press.

Sobchack, V. (2004) *Carnal Thoughts: Embodiment and Moving Image Culture*, Berkeley: University of California Press.

Stern, R. M., Botto, R. W., and Herrick, C. D. (1972) "Behavioral and Physiological Effects of False Heart-Rate Feedback: A Replication and Extension," *Psychophysiology* 9: 21–9.

Tan, E. S. (1996) *Emotion and the Structure of Narrative Film*, Mahwah, NJ: Lawrence Erlbaum.

Vickers, E. (2004) *Music and Consciousness*. Available at www.sfxmachine.com/docs/musicandconsciousness.html (accessed 19 May 2008). (Paper on the conscious effects of music on listeners.)

Walton, K. (1990) *Mimesis as Make-Believe: On the Foundations of the Representational Arts*, Cambridge, MA: Harvard University Press.

Williams, L. (1999) "Film Bodies: Gender, Genre, and Excess," in L. Braudy and M. Cohen (eds.) *Film Theory and Aesthetics: Introductory Readings*, 5th ed., Oxford: Oxford University Press.

Yanal, R. J. (1999) *Paradoxes of Emotion and Fiction*, University Park, PA: Penn State University Press.

Further reading

See chapter 6, "Affect and the Moving Image," in N. Carroll, *The Philosophy of Motion Pictures* (Malden, MA: Blackwell, 2008). Mette Hjort and Sue Laver (eds.) *Emotion and the Arts* (Oxford: Oxford University Press, 1997) is a solid collection of philosophical essays. C. Plantinga, *Moving Viewers: American Film and the Spectator's Experience* (Berkeley: University of California Press, forthcoming) offers a general theory of affect in cinema and its implications, concentrating on the theatrical experience of mainstream American films. C. Plantinga and G. M. Smith (eds.) *Passionate Views: Film, Cognition, and Emotion* (Baltimore, MD: Johns Hopkins University Press, 1999) is a collection of philosophical and theoretical essays on film and emotion by film scholars and philosophers. Although not dealing much with film, J. Robinson, *Deeper than Reason: Emotion and its Role in Literature, Music, and Art* (Oxford: Oxford University Press, 2005) offers an excellent analysis of emotion in relation to the arts.

9

EMPATHY AND CHARACTER ENGAGEMENT

Amy Coplan

Character engagement is a central topic in the philosophy of film that has implications for several other philosophical issues. Although discussions of character engagement in film studies and philosophy tell us a lot, they are often confusing for at least two reasons. First, a variety of explanatory concepts gets used in these discussions, and few of these are used uniformly. Second, the experience of character engagement itself is highly complex. It refers to all and any elements of spectatorial experience that are based on or relate to characters. This encompasses several distinct types of relationship, a number of additional types of response, and connections among all of the different experiences.

There are two major theoretical approaches to questions about spectatorship: psychoanalytic film theory and cognitive film theory. Psychoanalytic film theory, as the name suggests, draws extensively on psychoanalysis, particularly the work of Jacques Lacan, as well as on Marxist theory, Saussurean linguistics, critical theory, and the work of several recent postmodern and postcolonial thinkers. Cognitive film theory is based largely on research in empirical sciences related to the mind, such as cognitive psychology, developmental psychology, social psychology, and neuroscience. Most cognitive film theorists also share the assumption that our cognitive and perceptual experience when watching film is more or less like our cognitive and perceptual experience of events in ordinary life.

In this essay I will survey some of the leading explanations of character engagement developed in psychoanalytic and cognitive film theory. These explanations vary greatly in their operating assumptions, their theories of human psychology, and their sources of evidentiary support. What unifies them is that all are attempts to answer the question of how viewers engage with fictional characters in film.

Psychoanalytic film theory

During the 1970s, psychoanalytic film theory emerged as the leading framework in film studies for understanding film and our engagement with it. A central concern for theorists in this tradition is how film, the technology of film, and filmmaking conventions make film viewing a pleasurable experience that exploits unconscious desires, and reproduces the dominant ideology. Many of these theorists base their understanding of spectator psychology on a Lacanian model of human development and the formation of subjectivity.

Apparatus theory – Jean-Louis Baudry and Christian Metz

The apparatus theory of Jean-Louis Baudry and Christian Metz represents one of the most influential movements in psychoanalytic film theory, particularly on the issue of spectatorship (Baudry 1986a, b; Metz 1986). Apparatus theory asserts that in order to understand spectatorial response, we must first understand the nature of the cinematic apparatus, that is, the ways in which the organization and presentation of film interacts with human psychology, desire, and understanding. Baudry claims that the cinematic apparatus transforms the spectator into a transcendental subject "whose place is taken by the camera which constitutes and rules the objects in this 'world'" (Baudry 1986a: 295). The stream of on-screen images creates an impression of reality that locates the ideal viewer (or spectatorial position) at the center of vision as the creator of meaning, providing a sense of unity and control. It is from the privileged position of the camera that the spectator identifies with the on-screen characters.

Baudry describes two different processes of identification. First, there is the spectator's identification with the camera. This, in turn, makes possible the spectator's identification with the characters. On this view, then, just as during the mirror phase the child identifies with idealized images of himself, so the film viewer, from the perspective of the camera, identifies with idealized characters on screen. Following Lacan, Baudry argues that we all possess the desire to return to early stages of our development, during which we experienced moments of unified completeness, though we are not consciously aware of this desire. Nevertheless, this desire explains the natural appeal of the film viewing experience. Watching films does more than entertain us; it fulfills an unconscious wish by triggering an artificial regression back to a state of complete narcissistic fusion, which Baudry says is characterized by "a lack of differentiation between the subject and his environment" (Baudry 1986b: 313).

Identification, as characterized by Baudry, is a process that eliminates the boundaries between self and other, creating a type of all-encompassing fusion. The basis of this identification is an unconscious desire to regress that has far less to do with specific characters in a given film or features of an individual spectator's psychology than with the ability of the cinematic apparatus to fulfill this preexisting desire. This is one of the features of film form that Baudry points to in order to show how film is ideological.

Like Baudry, Christian Metz focuses on identification with the camera and likens this process to the mirror phase. Metz, however, emphasizes a key difference between the child's relationship to the mirror and the spectator's relationship to the screen. When the child gazes into the mirror, he sees himself reflected back. This does not occur in cinematic identification. The spectator is not part of what is perceived on screen. He is the perceiver but not the perceived. But he's more than this. He is an all-perceiving subject such that the world on screen appears to be there *for him*, as created *by him*:

> At the cinema, it is always the other who is the screen; as for me, I am there to look at him. I take no part in the perceived; on the contrary, I am *all-perceiving*. All perceiving as one says all-powerful (this the famous gift of "ubiquity" the film makes its spectator); all-perceiving, too, because I am entirely on the side of the perceiving instance: absent from the screen, but certainly present in the auditorium, a great eye and ear without which the perceived would have no one to perceive it, the instance, in other words, which *constitutes* the cinema signifier (it is I who make the film). (Metz 1986: 252)

The construction of the spectator as transcendental subject occurs through identification with the camera, which the spectator experiences as type of identification with the self as a pure act of perception.

Where does this leave identification with characters? Films give us opportunities to identify with characters, on Metz's view, but character identification is less central to his analysis. He writes that, "As for identifications with characters, with their own different levels (out-of-frame character, etc.), they are secondary, tertiary cinematic identifications, etc.; taken as a whole in opposition to the identification of the spectator with his own look, they constitute secondary cinematic identification" (Metz 1986: 259).

One of the aims of Baudry's and Metz's respective discussions of primary cinematic identification with the camera and its gaze is to shed light on the ideological structure of the cinematic apparatus. The all-perceiving, meaning-making subject position is revealed as an illusion. The spectator is not in fact creating the images on screen nor is he beyond the limits of space, time, and the body, as the created perspective suggests. It seems this way, as a result of the inherently deceptive nature of the cinematic apparatus, which, as Baudry explains, "uses the system but also conceals it" (Baudry 1986a: 289).

Feminist analysis – Laura Mulvey

Feminist theorist Laura Mulvey examines the source of our pleasure in watching films and analyzes its implications. She complicates Baudry's and Metz's account of spectatorial identification by using psychoanalysis to show how film fosters processes of identification that perpetuate oppressive patriarchal ideals.

Mulvey identifies a pattern in the cinematic conventions of standard Hollywood films. This pattern includes (1) the assumption of a male spectator; (2) the establishment and coding of a male protagonist as an active subject who controls the meaning of the narrative and of the female characters by being the "bearer of the look"; and (3) the establishment and coding of female characters as passive, weak objects of erotic desire, there to be "looked at" by the male characters and the male spectators (Mulvey 1986). This pattern exemplifies the "male gaze," a way of seeing, thinking about, and acting in the world that takes women as passive, weak objects to be looked at by male subjects (Devereaux 2002).

When a male spectator watches a standard Hollywood film, he identifies with the male protagonist who represents his ego ideal. Through this identification with the active controlling agent on screen, the spectator controls the unfolding of the narrative events and takes pleasure in looking voyeuristically at the female characters or fetishizing some parts of their bodies. This gives him the feeling of omnipotence and the pleasure associated with looking.

Mulvey's analysis aims to show that identification with male protagonists exploits unconscious desires and capitalizes on institutionalized sexism to generate pleasure. If Mulvey is right, then certain forms of character engagement, perhaps those that are most common, play an essential role in making film an instrument of oppressive ideological values.

Mulvey's original account of spectatorial identification has been challenged from all sides: feminist theory, psychoanalytic film theory, queer theory, and cognitive film theory. Feminist and queer theorists have charged that she exhibits covert heterosexism through her claim that the assumed spectator is a straight male and that she fails to address the female spectator, the role of race in representation, and the position of transgendered spectators (e.g., Creed 1998; White 1998; Friedberg 1990; Doane 1990). Many have also taken issue with Mulvey's characterization of the relationship between spectators and characters as fixed and thus not subject to resistance or to subversive viewing practices (e.g., Friedberg 1990; Smith 1995; White 1998). Mulvey is also criticized for failing to explore alternative cinematic forms and effects. However one evaluates Mulvey's particular account of character identification, it cannot be denied that she brought the topic of gender and oppressive practices from the periphery of film studies to its center. Prior to Mulvey's discussion, little attention was paid to gendered aspects of filmmaking, film, and character engagement. This is no longer the case.

Cognitive film theory

Cognitive film theory takes a very different approach to the question of character engagement. It appeals to research in empirical science and philosophy of mind to understand how engagement works, and concentrates not on the ideological influence of engagement but on how engagement explains viewers' emotional and affective responses to film. Moreover, most film theorists and philosophers in this tradition assume that we can use what we know about how psychological processes work in regular life to understand how they will work when we view films.

Identification

Although theorists in both the psychoanalytic and cognitivist traditions of film theory talk about identification with characters, they understand the concept very differently. Within cognitive film theory alone, a variety of psychological processes get referred to as identificatory, including empathy, simulation, sympathy, and mirroring processes. Some theorists have argued that, due to its vagueness and ambiguity, the term "identification" should no longer be used to characterize spectatorial response (Allen 2003). Along the same lines, some favor replacing identification with a more precise concept or set of concepts (Smith 1995). This is not because these theorists don't think something like identification occurs between viewers and characters but because they think that whatever this process is, it can be better explained some other way. Noël Carroll, by contrast, believes that identification, construed in any number of ways, is not a major part of character engagement and does little to explain spectatorial response (e.g., Carroll 2007, 2008: 161–77).

Despite these concerns, Berys Gaut considers identification a worthwhile concept for explaining our relationships to characters. He defends its use on two separate grounds (Gaut 1999). First, ordinary film viewers use the term more than any other to describe their experience. If they like a film, it is because they identify with one or more characters. If they don't like it, it is because they could not identify with any of the characters. For most spectators, films succeed or fail based on whether or not and to what extent they foster identification with characters (Gaut 1999: 200). Second, Gaut insists that the concept of identification is less confused than theorists suggest; it simply needs refining.

To do this, Gaut explains that when we talk about identifying with a character, we don't mean that we imagine being the character. Rather, we mean that we imagine being in the character's situation. This is the general meaning of identification, but there are many different aspects to any situation, and thus there are many different ways in which we can identify with a character. In short, identification is aspectual. It involves neither a total replication of another's experience, nor a loss of identity. Gaut is careful to point out that both the everyday use of identification by filmgoers and his use have little in common with the concept of identification employed by psychoanalytic film theorists.

Gaut enumerates four aspects of identification: perceptual, affective, motivational, and epistemic. Thus we can imagine seeing what the character sees, feeling what the character feels, wanting what the character wants, or believing what the character believes (Gaut 1999: 205). Identification with one aspect of a character's situation neither entails nor rules out identification with any other aspect; however, in some cases, identification of one kind encourages identification of another.

Gaut defends the concept of identification by clarifying, not replacing or redefining, its meaning. He regards as important the fact that, unlike most of the explanatory concepts offered to describe character engagement, identification is a term used by ordinary filmgoers. His analysis suggests that the ordinary filmgoer may not be as confused as theorists have believed.

The structure of sympathy – plural engagement

Murray Smith critiques standard accounts of character identification for their failure to capture the complexity of spectatorial responses to characters. He argues that the notion of identification does little to clarify the relationship between spectators and characters, since identification and related terms get used in so many different ways. Identification accounts based on Lacanian psychoanalysis make the additional mistake of focusing too much on film's visual appeal, at the expense of its capacity to involve spectators in imaginative and epistemological activities (Smith 1995).

Smith's alternative account of spectator engagement allows for multiple modes of character-spectator experience. Smith utilizes Richard Wollheim's distinction between central and acentral imagining. Central imagining refers to imagining a situation "from the inside," which is to say from a particular point of view. Acentral imagination, in contrast, refers to simply imagining *that* some situation is occurring without doing so from within the situation. According to Smith, acentral imagination plays a more important role in spectator engagement than central imagination. This goes against the standard identification accounts. Smith develops a model of spectatorial experience that comprises three distinct but related levels of engagement, a system he labels the "structure of sympathy." Empathic phenomena make up a separate feature of Smith's account that can work within or against the structure of sympathy.

The three levels of engagement in the structure of sympathy, which are all associated with acentral imagination, are recognition, alignment, and allegiance. Recognition is Smith's term for spectators' construction of characters as individuated and continuous human agents. Alignment refers to the way a film narrative gives viewers access to characters' thoughts, feelings, and actions; it is primarily about the communication of information. Allegiance describes the process by which film creates sympathies for and against characters.

Smith's model reveals how and why viewers experience plural identification, that is, how they can experience one level of engagement with a character but not another level, or different levels of engagement with a character during the course of a film, or different levels of engagement with different characters.

Empathy

Another relatively recent popular approach to character engagement focuses on empathy. Since empathy is believed to be one of the primary ways we emotionally engage with one another's experience in ordinary life, and most everyone agrees that we emotionally engage with film characters' experiences, theorists have reasoned that at least some of this engagement can be characterized as empathetic (see, e.g., Feagin 1996; Neill 1996; Currie 2004; Coplan 2004). One advantage empathy has over identification as an explanatory concept is that it refers to a psychological process that has been studied by empirical scientists (e.g., Decety and Sommerville 2003; Decety and Jackson 2004; Eisenberg and Strayer 1987; Hoffman 2000; Eisenberg 2000;

Batson *et al.* 2007), and yet is also a concept ordinary film viewers frequently employ to describe their reactions to characters.

Despite this advantage, accounts of spectatorial response that highlight empathy face many of the same difficulties that plague identification accounts, namely, multiple competing conceptualizations of empathy that refer to distinct psychological processes that vary, sometimes widely, in their function, phenomenology, mechanisms, and effects (see, e.g., Eisenberg 2000; Battaly forthcoming; Coplan forthcoming).

Only if we employ a more precise conceptualization of empathy will we make progress in our attempts to understand it. I have proposed such a conceptualization, based on current psychological and neuroscientific research (Coplan forthcoming; see also Coplan 2004). Under my proposed conceptualization, empathizing with a character is a complex imaginative process through which a spectator simulates the character's situated psychological states, including the character's beliefs, emotions, and desires, by imaginatively experiencing the character's experiences from the character's point of view, while simultaneously maintaining clear self/other differentiation. If understood in this more precise way, empathy does not risk dissolving the boundaries between self and other, nor does it require that spectators have only the emotions of the characters with whom they empathize, though it does require that they have at least these (Coplan 2004). It also fits with the most recent empirical findings (e.g., Decety and Sommerville 2003; Decety and Jackson 2004; Eisenberg 2000).

To empathize with a character, a spectator must accurately represent the character's relevant psychological states to a greater or lesser degree, but she may also experience additional states as part of her own separate response. A separate response is made possible by her clear self/other differentiation. Empathy allows spectators to connect to characters while remaining separate from them. Spectators' involvement in characters' experiences in this case is deep, but it does not come at the expense of a separate identity, which means that the spectator can continue to have a wide range of psychological experiences that do not match those of the character (Coplan 2004: 147–9).

Characterizations of spectatorial response as empathetic are common. We often talk about films allowing us to vicariously experience others' lives through an empathic process, and we point to various techniques filmmakers use to enable and encourage this. In addition, empirical research on text processing and narrative comprehension provides some evidence, though it is tentative, for thinking that empathy is a regular part of how we relate to characters (Coplan 2004; Harris 2000).

Simulation

In the past fifteen years, many of the discussions of empathy in philosophical aesthetics and philosophy of film have been tied to discussions of simulation theory (e.g., Smith 1995; Feagin 1996; Neill 1996; Currie 1995, 2004; Harold 2000). Simulation theory emerged in the 1980s as an alternative to "theory theory," the dominant view in philosophy and psychology of how we how we come to understand and predict others' mental states, or "mindread." According to theory theory, we do this appealing to our theories of folk psychology, which are made up of a set of law-like generalizations that connect various mental states with other mental states, with external circumstances, and with overt behavior. Simulation theorists explain things very differently. On their view, we attempt to determine what others think, feel, and desire by simulating their mental states, that is, attempting to adopt their perspective, using our own mind to model theirs under certain conditions (for recent formulations and defenses of simulation theory, see Currie and Ravenscroft 2002: 49–70; Currie 2004; and Goldman 2006; for a recent critique of simulation theory, see Stich and Nichols 2003: 131–42). To perform a successful simulation, it is not enough for us to experience the same emotions and thoughts as those of a target individual; we must come to have these emotions and thoughts through similar processes (Feagin 1996: 87–8). Soon after the emergence of simulation theory in philosophy of mind, philosophers and film theorists used it to explain our affective responses to art, including our affective responses to fictional characters.

How is simulation related to empathy? In both philosophy of mind and aesthetics, discussions of empathy and simulation are closely connected. In fact more often than not, either the concepts are used interchangeably or simulation is offered as an explanation of empathy and how it works. Despite their connections, it may be better at this point to keep these two models of character engagement separate. Neither the term empathy nor the term simulation is used uniformly, and the relations between them are rarely entirely clear. If we use simulation to define empathy or empathy to understand simulation, we risk confusing rather than clarifying what's happening during character engagement (for further discussion of the difficulty identifying simulation and empathy, see Goldie 1999; Nichols et al. 1996: 59–67; Stich and Nichols 1997: 299).

Mirroring processes

As the previous subsections show, cognitive film theorists and philosophers of film have focused primarily on modes of character engagement that involve high-level processing. This is in part a reaction to what they regard as an overemphasis in psychoanalytic film theory on unconscious processes and is in part a consequence of their theoretical frameworks. This pattern is beginning to shift, as a small number of cognitive film theorists and philosophers have begun to take seriously less sophisticated ways of responding to characters, such as motor mimicry, affective mimicry, low-level simulation, mirror reflexes, and emotional contagion (Smith 1995; Plantinga 1999, forthcoming; Choi 2003; Coplan 2006; Carroll 2007, 2008). Since each of these is an automatic process that causes mimicry or mirroring, it will be useful to collect them under the broad category of mirroring processes.

Mirroring processes are a set of innate mechanisms and feedback systems that under certain conditions cause us to have experiences that are the same in kind as those of a person whom we observe. We therefore end up "mirroring" that person. These processes are largely automatic and involuntary. They occur through direct perception and involve neither the imagination nor high-level cognitive processing. As such, they represent a much more primitive mode of character engagement than the types normally discussed in cognitive film theory.

Emotional contagion is one of the mirroring processes we know the most about. It's also one that is especially important for character engagement. Psychologists Elaine Hatfield, John Cacioppo, and Richard Rapson define emotional contagion as the "tendency to automatically mimic and synchronize expressions, vocalizations, postures, and movements with those of another person, and, consequently, to converge emotionally" (Hatfield *et al.* 1992: 153–4). As Stephen Davies explains, this "involves the transmission from A to B of a given affect such that B's affect is the same as A's but does not take A's state or any other thing as its emotional object" (Davies forthcoming). Due to our hardwired ability to mirror one another, our emotional experiences can be directly and immediately affected by others' emotions and need not depend on any conscious evaluation or interpretation of the other's emotions or external events.

Given the nature of emotional contagion, film is especially well suited to produce it. Carl Plantinga explains this in his discussion of the "scene of empathy," which refers to a scene in which the narrative slows down and a character's emotional experience becomes the locus of attention. Such scenes, which are typically shot in close-up and focus on a character's face, contain several eliciting conditions of emotional contagion. Most important is attention, since contagion responses require that a spectator's attention be fixed on a character's facial expressions. Filmmakers achieve this through the use of extreme close-ups, shallow focus, and various point-of-view structures and by using progressively closer shots of a character's face and expressions (Plantinga 1999: 239–55).

Although mirroring responses result from spectators' perception of characters, on their own they cannot provide deep understanding of characters, nor can they generate empathy or sympathy. Observation of a character's experience triggers the mirroring response, but the average film viewer will not be aware of this having happened. Nevertheless, these processes increase spectators' level of bodily excitement and can intensify their emotional responses (Carroll 2007, 2008; Plantinga 1999, forthcoming).

Since contagion responses can be triggered by direct sensory stimulation alone, they require neither involvement in a narrative nor investment in a character. This is one of the reasons why film often elicits emotional responses more easily than literature. Another interesting feature of emotional contagion is its ability to cause affective responses that are incongruent with a spectator's overall emotional experience of a film (Smith 1995).

Significantly, mirroring or mimicry responses are unique to our experience of film. Engagement with nondramatic literary fictions can produce empathy, sympathy, and emotions that result from cognitive evaluations. It cannot produce mirroring, since it does not appeal directly to readers' perception or senses. This makes mirroring responses all the more important, since they are part of what distinguishes film in general and our responses to film characters in particular from literature and our responses to (nontheatrical) literary characters (Carroll 2008: 185–91; Plantinga forthcoming: especially chapter 5; Coplan 2006).

Sympathy and criterial prefocusing

The most serious challenge to identification accounts of character engagement, including those that emphasize the roles of empathy and simulation, has come from Noël Carroll, who has repeatedly charged that such accounts fail to explain the majority of our reactions to fictional film characters (Carroll 2007, 2008: 177–84). Carroll doesn't deny that something akin to simulation, empathy, or identification can sometimes occur during the film viewing experiences, but he argues that when spectators' emotions match those of the characters, it is typically due to criterial prefocusing (which I'll explain below), not a process of identification or simulation (2008: 149–91).

Carroll offers several arguments to support his position. First, he says that spectators' emotions have different objects from those of the characters, and thus the emotions cannot be the same. This, he claims, is because we observe characters' situations from outside the narrative. Second, spectators often have different information or more information than the characters, and so they have a different experience of the narrative events. Finally, spectators often have different desires or preferences from those of the characters and ones that can be in conflict with those of the characters. If empathy, simulation, or some other form of identification were a major part of our interaction with characters, there would be greater symmetry than occurs between the characters' mental states and those of the spectators.

On Carroll's alternative view of character engagement, the majority of spectators' emotional responses to film are caused by one of two processes: (1) criterial prefocusing of the narrative; or (2) sympathy with film characters.

Criterial prefocusing is Carroll's term for the process by which filmmakers foreground certain events and actions in the presentation of the narrative so that audience members will recognize them as fitting into familiar schemas that are likely to elicit an emotional reaction. Carroll accepts a version of the judgment theory of emotion for standard emotions. On this view, emotion requires a judgment or belief, which causes some feeling state. For example, if I believe that X has wronged me or mine, then I feel anger toward X. The relevant judgment in this case is that X wronged me or mine, which corresponds to the emotion anger (for an overview and critique of the judgment, or cognitive, theory of emotion, see Robinson 2005, forthcoming). Filmmakers attempt to ensure that viewers will respond emotionally by highlighting or focusing on actions, events, and character traits that fit the standard criteria for specific emotions. This predisposes us to respond emotionally, yet is not sufficient to evoke a response. The viewer must also care about the relevant characters or the outcome of the story. Without this, viewers may recognize how the film's narrative events fit certain criteria but experience them dispassionately.

Sympathy, then, is essential for responding to characters, but it is even more than this. According to Carroll, sympathy is the "major emotional bond between audiences and leading fictional characters" (Carroll 2007: 103). Carroll uses the term "sympathy" in roughly the same way it is used by contemporary psychologists, namely, to refer to an other-oriented emotional process involving feelings of care and concern for another and the other's well-being (Carroll 2007: 101; Eisenberg 2000; Wispe 1991). Sympathy is not a synonym for empathy, nor is it a type of identification; when we sympathize with another, we feel *for* him or her, not *with* him or her.

Carroll's discussion of sympathy emphasizes that there is both a close relationship and an asymmetry between the feelings of the spectator and those of the character. We may occasionally experience the same feelings as a character, but when this happens, Carroll says, it is typically the result of criterial prefocusing, not a process of identification.

What reasons do we have for thinking sympathy is the primary mode of character engagement? Carroll claims that we respond sympathetically to the film's protagonists more than in any other way, and sympathy provides the "emotive optic" through which we survey the narrative events. In other words, we evaluate and respond to various characters, actions, and narrative events on the basis of our sympathy for a film's protagonists. As a result, the mistreatment of the protagonist will arouse our anger but only because of our sympathy. If we didn't care about the protagonist, we wouldn't care about his or her mistreatment.

Filmmakers establish sympathetic bonds, according to Carroll, by depicting protagonists as representative of values shared by the audience. The narrative reveals that the protagonists share some interest, project, or loyalty with the audience members. Another determining variable is moral character. Provided that a character, even an antihero, is morally praiseworthy in at least one significant respect, that character can arouse our sympathy (Carroll 2008: 181–2).

Effects of character engagement

I have now discussed some of the leading explanations of character engagement. The final section of this essay will briefly consider some of its effects. Psychoanalytic film theorists, such as Baudry and Metz, who characterize spectatorial response in terms of identification, have tended to focus on the harmful effects of engagement. Identification draws spectators into an illusion in which they feel more powerful and important than they actually are.

The social and political implications go beyond this. If Mulvey is right, then identification with male protagonists in standard Hollywood films leads to the adoption of the male gaze and the pleasurable experience of males as subjects and females as objects. Even though female characters are coded as weak and passive, they nevertheless represent a threat to male characters and male viewers. To neutralize this threat, standard Hollywood narratives foster either a sadistic voyeurism or the fetishizing of the female form, neither one of which recognizes women as subjects (Mulvey 1986). Standard Hollywood narratives punish female sexuality so that female characters who fail to fit stereotypical norms cannot survive and must be brought back into the dominant patriarchal structure. Alternatively, the threat female characters pose can be eliminated by reducing them to some body part and then fetishizing it.

Most cognitive film theorists and analytic philosophers of mind have explored the beneficial effects of character engagement. By increasing the stakes of the narrative events, character engagement heightens dramatic conflict. Certain forms of character engagement may do more than enhance aesthetic appreciation and enjoyment. Empathy and simulation can improve and expand our understanding of ourselves and others, including others whose experiences are very different from our own (Smith 1995, 1997; Neill 1996).

The beneficial effects of these sorts of character engagement are significant, but we need to be careful not to overstate their transformative power. Empirical research in social and developmental psychology shows that people are both more willing and better able to empathize with those whom they perceive to be like them in some significant respect; the more similar they in fact are, the more likely the attempt to empathize will succeed (Hoffman 2000). Dan Flory has carefully examined aspects of the relationship between race and film viewing and has shown that white viewers are often incapable of successfully empathizing with African American characters. Due to their ignorance of the life circumstances of nonwhite characters, they fail to appreciate those characters' situations and fail to deeply engage with them (Flory 2006).

Beyond this, the assumption that empathy will necessarily lead to altruistic or even prosocial behavior is flawed (Goldie 2000; Battaly 2008; Coplan forthcoming), and contrary to popular understanding there is no causal connection between empathy and sympathy (Eisenberg and Miller 1987). Heather Battaly's recent discussion of empathy clarifies this by classifying empathy as a skill rather than a virtue (Battaly forthcoming). Undoubtedly it is a skill with the potential to greatly impact the outcome of moral deliberation and action, but it cannot and should not be assumed that this is the only way or even the most common way it will be employed.

Keeping all of this in mind, engagement with characters still has the potential to benefit viewers in many ways. For example, through empathy or simulation, when it succeeds, we can gain a unique kind of experiential understanding of characters. While this is not tantamount to prosocial behavior, it's something much more than working out the features of the plot. It provides a representation, however partial, of another person's subjective experience – one that is not a representation of causes and effects but rather is a representation of what it is like to be another person.

See also Acting (Chapter 1), Emotion and affect (Chapter 8), Spectatorship (Chapter 23), Bertolt Brecht (Chapter 30), Noël Carroll (Chapter 31), Cognitive theory (Chapter 33), Gender (Chapter 13), Narrative closure (Chapter 19), Race (Chapter 21), Christian Metz (Chapter 36), and Psychoanalysis (Chapter 41).

References

Allen, R. (2003) "Identification in the Cinema: A Conceptual Investigation," unpublished manuscript, New York: New York University.

Batson, C. D., Håkansson, E., Chermok, V. L., Hoyt, J. L., and Ortiz, B. G. (2007) "An Additional Antecedent of Empathic Concern: Valuing the Welfare of the Person in Need," *Journal of Personality and Social Psychology* 93: 65–74.

Battaly, H. (forthcoming) "Empathy: Virtue or Skill?," in A. Coplan and P. Goldie (eds.) *Empathy: Philosophical and Psychological Approaches*, Oxford: Oxford University Press.

Baudry, J.-L. (1986a) "Ideological Effects of the Basic Cinematographic Apparatus," in P. Rosen (ed.) *Narrative, Apparatus, Ideology*, New York: Columbia University Press.

—— (1986b) "The Apparatus: Metaphysical Approaches to Ideology," in P. Rosen (ed.) *Narrative, Apparatus, Ideology*, New York: Columbia University Press.

Carroll, N. (2007) "On the Ties That Bind: Characters, the Emotions, and Popular Fictions," in W. Irwin and J. Garcia (eds.) *Philosophy and the Interpretation of Popular Culture*, Lanham, MD: Rowman & Littlefield.

—— (2008) *The Philosophy of Motion Pictures*, Malden, MA: Wiley-Blackwell.

Choi, J. (2003) "Fits and Startles: Cognitivism Revisited," *Journal of Aesthetics and Art Criticism* 61: 149–57.

Coplan, A. (2004) "Empathic Engagement with Narrative Fictions," *Journal of Aesthetics and Art Criticism* 62: 141–52.

—— (2006) "Catching Characters' Emotions," *Film Studies: An International Review* 8: 26–38.

—— (forthcoming) "Understanding Empathy: Its Features and Effects," in A. Coplan and P. Goldie (eds.) *Empathy: Philosophical and Psychological Approaches*, Oxford: Oxford University Press.

Creed, B. (1998) "Film and Psychoanalysis," in J. Hill and P. Church Gibson (eds.) *The Oxford Guide to Film Studies*, New York: Oxford University Press.

Currie, G. (1995) *Image and Mind: Film, Philosophy, and Cognitive Science*, Cambridge: Cambridge University Press.

—— (2004) *Arts and Minds*, New York: Oxford University Press.

Currie, G., and Ravenscroft, I. (2002) *Recreative Minds: Imagination in Philosophy and Psychology*, Oxford: Clarendon Press.

Davies, S. (forthcoming) "Music Listener Emotional Contagion," in A. Coplan and P. Goldie (eds.) *Empathy: Philosophical and Psychological Approaches*, Oxford: Oxford University Press.

Decety, J., and Jackson, P. (2004) "The Functional Architecture of Human Empathy," *Behavioral and Cognitive Neuroscience Reviews* 3: 71–100.

Decety, J., and Sommerville, J. (2003) "Shared Representations between Self and Other: A Social Cognitive Neuroscience View," *Trends in Cognitive Science* 7: 527–33.

Devereaux, M. (2002) "Oppressive Texts, Resisting Readers, and the Gendered Spectator: The 'New' Aesthetics," in A. Neill and A. Ridley (eds.) *Arguing about Art*, 2nd ed., New York: Routledge.

Doane, M. (1990) "Remembering Women: Psychical and Historical Constructions in Film Theory," in E. A. Kaplan (ed.) *Psychoanalysis and the Cinema*, New York: Routledge.

Eisenberg, N. (2000) "Empathy and Sympathy," in M. Lewis and J. Haviland-Jones (eds.) *Handbook of Emotions*, New York: Guilford.

Eisenberg, N., and Miller, P. (1987) "Empathy, Sympathy, and Altruism: Empirical and Conceptual Links," in N. Eisenberg and J. Stayer (eds.) *Empathy and Its Development*, Cambridge: Cambridge University Press.

Eisenberg, N., and Strayer, J. (eds.) (1987) *Empathy and Its Development*. Cambridge: Cambridge University Press.

Feagin, S. (1996) *Reading with Feeling: The Aesthetics of Appreciation*, Ithaca, NY: Cornell University Press.

Flory, D. (2006) "Spike Lee and the Sympathetic Racist," *Journal of Aesthetics and Art Criticism* 64: 67–79.

Friedberg, B. (1990) "A Denial of Difference: Theories of Cinematic Identification," in E. A. Kaplan (ed.) *Psychoanalysis and the Cinema*, New York: Routledge.

Gaut, B. (1999) "Identification and Emotion in Narrative Film," in C. Plantinga and G. M. Smith (eds.) *Passionate Views: Film, Cognition, and Emotion*, Baltimore, MD: Johns Hopkins University Press.

Goldie, P. (1999) "How We Think of Others' Emotions," *Mind and Language* 14: 394–423.

—— (2000) *The Emotions: A Philosophical Exploration*, Oxford: Oxford University Press.

Goldman, A. (2006) *Simulating Minds: The Philosophy, Psychology, and Neuroscience of Mindreading*, New York: Oxford University Press.

Harold, J. (2000) "Empathy with Fictions," *British Journal of Aesthetics* 40: 340–55.

Harris, P. (2000) *The Work of the Imagination*, Oxford: Blackwell Publishers.

Hatfield, E., Cacioppo, J. T., and Rapson, R. L. (1992) *Emotional Contagion*, Cambridge: Cambridge University Press.

Hoffman, M. (2000) *Empathy and Moral Development*, New York: Cambridge University Press.

Metz, C. (1986) "The Imaginary Signifier" (excerpts) in P. Rosen (ed.) *Narrative, Apparatus, Ideology*, New York: Columbia University Press.

Mulvey, L. (1986) "Visual Pleasure and Narrative Cinema," in P. Rosen (ed.) *Narrative, Apparatus, Ideology*, New York: Columbia University Press.

Neill, A. (1996) "Empathy and (Film) Fiction," in D. Bordwell and N. Carroll (eds.) *Post-Theory: Reconstructing Film Studies*, Madison: University of Wisconsin Press.

Nichols, S., Stich, S., Leslie, A., and Klein, D. (1996) "Varieties of Off-line Simulation," in P. Carruthers and P. Smith (eds.) *Theories of Theories of Mind*, Cambridge: Cambridge University Press, 39–74.

Nichols, S., and Stich, S. (2003) *Mindreading: An Integrated Account of Pretense, Self-Awareness, and Understanding Other Minds*, Oxford: Oxford University Press.

Plantinga, C. (1999) "The Scene of Empathy and the Human Face in Film," in C. Plantinga and G. M. Smith (eds.) *Passionate Views: Film, Cognition, and Emotion*, Baltimore, MD: Johns Hopkins University Press.

—— (forthcoming) *Moving Viewers: American Film and the Spectator's Experience*, Berkeley: University of California Press.

Robinson, J. (2005) *Deeper than Reason: Emotion and its Role in Music, Literature, and Art*, Oxford: Oxford University Press.

—— (forthcoming) "Emotion," in J. Prinz (ed.) *The Handbook of Philosophy of Psychology*, Oxford: Oxford University Press.

Smith, M. (1995) *Engaging Characters: Fiction, Emotion, and the Cinema*, New York: Oxford University Press.

—— (1997) "Imagining from the Inside," in R. Allen and M. Smith (eds.) *Film Theory and Philosophy*, New York: Oxford University Press.

Stich, S., and Nichols, S. (1997) "Cognitive Penetrability, Rationality, and Restricted Simulation," *Mind and Language* 12: 297–326.

White, P. (1998) "Feminism and Film," in J. Hill and P. Church Gibson (eds.) *The Oxford Guide to Film Studies*, New York: Oxford University Press.

Wispe, L. (1991) *The Psychology of Sympathy*, New York: Plenum Press.

Further reading

Barbara Creed, *The Monstrous Feminine: Film, Feminism, Psychoanalysis* (London: Routledge, 1993) offers a book-length treatment of the issue of how women are portrayed in horror films, based on psychoanalytic feminist theory. An edited collection on the topic of simulation theory is M. Davies and T. Stone (eds.) *Mental Simulation* (Oxford: Blackwell, 1995). Berys Gaut, "Film," in J. Levinson (ed.) *The Oxford Handbook of Aesthetics* (Oxford: Oxford University Press, 2003) is a survey article of key issues in philosophy of film, including spectatorial response. Jerrrold Levinson, "Emotion in Response to Art: A Survey of the Terrain," in Mette Hjort and Sue Laver (eds.) *Emotion and the Arts* (New York: Oxford University Press, 1997) is an overview article covering recent philosophical issues on the relationship between emotion and art. Aaron Meskin and Jonathan Weinberg, "Emotions, Fiction, and Cognitive Architecture," *British Journal of Aesthetics* 43 (2003): 18–34, offers a critique of simulation accounts of responding to fiction. Carl Plantinga, "Disgusted at the Movies," *Film Studies: An International Review* 8 (2006): 81–92, explores the topic of film-elicited disgust as a direct emotion, not an emotion triggered by spectators' relationship and response to characters.

10
ETHICS

Folke Tersman

> I know no great work of art in all of world culture that would not be linked
> to an ethical ideal, that is based on some other motives such as on the
> dark aspects of life. There are some talented works of such a nature, but no
> masterpieces.
>
> Andrei Tarkovsky (quoted in Lipkov 1988; translated by Robert Bird)

Many films address ethical questions and morally loaded situations, and this is part
of the reason why we find them interesting. Films occasionally also prompt moral
criticism. Some of such criticism focuses on events in the creation of the film.
Consider Herzog's masterpiece *Fitzcarraldo* (1982). The main character – the Irishman
Fitzgerald (who changed his name to Fitzcarraldo, when he reached South America
toward the end of the nineteenth century) – wanted to build an opera house in the
jungle town of Iquitos and planned to finance this endeavor by making a fortune
from rubber. To transport the rubber, he decided to move a ship from one part of the
Amazon River to another by crossing a large hill in between. The film is based on a
true story, and the real Fitzcarraldo had the ship dismantled and carried over the hill
in pieces. Herzog, however, decided to reenact the event by pulling a giant, three-story
boat over a large hill, using an ancient pulley system and the local Indians, and the
image of these Indians straining to pull a gigantic boat over the jungle hill became the
central one in the film. This project involved huge risks, as was pointed out to Herzog
many times in advance. And what people feared did in fact happen. A cable snapped,
sending the huge boat tumbling down back to the bottom of the hill. Miraculously,
none of the poorly paid Indians died, although three were injured. However, the mere
fact that the crew was put to such immense risks raises, of course, ethical questions.

From a moral point of view, there is nothing special about actions and decisions
that lead to an artwork. Like other, more domestic, activities, they can be evaluated
morally, and the considerations that are relevant to such evaluations are the same as
in other cases: the consequences of the decisions, the underlying intentions, whether
they represent breaches of important moral rules, and so forth. Of course, some
people might want to say that artists should be allowed a certain freedom that is not
acceptable for ordinary folks (*quod licet Iovi, non licet bovi*), at least when they act qua
artists. But, if this is reasonable (which I doubt), it can be accommodated by pointing

to the special circumstances involved, or to the special role that these people have. Just as teachers may have special obligations as a result of their role and responsibilities as teachers, there may be special rules applying to artists. This is compatible with thinking that, at a more general level, the same rules and principles apply to all agents, in the sense that it holds for everyone that if she *were* a teacher, or an artist, the special rules associated with those roles would apply to her as well.

In what follows, however, I shall largely ignore the kind of questions raised by filmmaking. Instead, I shall focus on questions regarding the outcomes of such activities, the films themselves. Can they too be evaluated from a moral point of view? The answer to this question may seem to depend on our view on the nature of a film when conceived as an artwork. On one view, what we are referring to is simply an "audio-visual display," detached from any connection with the manner in which it was produced and the agents who produced it. This does not rule out moral evaluation, but perhaps it limits the types of evaluations that can be made. Thus, we can presumably ask whether it is, from a moral point of view, a good thing that it exists, and whether we should encourage people to see it. But there are other moral properties (such as rightness or blameworthiness) that it makes less sense to ascribe. Only persons and actions can have certain moral properties. For example, consider a film that propagates racism and invites people to share that attitude. This is perhaps a reason to censor it, but not to consider it (as contrasted with the filmmaker or distributor) blameworthy.

However, on another view about the nature of an artwork, a film is not merely a bare, detached audio-visual display. Rather, it should be understood in relation to facts about the context of production, such as facts about the underlying intentions. Indeed, such considerations are constitutive of the very difference between a work and a type of display of lights and sounds. On this, more "contextualist," view, a work of art is an accomplishment, something somebody does (Levinson 1990; and Wollheim 1980; the view is also elaborated in Livingston 2005). This conception allows for more complex ethical evaluations of the film, evaluations informed also by facts about the process that led to the film, which slightly blurs the distinction between ethical criticism of films and of filmmaking.

In what follows, I shall consider various types of ethical criticism and praise that a film can be subjected to. This is not to say that the idea that it is appropriate to assess artworks from an ethical perspective is uncontroversial. On the contrary, it is often held that ethical criticism of art involves a kind of radical error, which is illustrated by a famous quote about literature by Oscar Wilde: "There is no such thing as a moral or an immoral book. Books are well written, or badly written. That is all." The plausibility of this attitude, however, is easier to assess once one has considered what ethical criticism could consist in.

If one grants that a film can have moral qualities, further questions arise. How do the supposed moral flaws or merits of a film interact with its artistic and aesthetic value? Can a moral flaw make a film worse, artistically or aesthetically speaking? If so, does a moral flaw always detract from the artistic value of a film, or could a moral flaw sometimes even enhance it? A number of different positions addressing such issues have emerged. I shall survey some of those positions, as well as some of the arguments used for or against them.

However, I shall also argue that what view we take on this issue does not necessarily settle the question of whether it may be appropriate for critics or scholars to engage in ethical criticism of film. Successful interpretation of a narrative such as a film often presupposes recognition of the moral virtues and vices of the characters in the film, and of the attitudes projected in the work toward these characters. It is probably difficult for a spectator to do this without engaging in a dialogue with the values thus projected, and to respond by forming ethical judgments. Whether the moral qualities of the film that may thus be discerned affect its aesthetic value or not seems to have little bearing on whether it might be worthwhile to communicate those judgments. At the end of the article, I shall also make some brief comments about why moral philosophers and others who engage in moral thinking might find films a useful tool in their explorations.

Can films be immoral?

Ethical criticism of art is as old as art itself, and in the history of philosophy it goes back at least to Plato. However, more recently, this attitude has come into disrepute. Indeed, I suspect that many think that talk of "moral qualities" of films has a slightly ridiculous ring to it. In the 1960s and 1970s, left-wing people in Sweden criticized literature and other cultural expressions as being reactionary, and as consolidating the allegedly unjust capitalist system of the day. One of the people who thus came under fire was the children's writer Astrid Lindgren. Lindgren is well known for the books and films about the girl Pippi Longstocking ("the strongest girl in the world"), who lived by herself in a big house (her mother had died and her father was far away), entirely self-sufficient and independent because of her strength, cleverness, and a huge chest of gold coins. According to the critics, these stories endorsed a fascist ideology that praises the strong and independent and loathes the weak. Today, this story is cited as an example of how incredibly silly and hysterical the radicals of the generation of 1968 could be.

Of course, there are more worrying examples of ethical criticism. These are cases where authoritarian regimes have banned books and films because they propagate the "wrong" values and subversive ideologies. It is probably association with those types of cases and a commitment to liberal values, such as free speech and freedom of expression, that underlies much of the skepticism toward the idea of ethical criticism of artworks. However, it is important to notice that by allowing for the appropriateness of such criticism one commits oneself neither to any particular moral views (such as the upper- and middle-class Victorian values that Wilde scorned or the authoritarian views that Plato is associated with) nor to the view that artworks should be censored or banned. One may well believe that there are good reasons for allowing freedom of expression and still think that some artworks have moral defects, just as one may hold that adultery is often morally problematic but that it should not be considered a legal offense. As John Stuart Mill has famously argued, there are good consequentialist arguments for allowing freedom of speech that do not presuppose any assumptions about the moral status of the speech thus being allowed.

If one does think that it may be appropriate to evaluate artworks morally, what could provide grounds for such evaluations? There are many possibilities. If a work records real acts of torture and violence, it might be argued that the immorality of these acts is inherited by the work itself. A work can also be held to be morally defective by the simple fact that it upsets people, such as when it mocks certain religious beliefs.

A criticism that needs more complex argumentation is when it is claimed that the work will encourage certain undesirable and antisocial types of behavior. Today, this type of criticism is probably more often launched against films than other cultural expressions, given the impact they currently have in society. The idea is that violence in films will lead to violence in the streets, if it is depicted in certain (glorifying) ways, and that similar things can be said about other types of undesirable phenomena (male dominance, racism, and so on). Arguments of this kind are in a wide sense consequentialist, but they do not rely on the assumptions about what makes an outcome better or desirable, usually associated with consequentialism. For example, by advocating such arguments, one does not commit oneself to the utilitarian view that the desirability of an outcome depends on how much "happiness" it contains.

However, an obvious problem with these arguments is that the truth of the empirical claims on which they rely – the claim that films will indeed affect people's attitudes and behavior in the way assumed – is very hard to determine. Indeed, their truth is even difficult to research, as people's attitudes and behavior are the complex result of many different factors. What reason do we have for thinking that it is the films that provide the (or a) crucial factor? The genre that has been the object of most research of this kind is probably pornography, as there are worries that consumption of pornography will lead to sexual violence and consolidate gender inequality. But the evidence that has been gathered through this research seems far from conclusive (for a survey of some research, see Donnerstein *et al.* 1987).

However, there is yet another type of ethical criticism, a type that does not rely on any far-reaching predictions about how films might affect general behavior. On this view, in order for a film to be morally defective it is not necessary for it to actually succeed in implanting morally flawed attitudes or perspectives in its audiences, at least not in any extensive way. It is enough if it endorses those attitudes. To use the word "endorses" in this context might seem awkward, as we usually believe that only agents or thinkers can endorse. However, given the wider concept of a film, mentioned above, the one that sees it as an accomplishment rather than a "bare audio-visual display," this objection has less force. The idea is that, given facts about the film and the making of it (the genre it belongs to, the creator's intentions, etc.), it can be seen as prescribing certain responses for the audience, such as feelings of sympathy or antipathy for certain characters. If these responses are morally problematic, that could be seen as a flaw in the film (such a view is defended in, e.g., Carroll 2000; and Stecker 2007). At least, this is so, it seems to me, if it is designed so as to secure or merit those responses – i.e., so that the formation of those responses is in a sense explicable or reasonable, given features of the film. If it does not have such a design, it might be more reasonable to think that the flaw lies (solely) with the filmmaker and not with the film.

Although this type of criticism does not rely on problematic empirical claims of the kind that the first type does, it raises other methodological issues, regarding interpretation. How can we determine that a film endorses a certain perspective? After all, we must distinguish between endorsing and merely depicting or representing or perhaps exploring a certain attitude (while remaining neutral toward it). The latter need not be a ground for thinking that the film is morally flawed. On the contrary, it might be considered a merit, as it increases an audience's understanding of the moral issues and attitudes addressed.

That is, a film may have features that superficially seem to indicate that it invites audiences to share a certain flawed perspective. However, a closer look that takes more factors into account may undermine our first impression. For example, consider the action comedy *Ocean's Eleven* (2001), in which the character Danny Ocean seeks revenge on an enemy, who previously has put him in jail and is courting his girlfriend, by robbing his casino. Given the sympathetic portrayal of the hero and his collaborators, the film might seem to endorse criminality. However, one must also take into account the special conventions that govern films belonging to the pertinent genre. In action films, people are hit in their heads and get thrown through glass windows without getting seriously hurt. This indicates that some of the worries that apply to the real world should not be applied to the fictional world that is portrayed. Indeed, in these films, we often see very little of the suffering and misery of the hero's victims. Those characters remain two-dimensional cut-outs, which sends the message that the spectator is expected to suspend some of her moral principles when judging what happens to them. It seems to me that judgments to the effect that a film endorses immoral perspectives are, for such reasons, often premature (see Davies 2006, for a discussion of the relevance of conventions of the kind discussed here).

If encouraging or endorsing ethically problematic attitudes and perspectives can be a moral flaw in a film, encouraging or endorsing admirable ones can presumably be a merit. Such judgments obviously face the same problems as those pertaining to their "negative" counterparts. However, more recently, much discussion has focused on another possible ground for valuing films and other artworks from a moral (or at least moral philosophical) point of view. And although the type of value that is thus ascribed to films is instrumental, so that the films are valued for the help they provide to some external aim (moral development), it does not rely on the kind of ambitious empirical claims that the other consequentialist arguments rely on.

These suggestions are often made in connection with the relatively recent renaissance of virtue-ethical and Aristotelian approaches to moral philosophy (see, e.g., Hursthouse 1999; and Slote 1992). Such approaches are suspicious toward attempts to codify moral obligations in general principles (such as utilitarianism) and stress that the basic moral questions concern agents and their characters rather than actions. More specifically, they stress the importance of developing and fostering certain stable character traits – virtues. These are traits that allow the agent to register and acknowledge the importance of ethically salient features of a situation and to act accordingly. That is, to acquire these traits is to develop a certain sensitivity, which allows one to perceive aspects of the situation that are morally relevant. It has been held that the appreciation of narrative art, such as literature and film, may have a crucial role for the development of such a sensitivity, in that they allow for representations of the complexity of the situations that raise moral questions and invite audiences to see these situations from different perspectives, by allowing them to "simulate" how it would be to be in such positions (see Currie 1995; Murdoch 1970; and Nussbaum 1990). It should be noted, however, that although this type of reasoning is usually used by virtue theorists, other theorists can adopt it as well. All viable moral theories stress that responsible action requires something like empathy and the ability to put oneself in the shoes of others to gather relevant information.

Moral and artistic value

If we grant that it is meaningful to say that films have moral qualities of the kind exemplified above, we might want to know how these qualities interact with their artistic value. A number of different positions addressing that issue have emerged.

These positions are often stated in a way that presupposes a distinction between artistic and aesthetic value. The aesthetic value of an artwork focuses on just some of its features – its gracefulness, beauty, unity, expressive subtlety, and on – whereas assessments of artistic value are all-things-considered judgments that take other evaluative dimensions into account, such as, perhaps, its cognitive value (what we can learn from it), or art-historic value. That is, artistic value is conceived as a "composite" value that includes, in addition to aesthetic value, other types of values as well (Dean 2002; Stecker 2005, 2007). Of course, it is possible to use "aesthetic value" in a wider sense, so that it includes the other dimensions as well, but I shall in what follows accept this terminology. How do the moral flaws and merits of an artwork affect its artistic value? This is the question that I take the positions to address. The idea is that although affecting the aesthetic value of a work would be one of the ways a moral flaw or virtue may alter its artistic value, it is at least conceivable there are other ways.

There are many possible views about the relationship between an artwork's moral qualities and its artistic value. The two extremes are "ethicism" and "autonomism." Ethicism is the view that moral defects or virtues always have an artistic significance, so that an ethical defect is always an artistic flaw (Gaut 1998). Autonomism, by contrast, denies that they have any artistic significance whatsoever (Isenberg 1973). Both these positions are incompatible with the "anti-theoretical" one that denies that there is a systematic relationship of any kind between artistic and ethical value. On that view, an ethical flaw can sometimes be an artistic defect, sometimes be insignificant, and can sometimes even be an artistic virtue (for some recent proponents, see Jacobson 1997; and John 2006). The position that allows for the latter possibility – that an ethical flaw may be an artistic virtue – is sometimes called "immoralism" (Kieran 2002). Another position that has recently received some attention is "moderate moralism" (Carroll 2000). Moderate moralism holds only that some ethical flaws are artistic flaws, and that some ethical virtues are artistic virtues. As it stands, it is possible to hold this view and also to think that ethical flaws can sometimes be artistic virtues. So, moderate moralism is compatible with the anti-theoretical view.

The assessment of these positions will depend on how we understand the concept of "artistic value." On one view, the idea that assessments of artistic value are all-things-considered judgments is to be taken literally. On this view, *all* possible grounds for evaluation should be taken into account. So, if artworks allow for ethical evaluation, it becomes trivial to say that moral flaws or virtues can affect artistic value (see, e.g., Dean 2002: 2). However, it is possible to adopt a narrower view of the concept of artistic value and to restrict the grounds and considerations that are relevant. For example, some insist that to make an assessment of the artistic value of an artwork is to assess it from a certain perspective, i.e., to assess it *as* art and not relative to some other role or function it may have, such as when it is viewed as an educational tool (John 2006). On such a view, whether a moral flaw can be an artistic flaw remains an open question, although one might wonder, of course, what it means to say that an artwork is evaluated *as* art. Anyway, the cases that have prompted most controversy are those where ethical flaws are supposed to affect the artistic value of a work, not directly (as ethical value is supposed to be built into the very concept of artistic value), but by affecting something else, such as its aesthetic value. It is on such cases I shall focus.

To adjudicate between ethicism and these other positions we also need to say something about what it means for a moral flaw to "affect," "enhance," or "detract" from the artistic value of a work. Thus, suppose that the filmmaker, in order to secure a response from an audience, makes certain moves that detract from a film's artistic value, for example by simplifying the story and its characters. Then, if the response is questionable from a moral point of view, this seems to illustrate how a moral flaw can affect the artistic value of a film. However, if the response could have been secured without taking such measures, the relationship between the moral flaw and the artistic one is merely contingent. Presumably, that moral flaws could affect artistic value in this sense is not anything controversial. So, if we want to find a meaningful topic for the debate, we must assume that the alleged relationship between moral and artistic value is stronger than that.

How could one try to establish that there is a more direct connection? One argument for ethicism takes as its point of departure the idea that if a film is not designed so as to mandate or justify the responses it prescribes, this represents an artistic flaw. For example, if a comedy is not funny, or a thriller is not thrilling, then the film has failed on its own terms and is thereby artistically flawed. Now, if a film is immoral in virtue of endorsing an immoral attitude, it prescribes that we should come to share that attitude. However, as the attitude is immoral, it can never be justified. Therefore, a moral flaw is also (always) an artistic flaw. This is called "the merited response argument" (Gaut 1998: 195; Carroll 2000: 375).

An obvious problem with this argument is that it exploits an ambiguity in the term "justified." One sense in which something could be justified is that it is morally acceptable (as when we say that violence in self-defense is justified). However, another sense is that it makes sense from a rational point of view (as when we say that a belief is justified by the available evidence). It might be argued that it is only when the responses fail to be warranted in the second sense that we should conclude that it has failed on its own terms and thus that the failure is an aesthetic flaw. So, if the fact that a response is not morally justified does not exclude its being justified in the second sense, the argument fails.

Another, but related, argument has been proposed by Noël Carroll (although he takes his argument to support moderate moralism, rather than ethicism). Carroll imagines a novel that invites audiences to respond by admiring a sadistic colonizer who "tortures every Indian he encounters" as he conceives of them as "vermin," an attitude with which the novel concurs. This makes the work morally defective. However, even if such a novel is skillfully designed, audiences will normally be unable to form the feelings of admiration toward the colonizer invited by the work, simply because we are disinclined to have admiration for such characters. In other words, the character fails or even contravenes "the morally relevant criteria for admiration." This makes the moral flaw an artistic one as well, as it represents "a failure to design the character in accordance with the warranting conditions for the emotional response prescribed." Or as Carroll puts it, "[T]he reason the work is aesthetically defective is that it is morally defective. Though the work prescribes admiration as part of its aesthetic agenda, it fails to secure it, precisely because it is evil" (Carroll 2000: 377–8). Like the argument for ethicism, this argument relies on the idea that a film is artistically flawed if it is not designed so as to mandate or secure the responses it prescribes. In this case, however, the question is not whether the responses are morally justified, but whether *we* can be justified in thinking that spectators will actually form those responses. The reason why the book about the colonizer does not satisfy this condition is simply that it prescribes responses (e.g., admiration for racist cruelty) that people with normal moral sensibilities are unable to form. And what explains why they are unable to form these responses is, exactly, that they are immoral.

Notice that I have now construed the argument as relying on claims about what responses audiences are in fact able to form. This means that, by accepting the argument, we commit ourselves to the idea that if people were to deteriorate morally (so that they *would* be able to admire cruelty), the artistic value of the work would, other things being equal, increase. This implication may seem a bit odd. One way to avoid it is to take the question to be whether spectators would be able to form the responses *insofar as* they are morally sensitive. But to count failure to merit prescribed responses in this sense as an artistic failure is to beg the question against the autonomist. Another possible objection to Carroll's argument relies on the suggestion made earlier, that when an artwork fails to secure or mandate the responses it prescribes the morally problematic character of those responses is more reasonably seen as a flaw of the artist behind the work, rather than of the work itself.

Can ethical flaws sometimes *enhance* the artistic value of a film? The fact that a film depicts a certain immoral perspective in a way that makes it intelligible and psychologically credible can presumably enhance the artistic value, for example by increasing an audience's understanding of the perspective. However, that it depicts such a perspective (while remaining neutral toward it) is not enough to make the film morally flawed. It must also endorse it. How could such endorsement contribute to the artistic value of the film?

The aesthetic literature does not abound with examples of films whose immorality is supposed to contribute to their artistic value. But one case that is often discussed is Leni Riefenstahl's *Triumph of the Will* (1936). This is a documentary where Hitler is represented as a visionary hero who is loved by the German people, to whom he in turn is supposed to bring fulfillment and self-respect. The film is often praised for its cinematic mastery and for its stunning scenes and powerful images and symbols. It is also condemned for its endorsement of Hitler and his ideas. That the film both has a high artistic quality and moral flaws is not enough, however, to prove the immoralist's thesis. It must also be shown that the artistic value somehow depends on (rather than simply outweighs) the moral flaw.

What difference does it make?

One may well wonder about the substance of the debate between autonomists, ethicists and so on. As the above discussion illustrates, given a sufficiently wide understanding of the concept of artistic value, autonomism becomes less promising, whereas, given a more narrow one, it is easier to defend. How are we to choose which conception of artistic value to adopt? It seems to me that there is no non–question-begging argument here, but that the discussion has to be decided by stipulation. After all, this question about how to delimit artistic value from others is largely a taxonomical question, and such questions are best answered by pondering the purpose the taxonomy is supposed to serve.

Accordingly, it seems to me that the outcome of the debate between autonomism, ethicism and so on will have only a limited significance. Suppose that autonomism comes out the winner. This does not exclude ethical criticism or evaluation being a worthwhile activity for a critic or scholar. After all, adopting such a critical perspective may be a crucial part in the process of trying to understand the film, by trying to discern what moral points of view, if any, it projects or endorses.

Nor would the victory of autonomism undermine the interest moral philosophers and others who engage in moral thinking take (and have reason to take) in films and other narratives. Artworks are uniquely able to represent human interactions, situations, and relationships in a way that can capture much of their complexity, or at least far more so than the simplistic stories used in the thought experiments by which moral philosophers "test" and explore their principles and moral theories. They can therefore be useful for allowing us to give substance to the concepts our moral theories invoke, as well as allowing us to perceive where distinctions need to be made, even if the theories posit none.

Having said that, however, it seems to me that there is rather little overlap between the films that prompt moral criticism and those that moral philosophers have most reason to take an interest in. In any narrative, the advocacy of a certain point of view is usually accompanied by a degree of oversimplification. This may manifest itself in the fact that some considerations that speak against the point of view being advocated are overlooked and that some of the complexity of the issues is ignored. So, if the main ground for morally criticizing (or praising) a film is that it endorses a certain moral perspective, the films that are most prone for such criticism tend also to be less interesting for a moral philosopher. We have enough oversimplification in moral philosophy as it is.

See also Censorship (Chapter 3), Emotion and affect (Chapter 8), Empathy and character engagement (Chapter 9), Race (Chapter 21), Stanley Cavell (Chapter 32), and Pornography (Chapter 47).

References

Carroll, N. (2000) "Art and Ethical Criticism: An Overview of Recent Directions of Research," *Ethics* 110: 350–87.

Currie, G. (1995) "The Moral Psychology of Fiction," *Australasian Journal of Philosophy* 73: 250–9.

Davies, S. (2006) *The Philosophy of Art*, Malden, MA; and Oxford: Blackwell.

Dean, J. (2002) "Aesthetics and Ethics: The State of the Art," *American Society for Aesthetics Newsletter* 22: 1–4.

Donnerstein, E., Linz, D., and Penrod, S. (1987) *The Question of Pornography: Research Findings and Policy Implications*, New York: Free Press.

Gaut, B. (1998) "The Ethical Criticism of Art," in J. Levinson (ed.) *Aesthetics and Ethics*, Cambridge and New York: Cambridge University Press.

Hursthouse, R. (1999) *On Virtue Ethics*, Oxford and New York: Oxford University Press.

Isenberg, A. (1973) *Aesthetics and the Theory of Criticism*, Chicago: Chicago University Press.

Jacobson, D. (1997) "In Praise of Immoral Art," *Philosophical Topics* 54: 155–99.

John, E. (2006) "Artistic Value and Opportunistic Moralism," in M. Kieran (ed.) *Contemporary Debates in Aesthetics and the Philosophy of Art*, Malden, MA: Blackwell, 331–41.

Kieran, M. (2002) "Forbidden Knowledge: The Challenge of Immoralism," in J. Bermudez and S. Gardiner (eds.) *Art and Morality*, London and New York: Routledge.

Levinson, J. (1990) *Music, Art and Metaphysics*, Ithaca, NY: Cornell University Press.

Lipkov, A. (1988) "Strasti po Andreiu" [The Passion according to Andrei], *Literaturnoe obozrenie* 9: 74–80.

Livingston, P. (2005) *Art and Intention*, Oxford: Clarendon Press.

Murdoch, I. (1970) *The Sovereignty of Good*, London: Routledge and Kegan Paul.

Nussbaum, M. (1990) *Love's Knowledge: Essays on Philosophy and Literature*, New York: Oxford University Press.

Slote, M. (1992) *From Morality to Virtue*, New York: Oxford University Press.

Stecker, R. (2005) "The Interaction of Ethical and Aesthetic Value," *British Journal of Aesthetics* 45: 138–50

—— (2007) "Interaction of Artistic and Ethical Value: Immoralism and the Anti-Theoretical View" (unpublished manuscript).

Wollheim, R. (1980) *Art and Its Objects*, Cambridge and New York: Cambridge University Press.

11
FILM AS ART

Robert Stecker

Question: Is film art? The question is ambiguous. It might be asking whether films are artworks, or, more cautiously, whether there are films that are artworks. Or, it might be asking whether film is an art form, or more cautiously, whether a kind of film medium is or contains an art form. A natural follow-up to the first question is, What makes an individual film an artwork? A natural follow-up to the second questions is, What makes a film medium (contain) an art form?

That there are distinct questions here may not be obvious. But the distinction is important and neglected. So is the philosophical investigation of art forms, which has always taken a backseat to artworks when people ask the question "what is art?"

The reason the distinction is important is this. Consider one film medium: still photography. There are lots of still photos, such as most family snapshots, that have no pretension to being artworks. There are others that almost certainly are artworks. But given that there are a vast number of nonart photos, someone might question whether still photography is an art form. Or, if they don't question this, they might still wonder what is responsible for the existence of an art form in a sea of nonart photographs.

The main focus of this essay is film in the sense of moving pictures as seen in the cinema, on television and on video or DVDs, though I will continue to pull in still photographs when it is helpful to do so. The majority view today is that film is an art form and, hence, many cinematic works are artworks. On this view, the main issues concern the nature of the art form, the nature of the film artwork, and the boundary between film art and film nonart. A further question, but one that we have space only to touch on, is whether there are important differences in the way we appreciate artworks and nonartworks that share the same medium?

Why should anyone care whether some films are artworks and whether there are one or more film art forms? The short answer concerning works is that, while asserting that a film is an artwork does not entail that it has any special value, it does entail it is the sort of thing capable of having great value. Regarding forms, the short answer is that asserting that there is a film art form entails that an institution exists for creating, distributing, interpreting, and evaluating a class of items, all of which are films, capable of having such value. Fuller answers will emerge from what is said below.

ROBERT STECKER

Skepticism about film as art

Before going further, we should face up to the fact that there is skepticism about film as an art form. As Noël Carroll (1988) and Berys Gaut (2002, 2003) have noted, much of classical film theory is an attempt to argue against such skepticism and in favor of a cinematic art form. The focus here will be on a more recent version of these skeptical arguments, forcefully advanced by Roger Scruton (1983).

Scruton's main conclusion is that photography and film are not representational arts, and by "arts" it is better to interpret him to mean art forms rather than artworks. In fact, Scruton does not deny that some photographs and some films are representational artworks but thinks that when they are, this is so in virtue of their using means borrowed from genuine art forms. In the case of photographs, the relevant art form is painting. Photographs become representational artworks, according to Scruton, only when they are "polluted" with painterly techniques. The relevant art form in the case of film is not painting but drama. There are films that are dramatic artworks, but Scruton seems to think that their existence in a film medium is merely contingent, rather than essential, to their being artworks.

Scruton also does not deny that photographs and films can have aesthetic value in virtue of their form, though he doesn't go so far as to claim (or explicitly deny) that they can be artworks in virtue of their formal interest. I suspect he would not be sympathetic to avant-garde filmmaking that attempts to get at the essence of film by emphasizing its formal dimensions – such as its basis in the projection of light or its creation of an impression of movement. Nor would he applaud other avant-garde works that emphasize film as a recording mechanism, though that is what Scruton thinks film essentially is. He just might not believe that the use of the film medium to tediously illustrate this "truth" makes the illustration an artwork.

Scruton believes that film is not a representational art form, because he thinks that film (or photography) does not create representations. The bare-bones argument for this conclusion is

1 A is a representation of B only if A expresses a thought about B.
2 Photographs (films) result from B causally interacting with a photographic mechanism in a way that does not require thought or intentionality.
3 Since A results from such a process, it does not express a thought about B.
4 Therefore, A is not a representation of B.

As it stands, this argument is not persuasive. First, what justifies the partial definition of representation in premise 1? If one looks at the literature on pictorial representation, one will not find in it any definition that has a condition as strong as Scruton's. Nor do all "handmade" pictures satisfy this condition. Suppose you ask me to make a picture of a man – any man – and I draw a stick figure. Have I expressed a thought about a man or men? It's not clear that I have. Have I depicted a man? Yes, I have, per instruction. Second, premise 3 looks to be false. Just because A results from a process that does not *require* thought, this does not imply that the photographic process is

122

never expressive of thought. It only implies that it needn't be (Gaut 2003: 631). But as we have seen, that is also true of handmade pictures.

Scruton might reply to the objection to premise 1, by claiming that we have misinterpreted it. All "expressing a thought" comes to is that there is an intentional relation, not just a causal relation, between the representation and its object. To put it another way, a genuine representation must always have an intentional object, which may or may not exist, and if it does exist, may or may not capture the object's true appearance. My stick figure meets this condition, and there are definitions of depiction in the literature that do so as well. Scruton replies to the objection to premise 3 by claiming that he is talking about ideal photographs (films), for which the premise is true. They can only have real objects that causally interact with the photographic process, and the result must at least roughly capture the objects' true appearance.

However, this is still not convincing. For one thing, we can imagine genres of painting which would seem not to count as representational on this account but surely are. I will call one such genre "ideal portraiture." To be an "ideal portrait," the following conventions must be met. First, like all actual portraits, there must be an actual person represented in the picture. There is no possibility that the portrait is not of something that exists. Second, A is an ideal portrait of B only if A at least roughly captures a true appearance of B. A painting that fails in this respect is not a bad ideal portrait; it is not an ideal portrait at all. This convention may not be true of all actual portraits, but it is a perfectly possible convention. Third, for A to be an ideal portrait of B, B must causally interact in the right way with the process that brings A into existence. Ideal portraits are like ideal photographs in the ways that purportedly disqualify the latter from representationality. Its intentional object is always identical to a real object, the true appearance of which is invariably captured in the painting, as a result of causal interaction between the objects and the production process.

Ideal portraits clearly are capable of expressing thoughts about their subjects, even though their subjects must exist and have an appearance not too different than the one represented. What about ideal photographs (films)? That depends on what Scruton means by this coinage. He sometimes seems to mean something brought about by a causal process devoid of intentionality. If so, ideal photographs (films) cannot express thought, but Scruton is then just making this true by definition. What he should mean by an ideal photograph (film) is one produced using only photographic or filmmaking techniques, and not ones imported from painting or drama. However, if this is what is meant, then ideal photographs (films) are not barred from expressing thoughts about their subjects and certainly do so. To give just one obvious example, consider the expressive potential of the close-up. This is not a technique available to theater, it only uses photographic resources, but it can be used in film for expressive purposes. For example, in Woody Allen's *Hannah and Her Sisters* (1986), at least two scenes end with Hannah (Mia Farrow) filling nearly the entire screen in close-up. This expresses various thoughts about the character – the central role she plays in her extended family, her conception of this role as the lynchpin of the family, and her Christ-like willingness to take on the burdens of all the other family members (represented tongue-in-cheek). (See Gaut [2002], King [1992], and Warburton [1988], for other examples of photographic and cinematic techniques that express thoughts about a subject.)

This same example illustrates what is wrong with another claim Scruton makes, namely, that our interest in a photograph (film) is in the subject shown in it, rather than in the representation in its own right. This is precisely not the case in the example just given. Our interest is not in what Mia Farrow looked like when these scenes were being shot, but in the meaning expressed in the way the scenes were shot.

There is one final charge that Scruton makes about photography and film that we should address. It is the claim that both photography and film are "fictionally incompetent," i.e., incapable in their own right of fictional representation. If this were true, it would be especially problematic for cinema, since so much of it is understood to be a type of fiction. (Fictions, roughly, are works a primary function of which is to authorize the *imagining* of various states of affairs. Whether the states of affairs do or do not exist in reality is a secondary matter, though it is also a mark of a fiction that it is capable of getting us to imagine what doesn't exist.)

Scruton's main argument for this claim is no more convincing than the previous one. Suppose I take a photograph of a denizen of skid row and entitle it "Silenus." Why wouldn't this be a fictional representation of the mythical old man? Scruton asks us to imagine a parallel case. I see an individual on skid row, and pointing to him utter "Silenus." Is my pointing a representation? Scruton rightly says no: my gesture at best makes the tramp into a representation, rather than being one itself, and he thinks the same is true of a photograph. However, there is a ready reply. First, Scruton does not deny that the pointing expresses a thought, and hence, so does the photograph, since it is after all "a pointing." So Scruton can't assert that the photograph lacks "intentionality." Second, you can't point to something that doesn't exist, so if the thought is "about" Silenus there must be more involved than pointing. Finally, the main reason the pointing is not a representation is that it is an act that results in no independent representational object. That is precisely what a representation is: an object that represents something else. But a photograph, which, *ex hypothesi*, expresses a thought intended by its maker, is such an object. Even if we see the tramp (or a surrogate) in the photograph as Scruton thinks, that is no bar to the photograph fictionally representing Silenus.

Underlying this argument is a simpler thought: that a photograph is not a fictional representation but a record of a preexistent fictional representation. Unfortunately, this is not true in the Silenus example (nothing is a representation of Silenus until the photo is taken), and it is even less plausible in the case of a movie. A film recording of a stage production approximates to what Scruton has in mind. But a movie, made by filming and editing many scene fragments, made significant by the use of many photographic techniques, is hardly the recording of a preexistent fictional representation.

The cinematic artwork

If films can represent actual people and things as well as fictions, they can do so in the rich and complex ways characteristic of artworks. In fact, even skeptics about the representational capacities of film, like Scruton, do not deny that there are artworks that happen to be films. Such works don't contingently exist in the medium in which we view them but are essentially cinematic works of art. This is so in two respects. First, the nature of the representational content of a film typically depends on the use of essentially photographic and other techniques peculiar to filmmaking and not available to live stage drama. Second, the modes of presentation and reception for film are distinctive of the medium, although it is interesting that there is not a unique format here. The same film can be viewed by projecting it onto a screen or by viewing it in VCR, DVD, or still other formats.

When is a film an artwork? The answer will depend on the conception of art one brings to the table. What is now known as classical film theory was concerned with this question and approached it in a way characteristic of the period in which it developed. It looked for established artistic functions that the film medium fulfills in virtue of resources peculiar to the medium – special ways of realizing standard functions. Two functions received the bulk of attention: expression and realistic representation. In part, the expressionist view is motivated by a desire to refute an objection to film art, much like Scruton's. Film cannot create artworks, because it is a mechanical recording device that only reproduces the reality in front of camera. "Expressionists" (Eisenstein 1988; Arnheim 1957; Münsterberg 1970) attempt to refute this picture by emphasizing the ability of film to manipulate and rearrange reality to manifest an attitude about its subject.

André Bazin (1967, 1997) is the most distinguished proponents of film as the art of realistic representation. However, it's worth noting that he is perfectly aware of the expressive and antirealist potential of film and is lucid in analyzing the two chief ways of realizing this potential: "the plastics of the image ... and the resources of montage, which ... is ... the ordering of the image in time" by means of editing (1997: 60). Nevertheless, Bazin views the history of filmmaking as an evolution to an aesthetically superior realism. This is realized by avoiding the most manipulative forms of montage, such the juxtaposition of distinct events by alternating shots, which Bazin described as "chopping the world into little bits" (1997: 70). Alternative techniques such as the deep-focus shot create an artistically superior spatial realism. Furthermore, Bazin seems to agree with Scruton and Kendall Walton (1984) that in a photograph, we actually see the objects photographed. However, it is not so clear what logical role this plays in Bazin's defense of realism in film. Like Walton and unlike Scruton, Bazin does not mistakenly infer from this belief about the presentational capacities of the photograph that it is not a representational medium, or that it is fictionally "incompetent." Nor does he infer that the purpose of film is just to present the reality in front of the camera. On the contrary he thinks of film as a medium for realistic fictional representation. The techniques allowing for greater realism also enhance the filmmaker's ability to manipulate reality (1997: 71), to create ambiguity, and it requires more active participation from its audience (1997: 68). It makes the filmmaker the "equal" not of the chronicler but of the "novelist" (1997: 71).

Theorists like Bazin and even to a greater extent Arnheim are reminiscent of philosophers who attempt to define art in terms of a single function or valuable property. Like Bazin's account of film realism, such philosophical accounts can be complex and highly nuanced, but the dominant view today is that simple functionalism will always fall to counterexamples of works in the relevant class that lack the function or valuable property in question. In recognizing masterpieces of montage, Bazin provides the counterexamples himself to a general theory of film art, based on realism. The rejection of simple functionalism leads some philosophers to offer accounts of arthood or art status, in self-consciously nonfunctional terms. However, it is not strictly necessary to eschew functions in explaining the nature of film as art as long as one is a pluralist about relevant functions. So we should recognize multiple functions that films can realize and be artworks in virtue of these. This includes evocative, expressive, and representational functions realized in both narrative fictional movies and documentaries. It also includes functions specific to the visual and pictorial nature of most films. Further it includes the function fulfilled by films that explore the nature of the film media themselves. The list should be left open ended. Functions evolve as a result of the evolution within a medium, of the larger art world, and of the culture at large.

The cinematic art form

Not only are there cinematic artworks, but it is plausible that there is a cinematic art form. We will discuss what makes this claim plausible, but before doing this, let us briefly consider a counting issue, namely, assuming there is at least one, how many cinematic art forms are there? (This issue is not trivial, because different art forms need to be appreciated in different ways and knowledge of form guides one's appreciative efforts.) Compare film with literature, which seems like a roughly analogous category within the arts. Poetry, the novel, and the short story are three different literary forms. Within each of these categories, there are different subforms or genres. So while the feature film has lots of genres perhaps it should be regarded as a cinematic art form, and similarly for the documentary and the short film. Cutting across this kind of classification are others. Animation seems like a different form than the live-action film, but both can be feature films or shorts. Silent film might be regarded as a different form than talkies. The technology used in creating a moving image also can have a much bigger impact on a final product than it does in literature, where it matters little to the reader whether the writer uses a pencil or a word processor. But whether one uses photography, video, digital technology, computer graphics, motion capture, or animation makes a difference to what one sees and the way one sees it. Sometimes this will just make possible modifications in already existing forms, but should we regard an entire film made using motion-capture technology such as A Scanner Darkly (2006) as a new form? While it seems plausible that within the broad category of cinematic art there are several proper forms, how they are to be individuated is an open question.

So is cinema an art form (in a broad sense in which literature is one too)? We have mentioned two grounds for doubting this. We have considered and rejected skepticism about film as a representational art. At the beginning of this essay we also mentioned the fact that many films (and photos) just aren't artworks. The underlying thought here is that if the typical product of a given medium is not an artwork, there is no art form, even if some works in the medium rise to the level of art. However, it turns out that the situation in film (and photography) is not unusual. Consider architecture. There are architectural artworks but a sea of buildings, many designed by architects, that have no pretension to art status. Again the question might be raised whether there is an architectural art form while admitting there are architectural artworks (Davies 1995). No one doubts that painting is an art form. However, there are lots of paintings – made for illustration or various commercial purposes that also exist outside the art form. One can say the same thing about musical and literary forms. These examples show that large numbers of nonartworks in a given medium is not evidence of the nonexistence of an art form

Given all this, we have no reason to deny that "architecture," "painting," "music," "poetry," and "film" can refer to art forms. It is true, though, that these terms can also refer to a class of items that include artworks and nonartworks, which I have been referring to as a medium. Perhaps all buildings belong to the medium of architecture, but not to the art form architecture. The same goes for films (and photos).

It is plausible, then, to see art forms as existing within wider media that get used for both artistic and nonartistic purposes. An art form typically encompasses a subclass of items in a medium, items made with certain intentions, or which achieve certain aims, which are capable (and possibly worthy) of receiving the attention of critics and audiences and being placed in certain institutional settings. Crucial to making something an *artwork* are the intentions with which it is made and the aims achieved. Crucial to the creation of an *art form* is the existence of institutional settings to organize the availability of such works to interested audiences, to interpret and evaluate them, and so on. Such institutions have developed in the film world. There are settings for the presentation or distribution of films in general: movie theaters, Cineplex, video stores, but there are additional venues that can be used to distinguish a set of films as artworks: film festivals, retrospectives of the work of certain directors, and film series. There is film criticism that exists in a number of forms ranging from five-minute television reviews to academic criticism. As we have noted already, there is film theory that has obvious similarities to literary and art theory. There is by now a canon of great movies, and there is a film avant-garde. All these items are indications that film is an art form.

It might be objected that these indications are insufficient. This is so for two reasons. First, there seems to be similar institutional arrangements for such things as fashion and food, for example, but this does not show that fashion designing or food preparation are art forms. Second, the film institutions I have mentioned do not do a very good job at segregating film artworks from film nonartworks. Just about any film can be grist for film criticism or film theory. Film festivals may try to show films that have artistic aims, but they also have a commercial rationale: to hook films up with distributors. This means that a film's presence at a festival could be a sign of its art status or its commercial potential.

There is no space to discuss the multiple issues raised by the first of these reasons. The second reason makes an important point about film as an art form. With respect to the distinction between the art form and the medium, where the line is to be drawn in the case of film is even more controversial than usual. Most home movies, and various "products" which use the film medium, such as film previews and advertising are presumably neither artworks nor in the art form. Beyond these, there is the large and diverse class of commercial films, and then avant-garde cinema. The latter clearly aspires to be art. The controversial question is how we sort out commercial cinema. Is it all part of the art form? Should we distinguish, within commercial cinema, entertainment from serious films, only the latter qualifying as artworks? Or do none qualify? The best way to explore the film art form is to turn to these questions.

Mass art

One category to which mass market, commercial movies might belong is that of popular art. A distinction between fine art and popular art is long-standing. But the point of the distinction varies among those who use it. For some, popular art is just a kind of art, to be studied alongside others that are put in the fine-art category. For others, to call something popular art is to deny it is really art (henceforth, Art) even if it resembles Art in some respects. On this usage, if it were Art, it would be fine art. This makes some sense because, among the many senses of "art" in English and other languages, it is the "fine-art" sense that is often assumed to be the one defining the subject matter of philosophy of art. However, because of the variable import of the distinction, the status of popular art as Art is perennially somewhat blurry.

Recently, Noël Carroll (1998) has introduced another concept related to popular art but intended to be sharper in its import: mass art. Mass art is Art. That is, it is an appropriate subject for the philosophy of art, for art criticism, art history, etc. It is to be contrasted with various categories of esoteric art, including avant-garde art, and with "middlebrow art" rather than fine art, a term that is absent from Carroll's discussion. What is distinctive of mass art is that it is a type of art produced and distributed by mass technology and is designed to be easily accessible to "the largest number of ... relatively untutored audiences" (1998: 196). Although mass art makes far fewer demands on its audience, its reception and appreciation is continuous with these other species of Art.

Carroll's proposal is attractive for two reasons. First, Carroll is right that there is some sort of continuity between the crassest commercial product such as the movie *Scooby Doo* (2002) and, say, *La Dolce Vita* (1960). Both attempt to fulfill representational, expressive, and other functions traditionally associated with narrative art, by making use of the potentialities of the film medium. Second, accepting the proposal appears to eliminate the need to make what inevitably will be a messy and uncertain distinction between commercial film Art and non-Art. All of it is film Art.

There are also reasons to question the proposal. One issue is whether it picks out mass art in the right way. With respect to cinema, since every work in the medium is made using a "mass technology," the whole burden of this falls to the condition that says that mass art is designed to be accessible to the largest relatively untutored audience. But it's not clear that this is so. Slasher films aim at a much smaller niche audience than blockbuster films like *Spider-man* (2002). It still should count as mass art, and Carroll would agree. He would claim that slasher films are accessible to, but just not enjoyed by, everyone in the *Spider-man* market. What probably is true is that most in that market could follow the narrative (such as it is) of a slasher film. However, with respect to appreciation – being able to say what makes one slasher film better than another – aficionados of the genre can make fine-grained distinctions quite unavailable to the larger public. Carroll's definition needs adjusting to account for the fact that different mass artworks aim at distinct audiences and are often not fully accessible to outsiders. Perhaps the task is not so hard. Mass art aims at a large, if not the largest possible, audience (Novitz 1992).

Finally, even if we accept it, it doesn't actually follow from Carroll's definition that all commercial films are Artworks. For we all know from the definition, *Scooby Doo* is not mass *art*. Remember, it is part of the definition of mass art that it is a type of Art. Since "art" appears on both sides of the definition, it won't help us decide which objects fall under it unless we already know which ones are Art. One might wonder whether there are some films where commercial intentions so overwhelm artistic ones that it is implausible to think of them as mass *art*. They may have a narrative form, but representational, expressive, and other properties of the production are just not guided by an artistic rationale. After all, advertisements can have a narrative form too, but not every commercial with such a form is an artwork. Just when one sort of intention does not merely constrain but overwhelms the other is hard to say, but it evidently sometimes happens. If so, the question that began this section simply gets transformed into the question, Which films are Art (mass, middlebrow, esoteric) and which are non-Art?

Conclusion

We have argued that there are film artworks and a film art form. Skepticism here should be rejected. We have been unable though to fix the boundary of the form. We leave it an open question. Let's conclude by pointing to an approach that may or may not help, but raises a question important in its own right. All film can provide some sort of aesthetic experience (good, bad, indifferent). They can be aesthetically appreciated and evaluated. Whether a film is art or nonart, we will look for many of the same features in seeking out an appreciative experience. We evaluate the fictional world it creates, the way it tells its story, the skillfulness of the camera work, the emotions it elicits, and the questions it raises, the integration of dialogue, visual elements, music, and so on. Is there something distinctive about the aesthetic appreciation of films that are art? Do only they, perhaps, have a style, and does appreciation require viewing the film with an understanding of its style? This is another issue that must be left for resolution on another occasion.

See also Authorship (Chapter 2), Medium (Chapter 16), Realism (Chapter 22), Style (Chapter 25), Rudolph Arnheim (Chapter 27), Sergei Eisenstein (Chapter 35), and Hugo Münsterberg (Chapter 39).

References

Arnheim, R. (1957) *Film as Art*, Berkeley: University of California Press.
Bazin, A. (1967) *What Is Cinema?*, trans. H. Gray, vol. 1, Berkeley: University of California Press.
—— (1997) "The Evolution of the Language of Cinema," trans. Hugh Gray, in P. Lehman (ed.) *Defining Cinema*, New Brunswick, NJ: Rutgers University Press.
Carroll, N. (1988) *Philosophical Problems of Classical Film Theory*, Princeton, NJ: Princeton University Press; New York: Oxford University Press.
—— (1998) *A Philosophy of Mass Art*, Oxford: Clarendon Press.
Davies, S. (1994) "Is Architecture an Art?," in M. Mitias (ed.) *Philosophy and Architecture*, Amsterdam: Editions Rodopi.
Eisenstein, S. (1988) *Selected Works*, ed. and trans. R. Taylor, London: British Film Institute; Bloomington: Indiana University Press.
Gaut, B. (2002) "Cinematic Art," *Journal of Aesthetics and Art Criticism* 60: 299–312.
—— (2003) "Film," in J. Jevinson (ed.) *The Oxford Handbook of Aesthetics*, Oxford and New York: Oxford University Press.
King, W. (1992) "Scruton and the Reasons for Looking at a Photograph," *British Journal of Aesthetics* 32: 258–65.
Münsterberg, H. (1970) *The Film: A Psychological Study*, New York: Dover.
Novitz, D. (1992) "Noël Carroll's Theory of Mass Art," *Philosophic Exchange* 23: 39–50.
Scruton, R. (1983) "Photography and Representation," in *The Aesthetic Understanding*, London and New York: Methuen.
Walton, K. (1984) "Transparent Pictures: On the Nature of Photographic Realism," *Critical Inquiry* 11: 246–77.
Warburton, N. (1988) "Seeing through 'Seeing Through Photographs'," *Ratio* 1: 64–74.

Further reading

Perhaps the most useful work for the project of linking film art and style is David Bordwell, *On the History of Film Style* (Cambridge, MA: Harvard University Press, 1997). Ian Jarvie, *Philosophy of the Film: Epistemology, Ontology, Aesthetics* (New York: Routledge and Kegan Paul, 1987), argues that film is art, and responds to arguments skeptical of this point of view. Another defense of the realist film aesthetic is Siegfried Kracauer, *Theory of Film: The Redemption of Physical Reality* (New York: Oxford University Press, 1960). A. Sesonske, "Aesthetics of Film, or a Funny Thing Happened on the Way to the Movies," *Journal of Aesthetics and Art Criticism* 33 (1974): 51–7, is a seminal philosophical work on the aesthetics of film, as is Francis Sparshott, "Basic Film Aesthetics," in G. Mast, M. Cohen, and L. Braudy (eds.) *Film Theory and Criticism: Introductory Readings*, 4th ed. (New York: Oxford University Press, 1992).

12
FORMALISM
Katherine Thomson-Jones

Film formalism is an unusual kind of formalism, for at least four reasons. The first reason is that, whereas in relation to other art forms – including painting, music, and dance – formalism has been a fairly dominant, mainstream view, in relation to film, formalism is a minority view overshadowed by a strong interpretive tradition. Moreover, it is not a minority view because it has gone largely unnoticed; on the contrary, formalism in its contemporary guise is seen by many film scholars as a threatening force to be vigorously resisted. The second reason film formalism is unusual is that it does not uphold many of the familiar formalist tenets. Most notably, film formalists deny the aesthetic significance of a sharp distinction between form and content, the existence of a distinctly aesthetic response to formal beauty, and the appropriateness of purely "immanent" and ahistorical criticism. The third reason that film formalism is unusual is that it is associated with a constructivist view of meaning, whereas classical formalism, in its commitment to the autonomy of art, would claim that the meaning of a work is determined by its intrinsic formal features. Finally, the fourth reason that film formalism is unusual is that it is derived from literary theory and yet finely attuned to the historical and technical possibilities of the film medium. As we shall see, it is precisely this attunement that explains the unusual features of film formalism. Yet film formalism remains part of a broader formalist tradition insofar as it is, in essence, a program for the structural analysis and appreciation of films as aesthetic objects.

The first formalist approach to film emerged in the 1920s, when the medium was still trying to legitimate itself as an art form. This approach was an attempt made by the Russian formalists to extend their literary poetics to cinema. In this attempt, they influenced the Soviet montage filmmakers, particularly Sergei Eisenstein. Both groups shared an interest in language and the technical construction of films. The influence of Russian formalism in the English-speaking world of film theory is comparatively recent, since the first translation of Russian formalist essays did not appear until 1965 (Lemon and Reis). In the mid- to late-1980s, David Bordwell and Kristin Thompson, frustrated with the established direction of film study, revived the methodology and key concepts of Russian formalism as part of an updated poetics of film. Thompson refers to this approach as "neoformalism," but Bordwell, while acknowledging his and Thompson's shared goals and interests, does not in fact consider himself a neoformalist. Nevertheless, the Russian formalists are arguably the greatest influence on Bordwell's work, and critics of neoformalism regularly take Bordwell as their primary target. For these reasons, I will treat the work of Bordwell and Thompson as belonging to the same broadly formalist tradition.

Neoformalism does not rely on the Russian formalists' own attempt to apply their ideas about literature to film, because the neoformalists are suspicious of the Russian formalists' reliance on an analogy between film and poetic language. Based on a much more extensive knowledge of film history and technique, the neoformalists attempt their own application of Russian formalist literary theory to film. In the process, they draw on other literary and film theorists (including Eisenstein, André Bazin, TzvetanTodorov, Gérard Genette, Noël Burch, the 1966–70 Barthes, and contemporary Israeli poeticians like Meir Sternberg) and add some important corollaries, most notably, a constructivist view of meaning. Bordwell and Thompson continue to practice neoformalist (or formalist-influenced) poetics today, as indicated by the most recent edition of *Film Art* (Bordwell and Thompson 2006), which continues to instruct the student of film, not to "read" the film as a symptomatic text but to analyze it as a complex structure.

Form and content

The defining characteristic of any formalist approach is its theoretical and critical emphasis on form. In relation to film, the neoformalists have a unique understanding of form, which is sensitive to historical context while revealing a methodological commitment to close analysis of the work. Whereas formalism is traditionally understood to uphold a strict distinction between form and content and to deny the aesthetic relevance of content, the neoformalists follow the Russian formalists in simply denying the aesthetic relevance of the distinction itself. They do this because they worry that insisting on the distinction encourages "extrinsic" criticism – assessing the work biographically, sociologically, psychologically, or politically but never on its own terms, *qua* art.

One way that the distinction between form and content is understood is in terms of form being the container for the work's content, which can thus be extracted for independent analysis. Rather than focusing on the conceptual problems with the container account, the neo- and Russian formalists focus on the way that such an account seems to prioritize content in analysis, as though the function of art is to convey a certain content to its audience. To discourage this disjunctive privileging of content, Bordwell and Thompson, in the first edition of *Film Art* (1979), refer to a film as an integrated "system." As we shall see, however, the neo- and Russian formalists ultimately reject the container account because they assign a different function to art. By doing so, Thompson thinks that they have "eliminated the need for the form-content split" (Thompson 1981: 11).

Another way that the distinction between form and content is understood is in terms of content being the work's subject matter and form being the mode of presentation for that subject matter. On this understanding, however, the Russian formalists claim that content is merely raw material for an artistic treatment, which results in a unified structural whole with a distinctly aesthetic function. Consequently, the Russian formalists substitute another distinction for the form/content distinction adopted for film by the neoformalists. This is the distinction between materials and devices.

The reason that the materials/devices distinction is supposed to be different from the form/content distinction is that, unlike content, materials are not alleged to be part of the artwork at all. This is because the same materials can be used to make both art and non-art objects. Whereas the Russian formalists identified words (and sometimes also ideas and emotions) as the materials of literature, Thompson identifies *mise en scène*, sound, camera framing, editing, and optical effects as the five kinds of cinematic material (Thompson 1981: 25–6). Further on, she also identifies as materials meanings or ideas from real life and artistic conventions (Thompson 1981: 51). According to the Russian formalists, words are the common material for both "practical" and poetic discourse, and this is the case even if particular ways of using words – say figuratively or literally, are more commonly associated with one form of discourse than the other. What distinguishes the work of literature, therefore, is not that it contains certain words with certain connotations but that those words are used in a certain way to serve a particular purpose. Similarly, framing, sound, editing, and so on are the common materials for both nonaesthetic films – for example, informational or promotional films – and aesthetic films, including narrative fiction, documentary, and experimental films. What distinguishes the work of film art is not that it exhibits technical features of the medium but that these features are used in a certain way for a certain purpose. Insofar as a device is any medium-specific technique for manipulating, transforming, and structuring materials, the neo- and Russian formalists understand the work of art simply as a set of devices.

The use of the term, "device," reflects the formalists' understanding of artworks as the products of craftsmanship, rather than as the product of inspiration or as vehicles for expression and communication. As Thompson points out, the Russian formalists reliably use a variety of craft metaphors in their analysis of the literary process – for example, metaphors of weaving and sewing. They also conceive of the work as a reassuringly solid and material construction – as seen, for example, with Viktor Shklovsky's description, embraced by the neoformalists, of narrative structure as a staircase. Essentially, the Russian formalists were interested in how a work *works*, both in terms of the technical possibilities and artistic conventions that shape the artists' constructional choices, and in terms of the purpose of all the various components in the work and the work as a whole. As we shall see further ahead, there is also a sense in which, for the neoformalists, a work *works* by working on us, or by achieving certain effects. Thus Bordwell's interest in the way a work cues our comprehension and interpretation is continuous with the neoformalist project, as is a shared interest in the way that the structures of a work can trigger affect. Thompson points out, however, that this interest in affect and structure does not mean that neoformalism posits a distinctly aesthetic emotion.

The Russian formalists assume that every component of a work has a purpose and thus it is a legitimate critical activity to consider the justification – or, in their own terms, the "motivation" – of any and all components of a work. The neoformalists adopt the Russian formalists' taxonomy of three kinds of motivation – compositional, realistic, and artistic – and then add a fourth kind of their own, transtextual motivation. As David Bordwell nicely illustrates, a single component of a film can be motivated in several ways: in answer to the question, Why does Marlene Dietrich sing a cabaret song at just this point in the film?, we could say that her character meets the hero at this point (story relevance), she plays a cabaret singer (realism), and Dietrich often sings these kinds of songs in her films (transtextual reference) (Bordwell 1985: 36). According to Thompson, every component of a film has at least an artistic motivation insofar as it contributes to "the work's abstract, overall shape," but we tend only to notice this motivation when the other kinds of motivation are lacking (Thompson 1988: 19). Given that a work can be broken down into its components in a number of ways, the analyst faces a practical difficulty in knowing where to focus his or her attention. To solve this problem, the Russian formalists introduce the concept of the "dominant," the structural component which organizes all other components and grounds the integrity of the work. To identify the dominant in a work, the analyst must know the overall function of the work. According to the Russian formalists, all art has the same primary function. The neoformalists' attraction to this view explains, in turn, how they conceive of the history of art and the relation between a work and its context.

The history and function of (film) art

The terms introduced by Shklovsky to characterize the function of art have become familiar catchwords for students and scholars of the arts: *ostranenie* is translated as either "defamiliarization" or "making strange"; and *zatrudnenie* is translated as "making difficult." By making its materials strange and more difficult to apprehend through the process of aesthetic transformation, the work of art renews and sharpens perception, breaking down "automatized" recognition and bringing us back to "the sensation of life" – for example, the "stoniness" of the stone (Shklovsky 1965: 11). This does not mean that art only has instrumental value, as a means for exercising our senses. According to Shklovsky, the way that art achieves its perceptual function is just by furnishing a perceptual experience that is fully absorbing and is had for its own sake. This explains how, despite the fact that Thompson explicitly distinguishes the neoformalists' historical conception of form from the narrower conception associated with the "art for art's sake" doctrine (Thompson 1981: 10–11), the traditional formalist idea that art should be created and consumed solely for its aesthetic value is preserved by neoformalism. The historically contingent aspect of defamiliarization is also emphasized by Bordwell, but in this case, such an emphasis may betray the influence of the early Czech structuralist, Jan Mukařovský, who recognized that even strangeness can become automatized within a particular cultural context (Burbank and Steiner 1977).

At first glance, there may appear to be a tension between conceiving of the work as the product of craftsmanship and claiming that the function of art is achieved by defamiliarization. Craftsmanship, after all, involves following technical rules to achieve a predetermined result whereas defamiliarization, as we shall see, is at least partly about challenging artistic conventions. The emphasis on craftsmanship may, however, serve simply to focus attention on the material structure of a work and the use of techniques to achieve defamiliarization. The interesting question, therefore, is how exactly defamiliarization is to be achieved by a work. In Thompson's application of Russian formalism, the options for defamiliarization become richly varied and context dependent. This is due in part to the variety of materials that can be manipulated or "deformed" by the filmmaker. But it is also due to when, where, and by whom a film is watched.

Any film is viewed in a particular context – or as the neo- and Russian formalists say, against a particular "background." The context of a work has several aspects to it, which the neo- and Russian formalists analyze in terms of three kinds of background: artistic conventions, real life, and the nonaesthetic uses of film. It is through our tacit awareness of these backgrounds that we can both make sense of works of art and appreciate the ways in which they achieve defamiliarization. A film like Alain Resnais' *Last Year at Marienbad* (1962) can be appreciated as subversive and challenging against the background of mainstream Hollywood-style cinema. Alternatively, a film like Jean Renoir's *Rules of the Game* (1939) may seem highly realistic against the background of German expressionist and Soviet montage cinema, but highly mannered against the background of Italian neorealism.

It is worth noting that this emphasis on "backgrounds" has prompted a general critique of neoformalism as relatively ahistorical. The argument is that, since history is mere "background" for the neoformalists, they fail to appreciate its active role in determining the range of stylistic options available to a particular filmmaker at a particular time. As Robert Stam explains, the neoformalist ignores "the historicity of forms themselves, i.e., forms as themselves historical events which both refract and shape a multi-faceted history at once artistic and trans-artistic" (Stam 2000: 197–8). This kind of criticism is widespread but rarely supported by close textual analysis. There is, after all, no logical barrier to the neoformalist adopting a more dynamic conception of the relation between form and history.

In addition, the emphasis on backgrounds does not imply that only experimental or highly original films can achieve the function of art. Thompson gives three reasons why any film, however generic or mainstream, can renew perception. The first reason is implied by the contextualization of film viewing. A generic film can be taken out of its familiar context and appreciated anew. This may depend on the critic scrutinizing the work and revealing its complex structures (Thompson 1988: 11), or simply on the temporal or cultural distance of a new audience from the work's generative context. As a result of this switch in backgrounds, the work can no longer be watched with mindless ease; we must pay attention, watching and listening carefully and thereby exercising and extending our perceptual capacities. The second reason why generic films can achieve the function of art is that they have "no immediate practical implications for us" (Thompson 1988: 8–9). It is not entirely clear why the nonpractical nature of film viewing would effect defamiliarization. But perhaps the idea is that since the depicted space in any film is separate from the space we occupy, any film is in some sense strange to our everyday, practical selves. If this is the case, it is noteworthy that art contributes to our lives – through defamiliarization and the renewal of perception – precisely by being removed from our lives.

The third reason why generic films can achieve the function of art is that to the extent that these films purposefully order depicted narrative events or simply have a structure, they activate our perceptual skills differently from unstructured everyday experience. Thompson then goes on to say that those films we consider highly original either defamiliarize reality more strongly, defamiliarize artistic conventions, or defamiliarize both reality and artistic conventions (Thompson 1988: 11). Thus defamiliarization seems to come in degrees, which suggests that works can achieve the function of art to a greater or lesser extent.

Does this mean that the more difficult and strange a work, the better it is? Perhaps not, since Thompson also recognizes that it is important for a critic to aid in the understanding of a work by providing key background information – for example, in the case of Ozu's films shown to a Western audience, background information about marital and familial practices in postwar Japan (Thompson 1988: 22–3). As well, we regularly criticize works for being unintelligible and praise others for their clarity, efficiency, or precision. These considerations suggest the need for clarification as to whether there is a limit to defamiliarization, either in terms of its efficacy for perceptual renewal or in some other terms of appreciation. There are also two further and more general questions about the function of art that the neoformalists leave unanswered: Can the perceptual function of art be achieved by means other than defamiliarization? And, does art really have a single (primary) function? Although these are important questions, the neoformalists may not feel the need to answer them, since they are not defending a theory of art but merely a functional mode of film analysis.

As well as having provocative implications for our understanding of aesthetic appreciation, the notion of defamiliarization has implications for our understanding of the history of art. One view of art history traditionally associated with formalist criticism is that each art form progressively purifies itself until it reveals its own unique essence. The Russian formalists do not hold this view, however. For them, the history of art is a constant overturning of artistic conventions for the sake of defamiliarization. This explains the Russian formalists' fascination with the avant-garde, since on their view the avant-garde is the mechanism of historical change. The neoformalists, however, are as much concerned with established traditions of filmmaking as with ground-breaking work. Nevertheless, they use the notion of defamiliarization to explain the historical contingency of a certain style being considered perspicuous, realistic, expressive, or properly cinematic. This suggests that there is something relative about the function of art, since a work may achieve its perceptual function with some people at a certain time but not with other people at other times, depending on their familiarity with the techniques used by the work. The neoformalists would not shy away from this suggestion, however, as they are deeply interested in the effects of a film, given its structure and context, on the audience. This is all part of their interest in how films work.

It is crucial to consider the effects of a work on an audience because, according to the neoformalist, the aesthetically significant features of a work are projected onto it by the audience in response to the work's devices. As Thompson explains, "all those qualities that are of interest to the analyst – its unity; its repetitions and variations; its representation of action, space, and time; its meanings – result from the interaction between the work's formal structures and the mental operations we perform in response to them" (Thompson 1988: 25–6). This brings us to the corollary that distinguishes neoformalism most sharply from other formalist approaches: a constructivist account of the activity of film viewing, or how viewers, both from a psychological and from a social perspective, comprehend and interpret films. This account is principally developed by David Bordwell in relation to narrative fiction film. According to Bordwell, the viewer constructs the literal meaning of a film through the activity of comprehension, and the more abstract meaning of a film through the activity of interpretation. Bordwell's "narrative science" is regularly criticized by film theorists for ignoring "subjectivity" – specifically, by conceiving of the viewer as a "hypothetical entity," rather than as an embodied, culturally defined individual (see, for example, Nichols 1992). In addition, Bordwell's account can be seen as a case study for the debate among philosophers about the intelligibility of constructivism: how it is that meaning can be given to an artwork which does not already have meaning (see, for example, Stecker 1997).

Neoformalism and constructivism

On Bordwell's account, there are at least four levels of construction in film viewing. First, the viewer must construct everything perceived – the sounds, shapes, and colors of the film, but also the two-dimensional images projected on the screen. Second, the viewer must construct the events and characters that he or she takes the two-dimensional images to represent. Third, the viewer must construct the unified causal history, not entirely shown on screen, of which the depicted events and characters are a part. And fourth, if the viewer is also an interpreter, he or she must construct the more abstract, thematic, or symptomatic meaning of the film as a whole. At every level, the viewer's constructive activity must have a degree of discretion; if the viewer constructs entirely according to the work's plan, he or she cannot be said to be the one making the work's meaning. This suggests that in order to determine whether constructivism is the correct theory of the viewer's activity, we will need to determine whether the discretionary requirement for viewer construction is compatible with the notion that construction is a structural effect of the work. First, however, we need to examine Bordwell's account more closely.

At the most basic level, the very act of perceiving a film is constructive. Bordwell embraces the dominant view in cognitive psychology that perceiving an object does not just require passively receiving visual, aural, or tactile data but also making an inference from the data in order to reach a perceptual judgment. Bordwell refers to such judgments as "hypotheses" to suggest that perception is always open to revision in the face of new data or a new application of relevant background knowledge. Even though our perceiving an object is an instantaneous and automatic process, it still involves the application of concepts in the making of inferences. Interestingly, film depends on our making the wrong inferences as a result of two physiological deficiencies in our visual systems. The raw perceptual data of a film consists in rapidly flashing light and a rapid display of static images, and yet what we see, based on inferences from this data, is a sequence of continuously lit, moving images. It is only because our eyes cannot keep up with the rapidity of changes, both in light intensity and in the image display, that a film is what it is experienced as, namely, a motion picture.

When Bordwell applies the general psychological theory of constructivism to aesthetic experience, he reintroduces the Russian formalists' notion of defamiliari-zation. By delaying, confusing, and complicating the making of perceptual judgments, works of art defamiliarize and thus bring us to a new awareness of the way in which perception is constructive. As Bordwell explains, in the context of aesthetic experience,

> what is nonconscious in everyday mental life becomes consciously attended to. Our schemata get shaped, stretched, and transgressed; a delay in hypothesis-confirmation can be prolonged for its own sake. And like all psychological activities, aesthetic activity has long-range effects. Art may reinforce, or modify, or even assault our normal perceptual-cognitive repertoire. (Bordwell 1985: 32)

Thompson corroborates this attempt to reconcile Russian formalist theory and constructivist psychology by distinguishing those cognitive processes in film viewing that are conscious, as opposed to preconscious or unconscious, and then suggesting that "[i]n a sense, for the neoformalist, the aim of original art is to put any or all of our thought processes onto this conscious level" (Thompson 1988: 27).

For most viewers familiar with the relevant representational, narrative, and cinematic conventions, once they have constructively perceived the two-dimensional images projected on screen, it is just as automatic for them to construct a three-dimensional, fictional world from those images. This is not to say, however, that the second level of construction is straightforward, since the viewer must draw on considerable background knowledge to determine the right configuration of three-dimensional objects captured in what is an inherently ambiguous two-dimensional image and to determine the fictional state of affairs represented by the image. Part of constructing the fictional state of affairs is constructing its spatial and temporal parameters, which extend beyond the image. Thus, for example, when an actor walks out of the frame of the shot, we do not think, without special reason, that her character has ceased to exist; rather we think that the character has moved into part of the fictional world that is not presently shown to us.

Insofar as the viewer is constructing fictional events and characters according to the order of images, he or she is constructing what the Russian formalists, and hence

Bordwell, call the *syuzhet*, or "plot." The *syuzhet* is the narrative just as it is shown on screen – as an incomplete and often out-of-order sequence of events. By filling in missing narrative information and reordering the depicted events into a causal sequence, the viewer then constructs the *fabula*, or "story," from the *syuzhet*.

Once the viewer has figured out what is going on in a film by constructing the *fabula*, he or she may wish to continue generating more abstract thematic and symptomatic meanings for the film. The process by which academic critics do this has, according to Bordwell, become highly regulated such that it is governed by institutional norms. Nevertheless, the interpretive process is constructive just as perception is, namely, by being actively inferential. On Bordwell's analysis, the critic maps concepts, which are structured as "semantic fields," onto those cues in a film that the critical tradition considers effective in viewers' comprehension and capable of bearing meaning. The mapping process is aided by "socially implanted hypotheses about how texts mean," in particular the hypotheses that the text is unified and related to an external world (Bordwell 1989: 133). The mapping process is achieved by the employment of heuristics, standard rules of thumb which have proved useful in generating novel and plausible interpretations. One popular heuristic is the punning heuristic, which involves, for example, taking the depiction of passageways in a film to suggest that the film is about the "passage" of life or certain "rites of passage," or taking the framing of certain shots to indicate that the film is about the "framing" of innocents. Once the critic has settled on and refined her semantic fields, and organized their application to suggest an overall meaning for the film, she must write up her interpretation in a way that is recognized as suitably persuasive by the interpretive institution. Not surprisingly perhaps, Bordwell's analysis of interpretation has been very unpopular among academic critics who do not like to think of themselves as something akin to assembly-line workers in "Interpretation, Inc." However, a deeper criticism of Bordwell's analysis can be found by examining his prior commitment to constructivism.

Although, as Berys Gaut (1995) points out, there may be more than one version of constructivism at work in Bordwell's account, the basic idea is that the film viewer's activities are constructive insofar as they are inferential and involve the application of concepts. Since perception, narrative comprehension, and interpretation are all constructive processes, Bordwell assumes that their objects are constructs. Hence his decisive and oft-repeated statement, "Meanings are not found but made" (Bordwell 1989: 3). Unfortunately, however, Bordwell is making a false assumption here. The fact that perception is an active, inferential process does not mean that the objects of perception – namely, the things we perceive around us – are constructed. After all, one can be a realist about the external world and a constructivist about the mind's activities. Furthermore, a critic who thinks, contra Bordwell, that meanings are not made but found in the text can still allow that the process of finding them is active and inferential.

The same critic can also allow that interpretation is governed by institutional norms, since many forms of detection, including criminal and scientific investigation, occur within institutions and yet retain independent objects of inquiry. Further evidence against interpretive constructivism is suggested by the fact that interpretation is constrained, not by the norms of the interpretive institution, but by the norms of the film and its generative context. A critic who fails to understand how certain techniques were standardly used in a particular filmmaking tradition is likely to misinterpret their significance. If the critic were the one constructing the interpretation, then there would be no possibility of his being wrong about what a film means. And yet critics are regularly shown to be wrong in light of the social and artistic norms governing a certain film.

Interestingly, these are just the kinds of norms to which the Russian formalists are so sensitive. Moreover, as we have seen, Thompson shares the Russian formalists' view that the backgrounds of a work (and not the critic's background) determine its formal significance. This suggests a deep tension between Bordwell's commitment to interpretive constructivism and neoformalism. Perhaps, however, Bordwell is not endorsing interpretive constructivism. Perhaps he is simply describing current interpretive procedure and could readily admit that this procedure often generates false interpretations (see Bordwell 1993). But if this is the case, we have no reason to count constructivism as related to neoformalism.

Without the constructivist corollary, what remains of neoformalism is a structural, technical, phenomenological, and historical mode of film analysis, which can be applied to any kind of film with diverse and highly particularized results. Film scholars have tended to spend most of their time figuring out what films mean. For the neoformalist, however, this is just part of a much broader task of figuring out how films work. Films work according to their formal structure, or how they are put together, but they also work differently in different contexts. The neoformalists' realization of this explains how they can breathe new life into formalism for the sake of redirecting film studies.

See also David Bordwell (Chapter 29), Film as art (Chapter 11), Interpretation (Chapter 15), Medium (Chapter 16), Style (Chapter 25), and Spectatorship (Chapter 23).

References

Bordwell, D. (1985) *Narration in the Fiction Film*, Madison: University of Wisconsin Press.
—— (1989) *Making Meaning: Inference and Rhetoric in the Interpretation of Cinema*, Cambridge, MA: Harvard University Press.
—— (1993) "Film Interpretation Revisited," *Film Criticism* 17: 93–119.
Bordwell, D., and Thompson, K. (1979) *Film Art: An Introduction*, Reading, MA: Addison-Wesley.
—— (2006) *Film Art: An Introduction*, 8th ed., New York: McGraw-Hill.
Burbank, J., and Steiner, P. (eds. and trans.) (1977) *The Word and Verbal Art: Selected Essays by Jan Mukařovský*, New Haven, CT: Yale University Press.
Gaut, B. (1995) "Making Sense of Films: Neoformalism and its Limits," *Forum for Modern Language Studies* 31: 8–23.
Nichols, B. (1992) "Form Wars: The Political Unconscious of Formalist Theory," in J. Gaines (ed.) *Classical Hollywood Narrative: The Paradigm Wars*, Durham, NC: Duke University Press.

Shklovsky, V. (1965) "Art as Technique," in L. T. Lemon and M. J. Reis (trans.) *Russian Formalist Criticism: Four Essays*, Lincoln: University of Nebraska Press.

Stam, R. (2000) *Film Theory: An Introduction*, Malden, MA: Blackwell.

Stecker, R. (1997) "The Constructivist's Dilemma," *Journal of Aesthetics and Art Criticism* 55: 43–52.

Thompson, K. (1981) *Eisenstein's* Ivan the Terrible: *A Neo-Formalist Analysis*, Princeton, NJ: Princeton University Press.

—— (1988) *Breaking the Glass Armor: Neoformalist Film Analysis*, Princeton, NJ: Princeton University Press.

13
GENDER
Angela Curran and Carol Donelan

"Gender" is a term that refers to the behavioral, social and psychological traits typically associated with being male or female. Since the early 1970s, film critics, theorists, and philosophers have taken up the study of gender in film, engaging theories rooted in psychoanalysis, cultural studies, feminist historiography, and cognitivism. Scholars in film studies and philosophy have been particularly interested in thinking about the relation of viewers and films and whether gender is a central factor in understanding this relation. In what follows, we survey various approaches to the study of gender in film, noting points of convergence and divergence between them.

Surveying the terrain of feminist film theory

Image studies

The feminist study of gender in film was launched in the early 1970s, with publications such as Marjorie Rosen's *Popcorn Venus* and Molly Haskell's *From Reverence to Rape* (Rosen 1973; Haskell 1974). These works chronicled the changing image of women in Hollywood and European art film, highlighting how the female characters related to the history of each era, how they were stereotyped – virgin or sex goddess – how active or passive they were, how much screen time they were allotted, and whether they served as positive or negative models for women in the audience. While acknowledged as groundbreaking, "image studies" such as these were also criticized as theoretically unsophisticated. Rosen and Haskell were accused of naïvely assuming that film mirrored or reflected reality without taking into account how film representations are constructed through the conventions of narrative, genre, camerawork, editing, lighting, and so on.

Influenced by a heightened political awareness brought on by worker and student revolts in France in 1968, and drawing on theories of structuralism and Marxism, critics associated with influential film journals such as *Les Cahiers du cinéma* in France and *Screen* in Britain, in particular, argued that mainstream film, like language and the bourgeois family, shaped the consciousness and beliefs of individuals. These complex theories suggested a more comprehensive analysis of how film works to support gender hierarchies. Feminist film critics drew on these analyses to provide a deeper account of how the formal conventions of film position viewers to accept the values of patriarchal society.

Mulvey on visual pleasure and the classical Hollywood cinema

One of the most influential essays to emerge out of this discussion was Laura Mulvey's "Visual Pleasure and Narrative Cinema," first published in 1975 (Mulvey 2004). In this essay, Mulvey advances a theory of gendered representation and the "masculini-zation" of spectatorship in the classical Hollywood cinema. Her theory was informed by the ideas of Marxist philosopher Louis Althusser and psychoanalysts Sigmund Freud and Jacques Lacan.

Althusser argued that ideology, which asserts itself through cultural and social institutions and practices, "hails" or "interpellates" us. Individuals do not exist prior to or apart from systems of ideology – they are produced as effects of it. Mulvey adapted Althusser's ideas to argue that the formal conventions of classic Hollywood cinema position the viewer to accept the patriarchal ideology articulated by films.

Mulvey also adopted the psychoanalytic theories of Freud and Lacan to argue that the classical Hollywood film is structured according to the logic of the "patriarchal unconscious" and privileges male desire. Men look and women are looked at. The central male protagonist advances the plot through his gaze and actions. The male spectator engages in a narcissistic identification with the male hero, a process that repeats the discovery of an image of oneself in the "mirror phase" postulated by Lacan. The female character is presented as a passive erotic object for the visual pleasure of both the male hero and spectator.

Gazing upon the female form – or "scopophilia," to borrow Freud's term – is posited in Hollywood films as pleasurable, but in psychoanalytic theory the sight of the female form for the male is also a potential source of displeasure. The female body represents sexual difference and provokes castration anxiety in the male unconscious. Mulvey argues that Hollywood narratives are thus structured to displace or mask the threat posed by sexual difference as exemplified in the female body, either by subjecting that body to voyeuristic punishment (Scottie's interrogation of Madeleine in Hitchcock's *Vertigo* [1958]) or fetishistic idealization (the stylization of Marlene Dietrich in Sternberg's films).

Mulvey ultimately calls for the "destruction of pleasure" associated with the realism of the classical Hollywood cinema. The aesthetic of realism is "illusionistic," performing the work of ideology in "interpellating" subjects to freely accept their subjectivity and subjection. Mulvey calls on feminists to create an alternative, antire-alist cinema that does not demean women.

Feminist film theory post-Mulvey

Critical responses to Mulvey's theory set the agenda for feminist film theory throughout the 1980s. Responses to Mulvey grappled with three problems with her theory. First, central to Mulvey's theory is her claim that the spectator is constructed as an effect of the text. This did not explain how it was possible for actual viewers to engage critically with a film and question its ideological viewpoint, something that feminist film critics clearly did in their responses to mainstream cinema. Second, Mulvey argues that it was not possible for viewers to take pleasure in the narrative structures of classic Hollywood cinema without participating in the gender hierarchies of patriarchy. Feminists argued that Mulvey's theory of the pleasure of Hollywood films was too general and did not account for the way that certain mainstream movies may subvert rather than support social structures of power. Third, in arguing that narrative Hollywood cinema constructs a normative male viewer, Mulvey's theory was universalizing and exclusionary. She did not account for how viewers who are excluded from the male norm of spectatorship respond to mainstream cinema. In attempting to analyze how Hollywood film functions as a tool of patriarchy, Mulvey's theory seemed to support the system of gender inequalities that she hoped to dismantle with her analysis.

Some feminist theorists attempted to modify some aspect of the psychoanalytic framework in order to address these problems. As we will see, a challenge for this line of reply is how to accept Mulvey's central claim – that mainstream cinema constructs the spectator as an effect of the text – yet still account for a range of responses that actual viewers can have to these films. Other responses to Mulvey came from cultural studies, critical race theory, and queer studies. These analyses argued that the relationship between a viewer and a text must be reconfigured if we are to address the problems with Mulvey's theory. In the following sections, we examine these responses to Mulvey's theory and analyze their success in proposing alternative accounts of the relationship between film, gender, and the viewer.

Psychoanalytic accounts of spectatorship

In an afterword to her "Visual Pleasure" essay, Mulvey proposed that the "woman in the audience" could either identify with the passive woman on screen or engage in "trans-sex" identification with the active male hero, neither of which seemed satisfactory as an explanation of women's cinematic pleasure (Mulvey 1989). Mary Anne Doane argued that certain genres, such as the "woman's film," posit a female spectator (Doane 1987a, b). The pleasurable tears of the woman seated in the audience signal her complicity with the film's organization of vision and desire. At the same time, Doane wants to argue that the feminist viewer, at least, is capable of a "critical moment" in which she steps back and questions the representation of gender in the film (Doane 2000).

Other critics working within a psychoanalytic framework challenged Mulvey's insistence that men cannot be the object of the "gaze." Steve Neale maintained that the homoeroticism implicit in the male gaze directed at the male body is repressed and disavowed, manifesting in the symptomatic violence accompanying so many representations of the male body in the Hollywood cinema (Neale 1993). In her analysis of the films of Rudolf Valentino, Miriam Hansen revealed how the star's persona oscillates between active and passive, sadism and masochism, opening up possibilities for alternative conceptions of visual pleasure while also posing a challenge to the myth of masculinity in American culture (Hansen 2004). More recent accounts by scholars such as David Gerstner and Peter Lehman examine and critique the way films characterize and enforce ideologies of masculinity (Gerstner 2006; Lehman 2007).

Some feminist critics argued that the positioning of the film viewer by the classical Hollywood film is not as monolithic as Mulvey supposed. Drawing upon the psychoanalytic theories of Nancy Chodorow, Linda Williams argued that female identity is formed through a process of double identification, first with her mother, her primary love object, and then also with her father (Williams 1990). A woman's film such as *Stella Dallas* (1937) mobilizes the female spectator's ability to take up multiple identifications, prompting her to empathize with a variety of conflicting points of view. The female viewer of *Stella Dallas* is not locked into accepting the viewpoint of a single character; she can use the viewpoint of one character to criticize that of another. Elizabeth Cowie turned to Freud's analysis of fantasy arguing, contra Mulvey, that identification is not determined according to gender and that films such as *Now, Voyager* (1942) and *Reckless Moment* (1949) offer multiple points of identification – father, mother, child, lover, wife, or husband – for the viewing subject (Cowie 1997).

Assessing psychoanalytic accounts

Throughout the 1980s, feminist film theorists used psychoanalytic theories to address a central problem in Mulvey's theory: her failure to account for the pleasures female spectators take in mainstream Hollywood film. At the same time, critical race theorists such as Jane Gaines and bell hooks argued that psychoanalytic feminist film theory had lost touch with the actual viewers' lived experience of film (Gaines 1990; hooks 2000). Psychoanalytic accounts primarily focused on the spectator "implied" by the film and did not consider the impact of race, ethnicity, and sexual orientation in an actual viewer's experience of film. Critics charged that in theorizing about an ahistorical, abstracted "female spectator," psychoanalytic accounts ironically helped perpetuate the same social arrangements of power that their analyses attempted to dismantle.

This neglect of the actual viewer's response to film has roots in the theoretical commitments of most psychoanalytic feminist film theories. Following Althusser, Mulvey posits that film assumes or "interpellates" a male spectator, producing him as an effect of the film. Feminist film theorists have challenged this account on multiple levels, but without critiquing the assumption that the viewing subject is an effect of representation and is caught up "within the language of patriarchy" (Mulvey 2004: 838). Indeed, as Jennifer Hammett argues, if women are "constituted as subjects by patriarchal representations," they "do not have the epistemic resources necessary to escape patriarchy" (Hammett 1997: 245). They are not able to adopt the critical standpoints identified by Doane and Williams.

In her analysis of *Stella Dallas* Williams seems to want to concede the point that Ann Kaplan makes in her reply to Williams' account: that as viewing subjects, women viewers are constituted as subjects within the discourses of representation, including those of film (Kaplan 1985). But she appeals to Chodorow to argue that patriarchy constructs women differently than men, as "fragmented" viewers who have a more complex and contradictory stance toward the world. It is not clear, however, how women viewers can develop a critical response to the representations they see on screen if Williams concedes the underlying assumption – made by Mulvey, Doane, Kaplan, and other psychoanalytic accounts – that the viewer is a product or construct of patriarchal "discourse."

Cultural studies, critical race theory, queer theory

Dissatisfaction with the psychoanalytic account of an ahistorical and abstracted spectator prompted feminist and other film theorists to turn to cultural studies in the late 1980s and 1990s. Central to cultural studies is the idea that cultural institutions, such as cinema, and cultural practices, such as textual interpretation, are sites of political struggle. Drawing on the work of Stuart Hall, among others, critics argued that meaning is not inherent in the film text but is produced in the interaction with viewers. Viewers are themselves constituted as subjects within a complex system of "discourses" circulating in society, including the representations in the film. Rejecting the ideas of Althusser in favor of those of the Italian Marxist Antonio Gramsci, critics argued that viewers are capable of resisting the dominant ideology presented in mainstream films. This is not so much because the viewer is a "free agent" who is not influenced by cultural and social forces, but for the reason that systems of representation like popular Hollywood films are not homogeneous in their meaning but are capable of multiple interpretations. An attentive viewer can "negotiate" with the film text and "read against the grain" to bring out strands or places in the film where the dominant viewpoints break down. Manthia Diawara, for example, developed a theory of black male "resisting" spectatorship, based on his own experience as a black man watching mainstream films (Diawara 2004). bell hooks made a case for the black female spectator's "oppositional" gaze as a basis for critical analysis and active resistance against racist representations in film (hooks 2000). Alexander Doty identified queerness as a viewing or reception position that could be taken up by queers and nonqueers alike in relation to homophobic texts (Doty 1993).

Criticisms informed by cultural studies, critical race, and queer theory were attempts to direct feminist film theorists to take account of viewing experiences excluded from Mulvey's analysis. In pointing to the wide range of response available to viewers of mainstream films, cultural studies theorists argue that a film can subvert gender norms if the viewer "negotiates" with the text in the right way. But not all films challenge social arrangements of power or do this in the same way. Feminists should be interested in analyzing which films and formal structures support social arrangements of power and which do not. The philosophers we examine in the third section of the paper argue that another analysis of the relationship between the viewer and a film is needed. Such an account would be able to show how formal features in a film can cue viewers to adopt an ideology implicit in the film, but also explain how a viewer is capable of an active, critical response to such a film.

The advent of feminist historiography

A "historical turn" in film studies in the 1990s prompted a new generation of feminist film scholars to investigate the historically specific relationships between viewers and films. The availability of digitized historical materials, especially those related to the era preceding the classical Hollywood cinema, have prompted feminist film scholars to rethink their assumptions about early cinema and women's participation in it (Rabinovitz 1998; Stamp 2000; Bean and Negra 2002). This work has also investigated the foundational position that women had in all roles in the beginning of the film industry, challenging conventional film histories.

While feminist historiography breaks with the psychoanalytic account of an abstracted spectator it also continues to be "catalyzed by questions of spectatorship, ideological coding, and cultural interpolations that persist from earlier conversations" (Bean and Negra 2002: 4). Film philosophers argue that a more direct examination of the basic theoretical assumptions of psychoanalysis, as well as of cultural studies, is needed in order to open up the analysis of gender and film to new directions of study. In the final section of the paper, we examine these criticisms as well as some other ideas of philosophers who have analyzed the topic of gender and film.

Philosophical approaches

As film studies came of age in the 1980s, philosophers and allies in film studies called "cognitivists" began to engage critically with the view that films mobilize unconscious processes in the viewer. Philosophers Thomas Wartenberg, Michael Ryan, and Douglas Kellner also interrogated the dominant view in film studies that the formal conventions of classic Hollywood films perpetuate social arrangements of power (Kellner and Ryan 1988; Wartenberg 1999). Although his analysis was not explicitly focused on gender, Stanley Cavell examined certain screwball comedies and women's melodramas from the 1930s and 1940s (Cavell 1981, 1996). His argument – that these films represent women in the pursuit of their desires – challenged Mulvey-influenced accounts that the conventions of classic Hollywood films do not allow for the representation of female desire (Scheman 1995). In this section we examine several of the salient criticisms and issues that have emerged out of these discussions.

Link of filmic conventions with ideology

Mulvey argued that the "gaze" of the camera in classic Hollywood film commonly aligns with the "look" of the central male protagonist so that the viewer adopts the desires of this character. The male characters in Hollywood film desire the woman as a passive recipient of male desire, making the viewer participate in the structures of patriarchy encoded in the film narrative.

Mulvey's argument about the gaze could be interpreted in two ways: that the male gaze is inherent to the formal structures of Hollywood film or that there is a historical *use* of these structures to position women as passive objects of male desire. The latter seems to be a more plausible construal of her argument. Mulvey seems to conclude that it is not possible to separate the historical use of Hollywood filmic conventions from the intrinsic features of film as an artistic medium.

Mulvey argues that feminist filmmakers must develop an avant-garde cinema that eschews narrative realism, emotional engagement with central protagonists, and so on. But it is not clear why the formal conventions of Hollywood cinema might not be able to prompt a pleasure in viewers that is not based in structures of domination. Noël Carroll has argued this in a discussion of women characters from Hollywood screwball comedies such as *Bringing Up Baby* (1938) and *His Girl Friday* (1940), as has Kathleen Rowe in her analysis of the "unruly woman" of the genres of comedy (Carroll 1995; Rowe 1995). Berys Gaut proposes that the sexism prevalent in mainstream film is explained by the "sexism of the surrounding society, the scarcity of women directors, [and] the almost total absence of female producers and financiers," not by "the structure of narrative, 'illusionistic' film *per se*" (Gaut 1994).

Gender and the viewer's emotional response to film

Some feminist philosophers of art have argued that Mulvey's account is useful because she exposes the way in which a dominant art is not epistemologically neutral but represents the social vantage point of the dominant (masculine) social class (Hein 1995). But others have been highly critical of Mulvey-influenced feminist film theorizing. Cynthia Freeland criticizes feminist film theorists' use of psychoanalysis (Freeland 1998; see also Shrage 1993). Like Noël Carroll, she argues that feminists interested in analyzing films' relation to a patriarchal society have appealed to psychoanalysis without arguing that this is superior to other theoretical frameworks (Carroll 1995). She also thinks an alternative is needed that enables us to understand how viewers are capable of active, critical responses to the ideological viewpoints in film.

Freeland proposes that new work being done in the philosophy of film can offer new, nonpsychoanalytic explanations for the pleasures of mainstream film. This work is grounded in the methodology of cognitivism, a dominant thread in the philosophy of film over the last fifteen years or so. Cognitivists propose to use current studies of perception and cognitive science to understand how films engage cognitive processes such as inference making, hypothesis testing, and perceptual and information processing. They hold, for the most part, that these theories offer a much better explanation of the way actual viewers engage and find pleasure in films than the theories offered by psychoanalysis. Cognitivists tend to argue that emotions are "cognitive appraisals" of situations and as such they need not be irrational; rather they are cognitive processes that we use to make sense of our everyday encounters with the world. We use these same cognitive processes in our response to film (Plantinga and Smith 1999).

Cognitivists have drawn on analyses of emotional response to explain some of the same issues with which psychoanalytic feminist film theorists engage. In an updated version of the "image studies" approach Noël Carroll has argued that emotions are forms of multifaceted behavior acquired from "paradigm scenarios" and that movies can be a source of these scenarios (Carroll 1995). From *Fatal Attraction*, for example, a male viewer might learn that the "scenario" for the appropriate emotional response to an ex-lover's demand for fair treatment is to distance her as irrational and not deserving of his attention. In her analysis of gender and the genre of the horror film, Freeland argues that horror films prompt the emotions of fear, sympathy, dread, anxiety, and disgust and in doing so provoke reflection about patriarchy and its institutions as well as the nature of evil (Freeland 2000). Looking at the subgenre of melodrama known as the woman's film, Flo Leibowitz analyzes how the response of pity and admiration that male and female viewers feel toward the characters can be part of a coherent assessment of the women protagonists' values and priorities (Leibowitz 1996).

These analyses are useful for several reasons. First, they point to an area that has for the most part been overlooked by feminist film theorists: the way that films mobilize emotions other than pleasure or desire (Plantinga and Smith 1999). Feminist film theorists have tended to think that all emotional engagement with characters in film must implicate viewers in submitting to structures of domination (as with Doane's analysis of women's melodrama). But emotional engagement with characters in film need not make us acquiesce to a questionable system of social arrangements. When emotions are engaged as part of a critical reflection on a movie's characters and their predicaments, they can lead to a rational reassessment of such an ideology (Curran 2005). Second, cultural studies theorists attempt to account for critical viewing, but they often neglect how the formal features of a film can prompt a viewer's critical engagement with what she or he sees on screen. A cognitive model of our engagement with film promises to help us understand how the formal features of film can either prompt viewers to accept the ideology implicit in the film or encourage the viewer to engage in a critical response to the characters and their situations. Future work on these issues of emotional engagement and critical viewing promises to open up discussions on several important but neglected aspects of feminist film theorizing.

Conclusion

There are no doubt sharp points of difference between feminist historiography and film philosophy. Most notably, there is a dominant trend in film philosophy that rejects the use of psychoanalysis as an overly general "grand theory (Bordwell and Carroll 1996)." On the other hand, arguably there is agreement between feminist historiographers and cognitivists that it is best to eschew generalizations about abstracted spectators and focus on theorizing that is more local and applicable to specific contexts of film viewing.

A charge often made in film studies is that cognitive theorists are, in effect, hoisted by their own petard. Cognitivists criticize the psychoanalytic accounts of abstracted "spectators" that bear little relation to active, cognizing viewers, but they also invoke the raceless, classless, and genderless "schemas" of an ahistorical mind as they theorize about viewer's engagement with film (Stam 2000: 241). It might then seem that cognitivist approaches to gender and film are at odds with feminist historiographers' emphasis on more historically and socially situated methods of investigation.

Coming from two different disciplinary perspectives, philosophy and film studies, we think there is much we can learn from one another. Cognitivists might take into consideration the emphasis in feminist historiography on a socially and culturally specific viewer. Feminist historiographers might study cognitivism to learn how recent theories of the mind and cognition can open up new avenues of investigation as we continue to explore the complex relationships between film, the viewer, and social arrangements of power.

See also Empathy and character engagement (Chapter 9), Psychoanalysis (Chapter 41), Race (Chapter 21), Stanley Cavell (Chapter 32), Spectatorship (Chapter 23), and Pornography (Chapter 47).

References

Bean, J. N., and Negra, D. (eds.) (2002) *A Feminist Reader in Early Cinema*, Durham, NC: Duke University Press.

Bordwell, D., and Carroll, N. (eds.) (1996) *Post Theory: Reconstructing Film Studies*, Madison: University of Wisconsin Press.

Carroll, N. (1995) "The Image of Women in Film: A Defense of a Paradigm," in P. Brand and C. Korsmeyer (eds.) *Feminism and Tradition in Aesthetics*, University Park, PA: Pennsylvania State University Press.

Cavell, S. (1981) *The Pursuits of Happiness: The Hollywood Comedy of Remarriage*, Cambridge, MA: Harvard University Press.

—— (1996) *Contesting Tears: The Hollywood Comedy of Remarriage*, Chicago: University of Chicago Press.

Cowie, E. (1997) *Representing the Woman: Cinema and Psychoanalysis*, Minneapolis: University of Minnesota Press.

Curran, A. (2005) "Stella at the Movies: Class Critical Spectatorship and Melodrama in *Stella Dallas*," in T. Wartenberg and A. Curran (eds.) *The Philosophy of Film: Introductory Text and Readings*, Malden, MA: Blackwell.

Diawara, M. (2004) "Black Spectatorship: Problems of Identification and Resistance," in L. Braudy and M. Cohen (eds.) *Film Theory and Criticism*, 6th ed., New York: Oxford University Press.

Doane, M. A. (1987a) "The Woman's Film: Possession and Address," in C. Gledhill (ed.) *Home Is Where the Heart Is: Studies in Melodrama and the Woman's Film*, London: British Film Institute.

—— (1987b) *The Desire to Desire: The Woman's Film of the 1940s*, Bloomington: Indiana University Press.

—— (2000) "Film and the Masquerade: Theorizing the Female Spectator," in R. Stam and T. Miller (eds.) *Film and Theory: An Anthology*, Malden, MA: Blackwell.

Doty, A. (1993) *Making Things Perfectly Queer: Interpreting Mass Culture*, Minneapolis: University of Minnesota Press.

Freeland, C. (1998) "Feminist Film Theory," in M. Kelly (ed.) *The Encyclopedia of Aesthetics*, New York: Oxford University Press.

—— (2000) *The Naked and the Undead: Evil and the Appeal of Horror*, Boulder, CO: Westview Press.

Gaines, J. (1990) "White Privilege and Looking Relations: Race and Gender in Feminist Film Theory," in P. Erens (ed.) *Issues in Feminist Film Criticism*, Bloomington: Indiana University Press.

Gaut, B. (1994) "On Cinema and Perversion," *Film and Philosophy* 1: 3–17.

Gerstner, D. (2006) *Manly Arts: Masculinity and Nation in Early American Cinema*, Durham, NC: Duke University Press.

Hammett, J. (1997) "The Ideological Impediment: Epistemology, Feminism and Film Theory," in R. Allen and M. Smith (eds.) *Film Theory and Philosophy*, Oxford: Clarendon; and New York: Oxford University Press.

Hansen, M. (2004) "Pleasure, Ambivalence, Identification: Valentino and Female Spectatorship," in L. Braudy and M. Cohen (eds.) *Film Theory and Criticism*, 6th ed., New York: Oxford University Press.

Haskell, M. (1974) *From Reverence to Rape: The Treatment of Women in the Movies*, New York: Holt, Rinehart, and Winston.

Hein, H. (1995) "The Role of Feminist Aesthetics in Feminist Theory," in P. Brand and C. Korsmeyer (eds.) *Feminism and Tradition in Aesthetics*, University Park, PA: Pennsylvania State University Press.

hooks, b. (2000) "The Oppositional Gaze: Black Female Spectators," in R. Stam and T. Miller (eds.) *Film and Theory: An Anthology*, Malden, MA: Blackwell.

Kaplan, A. (1985) "Dialogue: E. Ann Kaplan Replies to Linda Williams' 'Something Else besides a Mother': *Stella Dallas* and the Maternal Melodrama," *Cinema Journal* 24: 40–3.

Kellner, D., and Ryan, M. (eds.) (1988) *Camera Politica: The Politics and Ideology of Contemporary Hollywood Film*, Bloomington: Indiana University Press.

Lehman, P. (2007) *Running Scared: Masculinity and the Representation of the Male Body*, new ed., Detroit: Wayne State University Press.

Leibowitz, F. (1996) "Apt Feelings or Why 'Women's Films' Aren't Trivial," in D. Bordwell and N. Carroll (eds.) *Post-Theory: Reconstructing Film Studies*, Madison: University of Wisconsin Press.

Mulvey, L. (1989 [1981]) "Afterthoughts on 'Visual Pleasure and Narrative Cinema' inspired by King Vidor's Duel in the Sun," in *Visual and Other Pleasures*, Bloomington: Indiana University Press.

—— (2004) "Visual Pleasure and Narrative Cinema," in L. Braudy and M. Cohen (eds.) *Film Theory and Criticism*, 6th ed., New York: Oxford University Press.

Neale, S. (1993) "Masculinity as Spectacle: Reflections on Men and Mainstream Cinema," in S. Cohan and I. R. Hark (eds.) *Screening the Male: Exploring Masculinities in Hollywood Cinema*, London and New York: Routledge.

Plantinga, C., and Smith, G. M. (eds.) (1999) *Passionate Views: Film, Cognition, and Emotion*, Baltimore, MD: Johns Hopkins University Press.

Rabinovitz, L. (1998) *For the Love of Pleasure: Women, Movies, and Culture in Turn-of-the-Century Chicago*, New Brunswick, NJ: Rutgers University Press.

Rosen, M. (1973) *Popcorn Venus: Women, Movies and the American Dream*, New York: Coward, McCann, and Geoghegan.

Rowe, K. (1995) *The Unruly Woman: Gender and the Genre of Laughter*, Austin: University of Texas Press.

Scheman, N. (1995) "Missing Mothers and Desiring Daughters: Framing the Sight of Women," in C. Freeland and T. Wartenberg (eds.) *Philosophy and Film*, New York: Routledge.

Shrage, L. (1993) "Feminist Film Aesthetics: A Contextual Approach," in H. Hein and C. Korsmeyer (eds.) *Aesthetics in Feminist Perspective*, Bloomington: Indiana University Press.

Stam, R. (2000) *Film Theory: An Introduction*, Malden, MA: Blackwell.

Stamp, S. (2000) *Movie-Struck Girls: Women and Motion Picture Culture after the Nickelodeon*, Princeton, NJ: Princeton University Press.

Wartenberg, T. (1999) *Unlikely Couples: Movie Romance as Social Criticism*, Boulder, CO: Westview Press.

Williams, L. (1990) "'Something Else besides a Mother': *Stella Dallas* and the Maternal Melodrama," in P. Erens (ed.) *Issues in Feminist Film Criticism*, Bloomington: Indiana University Press.

14
GENRE
Brian Laetz and Dominic McIver Lopes

Genres like film noir, fantasy, and action are readily and reliably used by movie audiences and film scholars. Renting a DVD means navigating the genres, and genres belong in the tool kit of many film scholars. Genre criticism is a major mode of film studies, and it has spawned a rich literature that touches on theoretical questions of what movie genres are, how they function, and how they should best be studied (e.g., Grant 2003; see also Duff 2000). But although philosophers have written about specific movie genres like horror (Carroll 1990) and melodrama (Cavell 1996), they have paid little attention to the nature of film genre – or indeed of any art genre (the exception is Currie 2004). It is time to attempt a philosophy of movie genres that takes advantage of and potentially enriches related work in film studies.

Toward a philosophy of movie genre

The first step is to get a fix on what a philosophy of genre is intended to explain. That means understanding roughly how genre categories function, because a rough idea of the work that genre does in our thinking about movies can guide us as we work toward a philosophy of genre that explains genre as doing the job it does (see also Tudor 2003). Two tasks are obvious: genres help with interpretation and with appreciation. Movie audiences deploy genre concepts as they interpret and appreciate, and filmmakers also work with an eye to genre as long as they aim to make movies to be interpreted and appreciated.

Film scholars have documented in some detail how specific genres set audience expectations and thereby drive interpretation (e.g., Altman 2003; Sobchack 2003; and Neale 2003). A useful way to represent these expectations builds on David Lewis' (1978) account of truth in fiction, especially as it was developed by Kendall Walton (1990). Parts of the story a movie tells are not normally told explicitly, but are implied instead. When it shows her using a telephone, *Dial M for Murder* (1954) implies that Margot is speaking to someone. The implication is sustained by a

> Reality principle: a story represents that q if it explicitly represents that $p_1 \dots p_n$ and it would be the case that q, were it the case that $p_1 \dots p_n$.

In reality, people using telephones are talking to someone, so Margot is talking to someone. What a movie explicitly represents may join with a fact about reality to fill in the story. Not always, though. In some of her movies, Katharine Hepburn plays an independent woman and it is implied that her prospects of marriage are poor. (Exploiting this implication, the movies get the audience to worry for her.) Of course, in reality, independent women do not have poor marriage prospects. Another principle generates the needed implication:

> Mutual-belief principle: a story represents that q if it explicitly represents that $p_1 \ldots p_n$ and it is mutually believed among members of the story's original target audience that it would be the case that q, were it the case that $p_1 \ldots p_n$.

For much of the last century it was mutually believed by American movie viewers that an independent woman would probably not marry. This belief of the target audience joins with what the movies represent explicitly to imply that Hepburn's characters face a poor chance of marriage.

However, a third principle is also needed, and it brings in genre. Imagine a movie, *Dragon Story*, which represents a dragon, Snuffles, who is rather timid and never works up much anger. Snuffles breathes fire, although he is never explicitly shown engaged in this activity. What warrants the implication that he breathes fire? Not the reality principle, since it is not true in reality that a creature would breathe fire were it a large, flying serpent. Not the mutual-belief principle either, because movie audiences do not believe that a creature would breathe fire were it a large, flying serpent. What audiences do know is that the movie belongs to the fantasy genre and in this genre dragons breathe fire (see McArthur 1972: 23, for a detailed example). The third principle could be put roughly like this:

> Genre principle: a story belonging to genre K represents that q if it explicitly represents that $p_1 \ldots p_n$ and it is a feature of K that it would be the case that q, were it the case that $p_1 \ldots p_n$.

This formulation leaves it open what the feature in question is. Many film scholars follow Robert Warshow's (1962) view that the feature in question is a convention or a formula, though other views are available (e.g., Neale 2003). Any formulation must explain how we can miss the story a movie tells when we get its genre wrong. Put another way, the genre principle explains how a movie can be interpreted as telling different stories when it is viewed in different genres.

Genres also figure in movie appreciation. Part of appreciating a movie is attributing aesthetic properties to it. Walton (1970) showed in a famous thought experiment that attributions of aesthetic properties are category relative, and his argument can be adapted to genres. F. W. Murnau's *Nosferatu* (1922) is a classic horror movie. Imagine a genre – call it the "nosferatu" genre – which is made up of movies each edited together from the same shots as *Nosferatu*. By definition, *Nosferatu* is a nosferatu, but the aesthetic properties we attribute to *Nosferatu* depend on whether we view it as horror or as a nosferatu. Viewed as horror, it is provocatively, deliciously creepy. Viewed as a nosferatu, it is tediously linear and predictable.

So the aesthetic properties we attribute to any movie depend on the genre to which we assign it. Viewed as a buddy/road movie, *Thelma & Louise* (1991) is moving, though it stagnates when viewed as an action movie. As Walton points out, this means that we can rarely get a movie's aesthetic properties wrong. *West Side Story* (1961) is hilarious: true or false? True unless it is viewed as a musical, in which it is conventional for characters to burst into song. Otherwise, it might come across as silly that characters sing and dance in public. So we cannot be wrong in saying that *West Side Story* is hilarious – only in saying that it is hilarious *when viewed as a musical*. Walton solves this problem by identifying the aesthetic properties a work actually has with those it has when viewed in the correct genre. Thus appreciating a movie involves honing in on its genre and seeing what aesthetic properties it has in that genre.

Genre is not merely a cataloging scheme. It is a cataloging scheme that performs some useful tasks: recognizing a movie's genre helps the audience to fill in its story and it provides a background against which to view its aesthetic properties. In constructing a philosophy of genre, we are not in the difficult position of having to model inchoate, possibly irreconcilable intuitions generated from the folk concept of genre. A good philosophy of genre will explain the work that genre does in interpretation and appreciation.

Like a philosophy of art more generally, a philosophy of genre features three main elements: a theory, an ontology, and a value theory.

Theory: which categories are movie genres?

Some movies are animations based on computer-generated imagery (CGI), some are realistic, some are film noir, some are released in 1982, and some are Toho Company productions. Each of these categories belongs to a different metacategory. One metacategory is the art forms, whose subcategories are motion pictures, literary fiction, music, and the like. Another is art media like film, video, language, pastel, the chromatic scale. Going more fine grained, we get oeuvres like those of Eastwood and Fellini. Film and some other arts have traditions such as Hollywood and Bollywood; and some arts have styles like realism or postmodern mannerism. Standing apart from all of these is the metacategory of genre, which includes film noir, epic, satire, and many other genres. So, then, which categories belong to the metacategory of genres? Why is film noir a genre and the Toho backlist not? Why is satire a genre but not video? An answer to these questions is a theory of movie genre, which completes the schema:

Category *K* is a movie genre if and only if ...

A completion that gives individually necessary and jointly sufficient conditions is a definition. Anything else is a nondefinitional theory of movie genre.

A theory of movie genre is not the same as theories of the individual movie genres. What makes a movie a satire? A musical? A gangster movie? Answers to these and similar questions complete the following schema:

Movie x belongs to movie genre K if and only if …

As we will see below, theories of the movie genres must be worked out one at a time. A theory of movie genre does not deliver up a readymade theory of each individual genre.

An example of a nondefinitional theory of movie genre is a disjunctive theory, which states that something is a movie genre if and only if it is horror or suspense or romance or action, etc. This theory is a last resort, since it simply lists categories that are genres and refuses to say what makes them genres. This problem is especially serious if the list includes uninstantiated genres. No detective movies are set in ancient Egypt, but is the category of detective movies set in ancient Egypt a genre? If the answer is "yes" then the genre goes on the list. No detective movies feature murders in Iceland on a Tuesday, but is this category also a genre? If not, why not? It is hardly satisfying to be told nothing about why one category makes it onto the list of genres and the other does not. Perhaps, in the end, a disjunctive theory is the best we can do – some writers suspect as much (e.g., Buscombe 2003). Nevertheless, the first step is to seek something more ambitious – a definition (or a cluster theory modeled on Gaut 2000).

A definition of movie genre specifies conditions that are individually necessary and jointly sufficient for a category to be a movie genre. It specifies what horror, suspense, romance, and the other genres share in common and what distinguishes them from other categories. Specifying these features would explain what makes some categories movie genres.

To begin with, every movie genre has more than one member. This is not true of every movie category. For example, films that are identical to Midnight Cowboy (1969) is a category that has only one member. Indeed, any work belongs to a category of which it is the only member. We may not think of these as categories, but if not, let us be explicit about this.

Likewise, movies in a genre are made by more than one artist. This is not true of all movie categories. For example, movies directed by Alfred Hitchcock is a category but not a genre – it is an oeuvre. Complicating matters, movie artists include directors, producers, actors, cinematographers, and so forth (Gaut 1997), and movies can be categorized according to who occupies each of these artist roles. Rear Window (1954) belongs to the categories of movies-that-star-Jimmy-Stewart and movies-directed-by-Alfred-Hitchcock. However, movies-that-star-Jimmy-Stewart is not a genre, and neither is a complex category like movies-directed-by-Alfred-Hitchcock-starring-Jimmy-Stewart. So, a category is a movie genre only if more than one artist occupies any given role in making movies in that genre.

Artists from any background make movies in a genre. In principle, anyone can make a comedy or action film, but this is not true of every movie category. Only people who in some sense belong to Bollywood can make a Bollywood film. This difference between movie genres and traditions is sharply revealed by two explanatory asymmetries. Consider the genre of suspense and the tradition of Hollywood films. What makes *The Sixth Sense* (1999) suspense is not that M. Night Shyamalan made it. Rather, he is a suspense filmmaker because he makes suspense films. By contrast, what makes *The Sixth Sense* a Hollywood film is simply that Shyamalan made it under the auspices of Hollywood, and his doing so is what makes him a Hollywood filmmaker. Quite unlike traditions, movie genres are not defined in terms of social facts about their producers. Admittedly, there are tough questions regarding the nature of social facts and traditions, but since our focus is defining movie genre, we need not answer them here.

From here, things get tricky. A cursory glance at movie genres reveals much diversity. Some are partly defined by setting (western), some by subject (war), others by affect (comedy), some by format (musicals), and still others by style (film noir). Yet some settings (rural New Jersey), subjects (lawn mowers), affects (calmness), and styles (surrealism) do not help define any movie genre. What distinguishes these features from the features that do help define movie genres?

The answer is that the features of movie genres that help define them are ones that factor into their role in appreciation and interpretation. These features include ones that impact a large group of audience members' decisions about whether they want to view a film. Many people sometimes want to see movies with the historical setting that helps to define the western, but knowing that a film is set in New Jersey has little if any impact on most viewing decisions. Moreover, movie genres set audience expectations for purposes of appreciation and interpretation. War movies are partly defined by their subject matter because their subject matter factors in our appreciation of them. Knowing that *Saving Private Ryan* (1998) is a war movie, we do not judge its violence to be a flaw in it, as we would if we thought it was a screwball comedy. Since the Three Stooges' *Disorder in the Court* (1936) is a screwball comedy (and not a courtroom drama), you anticipate that justice will prevail, acquitting the innocent Gail Tempest, no matter how much mayhem occurs in the witness box. Comedies are partly defined by their happy affect because that affect helps set our interpretive expectations.

All this can be plugged into the schema for a theory of movie genre:

> Category K is a movie genre if and only if K has multiple members, which are made by more than one artist (for any given artist role), from any background, and K has features in virtue of which K figures into the appreciations or interpretations of K's audience.

This formulation does not imply that every movie belongs to no more than one movie genre – it allows for genre hybrids like action comedies and war film noir (Staiger 2003). It also allows for complex movie categories combining movie genres and other categories, such as thrillers directed by Hitchcock, Hong Kong action cinema, and classic comedies. Finally, it allows that a movie can migrate from one genre to another, if movie genres change over time.

This is a *proposal* for a definition of movie genre. It should be thoroughly tested to see if there are counterexamples. Movies that are three hours long, R-rated movies, movies with happy endings, and movies with foreign dialogue meet all the conditions laid out in the proposed schema, but it is a stretch to think of them as genres. One option is to bite the bullet and count them as genres, revising any contrary intuitions, so that the proposal states necessary and sufficient conditions. Another option is to side with intuitions, and admit that the definition only states necessary conditions and hence that more work is needed to identify sufficient conditions. This is not bad news so long as addressing counterexamples will refine and possibly complete the definition.

In evaluating the proposed definition, it is also helpful to note which questions it raises and which it rules out, since a good theory should raise the right questions. Thus this proposal quashes the question, "why do movie genres impact our aesthetic decisions or judgments?" After all, it just defines movie genres as categories that impact our aesthetic decisions and judgments about movies. At the same time, the proposal raises questions worth raising. For example, it accommodates variation in the kinds of features that help define movie genres – format helps define musicals, affect helps define horror, style helps define film noir, and setting helps define westerns. But why does the setting of the western impact aesthetic decisions and judgments? What is the interpretive and appreciative role of affect in horror movies? Of course, these are the very kinds of questions that interest film scholars and philosophers writing about the individual movie genres (e.g., Kitses 1969; Carroll 1990).

Ontology: Are there any movie genres?

What sort of entity is a movie genre? Is it a material object, a property, an event, or an abstractum, like a set or a type? Or maybe it is none of these? A theory of movie genre does not supply the answer. Suppose that movie genres are sets of movies. That does not tell us which sets of movies are genres – movies released in 1962 form a set which is not a movie genre. And suppose movie genres are defined in part by characteristic emotional effects. That says nothing about whether movie genres are sets or types or individuals – any of which can be defined by emotional effects. To find out what sort of entity is farce or horror we need an ontology of movie genre.

Ontologies of movie genre are readily adapted from the rich literature on the ontology of multiple-instance artworks, especially musical works (Rohrbaugh 2005). Philosophers have identified musical works with sets, types, and historical individuals; and some have even denied that there are any musical works. At the same time, a consensus has developed about how to choose among the options: a good ontology of art is implicit in sound appreciative practices (Thomasson 2005). A similar principle can help choose the correct ontology of movie genre: a conception of what movie genres are should reflect their role in interpretation and evaluation.

Ontologies of movie genre divide into realist ontologies, according to which movie genres exist, and nominalist ontologies denying that they exist (after Goodman 1976). According to nominalists, there is no satire or film noir. Of course, there are movies that we classify as satire and film, but "satire" and "film noir" are labels that we apply to some movies, so the movies exist and the labels exist but the genres do not. By denying that movie genres exist, this view deftly sidesteps the tricky problem of saying what kind of entity a movie genre is; but the viability of this view depends on its making sense of the role movie genre plays in interpretation and appreciation, and the prospects do not look good. A label like "satire" does not invoke conventions which carry us from what is represented explicitly to what is implied, and it does not delineate a comparison class as a background against which to attribute aesthetic properties.

According to a simple realist ontology, movie genres are sets. The trouble is that the members of a set make it the set that it is. Take the set of all satirical movies released before 1962. Add a new satire and you get a new set. Satire pre-1962 is not the same movie genre as satire post-1962. Again, this does not make sense of the role of movie genre in interpretation and appreciation. The comparison class for appreciating *The Great Dictator* (1940) is the same as the comparison class for *Dr. Strangelove* (1964). Indeed, the comparison class includes possible movies as well as movies that have been made. Part of appreciating *The Great Dictator* is seeing how bad similar movies might have been.

An improved realist proposal is that movie genres are types. Each type has a type-constitutive feature, a feature that items must have in order to be tokens of the type. Thus Richard Wollheim (1980) argues that musical works are types constituted by a sonic structure which any performance must have in order to be a performance of the work. Perhaps, then, movie genres are types whose tokens are movies having whatever feature constitutes the type. (What feature is that? A theory of each movie genre supplies the answer.) The advantage of this proposal is that the identity of a genre is secured not by its tokens but by a feature that they have. Movies actually made in a movie genre are not essential to it. Thus the comparison class in appreciating a movie in a genre may go beyond movies actually made in the genre.

These three proposals demonstrate how to go about developing an ontology of genre and how to argue for it by appealing to facts about the role of genre in interpretation and appreciation. They are merely starting points, however. Alternative proposals should be formulated and assessed. The process will net a better understanding of the role of genre in practices of film spectatorship and criticism, which may prove instrumental in reaching the right ontology of genre.

Value: what's worth got to do with it?

A theory of genre and value centers on at least three questions. First, some critics take the fact that a movie is a "genre movie" to be a mark against its quality. The best movies, they say, are not genre movies. Is this a sound critical principle? Second, some people rank movie genres: they typically rank action low and drama higher, comedy as lower brow than satire, and tragedy as higher brow than the tearjerker. Are such rankings justifiable? Finally, Charlie Chaplin's *The Great Dictator* is a superb instance of the genre of satire, whereas Jonathan Demme's 2004 remake of *The Manchurian Candidate* (1962) fails as a satire. This raises the question, what is it for a movie to be good or bad as a *K*, where *K* is a genre?

Sometimes auteur films, like those of Woody Allen, are contrasted with genre movies and the former are sometimes deemed better than the latter, because they are more creative and less formulaic. This argument is suspect on multiple grounds. Originality is just one meritorious feature of a film, so a formulaic movie may surpass more original fare on other grounds. Indeed, originality can mar a movie – a homage, for instance. Moreover, it is questionable whether genre movies are automatically less creative. The first movies in any genre can be just as innovative as any movie that allegedly lacks a genre, and creativity can thrive even when subject to constraints (Boden 2004). Adding to these general points, some film scholars have defended the merits of particular movie genres and of particular genre movies (e.g., Cawelti 1976; Braudy 1999; Sobchack 2003). Finally, and more fundamentally, it is not clear that any movie is in fact genreless. *Annie Hall* (1977) is still a comedy, albeit an exceptional one. Indeed, it is particularly exceptional when compared with other comedies. So perhaps every movie belongs to some genre, with drama currently acting as a sort of catchall for everything outside more fine-grained movie genres, like horror or action.

People commonly rank musical genres (saying that punk is better than disco, for example), and some also rank movie genres. Right off the bat, there is the problem of what sample of movies in a genre determines its ranking. We might look at the total number of good movies in each movie genre or the proportion of good to bad movies in the genre. Defenders of a movie genre will object that it is a matter of luck whether the true potential of a movie genre is exploited – maybe some genres attract less accomplished filmmakers. Alternative sampling methods use ideal or typical movies in each movie genre. But assuming that the sampling problem can be solved, is drama really better than action and comedy?

The answer to this question depends on how movie genres are evaluated. Obviously movie genres differ in instrumental value. Horror movies are better at frightening audiences than comedies, tearjerkers are better at saddening viewers than martial arts epics, and historical dramas are better at educating about the past than fantasies. Each genre wins when judged by its own ends.

One route to a genuine ranking evaluates these ends. If educating about the past is better than making people sad, then historical dramas are better than tearjerkers. However, both these ends are valuable in some circumstances and not others.

Another route to a genuine ranking judges movie genres by a common end. It judges each genre by the ability of sample movies to deliver an aesthetic experience. However, the danger is that our judgments simply echo our genre preferences. An action buff will claim that sample action movies get higher scores on the aesthetic standard than sample historical dramas, and a member of the highbrow crowd will give the nod to the historical dramas over action movies on the same standard. The only way to adjudicate incompatible rankings is to come up with a substantive theory of the aesthetic which all rankers should accept and which falsifies some of the incompatible rankings. Notoriously, no theory of the aesthetic meets both these conditions, and it is natural to suspect that theories of the aesthetic that do imply genre rankings smuggle in the theorist's own genre preferences (e.g., Horkheimer and Adorno 1972). Given this impasse, the best we can do is clarify debates about a hierarchy among movie genres.

The final question for a theory of value and genre concerns what it is to evaluate a movie as belonging to a genre. Unlike the 2004 remake of *The Manchurian Candidate*, *The Great Dictator* is a superb instance of satire. Viewed as film noir, however, Chaplin's masterpiece would come off rather poorly. So ideas about genre play into movie evaluations. The question is *how* genres play into these evaluations. One possibility is that evaluating a movie as a satire requires a belief that it is a satire. However, this cannot be the whole story. I may come to believe that a movie is a *jidaigeki* by reading the DVD case, but this belief alone cannot make a difference to my evaluation of it. To evaluate the movie as a *jidaigeki*, I must surely have some beliefs about the genre. The precise nature of these beliefs is an open question – one proposal is that I should believe that it is a samurai movie, governed by certain conventions (e.g., the villains have mussed-up hair). In sum, where K is a genre,

> S evaluates a movie as a K only if (1) S has some beliefs about K, and (2) the content of the evaluation counterfactually depends on S's beliefs about K.

Applied to the *jidaigeki* example, this says that I evaluate a movie as a *jidaigeki* only if I have some beliefs about the genre. In addition, these beliefs must make a difference to my evaluation – if I had different beliefs, I would evaluate the movie differently. Once again, though, the above principle is only a start. Here is something stronger:

> S evaluates a movie as a K only if (1) S has some *true* beliefs about K, and (2) the content of the evaluation counterfactually depends on S's *true* beliefs about K.

Considering the case for this stronger principle and for alternatives to it promises to shed light on the role of genre in evaluation (Lopes 2007).

That nobody has worked out a comprehensive philosophy of movie genre is not a sufficient reason to attempt one now. Some assurance is needed that genuine progress toward a philosophy of movie genre is possible. This chapter has sought to highlight the importance of genres in mediating our engagement with movies – something implicitly acknowledged in recent studies of individual movie genres. It illustrates how resources developed in other areas of the philosophy of art can be harnessed to make sense of the work done by genre in our engagement with movies. And it connects some proposals for philosophical accounts of movie genres to work in film studies. More should and can be said about the theory of movie genre, its ontology, and questions of value.

See also Dogme 95 (Chapter 44), Documentary (Chapter 45), Horror (Chapter 46), Pornography (Chapter 47), Avant-garde film (Chapter 48), Tragedy and comedy (Chapter 49), Noël Carroll (Chapter 31), and Authorship (Chapter 2).

References

Altman, R. (2003) "Genre," in B. K. Grant (ed.) *Film Genre Reader III*, Austin: University of Texas Press.

Boden, M. (2004) *The Creative Mind: Myths and Mechanisms*, London and New York: Routledge.

Braudy, L. (1999) "Genre: The Conventions of Connection," in L. Braudy and M. Cohen (eds.) *Film Theory and Criticism: Introductory Readings*, New York: Oxford University Press.

Buscombe, E. (2003) "The Idea of Genre in the American Cinema," in B. K. Grant (ed.) *Film Genre Reader III*, Austin: University of Texas Press.

Carroll, N. (1990) *The Philosophy of Horror, or Paradoxes of the Heart*, New York: Routledge.

Cavell, S. (1996) *Contesting Tears: The Hollywood Melodrama of the Unknown Woman*, Chicago: University of Chicago Press.

Cawelti, J. (1976) *Adventure, Mystery, and Romance: Formula Stories as Art and Popular Culture*, Chicago: University of Chicago Press.

Currie, G. (2004) "Genre," in *Arts and Minds*, Oxford: Clarendon Press; and New York: Oxford University Press.

Duff, D. (ed.) (2000) *Modern Genre Theory*, Harlow, UK; New York: Longman.

Gaut, B. (1997) "Film Authorship and Collaboration," in R. Allen and M. Smith (eds.) *Film Theory and Philosophy*, Oxford: Clarendon Press; and New York: Oxford University Press.

—— (2000) "'Art' as a Cluster Concept," in N. Carroll (ed.) *Theories of Art Today*, Madison: University of Wisconsin Press.

Goodman, N. (1976) *Languages of Art*, 2nd ed., Indianapolis: Hackett.

Grant, B. K. (ed.) (2003) *Film Genre Reader III*, Austin: University of Texas Press.

Horkheimer, M., and Adorno, T. (1972) "The Culture Industry," in J. Cumming (trans.) *Dialectic of Enlightenment*, New York: Herder and Herder.

Kitses, J. (1969) *Horizons West*, Bloomington: Indiana University Press.

Lewis, D. (1978) "Truth in Fiction," *American Philosophical Quarterly* 15: 37–46.

Lopes, D. M. (2007) "True Appreciation," in S. Walden (ed.) *Photography and Philosophy: New Essays on the Pencil of Nature*, Malden, MA: Blackwell.

McArthur, C. (1972) *Underworld U.S.A.*, New York: Viking.

Neale, S. (2003) "Questions of Genre," in B. K. Grant (ed.) *Film Genre Reader III*, Austin: University of Texas Press.

Rohrbaugh, G. (2005) "Ontology of Art," in B. Gaut and D. M. Lopes (eds.) *Routledge Companion to Aesthetics*, 2nd ed., London and New York: Routledge.

Sobchack, T. (2003) "Genre Film: A Classical Experience," in B. K. Grant (ed.) *Film Genre Reader III*, Austin: University of Texas Press.

Staiger, J. (2003) "Hybrid or Inbred: The Purity Hypothesis and Hollywood Genre History," in B. K. Grant (ed.) *Film Genre Reader III*, Austin: University of Texas Press.

Thomasson, A. (2005) "The Ontology of Art and Knowledge in Aesthetics," *Journal of Aesthetics and Art Criticism* 63: 221–9.

Tudor, A. (2003) "Genre," in B. K. Grant (ed.) *Film Genre Reader III*, Austin: University of Texas Press.

Walton, K. (1970) "Categories of Art," *Philosophical Review* 79: 334–67.

—— (1990) *Mimesis as Make-Believe*, Cambridge, MA: Harvard University Press.

Warshow, R. (1962) *The Immediate Experience: Movies, Comics, Theatre, and Other Aspects of Popular Culture*, Garden City, NY: Doubleday.

Wollheim, R. (1980) *Art and Its Objects*, 2nd ed., Cambridge and New York: Cambridge University Press.

15
INTERPRETATION
George Wilson

In her famous 1966 essay, "Against Interpretation," Susan Sontag asserts, "What the overemphasis on content entails is the perennial, never consummated project of *interpretation*. And conversely, it is the habit of approaching works of art in order to *interpret* them that sustains the fancy that there really is such a thing as the content of a work of art" (Sontag 1966 [1964]: 5). However, Sontag immediately grants that it is not just any concept of "interpretation" that she views as pernicious. The conception to which she objects is one in which the interpreter selects a set of elements from the targeted work and constructs an interpretation by claiming of each element that it really means *such and such* or stands for *so and so*. As she says herself, interpretation, so conceived, is virtually a task of translation – translating a part or aspect of the work into some proprietary content it purportedly expresses. However, Sontag's brief against interpretation is confusing. Most of the leading practitioners of close interpretation in the early sixties, the New Critics for instance, had themselves rejected the idea that interpretation consisted in the systematic translation or allegorization of the work to be interpreted. Interpretation grounded on the "translation idea" commits "the heresy of paraphrase," in Cleanth Brooks' well-known phrase (Brooks 1947). From the point of view of these critics, Sontag is really not objecting to the proper enterprise of inter-preting works of art, but to an insidious misconception of what practical criticism amounts to. For these critics, the "project of interpretation" is a tenable one, and it is important. What need to be repudiated are simply confusions about the proper aims and methodology of the project.

In the fifty years since Sontag's essay was published, the same confusing dialectic has recurred, and it recurs significantly in the study of film. On the one hand, film viewers, professional and otherwise, persist in prolifically producing interpretations of a great variety of films. On the other hand, Sontag's broad skepticism about "the project of interpretation" may well be the dominant view within the discipline (King 1998). Interpretation is commonly regarded as having at best marginal importance within film studies. And yet, as we'll see, various attempts to formulate the grounds for such skepticism often rest on tendentious notions of what is involved or presupposed in the actual interpretation of movies. For instance, generalizations and extensions of "the translation idea" still abound. On the other hand, when a less loaded conception is adopted, it is hard to see how interpretation could be avoided and why it cannot play a significant role in our overall understanding of movies. Without a better sorting out of a range of critical issues, there is the danger that the continuing debate will remain inconclusive, with each side arguing at cross-purposes with the other.

Sontag speaks as if there was some one identifiable enterprise that can legitimately be called "*the* project of interpretation," but it is unlikely that the messy mélange of interpretative works share any substantial common agenda, however broadly defined. Hence, questions about the nature and aims of interpretation are probably best relativized to one or another more specific interpretative project (Gaut 1993). Similarly, it is widely assumed that interpretation always purports to specify a *meaning* or a constellation of *meanings* for a work of art. First, however, interpretative work on film is frequently focused on understanding, e.g., aspects of style, tone, and point of view, and the detailed analysis of these matters need not issue in something that one would naturally refer to as "meaning" (Pye 2007). Second, the word "meaning" is used in English to cover such a range of diverse phenomena that it may not help much to insist on associating interpretation too closely with the retrieval or construction of some variety of "meaning." For example, we speak of the linguistic meaning of a word or sentence, the meaning a speaker intended to convey by an utterance, the symptomatic meaning of red spots on the skin, and the meaning of an important life-episode like the breakup of a friendship. Some or all of these concepts of meaning may have some bearing on some particular interpretative projects, but the concepts are quite different in import, and it assigns no higher unity to distinct interpretative projects to subsume them all under one or another of these senses of "meaning." In fact, the temptation to link interpretation with the exegesis of meaning probably has done a lot to reinforce the unfortunate conception of interpretation as some sort of decoding of the targeted text into an antecedently favored configuration of concepts and themes. If one wishes to insist that the interpretation of an element E in a work W always involves a claim that E, in the context of W, means *so and so*, then the thesis tells us very little about the character of the interpretation in question in the absence of an explication of the notion of "meaning" that one intends to invoke.

In his book, *Making Meaning*, David Bordwell also expresses a distinctly skeptical attitude toward interpretation, but at least he makes an attempt to draw some of the needed discriminations between different purported modes of understanding movies. He draws a distinction between what he calls, somewhat stipulatively, issues of "comprehension," "explicative interpretation," and "symptomatic interpretation." It is notable that he pairs each of these categories with a corresponding sort of "meaning." *Comprehension* is concerned with "referential" and "explicit" meanings, where these are the overt facts about story or theme that are directly presented as such within the film. Bordwell regards referential and explicit meanings, taken together, as the analogue of literal meaning in language. *Explicative interpretation* has "implicit meanings" as its object, and *symptomatic* interpretation aims at uncovering "repressed (symptomatic) meaning."

Very roughly, symptomatic interpretation attempts to explain a cinematic phenomenon as the manifestation (the symptom) in film viewers or in the film itself of some way in which social/cultural forces or unconscious psychological forces in the individual subject impinge significantly upon the construction of the movie or upon standard ways of watching and responding to it. This category of interpretation is meant to cover a great range of the interpretative strategies that were favored especially in the period of Grand Theory during the seventies and eighties. For example, in her widely read and highly influential essay, "Visual Pleasure and Narrative Cinema," Laura Mulvey (1990) argues that certain fundamental features of narrative and its presentation in classic Hollywood films are muted manifestations of unconscious and pathological male fascination and anxiety engendered in contemplating the erotically charged female body. However, in the present entry, I will focus on issues concerning explicative interpretation, beginning with Bordwell's conception of the enterprise and the sort of implicit meaning he thinks that it purports to specify.

According to Bordwell, implicit meanings satisfy two conditions.

1 An implicit meaning is one that is not overtly expressed or represented in the film. It is a content that the film merely implies, suggests, or otherwise communicates indirectly.
2 It is a general, abstract, or thematic content that is not included in referential meaning, although an implicit meaning is standardly conveyed, in part, by means of the exposition of narrative materials.

Thus, Bordwell suggests hypothetically that the proposition "Madness is indistinguishable from sanity" could be a part of the implicit meaning of Hitchcock's *Psycho* (Bordwell 1989: 9). The second condition, however vague, is important because, as Bordwell allows, referential meanings (aspects of the story) can very well be imparted in the movie only in an oblique manner as well. But the conception of explicative interpretation registered in 1) and 2) together is in danger of making explication the attempt to retrieve some general message or moral that is covert but somehow contained in the film. If this danger is not avoided, then Bordwell, like Sontag, describes explicative interpretation in a manner that is arguably untrue to the upshot of the best practical criticism of film and at odds with what the pertinent practical critics have taken themselves to accomplish. On the whole, *Making Meaning* tends to be dubious about, and even dismissive of, the products of Interpretation Inc., but Bordwell frames the basic issues about interpretation in such a way that some of his arguments are in danger of being aimed largely at a straw man.

This discussion of Bordwell points to two broad and basic questions about the nature and upshot of explicative interpretation. First, how is one to understand what it is for a film itself to *mean, imply, express*, or otherwise *convey*, whether directly or indirectly, certain content? Call this the question of *the grounding of meaning or implication relations*. Philosophers writing on film have discussed this question quite extensively. However, in doing so, they have commonly presupposed that (explicative) interpretation is to be construed as a kind of *exegesis* of the cinematic text. *The exegetical model* of film interpretation, as I will understand it, is the conjunction of 1) and 2) together with a realist or anticonstructivist view of meaning or implication relations in film. That is, the model assumes that

3 There are *objective* facts about what films or parts of a film mean, express, or imply, where those facts are determinately established in the making of the film and are not constructions projected by the viewer or the critic on the work.

This conception yields the second question. Is this the proper model, in general, of the practice and goals of explication? The idea is certainly not inevitable. Thus, consider thesis 2). When one attempts to make sense of some incident in a person's life, the outcome of the attempt will be a suitable pattern of explanation – an illuminating story – about the incident, concerning both its antecedents and consequences. (For a good overview of the connections between making sense of an event and constructing a narrative about it, see Williams [2002].) It is not as if there were some propositional content that the incident is supposed to have expressed, implied, or somehow come to signify. Nothing analogous to 2) holds in this case. It is a plausible conjecture that certain kinds of interpretation of films aim at patterns of explanation of this or a related variety. At any rate, we will also examine basic challenges to *the exegetical model* of explication.

Let us begin with the question of *meaning relations*. It is natural to believe that a film or a part or aspect of a film (X) can mean or imply a content only in a derivative sense. That is, it is natural to insist that X means or implies the content C only in virtue of the fact that the relevant filmmakers constructed X with the *intention* of expressing or invoking C for an appropriate audience. It is the actual intentions of the filmmakers in question that crucially determine whatever meaning or content that X may have. This is a form of *actual intentionalism* about meaning relations in connection with movies, a position that is familiar from debates about meaning relations in works of literature (Livingston 2005). The position models the meanings conveyed in literary works upon the meanings that speakers try to convey or communicate by the utterances they produce. There are various familiar objections to actual intentionalism as a general account of artistic meaning. First, it has commonly been argued that the critic is often in no position to know what the artist actually intended concerning interpretatively vital matters, and, partly for that reason, recovering intentions is not what the critic seems to be after. Second, it is possible for an agent to intend to communicate or express something, but fail utterly to do so.

Whatever one thinks about these common objections to actual intentionalism about meaning in literary criticism, the doctrine faces an immediate and obvious challenge in the case of film. Most movies are the product of collaborative work, and the fact of elaborate collaboration raises the question of *whose* intentions are supposed to be determinative of the film's content. The intentionalist may pick a single individual (the director, for example) as the putative source of the meaning-making intentions for the film, but any such choice seems wildly implausible in the general case. No *auteur* theorist ever went so far as to claim that the meaning or significance of any film was determined in detail by the intentions of its director. Of course, there are also shared or joint intentions. Two or more people may have the intention of robbing a bank together, and, more pertinently, they can coauthor a book or article. However, it is unlikely that the intentionalist about film can plausibly frame the account in terms of intentions about content that are shared among the various collaborators. There are simply too many cases in which an apparently coherent film was made despite the fact that the director, the screenwriters, and the actors had very different conceptions about what they were attempting to convey. (Actors sometimes hated working with Fritz Lang because he could be so demanding in his direction without being at all forthcoming about what it was that he was seeking to achieve.) Perhaps there is a way for the actual intentionalist to find a well-motivated multilayered version of the theory that allows properly for the complexities engendered by cinematic collaboration, but the problems faced by such an account are challenging (Gaut 1997).

The actual intentionalist likens the "meaning" of a movie shot, scene, or sequence to what speakers mean in producing their utterances, verbal or otherwise. However, when one considers the typical character of the sort of collaboration involved in fiction film, the implausibility of this comparison is especially striking. A verbal utterance is characteristically the product of a *single* agent, and it is the intentions of that agent that ground the particular content that the utterance conveys. A movie scene, by contrast, is normally the product of various agents operating at various levels of production, and all of these agents may well have had intentions, sometimes conflicting, about what the completed scene is supposed to achieve. Consider, for example, just the speech of a character in a fiction film. Although it will be the actor who literally performs the utterance, the intentions of various collaborators will have shaped and guided its content-relevant nature. For instance, the director, with his or her relevant intentions, may have done a lot to shape an actor's delivery of the lines, even in instances when the actor has not grasped the aims behind the director's instructions. And naturally, the actor's performance is significantly defined and structured from the outset by the words and instructions that the screenwriters have supplied. Where in this complicated intermeshing of artistic intentions in relation to the on-screen behavior of the character is the critical flash point that yields anything like an analogue of the relations that individual speakers bear to their own utterances? The situation becomes patently more complicated when all the diverse contributions that played a role in the construction of the completed scene are considered. In fact, philosophers have paid too little attention to the specific question of the ways in which screen performances concretely embody a detailed and nuanced dramatic significance (Livingston 1996; Klevan 2005). Correlatively, they have usually said little about the specific ways in which staging, photography, editing, and other procedures of postproduction contribute individually to the significance that is finally presented to the audience on screen. Treating a shot or sequence as an analogue of a speaker's utterance tends to discourage analysis of the distinct but interanimating dimensions involved in the construction of cinematic significance.

A number of philosophers writing on film have opted for some version of *hypothetical intentionalism* (Currie 1995; Levinson 1996). Here is one way of characterizing the view. In watching a fiction film, viewers know that they are seeing an audio-visual construction that is the product of a (collaborative) intelligence, personality, and sensibility. Knowing this to be so, viewers are disposed to imagine the characteristics of intelligence, personality, and sensibility that they find manifest in the detailed crafting of the film. They imagine a kind of "implied filmmaker" – an implied version of the filmmaker(s) expressed in the movie's detailed articulation. According to the hypothetical intentionalist, a shot or sequence in a movie expresses a content C just in case the film as a whole makes it maximally plausible to imagine that the implied filmmaker(s) intended that the designated shot or sequence was to convey or communicate C to a suitably attentive and responsive audience. What ground the ascription of meaning to a film segment, on this approach, are not facts about the intentions that some artist or group of artists actually had. They are putative facts about what the film's internal relationships prescribe concerning the content-relevant intentions justifiably imagined as part of a viewer's engagement with the film. As this formulation indicates, hypothetical intentionalism is a complex view, and its viability depends on how certain relations to which it appeals are ultimately to be spelled out.

For instance, does the hypothetical intentionalist about movies mean to appeal to the imagined intentions of an implied filmmaker (in the singular), and if so, is it an implied "director" to whom his theory refers? Or, perhaps, it would be better to appeal to the implied filmmakers (plural), imagining that they have effectively collaborated in the making of the film. However, this maneuver is likely to face objections in cases where there is plain evidence to the contrary. In addition, a great deal turns on the conception put forward about what *justifies* a viewer in *imagining* that a part or aspect of a movie was intended to be construed in such and such a way. For instance, if one knows as a matter of historical fact that no pertinent film artist had the intentions that the critic has been prompted to imagine, does that preclude the critic being justified in imagining otherwise? Or again, what is supposed to constitute a suitably attentive and responsive audience? In answering these questions, there is a danger of circularity.

It may be that an intention about meaning that one is justified in ascribing imaginatively is grounded upon the meaning that one supposes is manifested in the work, where "manifest meaning" is a factual matter, independent of anyone's actual or hypothetical intentions. This is the position of the *anti-intentionalist about meaning relations*. Many writers of a structuralist or semiotic persuasion seem to have supposed that meaning relations in a "semiotic system" are grounded in their quasi-conventional roles in social practices of signification and do not rely on individual communicative intentions. If this is their view, then these writers are anti-intentionalist in the sense delineated above. In any case, the hypothetical intentionalist and the anti-intentionalist differ about whether the imagined intentions of an implied filmmaker can serve as the source of the meaning of the work.

Bordwell holds that (implicit) meaning relations in the cinema are not objectively embodied in the work and are not discovered there by interpreters. Rather, they are something that interpreters *construct* by assigning contents of favored types on the basis of a rich assortment of audio-visual cues that the film supplies. In other words, Bordwell seems to reject thesis 3) of the exegetical model of interpretation. More specifically, for him, an explicative interpretation is projected onto the film by mapping a range of the salient cues it offers onto the elements of what he calls a "semantic field" – roughly, a conceptual framework that the critic has chosen as particularly suitable for an illuminating exercise in cinematic analysis. It is not that Bordwell contends that an interpreter's choice of cues, semantic fields, and the interpretative mappings between them is unconstrained. He maintains that the constraints that bear legitimately on a prospective interpretation are the interpretative practices and conventions endorsed by the critical community to which the interpreter belongs. To repeat, Bordwell's account of the critic's methodology repudiates the exegetical model of explicative interpretation, but it is striking that he accepts, with Sontag, a fairly strong version of the "translation" conception of interpretation. It is difficult on such an approach to avoid a counterintuitive relativism about acceptable interpretation.

The problematic character of the translation idea is highlighted if we consider an alternative to the exegetical model of interpretation. What is the sort of explanation that explicative interpretation aims primarily to produce? Given the vast range of explicative interpretations on the market, it is preposterous to suppose that there will be a single substantial answer to this question. Nevertheless, if we restrict the question to the understanding of narrative fiction film, we can narrow its scope to some degree. In *Film as Film* (1972), Victor Perkins asserts, "Our understanding and judgment of a movie ... will depend largely on the attempt to comprehend the nature and assess the quality of its created relationships" (118). Among the relationships to which Perkins is here referring are the dramatized narrative relationships between the characters. In trying to understand a movie story, we normally expect to achieve some overall understanding of the chief actions and reactions of its fictional agents. Working within the frameworks of genre, narrative exposition, and audio-visual articulation that inform the movie, viewers want to know why the characters have acted, thought, and felt in the ways depicted in the film. Similarly viewers also want to grasp a range of the consequences of the characters' actions, thoughts, and feelings. In other words, viewers seek to limn the relations of explanatory coherence and value assessment that the movie progressively reveals. So, *one* upshot of an interpretation can be a perspicuous representation of these purported patterns of explanation and evaluation in the narrative (Wilson 1997; Carroll 2002). Moreover, there is no reason to suppose that such a configuration must carry with it some general theme or thesis encapsulating, so to speak, a principle or lesson that the story covertly implies. In fact, the relevant patterns of causal and teleological explanations involve something more like an explicit elaboration of the details of the plot and the implied connections between them. The explication will be an especially cogent and specific reconstruction of the implicit fictional history presented in the film. On this line of thought, the challenge to the exegetical model turns on a rejection of thesis 2) above, and it contrasts sharply with the constructivist's rejection of 3).

To render the proposal here relatively concrete, it is worth working through an actual example, at least in outline. Toward the end of *Shadow of a Doubt* (Alfred Hitchcock, 1946), young Charlie (Teresa Wright) discovers that her uncle – also called Charlie (Joseph Cotton) – has in the past married and murdered a number of rich widows for their money. Although young Charlie has been thoroughly enthralled by the romantic mystery that she associates with her uncle, she comes eventually to learn that he is a profoundly evil man. She plans to let him know that she can prove that he committed the murders, because she possesses a ring that he has given her – a ring, she now realizes, that belonged to one of his victims. To convey this warning to him, she puts the ring on and displays it conspicuously when she enters a gathering of her relatives and friends at her home. Uncle Charlie sees the ring, grasps the message his niece is sending, and promptly announces that he has made a decision to leave town the next day. Young Charlie's mother is utterly distressed at his announcement, and she speaks movingly about her love for her brother and the value she places on her family. In the face of her mother's grief, young Charlie covers the ring and does not press the confrontation further. Since she has apparently effected her uncle's imminent expulsion from the town and because she is plainly dismayed by her mother's unhappiness, it may seem that her actions in this scene are perfectly in order.

But, there is a complication. The little gathering includes an attractive widow, Mrs Potter, and it is clear to everyone – to the people at the party, including young Charlie, and to the viewer – that if her uncle carries out the intentions he has just announced, then he will be headed out of Santa Rosa with still another widow who is thoroughly smitten with him. Therefore, young Charlie has every reason to know that by keeping silent about Uncle Charlie she is, at a minimum, placing Mrs Potter in mortal danger. So why does young Charlie suppress the damning information she possesses? Does she suppose that her mother's grief outweighs the dire consequences that the infatuated widow might face? Surely, that would be a questionable presumption! Earlier in the film, there have been strong indications that young Charlie and her uncle share some powerful but mysterious affinity. The nature of their affinity is never fully explained, although we learn early on that young Charlie is restless – bored and dissatisfied with the conventional outlook of small-town bourgeois life. Naturally, she comes to detest the utter nihilism about middle-class values that her uncle endorses, but is it possible that, even as the film moves toward its conclusion, she remains complicit with some facets of his distorted and disturbing outlook?

An answer to these questions would yield an interpretation of Charlie's action in the designated scene and an interpretation of other significant aspects of her actions elsewhere in the story. Such an interpretation would take the form of an imagined explanation of her fictional behavior – an explanation conjoined perhaps with some evaluation of the motives that are thereby deemed to have prompted her key decisions. One can rightly say that such an interpretation assigns a *meaning* or *significance* to Charlie's behavior, but this is the sort of meaning we are after whenever we attempt to *make sense* of an action or incident in a person's life by setting it in a plausible explanatory/evaluative framework. Call this "narrative meaning." The framework we aim at is an enlightening narrative about the action or incident in question. Hence, the narrative meaning of Charlie's behavior here is not something in addition to and more abstract and general than an account of the concluding scenes of *Shadow of a Doubt*. It is the product of the interpreter's attempt to give a more fine-grained specification of what he or she takes that story to involve when Charlie conceals the incriminating ring. The interpreter's version of the elaborated story may well suggest to some minds a comprehensive moral or abstract thesis that this version appears to them to illustrate. ("Everyone is corrupted by the temptation to disvalue the lives that one views as parasitical and useless.") Nevertheless, any such a generalizing gloss is a dubious add-on to the interpretation of narrative meaning, strictly construed. The gloss is not constitutive of the interpretation itself. These reflections demonstrate why it is implausible to separate, as Bordwell tries to do, the interpretation ("comprehension") of diegetic and narrative questions from the explicative interpretation that aims at what he calls "implicit meaning." In trying to understand young Charlie's somewhat surprising silence at the end of *Shadow*, one is trying to grasp the significance of her action, a meaning that *is* merely implicit in the context of this particular fictional narrative. But this is almost certainly not the sort of "implicit meaning" that Bordwell has in mind in his taxonomy of interpretation. And yet it is an important kind of meaning and is often the object of the puzzlement when viewers find themselves puzzled by the "meaning" of a scene.

Narrative meaning, as I have explained the notion, fails to satisfy the precepts of strong versions of actual intentionalism. That is, a fiction film or some segment thereof can have a narrative meaning that neither the director, nor the screenwriters, nor the actors intended to convey. Let us imagine (as I believe) that it is possible to argue convincingly and in detail that young Charlie, in failing to reveal that her uncle is the Merry Widow Murderer, is still somewhat tainted by her earlier complicity with aspects of his moral perspective. Thus, we stipulate, for the sake of argument, that her actions in the late scene make a compelling sense when they are explained along those lines. Suppose in addition, however, that it is also discovered that neither Hitchcock, the screenwriters, nor the principal actors intended that the end of the movie be understood in this way. They did intend, we might suppose, that the audience should notice the irony of the fact that, if Uncle Charlie gets away from Santa Rosa, he will leave in the company of a prospective victim. However, they did not intend, we'll imagine, that the audience was to focus upon the question of whether young Charlie has apprehended this potential consequence and, if she did, what considerations the knowledge might have provoked in her. Of course, this hypothetical discovery about the filmmaker's conception of the scene shows that the interpreter's postulated account does not capture a narrative meaning that the filmmakers *intended* to communicate, but it does *not* show that the interpreter has been wrong in holding that the episode naturally manifests, in its setting, the narrative meaning that he or she has proposed.

This observation highlights the need to be careful about the nature of the interpretative project that a given interpretation is meant to realize. The project of figuring out what narrative significance that, e.g., the director might have intended to express is a perfectly coherent one, although it is notoriously tricky to carry out the task successfully. Still, the narrative meaning that is manifest in a scene or segment need not coincide with whatever narrative meaning the relevant filmmakers intended to impart. Only confusion will result from running the two together. Moreover, it can be misleading to speak of *the* narrative meaning of a movie or a part thereof, since there will often be competing ways of constructing the explanations that ground narrative meaning, that tie in terms of overall plausibility and resonance.

The example of narrative meaning in film is necessarily a limited one. There are a host of movies (e.g., *Blowup* [Michelangelo Antonioni, 1961], *The Enigma of Casper*

Hauser [Werner Herzog, 1978], *Mulholland Drive* [David Lynch, 1999]) in which it is not expected that the audience make detailed sense of the narrative action in conventional psychological terms. This does not mean, of course, that the movies are not apt targets for systematic interpretation. It does mean that at least some of the interpretative questions one poses will have to shift their ground. Critics may ask about the "meaning" of the stylized acting and *mise en scène* and query the "significance" of the oddities and gaps in the cinematic exposition of events. The proper understanding of "meaning" and "significance" in these contexts will require elucidation on their own. Nevertheless, there is no reason to think in these cases that the results of the interpretative investigations will take the form of some general moral or theoretical doctrine imparted by the movie. An enlightening delineation of systematic patterns of narrative and narration should suffice.

Even in the case of narrative meaning, where the interpretation is directed at explaining incidents in the narrative, that explanation is guided and constrained by the host of features that define the manner in which the targeted incident has been portrayed. Hence, interpretative issues about style, tone, point of view, and so on will surely figure in an adequate explication of the narrative development (Pye and Gibbs 2005). In instances in which narrative meaning is only fitfully in focus, then issues of explanation about the forms and strategies of cinematic *narration* will assume greater prominence. There are many specific questions about the interpretation of various dimensions of narration (stylistic, epistemic, rhetorical) in fiction films that have been widely discussed, but there is not the space in this entry to pursue these topics. One hopes that in future research, there will be a more intimate collaboration between theoretical analysis and the most sophisticated and nuanced products of practical criticism.

See also Authorship (Chapter 2), Narration (Chapter 18), and David Bordwell (Chapter 29).

References

Bordwell, D. (1989) *Making Meaning: Inference and Rhetoric in the Interpretation of Cinema*, Cambridge, MA: Harvard University Press.

Brooks, C. (1947) "The Heresy of Paraphrase," in *The Well-Wrought Urn and Other Essays*, New York: Harcourt Brace and Jovanovich.

Carroll, N. (1998) *Interpreting the Moving Image*, Cambridge: Cambridge University Press.

Currie, G. (1995) *Image and Mind: Film, Philosophy, and Cognitive Science*, Cambridge: Cambridge University Press.

Gaut, B. (1993) "Interpreting the Arts: The Patchwork Theory," *Journal of Aesthetics and Art Criticism*, 51: 597–609.

—— (1997) "Film Authorship and Collaboration," in D. Allen and M. Smith (eds.) *Film Theory and Philosophy*, Oxford: Oxford University Press.

King, N. (1998) "Hermeneutics, Reception Aesthetics, and Film Interpretation," in J. Hill and P. C. Gibson (eds.) *The Oxford Guide to Film Studies*, Oxford: Oxford University Press.

Klevan, A. (2005) *Film Performance: From Achievement to Appreciation*, London: Wallflower Press.

Levinson, J. (1996) "Intention and Interpretation in Literature," in *The Pleasures of Aesthetics: Philosophical Essays*, Ithaca, NY: Cornell University Press.

Livingston, P. (1996) "Characterization and Fictional Truth in the Cinema," in D. Bordwell and N. Carroll (eds.) *Post-Theory: Reconstructing Film Studies*, Madison: University of Wisconsin Press.

—— (2005) *Art and Intention: A Philosophical Study*, Oxford: Oxford University Press.

Mulvey, L. (1990) "Visual Pleasure and Narrative Cinema," in *Visual and Other Pleasures*, Bloomington: Indiana University Press.

Perkins, V. (1972) *Film as Film*, New York, Penguin.

Pye, D. (2007) "Movies and Tone," in D. Pye and J. Gibbs (eds.) *Close-up 02*, London: Wallflower Press.

Pye, D., and Gibbs, J. (eds.) (2005) *Style and Meaning: Studies in the Detailed Analysis of Film*, Manchester, UK: Manchester University Press.

Sontag, S. (1966 [1964]) "Against Interpretation," in *Against Interpretation and Other Essays*, New York: Farrar, Straus, and Giroux, 3–14. Originally published in *Evergreen Review*, 34 (December 1964): 76–80, 93.

Williams, B. (2002) "Making Sense," in *Truth and Truthfulness*, Princeton, NJ: Princeton University Press,

Wilson, G. (1997) "On Film Narrative and Narrative Meaning," in R. Allen and M. Smith (eds.) *Film Theory and Philosophy* Oxford: Oxford University Press.

Further reading

Although not aiming at traditional modes of explication, the essays in Raymond Bellour, *The Analysis of Film*, ed. Constance Penley (Bloomington: Indiana University Press, 2000), include some striking and instructive frame-by-frame analyses of film segments. Edward Branigan, *Narrative Comprehension and Film* (London: Routledge, 1992), offers an unusually detailed study of the ways "narrative meaning" comes to be articulated in films. Stanley Cavell, *The World Viewed: Reflections on the Ontology of Film*, exp. ed. (Cambridge, MA: Harvard University Press, 1979), is a classic of philosophical writing about film – richly suggestive about the nature and importance of interpretation. Gilberto Perez, *The Material Ghost: Films and Their Medium* (Baltimore, MD: Johns Hopkins University Press, 1998) contains some of the best interpretative writing in recent years, combined with ample reflections on methodological and other theoretical issues. George M. Wilson, *Narration in Light: Studies in Cinematic Point of View* (Baltimore, MD: Johns Hopkins University Press, 1986) is an idiosyncratic book that joins close analyses of the narrative strategies of five classic Hollywood films with more theoretical considerations about point of view in film.

16

MEDIUM

Kevin W. Sweeney

Cinema – artistic film or movies – was the great new art form of the twentieth century. In its struggle to establish its artistic credentials, cinema inherited the nineteenth-century debate about whether photography was an artistic medium. The question now was: could film, involving a process that mechanically recorded whatever was in front of the camera's lens, be recognized as a medium of artistic expression? Was there a distinctive medium that allowed an artist or artists to create a cinematic work of art? As a developing narrative form, often adapting established theatrical works, film also prompted theorists to clarify the differences between theater and cinema. Exactly how was the film medium different from that of theater? This concern about the distinctive nature of the cinematic medium was not a new theoretical enterprise. Theorists of the arts had been engaging in similar debates about other artistic media for centuries.

One of the most famous earlier medium theorists was Gotthold Lessing, who in his book *Laocoön* (1968 [1766]) proposed distinguishing poetry from painting in terms of their different sign systems. "Since painting," Lessing claimed, "because its signs or means of imitation can be combined only in space, must relinquish all representations of time, therefore progressive actions, as such, cannot come within its range" (90). Painting, he argued, should only attempt to show bodies or objects in space and not try to show a temporally unfolding series of events. Because it presents its imitative signs sequentially in time, poetry should concentrate on representing actions or events and not the appearance of bodies in space.

What is important for later medium theorists about Lessing's theory is that Lessing connects a description of a medium with a prescription for how artists ought to use that medium. Because of its distinctive material and formal nature, each medium has its own special potential. Artists ought to produce works that recognize the formal restrictions and distinctive representational requirements of the medium; they ought not to employ stylistic strategies more appropriate to another medium. This two-part concern to identify a special functional character of an artistic medium and to prescribe certain projects appropriate to that medium has been referred to by Noël Carroll as "the specificity thesis" (Carroll 1988: 81).

This concern to identify the nature of an artistic medium and to prescribe a range of aesthetic features appropriate to that medium was a major formalist interest of *modernist* artistic theory. Beginning in the middle of the nineteenth century and continuing on into the middle of the twentieth century, modernist theorists questioned the imitative, illusionist aesthetic that had been the main direction of the arts since the Renaissance. In a classic statement of this position, Clement Greenberg in his essay, "Modernist Painting," claimed that an essential feature of the modernist project was that each particular cultural practice, such as an individual art form, should engage in a self-critical search for its own distinctive nature. Each art form should attempt to discover what is "unique and irreducible" about its nature. He asserts:

> It quickly emerged that the unique and proper area of competence of each art coincided with all that was unique to the nature of its medium. The task of self-criticism became to eliminate from the effects of each art any and every effect that might conceivably be borrowed from or by the medium of any other art. Therefore each art would be rendered "pure," and in its "purity" find the guarantee of its standards of quality as well as its independence. (1995: 120)

According to Greenberg, the essence of painting – the irreducible medium of painting – was a paint-covered flat surface. Realistic or illusory painting, he says, "had dissembled the medium, using art to conceal art" (ibid.: 120). Modernist painting that conformed to this effort at self-criticism revealed the art form's true or "pure" medium and proclaimed such works to be an honest expression of that medium, providing an experience for the viewer that no other art form could deliver.

Modernism had a profound effect on all twentieth-century art forms, leading theorists of the arts to search for the irreducible essence of each artistic medium so as to validate it as a genuine art form. Artists were encouraged to produce works which reflexively highlighted the medium employed and revealed to perceivers the distinctive nature of that medium. Theorists of modernist poetry, modernist dance, modernist architecture, modernist (Brechtian) theater – and many other art forms – all sought to discover the essential medium of their specific art form. One can see the attempt to search for the "true" medium of film as an endeavor in this same modernist spirit. It was also important to distinguish cinema from theater and to emphasize that artistic films should be true to their medium and not pretend to be works in some other medium, such as filmed plays.

An important issue in addressing the question of what is the true medium of film is the question of whether cinema is best thought of as a single medium. Or, because of its history of constant technological change, should film be better thought of as involving a process, where a newer medium constantly replaces an older medium? Or, is film better thought of as a composite medium – such as some might call opera – in which new features are added to established ones? To begin addressing these concerns, one might acknowledge that art forms often have several different, distinctive media. When speaking about painting, for example, one could say that water color is a different medium from oil paint. This way of speaking identifies a medium as a physical object or process with a distinctive set of properties or features. However, by emphasizing the properties of the manipulated physical object, this approach invites the question of whether changing the physical object (e.g., the paint) produces a new artistic medium. If because of advances in chemistry, contemporary oil-based paints are different than those used in seventeenth-century Holland, is that reason enough to say that contemporary oil painters and seventeenth-century Dutch genre painters were working in different media? Does each new advance in paint technology produce a new medium? While we might say that water color is a different medium from oil, is acrylic paint, which certainly has some unique properties, really a different medium from oil paint? Or, are they the same medium because they produce generally similar qualitative experiences?

If we insist that acrylic is a different medium from oil, important questions are raised about the nature of the cinematic medium, due to the continuous change in film technology. Such changes have often been dramatic (e.g., the introduction of sound), but there have also been minor changes whose accumulative effects have been equally dramatic (e.g., gradual changes in the design of the camera). Are 1920s silent films that used black-and-white nitrate film stock in the same medium as sound Technicolor films from the 1950s or contemporary films using computer-generated imagery? Is the film medium that D. W. Griffith worked with during the 1910s and 1920s the same medium that Steven Spielberg worked with at the end of the century? Has cinema changed from a single distinctive medium into a composite medium or multimedia (Carroll 1996)?

Some theorists have tried to find a common element across the myriad changes in film technology to identify as the essence of the medium. Gregory Currie finds the common element in cinema to be moving images (Currie 1995). Gerald Mast has proposed that cinema is essentially "an integrated succession of projected images and (recorded) sounds" (Mast 1977: 111). By emphasizing that cinema essentially involves projection, Mast distinguishes cinema from television, at least the cathode-ray-tube television technology that he was familiar with in 1977. The quality and resolution of the television and film images are quite different. The professional projected image in a theater has a much sharper resolution than that of a TV image in one's living room. The film image created by light projected through celluloid allows for a true black and white. "On a color television set," Mast points out, "black-and-white looks more like purple-gray-and-pale-pink, since the color dots still produce faint hues without any stimulus" (94).

Of course, lots of films are shown on television; however, Mast claims that one's experience of a film on a large movie theater screen is markedly different from that of watching even the same film on the little box in one's living room. Seeing those giant lips say "Rosebud" on a large screen, Mast thinks, is a very different experience from seeing Citizen Kane (1941) on a small television monitor (ibid.: 102). With film we can be overwhelmed by the size of objects in the image, fascinated by the detail of a close-up, startled by loud sounds, held in rapture by soft ones. These characteristics of the screen image, Mast says, "produce almost tactile, sensual effects on the nerves, stomach, even skin … on television they remain occasionally interesting" (ibid.: 102–3). Cinema can create an almost "hypnotic" effect on the perceiver; television in one's living room often competes with many distractions.

Like some other medium theorists, Mast approaches the problem of identifying the cinematic medium not just from the standpoint of the material features of the process. He closely identifies the nature of the film medium with providing a distinctive experience, one not afforded by other art forms. Even though film technology changed over the course of the twentieth century, Mast would claim that there is still a common store of experience that we would identify as cinematic experience.

One might challenge Mast's distinction between cinema and television by saying that future technological change might not preserve projection as the common, and hence essential, cinematic element. In distinguishing film viewing from watching television, Mast seems to discount the possibility of technological innovation changing TV. An improved high-definition image and larger monitors might narrow the difference between what, for Mast, are two different media. Mast anticipates such a challenge by replying to the following question: "Could television become as kinetically effective as cinema with sharp resolution, stereophonic sound, and an immense wall screen? Perhaps. (But then it would not be television as we know it today.)" (ibid.: 103).

Other theorists of the cinematic medium have also tied the conception of the medium to the distinctive experience that film viewers have, a kind of experience not shared by those attending to works in other art forms. French film theorist, André Bazin, denied that cinema as a medium has evolved through a series of different media or that it has become more and more composite with each new technological innovation. In his essay, "The Myth of Total Cinema," Bazin claimed that prior to any of the inventions of the early film pioneers, the cinematic medium existed as an ideal object in people's imagination. He asserted, "The cinema is an idealistic phenomenon. The concept men had of it existed so to speak fully armed in their minds, as if in some platonic heaven" (1967a: 17). Inventors of film technology tried to find the means to realize physically this ideal; each invention presumably brought them closer to achieving that goal. "In their imagination," Bazin claims, "they saw the cinema as a total and complete representation of reality; they saw in a trice the reconstruction of a perfect illusion of the outside world in sound, color, and relief" (ibid.: 20). Bazin thought that achieving this "perfect illusion" is the goal of cinema, the realization of the medium of cinema, and that only cinema has this experience as its goal.

Yet, Bazin's view on the cinematic medium yields a paradox, one that he was certainly aware of. He says, "Every new development added to the cinema must paradoxically take it nearer and nearer to its origins. In short, cinema has not yet been invented" (ibid.: 21). Since the cinematic work has not been produced that is the perfect embodiment of the ideal, paradoxically, true cinema, as a physical process, has not been invented. However, viewed in this way, the concept of a cinematic medium loses considerable value as a critical category useful for understanding and evaluating a director's achievement. Such a conception becomes a measuring stick that we can use only to measure how close, in an asymptotic convergence, a film comes to achieving an ideal representation of the world. Of course, all films will be found wanting when measured by this perfect standard, although presumably some films will be closer to perfection than others. Bazin thinks that De Sica's neorealist *Bicycle Thieves* (1948) approaches this ideal. Yet such a conception of the cinematic medium gives little room for appreciating the way in which directors in their films have created new visions of what cinema can be. Bazin conceives of the cinematic medium as being fixed and immutable, as are all ideal objects. There seems little room for aesthetic creativity in inventing, extending, or transforming our conception of film as a medium.

Nevertheless, the idea that cinema has an essential connection with the world and that cinema has a unique ability to make us experience either the world (reality) or a fictional world has had a powerful influence on many cinema theorists. A debate developed between the "realists," who claimed that film did have an essential connection with a world, and "formative" theorists, as Siegfried Kracauer has labeled them (Kracauer 1960), who denied this connection and held that film was a medium of the imagination. This debate could be said to have begun with the noting of the contrasting styles of two nineteenth-century pioneers of the cinema, the Lumière brothers with their films documenting events taking place in the world and the French magician, Georges Méliès, with his fanciful illusionistic films (Kracauer 1960). In the 1895 films such as *Workers Leaving the Factory* and *The Arrival of the Train*, the Lumière brothers showed actual events taking place in the world. Watching the films today, audiences – realists would say – see what the world actually looked like in 1895. As a magician, Méliès used stop-action and other photographic tricks to present not actual but imaginary events such as the live disembodied heads of *Le Mélomane* (1903). Cinema, formative theorists would say, has a distinctive technological capacity for this creative play.

The realists would often argue for their position by claiming that the mechanics of the camera and the projector guaranteed that the series of projected images would be a record of the world and that no other artistic medium could connect us to the world in this way. In his classic realist article, "Style and Medium in the Motion Pictures," Erwin Panofsky holds that the "medium of the movies is physical reality as such" (2004 [1934]: 302). The cinematic medium, he claims, is not an amorphous substance like the paint that a painter uses or the marble that a sculptor forms. Instead,

> the movies organize material things and persons, not as a neutral medium, into a composition that receives its style, and may even become fantastic or pretervoluntarily symbolic, not so much by an interpretation in the artist's mind as by the actual manipulation of physical objects and recording machinery. (302)

For Panofsky, film as an artistic project requires the filmmaker to shoot scenes in such a way that the camerawork creates the expressive or stylistic qualities of the film. To manipulate the scenery prior to filming, to construct the sets in a distorted way and paint in shadows, as occurs in *The Cabinet of Dr Caligari* (1920), is to "prestylize" the film. Not to use the camerawork in an expressive way, but instead to attempt to add stylistic features by manipulating the *mise en scène* prior to filming, violates Panofsky's realist aesthetic.

The use of the camera and film machinery to give style to the work means that cinema organizes "material things and persons" in a different way than does the theater.

Panofsky distinguishes cinema from theater by pointing out that the film medium has essential capabilities beyond the reach of theater, what he calls the *dynamization of space* and the *spatialization of time*. On the stage, space, Panofsky believes, is fixed and static – the theater audience is always the same distance from the stage space. Because of this static relation to the audience, stage space cannot become huge or very small or take on emotional characteristics. (Panofsky seems to discount the space-constructing powers of lighting on the stage.) In the cinema, the viewer's relation to space is not fixed, and film has the capacity to create a variety of different spaces. Space on the screen, Panofsky believes, is movable; the viewer "is in permanent motion as his eye identifies itself with the lens of the camera which permanently shifts in distance and direction" (ibid.: 292).

Time, he believes, can also work differently on stage and screen. On the stage, time can be separated from the space of the main dramatic action. The Shakespearean soliloquy presents an actor speaking lines that are understood by theatrical convention as not occurring in the time of the diegesis, but outside of the drama's narrative world. The thoughts expressed are "out of time," so to speak. Panofsky discusses Lawrence Olivier's soliloquy in the filmed version of *Henry V* (1944). Instead of presenting Olivier speaking Shakespeare's soliloquy as it would have been done on the stage, the film shows Olivier not speaking but sitting mutely by the campfire. The speech is given in voice-over.

Panofsky suggests that this presentation of a soliloquy in a filmed play is a compromise and that a film, true to the cinematic medium, would connect narrative time with narrative space. What he has in mind is that a film which cuts between two different events can show events taking place at two different times, or can show different events occurring simultaneously. When shown an event on the screen, the viewer can always ask when in the narrative a particular event is taking place. Although Panofsky does discuss the voice-over soliloquy in *Henry V*, unfortunately he doesn't draw out the ways in which a voice-over sequence can be extradiegetic – that voice-over narration can be understood as outside the time of the narrative.

Another prominent realist theorist of the film medium is Siegfried Kracauer. Film, he says, "is uniquely equipped to record and reveal physical reality" (1960: 28). Yet, it is not the totality of physical reality that Kracauer thinks film records and reveals, only the visible world (Andrew 1976: 111). Nevertheless, because of the recording technology of film, with its variety of lenses, different camera shutter speeds, and numerous other techniques, film can show us events that we would either ordinarily not notice or normally be incapable of seeing. It can show us very large events (the shape and movement of a hurricane) and microscopically small events. It can slow down very fast events and speed up very slow ones (a plant growing). As long as a film adheres to this recording function, Kracauer believes that it is true to the medium:

> Imagine a film which, in keeping with the basic properties, records interesting aspects of physical reality but does so in a technically imperfect manner; perhaps the lighting is awkward or the editing uninspired. Nevertheless such a film is more specifically a film than one which utilizes brilliantly all the

cinematic devices and tricks to produce a statement disregarding camera-reality. (Ibid.: 30)

On Kracauer's view, the cinematic medium should not be thought of as just having a recording function; it should also reveal the world to viewers. Contemporary life is saturated with theoretical abstractions about the world, and our acquaintance with the world is diminished by these abstract perspectives. Cinema can give the world back to us, so to speak, by revealing to us features of, and events taking place in, concrete reality that might otherwise be inaccessible. Contemporary urban living has disconnected us from the natural world; cinema can show us natural phenomena that are distant or hard to see in all their otherwise obscure detail. Cinema, for Kracauer, is a panacea for the alienation of contemporary living.

André Bazin also fits into the realist tradition because he believes that the photographic basis of film produces images that present the viewer with reality. Painters and sculptors can produce representations of the world that are surprisingly accurate; however, the image on the screen allows us to see the object photographed. Bazin claims, "The photographic image is the object itself … [I]t shares, by virtue of the very process of its becoming, the being of the model of which it is the reproduction; it *is* the model" (1967: 14). For Bazin, when watching a film, one does not just see a representational image of an object; one sees the actual model for the image.

Using some of C. S. Peirce's semiotic terms, one could say that the painting is an *icon*: it resembles the object it represents, and in so doing, Bazin says, "it may actually tell us more about the model" than a photographic image, if, for example, the photographic image is somehow degraded (ibid.: 14). A photographic image, even though it usually has high iconic value, is also an *index* of what it represents. It is the direct causal effect of a stimulus object, in the same way that a footprint is an index of the foot that made the impression, or an individual's visual image is an index of an object (caused by light waves bouncing off that object and stimulating the retina). Just as we say that we see the world in virtue of having a visual field, so Bazin would say that film allows us to see the stimulus object whose image is recorded in the camera and projected on the screen.

Yet Bazin ties the realist effect produced by the indexical film image to a distinctive experience that the viewer is capable of having with cinematic works. If cinema is identified as the vehicle to achieve the "perfect illusion" of the world, it should also provide viewers with experiences like those they have when they exercise their free choice to interpret and assign meaning to objects and events in the world. Bazin's reliance on the viewer's freedom derives from French existentialism, particularly Jean-Paul Sartre's view that human beings must choose how they act and assign meaning to what they experience in the world (Andrew 1976: 172). The world is an ambiguous place, existentialists believe. Rather than being restricted to a course in life that is preestablished or determined, we must choose our actions, the course of our lives, and ultimately the world in which we live. Bazin felt that cinema should also provide viewers with an ambiguous world in which to choose and to assign meaning. His famous advocacy of a filmmaking style emphasizing *deep space* and the *long take* was intended to support providing the cinematic occasion for such viewer agency and interpretive initiative.

In "The Evolution of the Language of Cinema," Bazin presents his defense of the deep-space and long-take style. He ties it to a vision of the active viewer facing an ambiguous cinematic world that calls for interpretation. The deep-space and long-take style is prominently associated with the films of Orson Welles and William Wyler, yet Bazin claims that it had been introduced by Jean Renoir and others. It proposes shooting in depth so that objects from the foreground to background of a long to an extreme long shot are in focus. Bazin advocates holding the shot long enough so that viewers have plenty of time to observe on their own terms the objects in the various focal planes. This, Bazin thought, made for a more active viewing experience. He claimed,

> [D]epth of focus brings the spectator into a relation with the image closer to that which he enjoys with reality … [I]t implies … both a more active mental attitude on the part of the spectator and a more positive contribution on his part to the action in progress … [The viewer] is called upon to exercise at least a minimum of personal choice … [D]epth of focus reintroduced ambiguity into the structure of the image … The uncertainty in which we find ourselves as to the spiritual key or the interpretation we should put on the film is built into the very design of the image. (1967b: 35–6)

Bazin contrasts this style of filmmaking, which mirrors an individual's active engagement with the world, with a *montage* style which he thinks promotes a more passive relation to a film on the part of a viewer. Montage, he thinks, predetermines the meaning of a sequence and eliminates viewers' active involvement.

Although very influential, Bazin and his fellow realists were opposed by formative theorists who proposed seeing the medium of film as having, not the capacity to reflect physical reality, but to construct a world. An early film theorist, Hugo Münsterberg, took a Kantian constructivist view of the cinematic medium. In perceiving the world, Kant held that we construct an interpersonal world with our common psychological faculties. Film, Münsterberg claimed, shares with our special psychological faculties a comparable means for world construction. Just as we construct an interpersonal world with a spatial-temporal framework and causal connections, Münsterberg saw film technology as supplying the means for constructing a narrative world with its own spatial, temporal, and causal relations. Film also has techniques comparable to other psychological faculties: memory is shown on the screen with the flashback; attention is indicated by an insert close-up (Münsterberg 1970 [1916]: 57–8).

Another formative theorist, equally famous as a filmmaker, was the great Soviet director, Sergei Eisenstein. As a Marxist, Eisenstein believed that the phenomenal world does not present human beings with the truth about history or economic and social reality. If one wants to learn the truth, one has to appreciate the dialectical struggle and class conflicts that go on behind the appearances. To get at the truth, film cannot just record the world as it appears. He is no realist. Long takes of "physical reality" do not give the spectator the truth. Only by showing the clash of elements within the frame or the clash of sequences in the editing (montage) does one create the dialectical oppositions necessary for stimulating the viewer in the search for truth. For Eisenstein, film does not reflect or record reality; it creates new cinematic relationships that provoke the spectator into realizing the truth.

The most prominent and systematic formative theorist was Rudolf Arnheim, who took pains to refute the realist view that film on the basis of its mechanical nature recorded physical reality. Arnheim points out that the world is three dimensional, but the film image is a projection of that world onto a two-dimensional plane. To suggest the missing depth, Arnheim thinks filmmakers have to make creative choices, as far as camera angles, the kinds of shots, and editing used to ensure that viewers see a sequence as having depth. In presenting a two-dimensional image, film does not automatically preserve the constancies of size and shape: a rectangular table would look trapezoidal, and objects closer to the lens would look much larger than those farther away (Arnheim 1966: 13–14). Again filmmakers have to exercise considerable inventiveness in choosing shots, camera angles, and kinds of editing to create a visual world on the screen that is understandable to the spectator. Arnheim identifies making such creative choices with artistic expression. Arnheim identifies a filmmaker's making creative choices, so that a particular film sequence exhibits qualities not conveyed by the automatic process of filmmaking, with using the cinematic medium in an artistic way. He places special importance on making these choices within the limitations of current technology. For example, in the silent era, Joseph von Sternberg used a visual sequence to give the impression of a sound. In *The Docks of New York* (1928), he added a visual insert of the sudden flight of a flock of birds to show the sound of a pistol shot. Arnheim considers the creative choices involved in making that sequence to be an especially expressive use of the cinematic medium (Arnheim 1966: 34).

Noël Carroll criticizes Arnheim's "specificity thesis," finding in Arnheim's formative theory a narrow and overly prescriptive view about the medium of cinema (Carroll 1988). Filmmaking has changed over the course of a century, and Carroll holds that one should not insist that cinema conform to a narrow and traditional format excluding new developments as authentic and interesting instances of filmmaking. Carroll labels the view that there is a single essential medium for an art form as "medium-essentialism" (Carroll 1996: 49–55). He rejects "medium-essentialism" and advocates a broader view which would accept a variety of media as equally worthy of cinematic use.

With the fading of the modernist urge to find each art form's "true" medium and adhere to the prescriptions for producing works of art in that unique medium, there has been a greater acceptance of artists bridging artistic disciplines and working in composite or multimedia forms. This postmodernist attitude of accepting a diversity of media suggests that theorists of cinema have moved away from a classical modernist period in which questions about the nature of the film medium led to principles for the evaluation of films. Stanley Cavell's film theory is representative of this theoretical shift. Instead of claiming that there is a single cinematic medium, he holds that there are "media" of film. He identifies these media with films made in different eras and grouped together as genres (e.g., screwball comedies from the 1930s and '40s). One of the advantages of this approach is that a medium becomes a set of common features determined by a natural historical grouping. There is no abstract essence with this approach: cinema has to be invented – and perhaps invented in different forms – rather than discovered by being matched to some ideal conception. Another advantage is its recognition of the role of technological change in transforming the processes of filmmaking and the invention of new acting styles and genres (Cavell 1979). However, essentialists like Gerald Mast would likely object that if one considers these to be different *film* media, one begs the question of why they are all *film* media. Isn't there some common cinematic element in virtue of which they are all *film* media rather than media of different art forms?

Finally, even if one adopts a multimedia perspective and recognizes different media corresponding to different film periods and genres, advocates of the classical realist and formative approaches (the heirs of the Lumière brothers and Méliès) are still alive and well, although they now pitch their arguments in narrower debates about the nature of individual genres and recent developments in filmmaking. For example, realist arguments abound about the nature of documentary filmmaking: Should documentaries be limited to a *cinema-verité* approach, which records actual events taking place, or should one allow the "re-creation" of these events in order to better inform the audience? Advocates of the formative approach can be found supporting new uses for computer-generated imagery in film.

See also Definition of "cinema" (Chapter 5), Film as art (Chapter 11), Formalism (Chapter 12), Ontology (Chapter 20), Rudolph Arnheim (Chapter 27), Walter Benjamin (Chapter 28), Noël Carroll (Chapter 31), Stanley Cavell (Chapter 32), Sergei Eisenstein (Chapter 35), Jean Mitry (Chapter 37), and Hugo Münsterberg (Chapter 39).

References

Andrew, D. (1976) *The Major Film Theories*, London and New York: Oxford University Press.

Arnheim, R. (1966) *Film as Art*, Berkeley: University of California Press.

Bazin, A. (1967a) "The Myth of Total Cinema," in H. Gray (trans.) *What Is Cinema?*, vol. 1, Berkeley: University of California Press.

—— (1967b) "The Evolution of the Language of Cinema," in H. Gray (trans.) *What Is Cinema?*, vol. 1, Berkeley: University of California Press.

Carroll, N. (1988) *Philosophical Problems of Classical Film Theory*, Princeton, NJ: Princeton University Press.

—— (1996) *Theorizing the Moving Image*, Cambridge and New York: Cambridge University Press.

Cavell, S. (1979) *The World Viewed: Reflections on the Ontology of Film*, exp. ed., Cambridge, MA: Harvard University Press.

Currie, G. (1995) *Image and Mind: Film, Philosophy and Cognitive Science*, Cambridge and New York: Cambridge University Press.

Greenberg, C. (1995 [1960]) "Modernist Painting," in A. Neil and A. Ridley (eds.) *The Philosophy of Art: Readings Ancient and Modern*, New York: McGraw-Hill.

Kracauer, S. (1960) *Theory of Film*, New York: Oxford University Press.

Lessing, G. (1968 [1766]) *Laocoön: An Essay upon the Limits of Painting and Poetry*, New York: Noonday Press.

Mast, G. (1977) *Film/Cinema/Movie: A Theory of Experience*, New York: Harper and Row.
Münsterberg, H. (1970 [1916]) *The Film: A Psychological Study*, New York: Dover.
Panofsky, E. (2004 [1934]) "Style and Medium in the Motion Pictures," in L. Braudy and M. Cohen (eds.) *Film Theory and Criticism*, 6th ed., New York: Oxford University Press.

Further reading

Dudley Andrew, *The Major Film Theories* (London and New York: Oxford University Press, 1976) is a survey of classical theories of film, with good analyses of realist and formative medium theories of film. Rudolph Arnheim, *Film as Art* (Berkeley: University of California Press, 1966) provides a major formative and expressionist theory of film as a medium. André Bazin, "The Myth of Total Cinema," in H. Gray (trans.) *What Is Cinema?*, vol. 1 (Berkeley: University of California Press, 1967), presents Bazin's theory that cinema is an idealist medium; and his "The Evolution of the Language of Cinema," in the same volume, presents his realist theory of the film medium and his advocacy of the long-take and deep-space style of filmmaking. Noël Carroll, *Philosophical Problems of Classical Film Theory* (Princeton, NJ: Princeton University Press, 1988) presents extended analyses of the medium theories of Arnheim, Bazin, and Perkins; Carroll also discusses and rejects the "specificity thesis." His *Theorizing the Moving Image* (Cambridge and New York: Cambridge University Press, 1996) argues against "medium-essentialism" and advocates an openness to new developments in filmmaking. Stanley Cavell, *The World Viewed: Reflections on the Ontology of Film*, exp. ed. (Cambridge, MA: Harvard University Press, 1979), rather than urging one cinematic medium, argues for various "media" of film. Greg Currie, *Image and Mind: Film, Philosophy and Cognitive Science* (Cambridge and New York: Cambridge University Press, 1995) offers a contemporary theory of the cinematic medium, requiring that film have moving images. A classical realist theory of the medium of film is Siegfried Kracauer, *Theory of Film* (New York: Oxford University Press, 1960). Gerald Mast, *Film/Cinema/Movie: A Theory of Experience* (New York: Harper and Row, 1977) emphasizes the projected image as an essential aspect of cinema as a medium, and contains a classical discussion of the difference between experiencing film and television. An early formative theory of film as a medium, emphasizing film as mirroring of human psychological faculties, is Hugo Münsterberg, *The Film: A Psychological Study* (New York: Dover, 1970), originally published in 1916. Erwin Panofsky, "Style and Medium in the Motion Pictures," in L. Braudy and M. Cohen (eds.) *Film Theory and Criticism*, 6th ed. (New York: Oxford University Press, 2004), originally published in 1934, is a classical realist theory of film as a medium. V. Perkins, *Film as Film: Understanding and Judging Movies* (Harmondsworth and New York: Penguin, 1972) offers a theory of film as a medium, melding formative and realist elements.

17
MUSIC
Jeff Smith

During the past two decades, the academic study of film music has emerged as a prolific and productive area of film scholarship. This wave of scholarship was initiated by Claudia Gorbman's (1987) pathfinding study of music in narrative filmmaking, *Unheard Melodies*, which inspired many scholars in both cinema studies and musicology to follow in its footsteps. Since then, the field of film-music studies has grown exponentially, with authors such as Caryl Flinn (1992), Royal S. Brown (1994), Kathryn Kalinak (1992), K. J. Donnelly (2001), Annahid Kassabian (2001), and Daniel Goldmark (2005) producing important monographs on the subject. In recent years, this intellectual ferment has reached a critical mass, with no fewer than four scholarly journals devoted to the study of music and media, and two series of books in the works at major university presses. Film-music studies has, thus, emerged from the shadows of its more prominent counterparts in cinema and music studies, drawing contributors from the fields of cultural studies, media studies, sound studies, and cognitive psychology.

Yet, while the study of film music has reached a sort of maturity in recent years, it remains a very marginal area within philosophy. Perhaps this is because the philosophical study of both film and music remain small subfields within the larger study of art, aesthetics, and communication. To date, only a handful of philosophers have tackled questions and issues related to music in film, and for the most part, even these works tend to focus on more localized queries. Peter Kivy, for example, has written on the aesthetic and filmic functions of film music, which he sees emerging from larger traditions of music and theater, such as opera and melodrama (1997). Noël Carroll proposes a definition of film music as "modifying music," suggesting that the scores in classical Hollywood films typically function analogously to the role of adverbs and adjectives in language (Carroll 1998: 213–23). For Carroll, music in film helps to characterize the people, places, things, and actions depicted within the diegesis it accompanies, by adding semiotic specificity to their representation. Jerrold Levinson (1996), by contrast, has attempted to define the role of music in its relation to the agencies of cinematic narrator and implied filmmaker entailed in the process of cinematic storytelling.

By far the most important work in the philosophical study of film music is Theodor Adorno's *Composing for the Films*, which he coauthored with composer Hanns Eisler

(Eisler and Adorno 1994). As a Frankfurt school theorist, Adorno, not surprisingly, offers a neo-Marxist critique of film-music practices as they have developed within the culture industry. Moreover, Adorno and Eisler argue that film music, like other kinds of mass culture, employs conventions and clichés rather than genuine invention. Decrying these "bad habits," Adorno and Eisler recommend an alternative model of film-music practice that utilizes the formal and stylistic properties represented within the new musical resources provided by Arnold Schoenberg, Igor Stravinsky, Alban Berg, and Anton Webern.

Because most of the work on the philosophy of film music has proceeded in a piecemeal fashion, it seems propitious to establish some "first principles" regarding film music's ontology and its relation to spectators. To that end, I will argue for two specific points in this essay: (1) that film music is best understood through a cluster account of the concept that identifies several possible criteria for its classification; and (2) that a cognitivist account of film-music audition offers the best explanation of the way music contributes to the viewer's perception and cognition of cinematic representations. While I do not propose to offer definitive answers to these questions, it is hoped that this brief exegesis of the relevant issues might provide a valuable framework for further debate and discussion.

The ontology of film music

As Nelson Goodman and others have acknowledged, the ontology of music has been a somewhat slippery concept for philosophers of art (1976). Within the tradition of Western art music, an individual piece, such as Brahms' First Symphony, exists as a kind of abstract program for performance, with each particular iteration of the piece being slightly different in terms of its interpretation. Although the printed score of the piece fixes its primary musical parameters, such as rhythm, melody, and harmony, secondary parameters, such as dynamics, tempo, and timbre, may vary subtly from performance to performance. The solution to this particular ontological problem has been to treat musical works in terms of a "type-token distinction" that can be traced back to the semiotics of Charles Sanders Peirce. Viewed in this way, a piece of concert music is an abstract sign system that exists as a type, with each performance or recording defined as a token of the type.

In contrast to music, film music avoids this ontological problem insofar as it exists as a recorded medium. Although film scores are frequently performed by symphonies in "pops" concerts around the country, the score itself has an independent existence as a component of the film's soundtrack, which also includes dialogue and sound effects. Soundtrack albums and live performances of film music offer certain advantages to listeners in that they eliminate competing visual and aural stimuli, but they are understood to be derivations of the original score, which exists in a separate physical form as an element in a larger audio-visual totality.

Film music, however, poses slightly different problems regarding its definition, having to do with the extent to which the category encompasses a widely divergent group of musical phenomena. Arguing that the study of music in film is marred by imprecise terminology, William H. Rosar examines the various ways in which the term "film music" has functioned in film-music scholarship. Noting its origins in earlier studies, such as Kurt London's landmark *Film Music* (1936), Rosar argues that the term was originally coined to describe a style or genre of music composition, making the concept analogous to that of incidental music composed for the theater. Over time, however, the concept of film music broadened to include a set of related concepts, such as score, source music, song scores, and compilation scores. For Rosar, the original designation of film music as a term intended to describe a specific approach to music composition has been superceded by academic definitions of film music that focus on the functions of music in films. The result, according to Rosar, is that the emerging field of film-music studies circulates two definitions of the concept that are more or less incommensurate.

Rosar suggests that the source of this terminological muddle can be traced to the interdisciplinary study of film music. Indeed, Rosar notes that scholarly inquiry over the last couple of decades has moved apace in the disciplines of both film and music, and further that these scholars have freely borrowed ideas from other domains, such as philosophy, psychology, semiotics, literary criticism, cultural studies, and even marketing research. Because this work has advanced through a "rapidly growing community of writers in various disciplines," the profusion of scholarship has produced the "potential for a veritable Babel" (2002: 1). Ironically, although scholars refer explicitly to film-music studies, the concept that ostensibly unites the field lacks a common domain of discourse.

As a corrective measure, Rosar proposes a conceptual distinction between "film music" and "music in film," as a means of sorting different types of musical phenomena in the cinema. Rosar suggests that we reserve the term "film music" to refer to the craft and technique of composing original music to accompany filmed scenes and sequences. All other types of musical phenomena, such as source music or interpo-lated songs, fall into the category of "music in film." In making this distinction, Rosar explicitly aims to clarify confusion that he believes "already exists in the literature resulting from two incommensurable uses of the term *film music*" (2002: 15). At the same time, though, Rosar implicitly hopes to place the study of film music on surer footing by providing scholars with a definition that is more specific, more coherent, and more discriminating than the one in current parlance within the field.

In advocating a definition of film music that refers to the craft and technique of film scoring, Rosar argues for a lexical designation derived from an understanding of the way the term is already used and accepted. In advancing the case for a *customary* or *reportive* definition of film music, Rosar offers an etymological defense of the concept that traces the origins of the term itself through its first usage in German and English publications. For Rosar, the innovation of sound technology had a significant impact on the meaning of film music insofar as it associated the term with scores specially composed for films. This more circumscribed meaning led to an *essential definition* that highlighted its unique and important characteristics. These characteristics arose out of the silent film's principle of using musical accompaniment as a form of musical illustration. Thus, for Rosar, film music came to be identified with a compositional technique for fitting music to pictures, rather than an understanding of the music's function. Perhaps more importantly, the promulgation of scores modeled on late nineteenth-century romanticism yielded a group style, a particular sound that listeners identified as "movie music," even in compositions not written for the screen.

At first blush, Rosar's essential definition of film music seems to offer both conceptual utility and elegant simplicity. By defining film music as music composed for films, Rosar's classification highlights its significant characteristics and distinguishes it from other types of music in film, such as "source music" and preexisting classical or popular music (about which I will say more later). The latter items are labeled as "music in film," a category that would include film music as a particular subset. Upon closer inspection, though, problems emerge from Rosar's insistence upon divorcing compositional technique from film music's functions. Rosar argues that this technique arose from the practice of musical illustration, but this simply begs the larger question of what the music is intended to illustrate. This question has no simple answer, but rather must be understood as a range of particular narrative functions that music played in the silent cinema. From a contemporary perspective, musical illustration in the studio era seemed to entail a particular isomorphism between music and image, one in which musical features of film composition are intended to match specific actions depicted in the narrative. Yet this compositional technique, which is sometimes described as "mickey-mousing," was not part of the repertoire of silent film accompaniment, since it depends on synchronized sound technology for its effect. Instead, the notion of musical illustration promulgated in the silent era was one that correlated musical features with narrative attributes, such as genre, characterization, setting, and mood. Viewed in this way, the compositional technique associated with film scoring in the sound era arose as a consequence of the particular narrative functions that music served in the silent era. Any attempt to define film music in a manner that brackets off those functions seems doomed to failure.

Similarly, Rosar's association of film music with the late romantic idiom is generally accurate as a historical descriptor, but it too fails as an essential definition. The evidence that Rosar cites to support this claim merely shows that the late romantic idiom is sufficient to summon the impression of "movie music," but hardly a necessary condition for film scoring. The predominance of original music composed in the style of the late romantics was the result of a variety of economic, cultural, and historical factors present during the studio era. These factors were historically contingent, and do nothing to suggest that the romantic idiom has inherent properties that make it more suited to film accompaniment than other types of music. Indeed, during much of the silent era, scores compiled from preexisting concert music or popular songs were easily as common as original compositions for films. By identifying film music with the late romantic idiom, Rosar treats a historical outcome as an essential property of film music, and thereby "freezes" the meaning of the term according to the way its connotations circulated more than sixty years ago.

While the problems already evident in Rosar's ontology of film music might be enough to reject the concept *tout court*, even more pressing difficulties emerge in his defense of his ontology in relation to competing definitions circulated among film-music scholars and historians. Rosar, for example, argues that film music is paradoxically, and perhaps illogically, distinct from *film score* as a term that refers to nondiegetic, background music. Film scores, unlike film music, need not be written directly for the screen, and may be adapted from preexisting sources. Citing examples, such as *The Black Cat* (1934) and *2001: A Space Odyssey* (1968), Rosar concludes that "score" is a more comprehensive term than film music.

Similarly, Rosar also argues against recent attempts to include popular music in the paradigm of film music. In perhaps his most contentious move, Rosar critiques K. J. Donnelly's claim that the pop music of *Performance* (1970) constitutes a model of film music that exists as an alternative to the classical Hollywood score. More specifically, Rosar critiques Donnelly's suggestion that the advent of popular music in films of the 1960s "as a replacement for film music" broke a "film music paradigm that had been weathered but had persisted since the 1930s" (Donnelly 2001: 153). Rosar claims that Donnelly's definition is caught in a logical contradiction insofar as a film-music paradigm can hardly replace itself. To put it mildly, though, Rosar is rather ungenerous in his reading of Donnelly in suggesting that the latter intends an ontological definition of film music rather than a historical one. Donnelly's claim about a "replacement for film music" might be clarified by voicing the implicit subordinate clause, "as it was understood historically prior to 1967." Donnelly's position advocates a historicized understanding of film music, while Rosar's paradigm, despite his claims to the contrary, seems fixed, immutable, and unresponsive to historical change. If we accept Rosar's assertion that the classical style of film music has changed, then his definition of film music needs to specify the reasons why certain types of music were assimilated, while others are consigned to the category of music in film.

Rosar's subsequent discussion of source music versus score and classical versus popular idioms only muddles things further in that he shifts his attention to properties and characteristics of film scores, rather than film music *per se*. For example, Rosar offers a fairly lengthy discussion of the way in which "As Time Goes By" and "La Marseillaise" appear as performed pieces of music within the diegesis of *Casablanca* (1942), but also function as musical themes within Max Steiner's score. Here Rosar's discussion cogently distinguishes between score and source music – that is, music which is heard by characters within the diegetic space of the film – but it evades a more salient question, namely whether or not Rosar defines Max Steiner's score as "film music." If we define film music as original music written directly for the screen, then there seems to be some equivocation about what is meant by original. A cue in *Casablanca* that features "As Time Goes By" is original in the sense that it did not exist before Steiner wrote it, but the theme itself is certainly not original. Does this commit us to the position that cues featuring themes specifically composed by Steiner are film music, while those cues that feature themes derived from preexisting sources are identified as music in film? If this is the case, then the distinction between film music and music in film seems specious and arbitrary.

Scores that emerged as an alternative to Hollywood classicism pose still another problem. As Rosar points out in his discussion of a "movie music" sound, the essential definition of film music derives some of its force from a cinematic character discerned in the music, and further that this cinematic character is heard in works written for the concert stage rather than the soundstage. Yet what are we to make of scores written outside of that late romantic idiom? Composers like Elmer Bernstein and Jerry Goldsmith appear to be worthy inheritors of the traditions disseminated by Steiner, Alfred Newman, Hugo Friedhofer, and Erich Wolfgang Korngold. Yet several of their scores do not employ melody and harmony in ways consistent with the late romantic tradition. Some cues in Goldsmith's scores, such as *Planet of the Apes* (1968) and *Chinatown* (1974), do not sound like "movie music" at all. Does each score's use of twelve-tone serial technique and jazz, respectively, place it outside the domain of film music? Likewise, does it make sense to identify Bernstein's score for *To Kill a Mockingbird* (1962) as film music, but treat his pioneering jazz score for *The Man with the Golden Arm* (1955) as music in film? Although part of Rosar's definition emphasizes a cinematic character to film music, perhaps it is not necessary for film music to sound like "movie music." But this simply opens the door to a range of cases that Rosar would likely reject as "film music." Can one legitimately include jazz scores like Leith Stevens' score for *The Wild One* (1953) or Henry Mancini's score for *Touch of Evil* (1958) in the category of film music, but exclude funk scores like Earth, Wind, and Fire's score for *Sweet Sweetback's Baadasssss Song* (1971), Isaac Hayes' score for *Shaft* (1971), or Curtis Mayfield's score for *Superfly* (1972)?

Rosar's model also encounters problems with films like *Out of Sight* (1998) and *Fight Club* (1999), which also appear to be borderline cases for his proposed definition of film music. On the one hand, these scores were specially created for their films and used established techniques to match music to visual action. On the other hand, however, the scores for *Out of Sight* and *Fight Club* are hardly composed in the usual manner. Rather DJs David Holmes and the Dust Brothers created these scores by sampling existing recordings to make new pieces of music.

Because of its difficulties in dealing with counterexamples and borderline cases, Rosar's "ordinary language" definition of film music unnecessarily rules out a number of instances that many film-music historians would likely identify as film music. As an alternative, I propose that we treat film music as a "cluster concept," following the example established by Berys Gaut in his description of art (Gaut 2000, 2005). Drawing inspiration from Wittgenstein's notion of "family resemblances" as a conceptual basis for categorization, Gaut says that a cluster account is one that cannot be defined in terms of individually necessary nor jointly sufficient conditions. Instead, Gaut suggests that a cluster account employs disjunctively necessary conditions, some of which must be instantiated if the object under investigation is to fall under the concept. That is, no single property is necessary or sufficient for an object to fall under a cluster concept. Rather, a cluster concept employs several criteria, and contains subsets of traits and functions that may be sufficient to count toward an object falling under the concept.

In developing his cluster account of art, Gaut offers several reasons why a cluster concept might be preferable to definitions organized around a single essential condition or a set of necessary properties: (1) cluster accounts are better suited for considering borderline cases and counterexamples; (2) cluster accounts are better suited to the inductive reasoning protocols employed in considering new objects; and (3) cluster accounts do a better job capturing the way we ordinarily think about the reasons for and against an object's inclusion in a particular category. Moreover, a cluster account is especially appropriate for a concept of film music, which is part of a creative enterprise that is itself engaged in large-scale processes of aesthetic and historical change. Like the concept art, film music is not rule governed, but is instead shaped by musical conventions and traditions, some of which may be revised or rejected as part of the creative process. A cluster account of film music is, thus, more capable of dealing with borderline cases and counterexamples that come about as a result of invention and innovation, including those that have not yet happened.

Following Gaut's precedent, I also wish to propose a provisional list of criteria to count toward an object's being film music. This list is not intended to be a definitive taxonomy of film-music properties, but rather should serve as a point of departure in illustrating the advantages of a cluster account of film music. The list contains some overlaps with similar lists offered by Jerrold Levinson and Noël Carroll. My criteria are (1) music specially composed for use as part of a recorded audio-visual medium; (2) music used to accompany cinematic depictions of peoples, places, things, ideas, or events; (3) music used to underline aspects of a film's setting; (4) music used to communicate a film character's traits; (5) music used to signify emotion or mood in a filmed scene or sequence; (6) music used to convey a film character's point of view; (7) music used to accent depicted actions in a filmed scene or sequence; (8) music used to reinforce a film's formal features, such as its editing; and (9) music that sounds like film music.

Armed with a cluster concept of film music, let us revisit some of the examples introduced earlier in the essay to see how they work. Scores composed for classical Hollywood films, for example, exhibit most, if not all, of these various criteria. Consequently, because they exhibit so many of these properties, we can readily see why Rosar tries to define film music in terms of a model exemplified by classical Hollywood composers. Much of the music used to accompany silent films, however, fits criteria 2–8, but not necessarily 1 or 9. This is because much of the music was not specifically written for films, but instead was culled from the literatures of concert music and contemporaneous popular music. The theme song for *Goldfinger* (1964), which was written specifically for the eponymous James Bond film, would fit criteria 1, 2, 4, 6, and 8. However, a song like "The Sounds of Silence," which was written before its appearance in *The Graduate* (1967), omits the criterion for originality. The scores for *Superfly*, *Out of Sight*, and *Fight Club* seem to fit criteria 1–8, but the style of these scores differs from the classical Hollywood paradigm, and thus they do not sound like film music in the sense described by Rosar. Thus, these pop scores would not count as film music under the last criterion insofar as film music has a normative definition that associates it with the romantic idiom of Wagner, Strauss, and Mahler. Finally, a cluster concept of film music can even deal with rather extreme limit cases, such as Alex North's rejected score for *2001: A Space Odyssey* (1967). North's score fits criteria 1 and 9, but since it was never used in Kubrick's film, it does not actually accompany images in the film, nor does it perform any of the narrative functions that it was expected to serve.

It is also worth noting that this cluster account of film music does not preclude the use of terms like "source music" or "underscore" according to their commonly understood denotations. The concept of source music is logically entailed in criterion 3, regarding music's role in a film's setting, but that does not exhaust the ways in which it might count as film music under a cluster account. Source music can, and frequently does, serve other functions, such as mood-setting or conveying a character's emotions. The same condition also applies to nondiegetic underscore, which routinely fits any of the criteria listed above.

Film music and psychology

Recent film-music scholarship has employed two paradigms for explaining the ways in which music in film engages the psychology of film spectators. The first model describes film music's emotional engagement and semiotic functions in terms of Freudian and Lacanian psychoanalysis. The second explicates film music's affective dimensions and narrative functions within a cognitive framework. Both paradigms, at least partially, are driven by a question that has bedeviled film-music theorists for ages, namely how does music in film fulfill its narrative functions while operating as something of which viewers are unaware. Film music, thus, seems to have a paradoxical status in terms of its audition; it offers some of the same aesthetic pleasures, formal structures, and emotional signification of other music but is attended to in a way fundamentally different.

Several scholars, such as Claudia Gorbman (1987), Caryl Flinn (1992), Annahid Kassabian (2001), and Samuel Chell (1984), employ a psychoanalytic account to explain film music's unconscious engagement of spectatorial processes. This model suggests that film music plays an especially important role in the constitution of a subject position that individual spectators inhabit when viewing a film. Gorbman analogizes film music's aural appeal to a hypnotist's voice that lures us into unconscious obeisance to a film text's ideological demands. This account is a variant of the "suture" theories that were popularized in film journals like *Screen* in the 1970s. According to this view, music, like other techniques of cinematic signification, works to "suture" the spectator's unconscious into that of the film, and music is specially equipped for this task, due to its direct pull on the viewer's emotions.

In contrast to this model, researchers in the subfield of psychomusicology have fleshed out a cognitive account of film-music perception. This paradigm developed through series of experiments that have measured, among other things, music's effect on our perception of the emotional meaning of depicted actions and characters, music's ability to enhance the viewer's memory of filmed events, music's ability to shape the viewer's interpretation of diegetic situations and to alter their expectations of future narrative outcomes (Marshall and Cohen 1988; Lipscomb and Kendall 1994; Boltz *et al.* 1991; Bullerjahn and Güldenring 1994).

In summarizing this research tradition, Annabel Cohen proposes a congruence-associationist framework for understanding film-music communication (2001). For Cohen, cinema is perceived through three parallel channels that are domain specific and that are used to process the meaning and structure of speech, music, and visual information communicated through the film's narration. From moment to moment, the viewer utilizes both bottom-up and top-down perceptual processes to extract the narrative information and emotional meanings necessary to form a coherent story in the diegesis. More importantly, perhaps, the ability to form a coherent story depends upon the viewer's understanding of crossmodal structural congruence that affects our perceptual groupings in visual and auditory domains in short-term memory. That is, film music works through the viewer's cognitive processing of perceived correspond-ences between musical and visual information. For Cohen, although the acoustical aspect of the music is encoded by sensory memory, it fails to be transported to short-term memory. Instead, because of inferences derived from long-term memory, the acoustical aspect of music falls away while the information about the narrative is stored. Cohen's associationist-congruence model, thus, explains how music in film communicates the emotional significance of narrative events and arouses low-level affects in viewers.

Within each of these paradigms, film music achieves its particular effects by operating at an unconscious level. For Gorbman, film music would cease to have its ideological effect if audiences were aware of its presence; if the subject hears the hypnotist's voice, the game is over. Likewise, Cohen cites empirical evidence to support the notion that film music is apprehended unconsciously. She references a survey conducted by Archie Levy in which subjects were asked while leaving the theater to evaluate the music's effectiveness in the film they just saw. Most individuals reported that the film's score was fine despite the fact that there was no music actually present in the film except for the opening credits (Cohen 2000: 366).

Yet it is clear that each paradigm has a different understanding of unconscious listening. For adherents of the psychoanalytic paradigm, the appeal of film music is grounded in processes of unconscious fantasy, more specifically the primordial fantasy of the *chora*. According to this theory, film music, like all types of music, engages the fantasy of the subject's unity with the mother's body insofar as music creates a sonorous envelope that is reminiscent of our experience prior to birth within the womb (Rosalato 1974; Anzieu 1976). In contrast, cognitive theorists typically take unconscious listening to simply mean that sound is apprehended below the threshold of our conscious attention. Cohen, in fact, suggests that film music's inaudibility is similar to the phenomenon of "inattentional blindness." In experiments conducted by Dan Levin and Daniel Simons, empirical research has shown that, due to limita-tions on our attention, subjects are "blind" to much of the information present within a visual field (cited in Cohen 2001: 256). Like the acoustical aspect of music, part of the visual field in these experiments is perceived unconsciously, but the information is not retained in either short- or long-term memory. While the relation between film-music audition and inattentional blindness is intriguing, Cohen suggests that a better parallel might be developed through research on the role of prosody in speech perception, which provides cues to listeners in the form of intensity and intonation of speech patterns, but which subjects generally ignore in favor of the semantic content of a message.

While I wholeheartedly endorse the model of film-music psychology elaborated in Cohen's congruence-associationist framework, I also propose that we might consider film-music audition to be a phenomenon akin to subliminal perception. Philip Merikle *et al.* define subliminal perception as something that occurs whenever "stimuli presented below the threshold or limen for awareness are found to influence thoughts, feelings, or actions" (Merikle *et al.* 2001: 123–4). Film music seems to fit both conditions for Merikle *et al.*'s definition insofar as music is perceived by film viewers, for the most part, without awareness, and clearly affects their perceptions and thoughts about the events depicted on screen. Although she does not describe it as such, Cohen's review of the psychological literature on film-music perception seems to support these necessary and sufficient conditions for subliminal phenomena.

Beyond this *prima facie* case, though, it seems to me that there is also some additional heuristic value in thinking about film-music audition as a type of subliminal perception. For one thing, it is a more precise descriptor than the notion of unconscious listening. The latter concept is perhaps too broad to be of much value. After all, George Lakoff and Steven Johnson point out that 95 percent of all thought is unconscious thought (Lakoff and Johnson 1999: 13). Treating film-music audition as part of that undifferentiated mass does little to communicate what is unique and specific about the phenomenon. More importantly, though, the notion of "unconscious listening" is tainted, especially in academic film studies, by its association with a psychoanalytic framework for analyzing film's effects on viewers. For that reason alone, it is perhaps better to reject the term "unconscious listening" outright so as to avoid the implication that Cohen's "associationist-congruence" framework somehow entails concepts like the Oedipus complex or the Mirror Stage.

Second, subliminal perception also better captures film music's ability to influence cognitive processes. Cognitive psychologists have performed several experiments that demonstrate the ways in which subliminal phenomena "prime" subjects' cognitive processes by influencing both what stimuli are perceived with awareness and how those stimuli are experienced. Many of these experiments tested the effects of masked stimuli on subjects' ability to recognize or complete letter strings. For example, in a 1998 study by Mack and Rock (1998), subjects were asked to complete the word stem *fla-* with the first two English words that came to mind. When the word *flake* was presented to them as masked stimuli, 36 percent of the subjects selected that as one of their two words. In contrast, among the control subjects, only 4 percent selected *flake* as one of their two completions. In another study by Moore and Egeth (1997), experimenters used subliminal stimuli to produce the famous Müller-Lyer illusion. For this test, subjects were asked to evaluate the relative length of horizontal lines against a random pattern of black-and-white dots. During the first three trials, the subjects correctly identified which line appeared to be longer. In the fourth trial, however, the lines were equal, but were set against a background pattern in which the black dots formed either inward or outward pointing arrows. Subjects identified the line with the inward pointing angle as longer than that with the outward pointing angle, but were unaware of any pattern in the black dots themselves.

This kind of priming effect does not seem to be a characteristic of the unattended stimuli in Levin and Simon's inattentional-blindness studies. In those experiments, the changed conditions that go unperceived do not seem to influence thought or behavior; the stimuli are simply there, but are unattended. Thus, although it is fair to say that viewers experience a kind of "inattentional deafness" with respect to film music, that descriptor does not positively capture the extent to which film music primes our conscious awareness of significant character traits, emotional subtexts, genre conventions, or our expectations of narrative outcomes. Think of the spooky music used to suggest the presence of the killer in the closet or the orchestral swell of romantic music that leads us to anticipate the couple's kiss. For these reasons, the notion of film music as a kind of subliminae offers the most heuristically useful concept for considering the ways in which film scores influence how viewers consciously perceive diegetic events.

Conclusion: the aesthetics of film music

Over the past several decades, the aesthetics of film music has been governed by a tacit concept of appropriateness. By appropriateness, critics and practitioners usually mean that the music matches well with the particular story that it accompanies, that the music effectively and efficiently performs its dramatic functions, and that it does so without distracting the viewer's attention from more salient narrative information. This provides a good rule of thumb for evaluating the aesthetic qualities of film music, but it is only a loosely articulated principle. Judgments about the worth of particular film scores or specific cues are themselves context dependent. Since every film poses its own problems and challenges, every film score must try to solve those problems and meet those challenges in its own way.

That said, even a loosely articulated notion of appropriateness presupposes some understanding of film music's ontology, as well as of the ways film music engages the psychology of film viewers. To offer conclusions about a particular score's effectiveness or greatness, one first must have a clear understanding of what film music is and what it is supposed to do. In this essay, I have tried to speak to those issues by sketching a cluster account of film music's ontology and the role of unconscious listening in film perception. As it turns out, music paradoxically may be most noticeable in its absence, during those moments in film when it is most commonly expected. Underlining its importance in cinematic storytelling, composer Bronislau Kaper averred, "Nothing is as loud in films as silence" (Karlin 1994: 11).

Acknowledgments

I'd like to thank Mark Minett for his comments on disc jockeys turned film composers.

See also Sound (Chapter 24).

References

Anzieu, D. (1976) "L'enveloppe sonore du soi," *Nouvelle Revue de Psychoanalyse* 13 (spring): 161–79.

Boltz, M., Schulkind, M., and Kantra, S. (1991) "Effects of Background Music on Remembering of Filmed Events," *Memory and Cognition* 19: 595–606.

Brown, R. (1994) *Overtones and Undertones: Reading Film Music*, Berkeley: University of California Press.

Bullerjahn, C., and Güldenring, M. (1994) "An Empirical Investigation of Effects of Film Music Using Qualitative Content Analysis," *Psychomusicology* 13: 99–118.

Carroll, N. (1998) *Mystifying Movies: Fads and Fallacies in Contemporary Film Theory*, New York: Columbia University Press.

Chell, S. (1984) "Music and Emotion in the Classical Hollywood Film: The Case of *The Best Years of Our Lives*," *Film Criticism* 8(2): 27–38.

Cohen, A. (2000) "Film Music: Perspectives from Cognitive Psychology," in J. Buhler, C. Flinn, and D. Neumeyer (eds.) *Music and Cinema*, Hanover, NH: University Press of New England, 360–77.

—— (2001) "Music as a Source of Emotion in Film," in P. Justin and J. Sloboda (eds.) *Music and Emotion: Theory and Research*, Oxford and New York: Oxford University Press, 249–72.

Donnelly, K. J. (2001) "*Performance* and the Composite Film Score," in K. J. Donnelly (ed.) *Film Music: Critical Approaches*, New York: Continuum, 152–66.

Eisler, H., and Adorno, T. (1994) *Composing for the Films*, London; and Atlantic Highlands, NJ: Athlone Press.

Flinn, C. (1992) *Strains of Utopia: Gender, Nostalgia, and Hollywood Film Music*, Princeton, NJ: Princeton University Press.

Gaut, B. (2000) "'Art' as a Cluster Concept," in N. Carroll (ed.) *Theories of Art Today*, Madison: University of Wisconsin Press, 25–44.

—— (2005) "The Cluster Account of Art Defended," *British Journal of Aesthetics* 45(3) (July): 273–88.

Goldmark, D. (2005) *Tunes for "Toons": Music and the Hollywood Cartoon*, Berkeley: University of California Press.

Goodman, N. (1976) *Languages of Art*, Indianapolis: Hackett.

Gorbman, C. (1987) *Unheard Melodies: Narrative Film Music*, London: British Film Institute; and Bloomington: Indiana University Press.

Kalinak, K. (1992) *Settling the Score: Music and the Classical Hollywood Film*, Madison: University of Wisconsin Press.

Karlin, F. (1994) *Listening to Movies: The Film Lover's Guide to Film Music*, New York: Schirmer Books.

Kassabian, A. (2001) *Hearing Film: Tracking Identifications in Contemporary Hollywood Film Music*, New York: Routledge.

Kivy, P. (1997) "Music in the Movies: A Philosophical Enquiry," in R. Allen and M. Smith (eds.) *Film Theory and Philosophy*, Oxford: Clarendon Press; and New York: Oxford University Press, 308–28.

Lakoff, G., and Johnson, S. (1999) *Philosophy in the Flesh: The Embodied Mind and Its Challenge to Western Thought*, New York: Basic Books.

Levinson, J. (1996) "Film Music and Narrative Agency," in D. Bordwell and N. Carroll (eds.) *Post-Theory: Reconstructing Film Studies*, Madison: University of Wisconsin Press, 248–82.

Lipscomb, S., and Kendall, R. (1994) "Perceptual Judgment of the Relationship between Musical and Visual Components in Film," *Psychomusicology* 13: 60–98.

London, K. (1936) *Film Music: A Summary of the Characteristic Features of Its History, Aesthetics, Technique, and Possible Developments*, trans. E. Bensinger, London: Faber and Faber.

Mack, A., and Rock, I. (1998) *Inattentional Blindness*, Cambridge, MA: MIT Press.

Marshall, S., and Cohen, A. (1988) "Effects of Musical Soundtracks on Attitudes toward Geometrical Figures," *Music Perception* 6: 95–112.

Merikle, P., Smilek, D., and Eastwood, J. (2001) "Perception without Awareness: Perspectives from Cognitive Psychology," *Cognition* 79: 115–34.

Moore, C. M., and Egeth, H. (1997) "Perception without Attention: Evidence of Grouping under Conditions of Inattention," *Journal of Experimental Psychology* 23: 339–52.

Rosar, W. (2002) "Film Music – What's in a Name?," *Journal of Film Music* 1: 1–18.

Rosolato, G. (1974) "La voix: entre corps et langage," *Revue Française du Psychoanalyse* 38 (January): 75–94.

18
NARRATION
Noël Carroll

Most of the motion pictures we encounter – whether nonfiction or fiction – are narrative in nature. Motion pictures, of course, are not the only medium in which narrative figures prominently. Nevertheless, narrative motion pictures are so pervasive that a discussion of cinematic narration is an unavoidable topic for the philosophy of the moving image.

Because it seems reasonable to presuppose that narration implies a narrator (Chatman 1990), a question naturally arises about the nature of that narrator. Who or what is the cinematic narrator? The answer might appear to you to require little thought. The narrator is just the motion picture maker or makers responsible for the work at hand. If we are talking about a nonfiction film, like *The Fog of War* (2003), then Errol Morris is the narrator. If we are speaking of a fiction film, such as *No Country for Old Men* (2007), then the narrators are the Coen brothers. However, even if the answer seems fairly straightforward when it comes to cases of nonfiction, many philosophers suspect that works of fiction are more complicated. To see why, it is useful first to take a brief detour into literary theory.

With respect to the study of literary fictions, distinctions are often made between the actual author, the implied author, and the narrator. The actual author is the real person who wrote the text and is presumably collecting royalties for it. The implied author is the author as he or she manifests him or herself in the text. The implied author may in fact share all her beliefs, desires, attitudes, allegiances, and so forth with the actual author, but, equally, she may not. The actual author – a romantic at heart – may don the persona or mask of a cynic for the purpose of telling her tale in a certain way. The implied author is the agent who is responsible for the way the fiction is written – its tone, structures, ellipses, emphases, etc. *qua* fiction.

Yet in addition to the actual and implied authors of a literary text, there may also be so-called narrators. These are fictional creatures. They are part of the fictional world as it is presented by the text. Indeed, they are the fictional presenters of the text. Often these presenters appear as characters in the story, as in the case of Henry James' *What Maisie Knew*. Watson is the explicit narrator with regard to the adventures of Sherlock Holmes. He, as a character, is overtly introduced in the fiction as its narrator; it is fictional, in the stories he inhabits, that he is presenting the story to us.

But in addition to overt or explicit narrators, like Watson, it is also argued that there may be implicit fictional narrators. For example, in Ring Lardner's classic short story "The Haircut," there is an explicit narrator, the barber, but it is not he, with his blinkered understanding of the situation, who lets us know that Jim Kendall was actually murdered. Yet, it is reasonable to suppose that we have been told that this is true in the fictional world of the short story. But if narration requires a narrator, who told us this was so? An implicit fictional narrator.

Why must we believe that there are such implicit fictional narrators? The argument goes like this: A fiction is something that we are mandated to imagine. We are mandated to imagine the events in the fiction as true – as obtaining in the world of the fiction. Where an explicit fictional narrator is telling the tale, we typically imagine what he or she reports as true in the world of the narrative (unless we have some reason to suspect the explicit narrator is unreliable or limited in one way or another). However, where there is no explicit narrator in evidence, it is argued that we still have reason to suspect there is an implicit one nearby – that is, a narrative agency that asserts or reports what is true from inside the world of the story.

Why? First, recall that it is being presupposed that there is no narration without a narrator. But when it comes to fiction, it is alleged that the narrator cannot be the actual author or the implied author. The actual author cannot report things as true in the story world; what the actual author does is establish that it is *fictional* that thus and such (rather than asserting that, or reporting that it is true that thus and such). Margaret Mitchell made it *fictional that* Scarlett O'Hara lived at Tara; Mitchell did not perform the illocutionary act of asserting "Scarlett O'Hara lived at Tara." Had Mitchell done that, she would have uttered a falsehood.

The same problem besets the implied author, since the implied author is responsible for *Gone with the Wind qua* fiction. Both the actual author and the implied author stand, so to speak, on the wrong side of the fiction operator (the "it is fictional that …" operator) with respect to making assertions or reports about what is the case in the fictional world. Implied authors can make assertions about what is fictional, but not about what is true in the narrative.

Yet it is a true narrative assertion in the fiction that Scarlett O'Hara lived at Tara. Who made this narrative assertion along with all the others we imagine to be true in the fictional world of *Gone with the Wind*? If there is no explicit narrator in view, we are urged to postulate an implicit fictional narrator, a narrational agency who (unlike the actual author) believes Scarlett O'Hara, Rhett Butler, Ashley Wilkes, and the rest exist, and who reports their trials and tribulations to us as facts which we then go on to imagine. Moreover, the implicit fictional narrator is, like explicit fictional narrators, a denizen of the fiction – a fictional character – even if he or she is unacknowledged by the other fictional inhabitants of his or her world.

The question for the philosophy of the moving image is which of these literary distinctions carry over to motion pictures and to what extent (i.e., if there are implicit fictional narrators, for example, how frequently do they occur: always, sometimes, or never?). Obviously motion pictures have actual authors – as Zhang Yimou is the actual author of *Ju Dou* (1990) – whose manifestation is implied in the film, whether sincerely or not. Motion pictures may also have explicit narrators – like Lester

Burnham in *American Beauty* (1999) – who are characters in the story, or explicit narrators in the form of voice-over commentators, as in the case of *The Magnificent Ambersons* (1942). But do motion picture fictions have implicit fictional narrators, and, if so, how extensive is the phenomenon?

There may be some reasons to deny the postulation of implicit fictional narrators across the board. Putatively, we are forced to posit the aforesaid narrator universally or ubiquitously because narration presupposes a narrator. But perhaps the possibility that the actual author is the narrator has been dismissed too quickly. Why suppose that there must be an act of asserting or reporting inside the fictional operator in order for such and such to be true in the fiction?

Rather, what makes something true in the fiction is that the actual author has mandated that we imagine (i.e., entertain as unasserted) certain propositional contents – for example: it is true in the fiction *Psycho* (1960) that Norman Bates is psychotic, just in case Alfred Hitchcock and his team of fictioneers have mandated that we imagine the propositional content "that Norman Bates is psychotic." In other words, there is no apparent pressure to presume that there are acts of assertion going on within the fiction. That appears to require of the viewer one thought too many or, at least, one thought that is not necessary.

Defenders of the implicit-narrator hypothesis argue that it is natural to imagine that there is a continuous activity of reporting going on as a novel unfolds (Wilson 2007). But claims of naturalness are not likely to carry the day here. Not only do I not find myself entertaining the report model, I see no necessity in doing so. When I watch a play, it would seem strained to think that I am watching a report, so why think that I am reading one upon encountering, for instance, a dialogue novel in the fashion of Ivy Compton Bennett?

That is, the report model hardly fits every case of narration. It does not fit what Plato called *mimesis* in books 2 and 3 of the *Republic*. Hence, claims on behalf of the report model will have to be made on a case-by-case basis, not summarily. And to the extent that the report model does not obtain comprehensively, there is no reason for the blanket postulation of implicit fictional narrators, since their postulation would appear to rest upon the report model. Yet, since the report model occurs at best occasionally, so will the need for introducing implicit fictional narrators.

Friends of the report model may find it natural because they endorse the notion that fictions are props in games of make-believe and that the consumption of a fiction involves the reader in making-believe that he or she is reading a report. But again, although some readers may behave this way, it is idiosyncratic enough that asserting that it is natural is immensely controversial. For how many of us are aware of playing this game? So the defender of implicit fictional narrators may be involved in attributing to audiences two more thoughts than are needed – the idea that there is a report before us and the idea that we are make-believing that we are reading one.

Another reason to be suspicious about the postulation of ubiquitous, implicit fictional narrators is that they often lead to self-contradiction. For example, readers often learn how things turn out in a story where, at the same time, it is given that no one in the fiction ever learnt what happened (Currie 1995). But if there is an implicit narrator who dwells in the fictional world, then there is someone or some agency in the fiction who knows what went down and who is reporting it to us. So, in cases like this, we are driven to the unhappy conclusion that no one in the fiction ever learnt the outcome of the story, and yet someone from the fiction is telling us the outcome. Of course, the way to avoid this logical contretemps is simply to abstain from postulating the existence of the implicit fictional narrator in the first instance.

Thus far, the arguments against the ubiquity of implicit fictional narrators have applied alike to both literary and cinematic examples. But it might be alleged that there is something about motion pictures that especially warrants hypothesizing them, and which so far our objections have left untouched. Specifically, some may contend that it has to do with the way in which we interact with the visuals in a motion picture.

On their account, when we see a house on screen, it is natural for us to suppose that "I imagine seeing a house" (or, that "I am seeing the house imaginarily"). So when presented with an establishing shot of the little house on the prairie, I imagine seeing the little house on the prairie. But for some philosophers, this raises the question of who in the fictional world is responsible for showing us the house; they maintain that reason demands an answer to this question (Levinson 1996).

Ostensibly, the actual filmmakers cannot be showing us the house, since the house is fictional, and they are merely showing us an actual house that is being used to represent the fictional house. So, it is argued, we must postulate some fictional presenter at work here. It is this implicit fictional presenter who makes it possible for us to perceive imaginarily the sights and sounds of the fictional world, something the actual filmmaker cannot do, since he/she only has access to the actual world.

Nevertheless, insofar as this argument rests upon the notion of seeing imaginarily, it falters. For the notion of seeing imaginarily does not seem very compelling. Watching a gun battle in *The 3:10 to Yuma* (2007) I find myself curiously unscathed, nor do I imagine myself ducking bullets. Yet if I were imagining that I was seeing a gunfight close up, wouldn't I have to imagine that my life was endangered? Can I be imagining that I'm seeing a gun battle from a vantage point inside the line of fire and not imagine bullets bursting midair around me? And if I were imagining that, would I continue eating my popcorn so nonchalantly? However, I do eat my popcorn nonchalantly, because I don't imagine myself amidst a blizzard of flying steel, and if I don't imagine that I am amidst the fire fight, how can I plausibly imagine that I am seeing it?

Similarly, many camera positions are such that were I to imagine myself to be an eyewitness inside the fictional world, I would also have to imagine myself in some very unlikely places. In *Casino Royale* (2006), a building in Venice sinks into the lagoon. Do I imagine myself submerged? Do I imagine myself wet, when I am dry? Of course, I don't imagine these things. But how then can it be the case that I am imagining that I am having a close encounter of the third kind within the world of the fiction?

And what do I imagine seeing when there is an on-screen dissolve or a wipe? That the world is immaterializing or erasing itself in my presence? Cuts are also a problem. One moment we are shown Paris and the next moment Moscow is before us. If we imagine seeing these two sights in rapid succession, then wouldn't the question of how

I moved across Europe so quickly arise? Yet it doesn't, nor do I feel any pressure to imagine how I pulled off this miracle – just because I wasn't seeing imaginarily in the first place.

In other words, if I were seeing imaginarily, I would have to perform a wealth of unlikely supplemental imaginings in order to account for how I came to be able to perform my primary feats of imaginary seeing (Currie 1995). But I do not appear to perform the requisite supplemental imaginings. So the notion of imagining-seeing appears dubious. Instead of seeing imaginarily, it seems that on a more plausible account of my relation to the visual array, I *literally* see representations of actors on screen, which I use to imagine the fiction. In other words, we may jettison talk of seeing imaginarily. And, if the hypothesis of imagining-seeing is supposed to support the hypothesis of the implicit fictional narrator/presenter, then the two ideas fall together.

Another problem, apart from that of improbable supplemental imagining, is that the hypothesis of the fictional presenters who guide our imagining-seeing can lead to self-contradiction. For example, in the TV series *Six Feet Under* (2001–5) the character, Nathan Fisher, buries his wife in the desert; in the fiction, it is given that no one sees this. Yet, if there is an implicit fictional narrator/presenter, who enables us to see the burial imaginarily, then someone has witnessed the event. But this yields the contradiction that it both is the case that, in the fiction, no one witnessed the burial and that someone witnessed the burial. To avoid this problem, the obvious solution is to eschew the notion of an implicit fictional narrator/presenter (Currie 1995).

However, not only does the implicit fictional narrator/presenter lead to untoward consequences, the reasoning in its behalf appears ill-motivated. Supposedly, we are in need of these fictional intermediaries because actual and implied authors lack the right metaphysical relationship to the world of the fiction. They cannot provide us with the proper metaphysical access to the fictional world, because they live on the wrong side of the fiction operator. But if the contents of the fictional world are inaccessible directly to actual authors, implied authors, and their audiences, why would not the same problem apply to the alleged fictional presenters as well as to the named fictional characters in the motion picture? If there is any problem with making contact with the fictional world from outside the fiction operator, that problem, *ex hypothesi*, would persist with respect to making contact with an implicit fiction narrator/presenter (Kania 2005).

That is, if we need a fictional intermediary to secure access to whatever is fictional, and the implicit narrator/presenter is fictional, then to make contact with the first implicit fictional narrator/presenter, we will need to postulate a second fictional narrator/presenter, and then, for the same reason, a third, and so on *ad infinitum*. The thinking behind the idea of such a narrator threatens to drag us in to an endless regress, such that we could never secure access to the fictional world. But we do have access to fictional worlds. Thus, so much the worse for the implicit fictional narrator/presenter (Carroll 2006).

One way to mute some of the objections to the notion of the implicit fictional narrator/presenter is to think of this narrative agency as a documentary motion picture

(Wilson 2006). Instead of imagining that we are seeing the world of the fiction under the guidance of an implicit narrator who beckons us to look here and then there, we are to imagine that we are viewing a documentary film produced in the world of the fiction. Just as we are supposed to imagine reading the novel A *Tale of Two Cities* as a report from inside the fiction, when we watch the movie adaptation of the novel, we are to imagine that we are seeing a nonfiction film about happenings that occurred during the French Revolution.

This will dodge many of the previous objections involving supplemental imaginings, for if what we imagine seeing is a movie, then we don't have to explain to ourselves why we weren't wounded during the gunfight, or dampened during *Casino Royale*, nor do we have to imagine a story about how we manage to get across Europe in less than a second or be perplexed about what we are to imagine seeing when confronted with visual effects like dissolves and wipes. We can account for all this and more on the supposition that it is a movie, albeit a nonfiction movie, that we imagine we are seeing.

Although the documentary version of the report model succeeds quite well with some of the problems of supplemental imagining, it has a number of liabilities. First, it seems plausible that many viewers encountered motion picture fictions before they were exposed to nonfictions. This may be true of children and people in remote areas. These viewers may not yet have the concept of nonfiction film or any idea of how such films are made. Thus, they would not be capable of imagining that they are seeing a nonfiction documentary. But they show no confusion over how they are to process the motion pictures in question.

Furthermore, there is the problem of historical films, like *Quo Vadis?* (1951), *Attila the Hun* (1954), or *Gladiator* (2000). Are we to imagine seeing a documentary centuries before moving-picture cameras were invented? And, in addition, the documentary hypothesis does not dispel the problem of motion picture events we are to imagine which were witnessed by no one. Surely we are mandated to imagine at the end of *Greed* (1924) that there are no onlookers when Marcus and MacTeague die in the desert. But this is incompatible with the documentary hypothesis, which would place a camera crew within spitting distance of the doomed men. Moreover, the documentary hypothesis not only incurs a logical problem here: it would force most viewers to raise ethical questions about the morality of the film, given the callousness of the supposed documentary filmmakers, who idly stand by as these two men perish.

One way to blunt these objections is to claim that we imagine that these documentaries are not human artifacts. They are naturally occurring objects – specifically they are naturally iconic representations or images, perhaps like mirrors (like the ones owned by wicked witches) (Wilson 2006). If we imagine that something of this sort is what transmits the images that we imagine seeing, then the problem of motion picture representations of witnessless events disappears, since these natural icons are not humans. Nor are movies whose events antedate the invention of cinema troublesome, so long as we presuppose that these natural iconic representations have been around since the dawn of time.

One might respond to the idea of natural iconic representations by objecting that imagining that we are encountering such entities has implications as unlikely as many of the implications involved in imagining we are confronting things like gunfights face-to-face. How do these naturally occurring iconic representations work? Exactly what are we supposed to imagine – simply that there are such things? But is that any less outlandish – or, at least, any less "magical" – than imagining that somehow, on a single cut, we can move across Europe faster than the speed of light? If the consequences of face-to-face imaginary seeing strain the bounds of sense, how much better off are we with these allegedly natural iconic representations?

Moreover, if these naturally occurring iconic representations are supposed to answer the question of who is narrating, then doesn't this process have to be an agent of some sort, like a human or, at least, an anthropomorphic person? But haven't natural iconic representations been introduced precisely to avert the problems that arise when we imagine we are dealing with the work of a human documentarian?

Of course, it might be stipulated that the natural iconic representations constitute some sort of imagemaker, but if that imagemaker is a person, then we are back to the problem of reports of putatively witnessless events. So, there appears to be a dilemma in the offing here: either the natural iconic representation is not an agent of some sort (violating the demand that narratives have narrators) or the natural iconic representation is an imagemaker (returning us to the problem of witnessless events) (Carroll 2006).

One way of attempting to repel this kind of criticism is to maintain that when we are mandated to imagine thus and so regarding the world of the fiction, we are not thereby mandated to imagine everything about how thus-and-so came to be, although we will suppose that it came about somehow. *The Son of Kong* (1933) features a scion to the one-of-a-kind King; we suppose the son to be legitimate and imagine he inhabits Skull Island, but we need not imagine how he got there with no Queen Kong in evidence.

Fictions leave much concerning that which we are mandated to imagine indeterminate and unexplained, but we are not mandated to fill in the gaps, it may be argued by the defenders of the implicit fictional narrators/presenters and/or natural iconic representations. Thus, we are not mandated to imagine how natural iconic representations work, nor whether they are agents. Nor are we prescribed to imagine everything such posits entail. We just imagine that, howsoever these things operate, they are producing the images of goings-on in the fictional world.

Indeed, in the old *Flash Gordon* (1936) serials, there was a viewing device that enabled one to see anywhere in the galaxy with no recording devices in evidence. Ours was not to reason why or how. We were simply to imagine that there were such machines in Flash's universe.

Thus, we may think likewise of the alleged naturally occurring iconic representations. The implicit, fictional presenter/narrating agency has access to or is identical with an equally unexplained and narratively underdeveloped mechanism which allows us to see imaginarily the pictures it produces, although we know not – and cannot even imagine – how. Just as you can imagine that you are in bed with your favorite celebrity – without imagining how you got there – so we may imagine seeing all sorts of images without imagining how we gained access to them. If such images appear to provoke certain anomalies – such as recordings of putatively unrecorded events – we need not imagine how the events were recorded in such a way that evades this apparent contradiction. We merely imagine that the images are somehow available, *sans* absurdity, for us to imagine seeing.

However, this suggestion will not do, for it is not true that when processing a fiction we are not mandated to imagine a great deal of what is presupposed or implied by what is given in the world of the motion picture. When assimilating a fiction, we constantly need to fill in many of the details that the creator of the story has left out, including things entailed by the narrative, although not stated outright or shown in it. For example, we are mandated to imagine that Philip Marlowe has a heart and that if he is shot in it, he will die.

This supplemental imagining is governed by a default assumption – unless otherwise instructed by the fiction, assume that the world of the fiction is like our world and imagine accordingly. Since this is a default assumption, it may be overridden. Some genres, for example, presuppose things at variance with the ways of the actual world – for example, that mummies can be brought back to life. And stories from other cultures and times may come with presuppositions at odds with the way we believe the world works and, in order to process these fictions, we will need to adjust our imaginings to alien views. However, our default response to a fiction is to fill it in in terms of our beliefs about how the world is. This is called the realistic heuristic. Moreover, this heuristic raises problems for the attempt to save the hypothesis of the implicit fictional presenter/narrator by means of the bold assertion that we are not mandated to worry, in our imaginings, whether natural iconic representations provoke contradictions.

For, insofar as there is a realistic heuristic, it is wrong to contend that we are not mandated to imagine altogether that which has not been said or shown in the fiction. We are mandated to imagine that Philip Marlowe has a heart, that a bullet can stop it, and that because of this, Marlowe will tread cautiously when a firearm is pointed his way. Similarly, when we deploy the realistic heuristic to the fiction of naturally occurring iconic representations, then, if there are salient implications such a device would have in the world as we know it, then we are entitled to imagine they prevail in the fictional world, *unless it is stipulated otherwise* by the actual author of the fiction or the presuppositions of the genre to which the fiction belongs. Just as J. K. Rowling establishes that owls can deliver mail to young wizards in the *Harry Potter* series, so it would fall to Chandler to alert us to Marlowe's invulnerability, should we be mandated to imagine it.

The realistic heuristic can be overridden. If it is stipulated by Chandler that we are to imagine that Philip Marlowe is invulnerable, then we will suspend the realistic heuristic and we will not be nonplussed when he survives repeated blastings. Likewise, we do not wonder about how the viewing device works in the *Flash Gordon* serials, because we have been told that it works and not to worry our pretty heads about it. But notice that in these cases, the realistic heuristic can be retired because the fiction has explicitly told us to do so. Flash Gordon's all-seeing television has been introduced into the story straightforwardly, and we have been overtly reassured that it works in the Flash Gordon universe. But the same is not true of the implicit fictional narrator/presenter or of the naturally occurring iconic representation. Therefore, if these postulations fall afoul of the realistic heuristic with respect to the supplemental imaginings they enjoin, then the disturbance they represent for our imaginings is genuine (Gaut 2004).

In fact, since the implicit fictional narrator is, by definition, *implicit*, no fiction tells us that it possesses an implicit fictional narrator/presenter or an implicit naturally occurring imagemaker. So, on the one hand, we have no reason to postulate the existence of one on the grounds of the default assumption of the realistic heuristic. On the other hand, if we are told that there are such things by some theorist, then, since within the fiction the realistic heuristic has not been suspended, we can, again by dint of the realistic heuristic, wonder whether the fiction is logically intelligible where it appears to violate the realistic heuristic.

That is, if these theoretical postulations concerning the implicit fictional narrator presuppose or entail any absurdity – such as an event given as unrecorded which has been recorded – the contradiction cannot be evaded by appealing to the idea that we need not imagine that which the recommended postulation entails *because*, without a stipulation to do otherwise, we are to imagine that the kinds of logical, physical, and psychological implications that obtain in the actual world obtain in the world of the fiction. And, of course, if these postulations are *implicit*, then it has not been stipulated that we should think otherwise.

Another consideration against the notion of the naturally iconic imagemaker is that it seems far too complex a posit to attribute to any viewers, save those steeped in analytic metaphysics. As we have seen, the notion of naturally occurring imagemaking emerges from an intense dialectic and is designed to deflect certain counterexamples and conundrums that beset the notion of ubiquitous, implicit, fictional narrators/presenters. Such a mechanism is extremely unlikely to occur to most viewers. It is not apt to be part of their imaginative processing of fictional motion pictures, since they lack the concept.

And yet most do assimilate such movies successfully. Thus, they must be doing it without the benefit of the various metaphysical hypotheses presented so far in the debate (Carroll 2006). Perhaps if normal viewers can do without such things, motion picture philosophers can do so as well.

Still another problem with the naturally iconic imagemaker as a solution to the perplexities raised by the implicit narrator/presenter is that even if we could imagine some natural process that might give rise to individual motion picture images, what conceivable natural process could edit them into a coherent story? The natural iconic imagemaker does not merely present single images; those images get organized into narratives. However, there is no Flash Gordon, Dale Arden, or Dr Zharkoff directing the imagemaker where to look and in what order. Even if naturally occurring iconic images were conceivable without too much effort, can entire naturally produced motion picture narratives be imagined as readily?

The friends of ubiquitous, implicit narrators/presenters with respect to fictional movies maintain as their starting point that if we get visual information about the fictional world from the movie, rationality compels us to ask how we get it (Levinson 1996). The implicit fictional narrator is their answer. But why do we stop there in our quest to learn about the provenance of this information?

Obviously, postulating the agency of an implicit narrator may lead us to ask what appear to be silly and irrelevant questions – such as, how does the implicit fictional narrator know that x when it is given by said narrator himself that no one within the boundaries of the fiction knows that x? For the sake of forestalling such questions, the defenders of the implicit narrators declare that our questioning about the way in which we learn about the fictional world should stop as soon as we surmise that the fictional narrator has informed us that x.

Yet isn't stopping just here arbitrary? Why has reason suddenly become so easy going? If we really felt driven to learn how we get the relevant information, won't we want an account of how the implicit narrator gathered it, especially where it conflicts with the assumption of the realistic heuristic?

But perhaps if we all agree that the pursuit of such questions is silly, then the best way to stop these questions before they start is by refraining from postulating the existence of an implicit fictional narrator/presenter, since once we get rid of him, these absurdities will disappear.

See also Interpretation (Chapter 15), David Bordwell (Chapter 29), and Noël Carroll (Chapter 31).

References

Carroll, N. (2006) "Film Narrative/Narration: Introduction," in N. Carroll and J. Choi (eds.) *Philosophy of Film and Motion Pictures*, Malden, MA: Blackwell.

Chatman, S. (1990) *Coming to Terms*, Ithaca, NY: Cornell University Press.

Currie, G. (1995) *Image and Mind*, Cambridge and New York: Cambridge University Press.

Gaut, B. (2004) "The Philosophy of the Movies: Cinematic Narration," in P. Kivy (ed.) *The Blackwell Guide to Aesthetics*, Malden, MA: Blackwell.

Kania, A. (2005) "Against the Ubiquity of Fictional Narrators," *Journal of Aesthetics and Art Criticism* 63: 47–54.

Levinson, J. (1996) "Film Music and Narrative Agency," in D. Bordwell and N. Carroll (eds.) *Post-Theory: Reconstructing Film Studies*, Madison: University of Wisconsin Press.

Wilson, G. (2006) "*Le Grand Imagier* Steps Out: On the Primitive Basis of Film Narration," in N. Carroll and J. Choi (eds.) *The Philosophy of Film and Motion Picture*, Malden, MA: Blackwell.

—— (2007) "Elusive Narrators in Fiction and Film," *Philosophical Studies* 135: 73–88.

Further reading

The following are further reading on this topic: Peter Alward, "Leave Me Out of It: *De Re*, But Not *De Se*: Imaginative Engagement with Fiction," *Journal of Aesthetics and Art Criticism* 64(4) (2006): 451–60; David Bordwell, *Narration in the Fiction Film* (Madison: University of Wisconsin Press, 1985), and "Three Dimensions of Film Narrative," in *Poetics of Cinema* (London and New York: Routledge, 2008), 85–134; Paisley Livingston, "Narrative," in B. Gaut and D. Lopes (eds.) *The Routledge Companion to*

Aesthetics (London and New York: Routledge, 2001), 359–70; Kendall Walton, *Mimesis as Make-Believe* (Cambridge, MA: Harvard University Press, 1990); George Wilson, *Narration in Light* (Baltimore, MD: Johns Hopkins University Press, 1986), "Narrative," in J. Levinson (ed.) *The Oxford Handbook of Aesthetics* (Oxford and New York: Oxford University Press, 2003), and "Transparency and Twist in Narrative Fiction Film," *Journal of Aesthetics and Art Criticism* 64 (2006): 81–96.

19

NARRATIVE CLOSURE

Noël Carroll

If by *narrative* we mean the mere recounting or representation of any event and/ or state of affairs through some interval of time, then the overwhelming numbers of motion picture shots, save for freeze frames, are narratives, albeit in many, many cases, minimal ones. However, in most usage, the concept of narrative is reserved for representations of states of affairs and events of a greater degree of complexity and structure.

Prototypically, most narratives involve at least two, but generally more, events and/or states of affairs which are related or arranged temporally and causally (where the causation in question may include mental states such as desires, intentions, and motives). "Charlemagne was crowned Holy Roman Emperor in 800 and, in 1945, Japan surrendered unconditionally to the Allies" is not a narrative in the afore-mentioned sense, although "After being tested in New Mexico, atomic bombs were dropped on Hiroshima and Nagasaki" is, since it comprises three events of which the first temporally preceded and was causally related to the second two. Most motion pictures – including most fictions, nonfictions, and even some abstractions – are narrative in the sense that they involve a number of events and states of affairs standing in temporal and causal relations to each other (Carroll 2001, 2007b).

Narratives may be very broadly sorted into two major categories: *episodic narratives* and *unified narratives*. Episodic narratives are composed of a string of smaller narratives or episodes, frequently connected by the recurring presence of a central character, but without strong causal linkage between one story and the next. In the ancient world, epic poems recalling the adventures of Hercules would be an example of this. Likewise, the *Odyssey* is another example of the episodic narrative. It is made up of individual stories of the wanderings of Ulysses, but one of his adventures – say his encounter with the Cyclops – does not figure causally in bringing about his encounter with Circe, or the Sirens, or Scylla and Charybdis. The movie serial *Rocketman* and the television series *Superman* are also episodic narratives, as are most sitcoms. So are soap operas; however, instead of rotating around one or a few central figures, their casts usually involve a larger revolving gallery of recurring characters.

A unified narrative, as Aristotle put it, has a *beginning*, a *middle*, and an *end* (Aristotle 1996). Although undoubtedly this sounds spectacularly uninformative – can't anything that is extended through space and/or time be subdivided in this way?

– these terms should not be understood in their bland, ordinary sense. Rather they are technical terms. By "the end," Aristotle means an event which secures the feeling of closure in an audience – the almost palpable sensation that the story has finished-up at exactly the right spot. Nothing that needed to be told has been left untold, nor has the story gone on superfluously. At most we learn that the prince and the princess lived happily ever after, but we are not informed of their subsequent adventures. That would be the stuff of other, further stories.

The *beginning*, in turn, is just what the audience needs to know in order to start to follow the story. We are introduced to a locale and a set of characters. We learn of their desires, aspirations, relations, struggles, and so forth. Perhaps we learn about certain conflicts between them, as when we witness the enmity between Achilles and Agamemnon at the opening of Wolfgang Petersen's 2004 *Troy*. The beginning typically supplies us with the background that we need to comprehend in order to track with understanding that which happens next.

Often the narrative of a motion picture begins with an establishing shot that depicts a state of affairs and tells us where and when the story will unfold. Then we meet a number of characters. Some change intrudes which calls for action, or reaction. Helen absconds with Paris to Troy. This complication generates a response – alliances are forged between various Greek forces in preparation for war. And with this complication, we enter the middle of the narrative, which concludes or ends when the problem that ensues from, or the questions (Who will win? Who will die?) that are provoked by the complications – in this case the Trojan War – are resolved.

A narrative of this sort is unified in as much as each part leads smoothly to the next. Given the situation and the people who inhabit it, the kind of change or complication introduced causes certain problems to be raised or questions to be asked; then these queries will gradually be further complicated and eventually answered by the action of the characters, and, precisely when all the presiding questions are settled, the story proper ends (though there may also be a brief coda). Such a narrative is unified insofar as it appears rhetorically to be held together tightly by the logic of questions and answers.

Of course, often in Hollywood movies, there is more than one story – there is frequently a problem to be solved (in *Casino Royale* [2006] James Bond has to entrap the international arms-merchant/gambler), while there is also a romantic subplot about whether 007 and his beautiful co-spy will become a couple (Bordwell *et al.* 1985). Nevertheless, these two stories usually get intertwined so that the romance often contributes to the solution of the problem. Indeed, as many as 60 percent of classical Hollywood films have been said to exhibit this structure (Bordwell *et al.* 1985).

Aristotle's theory of the unified narrative has influenced the way in which screenwriters construct narratives. Syd Field (1994) wrote an influential guide to popular screenwriting, in which he divided screenplays into three parts or *acts*: a beginning (often the first 25 percent of the motion picture), a confrontation (frequently, 50 percent of the movie), and a resolution (25 percent or whatever is left over after the first two acts), with turning points in-between. Paul Joseph Gulino (2004) thinks that the popularity of Field's book was a major influence on the notion of the Hollywood film possessing a "three-*act* structure," although the Danish director Urban Gad recommended that filmmakers construct their works in acts as early as in 1912 (Bordwell 2008).

Others have refined the three-part structure, not in a way that refutes Aristotle, but which instead limns with greater clarity the grounds for the interlocking coherence in the kind of story that Aristotle had in mind. For example, Kristin Thompson (1999) sees four acts, where Field says there are three. Hers include the setup, the complication, development, and climax; whereas David Bordwell (1985) describes the classical Hollywood plot as a six-part structure: introduction of setting and characters, explanation of state of affairs, complicating action, ensuing events, outcome, and ending. But despite the varying numbers, it seems fair to suggest that all these authors belong to the school of Aristotle; they do not contradict his *Poetics* as much as they make more explicit the interconnected elements that render such stories so unified.

Motion pictures articulated in the Aristotelian tradition not only are structurally unified: they feel unified or of a piece. That is, as mentioned earlier, when "The End" flashes on screen or, as is becoming more routine nowadays, when the credits start crawling up from the bottom edge of the image, the audience has a strong sense of finality and completeness. Unlike the episodic narrative, which, in principle, seems like it could keep going on and on, the unified narrative appears as though it has to end just where it does, rather like the sonnet that feels as though it concludes on exactly the right word, or the song that closes on just the correct note. Whereas the episodic narrative gives the appearance of an assortment of adventures, of which some might be subtracted with no irreparable loss to the feel of the saga, the unified narrative leaves us with the impression of one indissolubly integrated whole from which nothing can be left out, save at the cost of a tangible experience of perturbation. That is, once again, this sort of narrative engenders a powerful feeling of closure, the sense that every salient element that has been set in motion in the story has been, as they say, wrapped up.

This is not to say that closure is altogether an alien factor in episodic narratives. Within episodes in an episodic narrative, closure may obtain. In each episode of the television series, *Have Gun Will Travel*, for instance, Paladin's assignment for the week was successfully discharged. Of course, in some episodic narratives, like motion picture serials of the sort referred to as cliff-hangers, the closure of one adventure might be deferred to the beginning of the next installment to ensure that the audience returns in the subsequent week to discover the way the heroine escaped her fate worse than death. But, at the same time, very complicated episodic narratives with large storylines, like soap operas, over time become too intricate to wrap up. If they go off the air, they may have no other option but to leave viewers hanging, as the TV series *The Sopranos* did with stylish élan at the conclusion of its final season.

In one way or another, closure plays a role in our experience of the vast number of the motion picture narratives we encounter, including episodic and unified narratives. As we shall see, closure is not a universal feature of narrative motion pictures, and moviemakers may have important reasons to foreswear closure. Yet, it is reasonable to say that most motion picture narratives aspire to instill closure in spectators.

As already indicated, we signal our feelings of closure by saying of a movie that "it appears to wrap things up" or "it seems like it tied up all the loose ends." But can we be less metaphorical than this? Can we explain the narrative structures in the movie that account for these impressions?

In this regard, one important suggestion comes from David Hume's essay "Of Tragedy" (1993). Hume writes:

> Had you any intention to move a person extremely by the narration of any event, the best method of increasing its effect would be artfully to delay informing him of it, and first excite his curiosity and impatience before you let him into the secret. (Hume 1998)

That is, Hume recommends that the way in which a narrative can take hold of an audience's attention is to engender their curiosity about what happens next. He calls that which they want to know "a secret." Similarly, in his discussion of what he labels "the hermeneutic code," Roland Barthes dubs it "an enigma" (Barthes 1974: 18–20). For our purposes, we may adopt less inflated terminology and simply say that what Hume has in mind is that a story sustains our attention, often irresistibly, by presenting us with *questions* that we want answered – questions that the narrative implicitly promises to answer and which we expect will be answered. Hume, of course, was offering advice to playwrights; but it has been accepted even more eagerly by screenwriters.

What does this have to do with bringing about the impression of closure? Closure will obtain when all of the saliently posed questions that the narrative has served up are answered. For instance, recall this archetypal plot: boy meets girl and they are attracted to each other; enter some oily Lothario bent on seducing the girl – will the boy be able to unmask his rival and regain the girl's affections? This is what the audience wants to know. And, finally, the boy gets the girl. The End. Closure.

The movie does not go on to tell us that the couple then bought car insurance, because that was not part of the story. That is, whether or not the couple bought an insurance policy is not a question about which the movie has encouraged us to be curious. Were this episode to be added to the movie, the feeling of closure would be diluted; the movie would not strike us as having ended at the right spot. It would seem to ramble. It would have gone on beyond the point where closure would obtain.

However, if after establishing the existence of a happy family, their beloved infant is abducted, the audience will want to learn whether the child will be rescued. The complications that unfold contribute to sustaining or answering this question. The movie, then, is over when that question is answered one way or another. Suppose, as is usually the case, we learn that the infant has been saved. The impression of closure will correspond with that revelation. In ordinary suspense movies, we will feel frustration rather than closure if that answer is not forthcoming. And if the movie goes on to show us the child getting a flu shot, that will feel like a narrative non sequitur, since whether or not the baby needed a flu shot is not part of the story – not one of the forcefully advanced questions that have come to preoccupy our attention as spectators. That is, were the scene with the flu shot added, rather than things being wrapped up, a *loose end* would unravel.

It is to be hoped that this discussion of closure in the unified narrative suggests that a major source of the sense of the completeness and coherence evident in this species of narrative – to which, arguably, most motion pictures belong – is what we can call *erotetic*. "Erotetic logic" is the logic of questions and answers. By extension, there is also erotetic narration. This is narration that proceeds by generating questions that the narration then goes on to answer. Closure obtains when all of the pronounced questions the movie has elected to put emphatically before us have been answered. This hypothesis can be confirmed by turning off the projector as the last reel of the movie is about to wind onto the screen. Irritated, the audience will jump up and demand to know, for instance, whether the baby was rescued. They want their closure.

Erotetic narration not only imbues a motion picture with an aura of completeness and completion. The evolving network of questions and answers also holds the story together – renders it coherent – throughout the unified narrative. That is, scenes and sequences are connected to other scenes and sequences by a skein of questions and answers.

The motion picture standardly begins by answering the kind of questions we automatically ask whenever we are introduced to a novel situation. We want implicitly to know where the action is set and when, who these people are, what do they want, and why are they acting like this. The opening of the typical motion picture will answer these basic questions at least to the extent that we have enough information to understand the further questions that the subsequent changes in the initial states of affairs and their accompanying complications elicit.

Some scenes and sequences simply raise questions to be answered down the line by other scenes and sequences. In early American cinema, two-shot films, involving stories of kidnappings, comprised an opening shot in which a child was kidnapped, thereby raising the question of whether he or she could be recovered; and then the second shot, which delivered the answer, as the child was rescued from the clutches of some stereotypically swarthy Eastern or Southern European immigrant.

In other, more complex motion pictures, scenes and sequences may function to prolong, as Hume advised, the delivery of the answers to our questions. This may be the result of a subsequent scene only partially answering an ongoing question. For example, once we learn the child has been kidnapped, part of what we are apt to want to know, if we haven't witnessed the abduction, is "by whom?" This may be partially answered by learning that the kidnapper is a woman with a limp, but exactly which woman with a limp remains a live question.

Likewise, a later scene may sustain an earlier question by keeping our questions aloft. For instance, the escaped convict eludes apprehension in one scene, thereby iterating the question of whether he will be caught in the next scene or a subsequent one. Or, the fearless vampire killers close in on Dracula's lair, but he transforms himself into a bat and flies away, leaving us wondering if they will be able to stake him another day.

Sometimes when scenes answer one of our questions, they will replace one question with another. When King Kong is subdued on Skull Island, the inquiring minds in the audience want to know what Carl Denham intends to do with him. And, of course, new characters, forces, and situations can be established at any point in the diegesis, bringing in their tow new questions to be answered, as they interact with what has already been given about the story world up to that point.

Scenes and sequences in erotetic narratives function to raise and/or answer questions, to answer questions partially, to cause questions to be iterated, and to answer some questions in a way that opens onto others. Because scenes and sequences are bound together by this network of questions and answers, unified narratives give the appearance of coherence – everything seems to belong or to fit, specifically to fit into the network of questions and answers.

The questions and answers that hold together the typical motion picture narrative come in hierarchically differentiated orders of magnitude. For convenience sake, we can make the following rough distinctions. First, there are *presiding macroquestions*. These include the question that dominates the motion picture globally from one end to the other. Will the boy be able to get the girl? Can Goldfinger have his way with Fort Knox? Will the village survive in *Seven Samurai* (1954)?

Of course, a film may have more than one presiding macroquestion. Buster Keaton's 1927 *The General* has several, including the following: Will Johnny be able to enlist in the Southern army? Will Johnny be able to recover his locomotive, *The General*? Will he be able to rescue his love, Annabelle Lee? Will he be able to alert the Confederates of the encroaching Union attack in time? These are the interlocking, indeed, in this case, piggy-backed, macroquestions that keep us riveted to the story in the expectation that they will be answered. When they are answered, *The General* is effectively finished. We do not ask what Johnny will do after the Civil War, because that is not one of the presiding macroquestions that we have been invited to entertain. When all of the presiding macroquestions in a unified movie narrative are answered, closure is usually secured and we feel that Keaton's movie has been completed and is complete (Carroll 2007a).

However, motion pictures are not merely unified by overarching or presiding macro-questions. There are also more localized questions that call forth or propone answers of a more limited scope. In *The General*, in one scene, the Union hijackers pile debris on the rail tracks in order to derail Johnny, who is in hot pursuit. These activities raise the question of whether or not Johnny will be derailed in a subsequent scene or sequence. And, of course, subsequent scenes or sequences answer such questions. Johnny doesn't get derailed.

We may call these local erotetic networks *microquestions* and *microanswers*. They generally provide the glue that holds the trail of scenes and sequences together on a local basis, while not letting go of our attention. Moreover, these microquestions and answers are typically hierarchically subordinated to the presiding macroquestions that animate the narrative. For example, the question/answer network involving Johnny's possible derailment in *The General* provides information in the direction of answering the presiding macroquestions of whether he will save his engine, his love, and the Confederacy and ultimately whether he will win his uniform and enlist.

Finally, it should be added that there are erotetic structures that are neither presiding macroquestion/answer networks nor micro ones. These are question/answer complexes that span large parts of a motion picture, but not the entirety of the work. For example, the question of what is going to happen to Marion in Alfred Hitchcock's 1960 *Psycho* dominates the opening of the film but is resolved once Norman Bates kills her. The macroquestions about her fate organize a large part of the film, but not the whole of it, since once she is eviscerated in the shower sequence, questions about Marion's future are replaced by questions about whether her murder and her murderer will be discovered. Since the question about Marion is sustained over many micro-questions/answers – like, will the inquisitive-looking cop further investigate her? – it is a macrostructure, but since it is not sustained across the entire film, it is not a *presiding* macrostructure. It does not provoke closure. Answering presiding macroquestions is what educes closure.

Although I have spoken of the narrative organization of motion pictures in terms of its erotetic rhetorical address, narrative exposition is also importantly concerned with the temporal order of the depicted events. Events in films occur before, after, and simultaneously with each other. Nor need the procession of events in a film be that of a progressive linear movement. There can be flashbacks and flashforwards.

It is a fact about narration that the time of the telling or recounting of the tale (sometimes called *the discourse,* or in a related vein, *syuzhet)* need not follow the order of events as they occurred in the tale world (sometimes called *the story* or *fabula)* (Chatman 1978; Bordwell 2008). This is as true of movies as it is of other kinds of narra-tives. Although the story is told in a progressive fashion, moving forward in unbroken real time from the opening credits to the end credits, the events that comprise the tale in the story world need not be projected consecutively in our world, the world of the audience, outside of the fiction. *Mildred Pierce* (1945) begins in the present of the story world, with a man being shot, and then moves backward in the time of the fiction – that is, flashes back – to answer the questions of who shot the man and why.

Likewise, *Easy Rider* (1969) flashes forward to an image of a burning motorcycle in order to prompt the question of who is going to die. Or, if there is a flashforward to a shot of Petulia throwing something through a shop window, it primes us to ask "why?" That is, even though the temporal order of the narration is a level of plot structure distin-guishable from its erotetic organization, it is not altogether unrelated, since typically the manipulation of time by the discourse of the narration will be in the service of supplying the kinds of questions and answers that contribute to narrative closure.

Similarly, breaks out of the forward flow of the narrative and into the temporally suspended fantasies of characters – as in *Billy Liar* (1963), *Lord Jim* (1965), and *The Pawnbroker* (1964) – also serve to answer narrative questions, often concerning the desires of the characters, and thusly they can serve the designs of narrative closure by revealing the deepest wishes of these protagonists in a way that bids us to wonder whether they will be realized or not.

If so far I may have inadvertently suggested that all motion pictures that depict a series of events in time involve closure, then I have misled you, and not only because some motion pictures that strive for closure botch the job. For there are also things like home movies that show the major events in the life of a family – birthdays, vacations, weddings, etc. – in the temporal order in which they occurred. Yet, these – and comparably arranged, chronologically ordered event series – are best thought of as not yet fully prototypical narratives, properly so-called, but only chronicles, and are for that reason bereft of closure (Carroll 2001). And, in addition, even some full-fledged narratives, like the individual installments of cliff-hangers such as *The Perils of Pauline*, avoid closure at the end of each episode in order to drum up future business.

Moreover, there are unified narratives that eschew closure at the level of the depiction of the events and actions of the story world in order to achieve unity at a higher level or plane of organization or signification. For example, at the end of his 1950 masterpiece *Rashomon*, Akira Kurosawa refrains from announcing, from an omniscient viewpoint, what really happened when the bandit, the husband, and the wife met in the forest. Our questions about what actually went down in the story world go unanswered, but in a way that prompts us to ask about Kurosawa's artistic motivation or intention in withholding this information from us.

That is, the transparently purposive avoidance of closure at the level of the action of the story disposes us to attempt to interpret the significance of this decision on Kurosawa's part. It encourages what we might name "interpretive ascent." What is Kurosawa trying to communicate by this obvious subversion of the erotetic model? And once having ascended to that level of interpretation, thoughtful viewers regularly grasped that the point or theme of *Rashomon* is to suggest a form of epistemological perspectivism – which discovery provokes a kind of interpretive, as opposed to narrative, closure.

Likewise in *L'Avventura* (1960), Michelangelo Antonioni seems simply to drop the question of why the character played by Lea Messari has disappeared, in order to tantalize the viewer into inferring an other-than-narrative significance to the story – such as the insinuation of the existential meaninglessness of contemporary life, an acknowledgment, that is, of the possibility that life does not come – as unified movies do – with answers clearly stamped upon the face of it.

There are, of course, other objectives that may lead motion picture makers to forgo closure at the level of the story. It may be done to enhance the expressive unity of a film. That we never learn whether Irena in *The Curse of the Cat People* (1944) is a ghost or a psychological projection contributes to the eerie, ambiguous, uncanny feeling the film emits. Furthermore, realistic films like *Amarcord* (1973) often loosen the erotetic grip of the narrative structure in order to appear more "lifelike" – to contrive a rhythm more akin to the everyday flow of often directionless events, as opposed to the propulsive forward pace of erotetic narration.

Furthermore, reflexive films, such as *Last Year at Marienbad* (1961), pose questions they refuse to answer, in order to induce the viewer to reflect apperceptively upon the way in which this strategy discloses the degree to which we normally expect answers to the questions that narratives stimulate in us. Ordinarily those questions are tacit, despite the fact that they structure the way in which we follow movies with understanding. Modernist exercises like *Last Year at Marienbad*, in contrast, bring this tacit process of question formation to the surface, where the ambitious viewer may use it to flash a searchlight upon her own default motion-picture-processing dispositions and procedures.

Thus, not all motion picture makers intend closure, nor do they employ erotetic narration to its fullest natural advantage. Nevertheless a great many do – indeed, most do – including documentaries and narrative television. This, furthermore, is a major factor contributing to the surpassing clarity that most motion pictures possess, especially in contrast to our far more desultory and diffuse mundane lives. In this way, erotetic narration, and the closure it brings to the unified narrative, is a crucial element in accounting for the power of movies. As neurobiologists have begun to prove, the brain has a preference for clarity – for sharp distinctions such as black versus white and good versus evil. So in this regard, the kind of clarity associated with erotetic narratives – which represent the most common type of motion picture – are just the sort of brain food we crave.

Moreover, even motion pictures that defer the full effect of erotetic narration by forfeiting closure, nevertheless also frequently exploit it indirectly, since averting closure, where that evasion appears intentional, may inspire the viewer to ask "why?" And this may lead to an enhanced appreciation of the motion picture in terms of, among other things, its expressive and/or aesthetic qualities and/or its thematic and/or interpretive significance.

Although not all narratives are motion pictures and not all motion pictures are narrative, narration and the motion picture have come together so often that theirs would appear to be at least a common-law marriage, and therefore no philosophy of the motion pictures can be truly complete without a consideration of cinematic narrative and its most habitual, recurring structures, such as erotetic narration and closure.

See also David Bordwell (Chapter 29), Noël Carroll (Chapter 31), and Narration (Chapter 18).

References

Aristotle (1996) *Poetics*, trans. M. Heath, London and New York: Penguin Books.

Barthes, R. (1974) *S/Z*, trans. R. Howard, New York: Hill and Wang.

Bordwell, D. (1985) *Narration in the Fiction Film*, Madison: University of Wisconsin Press.

—— (2008) "Three Dimensions of Narrative Film," in *Poetics of Cinema*, London: Routledge.

Bordwell, D., Staiger, J., and Thompson, K. (1985) *The Classical Hollywood Cinema: Film Style and Mode of Production to 1960*, New York: Columbia University Press.

Carroll, N. (2001) "The Narrative Connection," in *Beyond Aesthetics*, Cambridge and New York: Cambridge University Press.

—— (2007a) *Comedy Incarnate: Buster Keaton, Physical Humor and Bodily Coping*, Malden, MA: Blackwell Publishers.

—— (2007b) "Narrative Closure," *Philosophical Studies* 135 (August): 1–15.

Chatman, S. (1978) *Story and Discourse: Narrative Structure in Fiction and Film*, Ithaca, NY: Cornell University Press.

Field, S. (1994) *Screenplay: The Foundations of Screenwriting*, New York: Dell.

Gulino, P. J. (2004) *Screenwriting: The Sequence Approach*, New York and London: Continuum.

Hume, D. (1998) "Of Tragedy," in *David Hume: Selected Essays*, Oxford: Oxford University Press.

Thompson, K. (1999) *Storytelling in the New Hollywood: Understanding Classical Narrative Technique*, Cambridge, MA: Harvard University Press.

Further reading

The following are further reading on this topic: David Bordwell, *The Way Hollywood Tells It: Story and Style in Modern Movies* (Berkeley: University of California Press, 2006); Noël Carroll, "Toward a Theory of Film Suspense," in *Theorizing the Moving Image* (Cambridge and New York: Cambridge University Press, 1996), and *The Philosophy of Motion Pictures* (Malden, MA: Blackwell Publishers, 2008); Paisley Livingston, "Narrative," in B. Gaut and D. Lopes (eds.) *The Routledge Companion to Aesthetics* (London and New York: Routledge, 2001); and Kristin Thompson, *Storytelling in Film and Television* (Cambridge, MA: Harvard University Press, 2003).

20
ONTOLOGY
David Davies

What kind of thing is a film? What kind of thing is a photograph? Philosophers who have pondered such matters have generally been moved by the following sorts of considerations. To appreciate an artwork or cultural artifact requires at least an experiential engagement of some kind with an instance of that work or artifact, whereby some or all of the properties bearing upon its appreciation are made manifest to the receiver. In the case of a painting, what is required is an experiential encounter with a particular physical object which is located at any given time in a particular gallery or museum, and this makes it plausible to identify the work itself with that object. In the case of a film or photograph, however, there seem to be many different locations where, at a given time, we might experientially encounter the work or artifact in the manner necessary for its appreciation. You may be watching *Citizen Kane*, or looking at a photograph by Diane Arbus, in Los Angeles at the same moment that I am watching the same film or viewing the same photograph in London. In this respect, films and photographs seem to resemble musical and literary works. Appreciating a musical work requires hearing it performed, and appreciating a literary work requires reading it, but people in different locations engaging with different objects or events can simultaneously have the necessary experiential encounter with a given musical or literary work.

Films and photographs, then, like literary works and works of music, must be the kinds of things that can have multiple instances, and such things are most naturally thought of as types or kinds. Just as the word "dog" is a word type that can have three instances, or tokens, on a given page, and just as the cocker spaniel is a kind of dog, of which my neighbor may have an instance, so, it is assumed, *Citizen Kane* (1941) is a type or kind whose tokens or instances are the entities with which viewers experientially engage in appreciating the film. If so, then our ontological understanding of film requires that we further clarify what more general type or kind *Citizen Kane* belongs to. If the cocker spaniel is a type of *dog*, what type of thing is a film like *Citizen Kane*? Answering the latter question should help us answer a further ontological question about films: how are films individuated, that is, when do we have two instances of the same film, and when do we have instances of two different films?

To ask "of what are films or photographs types or kinds?" is to ask about the distinctive features of their instances. Perhaps the most natural answer to this question is that they are types or kinds of *images*. Instances of photographs and films are still or moving images, and photographs and films themselves are types of still or moving images, it might be said. But this answer presupposes that we understand what, ontologically speaking, an image is, and also, perhaps, what is distinctive of the kinds of still images that are photographs and the kinds of moving images that are films. How do photographs, as images, differ from paintings, for example? Some have argued that the difference between paintings and photographs is not merely one of degree, but rather one of a more fundamental nature.

Understanding the ontology of film, then, requires that we address at least the following questions: (1) How is the multiple nature of films and photographs to be understood? (2) What kind of thing are instances of films and photographs? And (3) if filmic and photographic instances are images, do they differ in any fundamental way from the images we encounter in plastic arts, such as painting?

Film and photography as multiple art forms

We can think of an instance of a work of art or other artifact as something that has a distinctive place in the proper appreciation of that work or artifact in that it makes directly available to receivers manifest qualities that bear essentially on such appreciation. Then, as noted above, it is natural to distinguish between "singular" and "multiple" art forms (Wollheim 1980; Wolterstorff 1993 [1975]; Carroll 1998; S. Davies 2003). In the former, a work can, as a matter of necessity, have only one instance. Painting and carved sculpture are generally viewed as singular art forms in this sense. Some kinds of photographic processes also seem to result in singular works or artifacts – for example, the processes that produce daguerreotypes and Polaroids (Carroll 1998: 215). But photography and film of the more standard kinds are multiple art forms, as noted above, as are classical music, narrative and dramatic literature, silk-screening, and cast sculpture.

There are nonetheless significant differences between multiple art forms, and, of more significance in the present context, between film and photography, on the one hand, and music and literature, on the other. There are at least three ways in which multiple artworks can be brought into existence and made available to members of an artistic community (Wollheim 1980: 78–80; Wolterstorff 1980: 90ff.; S. Davies 2003: 159–63). First, as in the case of a literary work, such as a novel, an instance of the work an artist brings into existence may serve as an exemplar. Further instances are then generated through attempts to emulate the exemplar in those respects determined by relevant artistic conventions in place. Second, as in the case of cast sculpture, an artifact an artist produces may, when employed in prescribed ways, generate instances of the work. Such an artifact may be termed a "production artifact" (Wolterstorff 1980), an "encoding" (S. Davies 2003), or a "template" (Carroll 1998). As in the case of exemplars, conventions in place in the relevant art form determine how this artifact must be used if a properly formed instance is to be produced. Third, as in the case of classical musical works and dramatic works, the instructions an artist provides may, if properly followed by those aware of the relevant conventions and practices, result in well-formed instances of the work. In such cases, the instructions call for interpretation and the instances of the work count as performances of it.

Photographs and films clearly fall into the second of these categories. In the case of an analog photograph, the production artifact or encoding is the negative. In the case of a digital photograph, it is a computer file. In both cases, correct instances are images generated from the production artifact by appropriate means. Films, on the other hand, have as their production artifacts those entities used, in various cinematic media, to generate screenings of those films – film prints, videotapes, digital files, etc., which either are, or stand in a "copy" relation to, master encodings of the film.

But what is the ontological status of an artwork in a multiple art form? Or, more generally, what sorts of entities can have other entities as instances? Instantiation is merely one way in which an entity can be "generic" in the sense that it has elements falling under it (Wollheim 1980: 75ff.). The members of a set, for example, can be seen as elements "falling under" the set, but this seems an unpromising way of thinking about the relationship between multiple artworks or artifacts and their instances. Sets are individuated in terms of their members and any difference in membership entails a difference in set, but a given photograph by Cartier-Bresson could surely have had more or fewer instances than it actually has.

These reflections suggest that artworks in multiple art forms are types and their instances are tokens of those types. The distinction between types and tokens, first drawn by C. S. Peirce, is familiar in everyday contexts where we distinguish between, say, the letters in the alphabet and different occurrences of those letters. If asked how many letters there are in the word "sheep," we can correctly answer both five (there are five occurrences of letter-*tokens* in the word) and four (there are occurrences of four different *types* of letters). The identity and nature of a type is not changed as the number of its tokens changes. However, if multiple artworks and artifacts stand to their instances in the relationship of types to tokens, they are types of a special sort, for they are generally taken to admit of both correct and incorrect instances. For example, instances of a musical work arguably include not only performances that meet all the requirements for right performance of the work, but also performances containing at least some incorrect notes. Similarly, it would seem, a damaged print of Renoir's *Rules of the Game* (1939) can still provide an audience with an instance of the film, albeit an improperly formed one. Types or kinds that admit in this way of correct and incorrect instances can be termed "norm kinds" (Wolterstorff 1980, 1993 [1975]) or "norm types" (Dodd 2007). Whereas descriptive types are individuated by the condition that must be met by their tokens, norm types are individuated by the condition that must be met by their correct or properly formed tokens.

While many find attractive the idea that multiple artworks and artifacts are norm types and that their instances are well-formed or improperly formed tokens of those types, this view is not without its problems. Types, we have said, are generic entities that can have elements that "fall under" them, but what is the ontological status of such things? On pretty much every conception of such matters, types are abstract rather than concrete entities and do not have determinate spatial locations. It is therefore questionable whether they can enter into causal relationships with things that do. This raises concerns about our epistemic access to, and ability to refer to, types if we take knowledge and reference to require some kind of causal engagement with the entity known or referred to. However, it has been argued by some philosophers either that abstract objects can enter into causal relations (Burgess and Rosen 1997: 24ff.; Dodd 2007: 13–14) or that knowledge and reference do not require such relations with their objects (e.g., Brown 1991).

A further problem arises if we accept a particular account of the metaphysics of types (Dodd 2007: chapters 2–3), according to which types have a number of features that fit uneasily with our intuitions about films and photographs. Types, as we have seen, are individuated according to the conditions that must be satisfied by their (well-formed) instances. These conditions can be characterized as properties associated with the type – the property of being correctly instanced by strings of the form s-h-e-e-p associated with the word type "sheep," for example (Wolterstorff 1980; Dodd 2007). But, it can be argued, types exist just in case their property associates exist, and properties cannot be brought into or go out of existence – they exist eternally if they exist at all. If so, then it follows that types, too, cannot be brought into or go out of existence. So, if multiple artworks are types, it seems that they cannot be created by their artists, but only discovered. Furthermore, it can be argued, types, as abstract entities individuated by reference to their associated properties are modally inflexible – which is to say that they could not have had intrinsic (i.e., nonrelational) properties other than the ones that they actually possess. But we seem to think of multiple artworks as entities that could have differed in certain of their constitutive properties and still have been the same works. We certainly have no problem understanding such counterfactual claims about films – for example, the claim that *American Beauty* (1999) would have been a better film if the original ending had been retained rather than replaced as a result of feedback from focus groups. If films are types and if types are understood in the way just described, then we must take such a claim as pertaining not to *American Beauty* but to a cinematic counterpart that closely resembles *American Beauty*.

For some (Dodd 2007: chapters 4–5), these implications of identifying multiple artworks with types simply show that we must revise our intuitions about artworks (including films) in light of deeper metaphysical reflection. This line of thought has some plausibility in the case of musical works, where the idea that composers "creatively" discover possible sound sequences is perhaps, on reflection, no more absurd than the idea that mathematicians "creatively" discover novel proofs of theorems. But it seems very counterintuitive to think in this way about films, given both the very complex and collaborative nature of the filmmaking process and the fact that, as seen above, instances of films result from an extended process of manipulating physical media, resulting in the generation of the production artifact used to generate such instances. Some who wish to defend the idea of creatable multiple musical works have appealed to the normative element in such artworks if we construe them as norm types. While types of sound sequence may themselves exist eternally, musical creation, it can be argued, is a matter of making a particular type of sound sequence normative for a work, and this brings into being something that did not exist prior to the composer's activity. Musical works can then be thought of as "indicated sound sequences" created by their composers (Levinson 1980; for related proposals, see Wolterstorff 1993 [1975], and [in a more skeptical vein] S. Davies 2003: 170). But it can be responded that, if works are taken to be norm *types*, they will still be individuated in terms of a condition for correct instantiation that can be expressed as a property: being correct in successfully complying with the performance specifications set out by B in context C, for example. Then it can be argued that this property, like every property, must exist eternally if at all, so that we have not shown multiple works, as norm types, to be creatable or modally flexible (see Dodd 2007: chapter 5). Furthermore, the Levinsonian line of argument seems especially unattractive if applied to films and photographs, for it preserves the counterintuitive idea that the audio-visual structure of a film is itself discovered and becomes art through being made normative for the film.

Similar difficulties beset another strategy to which we might appeal in defense of the creatability of photographic and cinematic works in the face of arguments that appeal to the eternal existence of types. Some philosophers have argued that, in order to accommodate the contextually situated nature of artworks, we should view those works not merely as contextualized objects – indicated structures, for example – but as contextualized actions, indicatings of structures or generations of artistic vehicles. Works, then, are action types (Currie 1989) or token performances (D. Davies 2004). At least in the latter case, we can preserve our sense that photographs and films, and indeed all other multiple artworks, are brought into existence by the artist, since the act of generating the artistic vehicle – identified with the artwork – is itself performed by the artist. Whatever the merits of such an account, however, it fails to address the current concern, since it leaves unchallenged the idea that the artistic vehicle is itself discovered, which seems implausible for film.

A more radical response is to take the creatability and modal flexibility of multiple artworks such as photographs as given, and argue that, if types are indeed eternally existent and modally inflexible entities, this just shows that such multiple artworks cannot in fact be types (Rohrbaugh 2003). The challenge then is to say how an artwork can have multiple instances if it isn't a type. Rohrbaugh argues that talk of multiple artworks as types is harmless if it is merely part of a semantic account of the terms used to label such works, since all we are doing in saying that *Citizen Kane* is a type is distinguishing one use of that label from another use which refers to tokens of the type. Rohrbaugh rejects, however, the further contention that multiple artworks are types in the metaphysically freighted sense outlined above. Rather, he suggests, a multiple artwork like Steiglitz' *The Steerage* is a temporal and modally flexible entity that is both created by Steiglitz and may later be destroyed. Such historically situated and extended entities can be termed "continuants." A continuant is a higher order entity whose existence depends upon those lower order concreta that are its "embodiments." In the case of a traditional photograph, for example, the embodiments include both the negative and existing prints taken from the negative.

While the idea that multiple artworks are continuants whose instances figure among their embodiments preserves some of our intuitions about the creatability and possibly also the modal flexibility of films and photographs, by contrast the nature of continuants and the relationship they bear to those instances among their "embodiments" is far from clear (Dodd 2007: chapter 6). As a result, the ontological status of films and photographs, as multiple artworks, remains contested. Perhaps, however, we can establish some ground rules for resolving this issue. First, as a number of writers have stressed (Currie 1989: 11–12; S. Davies 2003: 155; Rohrbaugh 2003: 178–9; D. Davies 2004: 16–24), artworks of various kinds are things that have their place in certain human practices, and that have to be understood in terms of the ways in which they are treated in those practices. It is thus ill-advised to try to impose upon our understanding of artworks an a priori ontological framework. Artworks must be things of a kind that can function in the ways artworks function in our practices, and the fact, if fact it be, that we treat photographs, films, and other multiple artworks as creatable, modally flexible, entities gives us the best possible reason to seek a way of characterizing them, ontologically speaking, that explains how they can have such properties. Thus we must countenance, and even anticipate, that an ontology of art adequate to accommodate multiple artworks like films and photographs will be revisionary of our traditional ontological categories. So, even if Rohrbaugh's "continuants" are found to be unsatisfactory, we have reason to seek another way of reconciling the multiple nature of films and photographs with our sense that such artifacts are created and perhaps also modally flexible, if, as has been argued, no such reconciliation is possible if such entities are classified as norm types.

Filmic and photographic instances

Whichever kind of account we favor of the general ontological category to which multiple artworks like films and photographs belong, we must address a further question as to the nature of those *instances* of films and photographs an engagement with which is necessary for their proper appreciation. Answering this question will also clarify the manner in which films and photographs are individuated, that is, the conditions under which we have two instances of the same film or photograph rather than instances of two different films or photographs. In the case of another multiple art form, classical music, there is general agreement that an instance of a work is a realization, standardly in a performance, of a type of sound sequence or sound structure. Where there is disagreement over (a) whether realizations other than performances count as instances of a work; and (b) whether it is necessary, for a performance, that the sound sequence be realized on particular instruments and/or be consciously guided by a set of instructions for performance specified by a particular individual or in a particular musico-historical context.

In the case of films and photographs, we can expect a similar pattern of agreement and disagreement among theorists, although the literature here is much less developed than in the musical case. Take first the case of photographs. A well-formed instance of Stiegltiz's *The Steerage* is presumably what one gets if one processes the negative – the production artifact – in a manner determined by the relevant artistic practice. What one gets, in this case, is a print of the photograph which presents a particular image to the viewer. The print itself is a physical object, and the image is a visible aspect of that object. Given that what bears upon appreciating the photographic work is our engagement with the image, it might seem preferable to think of the image, rather than the object of which it is an aspect, as the instance of the work. Comparison with other artistic images, such as paintings, might suggest otherwise, however. For we standardly identify an instance of a painting with the physical object having as an aspect a particular visible array of pigment on canvas. But in the photographic case, the fact that photographs can be instanced not only in prints but also in screenings of slides and in digitally generated arrays on computer screens may favor a uniform treatment that takes the image, generated from a production artifact in an appropriate way, to be the instance. In any case, it seems open to someone to argue, as in the musical case, either that any realization of the visual design of the image is an instance of the photographic work, or that only those realizations generated by standard processing of a production artifact with a particular history so count. In fact, there seems to be general agreement here on the latter course of action. This may be because our sense of the well-formedness or ill-formedness of a photographic image is tied to its having been generated in this way, as in the case of other multiple artworks whose instances seem tied to a historically situated production artifact, such as works of cast sculpture or engraving.

In the case of film, instances are what can be seen (and, in sound films, heard) by appropriately qualified receivers at right screenings (Wolterstorff 1980: 924; Carroll 1998: 212; S. Davies 2003: 161). A right screening is one that uses an authorized production artifact and relevant decoding apparatus in the intended manner, where both the artifact and the apparatus are themselves in good working order. This may involve projection or computer realization, but nothing parallels the presentation of a photographic image through a print. There is therefore no reason to resist identifying an instance of a work with a sequence of images, usually synchronized with a sequence of diegetic and nondiegetic sounds. An instance of a film, then, is a series of two-dimensional moving images and, where relevant, correlated sounds. If, as Wolterstorff proposes, we think of a film as a norm type, the properties that are normative in the work are just those that are manifest to receivers in all right screenings as characterized above. Analogous notions of instance correctness are forthcoming on alternative construals of the ontological status of the cinematic work.

If instances of films and photographs are still and moving images respectively, what are the latter? The most obvious answer is that they are representations of whatever is thereby imaged, analogous in this respect to paintings and other representational images, but differing in the manner whereby the representation is produced. A number of writers on film and photography, however, have claimed that differences in the manner of production of photographic and pictorial images have more far-reaching implications as to the epistemological, ontological, and artistic status of those images. Key to these claims is the supposedly "mechanical" manner in which a traditional photographic or cinematic image is produced. What is imaged in such cases, it is claimed, is whatever played the appropriate causal role in a "mechanical" process leading to those features of the production artifact responsible for producing a given visible manifold in instances of the photograph or film. In the case of paintings, however, the intentions and beliefs of the painter also play a role in determining what is imaged. Some have argued that, in virtue of this difference in the manner of generating the image, photographic and cinematic images are not representations (Walton 1984), or are not representations in which we can take an artistic interest (Scruton 1983).

The most radical of these claims, at least on standard readings (Carroll 1988: 125ff.; Currie 1995: 48–50), is to be found in André Bazin's "The Ontology of the Photographic Image." Pictorial images represent through depiction. While the nature of pictorial depiction is a matter of dispute, it is generally taken to involve either some kind of intended resemblance between image and subject or our capacity to experience the image in certain ways that resemble how we would experience the things represented. Bazin, however, takes the relation between a photographic image and what it is an image of to be a matter of *identity* of some sort, rather than of intended or experienced resemblance. Contrasting pictorial and photographic images, Bazin writes that "the photographic image is the object itself ... It shares, by virtue of the very process of its becoming, the being of the model of which it is the reproduction: it *is* the model." Furthermore, this holds, according to Bazin, "no matter how fuzzy, distorted, or discoloured ... the image may be" (1967: 14). In virtue of this, traditional film for Bazin is by its very nature a "realistic" medium.

Given that Bazin's concern is to explain the distinctive psychological effects of photographs, the startling pronouncement that the photographic image *is* the imaged object might be seen as a claim about how photographs strike us, phenomenologically, rather than about their ontological status (Friday 2005). However, an ontological reading of Bazin's claim can be defended by reference to a further analogy that he draws between photographs and death masks. Just as the latter are moldings formed by "a certain automatic process," so "one might consider photography in this sense as a molding, the taking of an impression, by the manipulation of light" (1967: 12n). A death mask faithfully preserves, in virtue of its manner of production, the *shape* of its model, independently of the beliefs of the maker. In respect of its shape, then, it is identical with its model. Similarly, the process productive of a photographic or filmic image is "mechanical" or "automatic" in that it doesn't involve the subjectivity of the maker (ibid.: 12–13), and, as a result, re-presents, rather than merely representing, something of its model.

The problem with this claim, as critics have pointed out (e.g., Carroll 1998: 125ff.), is that the death mask analogy is difficult to sustain. Arnheim (1957), for example, argues at length that a photograph cannot re-present in some unique way the pattern of light rays emitted by an imaged object, but only preserve some of the visible information available. Which information is preserved, and how it is encoded, depends upon both the nature of the photographic equipment employed and choices that the photographer must make. But then we are left with the claim that light rays from imaged objects play some causal role in producing photographs – which, even if it might bear upon the psychological impact of photographs, merely reiterates what is distinctive about the process whereby photographic images are generated.

Kendall Walton, however, has argued that Bazin is right in thinking that there is an essentially "realistic" character to photographic images that is lacking in paintings. According to Walton (1984), the essential realism of photographs lies in the fact that photography is not simply a new way of producing pictures, but a new way of *seeing*. Photographic and filmic images of the traditional sort are *transparent*, in that we *see* the world *through* them. The camera, then, is properly analogized to glasses, mirrors, and telescopes, which are also media for indirect seeing, rather than modes of representation. Paintings, by contrast, are not transparent – in looking at a painting of a subject X, what we see is a representation of X, not X. Walton's argument presupposes a causal theory of seeing according to which to see something is to have visual experiences caused, in a certain manner, by what is seen. What is distinctive of seeing X is that the manner of causation is mechanical, or nonintentional, whereas in the case of seeing a representation of X our relation to X is mediated by the intentional states of X's producer. He claims that the manner in which a photograph causes my visual experience is also mechanical or nonintentional. A further necessary condition for visual perception, he maintains, is that, where we obtain information about X via a perceptual medium, our susceptibility to make mistakes reflects similarities among things of type X.

Critics have disputed Walton's account of perception, however, and thus his claim that photographic and filmic images are not representations. On the proposed account, a mode of access to information about X counts as perceptual just in case it is nonintentionally causally – and hence counterfactually – dependent upon X, and it preserves real similarity relations. It has been argued that these conditions are neither necessary nor sufficient for perception (e.g., Currie 1995: 61–9). A further necessary condition, it is argued, is that seeing, direct or indirect, furnishes us with "egocentric information" as to how X is related to us spatially and temporally, and "transtemporal" information that permits us to track X through time. In looking at a photo of X, however, I get neither egocentric nor transtemporal information. With moving images, I get transtemporal information, but not egocentric information. If so, this supports the idea that photographic and filmic images are indeed representations, but differ from paintings in that their content is determined *naturally* rather than, in part, by the intentional states of the imagemaker.

See also Definition of "cinema" (Chapter 5), Medium (Chapter 16), Rudolph Arnheim (Chapter 27), and Realism (Chapter 22).

References

Arnheim, R. (1957) *Film as Art*, Berkeley: University of California Press.

Bazin, A. (1967) "The Ontology of the Photographic Image," in H. Gray (trans.) *What Is Cinema?* vol. 1, Berkeley: University of California Press.

Brown, J. R. (1991) *The Laboratory of the Mind: Thought Experiments in the Natural Sciences*, London: Routledge.

Burgess, J., and Rosen, G. (1997) *A Subject with No Object*, Oxford: Clarendon Press.

Carroll, N. (1988) *Philosophical Problems of Classical Film Theory*, Princeton, NJ: Princeton University Press.

—— (1998) *A Philosophy of Mass Art*, Oxford: Clarendon Press, chapter 3.

Currie, G. (1989) *An Ontology of Art*, New York: St Martin's Press.

—— (1995) *Image and Mind: Film, Philosophy, and Cognitive Science*, Cambridge: Cambridge University Press.

Davies, D. (2004) *Art as Performance*, Oxford: Blackwell.

Davies, S. (2003) "Ontology of Art," in J. Levinson (ed.) *The Oxford Handbook of Aesthetics*, Oxford: Oxford University Press.

Dodd, J. (2007) *Works of Music*, Oxford: Oxford University Press.

Friday, J. (2005) "André Bazin's Ontology of Photographic and Film Imagery," *Journal of Aesthetics and Art Criticism* 63: 339–50.

Levinson, J. (1980) "What a Musical Work Is," *Journal of Philosophy* 77: 5–28.

Rohrbaugh, G. (2003) "Artworks as Historical Individuals," *European Journal of Philosophy* 11: 177–205.

Scruton, R. (1983) "Photography and Representation," in *The Aesthetic Understanding*, London: Methuen.

Walton, K. (1984) "Transparent Pictures," *Critical Inquiry* 11: 246–77.

Wollheim, R. (1980) *Art and Its Objects*, 2nd ed., Cambridge: Cambridge University Press.

Wolterstorff, N. (1993 [1975]) "Towards an Ontology of Art Works," in J. W. Bender and H. G. Blocker (eds.) *Contemporary Philosophy of Art*, Englewood Cliffs, NJ: Prentice Hall.

—— (1980) *Works and Worlds of Art*, Oxford: Clarendon Press.

21
RACE

Dan Flory

Ideas of race have shaped film since the medium's invention during the late nineteenth century. Some of the first works produced by Thomas Edison, Edwin S. Porter, and Georges Méliès contain demeaning portrayals of African Americans devouring watermelons, stealing chickens, or menacing innocent whites. Other early works show allegedly primitive "natives" living as "natural savages" in exotic settings, far from a presumed white viewership. One of the Edison Company's earliest major productions was *Uncle Tom's Cabin* in 1903, the first of many efforts to mount on film Harriet Beecher Stowe's flawed narrative concerning the injustices of racialized slavery. Perhaps not too surprisingly, prevailing conceptions of white supremacy, racial hierarchy, manifest destiny, ongoing contemporaneous projects of "race science," and the American theatrical tradition of blackface minstrelsy fundamentally influenced the depictions of race in these early films. However, similar conceptions or their successors also permeate many later cinematic landmarks, among them *Birth of a Nation* (1915), *Nanook of the North* (1922), *The Jazz Singer* (1927), *King Kong* (1933), *Gone With the Wind* (1939), *The Searchers* (1956), *Lawrence of Arabia* (1962), and *Chinatown* (1974).

While numerous filmmakers and social critics have examined the impact of race on film, philosophers have been somewhat slower to do so. The reason why is not especially difficult to identify: philosophers have typically thought of race as an empirical problem, resulting from the improper application of moral or political ideals, rather than a conceptual difficulty. Problems of race have not seemed central to the discipline but rather peripheral matters at best, to be dealt with after the theoretical complexities have been overcome. Recent work in the philosophy of race has shown, however, that this standard philosophical stance is nowhere near as clear-cut as many in the field have believed. As Charles Mills has argued, in the modern West "[r]acism and racially structured discrimination have not been *deviations* from the norm; they have *been* the norm." Moreover, philosophers such as Locke, Kant, and Hegel played fundamental roles in theoretically shaping modern ideas of race (Mills 1997: 93, 63–73, 94). The attitude of considering ideas of race and racism as mere unfortunate consequences accruing from misapplications of moral or political concepts has been further thrown into question by the erosion of a sharp distinction between the empirical and the conceptual that has taken place in philosophy during

DAN FLORY

the last half-century. However, some philosophers have taken the role of race seriously in cinematic imagery, narrative, and audience response, despite the more typical inclination to dismiss race as a nonphilosophical concern.

It is also crucial to make clear that while ideas of race themselves have undergone sea changes with regard to their standard meanings during the brief history of film, older, more rigid conceptions remain deeply influential. For example, even though superannuated research projects in biology, psychology, or other scientific disciplines no longer provide support for a hierarchical concept of race based in nature, outmoded senses of this idea as an essence-like "natural kind" continue to structure the social reality of many people's lives. Moreover, by virtue of being embedded in traditional social practices and ways of thinking, general forms of dealing with human life through the lens of permanent, unchanging, and inherited conceptions of graduated human difference have carried over into many audience members' viewing habits, making the function of such notions an issue for anyone interested in the role that standard presumptions and expectations play in our understanding of film – particularly their social, moral, political, and affective dimensions, but also at the level of cognition.

Lastly, I should note that although critics like James Baldwin (1976) and James Snead (1994) have analyzed race's role in film with striking perceptiveness, their discussions have typically been aimed as social criticisms, rather than as philosophical ones, by which I mean their analyses have been specific assessments of existing societies or cultural products and not meant as abstract, conceptual points. These discussions, in other words, ordinarily limit their scope to particular flaws in actual social arrangements or films. By contrast, philosophical criticisms aim more at the level of general truths; ideally, such criticisms would be universal, but in any event they would not be so closely tied to historical specifics as those usually offered by such critics. Of course, oftentimes these categories of criticism overlap, meaning that some forms of social criticism may also be philosophical ones, and vice versa, but the two categories remain distinguishable. My reason for noting this distinction is that it is crucial to grasp the differences between these forms of criticism, as well as their commonalities, when discussing race's operation in film. However, even as such discussions are best understood as not developing philosophical considerations of film *per se*, they nonetheless frequently contain insights that others have elaborated in ways more directly pertaining to philosophy.

Resisting standard forms of spectatorship

One way to begin understanding race's role in the philosophy of film is by means of the concept of the "oppositional gaze." The idea of "the gaze" itself is, of course, critically important to film studies, perhaps most famously through Laura Mulvey's "Visual Pleasure and Narrative Cinema" (1975). The concept, however, has roots in the work of Jean-Paul Sartre (1956) and Maurice Merleau-Ponty (1968). The relevant sense here denotes the way in which human beings often look at others and, rather than acknowledging their full humanity, impose oppressive misconceptions on them. As formulated by bell hooks, the idea of the oppositional gaze harks back to Fanon's

Sartrean-influenced discussion of the "white gaze" and his attempts to defend himself against it (1967: 109ff.). Frequently such attempts at self-defense force one to learn "to look in a certain way so as to resist" this commonplace mode of perceiving human beings and thereby develop a critical perspective that interrogates not only human relations, but visual media as well (hooks 1992: 116–17). Crucially positioned against more determinist theories positing a passive cinematic spectator (such as Mulvey's), the oppositional gaze argues for the possibility of an active agency that permits viewers to critically analyze representations of human beings, particularly with regard to race. hooks' concept is thus linked to the idea of the "resisting spectator" such that viewers may oppose racialized depictions that dehumanize and degrade through stereotype (Diawara 1988), as well as the idea that we possess the ability to "read through" filmic texts for alternative, nonracialized meanings (Bobo 1993). However, hooks goes to greater lengths than these critics to indicate that such stances amount to arguing for active critical *human* capacities that need to be developed, rather than being the essential characteristics of, say, black spectators, who, some have argued, possess such abilities merely because they are oppressed human beings. Whereas conditions of oppression would mean that one needed such capacities much more urgently, their actual development remains an independent, self-determined step that, in terms of general psychological capacities possessed by human beings, anyone could take.

Tommy Lott has further elaborated the importance of such resistant perspectives for philosophy of film by explaining how they not only permit one to better understand the concept of "black film" as more heterogeneous than often argued, but also enable us to better grasp the complicated interplay between aesthetics and politics in cinematic representations of racial blackness, such as the ways in which they often speak in complicated, "hybrid" voices that combine both mainstream and independent sensibilities (Lott 1991, 1997, 1998). Crucial to note here is what has been called the "politics of representation," the contingent, historically determined social meanings attached to racialized images in art forms like film, and how they may influence or reinforce ways viewers think about race without their even realizing it. According to this conception, stereotypes may play themselves out in cinematic narrative or characterization and sway us at a nonconscious level to think, act, or perceive according to rigidified hierarchical rankings of humanity. But these influences may be counteracted, particularly if we realize we may also develop the capacity to think critically and oppose them, even if developing that potential remains a daunting responsibility. Similar ideas have been discussed, although less fully, by Stuart Hall (1989). With their more generalized discussions of such matters, hooks and Lott have provided conceptual tools with which we might grasp not only the pernicious nature of racialized images in film, as well as the presumptions that give them currency, but also how to go about theorizing resistance to them.

Cavellian and cognitivist positions

Another place where serious discussion of race's role in film gains philosophical leverage is through Cavell's telling observation of more than three decades ago that:

> Until recently, types of black human beings were not created in film;
> black people were stereotypes – mammies, shiftless servants, loyal retainers,
> entertainers. We were not given, and were not in a position to be given,
> individualities that projected particular *ways* of inhabiting a social role; we
> recognized only the role. Occasionally the humanity behind the role would
> manifest itself; and the result was a revelation not of a human individuality,
> but of an entire realm of humanity becoming visible. (1979a: 33–4)

Through this and associated remarks Cavell argues that race's function in film is directly linked to the epistemological role of acknowledging the existence of others. Elsewhere Cavell asserts that one's full-fledged humanity depends fundamentally on its recognition and acknowledgment by other human beings (1979b). When these capacities are transferred over to film viewing, they become critically important to our understanding of certain types of cinematic characterizations, or "individualities," as Cavell refers to them – the kinds of characters that certain people are, such that we could imagine ourselves as having met or meeting them in other circumstances (1979a: 33, 35). Rather than thinking merely in terms of stereotypes, we may also consider other human beings as "well-rounded" characters like ourselves – for example, as full-fledged equals – provided that we are prepared to extend complete recognition and acknowledgment to their humanity. Cavell thus construes the problem of race in film as analogous to the problem of "other minds" and the attendant skepticisms we might entertain with regard to their existence, while at the same time evoking allusions to Sartre's, hooks', and Lott's discussions of various types of gazes. Although it would no doubt be appropriate to be slightly more reserved about the relative enlightenment of post-Civil Rights era spectators than Cavell is, he opens here a serious possibility for philosophically considering race in film.

Cavell's point about race is also an integral part of his overall argument about film's appeal. For him, its capacity to present individualities makes the medium attractive and aesthetically interesting in ways that, say, theater is not. Moreover, acknowledgment is "an act of the self" (1979a: 123), which underscores his efforts to integrate our general cognitive responses to cinematic characters with those we have to real human beings.

A number of philosophers have followed Cavell's lead here, including William Rothman, Thomas Wartenberg, and myself. Rothman analyzes specific representations of race in the "unknown woman" genre and other films, noting particularly some of these films' socially critical dimensions that are at the same time philosophical (2004: 98–109). Similarly taking seriously Cavell's conception of film as philosophy, Wartenberg outlines a genre he calls "the unlikely couple film," in which two individuals "transgress a social norm regulating appropriate partnering choice" (1999: xvi). These films may thereby express subversive, philosophical criticism of social hierarchies such as race by raising "questions that go to the very heart of how we imagine a life worth living" (xviii). "Interracial unlikely couple films are noteworthy for their assumption that racial hierarchy is illegitimate" as well as their focus on its eradication (238). Like Cavell, both these philosophers place reflective theorizing about race within particular shots or the narrative content of specific films, as well as in the discussions they generate in viewers.

Applying Cavellian methodology in combination with more cognitivist film theory, I have explored some of the asymmetries between audiences, based on their understandings of race. Divergent responses to racial representations, I argue, are significantly due to differing presumptions about the concept and their function in determining what one's aesthetic reaction will be (Flory 2005, 2006). Understanding such differences allows us to develop greater insights into audience response, concepts of human difference, and "critical cinema" – that is, films that raise explicit criticisms about society – as well as some of the ways in which such criticism may cross over into the philosophical. In particular, I have analyzed at length the use of film noir to influence audience members to reflect on racial injustice. By exploiting this film form's potential for making viewers think, a number of filmmakers have found ways to urge us to contemplate such matters as the gap between professed endorsements of full universal equality and moral actions that betray otherwise (Flory 2000, 2002, 2007, 2008). By linking our frequently unexamined background assumptions with their cognitive operation in film viewing, I bring to the surface often conflicting attitudes toward race and their effects on our lives as well as on aesthetic experience.

Noël Carroll's work provides a more squarely cognitivist response to cinematic presentations of race. He points, for example, to the frequent associations between racial whiteness, beauty, and morality, on the one hand, and racial "otherness," ugliness, and immorality, on the other, in cinematic uses of horror and humor (2000). These associations have frequently operated to reinforce racial stereotyping of groups that would otherwise be insupportable. In his analysis Carroll explicitly notes that he is analyzing the politics of representation (38). Similarly, he has examined films like *Nothing But a Man* and *The Cool World* for ways in which social contradictions may be made salient to viewers (1998: 203–13), as well as investigating some of the nuances regarding how moving images may or may not influence us with respect to race (2003: 114–20).

Like hooks and Lott, the philosophers of film described in this section presume an active spectatorship capable of critically regarding the cinematic representations they see. This presumption opens the possibility that viewers do not necessarily have to passively think or perceive according to racist preconceptions but may vigorously resist them. Clearly, such a presumption would be a crucial element of any philosophically respectable strategy for overcoming problems of race, whether in film or elsewhere. In addition, it is worth noting that the critical positions outlined above broadly conform to the guidelines of a "naturalized" epistemology – the theory that our knowledge of the world is most advantageously conceived as consistent with the best results that the sciences have to offer, such as Joshua Glasgow's recent assessment that ordinary conceptions of race have no basis in recent findings in biology (2003).

Psychoanalytic, Marxist, and existentialist perspectives

Other philosophical perspectives have contributed to a better understanding of race in film as well. Although some of these analyses are at times hampered by presuming overly deterministic conceptions of passive spectatorship, they frequently remain helpful investigations of standard racial preconceptions. For example, Kelly Oliver and Benigno Trigo argue that "both the narrative and style of [film noir] are motivated by anxieties over race and sex" (2003: xviii). Using the psychoanalytic concepts of condensation, displacement, and "abjection" (a term for that which calls into question or threatens human identity) to interpret film noir as "a type of Freudian dream-work" (xv), Oliver and Trigo excavate noir's "unconscious" for fears of "the other" and their determinations that shape such films. "Implicitly," they tell us, film noir "is always and everywhere about race ... racial ambiguity is [its] real anxiety" (4–5). Yet by essentializing this film form as they do, Oliver and Trigo preclude the possibility of resisting its characteristics. Spectatorship is presumed to be passive and without the capacity to critically analyze the racialized dimensions it "always and everywhere" contains. Thus, while their individual analyses of films often contain valuable insights, their overall philosophical perspective excludes the possibilities of transformation that they themselves advocate (e.g., 188, 234–6). Even though these authors seek to avoid having "totalized" their theory, that is precisely what they do. By contrast, Homi Bhabha's argument that racial stereotypes in film operate as Freudian fetishes largely escapes this criticism by introducing a sense of critical agency (1994: 66–84). Although weakened by its reliance on the nineteenth-century understanding of mind contained in typical Freudian perspectives, Bhabha's position accommodates the need to have the capacity for critically assessing race's role in film.

Working from a more Marxist stance, Douglas Kellner has used class-sensitive notions such as ideology and alienation to investigate how films may not only instill dominant myths and values, but also question them. Sensitive to the ways in which economic relations affect our sense of identity, both coauthors Michael Ryan and Kellner note that "cultural representations [such as those in film] not only give shape to psychological dispositions, they also play a role in determining how social reality will be constructed" (Ryan and Kellner 1988: 13). Thus control over the production of such representations importantly determines various forms of social power. In focusing on race, they praise works of black radicalism like *Sweet Sweetback's Baadasssss Song* (1971) and *The Spook Who Sat by the Door* (1973) for depicting structural problems of racial oppression (32–3). By the same token, they largely condemn other "blaxploitation"-era films because, despite frequent positive images, these works focused mainly on race as a problem to do with an individual's particular beliefs, rather than with structures of power and representation (122–6). In turning to an analysis of Spike Lee's work, Kellner employs Brechtian conceptions to argue that films like *Do the Right Thing* (1989) and *Malcolm X* (1992) are "morality tales rather than political learning plays in Brecht's sense" (1997: 96). While admittedly getting audiences to focus on some forms of structural oppression, Kellner argues that Lee's work ultimately fails to achieve its aim of making such matters clear by falling victim to "identity

politics" and the idea that racial beliefs are predominantly an individual's responsibility (99–100). I have contested this interpretation of Lee's work on the grounds that
it underappreciates his aim to make viewers think, rather than didactically presenting
them with an ideological *fait accompli* (Flory 2006, 2008). Nevertheless, through his
use of Marxist theory, Kellner brings to the surface important issues in analyzing philosophical dimensions of race in film.

In connection with the consideration of other philosophical perspectives, worth
noting is a controversy surrounding a more recent remark by Cavell about the role
of race in film. While analyzing an early sequence in 1953's *The Band Wagon*, he
asserts that actor Fred Astaire's "acknowledging his indebtedness for his existence as
a dancer – his deepest identity – to the genius of black dancing" is evident (1997:
35). This claim generated a spirited response from Robert Gooding-Williams, as well
as a rejoinder by Cavell. Despite the latter's immediate qualification that "[h]ow fully
such an acknowledgment is acceptable is a further question," Gooding-Williams
argues that numerous racial codings and references in the film reveal a "Jim Crow"
sensibility that Cavell's remark overlooks (Gooding-Williams 2006: 54ff.). By closely
analyzing the frequent appearances of black waiters and Pullman porters, as well
as numerous other references to blackness in *The Band Wagon*, Gooding-Williams
reveals a racialization of the melancholy that Astaire's character embodies in these
early scenes. Even as the film admittedly acknowledges its debt to black dance
(61–2), it also presumes racial blackness as a kind of "urbane, sophisticated … primi-
tivism" that holds the potential to rejuvenate melancholic white men such as Astaire
plays through imparting them with a nonthreatening "blackened masculinity" and
"swing" (151n49, 59, 151n53). As in his analyses of *Casablanca* (1942) and *The Lion
King* (1994) (17–41), Gooding-Williams takes pains to make clear that problems of
racial representation remain unresolved in Astaire's dancing routines. Working from
a broadly existentialist perspective, Gooding-Williams concludes that, rather than
feeling pleasure in viewing Astaire's routines in the early sequences of *The Band
Wagon*, as Cavell does, he feels "dismay" – something that he argues others should
feel as well, once they put aside their racialized viewing presumptions, because these
presumptions remain fundamentally unquestioned in the film's narrative (Gooding-
Williams 2006: 64).

In response, Cavell has argued that within the confines of mid-twentieth-century
America, Astaire went as far as he could in acknowledging his debt to black dance.
Invoking political philosopher John Rawls' conception of an imperfectly just society
that is nevertheless "good enough" to receive one's assent (1971), Cavell argues that,
analogously, Astaire's dance is "good enough to warrant praise" (2005: 82), even if,
from an ideal perspective, it remains tainted by the racial injustices of its era. The
dance, then, operates *partly* as a homage to African American dance, while recognizing the circumstances of injustice that prevent Astaire from dancing as a strict
equal for more than a moment with his partner in the second of the sequences, a black
shoeshine man played by Leroy Daniels. Thus, asserts Cavell, the dance is ambiguous,
even as it works through the circumstances of its own ambiguity, in particular the
circumstances of injustice that prevent full equality between Astaire's and Daniels'

characters (76–9). Still, the dance as "homage has presented itself as a step of change" (79), and with his outstretched arms to the shoeshine man during the finale Astaire declares "his willingness to change" (81), even if far more remains to be done and lone individuals such as Astaire represents could never accomplish these changes on their own. Yet this dancer's beckoning gesture holds out the as-yet-unfulfilled promise of equality (107–8), even as such a "claim is open to rebuke" and Astaire's gesture raises further questions of culture that remain difficult to resolve (82).

Although I do not propose to settle this controversy here, one thing its extended discussion reveals is the importance of being careful to determine who "we" are when analyzing "our" feelings and what "we" should judge. While Cavell seems accurate to point out the near-impossibility of Astaire expressing his desire for full equality within the confines of his circumstances and thus the difficulty of making the judgment Cavell proposes we make about it, I think Gooding-Williams is right to argue that his opponent's presumption about the viewing audience is that they are the "privileged ones," as Cavell describes "us" at one point (ibid.: 78), rather than referencing cinematic spectators in general. A crucial responsibility for philosophers of film that Gooding-Williams emphasizes in this disagreement, then, is the need to thoroughly inspect the foundations of one's viewing position, particularly for presumptions of racial privilege.

Rethinking the aesthetic

A suggestion made by Clyde Taylor directly relates to such a responsibility, namely, his challenge to philosophical theorists of film to rethink its aesthetics (1988, 1989). Synthesizing ideas from many of the positions described above as well as from the "Third Cinema" movement, "black aesthetics," and elsewhere, Taylor argues that standard Western conceptions of the beautiful and taste must be put aside and our sensibilities reconceptualized in order for us to escape the defects of racialized thinking. Clearly Taylor's challenge reaches far beyond philosophy of film into aesthetics itself, for he proposes a comprehensive program of research that breaks the prevailing "aesthetic contract," interrogates current systems of creating as well as discussing art, and elaborates ways in which "art and beauty can be approached with more even-handedness and less false consciousness" (1998: xiii). Also a project advocated by Sylvia Wynter (1992), such an overhaul of the aesthetic itself emphasizes an antiessentialist, pluralistic stance, the importance of attention to historical contingency, and possesses a striking consistency with naturalized epistemology. As Taylor notes, of special interest is "[t]he interplay between [Western aesthetics] and the representations of people of color in cinema," particularly "[t]he entrenched precept of aesthetic reasoning that white is equitable with beauty and black with ugliness" (2003: 400), a point that underscores one of Carroll's charges regarding the racialized politics of representation (2000).

In this context, one may see the relevance of Richard Dyer's *White* (1997) and Ella Shohat and Robert Stam's *Unthinking Eurocentrism* (1994). These works seek to rethink the aesthetics of Western visual media in ways that leave aside harmful conceptions of race and reimagine them from a perspective of full universal humanity. Although both works are somewhat marred by a tendency to essentialize their philosophical opposition and therefore miss subtleties in many conceptions of Western aesthetics as well as art objects, Dyer more successfully meets Taylor's challenge, perhaps because his goals are more modest and localized, and his method empirically based. This more "piecemeal" approach to theorizing philosophically about race in film has been further carried forward by many whose positions are described above.

This project of reimagining cinematic aesthetics so as to understand, as well as eliminate, the negative influences of modern racialized thinking will no doubt continue to be a focus for philosophers of film for some time to come.

See also Stanley Cavell (Chapter 32), Noël Carroll (Chapter 31), Cognitive theory (Chapter 33), Film as philosophy (Chapter 50), and Spectatorship (Chapter 23).

References

Baldwin, J. (1976) *The Devil Finds Work*, New York: Dial Press.

Bhabha, H. (1994) *The Location of Culture*, London and New York: Routledge.

Bobo, J. (1993) "'Reading through the Text': Black Women Spectators," in M. Diawara (ed.) *Black American Cinema*, New York: Routledge.

Carroll, N. (1998) *Interpreting the Moving Image*, Cambridge and New York: Cambridge University Press.

—— (2000) "Ethnicity, Race, and Monstrosity: The Rhetorics of Horror and Humor," in P. Brand (ed.) *Beauty Matters*, Bloomington: Indiana University Press.

—— (2003) *Engaging the Moving Image*, New Haven, CT: Yale University Press.

Cavell, S. (1979a) *The World Viewed: Reflections on the Ontology of Film*, exp. ed., Cambridge, MA: Harvard University Press.

—— (1979b) *The Claim of Reason: Wittgenstein, Skepticism, Morality, and Tragedy*, Oxford: Clarendon Press; New York: Oxford University Press.

—— (1997) "Something Out of the Ordinary", *Proceedings and Addresses of the American Philosophical Association* 71, no. 2: 23–37.

—— (2005) *Philosophy the Day after Tomorrow*, Cambridge, MA: Belknap Press of Harvard University Press.

Diawara, M. (1988) "Black Spectatorship: Problems of Identification and Resistance," *Screen* 29: 66–76.

Dyer, R. (1997) *White*, London and New York: Routledge.

Fanon, F. (1967) *Black Skins, White Masks*, trans. C. L. Markmann, New York: Grove Press.

Flory, D. (2000) "Black on White: *Film Noir* and the Epistemology of Race in Recent African American Cinema," *Journal of Social Philosophy* 31: 82–116.

—— (2002) "The Epistemology of Race and Black American *Film Noir*: Spike Lee's *Summer of Sam* as Lynching Parable," in K. Stoehr (ed.) *Film and Knowledge: Essays on the Integration of Images and Ideas*, Jefferson, NC: McFarland.

—— (2005) "Race, Rationality, and Melodrama: Aesthetic Response and the Case of Oscar Micheaux," *Journal of Aesthetics and Art Criticism* 63: 327–38.

—— (2006) "Spike Lee and the Sympathetic Racist," *Journal of Aesthetics and Art Criticism* 64: 67–79.

—— (2007) "Race, Empathy, and *Noir* in *Deep Cover*," *Film and Philosophy* 11: 67–85.

—— (2008) *Philosophy, Black Film, Film Noir*, University Park, PA: Pennsylvania State University Press.

Glasgow, J. (2003) "On the New Biology of Race," *Journal of Philosophy* 100: 456–74.

Gooding-Williams, R. (2006) *Look, A Negro! Philosophical Essays on Race, Culture, and Politics*, New York: Routledge.

Hall, S. (1989) "Cultural Identity and Cinematic Representation," *Framework* 36: 68–1.

hooks, b. (1992) *Black Looks: Race and Representation*, Boston: South End Press.

Kellner, D. (1997) "Aesthetic, Ethics, and Politics in the Films of Spike Lee," in M. Reid (ed.) *Spike Lee's "Do the Right Thing,"* Cambridge and New York: Cambridge University Press.

Lott, T. (1991) "A No-Theory Theory of Contemporary Black Cinema," *Black American Literature Forum* 25: 221–36.

—— (1997) "Aesthetics and Politics in Contemporary Black Film Theory," in R. Allen and M. Smith (eds.) *Film Theory and Philosophy*, Oxford: Clarendon Press; New York: Oxford University Press.

—— (1998) "Hollywood and Independent Black Cinema," in S. Neale and M. Smith (eds.) *Contemporary Hollywood Cinema*, London and New York: Routledge.

Merleau-Ponty, M. (1968) *The Visible and the Invisible*, ed. C. Lefort; trans. A. Lingis, Evanston, IL: Northwestern University Press.

Mills, C. (1997) *The Racial Contract*, Ithaca, NY: Cornell University Press.

Mulvey, L. (1975) "Visual Pleasure and Narrative Cinema," *Screen* 16: 6–18.

Oliver, K., and Trigo, B. (2003) *Noir Anxiety*, Minneapolis: University of Minnesota Press.

Rawls, J. (1971) *A Theory of Justice*, Cambridge, MA: Belknap Press of Harvard University Press.

Rothman, W. (2004) *The "I" of the Camera: Essays in Film Criticism, History, and Aesthetics*, 2nd ed., Cambridge and New York: Cambridge University Press.

Ryan, M., and Kellner, D. (1988) *Camera Politica: The Politics and Ideology of Contemporary Hollywood Film*, Bloomington: Indiana University Press.

Sartre, J.-P. (1956) *Being and Nothingness*, trans. H. Barnes, New York: Philosophical Library.

Shohat, E., and Stam, R. (1994) *Unthinking Eurocentrism: Multiculturalism and the Media*, London and New York: Routledge.

Snead, J. (1994) *White Screens/Black Images: Hollywood from the Dark Side*, ed. C. MacCabe and C. West, New York: Routledge.

Taylor, C. (1988) "We Don't Need Another Hero: Anti-Theses on Aesthetics," in C. Andrade-Watkins and M. Cham (eds.) *Blackframes: Critical Perspectives on Black Independent Cinema*, Cambridge, MA: MIT Press.

—— (1989) "Black Cinema in the Post-aesthetic Era," in J. Pines and P. Willemen (eds.) *Questions of Third Cinema*, London: British Film Institute.

—— (1998) *The Mask of Art: Breaking the Aesthetic Contract – Film and Literature*, Bloomington: Indiana University Press.

—— (2003) "Black Cinema and Aesthetics," in T. Lott and J. Pittman (eds.) *A Companion to African-American Philosophy*, Malden, MA: Blackwell.

Wartenberg, T. (1999) *Unlikely Couples: Movie Romance as Social Criticism*, Boulder, CO: Westview Press.

Wynter, S. (1992) "Rethinking 'Aesthetics': Notes towards a Deciphering Practice," in M. Cham (ed.) *Ex-Iles: Essays on Caribbean Cinema*, Trenton, NJ: Africa World Press.

Further reading

The classic scholarly history of blacks in American film to the Second World War is Thomas Cripps, *Slow Fade to Black: The Negro in American Film, 1900–1942* (New York: Oxford University Press, 1977). The continuation of Cripps' history is *Making Movies Black: The Hollywood Message Movie from World War II to the Civil Rights Era* (New York: Oxford University Press, 1993). Jim Pines and Paul Willemen (eds.) *Questions of Third Cinema* (London: British Film Institute, 1989) examines film-theoretical considerations of "Third Cinema." Sylvia Wynter, "Black Aesthetic," in M. Kelly (ed.) *Encyclopedia of Aesthetics*, vol. 1 (New York: Oxford University Press, 1998), provides a definition, historical survey, and discussion of the black aesthetic movement.

22
REALISM
Andrew Kania

The term "realism" has been put to almost as many uses in film theory as in philosophy. The basic idea in both areas of study is the same: something is realistic if it bears some sort of veridical relation to reality. Thus, in order to specify a particular sense of "realism" one must specify (i) what is being described as realistic; (ii) what one means by "reality"; and (iii) what relation is being posited between them. In film theory and criticism, one major concern has been with whether particular films, or kinds of film (e.g., film noir, neorealist cinema), veridically represent the true nature of the social or political order, or human nature or consciousness, or interpersonal relations. I largely ignore those questions here. Instead, I address more basic questions about the nature of film in general, and whether it can be said to be a realistic medium at some more fundamental level.

I also largely ignore the "classical" film theory of such figures as Arnheim, Bazin, and Panofsky, and contemporary film theory that draws on "continental" theories of psychoanalysis, structuralism, Marxism, and so on. Since these alternative approaches are well served by other chapters in this volume, I focus instead on more recent work in "analytic" philosophy of film and "cognitive" film studies, with their roots in Anglo-American philosophy of the twentieth century and empirical psychology. (On these distinctions, see Currie 1995: xi–xx; Bordwell and Carroll 1996: xiii–xvii; Bordwell 1996; Carroll 1988a, b, 1996c.)

There are a number of distinct ways in which film has been said to be realistic, even at a fundamental level. I address three of these claims: (i) that our experience of motion pictures engenders illusions about the reality of what we are seeing (what I will call "motion picture realism"); (ii) that we literally see the objects captured on film (photographic realism); and (iii) that our experience of film is like our experience of the world (perceptual realism). Finally, I briefly discuss the relation between these metaphysical claims and the aesthetics of film.

Motion picture realism

Some theorists argue that film is a realistic medium because it engenders an illusion in us that something is real, when in fact it is not. Gregory Currie has usefully divided such theses into two sorts (1995: 28–30). A *cognitive-illusionist* theory states that film engenders a *false belief* in us, such as that we are literally seeing the fictional events of a film unfold before us. A *perceptual illusionist* theory states that there is a difference between how film *appears to us* and how it really is, independently of our beliefs about it. For instance, film images may *seem* to move, even if we know that such motion is merely apparent and not real.

Cognitive-illusionist theories

A number of thoroughgoing cognitive illusions have been attributed to film. These claims are not usually explicitly linked to the illusion of movement (though see Baudry 2004a [1970], 2004b [1975]; and Panofsky 2004 [1934–47]), but such a link is perhaps implicit, given that the claims are exclusive to film, rather than being applied to other pictorial, dramatic, or narrative media. (Note, though, that not all films include moving images. See, for example, Derek Jarman's *Blue* [1993].) In some cases, cognitive-illusionist claims might plausibly be rejected as harmless hyperbole, but in others they seem central to a theory. In any case, as we shall see, they are all false.

Film has been claimed to engender the illusion that the *real things* we see on screen – Jeff Bridges pouring various nonalcoholic liquids into a glass during the shooting of *The Big Lebowski* (1998), for instance – are present to the viewer in the theater, or that the viewer is present to these things on the set (e.g., Bazin 1967b [1951]; Metz 1974: 1–15, 43). (These claims should not be confused with the thesis of transparency – that film enables us to see things that are *not* present – discussed below.) Alternatively, film has been claimed to engender the illusion that when the viewer sees *fictional things* on the screen – The Dude making a White Russian, for instance – she believes that they are really present to her, or she to them (e.g., Balázs 1970: 48).

All of these claims are untenable for the same sorts of reasons. First, they do not cohere with viewers' behavior. Depending on one's other beliefs, a person might act in various ways if she thought she was in the presence of Jeff Bridges or The Dude. But no one watching the movie asks for Bridges' signature, or inquires of The Dude whether there's enough Kahlúa for two. A familiar response to such objections is to weaken the claim. Is the viewer in a state of *partial* belief, or *uncertainty* about whether or not, she is in the presence of Bridges or The Dude? Again, no. Though someone might approach a stranger on the street if she suspected he were a famous actor, not even Bridges' biggest fan would ask for his signature while watching *The Big Lebowski*. Similarly, no one even considers attempting to intercede to stop the nihilists from dropping their ferret into The Dude's bath (Currie 1995: 24–5; Walton 1990: 197–200).

Second, these claims do not cohere with viewers' other beliefs about their abilities to move about in and perceive the world. If you believed you were present in the fictional world, or even at the shooting locations, of a film, then you would have to believe that you were able to jump from one place and time to another almost instantaneously with a cut from one scene to another; you would have to believe that you could perceive things in the manner of a zoom-dolly shot, or as if through different colored filters.

A slightly weaker form of cognitive illusionism holds that the viewer believes that the fictional things represented in the film are real but is not misled about the film's status as a representation. That is, the viewer knows he is watching a film but believes, at least while the film is playing, that it is documentary footage. One reason to doubt this hypothesis is that we are no more confused or forgetful about the status of the film we are watching (be it fiction or documentary) than we are about the fact that we are watching a film, as opposed to perceiving reality. Moreover, things are commonly presented on screen that we could not coherently believe to have been filmed in reality, such as the nihilists' threatening The Dude while he takes a bath.

More plausible than any of these cognitive-illusionist claims is the idea that the viewer *imagines*, rather than believes, what is fictionally represented on the screen (Walton 1990). But such a thesis requires no reference to the viewer undergoing any illusion.

Perceptual illusionism

Most writers on film argue or assume that the apparent motion of film images is an illusion. However, Gregory Currie, who rejects all forms of cognitive illusionism, also rejects perceptual illusionism; that is, he defends the view that film images *really do move* (Currie 1995: 34–47, 1996: 334–42). Currie thinks the burden of proof in these debates rests on the illusionist, since we should take things at face value unless we have reason to doubt them. The reason most people think that the motion of film images is illusory is that they understand that film projectors project a succession of still images, separated by moments of darkness, in such rapid succession that we seem to see a continuously projected image that moves. Thus there is no one film image that moves, any more than there is one image that moves in a "flipbook" (Kania 2002: 244, 246n8).

Currie responds with an analogy to colors. Colors are generally thought to be "response-dependent" properties, that is, there is no way to specify what "being red" is without reference to the way we experience the world. (A property such as "being square," by contrast, could be specified in purely geometric terms, without any reference to our experience of that property.) Nonetheless, colors are not illusory, since we are not wrong when we say that blood is red. Hence, we can say that the motion of film images is real, albeit response dependent.

This argument rests on a false analogy. Colors are response-dependent properties, but motion is not. Motion consists, at least, in a thing's being in contiguous spatial locations at contiguous moments in time. No film image meets that condition (Kania 2002: 254–7; Gaut 2003: 634–5). Currie can argue that film images have a distinct property that is related to motion – response-dependent motion – but this merely renames the illusion. A stick in a glass of water could be described as "response dependently bent," but this does nothing to militate against the fact that the stick is really straight, despite appearing bent, plainly speaking.

Currie has a number of ancillary arguments against perceptual illusionism: (1) If film images didn't move, then all we could see in a cinema would be static images (1995: 34–5). (2) If photography is transparent, and we see people moving in films, then the film images must be moving (1995: 38). (3) The identity of film images is response dependent, so we should expect their motion to be response dependent, also (1995: 40–2). However, each of these arguments either falsely assumes that there is a continuously existing image on the screen, or fails to acknowledge the vacuity of attributing response-dependent motion to images.

It is worth noting that the above arguments apply only to "moving pictures" produced by certain mechanisms (film, video, zoetrope, etc.). It is much more plausible to suppose that images produced by the uninterrupted projection of light can really move. A simple example would be a spotlight sweeping a prison compound. An example from art is the images on the screen of a shadow play. Furthermore, we can imagine a future technology where the projector's beam is continuously shone through a transparent cell, whose contents move. Nonetheless, it is not indisputable that such images move, since it is not clear what the identity conditions of images and shadows are (Currie 1995: 30–4; Cassati and Varzi 1994: 175–6). Suppose a searchlight is swept across a cloudy night sky. When the beam runs over a gap in the clouds, does the first spot end as the beam hits the gap and a new one begin when it hits the next cloud, or is this the same spot as before? If so, where was it in the meantime?

Photographic realism

Most people agree that seeing a photograph of something is quite different from seeing a painting or drawing of the same thing, and this difference is sometimes captured by saying that photographs are more realistic than paintings or drawings. Since most, though by no means all, films are photographic, many theorists have argued that film is a realistic art form on this basis.

The characteristic of photography that is appealed to in justifying this sort of realism is that photographs are mechanically produced, and thus the appearance of a photograph is "counterfactually dependent" on the appearance of its subject. That is, if the subject of a photograph had looked different, then the photograph would have looked different, no matter whether the photographer noticed the difference. This is to be contrasted with the case of painting or drawing where the image produced depends on the beliefs or intentions of the artist. That is, a change in the appearance of an object will only affect the appearance of a painting, if at all, by way of affecting the artist's beliefs about its appearance. (Sound recording is mechanical in the same sense, but has been little discussed, partly due to a tendency to focus on film images at the expense of film sound, and partly since sound synthesis – the sonic equivalent of painting or drawing – is relatively recent and postdates recording technology.)

Ontological realism

Sometimes the nature of photography is used to defend an extreme realism or illusionism of the kind put aside at the beginning of the previous section – that a photograph is identical with its subject, or that it gives the illusion that it is. Though we have dismissed these claims, the counterfactual dependence of a photograph on its subject does justify a related claim that we might call *ontological realism*, namely that a photograph of something, unlike a painting of it, guarantees the existence of that thing (Gaut 2003: 634; Walton 1984: 250). Of course, we must continue to distinguish between the real and fictional contents of an image. A photograph of Jeff Bridges shows that he existed at some time, but not that The Dude existed.

Transparency

A more controversial claim is that photographs are *transparent*, meaning that in looking at a photograph you literally see its subject (Bazin 1967a [1945]; Walton 1984). (If photography is transparent, but film motion is an illusion, then we really see the objects filmed but do not really see them move. If photography is transparent and film motion real, then we really see the filmed objects in motion.)

Almost everyone agrees that when you see something out of your window you literally see that thing, rather than seeing an image in the window. But this example sits at the top of a slippery slope. In which of the following examples do you literally see something? Seeing something while wearing glasses, in a mirror, in a distorting mirror, through a periscope, through a telescope, through night-vision goggles, on closed-circuit television, on a live television broadcast, on a delayed television broadcast, on a taped television show, in a mechanically generated drawing, in a person's drawing, in a mechanically generated description, in a person's description. Almost everyone denies that we see things through descriptions – even mechanically generated ones. Opinions differ about where to draw the line between the window and the description. What one needs is an argument for a principle according to which photography is ruled in or out of the class of transparent media.

Here are some arguments against photographic transparency that we can dismiss. It is irrelevant to the transparency claim that the object photographed may no longer exist. When we look at the night sky we see many stars that no longer exist (Walton 1984: 252). It is also irrelevant to the transparency claim that when we see a photo we may see no object. If you awake in the middle of the night and look around you may see nothing, though there are objects all around you. This doesn't show that you don't see things in ordinary vision (Currie 1995: 57). Another argument against transparency contends that photography is like painting after all, since photographs depend on the intentions of the photographer to choose a particular scene, frame it a certain way, expose the film at a certain moment, and so on. None of this is relevant to the key difference between photography and painting, though. A friend might blindfold you and take you to see a certain sight from a certain angle when the light is just right, even holding a frame up to the view so that you appreciate it in a certain way. Nonetheless, you still see the view, so the fact that photographers do equivalents of all these things does not show that we do not see the subjects of their photographs (Scruton 2006 [1983]: 29–30; Walton 1984: 261–2).

More recently it has been argued that the reason photographs are not transparent is that they fail to provide "egocentric information." That is, you do not know where the subject of a photograph is in relation to yourself. But the provision of such information is a central function of vision. Thus, photographs are not a way of literally seeing things (Currie 1995: 65–9; Carroll 1996d: 61–2). However, the relation between the function of vision and what counts as vision is not clear. The function of vision is to provide us with information in our immediate environment, yet we still literally see the stars. Also, if we see something in a mirror, then it seems we see something in a periscope, even if we don't know how the periscope is set up and thus have no idea where what we see is in relation to us (Walton 1997: 69–72).

Another recent concern in the debate over photographic transparency has been the continuity of the transmission of light. When you look at a star with the naked eye or through an optical telescope, the light that enters your eye comes directly from the star, though it may have been refracted through lenses and reflected off mirrors. Similarly, when you see an object in a mirror or through spectacles, the light that enters your eyes is the very light reflected off the object. When you see something on closed-circuit television or in a photograph, however, the light that enters your eyes may be *similar* to the light from the object that is responsible for the image, but it is not that very light. Some take this objection to be decisive (Gaut 2003: 637). Others argue that a transducer that acted just like a window, but collected light on one side and instantaneously emitted qualitatively similar light on the other, would be transparent (Currie 1995: 60, 70). It is difficult to see how this dispute could be resolved without begging the question.

A further kind of example is that of a three-dimensional model that is counterfactually dependent on some part of the world. Like a photographic film, the visual appearance of such a model is counterfactually dependent on its "subject," yet, also like a film, that appearance is not conveyed by the continuous transmission of light. Gregory Currie considers a clock that determines the positions of the hands of a second clock (1995: 64–5). Berys Gaut considers a model jungle that is richly counterfactually dependent on a section of real jungle, to which someone sells tickets, advertising the opportunity to "see real gorillas" (2003: 637; see also Noël Carroll's model rail-yard, 1996d: 61). Gaut rightly moves to the second example, since in the case of the clocks it is not clear that the information preserved from one clock to another is rich enough. (No matter how accurate your porch-light motion sensor is, you do not see the thing that set it off through seeing the light come on.)

Gaut is wrong to think that the model case is decisive, however. He argues that you could legitimately ask for your money back on discovering that you were seeing models rather than gorillas. There are three problems here. One is that there are different ways in which the term "see" is used. If someone sold you the opportunity to see Mars up close with your own eyes and then showed you to a telescope, you might legitimately ask for a refund. Nonetheless, it is true that you see Mars through a telescope. Another problem I suspect is a failure of imagination. It is difficult to imagine a model of a section of jungle that looks just like the section of jungle, gorillas and all, as opposed to a clunky animatronic. If a model of such, well, photographic realism could be achieved, it is not clear one could deny its transparency without begging the question. Finally, as Gaut says, our intuitions here are partly driven by "the abiding human desire to be in direct perceptual contact with objects" (Gaut 2003: 637). This muddies the waters, since it would be quite reasonable to believe that one was in the presence of a gorilla if one came upon a perfect robotic model of one, unlike the case of being in the presence of a photograph of a gorilla, and hence we are more likely to think of this case in terms of deception. Moreover, again, there are cases of our being in *indirect* perceptual contact with things that count uncontroversially as seeing, such as the mirror and telescope cases.

Given the vagueness or polysemy of "see," it may be that once we have figured out all the ways in which looking at objects in photographs is like and unlike ordinary vision, any decision to draw the line between literal and nonliteral seeing will be stipulative. Nonetheless, figuring out these similarities and differences is still of value if we want to understand the nature of photographic film. For if we can at least place film viewing with some precision on the spectrum between simply seeing and seeing in a painting (say), we can appeal to this *relative* immediacy in explaining one way in which photographic film is realistic.

Perceptual realism

Most films are (apparent) moving pictures, and pictures are one kind of representation. They differ from other kinds of representation, such as language, in being parasitic on ordinary perception. Unlike our understanding of language, we use the same capacities to recognize what a picture represents as those we use to recognize objects and events in the world (Carroll 1985: 82–8; Currie 1996: 327–30). As a result, pictures have been described as "perceptually realistic." One way of seeing the difference is that if you can understand a few pictures in a given style, say, you can understand any other picture in that style, while if you can understand a few words or sentences in a given language, it does not follow that you will understand other words or sentences in that language. Perceptual realism has something to do with the fact that we perceive pictures as resembling what they represent (Currie 1996: 328–30; Walton 1984: 270–3). For instance, if you are likely to confuse a rhinoceros with a hippopotamus, then you are likely to confuse a *picture* of a rhinoceros with a *picture* of a hippopotamus. But you are unlikely to confuse the *word* "rhinoceros" with the *word* "hippopotamus," since the words do not resemble each other in the way the animals (and pictures of them) do. Since resemblance is a matter of degree, and perceptual realism appeals to resemblance, so is perceptual realism a matter of degree. For instance, the stylized appearance of a cartoon donkey may be less realistic than a photographic film of a donkey, but the cartoon is nonetheless perceptually realistic, as opposed to, say, the *word* "donkey." To investigate the nature of pictures further is beyond the scope of this chapter. (See "Depiction" in this volume.) Instead, I will note a few ways in which perceptual realism relates specifically to film.

First, not all the visual elements of a film are pictorial. Even in standard narrative fiction films, titles announcing the time and location of scenes are common. These are linguistic rather than pictorial. But motion pictures are perceptually realistic with respect to more properties than still pictures. Since film is a temporal art, in the sense that the parts of a film have specific duration and ordering, it can be perceptually realistic with respect to the temporal properties of what it represents (Currie 1995: 92–6). Also, whether or not our perception of movement in film is veridical or illusory, it can be perceptually realistic. (It is perhaps worth noting that much "cognitive" film theory has focused on the nature of depiction in general, in reaction to the persistent notion in previous film theory that film is somehow linguistic. For a selection of such linguistic theories, see the first section of Braudy and Cohen [2004]. For arguments against such theories, see Currie [1992] and Prince [1993].)

Second, photographs are arguably the most reliably perceptually realistic kind of pictures we have (Cohen and Meskin 2004), and photographic film inherits that realism. Adding the points about film's perceptually realistic representation of time and movement, we can understand Currie's claim that "film is a realistic medium, and deep-focus, long-take style is an especially realistic style within that medium" (1996: 328). Deep focus allows us to perceive more easily or directly the spatial relations represented, and a long take allows us to perceive more easily or directly the temporal relations represented. More immersive formats, such as IMAX and 3-D film are presumably still more perceptually realistic.

Third, perceptual realism is not restricted to vision. Most films are also highly aurally realistic, at least with respect to diegetic sound (i.e., sound which "comes from within the world of the film"). We recognize the fact that a shot has been fired off screen by using the same aural perceptual capacities that we use to identify real gunshots (though, as with images, these sounds may be more or less stylized. Think, for instance, of the typical sound effect that accompanies an on-screen punch). Some theme-park movie rides represent the rocky progress of a spaceship by shaking the audience's seats, thus representing the feel of a rocky ride in a perceptually realistic way. There have also been experiments with olfactory realism, such as Smell-O-Vision and "odorama."

Finally, there is a synesthetic perceptual realism that comes from a matching of sounds and images (and movements, smells, and so on). Perceptually realistic images, coupled with perceptually realistic sounds, will result in a markedly less realistic film if the images and sounds do not *match* than if they do. (Note, however, that this simple idea calls immediately for qualification, since most film *music* is "nondiegetic," that is, unlike most sound effects, it does not represent sounds in the fictional world of the film. See Levinson [1996] for a consideration of such music.)

Aesthetic implications

The reason realism has been such a hot topic in film theory is twofold. Theorists have argued, first, that film is uniquely, essentially, or particularly realistic; and, second, that this has implications for how films ought to be made. I have investigated three ways in which the first of these claims has been defended, though it must be noted that I have focused on the extent to which film might be considered realistic. Whether what realism we have found is unique or essential to film is a further question, one to be quite skeptical about. For each kind of realism we have had to limit our discussion to certain types of film – those using traditional projection apparatus, photographic film, films employing a particular style, and so on. No such restricted realism can be taken as essential to film in general. But even if such a claim could be defended, it is not clear what implications this would have for what we might call the aesthetics of film – the study of what makes a film a good one.

Noël Carroll has argued persuasively against "medium-essentialism," the view that one ought to exploit effects of one's art form that are either unique to it, or that it achieves better than any other form (1996a [1984–5], 1996b [1985], 1996d). For one thing, it is doubtful that the most interesting effects achievable in film are achievable *only* in film. Further, it is difficult to know how we could judge whether films or novels, say, are better at telling stories – something at which they both excel. Supposing such a decision were made, it would be strange to decide that the inferior form should no longer attempt to tell stories.

So in general we should be suspicious of deriving aesthetic imperatives from claims about the nature of the medium, including claims about its realism. I end by considering some aesthetic issues specific to the types of realism we examined above.

Motion picture realism

Surprisingly few film theorists have focused on film's ability to produce (apparently) moving images (though see Arnheim 1957: 161–87; and Kracauer 1965: 41–5). Anyway, the idea that film should concentrate on the depiction of motion is questionable for the general reasons given above. Noël Carroll argues that the motion of film images should affect the aesthetics of film in a different way. He points out that the apparent motion of images is neither exclusive nor essential to film – there are films without motion and moving images in other media – but he argues that this suggests we should reorient the study of these media in an inclusive way. Film, television, video, etc., are all media in which the motion of images is possible, if not necessary. Thus it makes sense to study *motion pictures* or *moving images* in a broad sense, rather than focusing parochially on film (Carroll 1996d). (Note that it will make no difference in most cases whether the motion of the images is real or illusory.)

Photographic realism

The dispute over the transparency of photographs has been hotly debated in part because of its supposed implications for the aesthetics of photography and film. Roger Scruton (2006 [1983]) has argued that since a photograph is transparent, it cannot be a representation in the sense of expressing a thought about its subject. As a result, Scruton claims that a photograph or film cannot in itself be aesthetically valuable, though what we see through it may be aesthetically valuable.

If Scruton is wrong about the transparency of photographs, and if this implies that they are representations, then his argument will not go through. However, the implication is questionable, since it may be that the mechanical nature of photography is sufficient to prevent representation, yet insufficient to achieve transparency (Lopes 2003: 441). Nonetheless, Dominic Lopes argues that even given Scruton's restricted notion of representation, photographs can be aesthetically valuable despite their transparency, since there is still a difference between seeing an object face-to-face and seeing it through a photograph. We can take an aesthetic interest in a photograph, then, if we take an interest in (i) the object we see through it; (ii) the way in which the photograph enables us to see it; and (iii) the interplay between (i) and (ii) (Lopes 2003: 442–6).

Another way to defeat Scruton's argument is to show that transparency does not preclude a photograph's being a representation. Walton argues that photographs are representations since they are (usually) props in games of make-believe (1984: 253–4, 1990: 88, 330, 1997: 68). Stephen Davies argues that if photographs are transparent, then so too are some paintings and drawings. Both photographs and handmade pictures can be counterfactually dependent on their subjects, though the dependence is mechanical in one case and intentional in the other. Since paintings and drawings are paradigmatic representations, transparency cannot preclude representation. This does not open the door to all seeing being mediated by representation. What we see through windows, mirrors, spectacles, and so on is not only counterfactually dependent but *continuously* dependent on the thing seen. It is the spatiotemporal separation between image and object provided by the camera, the canvas, or whatever, that makes pictures representations distinct from the things we see through them (Davies 2006: 185–8). Note that cinematography does not violate this condition, despite the fact that it does not capture its object at one moment in time, like still photography. Whether or not you think that film images move, it is still the case that either each frame or the temporally extended image, once recorded, is no longer sensitive to changes in its subject.

Perceptual realism

Gregory Currie argues that films with a long-shot, deep-focus style are more perceptually realistic than others, since they represent spatial and temporal relations (between things) by means of spatial and temporal relations (between images). Our experience of such films is more like our experience of the world than is our experience of films with rapid editing, for instance (1996: 327–30). Should more films, then, employ this style? Clearly this is a matter for debate. Some (such as Bazin) will argue for the superiority of such a style on the basis of its ability to involve us in the world of the film, pointing to the success of films in a realist style. Others will argue that this is a dangerous seduction, and that filmmakers should work against it, alienating the viewer in order to force an awareness of the medium upon her, pointing to the success of films such as those of Jean-Luc Godard. It is not clear that one side must win this debate. Film, like every other artistic medium, is capable of employing many different styles for many different purposes (Carroll 1996b [1985]), and we are capable of appreciating many different kinds of films.

Conclusions

Some films are surely better than others, and perhaps some kinds of films are superior to others. However, it seems unlikely that we can discover which ones by measuring the degree to which they are realistic. Nonetheless, the different kinds of realism we have investigated here are relevant to the study of film for other reasons. Most simply, they allow us to describe the nature of film more precisely, in terms of its illusory nature, the extent to which it is transparent, and one dimension along which cinematic styles can be said to be realistic. These descriptions, in turn, may factor into a psychological explanation of the power and popularity of motion pictures in general, or specific films and styles (Carroll 1985). We should remain wary, however, of drawing conclusions about the value of those films, styles, and motion pictures in general, from premises about their power and popularity.

See also Consciousness (Chapter 4), Definition of "cinema" (Chapter 5), Depiction (Chapter 6), Film as art (Chapter 11), Formalism (Chapter 12), Medium (Chapter 16), Music (Chapter 17), Ontology (Chapter 20), Spectatorship (Chapter 23), Sound (Chapter 24), Style (Chapter 25), Rudolph Arnheim (Chapter 27), Bertolt Brecht (Chapter 30), Cognitive theory (Chapter 33), Edgar Morin (Chapter 38), and Phenomenology (Chapter 40), Dogme 95 (Chapter 44).

References

Arnheim, R. (1957) *Film as Art*, Berkeley and Los Angeles: University of California Press.

Balázs, B. (1970) *Theory of the Film: Character and Growth of a New Art*, New York: Dover.

Baudry, J.-L. (2004a [1970]) "Ideological Effects of the Basic Cinematographic Apparatus," in L. Braudy and M. Cohen (eds.) *Film Theory and Criticism: Introductory Readings*, 6th ed., New York: Oxford University Press.

—— (2004b [1975]) "The Apparatus: Metapsychological Approaches to the Impression of Reality in the Cinema," in L. Braudy and M. Cohen (eds.) *Film Theory and Criticism: Introductory Readings*, 6th ed., New York: Oxford University Press.

Bazin, A. (1967a [1945]) "The Ontology of the Photographic Image," in H. Gray (trans.) *What Is Cinema?* vol. 1, Berkeley and Los Angeles: University of California Press.

—— (1967b [1951]) "Theater and Cinema: Part Two," in H. Gray (trans.) *What Is Cinema?* vol. 1, Berkeley and Los Angeles: University of California Press.

Bordwell, D. (1996) "Contemporary Film Studies and the Vicissitudes of Grand Theory," in D. Bordwell and N. Carroll (eds.) *Post-Theory: Reconstructing Film Studies*, Madison: University of Wisconsin Press.

Bordwell, D., and Carroll, N. (eds.) (1996) *Post-Theory: Reconstructing Film Studies*, Madison: University of Wisconsin Press.

Braudy, L., and Cohen, M. (eds.) (2004) *Film Theory and Criticism: Introductory Readings*, 6th ed., New York: Oxford University Press.

Carroll, N. (1985) "The Power of Movies," *Daedalus* 114: 79–103.

—— (1988a) *Philosophical Problems of Classical Film Theory*, Princeton, NJ: Princeton University Press.

—— (1988b) *Mystifying Movies: Fads and Fallacies in Contemporary Film Theory*, New York: Columbia University Press.

—— (1996a [1984–5]) "Medium Specificity Arguments and the Self-Consciously Invented Arts: Film, Video, and Photography," in *Theorizing the Moving Image*, Cambridge and New York: Cambridge University Press.

—— (1996b [1985]) "The Specificity of Media in the Arts," in *Theorizing the Moving Image*, Cambridge and New York: Cambridge University Press.

—— (1996c) "Prospects for Film Theory: A Personal Assessment," in D. Bordwell and N. Carroll (eds.) *Post-Theory: Reconstructing Film Studies*, Madison: University of Wisconsin Press.

—— (1996d) "Defining the Moving Image," in *Theorizing the Moving Image*, Cambridge and New York: Cambridge University Press.

Cassati, R., and Varzi, A. (1994) *Holes and Other Superficialities*, Cambridge, MA: MIT Press.

Cohen, J., and Meskin, A. (2004) "On the Epistemic Value of Photographs," *Journal of Aesthetics and Art Criticism* 62: 197–210.

Currie, G. (1992) "The Long Goodbye: The Imaginary Language of Film," *British Journal of Aesthetics* 33: 207–19.

—— (1995) *Image and Mind: Film, Philosophy, and Cognitive Science*, Cambridge and New York: Cambridge University Press.

—— (1996) "Film, Reality, and Illusion," in D. Bordwell and N. Carroll (eds.) *Post-Theory: Reconstructing Film Studies*, Madison: University of Wisconsin Press.

Davies, S. (2006) *The Philosophy of Art*, Malden, MA; Oxford: Blackwell.

Gaut, B. (2003) "Film," in J. Levinson (ed.) *The Oxford Handbook of Aesthetics*, Oxford and New York: Oxford University Press.

Kania, A. (2002) "The Illusion of Realism in Film," *British Journal of Aesthetics* 42: 243–58.

Kracauer, S. (1965) *Theory of Film: The Redemption of Physical Reality*, London: Oxford University Press.

Levinson, J. (1996) "Film Music and Narrative Agency," in D. Bordwell and N. Carroll (eds.) *Post-Theory: Reconstructing Film Studies*, Madison: University of Wisconsin Press.

Lopes, D. (2003) "The Aesthetics of Photographic Transparency," *Mind* 112: 433–48.

Metz, C. (1974) *Film Language*, trans. M. Taylor, New York: Oxford University Press.

Panofsky, E. (2004 [1934–47]) "Style and Medium in the Motion Pictures," in L. Braudy and M. Cohen (eds.) *Film Theory and Criticism: Introductory Readings*, 6th ed., New York: Oxford University Press.

Prince, S. (1993) "The Discourse of Pictures: Iconicity and Film Studies," *Film Quarterly* 47: 16–28.

Scruton, R. (2006 [1983]) "Photography and Representation," in N. Carroll and J. Choi (eds.) *Philosophy of Film and Motion Pictures: An Anthology*, Malden, MA: Blackwell.

Walton, K. (1984) "Transparent Pictures: On the Nature of Photographic Realism," *Critical Inquiry* 11: 246–76.

—— (1990) *Mimesis as Make-Believe: On the Foundations of the Representational Arts*, Cambridge, MA: Harvard University Press.

—— (1997) "On Pictures and Photographs: Objections Answered," in R. Allen and M. Smith (eds.) *Film Theory and Philosophy*, Oxford: Clarendon Press; New York: Oxford University Press.

23

SPECTATORSHIP

Carl Plantinga

Film spectatorship, as I shall consider it here, is the experience of viewing and hearing fictional feature films, together with the psychological and social contexts in which such viewing/hearing occurs. A consideration of spectatorship leads to several difficult and fascinating philosophical issues about film viewing, including discussions of various models of the hypothetical spectator; the nature of spectators and their inter-action with films; models of the relationship between spectators, texts, and contexts; and how to think about differences between spectators in relation to interpretation and response.

Given space limitation, the discussion here will be limited to three broad approaches to spectatorship: (1) screen theory, by which I mean the amalgamation of Althusserian Marxism, Lacanian psychoanalysis, and Barthesian semiotics that dominated the field for over fifteen years, and which is still influential; (2) cultural studies, including historical-reception studies; and (3) cognitive film theory. All comprehensive film theories must consider spectatorship, and thus the reader is advised to examine related entries in this volume.

Hypothetical and actual spectators

Generalizations about viewer activities and responses, even those based on historical research (see below), require that the theorist construct or assume a model of the spectator. When scholars discuss the audience or the spectator in abstract terms, they invariably presume features of the spectator's psychology, relation to history and culture, and ways of responding to and interacting with moving images. In making theories about spectators, theorists have tended to characterize the spectator as either hypothetical or real. Of the real spectator I will say more below. The hypothetical spectator is typically a model of all spectators or some subset of spectators. Janet Staiger has noted several conceptions of the hypothetical reader in literary studies, among them "actual, authorial, coherent, competent, ideal, implied, mock, narratee, necessary, programmed, real, resisting, super, virtual, [and] zero-degree" readers (Staiger 1992: 24).

Among the most common types of hypothetical spectators are "ideal," "competent," and "implied." The ideal spectator meets a standard of perspicuity set by a filmmaker, critic, or theorist. As the word "ideal" implies, the standard is typically high, such that the ideal spectator is able to understand the subtleties and ambiguities of a film, or to appreciate its finer points of style and theme. The competent spectator, by contrast, who might also be called the typical or usual spectator, is thought to possess the basic competencies that enable comprehension of a mainstream text. Implied spectators, finally, are the spectators implied in the design and execution of the film. Film theory before 1960, for example, tended to hold some form of the "invisible observer" hypothesis, which claims that narrative films present story events from the perspective of an imaginary and invisible witness (Bordwell 1985: 9–12). V. I. Pudovkin, the Soviet filmmaker and theorist, claimed that a filmmaker, in constructing a scene, should imagine the perspective of an observer perfectly mobile in space and time, such that the finished scene will clarify the event through the selection and framing of shots and their careful editing. For Pudovkin, the filmic representation "strives to force the spectator to transcend the limits of normal human apprehension" (Pudovkin 1949: 90) with scenes of extraordinary clarity, efficiency, and force. It should be noted that the implied spectator is typically also an ideal and/or competent spectator.

Both screen theory and cognitive theory assume variations of the hypothetical spectator. David Bordwell, whose work has been singularly influential in the development of cognitive film theory, conceives of the spectator as a hypothetical entity, not an ideal but rather a competent spectator capable of "executing the operations relevant to constructing a story out of the film's representation." Bordwell explicitly states that his hypothetical spectator is "real," "at least in the sense that she or he possesses certain psychological limitations that real spectators also possess" (Bordwell 1985: 30).

Judith Mayne, in her book on film spectatorship, classifies the cognitive theory of the spectator as *empirical*, by which she means that it is about actual viewers rather than implied spectators, or "subjects" (Mayne 1993: 53–62). But this isn't quite right. We have already seen that Bordwell conceives of the spectator as a hypothetical entity, but one that is conceived to model empirical spectators in some regards. The question of how a theory of spectatorship could *avoid* claims about empirical spectators is a good one, and leads us to spectatorship as it is conceived in screen theory. Screen theory often uses the term "spectator" or what Mayne calls the "subject," in a confusing way. It conceives of the spectator not as a hypothetical person but as a "position," "role," or "space" (depending on the theorist) constructed by the text. The theory originally emerged from an interest in how "ideological state apparatuses" maintain mass control through what became known as "subject positioning" (Althusser 1971). For Althusser, an individual is "interpellated," assigned an identity and role by society's institutions. Thus the film is said to position the spectator much like ideological state apparatuses position "the subject."

The problem is that this position, role, or space is often described as though it were a person. In one prominent book about terminology in film theory, the authors write that in screen theory the spectator or "the viewer" is "an artificial construct produced by the cinematic apparatus" and a "space" that the cinema "constructs." Yet they go on to assign human characteristics to this constructed "space" or "position," claiming that in viewing a film a "state of regression is produced" and "a situation of belief is constructed" in the position or subject (Stam *et al.* 1992: 147). One wants to ask how a role or a position can regress or have beliefs. To take another example, theorists may claim that the spectator is a concept or a structural term constructed by the text (not a person), but then write that the classical stylistic system leads to various text–spectator relationships (relationships between texts and persons).

In his introduction to film theory, Robert Stam implicitly recognizes this problem (2000: 231); his somewhat telling solution is to distinguish between the "spectator" and the "actual spectator." One suspects that the better fix would be to restrict the word "spectator" to designations of persons rather than roles, terms, or positions. Mayne, for example, distinguishes between "subjects," which are roles or positions, and "viewers," or actual people. Yet the arch critic of screen theory might also point out that the theory depends precisely on this ambiguity in the meaning of "spectator." It gains its force by seeming to prescribe determinate effects of texts on viewers, claiming that the film "constitutes" or "produces" the "viewer as subject" (Pribram 1999: 149). Yet the screen theorist, when confronted by counterarguments to such determinism, can also disavow the implausibilities of the theory by claiming that it is really about positions, roles, or subjects, and not about actual people at all (Prince 1996). This is similar to Thomas Pavel's claims for what he calls Foucault's "l'esquive empirico-transcendentale," or "transcendental-empirical dodge," whereby the theorist, when confronted with empirical counterevidence to a historical argument, will counter that the argument is not about facts, but transcendental conditions of possibility (Pavel 1988: 16, 1992: 7).

Also interesting is the attempt by some scholars to bypass hypothetical spectators altogether to directly reach the real viewer. This has been a trend of historical-reception studies, which I consider here to be an offshoot of cultural studies. In the introduction to *Hollywood Spectatorship*, Melvyn Stokes writes that one of the book's central purposes is to "question the dominance of theoretical views of spectatorship" (Stokes and Maltby 2001: 1). *Hollywood Spectatorship* includes essays that investigate the actual and historical rather than hypothetical or possible reception of films. Janet Staiger writes that since historical-reception studies is history and not philosophy, it "does not attempt to construct a generalized, systematic explanation of how individuals might have comprehended texts, and possibly someday will, but rather [describes] how they actually have understood them" (Staiger 1992: 8). Staiger also claims that the historical-reception theorist would criticize the notion of the "ideal reader," by which I take her to mean any model of the hypothetical spectator, as "ahistorical" (Staiger 1992: 8). For Staiger, even theories that hypothesize spectators by identity (race, class, gender, sexual orientation, etc.) or historical period (pre- and post-sound, classical and postclassical, etc.) are deeply suspect and prone to "universalize" viewer experiences (Staiger 2001).

Yet any claim that spectatorship can be studied without the benefit of general psychological assumptions about spectators constitutes a naïve empiricism that most reception theorists and cultural studies proponents, Staiger included, would be loathe to embrace. Staiger's brand of historical-reception studies *does* make general theoretical claims about how spectators interact with texts. Staiger argues, for example, that spectators are "perverse" in the diversity of ways they interact with films. She also claims that the film text itself has no "immanent" meaning for the spectator, implying that the spectator constructs the film's meanings. Both of these are elements of a *de facto* model of the hypothetical spectator. The path to the "real" spectator runs through the fields of history *and* the formation of general hypotheses about spectator psychology and behavior. The historical-reception theorist may well ask that hypothetical models of the spectator meet some standard of plausibility or testability, but historical-reception studies cannot do away with hypothetical models of the spectator altogether. In arguing this, however, I am not claiming that scholars need a *comprehensive* a priori model of the spectator. A model of the spectator may describe only selected elements of the spectator's activities, psychology, or cultural influences.

Models of the spectator

How have screen theory, cultural studies, and cognitive theory modeled the spectator? Such a model could be very complex, but I will focus on three issues: (1) relations between text, context, and spectator; (2) degree of spectator activity or passivity; and (3) the spectator's motivation and psychology. I will also mention and in some cases discuss the major criticisms of each theory.

Viewing context, the characteristics of the film itself, and the spectator's particular subjectivity all must be taken into account in determining actual spectator responses and interpretations. Yet various theories seek to enlarge or diminish the role of one or the other. Screen theory is often thought to foreground the determinative powers of the film text at the expense of both context and spectator, but the issue is actually more complicated than this. If the spectator is constructed or positioned by the film text, then one analyzes the text to determine how such positioning occurs; this explains the focus on textual analysis prevalent in much screen theory. Now of course, the degree to which screen theory can be said to ignore the actual spectator depends on whether one takes this entity "spectator" to be a person or a position, as I have discussed above. But the theory is an empty shell if it does not assume that actual persons occupy the roles constructed by the text. That is why in screen theory the spectator is often described as having drives, an unconscious, desires, and fantasies; thus the "spectator" is not just a role or position, but a model for actual persons. In fact, textual analysis is a viable method of determining spectator response only if (a) actual viewers are thought to share important psychological characteristics; and (b) varied viewing contexts are relatively unimportant in relation to some (but not necessarily all) elements of viewer-text interaction.

Screen theory conceives of the spectator as passive, an unwitting victim of a system built to exercise hegemonic control of its capitalist subjects. The institutions and technologies of the cinema are often referred to as an "apparatus" that functions to acculturate subjects to structures of fantasy, desire, dream, and pleasure that fully conform to dominant ideology (Mayne 1993: 18). Since the supposed ideological effects of mainstream films are built into the apparatus and apparently irresistible, a viable strategy of resistance is the production of a "countercinema" and "progressive texts" that subvert the regressive pleasures of mainstream film (Comolli and Narboni 1976). It should be noted that the films of the countercinema, such as Jean-Luc Godard's *Weekend* (1967) and Sally Potter's *Thriller* (1979), were often influenced by Brechtian theory more than by psychoanalysis. Thus the idea of the progressive text does not necessarily depend on a psychoanalytic model of the mind (see Stam 1992; and Lovell 1982; for critiques of Brechtian theory as manifested in film studies, see Plantinga [1997] and Smith [1996]).

The psychological model of the spectator employed in screen theory is complex and varied, so this brief account risks overgeneralization (for a fuller description see "Psychoanalysis" in this volume). In screen theory, the viewer is taken to be hedonically motivated to watch films, the sources and workings of the spectator's desires being identified in the context of some version of the Freudian or Lacanian unconscious. The cinema is thought to be uniquely capable, among the arts, of eliciting unconscious processes similar to daydreaming, night-dreaming, voyeurism, fetishism, early psychosexual fantasies, and primitive oral narcissism, all of which engage "desire." The theory goes on to harness such processes to subject positioning, such that the subject's drives, or desires, channel him or her toward repression or socially acceptable patterns of subjectivity – toward the good capitalist subject.

Screen theory offers a controversial, yet in some ways seductive, theory of the motivations of the spectator – desire and the drive for pleasure – and of the unconscious processes put into play by film viewing. Few of its competitor theories have yet dealt with the vital issue of spectator motivations and pleasures in such depth (see Plantinga 2009, for an alternative account). Yet screen theory has received significant criticism. From the perspective of cultural studies, it has been critiqued for assuming a passive spectator, for ignoring differences between spectators, for minimizing history and more generally the contexts of film viewing, and for the determinism inherent in its use of psychoanalysis (Mayne 1993: 52). Cognitive theorists and analytic philosophers have critiqued the theory for its bad logic and reasoning. Noël Carroll, for example, has found fault with the protocols of reasoning instantiated in the theory, arguing that its "central concepts are often systematically ambiguous," often leading to equivocation and argument by pun (Carroll 1988: 226–34). David Bordwell has similarly criticized the reasoning methods of screen theory, such as its purported top-down inquiry impervious to empirical data, argument by *bricolage*, and associative reasoning (Bordwell 1996a: 18–26). In general, Bordwell and Carroll believe that psychoanalysis should be reserved for special cases, such as irrational spectator behavior, that psychoanalysis might be employed when "there is an apparent break-down in the normal functioning of our cognitive-perceptual processing" (Carroll 1996a: 64) and that "conscious and preconscious" spectator processes are better explained by cognitive science and associated methods (Bordwell 1985: 30). But it is not clear that reserving the application of psychoanalysis to irrational spectator behavior makes much sense. For either psychoanalysis is false as a general theory of the human psyche, in which case it doesn't apply to irrational or rational behavior, OR it is true, in which case it explains both!

Although screen theory does not hold the dominant position in film studies that it once did, its legacy is still substantial. For one, as David Bordwell convincingly argues, many of the dominant assumptions of what he calls "subject position" theory clearly remain in cultural studies (Bordwell 1996a). In addition, the claim for textual power over spectators has not been given up. In her book, which combines elements of screen theory and cultural studies, Michele Aaron argues that "the spectator's submersion in a submission to the text ... must be understood as an inevitable part of the act of engagement" (Aaron 2007: 3).

In contrast to screen theory, cultural studies seemingly offers a much more open and diverse account of possible film/spectator relationships. Cultural studies scholars, and especially historical-reception theorists, agree that the film text itself has been granted a larger role in determining spectator interpretation and response than it deserves. The focus must now be expanded outward to the film viewing context, and for some scholars, further yet. Rick Altman suggests that we think in terms of the "cinematic event," in which reception opens "onto an infinite cultural space ... neither beginning or ending at any specific point" (Altman 1992: 4). Cultural studies thus examines fan magazines, star images, film reviews, advertising and publicity, newspaper accounts of riots and disturbances at screenings, and in general any element of discourse and historical context that bears on viewing experiences. Historical-reception scholars offer case studies that show how contextual factors influence response, and that responses vary over time. They also argue that the film itself has no "immanent" meaning. Thus reception scholars will sometimes deny the distinction between the *comprehension* of what the film explicitly signifies, and the *interpretation* of implicit or ambiguous meaning (Staiger 1992: 20), which has the effect of draining the cinematic work of meaning and attributing meaning-making to the spectator. Taken together, the historical case studies, the discourses surrounding a particular film, and the denial of the distinction between comprehension and interpretation might be thought to minimize the importance of the film itself in determining or even influencing spectator interaction and response.

While space prohibits a full discussion of these issues, I will make two observations. The first is that the historical-case studies provided to demonstrate diversity of inter-pretation do not disprove the distinction between comprehension and interpretation, but rather affirm it. All of the diverse uses of and responses to films are grounded on basic agreements about first-level denotative meaning, the very elements that are comprehended rather than interpreted. Second, one might question the implicit assumption that spectators are wholly free to interact with texts in any way they wish and that they actually exercise whatever freedoms they do have. Using the framework of historical-reception theory, one might point out that for many viewing contexts, the most powerful available frameworks for the reception of movies will be limited and conventional, such that the spectator chooses a film, from a narrow range of possibil-ities, based on the kind of experience the film seems to offer. This choice of which film to view strengthens the impression that the viewing "contract" is freely entered into and increases the likelihood of a congruent or sympathetic viewing. In many cases, then, the spectator does not resist, but rather immerses herself in and *actively* enjoys, that experience, in effect opening herself to the film. This isn't the only "reading strategy" available, but it is arguably the most widespread and common, whether the film is viewed in a theater or at home. If this is right, it restores a more central place to the film text itself in making meaning and generating response because the conventional receptive context is assumed by filmmakers, exhibitors, and many audiences and is built into the design of films, marketing and advertising campaigns, and the institutions of exhibition and distribution. The spectator's response is never uniquely determined by the text, but contextual factors strongly support textual influence.

With regard to whether the spectator is active or passive, there is an unresolved tension in various strands of cultural studies between, on the one hand, the impetus to attribute a wholesale freedom to the spectator to interact with and respond to films in an infinite variety of ways (the perverse spectator or the "free" consumer) and, on the other, the claim that spectators are "constituted" in discourse, along with the recognition that any historical context prescribes a limited set of "possible" interpretive strategies for the spectator. The possibility of resistance to oppressive discourse is predicated on, for example, the spectator's ability to actively counter dominant "readings," yet such resistance implies agency and perhaps even free will. Culture studies proponents who insist that spectators are the products of sociocultural and ideological forces (including discourse) sometimes contrast such models of the spectator with the "humanist subject," who "creates 'himself'" and "controls the surrounding world" (Pribram 1999: 158). Yet the assumption of spectator agency and the possibility of resistance to social forces suggests a smaller difference between the cultural studies and humanist conceptions of the viewer than is sometimes assumed. Few humanists, after all, would deny that culture and ideology influence viewers. And any spectator with even a modicum of personal agency, one would think, could resist and affect "the surrounding world" and maintain at least some control of her subjectivity. Even if someone cannot exercise direct control over thoughts and feelings, she can exercise indirect control, for example, by leaving the theater or shutting down the DVD player.

Last, we come to the spectator as modeled in cognitive film theory. Cognitive film theorists foreground the film text and the spectator and usually minimize the viewing context. This stems in part from the assumption that spectators share certain psychological characteristics and viewing activities. Bordwell argues that for some purposes, film scholars can bypass the nature/culture debate by focusing on "contingent universals," that is, patterns of behavior and response that spectators share. Such patterns are contingent because "they did not, for any metaphysical reasons, have to be the way they are" and are universal because they are "widely present in human societies." For the cognitive theorist, diverse viewers approach films, to some extent, with similar psychic hardware. Many cognitive theorists embrace an evolutionary psychology that posits similar adaptive challenges in human history, resulting in common physical and psychological characteristics. As Bordwell writes, the "core assumption here is that given certain uniformities in the environment across cultures, humans have in their social activities faced comparable tasks in surviving and creating their ways of life" (Bordwell 1996b: 91). This has led to the development of common psychological characteristics that are neither wholly cultural nor wholly biological. Such contingent universals – for example, the startle response to loud sounds or inference-making when confronted with a narrative enigma – are assumed by filmmakers in the design of films. One project common to many cognitive theorists is the "naturalization" of film aesthetics, that is, the demonstration that various manifestations of film form and style have roots not only in cultural convention, but in human nature as developed in the broad span of human evolutionary adaptation (Anderson 1996: 23–5; Carroll 2003: 10–58; for a dissenting view, see Choi 2006). The assumption that spectators share characteristics universally is a controversial one, and will be addressed in the next section.

While screen theory modeled the spectator as a passive victim of ideology, Bordwell posits an active spectator. "A film," he writes, "does not 'position' anybody" but rather "cues the spectator to execute a definable body of *operations*" (Bordwell 1985: 29), such as making inferences and testing hypotheses. Bordwell's constructivism, moreover, posits a viewer who maintains a Gombrichian beholder's share, not only constructing the film's meanings but also its *fabula*, or story (Bordwell 1989: 1–8). Yet not all cognitive film theorists embrace constructivism. Gregory Currie, for one, argues that film viewers typically, or at least often, *find* rather than construct meaning. "From the point of view of stressing viewer activity, there is nothing to choose between saying that the viewer creates meaning and that she finds it" (Currie 2004: 160; see also Gaut 1995); both constructing and finding are active. Currie argues that Bordwell's constructivism is not central to cognitive film theory. With regard to spectator activity, it should also be noted that, although both cognitive theory and cultural studies posit an active spectator, the activities of interest differ. The former emphasizes the spectator's psychological activities in relation to the film text, while the latter focuses on identity formation in relation to films, as well as their political uses.

Screen theory holds that the spectator is motivated, and often at an unconscious level, by pleasure and desire. Cultural studies posits a spectator motivated primarily by identity politics, a spectator who finds and identifies with some representations and actively resists others. Cognitive theory in its early years tended to assume a spectator motivated by curiosity and anticipation to understand or comprehend a film. This resulted in various explorations of the means by which spectators comprehend narrative in film viewing (Bordwell 1985; Branigan 1992). Cognitive theorists have also explored the perception of images and the means by which viewers make sense of various film techniques (Currie 1995; Anderson 1996; Carroll 1996b, 2003; Persson 2003). More recently, cognitive theorists and philosophers have begun to explore character engagement or identification (Smith 1995; Gaut 2006; Coplan 2004; Neill 2006) and more broadly, the general emotional and affective responses elicited by films (Carroll 2008; Grodal 1997; Plantinga forthcoming). I have argued that pleasures and desires should be accounted for in any account of film spectatorship, and can be useful if the concepts are used in their folk-psychological senses (Plantinga forthcoming).

Cognitive film theory has been criticized from various perspectives. For one, it is said to "universalize" the spectator in much the same way as screen theory does, and has shown little interest in spectator difference. Some have found its model of spectatorship to be naïvely putting its faith in science and rational discourse (Stam 2000: 240–1) or to neglect the nonrational elements of spectatorship (Campbell 2005). Its concern with universal spectator psychology is sometimes thought to be trivial (see Robert Stam, as quoted in Quart 2000: 41) or narrow, while cultural studies, in contrast, is thought to be politically engaged. Bordwell and Carroll defend mid-level research on spectatorship that asks and attempts to answer researchable questions rather than engage in broad, top-down theory (Bordwell 1996a; Carroll 1996a). And the cognitive theorist might also answer that there is nothing in principle that would prevent the cognitive theorist from dealing with spectator difference or identity politics, despite the few attempts to do so thus far; in fact, various theories of social cognition would seemingly provide an excellent platform for such explorations.

Spectator difference and similarity

The study of spectator difference is a strong current in contemporary film and media studies. The issue deserves an essay unto itself, but here we must be content with a few remarks. Various accounts of spectatorship in film studies often begin with the homogeneous spectator of screen studies and count as a marked improvement the gradual recognition of heterogeneous spectators and the "multiple points of identification" possible in the viewing of any film. Laura Mulvey initiated the discussion of difference with her oft-cited essay "Visual Pleasure and the Narrative Cinema" (Mulvey 1992 [1975]), in which she argued that the spectator implied in mainstream films was male. This both instantiated gender as the major concern of studies of spectator difference for many years, and led to a good deal of scholarship attempting to theorize the place of female subjectivity in the film viewing experience (for an overview see Aaron 2007: 24–50; see also "Gender" in this volume). Subsequent scholarship has branched out to consider spectatorship from the perspective of race, class, ethnicity, and sexual orientation, sometimes in particular historical periods and contexts (see "Race" in this volume). Such studies are undeniably of great interest. If we wish to discover the place of films in the lives of actual persons, spectator difference will have to be taken into account.

Yet when the interest in spectator differences leads to a denial of similarities in viewers, there is a problem. As I argued at the essay's beginning, the study of spectatorship cannot proceed without a model of the hypothetical spectator. This issue has not been sufficiently discussed in film studies (or in philosophy). It is often presumed that the promotion of spectator difference is politically enabling and properly celebrates diverse human groups. Yet the study of difference in itself, like the search for human commonalities, is politically neither progressive nor regressive. The belief in presumed differences between races was the foundation of hundreds of years of racist oppression, and the idea that all people are in some sense equal or equally deserving of basic rights lay at the heart of the Civil Rights movement in the United States. Neither does the summary dismissal of "universals" in human nature derive from careful consideration of the issues. While "universalizing" the spectator is often assumed to be a BAD THING, one sees few discussions of just what this "universalizing" would entail. Are we to deny any similarities between spectators whatsoever? Moreover, in film and media studies, there have been very few discussions of the nature of universals themselves, nothing on the order, for example, of Patrick Colm Hogan's discussion of the concept (Hogan 2003: 133–9).

All of this is to suggest that the heavy promotion of spectator difference and the opprobrium attached to all discussion of universals or human similarities is something of an "idol of the tribe," a faulty habit of thought, a misplaced orthodoxy. In scholarship about spectatorship, both viewer differences *and* viewer similarities must eventually be accounted for.

See also Interpretation (Chapter 15), Emotion and affect (Chapter 8), Empathy and character engagement (Chapter 9), Consciousness (Chapter 4), Gender (Chapter 13), Race (Chapter 21), Psychoanalysis (Chapter 41), Cognitive theory (Chapter 33), and Phenomenology (Chapter 40).

References

Aaron, M. (2007) *Spectatorship: The Power of Looking On*, London and New York: Wallflower.
Althusser, L. (1971) "Ideology and Ideological State Apparatuses: Notes towards an Investigation," in B. Brewster (trans.) *Lenin and Philosophy*, New York: Monthly Review Press.
Altman, R. (1992) *Sound Theory Sound Practice*, New York: Routledge.
Anderson, J. D. (1996) *The Reality of Illusion: An Ecological Approach to Cognitive Film Theory*, Carbondale: Southern Illinois University Press.
Bordwell, D. (1985) *Narration in the Fiction Film*, Madison: University of Wisconsin Press.
—— (1989) *Making Meaning: Inference and Rhetoric in the Interpretation of the Cinema*, Cambridge, MA: Harvard University Press.
—— (1996a) "Contemporary Film Studies and the Vicissitudes of Grand Theory," in D. Bordwell and N. Carroll (eds.) *Post-Theory: Reconstructing Film Studies*, Madison: University of Wisconsin Press, 3–36.
—— (1996b) "Convention, Construction, and Cinematic Vision," in D. Bordwell and N. Carroll (eds.) *Post-Theory: Reconstructing Film Studies*, Madison: University of Wisconsin Press, 87–107.
Branigan, E. (1992) *Narrative Comprehension and Film*, London and New York: Routledge.
Campbell, J. (2005) *Film and Cinema Spectatorship*, Cambridge, UK; Malden, MA: Polity Press.
Carroll, N. (1988) *Mystifying Movies: Fads and Fallacies in Contemporary Film Theory*, New York: Columbia University Press.
—— (1996a) "Prospects for Film Theory: A Personal Assessment," in D. Bordwell and N. Carroll (eds.) *Post-Theory: Reconstructing Film Studies*, Madison: University of Wisconsin Press, 37–68.
—— (1996b) *Theorizing the Moving Image*, Cambridge: Cambridge University Press.
—— (2003) *Engaging the Moving Image*, New Haven, CT: Yale University Press.
—— (2008) *The Philosophy of Motion Pictures*, Malden, MA: Blackwell.
Choi, J. (2006) "Naturalizing Hollywood? Against the Naturalistic Account of Filmic Communication," *Film Studies: An International Review* 8: 149–53.
Comolli, J., and Narboni, J. (1976) "Cinema/Ideology/Criticism," in B. Nichols (ed.) *Movies and Methods*, vol. 1, Berkeley: University of California Press, 22–30.
Coplan, A. (2004) "Empathic Engagement with Narrative Fictions," *Journal of Aesthetics and Art Criticism* 62: 141–52.
Currie, G. (1995) *Image and Mind: Film, Philosophy, and Cognitive Science*, Cambridge and New York: Cambridge University Press.
—— (2004) *Arts and Minds*, Oxford: Clarendon Press; New York: Oxford University Press.

Gaut, B. (1995) "Making Sense of Films: Neoformalism and its Limits," *Forum for Modern Language Studies* 31: 8–23.

—— (2006) "Identification and Emotion in Narrative Film," in N. Carroll and J. Choi (eds.) *Philosophy of Film and Motion Pictures*, Malden, MA: Blackwell.

Grodal, T. (1997) *Moving Pictures: A New Theory of Film Genres, Feelings, and Cognition*, Oxford: Clarendon Press; New York: Oxford University Press.

Hogan, P. C. (2003) *Cognitive Science, Literature, and the Arts: A Guide for Humanists*, London and New York: Routledge.

Lovell, A. (1982) "Epic Theater and the Principles of Counter-Cinema," *Jump Cut: A Review of Contemporary Media* 27: 64–8.

Mayne, J. (1993) *Cinema and Spectatorship*, London and New York: Routledge.

Mulvey, L. (1992 [1975]) "Visual Pleasure and Narrative Cinema," *The Sexual Subject: A Screen Reader in Sexuality*, London and New York: Routledge.

Neill, A. (2006) "Empathy and (Film) Fiction," in N. Carroll and J. Choi (eds.) *Philosophy of Film and Motion Pictures*, Malden, MA: Blackwell.

Pavel, T. G. (1988) *Le mirage linguistic: essai sur la modernisation intellectuelle*, Paris: Minuit.

—— (1992) *The Feud of Language*, Oxford, UK; Cambridge, MA: Blackwell.

Persson, P. (2003) *Understanding Cinema: A Psychological Theory of Moving Imagery*, Cambridge and New York: Cambridge University Press.

Plantinga, C. (1997) "Notes on Spectator Emotion and Ideological Film Criticism," in R. Allen and M. Smith (eds.) *Film Theory and Philosophy*, Oxford: Clarendon Press; New York: Oxford University Press, 372–93.

—— (forthcoming) *Moving Viewers: American Film and the Spectator's Experience*, Berkeley: University of California Press.

Pribram, E. D. (1999) "Spectatorship and Subjectivity," in T. Miller and R. Stam (eds.) *A Companion to Film Theory*, Malden, MA: Blackwell.

Prince, S. (1996) "Psychoanalytic Film Theory and the Problem of the Missing Spectator," in D. Bordwell and N. Carroll (eds.) *Post-Theory: Reconstructing Film Studies*, Madison: University of Wisconsin Press, 71–86.

Pudovkin, V. I. (1949) *Film Technique*, trans. I. Montagu, New York: Lear.

Quart, A. (2000) "The Insider: David Bordwell Blows the Whistle on Film Studies," *Lingua Franca* 10(2): 34–3.

Smith, M. (1995) *Engaging Characters: Fiction, Emotion, and the Cinema*, Oxford: Clarendon Press; New York: Oxford University Press.

—— (1996) "The Logic and Legacy of Brechtianism," in D. Bordwell and N. Carroll (eds.) *Post-Theory: Reconstructing Film Studies*, Madison: University of Wisconsin Press, 130–48.

Staiger, J. (1992) *Interpreting Films: Studies in the Historical Reception of American Cinema*, Princeton, NJ: Princeton University Press.

—— (2001) "Writing the History of American Film Reception," in M. Stokes and R. Maltby (eds.) *Hollywood Spectatorship: Changing Perceptions of Cinema Audiences*, London: British Film Institute, 19–32.

Stam, R. (1992) *Reflexivity in Film and Literature: From Don Quixote to Jean-Luc Godard*, New York: Columbia University Press.

—— (2000) *Film Theory: An Introduction*, Malden, MA: Blackwell.

Stam, R., Burgoyne, R., and Flitterman-Lewis, S. (1992) *New Vocabularies in Film Semiotics: Structuralism, Post-Structuralism and Beyond*, London and New York: Routledge.

Stokes, M., and Maltby, R. (2001) "Introduction: Historical Hollywood Spectatorship," in M. Stokes and R. Maltby (eds.) *Hollywood Spectatorship: Changing Perceptions of Cinema Audiences*, London: British Film Institute, 1–16.

24
SOUND

Giorgio Biancorosso

The past three decades have seen the emergence of a wave of specialized scholarship that has greatly enhanced our understanding of sound in cinema and raised awareness of its significance to an unprecedented degree. This new development in film studies was very much needed. It was not until the work by Rick Altman and Tom Levin in the early eighties, for instance, that fundamental questions about the impact of sound technology on the perception of auditory events in cinema were first raised (Altman 1985–6; Levin 1984; see also Lastra 2000). Michel Chion's seminal work, too, emerged in the eighties, and its influence in the Anglo-American world crystallized in the nineteen-nineties (some of its most important implications, in fact, still await further development).

Framing much of the work produced in the wake of these authors' early, influential writings was a discussion of the relative importance of sound versus "the image." While crucial in instigating a debate on the marginalization of sound in film studies and investigating its causes, comparing sound with the image is in itself of little interest, however. The terms are too vague to be of any use, as both "image" and "sound" are at best approximations for complex, multifaceted phenomena. Moreover, the vastly different roles played by aural and visual cues in a film, despite their convergence in the mind of the spectator into something like a complex gestalt, make any attempt to establish a hierarchy between them simply uninformative. The significance of sound in cinema must be gauged in terms that are germane to hearing.

This need not be at the expense of vision, however. In fact, a fertile – indeed, urgent – question is whether it is useful to talk about film sound as a discrete area of inquiry in the first place. The history of filmmaking amply illustrates that sound is a specific area of praxis with its own specialized terms and practitioners. Separating out film sound as a category of the spectator's experience or an element in the production of meaning, however, is more problematic. For the more one addresses "sound" as a subject, the more one reaffirms the idea of its separation from the other elements of film. This not only legitimizes approaches to film analysis and interpretation that leave out sound as a matter of course but also endorses, however unwittingly, a view of "film sound" as a much more cohesive and unified field of experiences than it actually is.

As is well known, the term "sound" refers to dialogue, music, sound effects, and silence, while its cognate "soundtrack" refers to their strategic combination. These four broad categories further subdivide into many more types, reflecting a myriad of generic, stylistic, sociocultural, and personal factors at work in the shaping of a film. There is no one sound or sound dimension, but only concrete instances of recorded sounds mixed and reproduced in a certain way, and these can open up a complex, highly diversified world of its own (as the existence of radio dramas proves beyond question). In a film, an individual sonic occurrence may be best understood in relation not to other sounds but to a simultaneous visual shape or suggestion, dramatic lead, or symbolic meaning. Sounds, moreover, reach us in a physically overdetermined fashion, as they feature reverberation, time of decay, intensity of tone, relative loudness, and timbre (to name only a few of their characteristics). Not infrequently, one of these aspects stands out, reaching out, as it were, to an element of the *mise en scène*. Think, for instance, of how reverberation may link up to the shot of a particular place to conjure the impression of spatial depth, or how the rhythm and pace of a certain sonic pattern, synchronized to images of objects crossing the frame, helps convey the impression of motion. Criticism and analysis must bring out the finely textured connections between the visual and auditory elements of film as they pertain not only to different kinds of sounds but also to various aspects of those sounds.

Michel Chion is therefore right when he refers to cinema as a form of "audio-vision." One important corollary of his theory is the provocative claim that "there is no soundtrack," as "[e]ach audio element enters into simultaneous vertical relationships with narrative elements contained in the image (characters, actions) and visual elements of texture and setting" (Chion 1994: 40). The claim has been challenged on the grounds that sound-to-sound connections are just as important and are symptomatic of a holistic understanding of the soundtrack on the part of filmmakers (Altman *et al.* 2000: 341). But this seems to nuance and enrich, rather than fundamentally alter, the gist of his argument, especially as it pertains to the experience, as distinct from the production, of a film. Chion's analyses and neologisms, and above all his ideas of synchresis, causal listening, and the acousmêtre, are eloquent testimony to his attempt to read auditory and visual aspects of film in terms of their relationships, rather than spurious separateness. It is these relationships one must describe, if one wants to recover a full sense of the perceptual richness of the spectatorial experience. It is symptomatic of the formidable grip of old habits and prejudices that Chion's call for a truly integrated approach to the aural and visual dimensions of cinema has primarily informed scholarly work on sound, but not film analysis *tout court*.

The aptness of the term "audio-vision" notwithstanding, sitting through a fiction film amounts to more than just registering visual and auditory stimuli; rather, it is the active seeking of cues for the construction of a coherent story and parsing of a constantly evolving narrative. As such, it involves the interplay of seeing and hearing, not only with one another, but with previously acquired and newly accumulated knowledge. It is to this as yet unexplored area of the phenomenology of film that I would now like to turn. In the interest of space, I will do so by limiting the discussion to an important area of intense speculation in film theory: the relationship between sounds and their sources.

Edward Branigan observes that "[t]he perceptual difficulty of decoupling sound from a lighted object [understood as its source] is suggested by the fact that it is extraordinarily rare that a film spectator is led to interpret noise nondiegetically" (1997: 110 on unanchorable sounds, see Jost 1989). This difficulty, as we will see, lies at the heart of the art of dubbing as well. But let us stay with the example of noise and ask, what about offscreen noise? Examples are legion. How does one determine that noise is diegetic even when a source is not visible? The spectator may *know* that there is a source in the scene, either because he or she has previously seen it, or because a character has referred to it, or simply because it seems plausible or he expects it. He or she may *infer* that the noise is diegetic by its kind or because that *makes sense*, given the dramatic context at hand. Indeed, the determination may be made, to paraphrase psychologist Jerome Bruner, "before the information given" (1973). If the film has established a pattern of using certain types of sounds at recurring junctures then the spectator will instantly hear a noise as diegetic, simply by its *complying with* what in narratological jargon is called an infra-textual rule, that is, a pattern or figure that is distinctive of the film and the spectator's having learned to recognize and anticipate (for example, in his films, Jacques Tati flaunts the recurrence of certain sounds to tease the audience and help them recognize their strangeness).

The perception of a sound in film is imbued with beliefs, reminiscences, and expectations about its role in an imaginary construct, even when the source is clearly visible. This can be seen through a number of limit cases. In Woody Allen's notorious gag from *Bananas* (1971), the music underscoring Alvin's daydreaming about his meeting with Mr Vargas turns out to be played by a flesh-and-blood harpist hidden in the closet of his hotel room. One may be tempted to take the pun as paradigmatic of the ease with which music crosses the boundary between the diegetic and nondiegetic. In fact, the laughter with which the audience normally responds to the startling sight of the harpist suggests just the opposite. At issue is not whether music in film is used both diegetically and nondiegetically – it is, as we all know. The scene addresses a more specific question: Can the *same* music be both nondiegetic and diegetic within the same context? In the case of this excerpt, the answer is that it cannot. The harp glissandos may be plausible as nondiegetic background scoring – notwithstanding the parody implied therein – but it is entirely implausible as an occurrence in the film's story world, and that is why it cannot ultimately be anchored to a source without generating amusement, surprise, or outright laughter. No matter how much political truth there may be in the joke – if one was ever intended – harpists do not practice in closets. It's just not done, not even under the most fantastic and ridiculous Latin American dictatorship (the film is set in an imaginary Latin American country meant as a parody of both a fascist and a communist regime).

To be sure, Allen's conjuring trick demonstrates the power of seeing in guiding our understanding of music in film. Presented with the image of the on-screen harpist, one finds oneself forced to attach the music to a source known to be impossible or at best highly unlikely. But the success of Allen's conjuring trick also depends on the power of the knowledge of that very impossibility – for after all what he is after is a comical effect. Seeing the harpist in the closet, replaying the music in retrospect as if it were diegetic, and yet knowing that this is at best unlikely, creates a short circuit – the awareness of a contradiction – that plays itself out as laughter. As publicly observable behavior, laughter is the evidence of the complex interplay of hearing, seeing, and knowing that characterizes the perception of sound in film.

It may be argued that this interplay occurs only under very unusual circumstances, as one picks up information about the story world, much as a Gibsonian subject detecting invariants and building a picture of the on-screen world, irrespective of concepts and beliefs and the expectations that go with them (Gibson 1966). But whether dormant or concurrent, beliefs about the likelihood, plausibility, or artificiality of the coupling between a sound and an image are a central element of the phenomenology of the perception of sound in film, for they lie at the core of our relationship to film as representation. Whether understood as entertainment, narrative comprehension, or contemplation, the film experience needs a theory of imaginative response as much as a theory of perception to enable the richness of its phenomenology to emerge in full.

This is why it is important to distinguish between the perception of film sound and that of sound in general. Consider again the case of noise. While on-screen noise is nearly impossible to hear nondiegetically, due to the difficulty of "decoupling it from a lighted object," to use again Branigan's words, the instant recognition of noise as offscreen, as distinct from nondiegetic, is less easily explained (though it is equally common). It may well reflect the exercise of a certain kind of knowledge and thus result from a prediction of how films work (as already mentioned above). It may also reflect patterns of behavior common in everyday life. After all, sounds whose sources remain unseen not only reach us at all times, but are also crucial in guiding our sense of inhabiting a certain kind of space, specifying its properties and suggesting the kinds of activities taking place therein. It is fair to assume that we bring this ability to perceive the space around us through sound to bear on the construction of a diegetic space. Digital Surround Sound depends upon it. The experience of offscreen space, however, is layered in a special way, as it is informed by the awareness that it has been consciously left out of the frame and that this exclusion plays a specific role in an intentionally conceived entity (that is, the film as the product of a creative team working within a tradition and for a certain audience).

Whether seen or unseen, sources are of paramount significance for reasons that go beyond their role in determining the status of sounds within the narrative. Upon addressing the question of the perception of sound, Christian Metz argues that "the recognition of a sound leads directly to the question: "a sound of what? . . . In language as the metacode of sounds, the most complete identification is obviously that which simultaneously designates the sound and its source ('rumble of thunder')" (1980: 25, 26). Metz attributes this linguistic habit to what he calls "primitive substantialism," namely the tendency to distinguish "fairly rigidly the primary qualities that determine the list of objects (substances) and the secondary qualities which correspond to attributes applicable to these objects" (27). Descartes and Spinoza are mentioned as the beginners of this tradition, but in the Anglo-American philosophical tradition the *locus classicus* on the distinction between primary, secondary, *and tertiary* qualities is Locke's *Essay Concerning Human Understanding* (II.viii). This is, in any case, a metaphysics codified by Aristotle. Don Ihde, in what remains the most comprehensive and persuasive attempt to address the imbalance between vision and hearing in the field of philosophy, finds an anticipation of the doctrine of primary and secondary qualities in Democritus (1976: 9). Indeed, he traces the "visualism" of Western thought back to the Greeks and argues that its condition, one of philosophy's "original sins," is the separating of the senses (7).

Within the hierarchy of primary and secondary qualities, sound, like color, is ostensibly secondary, and so the auditory features of a sound are felt to be dispensable with the least loss of recognizability. This is more than a convention of language, according to Metz: it is through language, a condition of the perceptual experience itself. Therefore, Metz continues, "if I perceive a 'rumble' without further specification, some mystery or suspense remains (horror and mystery films depend on this effect): the identification is only partial. However, if I perceive 'thunder' without giving any attention to its acoustic characteristics, the identification is sufficient" (1980: 26).

Much has been made of the "adjectival" nature of sound as a symptom of a preference for the visual realm over the auditory one. One needs to be careful, however, in attributing the scarce attention to sound in film studies to a general inattention to sound in the wider culture. Rick Altman, for instance, has suggested that the reasons for the marginal role of sound in film theory and criticism can be found within the history of film, and film criticism, itself: the desire to distinguish cinema from the theater, the conditions of exhibition in the so-called silent era, and the belief that the medium must be defined in terms of an "essence" (which is inevitably identified with the image or an aspect of image manipulation, like editing) (1980: 12–14).

Practical factors have also come into play. Sounds unfold in time and they decay. In written commentaries, they can only be evoked or described rather than quoted. Though aspects of the moving image are also impossible to transpose – think of camera movement – others can be visually quoted or referred to without too obvious a misrepresentation of their original manifestation in a film (image composition, framing, the use of a certain camera lens, the costumes, the profile of an actor, his or her makeup, etc.). Citability and transposability, in other words, have played a major role in what writers and theorists have chosen to write about. More prosaically, but just as importantly, the tedious and enormously time-consuming tasks of arranging a set for shooting, positioning a camera, and achieving the most desirable conditions of light have slanted filmmakers' own jargon toward the visual. Anyone who has spent a day on a film set can testify to this. That so much effort is spent on capturing images does not mean that they are inherently more significant at the point of reception; still, it almost inevitably entails that film directors, when asked to talk about their craft, dwell primarily on the process of image production. To top it all off, the process of production and post-production appears to recapitulate the change of film from "silent" to "sound," reinforcing what Altman has dubbed the "ontological fallacy," namely the belief that cinema is essentially visual and that sound is an afterthought (1980: 14).

The bias for the visual in film studies has to some extent been exaggerated, however. In part, such a belief stems from a more liberal way of parsing linguistically the field of the visual *vis-à-vis* the auditory realm. No one refers to the notes of a Chopin ballade merely as the "sounds of the piano" or to an actor's soliloquy as "the sounds of a voice." It would be foolish to do so, though there is much of value in the process of sound production itself (the quality of the instrument, the acoustics of the venue, the physical efforts of the performer, the fullness of an actor's voice, and so forth). When it comes to music and language, we tend to equate "sound" with the acoustical. We don't seem to use the term "image" in the same way. Whether we talk about the optical features or representational content of a film shot we say that we are seeing an "image." Whether we remember props, facts, characters, or their specifically optical mode of presentation, we say of a film that we remember its "images." Should one restrict the field of the visual to the optical, just as that of sound is restricted to the acoustical, "images" would be understood as carrying considerably less weight in the process of film appreciation. It is to images as paths of access to people and objects that we pay attention, less so to images as such. After all, in everyday life, what sound is an adjective of – if at all – is not an image, but an object or a space. Heidegger puts it well when he says:

> Much closer to us than all sensations are the *things* themselves. We hear the door shut in the house and never hear acoustical sensations or mere sounds. In order to hear a *bare* sound we have to listen away from things, divert our ear from them, i.e., *listen abstractly*. (Quoted from Ihde 1976: 26; emphasis mine)

With this in mind, let us return to Metz's discussion of the relationship of a sound to its source. He argues that privileging the source object at the expense of the acoustical characteristics of the sound has shaped the way we talk about offscreen sound in film. Indeed, according to Metz, the very term "offscreen sound" reflects this bias, for strictly speaking a sound cannot be "off": "[E]ither it is audible or it doesn't exist … The situation is clear: the language used by technicians and studios, without realizing it, conceptualizes sound in a way that makes sense only for the image. We claim that we are talking about sound, but we are actually thinking of the visual image of the sound's source" (1980: 29).While suggestive, as every phenomenologist should know, the expression "offscreen sound" need not be taken as a transparent window onto the experience, let alone an accurate description of it. It is shorthand for a sonic occurrence that may well turn out to be appreciated and discussed in terms of its acoustical characteristics (despite the expression's emphasis on the fact that the source is not visualized). Understood descriptively, moreover, it does not suggest we "are actually thinking of the visual image of the sound's source," as Metz says; rather, it indicates that it is wrong to divorce sounds from their sources, in pursuit of the "purely acoustical," to begin with.

Whether inherited biologically or motivated culturally, our constant preoccupation with what a sound is a sound of is an established and fundamental component of the listening experience. To sever hearing a sound from knowing where it comes from and/or seeing its source is to offer a truncated picture of the listening experience; it is to talk about "bare sound" or "abstract listening," to quote Heidegger. Seeing the source helps project some of its qualities as an object back on to the sound through a process of mutual implication and enrichment; attributes of the lighted object are transferred on to the sound, and vice versa. Even the mere awareness of a source, in the case of offscreen sound, initiates a process of mutual implication (not between image and sound but between a concept, or idea, and the sound). Even in monophonic cinema, the offscreen sound of a crowd is the same sound as an on-screen one, only as far as their physical characteristics are concerned. Because of the inseparability of sound from image, they are, in fact, *perceived* differently. Faced with both the on-screen and the offscreen sound of a mumbling crowd, in other words, we are not dealing with the same sound, with or without the matching image of the source, but rather with two qualitatively different sounds. The expression "offscreen sound," then, does justice to the interdependence of seeing and hearing in the auditory experience.

So far I have spoken of sound as issuing from a source. Much of what we call sound, however, involves two or more physical objects or elements coming into contact in one way or another. The human voice, too, though seemingly generating from one point deep inside the body of the speaker, is the result of a complexly calibrated mechanism involving tissues, cavities, air, and energy. The fact that sounds are typically described with reference to a single or even simple source betrays the anthropomorphization they undergo in common speech, as if the rattling noise of an engine, like the human voice, came from some metaphorical "inside" rather than being produced by the friction of its mechanical components. It is in this respect that language does fail, for it makes us overlook the extent to which a sound, as Ulric Neisser suggests, informs the listener about an event or chain of events (1976: 155). Taking Neisser's intuition a step further, I want to suggest that as the product, however incidental, of an event, a sound – itself an event – is heard in terms of its sources because of a deep-seated need to read events causally. Think of how we perceive visible motion as the result of a physical cause, be it collusion, initial propulsion, or pull. Dancers exploit the compelling tendency to interpret events causally, inviting us to see their gestures and motion not only as a bodily equivalent or paraphrase of musical rhythm and melodies but also as their *effect*. By the same token, the anchoring of a sound to a source shown on a movie screen, or known to be offscreen, betrays a tendency to link a perceivable phenomenon to a *cause* (as distinct from a mere source).

Aristotle famously called the causing agent of physical phenomena their "efficient cause." The efficient cause is something that produces or brings about something else (its effect). In Aristotelian terms, then, the source is the efficient cause of the sound, and hearing a sound in terms of its source may be understood, after Chion, as a form of "causal listening" (1994: 25–8). One can describe the perception of film sound and music within the context of a more skeptical view of causality as the mere *relation* between two events. Within this conceptual framework, hearing diegetic sound can be described as nothing more than the forging of an imaginary relation between two (real) events: the playback of a sound and a moving image. Independent of whether one privileges the idea of "efficient causation" or that of "relation," reference to causality forces one to recognize that the source of a sound is not only its site of provenance but also *that which produces it*.

Upon listening to a character speak, a spectator is simultaneously constructing two kinds of causal relations, since he or she hears the sound of the actor's voice as springing from the source in the film's world, while knowing its physical genesis in the film production and playback processes. Attention is typically focused on the former, rather than on the latter, and for good reasons. Aware of the effortlessness with which audience members create imaginary relations between the objects and people they see on the screen and the synchronized sounds they hear, filmmakers have learned how not to worry about fidelity too much. The result of this state of affairs is a certain degree of stylization in the acoustical construction of the story world even in the most self-describedly "realistic" drama (a revealing foil to this is the use of harshly realistic sounds in cartoons). One reason for the considerable scientific and philosophical interest of blatantly intrusive dubbing, such as one finds in Italian, German, or Hong Kong cinema, is that it offers the illusion of a sumptuous, perceptually vivid impression of a causal relation which is known to be purely imaginary – one that is forced down our throats, in fact. As such, dubbing stands in spectacular contrast to our everyday experience of a great many causal relations that, though known to be scientifically true, cannot be grasped through our senses.

See also Definition of "cinema" (Chapter 5), Medium (Chapter 16), Music (Chapter 17), and Phenomenology (Chapter 40).

References

Altman, R. (1980) "Introduction," *Yale French Studies: Cinema/Sound* 60: 1–15.
—— (1985–6) "The Technology of the Voice," Pts. 1 and 2, *Iris* 3: 3–20; and 4: 107–18.
Altman, R., Jones, M., and Tatroe, S. (2000) "Inventing the Cinema Soundtrack: Hollywood's Multiplane Sound System," in J. Buhler, C. Flynn, and D. Neumeyer (eds.) *Music and Cinema*, Hanover and London: Wesleyan University Press.
Branigan, E. (1997) "Sound, Epistemology, Film," in R. Allen and M. Smith (eds.) *Film Theory and Philosophy*, New York: Oxford University Press.
Bruner, J. (1973) *Beyond the Information Given: Studies in the Psychology of Knowing*, New York: Norton.
Chion, M. (1994) *Audio-Vision*, trans. C. Gorbman, New York: Columbia University Press.
Gibson, J. J. (1966) *The Senses Considered as Perceptual Systems*, Boston: Houghton Mifflin.
Ihde, D. (1976) *Listening and Voice: A Phenomenology of Sound*, Athens, OH: Ohio University Press.
Jost, F. (1989) *L'œil-caméra*, 2nd ed. rev., Lyons: Presses Universitaires de Lyon.
Lastra, J. (2000) *Sound Technology and the American Cinema: Perception, Representation, Modernity*, New York: Columbia University Press.
Levin, T. (1984) "The Acoustic Dimension: Notes on Cinema Sound," *Screen* 25: 55–68.
Metz, C. (1980) "Aural Objects," trans. G. Gurrieri, *Yale French Studies: Cinema/Sound* 60: 24–32.
Neisser, U. (1976) *Cognition and Reality*, San Francisco: W. H. Freeman and Company.

25
STYLE
Noël Carroll

The notion of *style* in cinema plays a number of different roles in different contexts and serves a number of different purposes. In certain contexts, the purpose of the notion of style is to differentiate sets of motion pictures. In this regard, we might speak of the style of a period, a school, a movement, a genre, or even a nation. Likewise we might use the notion of style to differentiate one director in contrast to another – for example, to mark what distinguishes Jean Renoir from other directors, such as Sergei Eisenstein.

But the goal of stylistic analysis may not be descriptive and/or classificatory in the preceding sense. It may be explanatory. That is, we wish to explain why an individual motion picture is the way it is: why it has the elements it does and why they stand in the relations that they do. In this light, we are asking for an explanation of how the motion picture hangs together. Sometimes this sort of analysis might also be called close stylistic analysis or formal analysis. It is a matter of the analysis of the form of the motion picture – an explanation of the way in which the movie embodies its point or purpose.

Differentiating concepts of style

One view of style regards it as essentially a matter of differentiating works of art (Goodman 1978). Several of the prominent uses of the concept of style among cinema scholars aim at contrasting one group of motion pictures from other groups. Some of the leading kinds of cinematic groups that commentators have sought to distinguish include schools and movements (like Italian Neo-Realism, the French New Wave, Structural Film, Dogme 95 Film), period motion picture making (the International Style of Silent Filmmaking), genre style (slasher films, spy thrillers, musicals), national styles (Hong Kong Cinema, Bollywood), and personal or individual oeuvres (usually the body of work of a director, but one might also focus upon the work of a screenwriter, a cinematographer, a set designer, costumer, special effects artist, and so on). One thing that the aforesaid style groupings have in common is that their object typically involves groups of motion pictures greater than one (I say "typically," since there are examples of single film directors like Charles Laughton or Udi Shankar).

In addition, however, there are also stylistic descriptions of a general sort that operate upon the totality of motion pictures, dividing the entire corpus of cinema into different categories. For example, we may refer to certain films as surrealistic (with a small *s* as opposed to Surrealistic with a capital *S*, which is the label of a period-specific movement) in virtue of the oneiric shot transitions they exploit – as in the case of Busby Berkeley's dance numbers in *The Gang's All Here* (1943). We can call this kind of stylistic description *universal* because we can divide the totality of motion pictures into "surrealist" and "not surrealist" in this sense. That is, for any motion picture, speaking globally and transhistorically, it will fall into this category or not.

Similarly, we may call a shot "classical," if it is symmetrical or balanced, as are many of the compositions in Lang's *Siegfried's Death* (1924). Such stylistic descriptions are compatible with other stylistic descriptions because these other descriptions are being made relative to a more restricted category. So the compositions in Lang's *Siegfried* are classical in terms of one dimension of universal categorization, while the film is also an example of German Expressionist Cinema from the perspective of its membership in a specific school, movement, or tendency. Moreover, some of the aforementioned categories may overlap. A fifties' musical belongs both to a genre grouping and a period-specific category.

One thing to iterate here is that, although a motion picture may belong to a universal stylistic class, like that of the classical, it is also likely to belong to other categories of lesser generality, such as German Expressionism. We can call these latter categories *group*-stylistic categories, since they usually embrace a lower order of generality. Furthermore, many of the *group* categories mentioned above may intersect. For example, a thirties gangster film belongs to the genre category of the gangster film, while also inhabiting a class of period- and place-specific films. Although I admit that it sounds odd to classify the oeuvre of a single moviemaker, like Ida Lupino, under the rubric of a group category, nevertheless the body of work of such a director will be standardly made up of a group of more than one film.

In determining the style of a specific period, we concentrate on the similarities between the motion pictures under consideration. For example, we might describe the style of Soviet expressive realism of the twenties in terms of the recurring use of montage, naturalistic photography (with frequent use of low-key lighting and soft focus), epic compositions (often exploiting low-angle setups) and a tendency to favor the use of mass heroes – the collectivity as the protagonist (Huaco 1965). In addition, it is useful to clarify the profile of a period-specific style by contrasting it with other period- and place-specific styles, as Bazin does when he contrasts the montage style of Soviet Expressive Realism with the deep-focus realism of the sound cinema (Bazin 1967).

Since stylistic classifications are relative to different group categories, the same body of work may call for different directions of emphasis. For example, in discussing the work of Buster Keaton as a silent comic filmmaker, we notice features of his manner of filmmaking that correspond with the work of other directors of the period, like Chaplin. However, when analyzing Keaton's personal style, we look at what differentiates Keaton from his peers. Thus, the characterization of Keaton's personal style is likely to exclude a number of the features that comprise the characterization of Keaton as an example of a silent, comic film director.

Generally, a motion picture maker possesses a generic period style tacitly. It is presupposed. For example, Vincent Sherman did not self-consciously decide to adopt a thirties' studio style when he came to make his first film, *The Return of Dr X* (1939). He found the style readymade, so to speak.

Although typically period- and place-specific style is tacit, school or movement style is more a matter of conscious choice. Buñuel and Dali were quite deliberate in their adoption of a Surrealist (with a capital S) style of filmmaking in *Un chien andalou* (1929), extrapolating, as they did, from the disjunctive imagery of Surrealist poetry and then developing a comparable mode of abrupt editing in which sequences appear to be conjoined for no detectable reason.

Among the varieties of group style is genre style. Many motion pictures fall into certain categories with relatively fixed though still variable purposes, whose implementation most often involves recourse to certain reliable, recurring strategies for getting the job done. For example, comedies tend to be lit evenly and brightly in contrast to horror movies which tend to be lit darkly, often exploiting chiaroscuro effects. That is, genres come with certain enduring stylistic tendencies, and the analyst can use those tendencies to differentiate one genre from another.

Personal style differs from the other branches of group style canvassed so far in that it targets the work of specific motion picture artists. Although directorial style is the predominant focus, to date, of most cinema scholarship concerned with personal style, as indicated earlier, there is no reason why it cannot take up the oeuvres of screenwriters, cinematographers, etc. The preoccupation with the personal style of directors is often referred to as *auteurism* (Sarris 1985). Its influence since at least the 1960s has been enormous. As a result, it is perhaps the most common form of stylistic analysis currently practiced in cinema studies.

The goal of analyses of this sort is to pith what makes unique the characteristic approach of (usually) the motion picture director to his/her materials. This requires that the cinema analyst home-in on what differentiates how one director constructs his/her imagery from how others do it. Frequently, this involves pairwise comparisons, contrasting, for example, the monumentalism and architectonic nature of Stanley Kubrick's handling of the deep-focus shot with the more fluid, relaxed, and quotidian approach adopted by Robert Altman. In this, the motion picture analyst is searching for something like the "signature" of the auteur – the ways in which the motion picture maker's way of doing things sets him/her off from the rest. In this regard, Ozu's low-angle compositions are an important part of his signature, as are Martin Scorsese's rapid dolly zooms into close-up.

Since there are different orders of style – from the universal to the personal – the possibility for confusion is ripe. Indeed, analysts risk talking past each other, if they speak carelessly about motion picture style, *simpliciter*. Instead it is advisable that when speaking of style in cinema, analysts qualify their domain of inquiry – that they signal whether they are concerned with universal style or group style, and if group style, whether they are speaking of a generic period style, school or movement style, genre style, or individual style. Although this list of styles is not necessarily exhaustive, nor are the categories necessarily mutually exclusive, these classifications often serve a congruent taxonomic function, namely to describe bodies of motion pictures in such a way that we can differentiate certain groups of movies from others. Such categories are indispensable for connoisseurship.

However, to make matters even more complex, in addition there are forms of stylistic analysis that serve a different purpose than differentiation. Rather than aspiring to differentiate descriptively various groups of motion pictures from each other, a very central form of stylistic analysis is devoted to explaining why individual moving pictures have been put together as they have. This is a matter of attempting to identify and account for the form or style of the individual motion picture.

The concept of style in the individual work

Although a great deal of stylistic analysis is dedicated to differentiating groups of motion pictures from each other, stylistic analysis can also be directed at individual motion pictures and/or parts thereof. This type of analysis constitutes a large amount of what students are taught to do in introductory cinema appreciation classes.

Style is generally thought of as the way in which something is done. There is the action and the manner of its execution (Lang 1998). On this construal, the stylistic analysis of a motion picture addresses how a motion picture or a part thereof was constructed or *formed*, not in terms of its technological provenance (or material cause, as Aristotle would put it), but in terms of its design. In this respect, stylistic analysis is an interrogation of the form of the motion picture.

Unfortunately, this observation hardly clarifies the nature of the stylistic analysis of the individual motion picture, unless we can say something about the way in which the notion of form should be understood. That is, such stylistic analysis takes the form of the moving picture as its object of inquiry. But what is form?

A common approach to thinking about form, including cinematic form, is to contrast it with content. A motion picture has a content, something it is about, and the form of the motion picture is the way in which that content is articulated or embodied. This view of content, however, is inadequate because it is insufficiently comprehensive. For not all motion pictures have content in the requisite sense. Some films may not be "about" anything. For instance, a flicker film may only be aimed at provoking a certain perceptual experience and not have any subject matter. It is not about a certain perceptual experience: the film is what makes the perceptual experience happen. Nevertheless, I suppose, we would refrain from asserting that a flicker film like this lacked form.

Another popular way of thinking of form, in contrast to content, is to think of the form of a motion picture as that which contains the content of the movie after the fashion in which a bottle contains and gives shape to the liquid within it. However, this analogy raises significant problems when we attempt to extend it to motion pictures. It becomes difficult, for example, to determine whether or not we should call certain elements of a movie instances of the form or the content of the work in question.

Consider the point of view of a motion picture. Surely, in ordinary speech, it is natural to regard the point of view of a movie as part of its content. For generally it expresses an attitude toward whatever the movie or sequence thereof is about. And yet, it seems equally compelling to say that the content of a movie is both contained within and organized by its point of view. So the point of view of a motion picture would appear to count as an aspect both of the form and of the content of the work. This may be a view that certain theorists would be willing to endorse enthusiastically. But, be that as it may, such a view by dissolving the distinction from content gets us nowhere in terms of understanding the pertinent concept of form. We need another concept of motion picture form, one not hostage to the concept of content.

Returning to ordinary language for inspiration, one notes that two of the most frequent ways of discussing artistic form is to describe it in terms of unity and complexity (aka variety). Both these concepts imply that form is something that has parts. Obviously, something cannot be complex, unless it is made up of at least two diverse elements. To be complex is the contrary of simple – to be comprised of some single stuff. Likewise, to be unified, as opposed to being simple, requires parts that are related in a way that is organized or coordinated, as the recurring motif of clocks serves to reinforce visually the tight-knit structure of the flow of events in *The Set-Up* (1949). Indeed, most narrative motion pictures organize their diverse episodes in terms of an overarching unity of action through which the protagonists, across a varied series of events, discover a solution to some abiding problem, such as defeating Godzilla or winning the hands of seven brides.

Clearly the concepts of unity and complexity are complementary. If something is complex, as opposed to chaotic, the parts in question must be interrelated in some way, while, reciprocally, unity requires parts to unify. Therefore, since perhaps the most fundamental ways of characterizing form involve the concepts of unity and complexity, it seems reasonable to hypothesize that cinematic form has as among its basic ingredients *parts* and their *relations*. That is, when in the course of a stylistic analysis of a moving picture we make statements about its form, our statements are generally about the relations between parts of the movie in question.

When we say of the restaurant scene in Tati's *Playtime* (1967) that the composition of the comic incidents (the parts) is decentered, we are talking about the way in which they have been organized (intentionally interrelated by means of juxtaposition) such that none then has perceptual salience, thereby impelling the eye of the spectator to explore the frame in search of them. In general, it seems reasonable to conjecture that when we offer observations about the form or style of an individual motion picture, we are making statements about the relation or relations between its parts. For the style of the moving picture is a matter of how the parts are put together, or formed.

Form statements, then, appear to be ultimately translatable into statements such as "x bears such and such a relation to y" where x and y are parts, of some level of generality, of the motion picture. Even when the relation between the relevant parts is not made explicit, it can usually be fleshed out in terms of talk of parts and their relations.

If a motion picture's style is described as "jarring," then that implies that its parts are related discordantly, where, of course, this may be a commendable or unfortunate feature, depending on the goals of the moving picture.

Here it is important to keep in mind that motion pictures have many different kinds of elements and that these elements can stand in many different relationships. Sounds may repeat, functioning as leitmotifs, like the whistle of the child-killer in Lang's *M* (1931). Characters can stand in adversarial relationships to each other; this is a matter of dramatic conflict, which is a typical formal feature in narrative movies. Objects and their apparent scale can be juxtaposed to each other – like the gigantic kulak and the miniscule Marfa in Eisenstein's *The Old and the New* (1929). This too is a formal relation, as is the equilibrium or disequilibrium of the objects in a shot. Similarly, sequences can contrast with each other in terms of fast-cutting and slow-cutting, and this can supply the basis for a formal structure.

The form of an individual motion picture or its style, *ex hypothesi*, consists in how its various parts relate to each other. Motion pictures may have different parts related in different ways. Some of these ways may be coordinated, such as the way that most of, especially, the main characters are related to the plot in most narrative films. Or, the elements may be relatively uncoordinated. The color elements of a studio decor, though related to each other, may not have any significant relation to the dramatic conflict in the narrative. But regardless of whether the sets of relations in a motion picture are hierarchically organized, all of the relations are formal relations, and the style of the individual moving picture, it may be claimed, is a matter of how the parts of the film relate to each other.

This idea, then, suggests a conception of stylistic analysis almost naturally. The style or form of a motion picture is the sum total of its formal relations – the sum total of the ways in which all of the parts of the movie relate to each other and gather into further webs of relationships. Such is the object of stylistic analysis. Consequently, stylistic or formal analysis of an individual motion picture involves tracking all of the ways in which the parts of the movie are related to each other, and following the ways in which those relations become parts in larger networks of relationships.

This is a very liberal view of cinematic form or style. The way in which any part of a motion picture is related to another part is an instance of cinematic form on this view. Thus, any motion picture that has discriminable parts related in some way or other will have form of the sort that is subject to this kind of stylistic analysis. This approach might be called the *descriptive account* of form or style in the individual motion picture.

According to the descriptive account, any instance of a relation among elements of an individual movie is an instance of cinematic form. On this conception, in order to provide a full account of the form of a given motion picture, one would list or summarize all of the ways in which the parts or elements of the work are related. This approach can be called descriptive because it classifies any relation among elements of a work as an instance of cinematic form, irrespective of any principle of selection. On this view, the ideal stylistic analysis of a movie would be a long list of descriptions of all of the ways in which the elements of a given motion picture were related. Indeed, certain once popular strategies of cinema analysis, such as Raymond Bellour's notion of segmentation, have actually converged on the descriptive analysis of motion picture form (Bellour 1976).

An admirable feature of the descriptive approach to stylistic analysis is its comprehensiveness; it doesn't leave anything out. Nevertheless, I do not believe that the descriptive account delivers what we expect from an adequate approach to the stylistic analysis of the individual motion picture. For, the descriptive account is impracticable, precisely because its conception of form (the object of stylistic analysis) is, in effect, too broad.

Obviously, we rarely, if ever, encounter anything as exhaustive by way of stylistic analyses as what we would expect if the descriptive account sketched above crystallized our ruling conception of form or style in the individual work. Nor does the lack of such accounts seem purely accidental, or a function of the fact that virtually no one would have the energy to draw up such an account, let alone read one. For, more importantly, the aforesaid descriptive account does not seem as though it offers what we want from a stylistic analysis. For example, we want our stylistic analyses to be selective, whereas it is a mark of the descriptive account that it is nonselective.

But, furthermore, we do not want stylistic analyses to be selective because we are lazy. We want them to be selective in order to help us to understand and appreciate the motion picture at hand. A descriptive account of motion picture form is rather like the fantastic map that Borges imagines which is of the exact scale of its referent, while containing every one of its referent's details. Such a map is useless for guiding us through the territory since it is a mirror of the territory. For, if one cannot find one's way on the ground, then a perfect replica will be of no help. Likewise, the descriptive account of cinematic form is more like a duplicate of a motion picture's form than a guide to what is significant for understanding and appreciating the movie. And the reason for this is that it is not sufficiently selective.

Surely it seems promising to construe cinematic form in terms of how the motion picture's parts are related to each other. Yet not all of the relations between the elements of the motion picture are equal. Some are more important than others for the purpose of delivering an understanding of cinematic form. The trick is in determining which ones those are.

Form and function (Carroll 1999, 2003)

The descriptive account of cinematic form is inclusive and incorporative. It regards every way in which the elements of a motion picture relate to other elements as part of the form of the work. In this matter, it privileges no relations over others; it is – or would be – purely descriptive. However, this does not appear to be an apt characterization of our actual practices of stylistic analysis, since, in the ordinary run of things, we expect more of such analyses. Indeed, we expect them to be *analyses* – that is, to have an explanatory dimension. To this end, we are not interested in all the elements of the motion picture and their corresponding relata, but only those that contribute to the realization of the point(s) and purpose(s) of the individual work. For, it is just these features that will advance our understanding of the motion picture as a whole.

From this perspective, the formal elements and relations in the motion picture that are pertinent for stylistic analysis are those conducive to the realization of the point(s) and purpose(s) of the motion picture. The form of the moving picture, that is, is whatever functions to bring about whatever the movie is intended to achieve. The form of the moving picture is functional; the form of the movie is ideally determined by what the motion picture is supposed to do.

For example, in *The Lives of Others* (2006) there is an attempt to portray the bleakness of living conditions under the former communist regime in East Germany. To underscore viscerally the drabness of it all, the filmmakers shot scenes in which bright-colored objects were systemically removed. As a result, the screen is often continuously dominated by sequences of what feels like monotonous, institutional, unrelenting grayness – the expressive analog on the moviemaker's palette for existential hollowness. This way of articulating the color scheme of the *The Lives of Others* is a formal or stylistic choice, i.e., a choice designed to reinforce the point or purpose of the motion picture, which in this case amounts to the theme of the repressive tedium and life-crushing program of the German Democratic Republic.

This account of cinematic form can be labeled the *functional account*. According to the functional account of cinematic form, the form of an individual motion picture is the ensemble of choices intended to realize the point(s) or purpose(s) of the motion picture. Here the notion is that form or style follows function. This approach, of course, assumes that motion pictures have points or purposes. Yet this assumption appears scarcely controversial, once one realizes how very diverse those purposes can be.

In some cases, the purpose of a movie may be to propose a theme or point of view, or the purpose may be to foreground an expressive property, or it may be to arouse feelings, including feelings of visual pleasure, in audiences. A motion picture may be about communicating ideas – including ideas about the world or about the nature of film – or it may have no ideas or meanings, but might be merely devoted to promoting a certain sort of experience, such as repose, excitement, suspense, or perceptual delight. Motion pictures can make points, or they may simply have points – for instance, to encourage viewers to use their discriminatory powers keenly and perceptively. It should not be hard to concede that all or nearly all motion pictures have points or purposes – probably, in most cases, more than one – once we think of points and purposes in this broad way. The form or style of the movie comprises the ways in which the work realizes its purposes. And, in this regard, cinematic structure follows function.

In *The General* (1927), for example, Buster Keaton is committed to enabling the audience to seeing exactly how many of the large-scale physical events in the film – such as the decoupling, derailing, and swerving of railroad cars – transpire causally. That is one of the overarching purposes of the film. To this end, Keaton not only deploys highly determinate, deep-focus long shots, with internally pronounced perceptual pathways (such as uniformly articulated railroad tracks), but then rotates the array by means of long-shot field reversals to ensure that the viewer grasps all of the pertinent variables in the scene and their spatial and causal interrelations.

In the famous mortar sequence, he visually tracks the artillery piece from every side, shooting from in front of it and behind it, so that we see not only its probable trajectory, but, then, suddenly the curve in the roadbed that pulls Buster's locomotive out of the line of fire and saves him from being blown to smithereens. The choice here of long-shot field reversals not only communicates the information that Buster has been saved, but shows us how causally this came about (Carroll 2007).

Some commentators might be hesitant to call Keaton's directorial decision in the previous example a *choice* (Wollheim 1979). They reason that a choice involves the possibility that things might have been otherwise, but given Keaton's aims and his already established stylistic proclivities it would have been unlikely that he would have approached the mortar scene differently. Nevertheless, it still makes sense to call his decision a choice insofar as a director working in 1926 on a sequence like the mortar scene would have had a number of different ways of shooting it. One (though perhaps not the actual Keaton) could have done it in close-ups, as a Soviet filmmaker might have, albeit with different results. Call these alternative approaches a repertoire (Ross 2003). It is relative to such a repertoire that Keaton's decision counts as a choice – the decision to opt for one approach, out of a repertoire of contextually available alternatives, rather than others.

The form or style of the individual motion picture consists of the collection of formal choices enabling the realization of the points and purposes of the moving picture. Movies, needless to say, may have more than one point or purpose, and these may or may not be coordinated. Sometimes formal choices reinforce each other, often hierarchically, although sometimes they may not be related at all. Furthermore, formal choices themselves may have more than one function in a given motion picture. Cinematographer Dariusz Wolski's chalky/charcoal, black-and-white palette in Tim Burton's *Sweeney Todd* (2007) functions to underscore the griminess of London, and the moribund aspects of Sweeney Todd (Todd/Todt) and Mrs Lovat, while providing an eminently effective backdrop, colorwise, for all the gushing, red arterial explosions issuing from Sweeney's razors.

Generally, compared with the descriptive account, the functional account will regard fewer of the relations between elements of the motion picture as belonging to the form or style of the movie, since usually not all of the possible relations between elements contribute to the realization of its point or purpose. Of course, if all of the relations contributed to the point or purpose, then the functional account will take note of them all. But this will be the exception rather than the rule, since such cases are genuinely extraordinary. Typically, only some of the relations in the movie will function to advance the purpose of the work, and it is upon these that functional analysis concentrates. Moreover, insofar as these relations are understood in terms of the functions being discharged, this sort of analysis does not merely describe the motion picture but explains why it is the way it is, thereby augmenting our comprehension of the work at hand.

Similarly, the functional conception of cinematic form is superior to the notion of form as a container of content. For in speaking of form or style in terms of the intended realization of points or purposes, we are not committed to attributing meaningful content to a motion picture. A motion picture may not mean anything, but nevertheless do something, like stimulating a certain perceptual experience. Thus, the functional account is more comprehensive than the view that sees form as correlative to content, just because the functional account provides a way to discuss the forms of contentless motion pictures.

Style in an individual moving picture is a matter of form – a question of how the points or purposes of the work are implemented, manifested, or embodied. Something belongs to the form or style of the work if it belongs to the ensemble of choices intended to realize the point or purpose of the motion picture. A formal or stylistic choice has the intended function to realize the point or purpose of the movie, if the point in question is the intended result of the formal choice and if the formal choice occurs in the work in order to secure the point or purpose of the motion picture. In this respect, the form or style of the work is regarded as generative – as bringing to fruition the point or purpose of the work. Stylistic analysis, in this way, contributes to the explanation of how the motion picture achieves its points and purposes. This, of course, involves having a sense of the point or purpose of the work, a project that often involves interpretation, where the point of the work is to make meaning.

The explanatory concept of style with regard to group style

Although when applied to groups of motion pictures, the concept of style generally performs the function of differentiating descriptively one kind of movie from others, groups of motion pictures can be characterized functionally wherever and to the extent that it is feasible to assign points or purposes to the groups in question. If, for example, one can correlate an enduring project with a motion picture maker throughout his career, then it may be possible to identify the generative strategies he employs to those ends (along with their evolution over time) over his oeuvre, thereby isolating his style.

Stan Brakhage was, for instance, consistently engaged in championing alternative modes of perception and, to that end, he employed a panoply of techniques that subverted perspectival imagery, which he associated with conventional (and conventionally imposed) vision. Thus, his emphasis upon two-dimensional (such as perforations and scratches on an opaque background) and out-of-focus imagery were crucial to his generative style – to the realization of his point, the valorization of unacknowledged or underacknowledged realms of perception. Attending to these stylistic choices, in turn, helps viewers to understand and to appreciate Brakhage's production. Or, for a more mainstream example, consider the way in which Otto Preminger's roving camera movements, fluidly tracking scenes from every angle and thereby refraining from privileging the viewpoint of any character over others, serve to express his objective stance to the world of his fictions.

Similarly, if one can establish a point or purpose of a group of motion pictures – such as those that comprise a movement or school or genre, one can begin to suggest a functional account of the style of that group. This account of style will be explanatory, since the analysis of the relevant style explains how the works in question succeed in

277

realizing the points or purposes of the group. Generative accounts of style like this may not coincide with differentiating accounts of style for the same group of motion pictures, since the elements of style that explain how a group of motion pictures achieve their ends may not differentiate that group from other groups. For example, strategies of suspense are integral, generatively speaking, to most science fiction movies, but such structures of suspense do not differentiate science-fiction movies from other popular genres.

Of course, one may upon occasion succeed in marrying the differentiating approach to style in groups of motion pictures to the explanatory conception by focusing on the intersection of the generative or explanatory stylistic choices that, at the same time, differentiate the group of movies in question from the relevant comparison classes. Nevertheless, with sufficiently large and varied groups of motion pictures – like national cinemas – there may not be enough sharing of points or purposes among the group to allow for the application of the explanatory concept of style to the group.

See also David Bordwell (Chapter 29).

References

Bellour, R. (1976) "Segmenting/Analyzing," *Quarterly Review of Film Studies* 1: 331–53. Reprinted in P. Rosen (ed.) (1986) *Narrative, Apparatus, Ideology*, New York: Columbia University Press.

Carroll, N. (1999) *Philosophy of Art: A Contemporary Introduction*, London: Routledge.

—— (2003) "Film Form: An Argument for a Functional Theory of Style in the Individual Film," *Engaging the Moving Image*, New Haven, CT: Yale University Press.

—— (2007) *Comedy Incarnate: Buster Keaton, Physical Humor, and Bodily Coping*, Oxford: Blackwell.

Goodman, N. (1978) "The Status of Style," in *Ways of Worldmaking*, Indianapolis: Hackett.

Huaco, G. A. (1965) *The Sociology of Film Art*, New York: Basic Books.

Lang, B (ed.) (1979) *The Concept of Style*, Ithaca, NY: Cornell University Press.

—— (1998) "Style," in Michael Kelly (ed.) *Encyclopedia of Aesthetics*, vol. 4, Oxford: Oxford University Press.

Ross, S. (2003) "Style," in J. Levinson (ed.) *The Oxford Handbook of Aesthetics*, Oxford: Oxford University Press.

Sarris, A. (1985) "Notes on the Auteur Theory in 1962," in L. Braudy and M. Cohen (eds.) *Film Theory and Criticism*, 5th ed., Oxford: Oxford University Press.

Wollheim, R. (1979) "Pictorial Style: Two Views," in B. Lang, *The Concept of Style*, Ithaca, NY: Cornell University Press.

Further reading

The following are further reading on this topic: James Ackerman, "Style," in M. Philipson (ed.) *Aesthetics Today* (Cleveland, OH: World Publishing, 1961); André Bazin, *What Is Cinema?*, trans. Hugh Gray, vol. 1 (Berkeley: University of California Press, 1967); David Bordwell, *On the History of Film Style* (Cambridge, MA: Harvard University Press, 1997), together with his edited special issue of *Style*, vol. 32, on cinema, and his *Poetics of Cinema* (London: Routledge, 2007). See also David Bordwell and Kristin Thompson, *Film Art: An Introduction*, 8th ed. (New York: McGraw-Hill, 2006); E. H. Gombrich, "Style," in D. L. Sills (ed.) *International Encyclopedia of the Social Sciences* (New York: Macmillan, 1968); A. Harrison, "Style," in D. Cooper (ed.) *A Companion to Aesthetics* (Oxford: Blackwell, 1992); and Jenefer Robinson, "Style and Significance in Art History," *Journal of Aesthetics and Art Criticism* 40 (1981): 8–14, "General and Individual Style in Literature," *Journal of Aesthetics and Art Criticism* 43 (1984): 5–14, and "Style and Personality in the Literary Work," *Philosophical Review* 94 (1985): 227–47.

26

VIOLENCE

Stephen Prince

Depictions of violence have been an enduring feature of motion pictures since the inception of the medium. Violence has drawn filmmakers to explore its potential for cinematic stylization, and its presence on screen has fueled efforts to censor and regulate the medium. Movie violence has attracted audiences so deeply and incessantly that one might argue with much justification that depictions of violence constitute one of cinema's essential pleasures and appeals for viewers. Indeed, violent genres, such as westerns, war and gangster movies, emerged very early in cinema and have been with us ever since. Director Brian De Palma (*Dressed to Kill* [1980], *The Untouchables* [1987]) observed that cinema, as a medium emphasizing movement and action, is inescapably drawn toward violent action:

> Motion pictures are a kinetic art form; you're dealing with motion and sometimes that can be violent motion. There are very few art forms that let you deal with things in motion and that's why Westerns and chases and shoot-outs crop up in film. (Pally 1984: 14)

Because of its enduring presence throughout film history, movie violence has attracted the interest of scholars from diverse disciplines who have written substantial works about its psychological attractions for viewers (Bok 1998; Cerulo 1998; Goldstein 1998), its historical manifestation in the films of particular eras (Prince 2003), its economic functions in a modern media economy (Hamilton 1998), its prevalence in particular genres (Clover 1992; Lichtenfield 2007), and its symbolic functions in contemporary visual culture (Prince 2000; Sharrett 1999; Slocum 2001).

Much scholarly attention has focused on questions about the effects of viewing violent films, and anxieties about potential harmful effects have helped to fuel the controversies attaching to movie violence throughout the decades. Fears that viewing violence on screen may lead some viewers to behave violently in real life have motivated the long history of censoring screen violence. In this essay, I will trace some of that history and the assumptions about movie violence that lay behind it, focusing on the United States during Hollywood's Production Code era, which lasted until the 1960s, and the post-Code era that followed.

The effects of watching violence in film and on television have been extensively studied in the social scientific literature. More than two hundred studies, involving over 43,000 individuals as subjects, point to a link between media violence and aggressive attitudes and behavior in susceptible individuals, generally those who already harbor violent fantasies or have experienced abusive upbringings or have difficulty identifying the boundaries between real life and fictional media worlds (Paik and Comstock 1994: 516–46). Individuals predisposed to act violently are more likely to immerse themselves in violent films, most of which portray violence as an effective means of problem-solving and as being a behavior that does not cause lasting negative consequences in the form of bleeding, bruising, broken bones, emotional suffering, and so forth (McArthur *et al.* 2000: 164–8). The bulk of the violence shown in films and television is sanitized in this way; injury or death is quick and painless. For psychologists who work from a social learning orientation, such media content carries the lesson for viewers that violence works as an effective means of removing obstacles to one's goals (Bandura 1973). Paradoxically, violence sanitized of its overly negative components is the type often fingered by empirical research as offering the greatest potential harm:

> The contextual web of realistic, serious, painful action that surrounds graphic portrayals of violence serves both to outrage viewers to complain about these portrayals and at the same time protects them from negative effects, especially of disinhibition and desensitization. In contrast, it is the nongraphic violence that is surrounded by the much more antisocial web of context. While viewers are much less outraged by this "other" violence – which is much more prevalent on television – they are much more at risk of learning that violence is fun, successful, and non-harmful. (Potter and Smith 2000: 319)

The weight of the social scientific evidence tends to undercut the predominant critical framework that has infused popular thinking about violence in the movies, namely, that watching such violence produces a cathartic experience. There is little empirical evidence in support of this idea. The concept of catharsis derives from Aristotle's *Poetics* where, in a discussion of tragedy, he observed that by means of language and performance, a tragic play induces pity and fear in the spectator, emotions which the drama then effectively purges, a process denoted by the term "catharsis." Aristotle, however, was not talking about violence but about the emotions induced by tragedy as a theatrical genre. Nevertheless, although classical Greek drama contained little explicit violence on stage, the idea of catharsis has been absorbed into popular thinking about cinema, where it has furnished a template for thinking about the effects of movie violence. Director Sam Peckinpah (*The Wild Bunch* [1969]), for example, believed that the graphic bloodshed he put on screen would act as a safety valve for society, enabling viewers to work off their aggressions in the comfort of the imaginary screen world. Peckinpah, in turn, was influenced by Aristotle and by Antonin Artaud's "theatre of cruelty." In his influential essays on the place of cruel spectacle in theater, Artaud wrote that such dramatizations would be healthy; that they would drain social abscesses. "I defy any spectator," Artaud wrote, "to whom such violent scenes will have transferred their blood ... to give himself up, once outside the theater, to ideas of war, riot, and blatant murder" (Artaud 1958: 82). However, speaking as a social scientist, George Comstock observed that with respect to media violence:

> the catharsis hypothesis is often wrongly attributed to Aristotle, but in fact he proposed only that by arousing pity and fear, the dramatic genre of tragedy would lead to their catharsis. He said nothing about aggressive behavior, and he was prescient not to do so. (Comstock 1980: 130)

If there is scant empirical support for the idea that movie violence works in terms of catharsis, there is also no simple, one-to-one correspondence between screen violence and the behavior of viewers. Connections or linkages between the screen-world and real-world violence are complex, are not easy to disentangle from other variables, and are never without many forms of complex mediation. Despite this complexity, worries about the formative influences of screen violence are as old as cinema. Modern viewers looking at old movies are unlikely to feel that there is much violence in them, and yet audiences and critics in each historical period have found cinema to be excessive in its presentation of violence. Upholding Illinois state censorship of the western, *The Deadwood Coach* (1924), for example, an appellate judge condemned what he clearly felt was the film's excessive violence:

> The picture portrays, first, a killing, then a fight with the Indians and a stage-coach holdup, and an attempt to kill, then the shooting up of some kind of eating house, and a diving from a window, then a holdup of the Deadwood coach and its destruction, then a killing of the guard, the driver being beaten and tied to a tree, then an arrest, then a breaking of the jail by the roughest element of the town, then a release of a prisoner, and, finally, a so-called desperate fight to hold up the stage, then an attempt to escape, and, finally, a man plunges 1,000 feet to his death on the rocks. (Prince 2003: 18)

The classic Universal monster movies – *Dracula* (1931) and *Frankenstein* (1931) – may seem quite tame today, and yet, in their period, they were widely condemned for being unacceptably gruesome and horrific. State and municipal censor boards around the country made numerous cuts in *Frankenstein*, and these boards continued to delete shots and scenes from subsequent horror films, as well as from gangster movies. The latter were decried for having the excessive levels of killing that Tommy guns made possible and for showing the deaths of law-enforcement officers. When *Dracula* and *Frankenstein* were re-released as a double-feature in 1938, teachers complained that the films left those schoolchildren who had seen them agitated with fear and anxiety. One teacher wrote a letter of protest to the Hollywood industry's leading studios and distributors complaining that such films offered viewers an opportunity to feast on horror and murder (Prince 2003: 63–4). These examples suggest that violence on screen is governed by the representational conventions that operate within a given period and in relation to the sensibilities of viewers about the nature of what is real and where the thresholds lie that determine when a representation becomes excessive. Conventions for depicting violence change over time, as do assessments by audiences about what counts as real and convincing. *Dracula* and *Frankenstein* were excessive films in their day, just as *Saving Private Ryan* (1998) and *Hostel* (2005) have been in more recent periods.

Violence on the screen has two components, the depicted behavior and the stylistic means through which it is presented. The behaviors themselves have not changed awfully much over the course of film history. Characters have been beating on, shooting, stabbing, strangling, and mangling one another since film began. But the stylistic designs that filmmakers have employed to present these behaviors have changed considerably in ways that make violent behavior on the screen today more insistent and emphatic. A brief survey of changing conventions in screen violence can indicate how boundaries between acceptable and unacceptable content have shifted. First, an irony needs noting. Screen violence as a concept did not exist in earlier periods. "Violence" as a category of screen content emerges as a perceived phenomenon in the late 1960s, with the fall of screen censorship and the popularity of films that would have been deemed transgressive in an earlier period. Popular violent, sixties films that could not have been filmed in prior decades include *Bonnie and Clyde* (1967), *The Good, the Bad and the Ugly* (1967), *The Dirty Dozen* (1967), and *The Wild Bunch*. Before the 1960s and the greater creative freedoms for filmmakers which that period ushered in, the film industry had been very concerned about depictions of violence on screen, but this term never appears in memorandums about industry regulation or in the Production Code, which governed Hollywood filmmaking from 1932 to 1968. Instead of "violence" as a discrete category, Hollywood's in-house regulatory board, the Production Code Administration (PCA), used the terms "brutality" and "gruesome" to describe content that was considered excessive and in need of trimming for the screen. The PCA derived its understanding about what counted as unacceptably brutal content from its study of the kinds of scenes that regional censors had been deleting from films during the 1920s. These included knife violence and scenes of sharp weapons such as arrows or spears sticking in people; shootings in which law officers were killed or in which guns were fired at an excessive rate; beatings that were prolonged or that resulted in visible damage to the victim; scenes of torture, dismemberment or mutilation; and scenes in which the victim was shown to be suffering.

The PCA worked with filmmakers to reduce this type of content in Hollywood films. As a result, an elaborately coded visual system of representation emerged in which the camera averted its gaze from brutal violence or in which a symbolic substitute was offered for imagery that could not be shown explicitly. When the gangster Gaffney (Boris Karloff) is machine-gunned in *Scarface* (1932), viewers see, instead, a bowling pin that totters for a moment and then falls. A teddy bear on fire amid the wreckage of an aircraft tells viewers of *The High and the Mighty* (1954) that the young son of the film's hero (John Wayne) has perished in the crash. In *Sweet Smell of Success* (1957), a sudden cut to the drummer in a jazz band takes viewers out of a scene in which two brutal cops attack a musician, with the drummer's activity standing in for the beating that is off-camera.

The ideological assumption that guided this policy was that depictions of egregious violence to the human body were distasteful and loathsome and were to be off-limits to filmmakers. Thus, in the 1930s and 1940s, filmmakers might show gunfire blasting into masonry walls, shattering windows, and blowing holes in furniture, but they could not squib actors so as to simulate bullet strikes on the body. One of the anomalies of gangster movies in this period is that drive-by shootings wreak tremendous visible damage on buildings while shooting victims perish unmarked. The foundational convention of violence against people in this period was a representational statement that, far from producing anguish and pain, violent death merely signals the onset of sleep. In *The Strange Love of Martha Ivers* (1946), Walter O'Neil (Kirk Douglas) shoots Martha (Barbara Stanwyck) in the belly at close range, and she sinks peacefully out of the frame, as if she is falling asleep. This type of tranquil death is common in films of the period, and it strikes modern viewers as being quite unrealistic because they are accustomed to seeing signs of bullet trauma and spasms in the bodies of gunshot victims. Certainly Martha's narcotized response is a highly stylized manner of representing a violent assault. But as I will discuss in the last section of this essay, movies today are not much better at capturing essential truths about violence. What has changed is that viewers today expect to see visible evidence of physical trauma and pain. These signs, however, are often elaborated and embellished in contemporary film to a degree that becomes nonsensical, as when the villain in an action movie is punctured by scores of bullets, falls down seemingly dead, and then leaps back up to launch another attack on the hero.

While the PCA sought to impose limits on screen violence, filmmakers pushed in the opposite direction. They filmed scenes in which characters are skinned alive (*The Black Cat* [1934]), have a flaming fondue thrown into their face (*Raw Deal* [1948]), or are thrown down a flight of stairs in a wheelchair (*Kiss of Death* [1947]). The Second World War opened the door to greater violence in the era's combat films, such as *Bataan* (1943), which shows a partial decapitation. The PCA tolerated greater levels of violence in war movies than in gangster and horror movies, but across all action genres the push by filmmakers to do harder violence was unrelenting. Moviemakers were drawn to elaborate ever more stylish and intensified depictions of violence, and once knowledge of how to do gun violence for the camera or how to stage a convincing physical beating became part of the filmmaking community's stockpile of craft knowledge, such cinema accomplishments could not be unlearned. Thus, while montage editing and slow motion are not established as a normative template for gun violence until the late 1960s, the death of Tony Camonte in *Scarface* (1932) remained as an example to filmmakers wanting to take cinema further. As Camonte is machine-gunned by the cops, his death throes extend across several compositions taken with different camera setups. These prolong his death agony, and actor Paul Muni, playing Camonte, pantomimes the spasms produced by bullet hits, even though no squibs are employed. No slow motion is employed either, but the little montage shows very clearly how editing can effectively slow down, by extending, the temporal duration of a moment of violence. Once the sequence had been accomplished, it remained there for filmmakers to study in subsequent years. Thus, while it is doubtful that a history of screen violence can be written in terms of a movement toward ever more truthful depictions, it is the case that the evolution of screen violence has occurred in terms of a movement toward ever more intense and elaborated depictions.

These got their biggest boost in the 1960s, as the power of the PCA waned, along with the legal foundations on which regional censorship rested. Filmmakers rushed forward to pursue their long-nurtured visions of a bloody screen. Acts of violence and types of imagery that would have been censured in earlier decades now flourished. These included the extended beatings of Marlon Brando in *The Chase* (1966) and Eli Wallach in *The Good, the Bad and the Ugly*, graphic imagery of arrows penetrating victims in *Duel at Diablo* (1966), and the incineration of German officers and women in *The Dirty Dozen*. But it was the use by Arthur Penn and Sam Peckinpah of slow motion and multiple camera montages in *Bonnie and Clyde* and *The Wild Bunch* that established a stylistic template for gun violence that predominated for more than a generation. They also employed elaborate squibs to simulate bullet strikes on the characters, overturning a PCA prohibition in flamboyantly bloody fashion. When the Bunch and Bonnie and Clyde are gunned down, their flesh and clothing erupt with force that is both visual and visceral. Peckinpah even went so far as to rig squibs for entrance and for exit wounds and to put pieces of meat inside the explosive so that it would look like bits of the character were blown apart by the bullet.

Whereas the ideology governing violent representations during the PCA period in Hollywood stipulated that such representations be clean and sanitized and, oddly enough, that violence did no serious, visible harm to human beings even while killing them, the new approach emphasized the destructive power of violence, especially upon human flesh. Indeed, Peckinpah stated time and again that he wanted to put the sting, the pain, back into movie violence because he considered the existing Hollywood style to be false to reality. Ironically, however, critics and viewers regarded his slow motion and montage editing to be inherently more realistic as a style than the existing norms that he sought to overturn. Peckinpah, by contrast, always insisted that his style was artificial, but that through this artifice he could catch a truth about violence that Hollywood had avoided, namely, that it dehumanizes people, destroys their humanity. He sought to portray this by emphasizing the grotesqueness of a character's extended death throes.

With its lengthy, detailed massacre scenes, *The Wild Bunch* was the most elaborately violent film that had yet been made, and it had a terrific impact on audiences because it made them conscious of a new way of looking at, and filming, screen violence. There was nothing comparable to that impact until Steven Spielberg released *Saving Private Ryan*, which hit audiences with the same intensity and revolutionary force as Peckinpah's film had thirty years previously. Spielberg, too, sought to overcome the existing stylistic templates governing depictions of Second World War combat. Like Peckinpah, his solution was to create a novel way of seeing using a freshly calibrated formal design, one that audiences were not overly familiar with. In this case, it involved radical experimentation with the speed and angle of the camera's shutter, manipulation of the camera's lens, and methods of processing the film conjoined with extremely graphic depictions of bullet wounds and bodies blown apart by explosives. He also replaced the reassuring narrative conventions of Hollywood's combat films, in which the death scenes of secondary and major characters occurred at clear and preordained points in the story, with a more disturbing, existentialist acknowledgment that amid the chaos of combat death can come at any time for anyone.

This existentialist understanding that violent death is inescapable and threatens from all sides is a social perception that separates the contemporary period from earlier eras of screen violence, in which a violent event was understood to be exceptional and atypical. In the old horror movies, the monsters were always killed off unambiguously at the end. Horror, today, ends with the monsters still at large. Moreover, the graphic violence that Spielberg placed for the first time inside a Second World War combat movie had taken root in the horror film a generation earlier. In this respect, the horror genre is a key link between Peckinpah's experiment with the western in *The Wild Bunch* and Spielberg's experiment with the combat film in *Saving Private Ryan*. The widespread, ferocious, and indiscriminate killing that Peckinpah showed in *The Wild Bunch* flourished subsequently in horror movies, particularly the graphically violent ones that began to proliferate in the 1980s, where such violence constituted a statement about the essentially pitiless nature of the universe. As these developments suggest, films today are more unsparing of their audiences, are crueler, and are more assaultive, in part because the screen technologies of violence (prosthetic limbs, digital effects) make outré displays easier to achieve today, but also because viewers seem to regard such cruelty as offering a truer portrait of the world they inhabit. Indeed, this is why the brutality that shocked audiences in the 1930s seems pale today. In those earlier films it occurs less frequently and is staged with greater tact and indirection.

The cruelty on display in contemporary film is indeed breathtaking. In the horror genre, for example, a cycle of torture films has proven to be very successful at the box office. *Saw* (2004), *Hostel*, and their sequels construct narratives around the abduction and slow torture of characters whose physical torment is visualized in lurid and fascinating detail. Mel Gibson's *The Passion of the Christ* (2004) revivified the tale of Jesus' torture, by dwelling at length upon the tearing and rending of his flesh during scourging and crucifixion. Fans of the film reported this to be the most realistic depiction of these events, even though none ever had the misfortune to actually witness a victim scourged with a flagrum or nailed to a cross. Actually, much of what Gibson shows in the film is more in keeping with the conventions of movie violence than with the known facts of the physiological response to scourging and crucifixion. But despite this, the film's relentless cruelty seemed to provide its fans with what they regarded to be a truer account of Jesus' last days.

That contemporary films are more harsh and detailed in their presentation of violence seems clear enough. But what about the corollary assumption that such an approach offers a truer account of the phenomenon of human violence? While one may grant that viewers perhaps feel more unsettled about their world today than in generations past and that the higher level of cruelty in today's films is related to this anxiety, two qualifications need to be considered. In these key ways, the world of movie violence in mainstream films remains quite unreal. First, while viewers today are surrounded by media images of great violence – in the movies, on television, and in videogames – all of this is essentially fictitious violence. It is elaborated within a narrative framework that structures it according to moral formulas of punishment and reward, and viewers know at all times that it is fictitious. By contrast, imagery of actual, real-world violence is far more regulated, censored, and tightly controlled than are the fictitious images carried by the media. The killing and maiming of Iraqi civilians, often targeted by US forces, has been a widespread and enduring feature of the Iraq War, but it has been rarely photographed, despite extensive reporting in print media. The US government does not permit any filming of the returning caskets of American soldiers fallen in Iraq. Imagery of the planes hitting the World Trade Center on 9/11 and of the towers falling is readily accessible, but not images of the jumpers. Photos and footage of people falling from the towers have been widely suppressed, especially images of the mangled remains where these victims hit the street. Following Hurricane Katrina, hundreds of bodies littered New Orleans, yet the news media refrained from showing the scale of these deaths.

Fictional media violence is rampant in contemporary culture, yet imagery of real death is not, despite its abundance in the world that exists off screen. How then is a viewer to judge the veracity of contemporary cinema's visual language of violence? It becomes exceedingly difficult because of this paradox – violence as a fictitious construction is amplified and elaborated, while the visual record of actual violence in the world becomes a victim to political agendas that seek its suppression. As a result, viewers have a visual frame of reference that is skewed in terms of the representational conventions that predominate in contemporary media. A second problem must qualify any judgment that the movies today are better at depicting violence than in generations past. This problem is related to the attraction of cinema to action and to movement, which Brian De Palma noted. Cinema's privileging of action has meant that the representation of violence overwhelmingly occurs in terms of a stylistics of spectacle, in which the emotional buildup and explosive release of violent energy takes precedence. The western outlaws or the gangsters march dramatically toward their climactic confrontation with an antagonist; the viewer keys up with anticipation; and an exciting, extensive action sequence shows a glorious gun battle in which the characters find numerous opportunities for dramatic and heroic deaths.

Actual gun violence is different, and what the movies, fixated on the stylistics of spectacle, don't catch is the aftermath. Here I must speak more personally in order to describe this condition. I have been a professor at Virginia Tech for nearly twenty years, during which time the community has been a peaceful and quiet place to live and work. That changed on 16 April 2007, when a deranged student went on a rampage and shot to death thirty-two people. He killed two students at a dormitory early that morning and then, a few hours later, chained shut the doors to a building housing numerous classrooms. He prowled from room to room, slaughtering as many people as he could. He killed thirty in the building and wounded twenty-five. The shooting was over very quickly. His rampage in the building lasted about fifteen minutes, but the profound consequences, and indeed the meaning, of his actions were to be found in the aftermath. Stunned family members, friends, and members of the university community struggled to make sense of what had happened. Lives were changed forever, and the web of human relationships showed up as the densely constructed network that it is. In the movies, a killer's victims are quite discrete and are limited largely to those who are actually killed. Maybe a wife or a friend or a colleague is alive at the end of the story to reminisce about the character that has died, but movies don't capture the network of social interconnection upon which actual violence has such a terrible impact. In life, those affected are far more numerous because the fallen have families, friends, acquaintances, and those families and friends have other friends and families who are affected because they know someone who was involved. The movies don't get this web of effects very well, and they certainly don't get the aftermath of violence very well. The lingering pall that the loss of a loved one creates has never been as interesting for filmmakers as it is to stage and to stylize scenes of violent action. The aftermath is more inward, less visual. Filmmakers, especially in the action genres of popular cinema, are drawn to the mechanics of violence, less often to what violence leaves behind in the world after it is over. But in my community, that's where the meaning and effects of the killer's rampage were to be found.

Violence, then, is a fundamental category for expression in cinema, one that has always exerted great attraction for filmmakers and audiences, and yet the medium's grasp of this subject is partial, biased, and certainly misleading. Cinema attaches great stylistic hyperbole to its renditions of violent death, and, as style, violence is something the movies do extremely well. As a human phenomenon, however, violence retains a power and a complexity that film – popular cinema especially – has often failed to grasp.

See also Censorship (Chapter 3).

References

Artaud, A. (1958) *The Theater and Its Double*, trans. M. C. Richards, New York: Grove Press.

Bandura, A. (1973) *Aggression: A Social Learning Analysis*, Englewood Cliffs, NJ: Prentice-Hall.

Bok, S. (1998) *Mayhem: Violence as Public Entertainment*, Reading, MA: Addison-Wesley.

Cerulo, K. (1998) *Deciphering Violence: The Cognitive Structure of Right and Wrong*, New York: Routledge.

Clover, C. (1992) *Men, Women and Chainsaws: Gender in the Modern Horror Film*, Princeton, NJ: Princeton University Press.

Comstock, G. (1980) "New Emphases in Research on the Effects of Television and Violence," in E. L. Palmer and A. Dorr (eds.) *Children and the Faces of Television*, New York: Academic Press.

Goldstein, J. (ed.) (1998) *Why We Watch: The Attractions of Violent Entertainment*, New York: Oxford University Press.

Hamilton, J. (1998) *Channeling Violence: The Economic Market for Violent Television Programming*, Princeton, NJ: Princeton University Press.

Lichtenfield, E. (2007) *Action Speaks Louder: Violence, Spectacle, and the American Action Movie*, Middletown, CT: Wesleyan University Press.

McArthur, D., Peek-Asa, C., Webb, T., Fisher, K., Cook, B., Browne, N., Kraus, J., and Guyer, B. (2000) "Violence and Its Injury Consequences in American Movies: A Public Health Perspective," *Western Journal of Medicine* 173 (September): 164–8.

Paik, H., and Comstock, G. (1994) "The Effects of Television Violence on Anti-social Behavior: A Meta Analysis," *Communication Research* 21(4): 516–46.

Pally, M. (1984) "'Double' Trouble," *Film Comment* 20 (September–October): 12–17.

Potter, W., and Smith, S. (2000) "The Context of Graphic Portrayals of Television Violence," *Journal of Broadcasting and Electronic Media* 44(2): 301–23.

Prince, S. (ed.) (2000) *Screening Violence*, New Brunswick, NJ: Rutgers University Press.

—— (2003) *Classical Film Violence: Designing and Regulating Brutality in Hollywood Cinema, 1930–1968*, New Brunswick: Rutgers University Press.

Sharrett, C. (ed.) (1999) *Mythologies of Violence in Postmodern Media*, Detroit: Wayne State University Press.

Slocum, J. (ed.) (2001) *Violence and American Cinema*, New York: Routledge.

Part II

AUTHORS AND TRENDS

27

RUDOLPH ARNHEIM

Jinhee Choi

Since the turn of the twentieth century, the continuing attempt to elevate the status of film, artistic or otherwise, has taken various routes, through either an affiliation with or differentiation from previously established art forms. The *film d'art* movement in France and *Autorenfilm* in Germany, for instance, tried to lure the middle-class audiences through literary adaptations, the subject matter of which such middle-class audiences would find sophisticated. Classical film theorists, such as Rudolf Arnheim, André Bazin, and Sergei Eisenstein, took an opposite approach, claiming that there exists a set of characteristics distinctive of the film medium, and that film as art should explore these medium-specific qualities.

This essay examines Arnheim's film theory by tracing out his reasons for thinking of film as an independent art form. Since media convergence has become the norm within the global film industry, one may find the classical film theorist's urge to explore the peculiarities of the medium rather outdated. Media conglomeration might be an historically contingent phenomenon, one in which film plays a significant part, but aesthetic concerns still remain with regard to the relationship between cinema and other media. Arnheim has reservations about certain technological developments within the history of cinema because he believes that the artistic potential of film lies in its technological limitations. This reservation further invites us to consider and reconsider the relationship between film technology and aesthetics to counterbalance a tendency in the contemporary discourse on film technology that foregrounds the medium's limitlessness.

The real, the filmic, and the natural

Arnheim is concerned with film as art and characterizes his approach as *Materialtheorie*, according to which the aesthetic principles of a medium should be based upon its material properties (Arnheim 1957c: 2). Like other artistic media – such as pictures, music, dance, and literature – film can serve various functions, one of which is artistic. For Arnheim, not all films are art and they don't need to be. But to grant film an artistic possibility he had first to disprove the then common claim that the film medium lacks artistic potential. The major criticism leveled against film derived from a certain characterization of its representational capacity: as a photographic medium film is merely a reproduction of reality. One implication of such a criticism is that the mechanical processes involved in photography and film do not permit the operators' creative control or intervention. Painters, for instance, can intervene at any moment during the process of painting, from the decision of the subject matter, composition, drawing, and color of pigment, to the thickness of brush stroke. In contrast, filmmakers and camera operators have a limited range of control – such as lighting and the placement of objects during the filmmaking process – while the rest is rendered through a more or less automatic mechanical process. As Noël Carroll notes, such a charge comes from the growing artistic tendency in the late nineteenth and early twentieth centuries toward antimimesis (Carroll 1988: 21). From Baudelaire to Croce, the principal function of art, it is claimed, should not be found in the imitation of nature, and thus film, which excels in "re-presenting" reality, is considered too aesthetically inadequate to belong to the realm of fine art.

In his attempt to challenge the aesthetic criticism of photography and film, Arnheim first asks whether the filming process is indeed automatic. A photographic image of a simple object, such as a cube, notes Arnheim, is not automatically rendered. It can either succeed or fail in making an object recognizable to the viewer and thus requires the photographer's skill to find an adequate angle and proper lighting (Arnheim 1957a [1933]: 9–10). The representational capacity of photography and film, then, is not given, but is something that can be achieved by virtue of the photographer's skills. Arnheim does not construe the relationship between a photographic image and its referent as a matter of "truth," or correspondence. Rather, it involves the aesthetic sensibility of a photographer, which can provide an insight into the object. An artistic filmmaker should capture the essence of an object or an event, and there is no set of rules to follow. Arnheim argues, "There is no formula to help one choose the most characteristic aspect: it is a question of feeling" (Arnheim 1957a [1933]: 10). The then common assumption that photography and film cannot be art was the result of a misconception that the filmmaking process is automatic. As Arnheim asserts, it not only requires a level of skill from a filmmaker in order for the audience to discern the object filmed, but also involves an aesthetic sensibility in order to choose and foreground the most salient aspects of the object.

Arnheim further asserts that the film medium's tie to reality does not yield a filming process that is altogether automatic, nor does film replicate the perceptual experience of the real. Arnheim lists a set of attributes of film that differentiate filmic perception from natural perception. From (i) the reduction of depth, to (ii) lighting, to (iii) the delimitation of the screen, to (iv) the absence of the space-time continuum, and to (v) the absence of color and of nonvisual sensory coordination, filmic transformation of reality falls short of rendering an exact replica of natural perception. In filmic images, for instance, sizes and shapes of objects do not remain constant in the way we normally see two distant objects. Instead, the object in the background of a shot looks disproportionately small, due to the camera's monocular vision (Arnheim 1957a [1933]: 13–14). Moreover, a black-and-white film reduces the natural color scheme to a limited color palette, which results in the reconfiguration among colors and objects. The shade of tree leaves in a black-and-white film may be linked to that of a woman's lips through similar shades of gray, inviting the viewer to make a connection that he or she would not normally draw.

The characteristics that Arnheim attributes to cinema are not all specific to the medium. Many of them are shared with photography or derived from the fact that film is a photographic medium. Arnheim dwells on one aspect, though, which he believes distinguishes film from both photography and theater. Film produces in the spectator a distinctive spectatorial effect. Arnheim claims that the film image is neither completely two-dimensional nor completely three-dimensional, rendering a "partial" illusion of real space. By "partial," Arnheim refers to two different aspects: (i) the unreality of filmic space is often unnoticeable; and (ii) information gathered from filmic image is incomplete (Arnheim 1957a [1933]: 28–9). It is the first aspect that demarcates the film medium from the other competing media. I will come back to this point shortly. The second meaning of "partial" is in accordance with the major principles of gestalt psychology. Even the most elementary process of vision does not passively receive data from the real world but creatively organizes sensory raw materials in accordance with a set of principles. In natural perception, we do not need every detail to infer the whole. Likewise, with a few salient aspects of objects and events represented in a film, one can still have a strong sense of the real. But the partial illusion in the second sense is not unique to the film medium but can be shared with any type of art.

To what extent, then, does the perceptual experience of film involve an illusion? Arnheim postulates a continuum from abstraction to the real in representing space, with photography as the most abstract, film in the middle, and theater at the most real end. The film spectator does not have a false belief about what he or she sees. He or she does not mistake the film image for the real. But film has the spatial and temporal mobility that both photography and theater lack, without drawing much of the viewer's attention to it. A film image is bounded by its margins and can easily allow a montage, both within a scene and between scenes. Arnheim claims, "a result of the 'pictureness' of film is, then, that a sequence of scenes that are diverse in time and space is not felt as arbitrary. One looks at them as calmly as one would at a collection of picture postcards" (Arnheim 1957a [1933]: 27–8). He continues, "if at one moment we see a long shot of a woman at the back of a room, and the next we see a close-up of her face, we simply feel that we have 'turned over a page' and are looking at a fresh picture" (Arnheim 1957a [1933]: 28). Arnheim must have a specific editing system in mind, here, such as the continuity editing of Hollywood, in which the editing pattern is less noticeable. In contrast, theater employs "real" space to a certain extent, which disallows montage within a scene. But Arnheim does not further postulate the relationship between the spectator and the fictional space and/or its ideological implication, which becomes the focal point of the debates of postclassical film theorists, such as Jean-Louis Baudry and Christian Metz, of a psychoanalytical-semiotic bent.

Arnheim's ontological and epistemic observations about film lead him to refute the prevalent criticism of the medium. Film is far from a perfect copy of reality, rendering in the viewer a perceptual experience as an alternative to both natural perception and the perception given by other artistic media. For Arnheim, however, the imperfections of the "mechanical" reproduction process of the film medium should not be dismissed as technical flaws; instead, they should serve as the basis for the artistic use of the medium. In the chapter "The Making of a Film," Arnheim demonstrates how each "defect" or "drawback" of the film medium can yield artistic effects. His famous quote aptly captures this idea: "Art begins where mechanical reproduction leaves off, where the conditions of representation serve in some way to mold the object" (Arnheim 1957a [1933]: 57). According to Arnheim, the artistic possibility of the medium should be found in its very technical constraints. As Jon Elster notes, creativity comprises both "choice of constraints" and "choice within constraints" (Elster 2000: 176). The filmmaker's initial choice of the medium would impose certain intrinsic, technical constraints, within which he or she can pursue the medium's artistic potentials. Consider, for example, the reduced depth of field in the cinema, which can underscore a psychological state of a character. Arnheim takes an example from King Vidor's *The Crowd* (1928), which showcases an aesthetic inclination of the medium. A boy hurries home, as he sees a crowd gathering around his house drawn by the sound of ambulance. The camera is located on the second floor, looking down at the door, as the boy enters. As the boy nears the end of the stairs, he appears dispro-portionately large – an effect of the camera lens – which nevertheless artfully expresses his fear of hearing the dreadful news – his father is dead.

The delimitation of the visual field – another technical constraint, as well as aesthetic potential of the medium – carries one of the most significant functions of film: framing. Framing comprises a wider range of film techniques and devices – camera distance (especially close-up), angle, movement, and editing – in contrast to other limitation, such as absence of color or of the space-time continuum, which results from more or less a single device (film stock/development) or technique (editing). In theater, audiences have considerable visual freedom in terms of what to look at; film, by contrast, has a set of devices to direct and control the viewer's attention. The great silent comedies that Arnheim revisits throughout *Film as Art*, provide ample instances of gags created through framing. For example, in *The Cameraman* (1928), a female receptionist, who is the object of affection of the male protagonist, enters the office. The waiting area is not shown in its entirety, and as the camera reframes we see Buster Keaton sitting on a chair at the corner: he has been waiting for her all night. Such a narrative and spatial revelation can come as a pleasant surprise to the viewer, violating the viewer's expectation of space.

Given the artistic potentials of the medium, the goal of filmmakers is not merely to "re-present" reality, unfolding in front of the camera, but to transform its material constraints into cinematic expression. Arnheim does not clearly discuss the scope of "expression" in *Film as Art* and one must tease out his notion of "cinematic expression" in the light of his later work, *Art and Visual Perception*. In the latter, Arnheim empha-sizes the expressive nature of visual perception in general. Our perceptual mechanism does not merely register sense data but recognizes them as expressive:

> When I sit in front of a fireplace, I do not normally register certain shades of red, various degrees of brightness, geometrically defined shapes moving at such and such a speed. I see the graceful play of aggressive tongues, flexible striving,

lively color. The face of a person is more readily perceived and remembered as being alert, tense, and concentrated than it is as being triangularly shaped, having slanted eyebrows, straight lips, and so on. (Arnheim 1974: 454–5)

The perceptual processes Arnheim describes above differ from scientific observations. If the former translate the raw material into the rubric of expression broadly construed to include both expressive and nonexpressive qualities, the latter deal with the material conditions of objects – weight, shape, and size. Arnheim claims that expression consists of the recognition of the isomorphic relationship between the patterns of the stimuli and those of the expressive qualities (Arnheim 1974: 450). A drooping willow tree does not look sad because it looks like a sad person. Rather, the willow tree expresses sadness by virtue of the shapes of its branches that are structurally similar to that of the intended mood. For Arnheim expression is "an inherent characteristic of perceptual patterns," not a projection of and/or association with the expressive qualities of human and animate beings (Arnheim 1974: 452). A comparison or analogy with the physical manifestations of human expression comes as secondary (Arnheim 1974: 452). How can film express? In addition to the filming process transforming the real, a film reflects and registers the artistic vision and sensibility of the filmmaker. Arnheim continues, "If expression is the primary content of vision in daily life, the same should be all the more true of the way the artist looks at the world" (Arnheim 1974: 454–5). Cinematic representation is not a vehicle of transferring the real, not merely an instrument of observation, but a means to translate and communicate via the real.

The aesthetic appreciation of film should, then, encompass the understanding of content and its expressive appearance. As Arnheim notes, one should be aware that "there stands a policeman" and of "*how* he is standing" (my italics, Arnheim 1957a [1933]: 43). Film is a medium that displays both the generality and concreteness of the object filmed. A shot of a policeman should bring out the most characteristic aspect of policemen in general, as well as the peculiar aspect of that policeman. A carefully chosen angle will enable the viewer to see the unfamiliar within the familiar.

Arnheim's expressionist aesthetics, however, is heavily circumscribed by "naturalism." Film art is not an imitation but a transformation of nature: it "strengthens," "concentrates," and "interprets," but not to the extent that it completely "restructures" nature or imposes a new reality (Arnheim 1957a [1933]: 35, 57). With his emphasis on "nature," Arnheim does not align himself with any specific artistic movement, but rather uses it as an umbrella term, encompassing both his ontological assumptions about the medium and a general aesthetic principle. Arnheim views art as being located somewhere between nature and a complete replica of nature (the complete cinema). In order to be art, film should explore and foreground the formal as well as phenomenal gap between nature and film. But film still should remain faithful to nature. In his analyses of *Entr'acte* (1924), Arnheim claims that a shot of a dancer taken through the glass floor merely foregrounds the formal similarity between the dancer's tutu and a flower petal without increasing an artistic value of the film. Arnheim observes that Carl Theodor Dreyer's treatment of the court scene in *The*

Passion of Joan of Arc (1928) may be visually stimulating in an otherwise monotonous scene, but the camera angles are utterly unmotivated.

Arnheim raises a similar yet different criticism against the Soviet montage filmmakers, including V. I. Pudovkin and Sergei Eisenstein, for their use of intellectual montage. Some cases of intellectual montage "violate" reality by breaking both the narrative and spatial unity. In Pudovkin's *Mother* (1926), after the mother visits her imprisoned son, his hope of being rescued is expressed by a juxtaposition of shots of him in jail with images of children playing on the field and of ice thawing on a river. According to Arnheim:

> Putting actual pictures in juxtaposition, especially in an otherwise realistic film, often appears forced. The unity of the scene, the story of the prisoner who is rejoicing is suddenly interrupted by something totally different. Comparisons and associations like the brook and the sunbeams are not lightly touched upon in the abstract but are introduced as concrete pieces of nature – and hence are distracting. (Arnheim 1957a [1933]: 90)

Comparing intellectual montage with poetry, Arnheim claims that it is more challenging for the visual medium to convey abstract ideas than the verbal medium. The verbal medium readily allows a conceptual link between formally discrete ideas, due to their weak mental imageries. The concreteness of filmic images, however, would resist such an imposed unity.

Interestingly enough, Arnheim evaluates somewhat differently Eisenstein's use of intellectual montage in *The Battleship Potemkin* (1925). Although the stone lions seem to rise to roar through the juxtapositions of three successive shots of the three different statues, the apparent unity of the action created by montage is strong enough to make the montage convincing (Arnheim 1957a [1933]: 100). Arnheim does welcome the evocation of an abstract idea through cinematic means, insofar as it does not break the illusion of unity or produces the illusion of *a* reality. Arnheim praises the ingenuity of Chaplin's performance in *The Gold Rush* (1925), in the scene where Chaplin eats his boiled boot and shoelace as if it is a proper meal. Chaplin's performance effects the kind of expressive engagement with perceptual reality via a formal analogy manifest in the scene; it successfully translates the idea that poverty is a low grade of wealth through the formal similarity between the meal that Chaplin seemingly enjoys and a meal that the rich would consume (Arnheim 1957a [1933]: 144–5).

For Arnheim, film is first and foremost a visual medium. Although the artistic effects of the medium should be found in its departure from reality, film cannot completely do away with it. It is no surprise, then, that animation, which does not have any link to reality, is completely deleted from Arnheim's discussion of film art. However, one must note that Arnheim's criticisms of certain types of films or style, including abstract film and intellectual montage, are derived not only from his ontological assumption about the medium but also from the aesthetic code in art. Although Arnheim attempts to draw out a "naturalistic" aesthetic from the cinema's ontological commitment to reality, he equivocates on two different meanings of "natural": (i) natural in the sense that it is faithful to reality; and (ii) natural in the sense that it is "subtle" and "indirect." The latter sense of natural becomes apparent in his discussion of film acting.

Arnheim prefers "natural" acting to stylized silent acting. Cinema requires a type of acting different from what is desirable in theater, since the size of screen – and the close-up – increases the legibility of character action. According to Arnheim, everyday actions and gestures are often indeterminate, with their meanings assessed by recourse to the context. In contrast, film acting and gestures contain precision and clarity to the extent that they may be viewed as unnatural. "Naturalness" is a relative concept for Arnheim, judged in the light of convention. An appropriate acting style in slapstick comedy might be unsuitable for melodrama. Nevertheless, argues Arnheim, facial expressions and physical gestures should not be prioritized and serve only as one of the many ways in which character psychology is conveyed. In Les Nouveaux Messieurs (1929), for instance, Suzanne spills tea on the saucer when she learns that her lover will be transported abroad. As the simple phrase "That day we read no more" in Dante's The Inferno, condenses the love affair of Francesca and Paolo, Suzanne's behavior indirectly indicates her surprise and disappointment (Arnheim 1957a [1933]: 107, 142).

The indirect visual method that Arnheim endorses is, in part, possible by virtue of the cinematic devices – the close-up and framing. Inanimate objects can bear as much significance as actors do, as a result of the film's capacity to direct the viewer's attention to any element of mise en scène. But Arnheim's predilection for such an aesthetics does not necessarily result from the material base of the medium. Rather, Arnheim's approach to film aesthetics is deductive in the sense that he postulates a certain function and the principles of art in general, and then shows how film can meet such standards. Such an approach, however, has the risk of begging the question. One may legitimately challenge Arnheim's philosophical premises: Why is expression the principal function of all art? To what extent does the indirect visual method enhance such a function? The burden of proof is on Arnheim (Carroll 1988), and it seems fair to add that he did not ultimately shoulder that burden.

So far, we have examined how Arnheim builds his aesthetic theory of film on the medium-specific elements. As each artistic medium employs a distinct material, film should explore its material for artistic purposes. In the next section, I focus on Arnheim's conception of the "complete cinema," which is a neglected alternative to Bazin's (1967 [1945]) idea of the "total cinema." To what extent does the development of film technology circumscribe the artistic potential of the film medium? To what extent does Arnheim's rejection of the complete cinema further illuminate his film theory?

The notion of the complete cinema

The pursuit of the complete cinema, according to Arnheim, is a natural outcome of "the fulfillment of the age-old striving for the complete illusion" (Arnheim 1957a [1933]: 158). Technological developments would bring the film medium closer and closer to an exact reproduction of reality. Arnheim acknowledges that the history of visual art has been driven by the desire to create a replica of reality – what Bazin later calls the "mummy" complex, an impulse to immortalize an appearance against the passage of time (Bazin 1967 [1945]: 9). At the same time, he claims, there has been a countertendency "to originate, to interpret, to mold" (Arnheim 1957a [1933]: 157). But Arnheim is not concerned with whether the mimetic desire or the expressive tendency provides a better psychological explanation of the evolution of the visual art. His point is rather that in the case of film, the two are often in conflict, with the mimetic desire deterring filmmakers from exploring the expressive qualities of the medium.

Technological developments will enhance the medium's capacity to imitate nature. And the narrower is the gap between the filmic reproduction and reality, the slimmer are the chances for film to become an art. Arnheim's concern, however, is not that the introduction of technologies like sound, color, and widescreen will remove some of the constraints embedded in the medium. One should recall that, for Arnheim, technological imperfections manifest in the film medium are not, in and of themselves, aesthetic merits: instead they *can* be employed to produce artistic effects. Any technological novelty has its material constraints, and filmmakers can develop a new set of relationships between a newly developed device and the existing ones. Arnheim even grants an artistic possibility to sound film, although of an accidental kind. "By sheer good luck, sound film is not only destructive but also offers artistic potentialities of its own" (Arnheim 1957a [1933]: 154). Arnheim's rejection of sound films is based on both industry and aesthetic grounds. I will discuss the industry reason first, and the aesthetic one later.

Arnheim argues that when the sound film becomes the industry norm, there will be no room for the silent cinema to exist alongside the sound film (Arnheim 1957a [1933]: 159). This claim is a reflection on the practices of the film industry in general, but also has an aesthetic consequence. Arnheim argues that so long as silent film, sound film, and complete film can coexist, there is nothing inherently deplorable about the invention of the complete cinema. It can serve a function different from that of the silent cinema – such as filming a stage play. But the coming of sound has an aesthetic consequence as well, since it will alter the viewer's criteria for assessing the "naturalistic" film. As I have mentioned earlier, Arnheim construes "naturalness" as a relative concept. The viewer's conception of the natural would change in accordance with the introduction of new technologies. Sound film would make silent film feel artificial, as color film would make black-and-white film look unnatural (Arnheim 1957a [1933]: 160).

Arnheim's resistance to sound film is deep-seated and grounded in his conviction that film is a visual medium and that the introduction of sound will hamper the medium from expanding its expressive qualities. In his article entitled "A New Laocoön," Arnheim considers the artistic potentials of the hybrid arts, through which he attempts to demonstrate that sound film curtails, rather than strengthens, the aesthetic merits of the medium. Arnheim asserts that unlike human expression, which is anchored on the biological unity of a person, hybrid arts lack such a center.

The combination of two sensory modes – for instance, dance and music, or visual action and dialogue – does not automatically guarantee the artistic unity of a work. Artistic unity, according to Arnheim, is achieved at the secondary level, which presupposes both the separation and parallel between multimedia at a lower level. The fusion of two distinct media can be obtained by virtue of the expressive structure shared between the two modes. For instance, sadness of a dance can be expressed and enhanced through the perceptual kinship between the patterns of bodily movements and those of the melody. The two modes complement, yet reinforce the intended effect.

Sound film does satisfy the preconditions necessary for artistic unity. But Arnheim underlines the serious artistic drawbacks of sound film. First, film will lose the status of an independent art, indistinguishable from theater. One of the major differences between theater and film, according to Arnheim, is found in their principal material: the former is a verbal medium, while the latter is a visual medium. Even within the so-called hybrid art, they can be distinguished from one another by virtue of the "dominant medium" (Arnheim 1957b [1938]: 223) that's in place. In opera, although it incorporates dialogue, music still is its dominant form; in theater, it is the dialogue; and in film, visual action. But if both theater and film employ dialogue and visual action, the difference between the two will be a matter of degree, rather than of kind. Theater can use film projection as a backdrop, or emulate the traveling shot via rotating stages. Arnheim is concerned that dialogue in sound film would turn film into a verbal medium, diverting the viewer's attention from the visual components to the source of sound. Dialogue would center the action on the human figure, and the "homogeneous" relationship held between human figure and inanimate objects in the silent cinema would disappear with the coming of sound (Arnheim 1957b [1938]: 237).

Arnheim's approach to sound film is problematic on several grounds. He implicitly postulates a hierarchy among the characteristics of the medium. For example, cinematographic qualities – the effects produced through the camera – seem to bear more significance for Arnheim than the effects produced through means such as setting, costume, or even color. A quick look at the reason why Arnheim does not welcome color film will illustrate this point. Arnheim denies the artistic potential of color film, not only because they approximate reality more than black-and-white film, but also because the former decreases the artistic possibilities of the medium as a result of its lack of the homogeneity and harmony manifest in the latter (Arnheim 1997 [1935]: 19–20). Filmmakers' artistic freedom can be achieved only through the choice and configuration of color through *mise en scène*. Such a process, claims Arnheim, is merely a "transposition," not a "transformation," of reality (Arnheim 1957a [1933]: 155), and later discarded as inessential to the medium (Arnheim 1957b [1938]: 212).

Arnheim's adherence to the silent cinema reveals his conviction that each medium has one essence and that each medium should pursue its purest form in order to become an independent art. But the very assumption that Arnheim's theory operates on is questionable. Why is only "one" predominant medium assigned to each art form? The medium-specificity thesis can still be defended through a relational approach, instead of isolating the dominant medium in each art. The way image and sound are coordinated in film differs from that of theater or opera. Or one can further argue that the essence of the film medium can be found in its very hybridity of the multimedia.

One may find Arnheim's film theory rather extreme, given his rejection of all the subsequent cinematic forms after silent cinema. However, the significance of his theory lies in his attempt to systematically build a film theory based on film materials and to locate the source of artistic potentials in the very limitations of the medium. Although it is hard to find among contemporary film theorists a direct descendent of Arnheim, the heritage of Arnheim's gestalt theory can be found within the cognitive film theorists such as David Bordwell and Noël Carroll, who focus on how film form engages the perceptual and conceptual mechanisms of the viewer.

See also Film as art (Chapter 11), Medium (Chapter 16), and Sergei Eisenstein (Chapter 35).

References

Andrew, D. (1976) *The Major Film Theories*, London: Oxford University Press.
Arnheim, R. (1957a [1933]) "Film," in *Film as Art*, Berkeley: University of California Press.
—— (1957b [1938]) "A New Laocoön: Artistic Composites and the Talking Film," in *Film as Art*, Berkeley: University of California Press.
—— (1957c) "A Personal Note," in *Film as Art*, Berkeley: University of California Press.
—— (1974) *Art and Visual Perception*, Berkeley: University of California Press.
—— (1997 [1935]) "Remarks on Color Film," in *Film Essays and Criticism*, Madison: University of Wisconsin Press.
Bazin, A. (1967 [1945]) "The Ontology of the Photographic Image," in H. Gray (trans.) *What Is Cinema?*, vol. 1, Berkeley: University of California Press.
Carroll, N. (1988) *Philosophical Problems of Classical Film Theory*, Princeton, NJ: Princeton University Press.
Elster, J. (2000). *Ulysses Unbound: Study of Rationality, Precommitment and Constraints*, Cambridge: Cambridge University Press.

Further reading

Noël Carroll, "Medium Specificity Arguments and the Self-Consciously Invented Arts: Film, Video and Photography," in *Theorizing the Moving Image* (Cambridge: Cambridge University Press, 1996), examines the role of the medium-specificity thesis in emerging arts; Carroll's "The Specificity of Media in the Arts," in the same volume, gives a critique of the medium-specificity thesis. Jon Elster, "Less is More: Creativity and Constraints in the Arts," in *Ulysses Unbound* (Cambridge: Cambridge University Press, 2000), analyzes the aesthetics of constraints in the creation of artwork.

28

WALTER BENJAMIN

Stéphane Symons

The work of the German philosopher Walter Benjamin (1892–1940) ranges from art-theoretical books on German romanticism and the baroque tragic drama to an unfinished study on nineteenth-century Paris and religiously inspired and politically oriented writings. His overall philosophy was influenced by intellectual sources as diverse as Jewish messianism, historical materialism, modernism and surrealism. The texts he devoted to the topic of cinema are an illustration of this "Janus face" (Scholem 1981: 197) and remain remarkable in their capacity to combine an overall Marxist perspective with insights on the nature and reception of films relevant outside the Marxist political framework.

Early views on cinema

Around January–March 1927, during and immediately after a stay in Moscow, Walter Benjamin wrote two short essays devoted to Russian Revolutionary cinema. Preceding Benjamin's famous essay, "The Work of Art in the Era of Its Mechanical Reproducibility," by almost nine years, these early essays already contain some of the most important features of Benjamin's later, more systematically elaborated views on film in general. In his defense of *The Battleship Potemkin* (1925), for instance, Benjamin likens technical revolutions to "fracture points of artistic development" which bring out, like "deeper rock strata," tendencies that had up to then remained locked up (Benjamin 1999b: 17). Describing film as one of the most "dramatic" of these "points of fracture in artistic formations" (Benjamin 1999b: 17), he is clearly, in the first instance, interested in the potential of cinema as a *technological* invention, rather than as a purely artistic medium that could be believed to show beauty or to express emotions and ideas: "[T]he vital, fundamental advances in art are a matter neither of new content nor of new forms – the technological revolution takes precedence over both" (Benjamin 1999b: 17). On this level, i.e., reduced to the result of a purely mechanical process, film does not essentially differ from the entity that, at a pace of twenty-four frames per second, makes up its material support: the photograph. Benjamin adheres to the theory of realism in that he maintains that mechanically produced images are capable of rendering an immediate depiction of outside reality: "[F]ilm is the prism in which the spaces of the immediate environment – the spaces in which people live, pursue their avocations, and enjoy their leisure – are laid open before their eyes in a comprehensible, meaningful, and passionate way" (Benjamin 1999b: 17).

Benjamin's realist framework is tantamount to a discovery of cinema as a means of political consciousness-raising. This is on account of a supposed link between the mechanical essence of film, on the one hand, and the cause of the worker, on the other: the immediate representation of reality by the former is precisely what exposes the social and economic situation of the latter and should thus inspire people to political action. "[T]he complicity of film technique with the milieu that essentially constitutes a standing rebuke to it is incompatible with the glorification of the bourgeoisie" (Benjamin 1999b: 18). Film reveals the proletariat to be "the hero of those spaces" because it reveals "those spaces" for their part to be "collective spaces" (Benjamin 1999b: 18). What establishes this connection between film and the workers, and thus turns cinema into a tool for communist politics, is technology. In his review of *Potemkin* Benjamin does not just draw attention to the *nature* of film in general as a technological artifact, but to those genres (not only Russian Revolutionary film but also the American slapstick comedy) that *depict* the development and use of technology: "The obverse of a ludicrously liberated technology is the lethal power of naval squadrons on maneuver, as we see it openly displayed in *Potemkin*" (Benjamin 1999b: 17). The reason why film is a privileged medium to illuminate the situation of the worker is that it shares in the reality that it depicts: the outcome of the technological accomplishment to render a perfectly accurate representation of reality is a revelation of this reality as itself deeply penetrated by technology.

As an instrument for political consciousness-raising, film does not only express the modern, i.e., technological, mode of production, but it also exposes the social exploitation and psychological alienation that are, from a Marxist perspective, thought to be inherent in it. In the essays of 1927, Benjamin focuses on film as a mixture of both technology and art, capable of analyzing the truth about modern society and capitalist production in a scientific manner. The mechanical nature of cinema is here deemed important because it makes it possible to lay bare the *universal* social, economic, and psychological laws that are at work behind outside reality. It is for this reason that Benjamin considers the protagonists of *Potemkin* to be types, rather than historical individuals, i.e., transindividual subjects, with actions and ideas that cannot be understood independently of the societal framework in which they occur. "There is nothing feebler," writes Benjamin,

> than all the talk of "individual cases." The individual may be an individual case – but the uninhibited effects of his diabolical behavior are something else; they lie in the nature of the imperialist state and – within limits – the state as such. It is well known that many facts gain their meaning, their relief, only when they are put in context. (Benjamin 1999b: 18)

Benjamin's analysis, in 1927, of cinema as a political tool is based not only on this idea that film delivered an inherently new, i.e. mechanical and for that reason immediate, objective and scientific way of *representing* reality, but also on an intuition that film brought about a different manner of being *received*. In his mind, film is an innovative medium for both the artist and the spectator alike. That is, the perception of film is, first of all, *collective* and, second, from the start entangled with an initiation into *practice*. Benjamin rather optimistically announces that with cinema, a new collectivity takes shape: unlike traditional forms of art, film does not appeal to the individual in any private or museum-like isolated space, but brings about a public sphere of its own, thus reaching entire groups of people at a time. It is for this reason that in his essay "On the Present Situation of Russian Film," Benjamin applauds the *Wanderkinos*, or traveling cinemas, that go out to meet their audience in its own environment ("With our faces toward the village!" [Benjamin 1999b: 14]). In the same vein, he stresses the task of cinema to render workers politically active and to teach them how to come to terms with their place in the production process.

Later views on cinema

Throughout the thirties, Benjamin continued to think and write about the issue of mechanically produced art and the features that are supposed to be characteristic of it. In a 1931 text on early photography, he asserts that "[n]o matter how artful the photographer, no matter how carefully posed his subject, the beholder feels an irresistible urge to search such a picture for the tiny spark of contingency, of the here and now with which reality has (so to speak) seared the subject" (Benjamin 1999b: 510). This statement illustrates another side of the realist framework adhered to by Benjamin. What strikes his eye when seeing mechanically produced images is now not so much the scientifically laid out, universal laws at work "behind" outside reality as the details, singularities, and even "contingencies" that can be discovered within it. These lines betray the clear influence of his friend Siegfried Kracauer's 1927 article on photography. In that essay, Kracauer draws a connection between the "increasing independence of the technology" and a "simultaneous evacuation of meaning from the objects" (Kracauer 1995: 53), which makes photographs fascinating insofar as they lay bare precisely the sheer materiality and lack of scientific knowability of external reality. In Kracauer's view, photography explores the gap between meaning and world, disclosing a "ghostlike reality [that] is unredeemed ... consist[ing] of elements in space whose configuration is so far from necessary that one could just as well imagine a different organization of these elements" (Kracauer 1995: 56).

Benjamin's notion of the "optical unconscious" needs to be understood in relation to this context. Like Siegfried Kracauer, Benjamin maintains that "a different nature opens itself to the camera than [that which] opens to the naked eye – if only because an unconsciously penetrated space is substituted for a space consciously explored by man" (Benjamin 1999a: 230), thus clearing the path for the discovery of photographic images as media that not only *record* what is visible in reality but also – borrowing from Kracauer's later theory of cinema (see Kracauer 1997) – succeed in *revealing* what had hitherto gone unnoticed. "Even if one has a general knowledge of the way people walk," writes Benjamin, one knows nothing of a person's posture during the fractional second of a stride. The act of reaching for a lighter or a spoon is familiar routine, yet we hardly know what really goes on between hand and metal, not to mention how this fluctuates with our moods. Here the camera intervenes with the resources of its lowerings and liftings, its interruptions and isolations, its extensions and accelerations, its enlargements and reductions. The camera introduces us to unconscious optics as does psychoanalysis to unconscious impulses. (Benjamin 1999a: 230)

Characteristic of photographic images is that they are capable of blowing up the reality that they bear the traces of, both in the sense that they can magnify details that are invisible to the natural eye and in that they disrupt our spontaneous and unproblematic grasp of the outside world. This insight is Janus-faced. It means, on the one hand, that mechanically made images are for Benjamin not merely representations of outside reality, since they lay bare an alterity that seems to be at work in it: when seen through photographic images, the world becomes uncanny and symptomatic, having ceased to be always-already-meaningful. The images made by the French, nineteenth-century photographer Eugène Atget, for example, are likened to "scenes of crime ... deserted [and] photographed for the purpose of establishing evidence" (Benjamin 1999a: 220). In the view of Benjamin's friend and leading Frankfurt school philosopher, Theodor Adorno, this quality of the photographic image, i.e., its inability to sever its direct ties to outside reality, amounts to film's most "retarding aspect" (Adorno 1981/82: 202), since it makes it impossible for film to help spectators understand and criticize societal mechanisms: "Tending to reinforce, affirmatively, the phenomenal surface of society, realism dismisses any attempt to penetrate that surface as a romantic endeavor. Every meaning – including critical meaning – which the camera eye imparts to the film would already invalidate the law of the camera" (Adorno 1981/82: 202). Benjamin, however – and this is the other side of his notion of an optical unconscious – claims in his famous essay "The Work of Art in the Era of Its Mechanical Reproducibility" that this hitherto undiscovered dimension of reality does come together with a form of understanding, albeit an unpredictable and nonscientific one. The encounter with a reality that has only now become visible for the first time and is therefore not immediately perceived as meaningful entails for him not merely an experience of uncanniness, but also one of infinite possibility. "By close-ups of the things around us," writes Benjamin,

by focusing on hidden details of familiar objects, by exploring common place milieus under the ingenious guidance of the camera, the film, on the one hand, extends our comprehension of the necessities which rule our lives; on the other hand, it manages to assure us of an immense and unexpected field of action. (Benjamin 1999a: 229)

In a statement that he had already used, almost word by word, in his 1927 essay on *Potemkin*, he even goes as far as to link this renewed comprehension to a principle of hope, writing that

[o]ur taverns and our metropolitan streets, our offices and furnished rooms, our railroad stations and our factories appeared to have us locked up hopelessly. Then came the film and burst this prison-world asunder by the dynamite of the tenth of a second, so that now, in the midst of its far-flung ruins and debris, we calmly and adventurously go traveling. (Benjamin 1999a: 229)

What these words aim at now, however, is much more closely related to what Kracauer will, almost twenty-five years later, call a "redemption of physical reality" (Kracauer 1997) than to the rather naïve trust in a Marxist scientific rendition of laws and truths that Benjamin still seemed to endorse in 1927. In the opinion of both Kracauer and the Benjamin of the thirties, the cinematographic representation of a brute, i.e., unredeemed, reality is itself tantamount to the latter's redemption, since it restores our faith in it: mechanically produced images bring on display a richness in the world that continuously surpasses our expectations of it.

The idea that mechanically produced images redeem the world from its hopelessness by bringing out an unexpected form of comprehension is central to Benjamin's views on montage. In a 1930 review of Döblin's novel *Berlin Alexanderplatz*, he interprets montage as a means of revealing, within the very particularity and contingency of the outside world, a hitherto undiscovered order. "The material of the montage," writes Benjamin, "is anything but arbitrary. Authentic montage is based on the document. In its fanatical struggle with the work of art, Dadaism used montage to turn daily life into its ally ... The film at its best moments made as if to accustom us to montage" (Benjamin 1999b: 301). Montage is crucial in that it allows, according to Benjamin, the very *fragmentation* of our immediate understanding of outside reality to go hand in hand with the discovery of a new layer of *meaning* in these fragments. This idea will be severely criticized by Adorno in his 1966 essay "Transparencies on Film":

> Pure montage, without the addition of intentionality in its elements, does not derive intention merely from the principle itself. It seems illusory to claim that through the renunciation of all meaning, especially the cinematically inherent renunciation of psychology, meaning will emerge from the reproduced material itself. (Adorno 1981/82: 203)

The reasons for Benjamin's positive endorsement of montage, however, are made explicit in the above-mentioned photography essay, in the context of a brief discussion of Russian cinema. What becomes clear there is that, first, for Benjamin, the "hopelessness" in which we appear to have been "locked up" is due to a profound social crisis, and, second, that this social crisis is believed to remain unexpressed when it is merely *reflected* in imagination. Quoting from a text by his friend Bertolt Brecht, Benjamin writes that "[t]he reification of human relations – the factory, say – means that they are no longer explicit. So something must in fact be *built up*, something artificial, posed" (Benjamin 1999b: 526). In his opinion, Russian Revolutionary cinema is born from an awareness that it is experimentation, and not just immediate representation, which unmasks social reality: if it *instructs* about the social crisis, it is only because it *constructs* the image of reality anew through montage. The extended "comprehension of the necessities which rule our lives" and the "immense and unexpected field of action" (Benjamin 1999a: 229) that film will four years later, in the artwork essay, be credited with are thus first and foremost to be thought of in a communist-inspired, political sense. In Benjamin's view, it is only montage which allows cinema to ruthlessly expose the exploitation of the workers in a capitalist society and, moreover, to rearrange this material in such a way as to reveal how it might be abolished. It is on account of this two-sidedness – film stimulates comprehension *and* action – that he emphasizes, in the preface and epilogue of the artwork essay, that his ideas are "completely useless for the purposes of Fascism" and "on the other hand, useful for the formulation of revolutionary demands in the politics of art" (Benjamin 1999a: 212). His theses on a politicized aesthetics are meant as nothing less than an antidote against the fascist aestheticization of politics: in opposition to the latter's attempts to "organize the newly created proletarian masses without affecting the property structure which the masses strive to eliminate" (Benjamin 1999a: 234), Benjamin has clearly chosen the side of the revolutionary, seeking to understand the structure of capitalism only because he struggles to overthrow it.

The connection between cinema and politics that Benjamin had already established in 1927 is thus rendered more substantial in his writings from the thirties. The middle term which then allowed photographic images in general to become visible as indispensable allies to the revolutionary forces – their technological nature – is now further elaborated on through a discussion of the characteristically cinematographic procedure of montage. It is the first and second versions of the "Artwork" essay which explain most explicitly why it is exactly that this mounted or constructed nature of film can come together with both a new "comprehension" of, and "action" against, the flaws of capitalism. For Benjamin cinema is a privileged tool for communist politics because its very manner of being produced lays bare the essence of industrial capitalism: like mass-produced goods on a conveyor belt, films are assembled from different elements (shots) that will derive their meaning only from the context of the finished product. In a handful of paragraphs left out of later versions of the essay, Benjamin states that films only become artworks on account of montage, "[a]nd each individual component of this montage is a reproduction of a process which neither is an artwork in itself nor gives rise to one through photography" (Benjamin 2002: 110). The emancipatory potential of films, in other words, no longer revolves around their material support (photographic images that are supposed to represent reality in an immediate and scientific way), nor around their content (see, e.g., the educational value of the Russian *Wanderkinos*) but, in the first instance, around their form. For Benjamin, montage marks films with the same irreducible "capacity for improvement" (Benjamin 2002: 109) which characterizes all commodities as such, and cannot but destroy the traditional artistic aim of the production of "eternal value" (Benjamin 2002: 109).

The first and foremost consequence of this assembled structure of all films is that it is no longer the film actor alone who is responsible for his performance. He or she "performs not in front of an audience but in front of an apparatus" (Benjamin 2002:

111); performers are therefore doomed to become separated from the result of their acting, since the material that was shot in the studio is immediately handed over to a crew of producers who go on to finish the film on their own account. It is for this reason that Benjamin likens the performance by the film actor to the alienating experience of being "tested" in front of a mass audience that is, at the time of filming, yet to become visible:

> [N]ow the mirror image [*Bild*] has become detachable from the person mirrored, and is transportable. And where is it transported? To a site in front of the masses ... While he stands before the apparatus, [the film actor] knows that in the end he is confronting the masses. It is they who will control him. (Benjamin 2002: 113, see 1991b: 369–70)

In Benjamin's universe, the film actor figures among those typically modern personae that manage to retain their humanity in the face of a profoundly alienating world: like the flaneur, the collector, or the rag picker, the film actor refuses to repress the fragmentized state of his experience-world and succeeds in making it meaningful. Benjamin maintains that, in contrast to the stage actor, the film actor is denied the opportunity to identify himself with the character of his role and finds himself compelled to "operate with his whole living person" (Benjamin 2002: 112). Under the influence of Brechtian views on acting, Benjamin claims that, rather than attempting to understand the psyche of his character in order to "become one with it," the film actor ought to explore the possibilities of what is most properly his own, namely, his body. Having thus voluntarily surrendered himself to the naked eye of the camera, this body is to be brought on display as a mere prop. Benjamin credits film with an extended "comprehension of the necessities which rule our lives" (Benjamin 1999a: 229) because he sees the estrangement felt by the film actor in front of the machine as nothing less than an exemplification of the most common experience of the industrial worker: "The representation of human beings by means of an apparatus has made possible a highly productive use of the human being's self-alienation" (Benjamin 2002: 113). Following up on Marx's views on modern industry, Benjamin reads capitalism as a universe in which human beings have lost all overview on the production process and, not being able to follow the hellish rhythm of the machine, are forced to undergo an unceasing series of "tests." The inability of the film actor to "[oversee] the context in which his own test is exercised" (Benjamin 1991a: 453) is therefore, in Benjamin's mind, both an expression of the alienated condition of the modern laborer and an aid, for the latter, to come to terms with it:

> Film makes test performances capable of being exhibited, by turning that ability itself into a test ... [T]he majority of citydwellers, throughout the workday in offices and factories, have to relinquish their humanity in the face of an apparatus. In the evening these same masses fill the cinemas, to witness the film actor taking revenge on their behalf not only by asserting *his* humanity (or what appears to them as such) against the apparatus, but by placing that apparatus in the service of his triumph. (Benjamin 2002: 111)

Benjamin's views on cinema from the thirties testify to the same dual focus that was already present in the 1927 essays: film is in his opinion innovative not merely because it entails a wholly new way of *representing* reality, but also because it brings about a revolutionary manner of being *perceived*. If, for Benjamin, the "primary question" is not "whether photography is an art" but "whether the very invention of photography had not transformed the entire nature of art" (Benjamin 1999a: 220), it is precisely because the photographic/cinematographic, i.e., immediate, way of representing reality only allows for a response that is no less immediate. (In this vein, Benjamin asserts that "The painter maintains in his work a natural distance from reality, the cameraman penetrates deeply into its web" [Benjamin 1999a: 227].) In the first version of the artwork essay, Benjamin defines "the historic task, in the service of which film reaches its true meaning" as follows: "to make the colossal technical apparatus of our time the object of human innervation" (Benjamin 1991a: 445). Though this notion of "innervation" will disappear from later versions of the essay, including the fourth and, in Miriam Hansen's words, "dubiously canonic" one (Hansen 1999: 314), what it refers to is of crucial importance to an understanding of Benjamin's views on cinema. The statement that films *innervate* the spectator, i.e. have a direct, mobilizing influence upon his entire physical presence, is meant to illustrate the idea that their reception *is* itself already a form of political action, rather than – as seemed to be the argument in 1927 – an event that could possibly *lead* to political action. Susan Buck-Morss has described innervation most accurately as "a mimetic reception of the external world, one that is empowering, in contrast to a defensive mimetic adaptation that protects at the price of paralyzing the organism, robbing it of its capacity of imagination, and therefore of active response" (Buck-Morss 1992: 17n54). The references of the concept of innervation within philosophy and aesthetics are multiple, ranging from Freudian psychoanalysis to Eisensteinian reception theory, but what matters here is that it denotes a form of experience in which external stimuli (in this case photographic and cinematographic images) reach the spectator in such a direct way that they bypass the reflective process pure and proper. Referring to the photographs of Eugène Atget, for example, Benjamin writes that they "demand a specific kind of approach: free-floating contemplation is not appropriate to them. They stir the viewer; he feels challenged by them in a new way" (Benjamin 1999a: 220). In his opinion, the Dadaist work of art already appealed to a form of perception that is characteristically cinematographic in that it aimed for an immediate impact on the viewer's emotions, thoughts, and bodily behavior: "[The Dadaist work of art] hit the spectator like a bullet, it happened to him, thus acquiring a tactile quality" (Benjamin 1999a: 231). On account of the movement of its images, the reception of a film even surpasses that of a Dadaist work of art in its immediacy: films force their rhythm upon the viewer's sensory apparatus, thereby preventing him from reaching a frame of mind in which he isolates himself through contemplation. "The spectator's process of association in view of these [cinematographic] images," writes Benjamin, "is ... interrupted by their constant, sudden change. This constitutes the shock effect of the film, which, like all shocks, should be cushioned by heightened presence of mind" (Benjamin 1999a: 231–2).

The artwork essay retained the emphasis on the collective character of the reception of films that was already present in 1927, but the focus on the cinematographic image as a vehicle for knowledge has shifted to its discovery, as a means for what he terms "tactile appropriation" (Benjamin 1999a: 233). Benjamin diagnoses modern capitalism with an "emancipated technology [that] stands opposed to today's society as a second nature" (Benjamin 1991a: 444) which cannot any longer be mastered by man and which will therefore, ultimately, end up destroying mankind as such. Even so, however severe the symptoms of this modern malaise might be (Benjamin mentions "economic crises" and "wars" [Benjamin 1991a: 444]) a cure is not deemed impossible and, moreover, this solution is thought to lie contained within a renewed practice of technology itself. Films contribute to such an "instruction" (Benjamin 1991a: 444) to use technology as a reconciliation with, rather than as an alienation from, the environment: "The function of film is to train human beings in the apperceptions and reactions needed to deal with a vast apparatus whose role in their lives is expanding almost daily" (Benjamin 2002: 108). No doubt influenced by both the religious views on a redeemed universe of his friend and Kabbalah-specialist Gershom Scholem and the writings of the utopian socialists that he was reading at the time, Benjamin focuses on film as a manifestation of a "second" technology that "aims ... at an interplay between nature and humanity" (Benjamin 2002: 107). Cinema is here believed to help humanity reach the understanding that it ought not to try to dominate nature, since a revolutionary use of machines – through, e.g., mimetic practice, childlike play or improvisation – will realize the promise of a better world. Gertrud Koch therefore maintains that Benjamin endows the camera with a "Messianic-prophetic power" (Koch 1994: 210) that permits us "to forget anthropological lack" (Koch 1994: 209), whereas Miriam Bratu Hansen focuses on its ability to "unhinge experience and agency from anthropomorphic identity ... thus resum[ing] Fourier's project of 'cracking the teleology of nature'" (Hansen 1999: 323). In line with Kracauer's positive valuation, almost ten years earlier, of a "cult of distraction" which "convey[s] precisely and openly to thousands of eyes and ears the disorder of society" and thus "enable[s] them to evoke and maintain the tension that must precede the inevitable and radical change" (Kracauer 1995: 327), Benjamin claims that cinema disrupts the reactionary attitude of concentration and absorption through which classical works of art are received, replacing it with a not entirely cognitive formation of practical habits. In his opinion, films are like buildings in that they are, unlike paintings or theater, perceived in an absent-minded manner that appeals to both touch and sight and not in an attentive and merely optical one. It is for this reason that the movie theater is comparable to a training ground or rehearsal room for a nonalienating and creative mastery of machines. "The distracted person, too" writes Benjamin,

> can form habits. More, the ability to master certain tasks in a state of distraction proves that their solution has become a matter of habit. Distraction as provided by art presents a covert control of the extent to which new tasks have become soluble by apperception. Since, moreover, individuals

are tempted to avoid such tasks, art will tackle the most difficult and most important ones where it is able to mobilize the masses. Today it does so in the film. (Benjamin 1999a: 233)

The political relevance of cinema, however, can only be fully understood if films are not merely seen as the *cause* of a profound innovation of human perception but also as an *effect* of it. Benjamin's artwork essay is an assessment of what he elsewhere termed the "specific historical label" (Benjamin 1999a: 154) of human memory and, as such, an extensive elaboration of the statement that "the manner in which human sense perception is organized, the medium in which it is accomplished, is determined not only by nature but by historical circumstances as well" (Benjamin 1999a: 216). Retaining from Marx both the distinction between substructure and superstructure and the basic insight that it is the former which conditions the latter, Benjamin claims that the sensory apparatus of human beings is, no less than their artistic expression itself, to be understood as profoundly affected by the mode of production predominant in a specific society. Benjamin's famous statement that, in late modernity, human sense perception has become marked by a "desire ... to bring things 'closer' spatially and humanly" and a "bent toward overcoming the uniqueness of every reality by accepting its reproduction" (Benjamin 1999a: 217) is thus best understood as following from his views on the economic system that governed throughout that era: industrial capitalism. The ceaseless confrontation with mass-produced goods is believed to have affected the sensory apparatus of contemporary masses to such an extent that they have become oblivious to all sense of uniqueness. For Benjamin, the mass distribution of mechanically made art reproductions, e.g., photographs of paintings reprinted in art catalogues, is one of the most obvious symptoms of such a modern "poverty of experience." For what gets lost with the socially conditioned transformation of the human faculty of sense perception is the capacity to experience the remarkable constellation of distance, authority, and authenticity that he so famously termed "aura" (Benjamin 1999a: 215–17). Original artworks are believed to bring about a sensation of a "distance, however close it may be" (Benjamin 1999a: 216) that is tied to their unique existence and physical presence and therefore falls outside of the scope of reproducibility. Unlike manually made reproductions, technical reproductions gain an independence over the original, "substitut[ing] a plurality of copies for a unique existence" (Benjamin 1999a: 215) and thus transforming the art experience from within. With the destruction of the aura, to be understood as both a physical distance (the traditional artwork cannot be touched) and as a spiritual one (it comes together with a claim of wisdom), art is released from its embedment in tradition, religion, or cult but, by the same token, exposed as fully rooted in immanent societal processes. Moreover, since in mechanically produced art, e.g., artistic photography and cinema, the very distinction between original and copy has become almost entirely redundant, any cult value connected with a uniquely existing work of art has retreated, in favor of an enormous increase in social and political impact: "To an ever greater degree the work of art reproduced becomes the work of art designed for reproducibility" (Benjamin 1999a: 218).

This side of Benjamin's philosophy of cinema was meant to explain not only why films are deemed intrinsically valuable for all communist political goals, but also why they have not yet realized the utopian potential they are endowed with. As rooted in societal processes, that is to say, artworks can also be unmasked as expressions of what the Marxists have termed "false consciousness." Preceding Adorno and Horkheimer's analysis of the culture industry in *Dialectic of Enlightenment* (Adorno and Horkheimer 1997: 120–67) by nine years, the artwork essay already describes how, in late modernity, artworks themselves are being commodified and how they, when their production and mass distribution are in the hands of capital alone, end up being divested of their emancipatory features. "In western Europe today," writes Benjamin, "the capitalist exploitation of film obstructs the human being's legitimate claim to being reproduced ... [T]he film industry has an overriding interest in stimulating the involvement of the masses through illusionary displays and ambiguous speculations" (Benjamin 2002: 114). Through the exploitation of fake, auratic images (as in the star cult), an appeal to false forms of tradition and a revitalization of beautiful semblance, the film industry becomes serviceable for fascist aims, adding up to the alienated condition of the masses, instead of laying bare the social crisis that causes it.

Conclusion

In Benjamin's opinion the invention of the cinematographic image came together with an entirely new, immediate way of representing outside reality and the capacity, through montage, to reveal a hitherto undiscovered order in it. In addition to this, due to the public environment in which they are received and thanks to their quasi-infinite reproducibility, films were believed to have given shape to a new collectivity. With notions like the optical unconscious and innervation, Benjamin conceived of cinema as a medium that has modified the very nature of art, both on account of how it is produced and on account of how it is consumed. By thus combining the use of a realist framework to analyze the photographic image with an astute eye to the sociology of the reception of film, he cleared the path for two of the most influential strands of twentieth-century cinema studies. Although Benjamin's Marxist framework, realist assumptions, and emphasis on collective perception have lost some of their significance in an era in which digital (i.e., nonmimetic) technologies replace photographic images and the exposure to images takes place mainly in the private sphere of our living rooms, Benjamin's theory of cinema still provides insights into the nature of film that remain relevant, independent of his political conviction and historical context.

See also Realism (Chapter 22), Phenomenology (Chapter 40), and Medium (Chapter 16).

References

Adorno, T. (1981/82) "Transparencies on Film," trans. T. Y. Levin, *New German Critique* 24/25: 199–205.

Adorno, T., and Horkheimer, M. (1997) *Dialectic of Enlightenment*, trans. J. Cumming, London and New York: Verso.

Benjamin, W. (1991a) *Gesammelte Schriften*, vol. 1(2), eds. R. Tiedemann and H. Schweppenhäuser, Frankfurt am Main: Suhrkamp Verlag.

—— (1991b) *Gesammelte Schriften*, vol. 7(1), ed. R. Tiedemann and H. Schweppenhäuser, Frankfurt am Main: Suhrkamp Verlag.

—— (1999a) *Illuminations*, ed. Hannah Arendt; trans. H. Zorn, London: Pimlico.

—— (1999b) *Selected Writings*, vol. 2: 1927–34, ed. M. W. Jennings, H. Eiland, and G. Smith; trans. R. Livingstone *et al.* (various translators), Cambridge, MA and London: Belknap Press.

—— (2002) *Selected Writings*, vol. 3, 1935–8, ed. H. Eiland and M. W. Jennings; trans. E. Jephcott, H. Eiland *et al.* (various translators), Cambridge, MA and London: Belknap Press.

Buck-Morss, S. (1992) "Aesthetics and Anaesthetics: Walter Benjamin's Artwork Essay Reconsidered," *October* 62: 3–41.

Hansen, M. B. (1999) "Benjamin and Cinema: Not a One-Way Street," *Critical Inquiry* 25: 306–43.

Koch, G. (1994) "Cosmos in Film: On the Concept of Space in Walter Benjamin's 'Work of Art' Essay," in A. Benjamin and P. Osborne (eds.) *Walter Benjamin's Philosophy: Destruction and Experience*, London and New York: Routledge.

Kracauer, S. (1995) *The Mass Ornament: Weimar Essays*, ed. and trans. T. Y. Levin, Cambridge, MA: Harvard University Press.

—— (1997) *Theory of Film: The Redemption of Physical Reality*, Princeton, NJ: Princeton University Press.

Scholem, G. (1981) *Walter Benjamin: The Story of a Friendship*, trans. H. Zohn, New York: Schocken Books.

29

DAVID BORDWELL

Patrick Colm Hogan

David Bordwell was born on 23 July 1947. He received his BA in English from the State University of New York at Albany in 1969, then moved to the University of Iowa to pursue graduate work in Speech and Dramatic Arts with a concentration in Film. He received his PhD in 1974, completing a dissertation on French impressionist cinema (published in 1980). In 1997, he was awarded an honorary doctorate from the University of Copenhagen. After receiving his PhD, Bordwell taught in the Department of Communication Arts at the University of Wisconsin, Madison, retiring as Jacques Ledoux Professor of Film Studies. He has also been a visiting professor at New York University and the University of Iowa. Bordwell has received grants from the National Endowment for the Humanities, the American Council of Learned Societies, the Fulbright Foundation, and the Guggenheim Foundation. He earned two awards at the University of Wisconsin for excellence in teaching, as well as the Theatre Library Association Award for Outstanding Book in Film, Broadcasting, or Recorded Performance (for Bordwell 1993), the Anthology Film Archive Award for Film Preservation, and the Hong Kong Film Festival/Asian Film Forum Award for Excellence in Film Scholarship. He is the author or coauthor of sixteen books – with translations (published or forthcoming) into Chinese, Korean, Spanish, Hungarian, French, Persian, Italian, Slovenian, Greek, Japanese, Croatian, and Turkish – and over one hundred and thirty articles. He has been interviewed dozens of times for various media. He has delivered lecture series in Hong Kong, Beijing, Brussels, Budapest, Helsinki, Munich, Bruges, Cologne, and elsewhere – including the prestigious Gauss Seminars in Criticism at Princeton University. He is married to film critic, theorist, and historian, Kristin Thompson; they have collaborated on three books.

Along with Noël Carroll, Bordwell is widely considered to be one of the two major cognitive film theorists. Cognitive film theory draws on cognitive science and related fields to explore the creation, reception, structure, interpretation, and other aspects of film. However, only some of Bordwell's theoretical work is cognitive. He is also widely known as a formalist. "Formalism" is a fairly capacious term, including within its scope a range of theorists whose primary concerns are with literary "form" in some sense of the term. Paradigmatically, it refers to a set of theories developed in Russia and Eastern Europe in the early twentieth century. These theories treat a range of issues from the distinctiveness of poetic language to the narrative structure of folktales. Bordwell makes frequent reference to formalists. Moreover, he shares a deep and enduring interest in visual style in film (a rough parallel to the "literariness" of literary language) and narrative structure. However, Bordwell's intellectual formation took place in the context of structuralism and post-structuralism. One might argue that his work has a more consequential – and more illuminating – relation to that of such writers as Michel Foucault.

Beyond the large, theoretical issues of narrative (1985) and visual style (1997, 2001, 2005), Bordwell's writings range from analyses of national cinemas (American [Bordwell 1985, 2006], Hong Kong [Bordwell 2000]) to focused explorations of individual directors (Dreyer [Bordwell 1981, see also 1973], Ozu [Bordwell 1988], and Eisenstein [Bordwell 1993]). In addition, he has coauthored two textbooks, *Film Art* (Bordwell and Thompson 2006) and *Film History* (Thompson and Bordwell 2002). His most obviously philosophical book, *Making Meaning*, is also a major work of "metatheory" (theorization about film theories and criticism, rather than theorization about film *per se*).

Bordwell's discourse: a composite model

There is, of course, variety in the approaches and interests manifest in Bordwell's many writings. However, there is consistency as well. One way of organizing Bordwell's oeuvre is by separating the studies of individual directors from the treatments of broader patterns (e.g., in national cinemas). To use the structuralist division, we may say that the former are examinations of *speech*, while the latter focus on *language* – or, in a related terminology, *voice* and *discourse*. In this essay, I will concentrate on Bordwell's discursive studies, as they are more obviously relevant to philosophy.

As already suggested, one possible precursor for certain aspects of Bordwell's approach is Michel Foucault. Much of Bordwell's work involves analyzing how cinematic and critical practices are "discursively constructed" (Bordwell 1989: 205). Bordwell's discursive analyses recall Foucault, for they involve a non-Marxist and nonhermeneutic delimitation of institutionally defined discourses that constrain what topics are treated and how, who treats them through what apparatus, and so on, during specific historical periods. However, Bordwell places the phrase "discursively constructed" in scare quotes. As this suggests, Bordwell's analyses are not purely Foucauldian. First, they are inflected by a down-to-earth pragmatism. Bordwell repeatedly anchors the discourses of cinema in the problem-solving practicalities of real filmmaking. Bordwell also seems to accept a fairly sharp division between discourse – understood as an institutionally and to some extent arbitrarily constructed system of concepts, institutional positions, etc. – and science, understood (roughly) as complexes of empirically motivated hypotheses subjected to rigorous testing in the context of logically structured theories. Foucauldians, in contrast, commonly see sciences as prime instances of discourses. Of course, many writers adopt a position between these extremes – valuing scientific method as the only systematic way of improving our hypotheses, but simultaneously viewing the actual practice of science as pervaded by economic and ideological biases related to discrepancies in power. This leads to a final point of difference between Bordwell and Foucault. Power relations are central to Foucault's treatment of both discourse and institutions. However, Bordwell does not usually consider power, or other forms of stratification and struggle.

Leaving aside the specifics of his relation to Foucault, however, we might systematize and abstract from Bordwell's writings a general model for understanding film and "discursive construction" along the following lines.

First, every individual involved in the production or reception of films begins with a set of innate, evolutionary adaptations. These most obviously govern physiological processes such as perception. However, according to writers in evolutionary psychology, much admired by Bordwell, innate adaptations may govern a wide range of psychological tendencies.

Second, individuals producing and viewing films do so in the context of institutions, and do so during definable periods in the historical development of those institutions. On the productive side, these institutions (e.g., film studios) define tasks which generate problems in particular contexts. The tasks and problems may be divided into two categories, economic and aesthetic. Economic problems concern the film as an investment. By "aesthetic" problems, I do not mean problems of beauty or art, but simply problems relating to films as particular objects of experience. Bordwell tends to discuss aesthetic problems in terms of narrative (both the story itself and the techniques of presenting the story or "narration"), time, space, and style, particularly visual style. Most often, these aesthetic problems are, for Bordwell, a matter of communicating information, principally story information. Both economic and aesthetic problems arise at two levels. They arise at the systemic level as general issues of market structure or film technique and at the more specific level of daily, practical interactions, what Bordwell terms the "craft context" of the work.

Third, there are sets of devices – both conceptual and practical – that filmmakers employ to solve problems. The use of a device to respond to a problem gives that device a particular function. (Note that one problem may have several devices associated with it, and one device may be linked with several problems.) This analysis allows us to understand discourses in not only a (loosely) Foucauldian but also in cognitive way. Specifically, discourses have the following properties. They are complexes of conceptual and practical schemas. These schemas are employed by individuals located within institutions during particular historical periods. The schemas are used to resolve problems defined by practical situations. Finally, the situations generate problems only in the context of tasks set by the encompassing institutions during the relevant period. Note that, in filmmaking, the schemas necessarily incorporate technologies that allow the fulfillment of their functions. Technologies, then, are crucial here – not only to the implementation of a discourse in practice, but to its organization and conceptual specificity as well.

Finally, there are individual filmmakers operating on specific tasks in particular situations. Clearly, not all filmmakers are the same. So the question arises here as to just how they are different. Most often, individual differences are a matter of consistent patterns of selection within the options offered by the discourse. If the discourse allows a half dozen possible ways of resolving a particular problem (e.g.,

315

communicating story information in a dialogue), perhaps one filmmaker consistently chooses solutions based on editing, while another consistently chooses solutions based on staging. In some cases, however, filmmakers may go further. For example, an innovative filmmaker may combine available device-function pairs in new ways. Bordwell gives the example of Murnau's combination of shot–reverse shot (to indicate communication) with cross-cutting (to indicate simultaneity at a distance), when Murnau has the vampire turn away from his victim, as if he is responding to the cry of that victim's wife many miles away (Bordwell 1997: 152). A creative filmmaker might also draw devices and/or device-function pairings from other periods or traditions. (Such borrowing is possible, due to the cross-cultural constancies that result from human genetics, as well as to convergent social developments in diverse film traditions, termed "contingent universals" by Bordwell [1996].)

A fully developed Bordwellian account of a film, then, will involve the following:

1 The isolation of innate propensities relevant to the production and reception of film.
2 The analysis of institutional structures (in particular historical time periods) with their abstract/systemic and concrete/quotidian economic and aesthetic tasks and problems, particularly aesthetic problems of story, narration, time, space, and style.
3 The delimitation of conceptual devices, practical devices, and technologies available in those institutions during the relevant historical period, along with the mapping of devices onto problems (thus the assignment of functions to devices), often mediated by technologies.
4 The location of individual practices within this system and the explanation of apparent idiosyncrasy or creativity in terms of device/function alternatives offered within the system, the novel synthesis of already available device-function pairs, the borrowing of devices or device-function pairs from other traditions, etc.

An exemplary text on film

As already noted, Bordwell has published sixteen books. It is not possible to survey such a body of work in a short essay. In this section, then, I will consider one work that adheres well to the preceding model – *The Classical Hollywood Cinema: Film Style and Mode of Production to 1960* (Bordwell et al. 1985), coauthored with Janet Staiger and Kristin Thompson. I will make briefer reference to a later book, on Hong Kong cinema (2000), which manifests this structure as well. I will turn to Bordwell's metatheoretical book, *Making Meaning*, in the following section.

Though not solely Bordwell's work, *The Classical Hollywood Cinema* presents a clear instance of his approach to film. The preface explains that the book examines Hollywood cinema during a particular historical period (1917–60) as a "mode of film practice," which is to say, "a set of widely held stylistic norms sustained by and sustaining an integral mode of film production." This "determinate set" defines "what stories [a movie] tells and how it should tell them," as well as "the range and functions of film technique, and … the activities of the spectator" (Bordwell et al. 1985: xiv).

One can see hints of both Foucault and Marx in this project. (There are also elements of reception theory, which I will leave aside, as a result of limitations of space.)

The various sections of the book are attributed to their individual authors. Bordwell characteristically treats style, narration, and technology, rather than mode of production (the Marxist topic). When Bordwell does touch on conditions of production (e.g., at the end of chapter 7 [p. 84]), he speaks of them in a pragmatic vein, stressing such issues as whether or not there is a particular person on the crew who can address a certain problem (thus the craft context), whether one or another option costs more money, etc. He does not stress class differences or hierarchies in ownership relations (e.g., control over investment decisions), relations of production (e.g., divisions between mental and manual labor), or other standard Marxist topics. Indeed, at times, Bordwell seems to offer a sort of understated resistance to Marxist modes of analysis. For example, he and Staiger refer to "Comolli's concept of 'capitalist economics'," while in effect praising "corporate research" (251) as a source of modernization and advancement. (The general point is recognized, even stressed by Marxists, but in a context that is much more critical.)

Bordwell wrote the first seven chapters and begins the book by laying a theoretical foundation for what will follow. The opening chapter explores the system of norms that both constrained and – perhaps even more importantly for Bordwell – enabled the making of individual films. The subsequent five chapters explore the working-out of these norms in narrative and visual style (with some reference to sound). The final chapter takes up the issue of how much individual agency there is within this system. In keeping with a Foucauldian approach, there is not much. For example, regarding one set of films sometimes seen as involving "transgressive" elements, Bordwell remarks that "their most 'radical' moments" are "in fact codified through generic conventions" (71). He explains individual style as a matter of "habitually and systematically" choosing "one alternative" offered by the system.

More exactly, in the second chapter, Bordwell examines the ways Hollywood structures stories, focusing on causality. Here, too, it seems that Bordwell is at pains to avoid Marxist approaches. Thus he sets up the individualism of Hollywood cinema as a matter of one sort of causality – psychological causality – contrasting that with different sorts of causality found in other cinemas, such as the Marxist-inspired social causality of Eisenstein's *The Battleship Potemkin* (1925). However, this seems an odd way of explaining the differences. The more obvious approach would be to say that all cinemas have various sorts of causalities in their storylines – psychological, social, natural. The differences come in how the interactions among these are articulated. A standard Marxist view would not be that there is a simple difference in discourses between Hollywood and Eisenstein. In other words, it is not that Hollywood opts for personal causality while Eisenstein (in some films) opts for social causality. Rather, the divergence comes in the depiction of relations among diverse sorts of causality. Perhaps Hollywood repeatedly suggests that individual effort, if sustained through hard work, can result in personal success against great odds. Marxist-influenced films might be more likely to suggest that individuals are tightly constrained by social circumstances and that genuine success results only from the collective efforts of groups to better their conditions by changing the nature of social relations. In short, the classical Hollywood calibration of causal relations serves the ideological function of fostering individualism within the system of American capitalism.

One way of phrasing the difference here is in terms of epistemic criteria – what is true or what is most justified? Alternatively, what is false or motivated by class interests, rather than by evidence? Marxists would maintain that the ideas conveyed by Hollywood are often of the second ideological sort, fostered not by evidence but by the interests of dominant classes. Bordwell is deeply concerned with scientific validity. However, once he articulates a discursive structure, he often sets aside concerns about truth and treats all instantiations of the discourse as equal. In this case, that tendency may suggest that he sees the Marxist analysis as simply a product of discourse.

Following the discussion of story, Bordwell turns to the topics of narration (the ways in which the story is represented in a film), space, and time. In discussing narration, Bordwell focuses on the degree to which the film presents us with an overt or covert mediator in the communication of information, the degree to which that mediator is knowledgeable (thus whether he/she is or is not omniscient), and the degree to which he/she is willing to impart information. In his discussion of time, Bordwell explores order and duration; in relation to space, Bordwell focuses on composition within the frame and on editing (thus the system of continuity editing, in the case of classical Hollywood film).

I should stress that these concerns are not confined to a narrow period of Bordwell's work. Another exemplary text of this sort is Bordwell's *Planet Hong Kong*, published fifteen years later. The opening chapters of the work develop a history of Hong Kong popular cinema and the expansion of its market beyond Hong Kong. However, the rest of the book follows the structure outlined above. As Bordwell explains, chapter 5 "surveys local production methods and craft traditions," thus the broad institutional patterns and the quotidian practices that generate and contextualize tasks and problems. This is followed by a chapter on the standard devices and functions of Hong Kong cinema, with particular emphasis on "genre, stars, stories, and style" (17), a slightly different list from that just considered, but clearly along the same lines. The final chapter takes up the relation of experimental films to the institutionally embedded discourse of Hong Kong cinema. For example, this chapter considers Wong Kar-wai, "the most artistically adventurous director in current Hong Kong cinema," arguing that "[d]espite his avant-garde reputation, he came out of mass entertainment" and his films are "firmly rooted in genres" (270). *Planet Hong Kong* treats discourse more freely than earlier works, and it varies the constituents somewhat. But the approach and structure – thus the discourse it manifests in exploring discourse – are fundamentally the same.

Metatheory

Making Meaning (1989) is probably the most relevant of Bordwell's books to philosophy. In this book, Bordwell takes up his system of discourse analysis and applies it to film criticism. He explains his purpose early in the book, "to describe how an institution constructs and constrains what is thought and said by its members, and how the members solve routine problems by producing acceptable discourse" (xii). Bordwell rehearses some of the relevant institutional conditions facing teachers in colleges and universities. He then goes on to stress one central task of critical practice, defined by "the institution of criticism," as he calls it – "Produce a novel and persuasive interpretation of one or more appropriate films" (29).

Having established the task in its institutional context, Bordwell goes on to isolate the devices available to a critic in producing a piece of film criticism. These crucially involve a complex practical schema comprising four critical/discursive activities. First, one must indicate that the key meanings of a work are hidden or nonobvious. Second, one must isolate a "semantic field" (a semantic field is a complex of definitionally related concepts; for example, the semantic field of "temperature" includes "hot," "cold," "warm," and so forth). Third, one must map this semantic field onto the film in such a way as to indicate that the mapping reveals the hidden meaning. Finally, one must show that this interpretation is both novel and valid (41).

Bordwell is undoubtedly correct that academic film criticism is highly conventionalized, and he has greatly advanced our understanding of that conventionalization. However, one might question two aspects of his analysis. First, Bordwell distinguishes four types of meaning – referential, explicit, implicit, and symptomatic. Referential meaning is the constructed world of the film; explicit meaning is an abstract, usually thematic meaning stated in the film; implicit meaning is also thematic, but not stated overtly; and symptomatic meaning is some meaning unknown to the filmmaker. While this typology functions perfectly well to organize Bordwell's discussion, it is unconvincing as a semantic theory. First, as Bordwell acknowledges, referential meaning is not necessarily overt. We have to fill in a great deal of information to get from the images on the screen to what happened in the story world, even when we all agree about what happened. Second, that inference involves a great deal of abstract information – for example, about the moral beliefs of the characters. Third, abstract versus concrete information does not seem a crucial division anyway, nor does explicitly stated versus implicit information seem key. Nor is "symptomatic" meaning necessarily distinct from the other categories.

One can reasonably divide types of meaning in many different ways, depending on one's purpose. Given Bordwell's purpose, the first crucial division is not even between types of meaning, but between interpretive inferences commonly made by viewers and interpretive inferences not commonly made by viewers – most importantly, inferences that viewers would be likely to reject. These inferences may concern implicit moral or political themes, but they may concern explicit statements or even elements of the plot. For example, one interpretation of *Othello* might argue that the protagonist is not overly rash or prone to unreasonable outbursts of emotion but is driven to an extreme emotional state by social conditions, such as the casual racism of Desdemona. This interpretation would be of interest first of all because it treats the story world, thus referential meaning in Bordwell's typology. But Bordwell indicates that academic interpretations operate only at the levels of implicit and symptomatic meanings. Beyond the division between inferences commonly drawn by spectators and inferences that spectators would most often reject (or at least overlook), Bordwell might wish to isolate patterns or correlations of which the filmmaker was aware and those of which he or she was unaware. Even in a cognitive framework, it is clear that the overwhelming bulk of patterns in our speech and action (e.g., the complex grammatical patterns isolated by linguists) are not matters of which we are self-consciously aware. This division may be particularly consequential with respect to social ideology (e.g., in treatments of race or class).

One might also question the adequacy of semantic field mapping for understanding interpretation. For example, suppose I interpret Muzaffar Ali's *Umrao Jaan* (1981) as a Sufi allegory, suggesting the ways in which one's life is continually driven by a search for union with God. Certainly there are aspects of Sufism that it is reasonable to think of as a semantic field. But a semantic field is pre-sentential. It does not involve assertions, not to mind chains of theological inference. Suppose I say that Umrao's relationship with Nawab Sultan adumbrates the loss of self in God, and is even an instance of that loss, but that it is imperfect because Umrao maintains the illusion of individuality and separation. This is a relatively simple proposition. But could it be captured by mapping from a semantic field? Of course, one can expand the notion of a semantic field so that it includes complex propositional relations. But then it seems one has simply made "semantic field" mean "doctrine" or "belief system" – or "theory" – thereby losing the rigor and specificity of the concept.

In any case, Bordwell goes on to complicate this picture by introducing conceptual and procedural schemas, default presuppositions, and other elements of the governing discourse. Given that he is treating criticism, not fiction film, there is no clear place for story and narration here. However, two key "socially implanted hypotheses" form a rough parallel to the isolation of story principles. These are that the work is unified and that it "bears some relation to an external world" (133). Beyond this, his two basic types of schema are "category schemata," which bear most importantly on genre, and "person-based schemata" (146), which bear crucially on narrators and filmmakers – thus taking us from story to narration. Bordwell adds two further "text schemata": "One represents the text at a particular moment, 'frozen' synchronically; the other represents the film as a diachronic totality" (169). This moves us from story and narration to space and time, in keeping with the general pattern of Bordwell's discursive model. (The mention of "synchronic" and "diachronic" also links Bordwell's concern with space and time to standard structuralist and post-structuralist categories.) From here, Bordwell turns to the rhetorical aspect of film interpretation, an aspect analogous to style in films themselves (each being a manner of presentation that serves to enhance the intended effect). Again in keeping with his standard model, he then considers individual critics in relation to the discourse.

There is something of a "grab bag" to the list of devices isolated by Bordwell in this context. However, Bordwell's analysis suggests that the process of interpretation is driven by heuristics, not susceptible to strict formulation in terms of rules or necessary and sufficient conditions. Perhaps the grab bag is the critics' more than the metatheorist's.

Bordwell ends the book with an argument against the primacy of interpretation in film studies. Bordwell is certainly right that there is a lot of shoddy reasoning in interpretation – as in other areas of academic study. He may also be right that film studies pays excessive attention to interpretation. But part of this argument involves a fairly strict and, I believe, problematic separation of interpretation and science (see ibid.: 257). This takes up an argument from earlier in the book, where Bordwell drew on the philosophy of science to maintain that interpretation does not test or illustrate a theory, or even provide insights by way of a theory (4–6). Indeed, one peculiar aspect of Bordwell's discussion of the discourse of academic film interpretation – parallel to his discussion of Hollywood story devices – is that he does not seem to take up an epistemic criterion for interpretation. (He hedges his claims somewhat, but generally he does not view interpretation as yielding knowledge [see p. 257], despite the care and rigor of his own interpretations.) Interpretation is separated off from science and, as such, it is separated from evaluation by ordinary criteria of empirical support, explanatory simplicity, etc. But this seems wrong at two levels.

First, Bordwell's invocation of the philosophy of science in relation to interpretation appears misplaced. Interpretation is the examination of particulars. In, say, medical science, this is parallel, not to general theorization (theory formulation, testing, etc.), but to diagnosis. Diagnosis does not serve either to falsify or illustrate a theory. Moreover, like film interpretation, diagnosis is valuable to the degree that it reveals nonobvious meanings. If Bordwell's arguments segregate interpretation from truth concerns, it would seem that they must do the same for diagnosis.

Second, Bordwell draws on particularly implausible interpretations, such as the tendency of some Lacanians to take any image of a mirror as reason to invoke the Lacanian mirror stage. Bordwell's analysis suggests that the use of a mirror may be best explained by pragmatic factors of problem-solving on the set of the film. For example, perhaps the director wanted to shoot two characters in dialogue while one dressed. The mirror allows us to see both characters. It solves a practical problem. But the difficulty here is that there are many ways of solving that problem. The director presumably chose the mirror solution for a complex set of reasons, some self-conscious, some not. Consider, again, *Umrao Jaan*. It involves Sufi songs, explicated in relation to mysticism. It involves many narrative and stylistic elements that are commonly related to Sufism. Finally, within Sufism, the mirror is a common symbol, and mirrors appear repeatedly in the film, often without any clear pragmatic function. For example, one mirror shot includes just Umrao's face, with no mirror frame; only the left/right reversal of an ornament indicates that this is a mirror image. Bordwell's discursive analysis would seem to equate a Sufi interpretation of these mirror images with Lacanian interpretations of films, based on nothing more than the presence of a mirror in a single scene.

Conclusion

Bordwell has developed erudite and insightful discursive/institutional analyses of "modes of film practice." He has integrated these analyses with cognitive science in illuminating ways that have inspired many subsequent writers. Moreover, his explorations of visual style, national cinemas, and individual filmmakers have helped change the terms of discussion on these topics. Of course, no theories are beyond criticism. If the preceding arguments are valid, Bordwell's greatest fault may be the fault his own theory predicts. His discursive analyses are often too consistent with the professional discourses he rebelled against, the dominant discourses of structuralism and post-structuralism. However, Bordwell has not been determined by these discourses. Not only did he innovate brilliantly in his theoretical work, his writings on individual directors challenge any strict discursive model, exploring creativity, uniqueness, and interpretability. In this way, Bordwell repeatedly goes beyond the constraints of his own theoretical approach to further transform the way we view, understand, explain, and even interpret movies.

See also Noël Carroll (Chapter 31), Consciousness (Chapter 4), Cognitive theory (Chapter 33), Formalism (Chapter 12), Sergei Eisenstein (Chapter 35), Narrative closure (Chapter 19), Narration (Chapter 18), and Style (Chapter 25).

References

Bordwell, D. (1973) *Filmguide to* La Passion de Jeanne d'Arc, Bloomington: Indiana University Press.

—— (1980) *French Impressionist Cinema: Film Culture, Film Theory, Film Style*, New York: Arno Press.

—— (1981) *The Films of Carl-Theodor Dreyer*, Berkeley: University of California Press.

—— (1985) *Narration in the Fiction Film*, Madison: University of Wisconsin Press.

—— (1988) *Ozu and the Poetics of Cinema*, London: British Film Institute.

—— (1989) *Making Meaning: Inference and Rhetoric in the Interpretation of Cinema*, Cambridge, MA: Harvard University Press.

—— (1993) *The Cinema of Eisenstein*, Cambridge, MA: Harvard University Press.

—— (1996) "Convention, Construction, and Cinematic Vision," in D. Bordwell and N. Carroll (eds.) *Post-Theory: Reconstructing Film Studies*, Madison: University of Wisconsin Press.

—— (1997) *On the History of Film Style*, Cambridge, MA: Harvard University Press.

—— (2000) *Planet Hong Kong: Popular Cinema and the Art of Entertainment*, Cambridge, MA: Harvard University Press.

—— (2001) *Visual Style in the Cinema: Vier Kapitel Filmgeschichte*, Munich: Verlag der Autoren.

—— (2005) *Figures Traced in Light: On Cinematic Staging*, Berkeley: University of California Press.

—— (2006) *The Way Hollywood Tells It: Story and Style in Modern Movies*, Berkeley: University of California Press.

Bordwell, D., and Thompson, K. (2006) *Film Art: An Introduction*, 8th ed., New York: McGraw-Hill.

Bordwell, D., Staiger, J., and Thompson, K. (1985) *The Classical Hollywood Cinema: Film Style and Mode of Production to 1960*, New York: Columbia University Press.

Thompson, K., and Bordwell, D. (2002) *Film History: An Introduction*, 2nd ed., New York: McGraw-Hill.

30

BERTOLT BRECHT

Angela Curran

The camera is a sociologist.

Brecht, screenplay for *Die Beule* ("The Bruise")

Bertolt Brecht (1898–1956) is known as a German poet and director-playwright whose plays, innovative stage productions, and writings on the theater made him one of the most influential figures in theater in the twentieth century. But what is less widely known is that Brecht also had a lifelong engagement with film. As a young intellectual and artist with an interest in socialism, Brecht immediately took an interest in film as a new art form that had popular appeal (Brecht 2000: 3–5). During the course of his life Brecht was involved in the production of at least six films, and his diaries reveal that he had written as many as forty screenplays (Gersch 1975; Brecht 1979, 1993). Cinema also had a significant influence on Brecht's theory of epic theater, which in turn has influenced several generations of experimental filmmakers, most famously Jean-Luc Godard and Rainer Werner Fassbinder, starting in the 1960s and 1970s.

This entry has two main parts. In the first part, I examine Brecht's engagement with film, by looking at his writings on film and the films on which he worked. In the second part, I look at Brecht's influence on contemporary filmmakers and film theorists. I begin with a brief discussion of Brecht's views on theater and the role that film played in the development of his theory and practice of "epic theater."

Brecht's engagement with film

Epic theater

As a young man in the 1920s Brecht started out as a poet but soon developed an interest in Marxism, and he turned to writing and directing plays that provided social commentary (Kellner 1997). After the First World War, Germany was undergoing a state of economic collapse. As a Marxist, Brecht wanted to use drama to educate the working class and others about the role that the social environment played in shaping the course of people's lives and how it was open to criticism and change.

Brecht's development of a new type of theater, which he called "epic theater," was based on its contrast with the dominant theater of his day, which he called

"Aristotelian dramatic theater," a tradition which Brecht said was initiated by Aristotle's *Poetics* and found in Wagner's operas (Brecht 1964: 33–42). According to Brecht, Aristotelian drama pulls the audience into its representation through identification or "empathy" (*Einfühlung*) with a central character. Plot is the center of the drama and the other elements, such as music, staging, and lighting, recede into the background. The narrative is tightly organized to create a sense of a fixed causal order of events, prompting the idea that what happens to the characters is "inevitable" and due to some fixed "human condition" that is not open to change.

In epic theater, the audience is kept at a "distance" from the action and is encouraged to be critical of what it sees on stage. This is achieved through the use of "alienation devices" (*Verfremdungseffekts*, or V-effects for short) – such as characters talking directly to the audience, a "detached" style of acting, captions, projections, posters, songs, and choruses – that interrupt and comment on the action, allowing the viewer to see the action from multiple conflicting perspectives and prompting her or him to develop an "opinion" about what happens on stage (Grimm 1997; Brooker 2006). Production elements such as music, stage design, acting, and lighting are actively "separated out" and have an independent function. Epic theater is political, because it prompts the viewer to consider the underlying social causes of real-life events by considering how things might be different if social arrangements were to change.

Film and epic theater

Brecht's writings suggest that cinema was a formative influence on his developing theory of epic theater. During the early 1920s Brecht was an avid viewer of films and a prolific screenwriter. Brecht was attracted to film because, as a mass art, the film industry represented a challenge to the "high art" practices of his day, especially the novel and theater (Silberman 1997). From film Brecht developed some central principles of epic theater.

Brecht praised Charlie Chaplin's *A Face on the Bar Room Floor* (1914) and *The Gold Rush* (1925) because Chaplin used action to reveal social attitudes and not simply as an expression of a character's inner feelings (Brecht 1964: 50–1, 2000: 6). For the same reason, he admired the German comedian, Karl Valentin, and collaborated with him and the director Eric Engel on *Mysteries of a Hairdressing Salon* (*Mysterien eines Frisiersalons*) (1923), a comedy that uses the bizarre goings-on in a hair salon – including torture and beheading – as a form of social satire on bourgeois society. From Chaplin and Valentin, Brecht developed the idea of using acting to reveal what Brecht called *Gestus*. *Gestus* is a German word with Latin and Greek origins that Brecht introduced into his writings on drama starting around 1930 (Silberman 2006). It is difficult to give an exact translation of this term into English, but Brecht used this term to refer to the behavior and attitudes of a person in a socially typical situation, for example, as shown in Brecht's film, *Kuhle Wampe* (1932), the attitudes and behavior of a person who is unemployed in Germany after the First World War (Silberman 2006; Brecht 1964: 104–5; Brooker 2006: 219).

From film Brecht also took away ideas about how to structure the narrative in his epic theater. A basic principle of epic narration is to divide the action into discrete episodes so that the transitions, or "knots," between one scene and the next are easily noticed (Brecht 1964: 201). The breaking down of action into distinct units allows the audience to "interpose its judgment" on the action (Brecht 1964: 201). Brecht found that film was particularly suited for this kind of fragmented narration. He wrote that film should be treated like a series of two-dimensional "tableaux" and that its effect arises from "clear interruptions" in the transition from one scene to the next (Brecht 2000: 6–7). Here Brecht was likely influenced by the montage theory of Soviet film formalist Sergei Eisenstein, which involves the putting together of shots that noticeably have a lack of fit (Mueller 1989: 67–95; Willett 1984: 107–28).

The breaking down of a dramatic narrative into tableaux, along with Brecht's idea that each scene should foreground a *Grundgestus*, or socially typical action, became the basic building blocks of epic theater. Ironically, the introduction of sound into film would lead to the demise of the very features of film – expressive acting, the use of interscene titles, and a punctuated narrative – that Brecht admired. But his views on cinematic narration found their way into Brecht's three film scripts from the early 1920s, which have linear narratives, fragmented by the use of titles and captions, and focus on action and not the characters' inner psychology (Willett 1984: 111; Silberman 1997).

Influenced by his teacher, the German director, Erwin Piscator, Brecht wrote that film's ability to document social reality enables it to function in epic theater as a kind of "optical chorus" (Brecht 2000: 6–7). Here film footage and photography can be interjected into a theater production to display a contrastive reality and affect a comparison between the events on stage and real life. A contemporary example is the ending of Lars von Trier's *Dogville* (2003), which plays David Bowie's "Young Americans" as the film credits roll over iconic images of poor and disenfranchised Americans.

Brecht as filmmaker

In a footnote to *Beule* ("The Bruise"), Brecht's screenplay for the *Threepenny Opera* film, Brecht wrote that the camera was like a sociologist (Brecht 2000). The camera's ability to record and reproduce human behavior made film particularly suited for the critical social analysis that Brecht strove for in his epic theater. Brecht endorsed Marx's eleventh Thesis on Feuerbach: "The philosophers have only *interpreted* the world in various ways; the point, however, is to *change* it" (Brecht 1964: 248). To affect cultural and political change, Brecht joined with others in challenging the "apparatus," Brecht's word for the complex of artistic and production practices in theater, film, opera, and radio, which increasingly were at the service of commercial interests (Benjamin 1973).

Threepenny Opera film and *Hangmen Also Die*

Brecht's first major attempt to intervene in the film industry in Germany came in 1931, when he and his music collaborator, Kurt Weill, sued Nero Productions to gain control over the film rights to Brecht and Weill's play, *Threepenny Opera*, a satire of the bourgeois society in the Weimar Republic. In 1930 Brecht and Weill had signed a contract with Nero Productions to participate in a film production based on the play, to be directed by the German director, G. W. Pabst. Brecht reworked the play to bring out more strongly its critique of capitalism and private property. When Nero Productions learned of these changes, they completed the film without him, prompting Brecht and Weill to sue for copyright infringement. The court ruled in Nero's favor by arguing that the company had a right to demand fidelity to the play as a way of ensuring their financial investment in the film.

In response to the court's ruling, Brecht wrote a long essay, "The *Threepenny Opera* Lawsuit" (Brecht 2000: 147–202). One might think that Brecht's situation brings out the basic incompatibility of art and the commercial interests of the film industry. But Brecht rejected this analysis because, he argued, it relies on an outmoded view that art is autonomous from society and is an expression of the personality of the artist. In a capitalist society, he writes, art of any consequence is produced and marketed as a commodity to a mass market (168–70). Rather than thinking that art is incompatible with mass production, Brecht wrote that mass media like film opens up new politically progressive possibilities for artistic production, by creating art that is collectively produced and is intended for a mass distribution (Brewster 1975–6).

Brecht's other major contact with the commercial film industry came when he fled the Nazi regime and landed in Hollywood in 1941, where he stayed until 1946. During this time Brecht worked on numerous film projects, including his work as screenwriter on *Hangmen Also Die* (1943), a film about the real-life assassination of Reinhart Heydrich, the *Reichsprotektor* of the Nazi occupation forces in Czechoslovakia, directed by German exile Fritz Lang (Willett 1984; Gersch 1975). Because of aesthetic and political differences, Lang eventually cut Brecht loose from the film. The finished film was later criticized for presenting an unrealistic picture of the resistance in Czechoslovakia (Willett 1984: 122), but also defended because Lang's theme that appearances can be deceptive supports a Brechtian aesthetics (Elsaesser 1990a). Years later, in *Contempt* (1963), Jean-Luc Godard's examination of Hollywood, Lang plays a weary film director who quotes Brecht's poem about Hollywood, a place where Brecht hopes to "earn my bread" in the market "where lies are sold."

Kuhle Wampe

Despite his experiences with the *Threepenny Opera* film, Brecht went on a year later to work with others in an anti-capitalist film collective on an independently produced film, *Kuhle Wampe* (Murray 1990). We can turn to this film to see how to transpose the principles of epic drama into film. *Kuhle Wampe: To Whom Does the World Belong?* (1932), co-directed by Brecht and Slatan Dudow, examines the effects of the German economic crisis post-First World War on the German working class. Divided into four sections, the first two episodes look at the effects of the economic crisis in post-First World War Berlin through a look at the life of a working-class family, the Bönikes. The third and fourth episodes examine the Communist Party response to the crisis. The final scene is a spontaneous political debate in a Berlin subway. The film ends with a direct appeal to those who are "dissatisfied" with these social attitudes the film has examined, to "change the world."

Brecht and Dudow make extensive use of documentary materials that create a "realistic" effect, for example, recent headlines from Berlin newspapers, documentary shots of the Brandenburg gate, deteriorating slums in Berlin, as well as film footage from the actual Kuhle Wampe, which was a workers' tent camp in Berlin (Murray 1990; Silberman 1995). In addition, more than half of the film is also shot on actual locations (Alter 2004). This use of documentary techniques illustrates Brecht's view that epic drama should show "real-life incidents" for the purpose of "laying bare society's causal network" (Brecht 1964: 109). But in a discussion of painting, Brecht says that the best painters do not simply deliver "mere reflections"; they create a picture of a visible world and "one that is yet to be made visible" (Mueller 1989: 53). What needs to be made visible and what is hidden, on Brecht's view, are the essential contradictions of social life in capitalism. The alienation-effects in the film are designed to bring the underlying social processes to the viewer's attention by revealing the contradictions in the lives of the working class, who are the hardest hit by the economic crisis.

One often-discussed scene in the film illustrates this strategy. Here the film uses montage editing to contrast the *Gestus* of Mr Bönike, who is engrossed in reading a feature page story about the exotic dancer, Mata Hari, with the *Gestus* or viewpoint of Mrs Bönike, who is attending to her shopping list and how the family can afford to feed itself. The contradiction here is that the father is focused on the Mata Hari story when he should be concerned about his family's survival. Here the viewer is prompted to consider how mass media such as newspapers – images of which figure prominently in the early scenes of the film – function to entertain, but not instruct about the causes of the economic crisis (Murray 1990: 221).

We can also look at this film as an illustration of Brecht's views on empathy and identification in epic drama and film. *Kuhle Wampe* prompted a response from the film censors in Germany, whose central objection was delivered as an "artistic reproach": the film had not presented the story from the point of view of the "particular shocking fate" of one individual (Brecht 2000: 208). Brecht found that the censor had "penetrated far deeper into the essence of our artistic intentions than our most supportive critics" (Brecht 2000: 209). The film does not have a "hero" or central protagonist whose actions and viewpoint serve to structure the action. For Brecht, this means his epic cinema rejects "identification" or "empathy" (*Einfühlung*) with a character, which he defines as sharing one central character's feelings and seeing the action from his point of view (Curran 2001; Brecht 1964: 94, 192–3, 136–7). Brecht is clear, especially in his later writings, that this does not mean the rejection of emotion in epic drama. Rather, Brecht rejects the specific kind of engagement that the censor wanted – the following of the story by empathetically sharing the "fate" of a particular individual. It is this specific sort of response that Brecht sought to eliminate in *Kuhle Wampe* (Brecht 1964: 23, 87, 193–4).

Brecht's influence

Filmmaking and film theory

English-speaking film theorists in the mid-1970s "rediscovered" *Kuhle Wampe* when the British film journal *Screen* issued a special two-volume series on Brecht's writings and work on film. Scholarship on Brecht's ideas on film was made possible by the publication of his film writings for the first time, in a two-volume set, *Text für Filme* (*Texts for Films*) in Germany in 1969 (Brecht 1969; Silberman 1997: 198). But prior to this Brecht's dramatic theory and practice had a huge impact on filmmaking and film criticism in the 1960s. The interest in France in Brecht's work by French intellectuals Roland Barthes and Bernard Dort paved the way in 1960 for a special edition on Brecht in *Les Cahiers du cinéma*.

But more significantly, the social upheavals of the 1960s brought a desire for a socially conscious film theory and practice. A French and German new wave cinema emerged in the 1960s that was based on transplanting Brechtian ideas of dramatic theory and practice into film (Byg 1997). Jean-Luc Godard, in France, and Jean-Marie Straub and Danièle Huillet, in Germany, made films that broke with the practice of a unified narrative and a structure of identification. Films that show a strong Brechtian influence include Godard's *La Chinoise* (1967), *Le Vent d'est* (1970), and *Tout va bien* (1972), and Huillet and Straub's *History Lessons* (1972), based on Brecht's Caesar novel (Elsaesser 2004).

Brecht's notion of using film to foreground social *Gestus* has also greatly influenced a number of directors. Fassbinder, in films such as *In a Year of Thirteen Moons* (1978), *The Marriage of Maria Braun* (1979), and *Lola* (1981), uses Brechtian aesthetics to critique the post-Second World War "success story" of West German society. In the melodrama *The Cloud-Capped Star* (1960), Bengali filmmaker, Ritwik Ghatak, uses the conflicts between members of a refugee family as a reflection on the social effects of the partition of Bengal. In *Dogville*, Lars von Trier uses Brechtian staging practices in a film that presents the slide into cruelty of an isolated American community in the Rockies, as a critique of American attitudes toward labor, immigration, and the poor and disenfranchised. German director Harun Farocki looks at the social attitudes of a working-class neighborhood in Berlin in his *The Taste of Life* (1979) and investigates the social environment in post-First World War Germany in *Between Two Wars* (1977).

In 1968 Godard published a "battle cry" for a political cinema that would "start two or three Vietnams" and follow in Brecht's footsteps by challenging the film industry (Elsaesser 1990b: 172). The filmmaking practices used by Godard – a rejection of identification with characters, a dismantling of a classic, unified narrative, and a denunciation of "illusionist" cinema, in favor of techniques that foreground the film as a "construct" – have come to define the basic tenets of a "counter cinema" that sprung up in the 1960s and 1970s (Wollen 1985). The association of Brecht with Godard is so strong that this leads some to say that an adherence to these formal practices is the *sine qua non* of post-Brechtian filmmaking (Brady 2006). But others have argued that the emphasis on formal practices and anti-illusionist, "self-reflexive" cinema techniques has left us with filmic practices that have Brecht's form without his commitment to socially critical cinema (Polan 1985; Harvey 1982).

Film theory has also been greatly influenced by Brecht's writings on aesthetic theory and practice. Recently Thomas Elsaesser notes that there has been a radical shift in film theorists' attitudes toward Brecht (Elsaesser 1990b). He argues that Brecht was welcomed in the late 1960s by theory-conscious filmmakers such as Godard and the Straub–Huillet team, who wanted to revive Brecht's call for "intervention" in the film industry. Then in the late 1970s and 1980s, a shift away from Brechtian aesthetics took place. Film theorists, influenced by the ideas of Louis Althusser, argued that individuals do not exist prior to or apart from systems of ideology – they are produced as effects of it. According to this view, there is no stepping outside the influence of the dominant ideology; instead the film viewer is "constructed" as an effect of the film text.

Given these sweeping views on the power of cinematic representation, Brecht's idea that viewers can achieve a critical distance from a film text, even one with V-effects, then becomes questionable. Brecht's realism, his commitment to the idea that there is a real world that exists independently and outside of our minds, and his view that it is possible to represent this world in art, is also problematic for some theorists if one starts with a radical constructivist or antirealist premise (Lovell 1982; Moeller 1979). We can add that Brecht's idea that a socially conscious cinema can change social reality is also open to challenge. Elsaesser concludes, "In the age of post-modernism, or of post-modernist theory, Brecht's remarks on cinema, photography, and the media ... have not been invalidated, but their appeal to a reality outside representation ... has become problematic as a critical stance" (1990b: 183). However, does Elsaesser's conclusion follow? Many philosophers of film would say that his questioning of Brecht does not follow, for the postmodernist's across-the-board rejection of notions of "truth" and "reality" has not been sufficiently established (Allen and Smith 1997).

Philosophy of film

Although, for reasons to be explained shortly, philosophers of film have not warmly received Brecht's aesthetics, now might be the time for a critical reexamination of his views and their relevance for philosophy of film. A number of philosophers of film reject the determinism of Lacanian/Althusserian theory, reject the notion that film viewers are effects of a film text, but share Brecht's realist epistemology. So the impediments that Elsaesser notes to Brecht's current reception in film-theory circles would not be obstacles to his relevance to philosophy of film. In addition, many philosophers of film and art share Brecht's interest in investigating art as a vehicle for learning and knowledge. Brecht's idea that we can learn through a critical engagement with the representations of character and action in drama promises to add a new perspective to the investigation of this topic (Curran 2001).

But there are some theoretical stumbling blocks that also need to be addressed if Brecht's aesthetics are to be rehabilitated by philosophers of film. Here I address briefly three central issues: (1) Brecht's "anti-illusionism"; (2) his rejection of empathy; and (3) the linkage of form and socially critical content.

First, Brecht is widely known as a critic of "illusionist" film and a proponent of an "antirealist" aesthetic (Walsh 1981: 11; Wollen 1985). To clarify, there are several senses of realism, epistemological and aesthetic. Brecht's repeated insistence that drama can depict "real-life incidents" suggests that he accepts epistemological realism: the view that there exists a mind independent reality that we can represent and refer to in language (Brecht 1964: 109). But he has come to be a proponent of aesthetic antirealism. This is a rejection of classic narrative drama, on the grounds that it aims to pull the spectator into the fictional world of the film by presenting the "illusion" of reality. Illusionist films "absorb" or "immerse" the viewer by obscuring the fact that the film text is just a mediation of reality, so that the viewer loses sight of the fact that the film is a construction of reality and that she is outside the fictional world (Smith 1995; Plantinga 1997). Brecht writes of the importance of breaking down the "fourth wall" – the imaginary wall between audience and stage – and he is well known for saying that Aristotelian drama places the spectator under "hypnosis" and in a "trance" (Brecht 1964: 71, 91). Remarks such as these suggest that he accepts the view that narrative drama such as classic Hollywood film places viewers under the "illusion" that what they are watching on screen is real and that alienation devices are needed to combat the "narcotic" effects of narrative drama.

Contemporary philosophers of film have argued that illusionist theories of film spectatorship are incorrect, for it is clear that viewers of narrative film are consistently aware that the world of the film is artificial and that they stand apart from it (Smith 1995; Plantinga 1997). Given Brecht's influence on illusionist theories of film viewing, it is understandable that philosophers of film have criticized him on this score. But we also need to be careful in not reading Brecht's ideas through the lens of contemporary anti-illusionist film theories. For as the brief review of Brecht's relationship with film theory indicates, his theory has been both accepted and rejected by anti-illusionist film theorists, suggesting that Brecht's view on illusion in representational theater and film can be interpreted in various ways.

In Brecht's writings, he clearly states that what Aristotelian drama hides is the social causes of human actions, not the fact that it is a work of art. For example, he writes, "The object of the A-effect is to alienate the social gest underlying every incident. By social gest is meant the mimetic and gestural expression of the social relationships prevailing between people of a given period" (Brecht 1964: 139). As Dana Polan notes, in a chapter entitled, "The Modern Theater is the Epic Theater," "Brecht uses the example of opera to present his conception of art as possessing intrinsic qualities of distance from reality, to which the artist can *add* a sense of political engagement" (Polan 1985: 93). In these writings, Brecht makes it clear his concern in creating epic drama is not to disabuse spectators of the illusion that what they see on stage is real: his concern instead is to create drama that engages the viewer in active, political analysis.

A second major point of difference between Brecht and contemporary philosophers of film concerns his criticisms of "empathy" and his more general views about the role of emotions in aesthetic response, which to many have embodied a crude opposition between reason and the emotions (Smith 1996; Plantinga 1997). In an early work, Brecht writes, for example, "I aim at an extremely classical, cold, highly intellectual style of performance. I'm not writing for the scum who want to have the cockles of their heart warmed" (Brecht 1964: 14). This and similar writings have no doubt contributed to the negative response to Brecht's views on emotional engagement.

But Brecht's views on emotions in the theater changed over the years (Woodruff 1988). He came to think that there was an important role for a *critical* engagement of the emotions in epic drama. In the *Messingkauf Dialogues*, for example, he says, "Exercising one's critical faculties isn't a purely intellectual business, feelings also play a part" (Brecht 1965: 88) and that once we eliminate from Aristotelian aesthetics the notion that an individual is determined by fate, the emotions of pity and fear have a valuable place in epic drama (Brecht 1965: 26; Mueller 1989: 64; Brecht 1964: 227–9). More work needs to be done to clarify what sorts of emotional responses Brecht would think can aid in an understanding of the larger social reality that a film presumes. But Brecht's writings indicate that his considered view is not a rejection of an "entire class of spectator emotions" (Plantinga 1997: 374) but the rejection of a specific *kind* of engagement that blocks the viewer from a wider social analysis.

A third issue concerns the link that Brecht makes between specific dramatic or cinematic form and political attitudes. It may appear that Brecht is committed to "ideological formalism," the view that certain film forms or styles necessarily have certain political or ideological effects (Plantinga 1997: 376). His many statements, for example, that the narrative structures of Aristotelian drama create an uncritical viewer may suggest that he thinks there is an intrinsic connection between Aristotelian drama and the political attitude that social change is impossible. But there are many examples of narrative films, for example, Ermanno Olmi's *Tree of the Wooden Clogs* (1978) that encourage a social awareness of the problems of the working class.

However, Brecht strongly rejected the view that aesthetic forms can describe political attitudes for all times and instead took a more experimental approach, arguing that a socially conscious dramatist should "try out every conceivable artistic method which assists that end, old or new" (Brecht 1964: 229; see also Mueller 1989: 134). His willingness, noted above, to modify elements of an Aristotelian aesthetic is evidence of this view. For this reason, if Brecht were here today, he would resist any attempts to define a Brechtian cinematic method in terms of a set of formal practices, preferring instead to see what cinematic practices would work for today. A recent example of such a new direction is the "new media" piece *Cinema Like Never Before*, a video installation that uses a Brechtian method of breaking down and framing sequences from classic Hollywood films to get the viewer to rethink her response to these movies (Ehmann and Farocki 2006). The problems that Brecht worried about – the dominance of Hollywood-produced movies that allow little room for critical thinking or social analysis – are still with us today. For this reason there is much to be learned from Brecht as we attempt to understand the nature of our critical engagement with movies.

Acknowledgments

I thank the Bertolt Brecht Archive in Berlin for valuable access to films and print material and Carleton College for funding that made my trip to the archive possible. I am indebted to the editors, Paisley Livingston and Carl Plantinga, and to Carol Donelan and Valerie Weinstein, for many helpful comments. I owe a special debt to Julie Klassen and Marc Silberman for their generous assistance and invaluable suggestions for this essay.

See also Walter Benjamin (Chapter 28), Emotion and affect (Chapter 8), Empathy and character engagement (Chapter 9), and Acting (Chapter 1),

References

Allen, R., and Smith, M. (eds.) (1997) *Film Theory and Philosophy*, Oxford: Clarendon Press; New York: Oxford University Press.

Alter, N. (2004) "The Politics and Sounds of Everyday Life in *Kuhle Wampe*," in N. M. Alter and L. Koepnick (eds.) *Sound Matters: Essays the Acoustics of German Culture*, New York: Berghahn Books, 79–90.

Benjamin, W. (1973) *Understanding Brecht*, trans. A. Bostock, London: New Left Books.

Brady, M. (2006) "Brecht and Film," in P. Thomson and G. Sacks (eds.) *The Cambridge Companion to Brecht*, 2nd ed., Cambridge and New York: Cambridge University Press.

Brecht, B. (1964) *Brecht on Theatre*, trans. J. Willett, London: Methuen.

—— (1965) *The Messingkauf Dialogues*, trans. J. Willett, London: Methuen.

—— (1969) *Texte für Filme*, ed. W. Gersch and W. Hecht, Frankfurt am Main: Suhrkamp.

—— (1979) *Diaries 1920–1922*, ed. H. Ramthun; trans. J. Willett, London: Methuen.

—— (1993) *Journals 1934–1955*, eds. J. Willett and H. Rorrison, New York: Routledge.

—— (2000) *Brecht on Film and Radio*, trans. and ed. M. Silberman, London: Methuen.

Brewster, B. (1975–6) "Brecht and the Film Industry: (On the *Threepenny Opera* film and *Hangmen Also Die*)," *Screen* 16(4): 16–29.

Brooker, P. (2006) "Key Words in Brecht's Theory and Practice of Theatre," in P. Thomson and G. Sacks (eds.) *The Cambridge Companion to Brecht*, 2nd ed., Cambridge and New York: Cambridge University Press.

Byg, B. (1997) "Brecht, New Waves, and Political Modernism in Cinema," in S. Mews (ed.) *A Bertolt Brecht Reference Companion*, Westport, CT: Greenwood Press, 220–37.

Curran, A. (2001) "Brecht's Criticisms of Aristotle's Aesthetics of Tragedy," *Journal of Aesthetics and Art Criticism* 59(2): 167–84.

Ehmann, A., and Farocki, H. (curators) (2006), *Kino wie noch nie [Cinema Like Never Before]* (video installation), Vienna, Austria: Generali Foundation.

Elsaesser, T. (1990a) "Transparent Duplicities: The Three Penny Opera (1931)," in E. Rentschler (ed.) *The Films of G.W. Pabst: An Extraterritorial Cinema*, New Brunswick, NJ: Rutgers University Press, 103–15.

—— (1990b) "From Anti-illusionism to Hyper-realism: Bertolt Brecht and Contemporary Film," in P. Kleber and C. Visser (eds.) *Reinterpreting Brecht: His Influence on Contemporary Drama and Film*, Cambridge and New York: Cambridge University Press.

—— (2004) *Harun Farocki: Working on the Sight Lines*, ed. T. Elsaesser, Amsterdam: Amsterdam University Press.

Gersch, W. (1975) *Film bei Brecht*, Berlin: Henschelverlag Kunst und Gesellschaft.

Grimm, R. (1997) "Alienation in Context: On the Theory and Practice of Brechtian Theater," in S. Mews (ed.) *A Bertolt Brecht Reference Companion*, Westport, CT: Greenwood Press, 35-46.

Harvey, S. (1982) "Whose Brecht? Memories for the Eighties," *Screen* 23: 45–59.

Kellner, D. (1997) "Brecht's Marxist Aesthetic," in S. Mews (ed.) *A Bertolt Brecht Reference Companion*, Westport, CT: Greenwood Press.

Lovell, A. (1982) "Epic Theater and the Principles of Counter-Cinema," *Jump Cut: A Review of Contemporary Media* 27: 64–8.

Moeller, H. B. (1979) "Brecht and 'Epic Film' Medium: The Cineaste Playwright, Film Theoretician, and His Influence," *Wide Angle* 3(2): 4–11.

Mueller, R. (1989) *Bertolt Brecht and the Theory of the Media*, Lincoln and London: University of Nebraska Press.

Murray, B. (1990) *Film and the German Left in the Weimar Republic*, Austin: University of Texas Press.

Plantinga, C. (1997) "Notes on Spectator Emotion and Ideological Film Criticism," in R. Allen and M. Smith (eds.) *Film Theory and Philosophy*, Oxford: Clarendon Press; New York: Oxford University Press, 372–93.

Polan, D. (1985) *The Political Language of Film and the Avant-garde*, Ann Arbor, MI: UMI Research Press.

Silberman, M. (1995) *German Cinema: Texts in Context*, Detroit: Wayne State University Press.

—— (1997) "Brecht and Film," in S. Mews (ed.) *A Bertolt Brecht Reference Companion*, Westport, CT: Greenwood Press, 197–219.

—— (2006) "Brecht's Gestus or Staging Contradictions," *Brecht Yearbook* 31: 319–35.

Smith, M. (1995) "Film Spectatorship and the Institution of Fiction," *Journal of Aesthetics and Art Criticism* 53(2): 113–27.

—— (1996) "The Logic and Legacy of Brechtianism," in D. Bordwell and N. Carroll (eds.) *Post-Theory: Reconstructing Film Studies*, Madison: University of Wisconsin Press, 130–48.

Walsh, M. (1981) *The Brechtian Aspect of Radical Cinema*, ed. K. M. Griffiths, London: British Film Institute.

Willett, J. (1984) *Brecht in Context*, London and New York: Methuen.

Wollen, P. (1985) "Godard and Counter Cinema: *Vent d'Est*," in B. Nichols (ed.) *Movies and Methods*, vol. 2, Berkeley: University of California Press, 500–8.

Woodruff, P. (1988) "Engaging Emotion in Theatre: A Brechtian Model in Theater History," *Monist* 71: 235–57.

Further reading

See Gal Kirn, "*Kuhle Wampe*: Politics of Montage, De-Montage of Politics?," *Film-Philosophy* 11 (2007): 33–48; and James Lyon, *Bertolt Brecht in America* (Princeton, NJ: Princeton University Press, 1992). *Screen* (1975–6) is a special issue on Brecht.

31
NOËL CARROLL

Jonathan Frome

Noël Carroll (1947–) is one of the most influential philosophers of art of his generation. He has PhDs in both film studies and philosophy and has written about many
topics in aesthetics in addition to film, including other arts, such as literature and
dance, as well as more general topics, such as the definition of art. Although his work
is influential and frequently discussed in the realm of analytic aesthetics, it has been
harshly criticized or ignored in much of the mainstream film studies community, due
to Carroll's rejection of theories commonly utilized in that field. His early work focuses
on critiques of previous film theorists, including continental theorists who dominated
film studies in the 1970s and 1980s. By Carroll's own admission, his goal is to sweep
the table clean of these theories and encourage new film scholars to take a wholly
different approach. In *Post-Theory* (coedited with David Bordwell), Carroll criticizes
film scholars for their use of large-scale or "Grand" theories, such as Lacanian psychoanalysis and Althussarian Marxism. He argues that these theories are usually taken as
axiomatic and their frameworks are used to generate film interpretations rather than
to investigate the validity of the theories themselves. Carroll also argues that these
"Grand" theories have several problems per se. First, they are not only essentialist but
also have "every indication of being false" (Bordwell and Carroll 1996: 39). Second,
they are used dogmatically to exclude broad areas of inquiry from film studies. Finally,
they conflate film theorizing with film interpretation (albeit interpretation laden with
"theoretically derived jargon"), whereas the two are distinctly different activities.

For Carroll, film theorizing is a practice in which we should ask "middle-level"
questions and propose answers using limited theories that do not attempt to answer
every question about every type of film. He advocates a dialectical approach in which
smaller scale discussions of specific films are used to test larger theories and potentially
refine them. Those larger theories would be then used to generate (hopefully) better
answers to middle-level questions. Carroll argues that we should not start with a broad
theoretical framework we assume to be true, especially because the answers to middle-
level research questions will not necessarily all fit into one framework.

Due to his "piecemeal" approach, it is difficult to synthesize Carroll's writings into a
general theory of film. Nonetheless, his discussions can be said to have certain themes
running through them, as we shall see.

Film and antiessentialism

Carroll's view of film is distinctive in its critique of normative essentialism. His first book, *Philosophical Problems of Classical Film Theory* (1988a), offers detailed critiques of classical film theorists on the basis of their commitments to an essentialist concept of film. Specifically, he criticizes the influential theorists Rudolph Arnheim and André Bazin for basing their advocacy of certain film techniques on an erroneous view that film's nature legitimates the use of these techniques over others.

Arnheim's position was developed in a historical context in which it was commonly argued that film could not be art. After all, the argument goes, art is an expression of an artist's thoughts and feelings. When an artist creates a painting, everything on the canvas is there because the artist intended it to be there. In contrast, photography – and by extension, film – records reality automatically. Photographed images are a record of what was before the camera, not a view of the world as interpreted and expressed by an artist.

Arnheim's response to this position is to note that photography and film are not perfect recordings of reality. On the contrary, they necessarily transform reality (Arnheim 1957). An actual scene is three-dimensional, whereas a photographic image is two-dimensional. In real life, we experience time as smooth and uninterrupted, but a film can speed up, slow down, or skip over periods of time. These types of transformations of reality are based on choices made by the filmmaker, such as editing and framing. For this reason, Arnheim claims, film can be art. Further, since it is the essence of film to transform reality, Arnheim claims that the best films are those that transform reality in a meaningful and expressive way.

Although Bazin's position on praiseworthy filmmaking techniques almost directly opposes Arnheim's, Carroll argues that the structure of his position is similar. Bazin claims that one of the central functions of art is to immortalize the past (Bazin 1967). By this standard, film actually exceeds the capabilities of the traditional arts. Because it is an automatic recording device, it can more accurately capture the past than the other arts. Further, since the camera records without human intervention, film does not impose the preconceptions of the human mind on aspects of the world; it thus allows us to see the world in a new way. For Bazin, since film's essence is to capture and illuminate reality, the best films are those that exploit this capability through techniques such as the long take.

Carroll suggests that Arnheim's and Bazin's positions about the essence of film are the result of prior normative judgments about what types of films are to be preferred. For example, Bazin feels that long-take naturalistic films are praiseworthy in that they allow us to see the world in a new way. Thus, he identifies the essence of film as its recording capability, which justifies his advocacy of long-take films. But this preference for certain types of films is the result of the undefended assumption that there is value in seeing the world in the way that film allows. Carroll notes that film can be employed in many roles in our culture; it does not have one essential role that is more appropriate than others. Thus, it is unlikely that any theory based on a notion of film's essence will allow us to understand the many types and uses of film. A theory that answers questions about documentary film may be inappropriate for helping us understand why sight gags are funny, and vice versa. This argument forms the basis of Carroll's antiessentialism.

Carroll's antiessentialism also underlies his arguments against medium specificity, a view which holds that the arts each have certain unique capabilities, based on differences in their media (1996b). For example, sculpture is created with media that allow for certain three-dimensional effects not available to other arts, such as painting or dance. This view also holds that the best artworks are those that most fully exploit their unique capabilities, that is, capacities not shared with any other medium. Thus, one might think that the best sculptures are ones which most effectively use the three-dimensional capabilities of the medium. Carroll challenges media specificity, saying that it is not the case that the arts have distinctive media (Carroll, "Forget the Medium!" 2003b). It is difficult even to describe what counts as a medium. Is a medium the physical material used to create an artwork? Most arts are made with many types of materials; painting, e.g., requires paint, a tool to apply the paint, and something on which to apply the paint. It also seems wrong to say that the arts have unique media. A painting can be created using one's fingers as a primary tool, but a sculpture can as well. Thus, Carroll argues, there is no essential tie between an art form and any particular medium. Further, an art form's media can change. What we call "film" now comprises video and computer-generated images, in addition to images projected from film strips. For this reason, Carroll often uses the term "the moving image" rather than film (and all subsequent mentions of film in this essay should be read as meaning the moving image). But we would hesitate to say that film is now a different art simply because it includes different media than those present in its early years.

Based on these concerns about medium specificity, Carroll attempts to define film without recourse to the media that might be said to compose it ("Defining the Moving Image" 1996). He provides several necessary conditions for a representation or artwork to count as a film. The first is that the artwork must be a detached display. By "detached" Carroll means that an image is detached from the object it represents in a way that prevents a viewer from reliably orienting his or her body to the represented object. If I see an image of a horse on a movie screen, for example, I cannot orient my body toward the actual photographed horse. The image is detached from the object. Some might respond that, upon seeing an image of the Eiffel Tower, they can reliably orient themselves to the referent of the image, but this is true only if they already know where Paris is in relation to their current position. The orienting information is not provided by the image or the viewer's understanding of how the image is generated; it is solely based on the viewer's extrinsic knowledge of geography.

Another necessary condition for something to be a film is that it must have the potential to present moving images. A film might only present static images, and it might present only text rather than pictures, but we would still consider such works films if they had the potential to present images that appeared to move.

A third condition is that something can only be said to be a film if its token performances are generated by templates. What does this mean? Carroll defends an ontology of art that holds that some artworks, like the *Mona Lisa*, are particular objects, while other artworks, like *A Tale of Two Cities*, exist in thousands of copies. Two different editions of *A Tale of Two Cities* both count as instances of the artwork itself, because the artwork is not a physical book. There is not one physical copy of the novel which is the "real" artwork while others are merely duplicates of the original. Rather, every copy of the novel can be said to be a token of the artwork created from the same type (i.e., the same text). Similarly, every screening of *Goodfellas* can be considered a token performance of that film. A key feature of film is that its token performances are generated by the same type of template (typically a film print or a DVD) and are essentially similar. This is in contrast to theater, where the token performances differ substantially based on each theater company's interpretation of the script. A script and a film print are not templates in the same way, because to perform the play described in the script requires an artistic interpretation. Consequently, we can say that a theatrical performance is both a token performance of a play and an artwork in its own right. The play *Hamlet* can be an artistic success or failure, and a performance of that play can also be an artistic success or failure. In contrast, when a film is presented using a template, such as a film print, to generate a token performance, no similar artistic interpretation is required (excluding avant-garde films in which projection choices are part of the filmic performance). A film can only be said to be screened well or badly in a technical sense, not in an artistic sense. For this reason, an artwork can count as a film only if its performance tokens are not artworks in their own right.

Finally, a film must be two-dimensional. This apparently mundane requirement serves to exclude artworks such as music boxes from the domain of film. A music box with a spinning dancer is a detached display, presenting a moving image, where the performance is generated from a template but is not an artwork in its own right. But the music box is not two-dimensional, and thus cannot be considered a film.

Carroll's attempt to define film by positing necessary conditions may seem to contradict his antiessentialist positions. In response to this concern, Carroll notes that there are several different ways something might be considered essentialist. He argues that his definition of film is not essentialist in the sense used by medium-specificity theories because the definition does not define film in terms of any specific medium. Both the medium of a photographic film strip and the medium of videotape can count as a film. Another way something might be essentialist is by attempting to capture the essence of some kind of thing. Carroll argues that his definition of film cannot be said to describe film's essence because the conditions he proposes are not central to understanding how films function. This point seems questionable. For example, say we are trying to understand how people respond to films in ways that differ from their responses to actual objects. Whether films are two-dimensional or three-dimensional surely makes an important difference to our experience of them. Or, consider someone analyzing how films function in the world of aesthetic criticism. The differences between film and theater in terms of token-type relations would be an important part of that discussion.

In "Defining the Moving Image," Carroll (1996a) also argues that his definition is not essentialist, because he posits the conditions as necessary but not sufficient for classifying an artwork as a film, noting that a flipbook meets all of the conditions but is not what we normally mean when talking about films. In the more recent *The Philosophy of Moving Pictures* (2008), however, he proposes that these conditions are both necessary and sufficient. Carroll's definition invites a number of gray-area counterexamples – not only flipbooks but also historical antecedents to film, such as Mutoscope presentations, and possible future media, such as moving holograms. Carroll suggests that since he is defining "the moving image," rather than film proper, it is reasonable to include flipbooks and the like, although he thinks that moving holograms should be considered "moving sculptures," rather than moving images. Whether it is advantageous to include or exclude any particular example from the category of moving images presumably depends on the context of the discussion. However, Carroll does open himself to charges of essentialism in positing the conditions he presents as jointly sufficient for identifying what artworks count as films.

Comprehension and emotion

Another major dimension of Carroll's work is his attempt to understand how viewers comprehend and respond to films. In *Mystifying Movies* (1998b), Carroll criticizes the way that several strands of continental film theory dealt with the relationship between viewers and films. These theories, which dominated film studies in the 1970s and '80s, include semiology, which holds that filmic representation is a socially constructed symbolic system; Althusserian ideological criticism, which holds that film and many other institutions produce subjects to perform certain types of social roles; and Lacanian psychoanalysis, which holds that film's effect on the viewer is based on its ability to create or fulfill certain desires in his or her psyche. A common thread in the theories Carroll criticizes is the thesis that we can understand film as a language. Film scholars have combined these ideas to make various claims about how film affects viewers, such as the notion that film positions the viewer (often called the subject) through formal features such as shot/reverse-shot editing, and the claim that film's use of smooth-continuity editing allows it to surreptitiously present constructed aspects of society as natural.

In *Mystifying Movies*, Carroll harshly critiques these positions. He rejects Lacanian psychoanalysis in favor of models of the mind developed by cognitive psychology. In a number of his later works, he proposes alternate accounts of the viewer's relationship to film which rely on what he considers to be natural features of human beings (i.e., evolved or biological features), rather than on notions of social construction.

For example, in "Film, Attention, and Communication" (2003a), Carroll argues that although film is a major form of communication, it is not like a language. One reason is that there are no elements of film analogous to words, sentences, or rules of grammar. A shot is not like a sentence because it is not a compilation of discrete units. A shot does not have elements that function as a subject, predicate, or direct object does in a sentence. Further, the rules of grammar determine whether a sentence is well-formed. A sentence with subject/verb disagreement, for example, is not grammatical. The concept of grammaticality, however, does not apply to films or film sequences. Although there are sometimes said to be rules of film editing, such as the 180° rule, we cannot hold that a shot which violates this rule is "incorrect."

Finally, the words of a language have arbitrary connections to the objects to which they refer. The connection between the word "dog" and an actual dog is arbitrary. It could have been the case that we called dogs "elephants." Semiologists of film hold that the relationship between pictures and their referents are similarly arbitrary and also that pictorial conventions are culturally specific and must be learned. It is on this basis that semiologists say that we must learn to "read" a film. Carroll argues against this model by noting that film is a medium of *pictorial* representation, and, unlike words, film images do not have arbitrary connections to their referents. He cites an experiment by Julian Hochberg and Virginia Brooks, who raised their child in a picture-free environment for his first two years and thus formed no connections between pictures and words (Hochberg and Brooks 1962). When the child had developed a sufficient vocabulary, he was shown pictures without any labels and could identify what they were pictures of. He could identify the pictures based solely on a visual resemblance between the pictures and their referents. This and other pieces of evidence show that we primarily understand pictures by recognizing the objects in them based on our knowledge of what the actual objects look like, not by learning a system of codes.

Carroll similarly relies on folk psychology in understanding how other aspects of film function. For example, he argues that for films to communicate, they must direct the audience's attention to specific things on the screen. Several factors facilitate this process. The context of presentation (a darkened theater) encourages us to focus on the film. Movement also draws our attention because human beings have an adaptive sensitivity to movement in our environments. Many film techniques, such as shot scale, lighting, and framing can concentrate our attention on specific objects on screen, and drawing our attention allows the film to communicate information essential for us to understand the film.

Carroll discusses in detail a common technique in which we see a shot of a character looking off screen and then a shot of an object. This editing pattern communicates that the character is looking at that object (sometimes the pattern continues through several shots). This particular technique draws Carroll's attention because the notion that point-of-view editing has ideological implications has been influential in film studies. Some ideological theorists have claimed that this structure, which they call a "suture," simultaneously positions the subject in an ideological structure and masks its doing so (1982). Carroll argues to the contrary that point-of-view editing is not an unnatural construction with potentially pernicious effects; rather, it is popular because it effectively communicates information in a way that mirrors our natural perceptual and cognitive inclinations. When we see someone looking at something, the next thing we see is often what that person is looking at, because we have a natural tendency to follow someone's gaze. Point-of-view editing reflects this pattern by reproducing it on screen.

Our psychological tendencies also inform Carroll's account of how films tell their stories. Following George Wilson's (1986) discussion of narrative structure, Carroll proposes that most popular films have stories which proceed in a question/answer format. A movie's story proceeds when a movie scene poses or raises questions to be answered (or partially answered) in subsequent scenes. Carroll gives the example of a shot of an open door, which raises the question, "Why is the door open?" If a movie presents a scenario in which an asteroid threatens to destroy the Earth, it raises the question, "Will this disaster be averted?" We expect the film to answer this question, presumably at its climax. The process is driven by our natural thought processes, which encourage us to ask ourselves how events will proceed. Carroll calls this question/answer process *erotetic narration*.

Some movie scenes raise questions, others answer them, and some do both. As Carroll notes, the question whether King Kong can be stopped is answered when he is gassed into unconsciousness, but that scene also raises the question of what will happen once he is sent to New York. Further, we can understand questions as fitting into macro- or micronarrative structures. The microquestion, "will the 'launch missile' button be pushed in time?" organizes one scene in a film, but its answer also helps answer the macroquestion that organizes the movie as a whole: "will the asteroid destroy the Earth?" A movie has closure when all of the questions that have been posed by the narrative get answered. Most popular films aim for closure, while films of other types, such as art cinema, may intentionally avoid closure for aesthetic purposes.

Carroll also has written substantially on film and emotion. In his most recent work, he uses the term "affect" to refer to any bodily states associated with feelings. This includes reflexive states such as the state we are in when startled, sensory states such as pain, prototypical emotions like anger or joy, and general states of feeling such as moods. There are many ways film can create affect. At the most basic level, filmic stimuli such as loud noises or distasteful creatures such as spiders can generate feelings in the audience. Emotions, for Carroll, are a specific type of affective state that rely on appraisals of stimuli relative to our interests, and which incline us to act in certain ways. If you see a large creature and appraise it as threatening, you might feel a chill down your spine, and you might freeze in place. These elements constitute the emotion of fear.

A long-standing question in the philosophy of art is how fictional media, such as fiction films, can generate emotion. The so-called "paradox of fiction" is based on an apparent conflict between our emotions about fictions, such as a fear of a movie monster, and our knowledge that the monster, being fictional, poses no danger. The paradox extends beyond the emotion of fear. Why do we cry at a character's death, when we know that no one has actually died? Why do we want the good guy to beat the bad guy, when we know perfectly well that the good guy and bad guy do not really exist?

Carroll's solution to this quandary is what he calls the *thought theory*. Carroll argues that emotions are not necessarily responses to actual situations – they can be caused by thoughts as well. He gives the example of someone preparing to ask her boss for a raise. If she imagines her boss responding negatively, she may actually feel angry, even though the conversation has not yet taken place. Similarly, although we do not believe in the reality of a movie monster, just the thought of the monster can make us feel scared. Carroll ties this account to natural aspects of the human mind, saying that our ability to be emotionally aroused by imagination is evolutionarily advantageous because it assists us in planning future actions. For example, if we tell children stories about how strangers might kidnap and harm them, the very thought of wandering off with a stranger may cause a child to become scared. The emotion generated by the thought of wandering off thus encourages the child to act safely.

The concept of identification is typically used to explain how we relate to characters in films. Carroll notes that the term can be used in many ways. It can imply a type of mental projection in which a viewer imagines what it would be like to be a character. This type of imagination may be facilitated if the viewer and the character are similar in the right sorts of ways. For example, I might identify with a character who is a forklift operator because I once operated a forklift and thus can easily imagine what the character is experiencing. Or, I might imagine what it would be like to be a character very different from me who embodies qualities I admire – say, Superman. Carroll, however, says these situations should not be described with the term "identification." He says the former case is better described as feeling "affiliated" with a character and the latter as "wishful fantasizing."

Often, people think of identification as a process where we care deeply about a character in a manner that leads us to feel the same emotions the character feels. On Carroll's view, this is an appropriate use of the term identification because there is an identity relationship between the viewer's and character's emotions. But Carroll argues that this account is a poor description of the relationship between the viewer and character. In many situations, he notes, we may care deeply about characters but feel very differently than they do. Perhaps they are calmly walking down the road, not realizing (as we do) that there is a killer right behind them. We are scared for them, but they are not scared at all. In this case, our emotions are not identical.

Carroll argues that a better explanation of our emotional responses to film can be understood through the concept of *criterial prefocusing* – the notion that a filmmaker can focus the viewer on aspects of the story that address certain emotion-generating moral criteria. Filmmakers will often, but not always, present the story in a way that suggests the viewer should feel similarly to the protagonist. A character investigating a haunted house may be apprehensive, and the film's spooky soundtrack may encourage us to feel the same way. The film is structured to both generate our apprehension and to suggest the character's apprehension. Carroll believes that there is no reason to invoke the notion of identity in such a case.

Carroll presents a valid argument against identification as he understands it, but it could be argued that the narrowness of his definition blunts the force of the argument. He notes many situations in which people would say that they identify with a character even when their emotions do not match the character's emotion. He argues that other terms, such as affiliation, better describe those situations and that the term "identification" really only makes sense when used to describe a process where the character's emotions cause identical emotions in the viewer – a process that he then argues never actually occurs. If the goal is to describe and explain the feelings that ordinary people point to by using the term "identification," then it seems counterproductive to posit that many of those uses are not appropriate and that the word should be understood in only one sense.

Conclusion

Carroll's work is among the most cited in the field of aesthetics. In addition to the topics discussed above, he has made many substantial contributions to the philosophy of film which could not be discussed in this short entry. He has written genre analyses of horror, comedy, documentary, and the avant-garde; he has generated insightful critical essays on many individual films; and he has developed theories of narration, style, film evaluation, and the nature of art.

Carroll's keen skepticism and thorough critiques of theorists who aim to present comprehensive or overly broad accounts of how films work support his notion that the best approach to film theory is answering middle-level research questions. However, there is an irony here. Although Carroll argues against attempts at providing a comprehensive theory, the breadth of his writing and the consistency of his positions constitute a fairly comprehensive theoretical approach to film. His book *The Philosophy of Motion Pictures* belies the notion that middle-level research questions are in some way opposed to the construction of comprehensive theories. What this situation reveals is that, in fact, it is the top-down nature of most film theory that is the real target of his critique.

See also Definition of "cinema" (Chapter 5), Emotion and affect (Chapter 8), Empathy and character engagement (Chapter 9), Consciousness (Chapter 4), Gender (Chapter 13), Horror (Chapter 46), Psychoanalysis (Chapter 41), Cognitive theory (Chapter 33), Narration (Chapter 18), Narrative closure (Chapter 19), and Style (Chapter 25).

References

Arnheim, R. (1957) *Film as Art*, Berkeley: University of California Press.
Bazin, A. (1967) "The Evolution of the Language of Cinema," in H. Gray (trans.) *What Is Cinema?*, Berkeley: University of California Press.
Bordwell, D., and Carroll, N. (eds.) (1996) *Post-Theory: Reconstructing Film Studies*, Madison: University of Wisconsin Press.
Carroll, N. (1982) "Address to the Heathen," *October* 23: 89–163.
—— (1988a) *Philosophical Problems of Classical Film Theory*, Princeton, NJ: Princeton University Press.
—— (1988b) *Mystifying Movies: Fads and Fallacies in Contemporary Film Theory*, New York: Columbia University Press.
—— (1996a) "Defining the Moving Image," in *Theorizing the Moving Image*, New York: Cambridge University Press.
—— (1996b) "The Specificity of Media in the Arts," in *Theorizing the Moving Image*, New York: Cambridge University Press.
—— (2003a) "Film, Attention, and Communication," in *Engaging the Moving Image*, New Haven, CT: Yale University Press.
—— (2003b) "Forget the Medium!" in *Engaging the Moving Image*, New Haven, CT: Yale University Press.

—— (2008) *The Philosophy of Moving Pictures*, Malden, MA: Blackwell, 2008.

Hochberg, J., and Brooks, V. (1962) "Pictorial Recognition as an Unlearned Ability," *American Journal of Psychology* 75: 624–8.

Wilson, G. (1986) *Narration in Light*, Baltimore, MD: Johns Hopkins University Press.

32
STANLEY CAVELL

William Rothman

Stanley Cavell is the only major American philosopher who has made the subject of film a central part of his work. Film has figured centrally in four of his books and in numerous essays and occasional pieces. He has also reflected, philosophically, on other artistic media, such as theater, television, and opera, which bear an intimate relationship to film. To many philosophers, however, the relation of Cavell's writings on film to his explicitly philosophical writings remains perplexing. And within the field of film study, the potential usefulness of Cavell's writings – the potential usefulness of philosophy as he understands and practices it – remains generally unrecognized.

Cavell's philosophical perspective diverges in virtually every respect from the succession of theoretical positions that have gained most prominence in the field. Within academic film study, for example, it remains an all but unquestioned doctrine that "classical" movies systematically subordinate women, and, more generally, that movies are pernicious ideological representations to be decoded and resisted, not treated as works of art capable of instructing us as to how to view them. Film students are generally taught that in order to learn to think seriously about film, they must break their attachments to the films they love. Cavell's writings on film, by contrast, bespeak

> a sense of gratitude for the existence of the great and still-enigmatic art of film, whose history is punctuated as that of no other, by works, small and large, that have commanded the devotion of audiences of all classes, of virtually all ages, and of all spaces around the world in which a projector has been mounted and a screen set up. (Cavell 2005: 281)

It remains another largely unquestioned doctrine of academic film study that the stars projected on the movie screen are "personas," discursive ideological constructs, not real people; that the world projected on the screen is itself an ideological construct, not real; and, indeed, that the so-called real world is such a construct, too. By providing convincing alternatives to such skeptical positions, Cavell's writings on film are capable of helping academic film study free itself to explore regions that have remained closed to it – capable of inspiring the field to think in exciting new ways about film and its history.

What follows is a summary of the arguments of Cavell's best-known writings on film, *The World Viewed* (WV, 1979), *Pursuits of Happiness* (PH, 1981), and *Contesting Tears* (CT, 1996).

The World Viewed: Reflections on the Ontology of Film

The World Viewed incorporates reflections on film's origins, its historical development, its characteristic genres, the myths and human types around which those genres revolve; the medium's ability until recently to employ unselfconsciously traditional techniques that tap naturally into the medium's powers, and diverse other matters. Although it largely goes without saying, philosophy is central to Cavell's first book about film. In his view, it isn't possible to think seriously about film apart from philosophy. And philosophy cannot avoid film as a subject.

The World Viewed explores the ontological difference between film and painting by addressing the perplexing relationship between a photograph and the thing(s) and/or person(s) in that photograph. Photographs allow persons and things to reveal themselves. Yet it is misleading to suggest, as André Bazin did in "The Evolution of the Language of Cinema" (Bazin 1967: 30), that photographs satisfy painting's obsession with realism. First, because painting was obsessed with reality, not realism. So far as photography satisfied a wish, it satisfied the human wish – intensifying in the West since the Reformation – to escape the metaphysical isolation to which our subjectivity condemns us. "Apart from the wish for selfhood (hence the always simultaneous granting of otherness as well), I do not understand the value of art," Cavell writes (Cavell 1979: 22). Second, because photographs are not more realistic than paintings. Realistic as opposed to what? The world projected on the screen *is* real. Yet it does not exist (now). The world on film is a moving image of skepticism, as Cavell puts it, but the possibility of skepticism is internal to the conditions of human knowledge. That we don't know reality with certainty is a fact about what human knowledge is. It doesn't follow that we cannot know the world, or ourselves in it.

One of the book's guiding intuitions is that Hollywood westerns, musicals, romantic comedies, and melodramas of the 1930s and 1940s, no less than European master-pieces like *L'Atalante* (1934) or *Grand Illusion* (1937), are about the human need for society and the equal need to escape it, about privacy and unknownness, about the search for community. But a number of intuitions crucial to his later work hadn't yet occurred to Cavell. For example, that the combination of popularity and seriousness of "classical" American movies was a function of their inheritance of Emerson's and Thoreau's concerns, and his own, for human relationship. Those intuitions await the publication in 1979 of his first essay on Emerson, his reading of *The Lady Eve* (1941), and the monumental *The Claim of Reason*.

Pursuits of Happiness

In *The Postman Always Rings Twice* (1946) and *Double Indemnity* (1944), Cavell remarks in *The World Viewed*, the lovers die because they have killed, but also [because] they transgress the deeper law against combining sex and marriage. In a thousand other instances the marriage must not be seen, and the walk into the sunset is into a dying star: they live happily ever after – as long as they keep walking. (WV: 48)

Tellingly, Cavell invokes Thoreau's image, in the punning last sentence of *Walden*, of "the sun as but a morning" – and *mourning* – "star" (Thoreau 2002: 436, quoted in Cavell 1988: 54). For Thoreau, the morning of mourning, the dawning of grieving, is the alternative to what he calls "our present constitution," which must change (Cavell 1988: 54). Movies that end with a man and woman abandoned to a sexless marriage do not make explicit the necessity of transforming ourselves that Thoreau insists on. Cavell's invocation of movie couples walking into the sunset provides the penultimate image of a paragraph that singles out *The Philadelphia Story* (1940) and *The Awful Truth* (1937) as films in which "the marriage is established from the beginning and is worth having at the end" (WV: 49). All of *Pursuits of Happiness* can be glimpsed in *The World Viewed*'s linking of *The Philadelphia Story* and *The Awful Truth* to the culminating image of *Walden*. These are two of the seven films *Pursuits of Happiness* identifies as definitive "comedies of remarriage" (the others: *It Happened One Night* [1934], *Bringing Up Baby* [1938], *His Girl Friday* [1940], *The Lady Eve* and *Adam's Rib* [1949]). Remarriage comedies recount a story or myth about a woman and man who arrive at happiness not by overcoming societal obstacles to their love, as in classical comedy, but by facing divorce and coming back together.

Cavell understands the women of these films, played by the likes of Katharine Hepburn, Claudette Colbert, Irene Dunne, and Barbara Stanwyck, to be on a spiritual quest, like Emerson in his journals or the author in Thoreau's *Walden*. A non-American source Cavell cites is Nora in *A Doll's House*, who leaves her husband in search of an education he says she needs but she knows he can't provide. Unlike Nora, the woman in a remarriage comedy is lucky that her once and future husband is a man like Cary Grant or Spencer Tracy with the capacity to embrace her creation as a new woman, and lucky to have a father who, unlike the woman's father in classical comedy, wishes to award her to a man to whom she might freely award herself.

Such remarriage comedies, Cavell claims, exemplify a stage in the development of the consciousness of women at which the issue is mutual acknowledgment of the equality of women and men. The films' criteria for a marriage worth having – mutual trust and desire, as reflected in their conversation – have nothing to do with perpetuating patriarchal power. Neither church, nor state, nor society's need for children validates the marriage that the genre envisions, which also "marries" the realities of the day and the dreams of the night, the public and the private, and city and country. This last point is registered in the genre's insistence that the lovers at a certain moment find themselves in a location conducive to a new perspective. In *Anatomy of Criticism*, Northrop Frye influentially called this the Green World (Frye 2002: 85). Remarriage comedies usually call it Connecticut. "Connecticut" here means a perspective that discovers happiness here and now by living day and night in a spirit of adventure.

Each chapter presents what Cavell calls a reading of one comedy of remarriage.

The reading is guided by the claim that the film is an instance of a genre that inherits the preoccupations of late Shakespeare romance (*The Winter's Tale, The Tempest*). *Pursuits of Happiness* develops its understanding of genre when it asserts that instances of a genre do not share a set of features that can be completely specified. We may say they share *every* feature, so long as we remember, first, that what counts as a feature is not determinable apart from critical analysis; second, that a member of the genre may account for a feature's apparent absence by articulating a compensating circumstance (e.g., *It Happened One Night* compensates for lacking a Green World by the role played by the couple's being on the road). Cavell prefers to think of a genre's members as versions of a story or myth, or as sharing "certain conditions, procedures, and subjects and goals of composition." Each member *studies* those conditions, revises the ways other members have interpreted them, and earns membership in the genre by bearing the *responsibility* of its inheritance (PH: 28).

What a genre of film is, *Pursuits of Happiness* claims, is a matter internal to what remarriage comedies are, to what film is. What a reading of a film is, too, is such a matter. These last two facts bring home two further facts. First, although *Pursuits of Happiness* rarely refers to *The World Viewed*, it takes its reflections on film's ontology as its starting point. Second, *Pursuits of Happiness*, like *The World Viewed*, has a self-reflective dimension. What these readings enable us to know about film cannot be separated from what they enable us to know about *writing* about film. Not coincidentally, remarriage comedies, as they emerge in these readings, possess a self-reflective dimension, too.

In *The World Viewed*, Cavell argues that on film it is the human condition to be embodied, hence that film's emphasis on the bodies of women reveals that the medium singles women out as exemplars of the human. *Pursuits of Happiness* further develops this idea by insisting that each comedy has a way of "harping on the identity of the real woman cast in [the film], and each by way of some doubling or splitting of her projected presence" (PH: 64). This doubling or splitting is at once an emphasis on the *character's* identity and "an emphasis taken by the cinematic medium on the physical presence, that is, the photographic presence, of the real actress playing this part" (PH: 140). And each comedy also finds a way to declare its attention to the woman's projected presence as itself split or doubled. Thus the passage in *The Lady Eve* in which Jean first lays eyes on Hopsy virtually identifies the images on the screen with the images she sees in a mirror. "One plausible understanding of our view as Jean holds her hand mirror up to nature – or to society ... is that we are looking through the viewfinder of a camera" (PH: 66), Cavell writes. *The Lady Eve* presents the man as a stand-in for the viewer, the woman a stand-in for the director, and "as this surrogate she informs us openly that the attitude of the film begins with is one of cynicism or skepticism." By the end, this skeptical woman/artist becomes a member of this man's species, "the sucker sapiens, the wise fool; she has found what Katharine Hepburn at the end of *The Philadelphia Story* calls a human being; she has created herself, turned herself, not without some help, into a woman" (PH: 69).

The Lady Eve thus emerges as a story about a woman's overcoming or transcending skepticism. This helps us appreciate Cavell's observation in *Contesting*

Tears that looking back he sometimes sees *"Pursuits of Happiness* as an expression of the relief in completing the study of skepticism and tragedy in *The Claim of Reason"* (Cavell 1996: 11–12). *The Claim of Reason's* culminating reading of *Othello* fleshes out Cavell's discovery of the affinity between Cartesian skepticism and Shakespearean tragedy – as if what philosophy interprets as skepticism *is* what Elizabethan theater interprets as tragedy. Shakespeare's late romances discover a way of overcoming or transcending skepticism and thereby avoiding a tragic fate whose possibility is inherent in the condition of being human. In inheriting Shakespeare's concerns, but also transforming them (film is not theater), remarriage comedies discover their own ways – ways film makes possible – of overcoming or transcending skepticism.

Cavell writes:

> It is not news for men to try, as Thoreau puts it, to walk in the direction of their dreams, to join the thoughts of day and night, of the public and the private, to pursue happiness. Nor is it news that this will require a revolution, of the social or of the individual constitution, or both. What is news is the acknowledgment that a woman might attempt this direction, even that a man and a woman might try it together … For this we require a new creation of woman, call it a creation of the new woman … It is a new step in the creation of the human. (PH: 140)

Comedies of remarriage declare film's participation in this enterprise. The genre is committed to a way of thinking that affirms the possibility – and necessity – of radical change. Remarriage comedies affirm truths about the world, and about film, that Cavell too affirms, understanding himself thereby to be representative of the films' audience. Hence the special charm of *Pursuits of Happiness* – the sense that its author is enjoying a conversation with the reader as "meet and happy" as the conversation of a marriage worth having (even as these films enjoy such a conversation with their – our – culture).

Nonetheless, as Cavell anticipated, these readings have engendered resistance. The comedies *Pursuits of Happiness* addresses are (mostly) assumed to be escapist fairy tales for the Depression. And movie genres are (mostly) assumed to be formulas. "We seem fated to distort the good films closest to us, exemplified by the seven concentrated on in this book," he writes in a splendid passage:

> Their loud-mouthed inflation by the circus advertising of Hollywood is nicely matched by their thin-lipped deflation by those who cannot imagine that products of the Hollywood studio system could in principle rival the exports of revolutionary Russia, of Germany, and of France. This view … expresses, it feeds on, a pervasive conflict suffered by Americans about their own artistic accomplishments, a conflict I have described elsewhere as America's overpraising and undervaluing of those of its accomplishments it does not ignore. (PH: 39)

But something beyond that conflict keeps these films inaccessible to us. Remarriage comedies are films that many bear in their experience as memorable public events, segments of the experience, the memories, of a common life. So that the difficulty of assessing them is the same as the difficulty of assessing everyday experience, the difficulty of ... making oneself find the words for what one is specifically interested to say, which comes to the difficulty of finding the right to be thus interested ... This poses ... the specific difficulty of philosophy and calls upon its particular strength, to receive inspiration for taking thought from the very conditions that oppose thought. (PH: 41–2)

Contesting Tears

"Is it true in movies that virtue is always rewarded and vice vanquished?" Cavell asks in *The World Viewed* (WV: 48). Someone who draws the morals of movies too hastily might assume that movies condemn the "woman outside" for luring men to stray. Yet such a woman *is* "outside" because she rejects a marriage that would deny her nature, not because she is unworthy. It is a crucial datum in pondering the morals of movies that in films it is a moral imperative to pursue happiness. What Cavell discovered, in discovering this, is film's commitment to what in later writings, such as *Conditions Handsome and Unhandsome* and *Cities of Words*, he calls "moral perfectionism" or "Emersonian perfectionism" (Cavell 1990 and 2004: *passim*). In *The World Viewed* it is already a central theme that there is a serious moral philosophy internal to the stories movies are forever telling. In *Pursuits of Happiness*, Cavell doesn't use the term "perfectionism," but that way of thinking about morality is implicit throughout.

Cavell understands perfectionism not as a *theory* of morality, but as "a dimension or tradition of the moral life" (Cavell 1990: 2). Moral perfectionism is as internal to comedies of remarriage as it is to Shakespeare's late romances, Emerson's and Thoreau's writings, *A Doll's House*, or *Pursuits of Happiness* itself. "That there is no closed list of features that constitute perfectionism follows from conceiving of perfectionism as ... embodied in a set of texts spanning the range of Western culture" (4). *A Doll's House* is one. Nora's "imagination of her future, in leaving, turns on her sense of her need for education whose power of transformation presents itself to her as the chance to become human. In Emerson's terms, this is moving to claim one's humanness ... to follow the unattained" (115).

Cavell most fully develops the theme of a woman rejecting marriage to "follow the unattained" in *Contesting Tears: The Hollywood Melodrama of the Unknown Woman*. In the melodramas the book "reads" – *Gaslight* (1944), *Letter from an Unknown Woman* (1948), *Now, Voyager* (1942), *Stella Dallas* (1937) – the woman seeks fulfillment outside marriage. In comedies of remarriage, it is the man who claims the woman; he only needs prodding, while she undergoes a metamorphosis; and the woman's mother is absent, her absence underscored both by her father's role and by the fact that the woman herself is not a mother. In short, the creation of the woman is her own business, of course, but it is also the business of men, even though the creation is that of the so-called new woman, the woman of equality – as if there were a taint of villainy inherent in maleness. "This so to speak prepares the genre for its inner relation to melodrama," Cavell remarks in *Contesting Tears*, where he points out that *Pursuits of Happiness* predicted the discovery of a genre of melodrama adjacent to the comedy of remarriage, in which that genre's themes are negated in a way that hinges on the threats of misunderstanding and violence that dog the happiness of the comedies (CT: 5).

It is a claim central to *Contesting Tears* that the genre therein called the melodrama of the unknown woman is derived from the remarriage comedy by the mechanism of negation. For example, in these films

> the woman's father, or another older man (it may be her husband), is not on the side of her desire but on the side of law, and her mother is always present (or her search for or loss of or competition with a mother is always present), and she is always shown as a mother (or her relation to a child is explicit) ... [I]n the comedies the past is open, shared, a recurring topic of fun, no doubt somewhat ambiguous; but in melodramas the past is frozen, mysterious, with topics forbidden and isolating. Again, whereas in remarriage comedy the action of the narration moves ... from a setting in a big city to conclude in a place outside the city, a place of perspective, in melodramas of unknownness the action returns to and concludes in a place from which it began or in which it has climaxed, a place of abandonment or transcendence. (CT: 5–6)

The World Viewed claims that the most significant films are those that most meaningfully reveal the medium of film. *Pursuits of Happiness* develops this claim by arguing that comedies of remarriage reveal film's power of transfiguration, as expressed in the woman's suffering creation, where this refers both to the character's metamorphosis and to the transformation of the flesh-and-blood actress into projections of herself. *Contesting Tears* develops it further by reflecting on the fact that melodramas of the unknown woman register the woman's transformation less by revealing her body than by tracing its changes of costume and circumstance. Whatever role such a woman chooses to play at a given moment, she declares that in this role she is, and is not, herself, that her identity is not fixed. And she declares this with that "flair for theater, that theater of flair, exaggeration it may be thought, call it melodrama" that these films require of their leading women. Their star quality resides not in their beauty but their flair for declaring their distinctness, their freedom, their human *existence* (CT: 128). These women emblematize Cavell's intuition that "every single description of the self that is true is false, is, in a word, or a name, ironic" (CT: 134). So "one may take the subject of the genre ... as the irony of human identity as such" (CT: 134–5).

Cavell describes both remarriage comedies and melodramas of unknownness as "working out the problematic of self-reliance and conformity as established in the founding American thinking of Emerson and of Thoreau" (CT: 9). An earlier essay linked Emerson's idea of self-reliance with the Cartesian *cogito ergo sum*, Descartes' answer to philosophical skepticism (Cavell 1988: 10). Emerson's work, that essay claimed, proposes a new proof of human existence. And it linked Emerson's revision of Descartes' *cogito* to melodramas like *Now, Voyager*. The melodrama of the unknown woman, *Contesting Tears* argues, is an expression of a stage in the development of the skeptical problematic at which the theatricalization of the self becomes the main proof of the self's existence. And the book develops this suggestion by linking film with psychoanalysis. While men in movies primarily appear in contexts of mutual competition and of uniform or communal efforts, as *The World Viewed* argued, individual women have given film its depth. It is as if the role of women in originating both psychoanalysis and film – in psychoanalysis, as suffering subjects and in film, as subjects of the camera – reveals that by the turn of the twentieth century, psychic reality, the existence of minds, had become believable primarily in its feminine aspect. A star like Bette Davis reveals the affinity between film's interest in the "difference of women" and that of psychoanalysis, insofar as she

> taps a genius for that expressiveness … in which Breuer and Freud, in their *Studies in Hysteria*, first encountered the reality of the unconscious, the reality of the human mind as what is unconscious to itself, and encountered first in the suffering of women; a reality whose expression they determined as essentially theatrical, a theatricality of the body as such. (CT: 105)

In remarriage comedies, the woman's happiness depends on choosing the right man to educate her. Melodramas of the unknown woman, too, press the question of the woman's interest in knowledge, but "within their mood of heavy irony, since her knowledge becomes the object – as prize or as victim – of the man's fantasy, who seeks to share its secrets (*Now, Voyager*), to be ratified by it (*Letter from an Unknown Woman*), to escape it (*Stella Dallas*), or to destroy it (*Gaslight*), where each objective is (generically) reflected in the others" (CT: 13–4). In remarriage comedies, the "war between the sexes" is a struggle for mutual recognition. In melodramas of the unknown woman, the man struggles *against* recognizing the woman. The woman's struggle, as Cavell puts it, "is to understand why recognition by the man has not happened or has been denied or has become irrelevant, hence may be thought of as a struggle or argument (with herself) over her gender" (CT: 30). In each melodrama, the woman, unrecognized, isolated, is torn not simply over the conflicting desires or demands between being a mother and being a woman, say, but over questions

> as to what a mother does and what a woman is, what a mother has to teach, what a woman has to learn, whether her talent is for work or rather for the appreciation of work, whether romance is agreeable or marriage is refusable, how far idiosyncrasy is manageable. (CT: 198)

The ratifying of Stella's reliance on her own judgment – of her "taking on the thinking of her own existence, the announcing of her *cogito ergo sum* – happens without her yet knowing who this thinker is who is proving her existence (as in

351

Descartes' presenting of the *cogito*, it happens without his yet knowing who he is) (CT: 219). This woman's "walk toward us, as if the screen becomes her gaze, is allegorized as the presenting or creating of a star." As an interpretation of stardom, it "is the negation, in advance so to speak, of a theory of the star as fetish. This star, call her Barbara Stanwyck, is without obvious beauty or glamour ... But she has a future." Not only do we now know that this woman was to become the star of *The Lady Eve*, "she is presented *here* as a star (the camera showing her that particular insatiable interest in her every action and reaction), which entails the promise of return, of unpredictable incarnation" (two features of stardom *The World Viewed* singles out).

"The Emersonianism of the films I have written about as genres," Cavell writes,

> depict human beings as on a kind of journey ... from what he means by conformity to what he means by self-reliance; which comes to saying (so I have claimed) a journey, or path, or step, from haunting the world to existing in it; which may be expressed as the asserting of one's *cogito ergo sum* ... call it the power to think for oneself, to judge the world, to acquire – as Nora puts it at the end of *A Doll's House* – one's own experience of the world. (CT: 220)

For Cavell, acceptance of the woman's transfiguration in *Stella Dallas* provides "a certain verification of this philosophy, hence, of philosophy as such." *Contesting Tears* can be seen as part of his effort "to preserve that philosophy, or rather to show that it *is* preserved, is in existence, in effect, in works of lasting public power – world-famous, world-favored films – while the Emerson text itself, so to speak, is repressed in the public it helped to found" (CT: 220). Yet for all their popularity these films, too, are repressed in that public. Their thinking (mainly) remains unhonored and unsung (if hardly unwept):

> I assume that movies have played a role in American culture different from their role in other cultures, and more particularly that this difference is a function of the absence in America of the European edifice of philosophy. And since I assume further that American culture has been no less ambitious, craved no less to think about itself, than the most ambitious European culture, I assume further still that ... American film at its best participates in this Western cultural ambition of self-thought or self-invention that presents itself in the absence of the Western edifice of philosophy, so that on these shores film has the following peculiar economy: it has the space, and the cultural pressure, to satisfy the craving for thought, the ambition of a talented culture to examine itself publicly; but its public lacks the means to grasp this thought as such for the very reason that it naturally or historically lacks that edifice of philosophy within which to grasp it. (CT: 72)

The difficulty of grasping the thought of a remarriage comedy or unknown woman melodrama is the same as the difficulty of assessing everyday experience. Again, this difficulty calls for philosophy's capacity to receive inspiration for taking thought from the conditions that oppose thought. "Nothing much to me would be worth trying to understand" about a melodrama like *Now, Voyager*, Cavell writes,

> unless one cares for it, cares to find words for it that seem to capture its power of feeling and intelligence, in such a way as to understand why we who have caused it (for whom it was made) have also rejected it, why we wish it both into and out of existence. (CT: 117–8)

Cavell observes that despite most critics' condescension, *Stella Dallas*, *Gaslight*, *Now, Voyager*, and *Letter from an Unknown Woman* are worthy companions of the remarriage comedies. "They are of course less ingratiating," he adds. Indeed, they "are so often the reverse of ingratiating that it becomes painful to go on studying them. A compensating profit of instruction must be high for the experience to be justified" (CT: 7). The readings in *Contesting Tears* are worthy companions of those in *Pursuits of Happiness*, too, although they are less ingratiating, are indeed at times painful to study. In each melodrama, the woman suffers an isolation so extreme "as to portray and partake of madness," as Cavell puts it, "a state of utter incommunicability, as before the possession of speech" (CT: 16). The extremity of her isolation gives a woman like Stella a capacity to judge the world. But isolation so extreme is painful to think about. Less painful is to deny her power of judgment and fixate on the idea that she is oblivious of her own inadequacy. Not shrinking from the pain of thinking about Stella's thinking, Cavell's writing seeks to undo that fixation, to understand what is of value in such a woman, such a film. What, then, is the "compensating profit of instruction" in the understanding, the pain, exchanged in the writing, and reading, of *Contesting Tears*?

Cavell writes about these melodramas "as though the woman's demand for a voice, for a language, for attention to, and the power to enforce attention to, her own subjectivity, say to her difference of existence, is expressible as a response to an Emersonian demand for thinking" (CT: 220). What authorizes this supposition is his interpretation of Emerson's authorship as

> responding to his sense of the right to such a demand as already voiced on the feminine side, requiring a sense of thinking as reception ... and as a bearing of pain, which the masculine in philosophy would avoid. To overcome this avoidance is essential to Emerson's hopes for bringing an American difference to philosophy. (CT: 221)

Overcoming this avoidance, bearing the pain, is no less essential to Cavell's hopes to inherit philosophy, as received and founded in America by Emerson's (and Thoreau's) writings – essential to his hopes to preserve that philosophy, or rather to show that it *is* preserved, that it does exist.

Cavell ends the body of his reading of *Stella Dallas* by posing three questions. Does Emerson's idea of the feminine philosophical demand serve to prefigure the "difference of women" that film lives on? Does it articulate or blur the difference between the denial to women of political expression and a man's melancholy sense of his own inexpressiveness? And is the relation of the Emersonian and the feminine demands for language of one's own a topic for a serious conversation between women and men? "It is ... the logic of human intimacy, or separateness," Cavell writes, "that to exchange understanding with another is to share pain with that other, and that to take pleasure from another is to extend that pleasure. And what reason is there to enter this logic in a particular case?" (CT: 221). "No reason," Cavell concludes (with an echo of Wittgenstein's "Explanations come to an end somewhere").

In the words of *Contesting Tears*, *Pursuits of Happiness*, and *The World Viewed*, perhaps, the extremity of Stanley Cavell's own isolation can be glimpsed. But so can the way philosophy overcomes or transcends that isolation, finds its way to locate its author within the world, enables him to perform his own *cogito ergo sum*.

Contesting Tears does not shrink from the pain of thinking about the films it studies, but in most of his writings on film Cavell generously shares pleasures movies have given him, as well as pleasures philosophy alone is capable of providing (Are they the same pleasures?). Another way to put this is to say that there is poetry to Cavell's writing. In his writings on film, as in the films that move him to write this way about them, art and philosophy cannot be separated. "Unlike the prose of comic theatrical dialogue after Shakespeare," Cavell writes,

> film has a natural equivalent for the medium of Shakespeare's dramatic poetry. I think of it as the poetry of film itself, what it is that happens to figures and objects and places as they are variously molded and displaced by a motion-picture camera and then projected and screened. Every art, every worthwhile human enterprise, has its poetry, ways of doing things that perfect the possibilities of the enterprise itself, make it the one it is ... You may think of it as the unteachable point in any worthwhile enterprise. I understand it to be, let me say, a natural vision of film that every motion and station, in particular every human posture and gesture, however glancing, has its poetry, or you may say its lucidity ... Any of the arts will be drawn to this knowledge, this perception of the poetry of the ordinary, but film, I would like to say, democratizes the knowledge, hence at once blesses and curses us with it. It says that the perception of poetry is as open to all, regardless as it were of birth or talent, as the ability is to hold a camera on a subject, so that a failure so to perceive, to persist in missing the subject, which may amount to missing the evanescence of the subject, is ascribable only to ourselves ... as if to ... fail to trace the implications of things ... requires that we persistently coarsen and stupefy ourselves. (Cavell 1984: 12)

The study of film cannot be a worthwhile human enterprise, in Cavell's view, when it isolates itself from the kind of criticism Walter Benjamin had in mind when he argued, as Cavell paraphrases him, that "what establishes a work as art is its ability to inspire and sustain criticism of a certain sort, criticism that seeks to articulate the work's idea; what cannot be so criticized is not art" (Cavell 2005: 283).

Marrying film and philosophy, Cavell's writings do not miss the poetry of either subject, and thinking about film emerges as a worthwhile human enterprise, indeed. In these writings, the study of film achieves its own poetry, its own "ways of doing things that perfect the possibilities of the enterprise itself, make it the one it is." That is the "unteachable point" of Cavell's writings on film, the lesson they above all aspire to teach.

See also Ethics (Chapter 10), Gender (Chapter 13), Genre (Chapter 14), and Walter Benjamin (Chapter 28).

References

Bazin, A. (1967) *What is Cinema?*, Berkeley: University of California Press.

Cavell, S. (1979) *The World Viewed: Reflections on the Ontology of Film*, Cambridge, MA: Harvard University Press.

—— (1981) *Pursuits of Happiness: The Hollywood Comedy of Remarriage*, Cambridge, MA: Harvard University Press.

—— (1984) *Themes Out of School: Effects and Causes*, San Francisco: North Point Press.

—— (1988) *In Quest of the Ordinary: Lines of Skepticism and Romanticism*, Chicago: University of Chicago Press.

—— (1990) *Conditions Handsome and Unhandsome: The Constitution of Emersonian Perfectionism*, Chicago: University of Chicago Press and Open Court Press.

—— (1996) *Contesting Tears: The Hollywood Melodrama of the Unknown Woman*, Chicago: University of Chicago Press.

—— (2004) *Cities of Words: Pedagogical Letters on a Register of the Moral Life*, Cambridge MA: Harvard University Press.

—— (2005) *Cavell on Film*, ed. W. Rothman, Albany: SUNY Press.

Frye, N. (1957) *Anatomy of Criticism: Four Essays*, Princeton, NJ: Princeton University Press.

Thoreau, H. D. (2002) *Walden*, Mineola, NY: Dover.

33
COGNITIVE THEORY
David Bordwell

The cognitive revolution in linguistics, psychology, anthropology, and other social sciences had a profound impact on philosophy, but its effect on other areas of the humanities was far more muted. In particular, research into cinema was largely untouched by questions of information processing, metal representations, modularity, and other lines of research. But cinema has obvious psychological and social effects, and it was probably inevitable that some researchers would turn to the emerging cognitive sciences for assistance in answering questions of film theory.

The key intersection involves theories about how spectators respond to cinema. What accounts of human mental activity best help us understand the ways in which films stir our senses, arouse our passions, and provoke us to thought?

Precursors

Soon after cinema was invented, philosophers and psychologists, as well as filmmakers, proposed theories of how cinema related to the human mind. During the 1920s, for example, Sergei Eisenstein suggested that film functioned as a Pavlovian stimulus, triggering reflexes in its audience (see the "Sergei Eisenstein" entry in this volume). In 1933 Rudolf Arnheim proposed an account indebted to gestalt theories of mental activity. Other thinkers suggested, particularly in the 1940s, that cinema aroused responses that could best be explained by psychoanalytic concepts.

At least two theorists of the early years suggested what might be called protocognitivist theories of cinematic effects. In 1916, as American motion picture production was shifting toward the feature-length film we know today, philosopher and psychologist Hugo Münsterberg published *The Film: A Psychological Study*. In what was arguably the first book of film theory, Münsterberg argued that the distinctive feature of cinematic storytelling was its ability to mimic not only the content of the real world but also the processes by which we conceive it.

Münsterberg noted that perceptually, the cinematic illusion was at once supremely convincing and yet obviously artificial. Thanks to photography and continuous movement, we see a realistic world, yet we also perceive the projected display as a two-dimensional picture. Taking a somewhat Kantian and gestaltist line, he noted that movement was in effect "superadded" to the projected still frames in "a higher mental act" (2002: 77). From this foundation Münsterberg went on to survey a range of mental activities, from perception to more abstract processes of reasoning and inference. He argued that in all arts, the guiding of attention is crucial, and that cinema has unique means for doing this – not only through movement and performance (possible in the theater) but also through close-ups and composition. The cinema can also imitate the more cognitive activities of memory and imagination through flashbacks and fantasy sequences. And by cutting between actions taking place in different places, a film can integrate events "just as they are brought together in our own consciousness" (2002: 96).

In sum, Münsterberg argues, the modern photoplay creates a world designed to facilitate the exercise of our faculties. Freed from physical time, space, and causality, it provides experiences "adjusted to the free play of our mental experiences ... [in] complete isolation from the practical world" (2002: 138). Münsterberg's Kantian psychology corresponded to a somewhat Kantian aesthetic, whereby cinema offered a pure exhibition of the mind transforming the everyday world into a self-enclosed artistic experience.

Instead of explaining the psychological mechanisms that underpin cinema, Münsterberg offers a defense of an emerging film style, couched in terms of everyday psychology. Yet his focus on cinematic storytelling and his concrete attention to techniques that were still very new made The Photoplay a landmark in film aesthetics. It was not regarded as such at the time, largely because intellectuals of his day considered the cinema merely mass entertainment. His ideas were echoed, however, in nearly every study of film as an art form published over the next fifty years. For instance, Mitry's two-volume Esthétique et psychologie du cinéma (published in 1966 and 1968) put forth a mentalistic account reminiscent of Münsterberg's. Mitry suggests that the filmmaker solicits the "logic of implication," a set of universal perceptual and cognitive processes, but then exploits them in order to organize images and sounds into a unique whole more coherent than everyday reality (1997). Likewise, the philosopher George Wilson proposed that mainstream narrative cinema relied upon our ordinary capacities to perceive the world and understand others' behavior, but it goes on to create a patterned whole that extends "the meaningful perceptual experience of human obse͜vers" (Wilson 1986: 84).

͜e semiological tradition

In France after the Sec͜ ͜orld War, a group of thinkers gathered under the rubric of "filmologie," seeking ͜ ͜dy cinema with the tools of psychology and sociology. Distinguishing between ͜imic" facts, which bear on the expressive possibilities and effects of the medium, and "cinematic" facts, which involve the ways in which social institutions absorb and utilize films, several of the filmologists were concerned with the pedagogical uses of film, and this interest led them to conduct experiments on filmic comprehension in relation to the "mental age levels" differentiated by Jean Piaget. Filmologists also experimented with EEG monitoring of film viewing, with ambiguous results (Lowry 1985: 138–56). Filmology waned in the late 1950s, but in its insistence on a scientific approach to cinema it set the stage for a more long-lived line of thought.

Ferdinand de Saussure's *Course in General Linguistics*, initially published in 1915, began to lead several writers and scholars in mid-century Europe to revive his proposal to study "the life of signs in society" (1970: 16). Sympathetic accounts by Claude Lévi-Strauss, Roland Barthes, and Umberto Eco in the early 1960s put Saussure's ideas on the agenda. As students of art, literature, and music followed this line of inquiry, semiology emerged as an important area of the humanities. The Parisian academic Christian Metz became the leader of semiological thinking about cinema.

Influenced by both phenomenology and filmology, Metz set himself a crucial problem. "The fact that must be understood is that films are understood" (1974: 145). What enables us to grasp images, sounds, and the stories they tell? In a series of writings published during the 1960s and 1970s, Metz explored the possibility that the methods of Saussurean linguistics could furnish an account of cinematic meaning. Many theorists had looked for cinematic equivalents of grammar, metaphor, or morphology, but Metz denied that film had strong resemblances with verbal language. A shot was not equivalent to a word, as some Soviet theorists had maintained. It did not have that double articulation, between phonology and semantics, characteristic of a morpheme. Moreover, the image resembled what it showed, so it lacked the arbitrariness characteristic of the linguistic sign.

Yet the Saussurean frame of reference enabled Metz to posit that at certain levels, film was coded in the binary fashion of other semiotic systems. His most famous accomplishment was to show that at the level of the sequence, narrative cinema displays a systematic set of alternatives – what semiologists called a paradigm – that denote the temporal and spatial relationships among shots. For example, a filmmaker may present a scene in a single shot or in more than one shot. If the second option is chosen, the shots may be chronological or nonchronological in their temporal unfolding. Each of these possibilities harbors further alternatives (1974: 119–35). The result is a taxonomy of branching options.

This "Grand Syntagmatique," as Metz called it, is, like most aspects of cinematic expression, "codified but not arbitrary" (1974: 135). The shot combinations are conventional to some degree. But each type of sequence can be quickly learned, because all to one degree or another call upon practices of ordinary thinking. In an echo of Jakobson on phonology and Chomsky on grammar, Metz pointed out that of all the infinite combinations of shots that were possible, storytelling cinema called on very few – those which could be naturally grasped by ordinary adults.

Like Münsterberg, Metz was largely uninterested in the mental processes shaping this spontaneous uptake. Rigorously object-centered, determined to expose the structures underpinning cinematic expression, the first wave of cinema semiologists paid little attention to explaining filmic comprehension psychologically. When they turned in this direction, the sort of explanation they posited was psychoanalytic, not cognitive. In the 1970s, Metz and others began tying the play of cinematic signifiers to processes of identification and repression posited by Jacques Lacan (himself much influenced by Saussure). But Metz's initial impulse, to explain what made cinematic comprehension possible, was to be treated as both an aesthetic and psychological project by Anglophone academics and, somewhat later, other French ones.

New Look psychology in the lab and at the movies

One of the principal sources of the cognitive revolution was the so-called New Look trend in American psychology of the late 1950s. The reigning tradition of Behaviorism had declared mental life inaccessible to rigorous scientific experimentation and had posited human behavior as largely an affair of stimulus/response. Against this, several researchers argued that psychologists needed to open the black box and study principles that governed memory, thinking, and judgment. Jerome Bruner, George Miller, Irwin Rock, and R. L. Gregory were among this generation.

The New Look researchers proposed what has been called a constructivist research program, whereby the mind actively contributes to the shaping of experience. Mental processes are not wholly stimulus-bound. The mind goes "beyond the information given," in Bruner's famous phrase (1973), and fills in or extrapolates from what is supplied by brute experience. While the gestaltists had shown this to be the case for geometrical figures and abstract flashes of light, the New Look researchers posited that mental activity furnishes both structure and content. The mind is so made that it harbors assumptions – that lighting comes from above, that objects are bounded and are not infinitely plastic – and contextual expectations which it brings to every encounter with the world. We see what we expect to see; the very concept of surprise entails a violation of expectations.

Illustrating the point with ambiguous and illusory images, most famously the duck/rabbit drawing, New Look thinkers held that any sensory array is inherently ambiguous. Something like thinking, however quick and dirty, must go on at the perceptual level in order to interpret the world as three-dimensional, furnished with discrete objects, and so on. In this respect the New Look paradigm developed a broadly Kantian position and built upon Helmholtz's suggestion that mental experience, including low-level perceptual processes, is governed by "unconscious inference" (Gardner 1985: 100). This theory of cognitive constructivism, with its commitment to active information processing, was eventually to converge with a full-blown computational model of mind.

Julian Hochberg, a Columbia University researcher into psychophysics, with a strong New Look orientation (Hochberg 1964), became interested in how images represent the world. After conducting several studies with static pictures and movies, he published a comprehensive overview of how spectators perceive cinematic displays (Hochberg and Brooks 1978). This article became the basis of a robust research program updated over the decades (Brooks 1984–5; Hochberg and Brooks 1996; see especially Peterson *et al.* 2007).

Hochberg and his collaborator showed that viewers extract a rich, structured body of information from films, and that this information is predicated on assumptions about the regularities of our phenomenal world. With unprecedented care he analyzed illusory motion on the screen, showing that several processes, not simply "persistence of vision," are in play. Hochberg and Brooks also attended to the psycho-logical processes involved in seeing different shots of a locale. They suggested that making sense of a film's discontinuous views relies upon saccadic eye movements, our tendency to sample our environments, and our ability to remember landmarks. The practice of cutting, therefore,

> must tap abilities that we employ in the real world to guide our purposeful perceptual inquiries: The actions by which we obtain the perceptual infor-mation (e.g., ballistic saccades) to guide our larger actions (like locomotion) must themselves be guided by some expectations about what the eye will see. (1978: 297)

Hochberg and Brooks pointed the way toward a study of film using the experimental techniques of the social sciences. But as film studies developed in the academy during the 1970s, it moved into humanities departments and was resolutely separated from empirical psychology. A few humanities scholars developed New Look thinking in relation to the arts; E. H. Gombrich (1960, 1982) brought that framework to the study of art history, and cognitive musicology developed as a strong wing of music studies. By contrast, film scholars, like their counterparts in literature departments, were far more influenced by Continental trends toward social and political critique, largely of a neo-Marxist variety, and toward psychoanalytic theory, largely derived from Jacques Lacan's recasting of Freudian theory. These trends took virtually no notice of the cognitive revolution in psychology, linguistics, and allied fields.

The first book within film studies to offer an explicitly cognitive approach was David Bordwell's *Narration in the Fiction Film* (1985) (NiFF). The book fell within a recognizable tradition of film aesthetics, addressing familiar problems of how structure and style functioned in cinematic storytelling. But Bordwell also took a reverse-engineering approach, arguing that the regularities of narration revealed by film analysis indicated that films were designed to elicit particular activities from spectators. Many of those activities had already been identified by researchers in perceptual and cognitive psychology.

Narration in the Fiction Film thus sought a rapprochement between narratology and cognitive science. For instance, it suggested that Hollywood films' reliance on a certain plot structure, involving characters with goals that are definitely fulfilled or thwarted, tallied with what researchers in story comprehension had identified as the "canonical story format" (see Mandler 1984). Bordwell also sought to show how narrative strategies mobilize prototype thinking, the primacy and recency effects, and other reasoning shortcuts. In effect, he was proposing perceptual and inferential mechanisms underlying the "natural understanding" of cinematic expression posited by Mitry, Metz, and other theorists.

Influenced principally by the New Look school and by Gombrich's perceptual-cognitive approach to art history, Bordwell treated the film spectator as an active information seeker. The viewer was said to frame expectations about upcoming events, fit actions into larger frameworks, and apply schemas derived from world knowledge and cinematic traditions. NiFF went into considerable detail about narrative modes different from those of "classical" storytelling, ones that thwarted the canonical story to achieve other purposes.

In a later work, Bordwell applied a constructivist model to film interpretation. *Making Meaning* (1989b) analyzed how critics deployed institutionally sanctioned schemas, heuristics, and mental models. His argument relied particularly on George Lakoff's studies in prototype theory. Bordwell carried the cognitive framework into the analysis of film style by adopting rational-agent assumptions in his study of the Japanese filmmaker Yasujiro Ozu (1988) and of technical choices faced by filmmakers in certain historical circumstances (1997).

Related to Bordwell's enterprise was the effort of Noël Carroll to specify the sources of the cross-cultural reach of cinema. Carroll (N. Carroll 1985) argued that the analogy of film to verbal language failed because viewers could grasp the premises of cinematic imagery and storytelling far more quickly than they could learn a language. This led him to itemize factors, ranging from pictorial design to patterns of cutting that created "the power of movies." Carroll's project, reminiscent of Münsterberg's, anchored a great deal of cinematic expression in universals of human perception and inference, which made filmic conventions intuitive and easy to learn. In tandem, Paul Messaris (1994) reviewed the empirical research on the comprehension of films and television across cultures. He concluded that most of the pictorial conventions of mainstream moviemaking are grasped immediately or can be learned very easily. Neither Carroll nor Messaris pledged allegiance to as specific a theory of psychological activity as Bordwell had, but their arguments broadly supported the cognitive program.

During the 1980s Carroll pursued cognitively flavored research projects along other fronts. In Albert Michotte's studies in perceptual causality he found explanatory principles for the effects of certain practices of match-cut editing (1996: 169–86). In contrast with his investigation of cross-cultural communication, Carroll examined ways in which particular languages could inform cinematic images, as when a broken mirror calls to mind the idea of "shattering," which can in turn be attached to a protagonist's state of mind. He suggested that verbal images like this may owe more to illocutionary principles than to traditional notions of metaphor (N. Carroll 1996: 187–211). Such tightly focused studies exemplify what Carroll called "piecemeal" theorizing. In preference to proposing a sweeping account of all cinema and its effects, he urged researchers to concentrate on probing midrange problems in depth.

All of this work constituted a criticism, voiced or tacit, of the dominant psycho-analytic accounts of spectators' activities. In "A Case for Cognitivism" (1989a) Bordwell spelled out several divergences between the two perspectives. He and Carroll also edited *Post-Theory* (Bordwell and Carroll 1996), an anthology that, while not a manifesto of cognitivism, offered a variety of alternatives to the reigning psychoanalytic model. Despite these overtures, followers of Lacanian theory did not undertake a systematic critique of the cognitive program or respond to objections to their approach.

Although the cognitive approach remained confined to a small minority, dissatisfaction with the psychoanalytic program grew, and by the early 1990s it was largely supplanted. "Cultural Studies" became, and still remains, the dominant approach to understanding media. Bordwell's essay in *Post-Theory* (Bordwell and Carroll 1996) traced affinities between Cultural Studies and the psychoanalytic perspective and suggested that both rested upon weak accounts of how viewers respond to films. No replies were forthcoming, and a sustained conversation between the cognitive and Cultural Studies approaches has yet to occur.

Semiology revisited

The tradition just outlined treated cinema's effects as grounded in processes of perception, inference, and judgment as revealed by Anglo-American cognitive psychology. Elsewhere, an alternative line of thought continued Metz's exploration of the relations, both methodological and substantive, between language and cinema.

Metz's Saussurean account of filmic systems largely ignored the generative grammar revolution of the late 1950s. Saussure's theory centered on phonology and lexical semantics: the prototypical sign was the word, and its meaning was derived differentially from alternatives. So *cat* gains its meaning by virtue of differing from *cad* phonologically and *dog* lexically. Chomsky was far more interested in syntax and the way it could govern the production and comprehension of new well-formed sentences. His belief in the creative power of language and the tacit rules for sentence structure tallied with the New Look's mentalistic critique of Behaviorist psychology. More broadly, Chomsky's approach to linguistics offered support for computational and modular theories in cognitive science.

Very few theorists of the nonliterary arts drew on Chomskyan linguistics as a model. An early effort in film studies was made by John M. Carroll (1980), who proposed a "cinematic grammar" along the lines of transformational grammar, based on the assumption that a shot has a sentence-like structure. So, for example, a deletion rule in language (saying "The car next to mine was scratched," instead of "The car which was sitting next to mine, etc.") might also explain elliptical cutting in cinema. Carroll tested some of his theoretical claims experimentally with purpose-made films.

At the same time, some French researchers sought to revise semiology in the light of developments in linguistics. Like John M. Carroll, Michel Colin argued that a shot could be considered an utterance and that beneath film images and sequences we can find generative linguistic structures (Colin 1985). Colin's argument blended aspects of Chomsky's early syntactic theory, the generative semantics of George Lakoff and Ray Jackendoff, and the functionalist theories of M. A. K. Halliday and others (O'Leary 1999). Colin concluded that in important respects verbal language and writing systems shaped cinematic structure. For instance, he believed that shot composition in Western filmmaking followed the theme/rheme, left-to-right pattern of grammar and writing systems. Before his death, Colin was exploring Metz's Grande Syntagmatique with respect to mental representations of space and time as revealed in perceptual experiments (Colin 1992). Principal works by Colin and other Parisian researchers in the semiological vein have been translated and collected in Buckland (1995).

Cognition, evolution, and emotion

The 1990s and 2000s saw rapid expansion and refinement in Anglo-American cinematic cognitivism. Some scholars pursued the constructivist line of inquiry. Edward Branigan (1992) developed a multi-leveled model of cinematic narration, hinging on the multiple sources of narrative authority. James Peterson (1994) showed how two strains of American avant-garde cinema, pop and minimalist cinema, demanded viewing strategies based on distinct schematic rules. Murray Smith (1995) developed a theory of characterization in cinema that relied upon a conception of a person schema and showing how different genres and cinematic traditions revised it for various storytelling purposes.

In academic psychology, New Look theories had been countered by James J. Gibson's broadly evolutionist ecological approach. Gibson argued that perceptual activity was not as mentalistic as many had thought; it wasn't like solving a problem or drawing an inference. Instead, low-level, hardwired mechanisms had evolved by virtue of extracting information from regularities of the natural environment. Likewise, the constructivist initiative in film studies was countered by a broadly evolution-driven account of cinematic experience. Joseph Anderson's *The Reality of Illusion* (1996) argued that many aspects of cinematic technique could be understood as targeting capacities developed across the history of the human species.

Anderson argued that seeing an image as having depth, for example, is not the arbitrary imposition of bourgeois ideology, as some French-influenced theorists were maintaining. Nor does it rely upon an overlearned skill of applying the proper visual schema to resolve images' inherent ambiguity, as the New Look tradition had suggested. Images aren't in fact ambiguous because the sensory array isn't ambiguous, at least to creatures like us. We evolved in a three-dimensional world that permitted us to move freely, and our visual system is biased toward spontaneously seeing any slice of that world as providing reliable information about a three-dimensional space. No higher processes, of either ideological inculcation or schema-driven inference, are necessary.

The Reality of Illusion went on to apply ecological and evolutionary considerations to traditions of cutting, storytelling, and thematic interpretation. With Barbara Fisher Anderson, Anderson furthered a Gibsonian approach to cinematic communication by assembling an anthology of work by psychological researchers (Anderson and Anderson 2005).

By the late 1990s, cognitive film studies' range of inquiry paralleled some trends in cognitive science at large. Gregory Currie (1995) brought analytical techniques from the philosophy of mind to questions of the cinematic image. While a truly computational account of cinematic response was never developed, some scholars turned in another direction, toward neuroscience. This development was at least partly encouraged by a new attention to the problem of how films triggered emotions.

Narration in the Fiction Film had bracketed most emotions out of consideration, considering only the "cognitive" emotions of curiosity, suspense, and surprise. Carroll was far more concerned with feeling, putting forth theories of horror and suspense (N.

Carroll 1990). He argued for a version of appraisal theory, whereby people arrive at some judgment about the situation before being aroused emotionally. To feel anger, I must believe that someone has wronged me or mine. Likewise, we feel suspense during a film sequence because we judge that a desirable outcome of the events portrayed is far more unlikely than the undesirable outcome. In a study of characterization in film (1995), Murray Smith relied upon comparable concepts in showing that the flow of story information shapes our emotional response. At the same time, he drew upon studies of empathy, sympathy, affective mimicry, and other activities to study how filmmakers can create more visceral, less explicitly inference-driven emotions.

The reliance upon experimental evidence for emotional responses to film became a distinct trend in the late 1990s. Ed S. Tan was the first to propose a full-blown empirical account of cinematic emotion, in *Emotion and the Structure of Narrative Film* (1996). Tan linked the schema-based activities of the viewer, as proposed by Bordwell and others, to a central and overriding emotional state, that of interest. Interest involves cognitive processes, like expectation, attention, and problem-solving, but it also allows for "investment," a state of tension and resolution built around the viewer's concerns for the characters, such as their hopes and fears. Establishing interest as the center of the film's emotional effects allowed Tan to address matters of plot structure, the flow of story information, and characterization. Tan's work wove together several strands from film theory and from empirical studies of story comprehension in film and literature.

Like Tan, Gregory Smith (2003) sought to trace the affective arc involved in the viewer's ongoing comprehension of a narrative film. But Smith argued that the emotional dynamic of films was stronger than Tan's "interest," involving instead the maintenance of mood. The film's action and manner of telling establish fairly free-floating tenors or moods that prime us for vigorous but transient spikes of emotion proper. Whereas Tan remained agnostic about the brain events that underwrote the emotional appeals of fictional storytelling, Smith posited neural events, centrally in the amygdala, as primary causes for both moods and emotions. Smith also coedited an important collection of essays on emotion in cinema (Plantinga and Smith 1999).

Both Tan and Smith limited their inquiry to traditional story-based filmmaking. Torben Grodal's *Moving Pictures: A New Theory of Film Genres, Feelings, and Cognition* (1997) proposed a more comprehensive account of the interaction of cognition and emotion. Synthesizing constructivism and the Gibsonian approach in what he calls "ecological conventionalism," Grodal outlines a holistic theory. He argues that schematic structures, many of them the result of evolution, are not simply invoked by stimuli in the film. They are primed and elaborated by the viewer's affective states, which in turn are produced by the brain and the central nervous system.

According to Grodal, narrative sequences invite us to conceive objects in an "enactive" mode aimed at an object or goal, creating a rhythm of tension and relaxation. This activity is characteristic of the right brain hemisphere, with its bias toward active coping and the investment of hopes and fears. Lyrical film sequences, by contrast, tend to halt story time and create a network of metaphorical associations that appeal to passive emotions and left-hemisphere activity. In a Tarkovsky film, for instance, a scene of pounding rain might be narratively inconsequential but evoke qualities associated with cleansing and nourishment. Grodal further elaborated these ideas in *Embodied Visions* (forthcoming). The shift to questions of emotion had led Smith and Grodal to try to specify the brain processes underlying cinematic experience. The mental had become explicitly neural.

Current developments

Today film research shaped by the cognitive sciences may be said to have staked out a small but recognizable terrain within cinema studies. The publication of synthetic overviews such as Buckland (2000), Jullier (2002), Perron (2002), Persson (2003), Bordwell (2007), and Plantinga (forthcoming) indicates that the research program is consolidating and expanding. So too does a series of international conferences on the subject, sponsored by the Society for Cognitive Studies of the Moving Image. Although cognitive film studies has not yet reached maturity, they remain one of the principal areas in which ideas from philosophy and cognitive science have shaped research into the theory and analysis of the arts.

See also Consciousness (Chapter 4), Emotion and affect (Chapter 8), Empathy and character engagement (Chapter 9), Narrative closure (Chapter 19), Spectatorship (Chapter 23), Christian Metz (Chapter 36), Semiotics and semiology (Chapter 42), David Bordwell (Chapter 29), and Noël Carroll (Chapter 31).

References

Anderson, J. D. (1996) *The Reality of Illusion: An Ecological Approach to Cognitive Film Theory*, Carbondale: Southern Illinois University Press.

Anderson, J. D., and Anderson, B. F. (eds.) (2005) *Moving Image Theory: Ecological Considerations*, Carbondale: Southern Illinois University Press.

Bordwell, D. (1985) *Narration in the Fiction Film*, Madison: University of Wisconsin Press.

—— (1988) *Ozu and the Poetics of Cinema*, London: British Film Institute; Princeton, NJ: Princeton University Press.

—— (1989a) "A Case for Cognitivism," *Iris* 9: 11–40.

—— (1989b) *Making Meaning: Inference and Rhetoric in the Interpretation of Cinema*, Cambridge, MA: Harvard University Press.

—— (1997) *On the History of Film Style*, Cambridge, MA: Harvard University Press.

—— (2007) *Poetics of Cinema*, New York: Routledge.

Bordwell, D., and Carroll, N. (eds.) (1996) *Post-Theory: Reconstructing Film Studies*, Madison: University of Wisconsin Press.

Branigan, E. (1992) *Narrative Comprehension and Film*, London and New York: Routledge.

Brooks, V. (1984–5) "Film, Perception, and Cognitive Psychology," *Millennium Film Journal* 14–15 (fall–winter): 105–26.

Bruner, Jerome (1973) *Beyond the Information Given: Studies in the Psychology of Knowing*, New York: Norton.

Buckland, W. (ed.) (1995) *The Film Spectator: From Sign to Mind*, Amsterdam: Amsterdam University Press.

—— (2000) *The Cognitive Semiotics of Film*, Cambridge and New York: Cambridge University Press.

Carroll, J. M. (1980) *Toward a Structural Psychology of Cinema*, The Hague and New York: Mouton Publishers.

Carroll, N. (1985) "The Power of Movies," *Daedalus* 114 (fall): 79–103. Reprinted in *Theorizing the Moving Image* (Cambridge and New York: Cambridge University Press, 1996).

—— (1990) *The Philosophy of Horror, or Paradoxes of the Heart*, New York: Routledge.

—— (1996) *Theorizing the Moving Image*, Cambridge and New York: Cambridge University Press.

Colin, M. (1985) *Langue, Film, Discours: Prolégomènes à une sémiologie générative du film*. Paris: Klincksieck.

—— (1992) *Cinéma, television, cognition*, Nancy: Presses Universitaires de Nancy.

Currie, G. (1995) *Image and Mind: Film, Philosophy, and Cognitive Science*, Cambridge and New York: Cambridge University Press.

Gardner, H. (1985) *The Mind's New Science: A History of the Cognitive Revolution*, New York: Basic Books.

Gombrich, E. H. (1960) *Art and Illusion: A Study in the Psychology of Pictorial Representation*, New York: Pantheon.

—— (1982) *The Image and the Eye: Further Studies in the Psychology of Pictorial Representation*, Ithaca, NY: Cornell University Press.

Grodal, T. (1997) *Moving Pictures: A New Theory of Film Genres, Feelings, and Cognition*, Oxford: Clarendon Press; New York: Oxford University Press.

—— (forthcoming) *Embodied Visions: Evolution, Emotion, Culture, and Film*, Copenhagen: University of Copenhagen Press.

Hochberg, J. (1964) *Perception*, Englewood Cliffs, NJ: Prentice-Hall.

Hochberg, J., and Brooks, V. (1978) "The Perception of Motion Pictures," in E. C. Carterette and M. P. Friedman (eds.) *Handbook of Perception*, vol. 10: *Perceptual Ecology*, New York: Academic Press, 259–304.

—— (1996) "Movies in the Mind's Eye," in D. Bordwell and N. Carroll (eds.) *Post-Theory: Reconstructing Film Studies*, Madison: University of Wisconsin Press, 368–87.

Jullier, L. (2002) *Cinéma et cognition*, Paris: L'Harmattan.

Lowry, E. (1985) *The Filmology Movement and Film Study in France*, Ann Arbor, MI: UMI Research Press.

Mandler, J. M. (1984) *Stories, Scripts, and Scenes: Aspects of Schema Theory*, Hillsdale, NJ: L. Erlbaum Associates.

Messaris, P. (1994) *Visual Literacy: Image, Mind, and Reality*, Boulder, CO: Westview Press.

Metz, C. (1974) *Film Language*, trans. M. Taylor, New York: Oxford University Press.

Mitry, J. (1997) *The Aesthetics and Psychology of the Cinema*, trans. C. King, Bloomington: Indiana University Press.

Münsterberg, H. (2002) *Hugo Münsterberg on Film:* The Photoplay – A Psychological Study, *and Other Writings*, ed. A. Langdale, New York: Routledge.

O'Leary, B. (1999) *Michel Colin's Generative Semiology: A Post-Metzian Phase of Linguistics in Film Theory*, PhD thesis, University of Texas at Dallas.

Perron, B. (ed.) (2002) *Cinéma: Journal of Film Studies* 12(2) (special issue, cinema and cognition).

Persson, P. (2003) *Understanding Cinema: A Psychological Theory of Moving Imagery*, Cambridge and New York: Cambridge University Press.

Peterson, J. (1994) *Dreams of Chaos, Visions of Order: Understanding the American Avant-garde Cinema*, Detroit: Wayne State University Press.

Peterson, M. A., Gillam, B., and Sedgwick, H. A. (eds.) (2007) *In the Mind's Eye: Julian Hochberg on the Perception of Pictures, Films, and the World*, Oxford and New York: Oxford University Press.

Plantinga, C. (forthcoming) *Moving Viewers: American Film and the Spectator's Experience*, Berkeley: University of California Press.

Plantinga, C., and Smith, G. M. (1999) *Passionate Views: Film, Cognition, and Emotion*, Baltimore, MD: Johns Hopkins University Press.

Saussure, F. de (1970) *Course in General Linguistics*, trans. W. Baskin, London: Fontana.

Smith, G. M. (2003) *Film Structure and the Emotion System*, Cambridge and New York: Cambridge University Press.

Smith, M. (1995) *Engaging Characters: Fiction, Emotion, and the Cinema*, Oxford: Clarendon Press; New York: Oxford University Press.

Tan, E. (1996) *Emotion and the Structure of Narrative Film: Film as an Emotion Machine*, trans. B. Fasting, Mahwah, NJ: Erlbaum.

Wilson, G. M. (1986) *Narration in Light: Studies in Cinematic Point of View*, Baltimore, MD: Johns Hopkins University Press.

Further reading

See the Society for Cognitive Studies of the Moving Image website. Available at http://www.scsmi-online. org (archived here: http://www.uca.edu/org/ccsmi/index.htm).

34

GILLES DELEUZE

Ronald Bogue

At the time of his death on 4 November 1995, Gilles Deleuze was recognized as one of the leading French philosophers of his generation. Of his many books, his two volumes on film, *Cinema 1: The Movement-Image* (1986 [1983]) and *Cinema 2: The Time-Image* (1989 [1985]), are among his most impressive and challenging works – whose status, both within his own oeuvre and within philosophy and film studies in general, continues to be debated. He makes reference to hundreds of films from the silent era to the 1980s, discusses such specifically cinematic issues as framing, shot, montage, depth of focus, and so on, proposes a semiotic model of cinematic images, and yet insists that his is a work of philosophy, pure philosophy. For Deleuze, philosophy and the arts are both modes of creation, but philosophers create with concepts, whereas artists create with sensations. Hence, his theory of cinema "is not 'about' cinema, but about the concepts that cinema gives rise to" (Deleuze 1989: 280). Those concepts do not preexist within cinema, and "yet they are cinema's concepts, not theories about cinema. So that there is always a time, midday–midnight, when we must no longer ask ourselves, 'What is cinema?' but 'What is philosophy?'" (Deleuze 1989: 280). Deleuze's cinema books, then, might be regarded as a philosophical "thinking alongside" cinema, an exercise in opening philosophy's conceptual practice to cinema's "new practice of images and signs" (Deleuze 1989: 280).

Deleuze says that his study is not a history of cinema but a "taxonomy, an attempt at the classification of images and signs" (Deleuze 1986: xiv). These images and signs he divides into two broad categories, movement images and time images, *Cinema 1* devoted to the movement-image and the classic cinema, *Cinema 2* to the time-image and the modern cinema. There is a sense, however, even movement-images are images of time, for ultimately time is the fundamental element of all cinema. Deleuze identifies Charles Sanders Peirce and Henri Bergson as the chief guides in his inquiry. Peirce's semiotics provides Deleuze with an antidote to what he sees as the misguided Saussurean, language-oriented semiology of much French film theory, and Deleuze makes creative use of Peirce's categories of Firstness, Secondness, and Thirdness, as well as several of Peirce's classificatory schemes of individual signs. Despite such borrowings, however, Deleuze's approach to cinema is predominantly Bergsonian, rather than Peircean.

Deleuze follows Bergson in observing that we naturally tend to spatialize time, to treat time as a sequence of discrete states of solid objects in a static spatial container, the movement of such objects being merely a change of position affecting the objects from without. Bergson counters that time is not a sequence of points on a line, but a dynamic surge of a past thrusting through a present and into a future, such that the past is retained into the present and the present continues into the future. He also argues that movement cannot be separated from the object that moves, that movement is an indivisible time-space phenomenon. Finally, he observes that the very notion of stable things makes no sense in a world of becoming and indivisible time-space movement. Instead, the universe should be seen as a vibrational totality, a set of perturbations, flows, or modifications that form an indivisible oceanic Whole, which is open both spatially and temporally. Deleuze argues that the movement-images of cinema allow us to see time-space as modifications of such a vibrational open Whole. In the shot we see a *mobile cut*, a slice or chunk, of the open Whole, and through montage we have an indirect presentation of the open Whole. The various shots of the film in Deleuze's terminology are *expressions* of the open Whole. Deleuze takes the concept of "expression" from certain medieval neo-Platonists, who conceive of the relationship between the One of God and the many of the created world as a relationship of explication and implication. According to this model, the whole unfolds or explicates itself into the parts, and the whole remains enfolded or implicated in each of the parts. Thus, in Deleuze's understanding of the shot and montage, each shot is a kind of unfolding or ex-plication of the open Whole indirectly presented in montage, and the open Whole is enfolded or im-plicated in each shot.

The movement-image, then, manifests itself as mobile cuts of an open Whole, but movement-images also come in various types, which Deleuze organizes in an elaborate taxonomic system. Again, Bergson is his guide. In *Matter and Memory* (1911 [1896]), Bergson notes that realists and idealists argue endlessly whether reality is out there or just in our heads, and then after separating subject and object, they try futilely to put the two halves together again. He proposes instead simply to consider reality to be "images," or that which appears. In a sense, Bergson is doing what Husserl and phenomenologists do, and that is to insist that the object only appears *as perceived* by a consciousness, as an indivisible subject-object phenomenon. What is startling about Bergson's theory, as Deleuze points out, is that Bergson does not start with a perceiving subject, as does Husserl, but *derives* it from images. Bergson asks us first to imagine a universe of images, each one responding directly and immediately to the movements of all the images around it, the whole like a massive collection of particles jostling and bumping one another. Then we are asked to imagine a particle that, upon being struck by a neighboring particle, hesitates for a moment, or moves in an unpredictable direction. That particle, says Bergson, is a living image. A living image is a "center of indetermination" (Bergson 1911 [1896]: 28), and what we call consciousness is such a center of indetermination. We may differentiate three moments in the living image's response to its surroundings: a moment of *perception*, which is geared toward an antici-pation of what movements from outside will impinge upon it; a moment of *affection*, in which the living image feels impinging movements from within; and a moment of *action*, in which the living image responds to its environs through an act of some kind. The perception of a living image, according to Bergson, is always a *subtraction* of qualities from the perceived object. Perception is a matter of filtering out those qualities that do not interest the living image and are of no use to it in its survival. We humans, for example, do not perceive infrared and ultraviolet rays; our eyes filter out those rays, subtract them from surrounding objects.

Perception, then, gives rise to what Deleuze labels a *perception-image*, a kind of framing of the world that imparts a selection of elements in keeping with the interests and purposes of the perceiver. Bergson also observes that in living images all perception is inextricably tied to action. We anticipate surrounding events, we plan our actions and reactions, and in so doing our apprehension of the world around us takes on a shape, a sort of curvature of space and organization of its constituents according to our expectations, plans, habits, desires, and so on. Such a structured curvature of an environment around a living image Deleuze calls an *action-image*. Finally, the living image feels impinging movements within itself, and in a sense "translates" incoming movements of perception into outgoing movements of action. What Bergson calls "affection" is a "motor tendency on a sensible nerve" (Bergson 1911 [1896]: 56), which Deleuze rephrases as a "motor effort on an immobilized receptive plate" (or surface) (Deleuze 1986: 66). What the receptive surface of the living image does is to extract pure qualities that pertain both to the impingement of perceived motions on the body of the living image and to the future actions of the living image. From this affection arises the *affection-image*, which is an image of a pure quality. In a first approximation, Deleuze applies these three movement-images to cinema by associating the perception-image with the long shot, the action-image with the medium shot, and the affection-image with the close-up. But soon he complicates this simple system, finding different ways in which each of the three movement-images can be related to each of the three shots and then generating three additional movement-images, the relation-image (an image that discloses a mental relation between entities), the impulse-image (midway between the affection-image and the action-image), and the reflection-image (midway between the action-image and the relation-image). From these six movement-images, Deleuze formulates a taxonomy of cinematic signs, a sign being for Deleuze simply a specialized type of image. Every movement-image, Deleuze argues, may be viewed in three ways: as a function of a minimal interval of movement; as a function of the whole of the movement; and as a function of its genetic emergence from an undifferentiated chaos of movement. Deleuze defines the sign, then, "in a completely different way from Peirce," as "a particular image that refers to a type of image, either from the point of view of its bipolar composition [minimal interval or whole of movement] or from the point of view of its genesis" (Deleuze 1989: 32). Thus, since each of the six movement-images may be viewed in three ways, in theory there are eighteen kinds of movement-image signs. (Actually, Deleuze's nomenclature is rather casual, the number of signs he identifies ranging between fourteen and twenty-three, depending on what one counts as a separate sign or simply a subdivision of a single sign. See Bogue [2003: 65–105], for a detailed discussion of this taxonomy.)

The six movement-images and their corresponding eighteen signs are organized around "centers of indetermination," or living images, but those images only emerge from and remain part of a vibrational, oceanic Whole. Since movement cannot be separated from the moving entity, that Whole is a vibrational flux of matter-movement, and since the Whole consists solely of images, within that Whole "*movement-image* and *flowing-matter* are strictly the same thing" (Deleuze 1986: 59). Further, Deleuze argues, implicit in Bergson's equation of matter and image is the presupposition that the Whole "is entirely made up of Light ... The identity of the image and movement stems from the identity of matter and light. The image is movement, just as matter is light" (Deleuze 1986: 60). This oceanic flow of matter-movement-image-light, however, is not mere inert stuff. The living-image is a center of indetermination, whose perception/consciousness is a selective, subtractive filtering of influences. What this implies is that living images ultimately are not more perceptive than nonliving images, but less so. Nonliving images respond to all surrounding motions, and hence have a full perception of their surroundings (what Whitehead would term a "prehension"), whereas living images ignore some movements and recognize others. Diverse forms of consciousness and perception, then, are spread throughout all things, and the perception/consciousness of human beings is just a specialized filtering of images. Such a filtering consciousness, when conceived of in terms of light, may be thought of as a cinematic screen, which blocks the universal flow of light, selecting some elements for projection on that surface, allowing others to pass through the screen unimpeded. "In short, it is not consciousness which is light, it is the set of images, or the light, which is consciousness, immanent to matter" (Deleuze 1986: 61), for which reason we may view "the universe as cinema in itself, a metacinema" (Deleuze 1986: 59). The vibrational Whole of matter-movement-image-light is "a kind of plane of immanence" (Deleuze 1986: 58–9) from which various movement-images and signs emerge, but which remains immanent within them. The "plane of immanence or the plane of matter is: a set of movement-images; a collection of lines or figures of light; a series of blocs of space-time" (Deleuze 1986: 61).

Movement-images and time-images are both manifestations of the open Whole. What sets the movement-images of classic cinema apart from the time-images of modern cinema is that movement-images are regulated by a sensory-motor schema. In simple terms, this means that the time and space organizing movement-images is in accord with our commonsense categories of a uniform temporal succession in a Cartesian, Newtonian space. Such a time-space conforms to our everyday habits, practices, needs, desires, fears, and expectations, all of which are part of our embodied existence as *sensing* and *acting* beings in the world. These regular practices of sensing and acting form a sensory-motor schema that structures time-space for us; hence, though the classic cinema allows us to see time's dynamic thrust, the inseparability of movement and objects, and the perturbations of a vibrational Whole, it does so only in conformity with the commonsense structures of our sensory-motor schema. In the classic cinema, then, no matter how dreamlike, distorted, contradictory, or confusing the images, they are eventually naturalized and normalized, made sense of, in terms of our customary world of sensing and acting.

371

For Deleuze, the crucial divide in the history of cinema is not that between silent and sound cinema, but that between the classic cinema, both silent and sound, and the modern cinema, and that divide is marked by the collapse of the sensory-motor schema. That collapse Deleuze finds first in Italian neorealism, then in the French new wave and later still in German film of the late 1960s. What we see in these movements is the emergence of *opsigns* and *sonsigns*, visual images and sonic images, that cannot be readily assimilated within a commonsense space-time. With the collapse of the sensory-motor schema and the appearance of opsigns and sonsigns, movement and time reverse their relationship to one another. In the classic cinema, time is subservient to movement – that is, movement regulated by the sensory-motor schema generates a single uniform type of time. In the modern cinema, by contrast, movement is subservient to time. To put it another way, different forms of time generate movements that by commonsense standards are aberrant and irregular, but that are functions of the form of time that generates them. When in the cinema forms of time generate movements, we cease to see movement-images and begin to see time-images, images of forms of time that undermine our commonsense understanding of the world.

Deleuze divides time-images into two broad categories, those that concern the *order of time*, and those that involve *time as series*. The time-images related to the order of time fall into two groups, which Deleuze calls *sheets of the past* and *peaks of the present*. The notion of sheets of the past Deleuze develops from Bergson's conception of memory and the virtual past. Bergson argues that there is a qualitative difference between the present and the past, and that when we remember something, we do not simply bring back into our present a moment that was once present and has now faded into the past. Rather, we leap from the present into a different medium, the virtual past, a domain that is real without being actual. The virtual past is a realm in which all past events coexist, and that realm extends from the most ancient events into the present. Since the virtual past is qualitatively different from the actual present, that past cannot be formed out of the materials of the present, nor can it take form at some past moment, since then there would be a gap between the present and the beginning of the past. Therefore, he concludes, there must be a memory of the present. Every present moment is double, at once a moment of actual present and virtual past. (It is on the basis of this doubling of each moment as an actual present and virtual past that Deleuze delineates "crystals of time," or *hyalosigns*, which are images in which we see "an actual image *and* its own virtual image, to the extent that there is no longer any linkage of the real with the imaginary, but *indiscernibility of the two*, and perpetual exchange" [Deleuze 1989: 273]. Such crystals of time Deleuze examines at length in the films of Ophuls, Renoir, Fellini, and Visconti.) As that moment of the virtual past comes into existence, it immediately forms part of the entire expanse of the virtual past. In time's thrust from a past into a present and toward a future, there is a retention of the past into the present. Time automatically conserves itself in itself, and its retention into the present is that virtual past.

Bergson pictures the virtual past as a cone, with its apex the present. When we try to remember something, we plunge into that cone and alight on a plane of the cone, a slice or sheet of the past, and there we search out the specific memory. If we don't find it, we move to another sheet of the cone. Deleuze argues that in the modern cinema directors frequently present us with images that make visible this form of time. Alain Resnais is for Deleuze one of the great practitioners of this type of cinema, each of his films disclosing sheets of the past, folding and bending these sheets into one another, and passing transverse planes across the diverse sheets. Films like Resnais' are often treated as experiments with narrative or explorations of the psychology of memory, but Deleuze argues that in such films the narrative structures are secondary products of the form of time, and that the play of memory is not psychological. The virtual past itself is memory, a giant world-memory within which we move, like fish swimming in the ocean. And what directors like Resnais do is to create images of that memory ocean within which the characters float and swim.

In peaks of the present, another form of time is made visible, one that Deleuze takes from Leibniz and modifies via Borges. Essentially this time is one of a forking labyrinth of coexisting possible worlds. At each present moment I may decide to do one thing or another – to go home or to go to work, to kill someone or not kill someone – and following that decision other decisions in other present moments will take place, each decision connected to the previous decision. Each decision may be viewed as a fork in the road, a branching in time, and each branching sequence of decisions may be seen as belonging to a possible world. In one world, I decide to stay home, and then decide to watch television. In another, I go to work and kill my boss, and in yet a third, I go to work and decide not to kill my boss today. Some of these worlds are mutually harmonious, or compossible, others are in contradiction with one another, or incompossible. (For example, the world in which I kill my boss is incompossible with the world in which I do not kill him.) In Leibniz, all these possible worlds, whether compossible or incompossible, coexist within the mind of God. What Deleuze finds in modern cinema is a similar coexistence of compossible and incompossible worlds, not as a reflection of the divine mind, but as an image of time as a branching labyrinth of possible realities. In Robbe-Grillet's films, for example, a man strangles a woman, then later the same man stabs her, and later yet he spares her. Again, what might appear to be simply playful experiments with narrative, in which, say, the author is testing out various possible storylines, are actually images of time. The three scenes of the man and the woman are present moments of possible worlds, pointed peaks of cones of time, *pointes de présent*, and the film jumps from peak to peak as if from incommensurable present to incommensurable present of coexisting possible worlds.

The time-images related to time as series make visible the dynamic power of time. Bergsonian time, *durée*, or *duration*, is a thrust of a past into a present and toward a future, and what time-images of this sort do is to render visible the vital becoming of time, such that the before and after are brought within the present image. In movement-images, before and after are simply moments in an empirical sequence of instants, their position in the sequence determined from outside the sequence itself. In time-images, by contrast, the before and after are "the intrinsic quality of that which becomes in time" (Deleuze 1989: 275). This time-image of a vital becoming converts a sequence into a series. Deleuze defines a series as "a sequence of images, but images which tend in themselves in the direction of a limit, which orients and inspires the first sequence (the before) and gives way to another sequence organized as series which tends in turn towards another limit (the after)" (275). Time-images of time as series disclose time as a power or potency, a *puissance*, and these time-images are *puissances du faux*, "powers of the false." They are powers of the *false* in that they are powers of becoming, dynamic change, metamorphosis, and transformation, and hence powers that undermine fixed identities, thereby falsifying established truths and generating new forms.

These, then, are the basic time-images that come into existence with the collapse of the sensory-motor schema: sheets of the past and peaks of the present (order of time), and powers of the false (time as series). What is common to all these time-images is a method of film composition based on the *gap*, or the space *between* images. In the classic cinema, the physical world framed in a shot is in principle capable of being extended in space and time to merge with a single, unified cosmos. When the sensory-motor schema collapses in the modern cinema, images are disconnected from their customary sequences. Images that were once linked together in chains, are "disen-chained," and the problem is one of connecting them, or "reenchaining" them, in new combinations. In the classic cinema, the sensory-motor schema ensures that the gap between shots is merely a function of the first shot and/or the second, but in the modern cinema the gap takes on a value of its own. A *rational cut* between shots gives way to an *irrational cut*, a cut that privileges the space between shots. The principle that governs the composition of film in the modern cinema is one of selecting images that produce gaps. Given image A, what subsequent image will produce a dynamic force through its difference from the preceding image and allow a further juxtaposition of dynamically different images. The method is that of the *between*, of *and* – this *and* that *and* this other: A *and* M *and* H *and*, etc. In the modern cinema, the space between informs the framing of shots, camera angles and movements, and montage, but also the sonic elements and their relationship to the visual images. As Deleuze says, "inter-stices thus proliferate everywhere, in the visual image, in the sound image, between the sound image and the visual image" (Deleuze 1989: 181). In the modern cinema, visual and sonic images become fully separated from one another. Visual and sonic images interact with one another, in a back-and-forth coming-and-going, but they also turn in on themselves, as it were, as if two films were being constructed, one visual, another aural. But Deleuze stresses that modern films are not really double, that the problem of the modern cinema is to maintain the autonomy of sound and sight and yet to establish a necessary relationship between them based on their difference. Or, to put it another way, the object is to take two heterogeneous strata – one of sound, one of sight – and to *produce* a new relationship through their conjunction.

All directors, whether classic or modern, are like sculptors of time, light, sound, movement, and images. They shape "a plastic mass, an a-signifying and a-syntaxic material," a "*signaletic material* which includes all kinds of modulation features, sensory (visual and sound), kinetic, intensive, affective, rhythmic, tonal, and even verbal (oral and written)" (Deleuze 1989: 29). This material is part of the plane of immanence of "universal variation, which goes beyond the human limits of the sensory-motor schema towards a nonhuman world where movement equals matter, or else in the direction of a super-human world which speaks for a new spirit" (Deleuze 1989: 40). In the classic cinema, the sensory-motor schema organizes and regularizes images, but from the beginning disquieting elements are present – false continuities, aberrant camera movements, obsessive framings, camera-eyes in things, and so on. The time-image "is the phantom which has always haunted the cinema, but it took modern cinema to give a body to this phantom" (Deleuze 1989: 41). Deleuze could have emphasized the continuities between the classic and modern cinema, but he chose instead to stress their differences. Some commentators of Deleuze have suggested that the rift between classic and modern cinema is so great that each operates on a distinct plane of immanence (see Rodowick 1997: 175; and Martin-Jones 2006: 25), but this is true only in a limited sense. Deleuze concentrates on Bergson's theses concerning movement and images in *Cinema 1*, and on Bergson's theses concerning time in *Cinema 2*, but all these theses pertain to the same cosmos in Bergson and in Deleuze. When Deleuze introduces the concept of the plane of immanence in *Cinema 1*, he avoids the complexities of Bergsonian time, since they are not immediately relevant to a description of the movement-image, but when he engages those temporal complexities in *Cinema 2*, it is not to bring in an entirely new domain but to complete the picture only partially sketched in *Cinema 1*. The "*signaletic material*" of the plane of immanence, which directors sculpt and shape, includes movement-images and time-images alike.

The consequences of this concept of a common plane of immanence are significant. Many readers have remarked that several directors in *Cinema 1* reappear in *Cinema 2*, and some critics have seen this as a sign of confusion or inconsistency on Deleuze's part. But Deleuze's point is that aspects of the time-image have always been present in the cinema, partially and fleetingly in the classic cinema, more fully in modern films. Some directors straddle the divide, their work best considered as representative now of one cinema, and now of another. Perhaps Deleuze could have clarified this point further, but his concern is less to categorize directors than to classify images, and he is ready to make reference to illuminating examples of specific images wherever he may find them. We should note as well the implications of Deleuze's concept of the plane of immanence for a history of cinema. The modern cinema gives a body to the phantom of the time-image, but that phantom haunted cinema from the beginning. The history of cinema, then, is one of genuine creation, but also one of discovery. Cinema is always an inventive experimentation on the real. When modern directors fashion time-images, they produce entities that have never had an actual existence before, but what they disclose are forms of time that are immanent to the real, virtual rather than actual, but already "there" as part of the cosmos. Indeed, cinema as a whole is a mode of disclosure, the simplest movement-images of the classic cinema rendering visible those aspects of movement that commonsense tends to ignore. The cinema is a technological invention that arises at a specific point in human history, and directors make use of that invention in diverse, unpredictable ways. But what they disclose is the metacinema of the cosmos, the reality of matter = movement = image = light, of "prehensions" scattered throughout a vibrational, open whole that exhibits various forms of time, a metacinema of movement-images and time-images. Without the invention of the cinema, this metacinema might have remained merely an esoteric Bergsonian hypothesis, but with it the cosmic metacinema is made visible and audible. The phantom is given a body.

The assimilation of Deleuze's cinema texts within the English-speaking world has been understandably slow, given the difficulty of Deleuze's style and the demands he makes of readers in their familiarity with continental philosophy and French film criticism. Gradually, however, the books have drawn increased attention, and their reception has been mixed. Several film theorists have faulted Deleuze for his auteurism, his derivative readings of individual films, his crude delineations of historical periods, and his inattention to the recent interface of film and new media. There is some justice to all these charges, but his enterprise does not depend for its success on his stance on authorship, the originality of his analyses (whose sources he openly cites, and which at times can be quite illuminating), the film history he traces, or his approach to the technology of image reproduction (which, if one considers the conclusion of *Cinema 2*, is less naïve than his critics often allow). His taxonomy of images provides a single and original philosophical context for conceptualizing cinematic practice, and his dense commentaries on movement and time in hundreds of films offer a wealth of material for exploitation by other analysts. And in fact, in the last decade increasing numbers of film critics have made use of his concepts, with notable efforts including Rodowick's exemplary *Gilles Deleuze's Time Machine*, Kennedy's (2000) and Pisters' (2003) close readings of several commercial films, Powell's (2005) study of horror films, and Martin-Jones' examination of cinema and national identity. The problematic status of his project, which juxtaposes philosophy and cinema as complementary yet separate practices, prohibits any simple accommodation of his thought within either philosophy or film studies. But whatever the ultimate fate of the cinema books, the richness of their arguments and analyses suggests that their capacity for creative provocation has not yet been exhausted.

See also Semiotics and semiology (Chapter 42) and Edgar Morin (Chapter 38).

References

Bergson, H. (1911 [1896]) *Matter and Memory*, trans. N. M. Paul and W. S. Palmer, London: Allen and Unwin.

Bogue, R. (2003) *Deleuze on Cinema*, New York: Routledge.

Deleuze, G. (1986) *Cinema 1: The Movement-Image*, trans. H. Tomlinson and B. Habberjam, Minneapolis: University of Minnesota Press.

—— (1989) *Cinema 2: The Time-Image*, trans. H. Tomlinson and R. Galeta, Minneapolis: University of Minnesota Press.

Kennedy, B. (2000) *Deleuze and Cinema: The Aesthetics of Sensation*, Edinburgh: Edinburgh University Press.

Martin-Jones, D. (2006) *Deleuze, Cinema and National Identity: Narrative Time in National Contexts*, Edinburgh: Edinburgh University Press.

Pisters, P. (2003) *The Matrix of Visual Culture: Working with Deleuze in Film Theory*, Stanford, CA: Stanford University Press.

Powell, A. (2005) *Deleuze and Horror Film*, Edinburgh: Edinburgh University Press.
Rodowick, D. N. (1997) *Gilles Deleuze's Time Machine*, Durham, NC: Duke University Press.

Further reading

Gregory Flaxman (ed.) *The Brain Is the Screen: Deleuze and the Philosophy of Cinema* (Minneapolis: University of Minnesota Press, 2000) is an outstanding collection of essays on Deleuze and film. An illuminating application of Deleuze's theory to the analysis of individual films is Patricia Pisters', *The Matrix of Visual Culture: Working with Deleuze in Film Theory* (Stanford, CA: Stanford University Press, 2003). D. N. Rodowick, *Gilles Deleuze's Time Machine* (Durham, NC: Duke University Press, 1997) provides an outstanding introduction to Deleuze's philosophy of cinema.

35
SERGEI EISENSTEIN
David Bordwell

Few film directors venture into film theory, but Sergei Eisenstein was passionately interested in understanding how films worked – specifically, how they moved audiences. In 1917, when he was only nineteen years old, the Bolshevik party seized power in Russia and created a communist state. Although there was considerable debate about the role of art in the new society, many politicians and artists believed that it had a duty to promulgate a new set of political beliefs among the public. Several young directors, notably Lev Kuleshov and Vsevelod Pudovkin, began to write about the most effective ways to shape audience's experiences. This led them toward issues that had philosophical implications. Eisenstein, in both his theoretical essays and filmmaking practice, moved farthest in this direction.

The filmmaking career

Eisenstein began as a designer of theater sets and eventually moved to directing plays. His sensational stage productions of the early 1920s propelled him into cinema. His first film, *Strike* (1925), drew heavily on his theatrical efforts, notably what he called his "montage of attractions." *The Battleship Potemkin* (1925), a dramatized account of a 1905 mutiny, made him world famous, and thereafter he enjoyed both the honor and the pressures of being the USSR's most important filmmaker. He made two more silent films, *October* (1928), a commemoration of the Bolshevik revolution, and *Old and New* (1929), a tale of a peasant who establishes a collective farm. Formally experimental and even aggressive, his early films sought to galvanize audiences through their structure and style. "A work of art," he wrote, "is a tractor ploughing over the audience's psyche in a particular class context" (Eisenstein 1988c [1925]: 62).

The 1930s were a difficult period for Eisenstein. Sent to Hollywood to study how sound films were made, he found his proposed projects rejected by the Paramount studio. He began making an independent film about Mexican history, *Que Viva México!*, but the backer withdrew and the film was never completed. In 1932 Eisenstein returned to the Soviet Union, but circumstances had changed. Artistic experiment was discouraged. He became a teacher at the national film school and proposed several projects, all of them rejected, except *Bezhin Meadow*, which was halted in 1937 and destroyed.

Eisenstein came back into favor with *Alexander Nevksy* (1938), a historical spectacle about a Russian prince's battle against German invaders. Eisenstein followed this with plans for a multi-part film about Russia's most notorious tsar. In its own way as vigorously experimental as his silent films had been, the first part of *Ivan the Terrible* (1944) won considerable favor. More controversial was the sequel, which portrayed Ivan as both bloodthirsty and torn by uncertainties. The sequel was completed in 1946 but suppressed on Stalin's orders, and the planned third part was never finished. Eisenstein died of heart disease in 1948, and only a change in official ideology allowed Part II of *Ivan* to be released in 1958.

As if making some of the most important films in history were not enough, Eisenstein produced scripts, essays, and thousands of drawings. He planned a series of books, including one on film direction. His drafts of unpublished essays fill hundreds of archive files, and they bear witness to his unending search for the principles – he would have said "laws" – underlying cinema and artistic creation in general.

Eisenstein sought to unify theory and practice. His characteristic rhythm was to alternate between writing essays and making a film. An essay would propose some ideas, and he would try to put them into effect in the film. But while making the film, he would hit upon new ideas that demanded to be expressed in a new essay or two. As a result, the films don't fully exemplify the writing, and the writing doesn't always neatly fit the films. We have to study both together to get a sense of the range of Eisenstein's creative vision.

A bold thinker, Eisenstein was not a strict or systematic one. Endowed with a wide knowledge of culture, he tended to move freely among the world's art and literature, while making forays into anthropology, philosophy, social theory, and other areas of knowledge. Most of his essays are energetic but diffuse, providing a string of suggestive ideas that often remain undeveloped. Nonetheless, there are enough continuities and core assumptions to allow us to find some coherence in his thought. One way to make sense of his overall project is to see the silent films and the writings around them as tied to a world view somewhat distinct from the view he embraced in the 1930s and 1940s.

Eisenstein's film theory in the silent era

Eisenstein's films of the 1920s are, in both content and form, paradigms of Marxist art. He accepts the Bolshevik version of history, which places class struggle at the center of change. Capitalism is seen as an outmoded social system, and the proletariat, typically the urban working class, is the chief force for overthrowing it. Thus in *Strike*, the death of a machine worker in the factory triggers a walkout, which is eventually crushed by the police, working at the behest of the factory owners. *Potemkin* treats the mutiny as a microcosm of class struggle, with the ordinary sailors overthrowing the oppressive officers. The mutiny becomes a spark igniting the sympathy of the working class of Odessa and the crews aboard other ships.

Strike and *Potemkin* also exemplify a politicized conception of cinematic narrative. Other Soviet films of the period, notably Pudovkin's *Mother* (1926), center on a protagonist who comes to realize the need for revolutionary change. Eisenstein instead created a "mass hero." Individuals are picked out, such as the police spies in *Strike* and the sailor Vakulinchuk in *Potemkin*, but their actions are fitted into a larger dynamic of social upheaval. These films dramatize the Marxist idea that history is primarily made by social classes pitted against one another.

The same structure informs the two last silent films, but in these the Bolshevik party is presented as an active force, channeling revolutionary energy. While party officials are seldom individualized, it emerges as another historical force, the vanguard of the proletariat. *October* shows how a spontaneous uprising is guided by the strategic leadership provided by the Bolsheviks, personified in Lenin. In *Old and New*, the rural rebellion is triggered by the peasant Marfa, but she needs party representatives to realize her dream of a collective farm.

In creating a collective protagonist, Eisenstein relies on what came to be called typage. Workers are rugged, energetic, sensitive, and morally pure; capitalist figures are effete, brutal, and dissipated. In *October*, the compromising Menshevik leader Kerensky is a clown and becomes identified with feminine values. Eisenstein's stage work was influenced by the circus and caricature, making little effort to create the sort of realistic characterizations associated with the Moscow Art Theatre. He carried his use of broad types over into cinema, where such poster-like shorthand emphasized the social role of the individual over his or her unique qualities. Likewise, the performance style tends to be extroverted and unpsychological, based on metaphors and associations. The spies of *Strike* slink around like weasels, while the doctor aboard the *Potemkin* is characterized by means of a lordly pince-nez and, eventually, maggots. In Eisenstein's early films, personal identity is less important than class identity, which can be conveyed through vivid imagery.

Typage can create a strong effect in the viewer, Eisenstein believed, and his other artistic strategies were likewise based on stimulating the spectator. At the center of these strategies was what he called "expressive movement." Eisenstein held that the human body's manifestation of emotion was the prototype of expression in all the arts. In his early writings, he discussed how various methods of actor training could cultivate an exaggerated, acrobatic style of performance, one unrealistic in the narrow sense, but suited to "infecting" the spectator with powerful feelings (Eisenstein 1988b [1924]). He was fascinated by Asian acting traditions, which displayed a cinematic alternation of stillness and rapidity, what he called "transitionless acting" (Eisenstein 1988d [1929]: 148). This concern with stylized performances carried on throughout his life and is especially apparent in the performances of *Ivan the Terrible*.

The most famous of Eisenstein's strategies for arousing the spectator was what he called "montage of attractions." With the rise of constructivism, an artistic movement that compared artworks to machines, many Soviet artists spoke of creativity as a matter of *montage*, the French word for mechanical assembly of parts, like mounting a motor on a chassis. Eisenstein used the analogy to suggest that a theater performance should be assembled as a set of strong moments, vivid actions, and stage turns that would grab and arouse the audience. "Attractions" in this sense are something like circus or sideshow acts, often of a grotesque or shocking nature. In his first major essay, Eisenstein argued that attractions could be any "aggressive moment," from a burst of color in a costume to a roll on the kettledrums (Eisenstein 1988a [1923]). His production of the play, *The Wiseman*, ended with firecrackers going off under seats in the auditorium.

Eisenstein believed that the proper ordering, or montage, of such spectacular bits would affect the spectator on several levels. It would galvanize the senses, trigger the emotions, and lead to thought. Eisenstein accepted one role for art that was emerging in the new Soviet culture, that of "agitprop," agitation and propaganda – stirring up the public as a way of inculcating political messages. He conceived of attractions as agitational in the most literal sense, packing visceral and emotional force, "ploughing the spectator's psyche" (1988a [1923]: 34).

Eisenstein's first films provided plenty of attractions. *Strike* offered antics of dwarves and buffoonish spies, pathetic moments depicting the suffering of the strikers, and scenes of unprecedented violence – workers pounded by the spray from firemen's hoses, or a bull slaughtered before our eyes. *Potemkin* was less varied in tone, but every major part presented spikes of vivid stimulation. Still, Eisenstein realized that some attractions became more pallid on screen; a man howling in pain on the stage can horrify the audience, but in a silent film, the effect must be weaker.

Eisenstein concluded that simply showing an attraction was not enough. He had to magnify its impact by cinematic means – through lighting, through framing, and especially through the juxtaposition of shots. Cutting could intensify the sensory and emotional appeal of his attractions (Eisenstein 1988b [1924]). Throughout his career, Eisenstein would consider *montage* as both the technique of film editing and a broader artistic strategy for organizing the entirety of a work, its architectural dynamic.

Eisenstein did not halt his reasoning once he arrived at these craft considerations. He asked what enabled his montage of attractions, on stage or on film, to have an impact. He also explored how cinema could afford ever more precise ways to stimulate the senses, feelings, and thoughts of the viewer.

Throughout his career, Eisenstein held to an associationist model of mind. He believed that a successful artwork aroused the spectator's perception, as filmic or theatrical attractions did, and that organizing these appeals carefully allowed the artist to imbue them with emotional qualities. In his early writings, he appealed to the ideas of Pavlov and Bekhterev, who treated human behavior as at least partly governed by conditioned and unconditioned reflexes. Eisenstein proposed that a film could create a pattern of stimuli which would shape the spectator's unconditioned reflexes into new responses (Eisenstein 1988b [1924]: 49). For example, in *Strike*, Eisenstein intercut the butchering of a bull with a massacre of strikers. He believed that the spectator's revulsion at seeing the bull slaughtered could, through repetition and reinforcement, transfer to the situation of the police massacre.

Perceptual shock and emotional arousal were incomplete, Eisenstein believed, without some conceptual response as well. His cinematic montage of attractions aimed at transmitting ideas – not through words but through clusters of imagery. In his theory, he claimed a version of materialist monism that held that thought was simply nervous activity, on a par with sensory and affective experience. In his practice, the most famous experiment along these lines took place in *October*, when he sought to debunk the patriotic slogan "For God and Country" through editing. Shots of statues of Christ give way to pagan idols, as if by a reduction *ad absurdum*, and a montage of military regalia caricatures the idea of nation as merely empty symbols.

In sequences like these, Eisenstein sought a sort of pictographic equivalent of inferential reasoning. Several of his essays explore the idea that film communicated ideas through conventional images, making him a precursor of the semiotic conception of "film language." He stressed that many cinematic signs, such as the statues he employed in *October*, were comprehensible only through cultural training.

Eisenstein's most famous theoretical efforts sprang from his effort to find a theory of montage compatible with a Marxist world view. In the late 1920s, Soviet philosophers began to debate the notes by Engels published under the rubric *Dialectics of Nature* (1940 [1883]). There Engels argued that scientific research was inherently dialectical and it succeeded because nature's laws obeyed dialectical principles. Change in nature, he speculated, relied upon material conflicts, just as social change relied on class struggle. For instance, the fact that accelerating water molecules yielded steam exemplified the "transformation of quantity into quality."

Eisenstein picked up this idea and argued that cinematic style is inherently conflict-based. The individual shot displays pictorial conflicts of light and dark, foreground and background, clashing design elements. The juxtaposition of shots also displays conflict, which results in an effect that is implicit in neither shot, a "leap into a new quality." Drawing examples from *October*, he claimed that these conflicts could be organized to generate perceptual shock, emotional impact, and intellectual meaning (Eisenstein (1988e [1929])).

A similar impulse lay beneath his most ambitious essays at the end of the 1920s, where he sought to plot all the effects of shot-to-shot relations. He employs a musical analogy to explore the creative variables. The relative lengths of shots A and B are like musical meter, while the relations of movements within A and B are properly rhythmic. The continuity or discontinuity of image material from A to B is like melody, while the more intangible expressive qualities linking the two create something like harmony or "overtones." Finally, the qualities may not be sheerly emotional; there may also be "intellectual overtones," as in the "God and Country" sequence. As a final twist, Eisenstein asks us to imagine all these dimensions as harboring dialectical conflict (Eisenstein 1988f [1929]).

Obscure and contradictory, many of these writings are unsatisfactory as pure theory. For example, it appears that Eisenstein stretches the concept of dialectical form to the point of vacuity, treating any difference he can detect as a conflict. Still, his ideas about montage yielded heuristic insights into the implications of technical alternatives. In exploring his ideas, Eisenstein launched the most precise analysis of film style that we find in the silent era, and he brought out many aspects of technique that had never been noticed before.

Although Bolshevik Marxism remained an important reference point for him, Eisenstein was an eclectic thinker. He drew ideas from Russia's vigorous symbolist tradition and Russian formalist literary theory, and he was open to ideas from classical and romantic art theory. This intellectual diversity was to become even more accentuated over the next two decades.

Eisenstein's film theory in the sound era

In the 1920s Eisenstein's experimental filmmaking and theorizing could flourish in an atmosphere of relative creative freedom. With Stalin's takeover of the party and the state completed by 1930, the Soviet intelligentsia began to be subjected to a uniformity of thought and action. A version of "historical materialism," cobbled together out of ideas of Hegel, Marx, Engels, Lenin, and Stalin, guided academic research, from philosophy and history to the empirical sciences. Likewise, a homogenized "socialist realism" became the official Soviet style in painting, literature, and the cinema.

Eisenstein was in California and Mexico during the start of this overhaul of culture, working out his own ideas. Salient among these was a conception of "inner speech" that would, in various forms, shape his thinking for the rest of his life. After reading Joyce's *Ulysses*, he became convinced that our mental life consisted of a flow of ideas, images, and impressions that obeyed distinct laws of "syntax." At first his ruminations led him toward a notion of "stream of consciousness," in an effort to film Dreiser's *An American Tragedy* through what he called "inner monologue." He wanted to bring the anguish of the hero Clyde Griffiths to the screen in a burst of images, sounds, and snatches of dialogue that reflected his struggle with his conscience (Eisenstein 1988g [1932]).

Eisenstein continued to explore these ideas when he returned to the USSR after the debacles of the Paramount projects and *Que Viva México!* Unable to launch a film project, he turned to teaching (a set of his dazzling classroom sessions is preserved in Nizhny 1962). At a major filmmakers' conference of 1935, at which Soviet filmmakers pledged allegiance to socialist realism, Eisenstein proposed that the power of art lay not in the politically correct depiction of a world view but rather in formal processes of great primal force. Inner speech, understood now as prelogical thought most apparent in the rituals of primitive cultures, was the key to artistic expression. Eisenstein pointed to universal artistic devices, such as metaphor and synecdoche, as evidence of structural laws that, however faulty by the principles of science or formal logic, dominated the human mind (Eisenstein 1949 [1935]). The lecture was a slap in the face to Stalinist aesthetics and was harshly criticized by most of Eisenstein's peers.

For the next dozen years, while making *Alexander Nevsky* and *Ivan the Terrible*, Eisenstein's writings sought to grasp the deep expressive possibilities of the film medium. He abandoned the idea of intellectual montage, not only because there were political pressures against the extreme leftism of the montage school but also because he came to believe that cinema's power lay in its ability to engender overwhelming emotion. Impressed by the fiery mix of pagan and Catholic imagery he saw in Mexican rites, he saw art as a secular path to the ecstatic transport afforded by religion (Eisenstein 1991a [1939]).

He might have left it as vague as that. He remained, however, enough of an engineer to seek out basic principles, artistic strategies and tactics that could absorb the film viewer in an emotional experience. Abandoning the idea of montage as conflict, he posited that the viewer's inner speech could best be aroused and guided by a time-bound process of uninterrupted arousal and association. He called this "polyphonic montage" (Eisenstein 1988h [1934]).

Eisenstein starts from a conception of how we form concepts in life. Our idea of a familiar street isn't created by purely topographical information; we know the street by habitual exposure to its houses and shops and traffic patterns, its landmarks and distinctive features. Our idea of the street is composed of such accumulated impressions. To some extent this is an empiricist conception of mind, with ideas formed by what Hume called "constant conjunction." But Eisenstein adds that our sense of the street is emotional as well as intellectual, so feelings are born from the same process of repetition and association (Eisenstein 1991a [1939]).

To be truly effective, however, artistic form needs to replicate not merely the product of such mental activity, but the process. If we want the viewer to *feel* that Tsar Ivan is awe-inspiring, we must mount pictures and sounds that affirm that in varied, cumulative ways. So the film gives us Ivan's power in dramatic situations and in patterns of imagery reinforced by patterns of music. These stimuli weave together, building an encompassing "image" (*obraz*) of Ivan as awe-inspiring. By such a repetition and gradual accumulation of associations, Eisenstein claimed, the most powerful artworks mimic our basic thought processes.

Unsurprisingly, Eisenstein found precedents for this conception of film form. He turned to da Vinci, to Zola, to Dickens, and above all to Wagner. He saw the analogy between his aim for cinema and Wagner's idea of "synthetic spectacle," the blending of music, narrative, speech, light, architecture, and performance in the *Gesamtkunstwerk*, or total artwork (Eisenstein 1996 [1940]). In one of his most audacious theoretical essays he tried to show how a series of static shots in *Alexander Nevsky* imitated in their compositional design the trajectory of Prokofiev's accompanying score (Eisenstein 1991b [1940]). This was an instance of "vertical montage," the parallel between musical movement and visual movement, creating a "synchronization of senses." A similar desire to create an utterly through-composed film is evident in *Ivan the Terrible* (Thompson 1981). Unsurprisingly, the stylization of the film, which included a color sequence, owed much to Walt Disney, whom Eisenstein saluted as a pioneer in the audacious synchronization of pictures and music (Eisenstein 1986).

The idea of forming artistic images through the interplay of associations also had implications for artistic practice in general. In several essays he showed how literary texts were created by the weaving together of many motifs that rise and fall in prominence, building the spectator's emotional engagement with the work. And again, Eisenstein's close study of image design and its coordination with sound constituted an effort to analyze film style with a precision not equaled by film researchers until the 1970s.

Eisenstein's theoretical work has been interpreted in a variety of contexts. In his lifetime and in the years immediately following, his writings were usually taken as background to his own oeuvre or as general pronouncements on the nature and function of film. As more of his unpublished manuscripts became available in the

1980s and 1990s, he began to be seen as mounting a broad philosophy of art. From this perspective commentators have played down his early Marxist theorizing and emphasized the later, wide-ranging ruminations on literature, theater, and the visual arts. He remains the most important director to have written on the theory of cinema.

See also Acting (Chapter 1), Formalism (Chapter 12), Cognitive theory (Chapter 33), and Emotion and affect (Chapter 8).

References

Eisenstein supervised the collection and translation of his writings into English by Jay Leyda. These anthologies are *The Film Sense* (New York: Harcourt, Brace, 1942) and *Film Form* (New York: Harcourt, Brace, 1949). A more comprehensive, heavily annotated edition was completed under the supervision of Richard Taylor: S.M. *Eisenstein: Selected Works*, vol. 1: *Writings, 1922–1934* (London: British Film Institute, 1988), vol. 2: *Towards a Theory of Montage* (London: British Film Institute, 1991), and vol. 3: *Writings, 1934–1947* (London: British Film Institute, 1996).

Eisenstein, S. M. (1949 [1935]) "Film Form: New Problems," in J. Leyda (ed.) *Film Form*, New York: Harcourt, Brace, 122–49.

—— (1986) *Eisenstein on Disney*, ed. J. Leyda; trans. A. Upchurch, Calcutta: Seagull.

—— (1988a [1923]) "The Montage of Attractions," in R. Taylor (ed.) *S.M. Eisenstein: Selected Works*, London: British Film Institute, vol. 1, 33–8.

—— (1988b [1924]) "The Montage of Film Attractions," in R. Taylor (ed.) *S.M. Eisenstein: Selected Works*, London: British Film Institute, vol. 1, 39–58.

—— (1988c [1925]) "The Materialist Approach to Form," in R. Taylor (ed.) *S.M. Eisenstein: Selected Works*, London: British Film Institute, vol. 1, 59–64.

—— (1988d [1929]) "Beyond the Shot," in R. Taylor (ed.) *S.M. Eisenstein: Selected Works*, London: British Film Institute, vol. 1, 138–50.

—— (1988e [1929]) "The Dramaturgy of Film Form," in R. Taylor (ed.) *S.M. Eisenstein: Selected Works*, London: British Film Institute, vol. 1, 161–81.

—— (1988f [1929]) "The Fourth Dimension in Cinema," in R. Taylor (ed.) *S.M. Eisenstein: Selected Works*, London: British Film Institute, vol. 1, 181–94.

—— (1988g [1932]) "Help Yourself!" in R. Taylor (ed.) *S.M. Eisenstein: Selected Works*, London: British Film Institute, vol. 1, 219–37.

—— (1988h [1934]) "Eh! On the Purity of Film Language," in R. Taylor (ed.) *S.M. Eisenstein: Selected Works*, London: British Film Institute, vol. 1, 285–95.

—— (1991a [1939]) "Montage 1938," in R, Taylor (ed.) *S.M. Eisenstein: Selected Works*, London: British Film Institute, vol. 2, 296–326.

—— (1991b [1940]) "Vertical Montage," in R. Taylor (ed.) *S.M. Eisenstein: Selected Works*, London: British Film Institute, vol. 2, 327–99.

—— (1996 [1940]) "The Incarnation of a Myth," in R. Taylor (ed.) *S.M. Eisenstein: Selected Works*, London: British Film Institute, vol. 3, 142–69.

Engels, F. (1940 [1883]) *Dialectics of Nature*, trans. C. P. Dutt, New York: International Publishers.

Nizhny, V. (1962 [1958]) *Lessons with Eisenstein*, trans. and eds. I. Montagu and J. Leyda, New York: Hill and Wang.

Thompson, K. (1981) *Eisenstein's Ivan the Terrible: A Neoformalist Analysis*, Princeton, NJ: Princeton University Press.

Further reading

The following are further reading on this topic: Ronald Bergan, *Eisenstein: A Life in Conflict* (Woodstock, NY: Overlook Press, 1999); David Bordwell, *The Cinema of Eisenstein* (London and New York: Routledge,

2005 [1993]); Oksana Bulgakowa, *Sergei Eisenstein: A Biography* (Berlin and San Francisco: Potemkin Press, 2001 [1998]); Albert LaValley and Barry P. Scherr (eds.) *Eisenstein at 100: A Reconsideration* (New Brunswick, NJ: Rutgers University Press, 2001); Alma Law and Mel Gordon, *Meyerhold, Eisenstein, and Biomechanics: Actor Training in Revolutionary Russia* (Jefferson, NC: McFarland, 1996); Jay Leyda and Zina Voynow, *Eisenstein at Work* (New York: Pantheon, 1982); Joan Neuberger, *Ivan the Terrible* (London and New York: I. B. Tauris, 2003); Marie Seton, *Sergei M. Eisenstein: A Biography* (New York: Grove, 1960); and Yuri Tsivian, *Ivan the Terrible* (London: British Film Institute, 2002).

36
CHRISTIAN METZ
Francesco Casetti

Paradigms and freedom

Il y a une chose très importante dans la recherche, une chose très simple
(c'est peut-être ça qu'on l'oublie souvent): chacun doit étudier ce qu'il a envie
d'étudier. Et pour commencer, j'applique le principe à mon propre travail.
("There is something very important in all research, something very simple
(and that is perhaps what people often forget): everyone must study what they
want to study. And to begin, I apply this principle in my own work.")

Christian Metz, *Iris* (1990)

Christian Metz was born in Béziers in 1931 and died in Paris in 1933. He was
probably the most influential film scholar for almost three decades. Having initiated
film semiology with his essay "Cinéma: langue ou langage?" ("Cinema: Language or
Language System?") in 1964, he participated in its post-structuralist evolution with
his book *Langage et cinéma* (*Language and Cinema*) in 1971. With his *Le signifiant
imaginaire: psychanalyse et cinéma* (*The Imaginary Signifier: Cinema and Psychoanalysis*)
(1977), he offered a broad and complex picture of the relations between psychoanalytic
approaches and film studies. This work was highly influential in the elaboration of the
"Grand Theory" that dominated film studies for almost two decades and that would
later be criticized by David Bordwell and Noël Carrol in *Post-Theory: Reconstructing
Film Studies* (1996). Finally, with his last book, *L'Énonciation impersonelle, ou le site du
film* (1991), Metz explored ways in which a filmic text can display its own linguistic
devices, "opening" itself to reception and to its context: despite his doubts about this
opening, Metz faced the need for an approach that in some ways would be "post-
textualist." Thus in all three stages of his work, Metz was a leading figure, prone to be
loved or despised according to circumstances, but always a touchstone of reflection on
film. It is best to remember him as exemplifying freedom of research more than as the
advocate of a binding paradigm or doctrine. His remarkable combination of freedom
of thought and great rigor is the greatest legacy he has left to film scholars.

"Cinema: Language or Language System?" and the establishment of film semiology

The revolution in theory that took place in France in the 1960s began with the "linguistic turn." Structuralism, born from a rereading of the *Course in General Linguistics* by Ferdinand de Saussure (1983), affected many fields, and in particular anthropology (Lévi-Strauss) to psychoanalysis (Lacan). Semiotics, which was also predicted in the pages of Saussure's book, began to take shape, finding applications in architecture, music, the analysis of foklore, etc. In the field of cinema, the monumental work by Jean Mitry, *Esthétique et psychologie du cinéma* (*The Aesthetics and Psychology of the Cinema*) (1990 [1963]), had just been published. Mitry explored the nature of cinema as a language, but he did so using the classical tools of film theory, moving halfway between philosophy and psychology. His approach was "internal" to cinema, as he was intent on identifying an "essence," a "specificity." In his book, extraordinary as it may be, we cannot find any response to two demands that were making themselves felt at the time: the need for tools inspired by a scientific approach, and the need to connect the language of cinema to the broader field of the processes of signification. Christian Metz wrote a lengthy review of Mitry's two-volume work (collected in Metz 1972) and explained in depth the differences between his own approach and Mitry's. His own attempt to address the two needs just mentioned was developed in his essay, "Cinema: Language or Language System" (available in English in *Film Language: A Semiotics of the Cinema* [see Metz 1968]).

Metz's essay was published in the fourth issue of the French journal *Communications*, the same issue that by no coincidence featured "Eléments de sémiologie" ("The Elements of Semiology") by Roland Barthes. The goal of the essay was in fact to ask whether cinema could also become an object of semiotics. To approach an answer, Metz had to take up a second question, namely, the one that gave the essay its title. Only if cinema possesses a proper *language system* (a "langue," that is, an ordered set of codes, figures, or formulas which one can constantly refer to) and is not only a *fact of langage* (a "langage," that is, a mostly self-regulated and spontaneous discourse) can it be a part of semiotics, since the latter studies systems, and not single occurrences or particular instances of language use.

Metz's answer to the question opts in favor of *langage*. If we look at it carefully, cinema is not a *langue* – or more precisely, if a *langue* "is a *system* of *signs* used for *inter-communication*" (Metz 1968: 75), cinema does not have such a system or consist of signs or have intercommunication as a goal. First, a film does not rely on a system such as a dictionary, in which each term acquires its identity through its orderly opposition to others. On the contrary, it is the result of an alignment of different shots, relying more on the combination of scattered elements than on a selection of the elements of a paradigm. Besides, a film's images cannot be equated with signs in any strict sense (as can words). Each shot is already like a spoken phrase, a sentence, because what appears on the screen (e.g., a visual representation of a dog) means at least "here this is" (in this case, "here is a dog"). Finally, a film does not work at the level of communication, but of expression, or at a level where "meaning is somehow immanent to a thing, is directly released from it, and merges with its very form" (78). In other words, a film shows; it does not signify.

For Metz, cinema is therefore not a language system, a *langue*. It does not fully satisfy any of the "three elements of definition." Yet this should not discourage us. Even though the main object of semiotics is "strong" systems, such as language systems, we need to acknowledge that there is another legitimate attitude: "to look at the semiological endeavour as open research, permitting the study of new forms; 'language' (in the broad sense) is no simple thing – whole flexible systems may be studied as flexible systems, and with the appropriate methods" (89). In short, with felicitous intuition, Metz contradicts his initial conclusion to the effect that cinema lacks the features of a language system and therefore that semiotics must not be used to study film. On the contrary, he adds to its rigorous formulation a more open attitude so that even simple linguistic facts may be recovered. The essay ends with a sentence that clearly suggests hope: "The time has come for a semiotics of the cinema" (91).

The profound newness of Metz's essay resided not only in its opening up of a new field of research, but also in the way in which he arrives at this conclusion. In fact, he asked himself two questions, not one. He asked whether cinema could be an object of semiotics, and he asks whether it is a language system. The second question has meaning only from a semiotic perspective: being a language system is a condition for becoming an object of semiotics; and the specific notion of language system that Metz has in mind is a category valid only inside the semiotic approach. The result is that Metz ceases to investigate cinema in itself, in its intrinsic characteristics, as many scholars had done until then; on the contrary, he examined cinema from a certain perspective that tends to bring out certain traits instead of others, to underline certain compatibilities instead of others, to shed light on some connections instead of others. Here we find ourselves in a dimension of research profoundly different from the one that had ruled the scene in previous years, with scholars ranging from Béla Balázs to André Bazin. Rather than attempting to define the nature or essence of cinema, the inquiry starts from what is pertinent in the researcher's perspective. Also, a more natural way of looking and directly perceiving what appears before our eyes is replaced by a look, which strictly depends on the *methods* of the investigation. Furthermore, the way of looking that attempts to exhaust the global nature of the object in question is replaced by a look that *selects* the pertinent elements. Finally, Metz proposes to replace the way of looking that pursues the truth of things, as revealed in themselves, with a look concerned with the correctness of its inquiry.

Let us add that the success and relevance of Metz's essay depends not only on the dawning of a new way to conceive of theory, based on a pertinent, systematic, solid analysis. With Metz there also emerged a new kind of scholar in the area of film studies, namely, a scholar whose approach is more scientific than impressionistic, a scholar who works in research institutions instead of engaging in journalistic film criticism, a scholar who publishes in specialized academic journals and applies his/her new methods not only to film but also to discourses across a range of media. In short, "Cinema: Language or Language System?" introduced a shift in the approach to the filmic phenomenon. A new research *paradigm* was born, as well as a new *generation* of scholars.

Language and Cinema: structuralism and post-structuralism

During the second half of the sixties and the beginning of the seventies the semio-logical project moved forward with great success. Much of film theory was dominated by semiology of cinema, and the latter tackled a series of topics, ranging from the type of signs used by cinema to the way a film or a film genre works. Metz offered many contributions, both on cinema and other fields, later collected in *Essais sur la signifi-cation au cinéma* (Metz 1968; English translation, *Film Language*, appeared in 1974), *Essais sur la signification au cinéma – II* (1972), and *Essais sémiotiques* (1977b). Among his most famous contributions is a reconstruction of the editing forms of classical cinema, taking the name of the "Grande Syntagmatique."

However, in these same years, semiology also underwent significant changes. In the first place it gradually abandoned the idea of being simply the science of signs. Studying the way we signify and communicate means studying the ideology we are immersed in. Semiotics was increasingly seen as a "political" science, working to dismantle the underlying mechanisms of society, which guarantee the subjugation of men and women. Second, semiotics departed from linguistics and began to draw upon work from other disciplines, which were similarly reshaping themselves taking linguistics as a model. Among these disciplines was, on the one hand, structuralist anthropology, and, on the other hand, Lacanian psychoanalysis. The structuralist framework was put in question, and semiotics became open and more dynamic. Linguistic phenomena, it was thought, cannot be accounted for by the existence of a strongly structured formal organization, determining and replicating itself in every discourse. It is not only *langue* that exists; in fact *langage* exists too. And in *langage* what matters are *processes* brought into play by an addresser or an addressee, more than the *system* they each refer to. From the perspective of contemporary philosophy of language, we might say that film semiology began to discover pragmatics.

This latter point deserves to be underscored because it is central to *Language and Cinema*, a long and complex book in which Metz in some ways concludes the project expressed in the last lines of his first essay. In this book, Metz first of all tries to clarify the objects of semiotic research. There are four such objects. First, we have the *text*, which is a concrete and singular occurrence: the film. Then we have the *message*, which is a realized occurrence that intervenes in several productions and is therefore not singular: a play of light in a film, which is part of that text but is not exclusive to it. Third, we have the *code*, which is something constructed by the analyst and not singular: the "grammar" of lighting, for example. Fourth, we have the *singular system*, which is something that has been constructed, and is indeed something singular: the organization of a film text, the system of linguistic devices brought into focus by the analysis.

What is then the path that semiotics has to follow? As a rule it starts from the text and message and moves toward the code and singular system. In other words, it starts from what "precedes the analyst's intervention" and arrives at something that is "only a form of logic, a principle of coherence" (Metz 1971: 79). This path is typical of research inspired by structuralism, which tries to account for each phenomenon by uncovering its underlying structure and finding in that structure a principle of intelligibility. Metz follows this path and starts with the codes, i.e., the rules of the film grammar. He divides them according to their applicability: some cinematographic codes are general, common to all films; others are typical only of certain film groups; some are not exclusive, but shared by cinema with other "arts," etc. Then he lists the codes: the iconic-visual codes that give meaning to images and that cinema shares with painting and photography; the codes of mechanical duplication that regulate the mechanisms of reproduction of the world, which cinema shares only with photography; the codes of audio-visual composition, concerning the relationship between images and sounds, which cinema has developed on its own, etc.

As a result of these investigations, Metz derives an important idea: *cinematic language* is a two-sided reality. On the one hand, it is the set of the specific codes (only that which makes cinema what it is); on the other hand, it is the set of all the codes used to construct a film (a set that is part of cinema, even if a code may come from elsewhere). In short, the film language emerges from Metz's analysis as an aggregation of different elements: all previous attempts to define the cinema once and for all, separating it from the other media and arts, are put into question. Cinema is not characterized by one unique feature but by an ordered set of codes, some of these codes belonging only to cinema and others connecting it with other media and arts.

After examining codes, Metz moves on to the *singular system* or the structure that underlies a film. Here his point of view is slightly different. By uncovering the design behind each work, in fact, he realizes that what is at play is not only an ordered system of codes but also an operation performed on them. A singular system derives from the overlapping of elements (spatiotemporal organization, acting techniques, lighting procedures) that are ready to clash with one another, to redefine one another, to establish new connections. It is true that they later become integrated within a new, unified system, but while doing so, they also leave behind some areas of friction and disequilibrium. Most importantly, the tensions and reformulations they went through cannot be concealed. In other words, even before being an organic distribution of components, the singular system is above all a product of their intense interaction. Behind its design we perceive the presence of maneuvers consisting of constant moves and countermoves. To account for this aspect, it is necessary to place the idea of *writing* next to that of *structure*. In this way, we go back to the "work on the codes, which starts from them, goes against them, and the result of which – temporarily 'frozen' – is the text" (291). Thus, the structuralist theoretical stance gives way to a much more turbulent horizon: the underlying structure counts no more than the dynamics that brought about its development and that keep it moving. Concepts such as force, becoming, and energy enter the field and dominate discussions during the years that follow, partly thanks to reviews by scholars such as Stephen Heath (1973).

The Imaginary Signifier: psychoanalysis, semiotics, apparatus

As I said above, in the seventies semiotics adopted a more markedly political perspective, and connected with other disciplines such as anthropology and psychoanalysis. In the field of cinema, the study of the apparatus – a term that refers to the "technical-psychological machine" that presides over the construction of a film – gives theory a great opportunity, both to cast a critical glance at cinema and its ideological effects, and at the same time to build an approach combining different disciplines. Apparatus theory embraces the work of such scholars as Raymond Bellour, Jean-Louis Baudry, Jean-Pierre Oudart, Stephen Heath, and Colin MacCabe and intersects with the emerging feminist film studies of the period. Christian Metz intervened in this context with the very influential book, Le signifiant imaginaire (The Imaginary Signifier).

The present discussion of this work focuses on its first section. Metz contends that in the establishing of the cinematic signifier, three main psychoanalytical processes are brought into play: specular identification, voyeurism, and fetishism. With regard to specular identification, Metz asks himself whether the film screen functions as a mirror, that mirror in which, according to Lacan, the child finds his own image and, by seeing himself, learns to recognize himself. Metz dismantles this analogy: on the screen the spectator will never see his own body reflected; therefore, he will never be able to identify with himself:

> But with what, then, does the spectator identify during the projection of the film? For he certainly has to identify: identification in its primal form has ceased to be a current necessity for him, but he continues, in the cinema – if he did not the film would become incomprehensible, considerably more incomprehensible than the most incomprehensible films – to depend on that permanent play of identification without which there would be no social life. (Metz 1977a: 46)

At the movies the spectators may well identify with a character of the fiction, or with the actor playing the role, but they can also identify with themselves. This is an apparently impossible step (as we have seen, "contrary to the child in a mirror, [the spectator] cannot identity with himself as an object, but only with objects which are there without him" [48]). Still, it is fully understandable if we consider that cinema implies a double, although unitary, "knowledge." When I watch a film, "I know I am perceiving something imaginary ... and I know that it is I who am perceiving it. This second knowledge divides in turn: I know that I am really perceiving ... and I also know that it is I who am perceiving all this" (48). This is how spectators identify with themselves or, even better, with themselves "as a pure act of perception (as wakefulness, alertness): as the condition of possibility of the perceived and hence as a kind of transcendental subject, which comes before every there is" (49). The spectator is a transcendental subject, rather than an object, as well as identifying in turn with the camera eye or with the director's point of view.

On the subject of voyeurism, Metz observes that it "always keeps apart the *object* (here the object looked at) and the *source* of the drive, i.e., the generating organ (the eye)" (59). Hence, an interesting connection emerges:

> The voyeur is very careful to maintain a gulf, an empty space, between the object and the eye, the object and his own body: his look fastens the object at the right distance, as with those cinema spectators who take care to avoid being too close to or too far from the screen. (60)

With the exception of those spectators apart, cinema always widens the gap between desire and object. "Cinema only gives [its data] in effigy," thus placing them in the realm of the "inaccessible from the outset, in a primordial *elsewhere*, infinitely desirable (never possessible), on another scene which is that of absence" (61).

By showing the world in the form of images, cinema both makes it appear and deprives us of it. What is represented seems both to be there (or we would not recognize it) and not to be there (or we would not need its images). Indeed, it is exactly because we are deprived of the world that the latter's image may establish itself. This is what originates the desire that binds us to a film, our perceptive desire. "What defines the specifically cinematic *scopic regime* is not so much the distance kept, the 'keeping' itself (first figure of the lack, common to all voyeurism), as the absence of the object seen" (61). Consequently, cinema relies on some sort of voyeurism in its pure state, on the creation of an unbridgeable gap, on the impossibility of access. Of course, other conditions contribute to this phenomenon: "the obscurity surrounding the onlooker," "the aperture of the screen with its inevitable keyhole effect," "the spectator's solitude," "the segregation of spaces which characterizes a cinema performance, but not a theatrical one" (64). In the final analysis, what matters is that:

> For its spectator the film unfolds in that simultaneously very close and definitively inaccessible "elsewhere" in which the child *sees* the amorous play of the parental couple, who are similarly ignorant of it and leave it alone, a pure onlooker whose participation is inconceivable: (64)

After the mirror, the primal scene: the fundamental elements of an individual's psychic life penetrate deeply into the cinematographic machine.

With regard to fetishism, Metz reminds us that its object is mainly the cinematographic technique or cinema as technique. "The fetish is the cinema in its *physical state*" (75). How cinema comes into being is, therefore, the core of its interest:

> A fetish, the cinema as technical performance, as prowess, as an *exploit*, an exploit that underlines and denounces the lack on which the whole arrangement is based (the absence of the object, replaced by its reflection), an exploit which consists at the same rime of making this absence forgotten. (74)

FRANCESCO CASETTI

Sublime dolly shots, wonderful "plan sequences," extraordinary takes, all tell us about the reality we lost, while they present themselves as adequate substitutes for this loss. They both hide a lack and admit to it between the lines. According to Metz, this process blends a total love with the effects of knowledge.

Specular identification, voyeurism, and fetishism are therefore the elements through which a film on the screen actually acquires substance. Thanks to the dynamics underlying these phenomena, the *cinematographic signifier* comes into being. It is obvious that these points do not exhaust what psychoanalysis has to say about cinema. In the third section of his volume, Metz goes on to a review of the analogies between film and dream, while in the last section he analyzes the functioning of metaphor and metonymy, relating them to the mechanisms of condensation and displacement in Freud's analysis of the "dreamwork." But the essential thing is how the psychic machine of the spectator functions along with the functioning of cinema, to the extent that it becomes that which helps construct what the spectator sees, the image, the signifier.

L'Énonciation impersonelle: context and reflexivity

During the eighties Christian Metz devoted much of his energy to a book on witticism, which would never see publication. Meanwhile, around him cinema semiotics sought another road: it tried to unify the attention to the dynamics of language and the symbolic device through an analysis of enunciation. The latter term is used to refer both to the "making" of the film, that is, the way in which it establishes itself as a signifying object, and to the "giving" of the film, that is, the way in which it offers itself to its spectator and, by offering itself, shapes its reception. The topic of filmic enunciation is especially brought to light by a special issue of the French journal *Communications* (38, 1983), and by the work of Jean-Paul Simon, Francesco Casetti, Marc Vernet, and Nick Browne. Metz had already intervened on the topic of enunciation with an essay in honor of Émile Benveniste, the linguist whose work on this concept was extremely influential in the context of semiology. Metz returned to the theme with his last book, *L'Énonciation impersonelle, ou le site du film* (1991), in which he rethought and systematized the debate. He observes that one should not equate cinematic and verbal enunciation, which differ in many ways. Whereas a dialogue presents specific signs defining who is implied in the production or the reception of the text (deictics like "I," "you"), a film has no equivalent terms. Similarly, while a dialogue involves real people (the "I" and "you" define them), a film can only refer to generic and biased figures (the spectator reacting to a look into the camera is a typical, not an actual, spectator). Finally, while the sender and the receiver of a dialogue can trade places (so that the "I" becomes "you" and vice versa), a film is a predefined text, where no such exchange can take place. Hence, Metz suggests that cinematic enunciation should be seen not as the creation of one person for another person, but as the simple fact of the film's manifestation of itself (here enunciation is in fact *impersonal*). He also encourages us to perceive film not as a device that connects the text with its context, but as a moment of general self-reflection (here the enunciation involves above all the *reflexive* dimension).

This does not mean that the term *cinematic enunciation* is either incorrect or useless; on the contrary, it allows a useful exploration of the main filmic procedures. Metz gives an overview of them, dividing them into eleven groups. He isolates various "appeals" to the spectator (looking into the camera, a comment made by a character who appears on the scene, a comment made by an invisible spectator, written words that provide extra information, beginning and end titles, etc.). He also speaks of "internal references," such as a screen inside the screen, the presence of symptomatic objects such as mirrors, references to other films, close copies, etc. Metz mentions the display of the "device" – in this case, cameras, microphones, and other objects connected (perhaps metaphorically) with production and reception appear on the scene – the introduction of surreptitious "sources," such as characters who see or speak in subjective shots; the falsely neutral images, which make clear that they are constructs precisely by virtue of the way in which they are constructed; and so on. In all these cases, a film "bends" toward itself, sheds light on the principles that organize it, and makes of its self-presentation a term of comparison.

It is thus with a return to film and its procedures that Metz's scientific path ends. In this persistent centrality of film as a text we may also see the final weakness of Metz's approach: in the same years, there is a cultural studies move toward studying film within the main symbolic and economic processes, as well as in analyzing film language and narration in connection with the cognitive processes. Metz was not fully able to catch these new trends of research. But this return to text is also a sign of faithfulness to his starting project ("Il faut faire la sémiologie du cinéma") ("It is necessary to create a semiology of cinema"), along a path that never refuses to engage intellectually with the keywords of his place and time ("language," "code," "writing," "apparatus," "enunciation").

See also Empathy and character engagement (Chapter 9), Jean Mitry (Chapter 37), Psychoanalysis (Chapter 41), and Semiotics and semiology (Chapter 42).

References

Bordwell, D., and Carroll, N. (eds.) (1996) *Post-Theory: Reconstructing Film Studies*, Madison: University of Wisconsin Press.

Heath, S. (1973a) "Film/Cinetext/Text," *Screen* 14(1/2): 102–27.

—— (1973b) "The Work of Christian Metz," *Screen* 14(3): 5–28.

Metz, Christian (1964) "Le cinéma: langue ou langage," *Communications* 4: 52–90.

—— (1968) *Essais sur la signification au cinéma*, Paris: Klincksieck. Trans. M. Taylor, *Film Language: A Semiotics of the Cinema* (New York, Oxford University Press, 1974).

—— (1971) *Langage et cinéma*, Paris: Librairie Larousse. Trans. D. J. Umiker-Sebeok, *Language and Cinema* (The Hague: Mouton, 1974).

—— (1972) *Essais sur la signification au cinéma – II*, Paris: Klincksieck.

—— (1977a) *Le signifiant imaginaire: psychanalyse et cinéma*, Paris: Union Générale d'Éditions. Trans. C. Brittan, A. Williams, B. Brewster, and A. Guzzetti, *The Imaginary Signifier: Psychoanalysis and the Cinema* (Bloomington: Indiana University Press, 1982).

—— (1977b) *Essais sémiotiques*, Paris: Klincksieck.

—— (1990) Interview, *Iris* 10 (special issue, "Christian Metz et la théorie du cinéma").

—— (1991) *L'énonciation impersonnelle, ou le site du film*, Paris: Méridiens Klincksieck.

Mitry, J. (1990 [1963]) *The Aesthetics and Psychology of the Cinema*, 2 vols., trans. C. King, Bloomington and Indianapolis: University of Indiana Press.

Saussure, F. de (1983) *Course in General Linguistics*, trans. R. Harris; eds. C. Bally and A. Sechehaye, La Salle, IL: Open Court Press.

Further reading

Ça Cinéma (1975) 2(7–8) is a special issue on Christian Metz, including an interview with Metz. See also Dudley Andrew, "Film Analysis or Film Theory: To Step beyond Semiotics," *Quarterly Review of Film Studies* 2 (1977): 33–41; and Francesco Casetti, *Theories of Cinema: 1945–1995* (Austin: University of Texas Press, 1999). *Iris* (1990) 10 is a special issue, "Christian Metz et la théorie du cinéma," including an interview with Metz.

37

JEAN MITRY

Brian Lewis

How many of us could say, "I saw *Nanook of the North* for the first time (at least as far as I can remember) in September 1922"? How many more would still be thinking and writing about the cinema some fifty years later? Jean Mitry's life (1907–88) spanned a period which saw the flowering of cinema as a fully expressive art form. He must have relished his good fortune to have grown and developed intellectually and creatively along with the art he loved so much.

Mitry engaged with the cinema fully throughout his life. He was a publicist, a young camera assistant (e.g., *Napoleon*, with Abel Gance, 1927), a film society founder and director, and an experimental filmmaker. He reached his true glory in roles as film critic, historian, and theorist. In his books and articles on films and directors he developed a canon of classical cinema which is hard to refute. Mitry directed the development of a *Filmographie universelle* (1979) and wrote an encyclopedic, multi-volume *Histoire du cinéma* (1967–80). He participated in passionate academic and public debates around the nature and capacities of the new medium, expropriating the work of philosophers, psychologists, and art critics and historians to build a massive *Esthétique et psychologie du cinema* (1963–5). He purposefully dissected and sparred with competing views of earlier film theorists, as well as his contemporaries, and helped to legitimize an academic discourse around film. He was a pioneering professor of film history and aesthetics on two continents.

Mitry's aesthetic theory is still not very well known. *Esthétique et psychologie du cinema*, only translated into English in a condensed form by Christopher King in 1997, is long and often difficult to read in the original version. Mitry is largely understood through the journal articles and book chapters written about him. Nevertheless, he is a giant in the history of film theory.

I spent several months with Mitry when I was a young graduate student. Mitry lived, talked, and breathed the cinema. His intellectual project was ambitious, Aristotelian in nature. What are the material, efficient, formal, and final causes of the cinema? What is it made of? How does it work? To what effect? To what end? (For a description of the Aristotelian concept of "cause" in relation to film, see *The Major Film Theories* [Andrew 1976: 6–8].) Mitry intended to describe the cinema in all of its aspects: moving from the bare-bones experiential phenomenon, to its farthest extensions as a molder of the human spirit.

At the center of this project is the *Esthétique et psychologie du cinéma, 1: Les structures* and *Esthétique et psychologie du cinéma, 2: Les formes*. Orbiting these massive volumes, as planets orbit a sun, are additional works of criticism, history, and theory: books or monographs on Chaplin, Ford, Eisenstein, Sennett, the experimental cinema, semiotics, as well as his *Histoire* and *Filmographie*. Taken as a whole, this is a remarkably coherent and internally consistent conceptual universe. It is a powerful description of how the narrative cinema works its magic on us.

At the center of Mitry's critical theory lies a fundamental experience to which he remained devoted. Underneath it all, Jean Mitry was driven by a "wow!" experience. He loved the experience of sitting in front of the screen. He loved the movies. Driven by the "wow!," Mitry endeavors to explain the "whys, what ifs, and how comes?" Why the world on the screen is so compelling, and why, when leaving the theater, life can seem so pale and flat. Which films give us the deepest "wow!" experience? How do they work their magic? Which films fail, and why? This fundamental experience in front of a screen generated Mitry's lifework of observation, rationalization, intellection, and theory.

In his aesthetics, he would first describe the film experience in its multilayered complexity – the lived reality as it is experienced. Mitry's work is, at its core, a phenomenology of the narrative film experience; it is secondly an elaborate argument in defense of that experience, as opening up a new way of seeing and apprehending the world.

Mitry was born in Soissons, northeast of Paris, in 1907. (Mitry is a pseudonym for Jean-René-Pierre Goetgheluck le Rouge Rillard des Acres de Presfontaines, chosen, he claims, from a map of France.) He attended lycée in Paris, and seemed particularly interested in courses of a scientific nature, "how things work." He was sent to England for a year of high school, and described to me a regimented schedule relieved only by trips to Manchester's cinema. It was here he experienced *la photogénie* (a word later coined by Louis Delluc), that "magic power" of the cinema he would spend a lifetime trying to explain.

Returning to Paris a "cinema addict," he immersed himself in the rich film culture available there. In 1923, he began to work part time as an English-speaking publicist for the local Goldwyn-Mayer distribution company. His circle of acquaintances in the arts grew: the Prévert brothers, Breton, and Aragon were early influences upon his intellectual development. He joined a film discussion circle, meeting Louis Delluc and Marcel l'Herbier. He began to write film reviews for Parisian journals.

Entering university to study psychology and sciences, he continued to write reviews and find small jobs in the feature industry. He helped to found a ciné club with other fledgling film critics, La Tribune libre du cinéma. He tried to interest one of them, Jean Epstein, in writing together a history of film. Although the project never got off the ground, Mitry began collecting notes for a future work.

In 1929, Sergei Eisenstein was welcomed to Paris by Léon Moussinac and his film club, The Friends of Spartacus. The young Mitry, a member of the club, roamed Paris with Eisenstein. Through Notre Dame and the Louvre, Eisenstein expounded on art, the symbol, artistic strategy, and ecstasy. Mitry noted it all; these conversations, some of which are recounted in his book *S.M. Eisenstein* (Mitry 1955), would have a seminal influence on Jean Mitry the critic and theorist.

Mitry was by now earning a living as a film assistant, as well as by dubbing American films into French. With Henri Langlois and Georges Franju, Mitry helped found the Cinémathèque française in 1936. He became the archivist, an ideal position for a maturing film critic and historian.

Mitry was mobilized during the war, and spent the duration in the south, following the fall of France. Returning to Paris, in 1946 Mitry quarreled with Langlois and quit the Cinémathèque. He was soon hired as the first professor of film in France by the newly formed Institut des Hautes Études Cinématographiques. This was the start of an academic career which would continue at the Université de Paris and the Université de Montréal.

Mitry's academic positions provided time for research. His students provided stimulation. His archives provided data. His ceaseless readings in psychology, physics, and philosophy, as well as his years as film critic and technician, provided perspective. All of this he brought to his investigation of how films work in *Esthétique et psychologie du cinéma*.

Esthétique et psychologie du cinéma presents three major sets of interlocking goals and types of statements:

1 Mitry argues that there is a central core of phenomenal traits which define all film experience, the "basic structures." He goes on to describe "forms" of these structures, or styles of cinema, which work to evoke different psychological modes of that experience, but which do not define its "essence," as do the structures.
2 Mitry develops a vast poetics of the cinema: he describes the symbolic and expressive capacities of cinema as both an art and a language – as a language which works through concrete reality – and he argues a special status for the cinema among the arts on this basis. He develops a canon of great works, and standards by which to judge films, derived from the cinema's unique capacities and status.
3 Along the way, he confronts the great debates of film theory, which had been presented by the mid-1960s. Mitry's project was to write *the* definitive aesthetics of the cinema; in so doing, he consciously and consistently addresses all previous work. He additionally attempts to tackle many great issues in philosophy and psychology, and establish an original epistemology. (This latter objective makes the work extremely challenging for film students, and much of it has been dropped from the abridged English translation.)

Structures and forms: a phenomenology of film experience

With his "structures," Mitry sets out to describe the phenomenal core, the necessary, invariant, and defining features of our experience with film. Bracketing questions of use, taste, intention – what are the defining, the essential features, of the film experience as we live it?

Mitry starts with the photographic image itself. "The essential nature of the cinema is that it is a phenomenon of images" (Mitry 1963: 59). (Note: All translations are my own.) And the essential nature of the photographic image, the defining feature of the experience of the image, is its dual nature as a both a psychological double and an aesthetic rendering of the world. Mitry, as Bazin, insists upon the "earthly origins" of the photographic image, describing the photographic image as both icon and index of the world, analogous spatially and dependent on the reality of objects for its very existence. "The cinema originates in life, and in immediate reality" (Mitry 1963: 11). But he goes a step further. Because the photograph is as well perceived as a finite, framed, physical incarnation of a specific point of view, "the most ordinary image, by the very fact that it is an image, offers even in its immediacy, a *mediated* world ... a *formalized* double" (emphasis in original text – Mitry 1967: 145). This fundamental duality is the axiom of his aesthetic theory and everything flows from it: in our experience of the photographic image, "it happens that ... the reality represented is both *the same* and *an other*" (Mitry 1963: 178).

The second structure of film experience is the double nature of the frame. The frame delimits a finite, subjective, and potentially aesthetic field of play and creation, much as the frame of painting. At the same time, as image succeeds image in the movies, the frame becomes fluid, a "mask" Bazin would say, merely hiding and eventually yielding to the extensions of that defined space, as a world in constant exposition evolves. Here again Mitry goes beyond the positions of earlier theorists to insist that the key to the apprehension of the film is a tensive co-presence of the represented and the representation. The film frame is neither entirely centripetal nor centrifugal, but both, simultaneously.

The illusion of movement is the third defining structure of the film experience. To explain this effect Mitry embarks on a long description of the "phi phenomenon" and neurological and intellectual activity behind our perception of moving objects when faced with a rapid, distinct succession of static images. It is the perception of movement which gives volume, depth, and life to the film experience.

The fourth and final defining structure of film experience is the montage effect. Any film image, any sequence, any aspect of an image may acquire signification as a result of the implications of the relationships or the context in which it occurs. It may find itself "charged" with a signification or symbolic meaning it did not have before:

> [A] new power arises when we bring together two or more shots – *they acquire a value which they would not have except in this association*. Through montage, the shot functions in the sequence as words function in the sentence – where the subject and verb and adjective find full meaning only in their interrelationships. (Mitry 1963: 161)

Here again Mitry transcends earlier formalist (Eisenstein) versus realist (Bazin) debates in film theory, describing the montage effect as a basic, defining condition of all representational film experience, put into play (but to different psychological effect) by all styles of cutting, and camerawork.

The montage effect rounds out Mitry's catalogue of the basic cinematic structures. They describe our contact with film, how we are complicit with it, how we complete the circuit and make meaning. They define our experience in front of the screen: our experience of a *reality*, concrete, corporeal, evolving, which is, at the same time, an *other*, a signifying phenomenon confined within a segregated space and time. For Mitry, this is the *essence* of the film experience.

With his encyclopedic knowledge of film history and theory, Mitry goes on to describe at great length and with great insight stylistic elements and artistic approaches which can determine the qualities and types of our film experiences: the psychological and emotional effects of various styles of montage, the use of sound, of pacing and rhythm, etc. These nondefinitional elements he calls "forms."

Here, then, is a summary of Mitry's model of film experience: Indexical and iconographic qualities of the photographic image assure that reality is not merely represented but presented in the cinema. The perception of movement completes the feeling as the world detaches itself from the flat screen, acquiring volume and spatial extension. Film expression becomes tangible, corporal with the addition of rhythm and sound. But structures and forms of representation transform this reality, charging it with an ensemble of significations. The frame is already a kind of interpretation, delimiting time and space, and establishing a ground for the effects of lighting, camera positions, field sizes, and the arrangement of objects. Objects and actions lose more of their innocence when, united in a chain of events, they acquire dramatic, narrative sense and symbolic value. In the cinema, it is as if the world itself becomes rich, pregnant with meaning.

Mitry rightly argues that many of his predecessors confused film forms with structures, conflating a style or approach to filmmaking with the cinema itself, developing "stylistics" rather than true "aesthetics" of the cinema. From this perspective he successfully defuses many of the debates of presemiotic film theory, exposing them as formal or as tactical considerations within a basic set of defining conditions, and thus his work may be understood as the terminus for most of the lines of thought on the cinema before 1964.

But Mitry's model in fact privileges a certain form of cinema as well – representational narrative cinema, and more specifically a representational cinema which achieves a kind of deep symbolic and revelatory expression. Mitry's model cannot adequately describe the powers or pleasures of a cinema which is nonrepresentational or abstract, or a deconstructed cinema, except as vestigial forms. These cinemas are not overlooked in his work – he authored a book on experimental film and produced two experimental films himself – but they are largely excluded from his pantheon, as works of historical interest, capable of demonstrating certain interesting psychological effects of film, but incapable of fulfilling the full potential of the cinema as a unique art and language.

Film as art

Defining what film "is" from an experiential perspective is merely the starting point of Mitry's aesthetic theory. Mitry's ambitions are grand: a general aesthetics of film in a classical sense. He would situate the cinema among other modes of symbolic expression and discourse, comparing and explaining the expressive and experiential qualities of each. He would elaborate his own conceptions of reality, art, and language to better understand film and argue its significance, as a uniquely valuable human endeavor.

Long contextual passages, ranging into art history and criticism, epistemology, philosophy, psychology, aesthetic theory – even physics – are scattered throughout the books. These passages were regular targets of Mitry's critics. Too often they served his detractors as justification for blanket condemnation of his work and his ambitions. Perhaps the most conspicuous of these passages is a one-hundred-page chapter in the second volume of *Esthétique et psychologie du cinéma* called "La conscience du réel." Essentially, this homemade epistemology, borrowing heavily from, and yet critical of, gestalt psychology, the phenomenology of Merleau-Ponty, Sartrean existentialism, and others grounds Mitry's rejection of a transcendent reality, waiting to be revealed by film, and any notion of the "ontological realism" of the cinema. "That the image is a revelation, it is without a doubt, but of a reality which is more intensely perceived and signified, not of a transcendent reality" (Mitry 1963: 130).

The cinema is a vehicle which can reveal and allow us to share the experience of contingent, lived truths, rather than absolute truths. Here Mitry finds his answer to the mystery of *la photogénie*: it is a result of a presentation of a world which, on the one hand, is apprehended through the senses as if actually present, but which, on the other hand, is full of meaning and signification. The concrete world becomes saturated with a necessity and essentiality it normally lacks in everyday experience. This is the unique magic of the cinema.

Mitry defines the art experience generally as a kind of ecstatic possession and revelation effected through a new perception of the world (Mitry 1963: 17). He shares with his mentor Eisenstein a fundamental stance that the cinema marries the experiential possibilities of both the plastic and temporal arts, and goes beyond each.

Painting, sculpture, music, theater, and literature are discussed at length in *Esthétique et psychologie du cinéma*, from both historical and phenomenological perspectives. In a lengthy discussion of narrative literature, Mitry describes the history of film as an evolution away from forms of theater toward the novel (Mitry 1965: 281–361). Both present people engaged in events which seem contingent; both evoke open-ended significations, resonances which expand beyond the denotative sense; and both stimulate the creation in the viewer/reader's mind of an open, ongoing, developing concrete world in all of its complexities and ambiguities, yet infused with meaning. However, film and literature actually *work* in opposite directions: while literature works through abstract words, toward the concrete, toward an image of reality, film works from a perception of concrete reality, to the abstract, toward signification. "The novel is a story which organizes itself into a world, the film is a world which organizes itself into a story" (Mitry 1965: 354).

In a film we are invited to repossess the world in a perceptual process analogous to everyday experience. Among the arts it is, Mitry argues, the cinema which most fully engages the gamut of one's perceptual processes in contact with a mediating representation, providing, thereby, an experience which is uniquely complex as process, and uniquely compelling as possession.

Film as language

Finally, the film makes possible an experience which transcends the normal bounds of art, becoming language: "Spectacle like theater, image like painting, rhythm like music, [the cinema] is no less essentially language – or writing – like verbal expression. But language of a completely different kind" (Mitry 1965: 91). An interrogation of film language completes Mitry's aesthetics of the cinema. How does film signify? How does it speak? What can it say? This investigation is elaborated in various contexts across at least eight chapters of *Esthétique et psychologie du cinéma*, volumes one and two, as well as in his book on experimental film and in numerous articles. These arguments are extracted and brought together in his final work of theory, *La sémiologie en question: langage et cinéma* (Mitry 1987).

Mitry defines "language" as a means of expression based on the substitution of signs and symbols for things, and capable of organizing, constructing, and communicating ideas in time. Each language system has its own qualities and communicative capabilities. No language is entirely adequate to the expression of reality, and there is always a margin of indetermination between our experience of the world and our expression of it in a symbolic substitute.

In a tradition of aesthetic theory with roots in romantic and symbolist poetic theory, Mitry describes a typology of language systems, from those closest to our primary, imagistic, affective experience of the world to those farthest from it. Different types of language – the essay and the poem, for instance – provide access to different realms of experience and knowledge. Discursive language makes possible the communication of an objective, verifiable, consensus truth at the expense of a more ambiguous, suggestive, experiential truth. Lyrical language evokes physical and psychological participation in prelogical thought processes themselves, engaging a game of inferences and suggestions, at the expense of precision. Lyrical languages work through perception and suggestion and are limited in their capacities to tell, to name and to analyze. They offer "food for thought," rather than offering rational argument. But what they lose in precision, they gain in affective power.

As already mentioned, Mitry was deeply influenced by Eisenstein's descriptions of the power of artistic and religious symbols as embedded thoughts, inviting ecstatic participation and re-living. But painting, sculpture, music, and dance can never quite become language: they remain vehicles for feelings, emotions, and vaguely felt ideas. Film is the one art, argues Mitry, which can work through concrete perception toward language, providing a discourse about the world through perception.

It is how this discourse occurs that ultimately distinguishes film language from all other modes of symbolic expression, including poetry and the novel: "The essential magic of the cinema comes from the fact that concrete reality becomes the vehicle for the construction of its own imaginary" (Mitry 1963: 131). Cinematic signification is rooted, not in intellection, and not in the abstract sign which is the word, but in perception itself. Film language actually captures that aspect of the thought process to which symbolic poetry aspires: an understanding which begins in the association of images, and moves out from perception and sensations toward emotions and, ultimately to "felt ideas" – an ecstatic experience in which intelligence and affectivity remain fused, one to the other and each to sensation. "We believe, in effect, that the cinema is not only an art and a culture but a means of awareness – not merely a way of communication knowledge, but of opening thought to new horizons" (Mitry 1965: 437).

Mitry's symbolist poetics

Long before theorists trained in linguistic methodology began to examine film on the crest of the structuralist wave of the 1960s, Louis Delluc, Sergei Eisenstein, and Jean Mitry, among others, described film as a "language." It is precisely in their approach to film as language that the divergence is most obvious between the Aristotelian, presemiotic film theory which climaxes in Mitry and the first wave of semiotic theory following Christian Metz. Each evokes a different set of concerns and engages a different methodology. Mitry employs the notion of language as a general analogy, bound within the context of a philosophy of symbolic expression. He is concerned with demonstrating the perceptual, semantic, psychological, and revelatory potential of this language, as opposed to other forms of symbolic expression. And he maintains that while film may act, functionally, as a language, it remains, structurally, a free and creative aesthetic expression.

The publication in 1964 of Christian Metz's "Le cinéma: langue ou language?" – just a few months after the publication of Mitry's first volume – marked a watershed and offered a new approach: a methodology, vocabulary, and scholarly rigor borrowed from structural linguistics. It served as a model for a next wave of film theory: delimited studies of film as a signifying system and textual analyses of the codes at work in films and genres. Descriptive, nonnormative, largely reductive, these studies look through films or cinema toward the structures and codes underlying their intelligibility as a grammar underlies a language. These approaches, and the Marxist and psychoanalytic approaches which followed, break with traditions grounded in the primacy of perception, our experience of film. They would expose the social and psychological articulations and constructs underlying the cinema, examining the actual laws and patterns of production and consumption which, they argue, are merely masked and perpetuated by "idealist" notions of artist, free invention, artwork, and revelation.

Semiotics came into full force in the late 1960s, and Mitry was portrayed by Metz's disciples as a lumbering dinosaur born into the wrong decade. A typical editorial in the influential journal *Screen* reads, "Up until the time of Metz's intervention (about 1964) film/cinema had been used as an excuse to talk about something else, usually the moral views, the political beliefs and other prejudices of the critic himself" (Willeman

1973). Metz himself acknowledged a debt to Mitry, but it was a bitter period for Mitry, and while he responded in 1967 with a recapitulation of his ideas in an essay, "D'un langage sans signes" (1967), he largely turned away from theory to complete his *Histoire* and *Filmographie*. It would be two decades (1987) before he returned to theory with *La sémiologie en question: langage et cinéma*, shortly before his death. To the end Mitry argues the limits of the semiotic approach, defends artistic freedom, minimizes the significance of codes in filmic creation, and defends the power and the value of the cinema as a language of creative and unfolding, constitutive symbols.

The cinema is for Mitry no less than a solution to a quest for a mode of symbolic expression sought from the time of Coleridge: a system of symbols consubstantial with the truths they conduct. Film language returns to the intellectual process its vital concrete and emotional sources, opening an expanded consciousness of the world through a marriage of perceptual, affective, and intellectual processes:

> Let us say it again: it seems to us that the cinema is the only art, the only means of expression capable of achieving a synthesis of the two languages, capable of reconciling reason and emotion, attaining one by means of the other, in an interdependence which is always reciprocal. (Mitry 1963: 104)

This description of the cinema's unique capacities as both art and language founds Mitry's critical hierarchy. Mitry's measure against which he judges cinematic activity could be summarized as *to thine own means of signification be true*. A great film requires the presence of a concrete reality – a representation in full, concrete integrity, perceived as if real – imbued with deep human signification. Does the film fulfill the presentational possibilities of filmic expression (is it concrete and "alive"); does it fulfill the ecstatic and mediatory possibilities (does it evoke the physical and mental "transport" characteristic of great art); does it, finally, fulfill the prophetic and revelatory possibilities of language (does it have semantic density, resonance, and meaning)? Only such films fulfill the full potential of the cinema to allow us to experience and understand the world anew. And only cinema, among the arts – because of how it works through the perception of a concrete reality – makes this renewal fully possible:

> Today we can question ourselves on the reality of our world, in opposing our normal perception with a new perception, similar and yet different, the filmic perception. To this extent there is more philosophy in the least important film than in all of Aristotle and Plato, as there is more to ponder in Nature than in all universal thought. (Mitry 1965: 277)

In *L'Imagination symbolique* (1963), Gilbert Durand – following closely the thought of Paul Ricoeur – distinguishes among two general approaches to literary criticism and theory. "Reductive" hermeneutics "explore the symbolic imagination in order to integrate it into a pre-established intellectual system, reducing symbolization to a symbolic content without mysteries ... [reducing] the symbol to the sign." For "instaurative" or constitutive hermeneutics, on the other hand, "the problem of the symbol is hardly that of its substructure ... but rather ... the problem of the expression which is immanent to the symbol itself" (Durand 1963: 39–59).

The reductive-instaurative polarity reflects in fact dual aspects of a single phenomenon presented in the symbol, the symbol as a symptom, as a mask, requiring demystification, and the symbol as a key, constituting a new aspect of consciousness with an inexhaustible semantic resonance. In film theory and criticism this polarity is represented on the one side by the work of Christian Metz, and on the other by Jean Mitry. But these two great bodies of work should not be read as mutually exclusive paradigms. They may in fact be read as complements, describing the engagement, the psychological impact and semantic resonance of the film as it is perceived, together with the relational systems which circumscribe and bind these objects, and their significance.

Mitry's work rejoins in its aspirations and its general lines theories of artistic symbolism developed by Paul Ricoeur, Susanne Langer, and many great literary theorists. While Mitry's theory can be surveyed for various formative affinities and influences, including the writings of Eisenstein, gestalt psychology, and phenomeno-logical aesthetics, in fact it is appropriate to situate his work in a much larger tradition of aesthetic theory, dating back at least as far as the romantic poets, traceable through the French symbolists and then reaching forward to contemporary literary and film theorists – kindred souls with whom he shares a passion for the concrete symbol as an instrument of exploration, revelation, renewal, and discovery. (For a more detailed discussion of Mitry's links to symbolist poetics, see Lewis [1984].)

Esthétique et psychologie du cinéma is an extension into film theory of a general project which would defend the integrity of artistic freedom and genius, and defend and describe fully the revelatory powers of symbolic expression. Mitry's aesthetic theory is both a monumental theory of film, and a considered theory of the symbol which deals with film. As a compelling phenomenological encyclopedia of the film experience, and a synthesis of earlier film theories, it is uniquely valuable. As a fully elaborated defense of the aesthetic symbol written in relation to cinema, it is uniquely interesting.

See also Medium (Chapter 16), Sergei Eisenstein (Chapter 35), Christian Metz (Chapter 36), and Semiotics and semiology (Chapter 42).

References

Andrew, D. (1976) *The Major Film Theories*, London: Oxford University Press.
Durand, G. (1963) *L'Imagination symbolique*, Paris: Presses Universitaires de France.
Lewis, B. (1984) *Jean Mitry and the Aesthetics of the Cinema*, Ann Arbor, MI: UMI Research Press.
Metz, C. (1964) "Le cinéma: Langue ou langage," *Communications* 4: 52–90.
Mitry, J. (1955) *S.M. Eisenstein*, Paris: Editions Universitaires.
—— (1963) *Esthétique et psychologie du cinéma, 1: Les structures*, Paris: Editions Universitaires.
—— (1965) *Esthétique et psychologie du cinéma, 2: Les formes*, Paris: Editions Universitaires.
—— (1967) "D'Un langage sans signes," *Revue d'Esthétique* 20: 139–52.
—— (1967–80) *Histoire du cinéma*, vols. 1–5, Paris: Editions Universitaires.
—— (1974) *Le cinéma expérimental*, Paris: Seghers.

—— (1979) *Filmographie universelle*, Paris: Institut des hautes études cinématographiques.

—— (1987) *La sémiologie en question: langage et cinéma*, Paris: Éditions du Cerf.

—— (1997) *The Aesthetics and Psychology of the Cinema*, trans. C. King, Bloomington: Indiana University Press.

Willeman, P. (1973) Editorial, *Screen* 14: 2.

38
EDGAR MORIN
Dudley Andrew

Cinema, the very image of human complexity

Despite – indeed because – they comprise just two of the sixty books Edgar Morin (originally Edgar Nahoum) has published since the Second World War, *Cinema, or the Imaginary Man* (2005a [1956]), and *The Stars* (2005b [1957]) command attention. As a quintessential French intellectual, Morin could feel authorized to hold forth on the most important cultural phenomena of the twentieth century, despite being neither a film scholar nor a trained philosopher. He had been an inveterate filmgoer all his life and he had read and studied philosophy far beyond the norm. Besides, as a young, vagrant sociologist taken into the prestigious CNRS (Centre national de la recherche scientifique) by his Marxist mentor, Georges Friedman, he was intent to blend the high and the low, as well as to mix disciplines. In her careful and sympathetic introduction to the English translation of *Cinema, or the Imaginary Man*, Lorraine Mortimer paints him as an omnivorous thinker, striving to face up to human reality as a whole. Abandoning the secure results that standard "disciplines" promise, thanks to their delimited scope and reductive methods, Morin early on maintained a comprehensive social-anthropological perspective inspired by Karl Marx (Morin 2005a: xvi). It's hard to argue with his goal: currently President of the Association pour la Pensée Complexe, he has always vowed to approach behavior in all its aspects, including the irrational, and to formulate the laws by which human beings, singly and collectively, process their experiences. He also prides himself on being vigilant to the diversity as well as to the commonality of individuals and groups. Although he hadn't yet come up with the term, "complexity" is exactly what the cinema provided him early in his career, serving as a full field of investigation where he tested presuppositions he would later elaborate in his six-volume *La Méthode* (2004 [1977, 1980, 1986, 1991, 2001]).

Morin was educated during the Hegel revival in France and searches phenomena for embedded contradictory elements. However, after the war and in the throes of the Stalin scandals, he exchanged the fireworks of dialectical friction and sublation for a smoother, organic model of exchange, where opposites reciprocally and continually infuse one another. If Hegel's thought can be condensed into the formula "Master and Slave," Morin's would be "Man and his Shadow." The essential opposition of the former becomes the interrelated duality of the latter, a single reality with two aspects that perpetually proceed together. Attention to this sort of multidimension-ality leads to Morin's agglutinative rhetoric marked by the formulation "both x and y."

In his early career Morin concentrated on a couple of privileged examples of this duality: (a) man is *both* a rational animal *and* an irrational being; and (b) man *both* knows he will die *and* lives with a mythology of eternal endurance. Accompanied by feeling and shadowed by imagination, human experience is necessarily doubled. The ubiquity of belief in the afterlife is the chief among innumerable affective or spiritual "realities" addressed by undismissible practices and institutions like mythology, religion, and the arts. Sartre's hard-headed philosophical view had deemed emotions "unreal," but Morin pursues a social anthropology that accepts the genuine existence of the spiritual (or affective) shadow alongside the physical body, to which it is fundamentally related. And so he keeps both dimensions in view simultaneously. While a well-established discipline like economics, geography, or biology may make satisfying gains in knowledge of one area of mankind's existence, no single discipline can comprehend the complex phenomenon of human being. Instead of emphasizing a superior discipline that organizes all aspects, Morin gives priority to none; instead, every approach should be qualified by its neighbor or even by its opposite, just as the study of any material human experience or practice must be accompanied by a study of its spiritual counterpart in thought, feeling, or imagination, especially when these resist or contradict what is experienced.

Thus multidisciplinarity involves wielding a panoply of social scientific methods and instruments in an organized series. But it involves as well nonscientific "research" to gain access to the shadowland of myth and emotion that is equally present in human life. Morin proudly invokes poets and artists who take him into the midst of the phenomena that he investigates, transforming him into a "participant-observer," to use a much-debated anthropological stance. To scrutinize the human state, Morin insists *both* on scientific rigor with empirical (often quantitative) evidence *and* on inside knowledge of a qualitative sort.

At the cinema Morin encountered the modern era's most telling concentration of the duality of human experience. He was acquainted with sociologists who had scanned films as a reflection of human anxieties (Kracauer's *From Caligari to Hitler* [1947] had been excerpted in French in 1948, and Wolfenstein and Leites had used France as a case in their 1950 *Movies: A Psychological Study*). Although Morin's first book had dealt with Germany past and present, he now preached the need for a more general social anthropology that would rise above cultural difference. One of the attractions of cinema was its universality. In "Une sociologie du cinéma," coauthored with Georges Friedman for the *Revue Internationale de Filmologie* (1952), he identified the range of elements required to produce the common experience of the movies. The theater, first of all, is a protected chamber where human behavior, anxiety, and aspiration were on display for all classes and ages. Certain realist films may be so tied to the situations they depict that only the local populace can appreciate them, but most films operate, he believed, like myths, arching across individual and cultural distinctiveness.

Morin's position was strategic, since other social scientists writing in this same journal had argued that films target audiences according to the level of their "development." African viewers were more than once relegated to a lower stage of development, and thus probably incapable of following European or Hollywood films. Morin would not be immune from his era's belief in the evolution of cultures toward increasing sophistication, but he pointedly focused on shared structures and experiences. How are films structurally related to the psyche and how does the cinema bind audiences not just within the theater but outside it, in social life? In the cultures he was familiar with, evidence for the latter lay in the ubiquity of fan magazines, film festivals, award ceremonies, and the spin-offs that have made cinema less an industry than a network of franchises, a robust economy of the imaginary (1953). Morin set himself the task of getting to the bottom of this economy, to determine the basis of its currency, as it were, and the mechanism or system by which it projects its values into the real world.

The imaginary man and the magic of the movies

While he may disdain the "simple" as necessarily reductive and thus misleading, Morin nevertheless opens *Cinema, or the Imaginary Man* (IM hereafter) by calling up two elements (the photograph and the cinématographe) that are necessary precursors to his main topic, the cinema, "a phenomenon we must try to grasp in its fullness" (IM: 3). These kindred nineteenth-century machines of automatic image-capture put man into a stunning new relation to the world and to himself. Yet neither bears anything like the far more complex "spatial and temporal characteristics" of the cinema, when it emerged just prior to the First World War as a mass spectacle with mythic potential. Morin subscribes to "The Ontology of the Photographic Image" (Bazin 1967, cited in IM: 33), where André Bazin theorized the still image in advance of the cinema, for which it is a necessary though not a sufficient condition.

Following Bazin, whose essay had opened in the key of psychoanalysis, Morin claims that an innate "charm" is the photograph's chief attribute. While it usually represents a visual scene objectively (that is, with inhumanly even-handed attention to whatever stood before it), photographs bear some mysterious connection to the inner life (subjectivity). Charm is a modern locution for "magic," and Morin quickly establishes the fetishistic quality of photographs in relation to practices anthropologists have described among archaic peoples. "Magic is the image considered literally as presence and afterlife" (IM: 30), or as Bazin said of the photograph, "an image that is a reality of nature ... an hallucination that is true" (1967: 11). Scientific uses of photography may foreground its objective side, but popular uses often bring images into the heart of what are essentially rituals: photos at gravesites, in heart-shaped lockets, carried in wallets, kissed or torn to shreds, and so on.

Morin's reflections on the presence-absence-structure of the photographic image are explicitly indebted to Jean-Paul Sartre, whose *L'Imaginaire* (1940) also served as interlocutor for Bazin's famous essay. Sartre carefully distinguishes variants of the material image, which he termed the *analogon* (including photographs, paintings, mime, etc.), alongside the immaterial mental image; this he does on the basis, first, of what the imagination brings to perception, and, second, of how perception nourishes the imagination. In his first book, *L'Imagination* (1936), Sartre fretted over the impact of emotion in perception, something especially evident in the concentrated vision called for by the photograph as a framed analogon. Morin reminds us that it is by and large customary to "smile" at the camera, so as to communicate with those who will encounter one's image later on, although certain individuals – indeed entire ethnic groups – refuse to be photographed lest their smiles or their souls be sucked up by the lens. Here, as will be his custom, Morin puts abstract philosophical reflection into dialogue with anthropological discoveries (IM: 17, 37–41).

Because of its etymology, Morin fixates on the term *photogénie*, which the 1920s theorists – Delluc (1985) and Epstein (1974) above all – hijacked for cinema as "that extreme poetic aspect of being and things" (IM: 15) visible through the motion of certain mechanically recorded images. Morin returns it to its origin alongside the still image, where it can be found particularly in such literally uncanny nineteenth-century practices as "spirit photography" (IM: 21). Here belief in an afterlife finds itself confirmed in the objective world, at least in the objective image. Rather than a special case, "spirit photography" can be taken as the emblem of cinema's psychological structure, exhibiting the porous nature of mind and matter. "Spirit photographs" shocked viewers who looked at them and so come close to the experience of the *cinématographe*, the name the Lumière Brothers gave their invention for taking and projecting moving pictures. Where the charm of so many photos resides in the quasi-reality of a past moment kept vividly in view, the magic of the cinematographic image unfolds in the spectator's own time, i.e., the image of the onrushing train moves on the screen, while the spectator watches in astonishment or runs quickly away from the screen for protection.

To characterize this vitality of the material image, Morin resorts again and again to the rhetorical pattern of the chiasmus. "We cannot dissociate it [the image] from the presence of the world in man and the presence of man in the world. The image is their reciprocal medium" (IM: 23). This particular reciprocity may be an instance of the Sartrean live presence and a real absence, a presence-absence (IM: 17); but beyond Sartre, and in tune with Bazin's idea of "the mummy complex," Morin looks to the beliefs and practices of archaic peoples (and of children) that involve doubles of which photographic and cinematographic images are modern avatars. Morin deftly draws on a key chapter from his first important book, *L'Homme et la mort* (1951) to link contemporary aesthetic objects to occult practices involving the double, using the concept of "participation" that dates back to Lucien's publications in the twenties, particularly *The "Soul" of the Primitive* (1928). All people, Lévy-Bruhl argued – and Morin cautiously follows him (IM: 72–3) – retain vestiges of the magical, "participatory" thinking exhibited by undeveloped peoples and children. Inner fears and longings get projected onto shadowy chimeras that on occasion – as in sleep or art – can take us over, populating a world that involves us but is outside our control. In death these shadows detach themselves from their bodies altogether and live on as the ghosts and gods of religion and as the scenes and stories of myths. In the modern world, the mythology of the double can be found in all the arts, and is concentrated most in the genre of "the fantastic," in which an occult world takes shape ambiguously before the reader or viewer. The camera has a way of distilling the occult from objective images of faces and landscapes, "enhancing their moral character by filmic reproduction" (IM: 15). This is photogénie at work, the face seen as a landscape when properly filmed, while the *photogenic* (not the same as the picturesque) landscape becomes nature's face twitching with emotion (IM: 70).

Morin needs the chiasmus to express this elemental pattern where the double hovers as a figure (often as a literal character) of ambiguity, at once attached to and separate from the human. Especially when concentrated in the cinématographe, perception proceeds as a moebius strip across which subjectivity and objectivity, inner and outer, the self and the double, turn into one another, while remaining theoretically separate. As viewed on screen, the world is suffused with human sentiment, like an atmosphere or a liquid that has been seeping from inner to outer. This is why and how the cinématographe so astonished that first audience at the Grande Café; over the next century hundreds of millions of people around the world would regularly breathe the cinematographic atmosphere filling the liminal space between screen and imagination.

The cinema as artistic transformation

Yet all this discussion of the double is a mere prelude to Morin's real subject, the cinema, which is psychologically and anthropologically more profound than both photography and the cinématographe. For the cinema introduces a third dimension, so to speak, where the viewer actively participates in what is on screen rather than merely staring in marvel or in fear. Morin's anthropological investigations had taught him that the double constitutes but half of the enchanted world of the imagination (what he calls the "alienated" half), since the double is the self projected at a distance and reified. The complementary half works in the other direction, with the spectator pulled into an on-screen world through a process of identification. Identification is founded on image metamorphosis, not on the image as double. While Lumière supplied the cinématographe, it was Méliès who used it to produce, not a replica of reality, but reality as magically transformed. Within twenty years, the larvae that Méliès lodged within this new invention had burst forth as a different sort of creature altogether, becoming the cinema as we know it.

Morin here follows a common tale of cinema's birth and evolution, one that recent historians have done much to discredit. Just as his anthropology of "archaic peoples" sounds patronizing today, it is also politically incorrect to treat cinema's first years as necessarily prepubescent, or childlike, a primitive stage that the adult art of cinema would put behind itself. Yet we should not dismiss Morin's cleavage plane too quickly, for it underwrites among other things Gilles Deleuze's neglect of a cinema of attractions and it may explain the latter's apology for Bergson's disregard of this new invention (Deleuze 1986: 1). After all, in his notorious 1907 reference, Bergson wrote explicitly of "the cinématographe," not the cinema. Had he waited a few years, Deleuze implies,

412

had he seen how "the cinema" liberates the spectator and the camera from the mere doubling of the world, he would have found it a transformative apparatus, a thinking machine. André Malraux, whose *Sketch for a Psychology of Cinema* (1940) Morin cites, held precisely this view, which accorded perfectly with his evolutionary history of art (from primitive to classical, mannerist, and so on). Like Malraux and Deleuze, Morin sees a qualitative leap forward, when the spectator becomes more than a fascinated onlooker (as at the cinématographe of attractions) and instead participates in a world transformed on a white screen, "the magician's handkerchief" (IM: 62). It took the wiles of montage, of *mise en scène* (especially moving camera), and of music to lure the sedentary spectator into a mobile space and time made malleable through the magic of that white handkerchief. Francesco Casetti (1987) insists that Morin's chief concern was never the cinema as double (this terrain had been mapped by Bazin) but the cinema as alive within the imagination, alive nearly *as* the imagination.

Morin echoes the Bergsonism of Jean Epstein and predicts Deleuze in rhapsodizing on transformation. His vocabulary soars and melds as he describes "temporal dilation," "spatial dilation," and "techniques of movement [that] tend toward intensity" (IM: 99). These produce "fluid time subject to compressions and elongations … endowed with several speeds" (IM: 57). An overwhelmingly inclusive phenomenon, the cinema puts us within

> magical time, in a sense. But, in another sense, psychological time, that is, subjective, affective time whose dimensions – past, future, present – are found undifferentiated, in osmosis, as in the human mind, where past memory, the imaginary future, and the lived moment are simultaneously present and merged. This Bergsonian *durée*, this indefinable lived experience – it is the cinema that defines them. (IM: 60)

Morin's foregrounding the subjective effects of film through artistic play and viewer involvement mark a departure from Bazinian objectivity, but it runs the danger of murkiness. Mercifully, dead center in his study Morin summarizes his thesis: whereas the mechanically made *image* can be taken as the projection of a *double* out of our mental life and into the world, where it appears substantial, the manipulated film speaks to and inside the *imaginary*, partaking of the *metamorphoses* we associate with dreams, daydreams, myths, and fictions. Cinema requires a certain "regression," which occurs

> when the charms of the shadow and the double merge on a white screen in a darkened room, for the spectator, deep in his cell, a monad closed off to everything except the screen, enveloped in the double placenta of an anonymous community and obscurity, when the channels for action are blocked, then the locks to myth, dream, and magic are opened up. (IM: 97)

Within this framework (which includes not just the theater situation and the literal frame of the screen, but also credits and any framing story) the movie unrolls as an oneiric fiction, subject to psychological laws that distend and transform the charmed image. "The work of fiction is a radioactive pile of projection-identifications" whose energy source lay in the subjectivities of its creator but is "reconverted for the spectator into subjectivity and feelings, that is, into affective participations" (IM: 97). Morin falls short of claiming that spectatorial regression reaches an actual state of magical thinking, for the aesthetic attitude is "conscious of the absence of the practical reality of what is represented." Whereas archaic peoples lodge spiritual power in material objects, the spectator's processes of projection-identification transmute such reified powers into liquefied sentiments, thanks to the quasi-reality of shadows on a screen (IM: 155). Still, the spectator of the mid-twentieth century comes close to magical thinking when participating in near-hypnotic identification with the fiction film. Christian Metz owed Morin more than one footnote (though he is the first citation) for *Le signifiant imaginaire* (1977), a far more famous book that effectively elaborates through psychoanalysis the anthropological vocabulary of *Cinema, or the Imaginary Man*.

The projection-identification loop

Have greater claims ever been made for the ineluctable power of any art form? Because of its incomparable mix of objectivity (precise photography that doubles our world) and subjectivity (evocative music goes to our soul's sentiments), Morin comes right out and says that the cinema "corresponds to the great aesthetic mother who covers … the whole of the imaginary" and that "the cinema is the broadest aesthetic ever possible" (IM: 169). Innumerable genres, not just those Tzvetan Todorov (1973) would later associate with the Fantastic, are fertilized by the medium's constitutive interplay of real and unreal, where "the truthful, the seemingly truthful, the incredible, the possible, the idealized, the stylized, defined objects, undefined music, combine in a mixture with infinite possibilities" (IM: 167).

Just like Deleuze nearly thirty years later, Morin believes these "infinite possibilities" are conditioned, even determined by specific historical processes and national proclivities. While his anthropology finds the fiction film to be a "magical thinking" machine, his sociology knows that this machine thinks and dreams in a variety of distinctive ways, largely because the objective, photographic part of its makeup tethers it to precise, local situations. He claims that he had outlined but failed to complete an historical-anthropology of cinema to complement the more universal claims of *Imaginary Man* (IM: 225). *The Stars* gives us at least an idea of how beautifully he works with concrete social expressions. And he was prepared to look at such expressions across a differentiated cultural landscape through popular art rather than through documentaries, for, "even soviet cinemas, the Japanese, Hindu, South American, Egyptian, and very soon Black African cinemas … are going to develop with fiction films" (IM: 163).

André Bazin reviewed both of Morin's film books in depth and with gusto in the pages of *France-Observateur*. Of *Cinema, or the Imaginary Man* he wrote that he "generally subscribed to all its fundamental concepts" (1956: 17–18). He praised

Morin for refusing a claim that must have tempted him, namely that cinema introduced brand new processes of projection-identification into the world. Instead, more soberly, Morin argues that this medium exercises and exploits processes that have always been part of daily life. Likewise, he cheers Morin for overcoming popular occultism by demonstrating how a supple language of cinema has progressively evolved out of the magma of magic. Without losing its unconscious appeal, indeed banking on just this, filmmakers have learned to control unconscious effects, as when, for example, the superimposition has evolved from an eerie effect to a grammatical technique of narration in the lap dissolve. Indeed Bazin wishes Morin had introduced even more refined discussion of cinema-specific techniques based on conscious play rather than on unconscious participation. He suggests that to Morin's anthropology of magic be added an anthropology of play and game (he surely had Caillois' in mind, whose review of Huizinga's *Homo Ludens* appeared in the journal *Confluences* in March 1946, eight months after his own "Ontology of the Photographic Image" had come out of that same journal). *Le jeu*, he claims, underwrites theater and even television, while *la magie* is foundational for cinema. Yet audiences cross from one form of spectacle to the other, and so do actors, writers, directors, and many techniques. A comprehensive treatment of "Imaginary Man" in the twentieth century would require that cinema be put in dialogue with the other arts (Bazin 1956). Morin evidently agreed, for in *L'Esprit du temps* (1962) he identifies cinema as but one form of mass culture, though the most telling of all. As for play and game, Morin never relinquished his concern with the extraordinary way fiction films draw on the irrational, as well as the rational, side of the spectator. Ultimately, cinema is no game to him; it is the all-out exercise of the expansive human capacity to participate in a mysterious world: "anthropo-cosmomorphism," he called it (IM: 106).

Today Morin's rhetoric may sound overblown, since the spectacle of the fiction film is only one mode by which even the general public interacts with cinema. *Harry Potter* movies may appeal to worldwide audiences who flock to theaters to experience what Morin has described so well, but those same viewers also put moving pictures to other uses. DVDs have brought the movies into their homes and hands; computers encourage the routine and often irreverent alteration of experiences that producers no longer control. Irony and media-consciousness pervade even mainstream films, not just the few avant-garde and Brechtian works that Morin paid little attention to in the mid-fifties. Is projection-identification still the norm?

From filmologie to mass comm

Morin's ideas may seem dated because his subject, the cinema, has burst its frame to spread throughout culture in ways no universal anthropology can hope any longer to address. Also, his ideas, necessarily tied to their era, must suffer the fate of shifts in intellectual fashion. And Morin's orientation in sociology was heavily influenced by the dominant movements of the time, Marxism and phenomenology above all. In *Autocritique* (1959), a book that came out just after *Les Stars*, he himself amply documents his persistent but shifting relation to Marxism and communism (both of which he recognized were also undergoing change because of Stalinism). As we have noted, Marx first gave him the mission to strive for a total view of man, a true anthropology. As for existential phenomenology, Morin could hardly escape it in postwar France. Hence a vocabulary that credits "mystery" and "ambiguity"; hence the struggle to grasp things organically, and as a whole; hence the references to Sartre and Merleau-Ponty, whose efforts to understand man in his situations was a phenomenological version of Marx's "totality." *Cinema, or the Imaginary Man* blends these two idioms. So too would *Chronique d'un été*, which explicitly proposed a synoptic assessment of the state of French life in 1960.

It is easy to credit Morin's claim that Hegel was his earliest and most profound influence (1955, 1994: 70–1). This must be the source for Morin's "looping" pattern, the term he came up with in 1978 to characterize the chiasmus where opposites continually flow back into and refresh one another. Earlier I compared this to a moebius strip; but Morin's "genetic anthropology" operates as a loop in three dimensions, as each passage from the real to the imaginary spirals to more complex levels. His is a developmental study, diachronic as well as synchronic. Individual experiences as well as the history of the medium form an ever-widening spiral out of these loops, from the most juvenile uses of material images to the most sophisticated. In this way Morin aims to balance his Marxist leanings, his phenomenological attitude, and a standard history of cinema largely taken from Georges Sadoul (1946).

Morin's copious ideas about cinema derived only partially from prior theorists (especially Epstein 1946, 1981 [1923]; and Balázs 1962). His views were honed in discussion with colleagues in the emergent "Institute de Filmologie," a research venture started at the Sorbonne in 1946 by Gilbert Cohen-Séat. After 1951, Morin served as this group's principal socioanthropologist, introducing into their meetings and publication those effervescent terms that he adapted from Lévy-Bruhl like "participation," "projection," and "soul." He provided the *Revue Internationale de Filmologie* with a couple of scholarly articles on the global idea of a film sociology; then in 1955 and 1956 he summarized the point of departure of both his film volumes some months ahead of their appearance in bookstores. In *Imaginary Man* he defers to (and often cites) the group's experts in aesthetics (Etienne Souriau) and in the physiology/psychology of vision (René Zazzo and Michotte van den Berck).

Edward Lowry's fine study shows the main branch of filmologie adopting a scientific, generally positivist model, one at odds with fifties French film culture, known then and now for the cinephiliac humanism of *Les Cahiers du cinéma* and *Positif*. Both these journals actually monitored filmologie, ridiculing its supercilious rhetoric and characterizing its research as dry, pretentious, and missing the heart of its object. André Bazin was responsible for the most satirical view (Bazin 1951), writing under the pseudonym Florent Kirsch (his newborn son was named Florent and his wife's maiden name was Kirsch). Later, however, he softened, participating as a (still skeptical) respondent in the Institute's February 1955 conference. Morin, not in the least positivist in orientation, was one filmologist Bazin was happy to celebrate. As I noted, he praised both of Morin's books extravagantly (1956, 1957). Published by perhaps the two most adventurous presses in postwar Paris (Minuit and Seuil), these volumes reached a broad literate public, exemplifying the kind of cultural mission Bazin stood for. Lowry singles out Morin for having crossed over to a wide audience, while not compromising the discipline that characterized the filmologie group (1985: 269). *The Stars* was especially popular and even received a translation into English as early as 1960.

Morin made use of the filmologie movement to propel him toward grander ideas and a fuller engagement with his era. Filmologie provided him a place to absorb and test ideas about a phenomenon he took to be universal and mythic, ideas that absorbed him for a decade (1952–62). Ironically, making his own film, *Chronique d'un été*, seems to have dulled his appetite for cinema. Perhaps the new wave in which he participated brought cinema down from the stars to earth. No longer descending from its mythic source in Hollywood, the films worth talking about after 1959 were authored by individuals. Audiences began to fracture (elite versus popular), as Morin noted in an important article, "Le rôle du cinema" published in the June 1960 issue of *Esprit*, just as he was commencing his film. Drawing on his projection-identification loop, Morin catalogued films by genre and hero (from the most exotic ego projections like Tarzan to models one might identify with in realist dramas). He then categorized spectators according to class and political community. The resulting permutations of cinematic experience are nearly infinite as the ratio shifts between kinds and degrees of projection-identification. Cinema itself remains universal because every fiction film uses reality to activate the imagination through images while simultaneously using the imagination to thicken reality with human purpose and aspiration.

Increasingly concerned with large-scale issues at a time when TV loomed as the mass format of the future and when his friends in the new wave were scaling down spectacle in search of personal expression, Morin wrote *L'Esprit du temps* as a comprehensive theory of mass communication. Cinema still serves the heuristic role as his model cultural artifact, a spiritual-material entity containing undeniable financial and aesthetic (imaginary) value, but he doesn't subject its specific techniques and properties to analysis. Working at such a high level of generality, Morin had become something like France's version of Marshall McLuhan, who coedited *Explorations in Communications* in 1960, and then became a household word in 1962 with *The Gutenberg Galaxy*. In any case, in the new decade Morin had severed his relation to the filmologie movement and turned instead to an exciting and far more consequential new venture, the journal *Communications*.

From the outset *Communications* treated cinema as but one star in a huge constellation of processes and artifacts. And it determined to treat it in a disciplined manner, as an alternative to the proliferating "amateur" film journals of the new wave era. At the same time, *Communications* wanted to avoid merely applying traditional academic disciplines to popular culture, in the manner of the filmologie group. And it certainly wanted to overcome positivist research with something startlingly new. Indeed, it hoped to score the same kind of revolution within the academy that the new wave had scored in filmmaking. Actually, such a revolution had already begun in the late fifties, across many of what were now to be called "the human sciences." Lévy-Bruhl's terminology, for instance, which was archaic when Morin redeployed it, found itself completely inverted by Jacques Lacan, who twisted words like "projection" and "identification," in seminars that were all the rage. Morin's own domain may have been the site of the most telltale changing of the guard, when Lévi-Strauss' ascendant "structural anthropology" (1957) brashly overturned the Sartrean paradigm, a victory celebrated in the finale of *La pensée sauvage* (1962). Equally close to Morin's domain was Roland Barthes, who, in the same year as *Les Stars*, altered the definition and the study of "mythologies" in his famous book bearing that title (1957). While neither writer so much as mentions the other in print, and while the two are expressly opposed by Mortimer (IM: xxxii), Barthes joined the CNRS just in time to help Morin found the renegade Marxist journal *Arguments*. In 1960 they were thrown together once more, this time on the editorial board of *Communications*, where Morin remains a co-publisher to this day. Its very first issue featured articles by both men, Barthes contributing his well-known "The Photographic Message" and Morin writing on "The Culture Industry" (1960), as well as introducing a dossier on the current phenomenon of the Nouvelle Vague. The clean break of this journal, and of Morin, with postwar aesthetics and sociology, became unmistakable in the fourth issue, which carried the title, "Recherches sémiologiques." In it we find Bremond and Todorov writing on literary systems, while Christian Metz debuts with perhaps his most far-reaching essay, "Cinéma: langue ou langage?" (1964), Barthes appears twice, first with his crucial "Rhetoric of the Image" and then with the text of his "Elements of Semiology" (1964).

By 1968, Morin has been completely won over by the innovative style of thought, as is evident in *New Trends in the Study of Mass Communications*, the published lectures he gave at the Birmingham Centre for Contemporary Cultural Studies. There he summarizes the cutting-edge cybernetics of Abraham Moles, which must have appealed to him because of its structural use of the feedback "loop." Morin also tracks new developments in information theory and semiotics. He would try to stay literally atop this era over the next couple decades by articulating his increasingly abstract theories of method and complexity. And while he remained in the orbit of the radical developments in the human sciences (Lacan, Greimas, Althusser), his own orientation, cybernetics and systems theory, attracted him far more.

Looking back, keeping the faith

Looking back in 1978, Morin declared his film theory to be presemiotic, and in more than one sense. No doubt he was sheepish about his relative lack of sophistication in film semiotics and narratology, compared with Metz, Barthes, and their illustrious students at the École Pratique des Hautes Études, where he would have run into them. This was the apex of semiotics in cinema, after all, and Morin could easily have felt outmoded for having attempted a comprehensive understanding of the medium twenty years earlier, a genetic-anthropological investigation of man's imaginative interaction with the world through moving images. Semiotics had gotten its start in the mid-sixties with Metz's trenchant critiques of Jean Mitry's totalizing *Esthétique et psychologie du cinéma* (1963–5), whose grand vision grew out of much the same impulse as Morin's. Mitry had treated Morin with abundant praise, linking him to Epstein.

In the name of the tradition he felt they represented, Mitry lashed back at seventies theory in a 1987 book entitled *La sémiologie en question*. Morin, however, while never part of the *Tel Quel* group, was content to let the new scholars analyze cinematic discourse like a language, because, as he wrote:

> I can see that in principle my purpose is different. If it stops where semiotics begins, I think it begins where semiotics stops: it begins with ... the problematic of the human mind which secretes the "double" and effects *mimesis* through projections/identifications. In the same way that generative linguistics begins where structural linguistics stops ... my project is concerned with a generative anthropo-sociology. (IM: 227)

Morin had actually used the word "generative" in his 1955 prospectus for *Imaginary Man*, and so he was ready in this 1978 preface to a new edition of that book to latch onto Noam Chomsky's generative linguistics in order to defend his long-held belief that raw participation in images stands in advance of cinematic discourse and therefore that the mind-brain loop (genetically) precedes semiotics. Today Chomsky seems to me like an ill-chosen weapon, the convenient recourse of many who sought to skirt the imposing structuralist stronghold that commanded French intellectual terrain during the seventies. Chomsky may well have had a more advanced theory of language than Hjelmslev and Jakobson on whom film semiotics was based, but his linguistics failed to provide the basis of a theory of film signification. More germane and authentic by far is Morin's restatement, just two pages earlier in this preface of his own theory of images; here he betrays a profound debt to Bergson and he offers what turns out to have been a prophecy for Deleuze's film books that were incubating at just this time. In trying to characterize the incessant back-and-forth of the brain-mind loop, Morin says that the mind

> does not directly know external reality ... it is enclosed in a cerebral black box, and only receives, via the sensory receptors and neural networks (which are themselves cerebral representations), excitations (themselves represented in the form of undulating/corpuscular pathways), which it transforms into representations, that is, into images. One can even say that the mind is a representation of the brain but that the brain is itself a representation of the mind: in other words, the only reality of which we are certain is the representation, that is, the image, that is, nonreality, since the image refers to an unknown reality. Of course, these images are articulated, organized, not only according to external stimuli but also according to our logic, our ideology, that is to say also, our culture. All that is perceived as real thus passes through the image form. Then it is reborn as memory, that is, an image of an image. (IM: 223)

While Morin's wide reading and extensive interchange with scholars around the world put him in the orbit of Systems theory, cybernetics, and other discourses he might have conceived of as an anthropology of consciousness, he also stands in a line of French intellectuals for whom the cinema, while based on the insubstantial image, served as the twentieth century's most substantial cultural enterprise. Like André Malraux before him and Régis Debray after (the latter debuting in public life with a role in *Chronique d'un été*), Morin speculated on the cinema, directed an ambitious film, participated in leftist politics, and held a high-level administrative post. For all three, but perhaps for Morin above all, modern man is unthinkable without cinema; indeed, "real thought" in the twentieth century, if we can use that term, consists of an indiscernible circuit of perception-reflection, a cinematic circuit involving brain and mind, matter and spirit, etc., in short, involving a philosophical anthropology.

See also Gilles Deleuze (Chapter 34), Christian Metz (Chapter 36), Phenomenology (Chapter 40), and Semiotics and semiology (Chapter 42).

References

Balázs, B. (1962) *Theory of the Film: Character and Growth of a New Art*, London: Dobson.

Barthes, R. (1957) *Mythologies*, Paris: Seuil.

—— (1960) "Le message photographique." *Communications* 1: 127–38.

—— (1964) "La rhétorique de l'image" and "Éléments de sémiologie," *Communications* 4: 40–51; 91–135.

Bazin, A. (1951) "Introduction à une filmologie de la filmologie," *Cahiers du Cinéma* 5: 33–9. (Written under the name Florent Kirsch.)

—— (1956) "L'Homme imaginaire et la fonction magique du cinéma," *France-Observateur* 331 (13 September): 17–18.

—— (1957) "A propos d'un livre d'Edgar Morin: le star system est toujours vivant," *France-Observateur* 377 (August): 15.

—— (1967) "The Ontology of the Photographic Image," in H. Gray (trans.) *What Is Cinema?*, vol. 1, Berkeley: University of California Press.

Bergson, H. (1907) *L'Évolution créatrice*, Paris: Alcan.

Caillois, R. (1950 [1946]) "Jeu et sacré," in *L'homme et la sacré*, Paris: Gallimard, 208–24.

Casetti, F. (1987) "Edgar Morin et le cinéma," *Révue européenne des sciences sociales* 75: 217–24.

Colin, M. (1985) *Langue, film, discourse (reliure inconnue)*, Paris: Méridens Klincksieck.

Deleuze, G. (1986) *Cinema 1: The Movement-Image*, Minneapolis: University of Minnesota Press.

Delluc, L. (1985) "Photogénie," in *Écrits cinématographiques* I, Paris: Cinémathèque Française, 31–79.

Epstein, J. (1946) *L'Intelligence d'une machine*, Paris: J. Melot.

—— (1974 [1923]) "De quelques conditions de photogénie," in *Écrits sur le cinéma*, vol. 1, Paris: Seghers, 137–47. Trans. Tom Milne, "On Certain Characteristics of Photogenie," *Afterimage* 10 (1981): 23–31.

Kracauer, S. (1947) *From Caligari to Hitler*, Princeton, NJ: Princeton University Press.

Lévi-Strauss, C. (1957) *L'Anthropologie structurale*, Paris: Plon.

—— (1962) *La pensée sauvage*, Paris: Plon.

Lévy-Bruhl, L. (1928) *The "Soul" of the Primitive*, New York: Macmillan.

Lowry, E. (1985) *The Filmology Movement and Film Study in France*, Ann Arbor, MI: UMI Research Press.

Malraux, A. (1940) "L'Esquisse d'un psychologie du cinéma," *Verve* 8(2): 69–73.

McLuhan, M. (1962) *The Gutenberg Galaxy: The Making of Typographic Man*, Toronto: University of Toronto Press.

McLuhan, M., and Carpenter, E. (eds.) (1960) *Explorations in Communication*, Boston: Beacon.

Metz, C. (1964) "Le cinéma: langue ou langage," *Communications* 4: 52–90.

—— (1977) *Le signifiant imaginaire: psychanalyse et cinéma*, Paris: Union Général d'Éditions.

Mitry, J. (1963–5) *Esthétique et psychologie du cinéma*, 2 vols., Paris: Presses Universitaires de France.

—— (1987) *La sémiologie en question*, Paris: Éditions du Cerf.

Morin, E. (1951) *L'Homme et la mort dans l'histoire*, Paris: Éditions Corrêa.

—— (1953) "Recherche sur le public," *Revue Internationale de Filmologie* 12: 3–20.

—— (1955) "Cinéma ou l'homme imaginaire," *Revue Internationale de Filmologie* 20–24: 133–8.

—— (2005a [1956]) *Cinema, or the Imaginary Man*, Minneapolis: University of Minnesota Press.

—— (2005b [1957]) *The Stars*, Minneapolis: University of Minnesota Press.

—— (1959) *Autocritique*, Paris: René Julliard.

—— (1960a) "Le rôle du cinéma," *Esprit* (June): 1069–79.

—— (1960b) "L'Industrie culturelle," *Communications* 1: 38–59, 139–41.

—— (1962) *L'Esprit du temps*, Paris: Grasset.

—— (1968) *New Trends in the Study of Mass Communications*, Birmingham, UK: Centre for Contemporary Cultural Studies.

—— (2004 [1977, 1980, 1986, 1991, 2001]) *La méthode*, Paris: Seuil.

—— (1994) *Mes démons*, Paris: Éditions Stock.

Morin, E., and Friedman, G. (1952) "Une sociologie du cinéma," *Revue Internationale de Filmologie* 10: 95–112.

Sadoul, G. (1946) *Histoire généerale du cinéma*, Paris: Éditions Denoël.

Sartre, J. (1936) *L'Imagination*, Paris: Felix Alcan.

—— (1940) *L'Imaginaire*, Paris: Gallimard.

Todorov, T. (1973) *The Fantastic: A Structural Approach to a Literary Genre*, Cleveland, OH: Case Western Reserve Press.

Wolfenstein, M., and Leites, N. (eds.) (1950) *Movies: A Psychological Study*, New York: Hafner.

Further reading

See Sam Dilorio, "Total Cinema: *Chronique d'un été* and the End of Bazinian Film Theory," *Screen* 48 (2007): 25–43. *French Cultural Studies* 8 (1997) is an issue devoted entirely to Morin. Myron Kofman, *Edgar Morin: From Big Brother to Fraternity* (London: Pluto Press, 1996) is an intellectual biography that skirts the cinema but gives a rounded sense of Morin's trajectory and his constant concerns. Ivone Margulies, "*Chronicle of a Summer* as Autocritique: A Transition in the French Left," *Quarterly Review of Film and Video* 21 (2004): 173–85, relates Morin's film practice to his political ruminations. Jean Rouch, *Ciné-ethnography* (Minneapolis: University of Minnesota Press, 2003) is an anthology consisting mainly of Rouch's reflections, but it does have a section by Morin on the making of *Chronique d'un été*. Steven Ungar, "'In the Thick of Things': Rouch and Morin's *Chronicle of a Summer* Reconsidered," *French Cultural Studies* 14 (2003): 5–22, discusses the feedback loop that both men deployed in early work.

39

HUGO MÜNSTERBERG

Don Fredericksen

Hugo Münsterberg vis-à-vis contemporary film theory

To the question of where one might find a place in contemporary film theory for Hugo Münsterberg's *The Photoplay: A Psychological Study* (2002 [1916]), the answer at the most fundamental level has to be "nowhere." The early contribution to film theory of this distinguished German-American philosopher and psychologist might well have remained entirely tucked away in the shadow of history had it not been brought back into partial view by the development of cognitive film theory during the last twenty-five years. Some scholars involved in this latter endeavor see in Münsterberg's 1916 text as an insightful precursor and ally to their own interest in discovering the ways in which processes of the mind that are available for conscious reflection and empirical research interactively inform our perception and apperception of the conceptual, affective, and formal registers of film.

The first half of *The Photoplay*, in its own manner and for its own purposes, does just that. To assume, however, that this is Münsterberg's primary goal is to fundamentally misjudge what he is about. This is so because *the psychological study that takes up the first half of the book is explicitly nested within, and at the service of, a prior neo-Kantian aesthetic value theory*. In the latter, as we shall describe below, the governing and honorific concepts are those of disinterested interest, the isolation of the aesthetic object and of the aesthetic experience from the concerns of practical life and scientific knowledge, and the resultant claim for the aesthetic experience *sui generis* of harmony and beauty. The function of Münsterberg's 1916 study of the psychology of film is to reveal how the then new medium of film could find a legitimate place within the traditional arts that are taken to be exemplars of these qualities, as seen by him through the lens of neo-Kantian philosophy in general and its aesthetics in particular. This is not a task that contemporary cognitive film theory has set for itself. However much it finds of lasting and astute value in Münsterberg's psychology of film, it does not follow him in the aesthetic endeavors for which his psychological observations serve as support.

Three additional, often interrelated, aspects of contemporary film theory stand in direct conflict with Münsterberg's psychology and aesthetics of film: First, the emphasis upon unconscious factors in the creation of film, film spectatorship, and the structure and substance of films by psychoanalytic approaches based in Freud, Lacan, or Jung, among others; second, the devaluation of the honorific status of beauty by approaches based in analytical philosophy or feminism; and, third, the assertion of the primarily ideological character of film that underlies philosophical materialistic approaches to film which gained prominence after the seminal cultural turning point of May '68. The latter encompasses various Marxist and cultural studies approaches, including the sometimes useful, but quite reductive, lenses of race, class, and gender.

None of these salient aspects of contemporary film theory would have appealed to Münsterberg, because, in their separate ways, each of them violates axioms of his own system of thought. Regarding the unconscious, Münsterberg rather famously declares in his *Psychotherapy* that "the story of the subconscious mind can be told in three words: there is none" (Münsterberg 1909b:125). Although Münsterberg worked in part as a psychotherapist, his belief is that mental maladies are not symptoms of unconscious mental factors but are physiological malfunctions. His antipathy against Freud, in particular, was such that he reportedly left Boston when Freud visited Clark University in 1909, so as to avoid any possible meeting with him! (In passing we might note that cognitive psychology currently acknowledges the unconscious nature of some mental processes, although the intersection of the conceptions of the unconscious in cognitive psychology and depth psychology has not been worked out; in any case, it will most likely be found to be only partial.)

The devaluation of beauty because of its putative function in sexual politics, or because of doubts about its efficacy in the philosophical analysis of art, particularly modern art, would have been understood by Münsterberg as a rejection of the aesthetic value in life, attainable only in the isolated realm of the aesthetic, and necessary to the experience of harmony in human culture.

Equally misguided, from Münsterberg's perspective, is the assertion that film is always and most essentially an instrument – often unwittingly – of ideology. To make this assertion is to confound the realms of art (properly understood) and practical life and to miscast film as an essentially rhetorical medium, rather than as a new instrument, among others more traditional, for the experience of beauty. We will subsequently see how this argument rather awkwardly requires Münsterberg to eliminate documentary and educational film from his aesthetics of film, even while they obey the processes outlined in his psychology of film.

Perhaps we are in a position now to answer the initial question somewhat differently: Münsterberg's film theory can have an oppositional and compensatory function *vis-à-vis* contemporary film theory insofar as one or more aspects of the latter stands in need of a correction·or compensation of the kind suggested by him. Münsterberg has most likely come out the loser in the debate over the existence of an unconscious register of the mind, although this fact does nothing to prevent those who hold with the reality of the unconscious mind from uttering assertions that are often essentially speculative, and necessarily open to conceptual and empirical criticism. His opposition to philosophically materialistic theories of human culture and the high stature he gives to beauty and aesthetic value *sui generis* have more to contribute as compensation to film theories that champion the former and devalue the latter.

Münsterberg's scholarly life

Münsterberg was born in Danzig, Germany (now Gdansk, Poland), in 1863. He wrote three doctoral theses, at the universities of Leipzig (1885), Heidelberg (1887), and Freiberg (1887), respectively. The first was written under the guidance of Wilhelm Wundt, the founder of modern experimental psychology. The second earned him an MD, which led him into later work as a clinical psychologist and psychotherapist. The third was required by the German habilitation system for a position as a university lecturer. At this time psychology was still taught within philosophy faculties, which suited Münsterberg's own deepest propensities. He lectured on traditional philosophical subjects and was associated with the so-called school of Baden or Southwest school, one branch of the neo-Kantian movement that dominated German philosophy at the end of the nineteenth century. The school emphasized the investigation of value judgments, especially those with a claim to necessary, i.e., universal, status. It is this philosophy that informs *The Photoplay*.

Münsterberg's work caught the attention of William James, who first invited him to Harvard in 1892. He later moved permanently to Harvard in 1887 to head up the first experimental psychology laboratory. He published his systematic philosophy in German in 1908, as *Philosophie der Werte*, and in an English revision in 1909, as *The Eternal Values*.

Münsterberg is considered the father of applied psychology, for which he became a well-known lecturer throughout the United States. His writing in this area is voluminous, and includes *Psychology and Industrial Efficiency* (1913), *Psychology and the Teacher* (1909), and *Psychology and Social Sanity* (1914). Among his many accomplishments, he devised the first lie detector, used hypnotism to cure persons of alcoholism, investigated psychic phenomena, and devised tests for choosing safe trolley-car drivers *using film*.

Münsterberg's move to Harvard was partially motivated by his desire to improve German-American ties, for which purpose he wrote several books in German and English on the American character. The First World War defeated Münsterberg's hopes in this regard, and led to his being ostracized, even at Harvard, where one alumnus threatened to shoot him. He died in 1916, prior to the United States' entry into the war against Germany. There is some reason to believe that Münsterberg's interest in the photoplay during this period was partially motivated by his desire to be seen as engaging American popular culture. However, he was using film in his lab, as noted above, by 1912; and he was already familiar with films in the documentary, travel, educational, and newsreel modes. These types of film held no philosophical interest for Münsterberg – in contrast to their interest for European theorists in the near future – because they manifested values nested in practical life and science. Only the photoplay carried the potential for aesthetic values, which by definition within his neo-Kantian system were divorced from practical life and scientific endeavors.

Nonetheless, Münsterberg's practical use of film caught the eye of the film industry. At the time of his writing of *The Photoplay* Münsterberg was under contract with Paramount Pictures to contribute to its one-reel educational screen magazine,

Paramount Pictographs. He generated thirteen popular items, including "Are You Fit for Your Job?," which were simple psychological experiments requiring viewers' active participation in tests for vocational guidance. Left unrealized at his death were plans for the graphic presentation of history using film.

While relaxing during a Midwest scholarly conference, Münsterberg saw the photoplay *Neptune's Daughter*; this was apparently the seminal experience in his devotion to the photoplay. By 1916, he had written and published his lucid defense of the photoplay's aesthetic status, the first American film theory to be nested within a systematic philosophy, and by a distinguished philosopher.

Münsterberg's neo-Kantian philosophy: the Eternal Values

Münsterberg firmly held the belief that progress and greatness in philosophy are a function of inner consistency, a quality only possible in a close-knit system of thought. This belief manifests clearly in his general philosophy and in his film theory. Throughout both Münsterberg writes comfortably and with complete sincerity about absolute, universally valid, and eternal values – a tone very much out of step with postmodernism's pervasive irony and with the "hermeneutics of suspicion," grounded in Marx, Nietzsche, and Freud and currently pervasive in the humanities in general and film theory in particular.

Münsterberg takes his reasoning in this regard from Kant, whose transcendental logic moves in a vector opposite to that of empiricism's inductive logic. The latter moves from a collection of facts of experience to generalization(s), with the claim that the collected facts support the generalization(s). Transcendental logic, by contrast, moves from facts of experience to the description of the logically necessary presuppositions for the possibility of these facts. *Crucially, these facts consist of value judgments*. Induction cannot produce certainty, as Hume points out, because one can never know with certainty that the set "previous facts + new fact" will conform to the generalization(s) based on the "previous facts." Transcendental logic, on the contrary, yields certainties because it describes the logically necessary presuppositions for the very existence of those facts of experience, those value judgments. Transcendental logic's tone of certainty about the universal validity of the value judgments to which it is applied, for example scientific, ethical, and aesthetic judgments, is nested within the deeper certainty that the very existence of the value judgments in these areas is *inconceivable* without the logically necessary presuppositions transcendental logic finds. Thus, in the realm of aesthetics, both Kant and Münsterberg find it inconceivable that one would make a judgment that something is beautiful without the logically necessary presupposition that the judgment is universally valid. In this regard Kant's *Critique of Judgment* speaks for Münsterberg as well:

> It would ... be laughable if a man who imagined anything to his own taste thought to justify himself by saying: "This object ... is beautiful *for me*." For he must not call it beautiful if it merely pleases him ... If he gives out anything as beautiful, he supposes in others the same satisfaction; he judges

not merely for himself, but for everyone, and speaks of beauty as if it were a property of things ... We cannot say that each man has his own particular taste. For this would be as much as to say that there is no taste whatever, i.e., no aesthetic judgment which can make a rightful claim upon everyone's assent. (Kant 1951: 38–9)

Seen backward through the lenses of the various modes of skepticism and relativism that dominate today's culture, this Kantian claim would itself be laughable. Nonetheless, the claim remains a contestable one, and whatever one thinks about its credibility, if one is to understand Münsterberg "from the inside," then one must accept that it inheres in the tone of the claims he makes about the aesthetic character of the photoplay. To read Münsterberg's aesthetics of the photoplay without accepting the role of the Kantian claim in it is to miss its point.

Since Münsterberg's theory of the photoplay is firmly grounded in a prior systematic philosophy, it is crucial to become aware of just what kind of system of absolute values transcendental logic generates for him. He starts by postulating an ontological register called "immediate and individual life reality," in which individuals' relative, personal, and pragmatic experiences of will play out their myriad ephemeral trajectories. Coexistent with this "world of the will" is the world of objects, the "world of science." But, crucially, the will also *demands* a world that is more than the chaotic ensemble of individual desires and pleasures; this "pure will" demands a "true world" of absolute values, i.e., values that command everyone's allegiance. We can trust this demand because the will would not demand something that did not satisfy it. This "world of pure will" is the only basis for philosophy properly understood. From Münsterberg's perspective, pragmatism confuses the immediate and individual life reality with the true world. Naturalism and positivism likewise confuse the world of mere objects with the true world. Only a new articulation of philosophical idealism can generate a true philosophy, for it alone understands that only the true world demanded by the pure will can provide a basis for life that commands universal allegiance. This is so because only the values this idealism articulates are absolute, eternal, universal. This view must have made for lively debate in Harvard's philosophy department, which included the popular champion of pragmatism, William James, and an articulate defender of philosophical naturalism, George Santayana. Perhaps not surprisingly, James, who had initially invited Münsterberg to Harvard, eventually had a falling out with him.

Münsterberg's view was that, historically, culture, including philosophy, swings between nonidealistic and idealistic poles. Neo-Kantianism was an expression of a new idealistic period, weary of mere facts and the philosophical materialism and positivism that preceded it in Germany. The photoplays of 1916 are seen to have a potent, albeit nascent, function in this new swing toward idealism. Given Münsterberg's view in this regard, we can infer that he would reject philosophic materialist explanations for film's genesis and cultural function, including technological determinism.

In opposition to the contingent and ephemeral register of immediate and individual life reality, the fundamental absolute valuation is the assertion of identity among changing experiences:

Whatever secures for us a world, i.e., whatever allows us to transcend the isolated flashlike experience, must be valuable to us. Here we have the deciding factor from which everything else will follow. We must seek the identity of experiences. That is the one fundamental act which secures for us a world. It is the one act we cannot give up, and yet which has nothing to do whatever with personal pleasure and pain ... We demand that there be a world ... that [experience] assert itself in its identity in new experiences ... Only insofar as such identity offers itself is the experience at all a self-dependent [and self-asserting] world. Hence the world of values is the only true world. (Münsterberg 1909a: 74, 77–8)

This assertion of experience as a self-dependent world unfolds into four kinds of absolute values, both naïvely and culturally, and in three different registers.

It is useful for the reader of *The Photoplay* to see two sections of this system in their broad outline, and to see also the smaller parts of them activated for the book (Münsterberg 1909a: xii–xv):

I   The value of conservation (the logical values)
   A The naïve values: the values of existence
     1 Things (the outer world)
     2 Persons (the fellow world)
     3 Valuations (the inner world)
   B The cultural values: the values of connection
     1 Nature (the outer world)
     2 History (the fellow world)
     3 Reason (the inner world)
II The value of agreement (the aesthetic values)
   A The naïve values: the values of unity
     1 Harmony (the outer world)
     2 Love (the fellow world)
     3 Happiness (the inner world)
   B The cultural values: the values of beauty
     1 Fine arts (the outer world)
     2 Literature (the fellow world)
     3 Music (the inner world)
III The value of realization (the ethical values)
IV The value of completion (the metaphysical values)

Münsterberg's theory of the photoplay focuses upon only two sections of this exhaustive system. The psychological investigation engages the value of conservation (the logical values) at the level of the cultural values of connection, in the register of "Nature." This Nature is an abstract human construction that connects things principally through cause and effect. This abstraction is the work of the sciences, including what Münsterberg called "causal psychology." It is this psychology that he brings to bear upon the photoplay.

The aesthetic investigation engages the value of agreement (the aesthetic values) at the level of the cultural values of beauty, most particularly in the register of music. This placement of the photoplay in the company of music is part of Münsterberg's differentiation of the photoplay from literature and the theater, a common medium-purist rhetorical project in early film theory, and one that partially places him in company with some French film theorists of the 1920s, e.g., Germaine Dulac.

In this system the goal of psychology is the incorporation of the mental world into the causal system of Nature. The psychologist sees the mental world as the natural scientist sees the physical world, i.e., as a system of objects controlled by laws. Münsterberg's view was in basic agreement with the experimental psychology pioneered in Germany by Wundt. This "new psychology" broke down mental phenomena into elements and studied their combinations, as if they were a kind of "mental chemistry." It is essentially this kind of psychology that underlies Münsterberg's analysis of depth, movement, attention, memory, imagination, and emotions in the photoplay. The psychologist of the photoplay, like all scientists, must exclude the will in his investigations; therefore, he cannot simultaneously serve as an aesthetic investigator. The latter must exclude his *own* idiosyncratic will, but he acknowledges the manifold wills in the world that appears *on the screen*.

Münsterberg's atomistic psychology was opposed by the development of gestalt psychology's emphasis upon "wholes" that have "emergent qualities" not derived from the sum of their parts. Münsterberg knew and used Werthheimer's experiments in perception in *The Photoplay* but did not change his own conception of psychology in doing so. This has led some commentators to mistake Münsterberg as a proto-gestalt psychologist.

The knowledge and truth given by psychology are of a limited, particular kind that must be complemented by those given by art and other registers of human thought and culture. In Münsterberg's view, science does not give us knowledge of what a thing is in itself, but of what it can be transformed into by causal processes (the "thing in itself" under discussion here is *not* Kant's famous *Ding an sich*). The function of art is precisely to give us knowledge and experience of something in its isolation, not knowledge about its past or future, nor about its connections in a causal nexus. Thus the need for a separate psychological investigation of the viewers' "mental experience" of the photoplay, and an aesthetic analysis of the photoplay divorced from all wills, except those on the screen, that are brought into the agreement to constitute the absolute aesthetic value of beauty.

Both logical and aesthetic values are absolute because they do not adjust themselves to personal desires and because they must satisfy every person who wills a real world. By subordinating ourselves to scientific truth we grasp the outer world as an independent self-persevering *thing*. By devotion to natural and man-made or artificial beauty, we grasp the outer world as a self-agreeing *will*. Logical valuation demands that the thing remain identical as an object; aesthetic valuation demands that the wills of a thing remain the same – that they finally are one will, whose parts agree with one another. The wills reveal their identity by agreeing; therefore, aesthetic values isolate manifolds of agreeing wills from any and all upsetting factors. (In passing we might note that this view separates Münsterberg from the theory and practice of *dialectic film form*, as manifest, for example, in the pathos structures of Eisenstein's *The Battleship Potemkin* [1925] and *The General Line* [*The Old and the New*] [1929], Leo Hurwitz's *Native Land* [1942] and *Strange Victory* [1948], and Solanas and Getino's *Hour of the Furnaces* [1970].)

Scientific knowledge offers the means for action and moves from the given to the not-given via prediction. Beauty, by contrast, does not lead beyond itself; it is useless for practical activities. The scientific stance of psychology views the beautiful object as a thing in Nature. This violates the subjective experience of beauty, in which aesthetic objects confront us not as physical objects, but as will-manifolds. Aesthetic experience involves the interpretation of these wills, not the analysis of physical objects.

Münsterberg's conception of the aesthetic object, experience, and value are indebted to Kant and to eighteenth-century British aesthetics. In the latter, Lord Shaftesbury first expressed the view that the aesthetic contemplator does not connect the object of his or her contemplation with any purpose beyond the act of perception itself. Francis Hutcheson adds the idea that aesthetic experience has no concern with cognitive knowledge of the object being contemplated. Kant in turn asserts the autonomy of art from practical and cognitive concerns. The object of this so-called "disinterested interest" or satisfaction is called beautiful, and it has its own character- istic quality, which Kant characterized as "purposiveness without purpose." From this philosophical discussion Münsterberg himself emphasizes the isolation of the object of aesthetic contemplation, rather than the disinterested interest of the contemplator, although the latter is assumed. In his system the aesthetic object's purposiveness without purpose is expressed as the ultimate agreement of the object's wills, isolated from any purpose beyond their agreement. This isolation of the aesthetic object thus yields one of the absolute values. We see here the logic behind Münsterberg's exclusion of documentary, newsreel, and educational film forms, since they serve purposes beyond themselves.

The Photoplay: A Psychological Study

Münsterberg takes film's history to have an outer and an inner register; the former is essentially scientific and technical, and was initially motivated by the desire to analyze movement. The inner register is itself split into two: An outer-inner register is essen- tially cognitive and includes nonfiction film types. Such films stand for something outside themselves. The inner-inner register is essentially affective and moves through fiction and amusement, i.e., the photoplay. Such films do not stand for something outside themselves but are self-referential and isolated, in keeping with the require- ments of the aesthetic value of agreement.

Münsterberg's psychological study of the photoplay is motivated by the seminal questions of early film theory: Is the photoplay an independent art? If so, what aesthetic qualities give it its independence? These questions partake of the project of medium purism, which differentiates the expressive potentials of the various arts with the assumption that each should do what it does best in this regard, and not meddle in potentials better manifested in another medium. The result is usually prescriptive, giving such theorizing – including Münsterberg's – a strongly rhetorical tone, although the differentiation *per se* is, at least nominally, descriptive. In Münsterberg's case, the psychological study is the descriptive basis for the aesthetic prescriptions. Theater plays the major role in the differentiation of the photoplay from other arts. But when commonalities are discussed, music plays the major role. Münsterberg's approach differs from those of the supporters of early film who championed its putative realism or its potential for disseminating the values of the educated classes to the general public; his concern is the capacity of the photoplay to isolate itself in the service of the absolute aesthetic value of beauty. The psychology of the photoplay cannot answer the question of what constitutes aesthetic autonomy, but it can describe the mental means that function as that autonomy's means. Münsterberg's analysis intends to show that the spectators' experience of the photoplay results in a unique conjunction of unique inner experiences, thus providing the data for the subsequent aesthetic argument for the photoplay's independent status as an art.

Münsterberg begins with the perception of depth and movement. The crucial point is that both the perception of virtual depth in what we know to be a flat surface and the perception of apparent movement in what we know to be a series of static images require a kind of "filling in" by the spectator's mind. In theater both depth and movement are real, requiring no such filling in. Rather than claim, as others did, that this difference proves film's inferiority to theater, Münsterberg asserts that it marks one of the means of establishing the photoplay's aesthetic autonomy. Because of his knowledge of the extant scientific study of the perception of movement, Münsterberg knew that film's apparent movement has little to do with the persistence of vision, and much to do with the so-called phi phenomenon and fusion frequency, although this fact did not appear in most books on film until quite recently.

Moving from depth and movement to attention, memory, imagination, expectation, and suggestion, Münsterberg moves from perceptual psychology to what he calls the psychology of meaning. Now the essential distinction is not between fact and experience as it was regarding the former, but between the logic of the latter inner processes and natural, nonmental laws, especially physical causality. "The photoplay obeys the laws of the mind rather than those of the world" (Münsterberg 2002: 90). The goal is to demonstrate that salient cinematic devices and formal structures follow the logic of inner processes – even though the projected image is phenomenally objective.

Of these "psychical acts," attention is the most central. It constitutes stability in an ambience of flux because it partakes of the identity of anticipated and realized experiences that is the fundamental demand of the will for a real world rather than chaos. That is, we turn our attention to something in order to get more of it. In the process, the object of our attention becomes clearer, more vivid, separate from its environment, and a kind of magnet for feeling and impulse. In art the proper mode of attention is involuntary, because voluntary attention manifests one's personal will, not the ensemble of wills within the work. The photoplay's close-up is the objectification of the mental act of involuntary attention, and it is the aesthetic demarcation line between the photoplay and the theater. Many other early film theorists also assert the latter, but they do not necessarily find the same significance in it, e.g., Fernand Léger emphasizes the "plastic value" of objects obtained in the close-up, and Béla Balázs focuses on its ability to reveal the "micro-dramatics" of the human face (Balázs 1970).

In summary, the photoplay's objectification of these psychological processes is as follows (Fredericksen 1977: 155):

- the close-up objectifies attention;
- flashback objectifies memory;
- flashforward objectifies expectation or imagination;
- fades and dissolves objectify memory, expectation, or the imagination of a character in the photoplay;
- "cutting off" objectifies suggestion; and
- parallel editing objectifies the desire for an understanding of simultaneity.

Münsterberg asserts that "to picture emotions is the central aim of the photoplay" (Münsterberg 2002: 99). Initally the active role of the spectator takes a back seat to the emotions of the characters, manifest in "gestures, actions, and facial play," and by the "emotionalizing of nature," if judiciously employed. The spectator may imitate the emotions of the characters, thereby giving an affective tone to the former's grasp of the latters' actions. But this is a bit too passive for the active spectatorship for which Münsterberg is arguing. Therefore, he asserts that from the spectator's perspective, the emotion on the screen is a projection. This move sits uneasily with Münsterberg's prior philosophical claim that projection should not play a role in our experience of beauty. Later, Edgar Morin will struggle with the complexity of this process in a nuanced analysis of "projective identification" in his *The Cinema, or the Imaginary Man*.

The aesthetics of the photoplay

Münsterberg's aesthetics of the photoplay is not determined by the findings of his psychological study; rather, the latter is subsumed by the former. Because of this we encounter a troublesome and glaring *non sequitur* in Münsterberg's book. Münsterberg's psychological study, excepting perhaps his discussion of emotion, is applicable to the film medium *per se*, including all of the film types he excludes from his aesthetic analysis. Thus, it can be used equally well, albeit to different ends, in an analysis of what we can call in a general way the rhetorical function of film – including the rhetorical function of the photoplay itself. The structure of Münsterberg's book gives the mistaken impression that the psychological study is only relevant to the aesthetic function of film, as manifested in the photoplay alone. This *non sequitur* allows the critical reader to realize that the psychological study can be valued without accepting what Münsterberg does with it in his aesthetic theory. Nonetheless, if we wish to understand Münsterberg's own goals, then we need to understand and appreciate how *he* uses it.

Münsterberg restates his neo-Kantian view of the purpose of art in *The Photoplay* in the following manner:

> We find that the central aesthetic value is directly opposed to the spirit of imitation. A work of art may and must start from something which awakens in us the interest of reality and which contains traits of reality, and to that extent it cannot avoid some imitation. But it becomes art just insofar as it overcomes reality behind it. It is artistic just insofar as it does not imitate reality but changes the world, selects from it special features for new purposes, remodels the world and is through this truly creative. To imitate the world is a mechanical process; to transform the world so that is becomes a thing of beauty is the purpose of art. (Münsterberg 2002: 114)

Unlike science's transformation of reality into Nature, art's transformation brings desires to rest, not by eliminating them, but by satisfying them within the confines of the artwork. It does this through isolation:

> Only in contact with an isolated experience can we feel perfectly happy. Whatever we meet in life or nature [usually] awakens in us desires, impulses to action, suggestions and questions which must be answered. Life is a continuous striving. Nothing is an end in itself, and therefore nothing is a source of complete rest ... Such harmony [as we find in art], in which every part is the complete fulfillment of that which the other parts demand, when nothing is suggested that is not fulfilled in the midst of the same experience, where nothing points beyond and everything is complete in the offering itself, must be a source of inexhaustible happiness ... this is the aim of the isolation which the artist alone achieves. (Münsterberg 2002: 119)

Each art has its own means for effecting this isolation; indeed, the medium-purist argument to which Münsterberg subscribes demands that these means be different. Here is where the psychological analysis of the photoplay is utilized to support the aesthetic one, which Münsterberg states in several slightly different ways in the second part of his book. Here too is the crux of his entire argument:

> If this is the outcome of aesthetic analysis on the one side, of psychological research on the other, we need only combine the results of both into a unified principle: the photoplay tells us the human story by overcoming the forms of the outer world, namely space, time, and causality, and by adjusting the events to the forms of the inner world, namely attention, memory, imagination, and emotion. (Münsterberg 2002: 129)

> The photoplay shows us a significant conflict of human actions ... adjusted to

the free play of our mental experiences and which reach complete isolation from the practical world through the perfect unity of plot and pictorial appearance. (Münsterberg 2002: 138)

The richest source of the unique satisfaction in the photoplay is probably that aesthetic feeling which is significant for the new art ... The massive outer world has lost its weight ... and has been clothed in the forms of our own consciousness. The mind has triumphed over matter and the pictures roll on with the ease of musical tones. It is a superb enjoyment which no other art can furnish us. (Münsterberg 2002: 153–4)

Münsterberg's medium purism demands that the only medium of the photoplay be the moving picture; therefore, he argues against intertitles, color, sound effects, and synchronous sound. His aesthetic of isolation also argues against the last three, since they bring us too close to the practical world. This particular aspect of Münsterberg's book brought him back into fleeting prominence in the late twenties, when synchronous sound film was argued against by defenders of the art of the so-called silent film.

Münsterberg vis-à-vis classical film theory

Within the context of two canonical descriptions of differing approaches to the ontology of film, its nature and function(s), Münsterberg's theory resides in the tradition André Bazin calls the "faith in the image," as against the "faith in reality," and in what Siegfried Kracauer calls the "formative" tradition, as against the "realist" one. On one side Münsterberg, the Soviet masters of the twenties, Balázs, and Arnheim, among others; on the other, L'Herbier, Bazin, and Kracauer. Writing in 1917, L'Herbier makes clear the difference put forth again much later by Kracauer:

Isn't the contrast between the goal of the traditional Arts and the goal of the one we have nicknamed, in the cradle, the [seventh], sufficiently marked? Isn't it clearly apparent to all that the goal of the cinema, art of the real, is completely opposite: to transcribe as faithfully as possible, without transmutation or stylization, and by accurate means which are specifically its own, a certain phenomenal truth? (L'Herbier 1946: 205)

Apparent to L'Herbier – utterly mistaken, in Münsterberg's neo-Kantian view. Moreover, while Münsterberg's theory resides in the formative tradition, his aesthetic of isolation qualitatively separates him from the Marxist, rhetoric-driven Soviet masters and Balázs. Arnheim, whom he most closely resembles, is more deeply indebted to gestalt psychology, while Münsterberg remained indebted to the atomistic psychology of Wundt, against which gestalt rebelled.

See also Emotion and affect (Chapter 8), Film as art (Chapter 11), Medium (Chapter 16), Rudolph Arnheim (Chapter 27), and Psychoanalysis (Chapter 41).

References

Balazs, B. (1970) *Theory of the Film: Character and Growth of a New Art*, trans. E. Bone, New York: Dover.

Fredericksen, D. (1977) *The Aesthetic of Isolation in Film Theory: Hugo Münsterberg*, New York: Arno.

Kant, I. (1951) *Critique of Judgment*, trans. J. H. Bernard, New York: Hafner.

L'Herbier, M. (1946) *Intelligence du cinématographe*, Paris: Éditions Corrêa.

Münsterberg, H. (1909a) *The Eternal Values*, Boston: Houghton Mifflin.

—— (1909b) *Psychotherapy*, New York: Moffat, Yard.

—— (2002 [1916]) *The Photoplay: A Psychological Study*, in A. Langdale (ed.) *Hugo Münsterberg on Film: The Photoplay: A Psychological Study and Other Writings*, New York: Routledge.

Further reading

Dudley Andrew, *The Major Film Theories* (New York: Oxford University Press, 1976) places Münsterberg within the formative tradition in film theory. Monroe C. Beardsley, *Aesthetics from Classical Greece to the Present: A Short History* (New York: Macmillan, 1966) is a lucid discussion of the Kantian and eighteenth-century British aesthetics, from which Münsterberg's neo-Kantian aesthetics partially springs. Don Fredericksen, *The Aesthetic of Isolation in Film Theory: Hugo Münsterberg* (New York: Arno, 1977) is a detailed conceptual and logical analysis of Münsterberg's photoplay theory *vis-à-vis The Eternal Values*, including much that could not be contained in this short entry. See also Martha E. Hensley's MA thesis, *Hugo Münsterberg: Proto-cognitivist in the Classic Tradition* (University of Kansas, 1994). Allan Langdale (ed.) *Hugo Münsterberg on Film: The Photoplay: A Psychological Study and Other Writings* (New York: Routledge, 2002) contains the latest reprinting of *The Photoplay*, with a very useful introduction, updating some aspects of Fredericksen, and adding many post-1977 citations, including the cognitivists' interest in Münsterberg. The full English-language expression of Münsterberg's neo-Kantian philosophy is Hugo Münsterberg, *The Eternal Values* (Boston: Houghton Mifflin, 1909).

40
PHENOMENOLOGY
Vivian Sobchack

In 1978, at the height of structural, semiotic, and psychoanalytic film theory, Dudley Andrew published "The Neglected Tradition of Phenomenology in Film Theory," an essay critical of academic film theory's tendency to ignore the "peculiar way meaning is experienced in the cinema and the unique quality of the experience of many films" (1985 [1978]: 627–8). Providing a brief history of phenomenology's conjunction with the cinema and calling for reconsideration of a mode of inquiry that might describe the perceptual, sensuous, affective, and aesthetic dimensions of signification and meaning in the film experience, Andrew contrasted synthetic phenomenological description with the analytic search for cinematic codes and textual systems, and the purely structural or psychoanalytic readings of films.

Film theory's neglect of phenomenology was not surprising. From the mid-1940s to the present, the historical entailment of cinema and phenomenology has not been unified or always explicit – this, not only because of a notable variety of phenomenological perspectives on diverse aspects of the cinematic experience but also because, as a philosophy of experience, phenomenology has itself been transformed over time by various philosophers and practitioners. Nonetheless, however a particular orientation or application might emphasize them, there are certain invariant philosophical premises that ground all phenomenological inquiry and the practice of its descriptive method. What follows is, first, an admittedly rather crude gloss on phenomenology as philosophy and research method, as well as on its general relevance to the study of cinema. The subsequent section then addresses the history of phenomenology and cinema, with particular attention to specific works and debates.

Phenomenology and phenomenological method

Formally articulated in the early twentieth century by its "founding father," Edmund Husserl, phenomenology is the foundational study and description – a "first" philosophy – of phenomena in the "life-world" as they seem given and are taken up as conscious experience. The appropriate starting place for gaining knowledge of the world, ourselves, and the meaning of things is in rigorous reflection on experience itself – that is, on the activity and modalities of consciousness as it is engaged with (although differentiated from) *any* phenomena given to it in experience (whether material or imaginary, rationally or emotionally apprehended, or initially regarded as real or an illusion). Thus, however useful, various theoretical explanations of phenomena are regarded as "secondary," constructed *after* the experience we actively live (both objectively and subjectively) in a real world of phenomena and social others. Furthermore, following from this, all phenomenology is grounded on the premise that objective phenomena and subjective consciousness are entailed in an *irreducible correlation*. This correlation may be differentiated and described in its objective and subjective aspects but cannot be reduced further, as it constitutes meaning only as a synthetic whole. Called "intentionality," this correlation designates consciousness as never "empty" and always *directed* toward a present object (even when, in reflexive acts such as reflection, that intentional object is its own activity).

The phenomenological premise of intentionality also has methodological consequences. As Husserl emphasized, in our everyday lives and thought, the directedness and modes of engagement of our consciousness with meaningful phenomena are nearly always informed – and limited by – a host of mediating, yet transparent, presuppositions that make the way these phenomena "immediately" appear seem "given" and "natural" rather than taken up and constituted according to transparent historical, cultural, and scientific constraints and hierarchies. Thus, for Husserl, these presuppositions needed to be made explicit and then set aside so as to reveal the full possibilities or "essence" of the object otherwise limited by acculturation and habit (what he called the "natural attitude," but which might best be called the "naturalized attitude"). This "bracketing" of presuppositions to allow the full possibilities of the phenomenon under investigation to appear (its "fulfillment") was achieved through a rigorous critical method. Entailing a series of what phenomenology calls (after Husserl) "reductions," the method involves (1) recognizing and "bracketing" presuppositions about the phenomenon; (2) equalizing each feature of the phenomenon so as to undo habituated hierarchies of significance; (3) exercising a series of "imaginative variations" (or thought experiments) to test the "horizons" of the phenomenon and its modes of appearance so as to reveal the object's possibilities beyond its initial (or "naïve") appearance; and (4) interpreting the lived significance of the object as it has been shaped and limited by presuppositions and is now opened to further possibilities.

In this regard, phenomenology generates not only an *experiential* but also an *experimental* methodology that begins with a commitment to the openness of its object of inquiry, rather than to any *a priori* certainty of what that object already "really" is. Phenomenology thus has particular resonance in relation to cinema. The intentional directedness of subjective consciousness toward its intended object demands a description of the film experience that includes the "spectator" as well as the "text" – that is, it presumes an active (rather than passive) viewer and calls for focus not only on elements of the film viewed but also on possible modes of engaging and viewing it. In this conjunction of viewer and film, the dynamics, modulations, and effects of acts of visual and aural cinematic perception are correlated with the structures of cinematic expression. Indeed, from a phenomenological perspective, cinema becomes a philosophical exemplar of "intentionality," making manifest the directed and irreducible correlation of subjective consciousness (evidenced by the camera's projected and thus visible choice-making movements of attention) and its objects (whether "real" or "imaginary"). Furthermore, through editing, the cinema also demonstrates acts of reflection that organize and express the tacit meaning of its own and the world's explicit conjunction and movement. In effect, the cinema both enacts and dramatizes the intentional correlation as an actively lived structure through which meaning is constituted as such. Thus, as Andrew suggests, the cinema begs for explication of what it makes visible and audible, "those realms of preformulation where sensory data congeal into 'something that matters' and those realms of post-formulation where that 'something' is experienced as mattering" (1985 [1978]: 627).

Although best understood in its actual exercise, phenomenology's methodological approach and usefulness – particularly in relation to cinema – can be briefly suggested here through a concrete example. Derek Jarman's *Blue* (1993), made when the filmmaker was dying of AIDS and losing his sight, challenges ordinary notions of cinema. In the "natural attitude," it is described as monochromatic – "only" blue – with an unchanging, "empty" visual field of bright cobalt, this accompanied by a soundtrack woven of voices, sound effects, music, and first-person narration that eloquently describes Jarman's medical, social, and emotional journey toward blindness and imminent death. Phenomenological reductions, however, reveal that this initial description forecloses what is seen and how the film is actually experienced in the (theatrical) viewing situation. First, in experience rather than presumption, the image is not "empty"; indeed, not only does the field of blue become a figure in its own right against the darkness surrounding the screen (extending the viewer's usually more narrow focus on the screen's center), but there are also figures constituted within the blue field both objectively (i.e., scratches on the film print that appear and disappear, moving both independently and in seeming relation to the soundtrack) and subjectively (i.e., various afterimages that occur when one redirects one's eyes in relation to the visual field). Second, phenomenological method reveals that the "blue" that initially is presupposed as "constant" actually appears in many variations of hue and intensity: the afterimages appear superimposed on the blue in traces of orange and green; alterations in perceptual activity (narrow or diffuse focus, visual attentiveness or fatigue) make the blue more and less intense or dense; and, strikingly, the tonal and affective qualities of the blue field change with the soundtrack on which, in relation to his failing sight and fading life, Jarman evokes ever-mutable images of "blueness" (whether of "the blues," "bluebells," or "blue sky"). In sum, phenomenological method reveals *Blue* as not only objectively *about* the richness, complexity, and sensuality of visual perception (as well as its loss) but also as subjectively constituting for viewers an *experience* of extreme self-reflection on their own dynamics of vision – particularly as (akin to Jarman's experience) it is seemingly "deprived." Certainly, more can be said about *Blue*'s cultural context, generic status, aesthetic, thematic, and social significance, and its place in the filmmaker's oeuvre. However, as a "first philosophy," and particularly as amended by the existential philosophers who followed Husserl, what phenomenology demands is that we attend to the actual and possible experience that grounds the film's meaning, not merely as it is *thought*, but also as it is *perceived* (in this case by both Jarman and the viewer).

Husserl's goal was to reveal the "essence" of lived phenomena, not as they were apprehended in the "natural attitude" of the everyday life-world, but in the unbiased intentional structure of what he called the "transcendental ego." However, as suggested above, this construction of a unitary consciousness to which both its own modes of engagement and its intentional objects were fully disclosed was extremely problematic to many of Husserl's disciples. Ahistorical, acultural, and inherently static, the transcendental ego seemed a return to *metaphysical idealism*. That is, the goal of achieving a completely presuppositionless and all-encompassing description and interpretation of phenomena in the life-world ran counter not only to actual but also to possible experience with its countless ambiguities and variations of meaning and value. Thus, emphasizing consciousness as *embodied* and always *situated* in the world in an ongoing process of "becoming," Maurice Merleau-Ponty tells us in *Phenomenology of Perception* that "the greatest lesson of the [phenomenological] reduction is the *impossibility* of a complete reduction" (1962 [1945]: xiv; my emphasis).

Along with Martin Heidegger, Jean-Paul Sartre, and others, Merleau-Ponty transformed Husserl's *transcendental* (or constitutive) phenomenology into an *existential* phenomenology that embraced both consciousness and its objects as inherently variational and dynamic. Indeed, embodied consciousness can never quite catch up with or be fully disclosed to itself through acts of reflection, however rigorous – this not only because it is always situated but also because it is always both behind and ahead of reflection, always engaged in acting and "becoming" something other than it presently is. As a result, phenomenological description and interpretation can only be *provisional* – that is, qualified in embodied experience by the mutable possibilities and constraints of world, history, and culture that give the general structure of phenomena the particular value that makes them meaningful. Thus, most contemporary phenomenologists have rejected the idea of – or need for – a transcendental ego, while still embracing phenomenology's basic premises and method. Instead of seeking "essences," they seek to disclose, in a given case, both the general and particular structures, meanings, and ambiguities of phenomena as they are perceived and lived *in context*. Today, phenomenologists attempt not only to *correlate* the objective and subjective aspects of a given embodied experience but also to acknowledge their historical and cultural *asymmetry*. That is, while interested in describing the ontological functions that enable our general "being-in-the-world," they also focus on the epistemological functions that characterize our "being-in-a-particular-world." Attending rigorously to the *contents* of embodied experience (the "what" that appears), to its *forms* ("how" it appears), and to its *contexts* ("why" it appears as it does), the "proof" of a powerful phenomenological description and interpretation does not rest on totalizing claims. Rather, it rests on whether the description and interpretation of the experience's logical structure is sufficiently comprehensible and resonant to others who might possibly inhabit it.

Phenomenology of film/film as phenomenology

Phenomenology's explicit intersection with the study of cinema began in the mid-1940s in France with the inauguration of *filmologie*, a movement that lasted into the 1960s and took as its task the description not only of films but also of the existential, psychological, and institutional activities of filmmaking and film viewing. Although loosely organized and interdisciplinary, the movement published a journal, *Revue Internationale de Filmologie* (1947–60). While many of the journal's essays emphasized empirical research, many others were engaged in phenomenological research into the qualitative nature and psychology of cinematic perception (this particularly in the *Revue*'s early years, before filmologie became dominated by experimental psychology). This phenomenological work included differentiating cinematic perception from other perceptual productions of consciousness such as dreams, memories, and illusions, describing spatial and temporal perceptual gestalts such as the perception of movement and depth, and investigating spectator identification and affect. In 1948, for example, the *Revue* published A. Michotte van den Berck's "Le caractère de réalité des projections cinématographiques," an essay prescient in posing, perhaps for the first time, the still central question of what has been called the cinema's "reality effect."

Filmologie also provided a context in which interest in the cinema increased among philosophers and scholars not directly connected with the movement. A significant example was Merleau-Ponty, who, in 1947, published "The Film and the New Psychology," an essay relating gestalt psychology to the motion picture. "Let us say right off that a film is not a sum total of images, but a temporal *Gestalt*," he wrote (1964: 54); that is, a film is perceived not in its discrete cinematographic elements (visual, aural, and editorial) but in these elements' meaningful totality as a temporal and sensual *configuration* that is grasped as "a unique structure ... a unique way of being, which speaks to all [our] senses at once" (1964: 50). Merleau-Ponty emphasized that a film's meaning emerges not only in narrative and dialogue but also, and primarily, in our perception of lived conduct and behavior in the world (both the camera's and the actors'). The cinema was thus a phenomenological art, "peculiarly suited to make manifest the union of mind and body, mind and world, and the expression of one in the other" (1964: 58).

During the two decades of filmologie's popularity in Europe (the mid-1940s until the mid-1960s), there were a variety of phenomenological investigations of the cinema that described its "ontology" (most not translated into English except as indicated here by English titles). These, however, manifest two quite different interests, the one in an *existential* and *social anthropology* focused on the cultural effects of cinema as a radically new mode of representing our "life-world," and the other in a *transcendental aesthetics* focused on the cinema as a unique form of technologically mediated creation and expression.

Influenced by Merleau-Ponty, social anthropologist Edgar Morin (discussed elsewhere in this volume), in his *The Cinema, or the Imaginary Man* (2005 [1956]), was insistent on the cinema's corporeal and affective logic. Social and collective fascination with the medium emerged from its ontological ambiguity: on the one hand, its expansive perceptual capacity to bring human being to consciousness of itself as well as of a world previously unseen or taken for granted, and, on the other, its objectification of human being and the world in phantasmagoric images. Morin's work was phenomenologically inflected in his emphasis on embodiment and affect as co-constitutive of both social and cinematic meaning. Furthermore, his privileging of cinema rests on the central phenomenological premise of intentionality. That is, for Morin, the cinema provided an ongoing and historically open-ended "dialectic, where the objective truth of the image and the subjective participation of the spectator confront and join each other" (2005 [1956]: 147). Whereas Morin's work described the cinema as ontologically revelatory of human being's always social and historical inherence in the world, Roger Munier's *Contre l'image* (1963) was a great deal more negative about its essence and social effects. For Munier, cinema was a prelogical and alienating medium that mechanically represented and reified the world as autonomously – rather than socially – constituted. In sum, the medium was not only overpowering but also essentially inhuman.

A second strain of French phenomenology focused on the aesthetic qualities and experience of cinema, often articulated as a theologically inflected ontology. The medium was celebrated for its essential capacity to provide viewers an "immediate" apprehension of human being, as well as providing an "intuition" of spiritual and moral truths. Thus, Henri Agel suggested the cinema had a "soul." Greatly influenced by Gaston Bachelard's phenomenological writing on the "primordial" and "immediate" nature of the poetic image and highly critical of semiotics and structuralism, Agel's posthumously published work, *Poétique du cinéma: Manifeste essentialiste* (1973), described and privileged a cinema of "contemplation" that functioned aesthetically through analogy, rather than reason, to allow spectators access to the transcendental qualities of nature and human existence. Theologian Amédée Ayfre, a former student of Merleau-Ponty's, also focused on the medium's capacity to reveal transcendence in immanence: the openness of human consciousness and the world which – through its materiality – insists on the existence of more than merely meets the eye. Ayfre's *Le cinéma et sa verité* (1969) thus privileged "authentic" films that resonated in the viewer first intuitively and then reflectively, ultimately reorganizing the viewer's perception and behavior so that the life-world outside the theater was reengaged in a new and ethically enhanced relation of moral responsibility.

The best-known celebrant of the cinema's capacity for transcendence through perceptual "revelation" was French critic André Bazin (discussed elsewhere in this volume). Film's photographic ontology grounded the medium in a privileged existential and phenomenological relation to the world. Mechanical in nature, the camera "brackets" or puts out of play the habituated vision of human being, lets the world impress itself upon the film and our perception in its continual evolution, and leads us to a fresh awareness of human existence as contingent and ambiguous. Thus, although eclectic in subject matter, most of the essays collected in Bazin's influential *What Is Cinema?* (1967) privileged an aesthetic of "perceptual realism" – one that, through use of the long shot, deep focus, and the long take, revealed meaning as relational, and respected not only the spatial complexity of "being in the world" but also the temporal continuity of human being's continual "becoming."

The entailment of phenomenology and the cinema was at its height in the late 1940s and 1950s, when philosophers found the new medium both a challenge to and exemplar of phenomenological aesthetics. Thus, although film was not their central focus, several major philosophers paid attention to the cinema. For example, Roman Ingarden's influential 1947 *Ontology of the Work of Art* (1989) has a specific section on film, and Mikel Dufrenne makes numerous references to film in his 1953 *The Phenomenology of Aesthetic Experience* (1973). Interest in phenomenology waned, however, as research into perception and the cinema became increasingly influenced by the natural and social sciences. By the late 1960s, academic film studies, too, turned away from what it considered a less than "scientific" approach to its objects. Indeed, influenced by Christian Metz and Jacques Lacan, film studies took a semiotic and neopsychoanalytic "linguistic turn" and, influenced by neo-Marxist Louis Althusser, also emphasized the ideological structures of cinema as both apparatus and institution. In this context, phenomenology came under critical attack on both sides of the Atlantic. Not only were its transcendental (and often theological) leanings deemed "idealist" and "metaphysical," but also its foundational grounding in the description of "direct," "immediate," and "subjective" experience and its celebration of the cinema's "revelatory" capacity seemed evidence of "naïve realism." That is, the notion of film as enacting a phenomenological "bracketing" that removed habituated presuppositions (film *as* phenomenology) did not seem to take into account the specific mediations either of "film language" or of an ideologically informed technological apparatus. Indeed, the notion of cinema as "transcendental subject" was merely an illusion. Thus, although Jean Mitry (discussed elsewhere in this volume), in his masterwork, *The Aesthetics and Psychology of the Cinema* (1997 [1963]), engages in meticulous phenomenological description of forms of cinematic perception and expression, he also criticizes Ayfre, Agel, and Bazin for celebrating the cinema as "ineffable" or "transcendental." Indeed, this negative reference to the analogy made between Husserl's "transcendental ego" and the cinema is emphasized in Jean-Louis Baudry's seminal essay, "Ideological Effects of the Cinematographic Apparatus" (1974 [1970]), which elaborated the analogy to critique the ideology and spectatorial illusion of a visual mastery grounded in a cinematographic optics derived from Renaissance perspective.

Hence the "neglect" of phenomenology highlighted in Andrew's 1978 essay, at a time when, if referred to at all, it was identified with Husserl's transcendental phenomenology. It is not surprising, then, that works of existential phenomenology more relevant to contemporary semiotic and hermeneutic questions of cinematic signification and intelligibility were almost completely ignored. In Europe, Belgian psychologist Jean-Pierre Meunier published *Les structures de l'expérience filmique* (1969), which described and differentiated modes of viewer attention and relation to films "taken up" and perceived as home movies (*film souvenirs*), documentaries, and narrative fiction. (Elsewhere, I've glossed Meunier's still untranslated work; see Sobchack [1999].) Although more poetic than methodical, Italian filmmaker and theorist Pier Paolo Pasolini's *Heretical Empiricism* (2005 [1972]) combined a sensuous Marxism with existential phenomenology to acknowledge the subjective foundations of what is seen and lived as the objectively "real."

On the other side of the Atlantic, there were also several book-length attempts at a synthetic description of cinema and the film experience, the most well-known of them both ontologies: George Linden's *Reflections on the Screen* (1970) and Stanley Cavell's *The World Viewed: Reflections on the Ontology of Film* (1971). Linden is explicitly phenomenological: the ontology of film emerges in – and for – perceptual experience; intangible but constituted as a "real appearance," film creates "a kind of perpetual elsewhere that enters the presence of immediate experience" (1970: 279). Cavell (discussed elsewhere in this volume) echoes Linden's "perpetual elsewhere," in his description of the "material basis" of cinema as "a succession of automatic world projections" that are always already synthetic in their appearance (1971: 72). Furthermore, the cinema's reality appears "magical" insofar as it "automatically" satisfies our wish to see the world – unseen and outside it and yet in connection with it – through the very act of viewing. Not only does the medium fulfill this wish, but it also "takes the responsibility for it out of our hands," thus making the "movies seem more natural than reality" (1971: 103).

From the mid-1970s to the 1990s, and despite Andrew's rallying cry, interest in phenomenology was negligible. Nonetheless, it needs emphasis that phenomenology informed the early thought of many of its later critics, notably Jean Mitry, Christian Metz, and Gilles Deleuze (all discussed elsewhere in this volume). During this period, there were only sporadic attempts in the English language to bring phenomenology to bear on the cinema, these describing, on the one hand, essential structures such as cinematic time and space and, on the other, the particular aesthetics of specific films. Thus, essays such as Alexander Sesonske's "Cinema Space" (1973) and Edward Casey's "The Memorability of the Filmic Image" (1981) take on the general enabling structures and perceptual effects of the medium whereas essays such as Dudley Andrew's "The Gravity of *Sunrise*" (1977) and Frank Tomasulo's "The Intentionality of Consciousness: Subjectivity in Resnais's *Last Year at Marienbad*" (1988) focus more narrowly on particular films.

Renewed interest in phenomenology emerged in the 1990s, primarily in the United States. This occurred in the context of growing awareness of televisual and "new media" challenges to cinema's specificity as both medium and experience and of the need for a nondeterminist and synthetic method and vocabulary able to address aspects of cinematic experience such as spectatorial agency, pleasure, and affect, and the presence of the human body both on the screen and in the theater. In 1990, the *Quarterly Review of Film and Video* published an issue on "Phenomenology in Film and Television," with essays on representation, vision as embodied activity, cinematic "scopophilia," cinematic temporality, television reruns, the ontology of video technology, feminism and phenomenology, and a selective bibliography. Soon after, Allan Casebier and I (contributors to this special issue) published book-length phenomenologies of cinema – each quite different in approach and focus from the other.

Casebier's *Film and Phenomenology* (1991) follows Husserl in its "epistemologically realist" account of cinematic representation. Rejecting dominant idealist/nominalist notions of film and its figures as mentally produced by the spectator (even in the case of fiction), Casebier describes the film as having an existence independent of its viewing and referential – in its own modality – to reality. Engaging a film, perceivers "*transcend* their perceptual acts in recognizing what [the film] depicts" (1991: 9). The uses of particular cinematic elements (i.e., camera angle, editing) and representational elements (i.e., aesthetic or generic conventions) shape and constrain the dynamics of the viewer's apperceptive "looking through" some features (color or lines that make up an image, for example) and perceptive "looking at" others (the figures constituted by color and line, for example). A particular film thus limits a viewer's interpretive horizons; meaning is co-determined not only by the viewer's own intentional horizons but also by those of the film. Explicating Husserl's complex phenomenological vocabulary, Casebier goes on to consider a range of cinematic modes of representation, including documentary and Japanese film.

My own *The Address of the Eye: A Phenomenology of Film Experience* (Sobchack 1992) follows Merleau-Ponty to develop an existential and "semiotic" phenomenology. Rather than positing the film as constituting a "false" and "transcendental" consciousness that subsumes the independent vision of its viewers, it accounts for the spectator's "primary identification" with the cinema quite differently. The film experience is described as entailing a film and its spectator as two active and differently situated viewers viewing in intersubjective, dialectical, and dialogic conjunction. That is, both film and viewer are perceptive and expressive actors "being-in-the-world," the convergence and divergence of their visual and intentional interests dynamically constituting the general and particular significance of the visible and audible experience. A unique medium, the cinema "presents and represents acts of seeing, hearing, and moving as both the *original structures of existential being* and the *mediating structures of [film] language*" (1992: 11). This is achieved through the technological mediation of camera, projector, and screen – these transparently incorporated (by both filmmaker and spectator) so as to enable a given film's very existence and yet, as mediation, also opaque and requiring active interpretation. Describing our embodied and hermeneutic relations to cinematic technology, *The Address of the Eye* accounts for cinema's primary intelligibility as emerging in the technologically mediated conjunction of certain common perceptual structures, shared autonomously and together by filmmaker, film, and spectator.

Academic interest in phenomenology has increased greatly since the explorations of the early 1990s. Existential phenomenology, insofar as it is explicit in relation to the sensually meaningful embodiment of consciousness, has greatly informed Laura Marks' *The Skin of the Film* (2000) and *Touch* (2002) as well as more explicitly guiding my own *Carnal Thoughts: Embodiment and Moving Image Culture* (2004) and Jennifer Barker's forthcoming *The Tactile Eye*. Numerous essays in a variety of journals and anthologies have also brought phenomenology to bear on a variety of cinematic interests, including the oeuvre of particular filmmakers and the close reading of specific films. Laura Rascaroli, for example, has illuminated Kathryn Bigelow's cinema (1997) as Alex Cobb has Stan Brakhage's (2007); Elena del Rio has published on Michael Powell's *Peeping Tom* (2000), Michelangelo Antonioni's *Blowup* (2005a), and Godard's cinema (2005b); and Diane Pursley has explored Chantal Akerman's *Toute une nuit* (2005). (These two latter scholars also have put Merleau-Ponty and Deleuze into productive conversation.) Phenomenology has also been useful to understanding film genres – for example, aspects of animation (Boudin 2000; Bolton 2002; Riggs 2007) or horror (Zimmer 2004; Laine 2006). Furthermore, it has been significant to consideration of cinema and ethics (Stadler 2002; Sobchack 2004).

Indeed, major contemporary concern with moving image media and their variations across a broad range of screens and venues has raised many questions that seem the particular province of phenomenological inquiry: temporal and spatial configurations, embodied spectatorship, and the technological transformations of affects and effects. Thus, at the moment, phenomenology has been increasingly recognized as offering scholars both a rich vocabulary with which to articulate the dynamic correlations between moving images and spectators/users and a reflective method that is responsive to the viewing experience as it is variously lived, rather than only theorized.

See also Stanley Cavell (Chapter 32), Gilles Deleuze (Chapter 34), Christian Metz (Chapter 36), Jean Mitry (Chapter 37), Edgar Morin (Chapter 38), Consciousness (Chapter 4), and Emotion and affect (Chapter 8).

References

Agel, H. (1973) *Poetique du cinéma: Manifeste essentiale*, Fribourg: Éditions du Signe.
Andrew, D. (1977) "The Gravity of *Sunrise*," *Quarterly Review of Film Studies* 2: 356–87.
—— (1985 [1978]) "The Neglected Tradition of Phenomenology in Film Theory," in B. Nichols (ed.) *Movies and Methods*, vol. 2, Berkeley: University of California Press.
Ayfre, A. (1969) *Le cinéma et sa verité*, Paris: Éditions du Cerf.
Barker, J. (forthcoming) *The Tactile Eye*, Berkeley: University of California Press.
Baudry, J.-L. (1974 [1970]) "Ideological Effects of the Cinematographic Apparatus," trans. A. Williams, *Film Quarterly* 28: 39–47.
Bazin, A. (1967) *What Is Cinema?*, trans. H. Gray, Berkeley: University of California Press.
Bolton, C. (2002) "The Mecha's Blind Spot: *Patlabor 2* and the Phenomenology of Anime," *Science Fiction Studies* 29: 453–74.
Boudin, J. (2000) "Bodacious Bodies and the Voluptuous Gaze: A Phenomenology of Animation Spectatorship," *Animation Journal*, 2: 56–67.
Casebier, A. (1991) *Film and Phenomenology: Toward a Realist Theory of Cinematic Representation*, Cambridge and New York: Cambridge University Press.
Casey, E. (1981) "The Memorability of the Filmic Image," *Quarterly Review of Film Studies* 6: 241–64.
Cavell, S. (1971) *The World Viewed: Reflections on the Ontology of Film*, New York: Viking Press.
Cobb, A. (2007) "Cinema of Pre-Predication: On Stan Brakhage and the Phenomenology of Maurice Merleau-Ponty," *Senses of Cinema*, 44.
Available at http://www.sensesofcinema.com/ (accessed 27 August 2007).
del Rio, E. (2000) "The Body of Voyeurism: Mapping a Discourse of the Senses in Michael Powell's *Peeping Tom*," *Camera Obscura* 15: 115–49.
—— (2005a) "Antonioni's *Blowup*: Freeing the Imaginary from Metaphysical Ground," *Film-Philosophy*, 9(32). Available at http://www.film-philosophy.com/ (accessed 26 August 2007).
—— (2005b) "Alchemies of Thought in Godard's Cinema: Deleuze and Merleau-Ponty," *SubStance* 34: 62–78.
Dufrenne, M. (1973 [1953]) *The Phenomenology of Aesthetic Experience*, trans. E. Casey, Evanston, IL: Northwestern University Press.

Ingarden, R. (1989 [1947]) "Film," in *Ontology of the Work of Art*, trans. R. Meyer, with J. T. Goldthwait, Athens, OH: Ohio University Press.

Laine, T. (2006) "Cinema as Second Skin: Under the Membrane of Horror Film," *New Review of Film and Television Studies* 4: 93–106.

Linden, G. W. (1970) *Reflections on the Screen*, Belmont, CA: Wadsworth Publishing Co.

Marks, L. (2000) *The Skin of the Film: Intercultural Cinema, Embodiment, and the Senses*, Durham, NC: Duke University Press.

—— (2002) *Touch: Sensuous Theory and Multisensory Media*, Minneapolis: University of Minnesota Press.

Merleau-Ponty, M. (1962 [1945]) *Phenomenology of Perception*, trans. C. Smith, London: Routledge and Kegan Paul.

—— (1964 [1947]) "The Film and the New Psychology," in *Sense and Non-Sense*, trans. H. L. Dreyfus and P. A. Dreyfus, Evanston, IL: Northwestern University Press.

Meunier, J.-P. (1969) *Les structures de l'expérience filmique: l'identification filmique*, Louvain: Librarie Universitaire.

Mitry, J. (1997 [1963]) *The Aesthetics and Psychology of the Cinema*, trans. C. King, Bloomington: Indiana University Press.

Morin, E. (2005 [1956]) *The Cinema, or the Imaginary Man*, trans. L. Mortimer, Minneapolis: University of Minnesota Press.

Munier, R. (1963) *Contre l'image*, Paris: Gallimard.

Pasolini, P. (2005 [1972]) *Heretical Empiricism*, ed. L. K. Barnett; trans. L. K. Barnett and B. Lawton, Washington, DC: New Academia Publishing.

Pursley, D. (2005) "Moving in Time: Chantal Akerman's *Toute une nuite*," *MLN* 120: 1192–205.

Rascaroli, L. (1997) "Steel in the Gaze: On POV and the Discourse of Vision in Kathryn Bigelow's Cinema," *Screen* 38: 232–46.

Riggs, F. (2007) "The Infinite Quest: Husserl, Bakshi, the Rotoscope and the Ring," in A. Cholodenko (ed.) *The Illusion of Life II*, Sydney, Australia: Power Publications.

Sesonske, A. (1973) "Cinema Space," in D. Carr and E. S. Casey (eds.) *Explorations in Phenomenology*, The Hague: Martinus Nijoff.

Sobchack, V. (1992) *The Address of the Eye: A Phenomenology of Film Experience*, Princeton, NJ: Princeton University Press.

—— (1999) "Toward a Phenomenology of Non-Fictional Experience," in M. Renov and J. Gaines (eds.) *Collecting Visible Evidence*, Minneapolis: University of Minnesota Press.

—— (2004) *Carnal Thoughts: Embodiment and Moving Image Culture*, Berkeley: University of California Press.

Stadler, J. (2002) "Intersubjective, Embodied, Evaluative Perception: A Phenomenological Approach to the Ethics of Film," *Quarterly Review of Film and Video* 19: 237–48.

Tomasulo, F. P. (1988) "The Intentionality of Consciousness: Subjectivity in Resnais's *Last Year at Marienbad*," *PostScript* 7: 58–71.

van den Berck. A. M. (1948) "Le caractère de réalité des projections cinématographiques," *Revue Internationale de Filmologie* 1: 249–61.

Zimmer, C. (2004) "The Camera's Eye: *Peeping Tom* and Technological Perversion," in S. Hantke (ed.) *Horror Film: Creating and Marketing Fear*, Jackson: University of Mississippi Press.

Further reading

Dermot Moran and Timothy Mooney (eds.) *The Phenomenology Reader* (London and New York: Routledge, 2002) is a fairly comprehensive anthology of classic writings from many of phenomenology's seminal thinkers. David Stewart and Algis Mickunas, *Exploring Phenomenology: Guide to the Field and Its Literature* (Athens, OH: Ohio University Press, 1990) gives an overview of the history and development of phenomenology.

41
PSYCHOANALYSIS
Richard Allen

Psychoanalytic theory, a theory of the relationship between sexuality and unconscious mental states, has informed thinking about film almost from the inception of the medium, and this influence has been particularly profound upon film theory of the recent past. Orthodox psychoanalytic theories of art have focused on the relationship between the creation of art, sexuality, and unconscious mental life, and a great deal of both film and literary criticism has used psychoanalytic theory to interpret texts or genres of texts, but the distinctive contribution of film theory to psychoanalytic theories of art lies in its focus upon the nature and character of film spectatorship. The way a film spectator experiences a film has often been likened to the way in which a dreamer experiences her dream: movie images are said to be in crucial respects like dream images and to elicit the states of belief that are characteristic of dreams. At the same time, the film spectator, who unlike the dreamer, is an actual viewer, has often been compared to the voyeur, considered as someone who looks unseen into a private world. These characteristics of cinema have been celebrated by critics seeking to discern the unique appeal of film as form of entertainment and art, sometimes considered subversive of conventional moral values, but they have also grounded diagnoses of the manipulative nature of the medium and the gender-bound nature of voyeurism in the cinema. As Hortense Powdermaker wrote nearly sixty years ago: "Hollywood provides ready-made fantasies or day-dreams; the problem is whether these are productive or nonproductive, whether the audience is psychologically enriched or impoverished" (1950: 12–13).

Psychoanalytic theorists explain these aspects of film in the light of the specific theory of the mind, and by extension, human culture as a whole, that has developed out of the writings of Sigmund Freud. Freud, a physician by training, sought to develop a theory that would explain the irrational behavior manifest in hysteria and other forms of mental illness. He hypothesized the existence of powerful somatically driven wishes of a sexual nature that exist before the human mind is developed, which become channeled into the sexual desire for a parent (the Oedipus complex). The prohibition of this desire is experienced by the male child as the fantasy of castration at the hands of a punitive all-powerful father internalized as the superego. Psychic individuation – the formation of the ego – entails successful negotiation of the Oedipus complex and the repression of the infantile sexual wishes that animate it to form a reservoir of unconscious mental states. Since little girls do not experience the threat of castration like little boys (they are already castrated), their individuation is less complete, and the mechanism of repression is less rigorously installed in their psychic life.

Unconscious mental states are conceived by Freud as a mental stage upon which otherwise unrealizable wishes are realized as a result of the capacity of the human mind, most overtly manifest in dreams, to evoke the force or significance of events that we have actually lived through. This capacity is the residue of an infantile form of mental functioning where what is real is not yet differentiated from what is wished for. But the realization of our wishes in fantasy is not directly manifest, lest the wish break through to consciousness and its realization be undone. Instead, it is disguised through the pictures and symbols of the imagination, which thereby ensure that these wishes continue to be effective in the life of the mind. Under certain conditions the wish-fulfilling fantasy may break through the fabric of reality, and the agent's own body and actions become the stage upon which fantasy is acted out and projected, as in hysteria or obsessional neurosis. Alternatively, the mechanism of repression may fail and infantile sexual wishes become acted out in adult human behavior in the form of sexual "perversions."

Freud conceived psychoanalysis as a science that is at least in principle open to empirical verification, but equally influential upon psychoanalytic film theory are the writings of Jacques Lacan, who in reaction to the pragmatic operationalism of American ego psychology returned Freud to his roots in German romanticism and the "philosophy of nature" that culminates in the philosophy of Schopenhauer (Ellenberger 1970). Lacan attempted to create a unified view of psychoanalysis that connected Freud's earlier writings on individual psychology with his later reflections on civilization and culture through the central emphasis Lacan placed on the role of representation and language in shaping subjectivity.

For Lacan, the formation of the ego marks a moment of self-division that he characterizes in terms of the metaphor of the mirror stage (Lacan 1977). In the mirror stage (supposedly around six to eighteen months), the subject discovers who it is by looking in the mirror, and sees itself as a differentiated body. However, before encountering its self-image, that subject resides in what Lacan terms the Real, in which it did not (psychically) conceive itself as differentiated from everything else (Freud's primitive form of mental functioning). The true identity of the subject is thus as a no-thing. The subject's discovery of itself as a differentiated thing, as an essentially narcissistic ego, involves a fundamental misrecognition of its own no-thing-ness as a some-thing, albeit at this stage, one that resides in the realm of what Lacan terms the Imaginary, which is provisional, unstable, and informed by fantasy. The mirror is a literal mirror in Lacan's allegory but it stands for the mirror formed by "the other" in general, and archetypally the figure of the mother. For Lacan the Imaginary ego is stabilized by a third term, which is provided by the structure of meaning afforded by language and culture, in which the subject assumes a wholly fictitious, gendered identity and cements his self-alienation from the Real, that now forms the domain of that which is wholly unconscious. For Lacan, therefore, the castration of the subject refers not simply to the repressed fantasy of penile loss at the hands of the internalized castrating father figure that for Freud lay at the core of unconscious mental life. Instead, the fantasy described by Freud is a figuration of a quite general, metaphysical "lack in being" that is made permanent in the self-understanding achieved by the (male) subject, who begins to inhabit language and culture through identifying with the place of the father.

Psychoanalytic film theory in the traditions that came to be solidified in the 1970s and 1980s was inspired to a great extent by the contribution that film theorists believed that psychoanalysis could make to the understanding of film as ideology, that is, of how film works as an apparatus over and above any single story told in film, to shape the beliefs of its viewers. It consists of a promiscuous mix of the ostensibly empirical claims of Freudian theory and Lacan's philosophical myth of the formation of the subject in misrecognition (Allen 1999). Freudian theories were used to explain the ways in which cinema was said to mobilize the spectator's fantasy and "perversions." Lacanian theorists argued that beyond the singular messages conveyed by individual stories it told, cinematic narration exemplified and contributed to the self-division of the subject as it is shaped by language and culture.

Film and dream

It is important to note at the outset that the characteristics of cinema as dream or fantasy are capable of being articulated and defended without recourse to (formal) psychoanalytic theory. The analogy between film and dream, in particular, has a long pedigree. Surrealist critics and their commentators were the first to celebrate the affinities between film and dream, which were also explored in practice by surrealist-influenced filmmakers such as Jean Epstein, Germaine Dulac, and Luis Buñuel. As early as 1926, Jean Goudal wrote in an essay admired by Breton that "the cinema constitutes a conscious hallucination" (Hammond 1978: 51). The cinema spectator, like the theatergoer, sits in a darkened auditorium, but unlike the theatergoer, what he sees is not present to him but is rather a "simulacrum of a uniquely visual kind." In a later essay Jacques Brunius, compares dissolves, fade-outs, and fade-ins to transitions in dreams and writes that "the disposition of screen images in time is absolutely analogous with the arrangement thought or the dream can devise. Neither chronological order nor relative values of duration are real" (Hammond 1978: 61). Philosopher Suzanne Langer writes that "Cinema is 'like' dream in the mode of its presentation: it creates a virtual present, an order of direct apparition. That is the mode of the dream" (Langer 1953: 415). Christian Metz undertakes a detailed and subtle investigation of what he calls the "filmic state" of theatrical moviegoing "which in certain respect a kind of sleep in miniature, a waking sleep" (Metz 1982: 116). The spectator is relatively immobile; he is plunged into a relative darkness, and temporarily loses his concern with the outside world in favor of a perceptual and emotional absorption in a lifelike world of images.

Most recently, Colin McGinn has explored the film-dream analogy in a more systematic way, plausibly noting the way that our familiarity with dreams tutors our experience of film (McGinn 2005). Films, like dreams, are characterized by sensory/affective fusion, by which he means the manner in which emotional content is

purveyed through visual representations. Furthermore, like dreams, they are characterized by spatial discontinuity and by temporal fixation: the film viewer like the
dreamer is riveted to the sequence of "images" as they unfold in time. Films, like
dreams, are attention dependent. You can't be having a dream you are not attending
to. Movies too have a tendency to command our attention. Films, like dreams, are
often characterized by a heightened sensation of movement that is linked to the
solicitation of strong emotion. Films, like dreams, are characterized by the "salience"
of every element, at once compressing information and amplifying emotional impact.
In this sense every element in a dream or film is a "special effect." Objects in dreams
and films are often endowed with a heightened emotional significance, especially
through the use of the close-up, as French film theorist Jean Epstein first celebrated
in his theory of *photogénie*. Finally, and most contentiously, though again echoing
Epstein, McGinn claims that in films, like dreams, the minds of others seem peculiarly
transparent to the spectator. The body or face in a dream is designed to express a given
mind, in this sense it is a transparent portal to the mind in a way that the face of the
other usually fails to be. Likewise in films, the human mind is not merely inferred from
bodily criteria, but appears something we have transparent access to.

It is noteworthy that McGinn defends the analogy between film and dreams not
on the basis of psychoanalytic theory but on the basis of cognitive hypothesis about
the dreaming brain: films create in us a "filmic state," to borrow Metz's term, that is
analogous to the state of the brain when dreaming, though of course this hypothesis
has yet to be tested. Psychoanalytic film theorists have typically conceived the spectator's response to the cinema as a form of psychological regression congruent with
Freud's conception of dreaming, in which the spectator regresses to a more primitive
form of mental functioning. As Jean-Louis Baudry writes:

> Taking into account the darkness of the movie theater, the relative passivity
> of the situation, the forced immobility of the cine-subject, and the effects
> which result from the projection of images, moving images, the cinemato-
> graphic apparatus brings about a state of artificial regression. It artificially
> leads back to an anterior phase of his development – a phase which is barely
> hidden, as dream and certain pathological forms of our mental life have
> shown. It is the desire, unrecognized as such by the subject, to return to his
> phase, an early state of development with its own forms of satisfaction ...
> Return toward a relative narcissism, and even more toward a mode of relating
> to reality which could be defined as enveloping and in which the separation
> between one's own body and the exterior world is not well defined. (Baudry
> 1986b: 313)

Freud's theory of dreams as a form of mental regression remains a speculation.
However, even if it were true as McGinn contends, that the brain state is like the
"filmic state," it would still be unclear how this alleged identity actually impacts the
psychology of the spectator. As Noël Carroll has emphasized, the analogy itself is
vague, in part because we know so little about dreams (Carroll 1988). What exactly

are the psychological parameters of the alleged filmic state? Furthermore, there are many disanalogies between dreams and watching a movie, as Metz notes, the most important of which is that the spectator is wide awake and the images are real (Metz 1982). The analogy between film and dream at best provides a partial understanding of the film experience and an understanding that is probably not best cashed out in psychoanalytic terms.

Voyeurism and the male gaze

It is an axiomatic claim of psychoanalytic film theorists that cinema is a voyeuristic medium "almost by definition" (McGinn 2005: 55). Mulvey writes:

> the mass of mainstream film, and the conventions within which it has consciously evolved, portray an hermetically sealed world which unwinds magically, indifferent to the presence of the audience, producing for them a separation and playing on their voyeuristic fantasy ... conditions of screening and narrative conventions give the spectator an illusion of looking in on a private world. (Mulvey 1989: 17)

However, some consideration needs to be given to what exactly "voyeurism" means. In the "Three Essays on Sexuality," in the context of talking about childhood sexuality, Freud refers to scopophilia as the "pleasure in looking," meaning sexual pleasure derived from looking, which is not attached to any sense of shame and hence not hidden. But children may grow into voyeurs, where "this looking is connected with the overriding of disgust" (Freud 1977 [1905]: 70). Implicitly, for Freud, voyeurism derives from the shame attached to deriving sexual pleasure from looking and can be defined as the sexual pleasure taken from looking in a context in which the onlooker is concealed from view. In voyeurism, concealment is necessary for sexual pleasure; without it sexual pleasure is not possible, because it is inhibited. But this concealment is not sufficient, for it is not the concealment itself that yields sexual pleasure. Even granted the premise that cinema creates the necessary conditions of concealment one is still hard pressed to see how cinema is a voyeuristic medium "almost by definition." It would be at best a medium where the sexual pleasure derived from looking is not inhibited and thus can be used to encourage or exploit our sexual curiosity.

But in what sense do we gaze at a private world? Psychoanalytic theorists usually try and explain voyeurism by a theory of illusion. Illusions are perceptual tricks which drive a wedge between what we know to be the case and what we see. As we have seen, Metz argues that the cinematic image itself is such an illusion, which he calls "the imaginary signifier," where we confuse the cinematic image with what it represents (Metz 1982). He explains how this confusion occurs by recourse to Freud's theory of fetishism. For Freud the fetish object functions as a prop for a fantasy that denies sexual difference. In his imagination, the fetishist fills in the apparent gap caused by the perceived absence of the female phallus with the fetish. He disavows what he knows to be the case in favor of a primitive belief in sexual undifferentiation that the fetish serves to sustain. According to Metz, the cinematic image functions as a fetish because it allows us to *perceive* what is imaginary as being real and hence disavow our knowledge that what we see is only an image. But as Jacqueline Rose points out, Metz's assimilation of the fetish to a form of visual illusion is mistaken, for knowledge of an illusion functions to contradict our false belief in it and leaves us only with a perceptual confusion. We cannot know how a visual illusion works and sustain our belief in it. But the whole point of a fetish is that it allows us to maintain our false belief even when we know it is a fetish (Rose 1980). The film image thus cannot be both an illusion and a fetish. But it is not an illusion, precisely because we are not confused by its status into believing that it is real, and thus, as Noël Carroll argues, we do not need a complex theory of disavowal to explain our relationship to it (Carroll 1988). But neither is the film image obviously a fetish, because the fetish derives from the goal of realizing a sexual aim in relationship to a theory of sexual difference.

Metz argues that spectatorial voyeurism is further promoted by the keyhole effect of the screen that suggests we are looking through an aperture/apparatus upon the actors (a feature it shares with the television screen). This seems a more promising foundation on which to build the argument about the voyeuristic basis of the apparatus, because it depends, not upon a theory of illusion in which the cinema tricks us into seeing something as present to us which is not, but upon the idea that in some important sense looking at bodies on film is like looking at bodies. That is, upon the idea that in a some critical sense, cinema is, to use Kendall L. Walton's phrase, a "transparent" medium that allows us to see bodies in space even while they cannot see us (Walton 1984). This is not the place to argue for or against such a view, just to point out that it has a prima facie plausibility. What is important to point out in this context is that the salience of the keyhole effect to the idea of voyeurism seems to contradict Metz's overall argument that bases voyeurism upon the idea of the imaginary signifier, since the keyhole effect depends upon recognition of the aperture/apparatus that we are looking through, rather than a disavowal of it. It is an alternative, and better, explanation of, the same phenomenon. However, given the shifts in cultural norms in the western hemisphere with respect to the representation of sexuality since Freud, the kind of inhibitions that Freud identified that yield voyeurism may simply no longer be normative. The sexual pleasure derived from looking at bodies in film is arguably frank not furtive, neither explicable as a perversion nor derived from repression.

I have noted that Metz ignores the role of sexual difference in theorizing the imaginary signifier, but for feminist thinkers who sought to understand the gender-bound nature of the cinema, the psychoanalytic theory of sexual difference was of key importance. In her essay "Visual Pleasure and Narrative Cinema," which was published in the same year, 1975, as Metz's essay on "The Imaginary Signifier," Laura Mulvey concurs with Metz's view that the cinema is voyeuristic, yet she also proposes that this voyeuristic gaze is central to the gendering of cinema as a system of representation that objectifies and denigrates the figure of woman, for the gaze is both male and sadistic. Why is the voyeuristic look male and sadistic? One answer that seems to be implied by Mulvey is that the voyeuristic gaze is defined by Freud as being male and sadistic. A second answer she gives is that the look is contingently voyeuristic and sadistic because it is rooted through male characters who are voyeuristic and sadistic. A third answer is that the voyeuristic, sadistic gaze is entailed by the image of women in cinema. The image of woman threatens castration, but the threat is neutralized through the fetishization of female sexuality as the object of a voyeuristic gaze, together with scenarios in which the woman is humiliated and punished. But the claim that voyeurism is intrinsically male (as opposed to dominantly male), and presumptively heterosexual, is not supported by psychoanalytic theory and practice. Second, the claim that the voyeuristic gaze is intrinsic to the gaze of the camera not only seems false for the reasons cited, it leaves no space for the possibility of a nonexploitative looking position. Third, if the male gaze is merely contingent upon context, it cannot implicate the spectator in the manner required by the theory. Indeed, where the voyeuristic look is represented in a film like *Rear Window* (1954), discussed by Mulvey in support of her theory, it actually calls into question the spectator's adoption of that gaze. In this sense, camera voyeurism is quite unlike actual voyeurism.

In 1969, Raymond Bellour commenced a series of essays on American cinema, primarily on the work of Hitchcock, that also identified a gender hierarchy and inequality in narrative cinema, embodied in the male oedipal narrative. His analysis, however, unlike Mulvey's, is not predicated simply upon the hierarchy seen/being, nor does it simply deny female characters' control of the gaze (Bellour 2000). For example, in his detailed analysis of the Bodega Bay sequence from Hitchcock's film *The Birds* (1963), Bellour demonstrates the way in which a gender hierarchy is created across a series of formal contrasts, seen/being seen, close-up/long shot, stasis/movement. Furthermore, it is a hierarchy in which initially, at least, Melanie Daniels (Tippi Hedren), the heroine of the film, is in control of the gaze, brazenly seeking out Mitch Brenner (Rod Taylor) as a potential mate. If Bellour's analysis had become the paradigmatic example of how Hollywood narrative is gender bound, the history of feminist film theory may have been different, for his analysis is predicated upon the structure of visual fictions, not upon the putative character or the gaze or look in cinema. To be sure, Bellour assumes the ubiquity of a male-centered oedipal narrative, but this argument can be and was challenged by other critics, on the grounds that not all fictions have this structure and that even his interpretation of Hitchcock is only a partial one (Modleski 1988; Allen 2002/3).

Mulvey's argument, however, turns primarily not on the kind of stories narrated through the formal strategies of classical editing but upon the putative active, sadistic, masculine, voyeuristic quality of the gaze in cinema, and subsequent debates within feminist theory were framed by the question of how to conceptualize the place of the female spectator within a look, or a system of looks, that entailed her complete subordination. The most radical challenge to Mulvey's thesis came from Gaylyn Studlar, who argued that Baudry's comments about the psychic regression of the spectator in the cinema, and the analogy between cinema spectatorship and dreaming pursued by both Baudry and Metz, point in an altogether alternative direction to the idea of spectatorial voyeurism and sadism, and phallic fetishism, enshrined in the Metz–Mulvey model (Studlar 1985, 1988). Studlar suggests that the cinema spectator is characteristically not a sadistic voyeur but a masochist who swoons before the image which overwhelms him in its size and proximity. Since the origins of masochism lay in the child's fantasies of an all-powerful mother, rather than in the child's relationship with the father (an argument drawn from Deleuze), the perverse pleasures of cinema are undifferentiated according to gender, and therefore available (after all) for feminists and their antagonists alike. Carol Clover (1992) contests the putatively pre-oedipal character of masochism in Studlar's theory and, like David Rodowick, argues that spectatorial voyeurism cuts both ways: it can be both active and passive, masculine and sadistic, by turns (Rodowick 1991). However these revisionist theories, while they offered a fundamental challenge to the Metz–Mulvey paradigm, remained locked in the implausible assumption that perversion, whether masochistic or sadistic, male or female, is intrinsic to the experience of cinema (Gaut 1994).

Apparatus theory

The most ambitious use of psychoanalytic theory drew its inspiration from a threefold analogy: Lacan's story of the formation of the subject in front of the mirror, Louis Althusser's theory of ideology that Lacan's story inspired, and the idea of the cinema screen as mirror, like Lacan's. Christian Metz claimed that the cinema screen was akin to Lacan's idea of mirror-misrecognition, with the significant difference that one does not see an image of oneself in the cinema. Just as the subject in front of the mirror (of the other) is bestowed an illusory sense of identity, cinematic representation engenders in the spectator an illusory sense of himself as someone who "identifies" with the position of the camera and therefore authors and owns the visual field of the film, while both the visual field and the position he perceives it from are actually the product of the system of representation. Metz calls this "primary identification," as opposed to the "secondary identification" that takes place with the character (Metz 1982). But this idea was first suggested in an earlier essay by Jean-Louis Baudry, who drew his inspiration from Althusser's use of Lacan. For Althusser, ideology describes the process through which society cultivated compliant social subjects by appealing to their need to be recognized and to acquire a social identity (Althusser 1971). Individuals assent to the position they are invited to assume by institutions, believing that it is freely chosen though in fact the position they assume is determined in advance by the system that "interpellates" or hails the subject. Althusser compared this "error" to the "error" of the subject before Lacan's mirror who misrecognizes himself as an entity within it. For Baudry, the subject who misrecognizes himself in ideology is, canonically, nothing other than the film spectator himself. "What emerges here," Baudry writes, "is the specific function fulfilled by the cinema as support and instrument of ideology. It constitutes the "subject" by the illusory delimitation of a central location – whether this be that of a god or of an other substitute" (1986a: 295).

The task of psychoanalytic film theory became one of exposing the construction of the subject as an illusion and thereby revealing the truth of ideology from a cognitive standpoint that is outside it. Key to the development of apparatus theory was recognition of the effect played by cutting in undermining the spectator's sense of omnipotence before the image, that drew upon the metaphorical relationship between "the cut" and castration. Film theorists argued that while the cut cues a jarring and hence visible shift in viewpoint that seems to threaten the spectator's omnipotence and thereby metaphorically castrate him by suddenly making him aware that he is looking at an image, narrative cinema works to contain or "suture" (like stitches over a wound) the potentially catastrophic nature of this shift. Classical narrative cinema contains the effects of the cut through deploying strategies of reverse-field cutting, in which the visual field of an image that is lost to the spectator by the cut is restored to him vicariously through identification with the look of a character whom we see in the next image and who, its transpires, claims ownership to the visual field of the first. For suture theorists, the way in which cinematic narration stitches over the wound that is the subject's castration or lack serves as literalization of Lacan's theory of the subject's relationship to discourse. That is, it is at once an allegory of that story and a literal realization or enactment of it (Dayan 1976; Silverman 1983).

This theory has been thoroughly discredited for many different reasons, and from many different intellectual perspectives. Like so much psychoanalytic theory, apparatus theory mistakenly conceives analogies for identities (Carroll 1988). It also misunderstands the nature of character identification, for it assumes that identification is reducible to a perceptual point of view and neglects the way in which identification functions independently of it (Browne 1985; Smith 1995). It is based upon a naïve theory of representation as illusion that I have already criticized. It overlooks the preconscious and conscious aspects of the spectator's cognitive and emotional engagement with narrative film (Bordwell 1985). It relies upon a naïve, reductive analysis of film style that precludes the fine-grained distinctions the theory itself requires (Bordwell 1985). Finally it misconstrues the nature of Lacanian psychoanalysis, an error enshrined in Althusser's own appropriation of psychoanalysis, and this proves fatally self-contradictory for most versions of the theory. For Lacan, misrecognition is constitutive of the subject, there is no position from which the subject can recognize this misrecognition, but suture theory depends on the idea that the spectator can in principle recognize his own castration (by seeing the cut) and thereby be liberated from false consciousness.

This confusion derives from the fundamental misappropriation of Lacanian psychoanalysis by film theorists as a psychological theory of how film causally influences spectators rather than a philosophical myth. It is scarcely surprising then that what looks to cognitive theorists such as David Bordwell like bad science appears to Lacanian theorists like Joan Copjec and Slavoj Žižek as bad psychoanalysis (Copjec 1989). In Lacanian theory, looking that is informed by desire is defined by the gaze, which is counterposed to the mere act of looking (Lacan 1978). The gaze is not something that guarantees the subject's self-assurance, on the contrary it renders the subject paranoid, someone who is ensnared by a look that is imagined to come from the other but cannot actually be seen. The gaze is that which lies outside the field of what is perceived (whether representation or physical object), sustaining the fantasy of subjectivity, not by purporting to guarantee the subject a mastery of that visual field, but by ceaselessly engaging the subject's desire. Such a desire is necessarily mobilized by the world of appearances, whether or not those appearances take the form of visual representations, and whether or not those visual representations are fictional. However, Žižek argues that visual representations such as film, do afford the possibility of overtly symbolizing the gaze in the form of a stain or a grimace in the visual field that, so to speak, looks back at the observer and challenges their complacency in a manner that reveals the kernel of disorder and chaos beneath the calm surface of appearances in the fictional world. Žižek discovers this grimace of the real everywhere in Hitchcock's film and so he terms it the Hitchcockian Blot (Žižek 1991, 1992). Examples of this blot are the twitching face of the drummer toward which Hitchcock's camera moves in *Young and Innocent* (1937), or the drain that forms a vortex down which the blood flows from Marion Crane's corpse in *Psycho* (1960). In this way, for Žižek and others, Lacanian psychoanalysis continues to offer a powerful interpretative tool, though its success in this respect tells us nothing about its truth.

See also Consciousness (Chapter 4), Emotion and affect (Chapter 8), Empathy and character engagement (Chapter 9), Spectatorship (Chapter 23), and Christian Metz (Chapter 36).

References

Allen, R. (1999) "Psychoanalytic Film Theory," in T. Miller and R. Stam (eds.) *A Companion to Film Theory*, Malden, MA: Blackwell.
—— (2002/3) "Hitchcock after Bellour," *Hitchcock Annual* 11: 117–47.
Althusser, L. (1971) "Ideology and Ideological State Apparatuses," in B. Brewster (trans.) *Lenin and Philosophy, and Other Essays*, London: New Left Books.
Baudry, J.-L. (1986a [1970]) "Ideological Effects of the Basic Cinematographic Apparatus," in P. Rosen (ed.) *Narrative, Apparatus, Ideology*, New York: Columbia University Press.
—— (1986b [1975]) "The Apparatus: Metaphysical Approaches to Ideology," in P. Rosen (ed.) *Narrative, Apparatus, Ideology*, New York: Columbia University Press.
Bellour, R. (2000) *The Analysis of Film*, ed. C. Penley, Bloomington: Indiana University Press.
Bergstrom, J. (1979) "Enunciation and Sexual Difference" in C. Penley (ed.) *Feminism and Film Theory*, New York: Routledge; London: British Film Institute.
Bordwell, D. (1985) *Narration in the Fiction Film*, Madison: University of Wisconsin Press.
Browne, N. (1985 [1975]) "The Spectator-in-the-Text: The Rhetoric of *Stagecoach*," in B. Nichols (ed.) *Movies and Methods*, vol. 2, Berkeley: University of California Press.
Carroll, N. (1988) *Mystifying Movies: Fads and Fallacies in Contemporary Film Theory*, New York: Columbia University Press.
Clover, C. (1992) *Men Women and Chainsaws: Gender in the Modern Horror Film*, Princeton, NJ: Princeton University Press.
Copjec, J. (1989) "The Orthopsychic Subject: Film Theory and the Reception of Lacan," *October* 49 (summer): 53–71.
Dayan, D. (1976) "The Tutor Code of Classical Cinema," in B. Nichols (ed.) *Movies and Methods*, vol. 1, Berkeley: University of California Press.
Ellenberger, H. F. (1970) *The Discovery of the Unconscious*, New York: Basic Books.
Freud, S. (1977 [1905]) "Three Essays on Sexuality," in *On Sexuality*, vol. 7 of *The Pelican Freud Library*, Harmondsworth: Penguin Books.
Gaut, B. (1994) "On Cinema and Perversion," *Film and Philosophy* 1: 3–17.
Hammond, P. (ed.) (1978) *The Shadow and Its Shadow: Surrealist Writings on Cinema*, London: British Film Institute.

Lacan, J. (1977) "The Mirror Stage as Formative of the Function of the I," in A. Sheridan (trans.) *Écrits: A Selection*, New York: Norton; London: Tavistock Publications.

—— (1978) *The Four Fundamental Concepts of Psychoanalysis*, trans. A. Sheridan, New York: Norton.

Langer, S. K. (1953) *Feeling and Form*, New York: Scribner.

McGinn, C. (2005) *The Power of Movies*, New York: Pantheon.

Metz, C. (1982) *The Imaginary Signifier: Psychoanalysis and Cinema*, trans. C. Britton, A. Williams, B. Brewster, and A. Guzetti, Bloomington: Indiana University Press.

Modleski, T. (1988) *The Women Who Knew Too Much: Hitchcock and Feminist Theory*, New York: Methuen.

Mulvey, L. (1989) *Visual and Other Pleasures*, Bloomington: Indiana University Press.

Powdermaker, H. (1950) *Hollywood the Dream Factory*, London: Secker and Warburg.

Rodowick, D. N. (1991) *The Difficulty of Difference: Psychoanalysis, Sexual Difference and Film Theory*, New York: Routledge.

Rose, J. (1980) "The Cinematic Apparatus: Problems in Current Theory," in T. de Lauretis and S. Heath (eds.) *The Cinematic Apparatus*, New York: St Martin's Press.

Silverman, K. (1983) *The Subject of Semiotics*, New York: Oxford University Press.

Smith, M. (1995) *Engaging Characters: Fiction, Emotion, and the Cinema*, Oxford: The Clarendon Press; New York: Oxford University Press.

Studlar, G. (1985) "Masochism and the Perverse Pleasures of the Cinema," in B. Nichols (ed.) *Movies and Methods*, vol. 2, Berkeley: University of California Press.

—— (1988) *In the Realm of Pleasure: Von Sternberg, Dietrich, and the Masochistic Aesthetic*, Urbana: University of Illinois Press; New York: Columbia University Press.

Walton, K. (1984) "Transparent Pictures: On the Nature of Photographic Representation," *Critical Inquiry* 11(2): 246–77.

Žižek, S. (1991) *Looking Awry: An Introduction to Jacques Lacan through Popular Culture*, Cambridge, MA: MIT Press.

—— (1992) *Enjoy Your Symptom!: Jacques Lacan in and out of Hollywood*, New York: Routledge.

42
SEMIOTICS AND SEMIOLOGY

Joseph G. Kickasola

Though debates regarding signs and their referents go back to the Greek pre-Socratic philosophers, what we know as the contemporary "science" of signs and sign systems first solidified near the end of the nineteenth century. The intersection of semiotics with film studies has a short, intense history, the effects of which are still being felt today.

The fundamental question behind film semiotics is the extent to which semiotic research helps us understand the cinema. It is generally accepted that symbols and signs are in full operation in film, but to what degree do they determine the overall function of "the meaning" of a given film, and do they operate and function differently in the cinema than in other media (such as literature)? What should become clear is that semiotics developed and branched in numerous directions throughout the twentieth century. Some of these lines of semiotic inquiry were embraced by film theory, while others were/are important in other fields but remain largely neglected or underrepresented in film theory (e.g., the semiotics of Thomas Sebeok [1991 and 1994, among other works]).

It is, perhaps, most valuable to trace the modern history of semiotics, isolate some of the key issues in its evolution, and then conclude with some contemporary directions in film semiotics.

The birth of modern semiotics

Around the turn of the twentieth century, two primary thinkers were mulling over a science of signs, though they were doing so quite independently.

Ferdinand de Saussure (1857–1913), a Swiss academic, developed a "Course in General Linguistics," the lectures from which became a foundational book for the development of semiotics. Saussure primarily contended that signs were best thought of as conventional, referring not to the world but to other signs; as Dudley Andrew has pointed out (1984: 59), the French model of film semiotics (via Saussure) does not approach signs as access to any form of "reality," but only to other signs and the systems that make signs function. This would prove to be a central point of debate in twentieth-century thought, as it drove to the heart of what perception and communication really are, and the degree of relation between mind and world.

Similarly, Saussure claimed signs do not signify by their own positive content but by negative comparison, that is, by their place in the overall sign system, which is determined by what the signs are not. This idea proved remarkably influential on later "structuralists," such as the sociologist Claude Lévi-Strauss, who sought to explain all of culture in terms of differential relations in cultural sign systems (see his influential 1967 work *Structural Anthropology*). In addition, Saussure developed many other terms that would prove helpful for semioticians to come. Some of these terms include denotation (the simplest, most literal meaning of a sign, such as the "dictionary" definition of a word), connotation (the many subjective, cultural, and extended associations a term evokes, e.g., the color red means the Communist Party in China), *parole* (individual speech acts), *langue* (the "system" undergirding speech acts that generate meaning for a community), paradigm (the range of meanings of an individual sign), syntagm (the combining and assembling of signs into chains of meanings, such as sentences), signifier (the code or symbol being used to communicate), signified (the mental representation of the referent of the sign, in the mind of the speaker), etc. Saussure's most influential binary – synchronic versus diachronic – proved very influential on the approach to communication semiotics generally adopted, which was to stress the way the symbols are working as a "system" presently (synchronically) rather than how those symbols have evolved over time (diachronically). Various film theorists have taken these terms and attempted to find cinematic extensions of them (e.g., the shot as a paradigm, the sequence as a syntagm). The work of Louis Hjelmslev (1899–1965) provided a theoretical foundation for extending Saussure's concept of langue to govern all forms of sign production, not simply that which is functional in linguistics. In other words, he gave film theorists a reason to believe that there were master principles that governed all sign production, language and cinema included, though Saussure's linguistically focused terms were adopted to express these principles.

C. S. Peirce was an American philosopher working on similar problems to those of Saussure at roughly the same time. As a mathematician and philosopher, Peirce was rigorously working on formal logic and the ways in which semiotics and sign systems might be conceived through these paradigms. His astonishing body of work still remains to be fully applied to film theory, though scattered efforts have been made (e.g., the writings of Roman Jakobson [e.g., Jakobson and Halle 1971; and Jakobson 1987] and Peter Wollen's *Signs and Meaning in the Cinema* [1969–72], Johannes Ehrat's *Cinema and Semiotic* [2005]). Peirce's epistemological triad of the sign, object, and interpretant contrasts with Saussure's dyad of signifier/signified, in that the "object" is, in fact, that object to which a sign is referring, leaving room for the idea that we might have some access to reality outside the self. Realist film theorists have found value in Peirce's willingness to consider the sign a means by which we access the real world, as opposed to the isolationism of constructivist accounts (though careful readings of Peirce show a much more nuanced approach that resists exploitation from either camp).

By contrast, Saussure's placement of the "signified" in the mind sets him up for an ontological idealism he did not, perhaps, intend; his paradigm is devoted exclusively to signs and their functioning within a sign system. This "Saussurean" subjectivism has proved appealing to cultural theorists and postmodern film theorists, who see the most interesting realms of inquiry residing in the way codes and symbols play out in films as symptom and cause of ideology (i.e., not neutral facts about the world, but socially and personally constructed ideas posing as such).

The most cited Peircean terms in film theory abide in his most general typology of sign systems: icon (signs that signify by resemblance), index (signs that signify by causality), and symbols (signs that signify by social convention). Peter Wollen makes use of these categories in his classic work *Signs and Meaning in the Cinema*, saying that they not only provide a more exhaustive paradigm through which to study sign activity, but they reveal weaknesses in classic film theory, as most theorists before 1970 tended to focus upon one sign type in the cinema to the exclusion of the others (Wollen 1969–72: 141). Peirce's encyclopedic writings remain fertile ground for film theorists (1981–2000). For instance, Peirce's category of "Firstness" (1955: 80) is ripe for film theorists – particularly realists and phenomenologists – as it refers to the primary perceptive event and endows it with semiological significance, as opposed to relegating it to "mere" perceptual mechanics.

Throughout the twentieth century, semiotics moved on a parallel, complementary, and often overlapping path with "structuralism," a broader movement dedicated to the academic examination of the underlying structures of human life (e.g., Lévi-Strauss applying Saussurean principles to sociology, culture, and myth). As language is so fundamental to human activity, it became clear that Saussure's ideas on language were really the fountainhead for all these other streams of structuralist inquiry, as he himself envisioned linguistics as "a model for the whole of semiology" (Saussure 1972: 68). This approach would also prove limiting for film theory.

Semiotic film theory

The earliest film theories broached semiotic elements in the cinema (e.g., Sergei Eisenstein's considerations of the "hieroglyphic" form of communication inherent in film editing), but few (if any) of these early theorists focused exclusively on semiotics proper. They merely provided some foundation for film theorists to come.

Among classic "semioticians" of film, three names are most prominent: Roland Barthes (1915–80), Jean Mitry (1907–88), and Christian Metz (1931–93). Barthes carried his previous "cultural semiotic" ventures (e.g., semiotics of clothing, food), begun in *The Elements of Semiology* (1964), into film analysis. He approached semiotics, as a cultural critic, and was, therefore, very interested in what semiotics could reveal about the ideologies buried in culture, as well as being interested in the ways semiotics could help us understand new, challenging artwork (and vice versa). His 1966 work *Critique et vérité* (*Criticism and Truth*) also outlines the contrast between a kind of practical criticism and an investigation of the conditions of possibility of all such meaningful readings (Barthes 2007), and this proved to be a fruitful path for him to follow. For instance, in an interview with the journal *Les Cahiers du cinéma*, he praises Luis Buñuel's surrealist film *The Exterminating Angel* (1962), not for what it means or symbolizes (Buñuel himself denied any meaning to the film), but for how it toys with meaning-making itself, how it tinkers with the syntagm and so reveals the structure of meaning. In this way, the film is "full of significance" without signification (Barthes 1985: 21). In a later interview, he very clearly spells out the goal of the structuralist/ semiotic enterprise in optimistic terms, understanding of the systemic mechanics of meaning-making, particularly as it is demonstrated in film (1985: 36–7).

Barthes' thoughts on the cinema are typically presented in anthologies, along with essays on other areas of culture, but some of his most important essays on the cinema are in *Image-Music-Text* (1977). Barthes later moved from structuralism to what may be called post-structuralism (i.e., a term that may be loosely associated with postmodernism – and numerous other "posts" – that arise out of skepticism toward any universal structures of language, knowledge, or truth, discussed below). This is most clearly displayed in his book *S/Z* (1974).

Jean Mitry approached semiotics in the tradition of grand film theory, attempting to lay out and, to some degree, reconcile the large metaphysical questions of earlier theorists with the more particularized, operational analysis semiotics offered. His study *The Aesthetics and Psychology of the Cinema* (1997 [1963]) provides a comprehensive and thoughtful consideration of semiotics in light of the film theory that had gone before. He argues against the allegedly naïve transparency theories of André Bazin, stating that film does not provide us direct access to reality. Yet, film does give us access to a rich image, an "analogon" to reality, which bears in it traces of the real. His nuanced approach considers all the ways different elements of the cinema function to produce meaning through the power of the analogon, and so lays out one of the most thoughtful commentaries on the semiotic functions of film. Mitry insists on the limitations of a linguistic approach – there is no universal model for the language of cinema – but does argue for a sense in which the cinema could be seen as language: in a contextual way, where the elements of given films interact and create meaning with each other. Mitry's later work *Semiotics and the Analysis of Film* (2000 [1987]) is more specifically aimed at cine-semiotic issues, particularly as they were expressed by Mitry's contemporary Christian Metz and transformed by others in the late 1970s and 1980s. His essential position in this book (a collection of essays) is that "though semiology is capable of saying how something signifies, it has no way of saying why it does so," and all its "systemizations are after the fact" (2000: 21). Unlike Warren Buckland and David Bordwell (discussed below), Mitry is even suspicious of applications of Noam Chomsky's more broad generative grammar as a comprehensive structure for film because, in Mitry's mind, "images are never created to signify," but to create a "sort of discourse ... totally resistant to any rules of language" (21). However, he maintains that semiotics can remain useful because language, "though not a model, remains a basic term of comparison – an 'open' semiology, based on the constantly casual and contingent relationship between form and content" (23).

Christian Metz is the most prominent name in "classic" film semiotics or semiology. Metz's *Film Language* (1974a, from essays largely written in the mid-1960s) directly tackled the "structural" issue, that is, the material ways in which film embodies and conveys meaning, apart from the necessity of developing a comprehensive episte-mology. He addresses the specific elements of cinema (shot types, editing strategies, etc.) and, drawing on both Saussure and Peirce, attempts to discern the structure and function of them as signs. His project was less to describe what cinema means, but how it means. Though semiotics has been historically associated with linguistics, Metz the film semiotician spends a good deal of time itemizing the ways written/spoken signifiers are much more particular, flexible, and independent of their signifiers than cinematographic signifiers.

In fact, it was Metz's conviction that semiotics is only generally applicable to film, for a few key reasons. Film is not a two-way communication medium, hindering it from developing a "system" of communication. Likewise, there is no equivalent to "double articulation" in the cinema; that is, the first articulation (an idea) may be communi-cated, but there is no cinematic equivalent to a second articulation in spoken/written language (like a phoneme, or a letter), as the most basic unit of the cinema (the shot) is always composed of multiple elements that cannot stand alone. In linguistic terms, a shot might be comparable to a phrase, or a sentence, but never a letter. In short, Metz concluded that the cinema was not a comprehensive, two-way communication/language system (langue) but that it was a language (langage).

So, according to Metz, the analogy with written/spoken language is a red herring, but this did not dissuade him from seeking a film semiotic based on modified linguistic principles, a uniquely cinematic system of meaning (which, for him, began not with the analogical shot but with the sequence or syntagm).

The culmination of Metz's early semiotic efforts was his famous "Grande Syntagmatique du Cinéma," unveiled in chapter six of *Film Language*, a comprehensive "table of the codified orderings of various kinds used in film" (119). This table does not pursue Saussurean "paradigms," but "syntagms," that is, the ways in which various units of meaning (shots) are assembled together to create a chain of signifiers that cooperate to create meaning. It consists not of phonemes but primary syntagms, chains of fundamental cinematic utterances (shots) available to the filmmaker creating a narrative film. Metz believed this "table" to be the beginnings of a cinematic grammar; a list of the most basic units of time-space ordering available to the filmmaker. The syntagmas he lists are (1) the autonomous shot (of which there are several subtypes, unified by the fact that they stand alone in some respect); (2) the parallel syntagma (two motifs that are brought into relation but are not spatiotemporally related, such as images of the busy city versus tranquil country); (3) the bracket syntagma (shots ordered around a concept or theme, not a temporal unity); (4) the descriptive syntagma (shots presented as part of a coexisting spatial reality); (5) the alternating syntagma (shots presented as a synchronous temporal reality, e.g., "cross-cutting," to suggest things happening simultaneously, even if spatially separated); (6) the scene (diverse shots strung together to present a spatiotemporal unity, perceived as having no spatiotemporal breaks, despite the "breaks" of editing); (7) the episodic sequence (a syntagma which suggests the progress of an action through the presentation of various stages of the action, typically "compressing" time); and (8) the ordinary sequence

461

(syntagmas where details that supposedly "have no direct bearing on the plot" are skipped and masked by continuity editing).

Whether or not Metz had really boiled down cinematic expression to its most basic signifying units became a point of intense discussion among film scholars. Counterexamples (particularly from nonnarrative avant-garde films) were put forward, and the challenge to film semioticians was to improve upon Metz's initial, worthy effort. Others argued that the entire effort was ill-founded, as the categorization Metz was attempting was too enslaved to a linguistic mode of analysis.

Metz himself was central to the debate, and he immediately refined his position on the relationship between language and the cinema in his book *Language and Cinema* (1974b). In this work and subsequent essays, Metz aligned himself with a more general semiotic model – one applying to all communication systems – not a specifically linguistic one. Likewise, he shed any traces of Bazinian "realist" presuppositions, for which he was accused in his early work. *Language and Cinema*, while still a "structuralist" approach, showed the influence of post-structuralist semiotics, marking his movement toward the "second phase" of semiotic film theory, where semiotics proper really gives way to a number of suppositions regarding the nature of the spectator, the nature of interpretation, and the degree to which spectatorial experience can be generalized.

In sum, Metz attempted to describe – that is, create a useful paradigm for understanding – how films transmit their meanings via intermediate codes. He settled on the term "code" (over "linguistic unit" or "morpheme") precisely because it is a more general term that does not imply any concrete essence or linguistic determination, but rather serves as a flexible unit of signification that works through context and network. Metz quickly moved away from any inherent "Bazinian" suggestion of transparent reality in cinema, and insisted that the entire cinematic analogon is, at its core, a network of interacting codes (an argument throughout *Language and Cinema*); once this presupposition is made, the question of what a "code" is becomes broad and complicated indeed, as it presupposes that something is always standing in for something else in our experience. Indeed, the term "code" is then applied to everything from the mental representation to the materials of cinematic exhibition.

Some codes are specific to the cinema, conveying an undeniable message via film's unique means (such as multiple moving images, which all films possess). Other codes are nonspecific, shared with languages other than the cinema, and open to many connotations/interpretations (such as the significance of a character wearing the color black). The relationship of the cinematically specific code and the nonspecific code proves to be key, as it returns us once again to the question of signification: How is it cinema represents or conveys anything at all? It is not clear that Metz ever settled the question, though he did provide helpful terminology for addressing it. The relationship between these two realms of codes is often tenuous. Robert Stam, Robert Burgoyne, and Sandy Flitterman-Lewis give the following example: "color" is nonspecific, belonging to many arts and experiences, but the experience of 1950s Technicolor is a very specific type of code, referring only to a cinematic referent (Stam *et al.* 1992: 49). To further tangle the matter, the meanings of codes are often multiple, and best evaluated through subcodes, which are more particular examples of a code in a specific film, historical period, director's oeuvre, or all three. For instance, Metz would consider lighting a code, and a particular lighting style (such as high-key lighting) a subcode.

So, the term "code" has proved a point of criticism for Metz, as he has ambiguously employed it, and his commentators are left to discern much of what he meant. Stam, Burgoyne, and Flitterman-Lewis probably come closest to clarifying Metz's position: "The code, for Metz, is a logical calculus of possible permutations" (1992: 49), that is, all possible elements (codes) that come together into something that may still be called "a film." Given this very broad, unwieldy set of possibilities, it's not surprising that most of the profitable potential in Metz's semiotic system, then, lies at the concrete, historical subcode level.

Many film theorists were influenced by Metz's pioneering efforts. One in particular is worth discussing, if only for the fact that his work also emulates a transition from structuralist semiotics to a second, more nebulous phase. The British theorist and filmmaker Peter Wollen (in *Signs and Meaning in the Cinema* [1969–72]) chose to rely on both C. S. Peirce and Saussure for his film semiotics, and this has surely given us some profitable distinctions, as well as some valuable hybridized ideas. Most clearly, the Peircean distinction between index, sign, and symbol has helped us to understand the associations and references that the given shots and shot sequences yield. An icon (a sign that signifies by resemblance) goes to the heart of cinematic representation itself. An index helps us to understand the shorthand manner in which film can quickly communicate (e.g., a shot of a thermostat rising means hotter temperatures, though we do not actually see the heat "rising," we see the indexical, cause/effect sign of it). The common, arbitrary symbol helps us to understand a huge portion of cinema studies, that of cultural studies, which specializes in the ways different cultures at different times have interpreted and constructed the meanings of a wide variety of elements in films.

Yet, in Wollen's revised 1972 conclusion to the book, he states, "I no longer think that the future of cinema simply lies in a full use of all available codes. I think codes should be confronted with each other, that films are texts which should be structured around contradictions of codes" (173). A more radical, postmodern trace can be seen in this quote: "The text ... is not an instrument of communication but a challenge to the mystification that communication can exist" (163).

So, in the beginning of semiotic film theory there was a modernist idealist tendency to "totalize" our knowledge of human sign systems, and, in this case, the cinema. Labels were created to "hang" on elements of the cinema, with the goal of creating a universal "grammar" of the cinema that might assist us in analysis and understanding of films from every genre, nation, and time. Semiotics was nothing less than the effort to develop a model for the dissection and understanding of the "essence" of the cinema.

Such totalizing claims, however, proved difficult to substantiate, and, as with other "modern" projects in other areas of inquiry, strong doubts arose about universal structures of knowledge. As the "post-structuralist" thinkers (e.g., Jacques Derrida, Michel

Foucault) gained ascendancy throughout the 1970s, semiotics morphed into a useful (but limited) approach for the ideological criticism of this-or-that film in this-or-that culture at this-or-that time.

To keep their theories relevant and applicable beyond a radical, completely inaccessible subjectivity, many theorists in the 1970s and 1980s sought foundation for inquiry in the murky waters of psychoanalysis. They often attempted to use semiotic method – with post-structural "qualifiers" on its power – and give it "cultural studies" applications, that is, to issues of politics, gender, and identification. Since they assumed that connotations were too multiple and subjective to be "codified," they hoped an application of psychoanalysis would yield something of a universal mechanism by which connotations generally come into being. The resulting mode of criticism was to dominate film theory for the next twenty years.

Second phase: post-structuralism and psychosemiotics

Amid the political tensions of the late 1960s, the rise of other theoretical models began to compete with structuralism, provoking a tendency to morph structuralist methods with radical politics (e.g., Louis Althusser, who treated ideology as a structuring element in society) or psychoanalysis (e.g., Lacan, who said the unconscious is structured like a language). In relatively short order, "scientific" structuralism was left behind as a totalizing dream, but not before some influential ideas had been wrung out of it. As Robert Stam *et al.* have succinctly stated:

> The focus of interest was no longer on the relation between filmic and image and "reality," but rather on the cinematic apparatus itself, not only in the sense of the instrumental base of camera, projector, and screen, but also in the sense of the spectator as the desiring subject on which the cinematic institution depends as its object and accomplice. The interest shifts, in this phase, from questions such as "What is the nature of cinematic signs and the laws of their combination?" and "What is a textual system?" to questions such as "What do we want from the text?" and "What is our spectatorial investment in it?" (1992: 22)

It is in this phase where we see semiotics proper – that is, the systematic study of signs and signification – giving way to paths of inquiry that naturally flow from it. Many film scholars, encouraged by the thinkers at the influential film journal *Screen*, looked to the psychology of Sigmund Freud and Jacques Lacan for insight on the spectator. The term "subject" replaced "spectator," as the film viewer came to be seen not as an autonomous agent, but the site of multiple influences, from the deep irrational subconscious to formative cultural biases of dominant ideologies (e.g., capitalism) and gender construction (i.e., sexism, patriarchy, etc.).

Though psychoanalytic criticism is not semiotic study *per se*, it was predicated on semiological principles established by Saussure, as Lacan appropriated the notion of meaning-through-difference and "absence" in signification, in his theorization of the development of human identity. Indeed, Lacan perceived the Unconscious to be structured like a language, and he appropriated a number of Saussure's ideas. For example, his influential "Saussurean" idea of a binary "split subject" (i.e., between conscious and unconscious processes, where there is no "positive" subject, but such subject is produced by what it perceives itself not to be) proved very influential on those who would continue to "deconstruct" the Western humanist project. This also led to a host of ideas regarding how the "structured" subject and its Unconscious drives might inform the process of signification in film viewership. It is worth noting that Metz's "objective" scientific quest quickly turned toward post-structuralist concepts like "displacement" of signification (i.e., a constant dynamic evolution of meaning, as opposed to fixed meanings) and psychoanalysis in another book, *The Imaginary Signifier* (1982). This work is largely dedicated to the subject, rather than the "objective" structure or system of signification.

Lacan takes Freudian notions of desire and extends them to language use, seeing the child's entry into language as coterminous with the channeling of sexual energy. In this way, the psychoanalytic exploration of desire is also a semiotic enterprise, though not one concerned with systems of signification as much as with the hidden, pulsing, and unconscious foundations of signification. For instance, Lacan presumes that language use, art, expression, signification, etc., are all manifestations of the subject attempting to recapture a fantasy of totality and unity between self and world, experienced primordially while nursing as an infant. This has generated a lot of novel theory but has come under attack for providing a highly speculative foundation for "the subject," by cognitive theorists, who argue that it ignores a whole other tradition (i.e., cognitive psychology and analytic philosophy).

Lacan is famously quoted as saying we are "spoken by the culture," as opposed to speaking into it. At the heart of this statement is a radical culturalism bordering on determinism. It is precisely this determinism that leads the cognitivists to criticize so much of contemporary film theory (Stam *et al.* 1992: 132). With such a tight bond drawn between culture and perception, it did not take long for some theorists to designate the entire cultural/cinematic "apparatus" as a symptom of human neurosis, repression, and ideology. Though not an explicitly "semiotic" work, Jean-Louis Baudry's theory of "the apparatus" (1986) clearly flowed from the semiotic project as it diverted through psychoanalysis and critical post-structuralism.

As for semiotic study itself – focusing upon signification and its processes, not the subject – the post-structuralist and so-called postmodernist movements largely shut down its application to film studies (though semiotics continued on as its own discipline). Post-structuralist film theorists and critics (e.g., Stephen Heath 1981) pursued notions like "rupture," "fissure," and "play of signifiers" to highlight the difficulty (or impossibility) of any "totalizing" semiotic system. Yet, they often did so through many concepts set forth by structuralism, such as Saussure's notion that meaning is constructed through "difference," not "presence." As Sam Rhodie writes, in a post-structuralist spin on Metz's structuralist work *Film Language*:

> The cinesemiotics of Christian Metz marks a crucial beginning for a critical semiotics of the cinema. The gaps, the contradictions in his writings point to

the necessity for a genuine return to the text, not as a site of finalization, as ultimate goal, but as opening, initiation, commencement into an infinitude of difference, play and pleasure. (Rhodie 1975: 22–4)

For this reason, many have suggested that post-structuralism is really an extension, and natural end, of structuralism. Others argue that it is a radical critique and departure from it. This debate continues.

Other currents

Of course, this general survey does not do justice to all the nuanced thinkers who may not have fit easily within the camps described above. A few contemporary thinkers, all of them still influential today, are worthy of note. They indicate something of the diverse conversation semiotics has generated, as well as the different directions semiotic film theory could take in the future.

Umberto Eco is generally credited with taking film semiotics beyond its linguistic heritage into a more general science of signs. He is also credited with a rigorous defense of the importance of semiotics in the face of realists and phenomenologists, particularly in his detailed breakdown of the ways "iconicity" is actually "coded," as he takes the remarkable step of labeling dimensions of perception and experience as codes (Eco 1976: 590). This methodology – which presupposes convention and culture at every level of perception – leads him to analyze the most minute elements of the cinematic frame as constituent of a cinematic semiotic playground. He famously suggested, in the influential essay cited above, that cinema carries not only a double articulation (contra Metz), but a triple articulation of seme (an immediately recognizable unit of meaning [e.g., "tall, blond man stands here wearing a white suit"]), sign ("human nose, eye," "square surface," etc.), and figure ("angles," "light contrasts," "curves," "subject–background relationships") (in Nichols 1976–85: 601–2). Eco continues to write about semiotic issues and contemporary culture, though his original thought often defies categorization as a "structuralist" or "post-structuralist."

It is difficult to overestimate the importance of Gilles Deleuze (1925–95) to contemporary film theory. Deleuze's thought is more thoroughly examined in a dedicated entry to him in this volume. It is often difficult to summarize or pin down a wily theorist like Deleuze, but it may be safe to say, in short, that he pleases the semioticians by doing away with the "analogy" model of the realists, but he dismays them with his unique epistemology, which problematizes meaning, language, and systemization. Rather, Deleuze speaks in terms of the images' "signaletic material" (not codes, but material with potential for signification) which is in constant dynamic evolution throughout the meaning process (1989: 29). He sees cinema not as a language or language system, but as "intelligible content which is like a presupposition, a condition, a necessary correlate through which language constructs its own 'objects' (signifying units and operations)" (1989: 262).

Phenomenology has been a "neglected tradition" (Andrew 1985: 625) in recent decades, but some scholars in film studies have managed to combine the insights of

Deleuze and Metz with those of Maurice Merleau-Ponty and even Edmund Husserl. Phenomenology is the study of experience, and so the semiotic phenomenological process focuses upon the meaning "event," the experience of the body-self as it encounters meaning in the cinema. Some prominent thinkers along these lines are Vivian Sobchack (1992 and 2004) and Laura U. Marks (2000 and 2002). Interestingly, these theorists also show a willingness to consider ideas and discoveries from the "hard" sciences (e.g., neuroscience), forming a bridge over what has been, in recent decades, a large culturalist-scientific divide in film studies.

Those on the "other" side of that divide are roughly categorized as "cognitive theorists." See the entry on "Cognitive theory" in this volume for a more comprehensive understanding of this loose confederation of ideas, but it essentially sees language as one means of human communication among many, with the others not necessarily dependent upon it. Therefore, they are suspicious of the linguistic ancestry of semiotics and its theoretical progeny. They often look to biological structures to provide some universal epistemological basis for revisiting the question of signs, how they are developed, and the degree to which meaning is socially constructed, cognitively assembled, and/or biologically determined (e.g., David Bordwell's *Making Meaning* [1989], Noël Carroll's *Theorizing the Moving Image* [1995]). They do affirm the role of signs in the cinematic experience, but typically see the key to interpretation and sense-making in a cognitive "inferential" model, not a code/semantic model.

However, some recent voices have tried to reconcile the cultural studies and cognitivist camps. Warren Buckland's *Cognitive Semiotics of Film* chides some cognitive theorists (e.g., Gregory Currie [1995]) for making a straw man out of semioticians like Metz, and defends the idea of the semiotic enterprise. However, Buckland concedes that some of the criticism aimed at second-stage semiotics is legitimate (particularly the suggestion of a "passive," behavioristic view of the spectator as ideologically shaped subject without a will to resist). Buckland argues that semiotic film theory never really died after the second phase, just faded out of the limelight (particularly in America). Some students of Metz continued apace, even as they incorporated other neglected semioticians like Chomsky (Buckland surveys the work of Francesco Casetti, Roger Odin, Michel Colin, Dominique Chateau, and John M. Carroll as examples). Buckland argues specifically for a "cognitive semiotics," which balances between what he sees as the behaviorism of the "Language Analysis tradition" (i.e., Saussure, Metz, etc.) and the "overemphasis on the spectator as an autonomous rational self" in the cognitive tradition (Buckland 2000: 13).

Conclusion

Is film a language? Most theorists have, historically, come to the conclusion that it is not, or, at least, that such a conception is misleading. Even Metz argues that a strict analogy between the functions of written/spoken language and film breaks down at more particular levels. The debate arises, however, around the question "is there any profit from the analogy at all?" Is there a level where film is like a language, and does semiotics have anything to offer there? Many critics are coming around to a "yes" on this question, but with serious reservations about any totalizing claims. Semiotics, it should be clear, is no longer exclusively dedicated to written or spoken language, so there is certainly applicability here; one must simply recognize the linguistic bias from which the science emerged and identify those biases as problematic. The degree to which language structures our experience is still a matter of intense debate and interest. The degree to which metalinguistic semiotic concepts like "code" are helpful also remains an important discussion. However, the prominence of signs (language included) in "meaning" equation remains obvious, and so semiotics looks to survive in film studies for some time, even if only to provoke and set the terms of discussion.

See also Psychoanalysis (Chapter 41), Cognitive theory (Chapter 33), Christian Metz (Chapter 36), Gilles Deleuze (Chapter 34), Jean Mitry (Chapter 37), and Edgar Morin (Chapter 38).

References

Andrew, D. (1984) *Concepts in Film Theory*, Oxford and New York: Oxford University Press.

—— (1985) "The Neglected Tradition of Phenomenology in Film Theory," in B. Nichols (ed.) *Movies and Methods*, vol. 2, Berkeley: University of California Press.

Barthes, R. (1964) *Elements of Semiology*, trans. A. Lavers and C. Smith, New York: Hill and Wang.

—— (1974) *S/Z*, trans. R. Miller, New York: Hill and Wang.

—— (1977) *Image-Music-Text*, trans. S. Heath, New York: Hill and Wang.

—— (1985) *The Grain of the Voice: Interviews 1962–1980*, trans. L. Coverdale, New York: Hill and Wang.

—— (2007) *Criticism and Truth*, trans. K. P. Keuneman, new ed., New York: Continuum.

Baudry, J.-L. (1986) "The Apparatus: Metapsychological Approaches to the Impression of Reality in Cinema," in P. Rosen (ed.) *Narrative, Apparatus, Ideology: A Film Theory Reader*, New York: Columbia University Press.

Bordwell, D. (1989) *Making Meaning*, Cambridge, MA: Harvard University Press.

Buckland, W. (2000) *The Cognitive Semiotics of Film*, Cambridge and New York: Cambridge University Press.

Carroll, N. (1996) *Theorizing the Moving Image*, Cambridge and New York: Cambridge University Press.

Currie, G. (1995) *Image and Mind: Film, Philosophy, and Cognitive Science*, Cambridge and New York: Cambridge University Press.

Deleuze, G. (1989) *Cinema 2: The Time-Image*, trans. H. Tomlinson and R. Galeta, Minneapolis: University of Minnesota Press.

Eco, U. (1976) *A Theory of Semiotics*, Bloomington: Indiana University Press.

Ehrat, J. (2005) *Cinema and Semiotic: Peirce and Film Aesthetics, Narration, and Representation*, Toronto and Buffalo: University of Toronto Press.

Heath, S. (1981) *Questions of Cinema*, Bloomington: Indiana University Press.

Jakobson, R. (1987) *Language in Literature*, eds. K. Pomorska and S. Rudy, Cambridge, MA: Belknap Press.

Jakobson, R., and Halle, M. (1971) *Fundamentals of Language*, rev. ed., The Hague: Mouton.

Lévi-Strauss, C. (1967) *Structural Anthropology*, trans. C. Jacobson and B. G. Schoepf, Garden City, NY: Doubleday.

Marks, L. U. (2000) *The Skin of the Film: Intercultural Cinema, Embodiment, and the Senses*, Durham, NC: Duke University Press.

—— (2002) *Touch: Sensuous Theory and Multisensory Media*, Minneapolis: University of Minnesota Press.

Metz, C. (1974a) *Film Language: A Semiotics of the Cinema*, trans. M. Taylor, New York: Oxford University Press.

—— (1974b) *Language and Cinema*, trans. D. J. Umiker-Sebeok, The Hague: Mouton.

—— (1982) *The Imaginary Signifier*, trans. C. Britton, A. Williams, B. Brewster, and A. Guzzetti, Bloomington: Indiana University Press.

Mitry, J. (1997) *The Aesthetics and Psychology of the Cinema*, trans. C. King, Bloomington: Indiana University Press.

—— (2000) *Semiotics and the Analysis of Film*, trans. C. King, Bloomington: Indiana University Press.

Nichols, B. (ed.) (1976–85) *Movies and Methods*, 2 vols., Berkeley: University of California Press.

Peirce, C. S. (1955) *Philosophical Writings of Peirce*, ed. J. Butcher, New York: Dover.

—— (1982–2000) *The Writings of Charles S. Peirce: A Chronological Edition*, 6 vols., Bloomington: Indiana University Press.

Rhodie, S. (1975) "Metz and Film Semiotics: Opening the Field," in *Jump Cut: A Review of Contemporary Media* 7: 22–4. Available at http://www.ejumpcut.org/archive/onlinessays/JC07folder/Metz.html (accessed 13 September 2007).

Saussure, F. de (1972) *Course in General Linguistics*, trans. R. Harris; eds. C. Bally and A. Sechehaye, Chicago: Open Court Press.

Sebeok, T. A. (1991) *A Sign Is Just a Sign*, Bloomington: Indiana University Press.

—— (1994) *Signs: An Introduction to Semiotics*, Toronto and Buffalo: University of Toronto Press.

Sobchack, V. (1992) *The Address of the Eye: A Phenomenology of Film Experience*, Princeton, NJ: Princeton University Press.

—— (2004) *Carnal Thoughts: Embodiment and Moving Image Culture*, Berkeley: University of California Press.

Stam, R., Burgoyne, R., and Flitterman-Lewis, S. (1992) *New Vocabularies in Film Semiotics*, London and New York: Routledge.

Wollen, P. (1969–72) *Signs and Meaning in the Cinema*, rev. ed., Bloomington: Indiana University Press.

43
WITTGENSTEIN

Malcolm Turvey

Ludwig Wittgenstein (1889–1951) is widely regarded as one of the greatest philosophers of the twentieth century. Yet, his philosophy has had little influence on the study of film, at least until recently. This is due in part to the outsized influence of continental philosophy on film studies (Allen and Smith 1997: 1–41). Although Wittgenstein was born and grew up in Vienna, he received his philosophical training from Bertrand Russell, one of the pioneers of modern analytic philosophy, and his work was analytic in orientation. But it is also due to the fact that many analytic philosophers, including analytic philosophers of art and film, have themselves rejected central tenets of Wittgenstein's philosophy, principally his claim that philosophy is not continuous with the sciences and is not a theoretical or empirical discipline. While the philosophical topics he addressed – the nature of meaning, the mind, truth, etc. – are ones that have long preoccupied philosophers, unlike most of them he believed that the philosophical problems raised by these topics stem from misunderstandings of the workings of language. Thus, instead of trying to solve these problems by constructing theories or by investigating the world empirically as the scientist does, philosophers, he argued, should clarify the way our language works, thereby dissolving away these philosophical problems and the misunderstandings of language from which they derive. Although this conception of philosophy has been kept alive by philosophers such as Norman Malcolm, Anthony Kenny, and Peter Hacker, it is not widely adhered to in analytic philosophy today, which tends to be scientific – some would say scientistic – in character and to be dominated by post-positivist ideas, due largely to the influence of W. V. O. Quine (see Hacker 1996: 183–227). Wittgenstein's defenders claim that this state of affairs is not the result of Wittgenstein's arguments having "been shown to be flawed or inadequate, but simply because of the impact on philosophical fashion of variations in the prestige of a number of non-philosophical disciplines" (Kenny 1989: vi). If they are right, then his philosophy still has much to teach us, including those of us who study film and art.

Wittgenstein himself wrote very little about the philosophy of art even though he was a cultured man who remarked toward the end of his life that "Only *conceptual* and *aesthetic* questions [really grip me]" (CV: 79 [see the "Abbreviations" section, at the end of this chapter]). What we know about his views on the subject come primarily from notes taken by audience members at lectures he gave on aesthetics in the early

1930s and especially in 1938. The 1930s was a period of transition in Wittgenstein's philosophy, and the lectures on aesthetics are difficult to grasp without an understanding of the larger conception of philosophy Wittgenstein was moving toward when he gave them. In the first section of this entry, I outline this conception of philosophy. In the second, I explore some of the major arguments of the 1938 lectures, pointing to their potential significance for film studies. In the third and fourth, I examine other areas of his philosophy that have – and indeed have been shown to have – ramifications for the study of art and film.

Wittgenstein's conception of philosophy

Throughout his philosophical career Wittgenstein drew a sharp distinction between philosophy and science. "Philosophy is not one of the natural sciences" (TLP: 4.111), he wrote in the *Tractatus Logico-Philosophicus* (1921), his first masterpiece; and in *Philosophical Investigations* (1953), his second, he claimed: "It is true to say that our considerations could not be scientific ones" (PI: §109). According to Wittgenstein, the subject matter, questions, problems, and solutions of philosophy are fundamentally different from those of the sciences because they are not empirical in nature. Rather, philosophy is concerned exclusively with something that antecedes and is separable from empirical inquiry: meaning.

The basic distinction at stake here can be illustrated by invoking a simple, canonical example. The sentence "a bachelor cannot be married" seems to state a general proposition about bachelors that is akin to a general empirical proposition like "all cows eat grass." However, it does not state a general fact, one that can be proven or disproven by empirical research in the way that the claim "all cows eat grass" can be. Rather, the "cannot" of the first sentence is logical, not empirical. Someone who understands the English language knows in advance of any empirical investigation that a bachelor cannot be married, that empirical research will never turn up a married bachelor. And he knows this because it is part of the logic of the word bachelor, part of its sense that, if one says that a man is a bachelor, he cannot also be married. The sentence in question exhibits this aspect of the meaning of the word "bachelor" by specifying a necessary condition of its use, rather than making an empirical claim about the world.

Wittgenstein argued that philosophy is concerned purely with the type of subject matter this sentence exhibits, with what can be known about language in advance of any empirical research, namely, the meaning of the words, expressions, and sentences it contains. Philosophy, therefore, has nothing of an empirical nature to discover about language or anything else. In the *Investigations* he puts it this way:

> [Philosophical problems] are, of course, not empirical problems; they are solved, rather, by looking into the workings of our language, and that in such a way as to make us recognize those workings: in despite of an urge to misunderstand them ... Philosophy is a battle against the bewitchment of our intelligence by means of language. (PI: §109)

During his philosophical career, Wittgenstein changed his mind about the nature of meaning. According to the *Tractatus*, which Wittgenstein wrote in the 1910s, the only meaningful use of language is to "picture" or describe reality. Language is essentially a system for doing this, and the task of philosophy is to lay bare this system. This conception of meaning unifies the apparent diversity of meaningful uses of words, expressions, and sentences in ordinary language by reducing them to the same underlying function: "picturing," or describing reality. Furthermore, neither the system of language nor the reality to which this system supposedly corresponds is visible to the ordinary language user. They are something that must exist, a theoretical postulate, rather than something that is actually known and understood by the language user.

But why, Wittgenstein came to ask in the 1930s, must every sentence have the same essential function of describing a state of affairs, and every word have the same essential function of being a name? Why must all words or sentences have the same function at all? In his later philosophy, Wittgenstein points to the variety of ways words, expressions, and sentences are used by human beings, famously comparing language to a "tool box" containing many different tools. Language is used to give and obey orders, report, speculate, sing, guess, joke, ask, thank, curse, greet, pray, and many other things as well (PI: §23).

He also rejected the other fundamental feature of the *Tractatus*' conception of meaning, namely, that meaning is hidden from the human beings who use language and therefore needs to be laid bare by philosophy. For how can a linguistic expression be used correctly by users who have no idea how each word has meaning or what meaning is? An invisible system of representation of the sort postulated by the *Tractatus*, Wittgenstein came to believe, cannot account for how users of a language actually use language. Rather, the meaning of an expression must be visible to its user if he is to be able to use it correctly. Where, therefore, is it visible? The later Wittgenstein answered, "For a *large* class of cases – though not for all – in which we employ the word meaning it can be defined thus: the meaning of a word is its use in the language" (PI: §43). And the norms, standards, or rules that define its correct use in a specific context must in principle be ones its user can appeal to in justifying its usage, or in explaining how the expression is to be used correctly to others.

In the *Investigations*, meaning is no longer assumed to be something invisible that needs to be discovered by the philosopher through logical analysis, as it was in the *Tractatus*. Rather, philosophy now "simply puts everything before us, and neither explains nor deduces anything. Since everything lies open to view there is nothing to explain. For what is hidden is of no interest to us" (PI: §126). The philosopher's task, according to the later Wittgenstein, is to describe the correct use of language in practice: "Philosophy may in no way interfere with the actual use of language; it can in the end only describe it. For it cannot give it any foundation either. It leaves everything as it is" (PI: §124).

All problems of a properly philosophical nature, for Wittgenstein in his later philosophy, are the result of our failure to understand how we use language: "A main source of our failure to understand is that we do not command a clear view of the use of our words" (PI: §122). Hence, the philosopher's goal is to produce a "perspicuous representation" of its use (PI: §122). Rather than discovering new facts or constructing explanatory theories, the philosopher draws our attention to aspects of our use of language in practice that we have overlooked, or not paid sufficient attention to, thereby "assembling reminders" (PI: §127). Hence, philosophy is therapeutic. By clarifying the relevant segments of logical grammar, it dissolves away confusions about the workings of language that give rise to philosophical problems.

Wittgenstein's lectures on aesthetics

The first of Wittgenstein's 1938 lectures on aesthetics opens with an example of the importance of "assembling reminders" about the use of language in practice, and how this can dissolve away a philosophical problem. Much philosophy of art has aimed to answer the question "What is beauty?" Wittgenstein, however, argues that when we attend to the way the word "beauty" is taught and employed in practice in response to art, we discover that it is used first and foremost as an "interjection," an "expression of approval" much like a gesture of approval (say clapping), and not as an adjective that refers to a quality of an object (LC: I §5, §1). We also find that words like beauty play "hardly any role at all" in aesthetic judgments (LC: I §8). (Indeed, Wittgenstein suggests it is typically people who lack aesthetic expertise who employ such words in response to art [LC: I §9].) Instead, the words that we do use are "more akin to 'right' and 'correct'," as in this is the right transition in a piece of music, or the images in a poem are "precise" (LC: I §8). And when we do employ words like beauty, it is in order to capture the "character" of an artwork, to "give it a face" (this piece of music by Schubert is "melancholic") (LC: I §§9–10). Moreover, Wittgenstein points out, it is often by way of gestures, facial expressions, and the ways we behave, rather than words, that we manifest our aesthetic judgments, and he therefore concludes that "Aesthetic adjectives [play] hardly any role" (LC: I §12) in the appreciation of art. Thus, by describing the use of the word "beauty" in practice, not only is the philosophical problem "What is beauty?" potentially dissolved away – we realize that we employ the word "beauty" in other ways than as an adjective to refer to a quality of an object – but we discover that philosophers have attributed much more importance to the topic of beauty than it warrants. This is one reason why Wittgenstein begins the 1938 lectures by stating that aesthetics is "entirely misunderstood" (LC: I §1).

Another misunderstanding that Wittgenstein tackles in these lectures is "the idea that people have of a kind of science of aesthetics" (LC: II §1). By this, he means the claim that an aesthetic explanation is a causal explanation, one that seeks to identify the cause of an aesthetic reaction in the same way that the cause of a pleasant smell (LC: II §3) or a pain (LC: II §20) can be discovered. From this arises the view that "Aesthetics is a science telling us what's beautiful" (LC: II §2), a "branch of psychology" (LC: II §35) that, by way of "psychological experiments" (LC: II §36), can uncover the causes of aesthetic reactions. Wittgenstein calls this view "too ridiculous for words" (LC: II §2), and argues that there is a fundamental difference between reactions to causes and aesthetic reactions such as "discomfort," namely, that the latter are "directed" (LC: II §18). Genuine aesthetic reactions are not merely a matter of having a feeling "*plus* knowing the cause" (LC: II §11). Instead, they are "about" something; the object of the aesthetic reaction is bound up with or internal to the reaction itself. Reacting with delight to a piece of music, for instance, does not consist of feeling delight and knowing that the piece of music has caused this feeling, but taking delight *in* something about the music, such as its use of counterpoint. (Wittgenstein here means something similar to the now familiar philosophical claim that certain emotions are directed. For example, if someone is caused to be in the same physical state as an angry person, perhaps by way of an injection, this does not mean that he is angry, for to be angry also requires that there be someone or something to be angry at.) Wittgenstein concludes that no amount of empirical experimentation can explain why a work of art gives rise to a particular aesthetic reaction in the same way that such experimentation can determine the cause of a pain (LC: III §11). The scientific cause and effect model is the wrong one for aesthetic explanations. Instead, the "sort of explanation one is looking for" in aesthetics is one that "satisfies you," one with which "you agree" (LC: II §37), and this leads Wittgenstein into a discussion of the differences between reasons (or motives) and causes and the way Freud's theory of the unconscious traffics in a confusion between the two (LC: III §12ff.), a subject that he also addresses elsewhere in his philosophy of psychology (BB: 15).

Wittgenstein's arguments about beauty and aesthetic reactions in the 1938 lectures are not subject to the same painstaking elaboration that he devotes, say, to psychological concepts in the *Investigations*, and there is much about them with which one can disagree. However, other philosophers have sought to elaborate on them. Frank Cioffi has subjected to rigorous scrutiny Wittgenstein's distinction between the empirical investigation of causes and directed aesthetic reactions for which the only explanation is one that "satisfies you." He suggests that there are really two distinctions at work here, "a distinction between directed and non-directed feelings and between experimentally corrigible (prognostic) and non-corrigible (diagnostic) judgments," and he concludes that, while Wittgenstein is right to distinguish between directed and nondirected reactions in aesthetics, he is wrong to further assert that aesthetic explanations may not "proffer experimentally corrigible judgments about the objects of directed feelings" (Cioffi 1998: 54–5). Others have followed Wittgenstein's injunction to describe the language that we are taught and use in our responses to art (Hanfling 1996), as well as his claims about the role of nonverbal behavior in such responses (Lüdeking 1990). Others, still, have taken up further topics Wittgenstein addresses in the lectures, such as the role of rules in art-making and aesthetic judgments (Novitz 2004), and aesthetic competence (McFee 2001). In general, in addition to attempting to dissolve away traditional philosophical problems about art, Wittgenstein's application to aesthetics of the philosophical method of describing the way language is used in practice in his lectures of the 1930s lays the groundwork for a philosophy of criticism and artistic appreciation, one that is widely seen as standing in sharp contrast to the traditional philosophical enterprise of constructing theories of art (Johannessen 2004). It also stands in sharp contrast to the way film scholars have traditionally studied film. For they, too, have typically opted for constructing theories of film and our responses to it, instead of investigating the language people use, and the forms of behavior in which this language occurs, in their responses to film. Not only could such an investigation prevent film theorists from going down a theoretical dead end akin to the question "What is beauty?" – for example, trying to experimentally determine the causes of our aesthetic reactions to films as opposed to the reasons for them – but it could clarify what the nature of aesthetic judgment and appreciation in relation to film is, something that has been much too low on the agenda of academic film studies.

Art, film, and Wittgenstein's philosophy of language

Perhaps due to the provisional nature of the lectures on aesthetics, a number of analytic philosophers have mined other areas of Wittgenstein's later philosophy for arguments of relevance to the philosophy of art. The most influential of these is Wittgenstein's family resemblance argument, which is central to his later philosophy of language. When theorists attempt to define an entity of some kind, they often resort to an essentialist definition, one that identifies an essence, a property or set of properties, that all entities of that kind putatively have in common. As we have seen, Wittgenstein rejected the view that language has an essence, "something common to all that we call language" (PI: §65), such as the function of "picturing" the world. He also rejected the view that there must be something common to the various uses of individual linguistic items. Employing the example of "the proceedings we call 'games' … board-games, card-games, ball-games, Olympic games, and so on," he insisted:

> Don't say: "There *must* be something common [to all of them], or they would not be called 'games'" – but *look and see* whether there is something common to all. – For if you look at them you will not see something that is common to *all*, but similarities, relationships, and a whole series of them at that. (PI: §66)

Wittgenstein went on to clarify what he meant by similarities and relationships, using an analogy with family resemblances. Just as the members of a family can resemble each other in different ways rather than having one resemblance in common – a son's nose might resemble his father's and his hair his mother's – so games might have different things rather than the same thing in common, yet still "form a family" (PI: §67).

In the 1950s, a number of analytic philosophers of art applied versions of Wittgenstein's family resemblance argument to the enterprise that has dominated twentieth-century analytic aesthetics more than any other: defining what art is. They claimed that art cannot be defined by way of an essentialist definition, one that identifies a condition or set of conditions that something must fulfill in order for it to be an artwork. Morris Weitz, for example, argued that the concept of art is always open to change, due to innovations in artistic practice. Hence, an essentialist definition of the concept of art will always fail, because "its conditions of application can never be exhaustively enumerated since new cases can always be envisaged or created by artists, or even nature, which would call for a decision on someone's part to extend or to close the old or to invent a new concept" (Weitz 1978 [1956]: 127). Weitz suggested that art is like the concept of a game discussed by Wittgenstein (Weitz called it an "open" concept). "In elucidating [these concepts], certain (paradigm) cases can be given, about which there can be no question as to their being correctly described as 'art' or 'game', but no exhaustive set of cases can be given" (126). Hence, when we ask whether or not a new work is art, rather than looking to see whether it fulfills conditions common to all artworks, we compare it to paradigm cases of art. If there are enough similarities between it and the paradigm cases we conclude that it is an artwork.

Wittgenstein's family resemblance argument has certainly influenced post-Second World War analytic philosophy of art, but not in the way intended by its proponents, such as Weitz, for it has functioned more as an objection to be surmounted than a model to be followed, and it has not stopped philosophers from proposing essentialist definitions of art. Such philosophers point to what is commonly thought of as the argument's major weakness, that the concept of similarity it relies upon is too vague. For everything is like everything else in some respect, meaning that, without one or more necessary conditions on the sort of resemblances a new work must have to paradigm cases of art in order for it to be an artwork, everything would count as art. To propose such necessary conditions is, of course, to engage in the very definitional enterprise that is said to be impossible. Nevertheless, in a further twist of the dialectic, a few philosophers have responded to this criticism by returning to Wittgenstein's family resemblance argument, in the process exposing flaws in its original application to the concept of art by Weitz and others. Ben Tilghman has claimed that the real moral of Wittgenstein's family resemblance argument is not that some things, such as games and artworks, lack common, defining properties, as most philosophers have assumed, but that the very project of looking to see what games or artworks have in common is unintelligible in the absence of a context that determines what is to count as a candidate for the common property. "Without such a determination we don't know what we are looking for nor what would count as finding it" (Tilghman 1984: 30). More recently, Berys Gaut has pointed out that there is another way of construing Wittgenstein's family resemblance argument than the way Weitz and others understood it (or were imputed to have understood it). To replace the "resemblance-to-paradigm" understanding of family resemblance, according to which something falls under a concept if it resembles paradigm cases of the concept, Gaut advocates a "cluster concept" construal. By cluster concept is meant a concept for which there are multiple criteria for the concept's application, none of which is individually necessary. Instead they are *disjunctively* necessary. Something does not have to meet all of the criteria to fall under a concept, but only some, and there is a "great deal of indeterminacy in how many of these criteria must apply if an object is to fall under the concept" (Gaut 2000: 26). According to Gaut, such a construal of family resemblance avoids the major problem with the resemblance-to-paradigm construal, the fact that in the absence of one or more conditions on resemblance everything counts as art because everything resembles everything else in some respect. It does so by specifying "what the properties are that are relevant to determining whether something is art" (27–8). However, unlike essentialist definitions, the cluster concept construal of art does not lay down an exhaustive set of conditions that a work must fulfill in order to count as art. It instead proposes a number of conditions only some of which a work must fulfill, and Gaut proposes a number of such conditions, including being intellectually challenging and an act of creative imagination. In their work, Tilghman and Gaut show that Wittgenstein's family resemblance argument continues to provide the resources for challenging the philosophical project of defining art.

The rich postwar debate in analytic aesthetics about whether and how it is possible to define art, in which Wittgenstein's family resemblance argument has played a role, has had almost no influence on film studies. While the question of whether film is an art or not – a question which presupposes a definition of what art is – preoccupied film theorists prior to the 1960s, it has since been replaced by what is seen by many film scholars today as the far more important question of how film propagates ideology. Yet, given that film theorists prior to the 1960s proposed definitions of film art in ignorance of this debate about defining art among analytic philosophers, it may well prove fruitful to return to the question of whether and how film is an art, armed with the sophisticated resources this debate offers. The same is true of a definitional question that has remained on the agenda of academic film studies, if only barely, thanks largely to the work of philosopher of film Noël Carroll, namely, what is film? Carroll has argued forcefully in a number of works over a number of years that the medium of film does not possess an essential property or set of properties and that instead of speaking of film, scholars should speak of the art form of the moving image (see, for example, Carroll 1996). However, the work of Tilghman and Gaut may well offer film scholars the resources to challenge this view. Film, for example, might be a cluster concept, for which there are disjunctively necessary conditions for something to count as a film, none of which is individually necessary.

Art, film, and Wittgenstein's philosophy of psychology

The other area of Wittgenstein's later philosophy that has had some influence on post-Second World War analytic philosophy of art is his philosophy of psychology, particularly his partial analysis of the concept of seeing, in section xi of Part 2 of the *Investigations*, in which he uses an unusual visual experience he refers to as "noticing an aspect" (PI: 193) to make some general points about seeing. Although the duck-rabbit provides the most famous example of this experience, Wittgenstein gives many others, such as suddenly noticing a human shape in a picture puzzle (PI: 196). What makes noticing an aspect an unusual visual experience is that it appears to involve the beholder "seeing" more than the material properties of the object he is looking at. This is because the object of sight remains materially unchanged when the aspect is noticed. Yet, once the aspect has been noticed, the beholder seems to "see" something different about the object – what Wittgenstein calls an aspect – even though he knows there is nothing new to see about it, materially speaking. Wittgenstein tries to dissolve away this paradox by investigating the meaning of the concept of seeing, when and how it is employed correctly, in order to clarify precisely what the beholder means when he says that he "sees" something new about an object when he notices an aspect. He does so by showing that there are in fact "two uses of the word 'see'" in which two different "'objects' of sight" are at stake (PI: 193):

> If I saw the duck-rabbit as a rabbit, then I saw: these shapes and colors (I give them in detail) – and I saw besides something like this: and here I point to a number of different pictures of rabbits. – This shews the difference between the concepts. (PI: 196–7)

The first "'object' of sight" is material properties, such as shape and color. These can be pointed to, described, and represented using an exact copy. The second is the *kind* of object something is, in this case a rabbit depicted in a picture. The difference between the two types of object of sight is evident in the way they are represented by the beholder. Unlike material properties, the "rabbitness" of the rabbit in the picture, its *identity* as a rabbit, what Wittgenstein calls its aspect, cannot be pointed to, described, or represented using an exact copy. Instead, it can only be represented by pointing to other pictures that also depict rabbits. In general, one of Wittgenstein's goals in this part of the *Investigations* is to demonstrate that, like games, seeing involves "hugely many interrelated phenomena and possible concepts" (PI: 199).

A number of philosophers of art have turned to Wittgenstein's discussion of noticing an aspect to account for pictorial depiction, in particular how it is we see the depicted content of a picture in or through the configuration of lines and colors on its surface (see, for example, Wollheim 1968; Wilkerson 1991). This is because, while investigating the experience of noticing aspects, Wittgenstein points out that the fact that human beings identify the depicted content of pictures spontaneously and unhesitatingly and the fact that they do not treat their identifications as one among several possible interpretations constitute grounds for saying that they see what pictures depict. They do not just see the material properties of pictures – their surface lines and colors – and then infer what these pictures are supposed to represent (PI: 204–5).

Film theorists have also in recent years turned to Wittgenstein's discussion of noticing an aspect in order to explain cinematic depiction. Richard Allen, for example, has argued that the major theories of cinematic depiction to date – illusion, transparency, imagination, and recognition theories – are all dependent on an impoverished conception of seeing, which he refers to as the causal theory of perception, and which assumes that seeing is an experience caused by the object seen. Hence, in order to explain how it is that we see what a motion picture depicts, say an object, these theories either claim that we see the object itself or an illusion of it, or that we don't see the object itself but instead imagine or recognize it. Allen argues instead that "we require an understanding of seeing pictures that, contrary to imagination and recognition theorists, respects the fact that seeing what a picture is of is a genuine case of seeing, without commitment to the idea that what we see is the object itself or an illusion of it," and he finds just such an understanding in Wittgenstein's discussion of noticing an aspect, which shows that "the object of sight is not always a physical object" (Allen 1997: 77; see also Turvey 1997).

Wittgenstein's discussion of noticing an aspect involves clarifying the concept of seeing. However, Wittgenstein and philosophers such as Kenny and Hacker who have followed in his wake have also clarified other concepts employed by scholars of film and the other arts, such as intention, knowledge, belief, understanding, pleasure, emotion, and so on. This is why Richard Allen and I have argued that Wittgenstein's later philosophy has a *propaedeutic* role to play in disciplines that study the arts, such as film studies (Allen and Turvey 2001: 1–35). By this, we mean that it can help us clarify and therefore better understand the concepts, particularly the psychological concepts, we employ in theorizing about and studying film (see, for example, Turvey 2004 and 2008). For we routinely employ concepts, such as perceptual concepts, without a clear grasp of their meanings, with the result that our film theories can stray beyond the bounds of sense. Through clarifying the meaning of perception and other difficult concepts, Wittgenstein's later philosophy can be of considerable assistance to film theorists, helping them to avoid trafficking in conceptual confusion and nonsense.

Acknowledgments

Part 1 of this essay is a modified version of part 1 of an essay I co-wrote with Richard Allen, titled "Wittgenstein's Later Philosophy: A Prophylaxis against Theory" (in Allen and Turvey, 2001). I would like to thank Professor Allen for allowing me to use this material here, and for introducing me to Wittgenstein's later philosophy when I was his student in the Department of Cinema Studies at New York University. Thanks also to Paisley Livingston for his helpful comments on an earlier version of this entry.

Abbreviations

Throughout, the standard abbreviations for Wittgenstein's work are used. They are as follows:

BB   *The Blue and Brown Books* (Oxford: Blackwell, 1958)
CV   *Culture and Value*, ed. G. H. von Wright, in collaboration with H. Nyman; trans. P. Winch (Oxford: Blackwell, 1980)
LC   *Lectures and Conversations on Aesthetics, Psychology and Religious Belief*, ed. C. Barrett (Oxford: Blackwell, 1970)
PI   *Philosophical Investigations*, ed. G. E. M. Anscombe and R. Rhees; trans. G. E. M. Anscombe, 2nd ed. (Oxford: Blackwell, 1958)
TLP   *Tractatus Logico-Philosophicus*, trans. D. F. Pears and B. F. McGuinness (London: Routledge and Kegan Paul, 1961)

See also Depiction (Chapter 6).

References

Allen, R. (1997) "Looking at Motion Pictures," in R. Allen and M. Smith (eds.) *Film Theory and Philosophy*, Oxford: Clarendon Press; New York: Oxford University Press.

Allen, R., and Smith, M. (1997) "Introduction: Film Theory and Philosophy," in R. Allen and M. Smith (eds.) *Film Theory and Philosophy*, Oxford: Clarendon Press; New York Oxford University Press.

Allen, R., and Turvey, M. (2001) "Wittgenstein's Later Philosophy: A Prophylaxis against Theory," in R. Allen and M. Turvey (eds.) *Wittgenstein, Theory and the Arts*, London and New York: Routledge.

Carroll, N. (1996) "Defining the Moving Image," in *Theorizing the Moving Image*, Cambridge and New York: Cambridge University Press.

Cioffi, F. (1998) *Wittgenstein on Freud and Frazer*, Cambridge and New York: Cambridge University Press.

Gaut, B. (2000) "'Art' as a Cluster Concept," in N. Carroll (ed.) *Theories of Art Today*, Madison: University of Wisconsin Press.

Hacker, P. M. S. (1996) *Wittgenstein's Place in Twentieth Century Analytic Philosophy*, Oxford: Blackwell.

Hanfling, O. (1996) "Fact, Fiction and Feeling," *British Journal of Aesthetics* 36: 356–66.

Johannessen, K. S. (2004) "Wittgenstein and the Aesthetic Domain," in P. Lewis (ed.) *Wittgenstein, Aesthetics and Philosophy*, Aldershot, UK and Burlington, VT: Ashgate.

Kenny, A. (1989) *The Metaphysics of Mind*, Oxford: Clarendon; New York: Oxford University Press.

Lüdeking, K. (1990) "Pictures and Gestures," *British Journal of Aesthetics* 30: 218–32.

McFee, G. (2001) "Wittgenstein, Performing Art and Action," in R. Allen and M. Turvey (eds.) *Wittgenstein, Theory and the Arts*, London and New York: Routledge.

Novitz, D. (2004) "Rules, Creativity and Pictures: Wittgenstein's *Lectures on Aesthetics*," in P. Lewis (ed.) *Wittgenstein, Aesthetics and Philosophy*, Aldershot, UK and Burlington, VT: Ashgate.

Tilghman, B. R. (1984) *But Is It Art? The Value of Art and the Temptation of Theory*, Oxford and New York: Blackwell.

Turvey, M. (1997) "Seeing Theory: On Perception and Emotional Response in Current Film Theory," in R. Allen and M. Smith (eds.) *Film Theory and Philosophy*, Oxford: Clarendon Press; New York: Oxford University Press.

—— (2004) "Philosophical Problems Concerning the Concept of Pleasure in Psychoanalytical Theories of (the Horror) Film," in S. H. Schneider (ed.) *Horror Film and Psychoanalysis: Freud's Worst Nightmare*, New York: Cambridge University Press.

—— (2008) *Doubting Vision: Film and the Revelationist Tradition*, New York: Oxford University Press.

Weitz, M. (1978 [1956]) "The Role of Theory in Aesthetics," in J. Margolis (ed.) *Philosophy Looks at the Arts: Contemporary Readings in Aesthetics*, Philadelphia: Temple University Press.

Wilkerson, T. E. (1991) "Pictorial Representation: A Defense of the Aspect Theory," *Midwest Studies in Philosophy* 16: 152–66.

Wollheim, R. (1968–80) *Art and Its Objects*, Cambridge and New York: Cambridge University Press.

Further reading

Good introductions to Wittgenstein's philosophy are Anthony Kenny, *Wittgenstein* (London: Allen Lane, 1973) and P. M. S. Hacker, *Wittgenstein* (London and New York: Routledge, 1999). The best in-depth examination of the *Philosophical Investigations* is Hacker's monumental four-volume *Analytical Commentary on the Philosophical Investigations* (Oxford: Blackwell, 1980–96). A good overview of Wittgenstein's philosophy of psychology is Paul Johnston, *Wittgenstein: Rethinking the Inner* (London and New York: Routledge, 1993). The implications of Wittgenstein's later philosophy for the study of the arts are explored in depth in *Wittgenstein, Theory and the Arts*, edited by Richard Allen and Malcolm Turvey (London and New York: Routledge, 2001), and *Wittgenstein, Aesthetics and Philosophy*, edited by Peter Lewis (Aldershot, UK; Burlington, VT: Ashgate, 2004).

Part III

GENRES AND OTHER TYPES

44

DOGME 95

Mette Hjort

First announced by Danish director Lars von Trier, at a centennial celebration of film in Paris in 1995, Dogme 95 is a rule-governed, manifesto-based, back-to-basics film initiative that was intended from the outset to generate a movement. More than a decade later, the official Dogme website (http://www.dogme95.dk/menu/menuset. htm) provides evidence of the successful realization of von Trier's intentions, with more than two hundred films listed from countries (or subnational entities), including Australia, Denmark, Belgium, Brazil, Canada, Columbia, Chile, Estonia, France, Greece, Hungary, Israel, Korea, Luxembourg, Macedonia, Mexico, New Zealand, Norway, Quebec, Scotland, Singapore, South Africa, Sweden, Thailand, Turkey, the United States, and Wales. Spanning six continents, this list does not include the films by directors (in Hong Kong and mainland China, for example) who claim to have been greatly inspired by the Dogme program, without having felt compelled to abide by all of its rules in the production of bona fide Dogme films. In 2002 Ryan Gilbey called Dogme 95 "the most radical film-making movement since the French new wave" (Gilbey 2002: online) and more recently German filmmaker Wim Wenders claimed that "over time Dogme 95 will come to be seen as one of the most important developments in European film at the turn of the century" (Skotte and Møller 2005: online). Along with other aspects of its basic orientation, Dogme's manifesto-based and rule-governed nature makes it an inherently philosophical project, and the films and the now globalized movement to which they belong have in fact attracted the attention of a number of philosophers. Dogme 95 raises key philosophical questions having to do with rationality, creativity under constraint, rule-following, realism, and the psychology of fantasy and fiction. Before exploring the role played by some of these philosophical issues in the Dogme phenomenon, it is necessary to provide some basic information about Dogme and the various phases of its development since 1995.

The term "Dogme" refers both to a programmatic cinematic intervention targeting especially Hollywood filmmaking and to a film collective involving four "brethren": Lars von Trier, Thomas Vinterberg, Søren Kragh-Jacobsen, and Kristian Levring. The manifesto was coauthored by von Trier and the much younger Vinterberg, who describes the process as follows: "It was easy ... We asked ourselves what we most hated about film today, and then drew up a list banning it all. It took half an hour and it was a great laugh" (cited in Kelly 2000: 5). Printed in black on red paper and thrown into the audience at the Odéon theater in Paris by von Trier in 1995, the manifesto comprises three parts: an initial statement, rife with irony and hyperbole, that identifies the goals, and the targets, of the Dogme brethren's polemical initiative; a so-called Vow of Chastity, comprising ten rules that filmmakers wishing to produce a Dogme film must follow; and a coda, followed by the signatures of von Trier and Vinterberg, "on behalf of DOGMA 95." In the general statement Dogme 95 is described as a "rescue action," the goal of which is to counter "certain tendencies in the cinema today." The French new wave is evoked in connection with goals that were correct and "means [that] were not." The "auteur concept," in particular, is singled out as an instance of "bourgeois romanticism," as is the "individual film," which is described as "decadent by definition." Hollywood comes under fire in a series of phrases condemning "the decadent filmmakers" whose "task" it is "to fool the audience" by means of "illusions," "trickery," and "predictability" or "dramaturgy." With its ten rules, the Vow of Chastity is identified as the Dogme collective's proposed means of countering "the film of illusion."

Evoking the language and rituals of organized religion, the Vow begins as follows: "I swear to submit to the following set of rules drawn up and confirmed by Dogma 95." Many of the rules are highly specific and relatively transparent – "5. Optical work and filters are forbidden"; "6. The film must not contain superficial action (Murders, weapons, etc. must not occur)" – but the coda introduces a number of further prescriptions, some of which have proven difficult to interpret, let alone follow:

> Furthermore I swear as a director to refrain from personal taste! I am no longer an artist. I swear to refrain from creating a "work," as I regard the instant as more important than the whole. My supreme goal is to force the truth out of my characters and settings. I swear to do so by all the means available and at the cost of any good taste and any aesthetic considerations. Thus I make my VOW OF CHASTITY. (DFI 2005: 4–5)

Since it was first announced in Paris in 1995 Dogme 95 has evolved through a number of distinct, yet overlapping phases (Hjort 2003a). During the first of these phases, lasting from 1995 to 1998, when the first Dogme film, Vinterberg's *Festen* (*The Celebration*) (1998), won the Jury's Special Prize at Cannes, Dogme was often dismissed as a rather silly, attention-grabbing stunt. During this initial phase Dogme was also plagued by controversy having to do with the Danish Film Institute's decision *not* to provide block funding for the first four Dogme films, all of which were to be made by the brethren themselves. Dogme moved into a second phase in 1998, when *The Celebration* and von Trier's *Idioterne* (*The Idiots*) (1998) clearly established that abidance by the Vow of Chastity's rules could result in genuinely innovative and worthwhile cinematic works. French actor-turned-director Jean-Marc Barr released *Dogme 5: Lovers* in 1999, and this film marks the beginnings of a third phase involving an increasingly global circulation and appropriation of the Dogme concept in film milieus. This third phase overlaps with a fourth that sees the extension of Dogme's manifesto- and rule-based thinking to other areas of creative expression – to dance, computer game design, and literature, for example. During this period Lars von Trier seemed intent on sustaining the Dogme program for he himself extended it to a new area, that of documentary filmmaking, with the announcement of a new "Dogumentary" manifesto and a "documentarist code" consisting of nine rules. The point of these rules, the manifesto indicated, was to oppose "the documentary and television reality which has become more and more manipulated and filtered by camera people, editors and directors" (C. Christensen 2003: 186–7). Six films by Scandinavian directors have been made according to this code. The most well-known of these is Michael Klint's award-winning film entitled *Get a Life* (2004), a rather self-absorbed and in many other ways objectionable portrait of young Nigerian children suffering from a disease known as noma. By 2001, a fifth phase was clearly evident, and this one is characterized by the transformation of the term "Dogme" into a virtue term – often signifying opposition to oppressive realities and a related commitment to democratic practice – that could be mobilized in virtually any context. Hong Kong filmmaker Vincent Chui Wan-shun's *Youyou chouchou de zou le* (*Leaving in Sorrow*) (2001) can be seen as the start of a sixth phase, in which filmmakers consciously opt to align themselves with Dogme, but without feeling any obligation to follow all of the rules or any desire to seek formal Dogme certification. By 2002, in short, Dogme had become a well-established brand, a useful platform, especially for emerging directors. Dogme's reception in the People's Republic of China (PRC) brings to light yet another phase, one characterized by Dogme's transformation into something resembling a general philosophy of filmmaking. Ning Ying, for example, regards Dogme's normative claims about what film is and should be as having been a decisive influence during the making of the last film in her Beijing trilogy, *Xiari nuanyangyang* (*I Love Beijing*) (2001) (roundtable discussion, Szeto 2006). Ning's claim, possibly debatable, is that had she chosen to make *I Love Beijing* as a fully fledged Dogme film, the result would have been an underground film without the potential, as a result, to open the eyes of Chinese audiences to the impact of globalization and urbanization on contemporary Chinese life in a post-Mao era. Refusing such marginalization, the only choice, she insists, was to make the film in accordance with the established methods of state-sanctioned filmmaking. In the PRC, then, a perceived tension between Dogme's dicta and the requirements of state legitimacy has worked to transform Dogme from a rule-governed method and brand into an inspirational philosophy of filmmaking, in which concepts of truth, authenticity, realism, and contemporaneity figure centrally.

This brief sketch of Dogme's transformations over the years would not be complete without reference to the shifts that have occurred with regard to the issue of Dogme certification. At the outset, a given film's status as a bona fide Dogme film hinged on a successfully completed vetting process. Aspiring Dogme filmmakers were, in short, expected to submit their films to the Dogme Secretariat in Copenhagen (consisting of the brethren), who determined whether the rules had been observed and whether a Dogme certificate could be legitimately granted. This vetting practice was, however, abandoned when the brethren, after assessing and certifying Harmony Korine's film *Julien Donkey-Boy* (1999), realized just how difficult it was to ascertain rule abidance:

> To the best of our knowledge [they claimed on their website], *Julien Donkey-Boy* does, indeed, observe the Dogme criteria to a satisfactory extent ... Considering the fact that there are numerous problems connected with our review of aspiring Dogme films, we have decided on a change of practice when issuing Dogme certificates. In the future the director himself is solemnly to declare his adherence to the Dogme 95 Manifesto. (Cited in Kelly 2000: 33)

Vetting was thus replaced with a practice of solemn declarations of intent. On 20 March 2005 the brethren went one step further in a "Farewell [to Dogme] Manifesto," in which they announced that from Dogme's tenth anniversary onward the certificate would be available online, its use by various directors being entirely a matter of individual conscience, requiring neither vetting nor declarations of either intended or actual adherence to the rules.

There has been much discussion among film scholars and critics over the years of Dogme's antecedents. Von Trier's polemical gesture, it is often claimed, clearly recalls earlier moments in the history of film. Dziga Vertov's *Kino Pravda* is typically cited in this connection, as are Italian neorealism, Jean-Luc Godard's *Groupe Dziga Vertov*, and even the Oberhausen manifesto. For Scott MacKenzie, whose main interest is to determine the specificity and especially the unusual efficacy of Dogme's manifesto, Lindsay Anderson's Free Cinema movement provides an important reference point: "Like Dogma, Free Cinema functioned both as a new way to make films and as a *publicity stunt* [emphasis added] in order to garner recognition within the public sphere" (MacKenzie 2003: 51). Focusing on the "hand-held shooting style" that has come to be associated with Dogme, Murray Smith, by contrast, draws attention to "New American Cinema directors like John Cassavetes and Shirley Clarke" who pioneered this style in the area of fiction filmmaking some forty years before Dogme (Smith 2003: 114). For Peter Schepelern (2003) and Jack Stevenson (2003), these same figures are also an important part of Dogme's prehistory.

While Danish scholars acknowledge the relevance of all the sources just mentioned, they invariably emphasize a quite different trajectory of ideas, one centered on Lars von Trier himself and connecting different periods in his cinematic production. As Schepelern remarks, "Throughout his career, von Trier has set special rules for each production. The rules were usually a kind of production code used on the set and would typically establish some technical rules or aesthetic line to be followed" (Schepelern 2003: 58–9; see also O. Christensen 2004). The central concept of Dogme 95, which is that of creativity under constraint, is thus not one that Lars von Trier first adopted in connection with his cinematic "rescue action," but one that has informed his work as a director from the very beginning. In the context of von Trier's oeuvre, what is new about Dogme is the director's decision to *share* the rules with viewers in a metacultural Vow that was also an invitation to collectivism and a key factor in Dogme's globalization (Hjort 2003a).

Inasmuch as the concept of creativity under constraint lies at the heart of Dogme 95, this cinematic initiative directly contacts key areas of philosophical concern.

The Norwegian philosopher Jon Elster is largely responsible for putting "creativity under constraint" on the contemporary philosophical agenda, although the history of thinking about art, including artists' reflexive awareness of their practices, certainly recognizes the existence of the phenomenon. Elster's thinking about creativity under constraint has evolved over the years. In an early article on the topic, Elster (1992) focuses on technological, monetary, temporal, and self-imposed constraints, pursuing at all times the idea that such constraints need not be negative and can on the contrary enhance creativity. In *Ulysses Unbound: Studies in Rationality, Precommitment, and Constraints* (2000), Elster proposes a revised model of constraints, opting to work with a distinction among imposed, chosen, and invented constraints. In this new approach, technological, monetary, and temporal constraints all belong in the category of imposed constraints. Genre formulas serve to illustrate the category of chosen constraints, for the regularities that define specific genres cannot be invented by any single filmmaker or author but can instead be adopted as the overarching framework for a given work. The category of invented constraints is particularly important, given Elster's guiding concern, which is to understand how creativity is enhanced by constraints. An analysis of the different cases in which artists have chosen to invent constraints and reflexively to impose them on their own practices suggests, claims Elster, that the point of such exercises is to maximize inspiration and thus aesthetic value and creativity, the latter being "the ability to succeed in this endeavor" (2000: 200). Elster often returns to Georges Perec's decision to write the three-hundred page novel, *La disparition* (*A Void*) as a lipogram, in which the common vowel *e* would be systematically omitted. On Elster's view, Perec's invented and self-imposed constraint is entirely arbitrary, the point being simply to be constrained, but not necessarily in a particular way. The emphasis on the arbitrariness of invented and self-imposed constraints has been contested by the aesthetician Jerrold Levinson (2003), who, rightly in my view, points out that a ban on the letter *e* presents a far greater challenge than would the omission of any number of other letters, and in this and other ways Perec's choice cannot be viewed as entirely arbitrary. The point, it would appear, was to invent and reflexively impose a constraint that would genuinely pose difficulties with regard to the use of the French language.

In the context of Dogme, it is important to recognize that the rules outlined in the Vow of Chastity belong to different categories, depending on the identity of the filmmaker in question. In the case of von Trier and Vinterberg, the constraints are invented and self-imposed. In the case of the other two brethren the rules are largely chosen, inasmuch as Kragh-Jacobsen and Levring had no say in the initial articulation of the rules (although they were involved in the decision to interpret rule number 9 – "The film format must be Academy 35 mm" – as a distribution rather than production requirement). For all nonbrethren filmmakers the rules belong to the category of chosen constraints, in the sense that these rules constitute a preexisting framework with which filmmakers desiring to align themselves with von Trier's movement and/or brand, or with his approach to creativity, can *opt* to work.

A key question, relevant, as we have seen, to ongoing philosophical debates about the nature of invented constraints, concerns the extent to which Dogme's rules can be considered arbitrary. During the early phases of Dogme's reception, when von Trier's initiative was the butt of many a joke, the dominant tendency was to see the rules as motivated, rather than arbitrary, as fueled by a desire quite simply to create as much publicity as possible. If we are to understand the point of Dogme, it is in fact necessary to set aside the intuition, strong in Elster's work, that invented constraints are likely to be arbitrary. A careful examination of the Dogme rules reveals that they are "multiply motivated" (Hjort 2003a: 35). In Jesper Jargil's masterful documentary about the Dogme brethren and their films, *De lutrede* (*The Purified*) (2002), von Trier and Vinterberg suggest that emotions other than the aversion for standardized, commercialized, cinematic practices mentioned above played a role in the articulation of the rules. It was a matter, more specifically, of identifying, and then proscribing, the very techniques and technological devices for which these two filmmakers had demonstrated a clear preference in their earlier works. The goal, it is clear, was indeed to stimulate creativity, and in order to achieve this, it was necessary to prescribe an approach that would make it impossible to rely on comfortable habits, pregiven solutions, or on already existing expertise.

There is another sense, equally important, in which the rules are motivated rather than arbitrary, and this has to do with Dogme's anticipated (and now actualized) role as a "rescue action" aimed not only at film more generally, as the manifesto claimed, but at contemporary Danish film as a small, minor, and peripheral – all pertinent terms – cinema. In conversation with Richard Kelly on the topic of Dogme as a brand, Vinterberg claimed that the idea with Dogme was to "awaken" and "challenge" directors, and not "to make cheap films" (cited in Kelly 2000: 123). Yet, the rules were clearly formulated with the realities of small-nation filmmaking in mind (Hjort 2003b). And one of the defining features of such realities, as Vinca Wiedemann remarked in her capacity as director of New Danish Screen, is limited resources: "as a small nation, Denmark is completely limited by the available film subsidies … Every time someone makes a film they should be thinking low-budget" (Skotte 2006). Rules forbidding the use of props, proscribing "temporal and geographical alienation" and ruling out the use of "special lighting" all help to reduce costs significantly. As von Trier rightly says,

> Mainly it has made the process much cheaper which of course also pleases me. And it has led to a trend where people around the world have started making these cheap, cheap Dogme films … people who used to be limited by a notion of how a proper film should be … now feel that they can make films. (Rundle 1999)

The rules help to legitimate visual styles that depart noticeably from those, increasingly accepted as normative throughout the world, that require ultrahigh budgets. In keeping with its definition as a "rescue action" Dogme's invented rules are anything but arbitrary, involving instead a diagnosis of personal crutches and habits, of problems endemic to a global film system controlled largely by Hollywood, and of challenges associated with small-nation contexts. Dogme has much to contribute to the philosophical discussion of creativity under constraint, for it clearly shows that nonarbitrary constraints can facilitate the pursuit of creativity as an aesthetic goal while creating the conditions for achieving a number of other ends.

A second important point of contact between Dogme and key philosophical debates concerns the very concept, so central to the movement, of rule-following (Gaut 2003; Hjort 2003b). The Dogme brethren have made a number of pronouncements that highlight the difficulties of rule-following. Von Trier, for example, points out that "Many of the rules can't be kept or are as impossible to keep as the commandment 'Love your neighbour like yourself'" (Rundle 1999: 1). Reflecting on Dogme's rule-based approach, Vinterberg admits the possibility that none of the certified Dogme films merits its certificate:

> My film, Lars's film, all the films I've seen so far are definitely shot in accordance with Dogme 95 as a philosophy, and also as a set of rules – they follow them as closely as possible. I consider them Dogme films at heart. But then, if you apply the Rules strictly, there's a discussion left at the end of the day as to whether there have really been any Dogme films made yet? And my answer would be, "No." Not if you're truly rigid about it. (Cited in Kelly 2000: 122)

And in Jargil's *The Purified*, the brethren conclude that while von Trier's *The Idiots* comes closest to observing the rules, none of the brethren's films fully observes the rules. Rules, the brethren discovered during the process of making their respective films, may be difficult to interpret, for what is actually logically *entailed* by a given rule is not always clear. What is more, during the process of vetting Harmony Korine's film, they realized that the process of specifying what is to count as an instance of rule abidance is deeply problematic for evidentiary reasons and that a lot of audio-visual material may well be the result of either rule abidance or rule transgression. As Kristian Levring puts it,

> You can easily shoot in slow motion without breaking the Rules. But you'll still have people saying, "Is it Dogme?" Harmony's film looked to me like it had been shot according to the Rules. But if you really want to enforce this, you have to go on the shoot. (Cited in Kelly 2000: 56)

Many of the more successful Dogme films were accompanied by flamboyant, mock-serious confessions of transgressions, some of them highlighting momentary weaknesses in the form of avoidable departures from the rule-governed framework, others the impossibility of following some of the rules. Thus, for example, Vinterberg confessed to having constructed the reception desk in *The Celebration*, a transgression of the rule proscribing props not found on location. Kragh-Jacobsen confessed to violating the rule that prohibits "special lighting," by having worked creatively with fabrics. And Harmony Korine confessed to having violated the Dogme rules by simulating the pregnancy of Chloë Sevigny's character – after alleged attempts actually to impregnate his actress girlfriend. These confessions were, of course, entirely consistent with the reality of Dogme as an ingenious publicity stunt. Evoking the rules through the thematization of transgression, these absurd – but also quite amusing – confessions fueled talk about the individual films and the movement more generally, thereby contributing to Dogme's visibility and impact.

The Dogme brethren's various utterances about rules and rule-following suggest a certain philosophical naïveté about the matter. Indeed, whereas the Dogme phenomenon appears to rest on a coherent, and even incisive, conception of creativity under constraint, the underlying views on rule-following seem somewhat muddled. Indeed, the aesthetician Berys Gaut makes the perfectly valid point that "had the brethren read Wittgenstein, they might have saved themselves a lot of trouble" (2003: 98). Gaut is referring here to Wittgenstein's skeptical solution to the paradox of rule-following in *Philosophical Investigations* (1953: §143f.). The relevant passages have given rise over the years to numerous commentaries that have helped to make rules and rule-following a central issue in the philosophy of language. Most influential among these commentaries is Saul Kripke's not uncontroversial *Wittgenstein on Rules and Private Language: An Elementary Exposition* (1982), a text that itself has spawned considerable discussion. In the present context it is not possible, or necessary for that matter, to identify the various positions that have been adopted in response to these and other key texts. The point that needs to be made is that the Dogme initiative seems to have been developed without any real grasp of the following problems:

> any set of rules must fail to cover all aspects of every action, simply because there is an infinite number of properties that any action may possess; moreover, any rule is subject to interpretation, and thus can be complied with in any number of ways. And do not suppose that if one could agree on the rule's interpretation, all would be settled – any interpretation is itself a rule, which can itself be interpreted in different ways. (Gaut 2003: 98)

What the Dogme brethren's utterances, confessions, and shifting policies on certification jointly show, perhaps, is the necessity of bringing two separate philosophical discussions together: to the extent that creativity under constraint involves invented *rules*, scholars involved in theorizing the relevant phenomenon might usefully engage with the philosophical literature on rules and the conundra of rule-following.

Dogme 95, I have suggested, has the potential to contribute to the philosophical debate on creativity under constraint, just as the Dogme brethren and their followers stand to learn from the philosophical discussion of rules and rule-following. In conclusion, I would like to focus on philosophers' engagement with very particular aspects of the manifesto and films. In "Naked Film: Dogma and Its Limits," Berys Gaut looks closely at the first two Dogme films, Vinterberg's *The Celebration* and von Trier's *The Idiots* – the point being to show that "not only are the films instances of the rules … they are also *about* the rules" (Gaut 2003: 93). Drawing on Kendall Walton's concept of the "apparent artist," Gaut describes the "apparent director of von Trier's film" as follows:

He allows a cameraman and a sound boom to appear in some shots; many shots are out of focus, clumsily framed and sometimes mismatched; he seems not to have heard of standard shot/countershot techniques of filming; in conversations, the camera pans from one speaker to another, often without reaching the person who is speaking in time; the axis of action is crossed; the image often wobbles unsteadily; the editing is abrupt and badly handled; shots are composed with no apparent consideration as to their colour balance or formal qualities; and so on. The apparent director of this film is spectacularly incompetent and deeply ignorant of film-making. (Gaut 2003: 94)

Given that von Trier has an unassailable reputation as "one of the most accomplished film-makers of his generation" (Gaut 2003: 94), it is clear that there is a discrepancy here between the nature of the apparent artist and that of the actual artist. Von Trier, Gaut argues, is engaging in the very activity that is represented in his film – spassing or pretending to be an idiot, the point of which is to reveal the truth of a given situation, one of the central goals of Dogme 95 itself.

Gaut also contributes to a more fine-grained philosophical understanding of the manifesto by looking closely at the rules and the extent to which they secure the realism that the Dogme brethren are often held to be advocating. Dogme's rejection of the "film of illusion," best understood in Gaut's view as a type of filmmaking that encourages "false beliefs about the world" (2003: 90), provides yet another way of understanding the precise nature of the rules identified in the Vow of Chastity. While many of these rules do in fact support the aim of showing "how the world really is" (Gaut 2003: 91), Gaut contends that "there are limits on how well the rules secure realism" (98). In support of this line of argument, Gaut introduces an insightful distinction between what he calls "content realism" and "perceptual realism" (Gaut 2003: 98), two types of realism that can be pursued independently. Gaut goes on to show that there is nothing in the Dogme rules to stop directors from opting for "extremely odd characters and situations that depart from their real world counterparts" (Gaut 2003: 98) (and thus undermine content realism), just as there are no constraints requiring filmmakers to favor "unobtrusive editing and very long takes (which are more like our normal way of seeing)" (Gaut 2003: 99). In this instance, philosophical arguments and distinctions help to tease out some of the conceptual problems with Dogme's programmatic statements and rule-governed framework.

Paisley Livingston is another philosopher who has tried to clarify aspects of the manifesto's call for action. Focusing on the undefined concept of "film of illusion" to which Dogme is opposed, Livingston argues that illusion is best understood, not as "cinematic representation *per se*" (Livingston 2003: 103), nor as fiction, but as fantasy. Following Livingston, fantasy may be thought of as a type of fiction that involves certain hedonic rewards:

Although many fictions are like fantasy in that their imaginative contents involve radical departures from actuality, fantasy is unlike fiction in that it must in addition hinge upon a hedonically rewarding orientation towards events which are deemed by the fantasiser to be "out of reach." (Livingston 2003: 103)

On this reading of the manifesto, Dogme 95 targets a "hedonically motivated exploitation of cinematic artistry and rhetoric" (Livingston 2003: 104), which, once again, helps to explain the specific nature of the Vow's rules. Here too, the introduction of a clear (philosophical) distinction helps to make sense of some of the manifesto's key pronouncements.

Dogme 95's success in profiling the efforts of a number of small-nation filmmakers, in creating a globalized movement, and in producing a number of remarkable cinematic works guarantees this initiative a place in film history. With its manifesto and rules, Dogme 95 has also prompted filmmakers, critics, viewers, and philosophers to think carefully, and sometimes creatively, about the deeper purposes of filmmaking. As such its philosophical dimensions, and contributions, are undeniable.

Acknowledgments

The work described in this paper was partially supported by a grant from the Research Grants Council of the Hong Kong Special Administrative Region, China (Project No. LU340407). I am very grateful for this support.

See also Realism (Chapter 22) and *The Five Obstructions* (Chapter 58).

References

Christensen, C. (2003) "Documentary Gets the Dogma Treatment," in M. Hjort and S. MacKenzie (eds.) *Purity and Provocation: Dogma 95*, London: British Film Institute.
Christensen, O. (2004) "Nøgne billeder og usminkede fortællinger," in O. Christensen (ed.) *Nøgne billeder: De danske dogmefilm*, Copenhagen: Medusa.
DFI (Danish Film Institute) (2005) *FILM* (special issue, Dogme).
Elster, J. (1992) "Conventions, Creativity, Originality," in M. Hjort (ed.) *Rules and Conventions: Literature, Philosophy, Social Theory*, Baltimore, MD: Johns Hopkins University Press.
—— (2000) *Ulysses Unbound: Studies in Rationality, Precommitment, and Constraints*, Cambridge: Cambridge University Press.
Gaut, B. (2003) "Naked Film: Dogma and Its Limits," in M. Hjort and S. MacKenzie (eds.) *Purity and Provocation: Dogma 95*, London: British Film Institute.
Gilbey, R. (2002) "Dogme is Dead. Long Live Dogme," *Guardian* (London) (18 April). Available at http://film.guardian.co.uk/features/featurepages/0,,686645,00.html.
Hjort, M. (2003a) "The Globalisation of Dogma: The Dynamics of Metaculture and Counter-Publicity," in M. Hjort and S. MacKenzie (eds.) *Purity and Provocation: Dogma 95*, London: British Film Institute.
—— (2003b) "A Small Nation's Response to Globalisation," in M. Hjort and S. MacKenzie (eds.) *Purity and Provocation: Dogma 95*, London: British Film Institute.
Kelly, R. (2000) *The Name of this Book is Dogme 95*, London: Faber and Faber.
Kripke, S. (1982) *Wittgenstein on Rules and Private Language: An Elementary Exposition*, Oxford: Basil Blackwell.
Levinson, J. (2003) "Elster on Artistic Creativity," in P. Livingston and B. Gaut (eds.) *The Creation of Art: New Essays in Philosophical Aesthetics*, New York: Cambridge University Press.

Livingston, P. (2003) "Artistic Self-Reflexivity in *The King is Alive* and *Strass*," in M. Hjort and S. MacKenzie (eds.) *Purity and Provocation: Dogma 95*, London: British Film Institute.

MacKenzie, S. (2003) "Manifest Destinies: Dogma 95 and the Future of the Film Manifesto," in M. Hjort and S. MacKenzie (eds.) *Purity and Provocation: Dogma 95*, London: British Film Institute.

Rundle, P. (1999) *We Are All Sinners: Interview with Lars von Trier*. Dogme 95 website. Available at www.dogme95.dk/news/interview/trier_interview2.htm.

Schepelern, P. (2003) "'Kill Your Darlings': Lars von Trier and the Origin of Dogma 95," in M. Hjort and S. MacKenzie (eds.) *Purity and Provocation: Dogma 95*, London: British Film Institute.

Skotte, K. (2006) "New Danish Screen," *FILM* 50. Available at www.dfi.dk/tidsskriftetfilm/50/screen.htm

Skotte, K., and Møller, H. J. (2005) "Slut med dogme-filmene," *Politiken* (19 March).

Smith, M. (2003) "Lars von Trier: Sentimental Surrealist," in M. Hjort and S. MacKenzie (eds.) *Purity and Provocation: Dogma 95*, London: British Film Institute.

Stevenson, J. (2003) *Dogme Uncut: Lars von Trier, Thomas Vinterberg, and the Gang that Took on Hollywood*, Santa Monica, CA: Santa Monica Press.

Szeto, M. (2006) Roundtable discussion with Ning Ying, Hong Kong: University of Hong Kong.

Wittgenstein, L. (1953) *Philosophical Investigations*, trans. G. E. M. Anscombe, Oxford: Basil Blackwell.

45
DOCUMENTARY
Carl Plantinga

In the past twenty years documentaries have become an increasingly important element of the cultural mainstream. During this period scholarship on the documentary has also begun to flourish. In this essay I identify the most salient philosophical issues having to do with the nature of documentary, issues in documentary representation, and the ethics of documentary filmmaking.

What is a documentary?

To define the documentary would be to identify the necessary and sufficient conditions of a documentary film. To characterize the documentary, by contrast, would be merely to identify its typical or usual characteristics. The latter might be taken to be insufficiently ambitious by some, while the former is often seen as an impossible task, especially by those who consider the documentary to be an open or fuzzy concept. In any case, both defining and characterizing the documentary have proven to be difficult. While some prefer to eschew the making of definitions and categories altogether, the task cannot be easily dismissed because most relevant theoretical discussions eventually depend on foundational assumptions about the nature and kinds of documentary (Plantinga 1997: 7–39).

It is worth briefly examining the emergence of the word "documentary" for reasons that will become clear below. John Grierson, the early champion of the form, is thought to have been the first to use the term "documentary" in English, having done so in relation to Robert Flaherty's 1926 *Moana*. The word regularly appeared in English by the 1930s, by which time it designated a "higher" order of nonfiction film in which, as Grierson writes, "we pass from the plain ... descriptions of natural material, to arrangements, re-arrangements, and creative shapings of it" (Grierson 1932). Grierson established the tradition of elevating the documentary to a status above the broader category of nonfiction film, based on the documentarian's "creative shapings" of "natural material." Thus despite the fact that "documentary" seems to imply a film that is merely or primarily a "document," Grierson held that it is in fact an art form rather than the mechanical documentation of some bit of reality. The documentary, as he defines it, does not consist merely of "natural material," by which we might extrapolate that he means moving images as traces or unvarnished records of profilmic events (that is, whatever actually occurred before the camera). To take the documentary film as a mere photographic document ignores the "creative shaping" that is an ineluctable element of all documentary films, and that occurs in diverse registers such as narrative or rhetorical structure, editing, cinematography, sound design, and more controversially, reenactments and even the manipulation of profilmic events.

The ubiquitous-fiction and ubiquitous-documentary claims

Arguments have been made that all films are fiction films, and conversely, that all films are documentaries. The role of the documentary film as both a document and a creative shaping has been seen by some to be contradictory, and this has in turn been taken as somehow supporting the charge that all films are in fact fiction films. Jacques Aumont *et al.*, for example, follow the lead of Christian Metz in their claim that "every film is a fiction film" (Aumont *et al.* 1992: 77). Such an argument, as Noël Carroll notes, "posits the celluloid reproduction of a *ding-an-sich* as the goal of nonfiction, notes the impossibility of the task and declares all films fictional" (Carroll 1996: 237). The "ubiquitous-fiction" thesis holds, then, that all creative manipulations of the "documentary material" are necessarily fictional. And indeed this has been the position not only of some theorists but also a few documentary filmmakers. Thus direct-cinema filmmaker Frederick Wiseman, for example, has insisted that "reality fictions" is a more appropriate label for his films than "documentaries" because selection and editing are a "fictionalization" of the photographic materials that ostensibly qualify as documents in themselves (Benson and Anderson 1989).

The ubiquitous-fiction thesis would seem to take the surveillance video as the closest approximation to a documentary, in that it preserves the indexical nature of the moving image and involves little human intentionality or creative intervention. Yet this position would seemingly rule out all nonfiction communication. All of human communication involves the selection, omission, and arrangement of signs and decisions about what to show or say and how to show or say it. This is true of the documentary film just as it is for written journalism and history, instruction manuals, wedding announcements, political speeches, and indeed all forms of nonfiction discourse.

Other scholars have insisted that all films are in fact documentaries; we might call this the ubiquitous-documentary thesis. The first chapter of Bill Nichols' introductory textbook begins with this very claim: "Every film is a documentary" because it "gives evidence of the culture that produced it and reproduces the likenesses of the people who perform in it" (Nichols 1991: 1). *The Wizard of Oz* (1939), then, is a documentary because it features moving photographic images of Judy Garland and other actors and because it may serve as a kind of anthropological document providing clues about late 1930s Hollywood and American culture. The ubiquitous-documentary argument assumes that documentaries are essentially documents, notes that all films are documents of something or other, then declares that all films are documentaries. Yet documentary films cannot be reduced to the provision of documentation. When documentaries do incorporate photography for its value as evidence and proof, it is usually in support of some argument or claim that emerges not only from photographs and sounds, but also from their intentional organization. The overall project of a documentary film is to assert a kind of veridical or truthful representation that differs in significant ways from fiction (more on this later). Thus a documentary film resembles an illustrated historical essay or written journalism accompanied by photographs. To confuse a document with a documentary film is a serious error in categorization. The documentary film is not just a document, though it may make use of documents.

Documentary as a mode of reception

Closely related to the ubiquitous-documentary claim is the argument that "documentary" is a mode of reception. This argument seems to be that (1) all films can be comprehended nonfictionally or as documentaries; and/or that (2) the distinction between fiction and nonfiction is a function of audience reception. The strongest statement of this view would argue that the fiction/nonfiction distinction is a matter of reception rather than of text or context. Dirk Eitzen argues, for example, that the documentary is "not a kind of text but ... a kind of 'reading'" (Eitzen 1992: 92). Thus Eitzen argues that the audience can "read" Spike Lee's School Daze as a documentary (or as I would put it, as a document) or Ken Burns' The Civil War as "entirely make-believe," if it wishes. Ed Branigan claims that one can comprehend any film either fictionally or nonfictionally, the difference lying in the "method or procedure for making decisions about assigning reference" (Branigan 1992: 88). All films, the claim goes, have a nonfictional dimension and can provide evidence of their historical situation and effects. And Brian Winston has argued that the documentary suffers from a "crisis of legitimacy" because it falsely claims to "capture" the real. The documentary can be "justified" only by admitting that the difference between fiction and nonfiction film lies in "the mind of the audience" (Winston 1995: 253).

We may grant the "documentary-as-a-mode-of-reception" proponent that the documentary can never fully reproduce the Ding an sich and that all fiction films may be seen as documents of something or other. Yet the claim for documentary as a mode of reception faces problems (Plantinga 2000). First, it mistakes a document for a documentary film. Second, the position fails to take into account the social nature of definitions. That is, if the fiction/nonfiction distinction is all in the mind, or is a function of the way that individuals "read" a film, then the distinction becomes highly individualistic and subjective, as though the individual were the ultimate arbiter of a film genre or type. Consider an analogy. A culture often defines human artifacts according to their design and function. A screwdriver is designed to put in screws and a hammer to pound in and remove nails. Of course, I am free to use the hammer in my attempts to tighten a screw, but it wasn't designed for that function and my attempts may come to naught. Furthermore, although I am free to use the hammer for all sorts of purposes for which it was not originally designed, I cannot define the hammer in any way I see fit. This is because definitions are socially and not individually constructed.

In a similar way, I am free to use *Star Wars* in ways that were not intended, for example, as a soporific or as a religious devotional text. Yet I am not free to see it as a documentary, because its definition is not mine to alter. I cannot redefine a screwdriver as a hammer, a jelly bean as grilled halibut, or *Star Wars* as nonfiction. The status of a film as fiction or documentary is a social construction rooted in the communicative function documentaries are thought to play in social discourse. As I shall mention below, arguably the intentions of the relevant makers have a major role to play in the classification of artifacts, including symbolic artifacts like movies.

Trace accounts

The two most prominent attempts to define or characterize the documentary in the analytic tradition are the "documentary-as-trace" account of Gregory Currie and the various "communicative action" accounts. To understand Currie's theory, one must first understand his notion of the photograph as a "trace" and how traces differ from "testimonies." Both testimonies and traces are signs or communications that carry information. A testimony is the record of what someone thought about something; testimonies are belief dependent. Traces, by contrast, are records that are, to some extent, independent of belief. Photographs are traces, Currie claims, because they are independent of belief in a way that paintings (and other testimonies) are not. Documentary films, Currie claims, are films that are predominantly made up of traces. But most fiction films use images that are traces as well. A moving image of Cary Grant playing Roger O. Thornhill in *North by Northwest* (1959) is a trace, though it is a photograph that does not represent "what it is of," since it is a moving photograph of Cary Grant but it fictionally represents Roger O. Thornhill. What then distinguishes the fiction film from the documentary? The "Ideal" documentary, Currie argues, is "a filmically sustained narrative the constitutive film images of which represent only photographically: they represent only what they are of" (Currie 1999: 291). That is, a documentary film is a sustained discourse that makes use of moving or still photographs as traces to represent what the photographic images are of.

Currie's definition of the documentary is subject to various criticisms (Carroll 2003: 225–33; Choi 2001; Plantinga 2005). Like many before him, Currie closely identifies the documentary with documents and documentation, rather than taking the documentary to be fundamentally a structured rhetorical discourse. This is no doubt a lingering influence of the direct cinema or cinema verité movements of the late 1950s and 1960s. Cinéma vérité filmmakers emphasized the recording capacities of documentary filmmaking equipment and advocated an aesthetic of authenticity that eschewed the manipulations of the filmmaker. Yet the first sixty-five years of documentary were very different than this. Robert Flaherty, John Grierson, and Humphrey Jennings, for example, were not hesitant to employ stagings and re-creations of events under that banner of documentary filmmaking. Documentary filmmaking of the past twenty years has embraced a return to earlier forms and a rejection of the tenets and restrictions of cinéma vérité. To return to John Grierson's early characterization of the documentary, Currie's theory embraces the "natural material" – the traces – but discards Grierson's "arrangements, re-arrangements, and creative shapings of it" as nondocumentary material. Thus Currie's definition fits the cinéma vérité style of filmmaking better than documentaries that make use of voice-over narration and other creative techniques.

Communicative-action accounts

What I here call the "communicative-action" accounts characterize or define the documentary as a kind of speech act or communicative action. Communicative-action accounts draw from speech act theory and tend to find the distinguishing feature of the documentary to be a kind of illocutionary act (John Austin's term for that part of a speech act in which the person uses words, gestures, or some other expressive means to perform one of several kinds of actions, such as making an assertion, a request or an apology). In the case of documentary, the paradigmatic action is taken to be the making of an assertion about the actual world. Drawing on Nicholas Wolterstorff's theory of projected worlds, I have argued that through every representational work of art (and here I include documentaries under the rubric "art") an agent projects a "world" (Plantinga 1987, 1997: 16–19). In fiction the agent takes a fictive stance toward the world projected through the work, meaning that the state of affairs presented is not asserted to obtain in the actual world but rather that it is presented for the entertainment and edification of the audience. In nonfiction, the filmmaker takes the assertive stance, presenting states of affairs as occurring in the actual world. Thus the characteristic illocutionary act of the documentary filmmaker is to present the world of the work assertively.

Both Noël Carroll and Trevor Ponech have offered similar communicative-action accounts of the documentary. Carroll employs what he calls an "intention-response" model of communication that presupposes that the artist or maker of a work indicates that the audience is meant to respond in a certain way. Carroll calls the documentary a "film of presumptive assertion" because in presenting it the filmmaker intends that the audience entertain the propositional content of his film in thought as asserted (Carroll 1997). Carroll introduced the useful notion of "indexing" to demonstrate the means by which filmmakers (and the institutions of distribution) identify films for audiences as fictions or documentaries. Except in the case of hybrid films and docudramas (see the references in "Further reading" below), audiences typically view a film that is identified as fiction or nonfiction. Indexing cues the audience to undertake conventionally appropriate modes of reception and approach the film with certain expectations (Carroll 1996: 232).

Trevor Ponech argues that documentaries are "cinematic assertions" that consist at their core of "the action of indication." "To perform a cinematic assertion," he writes, "is to employ a motion picture medium ... with the expressed intention that the viewer form or continue to hold the attitude of belief toward certain states of affairs, objects, situations, events, propositions, and so forth, where the relevant states of affairs ... need not actually exist" (Ponech 1997: 204). Ponech's theory is intention-alist (as opposed to Carroll's intention-response theory) in that it locates the essence of documentary in the intentions of the filmmakers. Those intentions are discoverable in the plans the filmmakers develop in making the work, and in the manifestation of those plans in the finished films (Ponech 1999: 8–39).

Consider once more Grierson's definition of a documentary as a film that takes "natural materials" and creatively shapes and reshapes them. The documentary-as-trace definition takes this creative shaping and reshaping as not properly documentary. The communicative-action accounts, however, seem too beholden to a linguistic and "utterance" model of communication. How does making claims and assertions function in a medium of recorded images and sounds? Trevor Ponech suggests a distinction between linguistic and cinematic assertions. Cinematic assertion, for Ponech, is the determination of content and the expression of communicative force through the myriad techniques and devices available to filmmakers (Ponech 1999: 20–3). Yet although this gets us part of the way, it is not fully sufficient. Documentary moving or still images are not necessarily assertive in this way, but are sometimes used as traces in Currie's sense. They sometimes show rather than say, and thus leave some of the propositional content of their moving images and sounds unspecified (Plantinga 2005: 111). Such photographs and sounds, for example, may be used to communicate the look or feel of an event. The apprehension conditions for such phenomenological qualities may be nonlinguistic in nature; to grasp them we must view the scene. In response to this problem I have argued that we should take the documentary as an "asserted veridical representation." In the case of its propositional content, a documentary is meant to be taken as truthful; in the case of its recorded images and sounds and their ordering, it is designed to be taken as a reliable guide to relevant elements of the profilmic scene, without necessarily being taken as a particular account of the scene's propositional content (Plantinga 2005). The notion of asserted veridical representation would allow for diverse documentary styles and techniques, while holding that the illocutionary act characteristic of the typical documentary is to provide veridical, that is, an implicitly truthful, reliable, and/or accurate representation.

Issues in documentary representation

Some of the best-known scholars of the documentary approach the mode from the standpoint of a thoroughgoing skepticism about the ability of the documentary to represent reality with truthfulness, accuracy, or objectivity. Some would call this approach postmodernist or post-structuralist, but since those terms are vague, I will refer to the position as the skeptical position. The skeptical position may be opposed to "critical realism," the view that in some cases, the documentary can be truthful, accurate, and objective – or at the very least, its implicit epistemic claims can be rational and well justified.

The skeptical position derives from a general suspicion about any "optimistic" or positive accounts of knowledge (the target has various labels, including positivism, rationalism, scientism, but the core view can usually be characterized as some form of epistemic realism). Michael Renov, for example, identifies the mainstream documentary tradition's "self-assurance" with misplaced modernist certainty. He notes that much recent documentary theory, which could be called broadly skeptical, allies itself instead with "contingency, hybridity, knowledge as situated and particular, identity as ascribed and performed," and that these ideas are opposed to the ration-alist's "dreams of universal reason," predilection for "Truth in History," standards of objectivity, established protocols of inquiry, and the belief in disinterested knowledge (Renov 2004: 136–7).

The skeptical theorist rejects the possibility of objectivity in the documentary. The word "objectivity" is notoriously slippery, so it must be used with caution. Some believe that an objective documentary would be one in which all traces of subjec-tivity had been eliminated. Thus an objective film would eschew point of view, perspective, personal opinion, and, indeed, any mediation between filmmaker and actual world. Since such objectivity is impossible to achieve, Brian Winston holds that the entire project of documentary film can be questioned. Thus Winston finds a "profound contradiction" in the pronouncements of filmmaker Frederick Wiseman, who, on the one hand, claims to teach through his films, and on the other, admits that his editing makes his films subjective, or what he calls reality fictions. Shorn of their claim to objectivity, Winston believes that Wiseman's films become "mere opinion" and fall by the weight of Wiseman's admissions (Winston 1995: 48–9). What remains is Winston's questionable supposition that only objective documen-taries could have anything to teach, or that somehow the mediating presence of the filmmaker makes illicit all claims to veridical representation. This position assumes the very epistemic standards that Winston ostensibly opposes (Plantinga 1996: 313–14), and seems to hold that the admission of any sort of directorial manipulation or selection threatens all of the epistemic claims of the documentary film (Carroll 2003: 165–8). Surely Winston is right that if one defines an objective documentary as one that lacks any subjective or mediating element, then there are no objective documentaries. But we can safely reject the supposition that only documentaries objective in this very strong sense can provide information or serve a teaching function. Moreover, if objectivity cannot exist as an absolute if defined in this sense, it may still exist as a matter of degree or in some other, less other-worldly sense (Plantinga 1997: 212–13). Thus while no documentary film reaches the objective ideal of absolute realism, we might nonetheless find one documentary more objective than another.

Renov challenges objectivity by arguing, after Hayden White, that all documentary discourse resorts to tropes or rhetorical figures that are "added on," or in other words, that do not inherently exist in the reality being represented. The documentary makes use of narrative tropes such as irony, comedy, and tragedy, for example, devices such as closure and emphasis, and specifically filmic devices such as editing and flashbacks. None of these exists in the events being shown, and thus they are "distortions." Renov claims that "all discourse *constitutes* the objects which it pretends only to describe realistically and to analyze objectively" (Renov 1993: 7). Bill Nichols makes several arguments against documentary objectivity that are similar to Renov's and Winston's, and adds to these the charge that practices of objectivity often mask a political perspective (Nichols 1991: 195).

Noël Carroll has been the most ardent advocate for objectivity in the documentary. A piece of research or a documentary film, he writes, can be objective if it adheres "to the practices of reasoning and evidence gathering" in its field. It is objective "because it can be intersubjectively evaluated against standards of argument and evidence shared by practitioners" (Carroll 1996: 230–2). This definition of objectivity leaves the status of the objective documentary *vis-à-vis* reality undetermined, since a journalistic documentary, for example, might adhere to the standard practices of its profession (and thus qualify as objective) and yet be wholly mistaken or subtly biased in its claims. We may note, then, that Carroll's understanding of objectivity pertains more to justification than to truth. Yet Carroll also defends a more robust sense of objectivity (Carroll 2003: 165–92). At issue in these debates is the possibility of documentary veridicality and beyond that, of rational discourse itself.

Recently there has been much support for various notions of reflexivity and interactivity. The suspicion of epistemic certainty leads some to reject the traditional "voice of God" documentary in which the documentary speaks to what is conceived of as a passive spectator from a position of authority. What is promoted is an interactive or participatory text that makes meaning in collaboration with both subject and spectator (Renov 2004; Ruby 1988). Reflexivity is often promoted as a means of counteracting the tendency of documentaries to wear the mantle of epistemic authority, and to counteract the supposed gullibility of spectators. Winston claims, for example, that the discourses of science and evidence surrounding photography have become so pervasive that "the scientific and evidential ... are 'built-in' to the documentary cinematographic apparatus" (Winston 1995: 40–1) and that spectators will consequently tend to believe everything they see in a documentary. Thus skeptics often favor reflexive techniques that remind spectators of the mediated nature of documentary discourse, make the implicit perspectives of the filmmakers apparent, and perhaps even introduce a bit of epistemic humility into the film. These techniques can range from the overt presence of the filmmaker(s) in the film, to the showing of the camera and crew on screen, to collaboration with the film's subjects. I have argued that claims of epistemic benefits for reflexivity are exaggerated, in part because such claims depend on debatable assumptions about the documentary film (as pretending to "transparency") and the documentary spectator (as passive and gullible), and also because reflexivity guarantees neither a complexity of representation (what Nichols calls "magnitudes") nor accurate and sincere self-revelation on the part of the filmmaker (Plantinga 1997: 214–18).

The ethics of documentary filmmaking

Documentary films have the potential to significantly alter public perceptions and to seriously affect the lives of those whose images appear on film. Thus ethical concerns lie at the heart of documentary filmmaking, although ethics has sometimes been ignored or downplayed by theorists. The moral obligations of the documentary filmmaker extend to her- or himself, to the filmmaker's sponsoring institution or group affiliation, to the filmmaker's subjects, and to the audience. Ethical dilemmas often arise when obligations compete with or contradict one another, or strongly lead the filmmaker to consider unethical practices. This brief discussion of ethics in documentary filmmaking will confine itself to the ethical obligations of filmmakers to the audience and to subjects.

The documentary filmmaker's obligations to the audience are varied, but chief among them is the obligation not to deceive or mislead, or in other words, to strive for accuracy and truth (Plantinga 1997: 219–22). When a film is indexed as nonfiction, the audience is cued to receive the film as a vehicle for truth claims and a reliable photographic and aural account of its subject. Thus most audiences find something ethically unsavory, for example, about political advertisements that use blatantly unflattering photographs of political opponents, take quotes out of context, and present half-truths. It is worth noting from the outset that the skeptical position on the documentary, in its rejection of standards of evidence, truth-telling, and rational discourse, would arguably leave us with no method to determine whether a documentary is biased or deceptive, or even to distinguish between degrees of relative bias and deception. Without the appeal to such standards, how would we differentiate between blatant propaganda and objectivity? If objectivity does not exist, do all documentaries become equally propagandistic?

While blatant deception is clearly wrong, the most interesting cases are also the most subtle. Michael Moore's *Roger and Me* (1989) is at the center of one such controversy for the way in which it implies a false chronology of events for the purpose of creating a clear and entertaining narrative structure (Moore 1989). None of Moore's "white lies," however, compromises his overall argument about the bad citizenship of Roger Smith and General Motors in Flint, Michigan. Thus one might take the utilitarian position (with all of the problems that utilitarian ethics raises) that Moore's little deceptions are acceptable because his overall project leads to the greater good. One might also claim that Moore's manipulations of chronology in the film are standard documentary practice. For the documentary filmmaker, the smallest change of camera angle or lighting or composition, the selection of footage for inclusion, the music one chooses to accompany images – all documentary techniques come with a perspective. Thus one might claim that Moore's manipulation of historical chronology is one such inevitable manipulation. One might counter by arguing that the act of documentary filmmaking, however much it requires selection and creative mediation, is not inherently deceptive. Presumably Moore could have represented the chronology of historical events in his film *more accurately* had he chosen to do so. His decision was to sacrifice accuracy to make the film clear and entertaining, and such a decision is open to an ethical evaluation.

The chief ethical concern for documentary theorists has been the treatment of subjects by filmmakers. The presumption is that filmmakers owe a "duty of care" to those who appear in their films (Pryluck 1988). In both law and ethics, the "right to privacy" assumes that persons should be protected from intrusion, embarrassment, representation in a false light, and the appropriation of their image or words (Gross *et al.* 1988: 7–14). From an ethical standpoint, the interesting issues have to do with to whom the duty of care extends and in what contexts. For example, some would argue that Michael Moore was unethical in presenting some of the working poor in *Roger and Me* as buffoons, but nonetheless find no fault at all in his mocking portrayal of General Motors CEO Roger Smith or his footage of game-show host Bob Eubanks telling a racist joke. Context is also important; in some cases, the duty of care may be trumped by the public's right to know.

Central to these discussions is the idea of informed consent. Documentary filmmakers must typically have their subjects sign a release form allowing their image to be used in the film being made. Yet one cannot grant consent unless one has been adequately informed about the purposes and nature of the film and how the filmmaker will use the footage. Not only do filmmakers often have a vested interest in withholding information or misleading the subjects, but most subjects do not have a sufficient understanding of the documentary process to understand how their image might be used and what effect this might have on them (Anderson and Benson 1988). Thus documentary filmmaking inevitably leads to discussions of ethics that moral philosophy can illuminate.

See also Ethics (Chapter 10), Realism (Chapter 22), Spectatorship (Chapter 23), and Bertolt Brecht (Chapter 30).

References

Anderson, C., and Benson, T. (1988) "Direct Cinema and the Myth of Informed Consent," in L. Gross, J. Katz, and J. Ruby (eds.) *Image Ethics: The Moral Rights of Subjects in Photographs, Film, and Television*, New York: Oxford University Press.

Aumont, J., Bergala, A., Marie, M., and Vernet, M. (1992) *Aesthetics of Film*, rev. trans. R. Neupert, Austin: University of Texas Press.

Benson, T., and Anderson, C. (1989) *Reality Fictions: The Films of Frederick Wiseman*, Carbondale, IL: Southern Illinois University Press.

Branigan, E. (1992) *Narrative Comprehension and Film*, London and New York: Routledge.

Carroll, N. (1996) *Theorizing the Moving Image*, Cambridge and New York: Cambridge University Press.

—— (1997) "Fiction, Non-Fiction, and the Film of Presumptive Assertion: A Conceptual Analysis," in R. Allen and M. Smith (eds.) *Film Theory and Philosophy*, New York: Oxford University Press.

—— (2003) *Engaging the Moving Image*, New Haven, CT: Yale University Press.

Choi, J. (2001) "A Reply to Gregory Currie on Documentaries," *Journal of Aesthetics and Art Criticism* 59: 317–19.

Currie, G. (1999) "Visible Traces: Documentary and the Contents of Photographs," *Journal of Aesthetics and Art Criticism* 57: 285–97.

Eitzen, D. (1992) "When is a Documentary?: Documentary as a Mode of Reception," *Cinema Journal* 35: 81–102.

Grierson, J. (1932) "Documentary (1)," *Cinema Quarterly* 4: 67–72.

Gross, L., Katz, J., and Ruby, J. (1988) "Introduction: A Moral Pause," in L. Gross, J. Katz, and J. Ruby (eds.) *Image Ethics: The Moral Rights of Subjects in Photographs, Film, and Television*, New York: Oxford University Press.

Moore, M. (1989) "Michael and Me" (interview by Harlan Jacobson), *Film Comment* 25(6): 16–18, 20, 22–6.

Nichols, B. (1991) *Representing Reality*, Bloomington: Indiana University Press.

Plantinga, C. (1987) "Defining Documentary: Fiction, Nonfiction, and Projected Worlds," *Persistence of Vision* 5: 44–54.

—— (1996) "Moving Pictures and the Rhetoric of Nonfiction: Two Approaches," in D. Bordwell and N. Carroll (eds.) *Post-Theory: Reconstructing Film Studies*, Madison: University of Wisconsin Press.

—— (1997) *Rhetoric and Representation in Nonfiction Film*, Cambridge: Cambridge University Press.

—— (2000) "The Limits of Appropriation: Subjectivist Accounts of the Fiction/Nonfiction Distinction," in I. Bondebjerg (ed.) *Moving Images, Culture, and the Mind*, Luton, UK: University of Luton Press.

—— (2005) "What a Documentary Is, After All," *Journal of Aesthetics and Art Criticism* 63: 105–17.

Ponech, T. (1997) "What Is Non-Fiction Cinema?," in R. Allen and M. Smith (eds.) *Film Theory and Philosophy*, New York: Oxford University Press.

—— (1999) *What Is Non-Fiction Cinema?: On the Very Idea of Motion Picture Communication*, Boulder, CO: Westview Press.

Pryluck, C. (1988) "Ultimately We Are All Outsiders: The Ethics of Documentary Filming," in A. Rosenthal (ed.) *New Challenges for Documentary*, Berkeley: University of California Press.

Renov, M. (1993) "Introduction: The Truth about Non-Fiction," in M. Renov (ed.) *Theorizing Documentary*, New York: Routledge.

—— (2004) *The Subject of Documentary*, Minneapolis: University of Minnesota Press.

Ruby, J. (1988) "The Image Mirrored: Reflexivity and the Documentary Film," in A. Rosenthal (ed.) *New Challenges for Documentary*, Berkeley: University of California Press.

Winston, B. (1995) *Claiming the Real: The Documentary Film Revisited*, London: British Film Institute.

Further reading

The most comprehensive treatment of ethics in documentary is Larry Gross, John Stuart Katz, and Jay Ruby (eds.), *Image Ethics: The Moral Rights of Subjects in Photographs, Film, and Television* (New York: Oxford University Press, 1988). Steve Lipkin, *Real Emotional Logic: Film and Television Docudrama as Persuasive Practice* (Carbondale: Southern Illinois University Press, 2002) offers an intelligent account of the hybrid form lying in that fuzzy area between fiction and nonfiction, the docudrama. Jane Roscoe and Craig Hight, *Faking It: Mock-Documentary and the Subversion of Factuality* (Manchester and New York: Manchester University Press, 2001) provides an interesting discussion of the various "fact-fiction" forms, such as documentary parodies, docudramas, reality TV, and docusoaps. Paul Ward, *Documentary: The Margins of Reality* (London and New York: Wallflower, 2005) is a brief and thoughtful introduction to documentary theory and criticism.

46

HORROR

Aaron Smuts

Three questions have occupied much of the philosophical literature on cinematic horror: What is horror? How is it able to frighten and disgust? Why do we seek out horror if it horrifies? Although there are numerous other important topics, this entry will focus on these three general questions, since they motivate the overwhelming majority of the philosophical writing on cinematic horror.

What is horror?

In attempting to answer the question "What is horror?" many authors have pursued the goal of providing a definition of the genre. Although it would be something of a miracle if we could come up with a classical definition of any genre (comprising necessary and jointly sufficient conditions), especially of one as varied as horror, the task has not been unfruitful. Noël Carroll, in *The Philosophy of Horror, or, Paradoxes of the Heart*, offers a definition of horror that has been the subject of sustained controversy. Carroll's definition, roughly, is that a work should be classified as horror if it attempts to arouse fear and disgust directed at a monster, which he defines as a threatening creature not thought to exist by current science (Carroll 1990). It is important to note that Carroll's definition is centered on monsters. It is not enough for a work to merely arouse fear and disgust, as many slasher movies do; the fear and disgust must be directed at a monster. Given the further restrictions on what counts as a monster, this condition puts severe limitations on what can count as horror proper.

The second part of Carroll's definition concerns the nature of monsters. Carroll argues that to count as a horror monster the creature must be acknowledged not to exist according to contemporary science (Carroll 1990: 27). It is probably best to cash out "contemporary science" as the science in the world of the fiction, which typically maps onto or exceeds the science of the actual world, since we would not want the horror fiction of the past to become medical drama, if, say, biologists learn to revivify corpses. Regardless, this conception of "monster" has been thought to cause the most trouble for Carroll's definition. There are a few problems, most of which Carroll addresses directly.

The central issue is that this characterization of monsters is too restrictive. One particularly troubling case is that of Hitchcock's *Psycho* (1960). Although we might want to classify *Psycho* as a horror film, since it does not fit as cleanly into any other category, according to Carroll's criterion the movie lacks a monster and is thereby not a horror film. Psychopaths, such as Mark Lewis in *Peeping Tom* (Michael Powell, 1960) and Norman Bates in *Psycho*, are certainly acknowledged by science – they are not supernatural in any way – so they do not count as monsters in the strict sense. Carroll raises both of these cases as potential objections to his definition. In reply he argues that Norman is the exception that proves the rule: we are tempted to count Norman as a monster, since he shares so many attributes with genuine monsters, but he is not technically a monster. However, not everyone has been satisfied with the result: *Psycho* still does not count as horror according to Carroll's definition.

In *The Naked and the Undead*, Cynthia Freeland eschews the task of coming up with a formal definition for the genre, citing similar problems with Carroll's definition. Instead Freeland operates with the looser notion that horror is involved in exploring various forms of evil (Freeland 2000). We might be tempted to construct a revised notion of Carroll's definition, altering what it means to be a monster, by using a crude version of Freeland's criterion: monsters are evil. Although our new definition would certainly include *Psycho*, it would make the definition far too inclusive. *Goodfellas* (Scorsese, 1990), for instance, would be horror if we tried to construct a definition of monster based on this criterion, since many of the characters are unambiguously evil. Similarly, *The Sopranos* would count as horror under a theory that considered evil beings monsters.

Robert Yanal points out these potential difficulties with the evil theory of monsters and offers a third definition in response (Yanal 2003). Yanal's idea is inspired by Aristotle's discussion in the *Metaphysics* of a creature that fails to achieve its natural end. Aristotle's principal example is an ox with a human face, evincing the kind of categorical interstitiality that most monsters possess. We need not spend much time spelling out Yanal's proposal, since it is obviously underinclusive. Although Yanal's criterion may allow for Norman Bates, there are many kinds of monsters that have horrific natures. Hence, the problem is not that demons and aliens with acidic blood have failed to realize their natural ends that makes them into monsters; quite the opposite: these creatures are terrifying precisely because they have so effectively realized their horrific natures.

Given the problems that we have encountered in defining the genre, we are warranted in suspecting that it may not be possible to formulate an acceptable definition of horror that will map onto current usage. For the sake of argument, assume that it is acceptable, as I think it is, that *Psycho* would not count as horror proper according to Carroll's definition. This is only the tip of the iceberg: there are many other cases of what we often call horror that do not come close to meeting Carroll's criteria. For instance, slasher films would not count, even though the slasher movie is widely considered a horror subgenre. Some may find this consequence acceptable, but it points out that the definition is somewhat stipulative. And we have no reason to think that any nonstipulative definition could be created, since the borders of genres are just not neat enough to admit of classical definitions. Although a definition of the genre that meets our common usage might not be forthcoming, we might be able to provide a definition of a particular type of horror, perhaps even the paradigmatic type, and I think this is what Carroll has likely done. But one may still question the value of the entire definitional project. And, of course, the value of the project must be evident in its results: Having a definition has allowed Carroll to develop a theory of the appeal of horror, classify various common plot structures, and to explain why this type of horror is so effective. Narrowing the focus with a somewhat stipulative definition has made the related problems more manageable.

Fearing monsters

Why are vampires, werewolves, and other assorted horror monsters frightening for audiences that deny believing in such supernatural creatures? To appreciate the answers to this question, we must first look at a closely related puzzle. How are horror movies able to horrify when we are perfectly aware that what we are watching is fiction? We know that there is no such person as Marion Crane who is about to be stabbed by Norman Bates and no poolside party of teenagers about to be ripped to shreds by Freddy Krueger, but we are scared nonetheless. This puzzle is known as the paradox of fiction, which boils down to the question of how it is that we respond to fictional scenarios with genuine emotions (Radford 1975 and 1995).

It seems plausible to say that emotional responses require belief in the reality of their objects. To see why, consider this scenario: Imagine that you are at lunch with an old friend that you have not talked to in a while. Over the course of the meal, he describes in great detail how his wife of many years recently died after a painful battle with cancer. It is not controversial to think that you might feel sorry for your friend, depressed, and perhaps distraught. After paying the check, on the way out your friend tells you that he's been "pulling your leg" and that his wife, alive and healthy, would like to meet for drinks later. In this situation you might be angry with your friend: had you known that his wife was alive and well, it seems that you would not have felt painful sympathy for your friend, or so we assume (Carroll 1990). But knowing that many fictional narratives are merely make-believe has no dampening effect on our emotional responses.

Accordingly, Kendall Walton asks if an imagined horror fan named Charles is genuinely afraid of the Green Slime, or if perhaps Charles is only experiencing make-believe or pretend fear (Walton 1978). The "thought theory" is another compelling resolution to the paradox (Carroll 1990; Lamarque 1981). Carroll develops his version of the thought theory in reaction to both illusion and pretend theories. Unlike the pretend theorist such as Walton, Carroll argues that there is no reason to suppose that the emotions we feel in reaction to fictions are any less genuine than other real-life emotions. Contrary to the illusion theorists, who argue that a measure of belief in the reality of the fiction is necessary for emotional response, Carroll presents a thought theory, which states that "thought contents we entertain without believing them can genuinely move us emotionally" (Carroll 1990: 81). Given the plausibility of the analogy between our imaginative involvement with fictions that we create, in cases like those where we imagine the sudden death of a loved one, and our engagement with fictions not of our own construction, the thought theory is an incredibly intuitive, high-level account of how it is possible to be moved by fictions.

However, a complete explanation of our imaginative engagement with fictions will require, at least, an account of the role of belief. Perhaps the most fundamental questions about how we understand fictions are these: What beliefs must readers bring to fictions and how are they able to do it? No fiction could ever specify all the information required for even the most basic comprehension. For instance, Shakespeare did not have to specify that Hamlet has two eyes, a heart, and two kidneys. We bring to fictions a tremendous amount of beliefs about the world, genres, and the norms of the work's contemporaries.

There are obvious limits on the efficacy of the thoughts viewers are willing to entertain; and within the range of acceptable fictional situations, there are those that viewers will less readily consider and ones that effectively provoke strong responses. Carroll gives an example of a person standing stably near the edge of a cliff, in no danger of falling, but able to become frightened by thinking about dropping off. He argues that it is not the belief that we are about to fall that makes us scared, since we do not have that belief, but the mere thought of falling that provokes the fear response. However, one could argue, and the thought theorist could consistently agree, that the reaction to this thought scenario is highly influenced by various beliefs. We do not hold the one particular belief that Carroll mentions; however, we do believe (in the strong sense of the term) a great number of trivial things such as that things fall, that I can fall, that I could get hurt if I fall from high up. Thoughts about flying upward uncontrollably and hitting your head on the ceiling are less likely to scare you than they are to make you laugh, since the supporting beliefs are not available (Smuts 2003).

A useful test of the comprehensiveness of any theory of the imagination is to ask whether it explains why we are willing to entertain certain ideas and not others. Why are some thoughts so much more effective at arousing emotional responses than others? At a minimum, emotional response is both primed and partially constrained by our web of potentially acceptable beliefs, however minor they may seem. Though viewers do not have to confuse fiction and reality, the imagination cannot run wild and still pull the emotions, but serves best when fed by acceptable scenarios backed by supporting beliefs. It is common to hear people criticize a film by saying "It just wasn't believable. I couldn't get into it."

But just what kinds of supporting beliefs are optimal for horror viewing? Some psychoanalytically inclined theorists have attempted to explain the effectiveness of horror by recourse to Freud's theory of the uncanny (Freud 1953). Roughly, Freud argues that one experiences the uncanny when one recalls a repressed or surmounted belief that seems to be confirmed. In one of the more compelling psychoanalytic accounts, Steven Jay Schneider argues that horror monsters can be seen as metaphorical examples of repressed beliefs and desires (Schneider 2000). Although the effectiveness of some monsters might be attributable to repressed beliefs, there is no reason to think that repression funds most of the products of the genre. The uncanny is nearly the exclusive providence of the fantastic, where a supernatural explanation for the events in the fiction is tenuous. And there is some debate as to whether the fantastic should count as horror proper. What plausible repressed belief does the killer, mutant sea monster in *The Host* (John-ho Bong, 2006) represent, for instance? Although there is certainly more to be said about the role of the uncanny in the effectiveness of horror, there might be a more general way to explore the role of belief in the effectiveness of horror that does not carry with it psychoanalytic baggage, by focusing on surmounted rather than repressed beliefs.

In fact, based on a common response differential, a case can be made that audience reactions to some horror fictions provide evidence that they hold beliefs in the supernatural. A great deal of horror fiction is cross-culturally portable, that is, it is effective for audiences across the globe. However, much of the most effective horror fiction produced in the West is ineffective on those raised outside a Judeo-Christian culture. Many of my friends from India and China do not find *The Omen* (Donner, 1976) or *The Exorcist* (Friedkin, 1973) to be effective as horror movies, but these films are largely thought to be eerie, horrifying, and disturbing in the West. Similarly, I do not know many Americans who find the bouncing vampires in Chinese horror scary. What is particularly interesting about the situation is that the divide seems to work for even those who profess no religious beliefs. The apparent difference in effectiveness begs for an explanation.

One explanation of why *The Exorcist* is not scary for Buddhists is that the religious lore and mythology upon which the fiction draws is not familiar to those raised outside a Christian culture. If you are not familiar with the notion of possession by evil Latin-speaking spirits, then it might be difficult to become immersed in the story. However, this explanation radically overestimates the complexity of the folklore. Any audience can be brought up to speed and made fluent in the superstitions of a culture in minutes. I understand the properties of slow bouncing vampires, but they are not scary to me. Similarly, it is pretty simple to explain that in the world of *The Exorcist* there are powerful forces of good and evil; ancient evil spirits sometimes possess the bodies of humans; and Catholic priests are brought in to dispel the spirits when this happens. Overall, the situation is not very complicated and most of the subtleties are explained during the movie.

The difference in responses most plausibly has to do with our long-term affective inculcation into the mythology of our culture. It is uncontroversial to note that a few important things happen when we are immersed in a mythological tradition, things relevant to the effectiveness of some horror fictions. First of all, we become experienced in the mythology. It is not just that we understand a great deal about vampires and spirit possession, but that each subsequent vampire we encounter inherits something from those that came before. Monsters get a reputation, so to speak. This reputation undoubtedly contributes to their effectiveness. However, the reputation-building is not decisive: no matter how many times I encounter a bouncing vampire, they will never be terrifying monsters for me.

The second important thing that happens when we are immersed in a culture's mythology is that we develop beliefs. In the West, we can expect children to develop beliefs in vampires, werewolves, ghosts, evil spirits, zombies, and witches. This is not an outlandish claim. Just think of how many children will assent to a belief in Santa Claus, not to mention a variety of other magical beings. Similarly, there are few *de facto* atheists. Most atheists pass through an early stage of belief only to actively reject the religious tradition in which they were raised. Freud argues that "It seems as if each one of us has been through a phase of individual development corresponding to this animistic stage in primitive men" (Freud 1953). Assuming that such claims are plausible, one may wonder what the beliefs of children have to do with the effectiveness of horror on adults who deny believing in werewolves, ghosts, vampires, daemons, witches, and their kin.

Although we may not profess a belief in superstitions when the propositions are made occurrent, our responses to such fictions suggest that – like schoolchildren – many of us do indeed harbor beliefs, albeit partial, in the supernatural. It may seem as if this claim oversteps the evidence – the differential response – but an extremely plausible account can be given for how it is that rational adults could hold such beliefs. Simply put, it is not easy to shake off the kinds of beliefs that many of us develop as children. In fact, many Americans never shed their schoolyard superstitions. The reason these kinds of beliefs are so prevalent is due to a fundamental dissimilarity between believing in something and believing that something does not exist. Beliefs that things do not exist are easily corrected; all we have to do is see the thing. I might not believe that flying snakes exist, but show me one and I'll be converted to a believer in flying snakes. However, beliefs that things do exist are much harder to vanquish, since it is typically impossible to prove that something does not exist. How exactly would you get someone to stop believing in flying snakes? Needless to say, it would be much harder than proving that they exist.

The response differential between acculturated and nonacculturated audiences is not the only reason to think that horror fictions might be making use of audience beliefs in the supernatural. Many horror fictions enact a belief-revival process through the presence of a skeptical character. As Carroll has identified, one common horror plot structure involves the discovery and confirmation of the existence of a monster prior to its confrontation (Carroll 1990). Typically an extremely skeptical character, often in the guise of a scientist, will belittle accounts of the monster. Not only do skeptics end up converted, but often they are the first to die, as they are the least prepared to deal with a genuine threat. John Carpenter's *Prince of Darkness* (1987) follows a similar pattern. A group of physicists, mostly graduate students from Berkeley, are asked to investigate a mysterious canister locked away in the basement of a Catholic church. One of the students, a cocky Asian, repeatedly makes jokes about their assignment. Eventually it is revealed that the canister is filled with liquid Satan. Not only does the skeptical cut-up come to believe in the presence of Satan, he is one of the first characters to be dispatched by the dark lord's minions. The skeptic in horror fiction serves to chip away at the doubting audiences' certainty for the course of the fiction.

But, as with the psychoanalytic approach, the latent supernatural belief model has limited applicability. Many horror movies involve monsters that have little or no cultural funding, but the monsters are still frightening. Again, consider *The Host*

(John-ho Bong, 2006): the giant squid was largely unprecedented and audiences certainly did not have any latent beliefs in such creatures, but the monster was terrifying nonetheless. This should give us serious pause before claiming that any particular horror monster is effective because of latent audience beliefs in the supernatural.

The appeal of horror

Traditionally, the question of why people seek out experiences of putatively painful art has been presented as the paradox of tragedy, and recently, Carroll has introduced a related problem known as the paradox of horror. Both the paradox of tragedy and the paradox of horror arise as soon as we ask the question, why do people seek out or desire to see horror films or watch tragedies? More specifically, we might ask, why do people want to be scared by a movie or feel pity for a character when they avoid situations in real life that arouse the same emotions? An adequate solution to either problem will most likely require genre-specific considerations. However, the paradoxes of tragedy and horror are not simply questions about why people desire to see works in these genres: a question is not by itself a paradox. As they are typically stated, the two paradoxes ask how it is possible for audiences to feel pleasure at a horror movie or a tragedy.

If we do not assume that people derive pleasure from tragedy or that pleasure must be the sole motive for art experiences, the paradox of tragedy can be given a more general form that we can call the paradox of painful art. The paradox of painful art can be stated as follows:

1 People do not typically seek out situations that arouse painful emotions.
2 People have painful emotions in response to some art.
3 People routinely seek out art that they know will arouse painful emotions.

Since horror arouses fear and disgust, two reactions that are typically aversive, it maps neatly onto the paradox of painful art.

To clarify the various debates on the topic, it must be noted that there are two related questions that need to be answered. First, why is it that people seek out putatively painful art in general? And, second, why do people want to experience horror fiction in particular? We might be able to provide a perfectly general answer in resolution to the paradox of painful art without answering the horror-specific question. In evaluating answers to the second question, we must consider its explanatory scope. A theory might have universal application across the horror genre, or it might have a more limited explanatory domain, limited to, say, haunted house fictions. It is unclear how much weight should be given to scope when evaluating a solution to the paradox.

As to the first question, there are numerous competing accounts of how the paradox of painful art might be resolved. Control theorists argue that the putative painfulness of some artworks is mitigated by our ability to stop experiencing them at will (Morreall 1985). Compensation theorists argue that any painful reactions must be compensated for by other pleasures or values, either in the craft of the narrative (Hume 1985) or in the awareness that we are sympathetic creatures responsive to the suffering of others (Feagin 1983). Conversion theorists argue that the overall experience of painful artworks is not one of pain but of pleasure, as the pain is converted into a larger, more pleasurable experience (Hume 1985). Power theorists argue that we enjoy the feeling of power that arises from either the realization of the endurance of humanity (Price 1998), or through the overcoming of our fear (Shaw 2001). Rich-experience theorists argue that there are many reasons why people do things other than to feel pleasure. The overall experience of painful art may be unpleasant, but the experience can still be seen as valuable, and, as such, motivating (Smuts 2007).

As to the horror-specific question, some deny that horror fictions, unlike tragedy, do provide painful experiences that need special explanation (Neil 1992). In fact, we seek out horror fictions precisely for the combination of fear and disgust that Carroll calls art horror. But there are corresponding offerings that typically map onto one of the competing accounts of our desire to experience painful art. For instance, Carroll presents a compensatory theory, arguing that the reason why audiences seek out horror fictions, knowing full well that they will experience fear and disgust, is for the compensatory cognitive pleasures. Audiences, on Carroll's account, enjoy thinking about how one should go about confronting categorically interstitial monsters. The experience of horror is the "price we are willing to pay" for the pleasures of discovery (Carroll 1990: 186). This would explain why so many horror plots are structured in a four-stage model – onset, discovery, confirmation, confrontation. Carroll's explanation is intended to account for the appeal of narrative horror, but he also offers a curiosity-based account of nonnarrative works of horrific art.

Although there are certainly forms of pleasure available from the discovery plot structure, some would argue that Carroll's explanation leaves too much out, namely, the pleasures of identification with monsters (Shaw 2001). Daniel Shaw argues that horror fictions are often enjoyable because they allow audiences to identify both with a monster as it dispatches the more annoying teenagers, and with the victims, who often ultimately triumphant (Shaw 2001). Since the notion of character identification is suspect (Carroll 1990; Gaut 1999), we might want to revise the claim to state that audiences sympathize with or admire the monster. Shaw's principal example is Hannibal Lecter in *Silence of the Lambs* (Demme, 1999), whose cunning and wit bring him into sympathy with the audience. Elsewhere, Shaw argues that typical monster movies can encourage similar responses from audiences enamored with a killer's powers of destruction (Shaw 1997). Although Shaw's theory is intriguing and highlights an extremely important feature of the appeal of horror, it has yet to be worked out across a broad spectrum of the genre. But, yes, we can agree that some horror fictions are enjoyable because we like to see monsters vanquish their prey. Carroll's general reply to this line of argument (Hallie 1969) is that it has only limited applicability (Carroll 1990: 167–8). Perhaps the ferocity of the zombies in *28 Days Later* (Boyle, 2002) might arouse such reactions, but the slow masses of dumb walking corpses in *Night of the Living Dead* (Romero, 1968) certainly do not.

Many of the answers to the paradox of horror are simultaneously answers to the question addressed in the previous section, that is, what makes horror so effective? For instance, most Freudian accounts attempt to explain both how it is that horror fictions frighten us and why we desire such experiences. Robin Wood argues that repressed desires – oedipal and homosexual – drive much of the fear one experiences, while the punishment of transgression, affirming the normal moral order, is a source of much of the pleasure (Wood 1982). Similarly, fellow Freudian Carol Clover argues that female sexuality arouses fear that is vanquished in pleasurable scenes where "loose" women are punished (Clover 1992). Psychoanalytic stories can be fleshed out into highly persuasive accounts of the appeal of horror, explaining the prominence of certain themes found in much of contemporary horror. However, such explanations are typically unparsimonious, have difficulty explaining the attraction of horror to female audiences, and rest on the suspect foundation of psychoanalysis.

In one of the more popular accounts of the appeal of horror, H. P. Lovecraft argues that people enjoy horror, roughly because it allows them to combat scientific materialism and to engage in feelings of cosmic awe. One could construct a Lovecraft-inspired resolution to the paradox as follows: horror provides something of a religious experience that helps alleviate the deadening effects of living in a scientistic culture. The feeling of awe compensates for whatever negative reactions one might experience while fearing the unknown. Clearly, such an explanation would be very limited, since the bulk of the horror genre fails to inspire anything close to awe. For instance, Freddy Krueger inspires nothing similar to awe, and neither do Romero's clumsy zombies. Nevertheless, given the variability of the genre one suspects that the most compelling answers to "Why horror?" will have a limited scope – explaining the appeal of a certain type of horror movie rather than of the entire genre.

See also Emotion and affect (Chapter 8), Empathy and character engagement (Chapter 9), Genre (Chapter 14), Violence (Chapter 26), and Noël Carroll (Chapter 31).

References

Carroll, N. (1990) *The Philosophy of Horror; or, Paradoxes of the Heart*, New York: Routledge.
Clover, C. (1992) *Men, Women, and Chainsaws*, Princeton, NJ: Princeton University Press.
Feagin, S. (1983) "The Pleasures of Tragedy," *American Philosophical Quarterly* 20: 95–104.
Freeland, C. (2002) *The Naked and the Undead*, Boulder, CO: Westview Press.
Freud, S. (1953) "The Uncanny," in J. Strachey (trans. and ed.) *The Standard Edition of the Complete Psychological Works of Sigmund Freud*, vol. 17, London: Hogarth.
Gaut, B. (1999) "Identification and Emotion in Narrative Film," in C. Plantinga and G. M. Smith (eds.) *Passionate Views: Film, Cognition, and Emotion*, Baltimore, MD: Johns Hopkins University Press.
Hallie, P. (1969) *The Paradox of Cruelty*, Middletown, CT: Wesleyan University Press.
Hume, D. (1985) "Of Tragedy," in E. F. Miller (ed.) *Essays Moral, Political, and Literary*, Indianapolis: Liberty Classics.
Lamarque, P. (1981) "How Can We Fear and Pity Fictions?," *British Journal of Aesthetics*, 21: 291–304.
Lovecraft, H. P. (1973) *Supernatural in Horror Literature*, New York: Dover.
Morreall, J. (1985) "Enjoying Negative Emotions in Fictions," *Philosophy and Literature* 9: 95–103.
Neil, A. (1992) "On a Paradox of the Heart," *Philosophical Studies* 65: 53–65.
Price, A. (1998) "Nietzsche and the Paradox of Tragedy," *British Journal of Aesthetics*, 38: 384–93.

Radford, C. (1975) "How Can we be Moved by the Fate of Anna Karenina?," *Proceedings of the Aristotelian Society* 69: 67–80.

—— (1995) "Fiction, Pity, Fear, and Jealousy," *Journal of Aesthetics and Art Criticism* 53: 71–5.

Schneider, S. J. (2000) "Monsters as (Uncanny) Metaphors: Freud, Lakoff, and the Representation of Monstrosity in Cinematic Horror," in A. Silver and J. Ursini (eds.) *Horror Film Reader*, New York: Limelight Editions.

Shaw, D. (1997) "A Humean Definition of Horror," *film-philosophy*. Available at http://www.film-philosophy.com/vol1-1997/n4shaw.

—— (2001) "Power, Horror, and Ambivalence," *Film and Philosophy* 6: 1–12 (special issue, horror).

Smuts, A. (2003) "Haunting the House from Within: Disbelief Mitigation and Spatial Experience," in S. J. Schneider and D. Shaw (eds.) *Dark Thoughts: Philosophical Reflections on Cinematic Horror*, Lanham, MD: Scarecrow.

—— (2007) "The Paradox of Painful Art," *Journal of Aesthetic Education* 41: 59–77.

Yanal, R. (2003) "Two Monsters in Search of a Concept," *Contemporary Aesthetics* 1. Available at http://www.contempaesthetics.org/newvolume/pages/article.php?articleID=201.

Walton, K. (1978) "Fearing Fictions," *Journal of Philosophy* 75: 5–27.

Wood, R. (1982) *Hollywood from Vietnam to Reagan*, New York: Columbia University Press.

47

PORNOGRAPHY

Susan Dwyer

Pornography has attracted a good deal of academic and political attention, primarily from feminists of various persuasions, moral philosophers, and legal scholars. Surprisingly less work has been forthcoming from film theorists, given how much pornography has been produced on video and DVD and is now available through live streaming video over the Internet. Indeed, it is not until 1989, with the publication of Linda Williams' groundbreaking *Hard Core*, that pornography is distinguished, in terms of its content, intent, and governing conventions, as a filmic genre of its own. Still, not all pornography exists as film, and so a full discussion of it must encompass its other manifestations (e.g., magazines, websites, comics).

The central questions about pornography are these: (1) What is it? How is it to be defined? (2) What are its effects? (3) How, if at all, ought it to be regulated? While these questions are simple, providing answers to them, as we shall see, is complicated. There is plenty of disagreement about how to define pornography; research about pornography's effects is not univocal; and this in turn leads to substantial debate about what can and may be done about pornography. It is to these matters that the bulk of this essay is addressed. To begin, however, we will take a brief snapshot of the emergence of pornographic film and of the pornography business as it exists today.

The pornography business, film, and the Internet

Throughout history, as new representational and communication technology has emerged, each has been eagerly embraced by producers of sexually explicit material. The advent of the printing press made the mass production and circulation of sexually explicit images possible for the first time in the sixteenth century (Hunt 1993). Photography and then film were exploited early on. The Kinsey Institute at Indiana University has archived more than 1,500 8-mm and 16-mm black-and-white films, including the classic stag movies *Am Abend* (c. 1910), *El Satorio* (1907–15), and *A Free Ride* (c. 1915–17). During the 1970s sexually explicit material accounted for almost three-quarters of videos for home consumption in the United States (Tierney 1994); and, of course, pornographers have been major entrepreneurs in the digital age, leading the development of secure online transactions, database management, digital watermarking, and videoconferencing technology (Lane 2000).

From the perspective of film and cinema studies, perhaps the most interesting period is the so-called Golden Age of Porn, which is roughly coincident with the 1970s. Gerald Damiano's *Deep Throat* (1972) was the first full-length pornographic feature to garner mainstream success; wherever it was available in the United States men and women flocked to see it. Made for $25,000, the movie has now grossed, according to the most conservative estimates, over $100 million. In 1973, Art and James Mitchell released *Behind the Green Door*, and Damiano followed his earlier success with *The Devil in Miss Jones* (Lewis 2000).

Pornography producers at this time aimed to develop a technically better product than stag films and peep show loops, in order, in part, to gain mainstream legitimacy. Had it not been for the rise of video technology in the late 1970s, they may have succeeded. As it is, video technology made pornography cheaper to make and easier to get. It also pushed the viewing of sexually explicit film back into the private sphere, thereby allowing and encouraging the inclusion of more and more extreme content. Between 1992 and 2006, adult video sales and rentals in the United States rose from $1.6 billion to $3.26 billion; in 2005, more than 13,000 hardcore pornographic titles were produced (Ropelato 2006), in contrast to the approximately 400 titles produced by Hollywood (Williams 2004: 1).

The trend toward more and more extreme content in pornography is everywhere evident on the Internet, where it is now estimated there are some 420 million pornographic pages worldwide (Ropelato 2006). In addition to the usual fare of vaginal, anal, and oral sex between multiple partners, it is now very easy to access sites devoted to urination and defecation in a sexual context, sex with animals, and all manner of sexual bondage and torture. Thirty-five- to forty-nine-year-olds constitute the largest group of Internet pornography consumers, however, 80 percent of fifteen- to seventeen-year-olds report multiple exposures to hardcore pornography on line (Ropelato 2006).

The problem of definition

A large part of the difficulty in theorizing about pornography is due to persistent disagreement about how to define it and thus how to identify it in the world. The etymology of the word is of little help. The word pornography has its roots in the Greek *porne* (meaning prostitute) and *graphein* (meaning writing). But what most people today would identify as pornography is hardly merely documentary about sex workers.

Outside of logic and mathematics, definition is a tricky enterprise. For it is notoriously difficult to state the necessary and sufficient conditions for being a thing of a certain kind. What, for example, are the necessary and sufficient conditions for being a house? Is any structure with four walls a house? Need a structure have a front door to be a house? What if it lacks a complete roof? Matters only get more complex when we turn to something like pornography, about which people have very strong views. For those views – for example, that pornography is morally bad and ought to be banned – affect the ways in which pornography gets defined.

The words we use to talk about things can serve two functions. In the first place, they may be used to pick out things in the world, as in when I ask you to bring me the large, blue cat from the next room. Call this their identification function. In the second place, they may be used to bring about a certain effect, as in when I tell you that *The Lives of Others* (2006) is the best movie I have seen in a decade. Call this their strategic function. Part of your understanding me in the first case involves you bringing me the large blue cat and not the small red dog. And part of your understanding me in the second case involves you being motivated by my remark to see *The Lives of Others*.

In addition, the way we talk about things matters. It is useful here to distinguish between what we can call *normative* and *descriptive* characterizations of things. A normative characterization is one that employs evaluative terms, i.e., terms that assume particular value judgments. A descriptive characterization is one that does not employ such terms, i.e., is value neutral. We can characterize the very same thing either normatively ("That is an incredibly boring book") or descriptively ("That is a book about staplers in 1940s Toronto").

Let us now think about the relevance of these two distinctions to the difficulties involved in defining pornography. Pornography may be given either a normative or a descriptive characterization. Consider Brownmiller's remark that pornography is the "undiluted essence of anti-female propaganda" (1975: 394). There can be no mistaking that Brownmiller's view about pornography is negative. Her characterization of pornography presupposes a certain (negative) assessment of it. Another person might choose to convey a positive evaluation of pornography by characterizing it as the noblest expression of human creativity. Now, in contrast to both of these value-laden ways of talking about pornography, Williams provides a (relatively) value-neutral, descriptive characterization of the material: "the visual (and sometimes aural) representation of living, moving bodies engaged in explicit, usually unfaked, sexual acts with a primary intent of arousing viewers" (1989: 30).

The next step is to see that the choice to use a normative or descriptive characterization of pornography will depend on what a person's purpose is in talking about pornography at all. If I want you to bring me the big book of pornography from the next room, it will serve my purpose better if I tell you that by pornography I mean pictures of human sexual acts. You might well have difficulty identifying the undiluted essence of antifemale propaganda, or bring me a copy of *Cosmopolitan* instead! Hence, descriptive characterizations of things best perform the identification function of words. But suppose I want to motivate you to lobby your local officials to ban pornography from newsstands. In this event, I will want to use words that perform the strategic function of language well, and I will use a (negative) normative characterization of pornography. A person would be hard pressed to fail to be, at least a little, motivated to remove instances of undiluted antifemale propaganda from public view.

The fundamental point here is that if we want to inquire into the effects of pornography or to argue about whether pornography ought to be regulated, we need to begin by agreeing what we shall mean by the term pornography. It should be clear that a value-neutral, descriptive characterization will be best. No one should have any difficulty in finding material that satisfies Williams' definition above, and we can all agree that such material exists. Moreover, notice that Williams' definition will cover homosexual, heterosexual, and child pornography across all the media in which they appear.

It is worth noting that value-laden characterizations of pornography can get us to a conclusion about pornography's effects and about what should be done about pornography quite quickly. *If* pornography is the undiluted essence of antifemale propaganda, then it is likely that it has bad effects in society, and those bad effects ought to be eliminated or at least minimized. This is all well and good; but it is an empirical question whether any such material actually exists.

In this respect it is worth mentioning Longino's widely discussed definition of pornography, as "verbal or pictorial material which represents or describes sexual behavior that is degrading or abusive to one or more of the participants *in such a way as to endorse the degradation*" (1980: 43). Longino's purpose in proposing this definition is to draw a distinction between types of sexually explicit material. She wants to make clear that her objections to pornography are not conservative; they do not depend on the mere fact that pornography is sexually explicit. Longino's definition would appear to be a very detailed descriptive characterization of pornography, helping us to separate it from erotica (sexually explicit material that does *not* depict and endorse degradation or abuse) and from documentaries about sexual trafficking (sexually explicit material that does depict degradation and abuse but does not endorse them). Longino's characterization of pornography is very useful for critics of pornography, as we shall see, for it allows the critic to make a case for the regulation of pornography that does not impact *all* sexually explicit material. However, again, people will disagree about whether particular sexually explicit representations depict behavior that is degrading or abusive. For example, it is not obvious that the ubiquitous "money shots" (that is, scenes of a man ejaculating onto the face, breasts, or buttocks of a naked woman) of heterosexual pornography are instances of degrading or abusive behavior. And it is difficult to determine that degrading or abusive sexual behavior is endorsed in a particular film or photograph; it is not as if pornographers insert captions that read "Try this at home!"

In what follows, then, I shall for the most part assume something like Williams' descriptive characterization of pornography.

Pornography's effects

The most significant controversy surrounding pornography concerns its effects. Not its most obvious effect (sexual arousal), nor its allegedly good effect (of offering individuals a safe, because virtual, way to satisfy what would otherwise be dangerous sexual desires), but rather pornography's *bad* effects. These debates are crucial to arguments concerning what, if anything, should be done about pornography and about the role of the state in addressing pornographic material. Films, magazines, books, and websites – whether or not they have sexually explicit content – are typically considered forms of expression. And forms of human expression, and speech, in particular, typically enjoy very strong protection in democratic regimes.

The First Amendment of the United States Constitution states:

> Congress shall make no law respecting an establishment of religion, or prohibiting the free exercise thereof; or abridging the freedom of speech, or of the press; or the right of the people peaceably to assemble, and to petition the government for a redress of grievances.

Canada's Charter of Human Rights and Freedoms and the European Convention on Human Rights also guarantee liberty of expression. However, in contrast to the United States' *Bill of Rights*, the latter two documents explicitly state the conditions under which this liberty may be curtailed. In Europe, for example, freedom of expression may be restricted "for the prevention of disorder or crime, the protection of health or morals [and] for the protection of reputation or rights of others." This is not to say that the United States government is utterly prohibited from curtailing speech. So-called fighting words, libel, obscenity, seditious speech, and perjury are all forms of expression that the state may restrict. In addition, the state may regulate the time, place, and manner of expression. In any event, against this legal backdrop, anyone wishing to argue that pornography may and ought to be in some way seriously restricted or prohibited must show that pornography has harmful effects on the behavior and/or attitudes of its consumers – say, that it increases the incidence of sexual assault, the likelihood of child sex abuse, workplace discrimination, and so on.

Researchers have provided such conflicting evidence concerning pornography's effects that it is not possible confidently to assert any generalizations about pornography's connection to sexual violence. Nor has it been established that exposure to pornography is the cause of problematic attitudes about sex. Arguably, an interest in certain forms of pornography stems from preexisting attitudes about sex.

Investigation into the effects of pornography is subject to the difficulties that beset other social science research. Various biases operate in the design of experiments and questionnaires, and in the interpretation of their results (Bensimon 2007; King 1993); and the same expert testimony has been used in very different, often opposing policy arguments (Linz *et al.* 1987). Anecdotal, experimental, and criminological evidence concerning pornography's harmful effects is inconsistent, to say the least (Gunter 2002; Segal 1994). Hence, no sound argument has yet been made for state restriction or prohibition of pornography on account of its harmful effects.

In the mid-1980s, a very different antipornography policy argument emerged. Due to Catharine MacKinnon and Andrea Dworkin, this argument also employs a descriptive characterization of pornography; however, it claims that pornography does not so much cause harm as it *constitutes* a particular form of sexual discrimination. Specifically, MacKinnon and Dworkin claim that pornography just *is* the subordination and silencing of women and of those it treats as women (e.g., submissive partners in gay male sado-masochist pornography). Their definition is as follows:

> Pornography is the graphic sexually explicit subordination of women, whether in pictures or in words, that also includes one or more of the following: (1)

women presented as sexual objects who enjoy pain or humiliation; or (2) women are presented as sexual objects who experience sexual pleasure in being raped; or (3) women are presented as sexual objects tied up or cut up or mutilated or bruised or physically hurt, or as dismembered or truncated or fragmented or severed into body parts; or (4) women are presented as being penetrated by objects or animals; or (5) women are presented in scenarios of degradation, injury, debasement, torture, shown as filthy or inferior, bleeding, bruised, or hurt in a context that makes these conditions sexual; or (6) women are presented as sexual objects for domination, conquest, violation, exploitation, possession, or use, or through postures or positions of servility or submission or display ... [T]he use of men, children, or transsexuals in place of women in paragraphs (1) through (6) ... shall also constitute pornography. (MacKinnon 1987: 176)

This approach does not require denying that pornography is speech. Instead it aligns pornography with other types of speech that may be restricted on account of the discriminatory behavior such speech constitutes in certain contexts. Other examples include "'help wanted – male', 'sleep with me and I'll give you an A', and 'fuck me or you're fired'" (MacKinnon 1993: 12–14).

The idea that pornography is itself the subordination of women has encountered considerable skepticism, and some critics have argued that the claim is simply incoherent (Parent 1990). A sophisticated defense of the coherence, if not the truth, of MacKinnon and Dworkin's view of pornography is provided by Langton (1993). Very briefly, Langton draws on speech act theory to argue that in the right context a person with the right sort of authority in that context can indeed succeed in subordinating another just by speaking. For example, a white legislator in apartheid South Africa succeeded in subordinating Blacks simply by declaring, "Only whites can vote." Hence, pornography, as MacKinnon and Dworkin define it, can be a type of subordination if, as a matter of fact, pornographers have the requisite authority in the domain of sex. However, this is dubious. Pornographers are not like referees at baseball games, whose positional authority makes it the case that a runner is home safe, just by the referees signaling as much. There are no comparable "rules" about sex. So, whatever authority pornographers enjoy sufficient for their speech acts to be acts of subordination, that authority must be epistemic. That is, consumers of pornography must grant that pornographers have expertise regarding what sexual practices are desirable and acceptable such that their pronouncements are believed to be the truth about sex. Despite the sexist attitudes and biases of both men and women, especially when it comes to sex, it is really not very plausible to think that any consumers of pornography really do believe all that pornographers say (Saul 2006).

As mentioned above, most of the debate surrounding pornography's effects has concerned its allegedly harmful effects on others, especially women and children. Still, there are significant voices extolling the virtues of a free and open market in pornography and the value of sexually explicit material produced by women for women. The argument between feminists about pornography has been particularly interesting, with several feminist theorists and activists, some calling themselves anti-antipornography feminists, claiming that pornography can be a source of liberation for women (Califia 2000; McElroy 1995; Strossen 2000). Moreover, many women clearly do consume mainstream heterosexual pornography; Ropelato (2006) reports that one in three visitors to Internet pornography sites are women.

As we have seen, arguments for a particular policy regarding pornography's availability typically depend upon a moral analysis of pornography. According to some critics, pornography has harmful effects and *for that reason* should be legally restricted or criminalized. But it is important to remember that claims about the moral status of pornography are quite different from recommendations about what to do about pornography. It is perfectly consistent to believe that there is something morally problematic about pornography, without thereby being committed to its being restricted by the state. And indeed some moral critiques of pornography positively suggest that the state will be the least effective agent in dealing with whatever is morally suspect about the material. Two such accounts bear mentioning.

Both of these hold that the moral problem with pornography, insofar as there is one, is not so much its effects on others but its effects on the *consumer* of the material, in particular its effects on him or her. The first account is due to Roger Scruton (2003, 2006), who emphasizes the distinction between the mere experience of sexual pleasure and the satisfaction of genuine sexual *desire*. There is reason to believe that many animals can enjoy the former, however only human beings can have and seek to fulfill the latter. This is because, as Scruton puts it:

> [s]exual desire is not a desire for sensation. It is a desire for a person ... not his or her body conceived as an object in the physical world, but a person conceived as an incarnate subject, in whom the light of self consciousness shines and who confronts me eye to eye and I to I. (2003)

Sex without erotic love, that is, sex that is not in the service of fulfilling genuine sexual desire for another full person, is *just* sex. It can be no part of an individual person's flourishing and, pursued over the long haul, will diminish that person's sense of self and moral integrity. Thus, insofar as the consumption of pornography facilitates masturbation – typically a solitary activity – and glorifies the brute pursuit of what Scruton would call *just* sex, it facilitates a morally dangerous attitude toward others and one's self.

Dwyer (2005a) proposes a different account of what is morally problematic about some types of pornography. She focuses on the nature of some types of sexual fantasizing and on the role of pornography in developing and nurturing such fantasizing. Contrary to prevailing opinion, Dwyer argues that fantasizing is an action that is under a person's control and thus that a person can be held morally responsible for the content of his or her fantasizing. This is true equally of sexual and nonsexual fantasizing, as is evident in the fact that most people are quite adept at speeding up, slowing down, and rewinding fantasies they engage in during sex with others and during masturbation. Sexual fantasizing is not something that happens to a person;

it is something a person *does*. Dwyer then turns to the intuition that it is not good for a person's moral character if he or she persistently engages in bad thoughts about others. Imagine the person who regularly (albeit privately) celebrates the misfortunes of others or who fantasizes about the downfall of the justly successful. Over time, such toxic activities will negatively affect his or her moral character, and will do so, whether or not the person ever overtly behaves in ways prompted by those fantasies. Now, a good deal of pornography that is available on the Internet involves humiliating, degrading, and abusive treatment of others in a highly sexualized context. It is not possible to say whether the massive availability of this sort of pornography on our home computers has contributed to an increased prevalence of sexual fantasies involving this kind of treatment. And that does not affect the critique. For Dwyer's point is that sexual fantasizing with such content runs the risk of eroding moral character, no matter what its inspiration. Consumers of some types of pornography put themselves at moral risk in much the same way that a person who nurtures racist attitudes or deep feelings of envy toward others does. (It is interesting to note that Scruton has also launched moral objections to fantasy more generally. With respect to film, he argues that consumers of fantasy "will tend to have a diminished sense of the objectivity of his [*sic*.] world, and a diminished sense of his own agency within it" [1983: 131].)

Before we leave this discussion of pornography's nature and (alleged) effects and what these effects entail about what (if anything) ought to be done about pornography, it is worth noting two things. First, unlike MacKinnon and Dworkin's rather capacious definition of pornography, Longino's definition and Dwyer's critique identify a rather more circumscribed set of sexually explicit material as harmful. This matters, because critics of pornography are typically misinterpreted as being opposed to *all* sexually explicit material. Given the history of women's oppression, that is not a position any feminist should endorse.

Second, Dwyer's analysis of what is morally problematic about some types of pornography entails that the state is a particularly inapt agent of response to pornography. If the problem with some types of pornography resides in their effects on individual characters through persons' voluntary use of pornography, then the state will be the least effective avenue of redress. For the moral quality of a person's character is really a matter over which only he or she can exercise control (Dwyer 2005b).

Pornography and the law

Thus far we have considered distinctly philosophical analyses of pornography and its effects. And we have seen that none of the main critical approaches obviously supports state restriction or prohibition of pornography. Still, a good deal of sexually explicit material, whether we call it pornography or not, is as a matter of fact illegal. *Pornography* is not itself the name of a legal category. Rather, sexually explicit material typically falls under the rubric of *obscenity*.

The notion of obscenity has its roots in late nineteenth-century English Common Law. At that time, British courts determined whether some material was obscene, on the basis of the so-called Hicklin test, which asked whether the book or pamphlet in question had a tendency to "deprave and corrupt the minds of those whose minds are open to such immoral influences" (*R. v. Hicklin* [1868], L.R. 3 Q.B. 360). While we can read the Hicklin test as an attempt to protect children from certain kinds of material, it is almost certainly shot through with all manner of gender, race, and class assumptions. Arguably, we have in the Hicklin test the beginnings of what today is largely a class-inflected distinction between erotica and pornography (Kipnis 1996).

The current operative definition of obscenity in the United States stems from the Supreme Court's opinion in *Miller v. California*, 413 US 15 (1973):

> The basic guidelines for the trier of fact must be (a) whether the average person applying contemporary community standards would find the work, taken as a whole, appeals to the prurient interest; (b) whether the work depicts or describes, in a patently offensive way, sexual contact specifically defined by the applicable state law; and (c) whether the work, taken as a whole, lacks serious literary, artistic, political or scientific value.

While this definition appears to be an improvement over the Hicklin test, insofar as it does not require judges to speculate from their benches about whether something has a tendency to corrupt the morally vulnerable, it does rely on an equally problematic determination – that of contemporary community standards. It is not at all clear how a judge or jury is to know what prevailing community standards are. And it is notoriously difficult to specify the boundaries of the community upon whose standards the fate of a film or book depends. What may breach standards in Appleton, Wisconsin, might be perfectly acceptable in San Francisco. These problems continue to plague the application of obscenity law in the United States, especially with respect to material available on the World Wide Web. Given the reach of the Internet, any law that held Web-based material hostage to a particular, local, and conservative set of standards would be overbroad – that is, it would unfairly target material that is acceptable in other regions (*Ashcroft v. ACLU*, 535 US 564 [2002]).

Though a vast amount of currently available sexually explicit material is technically illegal in the United States, federal and state authorities have chosen to focus their legislative and prosecutorial efforts on restricting children's access to obscene material and on child pornography. Sexually explicit material that requires the sexual abuse of children for its production is not protected by the First Amendment (*New York v. Ferber*, 458 US 747 [1982]). In addition, over the past decade, the federal government has enacted a string of statutes, all of which have crumbled in the face of the constitutional challenges noted in the cases cited in parentheses: the *Communications Decency* Act of 1996 forbade the presentation of "indecent" material to minors on the Internet (*Reno v. ACLU*, 521 US 844 1997); the *Child Pornography Protection Act* of 1996, which would have made computer-generated representations of children engaged in sex acts illegal (*Ashcroft v. Free Speech Coalition*, 535 US 234 [2002]); and the *Children's Online Protection Act* of 1998 (*Ashcroft v. ACLU*, 542 US 656 [2004]). In September 2007, the US Supreme Court agreed to hear the appeal of Michael Williams, who was convicted under the *PROTECT Act* of 2003, which makes it a crime knowingly to advertise, promote, present, distribute, or solicit a visual depiction of a child engaged in sex, whether or not that material actually exists (*United States v. Michael Williams*, 06-694).

Pornography and culture

The proliferation of pornography on the World Wide Web and its literally immediate accessibility, together with the increased involvement of nonprofessional actors, photographers, and filmmakers in the production of pornography, raises two questions for further research. First, is Western culture becoming "pornified"? That is, has pornography now escaped the bounds of the private and slightly shameful to inflect major elements of culture, including music, advertising, and fashion? Levy (2005) and Paul (2005) each think so, arguing that our culture, led by young women, has come to accept, nay *embrace*, a pornographic view of women, as exemplified by *Girls Gone Wild* (1998) and by the celebrity-making potential of not wearing underwear.

Second, if there is any truth to the idea that pornography has evolved into just another genre in Western culture, does, and can, pornography remain in any plausible way transgressive? Theorists like Kipnis (1996) argue, quite persuasively, that pornography is of value because, in crossing boundaries of what is acceptable in a society, it illuminates the contours of those prevailing values and can point out double-standards and gender, race, and class assumptions. Everything that is "not allowed" in mainstream culture can find a home in pornography. If the line between the mainstream and the pornographic is no longer sharp, we may lose the sort of ironic vantage point on culture that pornography once provided.

Every society is to some extent governed by implicit norms, not all of which have explicit parallels in codified law. Implicit norms are often, but not always, maintained in the service of shoring up certain power hierarchies, many of which could not be kept in place by other more overt means. These are the norms that transgressive practices like pornography can reveal to us. However, not all transgressive practices are to be celebrated. Some are merely destructive, carried out just for their own sakes, or the amusement of particular individuals, and revealing nothing of value to us.

Kipnis has more recently made another claim in pornography's favor, one that might be contradicted by the arguments of Scruton and Dwyer, described above. She writes that, whatever else it does, it "insist[s] on a sanctioned space for fantasy" (2002). This might be true, but we can and should wonder whether this is necessarily a good thing and whether there are alternative practices that could provide a cultural sanctuary for things we would like to contemplate but not make real.

See also Censorship (Chapter 3) and Gender (Chapter 13).

References

Bensimon, P. (2007) "The Role of Pornography in Sexual Offending," *Sexual Addiction and Compulsivity* 14: 95–117.

Brownmiller, S. (1975) *Against Our Will: Men, Women and Rape*, New York: Simon and Schuster.

Califia, P. (2000) *Public Sex: The Culture of Radical Sex*, 2nd ed., San Francisco, CA: Cleis Press.

Dwyer, S. (2005a) "'Enter Here' – At Your Own Risk: The Moral Dangers of Cyberporn," in R. Cavalier (ed.) *The Impact of the Internet on Our Moral Lives*, Albany: State University of New York Press.

—— (2005b) "Caught in the Web: Sexual Fantasizing, Character, and Cyberpornography," in W. Cragg and C. M. Koggel (eds.) *Contemporary Moral Issues*, 5th ed., Toronto: McGraw-Hill Ryerson.

Gunter, B. (2002) *Media Sex: What Are the Issues?*, Mahwah, NJ; London: Lawrence Erlbaum Associates.

Hunt, L. (ed.) (1993) *The Invention of Pornography: Obscenity and the Origins of Modernity, 1500–1800*, New York: Zone Books; Cambridge, MA: MIT Press.

King, A. (1993) "Mystery and Imagination: The Case of Pornography Effect Studies," in A. Assiter and A. Carol (eds.) *Bad Girls and Dirty Pictures*, London and Boulder, CO: Pluto Press.

Kipnis, L. (1996) *Bound and Gagged: Pornography and the Politics of Fantasy in America*, New York: Grove Press.

—— (2002) "The Eloquence of Pornography," *Frontline*. Available at http://www.pbs.org/wgbh/pages/frontline/shows/porn/special/eloquence.html (accessed 28 September 2007).

Lane, F. S., III (2000) *Obscene Profits: The Entrepreneurs of Pornography in the Cyber Age*, New York: Routledge.

Langton, R. (1993) "Speech Acts and Unspeakable Acts," *Philosophy and Public Affairs* 22: 293–330.

Levy, A. (2005) *Female Chauvinist Pigs: Women and the Rise of Raunch Culture*, New York: Free Press.

Lewis, J. (2000) *Hollywood v. Hardcore: How the Struggle Over Censorship Saved the Modern Film Industry*, New York: New York University Press.

Linz, D., Donnerstein, E., and Penrod, S. (1987) "The Findings and Research of the Attorney General's Commission on Pornography: Do the Psychological Facts Fit the Political Fury?," *American Psychologist* 42: 946–53.

Longino, H. E. (1980) "Pornography, Oppression, and Freedom: A Closer Look," in L. Lederer (ed.) *Take Back the Night: Women on Pornography*, New York: William Morrow and Co.

MacKinnon, C. (1987) "Francis Biddle's Sister: Pornography, Civil Rights, and Speech," in *Feminism Unmodified: Discourses on Life and Law*, Cambridge, MA: Harvard University Press.

—— (1993) *Only Words*, Cambridge, MA: Harvard University Press.

McElroy, W. (1995) *XXX: A Woman's Right to Pornography*, New York: St Martin's Press.

Parent, W. A. (1990) "A Second Look at Pornography and the Subordination of Women," *Journal of Philosophy* 87: 205–11.

Paul, P. (2005) *Pornified: How Pornography Is Transforming Our Lives, Our Relationships, and Our Families*, New York: Times Books.

Ropelato, J. (2006) "Internet Pornography Statistics," *TopTenReviews.com*. Available at http://www.internet-filter-review.toptenreviews.com/internet-pornography-statistics.html (accessed 29 September 2007).

Saul, J. (2006) "Pornography, Speech Acts and Context," *Proceedings of the Aristotelian Society* 106: 229–48.

Scruton, R. (1983) "Fantasy, Imagination, and the Screen," in *The Aesthetic Understanding*, London and New York: Methuen.

—— (2003) "The Moral Birds and Bees," *National Review* 15 (September). Available at http://www.nationalreview.com/flashback/flashback200602140942.asp (accessed 14 October 2007).

—— (2006) *Sexual Desire: A Philosophical Investigation*, London and New York: Continuum.

Segal, L. (1994) "False Promises – Anti-Pornography Feminism," in M. Evans (ed.) *The Woman Question*, 2nd ed., London and Thousand Oaks, CA: Sage.

Strossen, N. (2000) *Defending Pornography: Free Speech, Sex and the Fight for Women's Rights*, New York and London: New York University Press.

Tierney, J. (1994) "Porn, the Low-Slung Engine of Progress," *The New York Times*, 9 January.

Williams, L. (1989) *Hard Core: Power, Pleasure and "The Frenzy of the Visible,"* Berkeley: University of California Press.
—— (ed.) (2004) *Porn Studies*, Durham, NC: Duke University Press.

Further reading

Susan Dwyer (ed.) *The Problem of Pornography* (Belmont, CA: Wadsworth Publishing Company, 1995) is a collection of essays representing a wide range of opinion about pornography. Tanya Krzywinska, *Sex and the Cinema* (London and New York: Wallflower Press, 2006) discusses the conventions governing the different ways real and simulated sex appears in film.

48
AVANT-GARDE FILM
Maureen Turim

Avant-garde films, along with modern and contemporary art, music, and theater, have long posed serious challenges to philosophy. Theorists of film have, for their part, turned to various schools of philosophy to theorize the functioning of these films that strive to reinvent sound and image composition, transforming film form and structure. In this essay, I will be describing primarily English-language considerations of the philosophical aspects of avant-garde film, though foundational and parallel work has been done in Germany, France, and other European countries.

Yet only certain theories of avant-garde film seem to enlist or imply philosophical concepts. Other ways of seeing and theorizing avant-garde film are poetic and subjective, purposely avoiding the discipline of philosophy, its historical references, and its terminology. Still, insofar as these approaches propose an expanded ontology for cinema or define subjectivity as an emotionally nuanced seeing, they can be seen as having philosophical resonances. Many of these are properly seen as so implicit and unreferenced as to be prephilosophical in the writing, never fully developed as a philosophical treatise or treatment.

Aesthetics may be the area of inquiry most often and directly addressed by the theorists of avant-garde film, particularly Kant's notions of the beautiful and the sublime. The power of nature and a notion of pure beauty constitute aspects of a Kantian investigation, while Kant's more conceptual notion of the sublime reaches toward ineffability, awe, and fear. This aesthetic tradition runs deeply through modern art and photography, often combining a strong relationship to nature with a romantic vision of the artist as one who expresses heightened sensitivities. In many cases, artists wrote about their own work as such a quest, as well as inscribing this framework in their films: consider such divergent film artists as Jean Cocteau, Maya Deren, and Stan Brakhage, each of whom write about their filmwork as seeking a pure beauty or transcendent poetics that has as its goal transforming the mind, the very process of thought.

P. Adams Sitney's *Visionary Film* (2002 [1974]: xiii), one of the most widely read volumes on the avant-garde, makes this point in his preface: "The preoccupation of the American avant-garde filmmakers coincides with those of our post romantic poets and abstract expressionist painters. Behind them lies a potent of romantic poetics." Naming the quest for visionary spirituality, for grounding in the American landscape, and for the magnification of the trials of everyday life abundantly present in the US avant-garde film, a romantic poetics may seem merely to name a citation. Such a citation indeed was subject to Peter Wollen's critique, in his (1975) essay "The Two Avant-gardes," of what he took as the lack of progressive ideological engagement in the US avant-garde. Yet it may also be read in a larger context, as it has by David E. James (1989) in his *Allegories of Cinema: American Films in the Sixties* as a reenergized poetics in which this American art movement strives to transform consciousness.

Sitney's naming of this romantic poetics echoed elements of Jonas Mekas' propositions in his *Village Voice* criticism. In a 1969 piece reproduced in his book, *Movie Journal* (1972), Mekas looked back at Ken Jacobs' *Little Stabs at Happiness* (1960): "His shapes and forms transmit to us, evoke in us, or rather produce in us the states and forms of radiance ... [of] Happiness in full consciousness" (351). Mekas writes of Bruce Baillie that he is "the eternal rider, superimposed on the map of the US ... but in the images of his films, he always seems to be going after some definite, and probably always the same, image" (417). If an impressionistic, subjective response to personal filmmaking such as that of Jonas Mekas seems to militate against a more philosophical investigation of phenomenology in film, it shares interest in heightened perception. Mekas strove to be a poet among poets, and was happy to have poets challenge philosophers, or breed new "natural" philosophers, as Mekas' filmic homage to Walden Pond evidences.

US avant-garde cinema proposed a renaissance of romantic poetry, tinged with its encounter with the Beats, abstract expressionism, underground sexual cultures, and street and group theater. The goal was philosophical, if nonlogocentric: to have visual forms of light and motion affect consciousness of the world by establishing a relay between the artist's vision and the audience openly affected by that vision.

Surrealist film historically had other philosophical *parti pris*: freeing imagination through the exploration of desire, especially sexual desire, and unleashing in its imagery the power of dreams. Antirational, explosive surrealist imagery constitutes a challenge to a more staid aesthetics, and in a larger sense challenges much of philosophy's investment in contemplation and logical argumentation. Parker Tyler becomes the American critic who in *Film Culture* carries over surrealism's philosophical challenge in his celebration of sexuality and eros as ongoing filmic fantasies that disrupt prevailing aesthetics.

Yet much of the US avant-garde's romanticism seems thoroughly tinged with surrealism; as surrealism challenged what could constitute beauty, aesthetics as a philosophical tradition struggled with some avant-garde film's affinity with strange and confrontational images of sex, death, and the void. As Matthew Kieran notes in "Aesthetic Value: Beauty, Ugliness and Incoherence" (1997: 386), philosophers need to rethink aesthetics so as to include the haunting appeal of such films as Luis Buñuel and Salvador Dali's *Un Chien Andalou* (1929); such assertions of course are taken for granted by avant-garde filmmakers and critics. Still, recourse to more traditional aesthetic judgment abounds in avant-garde criticism, sometimes from surprising quarters, as when Hollis Frampton simply speaks of Barry Gerson's films as beautiful, leaving aside Frampton's more usually conceptual approach to film practice.

The phenomenology of perception constitutes another major philosophical tack taken by critics of avant-garde film. Arthur Danto's phenomenological art criticism was a major precedent, steeped as it was in the work of Merleau-Ponty. A detailed formal explanation of the phenomenological approach is beyond the scope of this essay, but much writing about avant-garde film evinced elements of such an approach.

For phenomenological critics, perception, cognition, and being are three categories which film evokes, and many times when this terminology is used in addressing films, one has perhaps to recognize a popular induction of phenomenology. Avant-garde film, by self-consciously and creatively addressing perception, by troubling, challenging, and finally delighting cognition, and then by pointing back toward the artist-maker who laid down these processes on film, fundamentally asks that being be conceived as aesthetically heightened vision. Film time and space are construed in relationship to the human experience of time and space.

There is a streak of phenomenology running through P. Adams Sitney's *Visionary Film*, evident in such statements as these: "It is also a kind of demonstration or lesson in perception" (2002: 356), and in describing another work, "he compounded the paradoxes of reading and depth perception" (369). Annette Michelson made explicit, if brief reference to this branch of philosophy in her writing on Michael Snow: "In fact Snow's *Wavelength* in particular, but also *Back and Forth* and *La Région centrale* seem to bring out phenomenology in many of those who write about those films" (1978). Brakhage's famous dictum in "Metaphors on Vision" displays how romanticism may be tied to phenomenology: "Imagine an eye unruled by man-made laws of perspective, an eye unprejudiced by compositional logic, an eye which does not respond to the name of everything" (1963: 12).

More recently, Vivian Sobchack takes Merleau-Ponty on Husserl as key to her vision of phenomenology, one that connects perception to knowledge by way of desire and judgment: "or that which produces the natural and antepredicative unity of the world and of our life, being apparent in our desires, our evaluations and in the landscape we see more clearly than in Objective knowledge" (1992: 90–8). This becomes her means of discussing the writings and works of Stan Brakhage.

Semiotics, structuralism, and apparatus theory, as they came together in the 1970s, form another philosophical approach to and inspiration for avant-garde film. Or perhaps it is better to say that "theory" for a certain period trumped philosophy as a way of introducing serious thought about all forms of film, including the avant-garde.

The naming of objects may be an impoverished response to the visual signifier, especially if one's response is limited to this level of interpretation, but keen investigation of the process by which visual signifiers communicate when displayed in various contexts, of the means by which temporality and change affect presentation, or of how repetition and variation affect iterations, provides tools for examining the relationship between signifiers and structure that phenomenology often left vague. If phenomenology seemed consigned to descriptions of processes that more often translated films into descriptions of their operations, rather than analyzing their operations in any theoretical detail, semiotics and structuralism provided theoretical tools for moving beyond description. Attention to form becomes amplified in the "structural film," Sitney's term for the films of Hollis Frampton and Michael Snow. (Sitney seems mainly to have proposed the term "structural" in contradistinction to the way "formal," "abstract," or "cubist" had been used previously to describe primarily visual or montage innovation, and less in relationship to structuralism as an intellectual movement and method.) The films so designated developed formal structures and self-conscious gestures bent on calling attention to how meaning is made by images, how a series of images implies a narrative, and how concepts form out of the thoughtful serial arrangement of film images. "Minimalist" and "conceptual," terms from the art world, might also be usefully appropriated to discuss such films as Frampton's *Nostalgia* (1971) and *Zorn's Lemma* (1970) and Snow's *Wavelength* (1967) or his installation *Both Sides of the Story* (1974). The philosophical issues raised include their foregrounding of the absolute irreducibility of films to symbolic or narrative meanings, even though the richness of the signifiers suggestively arranged remains highly evocative of possible meanings. They defy a reading strategy of translation, even one that seems conceptual, such as calling *Zorn's Lemma* "a narrative mapping of human intellectual development." Though one might be tempted to see the slowly burning photographs in *Nostalgia* as simply an illustration, or conversely an expiation of what the title signifies, the process, as framed in the film, is more ironic and polysemic.

Given that, I took a different approach to semiotics and structuralism in *Abstraction in Avant-garde Films* (1985), by combining it with the more deconstructive philosophy of Jean-François Lyotard, particularly his *Libidinal Economy* (1993 [1974]). Here force is construed as a philosophical notion in ways similar to the early work of Jacques Derrida, Karl Abraham, and Maria Torok, thinkers who borrowed Freudian notions of charges attached to concepts as evident in notions of the symptom or dreamwork. Here the signfier can also be seen as part of a flow of energies, and the structures that frame them do less "mapping" than interacting and reinvigorating. Using Thierry Kuntzel's concept of the two films and "*l'émouvoir*" articulated in "Le défilement du film" (1973), I explore the fantasy evoked unconsciously by abstracted film images and sounds. Excess and lack form two polarities of experimentation, so that rate of change and motion can either pursue the extremely rapid or the very gradual as strategies. In a chapter entitled "Scanning landscapes and collapsing architectures: Shattering the Grounding of the Subject/Eye," I look at how Michel Foucault's sense of centering fictive subjectivity that occurs in *The Order of Things* provides a visual metaphor for philosophical grounding of thought. Fascination of landscape and architecture in experimental films lies in refusal to confirm place; the films induce a decentering. In "Sound: Beyond Distinctions between Music, Noise and Speech," the musical event and musical gestures become tied to a philosophy of the event and the gesture. If certain philosophers were thinking in reference to the structural findings of Freud, their insights on how thought might change were echoed by various praxes of filmmakers who were artistically shaping parallel shifts in their experimentation with sound and image compositions.

Many of these theoretical issues addressing semiotics and a philosophy of libidinal investment and circulation would later be used to address new media, as in D. N.

Rodowick's *Reading the Figural, or, Philosophy after the New Media* (2001), and video and installation work, as in essays by Turim and Timothy Murray's *Digital Baroque: New Media Art and Cinematic Folds* (forthcoming).

One complaint some critics such as Noël Carroll have with taking art to be doing or expressing philosophy has been the tendency to make the artwork fit a singular philosophic explanation held by the author. His grounding in analytical philosophy does not directly emerge in his writing about the avant-garde, writing he sees as descriptive criticism, except in this critique, analytical and empiricist in the way it tests a hypothesis against a base of examples. His writings in *Millennium Film Journal*, some of which are collected in *Theorizing the Moving Image* (1996), were aimed at underlining how films such as the early works of Yvonne Rainer established fresh image-to-sound relationships. Seemingly informed by new criticism's approach to poetry, his claims for the films are aesthetic.

Descriptive criticism may be consonant with the analytical philosopher's objection to grand theoretical schemas being forced on films, but it may alternatively fail to tease out concepts that filmic compositions evoke. Critics of the avant-garde have written about a variety of different works, using philosophical references keyed to the specificity of those works. Different works engage the terrain of contemporary philosophy by choosing particular takes on a problematic, and specific interventions, for example, with signifiers, the unconscious, fantasy, and energy flow. The ideas need not be imposed by a critic so much as evoked suggestively as potential, virtual possibilities in the films accessible to any attentive viewer and listener. So while some err by reading philosophy into works, and others err by stopping short of the philosophical implications of close descriptions, still others seek to balance close readings with carefully wrought and suggestive connections between films and philosophical ideas.

Malcolm Le Grice and Peter Gidal proposed thinking of the ideological potential of abstract expression in calling for materialist film as their avant-garde praxis. *Abstract Film and Beyond* (Le Grice 1977; Gidal 1974) sought to provide a philosophical context for both the British and European avant-garde cinemas. The idea of materialist film may be based on a misconceived pun that links "film material" as a formalist notion with the Marxist notion of materialism. Unlike Eisenstein's writings on dialectical materialism, in *Film Form*, that demonstrated how Marxian thought may be applied to film through dialectical montage and the interaction of graphically and conceptually opposing images, materialist film embraced the foregrounding of film's reflexivity concerning its own material praxis. Yet the concepts toward which they were aiming were far more significant than the terminology with which they branded their writing. Theirs was a deconstructive view of representation. Their avant-garde precedents could be found in a mixture of Eisenstein and Brecht, or perhaps Malevich, for like the constructivists and minimalists they clearly had a fondness for abstraction. They championed the material reflexivity of minimalism.

Malcolm Le Grice, in describing his film, *Sketches for a Sensual Philosophy* (1986–9), for a British website, marks his departure with his previous devotion to materialist film: "I have come to realize that my main interest is in creating experiences rather than concepts. Ideas emerge from sensation from colour, image, sound, movement and time" (Le Grice n.d.: online). In presenting *Critical Moments* (for Jean Piaget) (2004), his one-minute video work, he cites "psychologist Jean Piaget's work on the construction of reality in children," work deeply marked by phenomenology (Le Grice 2004).

Psychoanalytic, ideological, and feminist methodologies came to seek a different avant-garde project. Impatience with the personal and the privileging of the perceptual subject led theorists here to champion "theory films" that consciously articulated their positions through a more essayist structuration or in the foregrounding of performance (in a Brechtian learning-play sense of performance). Yvonne Rainer's films became the prototype for such inscription, especially as she was deeply engaged in citing Marxist media theory. One of the issues at stake was the representation of the woman's body, and the ever strong presence of Maya Deren's films reminded us that whatever momentum feminist theory gained by questioning the display and fetishization of the female body, one of the most powerful tropes in avant-garde films remains the quest of the female body for being and recognition. If there was a general sense of value assigned women avant-garde filmmakers making implicit feminist statements by overcoming what tended to be a male-dominated realm of expression, there were specific differences in women's emphases on embodiment. The prohibition on exploitation of the female body that shadowed the feminist reception of early Sally Potter films, such as *Thriller* (1979), gave way to an embrace of the performative female body and led to a recovery of the work of Eleanor Anton and Carolee Schneeman, together with the embrace of such emerging film artists as Abigail Child. Two recent anthologies, *Women and Experimental Filmmaking* (Petrolle and Wexman 2005) and *Women's Experimental Cinema: Critical Frameworks* (Blaetz 2007), represent the current trend for feminist criticism of women's work to focus on the body, sexuality, and desire; the theoretical and philosophical foundations of such criticism varies greatly among the authors.

Queer theory embraced the avant-garde as an exploration of queer identity in its most creative and fluid sense. Andy Warhol, Jack Smith, and Kenneth Anger are all seen as exemplars of a queer aesthetics, tied at once to popular culture and an underground pre-Stonewall existence, as well as to the legacy of Jean Genet's languid sexual imagery in *Un chant d'amour* (1950). Lesbian filmmakers such as Su Friedrich interlace the personal with the structural elements of conceptual filmmaking. Queer artistic filmmaking becomes its own philosophical statement of giving figuration to the long unspoken, underlining erotic qualities of the image and pose, opening once again the personal diaristic form, but this time with a sense that each personal story spoke to a sea change in conception of gender and sexuality. The human mind as queer and the queer film asked us to rethink the history of philosophy; despite its roots in a Greek culture, steeped in male-with-male love and exchange, philosophy had lost touch with its queer ontology.

One relatively recent turn that directly cites philosophy may be represented by James Peterson's *Dreams of Chaos, Visions of Order: Understanding the American Avant-garde Cinema* (1994), a book that embraces a cognitive-science approach that marries cognitive theories of perception to cognitive philosophy. The questions that

David Bordwell asks primarily of narrative film have been refocused on nonnarrative film by Peterson. In some ways Peterson returns to the question of phenomenology, but he uses a completely different vocabulary, with concomitant shifts in theoretical conclusions. Maybe this is why phenomenological approaches bear the brunt of his negative critique. As a counterweight, Ernst Gombrich becomes his touchstone in developing his theory of cognition. He shows how different forms of avant-garde films test schema of cognition by challenging normative expectations. One objection that could be made to this approach is to question its assumption of a normative viewer conforming to rigid schema expectations and priorities – rather than one more used to the more open expectations of art and music, even in its traditional forms surprising its spectator or listener with delightful little pleasures of deviation from the assumed to be universal or dominant schema. In other words, Peterson's book makes certain assumptions about the spectator. He assumes a viewer not predisposed to the delight of the avant-garde. He then suggests how such a naïve viewer might enjoy the cognitive experiments these films offer. This assumption may correspond to professors' experiences introducing students to avant-garde films but fails to consider how uninitiated spectators, even very young children, can be charmed or intrigued by these films. All spectators may not hold to Gombrich's schemas with the consistency Peterson claims they do.

Thus it is interesting to compare Peterson's concluding remarks on Brakhage with the thoughts of the phenomenologists:

> *Window Water Baby Moving* is a dense, complicated film whose structure and style will remain obscure for many viewers. But by establishing coherence at the level of surface structures of the images, the metaphorical connections among images, and the symbolic value of the events represented, the apparent violations of the principle of optimal relevance are recuperated. (1994: 56)

Peterson argues here that formal unity in a poetics outweighs Gombrich's principles of cognition. Yet recourse to those normative principles provides Peterson with a measure of how compositional experimentation is to be defined as breaking with the norm. Order then can be reconstituted by understanding departures within this system. Peterson will find visions of order in various experimental, apparently chaotic dreams.

It is clear that philosophical inquiry on visual and sonoric experimentation has much terrain left to explore, as video, installations, and computer interfaces perform their specific work on aesthetics, phenomenology, libidinal economies, feminist and queer philosophies, deconstruction, and cognitive science. If I see a common ground in these writings on experimental film and philosophy it is as an intellectual inquiry into the lines that so many filmmakers have articulated at discussions following screenings, about playing with time and space, exploring light, and rethinking writing, storytelling, listening, and perception. Philosophies provide a deepened awareness of what is at stake in such intuitively concise framings, yet much critical writing on the avant-garde remains descriptive, biographical, historical, and sociological, rather than theoretical and philosophical.

Still with the publication of many new volumes and essays on Deleuze in conjunction with avant-garde film and video, there is a clear new direction tracing the Bergsonian signs of our time-image machines. As Deleuze himself avoids addressing time-images, for example, forms other than the narrative films that largely comprise his corpus, his examples rarely are drawn from experimental filmmakers. Crystals of time might seem to be a useful construct for the multifaceted editing of experimental works, but for Deleuze we think time in the image within the parameters of narrative expansion, compression, refraction, and overlay. Still such writers as Laura U. Marks in *The Skin of the Film* (2000) and Jeffrey Skoller in *Shadows, Specters, Shards: Making History in Avant-garde Film* (2005) use Deleuze to speak to repetition and time in the essayist avant-garde cinema, though Marks does so by branching "from Bergson to phenomenology, and in turn to neurophysiology, in order to explain how sense memory is embodied" (xiv), while Skoller uses Walter Benjamin along with Deleuze to amplify his critical approach to the films. Let me close by noting a wonderful circularity to bringing Bergson via Deleuze back to bear on the experimental film, for Bergson's writings were referenced in cinephilic circles in response to early French avant-gardes as they reached toward the new philosopher of thoughts and images.

See also Phenomenology (Chapter 40) and Cognitive theory (Chapter 33).

References

Blaetz, R. (ed.) (2007) *Women's Experimental Cinema: Critical Frameworks*, Durham, NC: Duke University Press.
Brakhage, S. (1963) "Metaphors on Vision," *Film Culture* 30: 12–23.
Carroll, N. (1996) *Theorizing the Moving Image*, Cambridge and New York: Cambridge University Press.
James, D. E. (1989) *Allegories of Cinema: American Film in the Sixties*, Princeton, NJ: Princeton University Press.
Kieran, M. (1997) "Aesthetic Value: Beauty, Ugliness, and Incoherence," *Philosophy* 72: 383–99.
Kuntzel, T. (1973) "Le défilement du film," *La Revue d'Esthétique* 2–4: 97–110.
Le Grice, M. (1977) *Abstract Film and Beyond*, London: Studio Vista.
—— (2004) *Critical Moments (for Jean Piaget)* (video), Luxonline. Available at http://www.luxonline.org.uk/artists/malcolm_le_grice/critical_moments_(for_jean_piaget).html.
—— (n.d.) Artist profile. Luxonline. Available at http://www.luxonline.org.uk/artists/malcolm_le_grice/ (accessed 27 May 2008).
Lyotard, J.-F. (1993) *Libidinal Economy*, trans. I. H. Grant, Bloomington: Indiana University Press.
Marks, L. (2000) *The Skin of the Film: Intercultural Cinema, Embodiment, and the Senses*, Durham, NC: Duke University Press.
Mekas, J. (1972) *Movie Journal: The Rise of the New American Cinema, 1959–1971*, New York: Macmillan.
Michelson, A. (1978) "Towards Snow," in P. A. Sitney (ed.) *The Avant-garde Film: A Reader of Theory and Criticism*, New York: New York University Press.
Murray, T. (forthcoming) *Digital Baroque: New Media Art and Cinematic Folds*, Minneapolis: Minnesota University Press.
Peterson, J. (1994) *Dreams of Chaos, Visions of Order: Understanding the American Avant-garde Cinema*, Detroit: Wayne State University Press.
Petrolle, J., and Wexman, V. W. (eds.) (2005) *Women and Experimental Filmmaking*, Urbana, IL: University of Illinois Press.

Rodowick, D. (2001) *Reading the Figural, or, Philosophy after the New Media*, Durham, NC: Duke University Press.

Sitney, P. (2002 [1974]) *Visionary Film: The American Avant-garde, 1943–2000*, 3rd ed., Oxford and New York: Oxford University Press.

Skoller, J. (2005) *Shadows, Specters, Shards: Making History in Avant-garde Film*, Minneapolis: University of Minnesota Press.

Sobchack, V. (1992) *The Address of the Eye: A Phenomenology of Film Experience*, Princeton, NJ: Princeton University Press.

Turim, M. (1985) *Abstraction in Avant-garde Films*, Ann Arbor, MI: UMI Research Press.

Wollen, P. (1975), "The Two Avant Gardes," *Studio International* 190 (November–December): 171–5.

Further reading

The following are further reading on this topic: Paul Arthur, *A Line of Sight: American Avant-garde Film since 1965* (Minneapolis: University of Minnesota Press, 2005); Abigail Child, *This Is Called Moving: A Critical Poetics of Film* (Tuscaloosa: University of Alabama Press, 2005); Maureen Turim, "The Interiority of Space: Desire and Maya Deren," in A. Graf and D. Scheunemann (eds.) (2008) *Avant-garde Cinema* (Amsterdam: Editions Rodopi, 2007), 155–65; Malcolm Le Grice, *Experimental Cinema in the Digital Age* (London: British Film Institute, 2002); Dominique Noguez (1999) *Eloge du cinéma expérimental*, 2nd rev., exp. ed. (Paris: Éditions Paris Expérimental); and Edward S. Small (1994) *Direct Theory: Experimental Film/Video as Major Genre* (Carbondale: Southern Illinois University Press).

49
TRAGEDY AND COMEDY
Deborah Knight

This entry focuses on two of the master genres of narrative – tragedy and comedy – and will also offer thoughts about the other two master genres, romance and irony/ satire. By "master genre," I mean the most basic templates adopted and modified in the production of a variety of narratives, whether literary, filmic, dramatic, operatic, or other. Let me start with key points. Tragedy has held an extraordinarily privileged position among the master genres, not just in Western literary culture, but also in both analytic and continental philosophy. For example, Walter Kaufmann's *Tragedy and Philosophy* traces the connections between these two discourses from the ancient Greeks to the twentieth century, focusing admirably on key dramas in the tradition (Kaufmann 1992). It is noteworthy, but perhaps unsurprising, that philosophy does not have a companion volume titled *Comedy and Philosophy*. That said, there is a tension when discussing tragedy and comedy (and indeed romance and irony/satire) between treating them as literary modes having identifiable forms and conventional features and treating them as world views. This is the distinction between tragedy as a narrative form of the sort originally described by Aristotle, and modified over the centuries, and as a way of thinking about an author's or filmmaker's artistic vision. Another problem is that while there are twentieth- and twenty-first-century artistic examples of romance, irony/satire, and comedy, it is not entirely clear that there are many examples of tragedy. Even the usual suspects – for example, *Death of a Salesman* – bring the basic principles of what constitutes recent tragic drama into conflict with the Greek and Elizabethan tragedies that count as canonical. Of course, as Kaufmann notes, it is odd that some think tragedy should still be written in the style of Shakespeare when no one worries that music is no longer written in the style of Palestrina (Kaufmann 1992: 320). Willy Loman might be the antithesis of Oedipus. Nevertheless, like *Oedipus Rex*, at the core of *Death of a Salesman* is Loman's discovery of what he truly is (Kaufmann 1992: 322).

I begin by clarifying the relationships between tragedy and comedy, using as my key reference Northrop Frye's magisterial *Anatomy of Criticism* (Frye 1957). I then investigate the philosophical privileging of tragedy over comedy, consider the contrast between genre and world view, and conclude by proposing candidates for the status of paradigmatic film comedy and tragedy. In the course of the entry, I defend comedy against those who treat it as philosophically and artistically inferior to tragedy.

The master genres from the perspective of Northrop Frye

What exactly are tragedy and comedy, romance and irony/satire? At the heart of theorizing on this subject, and following a consistent arc from Aristotle to Northrop Frye, is the idea that these genres are most profitably construed as literary modes organized around recognizable conventions of plot and characterization, as well as certain anticipated audience responses. Frye takes from Aristotle the idea that the relationship between a literary work's central protagonists and its audience is in a broad sense an ethical one. It is a relationship characterized by different sorts of ethical regard, where the audience's attitude is in part determined by the perceived moral status of the various genres' protagonists. Thus as Aristotle notes, tragic protagonists are of a higher sociomoral standing than their audiences, whereas comic protagonists are base. Frye restates this point in terms of superiority. Accordingly, if a protagonist is "superior in *kind* both to other men and to the environment," then the dramatic or narrative mode at issue is myth, and the protagonist is a god. But if a protagonist is "superior in *degree* to other men and to his environment," then the mode is romance. If a protagonist is "superior in degree to other men but not to his natural environment," the mode is either tragedy or epic, and Frye notes that this "is primarily the kind of hero that Aristotle had in mind." The comic protagonist as well as the protagonist of most realist fiction is "superior neither to other men nor to his environment." Finally, the protagonist of works in the ironic mode as well as the satiric mode is "inferior in power or intelligence to ourselves." Given that myth is not much in vogue, we can posit a schema of the literary master genres focusing on the other four modes. Tragedy traditionally involves the fall of someone superior to us, romance the pursuit of a quest by someone superior to us, and comedy the welcoming into the community of someone lower than us who was initially an outsider. Irony differs from these three, since ironic works typically, as Frye would say, suppress moral judgments, which are not so much expressed as reflected by the ironic work (Frye 1957: 40).

How does all this relate to the current philosophical study of film? My suggestion is that we would do well to investigate the way master genres, which are themselves just schemas of possible narrative or dramatic works, underpin and direct the structuring of particular films and film genres. While it is true that some films, for example the *Thin Man* series (1934), *The Philadelphia Story* (1940), and *Groundhog Day* (1993) are popularly categorized as comedies, this is not just a matter of their humor but also the way they correspond to key features of the master genre, primarily in their overall narrative arc and the nature of their central characters. Few fictional films are categorized as tragedies, in part because, as Frye noted, the prevailing literary (and by extension, cinematic) tone has inclined toward irony over the last century or so, when it was not pursuing the modes of comedy or romance.

Indeed, the popular generic categories for fiction films are arguably quite different from the scheme of the master genres. Fiction films can fall into any number of recognizable genres: biopic, war film, western, espionage film, gangster film, romantic comedy, science fiction, costume drama, detective film, melodrama, murder mystery, and the list goes on. These are examples of popular or what I call *consensus* genres.

What is striking about works that fall into the categories of the consensus genres is that they are very often films which have features of more than one consensus genre or combine features taken from one (or more) consensus genre and one (or more) master genre. John Ford's *The Searchers* (1956), for example, is a western but also an example of the master genre of romance, given that the theme of the film is a quest undertaken by Ethan Edwards (John Wayne) and his part-native nephew, Marty (Jeffrey Hunter), to avenge the killing of Ethan's sister-in-law and true love, Martha (Dorothy Jordan), and to find Martha's daughter, Debbie (Natalie Wood), who has been abducted by the Comanche chief Cicatrice (Henry Brandon). John Madden's *Shakespeare in Love* (1998) combines the costume drama with the consensus genre of romantic comedy, but in the end, is it clear just what to say about the structure of the film? The separation of the lovers at the end of the film is not the stuff of the master genre of comedy but yet does not rise to the level of tragedy. In the film's final moments, Shakespeare (Joseph Fiennes) imagines his beloved emerging from the ocean and walking resolutely across a vast, empty beach in a new world. While this gives him the inspiration to write *The Tempest*, *Shakespeare in Love* seems to spin away from romantic comedy into something like the prolegomenon to an epic, which the film anticipates but does not deliver. *The Matrix* might look on the surface like a cyberthriller, but is, at least in its first installment, clearly an example of the master genre of romance, focused as it is on Neo's quest, which turns out ultimately to be a quest to discover his own identity as "the One."

So far I have only mentioned films obliquely, using them as examples, rather than offering detailed interpretive readings of them, and it is time to explain why I have chosen this course. Like Stanley Cavell, I take Northrop Frye to offer a model of how the master genres operate, their key themes and motifs, the distribution of typical characters, as well as the presumed relationship established between work and audience. As I construe them, none of the four master genres is ever purely instantiated in any particular film. In fact, Frye himself notes that some of our greatest works of literature combine different aspects of the four key master genres. But let me now turn to the appreciation of tragedy and comedy.

Tragedy, comedy, and the question of philosophical value

Tragedy and comedy have understandably been treated as opposites, as the sad and the smiling masks have depicted from ancient days, given that the narrative outcomes for tragic and comic protagonists are so strikingly antithetical. But tragedy and comedy have also been treated as opposites in terms of value, where tragedy is positively valued by many philosophers while comedy is valued much less highly. I would argue that tragedy has been attractive to philosophy because it can fairly straightforwardly lay claim to moral seriousness. Comedy, a much misunderstood genre, is considerably less appreciated, because the possibility that it could make an analogous claim to moral seriousness has largely gone uninvestigated by philosophers. Rather, comedy is typically thought to lack moral worth, to be unserious or frivolous, or to lack a suitable moral perspective. A selective review of handbooks and companions to aesthetics shows that many include entries on tragedy, whereas there are virtually none on comedy, which tends to be collapsed into the category of humor if it is treated at all. The standard philosophical approach to comedy presumes that dramatic or narrative comedy offers only momentary or superficial pleasure, expressed as laughter, and thus concludes that comedy does not offer the kind of contemplative, and therefore enduring, value associated with tragedy. Philosophers typically do not ask why happy endings might not tell us something important about our empathetic vision and our moral values.

In the tragedy-favoring philosophical tradition, it is argued that classical tragedies are philosophically significant because they illustrate for us the importance and value of empathy, yet the question whether perhaps comedy might not also do so goes unaddressed. Because of the concern that readers and viewers of classical tragedies experience on behalf of tragedy's unfortunate protagonists, Martha Nussbaum argues that we are reminded of the "fragility of goodness" and the dire consequences that can befall largely blameless characters when their moral luck fails them (Nussbaum 1986). Nussbaum and others of this persuasion maintain that our emotional response to the unfolding of the tragic plot – the experience of the so-called tragic emotions identified by Aristotle as pity and fear – marks our sense that in significant ways we are like the tragic protagonist. In particular, we are similarly vulnerable to the variableness of moral luck. Thus, as the Nussbaumian argument goes, our fear on behalf of the protagonist and our pity for the fate that befalls him or her is a sign of our participation in a broader and virtuous moral community. That the master genre of comedy is concerned with the rejuvenation and reinvigoration of the fictional community, and that audience engagement with comedies requires us to take this revitalization of the community as a morally positive end, tends to be passed over by the proponents of tragedy.

Additionally, philosophers including Nussbaum argue that engaging with dramatic tragedies encourages us to clarify our ideas about such important issues as justice at both familial and societal levels. Such concerns assume that one key value of dramatic tragedy is that it speaks to universally important themes, and that a closely related value concerns the way tragedies can impact us at an epistemological and conceptual level. At one and the same time, we develop our empathetic skills and clarify our sense of why the tragic events encountered matter to us in the way they do. Complementing Nussbaum's argument, Susan Feagin contends that our emotional response to tragedy has two components: a direct response and a meta-response (Feagin 1997). The direct response involves negative emotions, including pity and fear, as well as distress, sorrow, and so forth. The meta-response, however, is positive in the sense that we can be pleased at the metalevel that at the direct level we responded correctly to the gravity of the depicted events. Here again is the idea that in correctly responding to tragic drama, members of the audience identify themselves as part of a broader moral community. Such a view highlights the perception that tragic drama is philosophically significant because of its ability to help us reaffirm our moral commitments. The question whether our appreciation of dramatic or narrative comedy might not also occasion similar responses typically goes unexamined.

Occasionally, philosophers are explicit about their valuing of tragedy over comedy. Feagin argues that tragedy is superior to comedy, and by this I understand her to mean philosophically superior to comedy, as well as morally superior to comedy. She complains that "in comedy there must be a 'butt' of the joke" (Feagin 1997: 309). Feagin apparently subscribes to the superiority theory of humor, a view which says that audiences find humor because they feel themselves superior to the comic situation or protagonist. On my view of tragedy and comedy, the protagonist of tragedy is traditionally superior in virtue to members of the audience, while the protagonist of comedy is initially positioned below the members of the audience. But this does not ultimately entail that the superiority theory is the true account of the master genre of comedy. So I contest Feagin's claim that comedy "is skin deep" (Feagin 1997: 309). It is hardly the case that dramatic or narrative comedies must involve a central character who is the butt of a joke. By the same token, in many tragedies there is someone very much akin to the butt of a deeply malign joke – consider Oedipus or Romeo. Kaufmann notes how close certain tragedies are to black comedies (Kaufmann 1992: 320). Nor is it true that comedy invites only (or at least overwhelmingly) direct responses rather than meta-responses, as Feagin claims. The master genre of comedy paradigmatically features an outsider figure, who initially does not fulfill social expectations and may therefore be treated with derision. Yet the main thematic of the genre is the incorporation into society of the one initially rebuffed. This acceptance of the outsider is simultaneously the opportunity for the reinvigoration of the community, which is typically marked by a celebration, such as a wedding or a fête. Examples abound, but the conclusion of *Shrek* (2001) is wonderful, capped off as it is by Donkey's cover of "Livin' la Vida Loca." The comedy of, say, the stand-up comedian who specializes in put-down jokes is quite different from comic works in the narrative master genre of comedy. I am not sure that I subscribe to the direct-response/meta-response account of our engagement with either tragedy or comedy, but one who did subscribe could arguably see that comedies such as *Groundhog Day* and *Shrek* invite a meta- as well as a direct response.

I have suggested that tragedy is held in high regard because of its perceived moral seriousness, while comedy is assumed to be less morally serious and therefore less worthy of philosophical regard. If we are to challenge this view, we must have reasons, and it may not always be a philosopher who advances them. Julian Gough, an author and literary critic, suggests that perhaps we should look again at the privileging of tragedy over comedy. He writes:

> The Greeks believed that comedy was superior to tragedy: tragedy was the merely human view of life (we sicken, we die). But comedy was the gods' view, from on high: our endless and repetitive cycle of suffering, our horror of it, our inability to escape it. The big, drunk, flawed, horny Greek gods watched us for entertainment ... And the best of the old Greek comedy tried to give us that relaxed, amused perspective on our flawed selves. We became as gods, laughing at our own follies. (Gough 2007: online)

What Gough proposes is a view of comedy, derived as is our view of tragedy from the ancient Greeks, which suggests that comedy also has moral seriousness, despite the fact that it involves laughter. This is a minority view, but not an unreasonable one.

We might ask, along with Gough, how tragedy came to be valued more highly than comedy. One answer: that Aristotle's *Poetics* survived, giving us something like the definitive account of how a tragedy should be constructed, whereas there is no authoritative Aristotelian textbook for the construction of dramatic comedy. And there is another possibility. It is one thing for figures such as the Greek gods to laugh at mere humans. After all, they had their own foibles and worse, so their laughter is partly one of recognition, not condemnation. But it is impossible to imagine the God of the New Testament laughing at the human comedy. Tragedy, one might say, more closely captures what is thought to be the ethos of the Christian God.

Tragedy and comedy: genre or world view?

The philosophical defenders of tragedy over comedy have a rebuttal. They might argue that tragedy's superiority to comedy is not some idiosyncratic by-product of the history of the West from the Greeks to the present, but rather a fact about the subject matter and more importantly the perspective of dramatic tragedies – and here I mean something like the philosophical or moral perspective attributed to key examples of art tragedy. Some who defend this notion are inclined to collapse tragedy as a dramatic form together with tragedy as a world view. This creates many complexities, of which the most important are the following. The presumed perspective of the tragic drama need not correspond to the perspective of the dramatist. Someone with a tragic world view may not be any good at writing dramatic tragedy (perhaps accidentally writing melodramas instead). However, someone who writes brilliant tragedies might not have a tragic world view. Shakespeare could well be an example. A tragic world view might be experienced by any number of individuals who do not participate in the creation of artworks at all – those who are melancholy or depressive in real life are outside of the scope of this argument. In fact, also outside of this argument are cases of real-life catastrophe and mayhem. There are any number of odious incidents in real life that merit being described as "tragic," but this is not the sense of the term being used here. Certainly, as Kaufmann argues, such things as the Holocaust, the assassination of John F. Kennedy, and the Vietnam War are properly described as tragic, in the nonliterary sense. Indeed, Kaufmann argues that some nonliterary examples of tragedy actually take the form of something very much like classical tragedy. His example is the assassination of Kennedy. Nevertheless, I contend that what counts as tragic in cases of art tragedy is clearly very different from these real-life examples.

Aaron Ridley is someone who seems to conflate a tragic world view with tragedy as a master genre. Ridley writes, "Tragedy matters to aesthetics because it matters to philosophy, of which aesthetics is a part, and it matters to philosophy for one main reason. Tragedy engages more directly than any other artform with philosophy's own most fundamental question: How should one live?" (Ridley 2003: 408). I see why this idea is compelling, but I do not see why it is true, not least because I am not persuaded that Ridley is right that philosophy has a "most fundamental question," or that, even if it does, this is the one. But let us grant Ridley his point. It is simply false to suggest that the other master genres are silent on the question of how one should live. The master genre of comedy's answer is as follows: as a member of a welcoming community. Romance and irony/satire have their own answers, although less generally optimistic and more complicated to describe. Indeed, it is not at all obvious that the canonical tragedies, to restrict ourselves to those, answer the question about how one should live in anything like a clear and helpful way. Is there a general take-home lesson to be found in, say, *Antigone* or *Macbeth*? Even if there were, how are we to understand the sum of these take-home lessons? Ridley argues that we should treat art tragedy and real-life tragedy symmetrically because both share a common tragic vision. Yet surely this is not right. It is tragic, in the sense that it is the most awful and disheartening of cases, to learn, for example, that an infant has been shaken to death by a frustrated parent or that an innocent pedestrian has been killed by a drunk driver. But if we are thinking of tragedy as a master genre governing works of dramatic or narrative fiction, then arguably we are primarily concerned with certain sorts of plots featuring fairly clearly specifiable characters and situations, which is precisely the lesson taught to us by Aristotle and reiterated by Frye. Except in the very unusual sorts of cases that Kaufmann draws to our attention, real-life examples of tragedy bear little resemblance to art tragedy. And here I am concerned with art tragedy.

The idea that tragedy and morality are intimately connected has largely gone unchallenged, as has the idea that our engagement with works of dramatic tragedy encourages us to clarify our own moral concepts and commitments more than our engagement with works from other master genres. But perhaps things are not so straightforward. Sebastian Gardner has recently argued that we should question the historically well-entrenched conception of tragedy as being compatible with morality. Instead, Gardner argues that there is "a dissociation or discrepancy, or in stronger terms, a mutual antagonism, between tragedy and morality" (Gardner 2003: 218). In particular, Gardner argues that "the assumption that tragedy serves to enhance moral sensibility" is mistaken (Gardner 2003: 220). It is beyond the scope of this article to examine Gardner's argument in detail, but I will draw attention to two of his most striking claims. One is that the view "that tragedy awakens us to morality's demands by sharpening our sense of the fragility of goodness … is … superficial and misleading" (245). A central part of this claim is the recognition that the perspectives on the world offered by tragedy and by morality are at odds with one another: "moral consciousness regards human subjectivity as at home in the world in a way that tragedy says it is not, and it cancels the human antagonism with the world which tragedy presupposes" (245). The second, and clearly related, claim Gardner offers is that whatever makes tragedy valuable, it cannot be an example or type of moral value (248). If Gardner is right, then it would appear that some of the most cherished ways in which philosophy in general and philosophical aesthetics in particular have approached art tragedy are mistaken.

Vertigo: a modern tragedy?

In the opening scenes of Alfred Hitchcock's *Vertigo* (1958), Scottie (James Stewart), a police detective who suffers from the title affliction, is released from the force after an accident that causes the death of a colleague. He is then hired by an old friend, Gavin Elster (Tom Helmore), to follow Elster's wife, Madeleine (Kim Novak). Elster tells Scottie that he believes his wife is psychologically unstable and that he wants someone to keep an eye on her. What the first-time viewer cannot appreciate is that Elster is deliberately misleading Scottie. The woman Elster claims to be his wife is his lover acting as his wife's double. Her psychiatric problems are not real but feigned. Scottie, in short, is being set up by Elster as the "witness" to what Scottie will think is Madeleine's suicide. But the real Madeleine does not commit suicide, and the woman who has pretended to be Madeleine lives. It is the murdered body of Elster's wife which undergoes the fall that Scottie thinks is Madeleine's suicide.

Scottie succumbs psychologically, believing that Madeleine has died as a result of his inability to overcome his vertigo while ascending the steps to the bell tower in the mission of San Juan Bautista, where the apparent suicide takes place. After a lengthy recovery, during which he never forgets his infatuation, Scottie chances upon a young woman named Judy who reminds him of Madeleine. Judy is single, lives in a cheap hotel room, and is as different from Madeleine as could be: brunette rather than blonde, coarse rather than refined, apparently unattracted to Scottie as opposed to leading him on. The conceit of Hitchcock's film is that the coarse brunette living in the hotel room in San Francisco is the woman who played the role of Elster's wife. While it is true that Scottie, in the film, almost pathologically compels Judy to recreate herself as Madeleine – which involves changing her hairstyle, clothes, manners, and diction back to what Scottie remembers of Madeleine – the problem for Judy is that although she allows Scottie to turn her back into Madeleine, she wants Scottie to love her for herself, just as she loves him. When Scottie finally discovers that Judy is the person he believed to be Madeleine, he drags her up the vertiginous stairway of the bell tower at San Juan Bautista. When he compels her out onto the roof of the church, a nun unexpectedly comes through the rooftop door, scaring Judy enough that she plunges to her death, falling to the ground just as Elster's dead wife's body had done months before.

In *Vertigo* Hitchcock showcases his brilliant use of suspense, his ability to incorporate both comedy and irony into essentially serious plots, and his capacity to cast actors against type, as he does here with James Stewart. *Vertigo* is a film organized around the theme of falling: falling literally to one's death, as Scottie's partner does at the film's beginning and as Judy does at the film's end, and falling morally, as Scottie does when his obsession with Madeleine so consumes him that he forces Judy to let him make her over in Madeleine's image. Scottie initially represents law and order and is moreover a thoughtful and compassionate man who holds himself responsible for his partner's death, even though his vertigo is really no fault of his own. His moral fall is the stuff of tragedy as described by Aristotle and Frye. Indeed, the events that befall Scottie are really not ones for which he can be held at fault. That he has vertigo, that he trusts his old friend, that he becomes fascinated with the woman he believes to be Madeleine: these are as inevitable, narratively speaking, as that Oedipus should kill his father and marry his mother. His misunderstanding of Judy's true feelings for him when he finds her after Madeleine's death, his resentment at having been taken advantage of, his anger and desire for revenge, which lead to precisely what he did not want, namely Judy's death, are also the very ingredients of tragedy. In terms of such classic features of tragedy as reversal and recognition, *Vertigo* positions itself well as a modern tragedy. The reaction shot of James Stewart's expression as he witnesses Judy fall to her death illustrates this claim.

The Philadelphia Story: the romantic comedy meets the comedy of manners

Cavell's *Pursuits of Happiness: The Hollywood Comedy of Remarriage* makes the bold claim that a small group of films from the 1930s and the early 1940s form a coherent genre. What lends this genre its coherence is its debt to the structures and themes of Old Greek and Shakespearian comedy, its focus on the female rather than the male protagonist, and the task, not of marrying the heroine correctly, but of *remarrying* her correctly. The trick, Cavell notes, is not to get the central romantic couple together, but "to get them *back* together, together *again*" (Cavell 1981: 2). Another significant feature of the comedy of remarriage – not unique to it, of course (in comedy, think of *The Thin Man* and in drama, of *The Maltese Falcon* [1941]) – is the centrality of sharp, quick, sometimes stinging, often wry dialogue. *It Happened One Night* (1934), *The Philadelphia Story* (1940), *His Girl Friday* (1940): these are films that delight in talk, in verbal acrobatics and sparring, in nuance as well as in overt statements, in language which praises and condemns (for the right and wrong reasons), which entreats, scolds, and encourages, which allows for discovery and self-discovery. Cavell's decision to champion a philosophical conversation about Hollywood comedies was groundbreaking.

But *The Philadelphia Story* is also a paradigm example of the master genre of comedy. It takes place in a rarefied and somewhat fabulous world – the world of the Lord family's mansion. It features insiders to that world, notably Tracy Samantha Lord (Katharine Hepburn), her mother and her little sister, as well as a number of outsiders, including her ex-husband C. K. Dexter Haven (Cary Grant), who in the opening moments of the film is thrown out of the mansion, along with his suitcases and golf clubs. But all is not well on the inside, and it takes the outsiders to help bring about the return to order of the social world of the mansion.

In *The Philadelphia Story*, where language is so central and terms of praise and abuse so pointed, Tracy Lord discovers not so much who she is, but how she has been seen by others, and she discovers this from those who can also suggest who she could, and should, and can be. Shepherding her to this realization are her ex-husband, Dex, Macauley Connor (James Stewart), a journalist who, along with his photographer sidekick, has gained access to Tracy's home and wedding under false pretenses, her father, who has been very much in the tabloids through an alliance with a dancer in New York, and Tracy's current fiancé, George Kittering.

The primary motif of *Vertigo* was falling, and moral descent and actual death were the inevitable outcomes. The primary motif of *The Philadelphia Story* is arguably to be found in the various descriptions of Tracy Lord by the men in her life. She is often likened to a goddess, a statue, sometimes a queen. That she is regal and unfeeling is often mentioned. Specifically, she has not responded with feeling to her father or her first husband, who both have displayed weaknesses which she has met with scorn. The journey that Tracy undertakes is one of realizing three things. She need not be as cold and controlling (and self-controlled) as she has previously been. She need not be as angry toward those who love her. And she must actively determine how her life will proceed, specifically by sorting out who is and who is not her real partner in life. That decision depends on discovering who among those who either love her, think they love her, or are infatuated with her, most strongly want her to be herself.

At the conclusion of *The Philadelphia Story*, Tracy enters once again into marriage with Dex, the man who knows her best, has been most cruelly hurt by her, has been cruelest to her in an attempt to show her her own potential, and who loves her enough to risk a second chance with her. This reunification has depended on Tracy learning from others how she seems to them to be, and accepting the more positive view of herself that she has finally seen mirrored, both in the responses of Dex and in those of Macauley Connor. If tragedy is typically praised because it offers us a vision of characters who come to understand themselves, it isn't clear why we cannot also affirm comedies which offer us a similar vision of characters' self-recognition. That these modes of self-recognition take completely different tacks is not a result of moral significance, *per se*, but of generic convention.

See also Stanley Cavell (Chapter 32), Genre (Chapter 14), Emotion and affect (Chapter 8), and Empathy and character engagement (Chapter 9).

References

Cavell, Stanley (1981) *Pursuits of Happiness: The Hollywood Comedy of Remarriage*, Cambridge, MA: Harvard University Press.

Feagin, S. (1997) "The Pleasures of Tragedy," in S. Feagin and P. Maynard (eds.) *Aesthetics*, New York: Oxford University Press.

Frye, N. (1957) *Anatomy of Criticism: Four Essays*, Princeton, NJ: Princeton University Press.

Gardner, S. (2003) "Tragedy, Morality, and Metaphysics," in J. Bermudez and S. Gardener (eds.) *Art and Morality*, London: Routledge.

Gough, J. (2007) "Divine Comedy," *Prospect* 134 (May). Available at http://www.prospect-magazine.co.uk/article_details.php?id=9276.

Kaufmann, W. (1992) *Tragedy and Philosophy*, Princeton, NJ: Princeton University Press.

Nussbaum, M. (1986) *The Fragility of Goodness: Luck and Ethics in Greek Tragedy and Philosophy*, New York: Cambridge University Press.

Ridley, A. (2003) "Tragedy," in J. Levinson (ed.) *The Oxford Handbook of Aesthetics*, New York: Oxford University Press.

Part IV
FILM AS PHILOSOPHY

50
FILM AS PHILOSOPHY
Thomas E. Wartenberg

The twenty-first century has witnessed a growing recognition among both philosophers and film scholars alike that many films from a wide variety of genres and periods deserve and, in some cases, demand philosophical attention. In part, this realization stems from the growing trend of introducing students to philosophy through films. Perhaps because visual media are more accessible to young people than written ones, philosophy professors have realized that students can often more easily identify and understand philosophical issues when they are presented cinematically rather than in the literary texts generally taken to constitute the (Western) philosophical tradition.

There are other reasons for this trend as well. One can point to the rise of digital reproduction technologies as promoting changes in viewing practices that encourage the production of films – and I use this term in this entry to include what I call film's "cognate media" – television, video, DVDs, etc. – with philosophical content. One way to satisfy the demand for films that repay repeated viewing is to imbue them with a content that is not immediately available on a first viewing. And philosophy certainly fits that bill. So if it is true that films are increasingly made with a self-conscious philosophical content, we would expect this fact to be registered by philosophers and film scholars.

But whatever its sources, the validity of exploring the philosophical content of films depends, to a certain extent, on the prior question of whether film is a viable medium for presenting philosophical ideas. Although many people may find nothing problematic about this claim, an intense philosophical debate has arisen about the extent to which films are genuinely capable of doing philosophy, whether it makes sense to view (some) films as actually works of philosophy. Although all the participants in this debate acknowledge that films can, at a minimum, bring a philosophical issue to the awareness of their audiences, there is disagreement about how much more films can do philosophically. While some believe that film's philosophical contribution is limited to little more than raising philosophical problems in an accessible form for film audiences, others assert that films can actually philosophize, that films can be, to use Stephen Mulhall's pregnant phrase, "philosophy in action" (Mulhall 2001: 4).

In this entry, I address the question of whether films can do philosophy. After clarifying precisely what the issue is that fuels the debate over this question, I will consider a number of objections that have been raised to what I call the film-as-philosophy thesis. Once I have discussed possible responses to these objections, I canvas some of the ways in which films have been taken to be capable of doing philosophy.

The philosophy-as-film thesis

To assess the viability of the idea that films have the ability to do philosophy, it is crucial to have a clear understanding of what precisely is being asserted by the advocates of the film-as-philosophy thesis. There is general agreement between them and their critics about two claims. The first, which I have already mentioned, is that films can raise philosophical issues. But what makes an issue philosophical? This is a vexed question within philosophy itself. Here it will suffice to acknowledge two different sources of philosophical problems. First, there are certain basic questions that philosophy has traditionally attempted to answer, including "How is knowledge possible?," "What is real?," "Why be moral?," and "What makes something a work of art?" Second, any intellectual domain that faces issues about its own possibility thereby becomes philosophical. So, for example, science turns philosophical when it asks questions about its own practices, such as "What is an explanation?" This lets us understand why *The Matrix* (1999) is such a good example of a film that raises a philosophical problem, for it vividly presents the hypothesis of radical skepticism. Indeed, its presentation of this possibility has given rise to a great deal of discussion among philosophers (see, for example, the essays in Grau 2005). But many other films have also raised philosophical issues. Ingmar Bergman's 1956 art film, *The Seventh Seal*, clearly raises the philosophical questions of whether God exists and how faith might be possible in a world in which evil exists. Woody Allen's films are also generally recognized as posing for their viewers various philosophical questions, such as whether it pays to be moral. Thus, films made at quite different times and belonging to diverse genres are recognized as raising philosophical questions.

The second issue on which there is general consensus is that a film can do philosophy by simply recording the reading of a philosophical argument, but it is also agreed that this does not settle much in the film-as-philosophy debate. The idea is that a film that records a philosopher making a philosophical argument verbally would count as a genuine instance of philosophy on film. Although it involves more than simply the filming of John Berger presenting a philosophical argument, the BBC television series *Ways of Seeing* (1974) provides an actual example of a video in which philosophy is done on screen by a philosopher. Berger makes numerous claims about how techniques of mechanical reproduction of images, such as photography, have changed our appreciation of works of art. He supports these claims with evidence and argument, thereby making this series a paradigmatic instance of a film that *records* a philosophical argument. But the opponents of the film-as-philosophy thesis argue that films like this are a special case, for they do not settle the question of whether films that do not employ explicit argumentation, as *Ways of Seeing* does, can actually do the sorts of things that are generally taken to constitute doing philosophy, such as presenting a thesis or making an argument.

Once the consensus on these two ways in which philosophy can be done on film has been acknowledged, real disagreement surfaces. The crux of the debate is whether films within the standard genres of filmmaking – from fiction films to documentaries and even avant-garde films – can actually do more than raise a philosophical question or record a philosophical argument, whether some films should really be counted as doing philosophy on their own.

What fuels this debate is the conviction on the part of the opponents of the film-as-philosophy thesis that there are real obstacles to an artistic medium like film being philosophy. Proponents of the thesis argue that, on the contrary, there is no reason to preclude films from the category of philosophy. To gain more clarity on what fuels this disagreement, it will be useful to canvas some of the central objections that have been put forward to the film-as-philosophy thesis.

Objections to the thesis

I now examine four different objections to the film-as-philosophy thesis: the generality, explicitness, imposition, and banality objections. In each case, I present possible responses to these objections to give the reader a sense of what is at stake in the debate.

The generality objection

The generality objection to the film-as-philosophy thesis focuses on an alleged syntactic difference between philosophical claims and the content of films. According to this objection, philosophy is characterized by a search for general truths. If we think about the practice of Socrates, this objection points out, we find him searching for general definitions of such central philosophical concepts as justice, morality, and truth. In a dialogue like *The Republic*, attempted definitions of justice such as "the will of the stronger," are refuted by Socrates, who puts forward a radically new view of justice as "each part playing its role."

What stands out when the goal of philosophy is considered to be the discovery of general truths, the objection continues, is that this is not something that films, especially fiction films, are capable of doing. After all, fiction films present stories, narratives. A great fiction film like Orson Welles' *Citizen Kane* (1941) tells the story of Charles Foster Kane's rise and fall. As such, the film is inherently specific and particular. How could it possibly communicate the sort of general truths that are taken to be essential to philosophy?

One line of response to this objection points out that a film narrative can be an instance of a general truth. For example, parodying the famous quotation from the Gospel of Mark (8:36) – "For what shall it profit a man, if he shall gain the whole world, and lose his own soul?" – the influential film critic and theorist André Bazin claimed that *Citizen Kane* supported the general truth that "there is no profit in gaining the whole world if one has lost one's own childhood." If fiction films can make general claims like this, then it would seem that the generality objection loses its bite.

Still, opponents of the film-as-philosophy thesis retort that a single case cannot establish a general truth. As Aristotle said, one swallow does not a summer make. Although a film might lend some plausibility to a general claim by showing us one instance in which it is true, this is not adequate to justify it. No one would think of asserting, for example, that abortion was a legitimate social practice by pointing to a single example of a justifiable one. A philosophical defense of abortion requires that one establish the validity of the general claim that abortion is morally permissible. And it is just this that films cannot do, according to the generality objection.

There are a variety of moves available to proponents of the film-as-philosophy thesis in response. Here, I will just mention one: They can point out that it can be a genuine philosophical achievement to present a philosophical claim, even in the absence of an argument that supports it. One significant example is Saul Kripke's essay, *Naming and Necessity* (1980). There, Kripke outlined his theory of proper names as rigid designators, a theory that contradicted the then widely accepted view of proper names as concealed descriptions. Kripke does present objections to the accepted view, but, when it comes to his own theory, he does not so much *argue* for it as simply *present* it. Because this theory had not previously been on the table, so to speak, simply presenting it in a manner that shows it to be plausible counts as a major contribution to philosophy. But if this is so, why not admit that fiction films can sometimes present general claims in a way that makes them appear plausible, much as Kripke did in regard to the theory of proper names as rigid designators? The films will then not be seen as claiming for themselves an authoritative justification of the claims they support, but only as showing that the views they advocate should be taken seriously.

The explicitness objection

The generality objection was predicated on a recognition of a formal difference between philosophy and films. Philosophy is generally contained in written texts that are themselves composed of sentences that make assertions that say things like "beauty is a nonnatural property of objects" or "knowledge is justified true belief." Such sentences make claims that purport to be true. Films, by contrast, especially fiction films, tell stories. Although they may contain assertions – "That was a stupid thing to do!" – such assertions are made within a fictional world and don't apply to the real world.

The explicitness objection develops this difference between films and philosophy into the denial of the possibility of film-as-philosophy. It points out that the assertions that comprise a philosophical text are explicit and, as such, have a determinate propositional content. Even though films involve explicit claims, the explicitness objection maintains that they are not generally the ones that constitute a film's philosophical contribution. To stick with the example of *Citizen Kane*, it explicitly asserts, for example, that Kane built his mansion, Xanadu. But this assertion, explicit though it is, is about a fictional world and doesn't constitute an element in the potentially philosophical point that Bazin claims that the film makes. When it comes to such claims, the explicitness objection asserts that films lack the explicit content that allows the interpreter to maintain with precision what the content of the film's philosophical claim is. So when Bazin claims that *Citizen Kane* asserts that there is no profit in gaining the whole world if one has lost one's own childhood, what exactly is the film supposed to be asserting? That one should not sacrifice a childhood experience even if it gives one benefits in later life? Probably not. But what is the explicit assertion made by this claim? Bazin's statement reflects the ambiguity of the film's message, something that the explicitness objection takes to be characteristic of film in general.

One problem with the explicitness objection is that it uses ambiguities in the *interpretation* of a film to argue for the inherent ambiguity of the *film* itself and, hence, for its inability to do philosophy. But it is simply not clear that all films are ambiguous. It might be that the explicitness objection mistakes the source of the ambiguity, criticizing inadequate interpretations of films but then blaming it on the film itself. If so, then one could reinterpret this objection as a piece of methodological advice: Provide enough specificity and determinateness in a philosophical interpretation of a film so that the philosophy presented by the film is not inherently ambiguous.

The imposition objection

Another point of general agreement is that philosophical interpretations of films can be interesting and philosophically relevant. For example, Stanley Cavell's influential interpretation of Frank Capra's *It Happened One Night* (1934) as raising issues about the limits, not only of human knowledge, but also of our ability to know others, presents that screwball comedy as making a contribution to the discussion of the philosophical problem of other minds (Cavell 1981: 71ff.). But even if we grant Cavell's claim that an apparently trivial film can be seen to be making a significant contribution to philosophy, the imposition objection holds that that would be the result of Cavell's *imposition* of this philosophical claim upon the film, for the film itself is not capable of making such a sophisticated philosophical point.

What's interesting about this objection is that it admits that philosophical interpretations of film can count as philosophy. That is, the opponent of the film-as-philosophy thesis here admits that there may be philosophical interpretations of film that advance significant philosophical claims and make appropriate philosophical arguments. Indeed, Cavell's discussion of the films he calls "comedies of remarriage" – of which *It Happened One Night* is one example – is widely viewed as paradigmatic in its use of film in the service of a general philosophical position, namely Cavell's presentation of skepticism as a live option requiring what he calls "acknowledgment" for its overcoming.

Without getting into the specifics of Cavell's claims about the comedies of remarriage, some validity must be granted to the imposition objection to the film-as-philosophy thesis. It is certainly possible that a philosophical interpretation of a film might impose a philosopher's ideas upon a film that does not contain the sophisticated argumentation attributed to it by the interpretation. The charge often lodged against such problematic interpretations is that they *overinterpret* the film in question. I take this to mean that the philosophical interpreter is using the film to make a claim that the film cannot support on its own. Those who are skeptical that popular narrative films can really be philosophically significant thus object to the interpretive practice of the advocates of the film-as-philosophy thesis by saying that the interpreters are reading *into* the film more than is really there.

But even if we concede that philosophers may impose their own ideas upon films that do not exibit independent evidence of the presence of such concerns, this simply does not demonstrate that *every* philosophical interpretation of a film must be an imposition of the philosopher's concern onto the film. In order for the imposition objection to succeed, it would need to present an argument to support that general conclusion, something it seems not in a position to do.

Consider, for example, Ingmar Bergman's 1966 masterpiece *Persona*. At one point in the film, one character – a doctor – raises concerns that are easily recognizable as existentialist. She says that the film's main character has chosen to remain silent because she believes that any attempt to make a statement is subject to misinterpretation, so that all speaking is a form of inauthenticity. For her, silence is a strategy for achieving authenticity. Now issues of authenticity and inauthenticity are central to the philosophical tradition of existentialism. So an interpretation of *Persona* that credited the film with a concern for the existentialist question of how to achieve authenticity would not be imposing this concern on the film, for we can see that this issue is raised within the film's narrative itself.

Still, the advocate of the imposition objection could modify her claim by leaving art films like *Persona* out of the scope of the objection. The reformulated objection maintains that philosophical interpretations of *popular* fiction films are impositions, for such films lack the philosophical sophistication of art films like *Persona*. Insofar as these popular films – which are, after all, the subject of many philosophical interpretations, beginning with those of Cavell – are made to appeal to a wide public, they simply cannot address difficult and abstract philosophical issues on their own.

Here, the obvious counter is that the proof lies in the pudding. To see whether popular fiction films are not only amenable to, but also ask for philosophical interpretation, we need to turn to the interpretations of the films that have been put forward by philosophers to see whether they convince us that the film really raises those issues.

Once again, I suggest that a useful way to interpret the imposition objection is as regulative advice to the philosophical interpreter of a film: In proposing a philosophical interpretation of a film, be careful not to impose your own ideas upon the film. Be sure to show how the film itself raises the issue that you take to be presented by it, for philosophical film interpretations that do so are more likely to be convincing than those that do not.

The banality objection

The final objection to the film-as-philosophy thesis is the banality objection. This objection differs from the three previous ones in conceding that films can have philosophical content, but it asserts that whatever philosophical content films do have is trivial or banal. As a result, while agreeing with proponents of the film-as-philosophy thesis that films can philosophize, the banality objection simply minimizes the significance of the ideas presented by the films.

There are a variety of reasons why film has been thought to have only trivial philosophical content. One has to do with film's role as a popular art form. Insofar as film seeks to have a broad appeal to an international audience, it needs to adopt conventions that make it easy to understand. How, then, it is asked, could a film both have a serious philosophical content and also appeal to a wide audience? The presumed answer is that it could not.

Of course, there are genres of filmmaking that are not characterized by the desire for universal appeal. Various traditions of avant-garde films are one example, the art film another. Consider once more Bergman's film *Persona*. This is not an easy film to watch, and it is an even more difficult film to understand. Bergman made his film for a sophisticated international audience well-versed in the conventions of the art film. As a result, a film like *Persona* is simply not subject to the banality objection. And the same can be said for many films made in other avant-garde practices, such as structuralist films. The banality objection cannot get any purchase on such films, because their philosophical pretensions are not limited by a concern to attract as wide an audience as possible.

But the advocate of the banality objection could once again stage a strategic retreat and limit his or her claim to popular films. Since such films are created with the intention of attracting as wide an audience as possible, they will be limited to presenting nothing more complex than an easily understood philosophical message, one that appears banal from a philosophically sophisticated point of view.

And once again, the way to expose the weakness of this strategy is to invoke actual philosophical interpretations of films. Philosophers beginning with Cavell have presented interpretations of popular films that see them as making sophisticated philosophical points. So the advocate of the banality objection needs to explain what is wrong with such interpretations.

One difference between proponents of the banality objection and its critics may be their conception of philosophy. Those who see philosophy as a quasi-scientific discipline whose concepts and theories are only accessible to a narrow group of specialists will be hard pressed to see a popular art form as capable of the esoteric knowledge taken to be the proper domain of philosophy. But those, including myself, who see philosophy as addressing fundamental and often perennial concerns of human life will think it more natural that such issues find their way into all the popular arts. The roots of disagreement about the validity of the banality objection may run very deep indeed.

Let me end my discussion of the banality objection with one admission: Some philosophical interpretations of films do present films as making banal philosophical statements. But once again, what has not been proved is that this is the fault of the film, rather than the philosophical interpreter. So we can reformulate the banality objection as another piece of regulative advice for the philosophical film interpreter: Make sure that the philosophical point you attribute to a film deserves designation as philosophy and is not simply some banal or commonplace idea.

Modes of the philosophical in film

Having canvassed a range of objections to the film-as-philosophy thesis, I now want to consider some of the different ways that contemporary philosophers have seen films as capable of doing philosophy. In each case, I can only gesture at the interpretations that philosophers have presented of films. To fill out the interpretations I present, the reader is advised to read subsequent entries in this section of the *Companion* and to turn to the books listed at the end of this entry.

Film as illustrating philosophical theories

An overlooked and much denigrated way that films can be philosophy is by illustrating a philosophical theory. Even philosophers friendly to the film-as-philosophy thesis often compare films that *merely* illustrate philosophical theories with those that genuinely philosophize. But this is a mistake. A film that illustrates a philosophical theory can be doing philosophy in a similar way to a journal article: it can make the theory seem more plausible to its audience.

This way of interpreting the film-as-philosophy thesis pairs a film with a well-known philosophical theory. An example might be Charlie Chaplin's 1935 comedy, *Modern Times*. Chaplin was known for his left-wing views, so it makes sense to see the film as including some comic illustrations of Marx's theory of capitalist exploitation of the workers. Because the film presents viewers with an accessible way of understanding Marx's theory, it could be presented as an example of philosophy done on film (see Wartenberg 2007).

Film as counterexample

One central way in which *fiction* films have been held to be doing philosophy is by presenting thought experiments. Perhaps the simplest use of a thought experiment is as a counterexample to a general claim. Because fiction films also involve imaginary scenarios, some have been seen to function as counterexamples to philosophical theses.

Consider Woody Allen's 1989 film, *Crimes and Misdemeanors*. Its narrative could be considered to be a counterexample to the philosophical claim – dating all the way to Plato – that one should be moral because not doing so will make one unhappy. The film's narrative concerns Judah Rosenthal, a very successful ophthalmologist, who is regarded as a pillar of the Jewish community. When his mistress threatens to reveal his affair to this wife and the community in general, he takes out a contract on her life. But rather than suffer for this crime, he benefits from it, for his life and reputation remain intact. In effect, committing this immoral act brings him happiness. So Judah's story is a counterexample to the assertion that acting immorally will result in one becoming unhappy, for Judah thrives through his misdemeanor.

Films as making philosophical claims

Philosophers have investigated the phenomenon of memory in various different ways. One of the central claims about memory is that it plays a role in personal identity. This is a claim that at least one recent film, Christopher Nolan's 2000 film *Memento*, investigates. But one could also ask whether memory doesn't have other vital roles to play.

Michel Gondry's 2004 film, *Eternal Sunshine of the Spotless Mind*, also has something to contribute to the philosophical understanding of memory. Using a fictional technology for selective memory erasure, the film highlights the *educative function of memory on desire*. Consider how a young child learns not to fulfill his desire to touch a burning candle. Not only does he need to experience the pain of being burned, he also needs to remember that it happened. This memory then "educates" his desire by keeping the child from fulfilling it more than once.

Eternal Sunshine depicts the educative function of memory through an imaginary technology of selective memory erasure that offers people who have suffered traumas a way to recover by selectively erasing all their memories of the trauma. But attractive as this option might seem, the film warns us that it neglects the educative role of memory. Through a narrative in which three individuals who have had their memories of unhappy love affairs erased wind up pursuing the very relationships that had traumatized them, the film shows that, without the presence of memories, however painful they may be, no learning can take place. The film thus brings to our attention a philosophical claim that it makes plausible by means of its fictional narrative.

Film as self-definitional

Film scholars have routinely characterized avant-garde films as philosophical. One slogan that they have used to describe the achievement of such films is "form becomes content." The idea is that such films have such minimal content in a traditional sense that their form – that which viewers of traditional films generally pass over – becomes their content. But if the content of such a film is also one of the essential characteristics of film, then the film can be seen as making viewers aware that that specific formal feature is essential to the medium.

Tony Conrad's 1965 film, *The Flicker*, is an example of a film that does this. The film is composed of nothing but clear and opaque (black) film leader. Varying lengths of these are spliced together, giving rise to flickers of different frequencies. As the flickers increase their frequency, a range of optical effects arise in the viewer. For example, she notices swirls of color, moving rapidly in different directions. So what's unique about this film is that, without employing any photographic images, it can produce an awareness of motion in its viewers. But this lends credence to the idea that the film is thereby *asserting* that an essential characteristic of the film medium is its ability to present motion and that employing photography is not such a feature.

Film as social criticism

Our contemporary world is rife with social practices and structures that oppress and demean human beings. Classism, sexism, and racism are three forms that such oppression has taken. One of philosophy's basic tasks is to theorize such oppressive structures, namely to explain how they work and to explore the possibility of their supersession.

Films have also been seen as fulfilling these functions in a philosophical way. Consider, for example, Rainer Werner Fassbinder's 1974 film, *Angst essen Seele auf* (*Ali: Fear Eats the Soul*). The film is the story of an unlikely relationship between an elderly German cleaning woman and a young, handsome Moroccan guest worker. Against expectations, the relationship founders because of the racism of the elderly German woman rather than the younger man's pursuit of relationships with younger women. The film suggests that the reason why the woman's racism surfaces is that, despite her lowly social status in Germany, she actually enjoys a racial privilege in relation to her dark-skinned lover. Faced with losing that privilege, she chooses to betray her lover rather than accept that loss. The film thus contains an original insight into the persistence of racism: that one of its grounds is the threat of loss of social privilege for members of the dominant race who transgress racist norms.

Conclusion

The aim of this entry is twofold: on the one hand, to introduce the controversy surrounding the film-as-philosophy thesis; on the other, to show the fruitfulness of philosophical interpretations of film. Whatever one's stance on whether those interpretations actually constitute philosophy being done on film, it is clear that philosophers have found in film a fecund source for philosophical reflection.

See also Avant-garde film (Chapter 48), Documentary (Chapter 45), Phenomenology (Chapter 40), Stanley Cavell (Chapter 32), Race (Chapter 21), and Interpretation (Chapter 15).

References

Cavell, S. (1981) *Pursuits of Happiness: The Hollywood Comedy of Remarriage*, Cambridge, MA: Harvard University Press.
Grau, C. (ed.) (2005) *Philosophers Explore the Matrix*, New York: Oxford University Press.
Kripke, S. (1980) *Naming and Necessity*, Cambridge, MA: Harvard University Press.
Mulhall, S. (2002) *On Film*, London and New York: Routledge.

Further reading

Stanley Cavell, *Contesting Tears: The Hollywood Melodrama of the Unknown Woman* (Chicago: University of Chicago Press, 1996) offers interpretations of the companion genre to the comedies of remarriage that emphasize their philosophical significance. Cavell's *Cities of Words: Pedagogical Letters on a Register of the Moral Life* (Cambridge, MA: Belknap Press of Harvard University Press, 2004) is based on his lecture course at Harvard and the University of Chicago and pairs philosophical interpretations of films in the two genres Cavell explores in his earlier books with interpretations of philosophical texts. Their common aim is to investigate how the films and the texts supplement each other as explorations of moral perfectionism. Christopher Falzon, *Philosophy Goes to the Movies: An Introduction to Philosophy* (London and New York: Routledge, 2002) makes wide-ranging use of film to introduce philosophy to students. Cynthia Freeland, *The Naked and the Undead: Evil and the Appeal of Horror* (Boulder, CO: Westview Press, 2002) offers a feminist appraisal of horror films that claims the genre explores the nature of evil. Herbert Granger, "Cinematic Philosophy in *Le Feu Follet*: The Search for a Meaningful Life," *Film and Philosophy* 8 (2004): 76, gives an interpretation of the film that sees it as depicting a person confronting a deep philosophical issue. Joseph Kupfer, *Visions of Virtue in Popular Film* (Boulder, CO: Westview Press, 1999) is an exploration of film as a vehicle for developing a theory of virtue. Andrew Light, *Reel Arguments: Film, Philosophy, and Social Criticism* (Boulder, CO: Westview Press, 2003) is a series of essays exploring how films can present trenchant social criticism. All the authors in Rupert Read and Jerry Goodenough (eds.) *Film as Philosophy* (Basingstoke and New York: Palgrave Macmillan, 2005) engage with Cavell's account of film as making a contribution to philosophy. Bruce Russell, "The Philosophical Limits of Film," *Film and Philosophy* (2000, special issue): 163–7, gives an argument against the film-as-philosophy thesis that posits strict limits on film's philosophical contributions. The anthology edited by Murray Smith and Thomas E. Wartenberg, *Thinking through Cinema: Film as Philosophy* (Malden, MA: Blackwell, 2006) contains essays addressing the theoretical issues concerning the film-as-philosophy thesis, as well as philosophical interpretations of films from a variety of different genres. Kevin L. Stoehr (ed.) *Film and Knowledge: Essays on the Integration of Images and Ideas* (Jefferson, NC: McFarland, 2002) is a collection of essays that explore film as inquiring into the nature of, and basis for, our knowledge of the world. Thomas E. Wartenberg, *Unlikely Couples: Movie Romance as Social Criticism* (Boulder, CO: Westview Press, 1999) is a study of romantic films in which the couples violate social norms, arguing that the films present a critique of such norms and the societies that validate them. Wartenberg's *Thinking on Screen: Film as Philosophy* (London and New York: Routledge, 2008) is a theoretical brief in favor of the film-as-philosophy thesis that includes interpretations of specific films illustrating various forms of philosophy in film.

51

INGMAR BERGMAN

Paisley Livingston

Although Ingmar Bergman (1918–2007) figures on everyone's list of philosophical filmmakers, attempts to specify the philosophical implications of his films have yielded highly divergent results. One reason why this is the case is that interpreters disagree over how the philosophical content of a cinematic oeuvre is to be identified. Some interpreters clearly believe it best to work with their own philosophical views when interpreting a film's story and themes, while others contend that the content of a work is at least partly constituted by the filmmaker's own ideas and background, which the interpreter should try to reconstruct on the basis of the available evidence. This entry focuses on claims made by interpreters who share the latter premise. Such interpreters often disagree about the content of a given film because they do not have the same evidence about its context, or because they reason about the evidence differently. I survey such disagreements among Bergman's interpreters and then shed new light on his actual philosophical sources and ideas.

Various critics (e.g., Aristarco 1966; Blake 1978; Cohn 1970; Ketcham 1989) have attempted to situate Bergman's work within an existentialist philosophical tradition, which would appear especially appropriate insofar as many of Bergman's characters grapple with and articulately talk about death, illness, solitude, anxiety, and the meaning and value of life. Yet the case for reading Bergman as an existentialist, and his fictions as expressions of existentialism, rests on surprisingly flimsy grounds. For example, Bergman chose to stage Albert Camus' *Caligula* as his debut at the Göteborg City Theater in 1946 (Steene 2005: 530–2). Although this seems indicative of an interest in existentialism, Bergman appears to have prompted, or at least allowed, the flamboyant actor Anders Ek to characterize the emperor as a histrionic and suicidal madman, downplaying the more contemplative moments in Camus' text, such as Caligula's contemplative refrain that "Man dies and he is not happy." What is more, the long list of straightforwardly existentialist plays that Bergman never directed includes all of those written by Jean Genet and Jean-Paul Sartre. An existentialist director would presumably have been interested in staging at least some of these plays, such as *Huis clos* and *Le balcon*.

Another oft-cited piece of evidence thought to support an existentialist reading of Bergman is the scene in *Persona* (1966) where the doctor tells Elisabeth Volger that she is sympathetic to her "hopeless dream of being." Yet even though Bergman has explicitly endorsed some of what the doctor says in this scene, it is far from clear that any of this amounts to the expression of a genuinely existentialist philosophy. It is important to remember that the doctor is trying to impress the famous actress and fails to mention any of the less abstract and lofty reasons for her breakdown, which are far more central to the film's story and themes.

Another strategy adopted in support of existentialist interpretations of Bergman amounts to saying that Bergman's source was that "grandfather" of existentialism, Søren Kierkegaard. After all, both Bergman and Kierkegaard were Scandinavian, and both had a problematic relation to Lutheran orthodoxy and what Kierkegaard called "Christendom." It is true that on the occasion of his reception of the Sonning Prize, an eighty-one-year-old Bergman told a Danish audience that when he was sixteen he had been fascinated by the "dark streak and humour" in Kierkegaard's *Sickness unto Death* (cited by Steene 2005: 117). It is hard to believe, however, that the sixteen-year-old Bergman fathomed much of Anti-Climacus' intricate dialectical theology, nor is there any evidence to that effect in the movies. The first thing beginners in Kierkegaard need to learn about is his complex relation to Danish Hegelianism, and there is no reason whatsoever to believe that Bergman ever paid any attention to this topic.

Why should we think that any specific existentialist concepts, such as Sartre's notion of *la mauvaise foi*, are advanced in any of Bergman's cinematic fictions? In some studies describing Bergman's putative existentialism, reference is made to his connection with the *fyrtiotalist* movement in Swedish letters, which had vaguely existentialist tendencies. Yet Bergman's affiliation with the forties writers was both tenuous and temporary. The problem with the existentialist approach to Bergman is that there is no evidence that Bergman ever really engaged seriously with the theories of any of the existentialist philosophers, which suggests that if his works belong to such a tradition, this is a result of a mysterious osmotic process or *Zeitgeist* causation. In sum, the choice of existentialist premises in the interpretation of Bergman's films is *undermotivated*.

Another place to look for Bergman's intellectual sources is the Lutheranism preached in Bergman's milieu – beginning with the sermons delivered by his father. In a program note to *The Seventh Seal* (1956), Bergman recalls traveling with his father and sitting in church during his sermons, but he reports that the content of what was said was beyond his grasp; he was, however, fascinated by the interiors of small Swedish churches with their chalk paintings of angels and demons, and Death playing chess with a crusader. Only later did "faith and doubt" become his "constant companions" (Bergman 1972: 70). As Robert Lauder (1989) emphasizes, Bergman temporarily espoused a Pauline God-is-love doctrine, which surfaces explicitly at the end of *Through a Glass Darkly* (1961). Bergman also expressed this credo in an interview published in *Playboy* (1964: 68). Yet doubt seems to have won the upper hand, at least during Bergman's most productive decades. In the script of *Persona*, the actress Elisabeth Volger laughs derisively when she hears the God-is-love line delivered melodramatically in a radio play. And in the afterword Bergman wrote to his script for a TV film on the Crucifixion, he proclaimed that he was "not a believer" and added that he rejected "every form of otherwordly salvation" (Bergman

1975). Although Bergman no doubt remained under the influence of his Lutheran upbringing, to interpret his films as expressions of any species of Christian orthodoxy would be erroneous.

One conclusion that could be reached is that Bergman's sources and artistic intentions were literary and musical, not theoretical. By his own admission, he got nowhere when he tried to read Wittgenstein or Lacan (Bergman 1994: 10). Yet if Bergman's own word can be trusted, such a conclusion would be false because there is one specific philosophical book that was literally *foundational* for his work. One of Bergman's remarkable and seldom-heeded assertions to this effect was made at the end of his preface to the publication of an English translation of the screenplay of *Smultronstället* (*Wild Strawberries*) in 1957. Bergman wrote:

> Philosophically, there is a book which was a tremendous experience for me: Eino Kaila's *Psychology of the Personality*. His thesis that man lives strictly according to his needs – negative and positive – was shattering to me, but terribly true. And I built on this ground. (Bergman 1957: 12)

Although this striking remark has been briefly mentioned in passing by a few Bergman scholars (Cohen 1993: 439; Gado 1986: 225; Kalin 2003: 193), none of them appears to have read the philosophical source that Bergman identifies as the very ground on which he built. There may be various reasons why no one has followed up on Bergman's statement in trying to understand the philosophical implications of his films. One reason has to do with critics' understanding of "the intentional fallacy," which they take as entailing that an artist's attitudes and aims – whether they are stated or not – have nothing to do with what the artist's works actually mean. This is not a good reason (Livingston 2005). If an artist is skillful and successfully realizes his or her intentions (as was often the case with Bergman), intentions and the work's implications cohere, and the artist's statements about sources and intentions may then be indicative of what is actually expressed in the works. And even if the filmmaker failed to express his or her intended meanings, it is appropriate to understand the audio-visual display as the consequence of this failed attempt.

Another reason why few people have explored the Kaila connection when attempting to elucidate Bergman's themes and characterizations is that the treatise in question (Kaila 1934) was initially written and published in Finnish and has only been translated into Swedish and Danish. Those Scandinavian readers who were in a position to read Kaila's book, or who already knew about its influence on such prominent Scandinavian writers as Willy Kyrklund, may simply never have noticed what Bergman wrote in the preface to an English translation of the script of one of his films. Another reason why critics overlooked or discounted Bergman's statement could be that they were too committed to the project of applying other theoretical assumptions, such as Freudian ones, in the interpretation of Bergman's works (e.g., Gado 1986).

Although it would be a serious error to present a static picture of Bergman's lengthy career, an interpretative hypothesis worth exploring is that from the mid-1950s onward, Bergman often worked with some key philosophical ideas he had found – or found restated – in Kaila's book. To explore such a hypothesis, we need first of all to identify the ideas and arguments that Bergman could have taken over from the philosopher and/or his sources.

In his brief evocation of Kaila's influence, Bergman mentions the thesis that people live strictly according to their needs. The word "needs" here is quite misleading, as this is a translation of words in Finnish and Swedish (*tarve* and *behov*, respectively) that are ambiguous between what in English is called a "need," a "desire," or a "want." Kaila's point is that human behavior is determined by, and should be understood in terms of, the motivational states or "forces" that both prompt and orient activity. Kaila's insistence on the explanatory primacy of motivational forces is not linked to an attempt to reduce all behavior to a single kind of motive, such as elementary biological urges or needs. Nor does Kaila postulate erotic drives or the will to power as the unique or predominant motive. Kaila instead lays great stress on the plurality of motivational states and on conflicts between different kinds of needs or desires. In particular, he discusses ways in which a person's "high spiritual" and intellectual motives can come into conflict with that person's "lower" biological urges. This is the stuff of *Smiles of a Summer Night* (1955), where the young Henrik struggles with his lust, alternately lunging for the attractive servant girl and reading to her from Luther's shorter catechism. Bergman engaged in a more subtle and quasi-allegorical exploration of this kind of conflict in *The Silence* (1963).

Kaila thinks of a want, need, or desire as a "driving inner force in an organism" (Kaila 1934: 21). Living systems, he observes, have a tendency to move, or at least to attempt to move, from a state of disequilibrium to a preferred state of equilibrium; a want or desire is a "state of tension" that corresponds to a disequilibrium in this scheme. To a given want corresponds a "direction" or behavioral tendency, which targets a return to equilibrium. Kaila was influenced by Kurt Lewin's "field theoretical" psychology, and he at times employed that theoretical idiom in his characterization of motivation. A desire is, then, a "psychic vector," and everything that lies in the direction of its satisfaction takes on a corresponding valence, an "impulse character" that decreases to the extent that the desire is satisfied.

Kaila's main polemical target in his treatise on psychology is the philosophical thesis that "man" is the "rational animal." Drawing upon quite an eclectic range of sources (which include gestalt and empirical psychology as well as a variety of literary and philosophical authors, such as Nietzsche, Schopenhauer, and La Rochefoucauld), Kaila describes various forms of irrationality that contradict the philosophical idealization of human agency. Many literary works, he contends, offer a more plausible and insightful perspective on human behavior than the assumptions relied upon by rationalist philosophers. Kaila's central term, covering the several species of irrationality that he discusses, is best translated as "inauthenticity." Many people's desires, he contends, are inauthentic because they are in fact unacknowledged substitutes for another desire that could not be satisfied. Without the agent recognizing it, in the formation of a new desire, the motivational force of an earlier, frustrated desire can transfer "by analogy" to another representation. Kaila's examples include people taking out their frustration and anger on a surrogate object in an episode of humiliation or scapegoating, which is precisely the sort of behavior that Bergman has consistently identified as the specifically human form of "evil." This sort of thing is a central target in Bergman's critique of religious and other forms of fanaticism in *The Seventh Seal*, where a community terrified of the plague (read: death, violence, or any kind of major social crisis) copes with this fear by lashing out at a surrogate threat, namely, some accused party who stands in for the real (or apparent) danger. In *The Seventh Seal* the gruesome and pointless witch-burning, which is totally abhorrent to all of the sympathetic characters in the story, is Bergman's allegorical representation of this inauthentic and delusionary motivational process. A similar critique of the victimization and humiliation of surrogates is pursued in any number of Bergman's later films, such as *A Passion* (also distributed with the title *The Passion of Anna*) (1969). For detailed discussions of this theme in Bergman, see Livingston (1982) and Blackwell (1997).

One of Kaila's examples of inauthentic surrogate desire satisfaction that may have interested Bergman greatly is sadistic forms of moralism, and in particular the harsh punishment of children conducted self-righteously by deluded or hypocritical authorities in the name of some moral or religious authority. Kaila even mentions a case in which locking a child in a closet has a devastating, long-term impact on the victim. This is pure Bergman, as the horror and irrationality of punishment of this kind is driven home in at least four of his films: *Prison* (1949), *The Hour of the Wolf* (1967), *Face to Face* (1976), and *Fanny and Alexander* (1982–3). Bergman relates his own harrowing experience of such punishment in his autobiographical *Laterna Magica* (1987: 13–14), and repeats this very narrative at length in his second autobiographical tome, *Images* (1990: 38–41).

It might be protested that what Bergman found in Kaila was simply a convenient Scandinavian digest of Freudian psychology. Such a protest would be made, however, only by someone who has not actually read Kaila. Kaila was an experimentalist most heavily influenced by gestalt psychology, the positivist philosophy of science of the Vienna circle, and systems theory. His comments on psychoanalysis are overarchingly negative. He acknowledges that psychoanalysis has a suitably "dynamic" conception of motivational forces (i.e., one in which the force of a desire can transfer to a surrogate object), but this observation does not prevent him from classifying Freud's mode of thought more generally as an outdated "mechanistic associationist psychology" (Kaila 1934: 231). Kaila adds that what is true about motivation in psychoanalysis is what "we have always been perfectly aware of in our practical knowledge of ourselves and in our accumulated wisdom about life" (Kaila 1934: 237–8).

Problems of self-knowledge or awareness are central to psychoanalytic discussions of the unconscious and of the distinction between the manifest and latent content of a dream, action, or representation. As part of his polemic against psychoanalysis, Kaila casts doubt on the importance of the distinction between conscious and unconscious mental states. He lays greater stress on a contrast between inauthenticity and authenticity, which hinges instead on the quality of the subject's self-knowledge. In this regard Kaila frequently evokes the fable of the fox and the grapes, which provides a paradigmatic representation of a central species of irrationality. In Kaila's view, one of the reasons why the fox's shift in motivation is inauthentic is that the fox is unaware that the only reason why he ceases to want the grapes is that he has become convinced that he cannot acquire them. Kaila does not say that the fox cannot know what has gone on in his own psychic system because the relevant desires are repressed and belong to some deep "unconscious." What he says instead is that because an authentic self-awareness requires recognition of the key functional relations between various mental events occurring at different times, a complex cognitive representation is necessary to such awareness. And in cases where there is no motivation pushing the system in the direction of formulating, or even attempting to formulate, such a complex representation, no such self-awareness takes place. In place of the missing self-awareness, there may be some inauthentic self-conception that is the product of wishful thinking, which is another central type of irrationality in Kaila's conception. Only in cases where there is a special kind of motivation does authentic awareness emerge.

This philosophical perspective finds a complex illustration and exploration in several of Bergman's fictions; the characterization of the interaction between the nurse and her patient in *Persona* being an excellent example. Wishful thinking initially leads the nurse to believe that Elisabeth Vogler is a sympathetic person who reciprocates her affection; when she finds out what Vogler has written about her behind her back, this illusion collapses, and the nurse is motivated to engage in some lucid thinking about her relation to the patient. An even more complex and bleak exploration of problems of self-knowledge is achieved in Bergman's only German-language cinematic production, *Aus dem Leben der Marionetten* (*Scenes from the Life of the Marionettes*) (1982).

Why would the young Bergman have found Kaila's theses "shattering" and "terribly true"? As Bergman does not say, we can only risk a few conjectures. First of all, Kaila's theses about human nature constitute a serious challenge to the idea of human perfect-ibility that is so central to a range of idealistic and progressivist systems. Another possible reason is that Kaila is absolutely scathing with regard to the layers of wishful thinking and surrogate desire satisfaction at work in religion, by which Kaila meant the Christian faith and its institutions. Kaila calls religion the great cathedral of wishful thinking: instead of convincing himself that the grapes are sour, the frustrated fox decides that even better grapes will be his reward in heaven.

Many striking details in Kaila's work may have stirred the director's imagination. For example, Kaila discusses the meaning of the word "persona" in Schopenhauer and elsewhere. He extols literature's ability to explore mental illness, self-deception, and crises of faith. It seems highly likely that the author of *Through a Glass Darkly* (1961) and *Winter Light* (1963) found inspiration in such remarks.

There is one very explicit, and obviously intentional, allusion to Kaila in Bergman's cinematic oeuvre. This allusion bears a closer look, since far from indicating that Bergman was simply out to illustrate Kaila's ideas with his cinematic fictions, it raises the question whether Bergman did not also engage in some critical thinking of his own about the philosophical issues Kaila discussed. The allusion is to be found in *Wild Strawberries* in the context of a flashback depicting a heated discussion between Evald

Borg (Gunnar Björnstrand) and his wife Marianne (Ingrid Thulin). Marianne has revealed that she is pregnant, and Evald says he does not want to be a parent, because the world is terrible. He exclaims that it is absurd to bring children into the world, thinking that things could ever be better. He does not want to take on a responsibility that would require him to live a single day longer than he chooses. When Marianne protests that this is wrong, his Kailaesque réplique is, "There is nothing called right or wrong. One functions according to one's needs: you can read that in a schoolbook." This line recalls Kaila's emphasis on the primacy of motivation in the explanation of behavior, of course, but it also reflects his positivistic view of the ultimate status of value judgments, which he characterizes as subjective and unscientific. Yet in this regard, at least, Evald should hardly be taken as Bergman's *porte-parole* in the film, and this for several reasons. First of all, Kaila's views are hardly to be found in a "schoolbook" (this part was omitted in the English subtitles to the film). Second, Evald's blustery speech is an unpleasant and incoherent emotional outburst: if there is nothing right or wrong, as he claims, how would being a parent constitute a *responsibility* that could hinder any desire of his to commit suicide? A responsibility involves something that one ought to do, no matter what one's inclinations might be, and if there is no right or wrong, what could the basis of such an obligation be? Couldn't Evald simply "function according" to his need to kill himself? And although he categorically lays down that if Marianne insists on having the baby, their marriage is over, he subsequently changes his tune, telling his father that he cannot live without Marianne. When his father asks him whether what he really means is that he cannot face the prospect of living alone, Evald corrects him and says he cannot live without Marianne. It is hard to see how Evald's otherwise admirable attachment to Marianne as an individual person squares with his earlier nihilistic outburst to the effect that his most basic need was to be emotionally "dead."

The more general question raised here is whether Bergman's interest in Kaila's views about motivation and irrationality were accompanied by an equal enthusiasm with regard to the Finnish philosopher's extreme antirealist claims about value. In the absence of any theoretical assertions by Bergman on bedeviled topics in metaethics and axiology, it is hard to attribute to Bergman any fine-grained philosophical position in this regard. It is pertinent to point out that if Bergman had been interested in antirealism about value, the "Uppsala school," led by Axel Hägerström, would have been a far more obvious philosophical source (see Hägerström 1987 [1911]). What Bergman says on the subject does suffice, however, to cast doubt on the thought that he was persuaded by Kaila's claim that values are purely "subjective." Bergman writes, for example, that his "philosophy (even today) is that there exists an evil that cannot be explained – a virulent, terrifying evil – and humans are the only animals to possess it. An evil that is irrational and not bound by law. Cosmic. Without cause" (Bergman 1990: 306). This kind of specifically human evil, he had commented some twenty-five years earlier, is manifested, for example, when children viciously scapegoat one of their peers (Björkman *et al*. 1973: 40).

To sum up, Bergman's films are replete with characterizations informed by the perspective on human irrationality and conflict that Kaila codified in his treatise in philosophical psychology. Yet Bergman does not follow Kaila's call for a scientific, value-free perspective on the world. Strictly speaking, in Kaila's scheme of things, subjective valences attached to needs would fall outside the purview of a scientific understanding of human motivation. Bergman's films consistently diverge from any such perspective by expressing and soliciting sympathy for victims and repugnance toward victimization and cruelty. Whence, perhaps, the emphasis on both "positive and negative" needs in Bergman's phrase about the impact of Kaila's philosophy on him. For Bergman, the negative desires are the destructive and sadistic ones, while the positive desires to be affirmed include the longing for lucidity, authentic communication and togetherness, and an active, curiosity-driven exploration of the world. In this regard, we may discern the lasting influence of Bergman's Christian education. He indirectly affirmed that very thought in the afterword he wrote to the script for a film on the Crucifixion, for although he denied any belief in the supernatural, he extolled Jesus for the "wisdom" (of nonviolence and psychological insight) he represented, and which was passed along by the church's imperfect representatives. The climactic moment in the script involves the conversion of the Roman officer ordered to supervise Christ's torture and agony. When he can take the spectacle of suffering no longer, the centurion retreats to a nearby quarry and repeats the thought he has heard Jesus express: "Father, forgive them, they know not what they do."

Acknowledgements

The work described in this entry was supported by a grant from the Research Grants Council of the Hong Kong Special Administrative Region, China (Project No. LU3401/06H). I am very grateful for this generous support. Thanks as well go to Carl Plantinga for helpful comments.

References

Aristarco, G. (1966) "Bergman et Kierkegaard," Études Cinématographiques 46–7: 15–30.

Bergman, I. (1957) Wild Strawberries: A Film by Ingmar Bergman, trans. L. Malmström and D. Kushner, London: Lorrimer.

—— (1960) "Möte med Ingmar Bergman," SR (6 February). Typescript in Swedish Radio archives.

—— (1964) "Playboy Interview: Ingmar Bergman." Playboy (June): 61–8.

—— (1972) "A Program Note to The Seventh Seal," in B. Steene (ed.) Focus on The Seventh Seal, Englewood Cliffs, NJ: Prentice Hall, 70–1.

—— (1975) "Utkast till TV film om Jesu död och uppståndelse och några mänskor som deltog i dessa händelser" [Draft of a TV film about the death and resurrection of Jesus and about some people who took part in these events], unpublished ms. The Ingmar Bergman Archive, Swedish Film Institute, Stockholm.

—— (1987) Laterna Magica, Stockholm: Norstedts. Trans. J. Tate, The Magic Lantern (London: Hamish Hamilton, 1988).

—— (1990) Bilder, Stockholm: Norstedts. Trans. M. Ruuth, Images: My Life in Film (London: Bloomsbury, 1994).

—— (1994) Femte akten, Stockholm: Norstedts. Trans. L. Rugg and J. Tate, The Fifth Act (New York: New Press, 2001).

Björkman, S., Manns, T., and Sima, J. (1973) *Bergman on Bergman: Interviews with Ingmar Bergman*, trans. P. B. Austin, New York: Simon and Schuster.

Blackwell, M. J. (1997) *Gender and Representation in the Films of Ingmar Bergman*, Columbia, SC: Camden House.

Blake, R. A. (1978) *The Lutheran Milieu of the Films of Ingmar Bergman*, New York: Arno Press.

Cohen, H. I. (1993) *Ingmar Bergman: The Art of Confession*, New York: Twayne.

Cohn, B. (1970) "Connaissance de la voie," *Positif* 121: 34–40.

Gado, F. (1986) *The Passion of Ingmar Bergman*, Durham, NC: Duke University Press.

Hägerström, A. (1987 [1911]) *Moralfilsofins Grundläggning*, T. Mautner (ed.), Uppsala: Humanistiska Vetenskapssamfundet; Almqvist and Wiksell.

Kaila, E. (1934) *Personalisuus*, Helsinki: Otava. Trans. J. Gästrin, *Personlighetens psykologi* (Stockholm: Natur och Kultur, 1935).

Kalin, J. (2003) *The Films of Ingmar Bergman*, Cambridge and New York: Cambridge University Press.

Ketcham, C. B. (1986) *The Influence of Existentialism on Ingmar Bergman: An Analysis of the Theological Ideas Shaping a Filmmaker's Art*, Lewiston; Oueenston, NY: Edwin Mellen Press.

Lauder, R. E. (1989) *God, Death, Art, and Love: The Philosophical Vision of Ingmar Bergman*, New York: Paulist Press.

Livingston, P. (1982) *Ingmar Bergman and the Rituals of Art*, Ithaca, NY: Cornell University Press.

—— (2005) *Art and Intention: A Philosophical Study*, Oxford: Clarendon Press; New York: Oxford University Press.

Steene, B. (2005) *Ingmar Bergman: A Reference Guide*, Amsterdam: Amsterdam University Press.

Further reading

The following are further reading on this topic: Maaret Koskinen, *I begynnelsen var ordet: Ingmar Bergman och hans tidiga förgattarskap* (Stockholm: Wahlström and Widstrand, 2002); Paisley Livingston, *Cinema, Philosophy, Bergman: On Film as Philosophy* (forthcoming).

52

TERRENCE MALICK

David Davies

Terrence Malick is among the most celebrated and critically acclaimed contemporary American directors. Yet he is also a deeply enigmatic figure whose artistic career was punctuated by a twenty-year absence, during which time his whereabouts and activities remain unclear. Malick studiously avoids interactions with the media, giving no interviews since his first film, *Badlands*, in 1973. He has, in more than thirty years, directed only four feature films, the others being *Days of Heaven* (1978), *The Thin Red Line* (1998), and *The New World* (2005). His work has, from the first, been described as "poetic" and "visionary," qualities that relate to his often breathtaking use of natural imagery and to his cinematic explorations of human nature and our relationships with the natural world.

Malick was born in November 1943 in Ottawa, Illinois (or possibly in Waco, Texas), and grew up in Oklahoma and Texas. He studied philosophy at Harvard, working with Stanley Cavell, before going to Magdalen College, Oxford, on a Rhodes Scholarship. His intention was to work under the supervision of Gilbert Ryle on a thesis on the concept of world in Kierkegaard, Heidegger, and Wittgenstein, but, unsurprisingly perhaps, Ryle was not greatly enamored of the project. Malick returned to the United States without completing his thesis, and seemed destined for a career in academic philosophy. He taught phenomenology at MIT, as a leave replacement for Hubert Dreyfus, and published, in 1969, his translation of Heidegger's *Vom Wesen des Grundes*, as *The Essence of Reasons* (Northwestern University Press) (Malick 1969).

In the same year, however, he enrolled in the inaugural class at the Center for Advanced Film Studies at the American Film Institute in Los Angeles. There he produced an eighteen-minute film, *Lanton Miles* (1969), which was shown at an early screening of *Badlands* but subsequently withdrawn. For a couple of years, he worked in Hollywood as screenwriter and script doctor on a number of undistinguished films (see Morrison and Schur 2003: 2–8, for details of Malick's activities at this time). He received independent financial support to make *Badlands* (1973), a film loosely based on a series of apparently random killings carried out by Charlie Starkweather in the American Midwest in 1958. Drawing considerable praise when screened at the New York Film festival in autumn 1973, the film was bought and distributed by Warner Brothers. Malick's second film, *Days of Heaven*, set in the Texas panhandle during the First World War, went into production in 1976, with a much more substantial budget from Paramount, but was not released until 1978, after considerable editing in post-production.

After the release of *Days of Heaven*, Malick appears to have left Hollywood, possibly moving to France. He returned to cinema in 1998 with *The Thin Red Line*, based on James Earl Jones' novel chronicling the American battle for Guadalcanal in the Second World War. The film again underwent considerable changes during post-production. When released, it polarized reviewers – it was nominated for seven Academy awards but did not receive any – and there is wide critical disagreement as to its thematic content. Malick's most recent film, *The New World*, is a retelling of the story of John Smith and Pocahontas, which bears some close resemblances, stylistically and thematically, to Malick's previous film. It left both critics and supporters of Malick a little unsure of their ground, although serious critical readings are now starting to appear (see, e.g., Macdonald 2008; Morrison 2007; Cousins 2007; Martin 2007).

It is surprising, given Malick's elevated standing in the pantheon of modern directors, that there are to date only a few critical studies of his work – two critical monographs (Morrison and Schur 2003; Chion 2004), one forthcoming monograph (Martin forthcoming), an extended chapter of a book (Bersani and Dutoit 2004), a comparative assessment with other directors such as Lynch and Altman in a chapter of a book on contemporary cinema (Orr 1998: 162–87), and two collections of critical articles (Patterson 2003, exp. ed. 2007; Davies 2008a). However, given his philosophical training and the overtly philosophical material in his later films, many commentators have sought to locate his cinema in philosophical space. I shall begin by surveying the divergent conceptions of that location and, relatedly, of the role of images of nature in his films. I shall then briefly look at the ways in which Malick's films have been taken to play with generic expectations. In the final section, I shall relate the conflicting views as to the thematic content of Malick's cinema to the "polysemic" – semantically multilayered – nature of his films, and, in particular, to his use of voice-overs.

Philosophical dimensions of Malick's cinema

The first person to pay serious philosophical attention to Malick's work was his former teacher, Stanley Cavell, who discusses *Days of Heaven* in the introduction to the second edition (1979) of *The World Viewed*. Cavell maintains that Malick "discovered, or discovered how to acknowledge, a fundamental fact of the film's photographic basis: that objects participate in the photographic presence of themselves; they participate in the recreation of themselves on film; they are essential in the making of their appearances" (xvi). Malick thereby "found a way to transpose ... for our meditation" central Heideggerian themes (xv). According to Cavell, cinematic representation significantly resembles our metaphysical representation of the world, of the representational nature of which we have become unaware. Malick's film, in "foregrounding" and thereby making present to the viewer the self-referential nature of cinematic representation, also makes present the nature of our representation of the world, and thus can awaken us to "the question of Being." Since philosophy, for Heidegger, is a matter of "dwelling" in this question, *Days of Heaven* is itself a work of philosophy. Cavell's analysis has inspired others to offer Heideggerian readings of *The Thin Red Line*, describing it as "a film that aspires to the status of philosophy," and as "Heideggerian cinema" (Furstenau and MacAvoy 2003: 180). Through the voice-overs attributable to the central character, Witt, he can be seen to be "ask[ing] the question of Being in a decidedly philosophical manner" (182). An alternative Heideggerian reading of *The Thin Red Line* takes it subject, again most clearly articulated through Witt, to be "ontic wonder" (Clewis 2003).

While the temptation to uncover Heideggerian themes in Malick's cinema, and in particular in *The Thin Red Line*, is understandable, other commentators have rejected any attempt to reduce the film to a philosophical "message," while maintaining that Heideggerian or more broadly phenomenological themes can help to bring out philosophical dimensions of the narrative. For one such commentator (Critchley 2002), the key idea, represented both in his words and in his actions by Witt, is that one should strive to face death, and the vicissitudes of life, with a certain "calm" akin to that comprised by the Heideggerian conception of Angst when Dasein confronts its own being-unto-death. Witt recalls such a calm in the manner in which his mother confronted her own death and regards this as the true locus of immortality. An alternative reading of *The Thin Red Line* (Dreyfus and Prince 2008) takes as central a Heideggerian distinction between demise, as physical death, and dying, as ontological death, which involves a collapse of Dasein's world: it is the latter, and our ways of relating to it, rather than the former, that is the real subject of the film, on this reading. Another broadly phenomenological reading of Malick's later work (Davies 2008b) sees it as more indebted to Merleau-Ponty than to Heidegger, and as revolving around issues concerning the embodied nature of human perception and agency. This, it is claimed, accounts *inter alia* for Malick's notorious lack of interest in providing standard motivations for his characters' actions.

Other commentators, however, have located Malick's films in very different philosophical or spiritual terrain. Certain narrative elements in *Days of Heaven* – the "plagues" of locusts and fire that beset the farmer, for example (Mottram 2003; Silberman 2003) – and the overtly philosophical or religious dimensions to the voice-overs that punctuate the narratives of *The Thin Red Line* and *The New World*, have encouraged readings of these films in terms of Judeo-Christian symbolism and mythology. These features have led some to see at the core of Malick's cinema the expression of "an Edenic yearning to recapture a lost wholeness of being, an idyllic state of integration with the natural and the good both within and without ourselves" (Mottram 2003: 14). Other commentators have spoken of Malick's "Edenic mythologizing" (Silberman 2003: 165; see also Chion 2004: 8); and of *The Thin Red Line*, as "a reinvented myth of the Fall filtered through a Vietnam-era political consciousness" (Streamas 2003: 139). "Malick's narrative," according to one such reading, "preaches a sermon of the triumph of the spirit. The final monologue ... is a prayer for the indwelling spirit that begins with one more religious-spiritual question ... and ends with a kind of redemptive benediction that affirms Witt's position" (Silberman 2003: 170).

Closely allied to, and sometimes overlapping, such construals of Malick's cinema are readings that point to a different kind of spirituality present in the films that aligns them with American Transcendentalism of the sort expounded by Emerson (Power 2003) and Thoreau (Mottram 2003). For the Transcendentalists, the universe comprises two elements, Nature and Soul, and one can attain unity with the world soul through communing with nature. "Transcendentalist" readings point to various themes that can be found in Witt's voice-overs in *The Thin Red Line* – talk of all men having "one big soul," or as being part of "one self," of reaching out "to touch the glory," and, directly echoing Emerson, of "all things shinin'." It is in these terms, it is claimed, that we should understand the "calm" and "immortality" of which Witt speaks in discussing his mother's death. Furthermore, it is not hard to see how the voice-overs of Pocahontas and Smith in *The New World* might lend themselves to a similar reading. The place of natural images in the first two films has also been interpreted in this way.

Picking up on this idea of the "shinin'" of nature, it has been argued (Bersani and Dutoit 2004) that *The Thin Red Line* proposes a relational ethic, evidenced in Witt's talk of a man, taken by himself, as like a coal drawn from the fire. Witt's final voice-over in the film then expresses the possibility of attaining a kind of dispassionate yet compassionate seeing of life in all of its facets – an "implicated witnessing" – and the possibility of "a community grounded in anonymity and held together by an absence of both individuality and leadership" (165). Such a relationality, it is claimed, is mirrored in the physical rendition of nature in the film, which expresses an "ontology of universal immanence":

> The surfaces of all things "quiver" from the presence within them of all the other things to which they relate. There is, indeed, as Witt insists, another world, but it is *this* world seen as a vast reservoir of correspondences, of surfaces always ready to "open" in order to acknowledge, to welcome, to receive that which is at once their outer and their immanent being. (169)

Nature in Malick

This introduces a second and interrelated theme in the critical discussion of Malick's cinema – the place of nature in his films. What, for example, are we to make of the stunning visual representations of nature, especially shots of light filtered through high dense trees, water, long grass shaped by wind, the play of the sun on the landscape, and exotic fauna and flora that populate Malick's films after *Badlands*? Not surprisingly, the very different overall thematic readings of the films are accompanied by radically opposed interpretations of these representations of nature. On one broadly Heideggerian reading of *The Thin Red Line*, for example (Critchley 2002), the film expresses a naturalistic conception of nature. Nature, nonenchanted, is, as Tall remarks, "cruel," a warring force that frames the human drama of war but is utterly indifferent to human purposes and intentions. Human death is one more manifestation of the relentlessness of nature, in the face of which calmness is the only truly human response.

On a reading of the films as "Edenic myth," however, nature serves as "a powerful sign of a higher good," and natural images of light, wind, trees, and skies "function as a bridge to another world and as a sign of its existence" (Mottram 2003: 15). One commentator takes the central theme of *The Thin Red Line* to be the impenetrability of nature itself – is it cruel or kind, beautiful, or ugly? – and the problem of human action in the face of this impenetrability: "It is in the visuals of the landscape ... that Malick is able to most clearly express his vision of the world as paradise and paradise lost, caught up in darkness and death but open to redemption through the radiance of unselfish individual action" (Silberman 2003: 171). For Transcendentalist interpreters of the films, nature is presented as the spiritual realm, communion with which allows us to transcend the individual strivings expressed in war. In this respect, it has been claimed (Power 2003), Witt's ideas and those of the film as a whole echo Emerson's claim, in his transcendentalist manifesto *Nature*, that, through isolated communion with nature, one can achieve a communal spirituality and overcome egoism to become "a transparent eyeball."

Commentators who have written on Malick's cinema have generally assumed a continuity in his treatment of nature. For the Transcendentalists, as we have seen, Malick can be seen as using nature and natural beauty in his first three films as "a powerful sign of a higher good"; alternatively, it has been argued that natural images in Malick's first three films perform the function of providing "appropriate backdrops for movement from innocence to experience haunted by a dream of paradise" (Silberman 2003: 161). Others (Morrison and Schur 2003) see Malick's films as articulating a broadly Heideggerian philosophy of nature. *The Thin Red Line* is taken to be particularly concerned with what Heidegger calls "primordial nature," nature experienced as a powerful force which is both present to and absent from us.

Superficially, however, the role accorded to natural images in *The Thin Red Line* and *The New World* seems to differ from that accorded to such images in the earlier films. In *Badlands*, nature provides a frame for Kit and Holly's activities, but an indifferent frame. Shots of nature are firmly grounded in the diegesis. They can only rarely be interpreted as commenting in some way upon the narrative: this is perhaps the case with the presentations of nature during Kit and Holly's forest "idyll," where the images seem to express the subjective states of the characters rather than the natural setting of the action. In *Days of Heaven*, shots of nature, while luminescent and touched by the light of the "magic hour" just after sunset, are again diegetically anchored. But, rather than generally providing an indifferent frame for the actions of the protagonists, shots of animals and landscape often serve to anticipate or echo – provide an objective correlate for – their emotional states. In *The Thin Red Line*, however, shots of natural beauty punctuate the scenes in ways that are much less diegetically tied, as is especially the case with the opening and closing sequences. Nature as presented in these images seems even more removed from the unfolding human drama. While the images of nature in *The New World* are more closely tied to the narrative, their visual content and role is very reminiscent of *The Thin Red Line* – indeed, many of the natural images of light and water in the two films seem interchangeable. In both of these later films, images of nature seem to provide an additional semantic level that plays against both the narrative and the other semantic elements in the film, such as the voice-over (see below).

The most detailed examination of Malick's conception of nature in his later cinema is to be found in a recent study (Macdonald 2008) that identifies an overarching Malickian interest in the "nature" of human nature, and sees this interest as most fully explored in *The New World*. Macdonald argues that Malick's decision to follow Disney's *Pocahontas* in presenting the story as a *romance* between Smith and Pocahontas – a nineteenth-century embellishment having no basis in Smith's own historical accounts – is best understood by ascribing to Malick the desire that the audience largely prescind from an interest in the narrative so as to engage with the film at a deeper thematic level. He cites, as further evidence of Malick's intention to manifest such a desire to the viewer, the quotation of certain shots from the Disney film in *The New World* and the use in the latter of actors whose voices featured in related roles in *Pocohontas*. *The New World*, he argues, is not to be read at the "surface" level, as a revealing of human similarities underlying apparent cultural differences – the point of the Disney film – but as a meditation on the "nature of human nature," and, thereby, on the true "war in the heart of nature." The voice-overs by Smith and Pocahontas express a shared wish to understand how human nature stands in relation to nature in general. Malick's metaphysics, it is claimed, involves a materialism, roughly Nietzschean in character, that views reason and the idea of a rational subject that stands apart from nature as merely one more expression of nature. Human reason, then, turns out to be nothing more than an expression of the "blind" rationality of nature that Nietzsche terms the will to power.

Malick and genre

The manner in which natural images function as an independent semantic level in Malick's later films brings out one of the most striking stylistic features of his cinema – its polysemic character. As we shall see shortly, we need to balance the narrative and the images of nature against at least one further semantic element in the later films – the diegetically unanchored voice-overs – if we are to seriously assess competing thematic readings of these films. First, however, it is worth briefly remarking on another much discussed broadly stylistic feature of Malick's cinema, namely, the ways in which he both draws upon and critically engages with generic expectations in the audience.

It is not difficult to assign Malick's films to well-established cinematic genres, and to compare them with other contemporary films belonging to the same genres. *Badlands* and Penn's *Bonnie and Clyde* (1967) are readily ascribed to the "outlaw/road movie" genre (Campbell 2003; Orr 2003), and much was made, on release, of the relative virtues of *The Thin Red Line* and *Saving Private Ryan* (1998) as war movies (see Flanagan 2003). *Days of Heaven* seems to fall into the genre of the western; and

The New World, into that of grand historical drama with humanistic intent. But while all of Malick's films clearly presuppose certain generic expectations in the receiver, commentators have claimed that given how the films elicit and then fail to satisfy these expectations, this must be done in pursuit of some end other than the development or simple revision of the genre.

Days of Heaven, it has been claimed (McGettigan 2003), contains all of the elements required for the western genre, yet none of them plays its standard role in the overall narrative. We have the task of working the land, but here performed by migrant laborers; an "official" hero (the farmer) who fails to come good; and an "outlaw" hero (Bill) who is punished rather than redeemed. There is no indication in the final version of the film of the male camaraderie that is a feature of the western, and the foreman's revenge in the final scenes fails to bring the closure such acts usually bring in the western: it seems meaningless, rather than cathartic, both for the foreman and for the viewer. The point of thereby undermining the genre, it is further claimed (McGettigan 2003; Orr 2003), is to reveal the illusory nature of the "myth" of the western in the interests of bringing us to a clearer understanding of the history thereby mythologized.

A similar analysis can be given of *The Thin Red Line*. Our generic expectations of the "war movie" are that the narrative will be tightly structured and will present various scenes of combat action whose purpose is the attainment of some shared purpose that is realized, or fails to be realized, at the end of the film. We expect that the characters will be sharply individuated from one another in order to personalize them for the audience and that what is achieved will depend upon the different skills and the camaraderie of the "band of brothers" working together. In the case of *The Thin Red Line*, however, such expectations are constantly frustrated: "many of the characters are indistinguishable from one another. Then there is the great battle, which seems to resolve nothing and serves as an anti-climax" (McGettigan 2003: 50). As with the generic departures in *Days of Heaven*, the generic failings of *The Thin Red Line* can be seen as serving an ulterior interest in critically undermining the genre and providing a more realistic cinematic representation of the realities of modern warfare (Flanagan 2003).

Malick's polysemic cinema and the role of the voice-over

Malick's films are among the most celebrated contemporary examples of cinematic art, and it is perhaps to be expected that great works of art will support a plurality of interpretations. But the range and diversity of readings, in particular of his later films, calls for some explanation. A couple of factors may help to explain why the films have been read in such widely different ways.

First, even in the case of a relatively conventional film like *Badlands*, the ambiguous nature of Holly's voiced narrative requires that we assess how different kinds of contentful elements stand in relation to one another in determining the thematic meaning of the film. In the case of *The Thin Red Line* – the most stylistically and semantically complex of Malick's works – at least four different kinds of contentful elements are interwoven in the experienced fabric of the film, every sequence containing at least two of these elements in some kind of juxtaposition. There is, first, a "war narrative" of a not completely unfamiliar type, comprising a series of episodes in the battle for Guadalcanal. Second, as already noted, there are voice-overs, some of which raise philosophical or semi-religious questions about good and evil, the nature and origin of war in a number of senses, and how one should conduct oneself in the face of what life presents. In addition to, and sometimes accompanying, the voice-overs, there are flashbacks associated with particular characters. Third, as we have also seen, there are stunning visual representations of nature. Finally, there is the musical soundtrack, replete with leitmotifs and culturally resonant elements – for example, quotations from Charles Ives' *The Unanswered Question* and the development, in Hans Zimmer's score, of melodic ideas from the missionary song, which features early and very late in the film. The viewer trying to understand the thematic meaning of the film must seek to establish how these elements interact. For example, does the narrative exemplify, or call into question, the ideas expressed in the voice-overs, or do these ideas contribute in some other way to the workings of the film? Do the representations of nature frame, or comment on, or expressively embellish, the narrative and inter-rogatory threads? Or, indeed, are we mistaken in thinking that these often disparate threads are united in the service of articulating an overarching thematic meaning?

Second, it is difficult to reconstruct the filmmaker's intentions. The screenplays after *Badlands* leave much unclear, since major components of the films, such as the voice-overs in *Days of Heaven* and *The Thin Red Line*, were added only later in post-production (see chapter 4 of Morrison and Schur [2003] for very interesting insights into the making of Malick's films – I draw on this in the following paragraphs). Furthermore, Malick is notoriously reluctant to discuss the thematic content (or indeed other aspects) of his films. We have, as interpretive resources, only a couple of interviews following the release of *Badlands*, some biographies of, or interviews with, cinematographers and actors who have worked with Malick, and a DVD – with no direct contribution by Malick – on the making of *The New World*.

As a consequence, it is impossible to distance questions of thematic content in Malick's cinema from questions of style. Malick's films after *Badlands* are generated through the manipulation, in post-production, of material realized in the shooting – principally through the adding of voice-overs and the radical editing of the visual content. To illustrate the interpretive complexity of these films, we may focus on the contribution to content of one of the most distinctive elements in Malick's cinematic style, the voice-over. Voice-overs are not a staple of contemporary cinema, but when used they fulfill certain standard narrative functions – supplementing the visually presented narrative by filling in gaps, or providing deeper insight into the motivation and subjectivity of a character to whom a voice-over is attributable.

Remarkably, voice-overs are a prominent feature of all of Malick's films, although their function is increasingly idiosyncratic. The closest approximation to the standard use of cinematic voice-over is in *Badlands*, where Holly, from an unspecified location beyond the temporal span of the visually presented narrative, shares with the viewer her thoughts about the events portrayed. Even here, however, Malick's use of the voice-over is singular in two respects. First, he uses a female voice, self-consciously modeling this on child narrators in literary fictions, such as Huck Finn (Walker 1975). Second, like some literary narrators, Holly is not a "reliable" reporter on much that is going on, not because she misrepresents "what is going on" in a narrow sense, but because she fails to grasp "what is going on" in a moral or human sense. Some (Morrison and Schur 2003) have seen this as a key element in the ironic detachment and humor of the film with respect to the represented events.

Days of Heaven also features a young female voice-over, that of Linda, Bill's much younger sister. But the voice-over again fails to perform its customary functions, because of the quirky and sometimes (to the viewer) naïve perspective that Linda has on the events, and because of the absence of commentary on many significant parts of the action and the consequent failure to provide the kind of insight into motivation normally furnished through such a device. A further notable departure is that the voice-over was apparently only conceived and added in post-production, as the film underwent substantial changes prior to release.

In *The Thin Red Line*, however, Malick's use of the voice-over breaks more radically with the cinematic tradition. Indeed, what one takes to be the function served by these voice-overs will strongly influence one's interpretation of the film as a whole. Again, the voice-overs were with very few exceptions added in post-production. They are one of two prominent devices that stand in some kind of thematic relation to the visual narrative. The other device is the flashback, which is used to represent earlier episodes in the lives of specific characters. While it is always obvious which characters' experiences are represented in the flashbacks, it is only sometimes easily determined to which character, if indeed any, the voice-overs are attributable. Where the source of the voice-over is clear, this is because of the voice itself, or associated images, or the camera's dwelling on the character in question in a confirmatory way. In such cases, the function of the voice-over is also relatively clear – to represent the subjectivity of the character, thereby serving to provide psychological "thickness" that would otherwise be lacking. Bell's voice-overs combine with flashbacks to represent his very sensuous relationship with his wife. Tall's voice-overs represent his professional disenchantment, and Welsh's his personal view of the war – as all about "property," and of how one can survive it by making oneself "an island."

But many of the other voice-overs play a more ambiguous role, starting with the opening line of the film: "What's this war in the heart of nature?" This is usually attributed to Witt, as are most of the other voice-overs that do not obviously play the "character-thickening" roles just noted. But some voice-overs are difficult to attribute because the cues that serve us well in other cases lead here to conflicting attributions. For example, a very thematically significant voice-over comparing two ways in which we might see a dying bird seems to belong to Witt, given its content, but is visually accompanied by shots of Welsh walking through the camp dousing fires and is delivered in a voice that doesn't seem to match any of the other voice-overs. Some critics have nonetheless attempted attributions, based on the traditional idea that the voice-over belongs to the character we are (mostly) looking at, leading to some bizarre attributions that make no sense, given the rest of the movie (see, e.g., Clewis 2003).

Others have inferred that these voice-overs are not attributable to any particular character. It seems clear, however, that at least the majority of them are attributable to Witt. We may term these voice-overs, which are almost entirely interrogative in form and ask fundamental questions about the nature of evil and its presence in the world, "Witt" voice-overs.

What is the function of the Witt voice-overs? Are they ways of "thickening" Witt as a character by showing that, behind the calm exterior and demeanor, there is a stream of deep philosophical questioning? If so, it is strange that the role of philosophical questioning should be given to Witt rather than to Staros (Bersani and Dutoit 2004). Also, they seem to relate to the visually presented narrative differently from the character-thickening voice-overs, which are closely tied either to particular events in the narrative, or to flashbacks. The Witt voice-overs are only loosely diegetically anchored, and can occur when Witt is not present (the opening monologue) or is dead (the closing monologue).

If, in spite of these anomalies, we take the Witt voice-overs to be insights into his consciousness during the battle, we may be sympathetic to the Heideggerian reading of the film, according to which Witt is engaged in the primary philosophical activity of raising the question of Being. Alternatively, we may simply ascribe to all of the voice-overs the single function of contributing "to the construction of character, synthesising impersonal chronicle with stream-of-consciousness poetics" (Morrison and Schur 2003: 26). Others, however, are more skeptical, maintaining that the Witt voice-overs "are crucial to the film's sense, but they have very little intellectual weight" (Bersani and Dutoit 2004: 132). Their function is to provide a background of linguistically mediated questioning to which no linguistic answer is either provided or available: it is in the visual presentation of Witt's way of visually engaging with the world that the answer to these questions lies.

The voice-overs in *The New World* are enigmatic in a different way. There is, here, no difficulty in attributing them to characters. They are principally in the voices of Smith and Pocahontas, although Rolfe's closing voice-over describing the death of Pocahontas plays a crucial narrative role. And, even in their most abstract form, they seem to some extent rooted in what is happening to the characters. In their interrogative form, they are reminiscent of the Witt voice-overs, but they are much less evenly distributed through the film. Another difference between *The New World* and its predecessor is the absence, in the former, of both flashbacks and "character-thickening" voice-overs. The voice-overs in *The New World*, save for those by Rolfe, are, like the Witt voice-overs, very loosely anchored in the diegesis, generally interrogative in form, and provide a semantic level quite distinct from that furnished by the narrative. What is mysterious in *The New World* is the relationship between the voice-overs and the visually presented narrative, something addressed by Macdonald in the paper cited earlier (2008).

Is there anything that unifies these different uses of the voice-over device? In all of Malick's films, it is notable that the voice-overs present the viewer with a stream of reflective thinking that stands apart from the actions of the characters. It rarely motivates or illuminates those actions, however – a notable exception being Tall's "character-thickening" voice-overs in *The Thin Red Line*, although it represents, in many cases, the way in which a character experiences her or his engagements with the world. Indeed, as commentators have often noted, Malick also eschews the use of dialogue to make explicit his characters' motivations, excising, in production, such dialogue contained in the screenplays of *Days of Heaven* and *The Thin Red Line* (see Morrison and Schur 2003: chapter 4). This brings out a more general feature of agency in Malick's cinema. As a rule, characters are represented as acting in ways that are elicited from them by the world as it is given to them in experience, rather than as engaging in exercises of deliberation. Of course, we can always reconstruct their actions in terms of the sorts of psychological motivations familiar from intentional psychology. But, just as the characters generally perceive their actions as mandated by the experienced world, so we, as viewers have no difficulty understanding those actions prior to any attempts to reconstruct them in deliberative terms. This is apparent even in the case of the pathological agency of Kit, which strikes us as shocking but not unintelligible. It holds also in *Days of Heaven*, where we are offered, apparently intentionally on Malick's part, little in the way of explicit motivation for most of the actions of Bill and the farmer. Even though their more general beliefs and desires are clear to us, in general the intentionality of their actions is made manifest to us through the circumstances of their agency.

Arguably (Davies 2008b), a more developed view of embodied agency and embodied perception is central to *The Thin Red Line*, where, for example, Welsh's "courageous" action in administering morphine to a "gut-shot" fellow soldier completely contradicts his "philosophy," enunciated both in the dialogue and his voice-overs. But if the thought processes presented discursively in the voice-overs and visually, as memories, in the flashbacks do not in general provide us with insights into motivation, they do exemplify how human embodied agency differs from the embodied agency of the crocodile seen slipping beneath the surface of the water in the opening shot of *The Thin Red Line*. The images of physical intimacy with his wife elicited in Bell by the clinging of the grass as he snakes his way toward the Japanese bunker manifest the complex nature of our bodies' conscious entanglement in things. In this way, such devices play an essential part in Malick's cinematic presentation of the manner in which human agents encounter and respond to the world, a presentation that goes some way to explaining why viewers are so passionately engaged by his films.

References

Bersani, L., and Dutoit, U. (2004) "One Big Soul," chapter 3 of *Forms of Being: Cinema, Aesthetics, Subjectivity*, London: British Film Institute.

Campbell, N. (2003) "The Highway Kind: *Badlands*, Youth, Space and the Road," in H. Patterson (ed.) *The Cinema of Terrence Malick: Poetic Visions of America*, London: Wallflower Press.

Cavell, S. (1979) *The World Viewed*, 2nd ed., Cambridge, MA: Harvard University Press.

Chion, M. (2004) *The Thin Red Line*, London: British Film Institute.

Clewis, R. (2003) "Heideggerean Wonder in Terrence Malick's *The Thin Red Line*," *Film and Philosophy* 7: 22–36.

Cousins, M. (2007) "Praising *The New World*," in H. Patterson (ed.) *The Cinema of Terrence Malick: Poetic Visions of America*, 2nd exp. ed., London: Wallflower Press.

Critchley, S. (2002) "Calm – On Terrence Malick's *The Thin Red Line*," *Film-Philosophy* 6. Available at http://www.film-philosophy.com/vol6-2002/n48critchley.

Davies, D. (ed.) (2008a) *The Thin Red Line*, London: Routledge.

—— (2008b) "Vision, Touch, and Embodiment in *The Thin Red Line*," in D. Davies (ed.) *The Thin Red Line*, London: Routledge.

Dreyfus, H., and Prince, C. (2008) "*The Thin Red Line*: Dying without Demise, Demise without Dying," in D. Davies (ed.) *The Thin Red Line*, London: Routledge.

Flanagan, M. (2003) "'Everything a Lie': The Critical and Commercial Reception of Terrence Malick's *The Thin Red Line*," in H. Patterson (ed.) *The Cinema of Terrence Malick: Poetic Visions of America*, London: Wallflower Press.

Furstenau, M., and MacAvoy, L. (2003) "Terrence Malick's Heideggerian Cinema: War and the Question of Being in *The Thin Red Line*," in H. Patterson (ed.) *The Cinema of Terrence Malick: Poetic Visions of America*, London: Wallflower Press.

Macdonald, I. (2008) "Nature and the Will to Power in Malick's *New World*," in D. Davies (ed.) *The Thin Red Line*, London: Routledge.

Malick, T. (trans.) (1969) *The Essence of Reasons*, by M. Heidegger, bilingual edition, Evanston, IL: Northwestern University Press.

Martin, A. (2007) "Approaching *The New World*," in H. Patterson (ed.) *The Cinema of Terrence Malick: Poetic Visions of America*, 2nd exp. ed., London: Wallflower Press.

—— (forthcoming) *Terrence Malick*, London: British Film Institute.

McGettigan, J. (2003) "*Days of Heaven* and the Myth of the West," in H. Patterson (ed.) *The Cinema of Terrence Malick: Poetic Visions of America*, London: Wallflower Press.

Morrison, J. (2007) "Making Worlds, Making Pictures: Terrence Malick's *The New World*," in H. Patterson (ed.) *The Cinema of Terrence Malick: Poetic Visions of America*, 2nd exp. ed., London: Wallflower Press.

Morrison, J., and T. Schur (2003) *The Films of Terrence Malick*, London: Praeger.

Mottram, R. (2003) "All Things Shining: The Struggle of Wholeness, Redemption, and Transcendence in the Films of Terrence Malick," in H. Patterson (ed.) *The Cinema of Terrence Malick: Poetic Visions of America*, London: Wallflower Press.

Orr, J. (1998) *Contemporary Cinema*, Edinburgh: Edinburgh University Press.

—— (2003) "Terrence Malick and Arthur Penn: The Western Re-Myth," in H. Patterson (ed.) *The Cinema of Terrence Malick: Poetic Visions of America*, London: Wallflower Press.

Patterson, H. (ed.) (2003) *The Cinema of Terrence Malick: Poetic Visions of America*, London: Wallflower Press.

—— (ed.) (2007) *The Cinema of Terrence Malick: Poetic Visions of America*, 2nd exp. ed., London: Wallflower Press.

Power, S. P. (2003) "The Other World of War: Terrence Malick's Adaptation of *The Thin Red Line*," in H. Patterson (ed.) *The Cinema of Terrence Malick: Poetic Visions of America*, London: Wallflower Press.

Silberman, R. (2003) "Terrence Malick, Landscape, and 'This War at the Heart of Nature'," in H. Patterson (ed.) *The Cinema of Terrence Malick: Poetic Visions of America*, London: Wallflower Press.

Streamas, J. (2003) "The Greatest Generation Steps over *The Thin Red Line*," in H. Patterson (ed.) *The Cinema of Terrence Malick: Poetic Visions of America*, London: Wallflower Press.

Walker, B. (1975) "Malick on *Badlands*" (Interview), *Sight and Sound* 44(2): 82–3.

53

ANDREI TARKOVSKY

András Bálint Kovács

Even art films are not necessarily expressions of philosophical stances. In their way of representing a certain relationship between humans and the physical world, however, Tarkovsky's films are. Moreover, his films are philosophical not in the banal sense that they evoke "philosophical" ideas. They are philosophical in the very particular sense that they can be interpreted adequately against a specific philosophical background that is deeply rooted in Russian culture and of which most of Tarkovsky's films, in more than one respect, can be considered as another manifestation. Tarkovsky inserts himself into a cultural tradition of Russian Christian philosophy, and his films can be considered as a series of cinematic treatises on the question of how this tradition can be continued or revitalized in the civilization of the late twentieth century. In a unique way in the history of cinema, Tarkovsky does not merely develop a particular form or launch a particular idea; his seven long feature films can be lined up as various stages of the evolution in a particular train of thought. He was also among those rare filmmakers who did not take on a fashionable anti-intellectual mask by claiming that he was unable to comment on his own films. He seized every occasion to talk and write about the ideas developed in his films. So in many ways he claimed a theoretical status beside his filmmaker-artist status. In this essay I will follow the line of development of a certain idea central to this philosophical tradition: the construction of the *person*. I will compare the films of Tarkovsky with the ideas of Russian philosopher Nikolai Berdyaev (1874–1948) to show that Tarkovsky was indeed under the philosophical influence of Russian Christian Personalism, and that his films represent a particular renaissance of this thinking in a period in which these ideas were clearly unwelcome in the Soviet Union. Tarkovsky's films, of course, cannot be reduced to an adherence to personalist philosophy. This is only one aspect of Tarkovsky's work, but an important one, and this will be the subject of this essay.

I will distinguish two stages in the process of developing the personalist idea in Tarkovsky's films: (1) *The person as a mission*; and (2) *Transcending the person*. These stages can be considered as different aspects of this problem, but, with relation to the films of Tarkovsky, they represent chronological stages of an inner development of his personal and intellectual life.

What is the person?

Christian Personalism from the early twentieth century was the philosophical trend most influential in Tarkovsky's intellectual development. He most likely inherited this tradition from his father, Arseny Tarkovsky, a well-known poet and poetry translator in the intellectual circles of Russian symbolist poetry. We know that Tarkovsky read Berdyaev, since he mentions him several times in his published diary that he began writing in 1970. However, it is not clear how conscious his relationship with Berdyaev's ideas was, since his mention of Berdyaev does not contain any discussion or reflection on these ideas (Tarkovsky 1993: 15, 213, 274, 282). This kind of thinking was in currency within a certain Russian intellectual circle, even during the Communist era and even for a generation that was not under the direct influence of early twentieth-century intellectual life. Personalism, like existentialism, emerges from the idea of the condition of the alienated person, rather than from the exterior world. However, unlike existentialism, Personalism does not consider the human condition as a unified attribute of man. It splits man into two antagonistic entities. Central to the personalist thinking is the idea that man is partly integrated into the social-biological environment, but partly, and most importantly, alien to it. The integrated part of man is called the individual, and the alien part is called the person. The individual is determined by biological and social factors and is a product of those, while the person is independent of these factors and communicates only with God:

> Person is a whole, it is a totality, it is integral, it bears within itself the universal, and it cannot be part of any sort of the general, whether of the world or of society, or of universal being or Divinity. Person is not at all of nature nor does it appertain, like everything natural, to an objective natural hierarchy, nor is it able to be put into any sort of natural order. (Mounier 1935: online)

The person is therefore radically separated from its physical and social environment; it is even opposed to it:

> The person does not resemble anything in the world; it cannot be compared to anything. When the unique and unrepeatable person enters into the world, the process of the world is broken, and this process is obliged to change its course, although this is an imperceptible event. The person ... cannot be an element of world's evolution ... The person represents a breakthrough, a caesura in this world. (Berdyaev 1988: 191; note, all additional translations of Berdyaev are my own)

This makes the person for Berdyaev the most mysterious phenomenon in the world. The person is not a social, political, historical, racial category; it is an ethical one. The person is the ethical aspect of human beings, but its norms are suprapersonal. The person is not born automatically with a human being; it is not a given. It is rather a human being's task, it is a mission. The person is an absolute dimension for a human which elevates him or her over everyday material relations and relates humanity with another universe. Becoming a person is a process by which a human enters into a contact with the transcendental. The person "stands in front of the transcendental, and when it realizes itself, transcends" (Berdyaev 1988: 223). This transcending cannot be carried out alone. For the individual to turn into a person it is necessary that this happens with regard to a community. The person's independence from all exterior determination sets off a transcendental determination which is realized in the spiritual community of persons: "The person supposes that the transcendence is effectuated toward others; the person cannot breathe, it suffocates when closed into itself" (Berdyaev 1988: 214). The creation of this spiritual community, however, is not a communal task, and it is here that Christian Personalism differs from the revolutionary ideologies. It is rather everyone's duty toward oneself: "The lie of political and social revolutions consists in wanting to get rid of the evil from outside, whereas it continues to subsist inside. Revolutionists and counterrevolutionists never start by eradicating the evil within" (Berdyaev 1984: 183).

In sum, we can say that the person is not a natural given, it has to be reached. The person is the ethical aspect of the individual which is in direct communication with God and other ethical persons independently of the social and historical circumstances in which the person must realize itself. Since the person is the substance of humanity, one has no choice other than to struggle for the construction of one's ethical person. This is a task for everyone, and the more the circumstances are hostile the more this task becomes urgent, and the clearer the nature of the relationship between the person and the exterior world. In examining Tarkovsky's oeuvre one can clearly notice the central role of the idea of the conflict between person and individual or between the person and the world, as well as a certain evolution of this conflict. Each film elaborates the same problem from different angles: how is it possible for the person to be born and to subsist.

The person as a mission

In *Ivan's Childhood* (1962) and in *Andrei Rubljov* (1969) Berdyaev's ideas about the person's ethical independence are brought into the foreground. This can be explained, obviously, by the fact that Tarkovsky had to propose his particular point of view within the limits of the tradition of the war film and the historical film, a point of view alien to this tradition. Both films' fundamental question is to what extent the individual is dependent on his historical circumstances. This is clearly the independence at stake in these two films. In his first film, Tarkovsky shows what happens when the ethical person has no chance to develop in someone, while in his second he shows someone who comes to recognize the necessity of developing the person.

In *Ivan's Childhood* the protagonist is a twelve-year-old boy in the midst of the Second World War. He is a kind of volunteer in the Red Army who undertakes reconnaissance missions across the frontline. After returning from one of his missions, he meets a young lieutenant who is shocked at learning that this boy is serving in the army rather than going to school somewhere far away from the battle. The officers in charge also think that he should quit fighting and go to school. But Ivan is not willing to do that. He flees the headquarters to avoid being transferred from the front to a school. The officers have no choice but to concede, and give Ivan a last assignment – from which he never returns.

Ivan is an uncompromising character who ferociously hates the enemy and engages in fighting unconditionally. Yet that which is a virtue for an adult character in the tradition of the Soviet war film becomes an unnatural, even frightening trait in such a child. It is this aspect of this film Jean-Paul Sartre commented upon, when he stated that Ivan as a hero is really a monster (Sartre 1986). He is a "monster" because the war had killed the child in him, and only the unnatural hero remained, so his persona is entirely a product of the war. Tarkovsky shows Ivan's dreams, nightmares, and memories about his lost childhood, lost friends, and lost parents. His profoundly wounded soul becomes manifest only when he sleeps or is alone. Around others he is intransigent, forceful, and determined to an extent that even adult soldiers seldom are. In this film Tarkovsky presents a character whose experience of the exterior world does not allow him an opportunity to develop as a person. Ivan has no ethical independence from his environment; he is a creature of the war and acts accordingly.

Tarkovsky emphasizes this with the help of another character, the young lieutenant. This is a rather unlikely character and definitely an unusual one in the war-film tradition. He is an intellectual who is too tender and awkward to be a good soldier, and also keeps a Dürer album in his quarters. He is presented as someone clearly unsuited for war. However, he is the only one in the story who survives the war. Ivan and all of his commandants, professional and dedicated fighters, perish; only the one whose person is so conspicuously alien to this environment survives. This character clearly demonstrates the sharp opposition between the individual determined from outside and the person with ethical independence. There is Ivan, on the one hand, whose tragedy is that he has no chance to live his own life, follow his own way, develop his own ethical person. His life is taken by the war even before he died. He is too rigid, too strong to live. And there is the lieutenant, on the other hand, who on the contrary is too tender, too independent to be a good soldier, but that is his chance to survive the war.

In Tarkovsky's next film the protagonist is an icon painter from the fourteenth century, Andrei Rubljov. The real Rubljov lived the anonymous life of the orthodox monks, so there is very little known about his life. Even his paintings are not easy to identify, since at that time painters, especially the monk painters, did not consider their paintings as individual accomplishments, and they did not sign them. We know in which monasteries he lived, where he worked and with whom, but we don't know what ideas he had about painting or about his role as a painter. The only thing we know is that he was famous already in his lifetime for his very special, unorthodox style that broke the rigid uniformity of Byzantine icon painting of the time and initiated a Russian national style of icon painting. The faces, the gestures, and especially the colors on his icons were more lively and natural than those the Byzantine tradition prescribed. What Tarkovsky does in this film is to construct a hypothetical inner conflict in the character of Andrei Rubljov that in Tarkovsky's view could have led to the conscious recognition of his individuality, against the tradition, and to the acceptance of his spiritual personhood, against the exterior world. Clearly, we don't know whether Rubljov had any inner conflicts at all, and if so, what they were. It is very likely that Rubljov did not perceive his own character with the help of the categories of Christian Personalism inspired by the individualistic approach of modern existentialism of the twentieth century, which is why Alexander Soljenitsyne condemned this film as anti-Orthodox, even as anti-Russian. And the problem Tarkovsky depicts in relation to Rubljov is clearly Tarkovsky's own problem. But this is why Tarkovsky's fundamental ideas about the birth of the person can be clearly recognized in this film.

The central portion of the film's narrative concerns a debate and the events contributing to it. At the beginning, the debate goes on between two people: Rubljov and his old master, Feofan Grek. Feofan represents tradition, in which God is an almighty punitive power; and icon painting, a reminder of this power for the sinful man. From the point of view of religion, Feofan serves God, as he says, but from the point of view of art, he is hopelessly stuck with reality; his art is dependent on what he sees in the world. As Tarkovsky characterizes him:

> [T]he kind of artist like Feofan Grek reflects the world, his work is nothing more than the reflection of the world surrounding him. His reaction to the things around him is a result of his conviction that the world is fundamentally wrong. (Tarkovsky 1969: 8)

Rubljov's problem with this conception is not that it serves only God, but that it cannot display a difference between what one believes and what one sees. And from this point of view the servitude of God becomes, in a way, man's choice. One can decide whether icon painting reflects the inner conviction not about God but about the nature of man, or the exterior determinants of people's behavior. In Tarkovsky's view Feofan's attitude may seem deeply religious, but it is fundamentally empirically based: he sees man's wrongdoings, so he paints hell and the punitive God to deter man from wrongdoing. Rubljov's attitude is no less religious, but it is in no way dependent on the experience of visible reality. At least that is the position he puts against Feofan's stance. However, as he experiences more and more cruelty in the world, this very position seems more and more untenable for him as he loses belief in its foundation, the fundamental goodness of man. It turns out that even though he tried to see beyond superficial empirical experiences, so that his attitude was supported by an inner conviction, this conviction was still dependent on exterior influences. At some point, in order to save an innocent girl's life, Rubljov has to kill a soldier. The experience that he himself could not respect one of God's commandments finally was stronger than his belief in man's fundamental goodness. This experience becomes the source of his deep crisis, which leads him to suspend all communication with the world: he quits icon painting and refuses to speak. Unlike Ivan, Andrei already claims to be independent of the world and driven by inner convictions. Ivan did not have a chance to develop this independence; Andrei did, but this independence turned out to be too weak. It still depended on what happened outside. The cruelty of the world was able to influence it. That is what Andrei realizes in the last part of the film when he silently observes a young boy making a bell, by himself, without knowing the secrets of bell-founding. Andrei realizes that true creation comes entirely from within, and no exterior moral support should be necessary. Interior independence, the existence of the person, is the ultimate necessary condition of true creation. If *Ivan's Childhood* was about the lack of the person, *Andrei Rubljov* was about looking for the person.

How to become a person?

Starting from his next film, *Solaris* (1972), another dimension of the concept of the person becomes salient. Tarkovsky does not contemplate the definition of personhood or the necessity of the birth of the person, but rather the path that leads to the person and the changes that must occur for the ethical person to develop. *Solaris* and *Mirror* (1975) are films about the inner quest for this path. Berdyaev identifies the birth of the person with pain:

> The person not only experiences pain, but in a certain sense the person is the pain. The struggle for the person, the acknowledgment of the person, is painful ... The generation of the person, the struggle for its own image is the pain in the human world ... Freedom gives birth to suffering ... The dignity of man (i.e., the person, or freedom) supposes the acceptance of pain, the ability to live the pain. (Berdyaev 1988: 198)

Not surprisingly, the central category of these two films is *suffering* and *pain*. Unlike Ivan and Rubljov, both films' protagonists are in a deep interior crisis which is one step forward from Rubljov's recognition of the necessity of inner independence, and two steps forward from Ivan's lack of doubt and complete identification with the exterior world. Kelvin, the hero of *Solaris*, is an astronaut who is given a last chance to save the Solaris project from the authorities who want to close it down. It is believed that no useful information is coming from the space station observing the planet Solaris. Kelvin is allowed to travel to the space station to investigate personally what is happening there. As he arrives he immediately recognizes the weird behavior of the astronauts and scientists. He determines that their behavior is due to the fact that they are visited by the embodiments of the spirits of people from their past. These spirits of individuals, all of whom died one way or another by the astronauts' moral faults, haunt the astronauts. They cannot get rid of them as these ghosts have become immortal. The scientists have to live with the embodiments of their bad consciousness, and that is why they cannot continue their scientific mission. Kelvin also receives a visitor of his own – his wife, who committed suicide because he did not love her enough. Kelvin realizes that the big discovery about planet Solaris is not that this planet can "read" human consciousness and is able to impersonate its hidden sins, but that this is not something to be "resolved," to get rid of, or to overcome. To continue the practice of science, one has to face one's bad consciousness and live with the memories of those whose memories are the most painful. The autonomy of the person does not mean selfishness. The fact that the person can be created only from within and independent of exterior circumstances, which was the conclusion of *Andrei Rubljov*, has to be understood in the context of another important aspect of the person I mentioned above: the person cannot be closed in on itself, but can only subsist in a community. For this spiritual community to come into being, however, the person has to start with a most painful task, which is to eradicate evil from within.

The painful aspect of the person comes even more into the foreground in *Mirror*. While Kelvin in *Solaris* recognizes the necessity of accepting pain to become a person, the hero of *Mirror* lives in the middle of the pain. Here the narrative situation itself contains it. The narrator hero of the film is ill. He suffers from some undetermined illness which is diagnosed by a doctor at the end of the film as stemming from his psychological state. Even this psychological state is indeterminate in the film; the viewer has to infer from the narrator's memories, fantasies, and thoughts, the associative mixture of which builds up the film's texture. *Mirror*'s central problem is this: do the historical and personal life experiences, the memories and the remnants of a spiritual cultural tradition provide a sufficient background for a person to develop if inherent in this experience and tradition is constant rupture, abandonment, lack of communication, and oblivion? Here the most painful task for the person is no longer facing his or her bad consciousness, but facing the fact that the mere tradition of becoming a person is dying out; so the person whose only natural background is the spiritual community of other persons has to become not only the center of him- of herself but also the only keeper of a dying tradition of this community. To become a person it is not sufficient to join a community, for there such a community exists no more. The protagonist of the film realizes that he has to carry on this tradition by himself, hence his psychological and physical collapse. Transcendence of the person and transcending one's own person toward a supposed community becomes necessary, and this will be the next step one can observe in Tarkovsky's oeuvre.

Transcending the person

The way of becoming a person reaches its logical end in Tarkovsky's last film made in the Soviet Union, *Stalker* (1979). This film is about a journey undertaken by three people – the scientist, the writer, and the stalker – into a forbidden territory named the Zone. The Zone was closed down by the authorities because natural laws do not apply in it and therefore it cannot be controlled. In it lies the Room which is the main target of the illegal intruders, because as the popular legend has it, he who steps into the Room will see his deepest desires fulfilled. The stalkers are like guides who lead all kinds of adventurers to the Room. This is not only a job for the stalkers; it is a spiritual mission. For it turns out that the Room fulfills, not conscious desires, but the deep unconscious wishes of those who step inside. This makes the journey to the Room a journey to one's real self; and the stalker a spiritual leader. This time Tarkovsky's concern is not what can be found in the interior of the self but how someone – the stalker – who has already created his person can persuade others to do the same. With *Mirror*, Tarkovsky penetrated into the person's interior as far as he possibly could to reveal all the doubts and conflicts the person has to go through. The character of the stalker is already the embodiment of the ethical person who has gained maximum independence from the exterior world, who follows no other rules than those of his own moral convictions, against everybody and everything. He has no doubts at all in his mission, he identifies himself with it as much as Ivan did, only his mission is entirely spiritual, whereas Ivan's was entirely material. He has previously experienced all the recognitions, pains, and doubts that torment Tarkovsky's heroes from Rubljov through Alexei, the protagonist of *Mirror*. Paradoxically, the stalker is a somewhat frightening figure, as Ivan was. Both are entirely absorbed by their mission, and there is no human softness left in them. This is emphasized at the beginning of the film, when his wife, crying, tries to keep him from leaving. Stalker's mission is no longer directed toward his own self or person, but to the creation of other persons. Stalker is *the person* subordinated only to the transcendental mission of creating his personalist, spiritual community. Unlike *Solaris* and *Mirror*, *Stalker* is not a journey into the person; it is a journey into a world where the community of persons can be created. This world is the Zone. In *Stalker* Tarkovsky wants to lead not a single person but a cultural community – art and science – back to its spiritual foundations. In this film the subjective and interior universe of *Mirror* becomes a transcendental and exterior world. The interior world of a person opens up a possible transcendental world for others.

Clearly, this is a religious, even mystical, conception, and Tarkovsky could have stopped here or continued by fantasizing about another world: a supposed personalist community. It is very telling, regarding his attachment to the personalist tradition, that he did not go either way. In Berdyaev's view the realization of the unavoidable transcendence of the person is followed by a psychological crisis resulting from the fact that, in realistic terms, transcendence is impossible. The transcendence of the person is like a mental state rather than a real-life fact. "It is impossible for [the person] to transcend into the other world" (Berdyaev 1988: 224), says Berdyaev, which is to say that, not only is becoming a person painful, but once this mission is accomplished, the ultimate reward of it is the recognition of the person's loneliness and all the psychological distress resulting from that. At the end of *Stalker* the protagonist suddenly collapses psychologically, as he has experienced the ultimate faithlessness of the writer and the scientist. His wife puts him into bed and comforts him like a very sick man. This leads to new ideas which Tarkovsky explores in his two following films.

Nostalgia and Sacrifice

"It is impossible that the existence of the person does not go together with longing, because longing represents the break with the reality of the world ... The person exists in the gap of the subjective and the objective" (Berdyaev 1988: 224). Elsewhere Berdyaev puts this idea in even clearer terms: "In the spiritual experience man's nostalgia for God is manifested" (Berdyaev 1984: 192). This nostalgia, however, is not the usual calm and sorrowful feeling; it is rather a deadly sickness: "The wholeness of the person's life cannot be reached, the person's existence is running out and it is partial. The person's transcendence into the wholeness of eternity supposes death, catastrophe, a jump over a precipice" (Berdyaev 1988: 225). The stalker's answer to his wife forecasts the result of this spiritual way: the constant sickness from nostalgia for the unreachable wholeness, and finally the catastrophe.

Tarkovsky's next film's title is *Nostalgia* (1983), and the story is about a Russian writer, traveling in Italy, who desperately tries to understand his particular relation to this world. He is between two worlds and cannot find his home in either. He longs for each of them, but cannot find his spiritual home until he meets a fool and learns from him the ultimate authentic act for someone who has found his person and found by that an irreducible solitude. This act is self-sacrifice, a sort of condensation of all important categories of the person: nostalgia, pain, catastrophe, death. Not surprisingly, Tarkovsky's next and last film would be given the title *Sacrifice* (1986).

Just as in *Stalker* and in *Nostalgia*, in this last film the main issue is not the quest for the person. Nor is the issue of *Sacrifice*, unlike the preceding films, the quest for or the creation of a spiritual community. Tarkovsky dedicated this film entirely to giving sense to death, catastrophe, and self-sacrifice.

A note on Tarkovsky's style

Tarkovsky's "saturated," long-take style, which might be described as meditative or contemplative, cannot be explained directly by his personalist conviction. Personalism is a philosophical tendency that has different variations converging around one important idea. As Emmanuel Mounier put it, "We call personalist all doctrines, all civilizations that claim the precedence of the person over the material necessities and the collective institutions supporting its development" (Mounier 1936: 7). Tarkovsky's and Berdyaev's Personalism was a peculiar variation connecting Personalism to the Orthodox Christian religion through a common point: the person's independence from material constraints, which appears in Orthodoxy as man's resemblance to God – in other words, divinity emerging at least visually from earthly things. The person's direct communication with the transcendent and the pantheistic vision that comes with this idea made Orthodoxy open to personalist philosophy. Tarkovsky developed his style to represent this pantheistic perception of nature and society. In Orthodox religion, contemplating natural and human beauty brings man close to the perception of divinity. The icon is a concentrated form of this relationship. The icon is not only an image; it is also a "window" to the divine world through beauty. This idea is represented in the Orthodox churches by the icon wall, the iconostasis. The iconostasis that separates in the church the profane space from the sacred space, the sanctuary that remains invisible for the believer is like a big screen through which man achieves visual contact with the divine world. The visual contact is indirect and is mediated by the believer's imagination, prodded by his or her contemplation of beauty. This is how time becomes an important factor of visual perception. The viewer needs time to see "through" the object. The object's beauty only helps the vision's transcendence into the divine world. This is the conception that underlies Tarkovsky's slow-paced, long-take style that pans over natural and artificial objects, beautiful landscapes eliciting in every little visual detail the presence of divinity that remains intact despite whatever cruelty it might be surrounded by in the physical and social environment. (For a detailed discussion of Tarkovsky's style related to Orthodox Christianism, see Kovács-Szilágyi, 1987.)

Conclusion

According to Berdyaev, humans stand at the borderline between two worlds. Culture and nature, freedom and dependence, are fighting in them. One part of the self, the *individual*, is prone to exterior determinations and is opposed to the ethical person. The individual represents the influence of history, society, politics, and race in the self. The individual is an egoist and has an objectivist relationship to everything as it is objectively determined. The person's struggle with the individual is the struggle of the transcendental ethical world with historical and social determinations. The struggle between the person and the world has a double meaning in Tarkovsky's work. It means, on the one hand, the above opposition, following from the personalist approach, but, on the other hand, it represents the conflict between modern materialist civilization and this particular spiritualist tradition. Tarkovsky's biggest dilemma is that he cannot see this spiritualist tradition as unproblematic. He has an ambivalent relationship, not only to modern materialism, but to the personalist spiritualism too, simply because it doesn't persist as a communal tradition. He simply cannot disregard the existing world surrounding his beliefs. His films rest upon the conflict between the person and the world because it is this conflict, and not the unproblematic reality of the spiritualist tradition, that he wants to show. Cinema for Tarkovsky is a particularly vivid and powerful tool to represent the struggle of the spiritual person to prevail in a world where everything from politics to science and consumer culture denies its existence.

References

Berdyaev, N. (1984) *Esprit et liberté*, Paris: Desclée de Brauwer.
—— (1988) "A személy," *Az orosz vallásbölcselet virágkora* [The Golden Age of Russian Religious Philosophy], vol. 2, Budapest: Vigilia.
Kovács, A. B., and Szilágyi, Á. (1987) *Les mondes d'Andrei Tarkovsky*, Lausanne: Éditions L'Âge d'Homme.
Mounier, E. (1935) *Personalism and Marxism*, trans. Stephen Janos, Berdyaev Online Library. Available at http://www.berdyaev.com/berdiaev/berd_lib/1935_400.html.
—— (1936) *Le Manifeste au service du personnalisme*, Paris: Éditions Montaigne.
Sartre, J.-P. (1986) "Discussion sur la critique à propos de *L'Enfance d'Ivan*," *Etudes Cinématographiques* 46: 5–13 (special issue, Andrei Tarkovsky).
Tarkovsky, A. (1969) "L'artiste dans l'ancienne Russie et dans l'URSS nouvelle: entretien avec Andrei Tarkovsky" (interview by M. Ciment, L. Schnitzer, and J. Schnitzer), *Positif* 109 (October): 1–13.
—— (1993) *Journal (1970–1986)*, Paris: Cahiers du Cinéma.

54
WHY BE MORAL?

Chris Falzon

In philosophical discourse, one way of considering the question of why we should be moral has been through hypothetical scenarios in which being moral becomes an option, rather than simply a given. Most of the time, shaped as we are by our upbringing and culture, we do the right thing without giving it much thought. But when faced with a situation where we can do anything, no matter how wicked, without fear of punishment, or where doing the wrong thing seems more rewarding than doing the right thing, the question of why we should be moral naturally arises. Film, in a position to pose hypothetical scenarios of this sort, offers an opportunity for exploring such considerations. In addition, by posing these hypothetical scenarios in the form of concrete, emotionally engaging narratives, film can capture something else as well, the question's "existential" aspect. Whether to be moral is not simply an abstract theoretical question, but a deeply practical concern, of how one is to live, whether to commit oneself to a particular way of life.

That being said, certainly many films would seem to do no more than confirm conventional expectations about morality, namely that doing what one ought will inevitably take precedence over what one simply wants to do, should the two conflict. Even those who profess to be concerned only with their own interests typically come to recognize the force of moral considerations in the end. The transformation from someone who is only concerned to "get by," into a person of moral integrity, willing to make a stand, is a familiar cinematic theme. For the hero, moral behavior is expected somewhere along the line; incorrigible pursuit of one's own self-interest is strictly for the villain of the piece.

To the extent that films embody these views, we might see them as doing little more than offering a reassuring confirmation of the moral universe we already for the most part inhabit. But the very embodiment of these views in film also presents them for reflection, and even presents the opportunity to discern a rationale for being moral. In the most conventional narrative, the good eventually prosper, and those who lie, cheat, and kill get caught, are punished, suffer in some way. There's an implicit argument for being moral here: it is in the nature of the world that the bad pay the price and that the good are rewarded, and so it is in your interest to be moral. The problem with this of course is that the real world does not conspire to reward the good, and those who cheat don't always pay. Film can contrive to make things turn out satisfactorily, but precisely in virtue of that, the distance between the cinematic world and the real world is starkly illuminated.

Yet film itself also provides salutary counterinstances to the conventional narrative, more "realistic" scenarios where self-interest – even downright evil – is allowed to triumph. Such a scenario unfolds in Woody Allen's *Crimes and Misdemeanors* (1989). The doctor, Judah, arranges to have his mistress killed when she threatens to expose their affair, and he not only gets away with it but continues to prosper; while Cliff, the good person, ends up losing everything. As such it clearly raises the question – why should we live moral lives, when we can often get away with immoral actions it is in our interest to perform? And it seems to offer an uncompromising answer: there is no reason, it often pays to be morally bad. Even the possibility of suffering punishment at the hands of one's conscience is discounted. After a period of guilt, when the doctor comes close to breaking down and confessing all to the police, he gets over it and settles back into his privileged life. He finds that he might have bad moments, but can live with what he has done. The film even comments on the conventional Hollywood narrative it so conspicuously departs from. When Judah meets Cliff he recounts what he has done in the guise of a film plot. Cliff replies that it would be a better story if the murder were driven by guilt to give himself up. The doctor's reply is that this isn't what happens in real life: "If you want a happy ending, you should go see a Hollywood movie."

Invisibility, God, and society

As commentators have noted (e.g., Pappas 2004), *Crimes and Misdemeanors* provides a contemporary formulation of the challenge to provide a reason for being moral that found classical expression in Plato's *Republic*. There, the character Glaucon recounts the story of Gyges, the shepherd who finds a ring with the power to make the wearer invisible. He uses it to seduce the queen, kill the king, and become ruler. For Glaucon, Gyges is not exceptional. He does what anyone would do if they could act with impunity. None would be strong enough to remain moral:

> when he is able to take whatever he wants from the market-stalls without fear
> of being discovered, to enter houses and sleep with whomever he chooses, to
> kill and release from prison anyone he wants, and generally to act like a god
> among men. (Plato 1993: 360)

The import of the story is that the only reason we do the right thing is fear of being caught and punished, and that if we could do whatever we wanted without fear of discovery we would abandon all ethical standards and set about pursuing our self-interest. Glaucon challenges us to find some reason for being moral, even when the threat of punishment is removed.

Plato's hypothetical scenario in turn reappears in literal form in film. Invisibility is now effected through scientific rather than magical means, but similar behavior often becomes apparent and similar questions might be posed. The original *The Invisible Man*

(James Whale, 1933) embraces the opportunity his invisibility seems to afford him: "an invisible man can rule the world ... he can rob and rape and kill." Paul Verhoeven's *Hollow Man* (2000) offers an updated version. As the scientist Caine starts to explore his newfound freedom, one of his research team poses the inevitable question: "What would you do if you knew you couldn't be seen?" And once Caine realizes that he can get away with a good deal, he indulges in classic Gyges-like behavior – voyeurism, rape, and murder. On the face of it, what is again being suggested is that we only behave ourselves because of the threat of sanction, and if this is removed, we no longer have reason to behave morally.

What *Crimes and Misdemeanors* offers is a figurative version of this invisibility, free of fantastic magical and scientific devices. The doctor simply has the means, wealth, and power to conceal his crimes from the eyes of others and to maintain the appearance of being a decent person. The question remains: is there any reason for behaving morally if we can get away with being immoral, if we stand to benefit from doing so? The film itself refers us to one possible response to the challenge posed by invisibility, namely the religious perspective. One cannot hide from the eyes of God, and however successfully we might escape detection in this life, in the next we will be called to account; the good will be rewarded; and the unjust, punished. Thus there are good reasons to be moral; it is in our long-term interests. The view is represented especially by the doctor's father (in flashback). God sees everything, he says, and the righteous will be rewarded, while the wicked will be punished for eternity.

At the same time the doctor highlights a problem with the position, that it requires religious belief. As a creature of modernity, a scientist, he can no longer believe in a watching, judging God who rewards the good and punishes the wicked. Such thinking easily appears as wishful thinking, a comforting illusion in the face of a world where all too often the good suffer and the wicked prosper. It is portrayed as such in the film, where the religious view is espoused by a father who proclaims that, if there is a choice between God and truth, he will always choose God. Another character espousing similar views, the Rabbi Ben, goes blind. To rely on such belief is, it seems, to blind oneself to the truth of a godless reality. Some have suggested another message, that the cost of finding one can act without punishment is the "withdrawal of God," who does not punish the evil with retribution but by withdrawing from their lives, leaving them with an empty, pointless existence (see Nichols 1998: 158). This does not, however, seem to be Allen's view:

> I just wanted to illustrate, in an entertaining way, that there is no God, that we're alone in the universe, and that there is nobody out there to punish you, that there's not going to be any kind of Hollywood ending to your life in any way, that your morality is strictly up to you. (Quoted in Schickel 2003: 149)

It might be thought that, in the absence of a judging God, society could provide a reason for being moral. In the classic social contract account, going back to Hobbes, morality is understood not in terms of God-given rules but in terms of rules we mutually agree to lay down for ourselves. Here it is presupposed that we are essentially self-interested creatures, concerned only with satisfying our desires. It is in everyone's interests to live in a society in which these desires are constrained by moral rules, enforced by a sufficient authority. Without constraints, to adopt Hobbes' phrase, we would fall into a "state of nature," a nightmarish situation in which individuals, unrestrainedly pursuing their immediate desires, would come into conflict with each other and prevent one another from satisfying even their most basic needs (see Hobbes 1968: 163). Mutual agreement to play by the rules and curb one's desires serves to advance everyone's interests, since it removes the threat from others and allows everyone, within limits, to get what they want. So it is in everyone's longer-term interests to obey the rules, to be moral.

The state of nature represents another hypothetical scenario that by envisaging the removal of external sanction serves to pose the question of why we should be moral – now in the sense of "why abide by the rules of society?" film offers the possibility of realizing this apocalyptic vision of complete social breakdown, a memorable example being *Lord of the Flies* (Peter Brook, 1963). The schoolchildren shipwrecked on the island without adult authority descend into a competition for power and status, and those in the way are killed without remorse. Here it is supposed that there are bestial drives within us (the Lord of the Flies is the demonic "beast within") which it is in our interests to curb, whereas for Hobbes ordinary self-interested acquisitiveness is enough to lead to chaos if not held in check by society. But the essential idea of the need for rules is the same, and though the others are past listening by this stage, the weak, bespectacled Piggy still tries to make the case for a civilized social order, based on mutually agreed rules ("which is better, to have rules and agree, or to hunt and kill?"). Confronted by the state of nature as a terrible reality, Piggy can appreciate it as a reason not merely for the institution of morality in general but for an institution it is very much in his own interests to have in place.

So on this account there is a clear sense in which it is better for me, as a self-interested individual, to live in a society with moral rules than in a state of nature. However, it is society with moral rules that I normally find myself confronted with; and there is nothing in this account that provides me with reason to be moral if I can rely on everyone else to continue to be moral, on the institution of morality remaining in place. Certainly, if I choose to opt out of the contract, to violate the rules, I expose myself to the threat of punishment, not now by God but by society. That provides a reason for me to remain sociable, to continue to abide by the rules. However, if I can evade punishment by society, I have no reason to continue to obey society's rules. The challenge posed by the invisibility scenario thus remains: if I can pursue my interests without the threat of punishment, I no longer have any reason to cooperate with other people, to abide by the moral rules. It is thus far more reasonable, in keeping with his self-interest, for the invisible scientist in *Hollow Man* to return to his state of natural amorality; and in these terms the doctor in *Crimes and Misdemeanors* does even better, since he can secretly evade social constraints to pursue his interests, while also appearing to be part of society with all the benefits that this provides.

The social-contract view, then, does not provide an answer to the question – why be moral if we can act immorally without fear of punishment? It would seem that self-interest provides a relatively fragile incentive to be moral on this account. But we can also go on to question the very understanding of morality being presented, not only here but in the religious view noted above. In the religious account, our reason for being moral is to avoid eternal punishment, and this way of thinking might in fact be seen as a mark of moral immaturity and superficiality. Similarly, in the social-contract account, we only continue to do the right thing in order to avoid being punished by society, which again suggests moral underdevelopment. Indeed it might be argued that "to tie moral behaviour so closely to the threat of punishment is a sociopath's view of morality" (Rowlands 2003: 160). That Caine in *Hollow Man* is so ready to abandon all moral standards once he realizes he can do what he wants without fear of punishment might say less about a "natural amorality" that we all share than about Caine's own nature, that he is fundamentally lacking or flawed as a human being. A position that might appear plausible when considered abstractly does seem pathological when embodied in a concrete individual.

Equally, there is something flawed, sociopathic, about the doctor in *Crimes and Misdemeanors*, who once he realizes there is no possibility of divine punishment finds he has no reason to be moral. And he is an especially chilling kind of sociopath, one able to pass himself off as a respectable, morally upright pillar of society. And yet this manner of behaving is entirely consistent with an understanding of morality primarily in terms of self-interest. If the only consideration is self-interest, then it may well be that one's self-interests are best served by effecting an appearance of morality while being prepared to act immorally when one can get away with it (see Norman 1998: 173). The underlying suggestion being made here is that to behave morally merely to avoid external punishment (by God or society) is arguably not to be genuinely moral at all, but to only have a semblance of morality. It is bound up with a superficial conception of morality itself as something largely external to us, which we have to submit to, "a thin, conventional, easily dislodged veneer on human life" (Grayling 2002: 65).

Self, inner balance, and autonomy

This is not, however, the only kind of response we can give to the question of why we should be moral, and not the only response that can be explored through cinematic narratives. A second broad kind of approach moves away from tying being moral to the threat of external punishment. Instead of looking for an external inducement for being moral, for bringing us to do the right thing despite being essentially self-interested creatures, the "Why be moral?" question might be addressed in terms of the positive value that being moral has for the person. In other words, the question might be answered by bringing people to see that there is something inherently valuable in the moral life, something important that is lost if we reject morality, and thus to see that we should be moral, even if there is immediate advantage in being immoral, or significant sacrifice involved in being moral (see Powell 2006: 542–3).

This view need not preclude reference to our self-interest, but does require rethinking what self-interest involves, along with the underlying notion of the self.

Self-interest is usually understood in terms of egoistic hedonism, pursuing your desires, doing whatever increases pleasure or minimizes suffering, but we might understand the importance of being moral in terms of deeper human needs going beyond immediate desires, which being moral enables us to fulfill. There would a deeper conception of morality itself here, no longer a thin veneer on human life, but rather a "firm property of human social existence" (Grayling 2002: 65). The usefulness of film here lies in the way it can, not only present hypothetical scenarios to pose the "Why be moral?" question, but also chart responses offering concrete evocations of human experience to support claims about the importance of morality in our lives.

Plato offers a positive account of morality along these lines. The Ring of Gyges scenario posed to raise the question of why we should be moral if it is in our interests to be immoral is only the starting point. Plato goes on to argue that it is a mistake to think that it is in our interests to be immoral. The apparent conflict between morality and self-interest is really only a conflict with a false notion of self-interest in which the self is identified with immediate desires alone (see Irwin 1989: 102). Plato's own position turns on his conception of the self as composed of reason and spirit as well as desire, each with its proper function in the whole. In the healthy, properly balanced soul, reason with the help of spirit governs and directs desire, for the good of the self as a whole. So if I am really self-interested, I must be ruled by my reason; and for Plato, having this inner balance is what it is to be moral.

As such, being moral amounts to fully realizing ourselves, attaining the inner balance, the inner freedom of self-mastery, proper to ourselves as human beings. By contrast, the immoral life is one in which the self is deformed, dominated by the desiring part alone. Far from being able to pursue their interests, the immoral person is enslaved to their desires. The pressure of our desires also distorts relations with others. Unable to treat them as persons in their own right, we are driven to satisfy ourselves at their expense. What Plato wants to show, then, is that being moral, far from being opposed to self-interest, profoundly benefits us, and in these terms he justifies the value of the moral life. The moral person is better off than the immoral person. Even if we can get away with being immoral and are free to acquire all we desire, we are internally slaves to our desires, whereas no matter how much the moral person suffers in life, they have the freer, healthier existence.

In these terms we can come to a different assessment of Caine in *Hollow Man*. On this view, he has not been liberated by his invisibility. He may no longer be socially constrained, but he has become a slave to his desires, which he can no longer control once invisibility makes their unlimited satisfaction possible. His immoral behavior toward others is driven by this enslavement. His very descent into madness and monstrosity becomes emblematic of the cost of the immoral life. On the Platonic account the immoral person is unbalanced, at the mercy of their desires, and the thoroughly immoral person is virtually a madman. For the benefits of being a moral person, however, we need to turn to a different film. David Lynch's *Blue Velvet* (1986) offers a narrative in which the central character descends into immorality in the sense of spiritual disharmony, but also comes to recognize the worth of the moral life. Here, clean-cut Jeffrey, back in his hometown to look after his ailing father, discovers not only his town's dark, violent underworld but his own base appetites. Though involved with the equally innocent Sandy, he finds himself attracted to Dorothy, who represents the lure of perverse sex. He thus enters a depraved realm that is hidden, invisible to the everyday, sunlit world, a realm in which Jeffrey can freely gratify not only his sexual urges but also a taste for danger and violence (see Lee 1988: 573).

In this, *Blue Velvet* does not simply proclaim the virtues of the moral life. Indeed, it shows the enormous attractiveness of an immoral one, and it acknowledges the presence of desire, of often brutal desires within, which this life makes it possible to satisfy. But it also, in Platonic fashion, shows the cost, the inner slavery, the destruction of psychological peace – as Jeffrey finds himself driven yet also repulsed by his desires – as well as the corruption of his relations with others, for in the guise of trying to befriend and help Dorothy, he realizes he is exploiting her for his own satisfaction (see Lee 1988: 577). What Jeffrey is in danger of becoming is represented by his alter ego Frank, the gangster who is terrorizing Dorothy. Even more than Caine, Frank is the paradigm of inner imbalance and enslavement, utterly consumed by desire and impulse. The way forward for Jeffrey is to return to the good side, the moral life. But unlike Sandy, who remains innocent throughout, Jeffrey has had to confront his desires, to learn how to deal with them, to control them. He has recognized the costs of the immoral life, the inner corruption it involves, and the importance of being moral in terms of achieving psychological balance and tranquillity.

This kind of view is not confined to Plato. Although Kant is sometimes associated with the austere view that rational consistency alone demands we be moral, much more is at stake for him. Kant like Plato identifies being moral with the freedom of self-mastery, being ruled by the higher, rational part of our nature, and control of the desires. For Kant this means preventing desire and inclination from motivating us at all, in order to determine ourselves purely through the commands of our own rationality, identified with the moral duties. In rational self-determination, autonomy, we most fully realize ourselves. As Taylor puts it, the principle underlying Kant's ethical theory is "live up to what you really are – rational agents" (Taylor 1985: 324). Only rational beings, Kant argues, can act consciously in accordance with principles they themselves formulate. This is what sets us above nature, including our own desires, which are part of the natural order, governed by mechanical necessity. And as with Plato, the immoral life means becoming enslaved to the lower, desiring part of our nature. Kant grants that desires are not just self-seeking, that we can have altruistic impulses as well; nonetheless, to be moved by desire and inclination of any sort is to fall below one's proper status, to become just another thing determined by external forces, and thus to break faith with our rational nature.

So with Kant, as with Plato, there is something inherently valuable in being moral. To be moral, to determine ourselves in accordance with moral principles, is to live up to our proper status. To do otherwise is beneath our dignity. In addition, Kant thinks that we recognize the special importance of being moral in our ordinary experience. Because our rationality is something higher, we experience its commands, the moral principles, as higher than the demands of nature, the promptings of our merely natural desires and inclinations. We recognize the moral law as something we ought to obey, something that commands our respect, our reverence. And for Kant it is this feeling of respect for the moral law that provides an incentive to be moral, an interest capable of overcoming the seductions of desire and inclination (see Powell 2006: 540–1). In addition, we can be reminded of the motivating power of the moral law, Kant thinks, by contemplating tales of virtue, in which a man for instance rejects advantage and suffers great hardship, yet remains "true to his uprightness of purpose" (see Kant 2004: 148, cited in Powell 2006: 541).

The western *High Noon* (Fred Zinneman, 1952) is such a tale of virtue and arguably captures the core of what, for Kant, is at stake in our being moral. The recently retired town marshal, Will Kane, waits for the noon train and the return of the outlaw he sent to prison. Although deserted by his new bride and abandoned by the townspeople he has served for years, he remains to confront the outlaw and his gang. Why, despite the hardships, does he remain true to his uprightness of purpose? He is taking a heroic stance, but he does not act in order to be heroic, to impress others. As he puts it, "I'm not trying to be a hero. If you think I like this, you're crazy." Indeed, he has a strong inclination to go, to save himself, which he struggles with throughout the film. It is very much in his interests to leave. But there is the suggestion of an overriding motivation here – that it is a matter of preserving his integrity, his mastery over himself, which is bound up with doing his duty and remaining at his post.

Here, whether or not Kane is still officially town marshal is merely an external formality. Doing his duty, being moral, is an inner requirement. Being governed by his conception of where his duty lies is a matter of remaining true to himself. His selfhood, his self-possession, is what is on the line. And this arguably is what Kant sees as fundamentally valuable about being moral: "[w]hat Kant seeks is selfhood, individualism and dignity. These can be summed up in one word – autonomy" (Kreyche 1988: 224). For Kane to allow himself to be forced out of town by his fears and anxieties or by the urgings of others, or indeed to stay merely for glory, advancement, or some other external reward would be to succumb to the influence of external forces. His stance here is not automatic; after all, he is not superhuman. It involves struggle, particularly against his own feelings, his fears and anxieties. But he masters his feelings in order to stay true to himself and his "upright purpose." What is of overriding importance for him is that he act in a way that derives from his own sense of duty, to not break faith with himself.

Both Plato's and Kant's accounts of why we should be moral turn on the idea that being moral involves achieving a certain self-governance that is proper and fulfilling for human beings, in which we are free because the higher, rational part of our nature is in charge and is in control of the lower, desiring part. We may of course want to dispute the kind of picture of the proper relation of reason to desire and emotion being presented here. Kant in particular presents a highly repressive picture of the relationship between them. Being moral, fully realizing ourselves, it seems, requires us to exclude desire and emotion entirely from our motivation, to be guided entirely by reason, which might seem closer to a form of self-mutilation than to self-realization. Plato at least allows desire to have some place in the economy of the fully realized self, though he also thinks that the desires need to be firmly kept under control.

We may also ask whether being morally good can necessarily be equated with having a well-ordered self, as Plato in particular emphasizes. There is nothing in self-mastery itself that implies one has to be morally good, and immorality does not necessarily involve internal disorder or enslavement to desire. A person could single-mindedly, in an entirely self-controlled way, pursue evil. Indeed, this is what distinguishes *Crimes and Misdemeanors'* Judah from *Hollow Man's* Caine or *Blue Velvet's* Frank. In contrast to those out-of-control monsters, Judah is a wholly self-controlled individual, who engineers his wicked deed rationally and deliberately, and in the face of his feelings, fears, and anxieties. Indeed, it is his desires and feelings that urge him to turn himself in to the police, to face punishment for what he has done. It is precisely by controlling and subduing these feelings that Judah is able to get away with it.

Nonetheless, even if we can question the specific ways of conceiving the moral life in Plato and Kant, both point to another way in which we might respond to the question of why we should be moral, beyond merely saying that we need to be good in order to avoid external punishment by God or society. Instead, it turns on our seeing that being moral has a positive value for us, that it allows us to in some sense realize or fulfill ourselves, and that we have lost something important if we reject it, even if it is to our immediate advantage to behave immorally. And all of these ways of responding to the "Why be moral?" question, in terms of God, society, or self, find some purchase in the concrete narratives provided by film.

References

Grayling, A. (2002) *The Reason of Things*, London: Phoenix.

Hobbes, T. (1968) *Leviathan*, ed. C. B. Macpherson, Harmondsworth: Penguin.

Irwin, T. (1989) *Classical Thought*, Oxford and New York: Oxford University Press.

Kant, I. (2004) *Critique of Practical Reason*, trans. T. Abbott, New York: Barnes and Noble.

Kreyche, G. F. (1988) "High Noon – A Paradigm of Kant's Moral Philosophy," *Teaching Philosophy* 11: 217–28.

Lee, S. (1988) "The Essence of the Human Experience in David Lynch's *Blue Velvet*," in S. H. Lee (ed.) *Inquiries into Values and Ethical Views: The Inaugural Sessions of the International Society for Value Inquiry*, Lewiston, ME: Edwin Mellen Press.

Nichols, M. (1998) *Reconstructing Woody*, Lanham: Rowman and Littlefield.

Norman, R. (1998) *The Moral Philosophers: An Introduction to Ethics*, 2nd ed., Oxford and New York: Oxford University Press.

Pappas, J. (2004) "It's All Darkness: Plato, The Ring of Gyges, and *Crimes and Misdemeanors*," in M. Conard and A. Skoble (eds.) *Woody Allen and Philosophy*, Chicago: Open Court Press.

Plato (1993) *Republic*, trans. R. Waterfield, Oxford and New York: Oxford University Press.

Powell, B. (2006) "Kant and Kantians on 'the Normative Question'," *Ethical Theory and Moral Practice* 9: 535–44.

Rowlands, M. (2003) *The Philosopher at the End of the Universe*, London: Ebury Press.

Schickel, R. (2003) *Woody Allen: A Life in Film*, Chicago: Ivan R. Dee.

Taylor, C. (1985) "Kant's Theory of Freedom," in *Philosophy and the Human Sciences: Philosophical Papers*, vol. 2, Cambridge and New York: Cambridge University Press.

Further reading

Joseph Kupfer, "Virtue and Happiness in *Groundhog Day*," in *Visions of Virtue in Popular Film* (Boulder, CO: Westview, 1999), explores the significance of becoming a moral individual for Plato and Aristotle, in connection with *Groundhog Day*. C. Stephen Layman, "Why Be a Superhero? Why Be Moral?," in T. Morris and M. Morris (eds.) *Superheroes and Philosophy* (Chicago, IL: Open Court Press, 2005), looks at a number of responses to the "Why be moral?" question, in connection with the *Spider-man* film. Sander Lee (ed.) *Film and Philosophy* (special issue, Woody Allen) (Portsmouth, OH: Society for the Philosophic Study of the Contemporary Visual Arts, 2000) includes a number of discussions of the moral questions posed in *Crimes and Misdemeanors*, including Mark Roche, "Justice and the Withdrawal of God in Woody Allen's *Crimes and Misdemeanors*"; Robert Vigliotti, "Woody Allen's Ring of Gyges and the Virtue of Despair"; and Bruce Russell, "The Philosophical Limits of Film." Steven Sanders, "Why Be Moral? Amorality and Psychopathy in *Strangers on a Train*," in D. Baggett and W. A. Drumin (eds.) *Hitchcock and Philosophy* (Chicago: Open Court Press, 2007), discusses the "Why be moral?" question in connection with the willingness of the psychopath to reject moral restraints in Hitchcock's *Strangers on a Train*. Aeon Skoble, "Justice and Moral Corruption in *A Simple Plan*," in M. Conard (ed.) *The Philosophy of Neo-Noir* (Lexington: University Press of Kentucky, 2006), considers *A Simple Plan* in connection with Plato's account of why we should be moral.

55
SKEPTICISM
Richard Fumerton

Exotic thought experiments have often played a critical role in evaluating philosophical issues about the nature and epistemological significance of perception and memory. In raising initial concerns about what we know, Descartes (1999 [1641]) famously (if not originally) invokes the possibility that all of the experiences we take to be veridical (experiences we take to be of waking life) might instead be experiences of a vivid dream. He went on to suggest that it is at least conceivable that there exists a very powerful but evil demon exercising his power to induce in you hallucinatory experience qualitatively indistinguishable from the experiences you take to be veridical. On either possibility, your beliefs about your physical surroundings based on those experiences might involve massive error. Many contemporary epistemologists preoccupied with cognitive science often prefer invoking the possibility that your brain has been stolen and now lies in a vat, subject to the experiments of a mad neuroscientist. That scientist is stimulating your brain so as to produce the neuronal activity that either is (according to some philosophers), or is the immediate cause of (according to others), sensory experience in all of its glorious detail.

In stressing that apparent memory is a fallible source of information about the past, Russell famously suggested that we could make sense of a world in which we popped into existence a few moments ago, replete with vivid and detailed "memory" of a nonexistent past. Obviously, Descartes' evil demon or our mad neuroscientist would have no difficulty manufacturing such apparent memory. The immediate cause of apparent memory is, most would agree, just as dependent as other sensations on brain states that are, in principle, vulnerable to manipulation.

These skeptical scenarios (as they are often called) have worked their way into written works of fiction (like *The Martian Chronicles*), but have recently become increasingly well-known through the powerful medium of film. Television shows like *Star Trek* (in its various incarnations) and movies like *Total Recall* (1990), *The Matrix* (1999), and *The Sixth Day* (2000) have brought to cinematic life the thought experiments of philosophy. A few years ago, I was asked to talk to a seventh-grade class about the subject of philosophy. After wondering how best to illustrate a paradigmatically philosophical question to kids that young, I decided that I'd try talking about Descartes' dream and demon arguments. Almost immediately, a number of students shouted out excitedly – "It's just like *The Matrix*." I hadn't seen the movie at the time, but when I did, sure enough, it became immediately obvious that Cartesian thought experiments had been appropriated in the plot of the popular film.

In this paper, I want to explore a number of questions about the appearance of skeptical scenarios in plots of films. Do these films reinforce in a particularly vivid way that the skeptical scenarios are indeed possible, and do they reinforce in a particularly vivid way the skeptic's claims about the nature of the evidence upon which we implicitly rely in reaching commonplace conclusions? Do any of these films hint at solutions to the skeptical problems? Do some of the films raise new questions concerning the intelligibility of aspects of the plot lines?

Thought experiment and skeptical scenarios

Before we attempt to answer the above questions, it might be worth addressing in more detail precisely how the skeptic tries to make use of skeptical scenarios. As we noted above, Descartes raised the possibility of dreams and demon-induced hallucination primarily in the context of his search for an absolutely secure foundation of knowledge upon which we can safely build. Although Descartes was not ultimately interested in arguing for skepticism, the skeptic could easily embrace the intelligibility of Descartes' thought experiments to argue that there is a logical gap between the nature of our evidence for commonplace beliefs about the external world and the truth of the propositions we believe based on that evidence.

Consider the following arguments:

Argument from the Possibility of Hallucination:

1 The "phenomenologically given" character of experience is always logically and conceptually compatible with the experience being a part of an elaborate hallucination.
2 If 1), then we can't know with absolute certainty that any given sequence of sensory experience has not come to us as part of an elaborate hallucination.
3 If we can't know of any given sequence of sensory experience that it has not come to us as part of an elaborate hallucination, then we can't know on the basis of sensory experience any truth about our physical environment.

Therefore,

4 We can't know with absolute certainty (on the basis of sense experience) any truth about our physical environment.

Argument from the Possibility of Deceptive Apparent Memory:

1 No matter how vivid an apparent memory might seem, the fact that we *seem* to remember having done X (as opposed to actually remembering having done X) is logically and conceptually compatible with our not having done X. (We could be

the victims of demonic machination, or we could just be getting really old, for that matter).

2 If 1), then we can't know with absolute certainty that any apparent memory is veridical.

3 If we can't know of any apparent memory that it is veridical, we can't know on the basis of that apparent memory any truth about our past.

Therefore,

4 We can't know with absolute certainty (on the basis of apparent memory) any truth about our past.

It is an understatement to suggest that the above arguments are controversial. The second premises of both arguments do presuppose, I think, that our knowledge of the physical world and the past is in some important sense based on more fundamental knowledge of the qualitative character of subjective mental states (experience or apparent memory). Consider first the problem of perception. One might concede that the introspective character of experience never guarantees that experience is veridical but claims that one has perfectly good knowledge of the physical world *when the experience is veridical*. So, for example, some contemporary philosophers would argue that we get knowledge of the physical world when a belief about that world is caused (through perception) by the very fact that is the truth maker for the belief. The relevant causal connection is present in the case of veridical perception and absent in the case of nonveridical perception. If there is no requirement that we be able to introspectively discriminate between the character of the subjective experience in the "good" and the "bad" cases in order to get the relevant knowledge, the force of the above skeptical scenarios disappears. A similar argument might be made about knowledge of the past, based on memory. There may be no introspectable difference between "veridical" and "nonveridical" memory, but when one seems to remember having had an experience and when the apparent memory is caused by the earlier experience, there exists the right sort of causal connection to yield knowledge of the past.

But despite the rise of various externalist accounts of knowledge (as they are called), the internalist is surely right in suggesting that there is something very odd about the externalist's suggestion that we can gain knowledge through experience even when there is no "internal" indicator that the experience is veridical. If we admit that we can't tell the difference between a case in which we are deceived and a case in which we are not, why would we allow that the person nevertheless knows which case he is in? To be sure, we don't often think about evidence in the form of what we know about the subjective character of our experience. Outside of philosophy, it is very odd to suppose that there is anything like *inference* involved in our spontaneous beliefs and expectations about the physical world in which we live. But the internalist is surely right in suggesting that however seldom we think about the subjective character of experience, we surely realize upon reflection that we know such truths *better* than we know any truths about our physical environment. Although it has become increasingly common to deny it, there really is something common to both veridical and vivid hallucinatory experience, and the belief that the common element obtains is clearly "safer" than any belief that goes beyond a commitment to that common element. Once we retreat to that safer truth, it is only natural to wonder whether we are epistemically entitled to move beyond it to the riskier judgment about the physical world or the past.

Those who teach epistemology to undergraduates are familiar with the fact that it is not difficult to convince students that "knowledge" skepticism is true. While professional philosophers find outrageous the suggestion that we don't know much of what we casually claim to know, most of my students simply shrug their shoulders with an air of "What did you expect?" Knowledge, they say, and, in particular, knowledge with absolute certainty is very, very hard to come by. Contemporary contextualists try to explain this phenomenon with talk of context-dependent, shifting standards for knowledge claims (see, for example, David Lewis [1996] and Stewart Cohen [1999]), but it may be just as plausible to claim that the skeptical scenarios provide a reminder that when one gets serious about knowledge claims one must be much more careful than one typically is in casual conversation.

While knowledge skepticism may not be that unpalatable, the "gap" the skeptic exploits between evidence and conclusions drawn from that evidence can easily be exploited by the skeptic to argue for a much more dramatic form of skepticism. Hume famously argued that all we ever have to go on as ultimate evidence is what we know about perceptions, where "perception" is his generic term for fleeting, perceiver-dependent states such as sensations and apparent memories. Like Descartes, Hume thought it obvious that qualitatively similar sensations can have radically different causes. Also like Descartes, Hume assumed that the available premises for reasoning are restricted to those describing perceptions. But Hume argued (1958: 212) that if this is so, reason is impotent in establishing perceptions as evidence for anything other than perceptions. The only way to establish one kind of thing as evidence for the existence of another kind of thing is to correlate the two in experience. But if all we ever have to go on ultimately is knowledge of our perceptions, there is no way to step outside of our "perspective" to get a glimpse of the perspective-independent world that is supposed to causally explain perceptions. We can correlate perceptions with perceptions, but never perceptions with anything other than perceptions.

Cinematic thought experiments

We have already noted that the plots of some popular films seem to play on the very possibilities invoked by the skeptic. What significance, if any, does their portrayal in film have? At first blush, one might suppose that, at the very least, films like *The Matrix*, *Total Recall*, *Blade Runner* (1982), and *The Sixth Day* reinforce the intelligibility of the skeptical scenarios (where the latter two specifically invoke skeptical scenarios involving memory). Philosophical thought experiments are often criticized for their lack of detail. One can easily find oneself wondering whether we can really make sense of Descartes' demon-induced hallucination. But film fills in detail and seems to render unquestionable the *intelligibility* of the skeptical scenarios. As noted above, teenagers in junior high have no difficulty following the plots of such films.

One should, however, move slowly before one assumes that the apparent intelligibility of a plot line is real. In *Somewhere in Time* (1980), for example, the movie begins with an old lady giving a young playwright a watch. As it turns out, she got the watch from him after he goes back in time to meet her younger self. It is not until one starts thinking about the rather odd history of that watch that one begins to wonder whether the plot really makes sense. In the *Planet of the Apes* (1968) series of films, one of the apes turns out to be his own ancestor. Some plots of movies might be like Escher paintings – it is not until one looks closely that one discovers that the representation is of something that cannot be.

Perhaps one reason for being particularly cautious is that one can't, of course, film a hallucination. As one follows the plot of *The Matrix*, for example, one isn't even imagining that one sees (or seems to see) things from the very perspective of the characters undergoing the hallucination. I suppose that the filmmaker wants us to adopt a kind of sympathetic "alter perspective" of the characters depicted, where the "position" of the camera, in effect, constitutes that perspective. When we reach the conclusion that the character is undergoing a hallucination, we are simultaneously imagining that our own "camera perspective" is similarly hallucinatory. It does seem to me that we *can* do precisely that, but the intelligibility of what we are doing is parasitic upon the antecedent intelligibility of the skeptical scenarios. It is not as if the film does anything more than play on possibilities that we find antecedently intelligible.

What is particularly interesting, from a psychological point of view, is how easily we "accept" the transitions from hallucination to veridical experience and back again. Insofar as we are adopting a kind of alter perspective of Neo (the lead character in *The Matrix*), for example, why do we conclude as we take the pill and suddenly undergo the experience of seeming to be in a vat with countless rows of other envatted creatures, that *this* is the veridical experience? Why wouldn't it seem more natural for Neo (and us) to assume that the pill was some sort of hallucinatory agent playing a causal role analogous to that of Descartes' evil demon?

Interestingly, Descartes himself eventually suggests that his skeptical concerns were unfounded, and that there are infallible criteria for deciding whether or not we are dreaming. He rejects as "fantastic" his early speculation that our lives might be one long, vivid dream (though he rejects the skeptical doubts as unreasonable only after having established the existence of a perfect, nondeceiving God). Descartes, in effect, suggests that the clear mark of dreams (and one would assume other nonveridical experience) is the way in which the former don't "fit" with the rest of our experiences as we seem to remember them:

> I now notice that dreaming and being awake are importantly different: the events in dreams are not linked by memory to the rest of my life like those that happen while I am awake. If, while I am awake, someone were suddenly to appear and then disappear without my seeing where he came from or went

to (as happens in dreams), I would justifiably judge that he was not a real man, but a ghost – or, better, an apparition created in my brain. But, if I distinctly observe something's source, its place, and the time at which I learn about it, and if I grasp an unbroken connection between it and the rest of my life, I am quite sure that it is something in my waking life rather than in a dream. And I ought not to have the slightest doubt about the reality of such things, if I have examined them with all my senses, my memory, and my understanding without finding any conflicting evidence. (1999 [1641]: 139)

By Descartes' criteria for evaluating the veridicality of experience, I would have thought that it would be much more natural for Neo (and us) to conclude that the dramatic and abrupt change in experiences that followed the taking of a pill were the beginnings of hallucinatory-infected madness.

The problem of how to tell when experience is nonveridical is also represented nicely in the film *Total Recall*. In that film, the hero decides to take a hallucinatory "vacation." The future in which he lives allows one to visit the Recall center, where one's brain is stimulated so as to produce the experiences associated with one's chosen fantasy vacation. The protagonist wanted to be a spy who goes to Mars. In the film he either has the expected hallucinatory experience or he breaks free of Recall and actually discovers that he *is* a spy whose memory had been altered and who has to take the very trip to Mars that would have been the subject of his Recall hallucination. At various points in the film he is faced with the question of which of the two alternatives is real. In a particularly striking scene he is "visited" by "someone" who claims to be a hallucinatory representative of Recall inserted into his hallucination in an effort to bring him back to reality. The claim is that he is "stuck" in the hallucination, and the people running the "program" can't stop him from continuing to hallucinate. Our hero has to decide whether or not to "blow away" a real person pretending to be an apparition or to form the beliefs that will allow him to return to "reality." Not sure what to do, he finally notices that the "person" in question has begun to sweat, a decisive sign, he figures, that the experience is indeed of someone real. The usual carnage begins.

At first blush, our intrepid hero is on philosophically shaky ground. If I'm trying to figure out whether or not I'm hallucinating, the fact that the hallucination would be of a sweaty person seems neither here nor there. The "phenomenal" evidence is equally consistent with the experience being hallucinatory or veridical. However, as I seem to remember Mike Huemer once suggesting to me, the plot of the movie *artificially* restricts the hypotheses *entertained* by the protagonist. You will remember that he has, in effect, narrowed the two hypotheses down to the experience's being a hallucination programmed by Recall or a veridical experience (part of his life after he escaped the hallucination). As between *those* two hypotheses, one might suppose that there is an argument from analogy against the former. After all, if you were a programmer who alters the programmed hallucination to convince a person that he was hallucinating, why exactly would you bother to have the "hallucinatory" person sweat? After all, you are not interested in making the experience "realistic." In fact, it would be better if the experience induced were as if the person was shape-shifting or popping in and out of existence. That would be more likely to convince the person having the experience that something odd was going on. So, as between the two possibilities Douglas (the lead character) was considering, the veridical experience might be more plausible. There is no solace in any of this, however, for the philosopher looking for insight into how to reject skepticism. Once one takes seriously the logical gap between appearance and reality, there are indefinitely many ways in which appearance might fail to be veridical, and most of them won't allow the kind of reasoning from analogy discussed above. If, for example, a person were stuck in Recall and were "adding" details to the hallucinatory experience, there is no reason whatsoever to reject the hypothesis that one might add precisely the details that Douglas took to be indicative of veridicality.

Everything said about perception applies *mutatis mutandis* to memory. Indeed, *Total Recall* is a nice film to use in discussing skeptical scenarios, since on one hypothesis, the lead character has had his memory of his prior existence as a spy completely altered. On the hypothesis that he is in a Recall-induced hallucination, he is only having experiences of a sort that would lead him to believe (perhaps justifiably) that his memory was altered.

Problems of intelligibility and a (somewhat desperate) solution to skeptical doubt

In both *The Matrix* and *Total Recall*, the plot invites certain problems of interpretation. One might, in turn, wonder whether the puzzles may also suggest epistemological solutions to skeptical worries. In both movies, but particularly in *The Matrix*, we are invited to suppose that there is genuine action and interaction that takes place within the framework of a hallucination. In *The Matrix*, there are constant "fights" between the central character Neo and his "hallucinatory" nemesis Mr Anderson. These fights are won or lost, and we are asked to suppose that it is the skill, determination, courage, and so on, of the protagonist that secures the victory. Indeed, even before the plot involves characters leaving and entering the "Matrix World" of hallucination at will, the "pod people" were presumably hallucinating a life in which they were making all sorts of conscious decisions, which decisions were affecting their "behavior," or more carefully, the experiences one associates with that behavior. So for example, in his more mundane hallucinatory existence Neo was presumably under the impression that *he* was raising his arm – that his arm went up as a result of his conscious decision, his act of will. He certainly thought that he controlled in constant ways through his decisions his behavior. And even after he leaves his hallucinatory experience, he (and others) reenter the hallucinatory world and are again acting as if they were controlling what happens in the context of that hallucinatory experience. Can we make sense of all of this?

There are at least two ways of interpreting the plot. As I understand it, there is a huge computer inducing hallucinatory experience in countless numbers of people. On one view of what is happening, the hallucinatory experience *includes* acts of will, decisions, beliefs, and the illusion of a direct causal connection between those mental states and subsequent experiences associated with behavior. As such, the hallucination is no more puzzling than a dream. In dreams, we believe (falsely) that through an act of will we move our body. But whether or not the act of will occurs, the body certainly doesn't move, and it is not clear that the act of will causes even the *experiences* associated with bodily movement. The problem, however, is that on this first interpretation we can't make sense of the idea that the computer-generated hallucinatory antagonists can win or lose fights, or can succeed or fail to "find" their hallucinatory quarries.

There is a second interpretation of what the computer does in generating hallucinations that leaves more room for the exercise of some sort of causally effective acts of will. Presumably, it is intelligible to suppose that the computer can "read" the act of will (say the decision to raise one's hand) and within less than a millisecond induce the hallucinatory experience of one's hand going up. As soon as the computer notices a decision to lower the hand, the relevant experiences associated with that behavior occur. It might seem to the "actor" that the will is causally efficacious, and in a sense it is. But the causal connection is not "direct" in the way it was thought to be direct. That still leaves mysterious why the computer-generated programs would allow Neo to "win" a fight with his hallucinatory arch enemy. As Neo attempts the devastating drop kick, all the computer has to do is make an exception to the rule of generating the relevant experiences associated with the kick – inducing instead the experiences associated with a clumsy fall. But I suppose (and here the plot just gets a bit stupid), we might imagine that for all their sophistication the computers have loaded programs that can now only respond to acts of will in "standard" or "expected" ways. The computer has become something more like Berkeley's God, who has ordained (in advance) that experiences come and go in certain ordered ways (Berkeley 1954). Why it would "matter" to a computer that hallucinatory action results in hallucinatory victory, or, why it would matter to the person who *knows* that he is safely tucked away on a "ship" that he is "losing" a hallucinatory battle, is a whole other story – one that I won't try to explain here.

The second interpretation sketched above relies on a somewhat controversial view about the nature and epistemology of causal connections between acts of will and their effects. On one famous view of causation – the regularity theory of causation – one event causes another primarily in virtue of certain regularities existing between event kinds of which these two events are instances. Relations of temporal priority or spatial contiguity are also sometimes thrown into the mix of conditions necessary for causation, but the heart of the view is this idea that causation is nothing over and above the existence of regularities in the universe (thus the name, regularity theory). The regularity theory faces a host of serious objections. There is obviously a critical distinction between so-called accidental regularities (coincidences on a massive scale) and lawful regularities, and the regularity theorist better come up with a plausible account of the distinction. Despite the many problems the theory faces, however, it is still surprisingly popular, and one reason is the alleged phenomenology of causation. Hume, the first clear regularity theorist, famously claimed that he could find in experience nothing that was even a remotely plausible candidate for the "necessary" connection between cause and effect. The idea that there was such a connection, he concluded, was a confusion based on our disposition to virtually always think of an effect when we think of its cause, or our disposition to expect an effect when we experience its cause.

Against Hume, a number of philosophers claimed that we do sometimes have direct and unproblematic experience of the very necessary connection rejected by the regularity theorist. They have purported to find that necessary connection in a number of experiences. One candidate for direct confrontation with causation has been "pushes and pulls" – the experience of force exerted upon one's body. But another has always been alleged introspective awareness of the causal efficacy of will. Earlier, I suggested that computer-programmed hallucination could simply include an experience of causally inert will followed by sensations associated with movement, and could do so in a way that leaves the subject with the mistaken belief that the act of will caused the "movement." On the view we are considering here, one has direct and unproblematic access to the fact that the act of will was indeed the cause of subsequent motion. If, and this is a huge "if," one could have that kind of direct knowledge of a causally active will, then one might have direct knowledge that one is not the victim of a massive hallucination of the sort described in either *The Matrix* or *Total Recall*.

It is a standing joke in philosophy that one philosopher's *modus ponens* (If P then Q, and P – Therefore, Q) is another's *modus tollens* (If P then Q, but not-Q – Therefore, not-P). I'm inclined to take the above considerations to invite the *modus tollens* argument against any sort of direct apprehension of a causally efficacious will. While I warned earlier that one must carefully examine the superficial intelligibility of a plot line to make sure that it is, upon analysis, still without implicit contradiction, it does seem to me that the illusion of will producing behavior shouldn't be that hard to produce. Radical hallucination is perfectly compatible with the sense that one is in perfect control of one's actions, and, consequently, one can't do much with a sense of agency by way of eliminating skeptical scenarios.

Conclusion

In the final analysis, I think that the *ease* with which we follow the plots of films that invoke the possibility of massive and vivid nonveridical experience is an enormously powerful reason for thinking that there is indeed something common to both veridical experience and its nonveridical counterpart. It is almost impossible to deny the intelligibility of the so-called skeptical scenarios. Whether or not the intelligibility of such scenarios ultimately leads to skepticism depends on a host of fundamental controversies raging in contemporary epistemology on the conditions necessary and sufficient for knowledge and justified belief. If certain forms of externalism about justification are correct, then the intelligibility of skeptical scenarios, and even the fact that nonveridical experience is indistinguishable from veridical experience, has no obvious epistemic significance (unless we happen to be in a world in which most experience is nonveridical). We internalists who search for an internal mark of veridicality, however, have our work cut out for us.

References

Berkeley, G. (1954) *Three Dialogues between Hylas and Philonous*, ed. C. Turbayne, Indianapolis: Bobbs-Merrill.

Cohen, S. (1999) "Contextualism, Skepticism, and the Structure of Reasons," *Philosophical Perspectives* 13: 57–89.

Descartes, R. (1999 [1641]) *First Meditations on Philosophy*, trans. R. Rubin, in Perry and Bratman (eds.) *Introduction to Philosophy*, 3rd ed., New York: Oxford University Press.

Hume, D. (1958) *A Treatise of Human Nature*, ed. L. A. Selby-Bigge, London: Oxford University Press.

Lewis, D. (1996) "Elusive Knowledge," *Australasian Journal of Philosophy* 5: 49–67.

Further reading

The following are further reading on this topic: A. J. Ayer, *The Problem of Knowledge* (Harmondsworth: Penguin, 1956); Richard Fumerton, *Epistemology* (Malden, MA: Blackwell, 2006); William Irwin, *The Matrix and Philosophy* (Chicago: Open Court Press, 2002).

56

PERSONAL IDENTITY

Deborah Knight

Although Captain James T. Kirk never said the words that are burned into popular imagination – "Beam me up, Scotty" – Scotty often beamed Kirk and his crew up, or down, as the situation demanded, and every time the faithful Scotty complied, we witnessed a perfect illustration of a central puzzle in the philosophical study of personal identity. How can a person be destroyed in one place and put back together in another place, and still be the same person? When a mind-swap transplant misfires in *All of Me* (1984) causing both Lily Tomlin's mind and Steve Martin's to coinhabit his body, again we face a puzzle about personal identity. Can a single body house more than one person? Even when mind swaps (or body swaps, depending on how you look at things) go well, there are questions about just what counts as the same person, as for instance we see when Jamie Lee Curtis and Lindsay Lohan wind up having their bodies exchanged in *Freaky Friday* (2003). The obvious problems here are these: How can a teenager who is suddenly put into her mother's body act appropriately in the very foreign world of adulthood, and how can an adult learn how to act in a way appropriate to what she appears to be, namely a teenager? What should we say about personal identity in a situation where minds or bodies are swapped? These examples all encourage us to get clearer about what we think counts as the essence or nature of personal identity. Is it something primarily physical, or is it primarily mental? Is it some complex combination of the two?

Another, related set of questions is raised by films featuring serious problems with memory, for example, Leonard's short-term memory loss in *Memento* (2000) or Jason Bourne's amnesia in the *Bourne* franchise (2002, 2004, and 2007). These films challenge the idea that memory is a core component of one's personal identity, since both protagonists' memories are unreliable, and their ability to make sense of their identities is absolutely dependent on their bodies. Bourne learns about who he was prior to his amnesia by discovering what his body is capable of doing, while Leonard inscribes on his body information he needs to have available but will inevitably soon forget. A variation of the memory question is central to the plot of *Dark City* (1998), where John Murdoch and the other inhabitants of the city are the subjects of sinister experiments by a group of extraterrestrials who literally inject false memories into the citizens' sleeping minds, so that when they wake up, they have new identities, new pasts, new preferences, sometimes new surroundings, families, and friends. They proceed as if they enjoyed personal identity with past instantiations of themselves, and while it is true that their bodies persist, their psychologies and memories are newly reinvented with each experiment. The possibility that one's memories are both false and implanted is also, famously, a suspicion that dawns on Rick Deckard in *Blade Runner* (1992). In Deckard's case, the personal-identity question is particularly vexed. There is of course the question of *who* he really is, but it becomes increasingly clear that the more important question concerns *what* he really is. The evidence points to the very real possibility that Deckard is not what he all along believed himself to be, namely a human being working in a dystopian Los Angeles, but rather a replicant, a purpose-built piece of artificial life, with fabricated memories. In this chapter I trace the main lines of the debate about personal identity begun by John Locke. Along the way, I will pause to ask the question whether narrative fiction films, in treating the theme of personal identity, do so by means of presenting us with thought experiments of the sort so central to the philosophical study of this topic.

John Locke and the memory theory

John Locke inaugurated the modern debate about personal identity by first specifying the nature of personhood (Locke 1975). A person, Locke tells us, "is a thinking intelligent Being, that has reason and reflection, and can consider it self as it self, the same thinking thing in different times and places" (Locke 1975: 335). For Locke to maintain that a person must have reason seems the natural outcome of the philosophical tradition from Socrates to Descartes. To reason Locke adds the notion of reflection, which we can understand as a sort of second-order self-consciousness or self-awareness, captured by the idea of being able to consider oneself as oneself. The sort of identity characteristic of persons is one where we are aware from the inside, subjectively, of our thoughts, perceptions, and experiences, counting them as our own. As Locke puts it, it is "impossible for any one to perceive, without perceiving, that he does perceive" (Locke 1975: 335). Consciousness, Locke's preferred term for this second-order awareness – which he notes "always accompanies thinking" (Locke 1975: 335) – is what allows persons to recognize themselves as selves. Locke is not particularly concerned with whether or not persons enjoy personal identity at one time – a topic that some philosophers, notably Thomas Nagel, argue is more problematic than it might appear (Nagel 1971). Rather, Locke is interested in persons as entities persisting through time, capable of recognizing that they are now the same person they previously were, despite the sorts of changes that inevitably occur as children grow into young adults, young adults into the middle-aged, and the middle-aged into the elderly.

Locke endorses a memory theory of personal identity. That is, one is the same person now as one was previously in virtue of being able to remember previous actions and occurrences from the inside, as one's own. Locke declares that "as far as this consciousness can be extended backwards to any past Action or Thought, so far reaches the Identity of that *Person*; it is the same *self* now it was then" (Locke 1975: 335). The memory theory has a variety of peculiar consequences, many of which

Locke embraces. Perhaps the oddest is the idea that if I now remember, from the inside, being present with Noah at the flood, then I am the same person who was with Noah at the flood. Locke is willing to admit that personal identity does not depend on bodily or physical identity, since he is not claiming that my current body was present at the flood with Noah, even though my person was. Putting aside such odd consequences, one of the most incisive objections to Locke's theory is the thought experiment about the brave officer which is often attributed to Thomas Reid (Reid 2003: 114). A retired general recalls incidents of bravery earlier in his career, but not the flogging he received as a young man for stealing from an orchard, despite the fact that in mid-career he could remember the flogging. This would make the retired general the same person as the brave officer yet, counterintuitively, not the same person as his youthful self, despite the fact that the brave officer is the same person as the flogged youth. Reid's lovely example drives home a serious flaw in Locke's version of the memory theory.

To Locke we owe the first in a prolific string of puzzle cases or thought experiments designed to test our intuitions about personal identity. At issue is the question whether personal identity is primarily physical, based on our bodies or possibly our brains, or whether it is primarily mental, psychological, or even spiritual. Locke's thought experiment invites us to imagine a prince and a cobbler whose souls are rehoused in each other's bodies. Locke's intuition is that the person of the prince is preserved in the cobbler's body, and vice versa. The "body swap" has become something of a genre in the repertoire of philosophical thought experiments, and extends to include a range of brain transplant scenarios. While it does appear obvious that the prince's past memories are now domiciled in the cobbler's body, the question of the prince's personal identity surely becomes problematic after the body swap has occurred. This problem is neatly captured by Bernard Williams, who reimagines the prince and the cobbler as the emperor and the peasant. Williams asks us to "[s]uppose a magician is hired to perform the old trick of making the emperor and the peasant become each other" (Williams 1973: 11). Clearly, "after the smoke has cleared," the success of the trick will not reveal the emperor groveling in the corner previously occupied by the peasant and the peasant now seated on the emperor's throne. Rather, "the emperor's body, with the peasant's personality, should be on the throne, and the peasant's body with the emperor's personality, in the corner" (Williams 1973: 11–12). A main part of Williams' point is that it is hard to think that personal identity has been preserved through the body swap, since the peasant's vulgar mannerisms and speech are now presented through the emperor's aristocratic body and diction, while the emperor's diction and physical agility are compromised by the peasant's hoarse rasp and squat body (Williams 1973: 12). Intuitions seem to pull in two directions, with Williams arguing that to find oneself in a foreign body would throw off many aspects of oneself that previously contributed to one's sense of one's own identity. If the person, so to speak, of a prima ballerina were to be deposited in the body of a sumo wrestler, it is far from obvious that she would look upon this new composite as herself. It is, Williams concludes, not at all obvious that a person's personality can in fact be clinically detached from their body. This point is vividly illustrated in *Freaky Friday*, immediately after the body swap, when Jamie Lee Curtis smiles goofily at the boy Lindsay Lohan has a crush on, while Lindsay Lohan speaks and acts with stern maternal authority.

One of the things that motivated Locke was the need to sort out personal responsibility for past actions. To this end, he held that the concept of personal identity is fundamentally a forensic one. On his view of the prince/cobbler swap, the person of the prince, now domiciled in the cobbler's body, would continue to be responsible for everything the prince had done prior to the swap, and the same for the cobbler. This is a neat story but introduces some awkward moments, even if we abandon the question of body swapping. The prince's identity is preserved in the body of the cobbler because of his memory, and what the prince doesn't remember is not something for which he can be held responsible, since what he cannot remember is not part of his person. Is this a desirable approach to questions concerning an individual's responsibility for actions? Arguably not. Imagine that a drunk driver is involved in a hit and run which fatally injures a cyclist. The driver is a blackout drunk, and has no recollection of her action. Would we really want to say that the unremembered action does not count as, so to say, part of her person? Or would we want to say that the unremembered action is precisely part of her person, even if she has no memory of it, because part of her person is her excessive drinking? On the first view, she would doubtless not be held responsible, but on the second she would be.

Derek Parfit and teletransportation

Let us consider a more recent thought experiment. In *Reasons and Persons*, Derek Parfit asks you to imagine the following. You have a meeting on Mars, and one way of making it on time is to go by teletransporter. You have never been teletransported before, but those close to you who have been teletransported before assure you that everything will be fine, so you decide to go ahead. The teletransporter works in the following way: when you enter it, you press a button and fall immediately unconscious. A scanner records everything physical about you down to the exact nature of each of your cells, and then it destroys you. The information it has recorded is sent to Mars ("at the speed of light," as Parfit nicely notes). On Mars, a replicator produces a new version of you from entirely new material. When you wake up on Mars – or when the replica of you wakes up on Mars – you, or more precisely your replica, can detect nothing out of the ordinary about your body and remembers everything that you would have remembered up until pressing the button in the teletransporter (Parfit 1984: 199). Your situation is thus rather like that of Captain Kirk when he asks Scotty to beam him up. Perhaps the flow of the narrative in *Star Trek* prevents us from asking a main question about the use of the *Enterprise*'s transporter, something highlighted by Parfit. In Kirk's case, he tells Scotty to beam him up, and seconds later he emerges from the *Enterprise*'s transporter. It all appears so seamless in *Star Trek* that we might be forgiven for overlooking the fact that, in one sense, Kirk has been destroyed and replicated. If you pressed the button in Parfit's teletransporter and put the scanner to work, you would be destroyed, and later, on Mars, a different individual would be created.

Parfit's point is that although you have been destroyed, both body and brain, this experience somehow manages to go unrecognized. Your replica wakes up on Mars, and your replica's experience seems to be your continuing experience. But the "you" on Mars is in an important sense *not* you. It is a perfect duplicate, to be sure, but a different individual. Nevertheless, in Parfit's thought experiment, you don't feel as though you have died while a likeness of you has been put in your place. In this version of teletransportation, things are experienced as seamlessly as they are when we watch Kirk arrive back on the *Enterprise*. Because, as Parfit notes, you (on Earth) "do not co-exist with [your] replica," it is "easier to believe that this *is* a way of travelling" (Parfit 1984: 201). But Parfit offers another version of teletransportation to tweak your intuitions. He asks you to imagine that the technology of teletransportation changes so that after you press the button on Earth, everything else goes as before, except you are not destroyed. Rather, you wake up in the same teletransporter where you last recall pressing the button, while your replica wakes up on Mars. You learn that you will die very shortly, and that your replica will continue on in your place. But for a short period, you and your replica will coexist as distinct individuals. You might even talk to your replica, or see your replica by means of a video telephone call. Parfit's question, the point of the thought experiment, is this: In this second scenario, should you (the one on Earth) care that you are about to die and that you will be survived by a replica who is both physically and psychologically a perfect copy of you? In a bold move, Parfit will argue that having a replica is "about as good as ordinary survival," in other words, that we should not look at your situation on Earth as "almost as bad as ordinary death" (Parfit 1984: 201). Personal identity, for philosophers who subscribe to this notion – which David Hume notoriously did not – is for Parfit of considerably less importance than survival, and on both versions of the teletransporter thought experiment, Parfit argues, you survive. True, you survive as your replica, but aside from the fact that on the second scenario you do not have the subjective experiences your replica enjoys during those few days when you both exist, what matters about you continues with your replica, and Parfit argues that this sort of survival should be good enough.

The teletransporter thought experiment vividly illustrates a problem that can be easily overlooked by those caught up in the narrative flow of *Star Trek*. Certain films, by contrast, draw our attention to just the sorts of issues that can otherwise be developed by means of a philosophical thought experiment. Just what is the relationship between narrative fictions of the sort we find in fiction films and the sorts of philosophical thought experiments that proliferate in the philosophical study of personal identity? This is another way of asking the question, so often asked in the recent literature by philosophers of film: Do (at least some) films *do* philosophy? Should we treat *All of Me* and *Dark City* as contributing to the philosophical discourse on personal identity, or does something about the nature of narrative fiction films separate them from philosophy, so that they might serve as illustrations of philosophical problems but never direct interventions into philosophy itself? The primary recent spokesperson for the view that fiction films actually *do* philosophy, that is to say, actually *philosophize*, is Thomas Wartenberg, although Stanley Cavell's work in this area has in many ways been groundbreaking (Wartenberg 2006; Cavell 1981). Wartenberg captures his brief clearly with the following journal article title: "Beyond *Mere* Illustration: How Films Can Be Philosophy." But the question whether plot incidents or even entire narratives count as examples akin to philosophical thought experiments is challenged by Murray Smith, whose article on this subject cleverly discusses *All of Me* (Smith 2006; see also Livingston 2006). Smith's conclusion is that *if* certain fiction films can be treated as examples of thought experiments, they are very different in presentation and point from the sorts of philosophical thought experiments that ask us to consider body swaps and teletransportation. Smith offers the possibility that we might recognize philosophical thought experiments, such as Locke's and Parfit's, yet recognize another genre of fiction, namely the artistic thought experiment. Put another way, Plato's famous thought experiment concerning the ring of Gyges, which makes its wearer invisible and thus able to do anything the wearer wants, whether good or evil, shares similarities with (and could well have been the inspiration for) the One Ring in *The Lord of the Rings: The Fellowship of the Ring* (2001). This doesn't make the narrative function of the One Ring into a philosophical thought experiment, although it certainly develops the idea we owe to Plato, that even moral individuals might succumb to such a temptation, as clearly happens to Boromir and nearly happens to Frodo. Consider some other examples. *The Matrix* (1999) shares themes that are addressed philosophically by Hilary Putnam's famous thought experiment (Putnam 1982) of the brain in the vat, notably the idea that the experiences we believe are veridical are all in fact virtual. *The Bourne Identity* and its sequels ask how someone with only sporadic flashes of memory (which might of course be false memories) can possibly achieve a sense of personal identity, and so these films might honorifically be described as artistic thought experiments. But in all three cases, what compels our engagement with the films mentioned is a combination of plotting, character action, and psychology, suspense, mystery, and action – in short, the sort of thing Aristotle meant when he talked about plot. So, against Wartenberg and with Smith, it seems reasonable to admit that even if there is such a thing as an artistic thought experiment, it is different in structure and function from a philosophical thought experiment. And, returning to Smith's example, the primary function of what we might call the artistic thought experiment in *All of Me* is to allow Steve Martin to perform some very funny physical comedy, since his body is controlled by Lily Tomlin and therefore expresses her mannerisms.

The issue of personal identity, as originally presented, was to understand how we know that we are the same person over time, and that issue very much hinged on the unique first-person access we have to ourselves. Literally, our own experience is "first personal," whereas our understanding of others is either in the third person ("I saw him do this or that") or in the second person ("Tell me how you are"). Prose literature can give us a first-person perspective by means of first-person narration. There is nothing really comparable in filmmaking. Even if one adopted the device of having the camera assume the position of the central protagonist, as we find in Robert Montgomery's *Lady in the Lake* (1947), our access to what it is like to be that protagonist, understood from the inside, is still terribly limited. You might believe that what you see on screen is what the character sees as the character sees it (although as

Francis Sparshott has noted, what the film camera shows is very different from the way the human eye sees [Sparshott 1981]), and you might hear what the character says and possibly even what the character thinks (thanks to voice-over narration), but this is very different from the richness of detail available to novels and short stories written in the first person. And if the history of cinema can be used as a guide, there is little enthusiasm for constructing films, even so-called art cinema films, with the camera in the place of the main character.

Daniel C. Dennett and a post-Humean take on the self

But perhaps there is another way of approaching the question of personal identity that could bring its philosophical exemplars into a closer relationship with exemplars from narrative fiction films. One possibility is Daniel C. Dennett's (1988) suggestion that the self is not some entity in the world, on a par with tables and chairs. Rather, Dennett argues that the self is a theorist's fiction, functioning like a center of gravity. Dennett's idea is that when it comes to human lives and all the actions and events, beliefs and desires, thoughts and preferences that typify such lives, the self is in effect a center of *narrative* gravity. Instead of construing personal identity in terms of some temporally extended entity that serves as a ground or basis for all the changes that individuals typically go through in their lives, and certainly instead of construing personal identity in terms of the deliverances of memory which, notoriously, can be fallible, Dennett suggests that people are *confabulators*, that is, autobiographers, intent on telling the stories of their lives to themselves and anyone else who will listen. The sort of confabulation Dennett has in mind is a string of overlapping stories about events currently being lived, past events lived through, and anticipated future events and actions. The self is the upshot of such strings of self-narration, rather than being some sort of permanent feature of a person who goes through the normal sorts of temporal changes which, as Shakespeare remarked, flesh is heir to.

Dennett's theory is an updating of David Hume's "bundle theory" of personal identity (Hume 1985). Where Locke wanted to believe that memory could be the criterion of personal identity, Hume proposed that persons are composites of such things as memories, current beliefs and desires, and short- and long-range plans. For Hume, personhood cashed out in bundles: the amalgam of features of a given person as currently disposed. The bundle was certainly not a static collection that persisted unchanged through time, but was in flux given new experiences over time. Hume's idea, it seems, is that enough of the contents of the bundle continues from t_1 to t_2 to ensure that one is the same as one was before and will be the same one in the future. The bundle theory challenges the Lockean notion that there is something in which the self consists. As Hume argued, he could introspect as diligently and for as long as he liked, yet would never find his self there among the other contents of his mind. Dennett adapts Hume's insight and argues that the self is an abstraction.

A Dennettian view of the self as the center of narrative gravity offers another way of approaching the connection between the philosophical study of personal identity and film. It allows us to recognize some films as investigations into the mechanics of personal identity construed in Dennettian terms. We can track, as it were, Scottie's experiences in *Vertigo* (1958) as he meets and falls in love with Madeleine Elster and then see what befalls him after he witnesses what he thinks is her suicide. What we track, of course, is a story of love, loss, and in the aftermath of loss, the development of an emotionally crippling obsession. In *Citizen Kane* (1941), we try to untangle just what sort of man Kane was in life, given that his death makes his life both worthy of journalistic investigation and still extremely enigmatic. *Kane* does not give us the sort of direct access to Kane that we enjoyed with Scottie – understandably, since the first event of the film is Kane's death. Instead, *Kane* is constructed around the recollections of many who knew him intimately. What we find here are as many different views of Kane as the individuals who knew him. *Citizen Kane* does not offer the hope of a single right interpretation of Kane's life. Rather, the film suggests that, viewed from the outside at least, personal identity is as much an enigma as Kane's dying utterance, "Rosebud." By contrast, *Groundhog Day* (1993) might be seen as illustrating how Bill Murray's character comes to discover his identity, just what he is as a person, and indeed just what he wants to be as a person, as a result of becoming caught up in a comic version of the Nietzschean eternal return of the same. *Dark City* allows us to wonder whether personal identity might depend primarily on something other than memory – indeed, *must* depend on something other than memory, since everyone's memories are false. In *Dark City*, despite the fact that characters' memories are not veridical, they nevertheless provide the basis for a narrative account of the self which, in conjunction with individual plans and ambitions for the future, secure one's identity over time. For this reason, at the end of the film, John Murdoch, who has been able to destroy the extraterrestrials, continues in hope of winning the love of the woman who used to be his wife during a previous experiment, despite the fact that she has no recollection of that time. *Dark City* and *Groundhog Day* draw attention to the degree to which plans for the future matter in understanding just what constitutes personal identity.

Interestingly, the examples I have just cited to support the Hume–Dennett idea that the self is something like a narrative fiction also treat selfhood or personhood forensically, as Locke intended. Fictional narratives typically require us to determine who is responsible for what. So we discover that, in *Vertigo*, Scottie is not responsible for Madeleine's death, since the woman Scottie believes is Madeleine is deceiving him and in fact does not commit suicide at the mission in San Juan Bautista. But Scottie is certainly responsible for demanding that Judy, who deceived him as Madeleine, transform herself once again into Madeleine, and more importantly Scottie is morally if not actually responsible for Judy's death. *Citizen Kane* does not provide us with a clear understanding of Kane, since no singular view can be found among the various recollections of him, but that he is responsible for any number of actions, some of them underhanded, petty, and self-serving, is clear. While Bill Murray's character in *Groundhog Day* does not initially grasp the notion that he is responsible for his actions, his seemingly unending time spent in Punxsutawney teaches him to be morally responsible, despite the absurdity of reliving the same day over and over again. Examples of how he accepts moral responsibility in relation to others include his continuing to help the old ladies whose car develops a flat tire; his anticipation (since like everything else it has happened so often before) that a young boy will fall out of a tree; Phil's increasingly thoughtful treatment of his television crew, who appear to be stuck, for his sake, reliving Groundhog Day until Phil finally becomes a better person; and Phil's ongoing attempts to help an elderly street person in failing health. Both *Dark City* and *Groundhog Day* strongly suggest that our hopes and plans for the future are more important, forensically speaking, than our memories of the past. What these protagonists hope to achieve – in each case, the love of the woman they already love – is a clearer indicator of who these characters are than of anything as contingent of their psychological history.

Personal identity is perhaps not a topic that can be thoroughly tracked through narrative fiction films in exactly the way its primary philosophical advocates envisioned. Cinema typically does not allow us to enter into the subjective states of main characters, and to the extent that we might imagine that we see things from cinematic characters' perspectives, we are imagining what it is like to be them. The philosophical question of personal identity still lacks a definitive answer. John Locke argued for memory, which cannot be the whole or even the primary story. Clearly an account based on the persistence of the body is not satisfactory, as body-swap thought experiments illustrate. Dennett's rethinking of Hume's bundle theory has merit, but might not satisfy everyone. Cinema restricts access to first-person experiences; so, at best, filmic examinations let us see how personal-identity issues might look from a third-person point of view. Perhaps we should adopt the idea that, whatever we are talking about when we talk about personal identity, it cannot be something answered, as it were, entirely from the inside, but needs outside corroboration. If this is right, then films that closely track central characters can help us to understand the enigma of personal identity.

References

Cavell, S. (1981) *Pursuits of Happiness: The Hollywood Comedy of Remarriage*, Cambridge, MA: Harvard University Press.

Dennett, D. (1988) "Why Everyone Is a Novelist," *Times Literary Supplement* 4459 (16–22 September): 1016, 1028–9.

Hume, D. (1985) *A Treatise of Human Nature*, Harmondsworth: Penguin Books.

Livingston, P. (2006) "Theses on Cinema as Philosophy," *Journal of Aesthetics and Art Criticism* 64: 11–18.

Locke, J. (1975) *An Essay Concerning Human Understanding*, Oxford: Clarendon Press.

Nagel, T. (1971) "Brain Bisection and the Unity of Consciousness," *Synthese* 22: 396–413.

Parfit, D. (1984) *Reasons and Persons*, Oxford: Oxford University Press.

Putnam, H. (1982) *Reason, Truth and History*, Cambridge: Cambridge University Press.

Reid, T. (2003) "On Mr. Locke's Account of Our Personal Identity," in J. Perry (ed.) *Personal Identity*, Berkeley: University of California Press.

Smith, M. (2006) "Film Art, Argument and Ambiguity," *Journal of Aesthetics and Art Criticism* 64: 33–42.

Sparshott, F. (1971) "Basic Film Aesthetics," *Journal of Aesthetic Education* 5: 11–34.

Wartenberg, T. (2006) "Beyond *Mere* Illustration: How Films Can Be Philosophy," *Journal of Aesthetics and Art Criticism* 64: 19–32.

Williams, B. (1973) *Problems of the Self: Philosophical Papers 1956–1972*, Cambridge: Cambridge University Press.

57
PRACTICAL WISDOM AND THE GOOD GROUND OF GETTYSBURG

Joseph Kupfer

Practical wisdom, imagination, and narrative

The two-part film *Gettysburg* (Ronald Maxwell, 1993) is based on the novel *Killer Angels* (1974) by Michael Shaara. The title of the book alludes to Hamlet's soliloquy that begins "What a piece of work is man," and includes the phrase, "in action, how like an angel." The story of the famous Civil War battle provides us with two exemplars of practical wisdom, who exercise their virtue in various phases of war.

Practical wisdom is arguably the most valuable of virtues, since acting on any other virtue without it is liable to lead us astray or produce harmful consequences. We need practical wisdom, for example, to see that perseverance is passing into futile obstinacy or to know when justice should be tempered with mercy. Yet the virtue has received scant treatment, perhaps because it doesn't readily lend itself to generalization – dealing as it must with the details of concrete situations. Because what is practically wise is inseparable from particular situations, discussing this virtue in the context of a developed narrative may be more than a useful heuristic. It may be essential to our understanding.

Besides illustrating what we already know, cinematic and other narratives can extend and deepen our understanding of virtue. In what follows, I argue that the film's depictions of the decision-making of Colonel Joshua Chamberlain and General John Buford add crucial elements to the standard accounts of practical wisdom. The three vignettes we shall explore underscore the pivotal role played by imagination and its mobilization in narrative, in making practically wise decisions. By narrative I mean nothing more technical than an account that organizes people and events into a temporal whole. By causally connecting events with one another and persons with events, stories help make sense of what occurs and why it does. Narratives impart unity to episodes that are in themselves discrete and disparate, by integrating them with one another. Although valuable as an aspect of practical wisdom, narrative is not itself inherently good or bad. It can also be used to distort and misrepresent events, as well as persuade us to do vicious things. Let's begin by characterizing the virtue of practical wisdom, or *phronesis*.

Unlike many virtues, such as patience or generosity, practical wisdom depends on native intelligence and understanding (Aristotle 1962: 162). This partly explains why it is found in such small degree, when at all. The natural endowment includes the ability to learn from what is observed and to apply what is learned to experience as it unfolds willy-nilly. Phronesis involves the ability to hit upon the means to one's ends, being able to figure out how to get what we want. But what we want must be morally good; otherwise, we possess merely cleverness (Aristotle 1962: 169). After all, bank robbers and tyrants may know how to get what they want, but they lack wisdom, since what they want is not truly good. And someone who seeks fame or fortune for its own sake is not pursuing what ultimately makes life worthwhile. Therefore, the person of practical wisdom must be able to discriminate from among the multiplicity of ends those which are morally worthwhile. For example, the purposes of a war must be just and then the officers have to devise ways to win battles to achieve their morally worthy goals. The purpose of practical wisdom is to govern our action: "its end is to tell us what we ought to do and what we ought not to do" (Aristotle 1962: 164).

For Aristotle, phronesis turns on sound judgment, the process by which we reach good decisions in the determinate situations in which we happen to find ourselves. The judgment required by practical wisdom is uncommon because it is ever adapting generalizations (gleaned through intelligence) to particular situations. As Aristotle says, "A man of practical wisdom [must] take cognizance of particulars" (Aristotle 1962: 162). Rules may be helpful, but their application requires wise discrimination, since several rules may apply and, of course, we have to know when a rule ought to be violated. Therefore, besides knowing what is valuable in general, the individual must seize upon the particular means to attain the good in just the circumstances in which he finds himself.

The judgment concerning which action to perform is like perceptual discrimination. The apprehension is not, of course, sense perception, but rather seeing with the eye of imagination: seeing the concrete particular as an opportunity or an obstacle, as an opening or a quagmire. Following Aristotle's architectural analogy, good judgment is like the metal strip used to measure the contours of stone because the stone presents something like an "indefinite" situation (Aristotle 1962: 142). As with the strip, good judgment is flexible, able to bend to the lineaments of the particular context. The appropriate choice of action, then, is context dependent, and such contexts are both complex and open ended. Change and complexity flow naturally from the stubborn particularity of practical life.

Discussing the challenge posed by difficult circumstances that we may encounter, Martha Nussbaum argues that the concrete situation is liable to be characterized by "ultimately particular and non-repeatable elements" (1986: 304). Because rules or principles only cover what has previously occurred, they cannot be relied upon to guide our conduct without the exercise of judgment in novel situations. To sum up, practical wisdom enables people to make decisions that achieve morally desirable outcomes in unanticipated settings defying the unvarnished application of rules already in hand.

To deal with concrete particulars successfully, we are often called upon to use our imaginations to create narratives that contextualize our action. We need to imagine different scenarios for attaining the valued ends within the limits imposed by the concrete situation and the resources it affords. Think, for example, of burning forest or field in order to deprive a nearby fire of the fuel it needs to keep spreading. Although simple, the strategy requires a suppleness of imagination – to see the possibility of neutralizing the threat posed by a natural force, by employing that very force.

Where people are concerned, creating a story is needed to understand character, intention and motivation (MacIntyre 1981: chapter 15). Appreciating the experience of other people, moreover, requires a sympathetic imagination. The forgiveness or mercy we show wrongdoers, for example, "entails regarding each particular case as a complex narrative of human effort in a world full of obstacles" (Nussbaum 1993: 103). Taking a merciful attitude toward people requires putting ourselves in their place, with their history of hardships and resources, distorted experience, and harmful choice. Sheila Mullett describes this imaginative identification as apprehending the world through the eyes of another (1988: 122).

People with practical wisdom are adept at formulating possible narratives to guide future action. They then excel at weighing the advantages, risks, and likelihood of success of the various narrative possibilities. As if this weren't difficult enough, time is often at a premium – as in much of the wartime decision-making of *Gettysburg*. As the story unfolds, we see phronesis at work in three very different stages of war: rallying mutinous men to return to the fight; preparing strategically for battle; and improvising in the midst of fighting. In each stage, *Gettysburg* dramatizes the ability of the practically wise individual to cope with extreme adversity. For these officers, effectively resolving matters of life and death is in pursuit of ends – freedom and equality – that, the film argues, are morally worthwhile.

Rallying mutineers and the grounds of war

Because Colonel Joshua Chamberlain (Jeff Daniels) heads the Twentieth Maine Regiment, he is ordered to take charge of one hundred and twenty men from the Second Maine Regiment who refused to fight. Echoing the written dispatch, the captain delivering the men tells Chamberlain (a bit too enthusiastically for Chamberlain's sensibilities) that he can shoot the dissidents if he wishes. The problem for Chamberlain is clear: not only must he get his own troops ready to fight soon, but he also must deal with this large batch of recalcitrant soldiers, connected with him only through shared statehood.

Chamberlain dismisses the guard detail as unnecessary and then orders preparation of a meal for the men who have been denied food, as punishment. Instead of continuing to treat the mutineers harshly, as traitors to the Union cause, Chamberlain demonstrates trust and sees to their stomachs. The wise individual must be able to understand what other people are experiencing, in this case their needs and frustrations, by putting himself in their place. As noted, such understanding requires a sympathetic imagination. Martha Nussbaum's description of the impact of fiction captures Chamberlain's psychological acuity. "It is a form of imaginative and emotional receptivity," Nussbaum explains, in which the life of another penetrates "into one's own imagination and heart" (1993: 103). Chamberlain can identify with what these alienated soldiers are going through because, bearing out Nussbaum's observation about fiction, he has emotionally absorbed their narrative. Chamberlain wins over the mutinous soldiers because his sympathetic imagination enables him to respond with care to the needs of the men and the particularity of their offense.

The regiment's vexed spokesman, Joseph Bucklin, tells Chamberlain that the dissidents are tired: tired of fighting (in eleven engagements); tired of incompetent leadership; tired of being treated like animals. Bucklin points out that the regiment had its own flag, implying that the Second Maine are not slackers but have pride and patriotism. Having listened carefully to Bucklin's litany of grievances, Chamberlain tells him to get some food for himself. He then asks the men who are eating on the hillock to gather around and informs them that he knows of their mistreatment. Chamberlain indicates that he's been ordered to take them with him, adding, "I'm told that if you don't come, I can shoot you." He chortles at the idea, and says "Well . . . you know I won't do that. Maybe somebody else will, but I won't. So, that's that."

But how do the men know that he won't have them shot? They don't know anything about him except that he's from Maine. In one subtle but pointed phrase, Chamberlain establishes familiarity by presuming it, or by seeming to presume it. He has very quickly and effectively dealt with the main issues occupying the men. Chamberlain has seen to their hunger, displayed trust, heard out their grievances, and – all but laughing at the idea of executing them – relieved any fears of immediate reprisal. He has also intimated an intimacy, suggesting that the men know him, even as he understands their plight.

Chamberlain sees that the rebellious troops need to know that he understands their story and that he bears them no ill will. On the contrary, Chamberlain wants them to fight alongside his troops and has projected a scenario that will convert a burden (having to guard mutineers) into a resource, reinforcements for his depleted troops. His imagination yields a narrative for the men that encompasses their past trials and frustrations, includes their current straits, and envisions a restorative military future.

Chamberlain bends his thinking like the strip of metal used by the architect so as to take the "measure" of the practical circumstances that presently confront him. His flexibility of mind enables Chamberlain to adapt to these particular offenders in their concrete circumstances. No rule culled from past experience by itself is sufficient to guide someone facing precisely Chamberlain's pitfalls and possibilities. Rather, practical wisdom, informed by a lively and generous imagination, is needed to gain the support of the mutinous soldiers. Chamberlain must rekindle in the disaffected men the passion and sense of purpose that moved them to enlist in the first place.

Noting that the "whole Reb Army" is up the road, Chamberlain tells the mutineers that it is up to them whether they fight or not. He simultaneouly puts them in the driver's seat and affirms their value: "We could surely use you fellas. We're well below half strength." Initially one thousand strong, Chamberlain confides that "there are less than three hundred of us now." Further solidifying the bond between the recalcitrants and his men, he says, "All of us volunteered to fight for the Union. Just as you did." The sustained, inspiring speech that Chamberlain then delivers focuses on the uniqueness of the cause. Claiming that "this is a different kind of army," he offers an historical perspective. Men have fought for pay, women, land, power, because their king leads them or they like killing. By contrast, he argues, "We are here for something new. This has not happened much in the history of the world. We are an army [speaking of them as a collective unity] out to set other men free." Having entered into the narrative of the mutinous Maine Second, Chamberlain tells a moral story of the Union waging war, into which he folds a future narrative of the disaffected men as comrades-in-arms.

As Chamberlain speaks, the camera cuts back and forth between him and the men. They show little emotion, but listen quietly and intently. Soft music plays in the background, lending the scene a gentle air, as if distancing them all from the trials of war to reflect on its significance and purpose. Several shots focus on Bucklin who seems to be weighing Chamberlain's words. If Chamberlain can convince the embittered and despairing Bucklin, we are led to conjecture, he probably can persuade most of the malcontents to join with his regiment.

Chamberlain appeals to the ideals that he believes define their country and justify the war:

> America should be free ground. All of it. From here to the Pacific Ocean ...
> Here we judge you by what you do, not by who your father was [as in Europe].
> Here you can be something. *Here* is the place to build a home. But it's not the
> land ... It's the idea that we all have value. You and me. What we're fighting
> for, in the end, we're fighting for each other.

As he winds down, the camera slowly pans the faces of the men, somber but riveted by the threads of meaning and purpose Chamberlain weaves together.

Again, Chamberlain speaks the language of inclusivity. Not only have "we all" volunteered and seen men die, but we all have value and are "fighting for each other." Free ground, then, is the ultimate moral end which Chamberlain claims his army is trying to achieve. It is both the physical place to build a home and life, and the symbolic space in which men should be free – to pursue such building. Chamberlain has understood that the rebellious men are dispirited and in need, not merely of a good reason to fight, but of an ideal worth dying for. He crafts a response to this from his knowledge of history, moral ideals, and his imaginative resonance to the plight of the war-weary soldiers.

If the end for which the Union army is fighting is indeed a morally laudable one, then Chamberlain's attainment of it in precarious circumstances qualifies him as practically wise. The film presents a justification of the war in a philosophical exchange between Chamberlain and his doughty Sergeant, Buster (Kevin Conway).

Chamberlain finds no difference between negroes and whites because they both possess the "divine spark." To which Buster rejoins with skepticism, but nevertheless defends the war on the grounds of justice – giving everyone the chance to prove himself better. The wise man is thereby portrayed as ruminating over the moral nature of the ends for which he strives. For our discussion, I assume that the Civil War and the Union's ends (as articulated by Chamberlain and Buster) are morally defensible. I lack the space to consider objections to them or criticisms of violence raised by different strains of pacifism.

Chamberlain concludes by promising that if the men choose to join his regiment, they can have their muskets back and "nothing more will be said by anyone, anywhere." Such a simple offer, yet one that cuts to the heart of the history of the aggrieved soldiers and their potential future. In so many (or few) words, Chamberlain has offered amnesty. The men are being given a chance to exonerate and redeem themselves. Chamberlain forecasts a redemptive narrative in which the dissidents restore themselves to full status as honorable soldiers in the Union army. He somberly adds, "Gentlemen, I think if we lose this fight, we lose the war. So if you choose to join us, I'll be personally very grateful." Chamberlain boldly moves from the big picture, the fate of the war, to his own gratitude, implying that he has a personal stake in the outcome of the war (and perhaps that the men of the Second Maine do as well). In a medium shot, the camera frames Chamberlain (from behind) facing the mutinous soldiers. They are united in the composition of the picture, by their Maine heritage, and by the import of the words with which Chamberlain hopes to bind them to him.

When he speaks of the mutineers "choosing to join us," Chamberlain again alludes to their freedom (of choice) and value (as soldiers): the very moral ideals for which they all initially volunteered to fight. To the beat of drums and the piping of fifes, the men of Maine march out, taking the lead of this portion of the Union army. Chamberlain soon learns that an astonishing one hundred and fourteen of the one hundred and twenty rebellious troops have decided to fight with him. Having met the physical and emotional needs of these tattered soldiers, Chamberlain presents them with a narrative of reconciliation through which the men can rededicate themselves to the cause and restore themselves to honor.

Securing the high ground

The phronesis of General John Buford (Sam Elliott) concerns military strategy. Although less sweeping in scope than Chamberlain's, Buford's wisdom almost pictorially dramatizes the role of imagination in good judgment and decision-making. He witnesses a brigade of Confederate infantry on the march and perceptively infers that this is the front edge of Lee's army, not a mere scouting party. Inspecting the countryside around Gettysburg, Buford remarks to Colonel Devin that the terrain is "fine ground" on which to do battle. He then describes what he imagines is bound to happen, should the Confederate army be allowed to have its way. He pictures a series of military maneuvers and events that will prove disastrous to the Union forces: "You know what's gonna happen here in the mornin'? Whole damn Reb army's gonna be here … Lee'll have the high ground and there'll be the devil to pay!" Buford then shifts his Cassandra gaze to the newly appointed leader of the Union army, George Meade, who will be under pressure from Lincoln to take the battle to the Confederates. "Meade'll come in slowly, cautiously, new to command. They'll be on his back from Washington [DC]. [Telegraph] Wires hot with messages – 'Attack!' 'Attack!'"

By proceeding deliberately, Meade will give Lee's troops ample time to fortify their superior fighting position in the hills, one that will devastate the Union forces. Buford continues, fiercely:

> So he [Meade] will set up a ring around these hills. Then when Lee's army's all nicely entrenched behind *fat* rocks on the high ground, Meade will finally attack … Straight up the hillside, out in the open, in that gorgeous field of fire. And we will charge valiantly and be *butchered* valiantly!

Surveying field and hills, Buford envisions the narrative of the next day's engagement, including the psychology of the army's leaders, as well as the dynamic of the deployment of troops.

Buford marvels to Colonel Devin at the vivacity of his narrative imagination:

> Devin, I've led a soldier's life and I've never seen anything as brutally clear as this. It's as if I can actually see the blue troops in one long bloody moment, goin' up the long slope to the stoney top. As if it were already done, already a memory …

He bites off his words, spitting them out in frustration. Although speaking fatalistically, Buford wisely employs his perspicuous forecast of the Confederate army seizing the high ground (the hill, "Little Roundtop"), even as Chamberlain has seized the moral high ground in responding to the mutineers. Imaginatively extrapolating from the present twenty-five hundred Rebel troops to the likely twenty thousand men soon to arrive, Buford formulates an alternative strategic narrative to avert the foreseen disaster.

Buford envisions blocking the narrow, main road and bottling up the far superior Confederate forces. He hopes to hold Cemetery Ridge until the bulk of the Union army arrives, and growls, "We can deprive the enemy of the high ground." Buford projects a forceful assault temporarily throwing the Confederate troops into a scramble of defensive redeployment. In his alternative scenario, Buford's troops detain the Confederate soldiers until Union reinforcements arrive with cavalry and cannon. They will then be able to engage the two corps of Lee's soldiers that Buford foresees converging at Gettysburg.

Correctly anticipating a dawn attack, Buford has his cannon and guns preemptively fire on the Confederate soldiers marching along the vital road. Here, he must use his own judgment, as past experience and the rules garnered from it cannot provide enough guidance in such open-ended circumstances. To insistent military strains, we see Confederate forces approaching. They soon leave the narrow turnpike to regroup in the face of Buford's artillery barrage. Watching through binoculars atop an open-air cupola, Buford is pleasantly surprised that his foes have sent but one brigade against his soldiers who are occupying "the best damn ground around." Buford croons to himself, "Lovely. Lovely." The enemy has clearly miscalculated what awaits them. As he imagines, there is indeed a great Southern host on the move, coming his way. But Buford's sound judgment will enable him to thwart the immediate Confederate advance long enough to gain the advantage.

Learning that there is no action to the north, Buford swings another brigade into the turnpike fight. We watch as lines of Union and Confederate soldiers exchange fire. No music accompanies the pop-pop-pop of the shooting of muskets and pistols interspersed with cannonades. Having ridden about to take stock of the fighting, Buford resumes his perch atop the cupola. As he scans the battle, we hear a spurt of uplifting horns and synthesizer on the soundtrack, and see Reynolds arrive in the vanguard of his twenty thousand troops. His soldiers will prove just adequate enough to stem the tide of the much greater Southern forces merging at Gettysburg, because Buford has vouchsafed him the high ground.

Here the film deftly provides Buford with a less adroit foil. The Confederate general Heth lacks the imagination vital for practical wisdom. Unable to imagine the Union forces that will be arrayed against him, Heth is also bereft of rules or directives comprehensive yet precise enough to guide him successfully in this indeterminate situation. Even when rules are helpful, practical wisdom is needed to know which rule to apply, how it should be applied, and when an exception has arisen. Indeed, Heth had been explicitly told by Lee not to engage the enemy until joined by more troops – a directive or rule from which he should have deviated even more vigorously than he did!

Moreover, had Heth the visionary power of Buford, he might have understood the importance of pushing quickly through the Union resistance so as to secure the high ground. Grasping its importance, Heth would have thrown his full force into the fray and could not have been kept at bay. Because he underestimates the number of men he is fighting and the urgency of the moment, Heth sends too few men into combat. By the time he's mustered the requisite force, it's insufficient to meet Buford's realigned brigades, and the subsequent Union strength. Arguing against Buford's exceptional sagacity might be the apparent obviousness of the military advantage conferred by the high ground. However, either Heth doesn't value the elevated position enough or he fails to foresee how he can be stymied in attaining it. In either event, Heth is lacking in the practical wisdom with which Buford is blessed.

The good ground of which Buford speaks is literally good for unfettered battle, and the high ground is better still in affording a dominant fighting position. Yet there is also the high ground of moral ideals that Chamberlain offers the mutinous men as the reason for returning to the war. Recalling the dissidents to the good, free ground of America enables Chamberlain to enlist their help on the good fighting ground of the fields of Gettysburg. The good ground (for battle) is thereby fused with the high ground of the war's noble ends.

The references to ground naturally call to mind Lincoln's Gettysburg Address. He speaks of the ground being consecrated by the men who died in the battle, and even as he denies the power of those gathered on the day of his speech to hallow the ground, the phrase "hallowed ground" remains with us as definitive of the battle field. The makers of the film would seem to count on this resonance with Lincoln's famous speech to add depth of meaning, perhaps religious connotations, to the talk of ground by Chamberlain and Buford.

Holding to the high ground

In the third and last of our episodes of phronesis in action, Chamberlain must use his wisdom to hold the high ground with which Buford has so insightfully and painstakingly provided him. Where Buford's imagination played leisurely over the field of fire before the conflagration, Chamberlain's imaginative powers must work on the spur of the moment, when all about him his military position is collapsing. As his regiment occupies the extreme left side of the Union forces, they must hold their position just below the summit of Little Roundtop or the Confederate troops will outflank the entire Union army, pouring up over the hill and overrunning it from the rear.

In the ensuing battle, Chamberlain's regiment is besieged in its defense of the flank. The Confederate soldiers advance, inflict casualties, and fall back, only to advance again and again. With each assault, Chamberlain's forces are ground down and eaten away. The film implies the passage of war time with a montage of images of the Maine soldiers firing at the enemy accompanied by vaguely portentous, violin-laden music. We hear fusillades amidst exhortations to "Keep up your fire," and "Pour it into them." Smoke clouds the air, and Confederates scurry among the trees like a horde of hungry predators.

Chamberlain's men seem destined to die or be swallowed up, especially with the arrival of a fresh Confederate regiment readying to attack. Learning that no help is to be had from the neighboring Union regiment, Chamberlain instructs his officers to take ammunition from their dead and wounded soldiers. The situation grows desperate and the enemy closes to hand-to-hand combat in some segments of the line. The fighting is framed through the trees, burnished with light and smoke, the beauty of the cinematography making more poignant the falling of the slain and wounded.

During a brief lull, Chamberlain convenes his commanding officers and all tell the same story: munitions and men are all but spent. Clearly, the Twentieth Maine cannot stave off another wave of Confederate troops, yet they cannot pull out, or the rest of the Union forces will be swamped from the rear. Chamberlain discloses his *impromptu* plan to have all his troops charge down the hill, turning at an angle to "swing like a door." Up until this critical moment, Chamberlain's regiment has been on the defensive, just trying to protect the Union's left flank. Now he primes his troops to take the offensive, to "sweep them down the hill just as they come up." The men react with admiration and awe at the audacity of Chamberlain's improvisation – to attack when most vulnerable – captured by the image of a swinging door. Earlier the left side was pulled back, now it will dive down and toward the right. Chamberlain says, "When I give the command, I want the whole regiment moving forward, swinging down to the right."

Chamberlain soon bellows "Bayonets!" and the men head down the hill with fixed bayonets to strains of music triumphant. Scurrying over fallen comrades, the men of Maine yell, shoot, and pummel the Confederates, forcing them to retreat or surrender. In the midst of the mayhem, Chamberlain is confronted by a pistol-wielding enemy at point-blank range, only to hear a "click" when the trigger is pulled. We now know, with the plucky colonel, that the fates are on his side this day. The skirmish is over quickly; the Union soldiers gather in their prisoners; and Chamberlain sees to his seriously wounded sergeant. In the calm aftermath of the fighting, we sense that the victorious soldiers feel more relief than elation at the success of a maneuver born of desperation.

Although not possessed of the psychological breadth or depth of his earlier response to the malcontents of the Second Maine Regiment, Chamberlain's split-second decision to swoop down the hill at the oncoming Confederate soldiers is similarly invigorating. On the brink of defeat, the men are ordered to charge – "left wing/right wheel." Instead of continuing to defend until all their resources, personnel, and firepower, give out, Chamberlain decides to throw everything into the fight (as the Confederate general Heth did not, when approaching Cemetery Ridge and Buford's troops). To paraphrase Ecclesiastes, there is a time to defend and a time to attack, a time to fight incrementally and a time for all-out assault. It takes a bit of phronesis to know which is which. Chamberlain perceives that their only chance is to overwhelm the enemy more by the outlandishness of the maneuver than by numbers. Shortly after the furious Maine surge, the Confederate forces are routed, with many surrendering.

Conclusion

The three episodes from *Gettysburg* that we have examined develop our understanding of practical wisdom, particularly the dramatic role imagination plays in good judgment. Chamberlain and Buford are successful because they channel their imaginative powers into pairs of narratives that facilitate their wise decision-making. First, they discern *appreciative* narratives that disclose the implications of their current situations, then they create *pragmatic* narratives to fruitfully guide their future action. Let's review each episode with this in mind. Chamberlain first organizes the experience of the disaffected soldiers in an appreciative narrative of their initial patriotism, undermined by fatigue, mistreatment, and animosity; he then offers the mutineers a scenario of mutual trust, camaraderie, and redemption.

For his strategy on the fields of Gettysburg, Buford unfurls a narrative of disaster as implicit in the enemy's unimpeded, advantageous entrenchment of troops. His alternative pragmatic scenario is based upon delay, followed by reinforced fighting from the strategically superior position. Finally, for Chamberlain under siege, he frames the predicament of his troops as a tale of attrition culminating in imminent collapse. He then puts into action the narrative of swooping, surprise attack. Imagining appreciative and pragmatic narratives enables both officers to interpret what is problematic in their situations and devise effective responses to it – whether it's rousing dispirited soldiers, fending off a far superior fighting force, or improvising ingeniously in the hurly-burly of full-pitched battle. The narrative of *Gettysburg* itself, then, illuminates practical wisdom by portraying its imaginative thrust as embedded in narrative enterprise. We thereby see how practical wisdom turns on imaginative invention, in hitting upon the best means to its valuable ends.

References

Aristotle (1962) *Nicomachean Ethics*, trans. M. Ostwald, Indianapolis: Bobbs-Merrill.

MacIntyre, A. (1981) *After Virtue*, Notre Dame, IN: University of Notre Dame Press.

Mullet, S. (1988) "Shifting Perspectives: A New Approach to Ethics," in L. Code, S. Mullet, and C. Overall (eds.) *Feminist Perspectives: Philosophical Essays on Method and Morals*, Toronto and Buffalo: University of Toronto Press.

Nussbaum, M. (1986) *The Fragility of Goodness*, Cambridge and New York: Cambridge University Press.

—— (1993) "Equity and Mercy," *Philosophy and Public Affairs* 22 (spring): 83–125.

Further reading

Stanley Godlovitch, "On Wisdom," in C. Sommers and F. Sommers (eds.) *Vice and Virtue in Everyday Life*, 2nd ed. (Orlando, FL: Harcourt Brace Jovanovich, 1993), is a good general introduction to the nature of wisdom and the intellectual strengths it includes. John Kekes, *Moral Wisdom and Good Lives* (Ithaca, NY: Cornell University Press, 1995), gives a detailed analysis of the contingencies and adversities faced by practical reason.

58

THE FIVE OBSTRUCTIONS

Mette Hjort

Released in 2003, to considerable critical acclaim, *The Five Obstructions* (*De fem benspænd*) is a coauthored avant-gardist work that has intrigued philosophers on account of its philosophical dimensions. *The Five Obstructions* began as an e-mail invitation, issued by Danish filmmaker Lars von Trier to his former teacher and mentor, the older, quite accomplished, yet far less well-known filmmaker, Jørgen Leth. The invitation, more specifically, was to participate in a cinematic game, with general parameters established in advance and further rules to be unilaterally produced by Trier (while interacting with Leth) in the course of the game. The general parameters dictated that Leth would remake his celebrated twelve-minute modernist nonfiction film from 1967, *The Perfect Human* (*Det perfekte menneske*) five times, following obstructive rules laid down by von Trier. The aim of the rules, it was clear from the start, would be to trip up and thwart Leth, as the term "obstruction" itself suggests. While von Trier's e-mail says nothing about the ultimate purpose of the proposed collaborative project (although it does envisage a scenario that would generate "the most fun"), Leth's positive response points to a rationale having to do with creativity:

> I can see an interesting development between film one and six, the route around the obstacles, the conversations, I'm sure we'll get a lot out of this. It is exciting. I look forward to your obstructions. I really like the idea of having to change, adjust, and reduce according to given conditions in the process. (DFI 2002: 31)

The idea of undertaking a collaborative project was first discussed by von Trier and Leth during the celebratory launch of a new Zentropa subsidiary devoted to nonfiction filmmaking, Zentropa Real. As is the case with many of von Trier's initiatives, the establishing of Zentropa Real in 2000 was marked by manifesto-like statements, in this case not only by von Trier himself, but also by Leth, Børge Høst, and Toger Seidenfaden. Von Trier's pronouncements introduce a concept of "defocus," the point being to learn how to set aside "simple patterns," "solutions chosen in advance," and routine "techniques" in order somehow to reach and rediscover life that has not, as the director puts it, been "drain[ed of] life" (DFI 2002). The thrust of von Trier's text, as was the case with the Dogme manifesto in 1995, is polemical, the target here being "journalists," and the media more generally, who "kneel before the altar of sharpness, draining life out of life in the process" (DFI 2002), an admittedly ambiguous phrase. Much as in the case of Dogme 95, where dominant conventions were opposed to authenticity and truth, the point seems to be to point to the distorting role of practices that have become the norm. While Leth recently claimed that von Trier's concept of "defocus" played no decisive role in the making of *The Five Obstructions*, the manifesto's insistence on a search for "something between fiction and fact" does in fact have a direct bearing on the collaborative film. As Leth himself admits, the aim throughout was to work "*exactly* on the border between fiction and non-fiction" (Hjort 2008a: 147). For present purposes, suffice it to note that *The Five Obstructions* is framed by manifesto-like statements inviting reflection on the nature of fiction and nonfiction filmmaking, which reflection is further supported by many of the features of the collaborative film itself. This aspect of the film has not been lost on film critics, with Mark Jenkins pointing out, for example, that *The Five Obstructions* "contains much film-theory perversity" (2004). As we shall see, *The Five Obstructions* is a work that *itself* explores thoughts about, and thus prompts critical thinking about, a remarkable number of aesthetic and cinematic issues, including creativity and its conditions of possibility, style, and authorship. I shall return to these and other issues in a moment, in the context of a survey of the philosophical analyses to which *The Five Obstructions* has given rise, to date.

A recurrent worry in discussions focusing on film's possible philosophical dimensions is the thought, attributed to an imaginary skeptic by Noël Carroll, that "the moving image trades in a single case, and one case is not enough to warrant the sort of general claims that are the stuff of philosophy" (2006: 175). One of the unique features of *The Five Obstructions* is that this film thwarts the single-case approach of much filmmaking and effectively creates the conditions under which an inductive, and philosophical, process of thinking can emerge. Let us look a little closer at the various elements that make up *The Five Obstructions*. In this film, for which von Trier and Leth are jointly credited as directors, the viewer sees a series of excerpts from Leth's original film; the remakes in full, each lasting about five minutes and referencing a particular segment of the original film; scenes documenting the interaction between von Trier and Leth, von Trier's assessment of Leth's remakes, and von Trier's formulation of the various obstructive rules; and scenes documenting Leth's making of the remakes. The obstructive rules, many of them unwittingly suggested by Leth's casual and initially trusting expression of preferences, are as follows:

- Obstruction 1: "12 frames; answers; Cuba; no set" – That is, Leth is to remake *The Perfect Human* in Cuba, and without a set; takes are to be limited to twelve frames; and the questions articulated in the original film's voice-over narration are to be answered.
- Obstruction 2: "The most miserable place; Don't show it; Jørgen Leth is the man;

the meal" – *The Perfect Human* is to be remade by Leth in a place that he considers truly miserable; the misery of the place cannot be shown; Leth is to play the role played by Claus Nissen in the original film; the focus of the remake is to be the scene in which a tuxedo-clad Nissen consumes a gourmet meal.

- Obstruction 3: "Back to Bombay or Free-style film" – Von Trier rules that Leth has failed to observe the strictures established by Obstruction 2. The disjunctive Obstruction 3 is imposed on Leth as a punishment. While giving the semblance of choice, Obstruction 3 in fact imposes a freestyle film, since Leth has clearly indicated to von Trier that he cannot possibly remake the film yet again in the red-light district of Bombay, his choice of "most miserable place."
- Obstruction 4: "Animation" – Leth is required to remake *The Perfect Human* as an animated film.
- Obstruction 5: "Lars von Trier will make the last obstruction. Jørgen Leth will be credited as director. Jørgen Leth will read a text written by Lars von Trier."

What we have in *The Five Obstructions*, then, is what Livingston (2008: 58–61) calls a nesting work, which itself comprises a series of nested or embedded "artistic structures." As Livingston points out, "artistic nesting can be either complete or partial," and in the case of *The Five Obstructions* both forms of nesting occur. That is, the viewer sees each of the remakes in its totality, whereas only parts of *The Perfect Human* are excerpted for display in the nesting work that is *The Five Obstructions*. That this nesting phenomenon generates a film that involves multiple rather than single cases is clearly suggested by Murray Smith's (2008) discussion of *The Five Obstructions* in terms of David Bordwell's concept of "parametric narration." As Smith points out, "parametric" is used by Bordwell to refer to films that "make the systematic attention to and variation of style a primary focus (a 'parameter' being any dimension of style – shot scale, editing rhythm, film score, for example – which can be systematically varied)" (Smith 2008: 122). Whereas Bordwell insists that parametric films have "banality" of theme as one of their enabling conditions, Smith contends that in *The Five Obstructions* the thematic focus on "the nature of art" is not so much rendered banal as familiar through the device of repetition. The payoff of this kind of parametric narration in the context of *The Five Obstructions* is clear:

> We can best appreciate the stylistic variations on the original enacted by each of the five remakes by both considering the various "parameters" of style that are varied, as well as by tracking some of the particular motifs that recur across two or more of the films. (Smith 2008: 123)

With regard to the link between philosophizing and *general* claims based on analysis of *multiple* cases, we note that *The Five Obstructions* is a film that presents five strikingly different remakes, as well as a number of excerpts from the original film, for consideration in connection with a series of issues belonging to the philosophical fields of aesthetics, philosophy of mind, ethics, and epistemology. Some of these issues are clearly identified by von Trier himself, while others are strongly suggested by the basic setup or choice of obstructions. Parametric narration, in this instance, yields something resembling the multiplicity of cases, and their comparison in relation to hypotheses and contentions on which philosophical thinking typically relies.

Given its philosophical nature, it is not surprising that *The Five Obstructions* should have generated considerable interest among professional philosophers and philosophically minded film scholars. The first volume in Wallflower's *Dekalog* series is devoted to *The Five Obstructions*. The volume includes prefatory background information about the collaborative work, an interview with Leth, and seven articles, all but one of them written by either professional philosophers or film scholars with philosophical expertise acquired through formal philosophical training and/or through sustained dialogue over the years with philosophical research. Together these articles build a case for seeing the von Trier/Leth film as making contributions relevant to the following general areas of, and topics in, philosophy:

- Moral psychology: second-person perspectives and their role in self-understanding.
- Ethics: the ethics of art.
- Aesthetics: creativity under constraint; style; authorship; games and art; the role of nested works; the nature of authorship in the context of collaborative works with a nesting dimension; definitions of fiction/nonfiction.
- Epistemology: paradigms for thought.

The strongest claim made for *The Five Obstructions qua* philosophical work is made by moral philosopher Susan Dwyer (2008: 3), who identifies some of the difficulties involved in communicating what she calls "second-person perspectives," in order to argue "for the particular utility of filmic representation as a mode for such communication." There is a clear suggestion here that the specificity of filmic representation is such that films have the capacity to provide insights into the role of second-person perspectives that may be hard to arrive at by other means. In the context, then, of this particular issue in moral psychology, the role accorded to film goes beyond illustration and heuristics, evoking instead the activity of actually philosophizing through film.

But what exactly does Dwyer mean by second-person perspectives, why are they important, and how does *The Five Obstructions* engage with this particular issue in moral psychology? Dwyer begins by evoking the accepted view that human beings are both capable of introspection and are social beings, and goes on to draw out some of the implications of this for the nature of the self and self-consciousness. Her argument is that "an individual's self-understanding depends on the availability to that person of a genuinely second-person perspective on herself" (Dwyer 2008: 1). Put differently, to achieve self-understanding it is necessary to see oneself through the eyes of another person. What is more, the "other" person must stand in a certain relation to the individual seeking a deeper self-understanding. That is, if there is no identifiable relationship involving a substantial social bond – friendship, for example – then any perspective on the other generated through interaction qualifies only as "third personal," and this is not the kind of perspective that deepens self-understanding. Now, as Dwyer points out, second-person perspectives can be communicated verbally, as would be the case if von Trier, as Leth's friend and colleague, were to *tell* him things about himself that he has somehow managed to overlook. Yet, second-person perspectives are far more powerful and far more likely to bring about self-understanding, claims Dwyer, if they involve *showing* rather than mere *telling*. And this is where *The Five Obstructions* comes into the picture. *The Five Obstructions* stages a competitive game inscribed within a larger collaborative framework; it involves two individuals whose relationship is defined by friendship, respect, and trust; and inasmuch as the game consistently places Leth in situations that challenge his preferred self-understandings, one of its effects is to reveal him to himself. In Dwyer's view, this process of revelation counts as "second personal" rather than "third personal" because it ultimately flows from the kind of intimate and sympathetic understanding of the "other" that is made possible by a strong and mutually recognized social bond. Dwyer argues that Obstruction 2 is particularly important, inasmuch as the rule imposing a remake in the most miserable place imaginable confronts Leth with the rabidly third-person (or distanced and disengaged) perspective characterizing much of his work as a documentary filmmaker. What Leth learns, claims Dwyer, is one of two things: "that he is fully capable of exploiting the suffering of real persons in the service of what he himself says is just a 'game', or … that his view of himself as a sublimely cool observer is not in fact correct" (2008: 10–11). Dwyer's main point, then, is that:

> *The Five Obstructions* can be read as a sustained exercise about what we can learn – perhaps can *only* learn – from representations of ourselves produced by others. Von Trier succeeds, because Leth can trust the representation. It is *co*-produced, in a medium that is a common passion between them, and in the context of a palpably affectionate relationship. (Dwyer 2008: 6)

That selfhood is indeed an important feature of *The Five Obstructions*' philosophizing is also suggested by Hector Rodriguez (2008) and Smith (2008). In his "Constraint, Cruelty, and Conversation," Rodriguez evokes games involving a certain "display of the self" and designed "to put friendship, love, trust, confession, suspicion, betrayal and other aspects of *intimacy* and *self-disclosure* into play" (Rodriguez 2008: 46). And in "Funny Games," Smith notes that *The Five Obstructions* "functions as a means of argument within a serious dispute about the ethics of art, and the nature of self-knowledge" (Smith 2008: 135).

Style, as the references to parametric narration above indicate, is another key topic that is probingly explored in *The Five Obstructions*. This issue provides the focus for "Style and Creativity in the Cinema: The Case of *The Five Obstructions*" (Hjort 2008b), a discussion of the film drawing on the philosophical literature on style, creativity under constraint, and creativity. The claim is that the von Trier/Leth film takes seriously the idea, proposed by the aesthetician Richard Wollheim, that artists can suffer "a loss of style" (1979: 144). It is further argued that *The Five Obstructions* should be viewed as both *modeling* and *executing* an ingenious solution to this problem, which is not merely an individual but also a social problem in small-nation contexts, where every talented figure has collective value. Whereas the discussions of style in film studies tend to focus on regularities and discernible features, *The Five Obstructions* can be seen to adopt a deeper perspective, one that accords with the following insightful remarks by Wollheim:

> Some stylistic features may be such that they can be detected in a given work only with great difficulty. Stylistic features need not be obviously present when they are present, and the possibility should always be entertained that there will be some stylistic features that, so far from acting as clues to authorship, can be detected only once authorship has already and independently been established. (1979: 143)

The argument is that Leth is perceived by von Trier as having suffered a loss of style, a problem to which the creativity fostered by imposed constraints formulated by a knowing and sympathetic colleague provides a potential solution. More specifically, the experimental stance governing Leth's original and genuinely creative individual style appears to be viewed by the younger filmmaker as having been eroded over the years by a tendency to rely on style as mere manner or habit. The result of an increasingly routinized execution of a set of preferred protocols is an oeuvre with easily discernible regularities that function in the manner of a signature. Leth himself is lucid about the nature of these regularities, and has provided style descriptions of his own work that foreground the following: the long-take approach and (to use Dwyer's term) the third-person perspective that it supports; jarring relations between word and image; and strategies of defamiliarization (Hjort 2000). Many of the obstructive rules that von Trier imposes on Leth are designed to thwart the latter's artistic habits and routines, and thus to effectuate the transformation of conceptual space that philosopher Margaret A. Boden (1994, 2004) identifies as a necessary condition for genuine creativity.

As a solution to the problem of loss of style, *The Five Obstructions* can be said to succeed, for the remakes that Leth produces all register as innovative, partly, as we shall see, as a result of the nesting structure of the overall work. The success of von Trier's "therapeutic" "help Jørgen Leth project" (these are terms used by the obstructer himself) hinges to a significant extent on the two filmmakers' sophisticated understanding of what has become known in the philosophical literature as "creativity under constraint." As used by the Norwegian philosopher Jon Elster (1992, 2000), "creativity under constraint" refers to the idea that creativity can be stimulated by constraints that may be imposed, invented, or chosen. In the case of *The Five Obstructions*, we note, the constraints (or rules) are both invented (by von Trier) and imposed (inasmuch as Leth has no say in the matter). Another important feature of von Trier's therapeutic treatment for Leth's problem of style as manner has to do with the temporal horizon opened up by a general framework requiring *multiple* remakes. Von Trier makes reference in *The Five Obstructions* to Leth's bouts of depression, and as someone who has himself fought depression for years, he can be assumed to have been intensely aware of the impact of Leth's depressive tendencies on his ability to create. By requiring five remakes, the ground rules governing *The Five Obstructions* establish a context for prolonged interaction with a highly respected and motivating colleague who expects a sustained commitment to a series of creative projects. The paralyzing effect of certain psychological conditions is effectively countered by ongoing, serial collaboration, while the iterative nature of the game creates the conditions under which habits can be definitively broken, rather than just temporarily bracketed.

In many ways *The Five Obstructions* provides a demonstration of the philosophical thesis that creativity finds a condition of possibility in constraint. Inasmuch as the constraints that are operative here take the form of rules, *The Five Obstructions* also has relevance for the influential body of philosophical work on rule-following (Goodman 1965; Kripke 2007). Skeptical arguments about rule-following have been explored in connection with another of von Trier's rule-governed initiatives, the Dogme 95 movement (Hjort 2003), but have yet to be taken up in relation to *The Five Obstructions*. That it would be relevant to do so is clear, given that some of the most charged exchanges between Leth and his taskmaster concern the question of what exactly follows from a given rule and what is to count as a successful instance of rule-following. In this particular instance, the likely result of creating a dialogue between the film and relevant philosophical writings would be the discovery, as in the case of Dogme, of the filmmakers' philosophical naïveté about the complexities of rule-following and the cogency of various skeptical arguments.

"Gift" is a term frequently used by von Trier as he explains what he ultimately expects of Leth, or comments on the effect that a given rule had on Leth's cinematic practice (Hjort 2006). Von Trier is someone who time and again has used collaborative strategies involving gifts of reputation and talent as milieu-developing devices within the small-nation context of Denmark (Hjort 2007). In *The Five Obstructions* we see a concept of gift culture put to work in connection with an artistic crisis that can, as the film proves, be resolved. While philosophers have identified artistic problems such as loss of style, they have had little to say about how these problems might be dealt with, or about why it might be *socially* important to deal with them in the first place. In drawing attention to such issues, *The Five Obstructions* can be seen as putting a neglected topic on the philosophical agenda, a contribution that supports a characterization of this film as an instance of actual philosophizing.

Livingston's analysis of the function of nesting in *The Five Obstructions* sheds additional light on the film's significance as a project designed ultimately to boost rather than obstruct Leth's career as a filmmaker. According to Livingston "the film co-directed by Trier and Leth is designed to engage the spectator directly and immediately with Leth's achievement" (2008: 61), and nesting is the device used to prepare a favorable context of reception for Leth's cinematic efforts. To make this point, Livingston contrasts a counterfactual situation in which Leth spontaneously undertakes to make the very same remakes that we see in *The Five Obstructions* with the actual situation in which Leth's remakes are responses to von Trier's dictates. The "strong contextualist thesis" for which Livingston argues involves the conjunction of two ideas, "namely, the claim that the context not only makes a difference to the qualities of the embedded works, but ... makes them better" (Livingston 2008: 62). Focusing on Obstruction 1, *The Perfect Human, Cuba*, Livingston contrasts viewers' actual responses to Leth's nested, and thus contextualized, remakes with the likely effect of an identical film presented as a Leth-only initiative. Let me provide one example of the kind of divergence that Livingston's thought experiment brings to light:

> Looped or repeated shots constitute an ingenious way of obeying the rule while thwarting its limitations, allowing rhythmic editing with short and "longer" shots constructed through iteration of relatively static shots not longer than 12 frames ... [*The Perfect Human, Cuba*, in *The Five Obstructions*]

> Gimmicky. If the film-maker wants to use some longer shots to generate rhythm and to allow the observation of some apparently longer gestures, why imitate such shots through iterative construction alone? [*The Perfect Human, Cuba*, without the nesting framework of *The Five Obstructions*] (Livingston 2008: 64)

Livingston seems right to suggest that *The Perfect Human, Cuba*, would have seemed "irritating," "gimmicky," "superficial," and even "crude," had it been presented to viewers without the validating and valorizing context that von Trier's cinematic game effectively provides. Much like Dwyer, who attributes particular significance to Obstruction 2, *The Perfect Human, Bombay*, Livingston contends that the strong contextualist thesis is easiest to make with regard to this particular remake:

> It is one thing for Leth courageously to take up Trier's challenge and with some reluctance accept the task of staging the formal dinner in a setting of abject poverty and exploitation; it would be something different, and arguably far worse, had he spontaneously taken the initiative to film a staging of a whimsical ceremony of irrelevant gestures and bourgeois dining in such a context. (Livingston 2008: 62–3)

In sum, the overarching nesting work creates a "favourable context of reception" for Leth's remakes, in part because the invented, imposed constraints that get articulated and debated within that larger context set parameters for the nested works' evaluation by viewers.

I have been making reference throughout to *The Five Obstructions* as a kind of cinematic game, and this is a theme that is explored in great detail by both Hector Rodriguez (2008) and Trevor Ponech (2008), both of whom draw on Roger Caillois' influential *Man, Play, and Games* (1961) to make their points. Ponech makes a case for seeing *The Five Obstructions* as an "asymmetrically played agonistic game" that is "played in the spirit of cinéma vérité," with all of the latter's emphases on participation, provocation, and truth-seeking (Ponech 2008: 76). Referring to Jean Rouch and Edgar Morin's classic vérité work, *Chronicle of a Summer* (*Chronique d'un été*) (1961) Ponech shows that when it comes to "human realities" truth-seeking may involve elements of fictionalization. By construing *The Five Obstructions* as a cinéma vérité game, Ponech can shed light on the work's complex dynamics among various fictional and nonfictional elements. Ponech's approach also has the advantage of making sense of the last obstruction, which, as Smith (2008: 122) cogently puts it, amounts to "all rules and no play" for Leth. Referring to the critical and reflexive dimensions of *Chronicle of a Summer*, Ponech (2008: 88) provides a convincing description of Obstruction 5 as von Trier's "self-chastening ... moment of autocritique."

Rodriguez's discussion of *The Five Obstructions* is wide ranging and includes thoughtful reflections on the role and nature of constraints in art-making. With regard to *The Five Obstructions qua* cinematic game, Rodriguez aims to show that this particular film involves the kind of "receptivity and openness to the outside" that is a feature of a properly ludic approach to filmmaking. Rodriguez rightly attributes to von Trier the view that filmmaking should "extend the authors' and also the viewers' way of thinking and perceiving, leading beyond ordinary frames of expectation towards the new, the unseen, the unthought," and he goes on to endorse this approach as "the only model of filmmaking ... worth pursuing and celebrating" (2008: 40). According to Rodriguez "*The Five Obstructions* provides a model for creativity as ludic action" and ultimately expresses "an image of thought, a paradigm of what it means to think." Inasmuch as the film "tackles the possibility of thinking thoughts that defy clear-cut categorisation," its philosophical relevance is clear. As Rodriguez (2008: 55) puts it, "The making of *The Five Obstructions* is a work of thinking as problematising."

Acknowledgments

The work described in this paper was partially supported by a grant from the Research Grants Council of the Hong Kong Special Administrative Region, China (Project No. LU340407). I am very grateful for this support.

See also Dogme 95 (Chapter 44) and Documentary (Chapter 45).

References

Boden, M. (1994) "What Is Creativity," in M. Boden (ed.) *Dimensions of Creativity*, Cambridge, MA: MIT Press.

—— (2004) *The Creative Mind: Myths and Mechanisms*, 2nd ed., London and New York: Routledge.

Carroll, N. (2006) "Philosophizing through the Moving Image: The Case of *Serene Velocity*," *Journal of Aesthetics and Art Criticism* 64: 173–85.

DFI (Danish Film Institute) (2002) *Film* (special issue, Leth).

Dwyer, S. (2008) "Romancing the Dane," in M. Hjort (ed.) *Dekalog 1: On The Five Obstructions*, London: Wallflower Press.

Elster, J. (1992) "Conventions, Creativity, Originality," in M. Hjort (ed.) *Rules and Conventions: Literature, Philosophy, Social Theory*, Baltimore, MD: Johns Hopkins University Press.

—— (2000) *Ulysses Unbound: Studies in Rationality, Precommitment, and Constraints*, Cambridge and New York: Cambridge University Press.

Goodman, N. (1965) *Fact, Fiction, and Forecast*, 2nd ed., Indianapolis: Bobbs-Merrill.

Hjort, M. (2000) "Interview with Jørgen Leth," in M. Hjort and I. Bondebjerg (eds.) *The Danish Directors: Dialogues on a Contemporary National Cinema*, Bristol, UK; Portland, OR: Intellect Press.

—— (2003) "A Small Nation's Response to Globalisation," in M. Hjort and S. MacKenzie (eds.) *Purity and Provocation: Dogma 95*, London: British Film Institute.

—— (2006) "Gifts, Games, and Cheek: Counter-Globalisation in a Privileged Small-Nation Context: The Case of *The Five Obstructions*," in C. Thomson (ed.) *Northern Constellations: New Readings in Nordic Cinema*, Norwich, UK: Norvik Press.

—— (2007) "Denmark," in M. Hjort and D. Petrie (eds.) *The Cinema of Small Nations*, Edinburgh: Edinburgh University Press.

—— (2008a) "Interview with Jørgen Leth," in M. Hjort (ed.) *Dekalog 1: On* The Five Obstructions, London: Wallflower Press.

—— (2008b) "Style and Creativity in the Cinema: The Case of *The Five Obstructions*," in M. Hjort (ed.) *Dekalog 1: On* The Five Obstructions, London: Wallflower Press.

Jenkins, M. (2004) "Five Obstructions: Filmmaker Faceoff," *The Washington Post* (26 March). Available at http://www.washingtonpost.com/wp-dyn/articles/A24183-2004Mar25.html.

Kripke, S. (2007) *Wittgenstein on Rules and Private Language: An Elementary Exposition*, Cambridge, MA: Harvard University Press.

Livingston, P. (2008) "Artistic Nesting in *The Five Obstructions*," in M. Hjort (ed.) *Dekalog 1: On* The Five Obstructions, London: Wallflower Press.

Ponech, T. (2008) "Work and Play," in M. Hjort (ed.) *Dekalog 1: On* The Five Obstructions, London: Wallflower Press.

Rodriguez, H. (2008) "Constraint, Cruelty, and Conversation," in M. Hjort (ed.) *Dekalog 1: On* The Five Obstructions, London: Wallflower Press.

Smith, M. (2008) "Funny Games," in M. Hjort (ed.) *Dekalog 1: On* The Five Obstructions, London: Wallflower Press.

Wollheim, R. (1979) "Pictorial Style: Two Views," in B. Lang (ed.) *The Concept of Style*, Philadelphia: University of Pennsylvania Press.

59
GATTACA
Neven Sesardic

Imagine that you are on an intercontinental flight and that immediately after takeoff the pilot makes the following announcement:

> Dear passengers, I hope you will join me in celebrating a wonderful achievement of one of our navigators. His name is Vincent. Vincent's childhood dream was to become an airplane navigator but unfortunately he was declared unfit for the job because of his serious heart condition. True, he does occasionally have symptoms of heart disease, like shortness of breath and chest pain, yet he is certainly not the kind of person to be deterred from pursuing his dream so easily. Being quite convinced that he is up to the task and that everything would be fine Vincent decided to falsify his medical records. And indeed, with the clean bill of health readily forged and attached to his application, he smoothly managed to get the plum job and is very proud to take care of your safety today. Can we please get some applause for Vincent's accomplishment and perseverance in the face of adversity? And, by the way, keep your seat belts tightly fastened during the entire flight.

I somehow doubt that in such a situation you would clap enthusiastically, or that you would vote for Vincent as the airline employee of the month. I bet that, on the contrary, you would be outraged that he used deception and irresponsibly put other people's lives at risk to achieve his selfish goal. But why then do we react so differently when we are confronted with that other Vincent, the main character in the movie *Gattaca* (1997), who basically does the same thing? Why do we admire him? I will try to show that this is all the work of silver screen magic. The remainder of this essay will provide a detailed explanation of how this illusion of heroism has been produced. But just to pique your curiosity, let me just briefly describe the main trick that the Hollywood wizards pulled on us here. They first dramatized things by building into their science-fiction scenario some very strong assumptions about the power of genetic predictions, but later they did everything to suppress the awareness of clear logical implications of these very assumptions.

A triumph of recklessness?

The film *Gattaca* pictures a bleak future world in which members of the genetic underclass (the so-called invalids) are left with no good life prospects because their bad DNA profiles immediately disqualify them from all desirable careers. Vincent (Ethan Hawke) is one of the invalids. But instead of accepting his second-class status, he decides to fight the system. So he goes on to impersonate Jerome Morrow (Jude Law), a man with a superior genotype who became a paraplegic after a failed suicide attempt. By surreptitiously presenting Jerome's urine, blood, and other biological material as his own, Vincent creates a false genetic identity and in this way succeeds in becoming a navigator in a highly competitive astronaut team that Gattaca (the prestigious Aerospace Corporation) is sending on a one-year mission to Saturn's satellite, Titan.

In the last scene, we see Vincent entering the spaceship, apparently his crowning achievement and a triumph. But a triumph of what exactly? The admirable strength and invincibility of human spirit? Or inexcusable recklessness? The second possibility does not loom large on first watching, but it asserts itself later and gains plausibility on reflection.

Everything in the movie turns on the role of scientific knowledge and on the reliability and correctness of those pessimistic predictions that geneticists derive from the invalid people's DNA information. An important thing to notice here is that these predictions can be neither too strong nor too weak, for otherwise the whole point of the story will be destroyed.

On one hand, if predictions are too precise and too strict (e.g., "Vincent will surely suffer a fatal heart attack if he goes through all physical efforts involved in astronaut training"), then the truth of this prediction would simply leave no room for any heroic accomplishment. Interestingly, there is an unfortunate exaggeration in this direction in the movie's opening, when Vincent talks about his birth and says that "only seconds old, the exact time and cause of my death was already known." But of course if such a detailed knowledge had been already available at the time of his birth then it would have been simply foolish of him to engage in long-term life plans conflicting with this inevitable future.

On the other hand, if dire predictions are expressed in terms of vague probabilities (e.g., "Vincent will increase the likelihood of suffering a fatal heart attack if he goes through all physical efforts involved in astronaut training"), this will chip away from the heroism of his decision because now it will start to look as if the challenge was not really so formidable and that taking such a risk was almost part of "life as usual."

Moreover, it becomes very difficult to find an interpretation that will strike the right balance and that will resolve the tension in such a way that the film narrative continues to make sense. The assumption on which the whole plot is based is the advanced knowledge of the science of genetics, with its highly precise and reliable predictions about life, especially those based on people's health limitations. It is against this very background that Vincent's efforts are being gauged and are thought to deserve our admiration. Therefore the statistical estimates issued by genetic experts have to be true; otherwise, there is simply no story to tell. For if, say, scientists got things terribly wrong with their gene-based anticipations, then it would follow that Vincent was not really facing any internal obstacles, and because of this "lack of resistance" his deeds would cease to be particularly praiseworthy. (Of course, he would still deserve praise for resisting quack science and its arbitrary restrictions, but any relevance for deeper philosophical issues involving genetic engineering, responsibility, and freedom would be destroyed.)

This completes the proof that in analyzing the movie the claims of the futuristic science should be accepted as basically correct. It should be stressed, however, that apart from the above-mentioned infelicitous descent into fatalism ("the exact time and cause of my death was already known"), elsewhere gloomy forecasts are wisely couched in probabilistic terms. And yet, even in such a weakened form, they continue to be at odds with Vincent's hero status.

An accidental hero

The DNA test conducted immediately after Vincent's birth brings the bad news about the high likelihood of several serious disorders. The geneticist who informs the worried parents is clearly most alarmed about the following: "Heart disorder: 99 percent probability. Early fatal potential."

Even subjectively Vincent has always been acutely aware of his precarious health. For instance, speaking about his childhood relation with his "valid" brother Anton, he says: "By the time we were playing at blood brothers *I understood that there was something very different flowing through my veins*, and I'd need an awful lot more than a drop [of my brother's blood] if I was going to get anywhere."

We also see later that even an ordinary and undemanding physical exercise is enough to push Vincent to a dangerous limit. Only twenty minutes of running on a treadmill at a fairly moderate pace made him collapse in the locker room and gasp for air after suffering a frightening cardiac arrhythmia.

So there are at least three different lines of evidence indicating that Vincent's health did present a serious obstacle to the achievement of his dream: (a) the reliable DNA-based forecast of a highly probable early death from a heart attack *if he lived a normal life* (needless to say, this probability must increase considerably under the extremely harsh conditions of astronaut training); (b) his subjective awareness of his own limitations; and (c) the evidence that just a regular visit to the gym with no extraordinary exertion was sufficient to put him in the vicinity of death.

Now what reason could Vincent offer that would offset these strong grounds for believing that his whole project should not have been undertaken? Indeed, are there any considerations that could justify his decision to disregard so completely all these transparent warning signs? And what if there are actually no such considerations?

In his recent book on ethics in the age of genetic engineering Michael Sandel makes an obvious and well-known point: "The more the athlete relies on drugs or genetic fixes, the less his performance represents his achievement" (Sandel 2007: 26). Yet the same point applies to situations in which the athlete relies not on drugs or genetic fixes but purely on brute luck, associated with an extremely low probability of success. Here, too, if things turn out well *only* through some weird quirk of improbability, the "success" of the athlete would *not* represent his achievement. Any genuine accomplishment must at least partly be the result of some authentic personal feature of the agent, and this means that it cannot be wholly attributed to fluke chance. (For example, if desperately wishing to produce a wonderful mathematical proof I randomly type on a keyboard, and if against all odds I indeed miraculously manage in this way to churn out a new and amazing mathematical demonstration, I would earn no respect from my mathematical colleagues.)

A truly accidental hero is not a hero.

How he did it

So why was Vincent not moved in the least by the above three considerations, which all strongly urged him to abandon his venture? Is there anything else that he put forward as his justification for pressing on so persistently? Actually, yes, but strikingly he could muster only one piece of evidence in defense of his behavior: the fact that after a consistent and humiliating series of defeats in a game of "chicken" that he played with his genetically superior brother, he eventually achieved a one-off victory.

They used to swim as far from the shore as they dared, and the point was to see who would get scared and turn back first. As they both expected, Vincent was always the loser – until one afternoon at the beach when, as he recounts, something was very different that day, and "finally the impossible happened." He won, and it was this event that gave him that badly needed self-confidence and encouraged him to leave home and undertake the hazardous mission: "It was one moment in our lives when my brother was not as strong as he believed, and I was not as weak. *It was the moment that made everything else possible.*"

But could this feat really justify Vincent's embarking on the project? It all depends, of course, on how the feat was accomplished. If it were caused by what Vincent took to be a reliable perception of his hidden abilities or stamina unrecognized by others, this could indeed constitute a rational basis for his defiance. But this is not at all the account that he offers himself. When toward the end of the movie the brothers play chicken once more and when the again defeated and shocked Anton just cannot understand how Vincent pulled it off, Vincent gives the following explanation: "You want to know how I did it? This is how I did it, Anton: *I never saved anything for the swim back.*"

Well, it is hard to imagine a clearer example of a reckless action. Vincent's behavior is in fact far more reckless than the notorious game "chickie run" made famous in *Rebel without a Cause* (1955). There, two teenagers simultaneously drive their cars with great speed toward a cliff, and the one who loses his nerve and jumps out of the car first is the loser (the "chicken"). Neither of the two boys wants to die, but the best strategy of winning is to make the other guy believe that you are totally crazy and that you don't really care whether you will be killed or not. Note that the essential part of this strategy is *advertising* your indifference to death (regardless of whether it is genuine or not), in the hope that you will convince your opponent of your irrationality and in this way leave him with no other reasonable option but to "chicken out." If you really want to play with fire and experiment with this kind of strategy, the most stupid thing you could do under the circumstances would be to *hide* your (real or faked) madness. For if you make no effort to reveal your foolhardiness in any way, your rival would be unaware of the dangerousness of the whole situation. Consequently his ignorance of the extreme risk he is facing could easily get both of you killed.

But come to think of it, this is exactly what Vincent did. Competing with Anton and desperately wishing to prevail, he decided to swim as far into the open sea as it took, completely unconcerned about whether either of them would have enough strength to return to the shore – *and without disclosing any of this plan to his brother beforehand!*

Nothing succeeds like success

Can Vincent perhaps be vindicated by the fact that the swimming episode had a happy ending after all? Similarly, does his success in going through all the hurdles in *Gattaca* ultimately justify his decision to undertake this risky enterprise? Not necessarily.

With this suggestion, that a moral agent could be redeemed by merely being fortunate enough to have his project end up well by pure happenstance, we enter the murky waters of the philosophical literature on moral luck. In an article that started off the whole debate, Bernard Williams makes a highly significant statement for our purposes while discussing a case of a man who had to make a momentous moral decision under the conditions of great uncertainty: "I want to explore and uphold the claim that in such a situation *the only thing that will justify his choice will be success itself*" (Williams 1981: 23; italics added).

This is obviously not an appropriate place to discuss this claim in general, but let me narrow the focus and try to show that it cannot apply to Vincent's case. There are situations in which the mere outcome of an action does appear to affect our moral evaluation of that action, even if everything else is kept constant. Agent A succeeds, while agent B fails, and although every relevant consideration appears to be the same in both cases, we nevertheless judge A more favorably than B. Is there any way to claim coherently and simultaneously (1) that our different moral evaluation of A's and B's actions is justified; (2) that the only visible difference between the two cases is that A succeeded and that B failed; and (3) that mere success or failure of an action *cannot* be a relevant reason for a moral appraisal of that action?

The three statements do look mutually inconsistent but they are not. What opens the way to their reconciliation is the so-called epistemic solution to the problem of moral luck. Several authors have defended that view, but a particularly elegant exposition is to be found in Rosebury (1995). This approach can help us get a better grip on the *Gattaca* story.

The main point of the epistemic solution is to treat success not as a morally significant feature in its own right but rather as just signaling the presence of another currently *unknown* feature, which *is* morally relevant. Typically we judge people's behavior in moral terms, despite having only imperfect knowledge about all relevant aspects. So the fact of success can sometimes be used for making a fallible yet legitimate inference about some of those features that at a given moment lie behind the veil of ignorance. For instance, if an avid but not terribly good golfer manages, astonishingly, to beat Tiger Woods on one occasion, we will probably ascribe a great deal of that upstage to luck, simply because the skill difference between these two players is clearly enormous and manifestly goes against the actual score. Nevertheless, many people will feel that despite the undeniable impact of luck they should now upgrade their initial estimate of the winner's golfing ability, and this solely on the basis of his success. More precisely, the upgrade seems to be motivated by the awareness of two things: first, that very little is known about how exactly this unexpected outcome came about; and second, that such an astonishing event becomes at least slightly less astonishing if the true skill of the unlikely winner is somewhat higher than we thought in the first place. In other words, luck yes, but the praise for the subject is also thrown in for good measure.

Fanaticism of the will

The epistemic solution works quite well to explain how in situations of imperfect knowledge the mere success of an action can sometimes be a basis for inferring praise-worthy characteristics of the agent, for which there was little prior evidence. But the problem with applying this kind of reasoning to Vincent's case is that we know *too much* about him. Admittedly, our knowledge is still imperfect, but the sheer bulk of information available, especially from his own point of view, leaves little room for finding much commendable about his actions.

Both from Vincent's conversations with his friends (Irene and Jerome) and from his comments on his own past behavior in voice-over we learn a lot about his goals, deliberations, and decision-making. Yet he *never* says anything about why he believes that he will actually be able to overcome the limitations inscribed in his double helix. His words contain much resentment, bitterness, as well as daydreaming about success, but not a single positive reason is ever provided that would ground his consistent optimism. Given that the DNA so ominously casts a dark shadow over his future, it appears that he must be aware of something that counterpoises these really gloomy genetic predictions. But what is it? Is it maybe Vincent's exclusive insight into some of his hidden strengths? Or could it be some specific piece of information assuring him that depressing and otherwise reliable statistical generalizations do not in fact apply to his particular case? Or is it perhaps the reliance on a particular promising strategy that in his opinion gives him a reasonable chance to beat the terrible odds against him? Or what?

The answer is, nothing. The truth is that Vincent is consumed by a powerful and desperate desire to succeed, but at the same time he has absolutely no clue about how he is going to come through. When asked by Jerome how he intends to pull this off, he responds, "I don't know exactly." It seems, to invert the well-known proverb, that there's a will but there's no way. What is at work here is an uncontrollable and self-destructive will that is not accompanied by a vision of any minimally recognizable path to the goal. We are witnessing the phenomenon that Heinrich Heine in another context called "fanaticism of will, restrained neither by fear nor by self-interest" (Heine 1986: 159).

Lucking out

The take-home message is that success that just *happens* to a person does not deserve admiration. It has to be *brought about* by that person, at least to a certain extent. We should resist the temptation to infer admirability automatically from mere goal achievement. This kind of attribution error is encouraged by folk wisdom, reflected, for instance, in proverbs like *Audaces fortuna iuvat* ("Fortune favors the bold"). It suggests that courage is somehow associated with lucky outcome, and if this is accepted then, by the symmetry of statistical correlation, a chance success would indeed increase the probability that the subject deserves praise. But of course folk wisdom about such matters should not be trusted, if for no other reason than that it is flatly incoherent. It is easy to find proverbs with an outright contradictory advice, like *Fortuna favet fatuis* ("Fortune favors the foolish") or *Fortuna saepe indignos favet* ("The more knave, the better luck").

Despite all this talk of good fortune and luck it is perhaps time now to deconstruct the illusion of a happy ending in the final scene of the movie. As Vincent enters the spaceship and literally reaches the point of no return, we are flooded by a pleasing feeling of closure and a warm glow of satisfaction and accomplishment. But isn't this slightly premature? After all, this is actually just the beginning of a mission that will last one whole year. And remember, Vincent's worrying genetic predispositions are not magically switched off at this point. He is still the same person, for whom the best science of the day continues to predict a very high probability of a fatal heart attack. In all likelihood he will not return alive from Titan.

What will other crew members think if this happens, especially if they then also learn about all the details of his elaborate web of deception? How will they react when they realize that they lost a navigator on this dangerous and meticulously planned journey in which everyone's contribution is of pivotal importance – and all that just because one seriously ill man thought that he was entitled to use all means possible to realize his childhood dream, cost what it may? Although it is not made clear in the film what employment opportunities (if any) remain open for "invalids," surely even under the worst-case scenario Vincent could have attempted to cheat his way into some other attractive job that would not have put many human lives, including his own, at such high risk.

Conclusion

After all this dissection and critical comment, the reader will probably think that I do not find *Gattaca* to be a very good movie. But this is not true at all. On the contrary, I watched it at least five or six times, and on each occasion I was impressed with its subtlety, good dialogue, excellent acting and a very efficient buildup of the plot. Especially gripping is the creation of that chilling and menacing atmosphere of pervasive control and suffocating alienation. Besides, there is this almost palpable sadness in the main character's voice-overs and the accompanying music that emotionally sways the viewer to identify with Vincent entirely and consequently see him as nothing but a hapless victim of genetic discrimination. There is no denying that this is a powerful and masterfully crafted movie.

Yet my point is that a great movie need not necessarily have a fully coherent message or be defensible at a different level of analysis when it is no longer approached as a work of art. Despite all its forcefulness during the two hours of watching, on later reflection the story gives rise to some questions that cannot be resolved in a satisfactory way. Worse still, the more we try to make sense of all the events in the film, the harder it becomes to preserve that feel-good and uplifting attitude that engulfs us in the last minutes while we are watching the credits.

It is certainly gratifying to be told that people can continue to pursue their dreams in the same way, even after they become aware of their serious genetic limitations. But already on a surface level this claim rings false. Probing deeper, and thinking through all the consequences of the imagined advanced scientific knowledge, reveals only further cracks and makes the behavior of the main character less understandable and less admirable. Contrary to what the movie is trying to tell us, a more detached analysis leads us back to the common-sense belief that a more detailed knowledge of our genetic predispositions would indeed severely narrow our choices. Were this kind of information massively available, it would be rational for many people to abandon their previous career plans and reconsider what to do with their lives. Moreover, with such dramatic developments of science the whole way we currently see ourselves would probably undergo a radical change.

There remains an outstanding issue, which cannot be fully addressed in this context but cannot be completely ignored either. It is the relation between artistic and epistemic merit. A reader objected, "Isn't the epistemic foible also an artistic demerit? Wouldn't a basic inconsistency in a movie's thematic structure detract from its merit? Indeed, could there really be a philosophically incoherent masterpiece?"

I might actually concede that there will be an artistic loss connected with this type of logical incongruity. Perhaps it is true that there must be something artistically deficient in any such ineptly concocted story that consists of mutually incompatible fragments that just cannot make sense all together. And yet despite this inevitable artistic loss it is possible that in some cases, even after the "subtraction" of points for defects of logic, enough of aesthetic value will be preserved in the end and that, therefore, the piece will nevertheless qualify as great art. A masterpiece it may not be, but there is no principled reason why such a partially flawed film wouldn't still be regarded as powerful, gripping, and pleasing.

I hope that this defense clears a way for my somewhat odd advice to those who have not yet seen *Gattaca*: by all means rent it and enjoy this beautiful movie, but don't take it too seriously.

Acknowledgments

I would like to thank Steffen Huck, Paisley Livingston, and Carl Plantinga for useful comments on the first draft.

References

Heine, H. (1986) *Religion and Philosophy in Germany: A Fragment*, trans. J. Snodgrass, Albany, NY: State University of New York Press.

Rosebury, B. (1995) "Moral Responsibility and 'Moral Luck'," *Philosophical Review* 104: 499–524.

Sandel, M. J. (2007) *The Case Against Perfection: Ethics in the Age of Genetic Engineering*, Cambridge, MA: Belknap Press of Harvard University Press.

Williams, B. (1981) *Moral Luck: Philosophical Papers 1973–1980*, Cambridge and New York: Cambridge University Press.

60
MEMENTO
Andrew Kania

The sleeper hit *Memento* (2000), directed by Christopher Nolan, is a brilliantly structured contemporary film noir, focused through the main character, Leonard Shelby (Guy Pearce), who has a debilitating memory condition. Hit on the head during a home invasion – "the incident" – Leonard can remember his life as an insurance-claims investigator before the incident, but he cannot form new long-term memories. Thus, every fifteen minutes or so, he becomes a partial *tabula rasa* afresh. The audience comes to understand this condition through Leonard's recounting the story of Sammy Jankis (Stephen Tobolowsky) in order to explain his own condition to others and to himself. (Sammy, who suffers from a similar condition, was the subject of one of Leonard's pre-incident investigations.) One of the main narrative drives of the movie is Leonard's quest to find "John G" – the mysterious second assailant in the incident, who supposedly raped and murdered Leonard's wife – and to exact his revenge by killing him.

Nolan's stroke of genius, and initially the most striking feature of the film, is its structure, which places the audience in much the same epistemic position as Leonard, and contributes strongly to our identification and empathy with him. The majority of the film consists of scenes of about five minutes, presented in reverse chronological order. Thus, with each scene, we are thrown *in medias res*, and only at the end of the *next* scene does the action get put into context, as we come to understand the events that led up to it. Thus, unlike in most films, we are constantly witnessing events without knowing what has happened earlier. Of course, this means that, unlike Leonard, we soon know some things that will happen *later* than the fictional events now unfolding.

Memento's structure is more complicated even than this, though. The film contains forty-four scenes and covers a period of approximately thirty-six hours in the fictional world. (When I talk about the fictional world represented in the film, I will talk about "fictional time" and the "fictional world." When I am talking about the film itself, the representation or artwork, I will talk about "film time" and "the film." Thus, in *Memento*, though breakfast precedes lunch in the fictional world, lunch might well precede breakfast in the film. This distinction has various labels in narrative theory. Rough synonyms for what I call "the fictional world" include "story," *histoire*, and *fabula*, while what I call "the film" also goes by the general names of "discourse," "plot," *récit*, and *syuzhet*.) Twenty-one of the scenes are relatively short (averaging less than one minute) and shot in black and white. Their chronological order is the same in the film and the fictional world; that is, anything you see in a black-and-white scene fictionally occurs after anything else you have already seen in a black-and-white scene in the film (ignoring flashbacks). These scenes cover the first, much shorter period of fictional time covered in the movie (perhaps an hour or two). Twenty-one of the scenes are longer and shot in color. The fictional events they represent all occur after those of the black-and-white scenes, yet in the film they occur in reverse fictional chronological order and are interleaved with the black-and-white scenes. Labeling the black-and-white scenes 1–21, and the color scenes B–V, the fictional chronology can be represented as follows (Klein 2001a):

$$1, 2, 3, \ldots, 19, 20, 21, 22/A, B, C, D, \ldots, T, U, V, \Omega,$$

while the order of scenes in the movie runs as follows:

$$\Omega, 1, V, 2, U, 3, T, \ldots, 20, C, 21, B, 22/A.$$

There are two scenes in the above sequence that I have not yet discussed. 22/A is a pivotal scene, right in the *middle* of the fictional events, as divided into scenes (though quite *early* in the fictional time covered by the movie, since the black-and-white scenes are so short), and at the very *end* of the film. As its name suggests, scene 22/A begins in black and white and unobtrusively fades into color partway through, as one of Leonard's Polaroids develops (1:39:36–42). (I make a few references to the film by time elapsed in hours:minutes:seconds.) Scene Ω is another unique scene, the last fictional event represented, but the first scene in the movie – the credit sequence, in fact – which alerts the viewer to the "backward" structure of the movie. It is shot in color, and, unlike any other scene in the movie, it is actually shot in reverse; that is, fictional time is represented as flowing backward during this first (film time) and last (fictional time) scene. Blood oozes up walls, a pair of eyeglasses begins to tremble before flying up onto someone's face, and a bullet flies back into a gun, pulling the victim's brains back into his skull.

Memento as neo-noir

This structure, together with the lighting of the black-and-white scenes, Leonard's intermittent voice-over, the sleazy locations, sordid events, and so on, places *Memento* firmly within the category of "neo-noir" – films that draw heavily on elements of the classic film noirs of the 1940s and '50s. One classic film noir structure is the extended flashback: the film begins with the protagonist in some sorry state, followed by a flashback that comprises the rest of the film, showing how this came to pass. Through the protagonist's memories, the audience is introduced to characters who turn out to be quite other than they seemed at first, and the perpetrator of a central crime (legal, moral, amorous, or otherwise; often all three) is revealed (e.g., *Detour* [1945],

Double Indemnity [1944], and *Murder, My Sweet* [1944]). Literally every second scene of *Memento* is a microcosm of this classic structure. But there are idiosyncrasies in how the structure is fleshed out in *Memento* that amount to a reconsideration of some recurrent film noir themes.

First, the protagonist of a classic film noir has typically learned something important through his travails, even if it has cost him his peace of mind, livelihood, or even life. By contrast, it is not clear that Leonard is capable of learning anything of the sort. This is in part due to his condition, but the constant parallels drawn between Leonard's condition and the epistemic position we all inhabit perhaps imply a vision of our potential for enlightenment even more pessimistic than that of traditional film noir.

Second, there is typically a central betrayal of the protagonist, or a series of such betrayals. In *Memento* the protagonist is betrayed *by himself*, fooled into thinking that Teddy (Joe Pantoliano) is John G. One might say this metaphorically of traditional noir protagonists (betrayed by their hubris, for instance), but in *Memento* the self-betrayal is more literal (though see the discussion of personal identity, below, regarding the coherence of this claim). Together with the structure, which leads us to identify very strongly with Leonard, this confuses our emotional responses to Leonard. On the one hand, we sympathize with him as the betrayed vulnerable protagonist; on the other, we detest him as the betrayer. Thus there is an intensification of the usual ambiguity we feel toward noir protagonists.

Third, Natalie (Carrie-Anne Moss) seems to be the film's femme fatale, and most first-time viewers see her as a cold, self-seeking, manipulative character. She initiates a fight with Leonard by insulting his dead wife and manipulates him in order to escape her own dangerous situation. However, the structure of the film conceals that (i) she is in this situation only because of Leonard's actions, and knows it; (ii) she initiates the fight only to extricate herself from the situation; and (iii) she helps Leonard much more than is necessary to achieve her ends. In light of the fact that she has just learned that her partner is dead and that Leonard is somehow responsible for this, she is remarkably generous in offering him both her help in tracking down John G and a place to spend the night. (Though this place is her bed, it seems unlikely that Leonard and Natalie have sex, contrary to most people's initial inferences.)

Is *Memento* a film?

One of the reasons for *Memento*'s success is the challenge of simply figuring out what goes on in the film. Audiences went straight from theater to coffeehouse to try to answer the film's main narrative questions: Who is John G? Is Leonard Sammy Jankis? What is the true nature of his memory condition? Part of the difficulty of answering these questions is due to the film's confusing structure, but part of it is due to the underdetermination of the fictional facts by the movie. That is, the movie is ultimately ambiguous about some of these central questions, such as whether the tale Leonard recounts of Sammy Jankis is really about himself. Equally coherent and compelling interpretations provide mutually exclusive answers to these questions.

(For some consideration of different interpretations, see Klein 2001a, b; Zhu 2001; Mottram 2002: 21–77; and Duncker 2004.)

How coherent and compelling an interpretation is, though, depends on how much of the relevant data it accounts for. Like many recent movies, part of *Memento*'s release publicity was a website (http://www.otnemem.com/index.html). The website is even more enigmatic than the movie, since, of course, one of its prime functions was to intrigue people enough to buy a ticket to the film. But though the website was thus similar in function to the theatrical trailer, it was very different in one notable respect: the website provides a relatively large amount of new information about the fictional world – information that is not imparted, even implicitly, by the film. The main addition is the fictional truth that Leonard spent some time in a mental institution, beginning apparently nine months after the incident, and then escaped from it. There are fictional newspaper clippings, parts of psychological reports on Leonard from the institution, excerpts from Leonard's journal, and so on, all attesting to this additional piece of fictional information.

There is almost nothing in the movie itself to suggest that Leonard has spent time in a mental institution. There is a highly suggestive cut in one scene that shows Sammy Jankis in a mental institution. For a split second, Sammy is replaced by Leonard in the shot (1:29:56). But *throughout* the movie, parallels are being drawn between Sammy and Leonard. Without the additional materials from the website, an interpretation that claimed Leonard spent time in a mental institution following the incident – let alone that that time began long after the incident – would be unjustifiable. There is simply no information given in the movie about this fictional period. The action takes place over three days and two nights. Flashbacks and recollections of various characters give us information about two other periods: (1) the period before the incident, when Leonard was an insurance-claims investigator following Sammy's case; and (2) the night of the incident itself. (There are additionally a few short "projective" shots, which represent scenes Leonard is only imagining or entertaining.) The website gives information almost exclusively about the period between the incident and the "present" of the movie and, if taken into account, makes much more plausible the interpretation that there is in fact no Sammy Jankis as Leonard describes him, that Sammy's story is really a way Leonard (or some psychological part of him) has devised of representing parts of his past he cannot fully acknowledge. This has further ramifications for any interpretation of the film.

The question, then, is whether the information on the website has status equal to that of the contents of the film and must thus be taken into account in any interpretation of *Memento*. Of course, the website might reasonably be taken into account, even if it is *not* part of the artwork. Understanding any work of art requires more than simple sensory experience of it. However, two things should be noted. First, the website is unlike other background material (e.g., general knowledge of cinematic conventions, reviews of the film, even the short story on which the film is partly based) in that it seems to contribute to the content of the fictional world of the film. Second, whatever one's views on the relevance of background materials to the interpretation of a work, if the website material is *part of the work itself* it should surely play a more central role than if it were just background material.

There are good reasons to consider the possibility that the website material is part of the artwork we call *Memento*. First, the creation of the website was overseen by the director, who, for instance, seems to have removed some references to the date of Leonard's wife's death from earlier versions (Andy Klein, quoted in Zhu 2001). Second, in some interviews Nolan endorses the view that *Memento* is an extended artwork comprising website and film (Mottram 2002: 73). Third, not only is the website material included on all DVDs of the film but the limited edition DVD comes packaged as Leonard's file from the mental institution, and a psychological-test conceit governs its design. Even to get the movie to play, you need to select the right word from a selection of fifty formatted to look like a psychological test.

But there are also good reasons to reject the website material as part of *Memento*. For one thing, Nolan is inconsistent in how he regards the material. Sometimes he endorses it, but at other times he says that you can figure out what happens in the fictional world simply by watching the movie closely (Mottram 2002: 26). More importantly, though, there are reasons to think that an artist is not in sole control of the kind of thing she produces, especially in a popular mass art form such as narrative film. Theories of art interpretation tend to fall along a spectrum according to the extent to which they take the artist's intentions about the meaning of a work into account. Most fall somewhere between the extremes of simply equating the meaning of the work with whatever the artist intended and taking no account of the artist at all. However, when it comes to determining what kind of thing the artwork is (painting, symphony, etc.) most theorists, if not silent, are "actual intentionalists," claiming that the artist gets to determine what counts as the artwork, whatever their views on the implications of artists' intentions for interpretation (e.g., Levinson 1992: 232–3).

In most cases such a theory works well. After all, you do not get many painters insisting that the canvas in front of them is, literally, a string quartet. But it is the extraordinary cases that test a theory. If all educated audiences read some novel as a work of dark nihilism, for instance, it is difficult to defend a theory of interpretation according to which the novel's central theme is that love conquers all, simply because the author intended that reading. Cases like this suggest that an author's intentions only go so far in determining a work's meaning. Similarly, if all suitably backgrounded audiences take *Memento* to be simply a film, that is some evidence that it is and, by extension, that the kind of work an artist creates has to do with more than just the artist's intentions.

A theory that developed this idea might appeal to the social, public nature of art. One of the reasons that people work within a well-defined artistic category, such as painting, is that, due to a tradition of people producing objects of the same sort, and appreciating objects of that sort, there is a shared sense of what doing something with paint on a canvas amounts to. Such conventions often both provide an artistic language and restrict what an artist can meaningfully do (Davies 2003). In the twentieth century, avant-garde artists expanded the boundaries of art in such a way that, notoriously, now anything can be art. Philosophers have tended to focus on avant-garde and "high" art, but it may be that the popular mass arts, such as film, are more "conventional" in the sense that what is possible in an art gallery may not be possible in a cinema. Suppose, for instance, that Nolan insisted in a series of interviews that *Memento* was not just a film, but a film and a small pile of wood shavings in his garden shed. Though it would certainly be possible for an avant-garde artist to produce such a work for the avant-guarde art world, it is not obvious that Nolan can do so, given the overwhelming evidence that he is working within the tradition of popular narrative film.

Philosophical themes in *Memento*

Whatever the ontological nature of *Memento*, it does not contribute to any philosophical debate about the ontology of art, except by being an interesting *example* – part of the domain of inquiry. There has been some debate about whether, how, and the extent to which films can "do philosophy" (e.g., Livingston 2006; Wartenberg 2006; and Smith 2006). I tend to be sympathetic to Livingston's and Wartenberg's moderate views that some films can be insightful and useful pedagogical and heuristic illustrations of philosophical issues and theories. *Memento* is remarkable for the number of philosophical issues it raises. Unfortunately there is only space here to indicate some of those issues briefly. (I give few references in the text below; I refer the reader instead to the list of further reading at the end of this chapter.)

Mind and memory

Something that is very important to Leonard about Sammy Jankis' condition is that it is "mental" rather than "physical." Assuming, as is the majority view in contemporary philosophy of mind, that one's mind is, in some sense, simply one's brain – a physical organ – does this distinction amount to anything? That it does can be illustrated by the fact that exactly how to spell out the sense in which the mind is the brain is still a matter of much debate. This is not the place to recapitulate that debate. One way to think about it in connection with the distinction Leonard draws, however, is to think about the way the mind *represents* things. For instance, when you think about your mother, something in your head represents your mother in some way, just as her name written in your address book represents her in some way. Moreover, the representational system of your mind must be highly systematic, so that you can use your "mother representation" in thinking about different aspects of your mother, other people's mothers, and so on. How physical things can ultimately "be about" other things is one of the deepest mysteries about the mind, the problem of "intentionality." Taking intentionality for granted, though, we can consider two kinds of ways a mind or brain can malfunction. There are brute physical defects, such as those caused by massive physical trauma, like being hit in the head with a sap. Such an injury might simply stop your mind from functioning at all. But it might stop only part of your mind from functioning, such as your ability to read, to recognize familiar objects, or to form new long-term memories, particularly if such functions are localized in one part of the brain. Another kind of problem involves the representational content of your mind. For instance, some psychologists believe that in the face of horrific events, people sometimes involuntarily repress their memories of those events. The mechanism responsible for such repression would have to be sensitive to the representational content of whatever encodes the memory in the brain in order to repress *only* the memories of the horrific event.

This distinction allows us to think more closely about two aspects of *Memento*. First, it makes sense of the mental/physical distinction that Leonard and the insurance company he represents appeal to in considering Sammy's case. Second, it gives us one way to explain apparent inconsistencies in certain interpretations of the film. At first, it seems that the explanation Teddy gives of Leonard's situation in the final scene – namely, that the story Leonard tells about Sammy is really about himself – cannot be correct. If it were, Leonard would remember that his wife was diabetic, as she would have been diabetic prior to the incident. This assumes, though, that Leonard's condition is as he describes it throughout the film – a "physical" condition brought about by being hit on the head during the incident. If, rather, Leonard is repressing memories, his memories from before the incident may not be as reliable as he claims. This interpretation makes sense of some puzzling aspects of the film, such as the fact that none of Leonard's memories of his wife is happy. He even says twice that his wife called him "Lenny" and he hated it (0:17:43–52, 1:11:37–46). But it raises further questions, such as what his psychological condition was between the incident and his killing his wife, and how this could cohere with the repression of his memories of killing her.

Whatever the true nature of Leonard's condition, it is thankfully one not many of us suffer from, though our relief at this fact reminds us how much we rely on memory to make it through our everyday lives. However, Leonard claims that his "system" allows him to deal with his condition, often implying it is superior to ordinary memory, at least for certain purposes, such as his detective work. This is due in part to the alleged unreliability of memory, as opposed to other forms of evidence, such as Leonard's photographs and notes. There has been surprisingly little work on the epistemology of memory. Philosophers have been more concerned with the formation of beliefs than their maintenance (Senor 2005). Recently, however, it has been argued that the elements of a system like Leonard's (photographs, notes, etc.) qualify as parts of his memory – provided the system meets certain criteria, such as being reliable, accessible, and typically invoked (Clark and Chalmers 1998; Clark forthcoming). According to this "extended-mind" hypothesis, one's mind need not end at the boundary of one's brain. A big question in Leonard's case, of course, is how reliable his system is. But the fact that someone's biological memory is malfunctioning does not disqualify it from being part of his mind. Memory impairment is a psychological condition, after all. So if the extended-mind hypothesis is correct, it might be that Leonard's system is part of his mind after all, though it may be as faulty as his biological memory.

Freedom, personal identity, and moral responsibility

Teddy's death in the opening scene is one of the horrific results of the fallibility of Leonard's system. It seems clear that even if John G, the second assailant, exists, Teddy is not him. Yet we come to realize that Leonard kills Teddy *thinking* Teddy is John G. This raises a number of moral issues. Some revolve around the nexus of justice, punishment, and revenge: What punishment is appropriate for rape and murder? Is it ever acceptable to seek "vengeance" for a crime outside the law? Others revolve around Teddy's manipulation of Leonard: What is the relative culpability of someone who induces others to commit crimes? Can justice be served unintentionally? Whatever the answers to these questions, it is plausible that Teddy does not deserve to die at Leonard's hands. Does the fact that Leonard's actions are largely due to his false belief that Teddy raped and murdered his wife affect the extent to which Leonard is morally responsible for his actions?

Many people believe that you can only be responsible for actions performed of your own free will. If someone commits homicide robotically – as the result of hypnotic suggestion, for instance – we do not hold that person responsible. The nature of free will, though, is one of the most difficult and perennial of philosophical problems. Many philosophers take some sort of rationality to be a necessary criterion of free will. That is, if your actions are not counterfactually dependent on *reasons* (in other words if you would have done what you did no matter what reasons presented themselves to you), you are not free. Leonard's condition is cause for concern with respect to this criterion, since it prevents him from developing a coherent picture of the world that is sensitive to his experiences. If you first encountered someone with Leonard's condition you might consider him irrational, since he might, for instance, innocently offer you a cup of coffee fifteen minutes after you had told him you are fatally allergic to it. Learning about his condition would help *explain* the irrationality of this behavior, but it would not make it rational.

Another recurring theme in the discussion of free will is the relation between action and desire. Some philosophers hold that you act freely if your actions follow from your desires (e.g., Hume 1999 [1748]). Others argue that the relationship is more complex, for instance, that you act freely only if you act on a desire that you endorse at some fundamental level (Frankfurt 1971). Whatever the details, it seems questionable that Leonard meets any acceptable version of such a criterion. In a sense he is acting on his desire to kill Teddy – no one is holding a gun to *Leonard's* head – but in another sense he *has* been forced, or at least dishonestly led, to perform this action. For he has been tricked into thinking that Teddy raped and murdered his wife, and we might think that that is a mitigating circumstance, or at the very least that the person who so tricked him is partially morally responsible for Teddy's death.

Of course, one of the most chilling things about the dénouement of *Memento* is that we discover it is *Leonard* who has tricked *himself* into believing that Teddy is John G, knowing full well that he is not. This points to, among other things, the irony that it is precisely the condition that his system is supposed to compensate for that renders it fatally unreliable in the end. (You might wonder whether this is the right characterization of what is going on here, since Leonard obviously wants to kill Teddy, or he would not have knowingly set himself up to kill him. But Leonard could just as easily [and perhaps more securely] have written himself a note initiating a new quest to kill Teddy for what he really has done, or simply shot him then and there, rather than setting himself up to kill Teddy as John G.)

The fact that Leonard can be tricked by an earlier "temporal part" of himself raises a further question about the requirements for moral responsibility. Suppose Leonard had an identical twin brother. It would be grossly unjust to punish Leonard's twin for killing Teddy, since he is a different person from Leonard. The fact that they look the same is irrelevant. Given the nature of Leonard's condition, however, you might wonder whether the person we call "Leonard" the day after Teddy's death is any more Teddy's killer than Leonard's hypothetical twin. To settle this question we need a theory of "personal identity" – a theory of what makes one person (say, someone you point to on the street) the very same individual as "another" person (say, a child in a photograph).

The most popular kind of theory of personal identity is that the numerical identity, or sameness, of a person across time is a matter of a particular kind of psychological continuity. That is, the person you are right now is the same person as, for instance, the person in your high-school yearbook if, and only if, your current mental state – your emotions, beliefs, desires, and so on – depends in a certain way on the mental state of the person in the yearbook. How to spell out the exact nature of the connection is (again!) a matter of considerable debate. But this is enough to see what a strange position Leonard is in. Every time his memory "refreshes," he becomes the psychological continuant not of the person inhabiting his body ten minutes ago, but of Leonard Shelby the insurance investigator, as he was on the night of the incident. Thus Leonard's psychology is continually branching. The person "he" is every fifteen minutes is continuous with the person he was before the incident, but none of these continuants is continuous with any other!

There is *some* continuity between each post-incident "Leonard," however. For one thing, his pre-incident memories are somehow preserved continuously through the serial wipings of his short-term memory. For another, if he has been very active, and his memory is wiped, he still feels tired. Also, his emotional states seem continuous. As he says, "you feel angry, you don't know why; you feel guilty, you have no idea why" (1:26:42). One thing *Memento* provides us with, then, is an interesting test case for theories of personal identity. Does Leonard have the right sort of psychological continuity throughout his post-incident life to be considered a single person, in the sense that he can be held morally responsible for "his" earlier actions, such as killing Teddy?

As with many of the issues raised by *Memento*, it pays to reflect on the extent to which Leonard's situation is just our own, taken to the extreme. If you commit to achieving some goal, such as earning a degree, you might feel obligated by that commitment to try to reach that goal, even if you can't quite reconstruct the reasoning that led you to embrace the goal in the first place. But why should you? Why not rather see the goal as something imposed by someone you no longer are? As people go through their lives they can change their goals in quite radical ways, and they do not feel bound by their earlier desires. Leonard goes through this process at a greatly accelerated rate, thus leading us to question whether we might be as psychologically fragmented as he is, albeit on a larger scale.

Conclusions

Memento is a fascinating film on many levels. It is a compelling example of a puzzle film in the neo-noir tradition. The question of how we ought to solve its narrative puzzles raises questions about the ontology and interpretation of popular cinema and philosophical questions about the nature of the mind, moral responsibility, freedom, and the self. Here, I have only been able to make explicit some of the questions the film raises; answering them will require continuing the philosophical debate.

See also Definition of "cinema" (Chapter 5), Empathy and character engagement (Chapter 9), Genre (Chapter 14), Interpretation (Chapter 15), Narrative closure (Chapter 19), Ontology (Chapter 20), and Personal identity (Chapter 56).

References

Clark, A. (forthcoming) "*Memento*'s Revenge: The Extended Mind Revisited," in R. Menary (ed.) *The Extended Mind*, Kent: Ashgate.

Clark, A., and Chalmers, D. (1998) "The Extended Mind," *Analysis* 58: 7–19.

Davies, D. (2003) "Medium," in J. Levinson (ed.) *The Oxford Handbook of Aesthetics*, Oxford and New York: Oxford University Press.

Duncker, J. (2004) *Memento*. An unofficial *Memento* website. Available at http://www.christophernolan.net/memento.php.

Frankfurt, H. (1971) "Freedom of the Will and the Concept of a Person," *Journal of Philosophy* 68: 5–20.

Hume, D. (1999 [1748]) "Of Liberty and Necessity," section 8 of *An Enquiry Concerning Human Understanding*, Oxford: Oxford University Press.

Klein, A. (2001a) *Everything You Wanted to Know about "Memento."* An essay review of *Memento*. Available at http://dir.salon.com/ent/movies/feature/2001/06/28/memento_analysis/index.html.

—— (2001b) *Everything You Wanted to Know about "Memento."* Klein's responses to correspondence about his 2001a. Available at http://dir.salon.com/ent/letters/2001/07/04/memento/index.html.

Levinson, J. (1992) "Intention and Interpretation: A Last Look," in G. Iseminger (ed.) *Intention and Interpretation*, Philadelphia: Temple University Press.

Livingston, P. (2006) "Theses on Cinema as Philosophy," *Journal of Aesthetics and Art Criticism* 64: 11–18.

Mottram, J. (2002) *The Making of* Memento, London: Faber and Faber.

Senor, T. D. (2005) "Epistemological Problems of Memory," in E. N. Zalta (ed.) *The Stanford Encyclopedia of Philosophy*. Available at http://plato.stanford.edu/archives/spr2005/entries/memory-episprob/

Smith, M. (2006) "Film Art, Argument, and Ambiguity," *Journal of Aesthetics and Art Criticism* 64: 33–42.

Wartenberg, T. (2006) "Beyond Mere Illustration: How Films Can Be Philosophy," *Journal of Aesthetics and Art Criticism* 64: 19–32.

Zhu, D. (2001) Memento FAQ. An unofficial *Memento* website. Available at http://www.designpattern.org/mementofaq.htm.

Further reading

General
Andrew Kania (ed.) *Philosophers on* Memento (London and New York: Routledge, forthcoming) is a collection of essays exploring the philosophical aspects of *Memento*, including issues of memory, epistemology, and emotions; film noir, ontology, and narrative theory; and personal identity, moral responsibility, and the meaning of life. Jonathan Nolan, "Memento Mori," first published in 2001 in *Esquire* 135: 186–91, reprinted in J. Mottram (ed.) *The Making of* Memento (London: Faber and Faber, 2002), and available at http://www.esquire.com/fiction/fiction/ESQ0301-MAR_FICTION. Director Christopher Nolan's brother, Jonathan, came up with the original idea for the film. Christopher wrote the film, while Jonathan wrote this quite different short story.

Film noir, narrative, and interpretation
Greg Currie, "Travels in Narrative Time," chapter 7 of *Image and Mind* (Cambridge and New York: Cambridge University Press, 1995), 198–222, offers a discussion of the kinds of temporal properties film is capable of representing. Paisley Livingston, *Art and Intention* (Oxford: Clarendon Press; New York: Oxford University Press, 2005) contains an argument that an artist's intentions about the kind of work she is creating are inextricably bound up with her intentions for its meaning (pp. 148–65). Alain Silver and James Ursini (eds.) *Film Noir Reader* (New York: Limelight Editions, 1996) is a collection of classic essays on film noir.

Mind and memory
Christoph Hoerl and Teresa McCormack (eds.) *Time and Memory: Issues in Philosophy and Psychology* (Oxford: Clarendon Press; New York: Oxford University Press, 2001) is a collection of philosophical and psychological essays about time and memory – their representation, experience, epistemology, and metaphysics. Georges Rey, *Contemporary Philosophy of Mind: A Contentiously Classical Approach* (Cambridge, MA: Blackwell, 1997) offers a clear and detailed introduction to contemporary philosophy of mind, including discussion of intentionality and a defense of the computational/representational theory of thought. Oliver Sacks, *The Man Who Mistook His Wife for a Hat, and Other Clinical Tales* (New York: Summit Books, 1985) is an accessible collection of essays by a neurologist about people with bizarre psychological problems, including two with a problem very like Leonard's (chapters 2 and 12).

Freedom, personal identity, and moral responsibility
Robert Kane (ed.) *The Oxford Handbook of Free Will* (Oxford and New York: Oxford University Press, 2004) is an excellent collection of overview articles on a range of issues relevant to the problem of free will, including its relation to moral responsibility. Derek Parfit, *Reasons and Persons* (Oxford: Clarendon Press, 1984) contains the classic contemporary discussion of personal identity and its relation to rationality, morality, and our sense of our selves. Basil Smith, "John Locke, Personal Identity, and *Memento*," in M. T. Conrad (ed.) *The Philosophy of Neo-Noir* (Lexington: University Press of Kentucky, 2007), 35–46, is a nice consideration of how Leonard fares with respect to personal identity according to the theories of Locke and Parfit, and the implications for our selves.

INDEX